ENCYCLOPEDIA OF THE SUPREME COURT

David Schultz

Facts On File, Inc.

Encyclopedia of the Supreme Court

Copyright © 2005 by David Schultz

Facts On File, Inc.
132 West 31st Street
New York NY 10001

Library of Congress Cataloging-in-Publication Data

Schultz, David–
Encyclopedia of the Supreme Court/ David Schultz—1st ed.
p. cm.
Includes bibliographical references and index.
ISBN 0-8160-5086-4 (hardcover: alk. paper)
1. United States. Supreme Court—Encyclopedias. 2. United States.
Supreme Court—Biography. I. Title.
KF8742.A35S54 2005
347.73'26'03—dc22

Text design by Joan M. Toro

Cover design by Cathy Rincon

Printed in the United States of America

VB FOF 10 9 8 7 6 5 4 3 2 1

This book is printed on acid-free paper.

Contents

★ ───

LIST OF ENTRIES

iv

CONTRIBUTOR LIST

viii

ACKNOWLEDGMENTS

xi

INTRODUCTION

xii

ENTRIES A TO Z

1

CHRONOLOGY

536

SELECTED BIBLIOGRAPHY

541

INDEX

544

List of Entries

Abood v. Detroit Board of Education
abortion rights
Abrams v. United States
abstention
actual innocence
Adamson v. California
Adarand Constructors, Inc. v. Pena
Adkins v. Children's Hospital of District of Columbia
administrative law and decision making
affirmative action
Afroyim v. Rusk
age discrimination
Alabama v. Shelton
alienage
Allegheny County v. ACLU
Allgeyer v. Louisiana
Ambach v. Norwich
Anderson v. Celebrezze
anonymous political speech
antitrust law
appeal
Arizona v. Fulminante
Arlington Heights v. Metropolitan Housing Development Corp.
Ashwander v. Tennessee Valley Authority
Atkins v. Virginia
Austin v. Michigan State Chamber of Commerce
automobile stops and searches
bail, right to

Bailey v. Drexel Furniture
Baker v. Carr
bankruptcy
Barenblatt v. United States
Barnes v. Glen Theatre
Barron v. Baltimore
Batson v. Kentucky
Beauharnais v. Illinois
Belle Terre v. Boraas
Berman v. Parker
Betts v. Brady
bill of attainder
Bill of Rights
Black, Hugo Lafayette
Blackmun, Harry
Board of County Commissioners, Wabaunsee County, Kansas v. Keen A. Umbehr
Board of Education v. Pico
Board of Regents of State Colleges et al. v. Roth
Board of Regents of University of Wisconsin v. Southworth
Bob Jones University v. United States
Boerne v. Flores
Bolling v. Sharpe
Bork, Robert H.
Bowers v. Hardwick
Bowsher v. Synar
Bradley, Joseph
Bradwell v. Illinois
Brandeis, Louis Dembitz
Brandeis brief
Branzburg v. Hayes
Bray v. Alexandria Women's Health Clinic

Brennan, William
Breyer, Stephen Gerald
brief
Brown v. Board of Education of Topeka
Buchanan v. Warley
Buck v. Bell
Burger, Warren Earl
Burson v. Freeman
Burton, Harold
Bush v. Gore
Calder v. Bull
Cantwell v. Connecticut
capital punishment
Cardozo, Benjamin Nathan
Carey v. Population Services International
case or controversy
certification
Chaplinsky v. New Hampshire
Chase, Salmon
Chase, Samuel
Cherokee decisions
Chevron Inc., USA v. Natural Resources Defense Council
chief justice of the United States Supreme Court
Chimel v. California
Chisholm v. Georgia
cigarette advertising
Cipollone v. Liggett Group, Inc.
citizenship
City of Chicago v. Morales
City of Richmond v. J. A. Croson Company
civil liberties

civil rights
Civil Rights Act of 1964
Civil Rights Acts
civil rights of people with disabilities
Clark, Thomas
class action
City of Cleburne v. Cleburne Living Center
Clinton v. City of New York
Clinton v. Jones
Cohens v. Virginia
Cohen v. California
Coker v. Georgia
Colegrove v. Green
Collector v. Day
Colorado Republican Federal Campaign Committee et al. v. Federal Election Commission
comity
commercial speech
communists, rights of
commutation
compelling state interest
Complete Auto Transit v. Brady
Congress and the Supreme Court
constitutional interpretation
Continental TV v. GTE Sylvania
contraceptives
Cooley v. Board of Wardens
Cooper v. Aaron
Coppage v. Kansas

corporate speech
Court of Appeals, U.S.
court-packing plan
Coyle v. Smith
Coy v. Iowa
Craig v. Boren
cross burning
Cruzan v. Director,
    Missouri Department of
    Health
curator, office of the
Dartmouth College v.
    Woodward
Daubert v. Merrell-Dow
    Pharmaceuticals
declaratory judgment
Dennis v. United States
Department of Justice
Deshaney v. Winnebago
    County Social Services
    Department
Dickerson v. United States
dicta
die, right to
disability rights
docket
dormant commerce clause
double jeopardy
Douglas, William Orville
Dred Scott v. Sandford
drug testing
EEOC v. Arabian
    American Oil Co.
Eisenstadt v. Baird
Ellsworth, Oliver
eminent domain
Employment Division,
    Department of Human
    Resources of Oregon v.
    Smith
Engel v. Vitale
Equal Employment
    Opportunity
    Commission
equal protection clause
Equal Rights Amendment
Erie Railroad Co. v.
    Tompkins
Escobedo v. Illinois
establishment clause of the
    Constitution
Everson v. Board of
    Education

Ewing v. California
exclusionary rule
executive privilege
Ex parte Milligan
Ex parte Young
ex post facto law
Fairness Doctrine
Federal Communications
    Commission v. Pacifica
    Foundation
federal court system
Federal Election
    Commission v. Colorado
    Republican Federal
    Campaign Committee
Federal Election
    Commission v.
    Massachusetts Citizens
    for Life, Inc.
federalism
Ferguson v. Skrupa
fighting words
First English Lutheran
    Church v. County of Los
    Angeles
first Monday in October
flag burning
flag salute
Flast v. Cohen
Fletcher v. Peck
Florida v. Bostick
Food and Drug
    Administration v. Brown
    & Williamson Tobacco
    Corp.
Forsyth County v.
    Nationalist Movement
Fortas, Abe
Frankfurter, Felix
freedom of assembly and
    association
Frontiero v. Richardson
Frothingham v. Mellon
Fuller, Melville Weston
Fullilove v. Klutznick
fundamental rights
Furman v. Georgia
Garcia v. San Antonio
    Metropolitan Transit
    Authority
gay and lesbian rights
    (same-sex discrimination)
Geduldig v. Aiello

Gibbons v. Ogden
Gideon v. Wainwright
Ginsburg, Ruth Bader
Gitlow v. New York
Goldwater v. Carter
Good News Club v.
    Milford Central School
    District
Goss v. Lopez
Gratz v. Bollinger
Gravel v. United States
Gray v. Sanders
Green v. County School
    Board of New Kent
    County, Virginia
Gregg v. Georgia
Griggs v. Duke Power
Griswold v. Connecticut
Grove City College v. Bell
Grutter v. Bollinger
Haig v. Agee
Hammer v. Dagenhart
J. W. Hampton, Jr. & Co. v.
    United States
Harlan, John Marshall
Harmelin v. Michigan
harmless error
Harper v. Virginia State
    Board of Elections
Harris v. Forklift Systems,
    Inc.
Harris v. McRae
Hawaii Housing Authority
    v. Midkiff
Hazelwood School District
    v. Kuhlmeier
Heart of Atlanta Motel v.
    United States
Herrera v. Collins
Hodgson et al. v.
    Minnesota et al.
Hoke v. United States
Holmes, Oliver Wendell, Jr.
Home Building and Loan
    Association v. Blaisdell
H. P. Hood & Sons v.
    DuMond
Hughes, Charles Evans
Humphrey's Executor v.
    United States
Hurtado v. California
Hustler Magazine v.
    Falwell

illegal aliens
income tax
incorporation
Indian rights
inherent powers
In re Debs
In re Gault
In re Neagle
intermediate scrutiny
International Society for
    Krishna Consciousness,
    Inc. v. Lee
International Union, UAW
    v. Johnson Controls
Internet and censorship
Internet and the
    Worldwide Web
Internet taxation
interstate commerce
Interstate Commerce
    Commission
Jackson, Robert
Jay, John
J.E.B. v. Alabama
Jehovah's Witnesses and
    the Supreme Court
Jim Crow laws
Johnson v. Transportation
    Agency of Santa Clara
    County
judicial activism and
    restraint
judicial review
Judiciary Act of 1789
jury size and voting
justiciability
juvenile death penalty
juvenile rights
Katzenbach v. Morgan
Katz v. United States
Kennedy, Anthony M.
Kimel v. Board of Regents
Korematsu v. United States
labor union rights
Lamb's Chapel v. Center
    Moriches School District
land use
Lawrence v. Texas
lawyer advertising
Lee v. Weisman
Legal Services Corporation
    v. Velazquez
legislative standing

Lemon v. Kurtzman
liberty of contract
lie detector tests
Lochner v. New York
Locke v. Davey
Loving v. Virginia
Lucas v. South Carolina
    Coastal Council
Lujan v. Defenders of
    Wildlife
Lynch v. Donnelly
Madsen v. Women's Health
    Center, Inc.
Mapp v. Ohio
Marbury v. Madison
marriage, right to
Marshal, office of the
Marshall, John
Marshall, Secretary of
    Labor, et al. v. Barlow's,
    Inc.
Marshall, Thurgood
Martin v. Hunter's Lessee
Masson v. New Yorker
Mathews v. Eldridge
McCleskey v. Kemp
McConnell v. Federal
    Election Commission
McCulloch v. Maryland
McIntyre v. Ohio
Meritor Savings Bank v.
    Vinson
Metro Broadcasting, Inc.
    v. Federal
    Communications
    Commission
Meyer v. Nebraska
Miami Herald Publishing
    Co. v. Tornillo
Michael H. et al. v.
    Gerald D.
Michael M. v. Superior
    Court of Sonoma County
Michigan v. Long
Miller v. Johnson
Milliken v. Bradley
Minnesota v. Cloverleaf
    Creamery Company
minors, rights of
Miranda v. Arizona
Mississippi University for
    Women v. Hogan
Mississippi v. Johnson

Missouri v. Holland
Mistretta v. United States
Mitchell v. Helms
Mobile v. Bolden
moot
Morrison v. Olson
Mueller v. Allen
Muller v. Oregon
Munn v. Illinois
Murphy, Frank
music censorship
Muskrat v. United States
National Association for
    the Advancement of
    Colored People v.
    Alabama
National Labor Relations
    Board (NLRB) v. Jones
    & Laughlin Steel
    Corporation
National League of Cities
    v. Usery
National Organization for
    Women v. Scheidler
Nebbia v. New York
Nebraska Press Association
    v. Stuart
necessary and proper
    clause
New Deal constitutionality
new federalism
New Jersey v. T.L.O.
New State Ice Company v.
    Liebmann
New York Times Co. v.
    Sullivan
New York v. Ferber
New York v. United States
1983 lawsuits
Ninth Amendment
nude dancing
O'Connor, Sandra Day
O'Hare Truck Service, Inc.
    v. City of Northlake
Olim v. Wakinekona
one person, one vote
opinion writing
oral argument
original jurisdiction
overbreadth
overturning Supreme
    Court decisions
Palko v. Connecticut

pardon
parental rights
Paris Adult Theatre I v.
    Slaton
Payne v. Tennessee
Penn Central
    Transportation Co. v.
    New York City
Penry v. Lynaugh
peremptory challenges
Personnel Administrator of
    Massachusetts et al. v.
    Feeney
PGA Tour, Inc. v. Casey
    Martin
Pierce v. Society of the
    Sisters
plain view doctrine
Planned Parenthood of
    Missouri v. Danforth
Planned Parenthood of
    Southeastern
    Pennsylvania v. Casey
"plenary power" doctrine
Plessy v. Ferguson
Plyler v. Doe
Poe v. Ullman
police powers
political parties, rights of
political question doctrine
political speech
Pollock v. Farmer's Loan &
    Trust
pornography and obscenity
Powell, Lewis F., Jr.
prayer in school
precedent
preemption
Pregnancy Discrimination
    Act of 1978
prior restraint
prisoners, rights of
privacy, right to
Prize Cases
procedural due process
public forum
public trial
punitive damages
pure speech
racial discrimination
Racketeer Influenced and
    Corrupt Organizations
    Act (RICO)

Ragsdale et al. v.
    Wolverine World Wide,
    Inc.
rape and the death penalty
rational basis
reapportionment and
    redistricting
Red Lion Broadcasting v.
    FCC
Regents of the University
    of California v. Bakke
Rehnquist, William Hubbs
religion
religion, public displays of
Renton v. Playtime
    Theaters
Republican Party of
    Minnesota v. White
Reynolds v. Sims
Reynolds v. United States
Richardson v. McKnight
RICO and abortion
Ring v. Arizona
ripeness
Rochin v. California
Roe v. Wade
Romer v. Evans
Rosenberger v. Rector and
    Visitors of the Univ. of
    Virginia
Rostker v. Goldberg
rule of four
Rust v. Sullivan
Rutledge, John
Saenz v. Roe
San Antonio Independent
    School District v.
    Rodriguez
Santa Clara County v.
    Southern Pacific
    Railroad
Santa Fe Independent
    School District v. Doe
Scalia, Antonin
Schenck v. United States
Schlup v. Delo
Schmerber v. California
school prayer
school vouchers
scientific evidence
Scottsboro cases
search warrant
Second Amendment

selected exclusiveness
Selective Service
*Selective Service
    Commission v.
    Minnesota Public
    Interest Research Group*
self-incrimination, right
    against
Sell v. United States
separation of powers
sexual discrimination
sexual harassment
*Shapiro, Commissioner of
    Welfare of Connecticut
    v. Thompson*
Shaw v. Reno
Shelley v. Kraemer
Skinner v. Oklahoma
slander and libel
Slaughter-House Cases
Smith v. Doe
Souter, David H.
South Carolina v. Baker
South Dakota v. Dole
sovereign immunity
speedy trial
*Standard Oil Co. of New
    Jersey v. United States*
standing
stare decisis
Stevens, John Paul
Stewart, Potter
Stone, Harlan Fiske
stop and frisk
Story, Joseph
strict scrutiny
structure of the Supreme
    Court
student activity fees
student newspapers
students, rights of
student searches
substantive due process

summary judgment
Supreme Court and for-
    eign policy
Supreme Court and the
    constitutional amending
    process
Supreme Court building
Supreme Court confirma-
    tion
suspect classification
Sutherland, George
*Swann v. Charlotte-
    Mecklenburg Board of
    Education*
*Swift and Company v.
    United States*
Swift v. Tyson
symbolic speech
Taft, William Howard
takings clause
Taney, Roger Brooke
tax and spend powers
taxpayer suits
Terminiello v. Chicago
Terry v. Ohio
Texas v. Johnson
Thomas, Clarence
Thornburg v. Gingles
*Timmons v. Twin Cities
    Area New Party*
*Tinker et al. v. Des Moines
    Independent School
    District*
Title IX
Title VII of the Civil
    Rights Act of 1964
tobacco liability
Toyota Motors v. Williams
treaties
unenumerated rights
*United Public Workers of
    America v. Mitchell*
United States Constitution

United States Constitution,
    application overseas
*U.S. Term Limits, Inc. v.
    Thornton*
*United States Trust Co. v.
    New Jersey*
*United States v. American
    Library Association*
United States v. Belmont
United States v. Butler
*United States v. Carolene
    Products Co.*
*United States v. Curtiss
    Wright Export
    Corporation*
United States v. Darby
*United States v. E. C.
    Knight Co.*
United States v. Eichman
United States v. Leon
*United States v. Libellants
    and Claimants of the
    Schooner Amistad*
United States v. Morrison
*United States, et al. v.
    National Treasury
    Employees Union*
United States v. O'Brien
United States v. Pink
*United States v. Schechter
    Poultry Corporation*
United States v. Virginia
*United Steelworkers of
    America v. Weber*
Vacco v. Quill
Van Devanter, Willis
*Village of Euclid, Ohio v.
    Ambler Realty Co.*
Vinson, Fred M.
Violence Against Women
    Act of 1994
Virginia v. Hicks
Voting Rights Act

Waite, Morrison Remick
Wallace v. Jaffree
*Walz v. Tax Commission of
    the City of New York*
*Ward's Cove Packing
    Company v. Atonio*
*Ward v. Rock Against
    Racism*
war powers
Warren, Earl
Warth v. Seldin
Washington, Bushrod
Washington v. Davis
*Watchtower Bible & Tract
    Society v. Village of
    Stratton*
*Webster v. Reproductive
    Health Services*
Weeks v. United States
welfare benefit rights
Wesberry v. Sanders
*West Coast Hotel Co. v.
    Parrish*
White, Byron
White, Edward Douglass
Whren v. United States
Wickard v. Filburn
wiretapping
Wisconsin v. Yoder
women and the
    Constitution
writ of certiorari
Wyman v. James
Yates v. United States
Yick Wo v. Hopkins
Younger v. Harris
Youngstown Co. v. Sawyer
Zadvydas v. Davis
*Zobrest v. Catalina
    Foothills School District*
zoning
Zorach v. Clauson

Contributor List

Abraham, Jill, University of Virginia
Aichinger, Karen, freelance grants writer and administrator
Aichinger, Alex, Northwestern State University of Louisiana
Alcorn, Mark, Avon, Minnesota
Allen, Mahalley D., University of Kansas
Altman, Micah, Harvard University
Atwell, Mary Welek, Radford University
Baier, Gerald, University of British Columbia
Baker, William D., Arkansas School for Mathematics and Science
Baracskay, Daniel, Cleveland State University
Bardos, Andy V., University of Florida, Levin College of Law
Baumeier, Charlsey T., Greenbaum Doll & McDonald
Bierman, Luke, American Bar Association
Bishop, Sarah, Muskingum College
Bitzer, J. Michael, Catawba College
Bleich, Jeffrey, Munger, Tolles & Olson, San Francisco, California
Bowen, Rachel, Georgetown University
Bowers, Michael W., University of Nevada, Las Vegas
Brown, Greg, University of Texas, Austin
Brown, Scott M., Indiana University–Southeast
Byrd, Mason, Virginia Commonwealth University
Campbell, Patrick F., University of Massachusetts, Amherst
Campie, Patricia E., University of Arizona
Carey, Henry F., Georgia State University
Carobine, John P., Northern Michigan University
Charles, Robert, University of Louisville
Chasin, Andy, Baker & Hostetler, LLP, Washington, D.C.
Cheit, Ross E., Brown University
Chen, Jowei, Yale Law School
Chernyavskaya, Mariya, University of Louisville
Childs, Scott, University of North Carolina School of Law

Chilton, Bradley Stewart, University of North Texas
Christensen, Michelle D., Northwestern University
Claborn, David, University of Massachusetts, Amherst
Clark, Tom, Princeton University
Clouatre, Douglas, Kennesaw State University
Cocca, Carolyn E., SUNY, College at Old Westbury
Cody, Scott, University of Iowa
Coogan, William H., University of Southern Maine
Colucci, Frank J., Purdue University, Calumet
Covington, Jaeryl, University of Louisville
Coyle, Dennis, Catholic University of America
Cressman, Derek, USPIRG
Crowe, Justin, Princeton University
Culver, Amy-Marie, Boston College Law School
Davis, Jeffrey, University of Maryland, Baltimore County
Deardorff, Michelle Donaldson, Jackson State University
Dehnel, David, Augustana College, Illinois
DeMichael, Jen, Dickinson School of Law
Dempsey, Michelle L., Muskingum College
den Dulk, Kevin R., Grand Valley State University
Dennehy, Susan M., University of California, Berkeley
Dickman, Joshua M.
Dimino, Michael Richard, Sr., Widener School of Law
Donaghy, Ryan, Muskingum College
Doyle, Matthew R., University of Louisville
Dupuis, Martin
Dynia, Philip A., Loyola University, New Orleans
Eakins, Keith Rollin, University of Central Oklahoma
Erickson, Erick-Woods, Sell & Melton
Escoffier, Wendy, Northern Arizona University
Festa, Matt, Houston, Texas
Fisher, James Daniel, Edinboro University of Pennsylvania
Fowles, Jacob, University of Louisville
Flannery, Richard, University of Wisconsin Colleges
Fulks, Mark A.

Gear, John
Gerstmann, Evan, Loyola Marymount University
Gibson, Tobias T., Washington University, St. Louis
Gladstone-Sovell, Tracey L., University of Wisconsin, River Falls
Goetz, Jamie, University of Louisville
Gomez, Ernest Alexander, Chicago
Gordon, Elizabeth Ellen, Kennesaw State University
Goss, Robert P., Brigham Young University
Gossett, Charles W., California Polytechnic University, Pomona
Greenspan, Rosann, University of California, Berkeley
Groce, Wendy, University of Louisville
Gruberg, Martin, University of Wisconsin, Oshkosh
Haas, Kenneth C., University of Delaware
Hagan, Colleen, University of Louisville
Halpern, Justin, Northeastern State University
Hancock, Lauren, University of Minnesota
Hanratty, Kate, University of Louisville
Harper, Tim, University of Louisville
Hayler, Barbara J., University of Illinois, Springfield
Headley, James E., Eastern Washington University
Helfman, Tara, Yale Law School, New York University
Hemmens, Craig, Boise State University
Henson, Amy M., *Esquire Magazine*
Heumann, Milton, Rutgers University
Higgins, Temeka, University of Louisville
Hoffman, Daniel N., Johnson C. Smith University
Holland, Kenneth, Kansas State University
Howard, Charles C.
Hundsdorfer, Tim, University of Colorado
Hunt, Andrea, University of Louisville
James, Nicole M., University of Florida
Jarratt-Ziemski, Karen L., Northern Arizona University
Johnson, Lori A., Wellesley College
Johnson, Matthew A., Washington University, St. Louis
Jones, Steven, Brown University
Kalhan, Anil, Cleary, Gottlieb, Steen & Hamilton, New York
Kawar, Leila
Kersch, Ken I., Princeton University
Knull, Garret M., Muskingum College
Kradel, Adam, University of Wisconsin
Kubicek, Laurie M.
Lemieux, Scott, Hunter College
Lichtman, Steven B., Dickinson College
Malmsheimer, Robert W., SUNY College of Environmental Science and Forestry
Manna, Sharon A., University of Buffalo
Manweller, Mathew, Central Washington University
Mauldin, Marcus D., Florida State University
Maxwell, Jewerl, Miami University
McCall, Michael, San Diego State University

McCarthy, Osler, Texas Supreme Court
McIntire, Andrew C., Muskingum College
McLauchlan, Judithanne Scourfield, University of South Florida, St. Petersburg
Mezey, Susan Gluck, Loyola University, Chicago
Miller, Banks
Miller, Kenneth P., Claremont McKenna College
Miller, Rochelle, Muskingum College
Mitchell, Christopher G., University of Louisville
Monroe, Billy, University of Texas, Dallas
Moran, Mark, Abortion Debate Research Project
Morse, Adam H., Brennan Center, NYU School of Law
Morris, Stanley M., Cortez, Colorado
Mott, Kenneth F., Gettysburg College
Nazaretian, R. Nanette, University of Louisville
Niehaus, Benjamin, University of Louisville
Oliver, Amy, University of Louisville
O'Neill, Timothy J., Southwestern University
O'Sullivan, Deirdre, New York University
Owens, Ryan J., Washington University, St. Louis
Parrent, Blane, University of Louisville
Peach, Brett, Muskingum College
Pearce, Kevin G., Virginia Department of Health
Perry, George
Pender, Tassili, Claremont Graduate Center
Pershing, Stephen B., United States Department of Justice
Pesachowitz, Daniel J., Laura Margulies & Associates, LLC
Peters, Kylie, Muskingum College
Peterson, Steven A., Pennsylvania State University, Harrisburg
Pinaire, Brian K., Lehigh University
Pole, Antoinette, City University of New York, Graduate School & University Center
Provizer, Norman, Metropolitan State College of Denver
Purdy, Elizabeth
Raines, Julie
Ramos, Mitzi, University of Illinois, Chicago
Randazzo, Kirk A., University of Kentucky
Reeves, Andrew, Harvard University
Ricci, Elizabeth, Rambana & Ricci, Tallahassee, Florida
Riggs, William W., Texas A & M International University
Roberts, Gayle F., Barry University
Roberts, John L., North Carolina State University
Roberts, Patrick K., Webster University
Robinson, Robert
Ross, Jason, Georgetown University
Ruckman, P. S., Jr., Rock Valley College
Ruhl, Amber, University of Louisville
Rush, Mark, Washington and Lee University
Ryan, Paul S., Campaign Legal Center
Sabatello, Maya, University of Southern California

Sands, Eric C., University of Virginia
Saunders, Eugene L., Muskingum College
Schneider, Carrie A., SUNY Albany
Schultz, David, Hamline University
Scott-Hayward, Christine, New York University
Sears, Amanda B., Muskingum College
Shaw, Stephen K., Northwest Nazarene University
Shomade, Salmon A., University of Arizona
Shortell, Christopher, University of California, San Diego
Singel, Daniel J., University of Minnesota Law School
Singer, Rebecca
Skimmer, Daniel
Stangl, Christopher, University of Wisconsin, Madison
Stanko, Paul D., Indiana University, Northwest Campus
Steigerwalt, Amy, University of New Orleans
Steiner, Benjamin, University of Cincinnati
Strum, Nathan, Muskingum College
Sullivan, Kathleen S., Ohio University
Sutherland, Rosalyn S., University of Delaware
Swan, Robert, Portland State University
Swanson, Rick, University of Louisiana at Lafayette
Swartz, Beth S.
Sweet, Martin J., Dickinson College
Swenson, Karen, Eastern Illinois University
Toplak, Jurij, University of Maribor
Ulmschneider, Georgia Wralstad, Indiana
   University–Purdue University Fort Wayne
Vennum, Lindsay, Muskingum College
Vile, John R., Tennessee State University

Vining, Richard L., Jr., University of Delaware
Voigts, Anne M., Munger, Tolles & Olson
Wagner, Kevin M., University of Florida
Waite, Kendal, Muskingum College
Walker, Jason, Western Illinois University
Walker, Carol, Georgia State University
Wampler, Christina, Muskingum College
Ward, Artemus, Northern Illinois University
Waskey, A. J. L., Dalton State College
Wasniewski, Matthew, Washington, D.C.
Weber, Paul J., University of Louisville
Wermiel, Stephen, American University Washington
   College of Law
Whitney, Sharon G., Tennessee Technological University
Williams, Eric J., Rutgers University
Williams, Gwyneth I., Webster University
Williams, Terri D., Barry University
Williams, Zola-Mari, Jacksonville, Florida
Wilson, Amy P., University of Washington
Winford, Clenton G., II, University of Texas, Dallas
Woessner, Matthew, Pennsylvania State University
   Harrisburg
Worstall, Charlotte, Muskingum College
Wright, Christopher J., University of Arkansas,
   Monticello
Yasar, M. Murat, University of North Texas
Yung, John M., Muskingum College
Zinner, Susan, Indiana University, Northwest Campus
Zoeller, Lindsay B., University of Louisville

Acknowledgments

Encyclopedia of the Supreme Court is the product of many minds. More than 150 individuals penned the 400+ essays in this volume. To all those who contributed to this project, I give my warmest praise and thanks. Were it not for you, this volume would have never been produced. Not only did they contribute essays, but also ideas on terms that ought to be included in this volume. While my name goes on *Encyclopedia of the Supreme Court* as the editor, all of these contributors are the real heart and soul of this volume.

In editing this encyclopedia, I had to make many decisions regarding what terms to include, cases to discuss, and personalities to chronicle. Doing that and limiting the final project to one volume was difficult. No doubt some will find cases, or concepts, or names missing that they believe should be included. I acknowledge in advance that you are correct—many more essays should be here, and perhaps some which are here should not be. I have done my best to select essays that give the sense of the breadth of the Supreme Court's history and political significance. For those seeking more information, I hope *Encyclopedia of the Supreme Court* is not the last book you read on the subject but that it stimulates a curiosity that encourages you to read even more widely about the many subjects found in this volume.

Finally, while all effort has been made to acknowledge personally and individually everyone who contributed, no doubt I have missed a few people. To those unintentionally unacknowledged, I apologize for this error and any others in this volume.

Introduction

The Supreme Court is a powerful legal and political institution in the United States. In decisions such as *Bush v. Gore, Roe v. Wade, Brown v. Board of Education, McConnell v. Federal Election Commission,* and *Miranda v. Arizona,* the Court has determined the outcome of a presidential race, declared women have the right to abortions, struck down segregation, upheld campaign finance reform laws, and stipulated that police officers must inform those accused of crime their rights.

Yet this mighty power of the Supreme Court is not of recent origin. Instead, throughout American history it has often been a major player in American politics, deciding over time that states could deny women the right to vote in *Minor v. Happersett,* that African Americans were property and not citizens (*Dred Scott v. Sandford*), that gays and lesbians did not have the same rights as heterosexuals (*Bowers v. Hardwick*), and that Congress could create a national bank (*McCulloch v. Maryland*). In each of these opinions, the Supreme Court stepped into the middle of major legal debates, but it also issued decisions that addressed important political battles of the day. Yet this is not what the constitutional framers seemed to envision.

In 1787 in *Federalist Paper* 78 Alexander Hamilton described the Supreme Court as the "least dangerous branch" of the proposed national government. It would be an institution that would have the power of judgment and not will, such that it would not be able to substitute its views or opinions for that of Congress.

Yet despite this initial plan that envisioned the Supreme Court as perhaps a minor player in American politics, it has instead become a forceful and powerful branch coequal in many ways to that of Congress and the president. In its more than 200-year existence, the Supreme Court has ventured decisions on almost every aspect of American life, from the most intimate issues about abortion, procreation, and the right to die to major disputes over the power of the president to act in foreign affairs or the ability of Congress to regulate commerce.

Alexis de Tocqueville penned in *Democracy in America* (1841) that "There is hardly a political question in the United States which does not sooner or later turn into a judicial one." The history of the United States Supreme Court amply proves de Tocqueville correct—the courts, and especially the United States Supreme Court, is in fact often the final arbiter of many, if not all, of the major disputes in the country.

Encyclopedia of the Supreme Court is meant to provide readers an overview of the major cases, concepts, and issues and of the personalities who have shaped it and American politics. It is written in a style that seeks to demystify the Court, making what it does and how it works more accessible and understandable to the average citizen.

—David Schultz
Hamline University
Saint Paul, Minnesota

Abood v. Detroit Board of Education, 431 U.S. 209 (1977)

In *Abood v. Detroit Board of Education,* the Supreme Court unanimously held that a Michigan statute authorizing an "agency shop" arrangement between a local government employer and a union representing local government employees was constitutionally valid. The Court ruled that the arrangement under which nonunion employees represented by the union must pay a service fee equal in amount to union fees as a condition of their employment did not violate the First and Fourteenth Amendments rights of the employees. However, the Court prohibited the union from using the service fees for political and ideological purposes unrelated to the union's collective bargaining activities and for activities opposed by the employees.

Furthermore, the Court ruled that the nonunion employees may constitutionally bar the union from spending any part of their fees on those political activities unrelated to the union's collective bargaining work. But the Court emphasized that its decision does not bar a union representing public employees from spending money for the expression of political views or on behalf of political candidates. Rather, the Constitution, the Court surmised, requires that such expenditures be funded by union employees who do not object to advancing those views and who are not forced to contribute those funds based on the threat of employment loss with the government.

The plaintiffs in *Abood* were Detroit public school teachers who were unwilling or had refused to pay dues to the union representing all teachers employed by the Detroit Board of Education. They alleged that the union was engaged in political activities that they opposed and that were not related to any of the union's collective-bargaining purposes. Relying in part on the opinions in *Railway Employees' Dept. v. Hanson,* 351 U.S. 225 (1956) and *Machinists v. Street,* 367 U.S. 740 (1961), the Court argued that insofar as the charges required of the nonunion employees were used for funding union expenditures for collective-bargaining, contract-admin-istration, and grievance-adjustment activities, the agency-shop arrangement was valid. In *Hanson,* the Court held that requiring financial support for a collective-bargaining agency by those who received the agency's benefits was not a violation of the First Amendment. The Court in *Street* ruled that unions could not use agency shop funds for political purposes opposed by nonunion members.

Stressing that the crux of the First Amendment is the notion that each individual is free to believe as he/she will and that in a free society that belief should be shaped by the individual's mind or conscience rather than coerced by the government, the Court in *Abood* reasoned that the plaintiffs' constitutional rights were violated, irrespective of whether the plaintiffs were compelled to make, rather than prohibited from making, union contributions. Nonetheless, the Court rejected the plaintiffs' argument that the *Abood* case was different from its preceding cases because those precedents involved private sector employment.

The Court also rejected the plaintiffs' contention that collective bargaining in the public sector was inherently political, thus forcing the nonunion members to surrender their First Amendment rights by being forced to financially support the union. Concluding that the central constitutional question in *Abood* was whether a public employee had a First Amendment interest superior to a private employee's and thus was not required to financially contribute to the expenditures of exclusive union representation, the Court decided that a public employee had no such superior interest.

The *Abood* case is noteworthy because it became the foundational case for a later Court decision on STUDENT ACTIVITY FEES. In *BOARD OF REGENTS v. SOUTHWORTH,* 529 U.S. 217 (2000), the Court held that the First Amendment permits a public university to charge students mandatory student activity fees used to fund programs facilitating extracurricular philosophical, religious, or other student discussions, insofar as there is viewpoint neutrality in the allocation of funds to said organizations. *Abood* is also important because it was in this case that the Court extended the rule on agency shop arrangement to nonunion members in the public sector.

For more information: Schmedemann, Deborah A. "Of Meetings and Mailboxes: The First Amendment and Exclusive Representation in Public Sector Labor Relations." *Virginia Law Review* 72 (February 1986): 91; Wasserman, Howard M. "Compelled Expression and the Public Forum Doctrine." *Tulane Law Review* 73 (November 2002): 163.

—Salmon A. Shomade

abortion rights

Since 1973 when the Supreme Court handed down its landmark decision on abortion in ROE V. WADE, 410 U.S. 113 (1973), battle lines have been drawn between prochoice advocates who have labored to protect a woman's right to choose and antiabortionists who have determined to limit access to abortion in every way possible.

Before 1800, abortion laws evolved from English common law, and abortion prior to quickening was legal. Quickening, which involved the first perceptible movements of the fetus, was generally assumed to take place around the 12th week of pregnancy. Many women developed their own methods of abortion using various herbs. For example, herbal concoctions were frequently used by slave women to prevent the birth of children by slave owners.

By the mid-19th century, abortion services were regularly advertised in American newspapers. The early 19th century saw an increase in the number of abortions among married women who were beginning to realize both the health and financial risks of too many children. The American Medical Association (AMA), founded in 1847, created a Committee on Ethics that launched a campaign in 1857 to make abortion illegal at all stages. The campaign failed to stop abortions; it simply sent them underground. Scores of women died or became sterile from self-induced abortions or botched abortions—"back alley" abortions.

In the 1960s several events took place that changed the perceptions of abortion in the United States. The birth control pill was introduced in 1960, launching a sexual revolution. In 1965 the Supreme Court handed down a decision in GRISWOLD V. CONNECTICUT, 381 U.S. 479 that established the right to PRIVACY, which gave married couples access to birth control. The right was extended to single people in 1972 in EISENSTADT V. BAIRD, 405 U.S. 438. The women's movement gained momentum throughout the 1960s and 1970s, calling for women to be considered as more than "baby machines." Women were better educated, and they were more likely to postpone marriage to pursue a career and to delay childbirth after marriage.

Separate outbreaks of babies born with serious birth defects resulted from exposure to German measles and the use of thalidomide, and a number of states liberalized abortion laws. In 1973 the Supreme Court used the privacy standard of *Griswold* to determine in *Roe v. Wade,* 410 U.S. 113, that a woman has a constitutional right to an abortion without state interference up until the end of the first trimester. After that point, states have been assumed to have a "compelling interest" in protecting both the mother's life and the potential life of a fetus. Support for abortion rights had swung so far in the early 1970s that the medical profession and a number of churches and religious leaders supported the attempt to challenge existing restrictions on abortion rights. There is no doubt that *Roe v. Wade* was a turning point in the abortion battle. On the one hand, women throughout the country were able to request safe abortions from legitimate doctors who were concerned about their health, and both maternal deaths and the infant mortality rates decreased. Changes were most noticeable in the lives of poor and minority women since many middle- and upper-class women had been able to travel to other states, or out of the country if necessary, to obtain safe and legal abortions. On the other hand, abortion opponents were outraged and launched a concentrated campaign to have *Roe* overturned. The antiabortion movement gained momentum with the marriage of the Republican Party and the religious right in the 1980s.

After President Ronald Reagan was elected in 1980, his administration made it a top priority to overturn *Roe v. Wade.* These efforts were directed toward Congress through promoting legislation that restricted access to abortion for government workers, Medicaid patients, and patients in public hospitals. The Reagan administration extended its long arms over countries around the world through the practice of withholding foreign aid from any country that provided government access to abortion. From 1980 to 1988 it was common practice for both senators and representatives to add abortion riders to all sorts of bills. The Reagan efforts, and later those of George Bush, were particularly directed toward the Supreme Court, where views on abortion became the litmus test for nominating Supreme Court justices. Despite the appointment of conservative justices from 1981 to 1991, the Court adjusted itself toward balance, with Reagan-appointee Justice Sandra Day O'CONNOR frequently providing the pivotal swing vote.

In *Thornburgh v. the American College of Obstetrics and Gynecology,* 476 U.S. 747 (1985) the Supreme Court came within one vote of overturning *Roe.* Even though the Court surprisingly stopped short of overturning *Roe,* the Reagan/Bush appointees did limit access to abortion in a number of ways, and the move toward restrictive abortion rights was mirrored in many states. From 1995 to 2003, 335

Pro-choice demonstrators in New York City, 1977 *(Hulton/Archive)*

state laws were passed restricting access to abortion. In *WEBSTER V. REPRODUCTIVE HEALTH SERVICES*, 492 U.S. 490 (1989) the Supreme Court gave states almost total control of abortion rights.

In *PLANNED PARENTHOOD OF SOUTHEASTERN PENNSYLVANIA V. CASEY*, 505 U.S. 833 (1992) the ruling allowed states to impose "informed consent" and waiting periods on women who seek abortions. The *Casey* decision also replaced the trimester system of *Roe* with the "undue burden" test that prevents states from placing insurmountable obstacles to obtaining abortions. The Court overturned the spousal consent requirement in *Casey;* and in *Akron v. Ohio*, 462 U.S. 416 (1983) the Court refused to accept a parental consent law that required the consent of both parents and did not provide for judicial intervention for a minor who was unable or unwilling to obtain the consent of a parent. After the *Casey* decisions, the focus on abortion restrictions turned to banning so-called partial birth abor-

tions. The Partial-Birth Abortion Funding Ban Act of 2003 passed in the Senate but stalled in committee in the House of Representatives.

At the beginning of the 21st century, the United States Supreme Court has refused to withdraw *Roe*'s guarantee of a constitutional right to obtain an abortion. However, using the power granted under *Webster v. Reproductive Health Services,* 492 U.S. 490 (1989), the governors or legislatures of 25 states have restricted access to abortion through informed consent laws, waiting periods, and bans on all abortions after the viability except to save the mother's life. While the extent of antiabortion violence was stunted in 1994 with *NATIONAL ORGANIZATION FOR WOMEN V. SCHEIDLER*, 510 U.S. 249, which allowed family-planning clinics to recover damages from violent protesters, efforts toward restricting abortion rights continue. The violence directed toward abortion providers, which included the murder of two physicians, has left as many as 87 percent of all counties in the United States with no abortion services. It has been estimated that about one-third of women in the United States have been or could be affected by this restriction, although abortion continues to be protected as a constitutional right.

For more information: Mohr, James. *Abortion in America.* Oxford and New York: Oxford University Press, 1978; Reagan, Leslie J. *When Abortion Was a Crime: Women, Medicine, and Law in the United States, 1867–1973.* Berkeley: University of California Press, 1997.

—Elizabeth Purdy

Abrams v. United States, 250 U.S. 616 (1919)

In *Abrams v. United States* five individuals were convicted of violating the Espionage Act of 1917, and as amended in 1918, which allowed convictions for, among other things, conspiring to "utter, print, write, and publish disloyal, scurrilous, and abusive language about the form of government of the United States, or language intended to bring the form of government of the United States into contempt, scorn, contumely and disrepute, or intended to incite, provoke, and encourage resistance to the United States . . ." The defendants, Russian-born, non-naturalized residents of the United States, were avowed "anarchists" who, during the summer of 1918, circulated fliers around New York City criticizing the U.S. government and its leaders and urging resistance to the war effort underway against the Imperial German Government.

Affirming the convictions and reasoning expressed by the trial court, the United States Supreme Court looked to its recent PRECEDENT in *SCHENCK V. UNITED STATES*, 249 U.S. 47 (1919), *Frohwerk v. United States*, 249 U.S. 204 (1919), and *Debs v. United States*, 249 U.S. 211 (1919). Writing for the Court, Justice Clarke stressed the special circumstances and potentially pernicious consequences of such expression, explaining that, while the defendants' primary concern seemed to be the impact of U.S. troop movements on the ongoing Russian revolution, the practical effect of their efforts was to endanger the war effort in America by encouraging citizens not to support their government in a time of crisis. Importantly then, the Court offered, the "power [to punish speech that produces a clear and imminent danger] undoubtedly is greater in time of war than in time of peace because war opens dangers that do not exist at other times."

But the *Abrams* case is most famous for the dissent authored by Justice Oliver Wendell HOLMES, Jr. Distancing himself from his recent views in *Schenck, Frohwerk,* and *Debs,* Holmes held, in principle, to the "clear and present danger" doctrine but argued that the statutory requirement of "intent" had not been satisfied and, furthermore, the speech in question hardly amounted to the danger alleged by the government and accepted by the majority. In making his case, Holmes introduced to American constitutional law the concept of the "marketplace of ideas"—the notion that speech and ideas should be allowed to compete with one another in a PUBLIC FORUM that ultimately allows citizens to sort through the noise and arrive at the truth. "[W]hen men have realized that time has upset many fighting faiths," Holmes famously assured us, "they may come to believe even more than they believe the very foundations of their own conduct that the ultimate good desired is better reached by free trade in ideas—that the best test of truth is the power of the thought to get itself accepted in the competition of market, and that truth is the only ground upon which their wishes safely can be carried out." This, Holmes wrote, is the "theory of our Constitution"—the notion that life is an "experiment"—and his argument that citizens require increased liberty of expression in order to serve the greater social good is, to this day, the United States Supreme Court's preferred approach when assessing freedom of speech questions.

For more information: Chafee, Zechariah, Jr. *Free Speech in the United States.* Cambridge: Harvard University Press, 1967; Polenberg, Richard. *Fighting Faiths: The Abrams Case, the Supreme Court, and Free Speech.* New York: Viking, 1987.

—Brian K. Pinaire

abstention

Abstention is the principle that the federal courts should refrain from handling certain legal issues, even when they have appropriate jurisdiction, in order to prevent damaging intergovernmental relations. This concept is particularly applicable to relationships between federal courts and the states. The essence of abstention is in the guidelines that the federal courts consider when reviewing cases that impact parallel governmental processes. The guidelines help ease tensions that can develop between different levels of government. There are several types of abstention that the courts can refer to when applying the principle to a potential case. Two of these types of abstention are "Pullman abstention" and "Burford abstention."

The "Pullman abstention," developed in *Railroad Commission v. Pullman Co.,* 312 U.S. 496 (1941), holds that the federal courts, in particular circumstances, should abstain from deciding a case challenging state laws, either completely or abstaining until the state laws on the issue are clarified. As the Pullman abstention doctrine developed, it was applied in situations where the constitutionality of state law had yet to be decided. If clarification of the state laws would negate the need for the court to address the issue, the Pullman abstention was deemed appropriate. However, following *Meredith v. Winter Haven,* 320 U.S. 228 (1943), it was argued that the Pullman abstention's application may be denying a petitioner an opportunity to be heard in federal rather than state courts. Absent the exceptional circumstances mentioned in *Pullman,* abstaining under the guise of Pullman abstention may be violating a petitioner's rights.

Under the "Burford abstention," developed in *Burford v. Sun Oil Co.,* 319 U.S. 315 (1943), federal courts abstain from hearing court cases in which their review of a complicated state question might disrupt the ability of a state to establish a coherent policy on a substantial matter of public concern. The state does not have to be actively developing a policy for the Burford abstention to apply. This abstention has proven effective in several cases, keeping federal courts out of internal state disputes where neither the law nor policy is clear. Seemingly clear-cut, the Burford abstention is still as difficult to apply to a court case as Pullman abstention.

As of 2004, the FEDERAL COURT SYSTEM is in the process of merging the various forms of abstention into one standard form. The merger will help federal courts have a common guideline to follow when determining what action they should take. A currently popular view is that federal courts should avoid, whenever possible, interfering with the states on any level. Merging the various forms of abstention may allow application of the abstention doctrine to any case that may harmfully impact a state initiative.

For more information: Nash, Jonathan R. "Examining the Power of Federal Courts to Certify Questions of State Law." *Cornell Law Review* 88, no. 1627 (September 2003). Available online. URL: http://www.lexisnexis.com/universe; Norris, Daniel C. "The Final Frontier of Younger Abstention: The Judiciary's Abdication of the Federal Court Removal Jurisdiction Statute." *Florida State University Law Review* 31, no. 193 (fall 2003). Available online. URL: http://www.lexisnexis.com/universe.

—Jaeryl Covington and Anne M. Voigts

actual innocence

A persistent issue for the Supreme Court since the 1960s has been whether, and to what extent, it should matter to a court conducting federal habeas proceedings whether a state prisoner is "actually innocent." Historically, the fact that a prisoner may in fact be guilty of the crime has been irrelevant to whether he is entitled to federal review, because the concern of habeas has been whether some aspect of the prisoner's state court proceedings violated the U.S. Constitution or federal law. Beginning in the 1960s, however, some commentators and justices urged

that habeas relief be reserved only to those prisoners who could either show a colorable claim of innocence in addition to their constitutional claim or who at least presented the type of constitutional claim that "casts some shadow of doubt on [the prisoner's] guilt." While the Court to date has resisted these efforts, it has struggled with a different but related question: whether even without a valid constitutional claim "actual innocence" can be a basis for habeas relief, or should excuse an otherwise fatal bar to federal review. In doing so, the Court has also examined whether "innocence" can mean more than factual innocence of the alleged offense but can include innocence of death eligibility or innocence of habitual offender eligibility.

The Court has generally recognized only a very limited right to assert actual innocence alone as a basis for habeas relief. In *Herrera v. Collins,* 506 U.S. 390 (1992), the Court declined to let a capital prisoner present an "actual innocence" petition asserting that his now-deceased brother was the actual murderer. A majority of the justices reasoned that—while in a situation in which a "truly persuasive demonstration of actual innocence" was presented in a capital case, it may be cruel and unusual to execute that demonstrably innocent person—Herrera's belated claims about his brother did not meet this stringent standard. As a practical matter, most truly innocent prisoners are likely to tie their claims of innocence to a separate constitutional claim, and so the availability of this basis for habeas relief has rarely been tested and may be of limited practical value.

A far more significant use of "actual innocence" has developed in the context of procedural bars to habeas relief. Reform efforts since the 1970s produced a variety of limitations on the power of federal courts to review habeas petitions. Generally, a habeas petitioner must now show cause and prejudice before a court will reach the merits of a successive or abusive petition (petitions which raise the same claims repeatedly or different claims serially) or procedurally defaulted claims (i.e., claims that have been rejected in state court because the petitioner failed to comply with a rule of state procedural law). Even where a prisoner cannot meet this standard, however, the Court has carved out an exception in cases where refusing to hear the merits of the claim could result in a "miscarriage of justice." Thus, in *SCHLUP V. DELO,* 513 U.S. 298 (1994) the Court held that a prisoner who could not show cause and prejudice for not raising constitutional claims in his first federal petition was entitled to a hearing on the merits if he was able to show that this constitutional violation had "probably resulted in the conviction of one who is actually innocent." The Court also adopted a more demanding version of this standard for capital prisoners who claim that—while guilty of the underlying offense—they are innocent of the factors that would make them eligible for the death sentence. Specifically, in *Sawyer v. Whitley,* 505 U.S. 333 (1992), the

Court held that a prisoner may overcome a procedural default by showing through "clear and convincing evidence that but for a constitutional error, no reasonable juror could have found him eligible for the death penalty."

For more information: Steiker, Carol S. "Innocence and Federal Habeas." *UCLA Law Review* 41 (1993): 303, 377.

—Jeffrey Bleich

Adamson v. California, 332 U.S. 46 (1947)

In *Adamson v. California*, the Court affirmed the first-degree murder conviction of Admiral Dewey Adamson. In the process the Court upheld the ruling of an earlier decision, *Twining v. New Jersey*, 211 U.S. 78 (1908), which had held that the Fifth Amendment's guarantee against self-incrimination did not apply to the states. Adamson had not testified at his trial, and under procedures authorized by California law, the prosecuting attorney had commented to the jury on the defendant's failure to explain or deny the charges against him. Attorneys for Adamson had argued that this practice deprived him of his right against self-incrimination, in violation of both the privileges and immunities and the due process clauses of the Fourteenth Amendment.

The Court rejected the contention that the right against self-incrimination was applied to the states by either of these provisions of the Fourteenth Amendment. The privileges and immunities clause bars the states from violating "the privileges or immunities of citizens of the United States[.]" (Amendment XIV, Sec 1) Justice Reed, writing for the Court, reiterated the well established interpretation of this clause, which was based on the distinction between state and national CITIZENSHIP. Since *The Slaughter-House Cases*, 83 U.S. 36 (1873), the Court had maintained that the privileges and immunities of national citizenship were merely those contained in the Constitution, laws, or TREATIES of the United States. The Fifth Amendment includes the right against self-incrimination. However, this provision, like all of those in the BILL OF RIGHTS, was "inapplicable to similar actions done by the states." Therefore, this privilege could not be made applicable to the states by the privileges and immunities clause.

The Court also rejected the argument that the right against self-incrimination was made applicable to the states by the due process clause of the Fourteenth Amendment. Earlier decisions had concluded that some of the provisions in the Bill of Rights were made applicable to the states by the due process clause, because they were fundamental principles of liberty and justice. Based on this reasoning, the Court had concluded that the First Amendment's guarantees of freedom of speech and freedom of RELIGION did apply to the states. However, the Court had found that

when criminal proceedings were involved, the requirements of the due process clause were more flexible. They simply imposed on the states an "obligation to give a fair trial." Hence, Justice Reed reaffirmed the Court's position that the due clause did not make the Fifth Amendment's guarantee against self-incrimination applicable to the states. Furthermore, he found that the provisions of California law, which allowed both the prosecution and the court a limited right to comment on a defendant's failure to deny or explain evidence presented against him, did not deny Adamson's right to a fair trial.

This case is also noteworthy because of the lengthy dissent of Justice Hugo BLACK, which was accompanied by a 33-page appendix dealing with the history of the adoption of the Fourteenth Amendment. On the basis of his research, Black concluded that one of the chief purposes of the provisions of the amendment's first section "separately and as a whole . . . was to make the Bill of Rights applicable to the states." Black's position has never been adopted by a majority of the Court. However, the specific holding of this case was later reversed by *Malloy v. Hogan*, 378 U.S. 1 (1964), which held that the due process clause of the Fourteenth Amendment did apply the right against self-incrimination to the states.

For more information: Cortner, Richard C. *The Supreme Court and the Second Bill of Rights: The Fourteenth Amendment and the Nationalization of Civil Liberties.* Madison: The University of Wisconsin Press, 1981; Curtis, Michael Kent. *No State Shall Abridge: The Fourteenth Amendment and the Bill of Rights.* Durham, N.C.: Duke University Press, 1990.

—Justin Halpern

Adarand Constructors, Inc. v. Pena, 515 U.S. 200 (1995)

Adarand Constructors establishes that any government program, whether state or local, discriminatory or benign, that favors one group over another on the basis of race is presumptively invalid. The case is important because it signaled the Court's disagreement with economic affirmative action programs whereby governments provide an advantage to minority-owned businesses in order to remedy general past discrimination. *Adarand* does not hold that all such programs are automatically invalid; instead, these programs will be subject to STRICT SCRUTINY review, which has been described as "strict in theory, fatal in fact."

The facts of *Adarand* are relatively straightforward. The federal government issued a contract to build a highway in Colorado, which included a provision offering a monetary incentive for awarding subcontracts to minority-owned businesses. This type of provision was standard at the time in all Department of Transportation contracts. Adarand, a white male, submitted the low bid on a subcontract for guardrails but was not awarded the contract. Instead, Gonzales Construction Company, a minority-owned business, won the bidding. Because Gonzales was certified as a minority-owned—and therefore disadvantaged—business, the benefit provided by the government program made his bid the net lowest. Adarand sued, claiming that the race-based presumption in the program violated his right to equal protection and due process.

Before *Adarand,* the Court had already held that *states* could not offer benefits generally on the basis of race. Though a distinction can be made between legislation with the purpose of favoring disadvantaged races rather than discriminating against them, the Court had held that the Fourteenth Amendment guarantee of equal treatment under the law prohibits this favoritism. The Court had not held the same under the Fifth Amendment's guarantee of due process of law, which applies to the federal government. In *FULLILOVE V. KLUTZNICK,* 448 U.S. 448 (1980), the Court had in fact upheld, in a divided opinion, a 10 percent set-aside in a federal contracting provision. Relying on this PRECEDENT, both lower courts that reviewed the *Adarand* contract upheld the provision.

Justice O'CONNOR wrote the opinion for the Court. She said that previous cases had three common threads with respect to governmental racial classifications, even if the programs at issue were remedial: first, skepticism about any law treating people differently on account of race; second, consistency in strictly scrutinizing any racial classification; and third, congruence between analysis under the Fifth and Fourteenth Amendments for federal and state action. "Taken together, these three propositions lead to the conclusion that any person, of whatever race, has the right to demand that any governmental actor subject to the Constitution justify any racial classification subjecting that person to unequal treatment under the strictest judicial scrutiny." Under strict scrutiny, a racial classification will only be upheld if it is narrowly tailored to serve a compelling government interest. The Court also stated that the Fifth and Fourteenth Amendments "protect *persons,* not *groups*" because classification by groups has the potential to infringe on the *personal* right to equal protection.

Justice O'Connor did acknowledge the "unhappy persistence of both the practice and the lingering effects of RACIAL DISCRIMINATION against minority groups." Though government programs would be strictly scrutinized, they could be upheld if they were narrowly tailored to address specific evidence of past discrimination. Justice SCALIA concurred in the Court's judgment but argued that government could never justify discriminating on the basis of race in order to make up for past discrimination. "[U]nder our Constitution there is no such thing as either a creditor or debtor race. That concept is alien to the Constitution's focus upon the individual." Justice STEVENS dissented, arguing that there is a "significant difference between a decision by the majority to impose a special burden on the members of a minority race and a decision by the majority to provide a benefit to certain members of that minority notwithstanding its incidental burden on some members of the majority."

This decision did not mark the end of the controversy. *Adarand* continued in the courts long after this case was decided, bouncing between the district courts, the courts of appeal, and the Supreme Court eight times in trying to determine whether the government could in fact justify the program under strict scrutiny. In 2001, applying strict scrutiny, the COURT OF APPEALS upheld the government's revised program, which still provided some preference to minority-owned businesses, because the program was narrowly tailored to address the effects of past discrimination. However, the Supreme Court declined to hear the case, ruling that Adarand may have lacked STANDING to challenge the new regulations in place. Thus, the exact parameters of what race-based preferences are allowed under the Constitution remain unclear.

The case marks a turning point in that the Court for the first time firmly set strict scrutiny as the standard of review for all race-conscious government programs, even if those programs are remedial. *Adarand's* immediate result was to place most of the government's set-aside programs under review, and the Court made it unlikely that any federal or state government would adopt programs that offered a benefit on the basis of race, even if done in an attempt to remedy the effects of past discrimination.

For more information: Gentile, Leslie. "Giving Effect to Equal Protection: Adarand Constructors v. Pena." *Akron Law Review* 29 (Winter 1996): 397. Available online. URL: http://www.law.ucla.edu/faculty/bios/crenshaw/racerem/ contractarticles2.htm#Effect. Downloaded May 11, 2004; Ginsburg, Gilbert J., and Janine S. Benton. "One Year Later: Affirmative Action in Federal Government Contracting After Adarand." *American University Law Review* 45 (August 1996): 1,903. Available online. URL: http://www.law.ucla.edu/faculty/bios/crenshaw/racerem/ contractarticles2.htm#Year. Downloaded May 11, 2004.

—Andy Chasin

Adkins v. Children's Hospital of District of Columbia, 261 U.S. 525 (1923)

In *Adkins v. Children's Hospital of District of Columbia,* the Supreme Court struck down a law enacted by the Congress, which had established a minimum wage for children and women working in the District of Columbia. In

1918 Congress enacted the minimum wage law to address the problem of women in the workplace "receiving wages inadequate to supply them with the necessary cost of living, maintain them in health and protect their morals." The law was, according to Congress, a legitimate exercise of the broad police power.

In writing the opinion of the Court, Justice SUTHER-LAND maintained that legislation, federal or state, that regulates workers' wages violates the "freedom of contract" included in the "due process clause of the Fifth Amendment" guaranteeing "life, liberty, and property" from the arbitrary interference of government. Freedom of contract stipulates that, in general, "parties have an equal right to obtain from each other the best terms they can as the result of private bargaining." In effect, salaries are to be freely negotiated between the prospective employee and employer with no interference from government.

Despite this affirmation, Sutherland recognizes that that there is "no such thing as absolute freedom of contract." Some governmental regulation is justified by the Constitution, but "justified only by the existence of exceptional circumstances." First, it is permissible to establish fair "rates and charges" by businesses involved with the "public interest" such as regulation of grain elevator rates upheld in *MUNN V. ILLINOIS*, 94 U.S. 113 (1876). Second, governmental regulation is permitted "relating to contracts for the performance of public work." Third, laws may stipulate the "character, methods, and time for payment of wages." Fourth, statutes may set maximum hours worked as was the case in *Holden v. Hardy*, 169 U.S. 366 (1898), which upheld a Utah law that limited the number of hours worked by miners and smelters.

The first three of these exceptions do not apply to the present case according to Sutherland. However, the fourth example, setting maximum hours, comes closest to "the line of principle applicable to the statute here involved." The critical difference, the Court noted, is that the *Holden* decision upheld a legislative determination that "particular employments, when too long pursued, were injurious to the health of the employees . . ."

The Court argues that the minimum wage law under consideration has nothing to do with the health or working conditions of the employees, rather it is an all-encompassing regulation applying to all employees and all occupations. Justice Sutherland dismissed the idea that the minimum wage would provide women with a minimum standard of living since a person's cost of living depends on "individual temperament, habits of thrift, . . . and whether the woman lives alone or with her family." And finally, the Court stated, "It cannot be shown that well-paid women safeguard their morals more carefully than those who are poorly paid. Morality rests upon other considerations than wages, ..."

In concluding, Sutherland wrote that the element of the law that "perhaps more than any other" renders it invalid is its one-sided nature; the employer is required to pay a minimum wage, but the employee has no similar requirement to produce. There should be a notion of equal exchange, of equivalence, which is "The moral requirement implicit in every contract of employment, ..."

In a dissenting opinion, Chief Justice TAFT pointed out that legislatures enact minimum wage law based on the economic assumption that the employee and employer are "not upon a full level of equality" in wage negotiations. Taft believed this assumption to be reasonable and wrote that "it is not the function of this court to hold congressional acts invalid simply because they are passed to carry out economic views which the court believes to be unwise or unsound." In other words, in matters of social and economic regulation, the judiciary should defer to legislatively determined policy positions; that is, the Court should begin its deliberations with the idea that the law in question is constitutional unless proven otherwise. If a specific policy is not in violation of a "real" provision of the Constitution, the Supreme Court should not invalidate that policy simply because it does not agree with its underlying social or economic philosophy.

For more information: Friedman, Lawrence M. *A History of American Law.* New York: Simon and Schuster, 1973.

—Alex Aichinger

administrative law and decision making

The field of administrative law is a vast body of rules and regulations that govern the procedures and activities of government agencies. These rules and regulations consist of the agency charter granting the agency its power, other broader statutes that do not apply to a specific agency but which agencies must follow, court rulings, and internal rules and regulations established by the agency itself to control both its own conduct and the conduct of citizens or other entities coming under the agency's authority.

The Constitution established three branches of government, the legislative, judicial, and executive. It does refer to other elements of government but does not specifically define what those elements should be. Government agencies, however, were necessary from the birth of the nation to carry out functions of the government and conduct the day-to-day business and duties of government. Congress may have the power to make law and establish policy, but do they have the time to enforce each of those laws and policies? No. And the other two branches of government are similarly situated. They were established to deal with broad and major issues facing the nation, not the minutiae of day-to-day government function. And because there was a need for administrative agencies there also became a need for administrative law to regulate those agencies.

An example of an agency charter is the Reorganization Plan No. 3 of 1970. It was the brainchild of President Nixon and was submitted to Congress as the establishing instrument of the Environmental Protection Agency (EPA). It established the purpose and tasks of the EPA and defined what some of its broad powers would be.

The National Environmental Policy Act (NEPA) is an example of a broad policy that does not apply to a specific government agency, but which agencies must follow. Enacted in 1969, NEPA was designed to "to promote efforts which will prevent or eliminate damage to the environment" (Section 2, 42 USC § 4321). Among the many policies established by NEPA was the requirement for government agencies to create an Environmental Impact Statement whenever a governmental action may pose some risk to the environment. Since the enactment of NEPA, preparing Environmental Impact Statements in applicable situations has become a necessary duty for all government agencies.

CHEVRON INC., USA V. NATURAL RESOURCES DEFENSE COUNCIL, INC., 467 U.S. 837 (1984) is a recent example of how the courts can establish administrative law. In *Chevron* the Supreme Court held that in situations where Congress has not clearly indicated an intent that a law should apply in a particular situation, administrative agencies may exercise reasonable discretion in interpreting the law.

Administrative law prevents government agencies from running amok. It provides the regulations by which government agencies function and limits by which they must abide in dealings with the public. Without administrative law, agencies would lack the fundamental authority needed for competent decision making.

For more information: Reese, John H. *Administrative Law, Principles and Practice.* St. Paul, Minn.: West Group, 1995.

—John L. Roberts

affirmative action

Affirmative action means giving preference to members of some groups over others for admissions to universities and selection for jobs and business contracts. It is usually associated in the United States with giving preference to African Americans, but it also extends to other minority groups such as Native Americans, Hispanics, and occasionally to women, although the latter are not, strictly speaking, a minority. The original purpose of affirmative action was as a remedy for past segregation and discrimination. More recently the justification has been to enhance diversity. Not surprisingly, affirmative action has been a highly contentious issue.

The United States has a long, cruel history of RACIAL DISCRIMINATION. First came slavery, then JIM CROW LAWS and a reign of terror against blacks. Groups like the Ku Klux Klan aimed at refusing African Americans education, the right to vote, and all but the most menial of jobs. This exacted a terrible toll in terms of skill-development, self-confidence, and trust that hard work will be rewarded, to say nothing of equal opportunity. It is a toll that passed down through the generations. Affirmative action began in the early 1960s under President Kennedy as an effort to redress these evils. The idea was to create success stories, role models, and above all, hope for people who had been sorely abused.

Proponents of affirmative action argue that it has matured to include the goal of maintaining diversity. Globalization is changing everything. Proponents argue that we need to understand and get along with a greater variety of people than ever before. The 2000 census showed that the United States is more than 30 percent minority. Forty percent of public school students in the country are not classified as white. Ten percent of the population is foreign born. Fifty-six percent of college students are female. Diversity in classrooms and on the job helps Americans understand and work with people who are different, argue the defenders of affirmative action. Learning how to do that will keep the United States strong, united, and vibrant in the future. There is still effort to recover from past discrimination, but the goals are now broader—learning to put human faces on people who look different and to appreciate and work with them.

Opponents argue that affirmative action is simply reverse discrimination—that people who win admission, scholarships, jobs, and contracts *because* they belong to favored minority groups are not chosen on merit, and therefore their selection violates both the EQUAL PROTECTION CLAUSE of the Fourteenth Amendment to the UNITED STATES CONSTITUTION and also fundamental fairness. If race trumps merit, are we not back to where the nation was when discrimination was legal, only this time in reverse?

Even the question of whether affirmative action actually works is disputed. William Bowen and Derek Bok, one the former president of Harvard, the other a former president of Princeton, published a book, *The Shape of the River,* in 1998. Their research tracked 45,000 students admitted to elite colleges around the United States. They found that those admitted with the help of affirmative action had a high success rate and had more success after college than their white classmates in terms of becoming professionals, becoming active in their communities, and emerging as leaders. Opponents retort that this success came because the elite schools admitted and gave financial support mostly to middle- and upper-class blacks over more qualified whites.

The first affirmative action case decided by the Supreme Court, *REGENTS OF THE UNIVERSITY OF CALIFORNIA V. BAKKE* (1978) shows how divisive this issue can be. Four justices voted to uphold affirmative action while four voted to declare it unconstitutional. The fifth vote and deciding opinion by Justice POWELL upheld affirmative action as long as it is only one consideration for admissions, there is no quota or set number of seats reserved for minorities, and each applicant gets individualized attention. Remarkably, since *Bakke* was decided, the number of minorities enrolled in colleges has risen by 85 percent. Defenders also point to our achievements as a nation. When the Supreme Court rejected segregated schools in *BROWN V. BOARD OF EDUCATION* in 1954, between 5 and 10 percent of blacks were considered middle class. Only 50 years later that number is well over 50 percent. Affirmative action was an enormous help.

Opponents, on the other hand, argue that affirmative action has been a failure in most regards. It has increased the resentment of those who have been rejected for admissions, contracts, or employment opportunities, thereby increasing rather than decreasing racial tensions. It has placed a cloud of suspicion over the heads of those minorities who were actually admitted or employed strictly on the basis of merit, and it implants the seeds of doubt as to whether minorities are somehow inferior and could not succeed if the playing field were level.

At the heart of the affirmative action debate is the issue of "merit," but even this is not an easy issue. Merit is usually a primary consideration in hiring or admissions, but has rarely been the only consideration. Most proponents of affirmative action would agree that no one should ever be hired or admitted who does not have the qualifications to succeed, but they consider two additional facts: (a) merit is extremely difficult to predict or measure. For example, very few first round draft choices ever play in a Super Bowl and a high percentage of top CEOs were C students. Determining merit, whether in sports, business, or academia, is just sophisticated guesswork. (b) Individual merit is not, and never has been, the only consideration for admissions. For example, of all the elite schools in the nation none come closer to racial quotas than the military academies. They are unapologetic. Since 28 percent of Air Force and 44 percent of Army enlisted personnel are racial minorities, commanders know they need an integrated officer corps to build morale and trust. It is smart to have good relationships with people who carry big guns.

There is also the "affirmative action" given to children of alumni, donors, and athletes. Some colleges that are 60 percent female are now taking affirmative action to admit men. Businesses are noted for hiring the sons, daughters, and other relatives of their owners. Whatever else one might say, these are not of themselves merit based.

Protesters rally in front of the Supreme Court in support of affirmative action. *(Private collection)*

In 2003 the Supreme Court issued an authoritative statement on affirmative action in two cases, *GRUTTER V. BOLLINGER* and *GRATZ V. BOLLINGER,* both dealing with admissions policies at the University of Michigan. The Court upheld the law school's admissions policy because it took race into consideration as one of a number of factors but gave it no particular numerical weight and required individualized consideration of all applicants. The Court declared the undergraduate admissions policy unconstitutional because it assigned 20 out of a total of 150 points exclusively for racial minorities. Significantly, Justice O'CONNOR, writing for the majority in *Grutter,* agreed that affirmative action could not go on indefinitely and seemed to give a 25-year time frame to end it.

For more information: Bowen, William G., and Derek Bok. *The Shape of the River.* Princeton, N.J.: Princeton University Press, 1998; Babkina, A. M. *Affirmative Action: An Annotated Bibliography.* New York: Nova Science, 2003; Beckwith, Francis J., and Todd E. Jones, eds. *Affirmative Action: Social Justice or Reverse Discrimination?* Boston: Prometheus, 1997; Skrentny, John D. *Ironies of Affirmative Action.* Chicago: University of Chicago Press, 1996.

—Paul J. Weber

Afroyim v. Rusk, 387 U.S. 253 (1967)

In *Afroyim v. Rusk,* the Supreme Court held that Congress had no right to pass a law which had the effect of depriving an American of CITIZENSHIP without the citizen's voluntary and specific intent to renounce U.S. citizenship. Noting the special bond between Americans and their government, the Court overturned an earlier decision,

Perez v. Brownell, 356 U.S. 44 (1958), and held that only citizens themselves may voluntarily relinquish their citizenship, and that this principle applies equally to natural and naturalized citizens.

After immigrating to the United States from Poland in 1912, Beys Afroyim became a naturalized American citizen in 1926. He moved to Israel in 1950 and voted in that country's 1951 governmental elections. Afroyim applied for renewal of his U.S. passport in 1960, but the State Department refused on the grounds that he had forfeited his American citizenship by virtue of Section 401(e) of the 1940 Nationality Act, which stipulates that citizens of the United States shall "lose" their citizenship upon voting in a foreign state's political elections. Afroyim challenged the constitutionality of Section 401(e) and sued the State Department. On APPEAL from a district court's SUMMARY JUDGMENT favoring Secretary of State Dean Rusk, the Second Circuit COURT OF APPEALS affirmed. The Supreme Court granted Afroyim certiorari and ruled (5-4) that he was still a U.S. citizen.

The basic point of the Supreme Court's ruling in *Afroyim* was that the Fourteenth Amendment to the U.S. Constitution, which originally guaranteed citizenship to freed slaves and their descendants, effectively elevated citizenship to the status of a constitutionally protected right. Hence, a section of the Immigration and Nationality Act mandating automatic loss of citizenship for voting in a foreign election was invalid. Likewise, similar provisions for loss of citizenship, such as serving in a foreign army or swearing allegiance to a foreign country, were similarly invalid unless the action was accompanied by intent to give up U.S. citizenship.

The Supreme Court decision also pointed to a proposed (but never ratified) constitutional amendment, early in the 19th century, which would have revoked the U.S. citizenship of anyone who accepted a foreign title or gift, as proof that Congress was not believed at that time to have the power to do such a thing by means of ordinary legislation.

The *Afroyim* ruling did not definitively throw out all prohibitions against dual citizenship in the United States. Although the court clearly stated that loss of citizenship required the individual's consent, some uncertainty remained as to whether an actual swearing of allegiance to a foreign country would, by itself, constitute consent. This ambiguity is highlighted in debate regarding the recent draft legislation for the *Domestic Security Enhancement Act* (informally known as PATRIOT II), the proposed sequel to the *2001 USA PATRIOT Act*. Section 501 of the draft bill, titled "Expatriation of Terrorists," would allow the presumptive denationalization of an American citizen if, with the intent to relinquish nationality, an American citizen becomes a member of, or provides material support to, a group that the United States has designated as a terrorist organization, or if that group is engaged in hostilities against the United States.

The court also did not address the issue of what standard of proof would be required in citizenship cases—i.e., whether intent to give up citizenship had to be proved clearly and convincingly (as in a criminal trial), or by a preponderance of evidence (as in a lawsuit). Nor did *Afroyim* deal with Congress's right to require new citizens to renounce their prior allegiances as a prerequisite for naturalization.

For more information: Schuck, Peter H. *Citizens, Strangers, and In-Betweens.* Boulder, Colo.: Westview, 1998.

—Greg Brown

age discrimination

Age discrimination means denying an individual one or more of the rights guaranteed by the U.S. Constitution and state constitutions solely because of his or her age. Complaints of this nature most commonly originate in employment situations.

The American concept of government protecting individuals from discrimination originated in the Fifth and Fourteenth Amendments to the U.S. Constitution, both of which guarantee all individuals "equal protection of the laws."

The federal Civil Rights Law, U.S. Code, Title 42, Chapter 21, TITLE VII (hereinafter, "Title VII") contains provisions that specifically prohibit: private employers with at least 15 employees; the federal and state governments and all of their departments, agencies, bureaus, and offices; and local governmental units, such as county, parish, city, town, and village governments and their agencies, from discriminating against employees and applicants for employment because of individual characteristics such as age, race, creed, color, national origin, military status, or sex.

Another federal law, the 1967 Age Discrimination in Employment Act (hereinafter, "ADEA,"), 29 U.S.C. §§621 and 622, prohibits each governmental or private employer with at least 20 employees from discriminating against employees and applicants who are at least 40 years old (hereinafter, "age 40-plus"). ADEA prohibits an employer from discriminating against workers of age 40-plus and favoring those who are younger than 40. Additionally, the U.S. Supreme Court has interpreted ADEA as prohibiting discrimination among 40-plus employees, such as the hiring of a 40-year-old individual in preference to one who is 50 years old. Additional ADEA provisions prohibit employers from discriminating against older employees and applicants in help-wanted advertising, interviewing, hiring, compensating, promoting, disciplining, demoting, training, and terminating employees, job evaluations, and job assignments.

In cases dealing with employment discrimination of various kinds, the Supreme Court has noted that race is a "SUSPECT CLASSIFICATION" under the EQUAL PROTECTION CLAUSE contained in the Fifth and Fourteenth Amendments to the U.S. Constitution. Hence, the Constitution provides absolute protection from RACIAL DISCRIMINATION, preventing an employer from ever having a valid reason to justify racial discrimination. However, the U.S. Supreme Court has also held that unlike race, age, gender, RELIGION, and national origin are not suspect classifications, with the result that these traits are not absolutely protected by the U.S. Constitution.

Hence, when considering alleged violations of the ADEA, a court may find that an employer had a legitimate reason to discriminate on the basis of age. For instance, age discrimination may be legitimate if the very nature of the job requires the individual to be a member of a certain age group. Finally, the U.S. Supreme Court has held that it is possible for an employer to adequately demonstrate the existence of a legitimate reason to discriminate on the basis of age without matching age distinctions and the legitimate interests they serve with razor-like precision. The federal Older Workers Benefit Protection Act (hereinafter, "OWBPA"), 29 U.S.C. § 623, prohibits employers from discriminating against employees who are at least 40 years old with regard to the benefit and retirement plans available to them. Under this law, an employer cannot reduce health or life insurance benefits for older employees. OWBPA also protects individuals who choose to work past the previously common retirement age of 65 by requiring accrual of pension benefits until an employee actually retires. This provision prevents an employer from economizing by automatically cutting off pension accrual when an employee reaches age 65. Additionally, OWBPA contains provisions requiring seniority-based layoffs in most instances where layoffs are necessary. Without this provision, employers seeking to reduce their costs might be tempted to lay off older employees first, because older employees have usually worked for an employer for a longer time period than their younger counterparts and are generally paid more than younger employees because of their experience at the job.

OWBPA prohibits employers from cutting their costs by forcing higher-paid older employees to take early retirement. Under the law, an employer may encourage an employee's early retirement only by offering the employee an opportunity to choose between taking early retirement under a plan that would provide better benefits than the employee would receive under the employer's regular, non-early retirement plan; and refusing early retirement in order to continue working in his or her current position with the same benefit package he or she currently has. For instance, an employer's offer of early retirement would not meet the requirements of the OWBPA if one of the choices offered to the employee would provide less compensation or reduce benefits to a level lower than that provided by the employee's current salary and benefits package.

The Equal Employment Opportunity Commission (EEOC), created by 42 U.S.C. §2000-e, is responsible for interpreting and enforcing the Age Discrimination in Employment Act and Title VII of the Civil Rights Act of 1965 and for following the detailed guidelines and enforcement procedures created by 29 C.F.R. Pt. 1614.

Most states have enacted laws that mirror the salient provisions of the federal ADEA and OWBPA, with one major difference: The state laws are applicable to much smaller businesses. On average, the state employment discrimination laws apply to businesses with five or more employees, while the federal laws apply only to businesses with 20 or more employees. A few of the state employment discrimination laws protect workers of all ages, thereby prohibiting discrimination not only against older individuals but also against youths.

For more information: Nolo. "Age Discrimination in Employment." Nolo's Online Legal Encyclopedia. Available online. URL: http://www.nolo.com/lawcenter/ency/article.cfm/objectID/1DB0BA4D-38DC-41A0-A52E8F9ED-31E803E/catID/57153B2E-F39E-48DA-830ADA31F5A23325; Woodruff, Bryan. "Unprotected until Forty: The Limited Scope of Age Discrimination in the Employment Act of 1967," *Indiana Law Journal* 73, no. 1295 (1998).

—Beth S. Swartz
—Carrie A. Schneider

Alabama v. Shelton, 535 U.S. 654 (2002)

In *Alabama v. Shelton* a divided Supreme Court significantly expanded the Sixth Amendment right to counsel. In the 5-4 decision the Court ruled that suspended sentences cannot be imposed upon a defendant if the state did not provide the defendant with counsel at trial.

The Sixth Amendment to the UNITED STATES CONSTITUTION states that "in all criminal prosecutions, the accused shall enjoy the right to have . . . the Assistance of Counsel for his defense." In *Johnson v. Zerbst* (1938), the Supreme Court reaffirmed the right to counsel in federal proceedings. The landmark decision of *GIDEON V. WAINWRIGHT* (1963) extended the right to counsel to the states. Indigent defendants accused of felonies were entitled to state-appointed counsel. The ruling in *Shelton* is a further attempt by the Supreme Court to define what is meant by the Sixth Amendment right to counsel.

LeReed Shelton represented himself in an Alabama criminal trial. The court warned Shelton several times about the difficulties associated with self-representation, but at no time did the court offer Shelton state-appointed counsel. Shelton was convicted of a misdemeanor and sentenced to 30 days in jail. The sentence was subsequently suspended and Shelton was placed on two years probation. Justice GINSBURG delivered the opinion of the Supreme Court in which STEVENS, O'CONNOR, SOUTER, and BREYER joined. The Supreme Court found that a suspended sentence that may end up in imprisonment cannot be imposed upon a defendant if the state did not provide the defendant with counsel at trial. This significantly expanded the Court's previous decisions. The Court relied heavily on *Argersinger v. Hamilton* (1972) and *Scott v. Illinois* (1979). In *Argersinger,* the Court found that the right to counsel extended to all proceedings, misdemeanor and felony, that could lead to imprisonment. In *Scott,* the Court ruled that counsel is not required when a defendant's punishment is a fine, but only when the defendant's sentence is imprisonment. Accordingly, the Court found in *Shelton* that the Sixth Amendment does not allow the later activation of a suspended sentence when the defendant was not provided counsel at the trial where the sentence was imposed. If the suspended sentence was activated, the defendant would in actuality be incarcerated for the original offense although he or she did not have a lawyer at the trial. He or she would be facing actual imprisonment for the crime that was committed.

The dissent believed that the Court's ruling placed an undue burden on the states. Writing for the dissent, SCALIA found that the threat of imprisonment does not entitle a defendant to counsel. Several states were affected by the Court's ruling in *Shelton.* At the time of the ruling, 16 states did not provide counsel for a defendant facing the threat of imprisonment.

For more information: "Leading Cases: I. Constitutional Law: Sixth Amendment—Right to Appointed Counsel for Suspended Sentences." *Harvard Law Review* 116 (November 2002): 252–262.

alienage

The condition or state of being an alien. An alien is any person who is not a citizen or a national of the country of residence. Aliens are divided into two classes: immigrants, who are permanent residents, and nonimmigrants, who may have entered the country legally or illegally.

The UNITED STATES CONSTITUTION does not provide any rights for would-be aliens who have not entered the country. In cases such as *Knauff v. Shaughnessy* (1950) and *Shaughnessy v. United States ex rel. Mezei* (1953), the Supreme Court has ruled that Congress has full rights to disallow individuals from entering the country, especially when there were security concerns. Aliens who have not

entered the country may be denied entry without a hearing and do not have the right to contest that decision in court. Congress passes legislation about whom to allow entry into the country based on race, religious beliefs, economic needs of the country, social and cultural influences, foreign policy, and other factors deemed necessary for consideration. In *Nishimura Ekiu v. United States* (1892) the Supreme Court upheld Congress's right to determine immigration policy.

Legal nonimmigrant aliens include tourists, diplomats, students, and businessmen. Once they are in the United States, the Constitution partially protects their rights, including their right to due process. All persons located under U.S. jurisdiction have equal protection afforded by the Fifth Amendment. Their rights are also protected by international law. Nonimmigrant aliens may have restrictions placed on them, such as labor constraints and travel restrictions. They may be deported at the discretion of Congress.

Undocumented aliens, also known as ILLEGAL ALIENS, may enter the country illegally with either the intention to stay permanently or return to their home country or may enter the country legally but later violate the terms of their visa. In *Wong Wing v. United States* (1896) and in *Mathews v. Diaz* (1976) the Supreme Court ruled that the rights of undocumented aliens are protected under the Fifth and Fourteenth Amendments to the Constitution.

Congress also passes legislation about who may become a citizen. The basic requirements are five years residency, a CITIZENSHIP test, and a loyalty oath. Congress may restrict citizenship based on any number of factors. For example, until 1943 Chinese aliens were not eligible for naturalization. However, the Court ruled in *Wong Kim Ark v. United States* (1898) that any person born on U.S. soil is automatically a U.S. citizen, despite their parentage.

Resident aliens are eligible for naturalization. They are bound by all the laws of the United States including payment of taxes and, if called, service in the armed forces. They also have some rights to participate in American politics and are granted equal protection for employment and education. They are not, however, granted some of the privileges of citizens, including the right to vote or protection by the American government while traveling abroad. In several cases the Supreme Court has also ruled that Congress has the right to deport resident aliens for unlawful activities.

For more information: Hull, Elizabeth. *Without Justice for All: The Constitutional Rights of Aliens.* Westport, Conn.: Greenwood Press, 1985; LeMay, Michael, and Elliott R. Barkan, eds. *U.S. Immigration and Naturalization Laws and Issues: A Documentary History.* Westport, Conn.: Greenwood Press, 1999.

—Mariya Chernyavskaya

Allegheny County v. ACLU, 492 U.S. 573 (1989)

Allegheny County v. ACLU was a very fragmented decision dealing with the interpretation of the ESTABLISHMENT CLAUSE of the First Amendment by applying the endorsement test instead of the coercion test to allow religious symbols on public property if they are "secularized" or "pluralized."

The case of *Allegheny County v. ACLU Greater Pittsburgh Chapter*, 492 U.S. 573 (1989), and its companion case, *Chabad v. ACLU Greater Pittsburgh Chapter*, was argued on February 22, 1989, and decided on July 3, 1989. The case began when several private individuals and the Greater Pittsburgh Chapter of the American Civil Liberties Union (ACLU) sued the City of Pittsburgh and the County of Allegheny over two separate Christmas holiday displays claiming that the displays were violating the First Amendment ban against establishing a religion (see RELIGION, PUBLIC DISPLAYS OF).

The first display was a crèche in the Allegheny County Courthouse in a very prominent position on the "grand staircase" in full public display. The crèche was a familiar nativity scene that included figures of the Holy Family and of animals, shepherds, and an angel bearing a huge banner with the words *"Gloria in Excelsis Deo!"* emblazoned on it. Poinsettias were also placed in front and beside the crèche. The crèche had been donated by a Roman Catholic organization, the Holy Name Society. It was there by permission of the county government and without any governmental financial aid.

The second display was in another building, jointly owned by the county and the City of Pittsburgh, and was located a block away. This display included a 45-foot-tall Christmas tree, an 18-foot-tall Hanukkah menorah donated by Chabad Jewish organization of the Lubavitcher Hasidim (an ultraorthodox branch of Judaism), as part of its missionary work. There was also a sign that was put there by the mayor proclaiming a "Salute to Liberty." Beneath the motto the sign stated: "During this holiday season the City of Pittsburgh salutes liberty. Let these festive lights remind us that we are the keepers of the flame of liberty and our legacy of freedom."

The basic issue was did these displays have the effect of endorsing religion? The opinions of the justices were divided and hostile, demonstrating that the Court was struggling with the issue of displays of religious symbols on public property. The majority of the Court decided that the crèche inside the courthouse was an open endorsement of Christianity in violation of the establishment clause.

Justice Harry BLACKMUN announced the judgment and read the opinion of the Court, with Justice Sandra Day O'CONNOR concurring in part, Justices William J. BRENNAN and John Paul STEVENS concurring in part and dissenting in part, Justice Anthony KENNEDY concurring in part and dissenting in part. They voted 5-4 to strike the crèche and 6-3 to uphold the menorah. Blackmun's opinion declared the nativity scene to be unlike the crèche in the case of *LYNCH V. DONNELLY*, 465 U.S. 668 (1984), because there was nothing to deflect its religious message. In the *Lynch* case the city of Pawtucket, Rhode Island, annually erected a Christmas display in the city's shopping district. The display included such objects as a Santa Claus house, a Christmas tree, a banner reading "Seasons Greetings," and a nativity scene. The presence of plastic reindeer created the "plastic reindeer rule" for secularity in Christmas displays. However, the location of the crèche in the Allegheny County Courthouse was in effect an open endorsement of the Christmas message. The menorah, the Court held, in company with the other symbols of religious plurality and secularity, emphasized the secular side of the holiday, which the city could freely celebrate.

Justice O'Connor's concurring opinion wanted to use a "non-endorsement" rule for deciding the issue. This would be, she claimed, an improvement over the *Lemon test* [*LEMON V. KURTZMAN*, 403 U.S. 602 (1971)], where to avoid violating the establishment clause a law has to have a secular purpose, with its primary effect to neither advance nor hinder religion, and also avoid excessive entanglement between church and state. The justices found it difficult to apply this rule to the current case. Justice Kennedy, in dissent, wanted to apply a non-coercion test—unless forced to participate or believe then the establishment clause was not violated by the crèche or like displays.

For more information: Berg, Thomas C. *The State and Religion in a Nutshell.* St. Paul, Minn.: West Group, 1998; Flowers, Ronald B. *That Godless Court?: Supreme Court Decisions on Church-State Relationships.* Louisville, Ky.: Westminster John Knox Press, 1994.

—A. J. L. Waskey

Allgeyer v. Louisiana, 165 U.S. 578 (1897)

Allgeyer v. Louisiana, held that state law could be invalidated on the basis of the doctrine of SUBSTANTIVE DUE PROCESS. This case is important because it served as a direct precursor to a set of decisions, including *LOCHNER V. NEW YORK*, 198 U.S. 45 (1905), that set the Court against legislative bodies. The precursors to *Allgeyer* included the dissenters in the *Slaughter-House Cases*, 83 U.S. 36 (1873) and the majority who hinted at the power of courts to veto legislation based on substantive due process in *Mugler v. Kansas*, 123 U.S. 623 (1887).

The case began when the Louisiana legislature passed a law prohibiting obtaining property insurance from any insurance company not fully complying with Louisiana law. Allgeyer was convicted of violating this law. The United

States Supreme Court reversed lower courts, holding that the statute violated the Fourteenth Amendment ". . . in that it deprives the defendants of their liberty without due process of law." Judge Peckham delivered the opinion for a unanimous court.

Peckham and the Court developed the concept of "LIBERTY OF CONTRACT" in this opinion. Peckham noted that:

The liberty mentioned in that amendment [Fourteenth Amendment] means not only the right of the citizen to be free from the mere physical restraint of his person, as by incarceration, but the term is deemed to embrace the right of the citizen to be free in the enjoyment of all his faculties; to be free to use them in all lawful ways; to live and work where he will; to earn his livelihood by any lawful calling; to pursue any livelihood or avocation, and for that purpose to enter into any contracts which may be proper, necessary, and essential to his carrying out to a successful conclusion of the purposes above mentioned.

The specific holding of the Court with respect to insurance companies is not particularly important. The critical importance of this decision is its explicit enunciation of the principle of substantive due process through the medium of "liberty of contract." In future cases, this would serve to authorize courts to strike down state legislation aimed at regulating business and commerce. The state's police power would now be questioned by the courts under this doctrine. In the process, the Supreme Court began to substitute its judgment on the legitimacy and wisdom of public policy for that of the legislature.

For more information: Warren, Charles. "The New 'Liberty' under the Fourteenth Amendment." *Harvard Law Review* 39 (1926): 431.

—Steven A. Peterson

Ambach v. Norwich, 441 U.S. 68 (1979)

In *Ambach v. Norwich* the Supreme Court ruled that state laws preventing aliens who do not intend to become U.S. citizens from obtaining permanent teaching certificates do not violate the EQUAL PROTECTION CLAUSE of the Fourteenth Amendment.

Susan Norwich, a citizen of Great Britain, and Tarja Dachinger, a Finnish citizen, both resident aliens, were denied permanent teaching certificates because they consistently refused to obtain United States CITIZENSHIP. The two filed suit and won when the District Court ruled that the New York law violates the equal protection clause.

In the Court's opinion, Justice POWELL utilized the "rational-basis standard" from *Sugarman v. Dougall,* 413 U.S. 634 (1973), to explain that states have a right to disal-

low employment of noncitizens. The state has that right if it can show that there was a "rational relationship" between limiting employment to citizens and the interest that is protected by such limitation. Such restrictions apply to positions that "go to the heart of representative government." The Court based its decision on the PRECEDENT set in *Foley v. Connelie,* 435 U.S. 291 (1978), that New York had the right to not hire aliens for its police force because the nature of the job gives police "substantial discretionary powers." Justice Powell contended that public education does indeed fall under those types of jobs that are integral to a democratic government because education prepares individuals to become participating citizens and fill an integral role in preserving the values of society. Teachers play such a vital part in developing students that they directly influence individuals' attitudes and values. Therefore, the state has a valid interest in preventing noncitizens from becoming public school teachers. Because both appellees chose not to be naturalized and retained loyalty to their original country, there is a rational relationship between the state's interest and its limitations on the rights of aliens.

Justice BLACKMUN wrote a vigorous dissent. He examined the fact that the Court has ruled in favor of many resident aliens who were denied employment simply because they were not citizens and claimed that *Foley* was an exception. Instead, he thought that *In re Grifiths,* 413 U.S. 717 (1973), in which a lawyer from the Netherlands was allowed to practice law even though he refused to be naturalized, was more applicable to the case than *Foley.* Most of all he criticized the logic of the state's argument when he pointed out that individuals not eligible to obtain U.S. citizenship are allowed to be certified and that aliens are allowed to sit on local school boards.

As an ALIENAGE case *Ambach v. Norwick* influenced the decision in *PLYLER V. DOE,* 457 U.S. 202 (1982), which dealt with a Texas alienage law limiting the rights of undocumented alien primary and secondary school students. The law withheld funds from public school districts for the education of such students and gave local school districts the power to deny enrollment to undocumented alien children. The Court declared this law unconstitutional. Justice BRENNAN referred to *Ambach,* to support his position that education is a fundamental component of American society and denial of education to ILLEGAL ALIENS undermines society. In a higher education case, *Toll v. Moreno,* 458 U.S. 1 (1982), Justice Blackmun referred to *Ambach* to argue that while the differences between resident aliens and citizens are small, resident aliens should continue to be a "suspect class."

The most significant issue raised by this case is not alienage, however, but the role of public schools in a democratic society. Specifically, cases dealing with students' rights have often cited *Ambach.* The cases have been diverse, dealing with the establishment clause, freedom of speech, and equal protection. In *Board of Education of Westside Community School v. Mergens*, 496 U.S. 226 (1990), the Court ruled in favor of a federal law which allowed religious student groups to meet on school grounds during noninstructional times. In HAZELWOOD SCHOOL DISTRICT V. KUHLMEIER, 484 U.S. 260 (1988), the Supreme Court ruled that a high school principal can censor a school-sponsored student newspaper if he finds the material objectionable. Despite the holding, the Court cited *Ambach* to support students' right to expression as a "fundamental value necessary to the maintenance of a democratic political system. . . ." In all cases the Court referred to *Ambach* to reiterate the point that "[Public] schools are vitally important . . . as vehicles for inculcating fundamental values necessary to the maintenance of a democratic political system."

For more information: Boyd, Tamara M. "Keeping the Constitution's Promise: An Argument for Greater Judicial Scrutiny of Federal Alienage Classifications," *Stanford Law Review* 54, no. 319 (2001).

—Mariya Chernyavskaya

Anderson v. Celebrezze, 460 U.S. 780 (1983)

In this case, the Supreme Court struck down an Ohio law requiring independent candidates for president to register as such by mid-March. The law was challenged because the major parties were not required to declare their presidential nominees until midsummer (when their conventions had finished).

John Anderson ran as an independent candidate for president in 1980. He encountered one important hurdle however: The 50 states had different deadlines for submitting petitions and filing registration paper work for an independent presidential candidacy. Ohio required independent candidates to do this in March, even though the nominees of the two major parties would not be chosen till much later—via the Ohio primary and, ultimately, their respective nominating conventions. Anderson challenged the early filing requirement, arguing that it unconstitutionally infringed upon the First Amendment rights of candidates such as himself and his supporters.

The Supreme Court had to balance several competing rights claims. On the one hand, the Court noted that unjustified or unfair restrictions on independent or third-party candidates affected the speech rights of the candidates themselves and diminished the quality of the franchise to the extent that restrictions on candidacy limited the breadth of election day choices presented to the electorate. On the other hand, the court recognized as well that the franchise embodied the right to participate in an orderly, meaningful electoral process. If the process were confusing or disorderly, the vote would be diminished. Thus, the court noted:

> We have recognized that, "as a practical matter, there must be a substantial regulation of elections if they are to be fair and honest and if some sort of order, rather than chaos, is to accompany the democratic processes." To achieve these necessary objectives, States have enacted comprehensive and sometimes complex election codes. Each provision of these schemes, whether it governs the registration and qualifications of voters, the selection and eligibility of candidates, or the voting process itself, inevitably affects—at least to some degree—the individual's right to vote and his right to associate with others for political ends. Nevertheless, the State's important regulatory interests are generally sufficient to justify reasonable, nondiscriminatory restrictions.

In this case, however, the Court ruled that the early filing requirement for independent candidates violated the Constitution. While Ohio claimed that the early filing requirement was necessary to ensure political stability and keep the ballot clear of frivolous candidates, the Court ruled that the early filing requirement amounted to little more than an attempt by the Democrats and Republicans to suppress political competition. Insofar as Democrats and Republicans would not officially nominate their presidential candidates until July or August, the Court ruled that there was no justification for requiring other parties and candidates to complete their nomination processes five months in advance.

In their dissent, Justices REHNQUIST, WHITE, POWELL, and O'CONNOR saw the case in a different light. Was Anderson an aggrieved independent candidate or was he simply a "sore loser"? Thus, the dissents saw nothing unconstitutional about the challenged Ohio statute's essentially requiring all presidential aspirants to make a choice by March 20:

> the effect of the Ohio filing deadline is quite easily summarized: it requires that a candidate, who has already decided to run for President, decide by March 20 which route his candidacy will take. He can become a nonparty candidate by filing a nominating petition with 5,000 signatures and assure himself a place on the general election ballot. Or he can become a party candidate and take his chances in securing a position on the general election ballot by seeking the nomination of a party's national convention.

Viewed in this respect, the dissenters did not see any discrimination among political parties. Instead, they saw only a rule that required any candidate to decide which route he or she would use to pursue the presidential nomination.

Anderson thus raises important questions about the fairness of ballot access provisions. Cases such as *Anderson* confront the Court with the tension embodied in the fact that such restrictions are passed by legislatures comprised of the major parties and frequently work to the disadvantage of minor parties.

For more information: *Burdick v. Takushi*, 504 U.S. 428 (1992); *Timmons v. Twin Cities Area New Party*, 520 U.S. 351 (1997).

—Mark Rush

anonymous political speech

Anonymity has a long history in the American political tradition. Indeed, "Publius," the chosen pseudonym of James Madison, Alexander Hamilton, and John Jay, was the central advocate for the proposed Constitution during the debates over ratification in New York. The political pamphlet—whether affixed to lampposts or distributed on street corners—has historically been the chosen mode of expression for groups that desire to contribute to public debate. And, more recently, a prominent satire on modern presidential campaigns—the novel *Primary Colors*—was authored by "Anonymous."

Whether chosen for rhetorical purposes, or out of fear of reprisal, anonymity remains an option for political advocates due to the United States Supreme Court's decision in *McIntyre v. Ohio Elections Commission*, 514 U.S. 334 (1995). In this case, which involved a politically active mother distributing fliers in opposition to a proposed tax levy outside a school board meeting, the Court struck an Ohio law (as well as the laws of 48 states and the federal government) that required that a name and business address be included on all literature distributed in an electoral context. Writing for the Court, Justice Stevens portrayed Margaret McIntyre as just the latest entrant to a long line of dissidents, artists, and advocates who relied on anonymity to express themselves and whose speech would be unconstitutionally "chilled" were the state able to enforce such disclosure requirements.

But the dissenters in the *McIntyre* case, Justice Scalia and Chief Justice Rehnquist, vigorously stressed the competing social interests in question, arguing that the central issue was *society's* right to consider the range of available information, especially when voting on questions of public consequence. Furthermore, one need look no further than the state of modern political campaigns to see the scurrilousness that stems from a lack of accountability, both in terms of ads paid for by organizations with ambiguous, even cryptic, names and in situations where "anonymous

sources" routinely leak information that damages reputations and, arguably, sullies our political experience.

What degree of anonymity is, therefore, appropriate in our political life? Certainly anonymity is an essential feature of many of our political practices: Consider, for example, the fact that we vote in secret, self-contained booths and that we can, generally, write unsigned "letters to the editor," expressing our frustration with local officials. By contrast, within the domain of campaign finance, the United States Supreme Court has long held that the donor's interest in anonymity is not sufficient to outweigh the public's interest in knowing who is funding particular causes and candidates and the state's interest in regulating financial contributions. At what point does the individual's interest in expression yield to the public's interest in disclosure?

One forum where we are likely to see this tug-of-war take place on a grand scale is the Internet. The physical dimensions of a flier or leaflet bring with them certain assurances: The message can only be communicated as far as the paper can be distributed. Anonymity, under these conditions, increases in significance with changing technology: Publius' initial audience was limited to readers of the newspaper; Margaret McIntyre could reach only those exiting the school board meeting; but, with technology that can transport messages, postings, and "chat" around the world in a matter of seconds, suddenly anonymous political speech has, in the blink of an eye, a decidedly global *reach*. How will courts and communities respond to anonymous political speech in the future and how will changing technologies service this mode of expression?

For more information: DuVal, Benjamin. "Note and Comment: The Constitutional Right to Anonymity: Free Speech, Disclosure and the Devil." *Yale Law Journal* 70 (1961): 1084; Wieland, Jennifer. "Note: Death of Publius: Toward a World Without Anonymous Speech." *Journal of Law & Politics* 17 (Summer 2001): 589.

—Brian K. Pinaire

antitrust law

Antitrust law is derived from federal and state statutes that promote commercial competition and protect trade and commerce from monopolies, price fixing, price discriminations, and unlawful restraints. Federal antitrust law is articulated principally in the Sherman Act (1890), the Clayton Act (1914), the Federal Trade Commission Act (1914), and the Robinson-Patman Act (1936). Congressional authority to legislate these acts is found in Article I, Section 8 of the United States Constitution in which Congress is authorized to regulate commerce with foreign nations and between states.

The Sherman Act outlaws all contracts, combinations, and conspiracies that unreasonably restrain trade between states or with foreign nations. Included in the act's prohibitions are competitors' agreements to fix prices and allocate customers. The Sherman Act also forbids monopolizing any part of INTERSTATE COMMERCE. The Sherman Act prohibits a monopoly as defined as the power to exclude competition in the market by means other than business acumen or producing a superior product.

The Clayton Act outlawed specific practices designed to monopolize markets including price discrimination, and exclusive agreements, tying contracts, mergers, and interlocking directorates. The Clayton Act was designed to correct flaws of the Sherman Act. Clayton cleared up vague wording about what constitutes a monopoly as well as making practices that give rise to monopolies illegal.

The Federal Trade Commission Act was designed to prevent unfair competition methods and unfair or deceptive acts that may affect business commerce. Violation of the Federal Trade Commission Act can usually be proved by demonstrating fraud, oppression, violation of public policy, or bad faith. To supplement Federal Trade Commission regulations, many states have enacted antitrust laws to prevent strain on competition. The federal laws apply to foreign and interstate commerce, while the state laws apply to activities taking place within state borders. Congress's goal in passing the FTCA was to protect consumers from unfair methods of competition. According to the act, unfair or deceptive methods of business need only have the likelihood of deceiving the consumer. Actual deception does not have to take place. Businesses may also be liable for the unfair and deceptive acts of its employees, representatives, or agents.

The Robinson-Patman Act was passed by Congress as a supplement to the Clayton Act. The act forbade any person or firm engaged in interstate commerce to discriminate in price to different purchasers of the same commodity when the effect would be to inhibit competition or create a monopoly. The Robinson-Patman Act was aimed at protecting independent retailers from chain stores but was strongly supported by wholesalers hoping to prevent large chains from buying directly from the manufacturers for lower prices.

Supreme Court rulings in antitrust law cases normally have not focused on the constitutionality of antitrust acts. For the most part the Court has attempted to determine how and when the laws entailed in the acts should be applied. Examples of this approach are found in the cases of UNITED STATES V. E. C. KNIGHT COMPANY, 156 U.S. 1 (1895), SWIFT V. UNITED STATES, 196 U.S. 375 (1905), and NATIONAL LABOR RELATIONS BOARD V. JONES & LAUGHLIN STEEL CORPORATION, 301 U.S. 57 (1937).

At issue in the case of United States v. E. C. Knight Company was whether Congress has the authority to regulate manufacturing and whether the Sherman Antitrust Act outlawed manufacturing monopolies. In *Knight* the Court reasoned that the states, under the Tenth Amendment, have the right to regulate "local activities" such as manufacturing, thus limiting the scope of the Sherman Act. However, in *Swift v. United States* the Sherman Act's scope was broadened. At issue in *Swift* was whether the Sherman Antitrust Act could bar price fixing by meat dealers within a state. In *Swift* the Court reasoned that although the price fixing addressed in the case was related to activities occurring in one state, they were part of a "stream of interstate commerce" and, therefore, could be regulated by the federal government under the commerce clause of the U.S. Constitution. In *National Labor Relations Board v. Jones & Laughlin Steel Corporation* the Supreme Court considered how far Congress could go in the passage of antitrust law before crossing the bounds of Article I, Section 8 of the Constitution. In a 5-4 decision the Court ruled that Congress may enact all appropriate legislation to protect, advance, promote, and insure interstate commerce.

The case that best demonstrates the extent of antitrust law applicability is the case of HEART OF ATLANTA MOTEL, INC. V. UNITED STATES, 379 U.S. 241 (1964). At issue in *Heart of Atlanta* was whether Congress, under its authority to regulate interstate commerce, has the authority to require private businesses within a state to comply with the CIVIL RIGHTS ACT OF 1964. The Court found that the commerce clause of the Constitution empowers Congress to regulate both commercial and noncommercial interstate travel. Furthermore, the Court stated that since the hotel in question served interstate travel, its refusal to accommodate blacks hindered their freedom of movement across state lines. Congress, the Court concluded, has a constitutional right to regulate individual businesses in the interest of promoting interstate travel. *Heart of Atlanta* is significant for two reasons: (1) because antitrust law itself withstood what has been its most stringent constitutional challenge; and (2) because the Court clearly articulated its opinion that Congress has the power to uphold CIVIL LIBERTIES when exercising powers entailed in the commerce clause of the U.S. Constitution.

For more information: Benson, Paul R., Jr. *The Supreme Court and the Commerce Clause, 1937–1970.* New York: Dunellen, 1970; Corwin, Edwin S. *The Commerce Power versus States' Rights.* Princeton, N.J.: Princeton University Press, 1936; McClosky, Robert. *American Conservatism in the Age of Enterprise, 1865–1910.* Cambridge, Mass.: Harvard University Press, 1951; Wood, Stephen B. *Constitutional Politics in the Progressive Era: Child Labor and the Law.* Chicago: University of Chicago Press, 1968.

—Scott M. Brown

appeal

When a losing party to a lawsuit wants to have his or her case reconsidered by a higher court, he or she generally has the right to *appeal* the lower court's decision. Depending on the court in which the case was originally held, the type of case, and the jurisdiction, there are different procedures and rules for appealing a decision. However, many of the principles of an appeal are common throughout the United States. The Supreme Court has almost unlimited discretion over which appeals it will hear. Generally, appeals are brought to the Supreme Court through petitions for a WRIT OF CERTIORARI.

Within the FEDERAL COURT SYSTEM, a trial begins at the level of the District Court. There, trial is conducted. If a criminal defendant loses, he or she may appeal the decision to the U.S. COURT OF APPEALS for the circuit in which the district court is located. In a civil case, whichever party loses may appeal. The party appealing the decision is referred to as the appellant; the winning party is referred to as the appellee. At the Court of Appeals, a multimember panel of judges considers the case, with certain limits on what the parties may present. Namely, no new evidence can be entered; the judges make a decision based on the record from the District Court.

After the Court of Appeals decides the case, an appeal by the losing party may be made to the Supreme Court, usually in the form of a petition for a writ of certiorari. The procedures for filing an appeal with the Supreme Court are governed by the Rules of the Supreme Court. Under most circumstances, the appellant is referred to at the Supreme Court as the petitioner and the appellee is referred to as the respondent.

While the Supreme Court does have ORIGINAL JURISDICTION in some types of cases, most of the cases it hears are appeals. As noted above, the Supreme Court has almost complete discretion over which appeals it will hear, though there are some areas where its discretion is limited. The justices generally divide the petitions for writs of certiorari among each other in a system called the "cert pool." Their law clerks review the petitions and summarize the main elements of the appeal.

The justices then meet in conference and decide which appeals will be heard. The entire process is very confidential, and the justices and clerks have an exemplary record for maintaining the secrecy of these proceedings. However, we do know that there are certain factors the justices weigh when determining whether to grant a petition; the Court's Rules identify some of those factors, and political science has been able to ascertain which other factors tend to influence the Court. Some of those elements include whether there is a discrepancy among Courts of Appeals, the identity of the petitioner, and whether a state court of last resort or a Court of Appeals has issued a rule of law concerning the Constitution.

If the appeal is granted, the parties are notified, and the process of preparing briefs and for ORAL ARGUMENT (if granted) begins. If the appeal is denied, there is usually nothing more a litigant can do to further his or her case.

For more information: Baum, Lawrence. *The Supreme Court.* Washington, D.C.: CQ Press, 1998; Perry, H. W., Jr. *Deciding to Decide.* Cambridge, Mass.: Harvard University Press, 1991.

—Tom Clark

Arizona v. Fulminante, 499 U.S. 279 (1991)

In *Arizona v. Fulminante,* the court held that Fulminante's jailhouse confession to another inmate was coerced but that coerced confessions were no longer subject to automatic reversal. The *Fulminante* decision subjects coerced confessions to the HARMLESS ERROR rule on APPEAL. In upholding the state court's opinion that the confession was coerced, the Supreme Court upheld the ruling of an earlier case, *Blackburn v. Alabama,* 361 U.S. 199, 206 (1960), which said that "coercion can be mental as well as physical, and . . . the blood of the accused is not the only hallmark of an unconstitutional question." In applying the harmless error rubric to coerced confessions, the Court broke entirely new ground.

Fulminante had confessed to another inmate, while imprisoned, that he had murdered his 11-year-old stepdaughter. The inmate that he had confessed to was an informant to the Federal Bureau of Investigation, Anthony Sarivola. Fulminante also made a second confession to Donna Sarivola, then Anthony's fiancée and later wife. When Fulminante was taken to trial for the murder of his stepdaughter, he claimed that these confessions had been coerced and that due to this, the confession should be suppressed. Fulminante claimed his confession was coerced because Sarivola had promised Fulminante safety from other inmates while in jail in return for his confession. The trial court denied the motion to suppress the confessions on the basis of the stipulated facts; the confessions were voluntary. Both confessions were heard at court, and on December 19, 1985, Fulminante was convicted of murder. He was then sentenced to death.

Fulminante appealed that his confession to Sarivola was the product of coercion and that its admission at trial violated his rights to due process under the Fifth and Fourteenth Amendments of the U.S. Constitution. The Arizona Supreme Court ruled that the confessions were coerced but then decided that the admission of the confession at trial was harmless error. This decision was made because of the overwhelming nature of the evidence against Fulminante.

The Arizona Supreme Court then ruled that the Court's PRECEDENT precluded the use of harmless error analysis in the case of a coerced confession. The Court reversed the conviction and ordered that Fulminante be retried without the use of the confession to Sarivola. The case was then taken to the Supreme Court, due to differing opinion in the state and federal courts over whether the admission at trial of a coerced confession is subject to a harmless analysis.

The Supreme Court first dealt with the assertion that the court below had made an error in holding Fulminante's confession to be coerced. The State contended that it is the totality of the circumstances that determines whether Fulminante's confession was coerced, but instead of using this standard for the case they used the "but for" test. Under this the Court decided that but for the promise given by Sarivola, Fulminante would not have confessed. With this standard the Court found that Fulminante's statement to Sarivola had been coerced. The Arizona Supreme Court stated that "the ultimate issue of voluntariness is a legal question requiring independent federal determination."

The Supreme Court decided that although the question was a close one, they affirmed the Arizona Supreme Court's conclusion that Fulminante's confession was coerced because there was a credible threat of physical violence unless Fulminante confessed. The case makes clear that a finding of coercion need not depend upon actual violence by a government agent; a credible threat is sufficient. In DICTA, it establishes that coerced confessions are subject to harmless error analysis.

For more information: Charles J. Ogletree, Jr. "*Arizona v. Fulminante:* The Harm of Applying Harmless Error to Coerced Confessions." *Harvard Law Review* 105, no. 152 (1991): 152–175.

—Lindsay Vennum

Arlington Heights v. Metropolitan Housing Development Corp., 429 U.S. 252 (1977)

In this housing discrimination case, the Supreme Court ruled that ZONING regulations resulting in a disproportionately negative impact on a minority group do not violate the Fourteenth Amendment unless there is evidence of intent of racially discriminatory action.

The Village of Arlington Heights is a predominantly white Chicago suburb made up of mostly single-family housing. The Clerics of St. Viator, known as Viatorians, a Catholic religious order, owned 80 acres of land in the village. They had two buildings on the land, a high school and a novitiate. The rest of the property was unused. The area around the order's property is zoned for single-family residences. In 1970 the Viatorians decided to develop low- and

moderate-income housing on some of its unused land. They chose Metropolitan Housing Development Corp. (MHDC) as the developer.

MHDC is a nonprofit corporation organized specifically to build low- and moderate-income housing in and around Chicago. MHDC and the Viatorians signed a 99-year lease agreement and an accompanying agreement in which MHDC would buy 15 acres if a zoning change was approved and if MHDC received clearance for federal housing assistance. Building could not start until the lots were rezoned for multifamily housing. Because the project would receive federal assistance, the new community would be racially integrated.

The Village denied the request to rezone the property because the surrounding location had always been zoned single-family. Multifamily zones were only used as buffers between commercial or manufacturing districts and single-family zones. MHDC sued Arlington Heights, arguing that its denial of a zoning variation was racially motivated. Based on the evidence that historically the Village was overwhelmingly white, the COURT OF APPEALS ruled that the denial of a zoning change was racially motivated and violated the EQUAL PROTECTION CLAUSE of the Fourteenth Amendment. MHDC also contended that the Village's refusal to rezone violated the Fair Housing Act of 1968, while the Village challenged the right of MHDC to bring the suit. The Court of Appeals did not rule on these issues, but the Supreme Court did.

Justice POWELL wrote the opinion for the Court. He recounted the background of the case, determined that MHDC had STANDING, and then discussed how the Court might determine if the Village intended to be racially discriminating in its zoning ruling. Justice Powell relied heavily on *WASHINGTON V. DAVIS,* 426 U.S. 229 (1976), to conclude that an action is not necessarily unconstitutional "solely because it results in a racially disproportionate impact." There must be proof of intent to discriminate, even if that intent is not the sole basis for the decision. Examining the evidence from the lower courts, Justice Powell concluded for three reasons that the Village did not intend to discriminate when it refused to rezone the Viatorian property. First, the Village had a history, though not a perfectly consistent one, of denying rezoning because of its buffer policy. Second, the area around the Viatorian property had been designated single-family residential since the Village adopted zoning regulations. Finally, the minutes of the Village Board meeting at which MHDC's petition was discussed showed that the Board focused on the zoning factors used in other zoning decisions. These three factors lead Justice Powell to conclude that there was no racially discriminating intent behind the Village's zoning policy. He remanded the case to the Court of Appeals to decide about the alleged violation of the Fair Housing Act of 1968.

Justice MARSHALL, joined by Justice BRENNAN, concurred in part and dissented in part. He agreed with the Court's reasoning about what determines a petitioner's standing and how to determine a racially discriminating intent. However, he believed the entire decision should have been remanded to the Court of Appeals in light of the new reasoning from the Court.

Justice WHITE dissented, arguing that the Court should have remanded the entire case because *Washington v. Davis* had not been decided when the Court of Appeals was hearing *Arlington Heights v. MHDC*. He also believed the Court overstepped its bounds in reexamining the evidence accepted by a lower court.

This case is important because it reaffirmed the Court's view that the racially discriminatory impact of an action is not enough to declare it unconstitutional. There must be evidence of intent to discriminate. This case also established a three-part standard by which to judge such intent absent a clear-cut pattern of discriminatory action.

For more information: Mossey, Douglas, and Nancy Denton. *American Apartheid: Segregation and the Making of the American Underclass.* Cambridge, Mass.: Harvard University Press, 1993.

—Mariya Chernyavskaya

Ashwander v. Tennessee Valley Authority (TVA), 297 U.S. 288 (1936)

The *Ashwander v. Tennessee Valley Authority* case concerned some minority shareholders of the Alabama Power Company that wanted to void their contract with the TVA, who was selling electricity. The significance of this case is that the government was allowed to make money off of a by-product of their activities to better the Tennessee Valley by constructing and operating the Wilson Dam. The case was decided in favor of the TVA based upon the Constitution—specifically Article IV, Section 3. This part of the Constitution allows the government to sell property— used loosely in this context to include surplus power—it had lawfully obtained. The minority shareholders argued that the TVA and their actions were unconstitutional, but the Supreme Court thought that this case was not about the constitutionality of the TVA.

The Court believed it should avoid decisions that determined the constitutionality of legislation, it should not rule on the constitutionality of a law if there is another way to solve the dispute, and the courts should not anticipate questions of constitutional law. In the first and the second beliefs of the Court listed above, it has been argued that

these rules were to exclude frivolous lawsuits being brought to the Court with answers easily discernible. In other words, most cases probably could have a constitutional question answered within the context of the arguments, but the Court thinks that if the case is an argument where there is clearly a law to address the case, then the constitutional issue is moot. This does not always stand, but for the most part the superior court was looking to allow the lower courts to address the legal issues that pertain to their jurisdictions and then only address the big issues that could affect all of Americans.

Furthermore, in the third belief listed above of the Court, the Supreme Court thought that cases with facts must be established first and then the arguments made. This allows the Court to determine who could benefit and which aspect of society could be impacted by the decision. Once the Court accepts a case, groups could offer their opinions to the Court and these opinions are known as "friend of the court" briefs. In a matter of speaking, this gives the Court an opportunity to hear from those possibly impacted by the decision. If the Court were just to anticipate what society needed addressed, then certain groups or persons could be left out of the mix.

The Court also stated in their opinion that the Supreme Court will not create a decision broader than what is needed, the Court will not overturn a law by persons that benefited from the law previously, and the Court should consider that if there is a nonconstitutional way to address an issue, then the constitutionality questions would not be addressed. This fourth idea mentioned in their opinion offers an insight into the way the Court establishes their decisions. The Court is aware that if they formulate a rule, it becomes a law. If the law is too vague or too overreaching, then the law is unconstitutional. Various lower level laws, in the past, have been struck down because of this very circumstance. Another rationale behind this belief is that the impact upon society is unknown, and the courts are sometimes slow (as is evidenced by all of the etched turtles on their building) to make decisions because one decision could alter an entire business sector within society.

The last two ideas presented by the Court offer that the Court is not willing to overturn a law if the law benefited certain groups. For example, let us suggest that a group of people makes a lot of money performing in a business, and subsequently they develop resources in comparison to other persons in society. If these same people then complain and overturn the very law that afforded them so many riches—those people that made that money now could exclude others from the same opportunity. The suggestion focused on how the Court should address the issues presented to them. This last rule offered insight into how things are approached by the Court. Without this latter rule, persons might not know how the Court addresses decisions, and therefore bias might be perceived to be present in the result.

These affirmations by the Court established what would be called the "Ashwander rules." The sum total of the rules is that if there is a way to solve a legal question without making it the focal point of the decision, then the Court should provide a decision that avoids the question. In 1936 the law still was evolving and there were a lot of new cases being brought to the courts that needed constitutional questions to be answered; this case was not one of them that the Court thought needed the consideration of constitutionality. The rules established for cases were understood by the public as a means of providing that the Court was not inundated with too many cases that did not need a constitutional question answered.

The Court believed that the TVA should be allowed to sell extra power based upon rights enumerated in the Constitution. The agreement between the plaintiffs and the TVA, which was the underlying contract that was in question, was determined by the court to be a rightful agreement that the court should not interfere with. The results of this decision stretched far beyond the simple questions of fact within the case. The *Ashwander* decision set the standard for distilling which cases could be considered by the Court in regards to constitutional questions, and subsequently, there are thousands of cases that have used this case as a reference because of the Ashwander rules.

For more information: *Hatch v. Reardon,* 204 U.S. 152 (1907); *Arizona v. California,* 283 U.S. 423 (1931).

—Ernest Alexander Gomez

Atkins v. Virginia, 536 U.S. 304 (2002)

In *Atkins v. Virginia,* the Court ruled 6-3 that the execution of mentally retarded offenders violates the Eighth Amendment's provision against cruel and unusual punishment and is therefore unconstitutional. In so doing, and by applying the "evolving standards of decency" test, the U.S. Supreme Court reversed the Virginia Supreme Court's decision to affirm the death penalty sentence that was imposed against Daryl Renard Atkins by a lower trial court.

Atkins was convicted of abduction, armed robbery, and capital murder, and sentenced to death. At the state level Atkins did not argue that his sentence was disproportionate to penalties imposed for similar crimes but instead asserted that he could not be sentenced to death because he was mentally retarded. Before the original trial a forensic psychologist evaluated Atkins as being mildly mentally retarded with an IQ of 59.

The U.S. Supreme Court had addressed the constitutionality of executing the mentally retarded and upheld the practice more than a decade earlier in PENRY V. LYNAUGH, 492 U.S. 302 (1989). However, writing for the majority in *Atkins,* Justice STEVENS highlighted a shift in the legislative landscape noting that a growing number of states enacted provisions during the 1990s barring the execution of the mentally retarded. When *Penry* was considered in 1989, only two states and the federal government explicitly exempted mentally retarded offenders from the death penalty. By the time the Court heard the Atkins case, 18 states specifically prohibited executing the mentally retarded and 12 other states rejected CAPITAL PUNISHMENT completely. Justice Stevens also noted the consistent direction of change over time toward not executing such offenders despite the general popularity of anticrime legislation.

These trends led the majority in *Atkins* to conclude that a national consensus has formed against executing the mentally retarded. The perceived shift serves as the foundation of the Court's opinion in *Atkins,* which draws upon the guiding interpretation of Eighth Amendment protections against excessive, cruel, and unusual punishment as articulated by Chief Justice WARREN in *Trop v. Dulles,* 356 U.S. 86 (1958). In *Trop,* Chief Justice WARREN explained that the concept of human dignity underlies these protections and that the meaning of the Amendment is not static but rather derives from the "evolving standards of decency that mark the progress of a maturing society." In *Atkins,* the Court held relevant standards of decency indeed had evolved after *Penry* making the execution of the mentally retarded incompatible with contemporary societal values.

The majority in *Atkins* also reasons that deterrence and retribution as justifications for the death penalty as identified in GREGG V. GEORGIA, 428 U.S. 153, 183 (1976), possess less value in cases involving the mentally retarded because of the offender's impaired capacities and diminished criminal culpability. Furthermore, the Court notes the probability of wrongful conviction increases in such cases to the degree that the mentally retarded are less able to aid in their own defense, are typically poor witnesses, may find it difficult to adequately convey remorse, and are more likely to confess to a crime they did not commit. In short, based on the evolving standards of decency principle, the reduced culpability and capability of the offender, and the special risk of wrongful execution, the Court ruled the execution of the mentally retarded unconstitutional. Justices O'CONNOR, KENNEDY, SOUTER, GINSBURG, and BREYER joined Justice Stevens in the majority.

In strikingly bitter dissents, both Chief Justice REHNQUIST and Justice SCALIA authored opinions opposing the majority. Each joined the other's dissent and along with Justice THOMAS constituted the three-member minority. Chief Justice Rehnquist's dissenting opinion cautions the majority about the dangers of engaging in JUDICIAL ACTIVISM and criticizes the perceived lack of deference by the Court to state laws and principles of FEDERALISM. In a more caustic dissent, Justice Scalia characterizes the majority position as a feeble attempt to fabricate a national consensus in the absence of one. He argues that instead of recognizing the variety of approaches within state statutes and the diversity of community-state values these presumably reflect, the majority, according to Scalia, distorted the evolving standards of decency test to justify a decision predicated on little more than the justices's personal policy preferences.

Justice Scalia laments, "Today's decision is the pinnacle of our Eighth Amendment death-is-different jurisprudence . . . [which finds] no support in the text or history of the Eighth Amendment; it does not even have support in current social attitudes. . . . Seldom has an opinion of this Court rested so obviously upon nothing but the personal views of its members." Among the several issues Scalia takes with the majority position, he warns that an offender can readily feign the symptoms of mental retardation. He also chastises the Court for "riding a trend" especially when the move by states toward barring the execution of the mentally retarded in his view is incomplete and emerging only recently. Moreover, Scalia rebukes those who would consider prevailing global patterns and sentiments related to the subject as a partial basis for determining the meaning of protections within the U.S. Constitution.

While the highly publicized *Atkins* decision likely will continue to generate substantial debates in a number of spheres, three distinct implications beyond the specific issue of executing the mentally retarded warrant brief mention. First, several observers have questioned whether the protections afforded by *Atkins* to the mentally retarded might be extended logically to people with mental illnesses via an equal protection argument (Amendment XIV, Section 1). Second, some scholars and advocacy groups see the ruling in *Atkins* as a possible step toward eventually barring the use of capital charges against juvenile offenders. Adolescent offenders are frequently characterized as having the types of developmental limitations underscored by the Court's majority in *Atkins* regarding the mentally retarded. To date, however, the Court has not extended protections to include those facing the death penalty for crimes committed as juveniles. Indeed, just two months after the *Atkins* decision, the U.S. Supreme Court denied a stay of execution for Patterson, a Texas inmate facing execution for a crime committed as a juvenile. In a rare dissent from an order declining a stay of execution, Justices Stevens, Breyer, and Ginsburg asserted that an apparent consensus exists among states (and the global community) against the death penalty in cases involving juvenile offenders and encouraged the Court to reexamine the juvenile-offender issue in light of *Atkins*. [Stevens, J. dissenting, *On Application for Stay and Petition for Writ of Habeas Corpus,*

M. Patterson v. Texas, 536 U.S. 984 (2002), denied] Third, the *Atkins* case has shifted but not ended debate within the medical community on the appropriate role of psychiatrists and other forensic experts who evaluate the competency of death row and other inmates awaiting sentencing. In the past, several medical professionals have declined requests to assess the mental capacities of these prisoners. Often such experts have stated that playing this role might clash with the "Do no harm" mandate and cornerstone of medical ethics because a finding of competency might enhance the state's case for execution. For some, the ruling in *Atkins* removes the dilemma by prohibiting the execution of those found by experts to be mentally retarded.

For more information: Ellis, James W., and Victor L. Streib, Jeffrey Fagan, Douglas Mossman, MD, Christopher Slobogin, Michael L. Perlin, Elizabeth Rapaport. "Beyond *Atkins:* A Symposium on the Implications of *Atkins v. Virginia.*" *New Mexico Law Review* 33, no. 2 (2003); Stone, Alan A. "Supreme Court Decision Raises New Ethical Questions for Psychiatry." *Psychiatric Times* 19, issue 9 (2002).

—Michael McCall

Austin v. Michigan State Chamber of Commerce, 494 U.S. 652 (1990)

The Supreme Court upheld a Michigan law prohibiting corporations from making independent expenditures in support of or opposition to candidates for state political offices in *Austin v. Michigan State Chamber of Commerce.* The Court rejected arguments that the law violated the Chamber of Commerce's rights under the First Amendment or the EQUAL PROTECTION CLAUSE of the Fourteenth Amendment. While the Court agreed that the law implicated expressive rights, it concluded that the law should be upheld because it was narrowly tailored to serve a COMPELLING STATE INTEREST.

The Court began its analysis, in a majority opinion by Justice Thurgood MARSHALL, with the well-established principles that political expression is at the core of First Amendment protections and that speech by corporations is entitled to at least some protection. The Court applied the familiar standard of STRICT SCRUTINY, asking whether the law was narrowly tailored to serve a compelling state interest. The majority opinion relied on the government's interest in preventing corruption and stated that corporate expenditures raised a different danger of corruption than previous campaign finance cases had addressed: a danger from the "corrosive and distorting effects of immense aggregations of wealth that are accumulated with the help of the corporate form and that have little or no correlation to the public's support for the corporation's political ideas."

Justice Marshall stressed the role that the benefits conferred on corporations by the state had in shaping his conclusions. The Court also concluded that the law was narrowly tailored because corporations could establish segregated funds raised solely from contributions by individuals who intend to advance the political goals of the corporation. Those segregated funds could make independent expenditures to influence elections and could even make contributions to politicians' campaign committees. The law only restricted independent expenditures from the corporation's general treasury funds. Justice Marshall also rejected the argument that, as an ideological nonprofit corporation, the Chamber of Commerce should be exempt from the restriction on corporate political spending under the holding of *Federal Election Commission v. Massachusetts Citizens for Life, Inc.,* 479 U.S. 238 (1986). The Court noted that some of the Chamber's members sought economic benefits that were not tied to its political purposes, and that in any event that the Chamber accepts contributions from other corporations, thus creating the danger that an exception would allow it to serve as a conduit for political spending by ordinary business corporations.

Although the federal restrictions on independent expenditures by corporations also apply to unincorporated labor unions, the Court rejected the assertion that the Constitution required treating corporations and unions equally. Justice Marshall noted that corporations receive special state benefits and that employees who do not support a union's political goals can refuse to contribute to the union's political spending, even if they have a contract that requires them to pay their share of union expenses related to collective bargaining and contract administration. The Court also rejected the argument that an exemption for media corporations' ordinary publications and broadcasting created an equal protection violation, citing the special role of the press. Justices O'Connor, Scalia, and Kennedy dissented, arguing that the law violated the First Amendment.

Austin is an important campaign finance decision. It provides the constitutional basis for many laws requiring corporations to make political expenditures through segregated funds. It also represents an important step in the constitutional distinction between candidate elections and referenda: A prior case, *First National Bank of Boston v. Bellotti,* 435 U.S. 765 (1978), had struck down a similar law that applied to ballot measures. Some academics have criticized *Austin,* arguing that it misapplies the concept of corruption, but other academics have defended it. *Austin's* result has been defended by some based on principles of corporate law: Corporate decisions are made by management, but the corporation's wealth is owned by its shareholders, so political spending by corporations represents management spending other people's money on political goals that the owners may reject. While there was some

speculation that the Supreme Court would overturn *Austin,* the five-vote majority in *McConnell v. Federal Election Commission,* 124 S. Ct. 619 (2003), unambiguously reaffirmed its holding.

For more information: Issacharoff, Samuel, Pamela S. Karlan, and Richard H. Pildes. *The Law of Democracy.* 2nd ed. New York: Foundation Press, 2002: 513–524; Winkler, Adam. "Beyond Bellotti." *Loy. L.A. L. Rev.* 32 (November 1998): 133.

—Adam H. Morse

automobile stops and searches

Automobile stops and searches are also known as traffic stops, which are seizures of individuals and their automobiles and may include various types of searches depending on the circumstances. The legal concept of "automobile stops and searches" is governed primarily by the Fourth Amendment to the U.S. Constitution, and to some extent by the Fifth and Fourteenth Amendments, and by many decisions of the United States Supreme Court. The relevant portion of the Fourth Amendment which governs automobile stops and searches states: "The right of the people to be *secure in their persons, . . . and effects, against unreasonable searches and seizures,* shall not be violated. . . ."

It is important to distinguish automobile stops and searches from searches of homes. The Fourth Amendment protects citizens from unreasonable searches and seizures in automobiles and homes, but to different degrees. Historically, citizens and homes had been afforded the most protection as a citizen's expectation of privacy is highest in the home. From the beginning of the history of the automobile, the Supreme Court has recognized a much lower expectation of privacy of citizens in automobiles, because of the "ready mobility" of automobiles.

Automobile stops and searches by the government can occur in a number of situations and can vary in degree and duration. Searches and seizures normally must be based upon probable cause according to the Fourth Amendment. However, the Supreme Court has carved out exceptions to the requirement that searches and seizures be based on probable cause, and the Supreme Court has created exceptions allowing police officers to determine probable cause on their own and forgo the warrant requirement of the Fourth Amendment. At least police must have a reasonable suspicion or probable cause determined on their own to conduct a traffic stop and search. The least severe seizure of a person is called a "Terry" stop, after the Supreme Court decision in *Terry v. Ohio,* 392 U.S. 1 (1968). A *Terry* stop must be based on a reasonable articulable suspicion and limited in duration and scope. In the interest of officer safety, an officer conducting a *Terry* stop can conduct a "pat-down" search to check for weapons. *Terry* stop principles apply to traffic stop situations as well.

Officers, during a routine traffic stop, noticed a large hunting knife on the floorboard of the automobile. Officers conducted a pat-down search of the driver and further searched the passenger compartment, finding and seizing some marijuana. The Court stated "that the search of the passenger compartment of an automobile, limited to those areas in which a weapon may be placed or hidden, is permissible . . ." if based on a reasonable suspicion of the officer. Officer safety justifies the search by police.

It is sometimes difficult to determine what is an automobile. A home or residence is traditionally provided the most Fourth Amendment protection. Take a Dodge mini motor home for example. If the motor home is more like a home, then the law may treat it more like a home than an automobile. On the other hand, if the motor home is more like an automobile than a home, the law may treat it more like an automobile. The determination will depend largely upon the mobility of the motor home. If the motor home is readily mobile, law will probably treat it as an automobile. If the motor home is not readily mobile, i.e., it has no wheels and is on a foundation, then it will probably be treated more like a home for legal purposes.

If an officer makes a traffic stop which results in an arrest, the officer can ". . . as a contemporaneous incident of that arrest, search the passenger compartment of that automobile. . . . the police may also examine the contents of any containers found within the passenger compartment. . . ." This purpose of this rule is to protect officer safety and prevent the destruction of evidence.

If police have probable cause to believe that contraband is in an automobile, the police do not have to get a warrant to search the automobile. Police can conduct a warrantless search of the automobile, but the scope of the search must be limited. The scope of the search ". . . is defined by the object of the search and the places in which there is probable cause to believe that it may be found."

If police have probable cause to believe that contraband is in an automobile, police can search passenger's belongings for the contraband. ". . . police officers with probable cause to search a car may inspect passengers' belongings found in the car that are capable of concealing the object of the search."

Incident to a lawful custodial arrest, police may conduct an "inventory search" of a vehicle which is to be

Police search a vehicle for possible contraband. *(Henry County Sheriff's Office)*

impounded in accordance with reasonable procedures. This rule is meant to protect the police from dangerous material in the impounded automobile, and to protect the police from false claims of stolen property from the automobile, and to protect the individual's property interest.

Extraordinarily in some jurisdictions, like Texas, police may make custodial arrest of drivers that commit traffic infractions punishable by fines only. Police then can conduct searches incident to arrest and possibly impound and search the automobile.

Pretext stops occur when police conduct a traffic stop, but their real motivation is something other than the traffic stop. Pretext stops are quite controversial and hard to prove. Essentially, a police officer has to acknowledge the "other" motivation for the traffic stop. If the police have a valid reason for the traffic stop and do not admit some other motive for the traffic stop, a pretext stop is nearly impossible to prove. Police have tremendous power and discretion in conducting traffic stops.

A person can consent to an automobile stop and search if they do so knowingly, intelligently, and voluntarily.

For more information: LaFave, Wayne R., and Jerold M. Israel. *Criminal Procedure Constitutional Limitations in a Nutshell.* 6th ed. St. Paul: West Group, 2001.

—James E. Headley

B

bail, right to

The right to bail is a Constitution-based concept that affords all persons accused of a crime an equal and intrinsic citizen-based opportunity to maintain a presence within society until they have been proven guilty or innocent of the crime charged in a court of law.

The importance of a right to bail is that our very fabric of identity, that is the right to freedom, is protected, and any infringement upon such needs must be subject to an objective process. So, by taking away a person's right to freedom of movement, association, and action, the courts are in essence denying the freedom that is enumerated within the Constitution. The ability to do this has to be balanced, so the court must have a good reason and must follow a process so as to not allow for arbitrary decision making with someone's life.

The Eighth Amendment to the Constitution (1791), which was adopted as part of the BILL OF RIGHTS, offers that "Excessive bail shall not be required, nor excessive fines imposed, nor cruel and unusual punishments inflicted." A citizen's right to bail has its roots in the English Bill of Rights (1689), but the focus and the factors for consideration for the decision on who receives the right to be released after posting a bail has evolved over the years.

The posting of a bail amount offers a person an opportunity to remain a productive member of society while attempting to reconcile the need of the government to guarantee that the accused person appears at the next judicial proceeding. The charging of a crime or a tort does not necessarily mean that someone is guilty of the crime they are charged with. A decision of innocent or guilty first must be rendered before someone's freedom is restricted. Because of the adversarial process, which pits defense against prosecution, a person that is not defined innocent or guilty should not have his rights encumbered by restricted movement unless there are some extenuating issues attached. Once the proceedings are over, the bail amount is returned to the person or utilized for court costs—depending on the result. Historically, there were often considerations made by the judges of smaller towns for the accused. In a younger time in America, the person accused of a crime bore the brunt of being charged with that crime and the possibility of reputation damage. It was believed then that the shame of being accused of a crime in a court of law alone was enough to force someone to come to court in order to clear his name.

The right to bail often was viewed as an arbitrary gift of the court in some parts of the United States. In addition, some other collateral might be used as a bail substitute in some more rural areas. One theory to reduce the arbitrariness of posting a bail amount/collateral asset was to make the proper bail be solely a monetary amount. Often the accused person's money that was posted in order to "bond out" was viewed as an acceptable and reasonable assurance for the court that the court appearance would be met.

Eventually, the advancement in movement and technological change allowed for people to become more mobile, and thus came a need to limit the opportunity of some particular persons to flee from prosecution (aka "flight risk"). A little later as more cases came to court, it was recognized that there should be no standard time allotment set for the reasonable amount of time necessary to follow through with a criminal trial. The reasons behind not trying to set a time limit on a case were that the amount of time needed may vary, how long a person should be incarcerated or evaluated prior to the trial date, and even how long the prosecution needed to present their case. The gradual reforms implemented into the court system placed general limitations in order to speed up the court proceedings and also address the need of persons to mete out their responsibilities prior to coming to court.

Because a trial may take a long time period from the hearing and accusation stage to the final decision, a person accused of a crime may face pressure to place in order his personal matters, provide for his/her family, and even maintain his employment status. By allowing for this chance to meet his responsibilities, the accused also has an inherent opportunity to meet with his/her counsel.

The government is allowed to argue whether or not the accused should be given bail. The defense is also allowed to challenge those determining facts, and the judge then makes a decision based upon the totality of the circumstances involved. The judge has a duty to protect society from criminal behavior and from persons that could be a threat to society and subsequently, in order to make the decisions more uniform, certain things are looked by all judges; this was addressed in the case *United States v. Salerno* (1987). Some of the facts to be considered are whether or not a weapon was used, type of crime committed, history of the person accused when given other bond chances, whether or not the accused attempted to circumvent the arrest, history of violence of the accused, mental capacity, and even their other nonrelated criminal history. These are things that might be looked at when determining bond, and although the right to bail is available to everyone, some factors aforementioned may be utilized as a rationale to protect society from recidivist criminal behavior.

The burden to prove a person was worthy of bail was placed upon the accused and his legal counsel, historically. With the Bail Reform Act of 1984 (Title 18 U.S.C. Chapters 3141–3156), the understanding of bail changed, and the burden was shifted to the government to prove why the accused should remain in custody. Factors contributing to the change in philosophy were the increase of crime, the increased costs of housing prisoners, and also there was a social movement to humanize the bail process in order to allow people to correct their behavior when given a chance to contribute to society.

Opponents to the changing bail theory believed that the most serious criminals should be incarcerated. In addition, defendants who had committed nonviolent crimes and who could not afford to post a bond, should be allowed an opportunity to avoid trial-pending incarceration. This approach leads to a double standard, which is not commensurate with the rule of law theory. A few circumstances, where it was determined that some violent criminals were using the time off before a trial to go on a crime spree, fed the movement to change the bail rules. Although this was rare in relation to the number of persons brought before our courts, tough sentencing in some states contributed to the movement away from attempting to rehabilitate offenders and move more toward protecting society.

Denying the right to bail by setting unrealistic bond amounts became the fashion for those persons accused of very serious crimes, viewed to have had no measure of success or contribution to society, who had a history of criminal behavior, and perhaps who even had been convicted of certain other related crimes. Yet their aforementioned criminal rights were not violated. The advent was viewed as an adaptation of a tool within the law in order to create a buffer for society without denying a person his or her rights. Proponents of this approach within the criminal justice system have argued that the point has always been that the overall good for society outweighed the rights of a single person who has not been a good member of society. Judges often, because they were elected, did not want to upset their constituencies and were reluctant to let repeated criminals out on bond.

The opposition to these theories offered that each person should be given a new opportunity to face new charges brought against them because the person technically had not been proven to be guilty of the accused crime yet. In addition to the last mentioned theory, the argument was offered that there was no guarantee that the person accused would continue his negative behavior or that his previous behavior was a legitimate predictor of guilt in the recent case. Both theories have been points of contention within the Supreme Court.

The reformation of the bail rules gives each person the benefit of the doubt concerning bail matters. These reforms also limited the court's discretion in order to prevent judicial abuse and allow for more consistent decisions. In addition to those reforms, the judge could find alternate methods of guaranteeing a presence within the court. Now a judge may allow a person to be remanded into the supervision of another, has the ability to restrict movement and location, and has the ability to provide for witness or victim protection by limiting interaction. All of these ideas were allowed to stand in order to reduce the stress on our overcrowded prisons and yet still balance a person's rights versus unproven charges.

The founders of the country when writing the Constitution probably never envisioned the development of certain prohibited behaviors and societal restrictions to the level that they have currently risen to, but the generally accepted point of the Eighth Amendment was to provide persons with certain rights against excessive behaviors by the government in regards to bail. The balancing act that supports the right to bail is between society and the individual. Each individual municipality has varying processes of providing for bail but not for restricting who is allowed bail—everyone is allowed the right to a bail hearing. The judges and not the police decide such matters, and there are certain levels of proof that must be met in order to present a rationale for denying persons the right to bail.

For more information: Bail Reform Act of 1984; Title 18, U.S.C. Chapters: 3141–3156; *U.S. v. Salerno*, 481 U.S. 739, 750 (1987); *Stack v. Boyle*, 342 U.S. 1 (1951).

Bailey v. Drexel Furniture, 259 U.S. 20 (1922)

In *Bailey v. Drexel Furniture* the United States Supreme Court ruled that a federal tax on products made by child labor was an unconstitutional interference with INTERSTATE COMMERCE. The importance of this case resides in how the Supreme Court in the early part of the 20th century drew limits on the powers of Congress to use its taxing power to regulate commerce.

During the latter part of the 19th century Congress engaged in several attempts to regulate the economy and interstate commerce. It decided to do that because of the growth of businesses or trusts in the country and the impact they had upon commerce. In addition, as the United States industrialized during this time, the working conditions of many of the factories often raised health and safety concerns for the workers or consumers. One of the activities that Congress sought to regulate was the use of child labor in the manufacture of goods that traveled across state lines.

In *HAMMER V. DAGENHART*, 247 U.S. 251 (1918), the United States Supreme Court struck down the 1916 Keating-Owen Bill, which was passed by Congress. This law sought to ban the production of goods made by children under the age of 14 and also limit the transportation across state lines of products made by children between the ages of 14 and 16. The Court argued in this case that this law exceeded the powers of Congress to regulate interstate commerce and that it also interfered with the police power of individual states.

In response to this decision, Congress passed in 1919 the Child Labor Tax Act that imposed a 10 percent INCOME TAX on persons employing child labor, regardless of the number or amount of child labor used. However, the law exempted individuals from the tax if they did not know that the person employed was a child under the age of 14.

In striking down the law, Chief Justice TAFT wrote for the Court, arguing that this law was indistinguishable from *Hammer v. Dagenhart* in that both the laws in question in that case and in *Bailey* were directed at preventing or regulating child labor. As with the *Hammer* case, the Court saw this law as an unconstitutional infringement of state POLICE POWERS and, more importantly, that it exceeded Congress's Commerce Clause authority. Instead, the power to regulate child labor still resided with the states.

Moreover, Taft contended that this 10 percent tax was not really a tax but instead a penalty aimed at forcing states to do what Congress wanted. Thus, while the Court stated that the power to tax was fairly broad and that it would not generally second-guess Congress; here, the tax was really a penalty aimed at regulating interstate commerce beyond the scope of what the Constitution permitted for Congress.

Bailey v. Drexel Furniture was a controversial case in that for the second time within a few years the Court invalidated efforts by the federal government to regulate and ban child labor. This case can be seen as part of a series of Supreme Court decisions from the 1770s until the New Deal in 1936 where significant limits were placed upon Congress's ability to regulate interstate commerce or otherwise act in ways to regulate working conditions. It was not until cases such as *WICKARD V. FILBURN*, 317 U.S. 111 (1942) that the Supreme Court reversed itself and granted Congress more authority to use its taxing authority to regulate interstate commerce and working conditions. In many ways, *Bailey* serves as an example of one of the eras of Supreme Court jurisprudence that limited federal power over the economy and the states.

For more information: Benson, Paul Revere. *The Supreme Court and the Commerce Clause, 1937–1970.* New York: Dunellen, 1970.

—David Schultz

Baker v. Carr, 369 U.S. 186 (1962)

In *Baker v. Carr,* the United States Supreme Court held that the constitutionality of legislative restricting was a matter that the courts could review. Justice BRENNAN wrote the majority opinion for the Court. Residents of five Tennessee counties challenged a Tennessee law passed in 1901 arguing that the state's apportionment of legislative representatives violated the EQUAL PROTECTION CLAUSE of the Fourteenth Amendment. The district court dismissed the claim on the ground that it involved a political question over which the court had no jurisdiction. The case was appealed to the Supreme Court.

At the time the lawsuit was initiated, the general assembly of Tennessee consisted of a 33-member senate and a 99-member house of representatives. The Tennessee Constitution required that state legislators be apportioned among the state's counties based on a decennial census. The general assembly passed an apportionment law in 1901 allocating representatives among all counties in the state on the basis of the 1900 census. Between 1901 and 1961, all reapportionment proposals introduced to the general assembly failed to pass. Despite significant growth and geographic shifts in the state's population, political representation in 1962 was based on population distribution as recorded by the 1900 census. The plaintiffs argued that the state's outdated apportionment of political representation resulted in the underrepresentation of individuals living in more populous legislative districts and the "debasement of their votes."

The Supreme Court did not decide whether the challenged districts were, in fact, unconstitutional. Instead, in the words of Justice Brennan, "we hold today only (a) that the court possessed jurisdiction of the subject matter; (b) that a justiciable cause of action is stated upon which appellants would be entitled to appropriate relief; and (c) . . . that the appellants have STANDING to challenge the Tennessee apportionment statutes." The Court remanded the case back to the district court for a full trial.

The Court's ruling in *Baker v. Carr* is significant because it marks the first time the Supreme Court held that legal challenges to the apportionment of legislative districts brought under the equal protection clause of the Fourteenth Amendment should be heard by federal courts. *Baker v. Carr* made it clear that legal challenges to legislative districting plans should not be dismissed by district courts under the "political question" doctrine. The *Baker* Court distinguished this case from POLITICAL QUESTION DOCTRINE cases by noting that nonjusticiable political question cases involve distribution of power among the three separate branches of the federal government. This case, by contrast, involved a conflict between state politics and the federal Constitution.

Baker v. Carr opened the door for future voting rights lawsuits. Over the next two years, the Supreme Court established the principle of "ONE PERSON, ONE VOTE" with its decisions in *GRAY V. SANDERS*, *WESBERRY V. SANDERS* and *REYNOLDS V. SIMS*. Voting rights advocates have relied on *Baker v. Carr* and its progeny to challenge racially discriminatory redistricting and reapportionment schemes at every level of government throughout the nation.

For more information: Canon, David. *Race, Redistricting, and Representation.* Chicago: University of Chicago Press, 1999.

—Paul S. Ryan

bankruptcy

Bankruptcy refers to a legal proceeding that relieves a debtor from the obligation to pay debts or provides the debtor with protection from creditors while paying debts via a plan of repayment. The primary focus of the Bankruptcy Code is to balance a debtor's need for relief from burdensome debt with creditors' right to payment. Bankruptcy attempts to balance these conflicted needs by providing debt-plagued consumers or businesses with a "fresh start", i.e., relief from creditors and onerous debt that leave debtors financially debilitated and weaken the economy as a whole, while also recognizing the creditor's right to payment. Bankruptcy safeguards a creditor's right to payment by providing a court-supervised forum for the orderly distribution of the debtor's property.

Bankruptcy law is a federal statutory law contained in Title 11 of the U.S. Code. Congress passed the Bankruptcy Code under its constitutional authority provided in the U.S. Constitution Article I, Section 8. States may not regulate bankruptcy although they may pass legislation that governs how much property a debtor may protect from the collection efforts of creditors. Bankruptcy proceedings are supervised by and litigated in the U.S. Bankruptcy Courts. The Bankruptcy Courts are part of the District Courts of the United States. As part of the federal judicial system, the Supreme Court is the court of last review, and bankruptcy court decisions that are appealed may ultimately wind up before the Supreme Court. Supreme Court decisions help to formulate bankruptcy law by establishing legal PRECEDENT that must be followed by all lower courts. The Supreme Court has also established the Bankruptcy Rules of Procedure, which govern proceedings before U.S. Bankruptcy Courts.

A bankruptcy proceeding may be initiated voluntarily by the debtor or involuntarily by the debtor's creditors. There are two types of bankruptcy, liquidation and reorganization. Liquidation bankruptcy is called Chapter 7, referring to the chapter of the Bankruptcy Code that deals with liquidation. Reorganization bankruptcy is called Chapter 13 for consumer debtors and Chapter 11 for business debtors. Reorganization bankruptcy for family farmers is called Chapter 12.

Chapter 7 liquidation is the most common type of bankruptcy. In a Chapter 7 proceeding property owned by the debtor, except property protected from creditors by state law, becomes property of a bankruptcy estate. A person called a trustee is appointed by the bankruptcy court to administer the estate for the benefit of creditors. The trustee's job is to liquidate assets of the estate and distribute the proceeds to creditors in an orderly fashion based upon creditors' claims to payment. During the proceedings the debtor is protected, in most circumstances, from collection efforts by creditors. Upon completion of the proceedings the debtor is granted a discharge. The discharge order destroys the debtor's legal obligation to pay all dischargeable debts that were included in the bankruptcy proceeding.

In a Chapter 13, 11, or 12 reorganization bankruptcy, the debtor develops a plan to pay creditors over time. The amount of payments made to creditors depends on two primary components: the debtor's ability to pay, referred to as disposable income, and the aggregate value of the debtor's interest in property. The plan created by the debtor must be approved by the court and interested creditors. The debtor makes payments, according to the terms of the approved plan, to a court-appointed trustee who in turn distributes the payments to the debtor's creditors. Just as in a Chapter 7 proceeding, the debtor is protected from collection efforts by creditors during the case. Upon completion of the plan the debtor receives a discharge, which like a Chapter 7 destroys the legal obligation to pay creditors.

A bankruptcy case has an adverse effect on a debtor's credit rating and may prevent a debtor from obtaining credit in the future. However, the adverse consequences of filing for bankruptcy relief must be weighed in light of the advantages provided by the discharge and the idea that with renewed financial discipline a good credit rating can be reestablished in a reasonable period of time.

For more information: Warren, Charles. *Bankruptcy in United States History.* Buffalo, N.Y.: W. S. Hein, 1994; also, New York: Da Capo, 1972.

—Daniel J. Pesachowitz

Barenblatt v. United States, 360 U.S. 109 (1959)

Barenblatt v. United States is a significant United States Supreme Court decision from 1959 that upheld broad congressional powers to investigate alleged Communist infiltration of higher education in the United States. By a vote of 5 to 4, the Court ruled that Congress, and in particular the House Un-American Activities Committee, possessed "pervasive authority" to investigate Communist Party actions in the United States (360 U.S. 109 [1959]).

The case centered on Lloyd Barenblatt, a graduate student and teaching fellow at the University of Michigan from 1947 to 1950, and a professor of psychology at Vassar College from 1950 to 1954. He was called to testify before Congress; he appeared as a witness but refused to answer any questions, challenging the inquiry on several grounds, including and especially the First Amendment's speech and association clauses. He was charged with and convicted of contempt of Congress, and his contempt conviction was upheld by the Court in a majority opinion by Justice John Marshall HARLAN.

Justice Harlan employed a balancing test to resolve the conflict; he balanced Barenblatt's interest in free speech and association with national security and the country's "right of self-preservation." According to Harlan, the Communist Party in the United States was out to overthrow the United States, and virtually any congressional inquiry into real or alleged Communist infiltration, including and perhaps especially colleges and universities, was justified in the face of such a grave threat.

Justice Hugo BLACK wrote a scathing dissenting opinion, one joined by Chief Justice Earl WARREN and Justice William O. DOUGLAS, in which he attacked Harlan's balancing approach in principle and its immediate application to this case. According to Black, such a balancing approach invariably favored the interest of the government over the interest of the individual; in addition, for Black, the interest of the individual in fact represented broader and fundamental interests of the community. Black took the majority to task for failing to protect "the right to err politically, which keeps us strong as a nation." Moreover, according to Black, the Court needed to recognize and protect the role of universities for "the experimentation

and development of new ideas essential to our country's welfare."

This case came at a pivotal moment in our country's historic struggle between liberty and authority. The cold war was raging; McCarthyism still prevailed in many quarters, and divergent opinions, even as theories from the lectern, were not universally acclaimed. As a result of this decision, Congress continued to enjoy broad statutory and constitutional authority to investigate alleged Communist infiltration in the United States, and as a result, the First Amendment, as feared by the Court's minority and as expressed in Justice Black's eloquent dissent, was weakened.

For more information: Emerson, Thomas I. *The System of Freedom of Expression.* New York: Random House, 1971; Schrecker, Ellen W. *No Ivory Tower: McCarthyism and the Universities.* Oxford: Oxford University Press, 1988.

—Stephen K. Shaw

Barnes v. Glen Theatre, 501 U.S. 560 (1991)

This case deals with multiple respondents, all of which pertained to the same issue. These are in relation to the issues of NUDE DANCING, public indecency, and protected freedoms of expression. The Indiana establishments wished to provide totally nude dancing as entertainment without the restrictions imposed by the law in place. Glen Theatre Inc. showed nude and seminude performances and viewings of the female body through glass panels, and the Kitty Kat Lounge, Inc. sponsored go-go dancing. The Indiana statute regulating public nudity required the dancers to wear pasties and a G-string when they danced. The Court held that enforcement of Indiana's public indecency law to prevent totally nude dancing did not violate the First Amendment's guarantee of freedom of expression.

According to the Court, nude dancing of the kind sought to be performed here is expressive conduct within the outer perimeters of the First Amendment, although only marginally. The Court reasoned that through the four-part test of *U.S. v. O'BRIEN*, which rejected the contention that SYMBOLIC SPEECH is entitled to full First Amendment protection, the statute is justified despite its incidental limitations on some expressive activity. Outlined by the four-part test: The law is clearly within the state's constitutional power; it furthers a substantial governmental interest in protecting societal order and morality; public indecency statutes reflect moral disapproval of people appearing in the nude among strangers in public places; and this particular law follows a line of state laws, dating back to 1831, that banned public nudity. The public indecency statute follows a long line of earlier Indiana statutes banning all public nudity. It predates barroom nude dancing and was enacted as a general prohibition. As early as 1831, Indiana had a statute punishing "open and notorious lewdness, or . . . any grossly scandalous and public indecency." The Indiana Supreme Court filled a gap during which no statute was in effect in 1877, which held that the court could sustain a conviction for exhibition of privates in the presence of others. In 1881 a statute was enacted that would remain essentially unchanged for nearly a century.

This governmental interest is unrelated to the suppression of free expression, since public nudity is the evil the state seeks to prevent, whether or not it is conveying an erotic message. Likewise, erotic performance may be presented without any state interference, so long as the performers wear a scant amount of clothing and the incidental restriction of First Amendment freedom is no greater than is essential to the furtherance of the governmental interest. The statute, as a general law regulating conduct and not specifically directed at expression, either in practice or on its face, is not subject to normal First Amendment scrutiny and should be upheld on the ground that moral opposition to nudity supplies a RATIONAL BASIS for its prohibition. There is no intermediate level of scrutiny requiring that an incidental restriction on expression, such as that involved here, be justified by an important or substantial governmental interest. The asserted interest is plainly substantial, and the state could have concluded that it is furthered by a prohibition on nude dancing, even without localized proof of the harmful effects. The interest is unrelated to the suppression of free expression, since the pernicious effects are merely associated with nude dancing establishments and are not the result of the expression inherent in nude dancing.

Indiana has not banned nude dancing as such but had proscribed public nudity across the board. The Supreme Court of Indiana had construed the Indiana statute to preclude nudity in what are essentially places of public accommodation such as the Glen Theatre and the Kitty Kat Lounge. In such places, minors are excluded and there are no non-consenting viewers. While the state may license establishments such as the ones involved here and limit the geographical area in which they do business, it may not in any way limit the performance of the dances within them without violating the First Amendment. Indiana's restriction on nude dancing is a valid "time, place, or manner" restriction. The "time, place, or manner" test was developed for evaluating restrictions on expression taking place on public property which had been dedicated as a "PUBLIC FORUM."

Basically, nude dancing can be regulated only insofar as the regulation is not a regulation on the dancing or message within the dancing, but only a regulation on the level of nudity of the performers.

For further information: Fardon, Zachary T. "*Barnes v. Glen Theatre, Inc.*: Nude Dancing and the First Amend-

ment Question," *Vanderbilt Law Review* 45, no. 237 (1992).

—Amy Oliver

Barron v. Baltimore, 7 Pet. 243 (1833)

Barron v. Baltimore was a case in which the United States Supreme Court held that the CIVIL LIBERTIES and CIVIL RIGHTS protections included within the BILL OF RIGHTS restricted only the federal government and did not apply to the states.

The case began as a relatively pedestrian one in which the city of Baltimore, in the course of making street improvements, diverted water near Barron's Wharf, causing an accumulation of silt and sand. As a consequence, what had once been a wharf with deep waters that allowed even the largest ships to dock had now become virtually worthless. Barron filed suit against the city under the Fifth Amendment to the U.S. Constitution, which says in part that private property [shall not] be taken for public use, without just compensation. Given that his wharf was, as a result of the city's actions, now without value, Barron sued for just compensation. At trial, Barron was awarded $4,500 in compensation but the decision was overturned by the Maryland COURT OF APPEALS. Barron then appealed to the U.S. Supreme Court.

In his opinion for a unanimous Court, Chief Justice John MARSHALL examined both the text and history of the Bill of Rights and concluded that the nearly two dozen civil liberties and civil rights protections in the first 10 amendments were intended to apply only to the federal government and not to the states. Thus, although the First Amendment prohibited the federal government from infringing upon freedom of speech, freedom of press, and the like, that amendment did not in any way restrict the states. Similarly, the Fifth Amendment just compensation clause, which Barron relied upon in this case, applied only to the federal government and not to the states. To the extent that individual liberties were protected from state government intrusion, such protection would have to come from state constitutions and state bills of rights.

This situation began to change, albeit slowly, when, in 1868, the Fourteenth Amendment was added to the Constitution. That amendment provides in part that "No state shall make or enforce any law which shall abridge the privileges or immunities of citizens of the United States; nor shall any State deprive any person of life, liberty, or property, without due process of law." Unlike the Bill of Rights, then, the Fourteenth Amendment was a clear and emphatic limitation upon the power of the state governments to infringe upon civil rights and civil liberties. Although it was initially hesitant to do so, eventually the Supreme Court, in a series of landmark cases spanning several decades, held through the doctrine of selective INCORPORATION that the due process clause of the Fourteenth Amendment "incorporated" or "absorbed" most of the provisions of the Bill of Rights and made them applicable to the states as well as the federal government.

For more information: Abraham, Henry J., and Barbara A. Perry. *Freedom and the Court: Civil Rights and Liberties in the United States.* 7th ed. New York: Oxford University Press, 1998; Cortner, Richard C. *The Supreme Court and the Second Bill of Rights: The Fourteenth Amendment and the Nationalization of Civil Liberties.* Madison: University of Wisconsin Press, 1981.

—Michael W. Bowers

Batson v. Kentucky, 476 U.S. 79 (1986)

The Supreme Court held that a prosecutor may not use PEREMPTORY CHALLENGES to exclude potential jurors on the basis of race.

James Kirkland Batson, who was black, was tried for burglary and receipt of stolen goods. After the judge excluded some prospective jurors for cause, the prosecutor used his peremptory challenges to strike the four remaining African Americans from the jury. The all-white jury convicted Batson on both counts. In his APPEAL, Batson claimed that he had been denied a fair trial because his Sixth Amendment right to an impartial jury and his Fourteenth Amendment right to equal protection had been violated.

The Court had ruled on the discriminatory use of peremptory challenges in *Swain v. Alabama,* 380 U.S. 202 (1965). Although that opinion recognized that the deliberate exclusion of African Americans from juries on the basis of race violated the EQUAL PROTECTION CLAUSE of the Fourteenth Amendment, it required that a defendant prove the existence of a pattern of discrimination. The *Batson* Court overruled Swain, noting that expecting defendants to demonstrate that prosecutors repeatedly removed black jurors over a series of cases, forced the defense to assume "a crippling burden of proof." Instead, the accused could now raise the issue of discrimination based on the prosecution's use of peremptory challenges only in his own trial. In other words, it was not necessary that "several must suffer" before one could object. The Court described a process, which came to be known as a "Batson challenge," whereby a defendant could press his claim. In order to establish a *prima facie* (apparent) case of purposeful discrimination, the defendant must show that he was a member of a recognized racial group, that the prosecutor used peremptory challenges to remove members of that race, and that those prospective jurors were struck because of their race. The burden of proof would then shift to the prosecutor who would be required to show that he had removed the jurors

for a neutral, non-racial reason. The judge would ultimately rule on the merits of the defendant's claim.

The Court cited three reasons for addressing the issue of RACIAL DISCRIMINATION in the selection of trial juries as an equal protection claim. Although no one has a constitutional right to a jury made up of persons of his or her race, someone accused of a crime does have the right to an impartial jury. A state cannot choose jurors based on the false assumption that persons who are members of the defendant's racial group will not be fair and objective. Nor should prospective jurors be denied their opportunity to serve because their impartiality is suspect based on their race. The justices also claimed that excluding African Americans from juries undermines public confidence in the legal system. While they recognized that the peremptory challenge has been a valuable courtroom tool for centuries, the majority of the Court believed that procedures to prevent discrimination demanded its modification.

Justice Thurgood MARSHALL wrote a concurring opinion in which he argued that only elimination of the peremptory challenge would solve the problem. Under the *Batson* challenge, a prosecutor could devise a neutral reason to justify the exclusion of minority jurors. Marshall predicted that many prosecutors would, even unconsciously, believe that black jurors were unreliable and remove them. Few judges would accuse prosecutors of lying about their reasons for striking minorities, and therefore the discrimination would persist, even if it was clothed with a non-prejudicial rationale. There is evidence that Marshall correctly identified the difficulty with eliminating racial bias from the process. African Americans continue to face all-white juries, due at least in part to the continued discriminatory use of the peremptory challenge.

In *J.E.B. V. ALABAMA,* the Supreme Court extended *Batson* ruling that peremptory challenges could not be used to exclude prospective jurors on the basis of sex.

For more information: Cole, David. *No Equal Justice: Race and Class in the American Criminal Justice System.* New York: New Press, 1999; Kennedy, Randall. *Race, Crime, and the Law.* New York: Vintage, 1997.

—Mary Welek Atwell

Beauharnais v. Illinois, 343 U.S. 250 (1952)

In *Beauharnais v. Illinois,* the Supreme Court affirmed Joseph Beauharnais' criminal conviction for distributing leaflets containing derogatory statements about blacks in violation of an Illinois law. In the process, the Court determined that the Illinois statute did not violate his First Amendment rights of free speech and free press as guaranteed against the states by the due process clause of the Fourteenth Amendment. Beauharnais was charged and convicted of violating an Illinois statute which criminalized group libel. Specifically, the law made it a crime to publish materials which portray certain groups of citizens, including racial groups, as depraved or criminal or which exposes these groups "to contempt, derision or obloquy." Attorneys for Beauharnais argued that the law violated his First Amendment rights of free speech and press.

The Court rejected Beauharnais' claim that the law abridged his freedom of speech and instead affirmed its earlier holding in CHAPLINSKY V. NEW HAMPSHIRE, 315 U.S. 568 (1942), that certain types of speech, such as libelous or defamatory comments, are "of such slight social value as a step to truth that any benefit that may be derived from them is clearly outweighed by the social interest in order and morality." The Court held, therefore, that such speech is not "within the area of constitutionally protected speech" and may be punished by the state.

Writing for the majority, Justice FRANKFURTER outlined the history of libel law and noted that while some earlier decisions had decreased the reach of libel law, "nowhere was there any suggestion that the crime of libel be abolished." The Court relied on its earlier ruling in CANTWELL V. CONNECTICUT, 310 U.S. 296 (1940), that, "Resort to epithets or personal abuse is not in any proper sense communication of information or opinion safeguarded by the Constitution, and its punishment as a criminal act would raise no question under that instrument." The Court then extended this ruling to hold that criminal sanctions for group libel are just as constitutional as sanctions for libel directed at individuals and are necessary "to the peace and well-being of the State" given the history of extreme racial and religious propaganda in Illinois. Finally, the Court held that Illinois may require the defendant, in order to be found not guilty, to prove both that the utterance was factual and that the publication was made "with good motives and for justifiable ends." [Illinois Constitution, Article II, 4.] Interestingly, though, the majority opinion ended by stating that its finding of the statute's constitutionality "carries no implication of approval of the wisdom of the legislation or of its efficacy."

The dissents by Justices BLACK, Reed, and DOUGLAS reflect the criticism that the decision drew and that the majority attempted to deflect in its closing statements. Justices Black and Douglas, in particular, offered separate but related arguments that the Illinois law did not prohibit libelous speech but rather criminalized the actions of citizens who petitioned their elected representatives and expressed dissenting opinions on proposed policies and legislation, such as Beauharnais, who was protesting desegregation. As Justice Douglas famously noted, "Today a white man stands convicted for protesting in unseemly language against our decisions invalidating restrictive covenants. Tomorrow a Negro will be hauled before a court for denouncing lynch law in heated terms."

However, although the Court shortly thereafter struck down several state criminal libel laws as unconstitutionally vague (*Ashton v. Kentucky,* 384 U.S. 195 [1966]) and overbroad (*Garrison v. Louisiana,* 379 U.S. 64 [1964]), and curtailed the reach of civil libel, the Court has never expressly overturned *Beauharnais* or the concept of group libel. In fact, the Court has continued to cite *Beauharnais* as support for the concept that libelous or defamatory speech falls outside of the scope of speech protected by the First Amendment.

For more information: Freedman, Monroe H., and Eric M. Freedman, eds. *Group Defamation and Freedom of Speech: The Relationship between Language and Violence.* Westport, Conn.: Greenwood Press, 1995; Jones, William K. *Insult to Injury: Libel, Slander, and Invasions of Privacy.* Boulder: University Press of Colorado, 2003; Walker, Samuel. *Hate Speech: An American Controversy.* Lincoln: University of Nebraska Press, 1994.

—Amy Steigerwalt

Belle Terre v. Boraas, 416 U.S. 1 (1974)

In the *Village of Belle Terre Et Al. v. Boraas Et Al.,* the court held that a ZONING ordinance restricting LAND USE to particular circumstances is constitutional.

The Village of Belle Terre, New York, implemented a zoning ordinance that restricted land use to single-family households and households of no more than two unrelated persons. The ordinance defined a family as anyone related by blood, marriage, adoption, or no more than two persons that are not related. Persons related by blood, marriage, or adoption were permitted to live together with no limit on the number of persons in the home, while non-related persons in a single dwelling were limited to two. Multiple resident dwellings, such as fraternities or boardinghouses, were directly in violation of the ordinance. The owners of a home in Belle Terre, and three of six college students renting the home, filed suit claiming that their Fourteenth Amendment right to equal protection and their right to travel, privacy, and association had been violated by the ordinance. The district court held that the ordinance was constitutional because it protected the interests of the residents of Belle Terre and did not represent a hardship on the students' abilities to be housed. The appellate court reversed the decision based on the determination of a trend beginning in the Supreme Court toward a "new equal protection standard." The Supreme Court agreed with the district court's decision. However, by the time the case reached the Supreme Court, the students' lease had expired and they had vacated the home. This presented another aspect to be examined; was the case a MOOT case?

Justice DOUGLAS wrote for the majority and was joined by Chief Justice BURGER and Justices STEWART, WHITE, BLACKMUN, POWELL, and REHNQUIST. The majority opinion addressed several issues. First, the court examined the PRECEDENT set by *Euclid v. Ambler Realty Co.,* 272 U.S. 365 (1926). This particular case upheld a zoning ordinance as legitimate under state policing powers. As long as the ordinance is "fairly debatable, the legislative judgment must be allowed to control." The Supreme Court applied this standard to the case and found that the claims of the plaintiffs did not make the ordinance unconstitutional. The Court decided that the ordinance did not interfere with intra/interstate travelers; it did not discriminate against a particular group and not other groups; and it did not violate FUNDAMENTAL RIGHTS guaranteed by the Constitution.

In regards to the equal protection clause, the court relied on *Reed v. Reed,* 404 U.S. 71 (1971), stating that a law will be maintained if "the law is reasonable, not arbitrary, and bears a rational relationship to a permissible state objective." The court agreed that the community had the right to determine what type of environment they wanted to live in and to protect their interests with an ordinance. Lastly, they argued that the case was not moot because of the potential ongoing effects of the ordinance on the property owner.

Both Justices BRENNAN and MARSHALL offered dissenting opinions. Justice Brennan argued that the case had lost the element of controversy necessary to file suit. The students who filed suit moved out; therefore, the new question was whether the landlord had the right to file suit on behalf of his tenants. When approached this way, Justice Brennan stated the landlord would have STANDING to sue and the case should be dismissed.

Justice Marshall dissented on the grounds that the ordinance violated the students' First and Fourteenth Amendment rights to association and privacy. He suggested that this case is comparable to cases where neighborhoods discriminate against certain races and religions. Justice Marshall thought that the ordinance would accomplish the same goals if it were to limit the size of the dwellings or the number of occupants allowed in each dwelling as opposed to the current system of limitation.

For more information: Lockhart, William. *The American Constitution.* St. Paul, Minn.: West Group, 1999.

—Jaeryl Covington

Berman v. Parker, 348 U.S. 26 (1954)

The controversy that resulted in the lawsuit in *Berman v. Parker* arose when a citizen objected to a governmental agency's plan to make major changes in an urban area, with the intended result of long-term benefits to both businesses and residents of the community. Mr. Berman, the plaintiff in the case, owned and operated a business located in a block of buildings, all of which were scheduled for demolition pursuant to the urban renewal project. When Mr. Berman realized that effectuation of the project required demolition of the building in which his business was located, he sued the government agency that administered the project and requested that his building be exempt from the demolition plan. If Mr. Berman had won the lawsuit, his business would have remained standing while every other building located in the same square block would be demolished.

When *Berman v. Parker* reached the Supreme Court, the justices considered all of the legal concepts underlying the controversial situation, beginning with the power of EMINENT DOMAIN, which grants a government or governmental agency limited power to seize privately owned property. The Fifth Amendment to the U.S. Constitution grants the federal government limited authority to require landowners to sell their real estate to a government representative:

No person shall . . . be deprived of . . . property, without due process of law; nor shall private property be taken for public use, without just compensation.

While this constitutional amendment clearly authorizes the federal government to seize private property, the amendment equally clearly limits that power by establishing two prerequisites to actual transfer of the property. First, the government must pay the landowner "just compensation," for the property. Second, the government must intend to put the seized land to "public use."

Unfortunately, neither the Fifth Amendment nor the remainder of the Constitution and its Amendments contains definitions of the phrases *just compensation* and *public use.* Supreme Court PRECEDENT provided the justices with a definition of the first phrase. For over a century, the justices consistently interpreted "just compensation" as synonymous with "fair market value." In *Berman v. Parker,* the Supreme Court remained aligned with this precedent and defined "just compensation" as "fair market value."

The more problematic of the Fifth Amendment's undefined but important phrases was *public use.* The *Berman v. Parker* plaintiff had two arguments that involved this phrase. First, the plaintiff argued that his store should not be demolished because its longevity combined with its record of ongoing profitability proved that this business served a "public use." Second, the plaintiff stated that the urban renewal project's goals exceeded the limitations inherent in any reasonable interpretation of the Fifth Amendment's "public use" clause.

To form a coherent opinion in the case of *Berman v. Parker,* it was necessary for the Court to define "public use." Precedent was not helpful in this instance, since previous Supreme Court decisions attributed a variety of meanings to this phrase. Eventually, the justices decided to treat their opinion in the case as an opportunity to provide a definition of "public use" that would be helpful in future EMINENT DOMAIN cases. The Court found that the stated purposes of the urban renewal project that provoked this lawsuit would be useful in concocting a modern definition of "public use."

The urban revitalization project at the root of *Berman v. Parker* sought to: beautify a specific neighborhood by demolishing substandard, unsanitary housing, and building safe, sanitary, building-code compliant residences; and encourage ongoing community pride and vitality by improving the area's balance of residential, educational, religious, municipal, and commercial land uses. In its opinion in the case, the U.S. Supreme Court defined *public use* as utilization of property for one or more of the urban renewal project's purposes.

In its *Berman v. Parker* decision, the Supreme Court found that a community's interest in completion of an urban revitalization project far outweighed a proprietor's interest in continuing the affairs of a single, preexisting business within the boundaries of a project area, particularly where inclusion of this business: provided a reminder of the blight that previously existed in the neighborhood; detracted from the community's self-image, when improvement of this image was crucial to the success of the project; and impaired the urban revitalization project's prospects for long-term success by upsetting its carefully planned balance of residential, educational, religious, municipal, and commercial land usage. Hence, the Court held that completion of the entire urban renewal project, including demolishing the plaintiff's store, constituted a "public use" within the meaning of the Fifth Amendment to the U.S. Constitution.

Since its 1954 decision in *Berman v. Parker*, the Supreme Court has continued to broaden the scope of the Fifth Amendment's "public use" clause. The current, 21st-century interpretation of "public use" of land seized pursuant to exercise of eminent domain includes construction of factories, casinos, shopping malls, parking lots, high-rise office buildings, and residential property.

For more information: Klop, Jeremy R. *Eminent Domain*. Raleigh: University of North Carolina Press, 1998; Sinnitt and Sinnitt, Inc. "Condemnation." Findlaw. Available online. URL: http://library.lp.findlaw.com/articles/file/00512/008398. Downloaded May 11, 2004.

—Beth S. Swartz

Betts v. Brady, 316 U.S. 455 (1942)

In *Betts v. Brady*, the Supreme Court of the United States held that the Constitution does not require states to provide an attorney to represent indigent defendants who are accused of serious crimes. Betts, an indigent man residing in Mary-land, was indicted for robbery and held in jail. After asserting his innocence, Betts told the judge that he had no money to hire an attorney and asked if the court could appoint an attorney to defend him. The judge denied his request, telling him the practice of the local courts was to appoint counsel only to defendants charged with rape or murder.

Betts stuck with his plea of "not guilty" but chose not to have a jury trial. Instead, he proceeded to represent himself in a trial before a judge. Betts cross-examined the witnesses brought by the prosecution and presented witnesses of his own who provided him with an alibi during the time he was alleged to have committed the robbery. Nevertheless, at the end of the trial, the judge pronounced Betts guilty and sentenced him to eight years in prison.

While in prison, Betts filed court petitions seeking to overturn his conviction. He argued that since he had been accused of a serious crime, the Fourteenth Amendment to the Constitution guaranteed him a right to counsel. And because he had been tried and convicted without an attorney for his defense, Betts claimed his conviction was unconstitutional. Betts was denied relief in the state courts, and eventually the Supreme Court of the United States agreed to consider his case.

The Court, in a divided, six-to-three opinion, held that there is no constitutional right to counsel for criminal defendants. In justifying its decision, the Court noted that most of the states did not consider appointed counsel a fundamental right necessary for a fair trial. Justice Roberts, writing the opinion of the Court, asserted that Betts's trial was fair for several reasons. First, as was typical for defendants without counsel, Betts had not faced a jury trial. "Bench trials"—conducted by a judge—are much less formal and give the judge greater control over the proceedings to ensure impartiality. Second, Betts was capable of providing an adequate defense, the Court claimed, because the only issue raised at trial was the truthfulness of the witnesses presented. Betts was 43 years old, of average intelligence, and able to defend himself on the simple question of the veracity of his alibi, the Court reasoned. Moreover, he had pled guilty in a prior felony case, so he was somewhat familiar with the operations of the criminal justice system.

Three justices dissented from the majority opinion and challenged its reasoning. Justice BLACK, writing for the dissenting justices, argued that the majority opinion was wrong and violated Supreme Court precedents. Black asserted that the denial of legal representation to poor defendants had long been viewed as "shocking to the universal sense of justice throughout this country."

Twenty years later, in the case of *GIDEON V. WAINWRIGHT*, 372 U.S. 335 (1963), the Supreme Court overruled its decision in *Betts v. Brady*. Justice Black now wrote for the majority of the Court and stated that the Sixth Amendment to the Constitution required the provision of counsel to defendants accused of serious crimes, and that defense lawyers were "necessities not luxuries."

For more information: Epstein, Lee, and Thomas G. Walker. *Constitutional Law for a Changing America: Rights, Liberties, and Justice.* 4th ed. Washington, D.C.: CQ Press, 2001; Israel, Jerold H., Yale Kamisar, and Wayne R. LaFave. *Criminal Procedure and the Constitution: Leading Supreme Court Cases and Introductory Text.* St. Paul, Minn.: West Wadsworth, 2003.

—Keith Rollin Eakins

bill of attainder

The United States Supreme Court has defined bills of attainder as legislative acts that inflict punishment on named individuals or members of an easily ascertainable group without a judicial trial. The U.S. Constitution forbids bills of attainder, at both the state and federal level, ensuring that only judges can punish individuals, not state legislatures or the U.S. Congress.

Under medieval English law, Parliament would pass bills of attainder for a variety of reasons: to execute individuals, seize property from individuals, or to prevent them from inheriting property—a condition known as "corruption of blood." In effect, the English Parliament used bills of attainder to punish political enemies who would be difficult to convict in a court.

Bills that were limited to seizing property were called "bills of pains and penalties" whereas bills of attainder included execution. Bills of pains and penalties were widely used during the American Revolution in order to confiscate the property of English loyalists. Seeing how legislatures might abuse bills of attainder, the Framers abolished them in the U.S. Constitution. The framers worried that passionate public bodies might usurp judicial powers and thereby abuse minority factions or individuals. After the adoption of the Constitution, the U.S. Supreme Court, in *FLETCHER V. PECK,* 10 U.S. 87 (1810), eliminated the difference between bills of attainder and bills of pains and penalties, ruling that the bill of attainder clause in the Constitution also refers to bills of pains and penalties. In general, the Court accepts any punishment, whether it takes the form of death, fines, or denial of a specific right, as grounds for an attainder claim.

Bill of attainder case law began developing after the Civil War, when some states started requiring public employees to take loyalty oaths swearing that they had never aided the Confederacy. Those who refused to take the oath were considered de facto guilty by law. In *Cummings v. Missouri* and *Ex Parte Garland,* 71 U.S. 333 (1866), the Supreme Court struck down oath requirements as bills of attainder. For 80 years after *Cummings,* the bill of attainder clause remained nearly dormant. Then, in the 1940s and 1950s, the Red Scare provided fertile ground for its reemergence.

The first modern attainder case was *United States v. Lovett,* 328 U.S. 303 (1946). In 1943 Congress passed an appropriations rider denying salaries to three government officials who were suspected of being communists. For the first time in American history, Congress had subjected specifically named individuals to a statutory penalty. The Supreme Court nullified the rider.

After the hysteria of the Red Scare subsided, the Court developed a more expansive view of punishment. In *Communist Party of the United States v. Subversive Activities Control Board,* 367 U.S. 1 (1961), the Court began to examine Congress's intent in passing legislation. The justices concluded if the intent was to create a hardship, then the act constituted a punishment, and it was therefore a bill of attainder.

In *United States v. Brown,* 381 U.S. 437 (1965), the Supreme Court continued to broaden its definition of punishment and developed a "functional" approach to attainder cases. In *Brown* the Court declared that "legislative punishment of any form or severity, of specifically designated persons or groups (381 U.S. 437 at 447)" constitute a bill of attainder: The Court argued that any bill that functioned as a punishment should be considered a bill of attainder, continuing, "It would be archaic to limit the definition of punishment to retribution. Punishment serves several purposes: retribution, rehabilitative, deterrent, and preventive (381 U.S. 437 at 458)."

The most important modern attainder case is *Nixon v. Administrator of General Services,* 433 U.S. 425 (1977). President Richard M. Nixon challenged a congressional edict that required him to turn over his papers and tape recordings to the General Services Department. He claimed that Congress had violated the attainder clause because it had singled him out as a specific individual. The Supreme Court disagreed, arguing that turning over papers is not a punishment and therefore that Congress's specifically naming him was irrelevant. In the *Nixon* case, the Court sought to establish standards for determining if Congress had imposed a bill of attainder. The Court ruled that if any of the following criteria were met, Congress had enacted a bill of attainder: (1) if "the challenged statute falls within the historical meaning of legislative punishment"; (2) whether the statute, "viewed in terms of the type and severity of burdens imposed, reasonably can be said to further nonpunitive legislative purposes"; and (3) whether the legislative record "evinces a congressional intent to punish."

For more information: Levy, Leonard W. *Origins of the Bill of Rights.* New Haven, Conn.: Yale University Press,

1999; Manweller, Mathew. "Can a Reparations Package Be a Bill of Attainder?" *The Independent Review* 6, no. 4 (2002): 555–571.

—Mathew Manweller

Bill of Rights (1791)

The Bill of Rights refers to the first 10 amendments to the U.S. Constitution. These amendments guarantee important rights and freedoms and establish safeguards against tyranny. Originally the Bill of Rights applied only to the federal government. However, over time, the Supreme Court has held, through a process called selective INCORPORATION, that most clauses of most of the Bill of Rights apply to the states as well as the federal government.

The First Amendment guarantees free speech and freedom of RELIGION. However, these freedoms are not absolute. The government can regulate the time, place, and manner of speech in order to protect the health, safety, and welfare of society. In other words, the government can make it illegal to yell "fire" in a crowded theater, to quote a famous example from Justice Oliver Wendell HOLMES. Religious freedom is not absolute either, as human sacrifice is obviously illegal, animal abuse is illegal, and the use of many drugs is illegal. Notably, there is no express provision in the First Amendment, or the Constitution for that matter, that prohibits government involvement with religion. "In God We Trust" on the money of the United States is allowed, and Congress can employ a chaplain. The First Amendment only prohibits the government establishment of religion and excessive entanglement between government and religion. The First Amendment also guarantees the freedom of the press and the right of the people to petition the government to address grievances. First Amendment issues are frequently litigated, and there are numerous Supreme Court decisions regarding the First Amendment.

The SECOND AMENDMENT is only one small sentence, but its meaning is vague and controversial. The Second Amendment states "A well regulated Militia, being necessary to the security of a free State, the right of the people to keep and bear Arms, shall not be infringed." Gun owners cite this amendment as establishing the right of citizens to own firearms. Others read the amendment as allowing states the ability to provide arms to militias or national guards. Both interpretations are to some extent correct, and these rights are not absolute. The government—through its police power to legislate to protect the health, safety, and welfare of citizens—can prohibit various firearms like fully automatic machine guns. The federal government can federalize or take control of state national guard units when necessary to respond to national emergencies. Compared to the other Amendments in the Bill of Rights, the Second Amendment has not received much attention from the Supreme Court.

The Fourth, Fifth, Sixth, and Eighth Amendments are crucial to criminal procedure and protecting the accused from wrongful prosecution. These amendments are the subject of many Supreme Court decisions. The Fourth Amendment prohibits unreasonable searches and seizures and requires that warrants be based on probable cause. These requirements protect citizens from random, arbitrary, abusive invasions of privacy and illegal seizure of property by the government. Questions of technology and how the Fourth Amendment applies to that technology are questions frequently addressed by the Supreme Court.

The Fifth Amendment contains important provisions for criminal procedure. The Fifth Amendment requires criminal indictment by a process of a grand jury, prohibits being tried twice for the same crime (the DOUBLE JEOPARDY clause), allows an accused to not be a witness against himself, and requires due process of law.

The Sixth Amendment also contains important criminal procedure safeguards. It guarantees the right to have a speedy and public trial and to be informed of the charges against the accused. The Sixth Amendment also guarantees the right to counsel and the right to confront or cross-examine adverse witnesses.

The Eighth Amendment is another important rule regarding criminal procedure. The Eighth Amendment states "Excessive bail shall not be required, nor excessive fines imposed, nor cruel and unusual punishment inflicted." Interpretation of this Amendment by the Supreme Court has evolved, for better or worse, as society has evolved. Many scholars and judges believe that the Eight Amendment requires reasonable proportionality—that the punishment fit the crime. However, the Supreme Court, largely following Justice Scalia's lead, has interpreted the Eighth Amendment not to include a reasonable proportionality requirement.

The Tenth Amendment assists in defining the power relationship between the federal government, state governments, and the people. More specifically, powers not granted to the federal government, or prohibited to the states, are reserved to the states or the people. Power is specifically divided among the federal government, the state governments, and the people. In an attempt to prevent tyrannical exercise of power by the government, power is divided among various levels of government.

The Third, Seventh, and NINTH AMENDMENTS deserve mention, though they are not the subject of the most significant Supreme Court decisions. The Third Amendment prohibits the government from quartering soldiers in one's house in times of peace; the Seventh Amendment guarantees the right to a trial by jury; and the Ninth Amendment guarantees rights not specifically mentioned.

The Bill of Rights limits the power of government to exercise arbitrary and tyrannical power. It represents an important mark in human history, as crucial rights were recognized as necessary to prevent tyranny by the government and in order to ensure that certain basic rights were afforded to citizens. The Supreme Court over time has interpreted and applied provisions of the Bill of Rights to an evolving society, and the Supreme Court will continue to interpret and apply the Bill of Rights to our evolving society.

For more information: Tribe, Lawrence. *American Constitutional Law.* Mineola, N.Y.: Foundation Press, 1988.

—James E. Headley

Black, Hugo Lafayette (1886–1971) *Supreme Court justice*

Hugo Black served on the United States Supreme Court from 1937 to 1971, a tenure that ranks second only to William O. DOUGLAS, his colleague for more than three decades on the Court, and one that ties Black with the likes of Chief Justice John MARSHALL and Justice John Marshall HARLAN. In his time on the Court, Black authored almost 1,000 opinions, more than a few of which played their own role in garnering for Black the label "great" as an American jurist.

Justice Black was President Franklin Roosevelt's first appointment to the Supreme Court, an appointment that came on the heels of FDR's ill-fated COURT-PACKING PLAN announced in February 1937. As a member of the U.S. Senate, then-Senator Black, Democrat of Alabama, was one of the principal supporters of the president's plan to reshape the federal judiciary. President Roosevelt's plan went nowhere in the Senate, but when he finally had an opportunity to nominate someone for the Supreme Court, in the summer of 1937, FDR chose his loyal New Deal supporter from the South. Upon hearing of Roosevelt's selection, his press secretary, Stephen Early exclaimed, "Jesus Christ." In the eyes of many political insiders, Black was not qualified for the Court; however, Roosevelt's selection of Hugo Lafayette Black proved to be one of his most masterly deeds, for Black would carve out a judicial legacy rivaled by only a few justices in the history of the Supreme Court.

After being confirmed by his colleagues in the U.S. Senate, and in the process allaying fears about his one-time and brief membership in the Ku Klux Klan in Alabama, Justice Black became the first justice on the Supreme Court to take up offices in the newly constructed "marble palace" across from Capitol Hill. Black would occupy this office, and a highly influential role in American law, until his resignation from the Court on September 17, 1971. Black died

Justice Hugo Black *(United States Supreme Court)*

a week later and was buried in a $165 pine casket along with several copies of his cherished Constitution.

Justice Black's contribution to American jurisprudence in the 20th century (a contribution still felt today) is virtually unequaled. He wrote the Court's major decisions in cases concerning the establishment clause, enshrining Jefferson's "wall of separation" between church and state into American constitutional law. He authored his famous dissent in the case of *BETTS V. BRADY* in 1942 and lived to write the Court's opinion in *GIDEON V. WAINRIGHT* in 1963, overruling Betts and establishing the right of counsel for indigent defendants. Black wrote the majority opinion in the famous "Steel Seizure Case" concerning presidential powers in wartime, and his last major opinion, his swan song from the Court, was a moving concurrence in the Pentagon Papers case concerning freedom of the press and national security.

Perhaps Black's crowning achievement in American constitutional law concerns the absorption of the BILL OF RIGHTS into the Fourteenth Amendment's due process clause, as seen in his *ADAMSON V. CALIFORNIA* opinion. Black referred to the Constitution as his "legal bible," and his constitutional fundamentalism led him to an absolutist approach to the First Amendment and a leading dissenting opinion in the *Griswold* case in which the Court discovered the right to marital privacy, a right rejected by Black for it did not appear specifically in the text of our founding document.

Justice Black penned nearly 1,000 opinions during his tenure on the Court. Perhaps his opinion in *Gideon* is his touchstone as a jurist. An autodidact, Black firmly believed the Constitution itself was a teaching instrument if one but consulted it regularly.

For more information: Black, Hugo L. *A Constitutional Faith.* New York: Alfred A. Knopf, 1968; Newman, Roger K. *Hugo Black: A Biography.* New York: Random House, 1994.
—Stephen K. Shaw

Blackmun, Harry (1908–1999) *Supreme Court justice*
Harry Blackmun (November 12, 1908–March 4, 1999), Supreme Court justice (1970–94), a Nixon appointee, was known for his thoughtful and scholarly opinions, the most famous of which was *ROE V. WADE,* 410 U.S. 113 (1973). A nominal Republican, he left the Court as its most liberal member.

Blackmun attended Harvard College and Harvard Law School. He was for 16 years a member of a prestigious Minneapolis law firm. He also taught at William Mitchell College of Law. Blackmun served as general counsel for the Mayo Clinic.

In 1959 he was appointed by President Eisenhower to the U.S. COURT OF APPEALS. Blackmun was among the first federal judges to declare prison conditions were violating the Eighth Amendment. (He struck down the use of whips for punishing prisoners in the Arkansas prison system.)

In 1970 Blackmun was appointed to the U.S. Supreme Court after President Nixon's two previous nominees had been rejected by the Senate. Blackmun had gone to kindergarten with Warren E. BURGER and they became lifelong friends. It was Chief Justice Burger who recommended Blackmun to Nixon for the Court. (Lazy journalists called them the "Minnesota Twins," assuming that Blackmun was a clone of Burger.)

Initially the freshman judge relied on his friend for guidance. In his first term Blackmun had 95.8% concurrence with Burger's votes. By 1977 just over half the time their votes coincided. By 1981 it was down to 40.9% in nonunanimous cases. The chief justice rarely asked Blackmun to write opinions in important or even interesting cases.

Blackmun was a conservative in the criminal justice area. He favored victims' rights over criminals' rights and deferred to criminal justice officials (prosecutors, police, prison administrators).

He voted with Burger in the Pentagon Papers case and in death penalty cases. Though Blackmun personally opposed CAPITAL PUNISHMENT, he did not think that judges should make such a policy decision. In the 1994 case of *Callins v. Collins,* 510 U.S. 1141, he reversed his longtime support of decisions upholding executions. He thought attempts to endure fairness in applying the death penalty had failed.

Blackmun's reputation is tied to his authorship of the abortion decision, *Roe v. Wade.* His understanding of the medical community (at Harvard he was premed and later counseled the Mayo Clinic) and his being the father of three daughters may have given him the orientation to overrule laws banning abortions. He devised a trimester formula for when a decision to abort a fetus would involve more than the woman and her physician. Despite receiving 60,000 pieces of hate mail, he never retreated from his position.

Blackmun had a sympathy for the disadvantaged. He consciously sought to hew to the Supreme Court's center. He upheld AFFIRMATIVE ACTION and championed a strict separation of church and state. In a case of an abused child and an unresponsive child protection agency, he dissented at the consequences of indifference.

Blackmun also dissented in the 1986 case of *BOWERS V. HARDWICK,* 478 U.S. 186, regarding extending the right of privacy to cover consensual homosexual acts. When the Court in 1993 ruled that U.S. authorities need not give

Justice Harry Blackmun *(United States Supreme Court)*

hearings before seizing and returning Haitians who had fled their country by boats, Blackmun was the lone dissenter.

One of Blackmun's great loves was baseball. In an early opinion, *Flood v. Kuhn*, 407 U.S. 258 (1972), he reaffirmed professional baseball's immunity from federal ANTITRUST LAW.

Blackmun retired from the Supreme Court at 85, the third oldest person ever to have served on the Court.

For more information: Schneider, Mark. "Justice Blackmun: A Wise Man Walking the Corridors of Power, Gently." *Georgetown Law Journal* 83, no. 1 (November 1994): 11–15; Wasby, Stephen L. "Justice Blackmun and Criminal Justice: A Modest Overview." *Akron Law Review* 28, no. 2 (Fall/Winter, 1995): 125–186; ———. "Justice Harry A. Blackmun: Transformation from 'Minnesota Twin' to Independent Voice." In *The Burger Court: Political and Judicial Profiles,* edited by Charles M. Lamb and Stephen C. Halpern. Urbana and Chicago: University of Illinois Press, 1991; Yarbrough, Tinsley. *The Rehnquist Court and the Constitution.* New York: Oxford University Press, 2000.

—Martin Gruberg

Board of County Commissioners, Wabaunsee County, Kansas v. Keen A. Umbehr, 518 U.S. 668 (1996)

In *County Commissioners, Wabaunsee County, Kansas, v. Umbehr,* the Supreme Court ruled, in a 7-2 vote, that the same free speech protections that prevent the arbitrary dismissal of government employees for expressing political views also protect independent government contractors from having contracts terminated. This case was a companion case to O'HARE TRUCK SERVICE, INC. V. CITY OF NORTHLAKE, 518 U.S. 712 (1996), which was decided on the same day.

Keen Umbehr ran a trash hauling service in rural Wabaunsee County, Kansas, and he had an exclusive contract for collecting trash from several locations in the county from the early 1980s until 1991. During this period, Umbehr not only hauled trash; he also was one of the loudest and most persistent critics of the Board of Commissioners for a variety of alleged sins, including financial mismanagement and secret (and illegal) meetings. He ran for one of the Commission seats, and he sued the commissioners over a change in the rates charged for dumping the trash he hauled in 1990. The commissioners voted in 1991 not to approve the renewal of the contract. Umbehr then sued the two commissioners who voted against the renewal as individuals and against the Commission as a whole. The suit against the individual commissioners was thrown out because of their "qualified immunity" as public officials acting in their official capacity. The District Court ruled that

the county was free to consider the contractor's public statements in making a decision about renewing the contract and that contractors did not have the same First Amendment protections that are provided to employees.

The 10th Circuit COURT OF APPEALS overturned the District Court and said that contractors did have First Amendment protections and that the court should apply a "balancing test" in determining whether or not the interests of the government as a contracting agency outweighed the free speech interests of the contractor. Specifically, they argued that the test established in *Pickering v. Board of Education of Township High School Dist. 205, Will County,* 391 U.S. 563 (1968), should be applied, recognizing that the rights of a contractor might not have quite as much weight in this balancing act as would the rights of an employee. The Supreme Court affirmed the decision of the 10th Circuit.

This case is particularly important as many governments—local, state, and federal—increasingly turn to private contractors to perform government functions. The Court majority was very clear that they saw little difference between employees who worked for government employers directly and those who held government contracts (though they did not address the issue of whether or not those protections extend to the employees of the contractor). The Court did say, however, that it is generally easier for the government, because it is acting as an employer or contracting agency, to establish that its interests outweigh those of an employee or independent contractor than it would be to say that their interests outweighed those of a citizen or interest group where government is acting as a sovereign power.

The dissenters, Justices SCALIA and THOMAS, vehemently opposed the majority's decision in this and the *O'Hare Truck Service v. Northlake* case (they responded to both cases in a single dissent). The principal basis of their objection is that there is no specific prohibition against considering the political opinions or political party affiliation of persons or corporations seeking to do business with the government. To the dissenters, awarding of government contracts on the basis of political position or support is a practice as old as the country itself. They see this case as another example of where the "slippery slope" that began with cases like *Elrod v. Burns*, 427 U.S. 347 (1976), and *Rankin v. McPherson*, 483 U.S. 378 (1987), which began the process of reducing the authority of governments to act completely as "at will" employers. Also, the dissenters feared that this would open a Pandora's Box and that because it would be necessary to balance the government's interests against the contractor's interests separately in each case, the floodgates would open and the courts would become inundated with claims from unhappy contractors who lost their contracts.

The case was returned to the lower courts for a trial on the facts of the case where a settlement was eventually reached.

For more information: Bresser, Bonnie. "Freedom: A Fight for Everyone." *Quill* 89 (October 2001): 19–23.

—Charles W. Gosset
—Daniel Baracskay

Board of Education v. Pico, 457 U.S. 853 (1982)

In *Board of Education v. Pico,* the Supreme Court held that school boards may limit curriculum based on community standards; however, they cannot limit freedom of speech in a voluntary environment such as the library.

In 1975 three members of the Island Trees Union Free School District No. 26 attended a conference at which they obtained a list of books deemed controversial and unsuitable for students. The group found that nine of the books on the list were in the high school library and that another was in the junior high library. The board ordered these books removed stating that they were "anti-American, anti-Christian, anti-Semitic, and just plain filthy." The school board further asserted that it was their duty to "protect the children in our schools from this moral danger as surely as from physical and medical dangers." The superintendent objected to the board's removal of the books. As a compromise they formed a "Book Review Committee" on which four teachers and four parents would review the content of the books and recommend further action concerning them. The committee found that five books should remain in the library, citing their "relevance," "educational suitability," and "appropriateness to age and grade level." They recommended that two books be removed. The committee took no position on one of the books and recommended that one book be available to students with parents' approval. The school board rejected the committee's proposal, returning only one book to the school library and allowing one to be available with parents' permission. The original petitioners in the case claimed that the school board's removal of books was a denial of their First Amendment rights.

Justice BRENNAN wrote for a five-person majority that included Justices MARSHALL, STEVENS, BLACKMUN, and WHITE. He observed that while school boards have broad discretion in school affairs, it does not transcend rights protected by the First Amendment. Brennan relied on *TINKER V. DES MOINES INDEPENDENT SCHOOL DISTRICT,* 393 U.S. 503 (1969), quoting the phrase "students do not shed their constitutional rights to freedom of speech or expression at the schoolhouse gate." Brennan acknowledged that school boards have discretion in limiting school curriculum based on community values and standards due to the compulsory nature of the classroom. However, this right does not extend to the school library where the use of its content is voluntary. Granted that school boards hold considerable discretion in determining the contents of their district libraries, that discretion may not be narrowly partisan or political. Whether the removal or withholding of specific books in a school library violates the First Amendment is dependent upon the motivation behind the removal. The irregular circumstances surrounding the removal of these books from the library tends not "to allay suspicions regarding the petitioners' motivation."

Justice Blackmun concurred to emphasize that school boards cannot remove books simply because they disapprove of the values in them. Justice WHITE, also concurring, stated that there is no necessity for "discussing the extent to which the First Amendment limits the school board's discretion to remove books from school libraries."

Justice BURGER, joined by Justices POWELL, REHNQUIST, and O'CONNOR, dissented on FEDERALISM and JUDICIAL RESTRAINT grounds. This is an area typically left to the states, not the federal judiciary. The court, said Burger, is running the risk of becoming the "super censor of school board decisions" and the Constitution does not dictate that judges determine the standards of morality. Justice Powell, who once served on a school board, wrote that locally elected school boards are "uniquely local and democratic" and should have the authority to determine the educational standards of their district. Rehnquist, joined by Burger and Powell, wrote that the actions of educators do not raise the same First Amendment questions as those of the government and that this decision is inconsistent with past court decisions. Justice O'Connor stated that a school board can limit books in a school library as long as it does not forbid students from reading or discussing the ideas in them. She also agreed that it is not the function of the court to regulate the decisions of local school boards.

This decision is important for determining the limits of censorship and rights of STUDENTS. It further defined that students' constitutional rights to Freedom of Speech are not to be forgotten when they enter school. It restricts a school board's ability to limit the rights of students to read books even if the board deems them immoral or disagreeable.

For more information: Supreme Court Opinions. "*Board of Education v. Pico,* 457 U.S. 853 (1982)." Find Law. Available online. URL: http://laws.findlaw.com/us/457/853.html. Downloaded on May 11, 2004; Gold, Susan Dudley. *Board of Education v. Pico.* New York: 21st Century Books, 1997.

—Andrew C. McIntire
—John M. Yung
—Lindsay B. Zoeller

Board of Regents of State Colleges et al. v. Roth, 408 U.S. 564 (1972)

In *Board of Regents v. Roth*, the Court held that employees who speak unfavorably about their employer and do not have their contracts renewed cannot claim their First Amendment right to freedom of speech has been violated if the employer did not clearly base the decision not to rehire on the speech in question. This is important because it signals that the Constitution only protects interests and property that exist in the present, not interests or property that might hypothetically exist.

In this case David Roth was hired by Wisconsin State University in Oshkosh in 1968 to teach political science for one year. At the end of this year he was released without a reason for his not being rehired or a hearing to perhaps be rehired. Roth, feeling he was not rehired due to his speaking out about school policies, thought this was a violation of the First Amendment. He had spoken against the school's wrongful dismissal of a group of students; "Congress shall make no law . . . abridging the freedom of speech" [Amendment I]. The Court found no evidence that the University of Wisconsin was acting to deny freedom of speech to Mr. Roth.

This case demonstrates that the Fourteenth Amendment does not protect interests or property that could hypothetically exist, rather just property that exists now. For instance, before you invent something you do not have any legal rights to that invention.

The Supreme Court did however uphold the first section of the Fourteenth Amendment that states, ". . . nor shall any State deprive any person of life, liberty, or property, without due process of law; nor deny to any person within its jurisdiction the equal protection of the laws." They found that David Roth could not be given SUMMARY JUDGMENT when it pertains to his job as an employee of University of Wisconsin–Oshkosh, which is in fact working for the state of Wisconsin as a teacher of political science. The problem arises when you realize that Roth did not work long enough to accumulate enough experience to receive tenure. If Roth had tenure it would, among other things, provide him with more job security. The court found five to four against David Roth, feeling that the Board of Regents did not owe Roth a hearing and an explanation.

Writing the lead opinion for the majority Justice STEWART said, "Procedural due process applies only to the deprivation of interests encompassed within the Fourteenth Amendment's protection of liberty and property, and the range of such interests is not infinite." Here he is saying that due process only applies to the loss of interests regarding the Fourteenth Amendment's protection of liberty and properties have boundaries. He then holds that due process only protects interests that a person already has, not what he could in theory get. For instance, Stewart claims that due process can protect your house that you built but not the houses you could build in the future.

For more information: Roosenbloom, David H. *Administrative Law for Managers*. Boulder, Colo.: Westview, 2003; Drake, W. Avon, and Robert D. Holsworth. *Affirmative Action and the Stalled Quest for Black Progress*. Urbana: University of Illinois Press, 1996.

Board of Regents of University of Wisconsin v. Southworth, 529 U.S. 217 (2000)

A unanimous Supreme Court held, in *Board of Regents of University of Wisconsin v. Southworth*, that public university students may not be exempt from paying a compulsory student activity fee, even if the money is distributed to groups engaging in political and ideological speech to which they object. Several past and present students of the University of Wisconsin-Madison objected to the university's policy of disbursing allocable funds (approximately 20% of the total activity fees collected) to support various extracurricular endeavors pursued by registered student organizations (RSOs). According to Southworth and others, the compulsory fees amounted to "compelled speech" and were thereby unconstitutional.

Finding for Southworth, the district court relied on two cases involving the linkage between professional membership fees and political expression (*ABOOD V. DETROIT BOARD OF EDUCATION*, 431 U.S. 209 [1977], and *Keller v. State Bar of California*, 496 U.S. 1 [1990]) and reasoned that the university violated students' First Amendment rights by denying them the choice not to fund certain organizations. Affirming the trial court decision in relevant part, the 7th Circuit COURT OF APPEALS further enjoined the university from requiring students to pay the allocable funds portion of the student activity fee, given its conclusion that "the program was not germane to the university's mission, did not further vital policy of the university, and imposed too much of a burden on respondent's free speech rights."

Writing for a unanimous United States Supreme Court, Justice Anthony KENNEDY reversed the judgment of the lower court, emphasizing the special significance of the university setting—an environment that properly took as its mission the encouragement of a free, open, and vibrant exchange of speech. So long as the disbursement of moneys was carried out in a "viewpoint neutral manner"— that is, so long as the allocation was evenhanded and not contingent on the *content* of a particular group's message— then the program could pass constitutional muster. Indeed, the Court remanded the case on this point, in order that the university may ensure that all three of its possible methods of allocation were consistent with this requirement. Concurring in the Court's judgment, Justice SOUTER reasoned that the majority should have decided the case on narrower grounds—avoiding the rigid, indeed "cast-iron" requirement of viewpoint neutrality in this context—and preserved the university's programs as consistent with PRECEDENT involving academic freedom and the discretion of educational institutions.

The *Southworth* decision embodies the classical "marketplace of ideas" approach to speech regulation, especially in its assumption that, given a forum for all ideas, theories, and expression, a contest for acceptance will take place and ultimately the "truth," or the best possible results, will emerge. In doing so, the Court offered an important commentary on the *mission* of the university: The exposure to difficult and perhaps troubling notions is part of the college experience, and rather than *enervating* speech rights by not allowing individuals to "opt out" of the indirect subsidization of groups or expression with which they might disagree, the disbursement program actually *energizes* speech by increasing the amount of public discourse on campus and affording virtually all groups (RSOs) the opportunity to receive funding so that they may offer their own communicative contributions.

For more information: O'Neil, Robert M. *Free Speech in the College Community.* Bloomington: Indiana University Press, 1997; Walker, Scott. "I'll Speak for Myself: Compulsory Speech and the Use of Student Fees at State Universities." *Rutgers Law Review* 52 (Fall 1999): 341.

—Brian K. Pinaire

Bob Jones University v. United States, 461 U.S. 547 (1983)

In *Bob Jones University v. United States*, the Supreme Court held that the new IRS code established in 1970, which withholds tax-exempt status from institutions that discriminate on the basis of race, was not in violation of the freedom of religion clause of the First Amendment.

Bob Jones University is a private, Christian college in South Carolina that prohibits any advocacy, or action, that involves interracial dating or marriage. The college does not allow any interracial couples to attend the University, nor can anyone promote the idea of interracial couples on the campus. Until 1970, Bob Jones University had a tax-exempt status with the IRS. Contributions to the school were considered "charitable donations," which could be listed as tax deductions.

After *Cannon v. Green*, 398 U.S. 956 (1970), a case involving private schools in Mississippi that had discriminatory admission standards, the IRS concluded that it would no longer grant tax-exempt status to private schools adhering to such policies. This caused Bob Jones University to lose its tax-exempt status, which meant that donors could

no longer deduct donations from their income taxes. *Coit v. Green*, 404 U.S. 997 (1971), was the first court case to challenge this change, but the Supreme Court ruled in favor of the IRS, so the change remained in effect. Bob Jones University then filed a lawsuit in 1983 against the IRS for violating the freedom of religion clause of the First Amendment. *Christian Schools, Inc. v. United States* was decided along with this case and the result was an 8-1 vote for the IRS.

Chief Justice BURGER wrote the majority opinion, joined by Justices BRENNAN, WHITE, MARSHALL, BLACKMUN, STEVENS, and in part by POWELL. Justice Powell also wrote a concurring opinion. Chief Justice Burger acknowledged that Bob Jones University is a private, Christian institution with the rights to freely teach what it believes. He then states that this freedom changes when the institution receives governmental funding. When government funds are involved, the institution must "serve a public purpose and not be contrary to established public policy." The public policy to which he was referring is that which prohibits RACIAL DISCRIMINATION. He takes a brief moment to criticize the Congress for not passing legislation on this matter and then moves to the core of the case: If the government has a compelling interest, then it is possible to restrict an institution's freedom of RELIGION without violating the constitution. The CHIEF JUSTICE concludes that Bob Jones University is practicing racial discrimination, and that this policy interferes with a compelling government interest. That interest is eliminating all forms of discrimination. He therefore upholds the IRS decision to eliminate Bob Jones University's tax-exempt status.

Justice Powell agrees with the majority because he believes that the IRS decision to eliminate the tax-exempt status and tax deductions for donations to the university is not unconstitutional. However he does not agree that the IRS has the right to determine what public policies are "fundamental" to society. His other argument is that he believes that the majority of schools, public or private, do not always conduct themselves in ways that promote public policy, so it is not just the private institutions that need to be reprimanded.

Justice REHNQUIST wrote the lone dissent, arguing that the "Court should not legislate for Congress." He is very uneasy about this Court ruling because he believes that the Congress should be the one to pass this kind of legislation. He believes such IRS initiatives will lead to increasing tension between it and Congress. Justice Rehnquist agrees that there is a national interest in eliminating discrimination, but this is the responsibility of Congress. He cites *United States v. Wise*, 370 U.S. 405, 411 (1962), as PRECEDENT because it shows the court deferring to Congress. This is the only case that truly supports Justice Rehnquist's views.

For more information: Miller, Robert T., and Ronald B. Flowers. *Toward Benevolent Neutrality: Church, State and the Supreme Court.* 5th ed. Waco, Tex.: Baylor University Press, 1996.

—Christopher G. Mitchell

Boerne v. Flores, 521 U.S. 507 (1997)

The United States Supreme Court declared the 1993 Religious Freedom Restoration Act unconstitutional in *Boerne v. Flores.* The case is one of several recent decisions narrowing the constitutional protection for the First Amendment's free exercise of RELIGION guarantee.

St. Peter Catholic Church in Boerne, Texas, had grown too small for its parishioners. The city of Boerne denied a request by the archbishop of the San Antonio Diocese, Patrick Flores, to expand the building. The city cited an ordinance protecting the town's historic preservation district in which the 74-year-old church was located. Archbishop Flores sued the city, arguing that the ordinance prevented his parishioners from exercising their First Amendment right to the free exercise of religion and that it violated the Religious Freedom Restoration Act of 1993, 42 U.S.C.A section 2000bb.

Prior to 1990, the courts had applied a COMPELLING STATE INTEREST test to laws affecting the exercise of religion. This test obliged government to demonstrate that its goal was an essential ("compelling") public interest and that its efforts to accomplish that goal were least intrusive on an individual's exercise of religion. In 1990 the Supreme Court discarded this test. It rejected a claim made by members of the North American Church that Oregon had unlawfully denied them unemployment benefits. They had lost their jobs because they used peyote, a hallucinogenic drug smoked for religious purposes. The Court in *Oregon v. Smith,* 494 U.S. 872 (1990), held that a state can impose a valid and neutral law regulating religious activities provided that the law applies to all citizens regardless of their religion.

In 1993 Congress sought to overturn the *Smith* decision by passing the Religious Freedom Restoration Act. The law sought to reimpose the compelling state interest test in order to protect free exercise of religion rights. Congress relied on its enforcement power, granted by the Fourteenth Amendment, to prevent states from depriving individuals of their constitutional rights. It was a highly popular congressional statute, supported by groups as diverse as the Christian Coalition and the American Civil Liberties Union.

Justice Anthony M. KENNEDY, writing for the majority in *Boerne v. Flores,* struck down the Religious Freedom Restoration Act. Congress's power to enforce the Fourteenth Amendment could only be used to prevent or remedy actual violations of individual rights. Congressional

hearings on the act had not revealed recent examples of laws targeting religious practice or motivated by an antireligious intent, and therefore there was nothing for Congress to constitutionally remedy. The Court held that the act was not remedial in nature but rather an attempt to change the Constitution without going through the required amending process and thus was unconstitutional.

Justice Sandra Day O'CONNOR, in a dissent joined by Justice Stephen G. BREYER, agreed with the majority about Congress's powers under the Fourteenth Amendment. But O'Connor believed that *Smith* was wrongly decided and that the Court should return to the compelling state interest test. Justice David H. SOUTER dissented on procedural grounds.

Congress continues to pass laws seeking to overthrow the *Smith* and *Boerne* cases. It unanimously passed the Religious Land Use and Institutionalized Person Act in 2000. By mid-2003, more than a dozen states had enacted religious freedom restoration acts of their own. Both the state and federal laws seek to reintroduce the compelling state interest test.

For more information: Fowler, Robert Booth, et al. *Religion and Politics in America.* Boulder, Colo.: Westview Press, 1999.

—Timothy J. O'Neill

Bolling v. Sharpe, 347 U.S. 497 (1954)

Bolling v. Sharpe was a companion case to BROWN V. BOARD OF EDUCATION, 347 U.S. 483 (1954). Decided on the same day as *Brown,* it declared racial segregation in the District of Columbia schools unconstitutional. Earlier the Court had declared that segregation in state public schools violated the EQUAL PROTECTION CLAUSE of the Fourteenth Amendment. However, the Fourteenth Amendment only applies to the states. Since the District of Columbia comes under federal jurisdiction, the Court relied instead on the due process clause of the Fifth Amendment.

In his opinion for the Court, Chief Justice WARREN argued that the concepts of due process and equal protection have a common dimension that addresses the issue of discrimination. This overlap between the due process and equal protection clauses exists because both are based on what he refers to as "our American ideal of fairness[.]" Therefore, Warren argued that "discrimination may be so unjustifiable as to be violative of due process." This is particularly likely to be the case when discrimination is based on race. According to Warren, racial classifications "must be scrutinized with particular care, since they are contrary to our traditions and hence constitutionally suspect." When Warren applied this scrutiny to the segregated schools in the District of Columbia he found that since it was "not reasonably related to any proper governmental objective, . . .

[it] constituted an arbitrary deprivation of liberty . . . in violation of the Due Process Clause."

Although this case is not as well known as the *Brown* decision, it has had a lasting effect on federal CIVIL RIGHTS law. The status of racial classifications as constitutionally suspect has become one of the bedrock principles of American constitutional law. In the years since *Brown v. Board of Education* and *Bolling v. Sharpe*, a STRICT SCRUTINY test has been developed and applied to these SUSPECT CLASSIFICATIONS. Under this test, a law containing a racial classification can only be considered constitutional if it is the least restrictive means to achieve a compelling governmental interest.

On the federal level, the application of strict scrutiny under the due process clause to racial classifications has come to be a double-edged sword as federal programs designed to benefit minorities have been challenged as violations of due process rights. For example, in the recent case of *ADARAND CONSTRUCTORS, INC. V. PENA*, 515 U.S. 200 (1995), the Court dealt with the constitutionality of a federal law which provided financial incentives for primary contractors on federal highway construction contracts to hire subcontractors that were controlled by individuals found to be socially and economically disadvantaged. This disadvantaged status was presumed for certain racial and ethnic minorities. The Court held that standards for determining the constitutionality of racial classifications were the same for the states and the federal government. Hence, Justice O'CONNOR's opinion for the Court declared that "any person, of whatever race, has the right to demand that any governmental actor subject to the Constitution justify any racial classification . . . under the strictest scrutiny."

The Department of Transportation ultimately redesigned its minority subcontractor program so that the determination of minority status was more narrowly tailored to achieve its purpose. However, this case demonstrates the continuing relevance of the Court's ruling in *Bolling v. Sharpe*. It is now an established principle of American law that both state and federal programs will be subjected to strict scrutiny when they employ racial classifications.

For more information: Epstein, Lee, and Thomas, G. Walker. *Constitutional Law for a Changing America: Rights, Liberties, and Justice.* 4th ed. Washington, DC: Congressional Quarterly Press, 2001; O'Brien, David M. *Constitutional Law and Politics.* Vol. 2, *Civil Rights and Civil Liberties.* New York: W. W. Norton, 1997.

—Justin Halpern

Bork, Robert H. (1927–) *attorney general, Supreme Court justice*

Born March 1, 1927, Robert H. Bork is a renowned legal scholar having earned a law degree at the University of Chicago in 1953. Bork joined a Chicago law firm and then the Yale Law School faculty before serving as solicitor general from 1973 until 1977. During this period he also served as acting attorney general in 1974. He taught at Yale from 1977 until 1979 and served as a U.S. COURT OF APPEALS judge from 1982 to 1988. He became a fellow at the American Enterprise Institution for Public Policy Research in 1988. His many publications include *Slouching Towards Gomorrah,* Harper Collins, 1997; *The Tempting of America,* Simon & Schuster, 1997; and *Coercing Virtue,* Aei Press, 2003.

He is first known for his dark role in the Watergate scandal and his willingness to carry out President Richard Nixon's order to fire Watergate Special Prosecutor Archibald Cox following Cox's request of tapes of Oval Office conversations, the existence of which had been revealed by Nixon presidential assistant Alexander Butterfield. Nixon's attorney general, Elliot Richardson, and next in line deputy attorney general, William Ruckleshaus, resigned rather than carry out that order. Bork, as next in line promptly fired Cox. Public reaction to the chain of events became popularized as "The Saturday Night Massacre." The subsequent appointment of Leon Jaworski as another special prosecutor ultimately led to public knowledge of Nixon's role in the Watergate cover-up when the Supreme Court ordered the tapes to be reviewed. Rather than confront impeachment proceedings stemming from his role in the Watergate cover-up, Nixon resigned the presidency.

Bork's second foray into the public spotlight involved his 1987 nomination to the Supreme Court by President Ronald Reagan. Throughout his career, Bork has remained critical of the JUDICIAL ACTIVISM practiced by the Supreme Court in landmark cases involving abortion, CIVIL RIGHTS, and AFFIRMATIVE ACTION. A self-proclaimed strict constructionist, Bork is critical of judges applying broad interpretations of constitutional intent and vowed he would exercise judicial restraint and not be complicitous in Supreme Court decisions that thwarted the will of popularly elected lawmakers. Bork believes judges should not substitute their values for the original intent of the framers of the Constitution. Bork's contrary public position in cases such as *GRISWOLD V. CONNECTICUT*, 318 U.S. 479 (1965), that had provided the constitutional foundation for the right to PRIVACY and *ROE V. WADE*, 410 U.S. 113 (1973), which established a woman's right to an abortion, was characterized by Bork as "a serious and wholly unjustified usurpation of state legislative authority." Bork also criticized the public accommodation provision in the 1964 CIVIL RIGHTS ACT for being a violation of the proprietor's freedom of association and its principle one of "unsurpassed ugliness." Comments like these ignited a firestorm of controversy at his confirmation hearings and placed him at the center of a jurisprudence maelstrom when he appeared before the 14-member judiciary committee. Throughout his five days of testimony, the longest confirmation hearing since hearings began in 1939, Bork surprised everyone by providing testimony that revealed a moderation of his controversial views.

However, despite Bork's attempt at conciliatory and nonideological testimony, his confirmation hearings became so vituperative and vitriolic that his ultimate defeat in the judiciary committee (9-5) and a floor vote in the Senate (58-42) has possibly forever scarred, politicized, and tainted the advise and consent role of the Senate. The Bork confirmation experience established a new verb, "borked," to describe the rough treatment of presidential nominees at Congressional hearings.

For more information: Vieira, Norman, and Leonard Gross. *Supreme Court Appointments and the Politicization of Senate Confirmations.* Carbondale: Southern Illinois University Press, 1998.

—William W. Riggs

Bowers v. Hardwick, 478 U.S. 186 (1986)

Bowers v. Hardwick upheld the constitutionality of a Georgia sodomy statute applied to consensual homosexual sodomy performed in the privacy of one's home. The Georgia statute, which made such acts a felony punishable by up to 20 years in prison, defined sodomy as "any sexual act involving the sex organs of one person and the mouth and anus of another."

Michael Hardwick was arrested in 1982 in Atlanta in his bedroom, where he was having oral sex with another man. A police officer had entered the house to serve an arrest warrant on Hardwick for another (minor) offense and discovered the two men when he pushed open the bedroom door. Hardwick challenged the Georgia sodomy statute on constitutional grounds, arguing that the law violated the right to PRIVACY protected by the due process clause of the Fourteenth Amendment, that it served no legitimate government purpose, and that it violated the First Amendment's protections for freedom of expression and association.

In 1983 a federal district court dismissed the case, relying on a 1976 U.S. Supreme Court decision (*Doe v. Commonwealth's Attorney,* 425 U.S. 901) upholding a Virginia sodomy law similar to Georgia's statute. But in 1985, a three-judge panel of the 11th Circuit COURT OF APPEALS reversed the district court. The two-judge majority held that Hardwick's "fundamental constitutional rights" were infringed. In 1985 Georgia Attorney General Michael J. Bowers petitioned the U.S. Supreme Court to intervene and reverse the Court of Appeals.

The Supreme Court's decision was handed down June 30, 1986. By a 5-4 vote, the Court, in an opinion written by Justice Byron WHITE, rejected Hardwick's claims. White argued that Hardwick's situation was different from earlier privacy decisions that protected families and marriage and rights of procreation, matters in no way connected to homosexual activity. The argument that a right to engage in such conduct is a fundamental right was dismissed by White as "at best, facetious." White stressed that as late as 1961 all 50 states outlawed sodomy, and that in 1986 24 states and the District of Columbia had such laws on the books.

Justice Harry A. BLACKMUN wrote an eloquent dissent in which he argued that the majority had wrongly characterized the case as being about a fundamental right to engage in homosexual sodomy when in fact "this case is about 'the most comprehensive of rights and the right most valued by civilized men,' namely, 'the right to be let alone.'" Blackmun also suggested that the Georgia law might violate the Eighth or NINTH AMENDMENTs as well as the EQUAL PROTECTION CLAUSE of the Fourteenth Amendment.

In a concurring opinion, Justice Lewis POWELL stated his belief that a 20-year prison sentence for sodomy would create a serious Eighth Amendment problem. But for technical reasons Powell believed Hardwick could not raise the Eighth Amendment issue.

Justice Powell was the crucial fifth vote in this case, and several accounts indicate that he initially voted with the four dissenters to overturn the Georgia statute, but then changed his mind. In 1990 he told a group of law students that he believed he made a mistake in voting the way he eventually did (to uphold the Georgia statute).

The case was bitterly criticized by academic observers, as well as by gay rights groups, who referred to it as "our Dred Scott case." In 2003, in the case of LAWRENCE V. TEXAS, the Supreme Court overruled *Bowers v. Hardwick.*

For more information: DeCew, Judith Wagner. *In Pursuit of Privacy.* Ithaca, N.Y.: Cornell University Press, 1997; Murdoch, Joyce, and Deb Price. *Courting Justice: Gay Men and Lesbians v. the Supreme Court.* New York: Basic Books, 2001.

—Philip A. Dynia

Bowsher v. Synar, 478 U.S. 714 (1986)

In *Bowsher,* the Supreme Court held that Congress cannot assign executive functions to a subunit of itself.

As background it is important to note that the Constitution divided the delegated powers of the federal government into three defined categories: legislative, executive, and judicial. The purpose of dividing the powers of government was to diffuse power to better secure liberty. This system of dividing power among the three branches of government was deliberately structured to provide checks and balances on governmental power.

In *Bowsher,* a complaint was filed seeking a judgment that the Balanced Budget and Emergency Deficit Control Act of 1985 was unconstitutional as violating the doctrine of SEPARATION OF POWERS.

Under the act, the comptroller general was responsible for keeping the federal budget in accord with the maximum deficit amount set by the act. The comptroller general was nominated by the president from a list of three individuals recommended by the Speaker of the House of Representatives and the Speaker *pro tempore* of the Senate and confirmed by the Senate. The comptroller general, however, could not be removed by the president. Removal required a joint resolution of Congress or impeachment.

If budget cuts in federal spending were needed in any given year, the comptroller general would report his conclusions to the president. The president in turn would be required to issue a sequestration order mandating the spending reductions specified by the comptroller general. There would follow a period during which Congress, by legislation, could reduce spending to obviate, in whole or in part, the need for the sequestration order.

Since the comptroller general could only be removed by Congress, he was thus operating under the sole control of Congress. In fact, over the years comptrollers general had viewed themselves as part of the legislative branch.

The Court reasoned that the structure of the Constitution did not permit Congress to execute the laws, therefore it followed that Congress could not grant to an officer under its control what it did not possess—control over the execution of the laws. After a review of the evidence, the Court determined that the comptroller general was exercising executive functions under the act.

The Court thus held that to permit the comptroller general, who was answerable only to Congress, to exercise executive powers under the act, would in practical terms reserve in Congress control over execution of the laws. That would be an intrusion into the powers vested in the executive branch of government and a violation of the doctrine of separation of powers.

It has been argued that Bowsher is one of the BURGER Court's (Chief Justice Warren Burger) most important separation of powers decisions. *Bowsher* has been lauded by some commentators and criticized by others as establishing a bright line, impermeable separation of powers and as being contrary to the intent of the Constitution. Some criticizers emphasize that the *Bowsher* decision ignores the great truth contained in the famous Oliver Wendell HOLMES statement: "The great ordinances of the Constitution do not establish and divide fields of black and white."

For more information: Schwartz, Bernard. "Curiouser and Curiouser: The Supreme Court's Separation of Powers Wonderland." *Notre Dame L. Rev.* 65 (1990): 587; *Mis-*

tretta v. United States, 488 U.S. 361 (1989); *INS v. Chadha,* 462 U.S. 919 (1983); *Yakus v. United States,* 321 U.S. 414 (1944).

—Zola-Mari Williams

Bradley, Joseph (1813–1892) *Supreme Court justice*
Joseph Bradley was a justice on the United States Supreme Court from 1870 to 1892. Bradley was born on his parents' upstate New York farm on March 14, 1813. His exceptional intellectual abilities became apparent when he was a child, and by the time he reach 15 years of age, he had not only graduated from the local school but also accepted a job as a teacher there. After four years of teaching in rural New York State, Bradley moved to Newark, New Jersey, to accept a scholarship to attend Rutgers College. After graduating in 1836, Bradley worked as a law clerk in a Newark law office for three years. After his admission to the New Jersey bar in 1839, Bradley began his legal career in Newark. He soon developed a lucrative practice and during the next 31 years became well known and widely respected for his intellect and for his expertise on laws concerning railroads.

In early 1870, soon after he took office, President Ulysses S. Grant's first significant official action was to fill two vacancies on the U.S. Supreme Court by appointing Joseph Bradley and William Strong as justices of the U.S. Supreme Court. Bradley, one of only two justices appointed prior to 1916 who had never before held public office, was brought to the president's attention because of his distinguished record as an advocate for railroad companies and related businesses involved in highly complex commercial transactions. Because Bradley had extensive experience in the business world, Grant believed the new justice would agree that the nation's economy could recover from its post-Civil War slump only if wartime debt could be repaid with paper currency.

Unfortunately, effectuation of Grant's plan would be possible only if the U.S. Supreme Court overturned its recent decision in *Hepburn v. Griswold,* 8 Wall. 603 (U.S. 1870), in which the Court held that the Constitution did not empower Congress to authorize printing of paper money or to declare that paper money could be used to satisfy debts. Grant obviously chose his new justices well, because in the legal tender cases, 12 Wall. 457 (U.S. 1871), the Supreme Court accomplished the change Grant desired by overturning *Hepburn v. Griswold* and holding that the Constitution authorized Congress to draft laws that gave value to paper money and enabled repayment of debts with paper money instead of gold.

In 1873 the U.S. Supreme Court decided the landmark *Slaughter-House Cases,* 16 Wall. 36 (U.S. 1873). In that case, the Louisiana state legislature, which was then rife with graft and political corruption, granted a monopoly on all livestock-slaughtering business in the city of New Orleans to one slaughterhouse, allegedly in the interests of public health. Owners of other local slaughterhouses, who were put out of business by this action, protested that the state-granted monopoly violated the Fourteenth Amendment to the U.S. Constitution because it deprived them of their property without due process. In deciding against the plaintiffs, the majority of the Supreme Court stated that the Fourteenth Amendment was concerned with the rights of former slaves and was not meant to be stretched to protect the rights of the other slaughterhouse owners. Justice Bradley, in dissenting from the majority opinion, found that as a result of the state legislature's enactment of the law that granted a monopoly on slaughterhouse business to only one owner, the other slaughterhouse owners were deprived of their livelihood without due process. It is interesting to note that during the next 25 years, the majority of the Court broadened its perspective on due process to align with Bradley's viewpoint in his dissent from *Slaughter-House.*

Three weeks after the U.S. Supreme Court issued its decision in the *Slaughter-House Cases,* Chief Justice CHASE died. The new chief justice, Morrison WAITE, was chosen as a result of political compromise and was generally acknowledged to be a competent lawyer but to not be of the intellectual caliber of previous chief justices. Fortunately, Waite was aware of his shortcomings and soon befriended Justice Bradley, whom the other justices considered to be the most intelligent of their group. Waite remained chief justice until his death in 1888, and he readily acknowledged that many of the opinions to which he signed his name were actually written by Bradley.

In early 1877 Joseph Bradley was picked to serve on the presidential electoral commission that Congress created to resolve problems with disputed electoral votes, in order to decide the outcome of the disputed 1876 presidential election. Bradley's vote was crucially important because the remainder of the commission was evenly divided along party lines. When he voted with the Republicans, Bradley guaranteed that Rutherford B. Hayes would win the race by a margin of one electoral vote.

The most significant decision to which Bradley signed his own name was the Civil Rights Cases, 109 U.S. 3 (1883). The Civil Rights Act of 1875 prohibited RACIAL DISCRIMINATION in inns, public transportation, and sites at which people enjoyed recreation during their leisure time. Bradley's opinion held that this law violated the EQUAL PROTECTION CLAUSE of the Fourteenth Amendment to the Constitution because the law attempted to reach discriminatory action taken by private individuals, while the equal protection clause was applicable only to action taken by a state.

Joseph Bradley continued to serve as a justice of the U.S. Supreme Court until his death in Washington, D.C., on January 19, 1892.

For more information: Ariens, Michael. "Supreme Court Justices: Joseph Bradley (1813–1892)." Michaelariens.com. Available online. URL: http://www.michaelariens.com/ConLaw/justices/bradley.htm. Downloaded May 11, 2004; Miller, Ralph. "Supreme Court Justice Joseph P. Bradley." The Berne Historical Project. Available online. URL: http://www.bernehistory.org/area_history/bradley_bio.htm. Downloaded May 11, 2004; Schwartz, Bernard. *A History of the Supreme Court.* Oxford: Oxford University Press, 1993.
—Beth S. Swartz

Bradwell v. Illinois, 83 U.S. 130 (1873)

Bradwell v. Illinois was the first United States Supreme Court case to deal with women's rights. The Court held that the state of Illinois was not required to admit women into the practice of law. *Bradwell v. Illinois,* along with its companion, the *SLAUGHTER-HOUSE CASES,* 83 U.S. 36 (1873), stripped protection for individual rights from the privileges and immunities clause of the Fourteenth Amendment to the Constitution.

Myra Colby Bradwell was a politically active Chicago businesswoman. She founded the first legal newspaper in the United States and authored some of the most important Illinois state statutes granting married women control over their property and personal earnings. Bradwell applied for a license to practice law, invoking an Illinois statute declaring any "person" of good character and having the proper training eligible to be an attorney. The Illinois state supreme court denied the license, explaining that "God designed the sexes to occupy different spheres of action, and that it belonged to men to make, apply and execute laws."

Bradwell appealed to the U.S. Supreme Court. She asserted that the Illinois court had violated her rights under the Constitution's Fourteenth Amendment. The Illinois court had denied her one of the privileges of CITIZENSHIP, the privilege of practicing law. The Fourteenth Amendment, ratified in 1868, declared that no state could make or enforce any law that abridged the privileges and immunities of U.S. citizens.

Justice Samuel Miller, writing for the Supreme Court, with only Chief Justice Samuel P. CHASE dissenting, held that admission to law practice was not a privilege of citizenship. Following the PRECEDENT in the *Slaughter-House Cases,* he argued that the Fourteenth Amendment did not limit the state's traditional power to determine who could be an attorney.

Justice Joseph BRADLEY wrote a concurring opinion that echoed a common 19th-century belief. He contended, "Man is, or should be, women's protector and defender. . . . The paramount destiny and mission of women is to fulfill the noble and benign offices of wife and mother. This is the law of the Creator."

Anticipating the failure of her APPEAL to the Supreme Court, Bradwell turned to the Illinois state legislature. Working with Alta Hulett, she wrote and helped pass a bill that opened all occupations in Illinois, except the military, to women.

Women's road to equality as attorneys was a long one. The American Bar Association did not permit women to join until 1920. Harvard Law School did not admit a woman until 1950. It was not until 1971 that the U.S. Supreme Court challenged barriers to gender equality. Relying upon the Fourteenth Amendment's equal protection clause, the Court held in *Reed v. Reed,* 404 U.S. 71 (1971), that men could not be automatically preferred over women as administrators of an estate. No court has treated gender discrimination like RACIAL DISCRIMINATION, which requires a COMPELLING STATE INTEREST to sustain it. The courts developed instead an INTERMEDIATE SCRUTINY test requiring government to prove its gender-based distinctions serve important goals and that the means used substantially attain those goals.

For more information: Olsen, Frances. "From False Paternalism to False Equality: Judicial Assaults on Feminist Community, Illinois 1869–1895." *Michigan Law Review* (June 1986): 1,518–1,541.

—Timothy J. O'Neill

Brandeis, Louis Dembitz (1856–1941) *Supreme Court justice*

Louis Dembitz Brandeis was a lawyer who practiced a fact-oriented approach to law, an advocate of individual rights, and the first Jew appointed as an associate justice of the United States Supreme Court, in 1916 by President Wilson.

Brandeis was born November 13, 1856, at Louisville, Kentucky. In 1878 he graduated from Harvard Law School. After graduating Brandeis settled in Boston and formed a law partnership. In the years that followed Brandeis developed his legal philosophy in response to the needs of his small business and laboring clients. He came to believe that it was necessary to understand both the immediate legal problem of a case at hand and the socioeconomic context in which that case arose. To Brandeis, law was not a set of inherited legal principles but an instrument for meeting societal needs. Moreover, law needed to be part of a moral

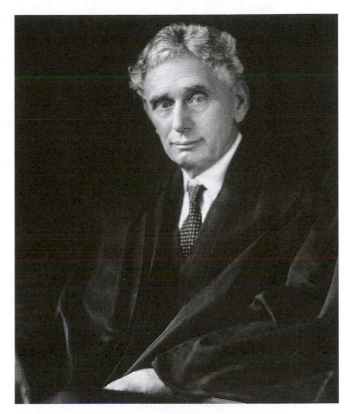

Justice Louis Brandeis *(United States Supreme Court)*

order to be legitimate. This meant that the practice of law was to be a work on behalf of the whole people, rather than a tool for serving the interests of the wealthy.

These beliefs led Brandeis in 1893 to expand his practice by taking some cases as a public service, or *pro bono.* This was a novel action at the time, and it started a new legal tradition in American jurisprudence.

Brandeis's public service involved him in a decade-long struggle with the Boston Elevated Railway to prevent its attempt to achieve a transportation monopoly in Boston. The news media eventually nicknamed Brandeis "The People's Attorney" for his public service.

In many cases Brandeis represented small companies, small shareholders, or labor unions suing large corporations to block monopolistic practices. His legal experiences led him to advocate antitrust legislation, minimum wages, laws for improving working conditions for women, and a Saving Bank Life Insurance program. He also helped to design Massachusetts' utilities laws.

In 1908 Brandeis accepted a case centered on the state of Oregon's progressive attempt to regulate the working hours of women. The case, *MULLER V. OREGON*, 208 U.S. 412 (1908), gave him a chance to apply his fact-oriented approach to law. At that time most legal briefs were composed of citations from PRECEDENT-setting cases. Brandeis realized that his only chance to win the case was to overwhelm the Supreme Court's justices with facts. To defeat the precedents he presented a BRIEF that had only two pages devoted to legal precedents and about 100 pages focused on statistical, sociological, economic, and physiological facts. The resulting "BRANDEIS BRIEF" made legal facts of major importance to future cases.

Brandeis was also an early advocate of nature conservation and opposed to exploiters. In 1910 he served as a counsel in a congressional investigation of Richard A. Ballinger. He was able to expose the anticonservationist views of President TAFT's Secretary of the Interior.

In 1910 Brandeis arbitrated a strike in New York City's garment district. Since most of the garment workers were Jewish, he acquired a new awareness of Jewish problems. This led him to become a leader of the Zionist movement in America. During the First World War he served as chairman of the Provisional Executive Committee for General Zionist Affairs.

As a progressive, Brandeis supported Woodrow Wilson's nomination for presidency in the election of 1912. Brandeis's views on economic matters influenced Wilson's thinking and contributed to Wilson's New Freedom doctrine.

Brandeis put many of his economic ideas into print in 1914 when he published essays favoring business competition in *Other People's Money: and How the Bankers Use It*. That year he also published *Business—A Profession*.

On January 28, 1916, President Wilson nominated Brandeis to the Supreme Court. His appointment was bitterly contested in the Senate by vested interests Brandeis had offended as the "People's Attorney," and by anti-Semites. However, the Senate confirmed his nomination and he took office on June 5, 1916.

When Brandeis took his seat he resigned his official Zionist position. However, at times he worked behind the scenes to influence President Wilson to support the Zionist cause. After World War I ended he led a delegation of American Zionists to London. In 1937 he appealed to President Roosevelt to oppose the British partition scheme of 1937 calling instead for all of Palestine to become a Jewish national home.

Long an advocate of social and economic reforms, he maintained a position of judicial liberalism on the bench. With Oliver Wendell HOLMES, he often dissented from the majority. He was opposed to the wartime Espionage Act (1917) because he considered it to be an unconstitutional restriction of freedom of speech. Brandeis believed in "the right to be let alone" from unwarranted government intrusion. In a major wiretapping case, *Olmstead v. United States*, 277 U.S. 438 (1928), he delivered a stinging dissent declaring that privacy was a constitutional right.

After Franklin Delano Roosevelt took office as president in 1933, Brandeis was one of the few justices who voted to uphold most of Roosevelt's New Deal legislation. While he favored government intervention to control the economy, he voted against the National Recovery Act (NRA), siding with other justices to declare it unconstitutional.

One of Brandeis's most important decisions on the Court was the case of *ERIE RAILROAD COMPANY V. TOMPKINS*, 304 U.S. 64 (1938). He wrote for the Court that in cases of diversity of CITIZENSHIP federal courts must enforce the appropriate state law rather than invoke a "federal common law."

Brandeis served as an associate justice of the Supreme Court until 1939. He retired February 13, 1939, and died October 5, 1941, at Washington, D.C. Both Brandeis Law School at the University of Louisville, Kentucky, and Brandeis University at Waltham, Massachusetts, are named for him. The Brandeis Award is given to outstanding champions of the right of privacy.

For more information: Strum, Philippa. *Louis D. Brandeis: Justice for the People*. New York: Alfred A. Knopf, 1990; Strum, Philippa, ed. *Brandeis on Democracy*. Lawrence: University Press of Kansas, 1994; Woloch, Nancy. *Muller v. Oregon*. New York: Bedford Books, 1996.
—A. J. L. Waskey

Brandeis brief

Louis D. BRANDEIS, then a private attorney in private practice and social activist—in arguing a case before the U.S. Supreme Court, *MULLER V. OREGON*, 208 U.S. 412 (1908)—added a new and revolutionary dimension to the practice of law. He emphasized the facts to which the law applied, and this has, since 1908, been known as the "Brandeis brief" and has led to important changes in legal analysis and Supreme Court litigation.

In February 1903, Oregon passed a statute, much like those passed in other states during the Progressive Era, setting a maximum of 10 hours work in a day for women employed in laundries and factories. In *Holden v. Hardy*, 169 U.S. 366 (1898), the Supreme Court upheld a similar law for miners in Utah but seven years later struck down a 10-hour limit for bakery workers in *LOCHNER V. NEW YORK*, 198 U.S. 45 (1905). After the decision in *Lochner* some workers at Muller's Grand Laundry in Portland, Oregon, were required to exceed this limitation. A local court fined the laundry for violating the state statute; Muller appealed the conviction and the Oregon State Supreme Court upheld the law in 1906. A year later the U.S. Supreme Court agreed to hear the case and the National Consumers' League secured the services of Brandeis to represent the state of Oregon before the Court.

As counsel for the state in *Muller v. Oregon,* Brandeis submitted a BRIEF of more than 100 pages with only two of those pages devoted to the argument on the law. In the early 20th century the approach to judging, and particularly constitutional litigation, taken by most courts was based on what judges thought the statute's writers meant or what judges believed to be the plain meaning of the words. Brandeis's approach to oral arguments in the Muller case was a drastic departure from the norm of the day.

Brandeis believed it was the task of judges to understand society sufficiently to permit the Constitution to be adapted accordingly. If a law was passed because people considered it useful in light of current circumstances, the courts could not strike it down unless it clearly violated a constitutional provision. The litigator in him recognized that although judges did not accept the doctrine of sociological jurisprudence, they might be persuaded to accept its application on certain occasions. He found one in *Muller v. Oregon.* He was aware that the Supreme Court and lower courts had written that maximum-hours statutes might be constitutional where the state demonstrated that specific injury to the workers could result from long hours.

To persuade the Court to uphold the Oregon statute, Brandeis gathered a remarkable body of statistics to demonstrate there was reasonable ground for deciding in Oregon's favor. The brief was based on the fact-oriented sociological jurisprudence of the Progressive Era and attempted to force the Court to consider data state legislators considered in drafting reform laws. In addition to the two pages devoted to the conventional legal arguments, 15 pages were devoted to state and foreign laws that limited women's hours. A 95-page section was entitled "The World's Experience upon which the Legislation Limiting the Hours of Labor for Women is Based." This section contained subsections with titles such as "The Dangers of Long Hours," "Laundries," and "The Reasonableness of the Ten-Hour Day." It introduced quotations from reports by American and English commissions, bureaus, committees, and authors. Virtually the entire 95-page section was intended to demonstrate both the social utility of maximum-hours legislation for women and the general acceptance of the idea.

Brandeis's approach succeeded. Justice David J. Brewer, writing for a unanimous Court, upheld the law and, in doing so, made positive mention of the data compiled in the brief for Oregon.

The brief became a model of how lawyers could effectively introduce economic and sociological evidence into a case. Thereafter, legal arguments on significant social issues have brought forth extensive briefs patterned after the Brandeis brief in an attempt to persuade the Court.

For more information: *Muller v. Oregon,* 208 U.S. 412 (1908); Schwartz, Bernard. *A History of the Supreme Court.* New York: Oxford University Press, 1993; Strum, Phillipa. *Brandeis: Beyond Progressivism.* Lawrence: University of Kansas Press, 1993; Urofsky, Melvin, and Paul Finkelman. *A March of Liberty: A Constitutional History of the United States.* New York: Oxford University Press, 2002.

—Mark Alcorn

Branzburg v. Hayes, 408 U.S. 665 (1972)

In *Branzburg v. Hayes,* the Supreme Court held that requiring a reporter to testify before a grand jury does not abridge First Amendment freedoms of speech and press.

Petitioner Paul M. Branzburg was a reporter for the *Courier-Journal,* a newspaper published in Louisville, Kentucky. On November 15, 1969, the newspaper carried a story by Mr. Branzburg that described his observations of two Jefferson County residents "synthesizing hashish from marijuana." The individuals claimed to have earned about $5,000 in three weeks of doing this and had asked the petitioner not to reveal their identity. Branzburg was subpoenaed to appear before the Jefferson County grand jury but declined to identify the individuals whom he interviewed for the article. On January 10, 1971, Branzburg published an article describing the "drug scene" in Frankfort, Kentucky. Branzburg wrote that he had "spent two weeks interviewing several dozen drug users" and observed them using drugs. He was subpoenaed to appear before a Franklin County grand jury "to testify in the matter of violation of statutes concerning use and sale of drugs." He again refused to disclose the identities of his sources but this time was charged with contempt of court. He appealed.

Justice WHITE wrote for the majority, joined by Chief Justice BURGER and Justices REHNQUIST and BLACKMUN. The Court held that the First Amendment rights of Branzburg had not been violated because there was a COMPELLING STATE INTEREST in the grand jury testimony of Mr. Branzburg. Because there was no prior restrain on what Branzburg published, his First Amendment rights had not been violated. While a member of the press is free to seek information by any legal means, Justice White argued, during a criminal investigation he must comply with government officials just as any other citizen.

Justice POWELL's concurring opinion stated that there are circumstances under which a reporter could refuse to testify before a grand jury and that a reporter should have access to a protective court order if he believes that his testimony does not bear a direct relationship to the matter being investigated. Justice POWELL suggested a test to balance the freedom of the press against the obligation to give relevant testimony.

Justice STEWART wrote a dissenting opinion joined by Justices MARSHALL and BRENNAN. These justices contended that compelling a member of the press to testify against his sources before a grand jury deprives the press of its historic independence from the government. Such a lack of independence impairs the constitutionally protected freedom of the press and may also impair justice administration by drying up sources.

Justice DOUGLAS, dissenting separately, argued that the majority's judgment in this case would cause the press to become a tool of government if its reporters are forced to testify before a grand jury.

This case is important because it established the PRECEDENT that there is no such thing as a "reporter's privilege." Newspapers have no special protection under the First Amendment that is not available to all other citizens.

For more information: Kalven, Harry, Jr. *A Worthy Tradition: Freedom of Speech in America.* New York: Harper and Row, 1988.

—Andrea Hunt

Bray v. Alexandria Women's Health Clinic, 506 U.S. 263 (1993)

In *Bray v. Alexandria Women's Health Clinic,* the Supreme Court held that antiabortionists were not prevented by federal CIVIL RIGHTS laws from obstructing entrances to family-planning clinics. From the late 1980s to the early 1990s, antiabortion groups regularly prevented individuals from entering family-planning clinics. In the early days of the antiabortion movement, most protestors contented themselves with picketing, leafleting, verbal harassment, and physically blockading clinics. However, as the movement gained momentum, and with the at least tacit support of police and government authorities, antiabortionists expanded their activities to include stalking, assault, battery, bombing, chemical attacks, death threats, and murder.

Jayne Bray, the plaintiff in *Bray,* argued that clients and workers who were prevented from entering an Alexandria, Virginia, clinic had the right to sue for civil rights damages under an 1871 civil rights law directed at the Ku Klux Klan. What became known as the Ku Klux Klan Act established protection for "person or classes of persons against conspiracies to keep them from exercising their constitutional rights." In *Bray v. Alexandria Women's Health Clinic,* Justice SCALIA, writing for the Court, declared that "respondents have not shown that opposition to abortion qualifies alongside race discrimination as an otherwise class-based, invidiously discriminatory animus." The Court also rejected the argument that out-of-state clients had been deprived of the right to protected interstate travel. Nor, according to Justice SOUTER, had the plaintiffs proved a private conspiracy or been denied their right to equal protection. The justices suggested that state governments could provide an avenue of relief for family-planning clinics.

Justices STEVENS, Blackmun, and O'CONNOR dissented in the *Bray* decision and argued that the majority had misunderstood the issue at hand. In his dissent, Justice Stevens insisted that the actions of many antiabortionists had indicated that they were "not mere opponents of abortion" but "defiant lawbreakers who have engaged in massive concerted conduct that is designed to prevent all women from making up their own minds about not only the issue of abortion in general, but also whether they should (or will) exercise a right that all women—and only women—possess."

Abortion rights activists around the country declared that the *Bray* decision would result in open season on family-planning clinics. Their fears were borne out when on March 10, 1993, Dr. David Gunn was shot three times in the back by Michael Griffin of Rescue America at the Pensacola Women's Medical Services Clinic. Dr. Gunn later died in surgery. In response to the murder and to the *Bray* decision, Congress passed the Freedom of Access to Clinic Entrances Act (FACE), which established criminal and civil penalties for individuals and groups that obstructed or damaged abortion clinics and interfered with the right to provide abortion services. The new law did not stop the violence. In Pensacola, Florida, on July 29, 1994, Paul Hill, an Operation Rescue antiabortionist and former Presbyterian minister, shot and killed Dr. John Britton and James Barrett, a volunteer escort, at The Ladies Center. Most antiabortion protestors insist that their right to harass individuals entering abortion clinics is protected by the First Amendment of the U.S. Constitution.

Few protestors are willing to go so far as murder, but some antiabortionists justified Griffin's and Hill's actions on the grounds that they stopped more babies from being "murdered." Most abortion providers were justifiably afraid for their own lives and for those of their families who had also been threatened by antiabortionists. Some providers hired bodyguards and donned bulletproof vests. Others chose not to continue offering services, leaving some areas without access to abortion services. Subsequent actions of the Supreme Court responded to the realities of antiabortion protests rather than to the ideology behind the attacks and placed limits on antiabortion activities.

For more information: LaPlante, Nona. "Clinic Blockades: What Is the Problem? What Is the Harm? What Is the Solution?" on "Abortion: Medicine, Ethics, and Law." Douglas Butler. CD-ROM, 1997; Lindgren, J. Ralph, and Nadine Taub. *The Law of Sex Discrimination.* Minneapolis and St. Paul: West, 1993.

—Elizabeth Purdy

Brennan, William (1906–1997) *Supreme Court justice*
William Joseph Brennan, Jr., served as a United States
Supreme Court Justice from 1956 until 1990. Brennan was
born April 25, 1906, to a working-class Irish Catholic family in Newark, New Jersey. His father was a coal heaver who
became a labor union activist and then went on to serve
three terms as director of public safety and police commissioner in Newark. Brennan graduated from a public high
school and went on to earn an economics degree with honors
from the University of Pennsylvania. He then attended Harvard Law School on a scholarship and graduated in the top
10 percent of his class in 1931. He entered private law practice and became partner in a firm specializing in manage-
ment-side labor law. During World War II, Brennan served
as an army officer and was discharged as a full colonel.

Brennan returned to private law practice after the war
and was appointed to the New Jersey superior court in
1947. He was elevated to the appellate division in 1950 and
then to the New Jersey Supreme Court in 1952.

Republican President Dwight D. Eisenhower
appointed Brennan to the U.S. Supreme Court in 1956 to
succeed Justice Sherman Minton. Over time, Brennan

Justice William Joseph Brennan, Jr. *(United States Supreme
Court)*

became known as a liberal judicial activist, prompting
Eisenhower to admit publicly that appointing Brennan to
the Court was one of his worst mistakes ever. Brennan's constitutional philosophy is best described in his own words:

> I approached my responsibility to interpret the Consti-
> tution in the only way I could—as a twentieth-century
> American concerned about what the Constitution and
> the Bill of Rights mean to us in our time. The genius of
> the Constitution rests not in any static meaning it may
> have had in a world that is dead and gone, but in the
> adaptability of its great principles to cope with current
> problems and present needs.

Brennan employed an expansive interpretation of the
BILL OF RIGHTS and the CIVIL RIGHTS Amendments to
the Constitution. The Constitution was, in his mind, a tool
for advancing civil rights and social justice.

Brennan is one of the most influential and prolific
Supreme Court justices of all time. He wrote 1,360 opinions. Although Brennan became known as the Court's
"greatest dissenter" in his latter years on the bench, he
authored more majority opinions than dissents.

Brennan served under the liberal Chief Justice Earl
WARREN from 1956 until Warren's retirement in 1969.
Many of Brennan's most significant majority opinions were
written during this period. Warren's retirement began a
long period of conservatism on the Court under Chief Justices BURGER and REHNQUIST. Brennan's dissents averaged four per term during the Warren era but increased to
more than 20 per term under Burger and Rehnquist.

Brennan's landmark majority opinion in *BAKER V.
CARR*, 369 U.S. 186 (1962), dramatically expanded the voting rights of people of color throughout the United States.
In *Baker*, the Court established the Fourteenth Amendment's EQUAL PROTECTION CLAUSE as a constitutional basis
for challenging the unequal distribution of political representation common throughout the South at the time. *Baker*
opened the door for later lawsuits that established the principle of "ONE PERSON, ONE VOTE" and led to the election of
unprecedented numbers of people of color at every level
of government throughout the nation.

Brennan's opinion for the unanimous Court in *NEW
YORK TIMES CO. v. SULLIVAN*, 376 U.S. 254 (1964), is perhaps his most well-known decision. In *New York Times*,
the Court declared that the First and Fourteenth Amendments limit a state's power to award damages for libel in
actions brought by public officials against critics of their
official conduct [376 U.S. at 283]. Brennan wrote that
"debate on public issues should be uninhibited, robust, and
wide-open" [376 U.S. at 270]. As a result of *New York
Times*, honest journalists may report the news without fear

of lawsuits by public officials. A state may only award libel damages related to the conduct of public officials if the false statement was made with "actual malice"—knowledge of its falsity or reckless disregard of whether it was true or false.

Brennan relied on the equal protection clause to uphold the use of race as a university admissions criterion in *REGENTS OF THE UNIVERSITY OF CALIFORNIA V. BAKKE*, 438 U.S. 265 (1978). A white student who was denied admission to the U.C. Davis Medical School filed a lawsuit arguing that the school's AFFIRMATIVE ACTION admission policy violated the equal protection clause of the Fourteenth Amendment. Brennan, writing for a plurality of the Court, reasoned, "Our Nation was founded on the principle that 'all Men are created equal.' Yet candor requires acknowledgment that the Framers of our Constitution . . . openly compromised this principle of equality with its antithesis: slavery." Brennan continued,

> even today officially sanctioned discrimination is not a thing of the past. Against this background, claims that law must be "color-blind". . . must be seen as aspiration rather than as description of reality. . . . [W]e cannot . . . let color blindness become myopia which masks the reality that many "created equal" have been treated within our lifetimes as inferior both by the law and by their fellow citizens.

Brennan concluded in *Bakke* that federal law "does not bar the preferential treatment of racial minorities as a means of remedying past societal discrimination to the extent that such action is consistent with the Fourteenth Amendment."

One year before retirement, Brennan authored yet another landmark free speech decision in *TEXAS V. JOHNSON*, 491 U.S. 397 (1989), declaring that the First Amendment protects an individual's right to burn a flag as a form of political expression.

Brennan retired from the Supreme Court in 1990, with more than 1,300 opinions demonstrating his intellectual leadership and commitment to the creation of a just and humane society. Brennan passed away July 24, 1997, at the age of 91.

For more information: Rosenkranz, E. Joshua, and Bernard Schwartz, eds. *Reason & Passion.* New York: The Brennan Center for Justice at NYU School of Law, 1997.

—Paul S. Ryan

Breyer, Stephen Gerald (1938–) *Supreme Court justice*

Justice Stephen Gerald Breyer, a Democrat, was appointed to the United States Supreme Court by President Bill Clinton after a distinguished career as a law professor, government lawyer, high-level congressional staff member, and federal judge. A San Francisco native, Breyer was educated at Stanford, Oxford, and the Harvard Law School. After law school, Breyer clerked for Supreme Court Justice Arthur Goldberg and subsequently returned to Harvard where he taught courses on antitrust, regulatory, and administrative law. Breyer served as chief counsel to the Senate Judiciary Committee and aide to Massachusetts Senator Edward Kennedy, where he was an architect of the deregulation of the airline industry. President Jimmy Carter subsequently tapped Breyer to be a judge of Boston's First Circuit COURT OF APPEALS, where he served until his elevation to the Supreme Court.

President Clinton named Breyer to the Court in the wake of a series of bitterly partisan and ideologically charged fights over a number of judicial and executive branch appointments. Like Justice Ruth Bader GINSBURG, Clinton's first appointment to the Court, Justice Breyer was chosen to diffuse these tensions. A leading authority on the economics and law of regulation, Breyer had said very little about contentious constitutional issues such as abortion or AFFIRMATIVE ACTION. His command of economics, and understanding of (and sympathy for) business won him the goodwill of pro-business Republicans. The limited opposition to his appointment that did arise came from the public interest and consumer movements within the Democratic Party itself.

Justice Breyer is generally considered a judicial moderate. His reasoning is not sweeping and categorical, like that of the classically liberal justice of the WARREN Court (1953–69), but measured, fact-specific, and pragmatic. Reflecting the "legal process" conception of the judicial role in which he was steeped at Harvard, Breyer believes that judging is a purposive task in which judges, mindful of the limits of judicial authority and expertise, collaborate with the other governmental institutions to formulate rational, goal-directed and empirically grounded public policy.

Justice Breyer's rulings, however, hew to the commitments of modern constitutional liberalism. Breyer has defended an expansive understanding of federal power under the commerce clause. He has adopted a flexible, pragmatic approach to SEPARATION OF POWERS questions, voting in dissent, for example, to uphold the constitutionality of the line-item veto. Breyer supports a "cooperative" FEDERALISM in which the respective roles of the states and the national government are perpetually renegotiated in light of perceptions of the evolving needs of the governing system. Accordingly, he has voted in favor of the federal government's authority to commandeer local sheriffs to conduct background checks on gun buyers. He has criticized the use of the doctrine of SOVEREIGN IMMUNITY to shield state governments from federally authorized lawsuits. In his government powers decisions, Breyer gives due weight to the way in which changing contexts alter the constitutional calculus. For example, in *CLINTON V. JONES*, 520 U.S. 681

Justice Stephen Gerald Breyer *(United States Supreme Court)*

(1997), Breyer voted to stay a SEXUAL HARASSMENT lawsuit against a sitting president because of what he saw as new and highly litigious legal landscape. In campaign finance cases, similarly, Breyer has attached significant weight to the way in which alterations in the electoral system have allowed money to skew the modern electoral process.

With a few notable exceptions, Breyer's votes on CIVIL RIGHTS and CIVIL LIBERTIES issues are also quintessentially liberal. He has supported the right to PRIVACY, including expansive understandings of ABORTION RIGHTS, the RIGHT-TO-DIE, and gay rights. He has voted to affirm the constitutionality of racially gerrymandered electoral districts and the use of race in university admissions. He has defended sweeping readings of statutory sexual harassment and DISABILITY RIGHTS, as well as the equal protection rights of women. His free speech decisions, while generally liberal, are distinctively fact-specific and technical in style.

There are some areas in which Justice Breyer has voted with the Court's conservatives. He tends to be more deferential to the government in search and seizure cases than quintessential constitutional liberals. He sometimes evinces more flexibility in his ESTABLISHMENT CLAUSE decisions than the Court's "strict separationist" justices. Moreover, like many conservatives, Breyer believes in the importance of "economic" rights.

The most innovative aspect of Justice Breyer's jurisprudence involves his belief that the Court should devote greater attention in resolving future cases to the ways in which other nations and foreign and international courts have approached similar problems of law, governance, and public policy. Breyer has even suggested in extrajudicial speeches that this may involve American judges working to integrate the U.S. Constitution into the governing documents of other nations. Breyer's transnationalism has already exerted considerable sway over many of the Court's other justices and has influenced both the Court's practices and its decisions. Over time, it may very well help define a new form of constitutional liberalism for the 21st century.

For more information: Kersch, Ken I. "The Synthetic Progressivism of Stephen G. Breyer." In *Rehnquist Justice: Understanding the Court Dynamic,* edited by Earl M. Maltz. Lawrence: University Press of Kansas, 2003.

—Ken I. Kersch

brief

Parties to a lawsuit usually submit their arguments to the Supreme Court in the form of a legal *brief.* Briefs are written summaries of lower court proceedings and the factual and legal basis of a litigant's case and position. The brief must also state the question of law posed to the Court. Aside from the individual litigants to a case, other interested parties, referred to as amicus curiae, may petition the Court for permission to submit a brief as well.

The specific requirements of the brief and the proper form of the document are governed by Supreme Court Rule 24. There are rigid requirements for citations, spacing, paper color, number of copies, date, time, and manner of filing, to which a party to a case before the Supreme Court must adhere religiously. Failure to meet the formal requirements of a brief can result in the document being rejected by the Court. In cases involving an indigent litigant, however, the Supreme Court may allow a party to submit a brief *in forma pauperis,* which means that, because the individual is poor or otherwise unable to have the benefit of an attorney or legal assistance, the brief may be submitted without conforming to the official requirements.

The brief is a very important document because it is the key to whether the Court agrees to hear a litigant's case and can often form the basis of the Court's decision. Thousands of briefs are submitted to the Supreme Court each year, and the justices' law clerks are charged with the duty of reviewing and summarizing the briefs for them. When the Court accepts a case for review, the justices rely heavily on the briefs to understand the legal arguments and factual bases for each party's claims.

As mentioned above, individuals or groups holding a special interest in a case may obtain permission to submit an amicus curiae brief to the Court. These briefs support one side or another in a case and often provide insight into the broader implications of the case before the Court. They allow the Court to learn how its holding may affect the issue at hand with respect to various special interest groups and often supply valuable information not available through the litigants' briefs. Certain groups serve as repeat players before the Court (the U.S. solicitor general, for example) and therefore have better credibility in their briefs and better chances of influencing the Court.

Briefs submitted to the Supreme Court are public records. With the advent of modern technology, briefs for recent and current cases have become readily available through the Supreme Court's Web site. However, briefs for older cases are not, though they may be obtained through the clerk at the Court. Additionally, lawyers and researchers can use any one of a number of private services that will go to the Court and copy the briefs for a fee.

For more information: Baum, Lawrence. *The Supreme Court.* Washington, D.C.: CQ Press, 1998; Perry, H. W., Jr. *Deciding to Decide.* Cambridge, Mass.: Harvard University Press, 1991.

—Tom Clark

Brown v. Board of Education of Topeka, 347 U.S. 483 (1954)

In 1954 the United States Supreme Court agreed to hear a set of five school discrimination cases that came to be known collectively as *Brown v. Board of Education of Topeka.* In this landmark case, the Supreme Court overturned the "separate but equal" doctrine that had prevailed in the United States for almost a hundred years on the grounds that "separate but equal" violated the Fourteenth Amendment's guarantee of equal protection of the law. The concept of "separate but equal" meant that as long as states provided relatively "equal" access to public facilities, they could be completely "separate" in practice. In reality, this meant that throughout segregated states, blacks and whites attended separate schools, sat in separate sections on public transportation, drank from separate water fountains, sat in separate waiting rooms in doctor's offices, and so on. When only a single facility was available, "whites only" requirements were often established. Owners and managers of restaurants, hotels, apartment buildings, and other privately owned facilities were given the right to deny services to blacks. Because of this discrimination, "equality" for blacks in segregated states was a myth.

In theory, discrimination on the basis of race had been illegal since the CIVIL RIGHTS Amendments passed by Congress in the aftermath of the Civil War. The Thirteenth Amendment of 1865 abolished slavery; the Fourteenth Amendment of 1868 provided for civil rights for former slaves; and the Fifteenth Amendment of 1870 granted suffrage rights to black males. After Reconstruction ended with the compromise election of Rutherford B. Hayes in 1876, the "separate but equal" doctrine provided for legal discrimination in the former slave states. The Supreme Court upheld the "separate but equal doctrine" in *PLESSY v. FERGUSON,* 163 U.S. 537, in 1896. In public schools, this meant that black children were channeled into separate schools that were often ill equipped with teachers who may have been inadequately trained, and where school transportation was usually limited to white students.

Four of the five cases included under the *Brown* umbrella included *Brown v. Board of Education* from Kansas; *Briggs v. Elliott* from South Carolina; *Davis v. Prince Edward County* from Virginia; and *Gephardt v. Beldon* from Delaware. The Court contended that in all four states segregated schools violated the EQUAL PROTECTION CLAUSE of the Fourteenth Amendment. In the fifth case, *BOLLING V. SHARPE,* 347 U.S. 497, the Court decided that Washington, D.C.,'s failure to admit black children to all-white schools was a denial of the due process clause of the Fifth Amendment because the equal protection clause of the Fourteenth Amendment applied only to states. Four of the five cases had been appealed to three-judge panels that determined that the "separate but equal" doctrine of *Plessy* applied as long as the separate schools were "substantially equal." In the fifth case, the Delaware court found that the black schools were not "substantially equal." The plaintiffs in all five cases contended that the black schools were not equal and could not be made equal. In an unprecedented move, the Supreme Court allowed psychological evidence to be introduced that illustrated the devastating results of school segregation on black children.

The Court first agreed to hear arguments on the school segregation cases in 1952, but a divided Court was unprepared at that time to render a decision that was destined to result in sweeping legal, political, and social changes throughout the country. By 1954, when the *Brown* case was reargued, former governor of California Earl WARREN had accepted the position of CHIEF JUSTICE of the Supreme Court, and Warren believed the Court could be the instrument that brought about substantial legal and societal reforms. In a unanimous decision, the Supreme Court unequivocally rejected *Plessy:* "We conclude that in the field of private education the doctrine of 'separate but equal' has no place. Separate education facilities are inherently unequal."

In the following year, *Brown II,* 349 U.S. 294 (1955), was concerned with how to implement the changes brought about by *Brown I.* Attorney Thurgood MARSHALL asked the court to order immediate desegregation of the public schools. While the Court failed to do this, they did call for "all deliberate speed" in ending "separate but equal" in public education, providing for oversight of local school boards who directed the move toward compliance. The Court recognized that implementing the *Brown* decision required the cooperation of reluctant states that were dedicated to the concept of white supremacy.

Although the *Brown* decision was generally praised outside the South, much criticism was leveled at the Court from both supporters and opponents of the decision. Supporters argued that the Court should have provided a method of enforcement in 1954 that would have speeded up the process of desegregation and circumvented the bitter rebellion and open defiance that took place over the next two decades in many parts of the country and particularly in the South. Opponents of *Brown* contended that states and not the federal government were in control of public education and that states were within their legal rights to continue segregation of the schools. The decision in *Brown* was a compromise among the nine justices who fully understood the implications of the decision. Over the next two decades, sweeping reforms at the federal level, which included the passage of the CIVIL RIGHTS ACT of 1964 and the VOTING RIGHTS ACT of 1965, ended most legal forms of segregation in the United States.

For more information: Grossman, Joel B., and Richard S. Wells. *Constitutional Law and Judicial Policymaking.* New York and London: Longman, 1988; Williams, Juan. *Eyes on the Prize: America's Civil Rights Years, 1951–1965.* New York: Penguin, 1987.

—Elizabeth Purdy

Buchanan v. Warley, 245 U.S. 60 (1917)

In *Buchanan v. Warley,* the Supreme Court struck down the use of ZONING for racial purposes.

During the time between the 1875 CIVIL RIGHTS bill and the 1964 Civil Rights bill, no meaningful civil rights legislation passed Congress. Enforcement of the rights found in the Fourteenth and Fifteenth Amendments was left to the federal courts, which found themselves inundated with a challenges to the segregation laws of the southern states. During the first two decades of the 20th century, the U.S. Supreme Court issued several decisions striking down laws that discriminated on the basis of race. One of those laws, dealing with forced segregation of neighborhoods, was *Buchanan v. Warley* (1917). The Court's decision in *Warley* struck a blow at laws that forced people to sell their property only to people of the same race.

The Buchanan case involved a challenge to a Louisville, Kentucky, ordinance forbidding blacks from buying houses in a white majority neighborhood. White residences of those neighborhoods were also prohibited from selling their property to those of a different race. It also prohibited the gathering of people of one race in a neighborhood that was occupied by members of the other race. All of this was done, according to the ordinance, to preserve peace and good order in the city of Louisville. The Democrat-controlled city council passed this draconian law to extend segregation from public facilities such as water fountains and bathrooms to include private residences.

The head of the local NAACP chapter challenged the law as a violation of the Fourteenth Amendment's due process clause. That clause forbids states from taking its citizens' life, liberty, or property without due process of law. The NAACP also claimed the law violated the EQUAL PROTECTION CLAUSE, arguing the clause forbade states from discriminating on the basis of race. The Supreme Court agreed with the arguments but chose the due process clause to decide the case.

Justice William Day wrote for a unanimous Court in striking down the law. Day ruled that the Louisville ordinance violated Warley's rights to buy, sell, and own property, all of which was protected under the due process clause. According to Day, the state could not force people to sell their property to others based on race and could not forbid the sale of property based on the race of the seller or the buyer.

During this period in its history, the Court tended to protect property rights more than other individual rights. By framing the case in terms of Warley's right to buy, sell, and own property, the NAACP had hit a nerve with the justices. Yet while *Warley* did prevent the type of laws banning residential segregation, southern governments responded with the use of restrictive covenants within the deed of a property. Such covenants prohibited the sale of property to certain races. The enforcement of these covenants would not be struck down by the Court until the 1950s.

For more information: Bickel, Alexander, and Benno Schmidt. *The Judiciary and Responsible Government.* New York: Macmillan, 1985; Meyer, Stephen. *Segregation and Racial Conflicts in American Neighborhoods.* Lanham, Md.: Rowman and Littlefield, 2000.

—Douglas Clouatre

Buck v. Bell, 274 U.S. 200 (1927)

The Supreme Court ruled that Carrie Buck's Fourteenth Amendment right to equal protection was not violated when she was forced to undergo involuntary sterilization at the Virginia Colony for Epileptics and Feeble Minded.

Buck was an institutionalized 18-year-old "feebleminded" woman, described as the daughter of a feebleminded mother, and the mother of an "illegitimate feebleminded child." The state of Virginia argued that its interest in preventing Carrie Buck from giving birth to additional, presumably defective, children took precedence over her personal liberty to make decisions about reproduction. Justice Oliver Wendell HOLMES wrote the opinion for the Court in which he considered several points. Procedurally, the sterilization operation could not be challenged. The superintendent of the state facility had followed the rules for deciding to perform the surgery and had seen that it was done safely. The Court apparently agreed with the assumptions that were used to justify the procedure—that heredity played an important part in transmitting "insanity, imbecility, etc." They believed that Carrie Buck was likely to produce more "socially inadequate offspring," thus causing a concern for society as these potential children created a potential menace. The justices feared that society would become "swamped with incompetents." Essentially the Court claimed that the state was furthering its interest in preventing crime and in limiting the number of people who would become a drain on the public funds. "Three generations of imbeciles are enough," Holmes wrote.

Finally, the Court dismissed Buck's argument that she was denied equal protection because similarly situated "feebleminded" persons outside the institution were not subjected to forced sterilization. They held that after the operation, someone like Buck could be released. That would "open the asylum to others" and "the equality aimed at will be more nearly reached." In other words, sterilization would make some inmates eligible for release, letting others into the institution to be sterilized.

In 1927, when *Buck v. Bell* was decided, it reflected the widely held view that "feebleminded" girls were more likely than those with average intelligence to be sexually active and that they would transmit this promiscuity, with its potential for social disruption, to future generations. The Court expressed a somewhat modified view toward compulsory sterilization in SKINNER V. STATE OF OKLAHOMA EX REL. WILLIAMSON, 316 U.S. 535 (1942). Here they found that the Fourteenth Amendment's guarantee of equal protection was violated when "habitual criminals" who had committed certain felonies, such as robbery, could be sterilized by the state, while those who committed white collar crimes were not eligible for the procedure. In the opinion, the Court referred to the right to have offspring as "fundamental to the very existence and survival of the race."

Although the laws authorizing states to control the reproductive capabilities of those deemed "defective" historically applied to both males and females, they have been most commonly invoked against poor women and members of minority groups.

For more information: Atwell, Mary Welek. *Equal Protection of the Law? Gender and Justice in the United States.*

New York: Peter Lang, 2002; Gordon, Linda. *Woman's Body, Woman's Right: A Social History of Birth Control in America.* New York: Penguin, 1977.

—Mary Welek Atwell

Burger, Warren Earl (1907–1995) *chief justice of the United States*

For more than 17 years on the U.S. Supreme Court (June 23, 1969, to September 26, 1986) Warren Earl Burger served the longest term as CHIEF JUSTICE in the 20th century, with highest praise for his unmatched achievements in judicial administration.

Warren Earl Burger was born September 17, 1907, in St. Paul, Minnesota, and was pleased to share his birthday with the Constitution. He was the fourth of seven children born to Charles Joseph and Katharine (Schnittger) Burger. His father worked as a railroad cargo inspector and salesman. His father's father, Joseph Burger, was a Swiss immigrant who joined the Union Army at age 14 and was a Civil War hero. His mother's parents were German and Austrian immigrants. Burger described his mother as one who ran an "old-fashioned German house" instilling "common sense" in her children. Burger always loved the U.S. Constitution and wanted to be a lawyer, even as a young boy. Suffering from polio at age eight, he was kept home from school for a year and his teacher brought him many biographies of great judges and lawyers.

In high school Burger was president of the student council, editor of the school paper, and a letterman in hockey, football, track, and swimming. Awarded a scholarship from Princeton, he turned it down to stay at home and help support his family. Attending night school at the University of Minnesota from 1925 to 1927, he was president of the student council where he met his future wife, Elvera Stromberg. He attended night classes at the St. Paul College of Law, now the William Mitchell College of Law, and graduated with his LL.B. magna cum laude in 1931. He sold life insurance while attending evening classes in college and law school. Burger married Elvera Stromberg in 1933, and they had two children, Wade and Margaret, and grandchildren.

Burger won a legal job in the depression year of 1931, made partner in 1935, and taught law at his alma mater. He built his law practice with civic work and met Harold E. Stassen. Burger organized the Minnesota Young Republicans in 1934 and Stassen's successful campaign for governor in 1938. Although rejected from World War II military duty due to spinal injury, he served on Minnesota's Emergency War Labor Board from 1942 to 1947.

In 1948 Burger went to the Republican (GOP) National Convention, where he met Richard M. Nixon and the two were "great Stassen men." At the 1952 GOP convention, when Dwight D. Eisenhower emerged as a leading presidential hopeful, Burger was the key figure in a floor decision shifting Stassen support to ensure Eisenhower's nomination on the first ballot. Eisenhower was favorably impressed and, in 1953, Burger was appointed U.S. assistant attorney general.

On June 21, 1955, Eisenhower nominated Burger to a judgeship on the D.C. Circuit COURT OF APPEALS. His confirmation was stalled when discrimination charges were made, without basis, by employees that Burger had fired for incompetence. Burger was finally sworn in on April 13, 1956. Burger developed an early interest in court administration and was actively involved with the American Bar Association (ABA) to promote an effective judiciary. Further, his critique of Supreme Court decisions on insanity and self-incrimination gained him national attention.

On May 21, 1969, Burger was nominated as chief justice by President Nixon. Burger was to be the "law and order" appointee Nixon had campaigned for. He was confirmed by a Senate vote of 74 to 3 on June 9, 1969, with endorsements by 50 past presidents of the ABA and other bar groups. Chief Justice Earl WARREN swore in his successor, Warren Earl Burger, on June 23, 1969.

Burger served 17 terms as chief justice, a tenure as chief justice exceeded by John MARSHALL, Roger TANEY, and Melville FULLER. On June 17, 1986, Reagan announced Burger's resignation and his nomination of William REHNQUIST to succeed Burger, with Antonin SCALIA to replace Rehnquist. On September 26, 1986, at age 78, Burger moved most of his personal belongings from the SUPREME COURT BUILDING and undertook his role as Chairman of the Commission on the Bicentennial of the United States Constitution.

Judicial Administration

Even Burger's critics admit that he accomplished more in the area of judicial administration than anyone in American legal history. Burger insisted he was Chief Justice of the United States, not simply Chief Justice of the Supreme Court. He had more than 64 proscribed duties, including presiding over the Federal Judicial Center, Judicial Conference of the United States, Smithsonian Institution, National Gallery of Art, and so forth. But his greatest accomplishment was his innovation of improvements in judicial operations. While we cannot list all his many achievements, Burger contributed to judicial administration in at least six major areas. First, Burger added new administrative support to the Court with an administrative assistant to the chief justice, judicial fellows, public relations professionals, librarians, clerks, and vast improvements to the law library and technology of the Court. Second, he continued his efforts with the ABA in judicial education programs with the National Judicial College and

Chief Justice Warren Burger *(United States Supreme Court)*

so forth. Third, he developed the *Federal Judicial Center, National Center for State Courts,* and promoted related organizations to gather data on courts, research judicial reforms, and train and inform the judiciary. Fourth, Burger convened lectures and colloquia, such as the *Seminar on the Administration of Justice,* to bring together key decision makers to discuss judicial administration. Fifth, Burger urged training in actual legal skills and litigation practice in law schools, continuing education for lawyers, and programs such as the American Inns of Court. And finally, Burger is considered the father of alternative dispute resolution (ADR) and court mediation, arbitration, and other alternatives to litigation.

As the Court's judicial administrator, Burger's opinion in *United States v. Nixon,* 418 U.S. 683 (1974), turned away a potential public attack against the Court when Burger decided against his appointing president. Yet Burger believed the greatest threat to the Court was its case DOCKET overload, which had climbed from 4,202 cases and 88 signed opinions in the 1969 term to more than 5,158 cases and 161 signed opinions in the 1985 term. Burger was successful in lobbying Congress to limit the Court's mandatory jurisdiction docket, narrow federal three-judge court jurisdiction, place sanctions against attorneys for abuse of process, and create a special *Court of Appeals for the Federal Circuit* for expertise in patent, copyright, trademark, and so forth. He was not successful in such reform proposals as an Intercircuit Tribunal to take a burden off the Supreme Court for resolving conflicts between the federal circuits. Burger wanted a central federal judicial administrator like the lord chancellor of England, which never came to fruition.

Jurisprudence

Burger proved to be difficult to categorize as a jurist. He was supposed to have been "Nixon's man" and lead the Court in a conservative revolution. Instead he rejected Nixon's arguments for EXECUTIVE PRIVILEGE, limited congressional oversight of the bureaucracy, joined to establish ABORTION RIGHTS, upheld school busing, and defended freedom for religious minorities. The most perceptive analyses conclude that Burger was neither conservative or liberal but was pragmatic and concerned with street-level implementation and administrative aspects of decisions. He was more concerned with efficiency and democratic accountability than in preserving tradition or some other conservative impulse.

As Chief Justice, Burger wrote 265 opinions of the Court, averaging 15.6 per year, in addition to separate concurring and dissenting opinions. Although this was a high output, most have not endured as landmark decisions. This was because he was distracted by judicial administration matters, and he tended to assign the landmark decisions to others on the Court; he believed in a limited role of the judiciary in resolving public controversies. However, Burger's lifelong love for the Constitution is marked by three landmark decisions recited in most constitutional law textbooks. In *United States v. Nixon*, 418 U.S. 683 (1974), a unanimous Court ruled against President Nixon and ordered him to comply with subpoenas of the special prosecutor investigating the Watergate Hotel burglary and other crimes. Burger rejected Nixon's argument of executive privilege to keep confidential the tape recordings of White House discussions. SEPARATION OF POWERS was preserved by the Court by affirming the special prosecutor's power of subpoena over the president, and also in this "declaration of independence" of the Court by Burger and three other justices appointed by Nixon.

In *Immigration and Naturalization Service v. Chada*, 462 U.S. 919 (1983), Burger preserved separation of powers between Congress and the federal bureaucracy by striking down the legislative veto. Although used by Congress in more than 200 statutes since the 1930s, Burger reasoned that separation of powers did not allow Congress to take back agency decisions in this piecemeal fashion. *BOWSHER*

v. SYNAR, 478 U.S. 714 (1986), was Burger's last opinion of the Court. The Gramm-Rudman-Hollings Act of 1985 had created the office of comptroller general to identify spending reductions as mandated by the statute and balance the federal budget, an executive function. However, the comptroller general was removable from office by Congress. Burger concluded this crossover of function and removal powers was unconstitutional.

Burger defended the freedom of religious minorities in *WISCONSIN V. YODER*, 406 U.S. 205 (1972), refusing to require Amish parents to send their children to public high schools. His definition of obscenity in *Miller v. California*, 413 U.S. 15 (1973), endures today and allows for local "contemporary community standards," rather than national definitions of obscenity. Other landmark decisions by Burger are not as popularly known to the general public, but concern more technical court procedures, such as jurisdiction, and are in keeping with his intense interests in judicial administration.

Burger gathered many critics in his long tenure as chief justice. Scholars such as Vincent Blasi, in *The Burger Court: The Counter-Revolution That Wasn't*, described him as a man of limited capacity with no discernable coherent philosophy. Burger's working-class background, night school legal education, and pragmatic philosophy have all been subject to intense personal attack. Bob Woodward and Scott Armstrong in *The Brethren: Inside the Supreme Court* present a dismal portrait of Burger's leadership on the Court, alleging that even the old friendship between BLACKMUN and Burger went sour. Justices Marshall, STEVENS, STEWART, and Blackmun publicly aired their complaints about the Court's conflicts with bitter personal criticisms of Burger.

Yet Justice BRENNAN credited Burger with "boundless considerateness and compassion for the personal and family problems of every member of the Court" that kept relations cordial between justices of sharply divided philosophies. Justice POWELL also claimed that good relations and comradeship existed between justices. For example, Justices DOUGLAS and Rehnquist, of opposing ideologies, were the best of friends and their families vacationed together. And Justice Blackmun claimed to remain Burger's best friend to the end.

Before resigning from the Court, Burger had been appointed the chairman of the Commission on the Bicentennial of the Constitution of the United States by President Ronald Reagan in 1985. After resigning as chief justice, he regularly worked double shifts on the commission through to the bicentennial of the ratification of the BILL OF RIGHTS in 1991. Burger took special delight that the 200th birthday of the Constitution on September 17, 1987, was also his 80th birthday. He continued his work and wrote a book about the greatest decisions of the Court, *It Is So Ordered: A Constitution Unfolds.* After the 1994 death of his wife Elvera, Burger's health declined and he died of congestive heart failure on June 25, 1995. He was laid in state in the Great Hall of the Supreme Court, memorialized at the National Presbyterian Church, and buried next to Elvera at Arlington National Cemetery near other justices.

For more information: Halpern, Steven, and Charles Lamb, eds. *The Burger Court: Political and Judicial Profiles.* Urbana: University of Illinois Press, 1991.

—Bradley Stewart Chilton

Burson v. Freeman, 504 U.S. 191 (1992)

Burson v. Freeman was a Supreme Court decision that upheld a Tennessee statute prohibiting the solicitation of votes and distribution of campaign literature within 100 feet of the entrance to a polling place. The question in the case was whether this provision violated the First and Fourteenth Amendments to the United States Constitution. The First Amendment guarantees the freedoms of speech, RELIGION, press, peaceful assembly, and governmental petitions, while the Fourteenth Amendment makes part of the BILL OF RIGHTS applicable to the states and guarantees due process and equal protection.

Tennessee has set up a "campaign-free zone" statute in its election code. This code stated that the display of campaign posters, signs, or other campaign materials, distribution of campaign materials, and solicitation of votes for or against any person or political party or position on a question are prohibited within 100 feet of the entrance and within the building where the polling place is located. Mary Rebecca Freeman was a candidate for office in Tennessee, had managed local campaigns, and worked actively in statewide elections. She claimed that the statutes limited her ability to communicate with voters and brought a challenge in Davidson County court. This court ruled that the statutes did not violate either the United States or Tennessee Constitutions and dismissed her lawsuit. The Tennessee Supreme Court reversed, finding that the state had shown a compelling interest in banning solicitation and distribution of campaign materials within the polling place itself but had not shown a compelling interest in regulating the premises around the polling place.

On APPEAL the United States Supreme Court overturned the Tennessee Supreme Court. Writing for the majority, Justice BLACKMUN concluded that while the Tennessee statute was not a content-neutral time, place, or manner restriction, it violated neither the First nor the Fourteenth Amendment. Whether individuals may exercise their free speech rights near polling places depends entirely on whether their speech is related to a political campaign. The statute does not reach other categories of speech, such as commercial solicitation, distribution, and display. Therefore, to survive STRICT SCRUTINY a state must do more than assert a COMPELLING STATE INTEREST—it must demonstrate that its law is necessary to serve the asserted interest. While laws rarely survive such scrutiny, this one does. An examination of election reform efforts demonstrates the need for restricted areas in and around polling places. The United States has experienced such a large and varied kind of voter intimidation, election fraud, and disenfranchisement that it is very important to keep the places near where the people will vote safe from these kinds of problems so that no voter is so intimidated as to deny them the right to vote for candidates of their choice. Blackmun added that while 100 feet may seem arbitrary, the state statute does not have to designate the perfect distance, just be consistent and reasonable.

Justices SOUTER, STEVENS, and O'CONNOR dissented. Justice THOMAS did not participate.

For more information: Legal Information Institute: Supreme Court Collection. "Charles W. Burson, Attorney General and Reporter for Tennessee, Petitioner v. Mary Rebecca Freeman." Cornell Law School. Available online. URL: http://supct.law.cornell.edu/supct/html/90-1056.ZO.html. Downloaded May 11, 2004.

—Amy Oliver

Burton, Harold (1888–1964) *Supreme Court justice*

Harold Burton, the only Republican appointed to the Supreme Court between 1933 and 1953, was born and raised in Boston, Massachusetts, where his father served as dean of faculty at the Massachusetts Institute of Technology. Graduating summa cum laude from Bowdoin College in 1909, Burton went on to receive a law degree from Harvard Law School in 1912 before moving to Cleveland, where he would establish a successful law practice. In 1917 Burton enlisted in the U.S. Army and served in France and Belgium during World War I, where he would rise to the rank of captain and receive the Purple Heart.

Returning to Cleveland after the war, Burton resumed his corporate law practice and taught law at Western Reserve University Law School from 1923 to 1925. He was unsuccessful in his attempts to secure an appointment to the U.S. District Court for the Northern District of Ohio but was elected to the Ohio legislature in 1929 as a Republican. He also served as chief legal counsel for the City of Cleveland from 1929 to 1932, and in 1935 he was elected to the first of three two-year terms as mayor of Cleveland. In 1940 Burton was elected as a Republican to represent Ohio in the U.S. Senate, where he developed a reputation as a moderate and was an early advocate of U.S. participation in what would become the United Nations.

Soon after taking office on the death of President Roosevelt in 1945, President Harry S Truman had his first opportunity for a Supreme Court appointment with the retirement of Justice Owen J. Roberts. Faced with considerable pressure to appoint a Republican to the seat, Truman turned to Burton, his former Senate colleague, in part because Ohio's Democratic governor would then be able to appoint a Democrat to Burton's Senate seat. The Senate unanimously approved Truman's nomination of Burton just 24 hours after the nomination was submitted.

During his 13 years on the Supreme Court, Burton developed a reputation as a hard-working and principled jurist, often working 80- or 90-hour weeks and eating lunch at his desk. He generally took moderate positions on the legal issues that came before the Court, and he was an early advocate of extending constitutional protections to African Americans in segregation cases, voting to declare the doctrine of "separate but equal" unconstitutional in 1954's BROWN V. BOARD OF EDUCATION and to strike down racially restrictive housing covenants in 1948's SHELLEY V. KRAEMER. On issues of CIVIL LIBERTIES, however, Burton was more willing to favor governmental efforts to limit potentially subversive speech over individual First Amendment claims, as in 1951's DENNIS V. UNITED STATES, in which the court upheld the conviction of 11 top members of the Communist Party.

Diagnosed with Parkinson's disease in 1957, Burton stepped down from the court in 1958 but continued to serve on the D.C. Circuit COURT OF APPEALS until his death in 1964.

For more information: Berry, Mary Frances. *Stability, Security, and Continuity: Mr. Justice Burton and Decision-Making in the Supreme Court, 1945–1958.* Westport, Conn.: Greenwood Press, 1978.

—William D. Baker

Bush v. Gore, 531 U.S. 98 (2000)

In *Bush v. Gore*, the United States Supreme Court ended the presidential election controversy by issuing an unsigned per curiam opinion on December 12, 2000, ordering an end to ballot recounts in the state of Florida. The end result was the awarding of the presidency to George W. Bush. In doing so, the Court held that the recount had to be halted because it could not be conducted in compliance with the requirements of equal protection and due process. Four justices dissented.

The case arose because of the closeness of the election totals in Florida. The initial count by the Florida Division of Elections reported that Governor Bush had defeated Albert Gore by a margin of 1,784, or less than one-half of 1 percent of the votes cast. As a result, Gore sought manual recounts in Volusia, Palm Beach, Broward, and Miami-Dade Counties, pursuant to Florida's election protest provisions.

Because of the narrow margin, 11 different and significant court challenges were filed, not only by the candidates but by voters and interested parties. The cases alleged an assortment of illegalities, including claims about the validity of the butterfly ballot in Palm Beach County, *Fladell v. Palm Beach County Canvassing Board*, 772 So. 2d 1240 (2000), and the standard for manual ballot counting, *Florida Democratic Party v. Palm Beach County Canvassing Board*, No. 0011078AH (15th Circuit of Florida, November 4, 2000).

Though there were multiple legal strategies, supporters of Gore were unable to get a court to order a new vote because of the allegedly confusing and illegal butterfly ballot, or to have a decisive number of Republican ballots rejected because of irregularities. [*Taylor v. Martin County Canvassing Board*, 773 So.2d 517 (2000); *Harris v. Florida Elections Canvassing Commission*, 235 F.3d 578 (11th Cir. 2000), respectively.] However, the Florida Supreme Court in *Gore v. Harris*, 772 So.2d 524 (2000), ruled that the appropriate remedy was to have a manual recount of all possibly missed legal votes, or "under votes," based on the Florida contest statute. [Florida Statutes § 102.168 (2000).]

The recount was stopped a day later when, by a 5-4 vote, the U.S. Supreme Court issued an emergency injunction halting the recount because the recount might irreparably harm George W. Bush. Four justices dissented from the order, arguing that counting every legal ballot cannot constitute irreparable harm. Subsequently, in a 13-page unsigned opinion, the same majority ruled that the recount would be stopped permanently because it violated the EQUAL PROTECTION CLAUSE of the Fourteenth Amendment to the U.S. Constitution, since the manual recount standard was viewed as inconsistent and arbitrary.

Though the ruling ended the election controversy, it left a number of questions. It was not clear why the Supreme Court was concerned about unequal treatment of the ballots during the recount, but not during the original count where various counties used different ballot-counting procedures. Dissenting from the opinion, Justice SOUTER argued that even with equal protection concerns, the Court simply could have remanded the case back to the Florida Supreme Court with instructions to use a clear standard for the recount.

The case raises difficult questions about the role of the courts in elections and whether judicial decisions are as political and partisan as any other. The justices denied that politics played a role. Even justices who authored forceful dissents in *Bush v. Gore* claimed that neither ideology nor politics drives the Court. Though there are criticisms of the various courts from both sides throughout the convoluted legal process, the record is not as stark. Though the Florida Supreme Court took the brunt of the criticism from conservatives for allegedly favoring Gore, Florida's highest court actually ruled for George W. Bush three times out of five. Ultimately, whether the decisions are seen as political or based on objective legal principles depends entirely on one's point of view.

Bush v. Gore is unique in American history in deciding a presidential election and is the only U.S. Supreme Court case with the names of the presidential candidates in the title. The opinion also is distinguished by the Court's very unusual holding that the opinion should not be used as PRECEDENT or authority in the future. Despite the Court's desire to limit the implications of the decision, *Bush v. Gore* may have some unintended consequences, including an increased involvement of the courts in monitoring and policing election disputes as well as a less favorable view of judges or justices as objective players in the political system. Regardless, the case will generate discussion and argument within the legal community and the nation for many years to come.

For more information: Ackerman, Bruce, ed. *Bush v. Gore: The Question of Legitimacy.* New Haven, Conn.: Yale University Press, 2002; Bugliosi, Vincent. *The Betrayal of America: How the Supreme Court Undermined the Constitution and Chose Our President.* New York: Thunder's Mouth Press/Nation Books, 2001; Dershowitz, Alan M. *Supreme Injustice: How the High Court Hijacked Election 2000.* New York: Oxford University Press, 2001; Gillman, Howard. *The Votes That Counted: How the Court Decided the 2000 Presidential Election.* Chicago: University of Chicago Press, 2001; Greene, Abner. *Understanding The 2000 Election: A Guide to the Legal Battles that Decided the Presidency.* New York: New York University Press, 2001; Posner, Richard A. *Breaking the Deadlock: The 2000 Election, the Constitution, and the Courts.* Princeton, N.J.: Princeton University Press, 2001; Rakove, Jack, ed. *The Unfinished Election of 2000.* New York: Basic Books, 2001; Sunstein, Cass R., and Richard A. Epstein, eds. *The Vote: Bush, Gore, and the Supreme Court.* Chicago: University of Chicago Press, 2001.

—Kevin M. Wagner

C

Calder v. Bull, 3 U.S. 386 (1798)

The major reason why *Calder v. Bull* has such a prominent place within history is because it represents the first decision of the Supreme Court of the United States to regulate the power of the government in terms of the Constitution.

The point of contention came on Article 1, Section 10 of the Constitution, specifically the references to EX POST FACTO LAWS. The Constitution contains wording to the effect that Congress shall not pass any "ex post facto Law, or Law impairing the Obligation of Contracts." By this it was understood to mean that any new law that penalizes or criminalizes someone for a behavior, or that makes some behavior or action illegal, that was legal at the time of performing the behavior or act. In essence, one cannot go back and make actions illegal now that were done before the law was established. The time period of this case was only eight years after the ratification of the BILL OF RIGHTS to the Constitution. Most states were just getting the rewriting of their state constitutions affirmed.

In *Calder v. Bull,* a couple, Mr. and Mrs. Caleb Bull, were denied an inheritance from a Mr. Norman Morrison by a mid-level Connecticut court. The Connecticut state supreme court was not in working order because the state had not accepted a new state constitution. Therefore, the legislature was acting as the high court for the state and had been for some time.

The underlying facts of the case were that the Bulls appealed the decision more than a year and a half after the decision. In the interim, the state had passed a law making any appeals that came after 18 months to be without merit and thus had no grounds for bringing the APPEAL to the emerging court system. The legislature was persuaded to change their focus and allow for the Bulls to bring their case to the legislature for hearing. Mr. Calder had inherited the money initially, and it was he that took the case to the Supreme Court.

As mentioned earlier, the point in contention was whether the Connecticut legislation was a direct or indirect violation of the ex post facto exclusion in the U.S. Constitution. In a 4-0 decision, with two justices abstaining, the court determined that the Connecticut legislation was not in fact an ex post facto law in terms of the meaning within the Constitution. The court believed that the ex post facto law exclusion only applied to the criminal laws and not civil laws.

This demarcation point was whose rights were to be affected, and the value was that there was a basis for protections in the rights of people when faced with criminal laws. For civil protections, ex post facto laws do not impact the contractual rights of persons. Chief Justice Samuel CHASE, who wrote one of the four opinions for the court, thought that although retrospective laws (laws that apply backward) are all ex post facto laws, not all retrospective laws are ex post facto laws. Justice Chase and Justice William Patterson thought that the basis of the term, *ex post facto law* had its roots in the history of the laws, even before the American Revolution, in both English parliamentary law and within the writings of the Federalist Papers.

Justice Chase imposed these limitations on the kind of laws that the courts and the legislatures could impose, and this decision still is a point of controversy. More modern interpretations think that the justices erred in their strict adherence to an interpretation of the Constitution. The precedence of the court is this area has been challenged many times, and the interpretations that stem from whether a court has the power to make statutes invalid are the flash point, it seems.

The courts themselves have since continued the interpretation of the power that was established in the Calder court's decision. The impact upon society has been profound, and the precedence has had a positive effect on the importance and reliance upon the court by other branches within the government to address issues of legislative power.

For more information: Friedman, Lawrence M. *A History of American Law.* New York: Simon and Schuster, 1972.

—Ernest Alexander Gomez

Cantwell v. Connecticut, 310 U.S. 296 (1940)

Argued March 29, 1940; decided May 30, 1940. In *Cantwell*, the Court reversed the defendant's conviction for unauthorized soliciting and inciting a breach of the peace. More significantly in the long term, the Court incorporated the free exercise clause of the First Amendment and applied it to the states.

The Cantwells were members of a religious group known as the Jehovah's Witnesses. This group regularly went door-to-door and held public meetings attempting to sell their publications and convert people to their RELI-GION. Newton Cantwell and his two sons, Jesse and Russell, had been trying to distribute religious materials and message in a heavily Catholic neighborhood of New Haven, Connecticut. They played a phonograph record describing a book entitled *Enemies,* which included an attack on the Catholic religion. Two residents complained to the police, and the next day the Cantwells were arrested for soliciting without a license issued by the state's secretary of the Public Welfare Council.

Each of the Cantwells was charged with, and convicted of, five offenses related to soliciting without a license. The Connecticut Supreme Court of Errors upheld the conviction and the case proceeded to the U.S. Supreme Court. A unanimous Court, with the opinion written by Justice Owen Roberts, held that the Cantwells' free exercise of religion rights had been violated because of the arbitrary authority the statute placed in the hands of the state official in setting criteria for the license.

In the opinion, Roberts stated—reminiscent of Chief Justice WAITE in *REYNOLDS V. U.S.* (1879)—that the right to believe is absolute, but the right to act on those beliefs is not; noting that state and local authorities could require "certificates of approval" prior to solicitation whether religious or secular in nature. If there was not the absolute right to act in accordance with one's religious belief, the question then raised was how the Court would differentiate between protected and illegal actions. What developed in *Cantwell,* though it lasted less than 25 years, was the "valid secular policy" test. That is, if the policy of a government served a legitimate nonreligious goal and was not directed at any particular religion, the Court could uphold it regardless of whether the statute in question conflicted with religious practice.

In addition to the long-term importance of *Cantwell* due to INCORPORATION, or making the BILL OF RIGHTS applicable to actions of state and local governments, it is also significant as the case wherein the Court began to distinguish between the religion and speech clauses of the First Amendment.

For more information: Epstein, Lee. *Constitutional Law for a Changing America: Rights Liberties, and Justice.* 3rd ed. Washington, D.C.: Congressional Quarterly Press, 1998; Urofsky, Melvin I. *"Cantwell v. Connecticut."* In *Religion and American Law,* edited by Paul Finkelman. New York: Garland, 2000.

—Mark Alcorn

capital punishment

Capital punishment, allowing governments to put convicted criminals to death, is one of the most controversial subjects ever to roil American politics. The death penalty has been imposed for grievous crimes since colonial days. When the Eighth Amendment, prohibiting cruel and unusual punishment, was passed as part of the BILL OF RIGHTS in 1789, the death penalty was not considered to be within its scope. The death penalty was also common in Europe, but that changed in the late 20th century when all industrialized Western countries except the United States ended it.

Since the 1970s the death penalty has been imposed in the United States only for crimes that involve murder plus aggravating circumstances such as premeditation, heinousness, and cruelty. Two purposes are given for imposing capital punishment—deterrence of other potential criminals and vindication of victims. No evidence has been developed to prove that the death penalty deters other criminals, although it certainly stops the convicted from committing further crimes! Nonetheless, vindication is a powerful motive people give for continuing the death penalty.

Numerous attempts have been made to have the courts declare that capital punishment is cruel and unusual punishment, or at least that it violates the due process clause of the Fourteenth Amendment. Opponents, led by the Legal Defense Fund of the National Association for the Advancement of Colored People (NAACP), scored a near victory in 1972. In *FURMAN V. GEORGIA* the Supreme Court, with a bare 5-4 majority, declared the death penalty unconstitutional *as applied* because it was imposed arbitrarily and disproportionately on black defendants. However Chief Justice BURGER, writing in dissent, noted that states might rewrite their capital punishment statutes to minimize arbitrariness and pass constitutional muster. A number of states, including Georgia, did just that. Four years later the issue came before the Supreme Court again in *GREGG V. GEORGIA,* 428 U.S. 153 (1976). This time a 7-2 majority ruled that Georgia had eliminated the arbitrariness from its procedures and that its death penalty statute was constitutional.

In a later case, *MCCLESKEY V. KEMP,* 481 U.S. 279 (1987), the Legal Defense Fund tried again, this time using a massive statistical study of Georgia capital punishment cases, called the Baldus Report after one of its authors, to show the disproportionate treatment of African Americans in death penalty cases. Among the Baldus Report conclusions were that those convicted of murder were 4.3 times more likely to receive the death penalty if their victims were white rather than black. Also, 108 of 128 cases, or 87 percent, in which the death penalty was imposed involved white victims. Finally, prosecutors sought the death penalty in 70 percent of cases with black defendants and white victims, but in only 32 percent in which both defendants and victims were white. Writing for another 5-4 majority, Justice POWELL did not dispute the findings of the Baldus Report. Rather he argued that McCleskey had to prove that there had been racial bias in his own trial, and this he had not been able to do. Under the Georgia statute each jury considers the circumstances of each crime before sentencing a defendant to death. The state Supreme Court automatically reviews the sentence, a process the court majority found to be neither arbitrary nor capricious. Nonetheless, controversy continues.

Since the Supreme Court approved capital punishment in 1976 and the summer of 2003, some 850 people have been put to death in the United States. However, in the year 2000, Governor George Ryan of Illinois commuted all death sentences when it was discovered that 13 people on Illinois' death row had been wrongly convicted. Nationwide more than 100 death row inmates had been released since 1973 after having been found innocent, many as the result of research done by students at the Center on Wrongful Convictions at Northwestern University School of Law. Several issues continue to be controversial in the United States. Can defendants who committed crimes as juveniles be executed? How young is too young? Can mentally retarded defendants be executed? How retarded is too much?

Of increasing concern is the split between Europe and the United States over capital punishment. Protocol #6 of the European Convention on Human Rights prohibits member nations from imposing the death penalty. The Council of Europe now requires new members to abolish capital punishment, effectively expanding its prohibition to Eastern Europe nations seeking to join the European Union. The protocol also prohibits extradition of suspects to nations in which they would face the death penalty, setting up a potential conflict with the United States over the fate of terrorist suspects. In addition, in 1999 the United Nations Human Rights Commission proposed a moratorium on the death penalty. Only 10 nations opposed the proposal, including China, Pakistan, Rwanda, Iran, and the United States. Currently more than half the world's nations have abolished the death penalty. Russia, Ukraine, and South Africa, nations that previously had high execution rates, have imposed moratoriums. Can the United States be far behind?

The answer may be "yes." Public opinion in both the United States and Europe has consistently supported capital punishment by margins of 60 to 70 percent. However there are differences in culture and political structures that have led to the split in actual legislation. European nations are more centrally governed. In the United States each of 50 states is able to make its own decisions about capital punishment, as can the federal government and the District of Columbia. Therefore opponents must wage their campaigns in 52 different venues. Second, European nations have parliamentary governmental structures, meaning that individual politicians do not need to be as sensitive to public opinion as do politicians in the United States. Being "soft on crime" is a deadly charge in American political campaigns. Finally, race is an issue. States with a high percentage of minorities support the death penalty. Those with few minorities have abolished capital punishment or rarely carry it out. Capital punishment elicits strong emotions from both defenders and opponents.

For more information: Galliher, John F., et al. *America Without the Death Penalty: States Leading the Way.* Boston: Northeastern University Press, 2002; Garvey, Stephen P. *Beyond Repair? America's Death Penalty.* Durham: Duke University Press, 2003; Hood, Roger. *The Death Penalty: A World-wide Perspective.* Oxford: Clarendon Press, 1996; Lifton, Roger, and Greg Mitchell. *Who Owns Death? Capital Punishment, the American Conscience, and the End of Executions.* New York: Harper-Collins, 2002.

—Paul J. Weber

Cardozo, Benjamin Nathan (1870–1938) *Supreme Court justice*

Benjamin Nathan Cardozo was a Supreme Court justice who was born on May 24, 1870, in New York City, New York, and died on July 9, 1938, in Port Chester, New York. He was known and often currently cited as one of the most prominent legal minds of the first half of the 20th century. His reputation grew as a great common law jurist and through the interpretations of his opinions—both legendary for quality and clarity. Cardozo's understanding of the law was based upon his experience and historical research. The depth and breadth of his understanding of the law was recognized in tort law and commercial contract law. The rare combination of skills made him very qualified to be appointed by Herbert Hoover to the Supreme Court of the United States in 1932 where he served as an associate justice until 1938. Justice Cardozo was chosen to replace Justice Oliver Wendell HOLMES—a legendary justice in his own right.

Justice Cardozo was only the second Supreme Court justice of the Jewish faith to be appointed to the Court, with Justice Louis BRANDEIS being the first. Cardozo's accomplishment came about during a time of social exclusion for members of the Jewish faith within the upper echelons of the American social economic classes. The appointment by President Hoover came despite the fact that Cardozo had supported the presidential campaign of Al Smith in 1928.

By the time that Cardozo had been elected to the Supreme Court in 1932, he had written four volumes of essays upon the philosophy of law. Justice Cardozo was known to have read the original texts of legal philosophers in their native languages. His philosophical underpinnings could be understood in his support for the ideas of Alexander Hamilton. Cardozo wrote that, ". . . the great generalities of the Constitution have a content and a significance that vary from age to age. The method of free decision sees thru the transitory particulars and reaches what is permanent behind them."

Cardozo's ability to clearly pen opinions and draft a focus for the Court allowed his ethical desires and respect for the law to be recognized, and through his efforts he recovered the Cardozo name. Benjamin's father, Albert Cardozo, was of a prominent family with a long tradition of respect within the community on the East Coast. One of Benjamin Cardozo's ancestors was a trustee of Columbia University and his father was a judge. Another relative, Emma Lazarus, had her poetry hung in front of the Statute of Liberty in New York Harbor.

Yet, this notoriety could not keep the elder Cardozo—a Tammany Hall appointee—from being brought up on nepotism charges. In 1872, when Benjamin was two years old, his father resigned from his New York Supreme Court judgeship prior to being impeached because of the allegations of the Association of the Bar of New York City—an organization that he started. The Erie Railway takeover wars sparked a scandal that implicated some judges, one of whom was Albert Cardozo. Judges were responsible to remain free from subjective decision making, and for a judge to be impeached was a recognition of an egregious act of trust compromise. Politically, some have argued that the climate of those times dictated that minorities within the government were not able to follow practices that were very common, but that were normally reserved for the majority. Such being the case, some have felt that elder Cardozo's pending impeachment was politically motivated. This result may have shaped the younger Cardozo and his ethical stances on the common law as well.

Benjamin Cardozo attended Columbia University at age 15 and later attended the Columbia School of Law for two years of a three-year program (he did not obtain his law degree then because it was not required to do so in New York at the time). Promptly thereafter, he entered his father's law firm. This was either a clear message to society that either Benjamin thought his father was wrongly accused or that his character was of such metal that it could not be corrupted. Benjamin quickly became known for his

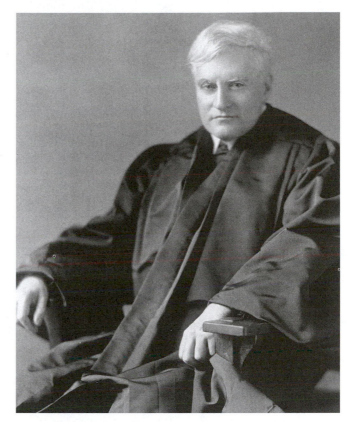

Justice Benjamin Cardozo *(United States Supreme Court)*

oratories in the court and his calm demeanor outside of court. In addition, his knowledge of the law made him a favorite of the other lawyers in New York where he acted as both mentor and stalwart for common law. It became commonplace for even the brightest lawyers of the time to consult Cardozo or bring him their most challenging cases while he practiced law in 1891–1914. Later as a trustee for Columbia University, and in spite of the infamous reputation of his father, his integrity was unchallenged, and in this way he succeeded his father in many ways and reaffirmed the Cardozo name.

Prior to appointment to the Supreme Court Benjamin served on the New York Supreme Court, and shortly thereafter rose to chief justice on the COURT OF APPEALS where he earned his reputation as a celebrated common-law judge. Cardozo's famous opinions span a wide range of legal precedence. Maybe his most famous opinion came in the area of tort law in the *MacPherson v. Buick Motor Company* case in 1916. This case in particular expanded the definitions that were assumed to be apparent in to whom a duty was owed within commercial contractual obligations. The Cardozo opinions in that case and others shaped commercial product liability and expanded the focus of the law in those areas. His impact was also felt within the field of fraud, as his opinion in the *Ultramares Corporation v. Touche* in 1931 changed who could be protected in contractual obligations.

Cardozo believed that wherever a contract existed, so did the presumption of rules that should govern typical contracts. His contributions to the law did not only apply to cases. In fact his speech at Yale in 1921 (The Storres Lectures) is often regarded as the treatise on judging from a philosophical and a decision-making functional standpoint. As a justice within the Supreme Court of the United States, Cardozo often stood against a small majority of justices named the Four Horsemen on many issues. Despite this pressure, he retained a legal focus that deferred powers to the states and the legislative bodies, thereby making him one of the most prominent federalists of the time and a strong Hamilton-style supporter of the Constitution.

Cardozo supported government regulation of industry and supported the famous "Black Monday" rulings which made the New Deal provisions unconstitutional. During this time, though, his most famous case may have been in the Constitutional area in *Helvering v. Davis* (1937), where he combined with Brandeis and others to reverse a previous ruling. This was a colorful time in the Court, and the newspapers referred to these actions as the "Switch in Time That Saved Nine" (referring to the number of justices on the high court and the atypical decision for the Court).

In summation, Cardozo stands as one of the great minds of the Supreme Court and of legal theory. His challenges to the way that jurisprudence was approached made him a leader and a firebrand for correcting and clarifying the law. His proved his grasp of justice from a social standpoint, from a commercial approach, and as a supporter of the Constitution he distinguished himself as one of the strongest champions for democracy.

For more information: Cardozo, B. N. *The Growth of the Law.* New Haven, Conn.: Yale University Press, 1924; O'Brien, David M. *Constitutional Law and Politics: Civil Rights and Civil Liberties,* Vol. 2, 4th ed. New York: W. W. Norton, 2000.

—Ernest Alexander Gomez

Carey v. Population Services International, 431 U.S. 678 (1977)

In *Carey v. Population Services International,* the Supreme Court considered whether access to CONTRACEPTIVES was protected as part of the right to privacy recognized earlier in *ROE V. WADE,* 410 U.S. 113 (1973). New York State had enacted a law that made it a crime for anyone other than a physician to sell or distribute contraceptives to minors younger than 16, allowed only licensed pharmacists and physicians to sell or distribute contraceptives to those 16 or older, and prohibited all advertising and display of contraceptives. State officials were sued by several individuals and organizations, including Population Services International, which sold nonprescription contraceptives through the mail and advertised its products in periodicals in New York.

A three-judge federal district court unanimously found the law unconstitutional under the First and Fourteenth Amendments. On APPEAL the Court affirmed this decision, striking down all provisions by a 7-2 vote. Justice William BRENNAN, writing for the Court, cited the holdings in *Roe v. Wade* (1973) and *EISENSTADT V. BAIRD,* 405 U.S. 438 (1972), that the liberty protected by the Fourteenth Amendment due process clause includes "a right of personal privacy," and that "the decision whether or not to beget or bear a child" is clearly part of that right. Any restrictions on the availability of contraceptives, which limit the freedom to make choices regarding childbearing, are constitutional only if they are justified by "COMPELLING STATE INTEREST" and are "narrowly drawn to express only those interests." Noting that the state cannot claim to be protecting health when it regulates the sale or distribution of nonhazardous contraceptives, the Court concluded that New York had failed to demonstrate a compelling interest.

The Court also struck down the prohibition on distributing nonprescription contraceptives to minors under the age of 16. However, there was no majority opinion. Justice Brennan, writing for himself and three others, stated that the right to privacy in connection with decisions affecting procreation (including contraception) extends to minors as well as adults. Even partial restrictions on access to contraceptives that "significantly burden" the right to decide whether to have a child must pass constitutional scrutiny.

When a state burdens this right for minors, it must show that the burden is connected to a significant state interest. New York argued that the law was a legitimate way to regulate "the morality of minors," part of the state's policy against "promiscuous sexual intercourse among the young." The state argued that it could restrict the availability of contraceptives to deter sexual activity "by increasing the hazards attendant on it." Justice Brennan pointed out that New York had conceded in the district court that "there is no evidence that teenage extramarital sexual activity increases in proportion to the availability of contraceptives." He quoted from the earlier opinion in *Eisenstadt v. Baird,* where the Court concluded: "It would be plainly unreasonable to assume that [the State] has prescribed pregnancy and the birth of an unwanted child [or the physical and psychological dangers of an abortion] as punishment for fornication."

Three justices wrote concurring opinions on this issue. Justice POWELL suggested that the state might design a law that "encouraged adolescents to seek the advice and guidance of their parents" by requiring parental consultation before contraceptives could be distributed. Justice STEVENS acknowledged that New York had a significant interest in discouraging sexual activity among unmarried minors, but he insisted that subjecting minors to increased risk of unwanted pregnancy and sexually transmitted disease was not a legitimate way to promote this interest. Characterizing such an attempt to persuade by inflicting the risk of harm as "irrational and perverse," Justice Stevens concluded: "It is as though a State decided to dramatize its disapproval of motorcycles by forbidding the use of safety helmets."

Courts have relied on *Carey v. Population Services International* to strike down laws requiring parental consent or notification as a condition of access to contraceptives for minors. *Carey v. Population Services International* has been cited primarily in support of two positions: that a state-created obstacle to exercising the right to privacy need not be absolute to be constitutionally impermissible, and that the constitutional significance of state interests may differ for adults and minors.

For more information: Hofman, Brenda D. "Note: The Squeal Rule: Statutory Resolution and Constitutional Implications—Burdening the Minor's Right of Privacy." *Duke Law Journal* 34 (1984): 1,325–1,357; Luker, Kristin. *Dubious Conceptions: The Politics of Teenage Pregnancy.* Cambridge, Mass.: Harvard University Press, 1996; Arons, Jessica R. "Misconceived Laws: The Irrationality of Parental Involvement Requirements for Contraception." *William & Mary Law Review* 41 (2000): 1,093–1,131.

—Barbara J. Hayler

case or controversy

Article III of the UNITED STATES CONSTITUTION limits the jurisdiction of federal courts to actual "cases or controversies" but does not provide specific definitions for these concepts. Before judges reach the merits of a dispute they must resolve any jurisdictional issues; yet, determining if an actual case or controversy exists is often left to the discretion of the judges without clear guidelines.

Chief Justice WARREN claims these concepts possess "an iceberg quality, containing beneath their surface simplicity submerged complexities which go to the very heart of our constitutional form of government." Thus, trying to determine the definition of "case or controversy" involves examining several, potentially complex, aspects. According to Warren, the term *case or controversy* limits federal courts to deciding cases presented in an adversary context and in a form capable of resolution through the judicial process, so that the courts will not intrude into areas committed to the other branches of government. Warren states "justiciability is the term of art employed to give expression to this dual limitation placed upon federal courts by the case-and-controversy doctrine." The term *justiciability* involves several aspects, as per the iceberg analogy given by Chief Justice Warren. The Supreme Court has ruled that cases are nonjusticiable when they present a political question (*BAKER V. CARR,* 369 U.S. 186 [1962]), when the litigants request an advisory opinion (*Bellotti v. Baird,* 443 U.S. 622 [1979]), when the issue is MOOT or not ripe for review, and when the litigants do not possess STANDING. Unfortunately, determining the existence of one of these aspects is not clear, leading some legal scholars to conclude that the definitions are based more on political concerns than on legal doctrine. Whether one believes definitions of justiciability involve political or legal facets, it is obvious that determining the existence of a case or controversy often involves subtle interpretations of the Article III requirement. Warren's characterization of justiciability, with its "submerged complexities," provides an accurate illustration of the difficulties judges encounter when presented with a case or controversy issue.

For more information: King, J. Brian. "Jurisprudential Analysis of Justiciability Under Article III," *Kansas Journal of Law and Public Policy* 10 (2000): 217; Nichol, Gene R. "Is There a Law of Federal Courts?" *West Virginia Law Review* 96 (1993): 147; Pierce, Richard J., Jr. "Is Standing Law or Politics?" *North Carolina Law Review* 77 (1999): 1741; Stradling, Tyler R., and Doyle S. Byers. "Intervening in the Case or Controversy: Article III Standing, Rule 24 Intervention and the Conflict in Federal Courts," *Brigham Young University Law Review* 419 (2003).

—Kirk A. Randazzo

certification

The Supreme Court has considered and dealt with certification as a legal concept connoting corroboration, authentication, and credentialing. Certification may represent some act of certifying or confirmation that a statement or fact is accurate and true, or the process of validation or authentication of something or some person, or it may refer to a document that attests to the accuracy and truthfulness of certain stated facts.

In a famous case involving election of the president of the United States, *BUSH V. GORE,* 531 U.S. 98 (2000), the court recognized that state and county officials certify election results—those votes eligible for inclusion in the certification because they meet properly established legal requirements. Specifically, the Florida Elections Canvassing Commission certified the results of the election and declared Governor Bush the winner of Florida's 25 electoral votes, and the next day Vice President Gore filed a complaint contesting that certification, thereby challenging such validation and authentication. In turn, the vote certification issue was then taken up by a Florida Circuit Court, a district court of appeal, and then the Florida Supreme Court, which enjoined the commission from certifying results and directed vote recounts to be included in the certified total. But the U.S. Supreme Court reversed that decision as a violation of the EQUAL PROTECTION CLAUSE of the Fourteenth Amendment, thereby permitting the commission's certification to become final.

The work of the Court also requires certification of a lawyer applying to join the U.S. Supreme Court Bar. An attorney must complete a written application for admission to practice that he or she must sign and date, with a signature following this statement: "I certify that I have read the foregoing questions and have answered them fully and frankly. The answers are complete and true to the best of my knowledge." Both his or her act of certifying and the attesting signature properly represent the meaning of certification. Similar common acts of certifying or attesting by others who fill out, sign, or submit such applications required by government agencies, businesses, and voluntary associations and clubs are considered certifications by applicants.

The Court has also decided cases dealing with the certification of individuals—meaning recognition that such individuals have met predetermined qualifications to use a title or trademark. In *Ibanez v. Florida Dep't of Business & Professional Regulation*, 512 U.S. 136 (1994), the Florida Board of Accountancy sought to ban Ms. Ibanez from advertising the certifications that she had achieved—Certified Public Accountant (CPA) from the Florida Board of Accountancy and Certified Financial Planner™ (CFP™) from the Certified Financial Planner Board of Standards, Inc. Because Ms. Ibanez had received these certifications from both the government agency and the nonprofit organization, the court found that her truthful, nondeceptive COMMERCIAL SPEECH could not be banned under the First Amendment.

Most individual certifications are issued by nonprofit organizations, including specializations for physicians and other professions or occupations, which often involve requirements of education, examination, experience, and ethics. Under an earlier Supreme Court decision, *Peel v. Attorney Registration and Disciplinary Comm'n of Ill.*, 496 U.S. 91 (1990), the Court decided that truthful, relevant certification disclosures may help consumers select attorneys best able to help them. Accordingly, many state bar organizations have approved certifications from private certifying organizations as well as the state bar itself.

For more information: Jacobs, Jerald A. *Certification and Accreditation Law Handbook.* Washington, D.C.: American Society of Association Executives, 1992.

—Robert P. Goss, J.D., Ph.D.

Chaplinsky v. New Hampshire, 315 U.S. 568 (1942)

The case of Walter Chaplinsky was a seminal free speech decision for the United States Supreme Court. The case delineated two separate categories; protected and unprotected types of speech. This decision established three basic categories of "unprotected" speech that still exist.

Walter Chaplinsky had come from a coal-mining family who had converted to the Jehovah's Witness RELIGION. Chaplinsky became an active and experienced proselytizer in Manchester, New Hampshire, and surrounding communities.

In 1940 Chaplinsky began preaching on street corners in Rochester, New Hampshire, a small mill town. He had several run-ins with local police as well as mobs of citizens who objected to his preaching and attacks on the Catholic Church. On one occasion a group of men began shoving and shouting at Chaplinsky and the other witnesses; when the police tried to break up the melee they arrested him and the other Witnesses. While being taken to jail Chaplinsky reportedly said to the police, "You are a God damned racketeer" and "a damned Fascist and the whole government of Rochester are Fascists or agents of Fascists." Chaplinsky was charged under a local statute that prohibited "offensive derisive or annoying" language spoke in public places. He was convicted in Superior Court and his conviction was affirmed by the New Hampshire Supreme Court and then appealed to the United States Supreme Court.

Chaplinsky's case was argued on March 5, 1942, and the unanimous decision was handed down less than five weeks later. Written by Justice MURPHY, the decision states emphatically that the First Amendment is not absolute. Murphy wrote, "There are certain well-defined and narrowly limited classes of speech, the prevention and punishment of which have never been thought to raise any Constitutional problem." He then describes these classes of speech as "the lewd and obscene, the profane, the libelous, and the insulting or 'fighting' words—those which by their very utterance inflict injury or tend to incite an immediate breach of the peace."

Murphy's brief (less than four pages) opinion and unanimity of the Court were devastating to Chaplinsky's cause. He served six months on a state prison farm and continued to preach and witness well into his 80s.

Chaplinsky's case is important to legal scholars for its establishment of a two-tier system of free speech and its creation of the "FIGHTING WORDS" doctrine. In the decision Murphy states that words that inflict injury or incite others to breach the peace are not covered by the First Amendment. Without definitions or explanatory footnotes this argument creates a large hole in First Amendment protection, yet none of the other justices saw fit to challenge Murphy on a single point. In later years some of the justices would change their minds and start to limit the fighting words doctrine in cases such as TERMINIELLO V. CHICAGO (1949) and COHEN V. CALIFORNIA (1971).

Chaplinsky's arrest and trial might best be understood as a part of a large movement by Jehovah's Witnesses in the 1940s and the effort made to suppress them. But the case he brought before the court had implications reaching much further than one man in a small town.

For more information: Kalven, Harry, Jr. *A Worthy Tradition: Freedom of Speech in America.* New York: Harper and Row, 1988.

—Charles Howard

Chase, Salmon (1808–1873) *chief justice of the United States*

Salmon P. Chase (January 13, 1808–May 7, 1873), sixth CHIEF JUSTICE (serving 1864–73, appointed by Abraham Lincoln), secretary of the Treasury, a foe of slavery, was a perennial presidential hopeful. He learned law under William Wirt, who was Monroe's attorney general. Chase began in politics as an admirer of Calhoun and Clay. In 1836 he helped defend abolitionist James G. Birney during a riot and became an antislavery hero. He also defended a number of escaping slaves.

Until 1841 Chase was a Whig. Then he became a leader of the Liberty Party. In 1848 he supported the Free Soil slate and in 1849 was elected to the U.S. Senate as a Free Soiler (though in alliance with the Democrats). Chase opposed the Compromise of 1850 and the Kansas-Nebraska Act. His break with the Democrats cost him his Senate seat. In 1855 he was nominated by the Republicans and the Know-Nothings for governor of Ohio and was reviled by many a Democrat and Whig as a renegade for having changed parties five times. Chase was elected and was reelected in 1857. In 1860 he returned to the Senate but his stay was brief.

Chase sought the presidency in 1856, 1860, and 1864. He was a "sculptor's idea of a president." Yet his extremism and inflated idea of his own worth made him a difficult person to work with. He became Lincoln's secretary of the Treasury but repeatedly threatened to resign.

Chase was instrumental in establishing the national banking system in 1863. His scheming forced Lincoln to accept his resignation in 1864. However, recognizing his worth and seeking to contain Chase, Lincoln nominated him to be chief justice.

As chief justice, Chase avoided tangling with the Radical Republican Congress over Reconstruction measures. In 1868 he presided fairly over the impeachment trial of Andrew Johnson. He returned to the Democrats in 1868, unsuccessfully seeking their presidential nomination.

As secretary of the Treasury, Chase had issued greenbacks (federal paper money) but in the 1870 case of *Hepburn v. Griswold* (8 Wall. 603) he voted against their being legal tender. This decision was soon reversed.

In 1872 he became an early enrollee in the Liberal Republican Party. As Herbert Eaton put it, "It would, after all, hardly seem a presidential year without Chase coming forward for one nomination or another." He was ill and was passed over by that party.

Chase dissented in the 1873 *Slaughter-House Cases* (83 U.S. 36), which limited the applicability of the Fourteenth Amendment in CIVIL LIBERTIES and CIVIL RIGHTS cases. His dissent eventually became the Court's position.

For more information: Blue, Frederick J. *Salmon P. Chase: A Life in Politics.* Kent, Ohio: Kent State University Press, 1987; Niven, John. *Salmon P. Chase: A Biography.* New York and Oxford: Oxford University Press, 1995.

—Martin Gruberg

Chase, Samuel (1741–1811) *Supreme Court justice*

Samuel Chase (Somerset County, Maryland, April 17, 1741–Baltimore, Maryland, June 19, 1811) was appointed to the Supreme Court by President George Washington in 1795 and served until 1811.

Revolutionary War leader, signer of the Declaration of Independence, and U.S. Supreme Court associate justice, Chase is best remembered as the only justice of the high court to be impeached by Congress. Chase's partisan and inflammatory style cultivated many enemies and obscured his significant contributions to legal thought. Scholars now rate Chase as one of the early Supreme Court's formidable jurists.

Educated by his father, the Reverend Thomas Chase, rector at St. Paul's Church in Baltimore, Chase eventually studied law with a firm in Annapolis, Maryland. In 1761 he was admitted to the bar. As a young lawyer, Chase delivered fiery speeches against Maryland's royal governor and led local opposition to the Stamp Act. From his seat in the Maryland Assembly, where he served from 1764 to 1784, Chase was a militant supporter of colonial rights. An enthusiastic member of the "Sons of Liberty," he denounced his pro-British rivals as "despicable tools of power, emerged from obscurity and basking in proprietary sunshine." From 1774 to 1778 he represented Maryland as a delegate to the Continental Congress, until accusations of business improprieties forced him to retire and return to Maryland. In 1788 Chase was appointed chief judge of the criminal court in Baltimore. In 1791 he was named chief judge of the general court of Maryland. Chase's confrontational manner generated controversy—as well as several charges, later dismissed—that he had abused his power as a judge.

Having spent his early adult life fighting British control of the colonies, Chase at first believed in a weak, decentralized government after U.S. independence in 1783. In 1787 he opposed ratification of the U.S. Constitution on the grounds that it concentrated too much power in a federal government dominated by mercantile interests. But by the 1790s, Chase reversed course and became a firm Federalist—supporting a powerful, centralized government. His exposure to English conservatism during the 1780s, antagonism toward Jeffersonian Republicanism, and concerns about the violent French Revolution and the excesses of democracy drew him to FEDERALISM.

In 1796 President George Washington appointed Chase to a seat on the U.S. Supreme Court, where he soon wrote several opinions that distinguished him as one of the early Court's leading legal theorists. Only later did his partisanship undermine his influence.

In three cases—*Hylton v. United States,* 3 Dall. (3 U.S.) 171 (1796); *Ware v. Hylton,* 3 Dall. (3 U.S.) 199 (1796), and CALDER V. BULL, 3 Dall. (3 U.S.) 386 (1798)—Chase helped establish the PRECEDENT for JUDICIAL REVIEW and also shaped the notion of "SUBSTANTIVE DUE PROCESS." In *Hylton v. United States,* the Supreme Court, in considering the carriage tax of 1794, determined for the first time whether a law passed by Congress was constitutional (it upheld the tax). The opinion Chase delivered in *Ware v. Hylton* determined that federal TREATIES superceded state laws that contradicted them. *Calder v. Bull* was Chase's most influential opinion. In it, he argued that the due process clauses of the Fifth and Fourteenth Amendments conferred "natural law" rights not explicitly stated in the Constitution. Natural law, he explained, placed limits on legislative actions. Chase wrote, "An Act of the legislature . . . contrary to the great first principles of the social compact, cannot be considered a rightful exercise of legislative authority." Several years later he declared more pointedly, "If the Federal Legislature should, at any time, pass a Law contrary to the Constitution of the United States, such Law would be void." Chief Justice John MARSHALL followed this line of reasoning in MARBURY V. MADISON, 1 Cranch (5 U.S.) 137 (1803), which established the principle of judicial review.

By that time, Chase had become an outspoken critic of President Thomas Jefferson and his allies in Congress. In two 1800 circuit cases over which Chase presided, the associate justice acted in a flagrantly prejudicial manner, causing defense counsel in both cases to quit. In 1803 he denounced the repeal of the Judiciary Act of 1801, as well as Maryland's adoption of universal suffrage. These miscues provided Chase's enemies the opportunity to remove him from the bench.

In early 1804 Virginia Representative John Randolph, a member of the Jeffersonian-Republican majority, urged the House of Representatives to raise articles of impeachment against Chase. A majority voted to impeach Chase on seven counts and a trial was set in the Senate in 1805. For Chase to be removed, two-thirds of the senators needed to vote for conviction on any one of the counts, but the Jeffersonian-Republican majority was divided over what constituted an impeachable offense. The Constitution vaguely described this threshold as "high crimes and misdemeanors." Some senators believed unbecoming personal conduct and partisan actions applied. Another faction determined that the Constitution implied only criminal actions. The latter view prevailed and the Senate acquitted Chase on all counts.

The failed impeachment gave the Supreme Court independence from legislative intervention. However, it also reinforced the idea that the bench was no place to express political opinions and, accordingly, Chief Justice Marshall steered the court toward a more impartial course. Though Chase survived and served until his death in 1811, the impeachment turmoil greatly diminished his role.

For more information: Haw, James, et al. *Stormy Patriot: The Life of Samuel Chase.* Baltimore: Maryland Historical Society, 1980; Presser, Stephen. "The Original Misunderstanding: The English, the Americans, and the Dialectic of Federalist Constitutional Jurisprudence." *Northwestern University Law Review* 84 (1989): 106–185.

—Matthew Wasniewski

Cherokee decisions, 21 U.S. 543 (1823), 30 U.S. 1 (1831), & 31 U.S. 515 (1832)

The series of three monumental Supreme Court decisions written by Chief Justice John MARSHALL concerning disputes between the Cherokee Nation and the State of Georgia had wide-ranging implications for government relations with Native Americans ever since.

The first case of the trilogy, *Johnson v. McIntosh,* attempted to make sense of U.S. title to lands belonging to the native peoples. Marshall decided that the Congress holds the legal title to all Indian lands. The Indians could use the lands, but the use was limited to what Congress allowed.

The second and perhaps most important of these decisions was *Cherokee v. Georgia.* In 1828 Georgia passed a series of laws that eliminated Cherokee sovereignty and imposed Georgia law over Cherokee lands. Marshall here decided that while the Indians represented domestic dependent nations, owing no allegiance to the United States, they were not "foreign nations." In order to bring a case directly to the Supreme Court, Indian nations had to be considered foreign nations. As such, Marshall declined to protect the Cherokee from the Georgia statutes. In effect, while Marshall said Georgia was wrong to pass laws over the Cherokee, he declined to take their case.

A year later Marshall reversed his own direction on the rights of Indian nations in deciding *Worcester v. Georgia.* Samuel Worcester, a Massachusetts missionary, went to the Cherokee Nation and did not first swear loyalty to Georgia under the 1828 laws. He was convicted and sentenced to four years. The Court found for Worcester, deciding that only Congress was empowered to make laws regulating Indian tribes and therefore nullifying the Georgia requirement for a loyalty oath. The decision marks a change in outcome for Indian nations because it held that states were not empowered to override their sovereignty.

The tribal victory was short-lived, however. President Andrew Jackson declared: "John Marshall has made his decision, now let him enforce it." Jackson refused to seek Worcester's release, and Georgia retained him in prison in defiance of Marshall's decision. The decision simply went unenforced.

By inventing the ambiguous status of dependent domestic nations, Marshall created a legacy for colonized people throughout the world. The outcome of the *Cherokee decisions* for the Native American tribes was disastrous. The official policy of removal from the Eastern United States commenced in 1838, and the Cherokee embarked on the "Trail of Tears." On the way to eventual resettlement in the Oklahoma Territory the Cherokee suffered more than 8,000 documented deaths.

Because the United States was the first independent nation-state in the New World, later nations would take their cue from the U.S. legal policy on the rights of indigenous peoples within their borders. The Cherokee decisions would help form the basis of national laws throughout North and South America and, later, human rights international law.

For more information: Norgren, Jill. *The Cherokee Cases: The Confrontation of Law and Politics.* New York: McGraw-Hill, 1996.

—Tim Hundsdorfer

Chevron Inc., USA v. Natural Resources Defense Council, 467 U.S. 837 (1984)

In *Chevron Inc., USA., v. Natural Resources Defense Council,* the Supreme Court held that where Congress has not clearly expressed its intent in an area of law the only determination to be made by the courts is whether the agency interpreting the law did so in a reasonable manner.

Under the Clean Air Act, states that have not achieved national ambient air quality standards set by the Environmental Protection Agency (EPA) must establish a program regulating stationary sources of air pollution. In 1981 the EPA put in place regulations that allow states to use a "bubble" approach to achieving air quality standards. It is known as the "bubble" approach because under the regulations states may allow plants within which there may be multiple sources of pollution to modify one source at a time so long as there is not an increase in total emissions from the plant.

The Natural Resources Defense Council filed suit to challenge this agency regulation, alleging that its interpretation of the Clean Air Act was contrary to the law. The COURT OF APPEALS held that in the court's view the agency's interpretation was not reasonable.

On APPEAL to the Supreme Court the main issue was whether the EPA had acted reasonably in its attempt to define what constitutes a "stationary source" under the Clean Air Act. In its opinion the Court acknowledged that there was no definition of what Congress had intended by the words *stationary source.* The Court also found that there was no evidence in the legislative history of the Clean Air Act or its amendments that Congress had addressed the "bubble" theory of what could be a "stationary source." Absent evidence of congressional intent, the court turned to whether the EPA's interpretation of the term *stationary source* was reasonable.

In its opinion the Court took note of the fact that it has always been the function of the courts to say what the law is. The Court, however, stated that where there is an administrative agency responsible for implementing the law, the agency may use reasonable discretion to interpret elements of the law not addressed by the legislative body. The Court held that in situations where there is such an agency, the decision on whether an interpretation is appropriate is whether the "Administrator's view that it is appropriate in the context of this particular program is a reasonable one." In its holding, the Court further stated that policy arguments concerning whether the "bubble" theory was appropriate "should be addressed to legislators or administrators, not to judges."

In the area of administrative law *Chevron* has become one of the most cited cases in recent decades. The Court's decision has allowed for greater freedom of government agencies in interpreting the law. Traditionally, interpreting the law was the job of the courts alone. However, after the holding in *Chevron,* in situations where Congress has not clearly addressed a subject, government agencies are free to interpret the law in that subject area so long as their interpretation is reasonable.

For more information: Reese, John H. *Administrative Law, Principles and Practice.* St. Paul, Minn.: West, 1995.

—John L. Roberts

chief justice of the United States Supreme Court

The chief justice is the presiding officer of the United States Supreme Court. The only power assigned to the chief justice in the Constitution is the duty to preside over the Senate when the impeachment of the president is at issue. Otherwise, the role of the chief justice is left to be defined by Congress or by the Court itself. Like other members of the Court, the chief is appointed by the president, subject to approval by the Senate, and serves for life unless removed by impeachment.

Although it is an office of great prestige, the formal powers of the chief justice are limited. The Supreme Court decides cases collectively, and the chief is "first among equals" in that he or she has no extra vote or veto power. The chief presides over public sessions of the Court, including hearings in the cases before it (called ORAL ARGUMENT). The chief also plays an enhanced role in the internal operations of the Court, conducting the private conferences during which the members of the Court discuss and vote on cases. The chief and his or her clerks also do a preliminary screening of potential cases for the Court's DOCKET. Other members of the Court are, however, free to place on the Court's agenda a case not on the chief's "discuss list."

The most important power of the chief inside the Court is the assignment of the majority opinion. After the initial, private vote in a case, the chief chooses one of the justices who voted with the majority to write an opinion that explains the Court's ruling and defines the legal PRECEDENT set by the decision. This enables the chief to assign important cases to himself or herself, or to another member of the Court with similar views. If the vote in a case is close, the chief may choose to assign the case strategically to a moderate member of the Court in order to dissuade wavering justices from switching sides. If the chief justice is in the minority in a case, the power to assign the majority opinion passes to the senior member of the majority.

Although the chief justice cannot control how other justices vote, the various duties assigned do give the chief some advantages when it comes to persuasion. Some chief justices have emerged as effective leaders inside the Court, such as John MARSHALL (chief justice in 1801–35) and Charles Evans HUGHES (served 1930–41). Others, such as Harlan STONE (1941–46) and Warren BURGER (1969–86) have struggled in their attempts to lead.

Despite the fact that the chief justice has little power over other members of the Supreme Court, the office nonetheless is one of considerable symbolic significance. It is common to refer to historical eras of the Supreme Court by the name of the chief justice, such as the "WARREN Court" (after Earl Warren, who served 1953–69) or the "Rehnquist Court" (1986–present).

For more information: Danelski, Daniel. "The Influence of the Chief Justice in the Decisional Process." In *Courts, Judges and Politics, An Introduction.* 5th ed. Edited by Walter Murphy, C. Herman Pritchett, and Lee Epstein, pp. 662–670. New York: McGraw-Hill, 2001; Rehnquist, William. *The Supreme Court: How It Was, How It Is.* New York: William Morrow, 1987.

—David Dehnel

Chimel v. California, 395 U.S. 752 (1969)

In *Chimel v. California* the United States Supreme Court ruled that a warrantless search of a person's entire house after his arrest was unreasonable and a violation of the Fourth Amendment. This decision was important because the ruling established the scope of a search that police may conduct of a person incident to or after an arrest.

The Fourth Amendment declares that individuals and their homes generally cannot be searched unless a warrant has been issued by a judge, upon showing that there is probable cause. First in *WEEKS, V. UNITED STATES,* 232 U.S. 383 (1914), and then in *MAPP V. OHIO,* 367 U.S. 643 (1961), the Supreme Court articulated what has come to be known as the EXCLUSIONARY RULE. This rule states that evidence illegally obtained in violation of the Fourth Amendment should be excluded from use in proving the guilt of a person accused of a crime. Thus, the Fourth Amendment, *Weeks,* and *Mapp* establish the general rule that warrants are required to undertake searches.

However, over time the Supreme Court has established several exceptions to the warrant requirement. *Chimel v. California* addresses one of these exceptions. In *Chimel,* three police officers had a warrant for Ted Chimel to arrest him in connection with a burglary of a coin shop. When police arrived at his house Chimel was not present, but his wife let them in to wait for him. When he arrived the police arrested Chimel and asked for permission to search the entire house. They were denied permission but nonetheless searched the entire place, including the attic, the garage, and a workshop, and they opened drawers and moved objects around. They seized several objects, including coins. These items were introduced in the burglary trial to convict him, over the objection of his attorney that they were obtained in violation of the Fourth Amendment. Both the California Court of Appeals and the state Supreme Court upheld his conviction and the introduction of the coins obtained from the search. The case was appealed to the U.S. Supreme Court, which reversed his conviction and the introduction of this evidence.

Writing for the Court, Justice STEWART first noted that the arrest in the case was valid and that the real question in the case was whether the search incident to or subsequent to the arrest was constitutional. Stewart noted that in *Weeks v. United States* the Court had first discussed the constitutionality of searches incident to arrest. In that case and in subsequent opinions the Court noted that when individuals are arrested, the police are entitled to search their persons and they may use whatever they find on them as evidence.

Moreover, Justice Stewart contended that the basis for allowing a search of persons arrested is to look for guns or other weapons and to ensure the safety of the police. Yet in cases such as *Harris v. United States,* 331 U.S. 145 (1947), and in *United States v. Rabinowitz,* 339 U.S. 56 (1950), the Court appeared to have endorsed searches that extended beyond the person incident to arrest. Not made clear in these decisions was how broad was the scope of the search. Could the search extend to any entire house, for example, where the arrest took place, or was it limited to where a gun or weapon might be hidden and which could be accessed by the person arrested? Moreover, what justification did the police need to have to do this search?

What *Chimel* did was to clarify these questions. The Court indicated that a search incident to arrest could extend to the immediate surroundings, or to the area near where a person arrested could grab for a gun or other weapon or destroy evidence. The justification for this search would not need additional probable cause, but instead would be part of or incident to the original arrest, viewed as necessary to protect the police and prevent the destruction of evidence. Given this rule, Justice Stewart ruled that the search of Chimel's entire house was an unconstitutional violation of the Fourth Amendment because it was beyond the immediate surroundings or area where he could have grabbed a weapon or destroyed evidence.

Chimel v. California is an important Fourth Amendment case. It established both an exception to the exclusionary rule and warrant requirement while at the same time defining the zone incident to a lawful arrest could be searched by the police.

For more information: Cassak, Lance, and Milton Heumann. *Good Cop, Bad Cop: Racial Profiling and Competing Views of Justice.* New York: Peter Lang, 2003.
—David Schultz

Chisholm v. Georgia, 2 U.S. 419 (1793)

Chisholm v. Georgia was the first major case decided by the U.S. Supreme Court, with important contemporary constitutional implications. The issue was states' rights: whether U.S. states enjoyed SOVEREIGN IMMUNITY under the Constitution. The decision was highly controversial; no less so because Chief Justice John JAY, voting with the majority, had helped write the *Federalist Papers,* an argument for extended federal powers.

When reading *Chisholm,* students should be aware that modern procedure of judicial decision writing did not apply. At that time, each justice wrote an opinion and delivered it in order of seniority, with no justice delivering an "opinion

of the court." This unwieldy system created problems in cataloging cases and was fortunately dropped years later.

Traditionally, the concept of sovereignty implies that the sovereign is not answerable to anyone for his/her actions. The sovereign is immune from civil or criminal liabilities resulting from the decisions he/she lawfully makes. The legal purpose behind this is to remove this consideration from the decision-making process. For example, if a representative could be sued because a business lost part of a market due to the representative's vote, the representative may be reluctant to vote against the business' interests. The question addressed in *Chisholm* is how far the immunity goes.

In 1777, the state of Georgia purchased some military supplies from Alexander Chisholm in South Carolina but never paid for them. After his death, the executor of his will pressed the state for payment. Georgia claimed sovereign immunity and refused to answer the charges, refusing to appear in court or file an argument.

Under the constitution, the U.S. Supreme Court could claim ORIGINAL JURISDICTION because the dispute involved a state and the citizen of another state (Article III, Section 2). Jay and the Federalist majority on the Court rejected Georgia's claim of sovereign immunity. The decision was made on the basis that the Court is charged in the Constitution with settling claims between the states and citizens of other states and the founders could not reasonably have bestowed such a responsibility if they had meant to absolve states of liability under such proceedings. In other words, the founders would not have given the Court the responsibility if they never expected states to be sued. The court examined and rejected a wealth of English case law on the subject of sovereignty.

The decision was highly controversial. The battle between Federalists and States' Rights advocates were not settled by the ratification of the Constitution. The Chisholm decision stoked the fires of this debate. The next year (1794), a constitutional amendment was proposed to overturn *Chisholm* and restore to the states protection against lawsuits from the citizens of other states. Within a year enough states had ratified the Eleventh Amendment to make it part of the Constitution, though President John Adams did not certify its ratification until 1798. Under the terms of the Eleventh Amendment, the Constitution did not allow the Court to claim original jurisdiction in these cases. Almost certainly, at some point the Eleventh Amendment, or something like it, was necessary, if for no other reason than to restrict the Court's DOCKET to a reasonable level.

The Eleventh Amendment was the direct response to *Chisholm,* and the swiftness of its passage is reflective of a Congress and state legislatures that, despite ratification of the Constitution, were not prepared to let go of state sovereignty to the extent desired by the Federalist

Supreme Court and President Adams. In *Chisholm,* the Federalists had overplayed their hand and handed the Democratic-Republicans another issue around which to organize. This brief triumph for a Federalist Supreme Court was a political reach that would be rejected by federal and state lawmakers and help fuel the rise of the Democratic-Republicans highlighting the wedge issue of states' rights.

For more information: Orth, John V. *The Judicial Power of the United States: The Eleventh Amendment in American History.* Oxford and New York: Oxford University Press, 1987.

—Charles C. Howard
—Tim Hundsdorfer

cigarette advertising

Cigarette advertising was banned from television and radio more than three decades ago, as a result of the release of the U.S. surgeon general's widely publicized report linking cigarette smoking to lung cancer and heart disease. Today, cigarette advertising remains banned from broadcast media throughout the United States, yet the tobacco industry is spending record sums of money advertising in print and other visual media, such as billboards; or banners lining the interior of skating rinks, basketball and tennis courts, and baseball and football fields from which events may be televised; or the Internet. The Supreme Court has allowed these disparate rules on cigarette advertising to coexist partly because broadcast and print media are so different from one another that there should be separate rules tailored to each type of medium; and partly because of the U.S. Supreme Court's stance on the question of extending First Amendment protection to advertising.

Historically, the Supreme Court found no conflict between the First Amendment and state laws or regulations that prevented advertising of a commercial product. To the high court, all advertising, or any other communication made in pursuit of personal profit, was automatically entitled to less First Amendment protection than communication made without a profit motive.

During the last quarter century, the Supreme Court has gradually phased in some First Amendment protection for COMMERCIAL SPEECH. In 1976 the U.S. Supreme Court began to back away from its general rule that provided no First Amendment protection for commercial speech. In *Virginia State Board of Pharmacy v. Virginia Consumer Council,* 425 U.S. 748 (1976), the plaintiffs argued that a state law that completely prohibited certain types of commercial speech was overly broad. The high court's decision noted that in a case where the constitutionality of a law or regulation was questioned, it was par-

ticularly important to consider the specific facts before deciding whether commercial speech should be entitled to First Amendment protection. The high court concluded that the plaintiff's argument was valid, and that certain speech could be entitled to some First Amendment protection, although not the complete protection afforded to noncommercial speech.

Four years later, in a landmark decision, *Central Hudson Gas & Electric Corp. v. Public Service Commission of New York,* 447 U.S. 557 (1980), the Supreme Court extended First Amendment protection of commercial speech. In that case, the Court held that a state law restricting truthful commercial speech would be found valid only if the state could demonstrate that the restriction was drawn as narrowly as possible, and that the restriction was necessary to maintain progress on a matter that was more important to the state.

In 1993 two Supreme Court decisions held that commercial speech was entitled to at least some First Amendment protection from state restriction or regulation: *Edenfield v. Fane,* 123 L. Ed. 2d 543 (1993), and *U.S. v. Edge Broadcasting Co.,* 125 L. Ed. 2d 345 (1993).

Finally, in *Lorillard Tobacco Co. v. Reilly,* 533 US 525 (2001), the Supreme Court was faced with a commercial speech question relevant to cigarette advertising. In *Lorillard,* the state of Massachusetts adopted regulations applicable only to advertising and promoting the sale of tobacco products. The regulations banned, among other things, cigarette advertisements on billboards appearing within 1,000 feet of schools or playgrounds. Predictably, Lorillard, a major tobacco company, sued the state. Their lawsuit challenged the constitutionality of several newly adopted state regulations, one of which was so restrictive that it effectively banned all outdoor advertising for cigarettes in the entire state.

The Supreme Court found that Massachusetts had a valid interest in preventing children from becoming smokers. Hence, the state regulation that prohibited placing cigarette advertising material within the line of sight of children under five feet tall was valid. However, another regulation prohibited cigarette advertisements from appearing on billboards that were visible within 1,000 feet of any school. The high court referred to statistics demonstrating that compliance with this provision would mandate that Lorillard remove more than 90 percent of its pre-lawsuit billboards and signs from the entire densely populated Boston–Worcester–Springfield area. Although cigarettes were admittedly dangerous, and children should not be faced with materials advertising such a product, it was legal to sell cigarettes in Massachusetts. The Constitution could not condone state regulations that effectively banned a legal enterprise from operating in the state. The regulation that dealt with billboard placement was struck down, since it clearly violated Lorillard's right to free speech.

In *Lorillard,* faced with a situation involving the most controversial type of commercial speech possible, the Supreme Court's decision clearly acknowledged that as long as cigarette advertising complied with a valid state regulation that prohibited placing such material within the line of sight of children under five feet tall, cigarette advertising deserves the same type of First Amendment protection as advertising for any other product. In the future, if the high court is faced with a situation involving state regulations or laws that place limits on or prohibit cigarette advertising, it is unlikely that the court will support state regulation unless the state has a truly compelling reason for imposing the rule. Eventually, it appears likely that the high court will decide that all commercial speech is entitled to First Amendment protection.

For more information: Columbia Encyclopedia, 6th ed. "Cigar and Cigarette." Columbia University Press. Available online. URL: http://www.encyclopedia.com/html/c1/cigarn1ci.asp. Downloaded May 11, 2004; National Center for Chronic Disease Prevention and Health Promotion, Office on Smoking and Health. "Selected Actions of the U.S. Government Regarding the Regulation of Tobacco Sales, Marketing, and Use." U.S. Department of Health and Human Services, Centers for Disease Control and Prevention. Available online. URL: http://www.cdc.gov/tobacco/overview/regulate.htm. Downloaded May 11, 2004.

—Beth S. Swartz

Cipollone v. Liggett Group, Inc.

In *Cipollone v. Liggett Group, Inc.,* the Supreme Court ruled that the tobacco industry could be held liable for the health affects due to cigarette smoking. Rose Cipollone began smoking in 1942. In 1983, after she was diagnosed with terminal lung cancer, she and her husband initiated a lawsuit against the three companies that manufactured, marketed, and sold the brands of cigarettes she smoked, *Cipollone v. Liggett Group, Inc.,* 593 F. Supp. 1146 (N.J., 1984), based on the New Jersey common law concept of product liability. The couple claimed that the manufacturers were liable for Mrs. Cipollone's illness and death because they had knowingly produced, marketed, advertised, and sold an inherently dangerous product that was the direct cause of her illness and death.

Liggett and the other tobacco companies denied responsibility. They claimed that since they printed, on each cigarette pack they manufactured, the warning label required by federal law, they had fulfilled their legal obligation and had no need to give smokers additional information. The defendants also asserted that an individual

who decided to smoke after reading and understanding the warning label assumed responsibility for all of the risks associated with smoking. Finally, the tobacco companies argued that when Congress specified the wording and appearance of the warning labels, they prevented the tobacco companies from amending the labels to provide smokers with additional information about newly discovered hazards inherent in smoking and also foreclosed smokers from suing cigarette manufacturers for injury, suffering, and/or death resulting from smoking.

After an extensive jury trial, the Federal District Court for the state of New Jersey decided that prior to 1966, when the federal law requiring warning labels on cigarette packs took effect, Liggett had known that cigarettes posed serious health risks and had breached its common law duty to warn smokers of these dangers. The court denied Mrs. Cipollone's estate's claim for compensatory damages, because the court found that by continuing to smoke after receiving the mandatory warnings on every cigarette pack she bought between 1966 and 1984, she was 80 percent responsible for her illness and death. The court awarded Mr. Cipollone $400,000 as compensatory damages, because prior to 1966, the cigarette manufacturers breached their duty to warn consumers about the risks associated with smoking. The court concluded that Liggett was not responsible for any smoking-related problems that occurred after they commenced printing warnings on cigarette packages, since compliance with federal law's warning provisions preempted the Cipollones' state common law-based claim of product liability.

Mr. Cipollone appealed this ruling in the U.S. COURT OF APPEALS, claiming that Liggett was liable for compensatory damages not only to him but also to his wife's estate. The decision in that case, *Cipollone v. Liggett Group, Inc.,* 893 F. 2d 541 (Third Circuit Court of Appeals, 1990), affirmed the salient points of the district court's decision and once again denied Mrs. Cipollone's estate's claim for compensatory damages.

When the parties appealed to the U.S. Supreme Court, it stated that it would hear the case only to decide whether a cigarette manufacturer's compliance with federal CIGARETTE ADVERTISING and labeling laws (14 U.S.C. §1333, *Labeling; requirements; conspicuous statement,* as amended July 27, 1965, and April 1, 1970; and 14 U.S.C. §1334, PREEMPTION, as amended July 27, 1965, and April 1, 1970) prevented individuals harmed by cigarette smoking from suing cigarette manufacturers for damages based on state law. The Supreme Court's reason for making this unusual type of decision was that federal courts disagreed on the correct interpretation of the labeling laws, so that some states provided manufacturers with immunity from lawsuits by injured smokers, while other states allowed such lawsuits. As the result of this inconsistency in interpretation, if a smoker sued a manufacturer in a state that permitted such lawsuits to proceed, the manufacturer might be able to "forum shop," i.e., concoct a reason to request that the case be transferred to another venue in which: (a) the manufacturer has an office or other business address; and (b) such lawsuits are prohibited. Clearly, if the manufacturer succeeds in this type of forum-shopping situation, the plaintiff will be unable to sue in the new forum, whereas he/she might have prevailed in a lawsuit in the first jurisdiction.

Hence, instead of making a decision specific to the unique facts of *Cipollone,* the Supreme Court planned to make a more general decision to prevent the occurrence of inequitable forum-shopping situations. While the Supreme Court would *not* decide whether the Cipollone family should receive compensation for smoking-related suffering and death, the Court would establish the rights of the parties and other criteria relevant to future lawsuits similar to *Cipollone.*

Under current product liability law in the United States, if a manufacturer knows or suspects that one of its products presents some type of hazard, a consumer injured by the product has the right to sue the manufacturer for monetary damages. The risk of susceptibility to this type of lawsuit provides a strong incentive for manufacturers to either: (a) be absolutely certain that they have removed the hazard from the product prior to marketing it; or (b) provide the consumer with easy-to-find, clearly written and/or diagrammed, highly precise information about the hazard so that the average consumer will know exactly what magnitude and type of risk he/she will assume when using the product. If Congress intended the current cigarette package labeling laws to preempt consumers from initiating a product liability lawsuit, when confronted by an injured smoker, a cigarette manufacturer would have the legal right to say, "Under federal law, we are only allowed to tell you exactly what appears on the cigarette package. We would like to give you additional information about the hazards inherent in cigarette smoking, but the federal government prohibits us from providing more information than we have already printed on the package."

The Supreme Court found that when Congress passed the current cigarette package labeling laws, it did *not* intend to preempt all lawsuits by injured smokers. The labeling laws are of very limited scope. They specifically prevent lawsuits based on state law with respect to advertising or promotion of cigarettes. These federal laws do not prevent legal actions for monetary damages based on: (1) harm to an individual due to detrimental reliance on a cigarette manufacturer's testing or research practices; (2) breech of express warranty, or a situation in which a buyer is injured because goods that he believed would measure up to a standard promised by the seller fail to meet that standard; (3)

detrimental reliance of a buyer on a seller's false representation or concealment of a material fact, where the untrue communication is in any form other than advertising; (4) conspiracy among sellers to misrepresent or conceal material facts concerning the health hazards of smoking.

Cigarettes are inherently hazardous; they can cause serious health problems when put to their intended use. There are no other products that are currently legal and available in the United States that are as dangerous as cigarettes. Because of cigarettes' unique status, those who profit from manufacturing, advertising, or selling cigarettes must be very cautious about the manner in which this product is presented to the public. The Supreme Court's policy statement in *Cipollone* served as a warning to cigarette manufacturers that their continued existence is dependent upon strict compliance with all federal and state statutes and common laws.

For more information: Frontline. "Inside the Tobacco Deal." Frontline/PBS online (May 1998). Available Online. URL: http://www.pbs.org/wgbh/pages/frontline/shows/settlement/. Downloaded May 11, 2004; Encarta Online Encyclopedia 2004. "Tobacco." Microsoft MSN. Available online. URL: http://encarta.msn.com/encyclopedia_761562287/Tobacco.html. Downloaded May 11, 2004.

—Beth S. Swartz

citizenship

Citizenship refers to the country in which individuals have legal rights such as to vote. Congress has the power to establish a uniform rule of naturalization, as established in the Constitution, Article I, Section 8, clause 4. In general, a person may become a U.S. citizen by one of two ways, operation of law or naturalization.

Benefits of being a citizen include the right to vote and hold public office, a U.S. passport, and certain federal government jobs ranging from aerospace engineers to airport screeners. A citizen enjoys travel privileges, the ability to petition for permanent residence for immediate family members, and eligibility for U.S. citizen services including protection while abroad.

Responsibilities of citizenship include promises to give up prior allegiances to other countries, support and defend the Constitution and the laws of the United States, and perform service when required. Other responsibilities include serving on a jury and participating in the political process by registering and voting in elections.

Most commonly, citizenship is conferred by right of birthplace, *jus soli,* to those born in the United States and its territories. Subject to some limitations, a child born abroad to one or more U.S. citizen parents may generally acquire citizenship by right of blood, *jus sanguinis,* at birth. In some instances, a nonmarital child born abroad may also be entitled to citizenship. However, such a person does not have a constitutional right to citizenship.

Citizenship may also be acquired through naturalization petition, naturalization of one parent, or military service. No person's right to be naturalized may be denied because of race, sex, or marital status. (See 8 USC §1422.)

Naturalization applicants must file Form N-400 Application for Citizenship with the Bureau of Citizenship and Immigration Services (BCIS), an agency of the U.S. Department of Homeland Security created in 2003. Although the BCIS's stated processing goal is six months, naturalization applications generally take approximately three years due to the bureau's limited resources and high number of pending naturalization applications.

In general, the Immigration and Nationality Act provides that naturalization applicants must be at least 18 years of age, possess good moral character, be literate and conversant in English, have continuously resided in the United States, and demonstrate attachment to the principles of the U.S. Constitution and a favorable disposition toward the United States. Some exceptions to these requirements can include honorably discharged members of the armed services, Philippino and Persian Gulf veterans, Hmong tribe members, and those individuals who make extraordinary contributions to national security or intelligence activities.

One becomes a citizen upon taking the Oath of Allegiance to the United States. The oath can be taken without the words "to bear arms on behalf of the United States when required by law . . ." if the applicant can evidence strong religious opposition to bearing arms. The oath can be administered by the BCIS on the same day as the naturalization interview or by a U.S. district or state court at a later date. Although long concerned with allegiance problems attendant to dual nationality, a U.S. citizen may possess dual citizenship.

An applicant denied naturalization may APPEAL to the BCIS by filing Form N-336 Request for Hearing on a Decision in Naturalization Proceedings under 336 of the act. Such an applicant may have a denial reviewed *de novo* by the U.S. district court of jurisdiction.

Citizenship can be lost through expatriation, revocation, or denaturalization by performing certain acts such as bearing arms against the United States. Cases of revocation and denaturalization are governed by the DEPARTMENT OF JUSTICE.

Recent changes in naturalization practices include the passage of the Child Citizenship Act of 2000 which automatically confers citizenship to qualifying orphans adopted abroad and allows for the expeditious naturalization of adopted children residing outside the United States. The act also allows for automatic naturalization for those adopted children who adjust their status to that of lawful permanent resident prior to the age of 18.

More notable is the Domestic Security Enhancement Act, also known as the USA PATRIOT Act, enacted in 2001, which broadened the U.S. Supreme Court's ability to revoke citizenship, especially within the first two years of naturalization.

Seemingly in contrast to the Constitution, the Justice Department is contemplating the enforcement of the USA PATRIOT Act II, a measure that would give the federal government unprecedented antiterror powers including the authority to revoke American citizenship of native-born Americans.

For more information: *A Guide to Naturalization,* Form M-476. U.S. Department of Citizenship and Immigration Services; U.S. Department of Justice. "The USA Patriot Act: Preserving Life and Liberty." Department of Justice Web site. Available online. URL: http://www.lifeandliberty.gov. Downloaded May 11, 2004.

—Elizabeth Ricci

City of Chicago v. Morales, 527 U.S. 41 (1999)

In *City of Chicago v. Morales,* a divided Supreme Court struck down a city law that made it illegal for several youths to loiter on public streets. The Court struck the law down as unconstitutionally vague and as an infringement of the Fourteenth Amendment right of individuals to freely associate with others.

In an effort to combat street gang activity, the City of Chicago, Illinois, enacted an ordinance in 1992 that prohibited criminal street gang members from loitering with one another in any public place. The concern was that gang members often hung out on city streets, intimidating members of the public, and committing many of their crimes in these locations. In order to lessen this intimidation and to prevent street crime, the Gang Congregation ordinance defined loitering as "remaining in any one place with no apparent purpose." It then made it illegal for any member of a street gang, whether it be formal or informal, to loiter in any public place such as a street, public sidewalk, or park. If a police officer suspected an individual or individuals whom she reasonably believed to be loitering in violation of this ordinance, the officer could order them to leave the area. If they did not disperse, they could be arrested.

Before lower courts found the law unconstitutional in 1995, police had issued more than 89,000 dispersal orders and arrested more than 42,000 individuals for violating the Gang Congregation ordinance. In that time, several courts had upheld the ordinance as constitutional, while others had ruled the opposite, contending that the law was vague and that it had violated the Fourth Amendment. One individual who was arrested challenged the case up through the Illinois court system where the state supreme court found that the law violated the Illinois and federal constitutions. The United States Supreme Court accepted certiorari, affirming the decision of the Illinois Supreme Court.

In writing for the Court, Justice STEVENS contended that the Gang Congregation ordinance was unconstitutionally vague and therefore in violation of the due process clause of the Fourteenth Amendment. First he argued that the definition of loitering was vague, drawing no clear distinction between innocent conduct and activities that may result in criminal harm. For criminal laws to be upheld as constitutional, they must give a clear warning to citizens regarding what behavior was illegal so that they could comply. Instead, the law here failed to give individuals proper notice regarding what type of activity was illegal, leaving instead too much discretion in the police to decide what constituted loitering or a violation of the law. Thus, individuals would be subject to arrest only when they failed to comply with a police order to disperse and, lacking this order, the Court contended, individuals may not know when they may be in violation of the law.

Critical to its reasoning was an assertion by the Court that individuals do have a constitutional right to loiter or simply just move about freely from one place to another. Justice Stevens contended that the right to innocently be on the streets is one of the basic rights protected by the Fourteenth Amendment.

In concurring with the decision, Justice O'CONNOR indicated that while she agreed that the current law was unconstitutional, it would be possible to draft new laws that were less vague and might be upheld by the Court. She suggested that loitering ordinances that required a harmful purpose associated with loitering, such as intimidation of the public, or laws that limit the areas and manner regarding its enforcement, might be constitutional. As a result of her comments, Chicago and other cities did draft new laws making loitering illegal, and they have again been challenged as unconstitutionally vague.

Overall, *City of Chicago v. Morales* is an important affirmation of the right of individuals simply to be on the streets, free from being hassled by police officers. The case is also important since it seemed to reaffirm the rights even of minors to enjoy basic constitutional rights, such as the freedom of association.

For more information: Cassak, Lance, and Milton Heumann. *Good Cop, Bad Cop: Racial Profiling and Competing Views of Justice.* New York: Peter Lang, 2003.

—David Schultz

City of Richmond v. J. A. Croson Company, 488 U.S. 494 (1989)

In *City of Richmond v. J.A. Croson Company*, 488 U.S. 494 (1989), the U.S. Supreme Court found the City of Richmond's AFFIRMATIVE ACTION program used in city contracts unconstitutional. The Court ruled that the City of Richmond's "Minority Business Enterprise" (MBE) program violated the Constitution's Fourteenth Amendment clause providing for "equal protection of the laws." In doing so, the Court established that all nonfederal "Minority Business Enterprise" programs would be evaluated by the courts under the "STRICT SCRUTINY" standard of review.

Richmond, Virginia, like hundreds of other state and local governments around the country, had enacted an affirmative-action statute designed to increase the rate of minority participation on government-funded work projects. While many of these programs contained provisions focusing on direct contracts between the government and minority-owned businesses, Richmond's MBE program called for successful bidders on government contracts to subcontract 30 percent of the dollars in the contract to minority-owned firms. Richmond based the majority of its MBE program on the federal MBE program upheld by the Supreme Court in *FULLILOVE V. KLUTZNICK,* 448 U.S. 448 (1980).

The City of Richmond refused the low bid of J. A. Croson Company because it did not provide for minority subcontractors, and J. A. Croson sued the city for "reverse" RACIAL DISCRIMINATION. Richmond argued that its program was designed (1) to help minorities and (2) to remediate discrimination against minorities, both points critical to the Court in *Fullilove*. The Court, however, ruled that any distinction between benevolent and malevolent discrimination was misguided and that remedial programs must be targeted to proved discrimination against minorities within the Richmond area. The Court in *Croson* did not overrule *Fullilove* but rather argued that there is a constitutional difference between federal and state or local race-based legislation. This distinction was subsequently overruled in *ADARAND CONSTRUCTORS, INC. V. PENA,* 515 U.S. 200 (1995).

Though the outcome of *Croson* was a seeming defeat for affirmative-action proponents, the opinion in *Croson* established how governments could create a constitutional affirmative-action program. To do so, a government must establish that its program is "narrowly tailored to a COMPELLING STATE INTEREST." As the Court elaborated, this means that governments seeking to create an MBE program must prove that there is a significant disparity between the availability and utilization of minority contractors in the area. Further, (1) the government must consider race neutral methods toward addressing the disparity; (2) the MBE program targets must correspond to the respective populations in the area; (3) the statute must be flexible; (4) the burden on excluded groups must be minimized; and (5) MBE programs must be of limited duration.

In the decade following *Croson,* the lower courts have consistently followed the dictates set out by the U.S. Supreme Court. Local governments, however, have responded to political demands and actually created more than 100 new MBE programs. Many of these new programs have been created based on the Court's opinion in *Croson.*

For more information: Drake, W. Avon, and Robert D. Holsworth. *Affirmative Action and the Stalled Quest for Black Progress.* Urbana: University of Illinois Press, 1996; Sweet, Martin J. *Supreme Policymaking: Coping with the Supreme Court's Affirmative Action Policies* (forthcoming).

—Martin J. Sweet

civil liberties

Civil liberties involve limits imposed on government power with the aim of preserving individual freedom. Such limitations are placed on governments both in the bodies of state and the federal constitutions (which set out specific liberties and limit government powers through checks and balances and the SEPARATION OF POWERS) and in their bills of rights.

The U.S. Constitution's BILL OF RIGHTS (1791), comprising the Constitution's first 10 amendments, sets out guarantees for (among others) the freedom of speech and press, the free exercise of RELIGION, the right to keep and bear arms, rights against unreasonable searches and seizures, and a broad array of procedural rights applying to those charged with crimes. The Bill of Rights preserves civil liberties by serving as a touchstone for political argument concerning government actions and policies and by setting judicially enforceable legal requirements. Civil liberties, which involve limiting government power to preserve individual freedom, are commonly distinguished from CIVIL RIGHTS, which involve the affirmative rights of similarly situated people to be treated equally under law.

Americans have been famously suspicious of government power and jealous of their liberties since their inception as a nation. Indeed, the American Revolution was sparked in considerable part by their conviction that the British were repeatedly violating their rights as Englishmen, guaranteed (among other places) by the English Bill of Rights (1689). But the era in which the Supreme Court (and other federal courts) served as the primary protector of civil liberties is relatively recent.

For much of American history, the Bill of Rights were understood to be legal restrictions on the distant and suspect national government only, and not the states. As government power grew rapidly in the early 20th century, however, the Court developed a sustained interest in protecting civil liberties. Although the Court did deal with scattered civil liberties issues throughout the 19th century and developed a sustained interest in issues of freedom from certain forms of economic regulation in the late 19th century, its modern civil liberties jurisprudence began with a series of free speech decisions involving political radicals opposed to U.S. entry into World War I.

Over the course of the 20th century, while grappling with altering social and political contexts, the Court was confronted with diverse arguments concerning the proper scope of civil liberties, given the legitimate authority of government to enact laws that advance peace and good order and the public health, safety, and morals. The Court wrestled with the countervailing claims of liberty and good order in free speech cases involving radical politics (including anarchism and communism) in times of crisis, aggressive religious proselytizing by Jehovah's Witnesses, labor marches and strikes, civil rights and antiwar protests, a new sexual openness and expressiveness, and other areas. In the process, it developed constitutional doctrine (or a framework for interpreting the broad and vague provisions of the Bill of Rights that would help resolve highly specific cases) that protected a variety of types of speech—from "pure" verbal speech to "expressive conduct" and "symbolic speech," in an expanding variety of settings. The Court expanded press freedoms significantly in the early 1960s.

In a series of cases involving schools which stuck down both prayer and (voluntary) Bible reading in the public schools, the Court inaugurated the modern understanding of the separation of church and state under the First Amendment's establishment clause. In cases involving requested religious exemptions from laws involving conscientious objectors, public education, taxation, military dress, and religious rituals involving animal sacrifice and illegal drugs, the Court refined its doctrine concerning the individual right to the free exercise of religion. In part reacting to police excesses during Prohibition and the often brutal treatment of blacks by southern courts and police forces, the Court fashioned a complex web of constitutional doctrine constraining the power of prosecutors and the police pursuant to the criminal process provisions of the Bill of Rights.

The modern Supreme Court approaches civil liberties cases by asking first whether the challenged law impinges on a fundamental right or a "preferred freedom," whether that right or freedom is set out expressly in the constitutional text or not. If it does, the Court applies a highly skeptical "STRICT SCRUTINY" to the laws, which inclines toward striking it down, upholding only if it concludes the law is narrowly tailored in service of a compelling government interest. Arguments about the status of particular freedoms under the Constitution and about the respective claims of government and the individual are at the heart of the modern civil liberties law. The Supreme Court's decisions in weighing these arguments are an important part of American politics, and have become a touchstone of the American constitutional tradition.

For more information: Gillman, Howard. "'Preferred Freedoms': The Progressive Expansion of State Power and the Rise of Modern Civil Liberties Jurisprudence." *Political Research Quarterly* 47 (September 1994): 623–653; Kersch, Ken I. *Constructing Civil Liberties: Discontinuities in the Development of American Constitutional Law.* Cambridge: Cambridge University Press, 2004; Klarman, Michael. "Rethinking the Civil Rights and Civil Liberties Revolution." *Virginia Law Review* 82 (1990): 1–67; Powe, Lucas S. *The Warren Court and American Politics.* Cambridge, Mass.: Belknap Press/Harvard University Press, 2000.

—Ken I. Kersch

civil rights

Civil rights guarantee similarly situated persons that they will be treated equally under law. Constitutional rights to equal treatment by the government are set out in the U.S. Constitution's Thirteenth (1865), Fourteenth (1868), and Fifteenth (1870) Amendments (the "Civil War Amendments"), which, respectively, outlaw slavery, guarantee all persons the equal protection of the laws, and vouchsafe equal voting rights regardless of race, color, or previous condition of servitude. Statutory rights to equal treatment by either governments or private entities (such as businesses or private schools) are also part of modern civil rights law. The Supreme Court protects civil rights both through its power to void laws that violate the Constitution (the power of JUDICIAL REVIEW) and through its power to interpret the nation's civil rights statutes. Although the terms are sometimes used interchangeably and the conceptual distinction is far from pristine, civil rights refers to affirmative guarantees to equal treatment, while CIVIL LIBERTIES refers to freedom-preserving negative limitations on government power.

The principles of civil rights law were forged with a single problem foremost in mind: the unequal treatment, by government and private entities alike, accorded to African Americans because of their race. Before the Civil War, most African Americans were enslaved, and (as the Supreme Court noted in its infamous *DRED SCOTT* case decision) were considered property with "no rights which the white man was bound to respect."

In the war's aftermath, northern initiated efforts were made to alter this status by passage of federal statutes like the Civil Rights Act of 1866 (guaranteeing blacks equal rights to make and enforce contracts, to sue, be sued, and appear as witnesses in court, to purchase and own property, and to be protected against physical violence), the Civil Rights Act of 1875 (which sought to protect blacks against discrimination in public accommodations like parks, schools, public transportation, and hotels), and the First Military Reconstruction Act of 1867 (protecting the right of blacks to vote). The Civil War Amendments were passed both to provide their own list of guarantees and to make clear that the unprecedented national efforts to enforce civil rights were consistent with the Constitution, which heretofore had placed strict limits on federal power.

Over time, however, southern resistance mounted and northern will flagged. The Supreme Court at the time drew a distinction between less controversial "civil rights" of the sort protected in the 1866 Civil Rights Act from "political rights" (like the right to vote and hold office) and the most controversial "social rights" (like public accommodations, education, and intermarriage). The Supreme Court held that Congress had no authority under the Civil War Amendments to enforce social rights. As the southern Jim Crow regime was consolidated, blacks were denied their voting rights and segregated from whites, and the Supreme Court sanctioned these developments.

Although rooted in the Civil War Amendments, modern civil rights law began to take shape only in the mid-20th century, in the aftermath of a massive black migration north to cities in the 1920s (where they could vote), intense political and legal pressure from the civil rights movement, and an ideological context altered by a war against an overtly racist Nazi enemy. It was at this time that, reinforcing tentative first steps taken by the Roosevelt and Truman administrations, the Supreme Court began to consider the formerly separate categories of civil, political, and social rights as a single category of "civil rights" and adopt increasingly expansive understandings of those rights.

In the aftermath of the Kennedy assassination and under the leadership of President Johnson, Congress passed major civil rights legislation: the CIVIL RIGHTS ACT OF 1964 (outlawing discrimination on the basis of race, color, RELIGION, sex, and national origin in employment, education, labor unions, and public accommodations); and the VOTING RIGHTS ACT of 1965, which the Court subsequently interpreted broadly.

Although civil rights law was initially formulated with African Americans in mind, even before the Civil War, other groups, often drawing analogies between their own unequal treatment and the unequal treatment of blacks, argued on behalf of their own civil rights. In the 19th century, women, many of whom were active in the abolitionist movement and faced discrimination within it, argued that

President Lyndon Johnson signs the Civil Rights Act of 1964 as Martin Luther King, Jr., looks on. *(Johnson Library)*

in being denied the right to vote, to own property, to make contracts, to sue, and to serve on juries, and in being barred from professions like law and medicine, their constitutional rights to equal treatment, like those of African Americans, were being denied.

In the 19th century, the Supreme Court rejected these assertions out of hand. The situation remained relatively unchanged, despite women winning the right to vote with the adoption of the Nineteenth Amendment in 1920, until women were granted statutory protection against SEX DIS-CRIMINATION alongside blacks in a provision of the Civil Rights Act of 1964; and at the behest of women's rights organizations, the Court inaugurated its modern constitutional and statutory sex-discrimination jurisprudence in the 1970s. Following these successes, other groups like gays and lesbians and the disabled, sought and won similar protections from courts, legislatures, administrative agencies, and private organizations. Other groups, such as the poor, sought, and continue to seek, similar civil rights.

In civil rights cases invoking the Fourteenth Amendment's EQUAL PROTECTION CLAUSE, the Court evinces spe-cial vigilance when confronted with laws imposing disabilities on certain "discrete and insular minorities."

The modern Court applies different "tiers of scrutiny" to different groups in its equal protection analysis. It applies minimal scrutiny to laws which do not involve "sus-pect" or "semi-suspect" classifications (or FUNDAMENTAL RIGHTS such as marriage and procreation), upholding such laws if it finds them to be rationally related to a legitimate government interest. In cases involving "SUSPECT CLASSI-FICATION" like religion or race, however, the Court applies "STRICT SCRUTINY" by which it holds the law unconstitu-tional unless it finds it to be narrowly tailored in service of a compelling government interest. The Court has devised an "intermediate" tier of scrutiny applicable to "semi-sus-pect" classifications like sex or illegitimacy, upholding only those laws that are substantially related to an important government interest.

While this framework for analysis has guided the Court in much of its civil rights jurisprudence, some have begun to question whether the Court has begun to depart from it in recent years. Despite its refusal to designate the mentally retarded or gays and lesbians—or even "hippies"—suspect classifications, the Court has invalidated laws burdening them under the ostensibly highly deferential RATIONAL BASIS test. In AFFIRMATIVE ACTION cases, the Court has upheld racial classifications, despite a strict scrutiny standard, drawing a relatively new distinction between "benign" and "invidious" discrimination and citing "diversity" as a "compelling government interest."

For much of American history, civil rights disputes involved open and patently invidious discrimination, such as the forthright denial of jobs to people on account of their race or sex. Many contemporary arguments concerning civil rights, however, involve allegations of hidden or subtle discrimination, such as claims that the reasons offered for failing to hire someone or sell him a house were offered as covers for a discriminatory motivation, or that ostensibly neutral or reasonable laws have a "disparate impact" on disadvantaged minority groups.

Contemporary civil rights issues are raised in cases involving racial profiling, racial preferences, and the use of racial classifications in hiring and college admissions, proportionality in funding of men's and women's college sports teams (TITLE IX), the racial gerrymandering of electoral districts, differential treatment of ILLEGAL ALIENS in access to public services such as schools and health care, same-sex marriage, adoption, and visitation, and the provision of special accommodations for the disabled in sports and employment. In many of these disputes, both sides claim to be fighting for "civil rights." In the future, the meaning of the term itself will be shaped in significant part by rulings of the U.S. Supreme Court.

For more information: Eskridge, William N., Jr. *Gaylaw: Challenging the Apartheid of the Closet.* Cambridge, Mass.: Harvard University Press, 1999; Hoff, Joan. *Law, Gender, and Injustice: A Legal History of U.S. Women.* New York: New York University Press, 1991; Klarman, Michael J. *From Jim Crow to Civil Rights: The Supreme Court and the Struggle for Racial Equality.* New York and Oxford: Oxford University Press, 2003; Nelson, William E. *The Fourteenth Amendment: From Political Principle to Judicial Doctrine.* Cambridge, Mass.: Harvard University Press, 1988.

—Ken I. Kersch

Civil Rights Act of 1964

The Civil Rights Act of 1964 was a major piece of legislation passed by Congress to ban discrimination in many private establishments. Yet once passed, its constitutionality was open to question.

The Civil Rights movement brought the discriminatory treatment of African Americans to the forefront of the American psyche. President Lyndon B. Johnson, seeking to eradicate the vestiges of centuries of oppression, asked Congress to create a law that would move African Americans from a disenfranchised minority to an empowered class. After the longest debate in Senate history and an unsuccessful filibuster led by Senator Strom Thurmond, Congress passed the Civil Rights Act of 1964. This act was the first major piece of legislation dealing with Civil Rights in the nearly hundred years since Reconstruction. In writing the Civil Rights Act, Congress invoked its powers under the Interstate Commerce Clause instead of power emanating from the Fourteenth Amendment since the latter applies to the states. The decision to use the Interstate Commerce Clause gave Congress wide latitude in setting the specific requirements and enforcing the act, as well as allowing the act to pass constitutional muster.

The Civil Rights Act of 1964 sought to create a more egalitarian society through government standards and legislation. The act prohibited the use of literacy tests and other discriminatory tactics in voter registration, called for desegregation of public facilities and education, and established the EEOC, the EQUAL EMPLOYMENT OPPORTUNITY COMMISSION. The most controversial aspect of the act was Title II, a ban on discrimination in public accommodations that have a substantial relation to INTERSTATE COMMERCE. This facet proved to be controversial because it dictated how private property could be used.

HEART OF ATLANTA MOTEL V. UNITED STATES, 379 U.S. 241 (1964), was the first challenge to the newly passed law. An Atlanta motel, which derived the majority of its business from interstate travelers, steadfastly refused to serve African-American patrons. The owner of the motel claimed that Congress had exceeded its authority under Article II of the Constitution and had violated his Fifth Amendment due process rights by effectively taking his property out of his control. He further claimed that Congress' forcing him to rent to African Americans amounted to forcing him into slavery, a violation of the Thirteenth Amendment. The Supreme Court did not agree.

In a unanimous opinion written by Justice Arthur Goldberg, the Court ruled in favor of the federal government. Congress, the Court said, was well within its rights to invoke the Interstate Commerce Clause in passing this sweeping legislation. Since the motel derived more than 70 percent of its revenue from interstate travel, Title II could be applied specifically in this case. The Court dismissed assertions of violations based on the Fifth and Thirteenth Amendments.

A companion case, *Katzenbach v. McClung*, 379 U.S. 294 (1964), established the same principle for restaurants. Ollie's Barbecue in Atlanta, Georgia, refused to serve Negroes. Justice Thomas CLARK, writing for a unanimous court, held that restaurants were involved in interstate commerce and therefore covered by the act. He further argued that discrimination by restaurants was a significant burden on Negroes traveling in interstate commerce.

Title VI of the Civil Rights Act authorized cutting off federal funds from states and local governments that practiced discrimination. This was undoubtedly the most effective provision of the act. It resulted in a major step toward desegregating public schools. Some have argued that it had more of an impact than did the famous court case, *Brown v. Board of Education,* 347 U.S. (1954), that declared "separate but equal" schools to be inherently discriminatory.

In addition, all agencies within state governments that received federal funds were now required to submit "assurance of compliance" forms that stated the extent to which they were in compliance with the Civil Rights Act of 1964. Since roughly 20 percent of all state and local revenues came from federal sources, this too proved to be an extraordinarily effective incentive to end segregation.

Little noticed at the time was a provision prohibiting discrimination based on race, color, RELIGION, national origin, and in employment, sex. Thus the act, intended primarily as a law prohibiting RACIAL DISCRIMINATION, became a major resource in the subsequent battle for gender equality.

A major area not covered by the act was discrimination in housing. The resolution to that problem had to wait for the Civil Rights Act of 1968.

For more information: Cortner, Richard C. *Civil Rights and Public Accommodations: The* Heart of Atlanta *and* McClung *Cases.* Lawrence: University Press of Kansas, 2001; Epstein, Lee, and Thomas G. Walker. *Constitutional Law for a Changing America: Rights, Liberties and Justice.* 5th ed. Washington, D.C.: CQ Press, 2004.

—Temeka Higgins

Civil Rights Acts

The Civil Rights Acts refer to legislation passed during the Reconstruction to provide rights and liberties to the freed slaves.

During the Reconstruction period following the Civil War (1861–65), idealistic legislators believed they could secure the rights of freed slaves to prove that the bloody conflict had not been fought in vain. Their first priority was ratification of three amendments to the U.S. Constitution.

The Thirteenth Amendment, enacted in 1866, one year after the end of the Civil War, quite simply abolished slavery throughout the United States. It added to the Constitution, which otherwise included substantial restatement of the Declaration of Independence, the previously conspicuously absent word *equality.* Unfortunately, in response to this amendment, many states enacted "black codes" that codified limitations to the CIVIL RIGHTS of the newly freed slaves.

One of the reasons behind the 1868 enactment of the Fourteenth Amendment was an effort by some members of Congress to counter the "black codes." In retrospect, it is clear that the provisions of this amendment had far more impact than the black codes had had. The Fourteenth Amendment: (1) granted CITIZENSHIP to former slaves and other individuals born or naturalized in the U.S.; (2) prohibited states from (a) depriving any person of life, liberty, or property without due process of law, or (b) denying any person equal protection of the laws; and (c) enacting or enforcing any law that would diminish the privileges associated with U.S. citizenship; and finally (and perhaps most important) (3) to insure that its provisions would be effectuated, gave Congress explicit authority to pass any laws needed to enforce its provisions.

The Fifteenth Amendment, enacted in 1870, prohibited anyone from using race as a reason for depriving a citizen of the right to vote.

The 1871 Civil Rights Act prohibited anyone from using force, intimidation, or threat to deny any citizen equal protection under the law and provided criminal penalties for violators of its provisions. The 1875 Civil Rights Act, which was later declared unconstitutional by the Supreme Court, guaranteed former slaves the right to use public accommodations.

To effectuate the intentions behind the Thirteenth through Fifteenth Amendments, Congress passed four Civil Rights Acts, one each in 1866, 1870, 1871, and 1875. The latter was by far the most significant of these acts, in that its goal was achievement of equal access to inns, public conveyances, and places of amusement.

The Supreme Court declared the 1875 Civil Rights Act unconstitutional in the 1883 Civil Rights cases, on the ground that the act sought to bar discriminatory action between individuals, while the Fourteenth Amendment's EQUAL PROTECTION CLAUSE was applicable only to state action. Although certain groups and individuals throughout the United States had an ongoing interest in integration of public facilities, such as schools, and development of social as well as legal equality, they were a small and poorly funded minority and were able to convince neither Congress nor state legislative bodies to implement these ideas. Reintroduction of legislation with intent and reasoning similar to the 1875 act's equal protection clause argument became increasingly unlikely as subsequent Supreme Court decisions and congressional actions further narrowed interpretation of the equal protection clause. Even today, the current Supreme Court continues to interpret the equal protection clause as applicable only to state, and not individual, actions.

New legislation regarding equal access to public accommodations was finally introduced in Congress more than 80 years after the Supreme Court found the 1875 Civil Rights Act unconstitutional. The new bill, which became the CIVIL RIGHTS ACT OF 1964, sought to create equal access to public facilities and accommodations through use of Congress' commerce power, rather than the Fourteenth Amendment's guarantee of equal protection.

Despite multiple challenges to the constitutionality of the 1964 law that began as soon as the law was passed, the Supreme Court has continued to find the law constitutional *HEART OF ATLANTA MOTEL V. U.S.*, 379 U.S. 241 (1964); *Katzenbach v. McClung*, 379 U.S. 294 (1964); *UNITED STATES V. MORRISON*, 529 U.S. 598 (2000). It is apparent that Congress' commerce power provides a more sound basis than the Fourteenth Amendment's equal protection clause for legislation that prevents discrimination based on race, creed, color, RELIGION, or sex, or age.

For more information: Schwartz, Bernard. *A History of the Supreme Court.* New York and Oxford: Oxford University Press, 1993; Legal Information Institute of Cornell University Law School. "Civil Rights: An Overview." Cornell University Press (2002). Available online. URL: http://www.law.cornell.edu/topics/civil_rights.html. Downloaded May 12, 2004.

—Beth S. Swartz

civil rights of people with disabilities

CIVIL RIGHTS refers to the body of individual liberty and equal opportunity protection that insures the legal ability of people to participate fully in societal life—without discrimination. In the United States the civil rights of people with disabilities are ensured by the "due process" and "equal protection" clauses of the Fourteenth Amendment to the Constitution. In addition, the last four decades have seen landmark national legislation aimed at codifying specific rights and antidiscrimination protection in areas such as education, employment, and access to public services and accommodations. The seminal statutes in these areas are: the Individuals with Disabilities Education Act, the Rehabilitation Act, and the Americans with Disabilities Act. While one might suppose that civil rights are always both morally and legally absolute, in the area of disability, questions over the cost of strict implementation and the interpretation of statutory provisions often make these rights uncertain.

Individuals with Disabilities Education Act (IDEA)

IDEA, originally the Education for All Handicapped Children Act of 1975, broadly defines the manner in which local school districts are obliged to serve students with disabilities. The U.S. Congress found that "improving educational results for children with disabilities is an essential element of our national policy of ensuring equality of opportunity." Hence, IDEA was enacted to protect the educational rights of children with disabilities and their parents. This congressional action to eliminate discrimination in education was precipitated by court cases, which held that children with disabilities have the right to a free and adequate public education. IDEA mandates that this education be provided in the "least restrictive environment" (LRE).

Rehabilitation Act

The Rehabilitation Act of 1973 was enacted "to promote the rehabilitation, employment, and independent living of people with disabilities." The act was proffered with no significant commitment of federal authority. Section 504, a somewhat routine inclusion, was but a tip of the hat to equal access for people with disabilities—physical and mental. Simply, 504, which was modeled after TITLE VII of the CIVIL RIGHTS ACT OF 1964, prohibits employers who receive federal financial assistance, federal employers, and employers having certain contracts with the federal government from discriminating against people with disabilities. Section 504 represents a significant departure from the assumptions of dependency and incapacity inherent in much of the earlier U.S. vocational rehabilitation policy.

Americans with Disabilities Act (ADA)

With the ADA of 1990, Congress acted in order "to provide a clear and comprehensive national mandate for the elimination of discrimination against individuals with disabilities." Similar to the Rehabilitation Act, the ADA defines disability as: (1) a physical or mental impairment that substantially limits an individual's major life activities, (2) a record of such an impairment, or (3) being regarded as having such an impairment. The ADA expands the employment coverage of the Rehabilitation Act to include entities in the private sector. Further, the ADA significantly expands the scope of antidiscrimination protection for people with disabilities to include public services and public accommodations and services operated by private entities.

Limitations on Civil Rights

As noted supra, one might assume that all civil rights are absolute. Regrettably, for people with disabilities this is not the case. Myriad issues militate against strict enforcement of all supposed rights. In the area of education, the proper identification of special education students posed an early problem. While this seems to have been rectified, recent questions over the form of educational grants seemingly threaten the current system of special education. One cannot foreknow the ramifications for the civil rights of special education students if block educational grants are substituted for the categorical grants currently awarded.

Conceivably, IDEA's mandate to educate in the LRE would be significantly diminished.

The ADA, which dramatically expands the rights delineated in the Rehabilitation Act, defines people with disabilities as an "insular minority." Yet the civil rights of these people are far less absolute than those for other groups considered insular minorities. Amendments to the Rehabilitation Act allow investigation of what is "reasonable." Similarly, "undue hardship" is the safe harbor that prevents many accommodations from being deemed "reasonable" under the ADA's Title I employment protection. In *Olmstead v. L.C., by Zimring*, 527 U.S. 581 (1999), the ADA's Title II protection was also interpreted to permit cost to be a consideration in a municipality's provision of public services.

The federal courts play a central role in interpreting the protection found within the ADA. The lower level of scrutiny employed by these courts often leads to interpretations that are inconsistent with the civil rights tradition within the United States and go against congressional intent. This is especially the situation with cases brought by individuals seeking ADA Title I employment protection. As if an ad hoc system of financial consideration were not enough, there appears to be no clear understanding of just who may seek Title I protection. Several cases have addressed the question of whether an individual has a disability for purposes of ADA protection. Illustrative are three cases known as the "Sutton Rulings."

In 1999 the Supreme Court issued a trio of opinions that established PRECEDENT for a dramatic narrowing of the ADA's Title I employment protection. In *Sutton v. United Air Lines, Inc.*, 527 U.S. 471 (1999), the Court affirmed a lower court decision which held that the petitioners, commercial airline pilots with correctable vision, were not substantially limited in any major life activity. Thus, the twin sisters had no claim of disability under the ADA, as they were precluded from one specific job, not a class of jobs. Using similar reasoning, in *Murphy v. United Parcel Service, Inc.*, 527 U.S. 516 (1999), the Court held that a mechanic with controllable high blood pressure was not precluded from a class of mechanic jobs, as necessary for ADA protection, rather only from mechanic jobs that required driving commercial vehicles. In *Albertsons, Inc., v. Kirkingburg*, 527 U.S. 555 (1999), the Court found that the appellate court was in error when it found a monocular truck driver disabled for purposes of ADA protection, as he continued to work in a mechanic position that he had held for more than 20 years.

The concept of FEDERALISM has also come to play an important role in the judicial application of the ADA's protection. In *Alden v. Maine*, 527 U.S. 706 (1999), the Court held that state sovereignty reaches far beyond the Eleventh Amendment's "citizens of another state." In *Board of Trustees of the University of Alabama v. Garrett*, 531 U.S.

356 (2001), the Court extended this reasoning to an ADA claim. An appellate court had ruled that a nurse and a security guard could sue the state of Alabama under the ADA's Title I. However, in a 5-4 decision, the Court held that state sovereignty prohibited the state employees from being able to sue under the ADA. Given the Court's lower level of scrutiny in disability cases and the Court precedent on federalism, the implications for other areas of protection for people with disabilities remain unclear.

For more information: Freilich, Robert H., Adrienne H. Wyker, and Leslie Eriksen Harris. "Federalism at the Millennium: A Review of U.S. Supreme Court Cases Affecting State and Local Government." *Urban Lawyer* 31, no. 4 (Fall 1999): 683–775; Krieger, Linda Hamilton, ed. *Backlash Against the ADA: Reinterpreting Disability Rights.* Ann Arbor: University of Michigan Press, 2003; Scotch, Richard K. *From Good Will to Civil Rights: Transforming Federal Disability Policy.* Philadelphia, Pa.: Temple University Press, 1984; Terman, Donna L., Edwin W. Martin, and Reed Martin. "The Legislative and Litigation History of Special Education." *The Future of Children* (Special Education for Students with Disabilities) 6, no. 1 (Spring 1996): 25–39.

—Clenton G. Winford II, Ph.D.

Clark, Thomas (1899–1977) *Supreme Court justice*
Thomas Clark served as a justice of the United States Supreme Court from 1949 to 1967. Although generally seen as a lesser justice, his term included many controversial issues. He also wrote some of the most important decisions of the 1960s and generally supported CIVIL RIGHTS and political equality.

Born in Dallas, Texas, in 1899, Clark came from a family of prominent lawyers. His father served as president of the Texas Bar Association in 1896–97. He received a bachelor's and law degree from the University of Texas. Clark joined his family's law firm in 1922 and in 1927 was named Dallas County's civil district attorney. In 1937 Clark joined the U.S. Justice Department and spent several years there. During World War II Clark worked with Sen. Harry S Truman on defense contractor waste and abuse. When Truman became president in 1945 he promoted Clark to attorney general.

As attorney general, Clark pursued legislation favorable to civil rights but harsh on suspected subversives. In 1949, after the death of Justice Frank MURPHY, Truman appointed Clark to the U.S. Supreme Court.

Clark had come from a background of politics more than law and was somewhat distrusted by the legal establishment in Washington, D.C. He dressed somewhat flamboyantly, with a bow tie he wore under his robes. Clark's informal style and his occasional Texas braggadocio made him a subject of humor among refined legal circles.

Many of Truman's appointments have been criticized as mediocre justices. Clark's record, however, is much stronger than some believe. He strongly opposed segregation and voted for all the major civil rights cases in the 1950s. In 1961 he authored the opinion in *Mapp v. Ohio* that prohibited law enforcement officials from using illegally obtained evidence, and in 1963 he wrote the majority opinion in *School District of Abington Township v. Schempp*, which specifically outlawed school-sponsored Bible readings in public schools. Clark's refusal to support President Truman's seizure of the steel industry in 1952 caused a break with the president.

Clark was particularly outspoken in a series of cases in the 1960s concerning voting rights. In the celebrated *Baker v. Carr* case he wrote a concurring opinion urging the court to provide an immediate remedy for the plaintiffs. He also supported the Court's decision in *Gray v. Sanders*, moving toward the one-man, one-vote principle.

Clark's son Ramsey followed in his family's tradition and also became a lawyer. He was prominent in the John Kennedy and Lyndon Johnson Justice Department and was named attorney general in 1967; this led to his father's resignation from the Court in the summer of that year.

In retirement, Justice Clark served as visiting justice for different courts of appeal. In the summer of 1977 he died in his sleep in New York City while serving on the bench for the 2nd Circuit COURT OF APPEALS.

Clark's tenure on the Court covered many some of the most tumultuous years in American history. What Clark lacked in legal scholarship and sophistication he made up for in common sense and political decency.

For more information: Srerer, Mark. "Justice Tom C. Clark's Unconditional Approach to Individual Rights in the Courtroom," *Texas Law Review* 64, no. 421 (1965).

—Charles C. Howard

class action

Class action refers to a lawsuit in which a person or a small group serves as plaintiff or defendant representing the interests of a larger group, or class. *Federal Rule of Civil Procedure* 23 sets forth the procedures for bringing a class action. A court generally maintains a class action where it is not possible to join all persons a lawsuit affects. Subjects of class actions range from CIVIL RIGHTS, *Brown v. Board of Education of Topeka*, 347 U.S. 483 (1952), and *Roe v. Wade*, 410 U.S. 113 (1973), to real estate issues, *Hansberry v. Lee*, 311 U.S. 32 (1940), to gas and oil leases, *Phillips Petroleum Co. v. Shutts*, 472 U.S. 797 (1985), and to products liability, *Stephenson v. Dow Chemical Co.*, 123 S. Ct. 2161 (2003).

Rule 23 authorizes a party to sue or be sued as a representative in a class action if the party shows four prerequisites. First, the class must be so large that individual suits would be impractical. Thus, the party must produce evidence of both impracticality and a large number of class members. Second, legal or factual questions common to the class must predominate. Sufficient common questions do not exist where the class members' claims depend on issues specific to each individual.

The third prerequisite concerns the qualifications of the representative party. It must have claims or defenses typical of the class arising from the same event or theory as the other members. The fourth prerequisite also concerns the class representative. The representative must adequately protect the interests of the class. This requirement reflects the principles of due process in the protection of absent class members' rights. The court must determine the adequacy of a representative under the circumstances of each case, considering that the representative must represent the class's varied interests and present an interest sufficiently adverse to the opposing party's so that the parties actually litigate the issues.

In order for a trial court to maintain, or certify, a class action, the representative must prove one of three further requirements. Rule 23 requires the court to determine whether to certify a class action "as soon as practicable" after the action commences. The first of these involves the difficulties that would likely arise if class members resorted to separate actions. A representative may prove either one of two things. The representative may prove a person or entity may have rights for which separate judgments might create conflicting standards for the other party's conduct. Alternatively, the representative may prove an individual judgment, without a class action, might, as a practical matter, dispose of the other class members' potential causes of action or impair their ability to protect their interests. Second, the representative may prove a party has taken action or refused to take action regarding a class, making injunctive or declaratory relief appropriate. Third, the representative may show that common questions of law or fact outweigh questions involving individual members and that a class action is a superior method for fair and efficient judicial decision of the issues. This option covers those cases in which a class action would save time, effort, and expense and promote uniform decisions for similarly situated persons, without sacrificing procedural fairness or causing undesirable results.

The trial court closely controls the progress of a class action lawsuit and may make orders concerning its development. The parties must obtain court approval of a proposed settlement or dismissal of a class action. In addition, the parties must give each class member notice of a proposed settlement or dismissal.

State courts also have rules of procedure, similar to Rule 23, which permit class actions.

For more information: Coyne, Thomas A. *Federal Rules of Civil Procedure.* 2nd ed. St. Paul, Minn.: West Group, 2001; Federal Judicial Center. *Manual for Complex Litigation.* 3rd ed. St. Paul, Minn.: West Group, 1995.

—Patrick K. Roberts

City of Cleburne v. Cleburne Living Center, 473 U.S. 432 (1985)

In the *City of Cleburne v. Cleburne Living Center,* the Supreme Court struck down a city ordinance requiring a special use permit for a group home for the mentally retarded. In a plurality opinion authored by Justice White, the Court held that the mentally retarded do not constitute a quasi-suspect group of people entitled to a more demanding standard of JUDICIAL REVIEW than the RATIONAL BASIS test associated with economic and social legislation. The EQUAL PROTECTION CLAUSE of the Fourteenth Amendment is violated when a municipality requires a special use permit for a group home for the mentally retarded but not for other types of group homes if there is no rational basis to believe that these facilities will pose a threat to the legitimate interests of the city.

The Cleburne Living Center (CLC) applied for a special use permit from the City of Cleburne after the city concluded that the home should be classified as a "hospital for the feebleminded." The home would accommodate 13 retarded men and women and the resident staff. After a public hearing, the city denied the permit. The city claimed to be concerned about the safety and the fears of people in the adjoining neighborhood. The CLC sued in federal court alleging that the ordinance violated the equal protection clause. The district court found the denial of the permit constitutional, but the COURT OF APPEALS reversed, holding that mental retardation is a "quasi-suspect" classification. Under this "heightened-scrutiny" standard of judicial review, a government regulation has to substantially further an important governmental objective. Most legislation is reviewed under the "rational basis" test, which assumes that our elected officials act in a way reasonably related to a legitimate government purpose. When groups of people who have historically been discriminated against are the basis of a governmental category or when FUNDAMENTAL RIGHTS are implicated, the Supreme Court takes a skeptical view of the law and requires the government to show a compelling reason for the regulation. This level of review is known as "STRICT SCRUTINY." In previous Court decisions, heightened scrutiny has been extended to cases involving SEX DISCRIMINATION and illegitimacy but not to

the aged. This case is significant because the Supreme Court chose not to expand the application of heightened scrutiny to the mentally retarded.

Justice WHITE, with Justices BURGER, POWELL, REHNQUIST, STEVENS, and O'CONNOR, held that the city's denial of the use permit was based on an irrational prejudice against the mentally retarded. The mentally retarded have a history of "unfair and often grotesque mistreatment." The city failed to show how this home would be different than other types of group residences that were allowed without a permit. Group homes provide the mentally retarded with the means to be integrated into the community. Since there was not even a rational basis to believe the city would be threatened by the home for the mentally retarded, the Court did not have to decide whether the mentally retarded were a quasi-suspect class of people. In addition, the mentally retarded have not lacked political power since there is a great deal of legislation protecting them. Justices MARSHALL, BRENNAN, and BLACKMUN concurred in the outcome of the case but disagreed with how the Court reached its decision and with the narrow, as-applied remedy against the city. They would have used the more demanding standard of heightened scrutiny, and they felt that the city should not have prevailed under the rational-basis test.

For more information: Perlin, Michael L. *Mental Disability Law.* 2nd ed. Durham, N.C.: Carolina Academic Press, 1999.

—Colleen Hagan
—Martin Dupuis

Clinton v. City of New York, 524 U.S. 417 (1998)

In *Clinton v. City of New York,* the Supreme Court struck down the Line Item Veto Act of 1996 in which the Congress had given the president permission to selectively cancel certain spending items or tax breaks. The movement to pass legislation to allow the president the power to selectively veto provisions from legislation has occurred since the late 19th century. The movement gained strength when President Reagan in the 1980s and then the newly Republican-controlled Congress in the 1990s advocated the line item veto to balance the budget or to limit the spending of the federal government. Article I of the Constitution, however, contains the presentment clause, in which the president is required either to sign the proposed bill into law or return the whole proposal to Congress (i.e., the veto power). The Constitution has never been interpreted to allow selective vetoing so this was the main question the Court had to answer.

Large majorities in both chambers of Congress passed the legislation but its opponents had worked quickly to overturn it. This was actually the second case where the law was challenged and the Supreme Court granted quick review. Senator Robert Byrd and five other members of Congress sued in federal court in *Raines v. Byrd*, 521 U.S. 811 (1997). The Supreme Court decided that these members of Congress did not have the ability to sue because the act had not caused them any direct harm or injury. The Clinton case would be the second legal challenge when it was brought by a group of hospitals in New York City and a group of potato farmers in Idaho who had lost money, as well as other benefits. The Clinton administration, through Solicitor General Seth Waxman, argued that this legislation was not a true line item veto because Congress had reserved the right to exempt measures from being vetoed and also because Congress had given the power to the president to use as he sees fit. The argument was also made that the president was allowed some discretion in spending the money appropriated by Congress in *Field v. Clark*, 143 U.S. 649 (1892), so this line item veto power would be similar to that authority.

The Supreme Court rejected this logic. Justice John Paul STEVENS, writing for the majority of the Court, determined that this law was a clear violation of the presentment clause of the Constitution in Article I. The Court believed that the president must either accept or veto a proposed law in its entirety or not at all. The Court majority made a clear distinction between the veto power and the cancellation of part of a bill, as was outlined in the Line Item Veto Act of 1996. The veto power given in Article I occurs before a proposed bill becomes law, while the cancellation would occur afterward. The final argument regarding the discretionary spending power of the president was also rejected in this decision because the 1996 law contained major differences to previous laws or cases dealing with this presidential power and would basically give the power to repeal laws to the president. *INS v. Chadha*, 462 U.S. 919 (1983), decided that the repeal of any law must conform to the provisions of Article I. Allowing this law to be considered constitutional would violate the SEPARATION OF POWERS set forth in Article I, Section 7 of the Constitution because it would give the president the authority to modify law, and the Court argued that this power must remain completely with Congress.

The three dissenters, led by Justice Antonin SCALIA, believed that the proposal is constitutional. They argued that there was no major difference between using the line item veto and simply choosing not to spend money that Congress had appropriated, which occurs all the time. The Congress had also clearly chosen to give this power to the president so it could not be a violation of separation of powers in their minds.

It is also very important to note that several similar options to the line item veto have been proposed but never

passed and that 40 states allow their governors to have this special veto power. The decision of the Supreme Court in this case has made the answer to this important constitutional question clear for the time being and has made it likely that a constitutional amendment would be necessary to give the president the power of the line item veto in the future.

For more information: Stephens, Otis H., Jr., and John M. Scheb II. *American Constitutional Law*. 2nd ed. Belmont, Calif.: Wadsworth, 1999.

—Billy Monroe

Clinton v. Jones, 520 U.S. 681 (1997)

In *Clinton v. Jones*, decided on May 27, 1997, the Supreme Court unanimously ruled that the Constitution does not provide a sitting president with immunity in a civil lawsuit.

Paula Corbin Jones, a 24-year-old state employee of the Arkansas Industrial Development Commission, charged that then-Arkansas Governor Bill Clinton had been guilty of lewd conduct in a Little Rock hotel room on May 8, 1991. She claimed that he made "abhorrent" sexual advances to her and, when she rejected them, she was punished by supervisors in her state job. In May 1994, after Clinton had been in the White House for two years, she filed a lawsuit against him in federal court, alleging that he had sexually harassed her and seeking $700,000 in damages.

Clinton argued that he was entitled to immunity from suit, contending that barring extraordinary circumstances, the Constitution requires that a lawsuit against a sitting president for conduct that occurred before he took office be postponed until after he leaves office. In December 1994, Arkansas District Court Judge Susan Webber Wright decided in his favor, ruling that the trial must wait until he was out of office; she did, however, allow lawyers to begin interviewing witnesses. In part, the judge was unwilling to order the trial to proceed because Jones had waited to file suit until three days before the deadline for filing such claims. Wright concluded that the need to go forward with the trial was less important than the public's interest in allowing a president to carry out his duties without being hindered.

A year later, the Eighth Circuit COURT OF APPEALS reversed Wright, explaining that a president is not immune from suit for unofficial conduct while in office. The case went to the Supreme Court to decide the extent of a president's immunity. Because there was a rule that presidents were immune from civil liability for their official acts, Clinton hoped the Court would dismiss the suit.

The Supreme Court agreed with the circuit court that a sitting president is not entitled to immunity from civil suit and that the Constitution does not bar a plaintiff from proceeding to trial against a president. A president's immunity from suit for official conduct does not extend to Clinton's situation of immunity from suit for unofficial conduct, in this case, conduct that occurred before he assumed the presidency. The Court ruled that Wright had given insufficient weight to the importance of bringing a plaintiff's case to trial in a timely manner. Refusing to rule on the extent to which the president's duties would excuse him from the normal trial procedure, the Court specifically held that it was not deciding how the case should proceed. Thus, stating that it assumed that the president's testimony could be taken at the White House at a time convenient to him, the Court avoided the question of whether a trial court may compel a president's appearance during the course of the trial proceedings. Later events proved that the Court committed a great error in judgment by rejecting the president's argument that the decision would unduly interfere with the duties and office of the presidency and would "generate a large volume of politically motivated harassing and frivolous litigation."

When the case finally came to trial, a year later in May 1998, Wright decided that even if Clinton were guilty of what Jones accused him of, there were no legal grounds for a SEXUAL HARASSMENT suit. The judge explained that, although the encounter might have been "odious," it was brief; moreover, there was no force or threats involved, and, as soon as she made it clear his conduct was unwelcome, he ceased his behavior. Wright rejected Jones's evidence that she suffered adverse job consequences after the incident took place, including the fact that she was not given flowers on Secretary's Day. The judge wrote that although she did not know the reason for this omission, unless there was evidence of a tangible change in her duties or working conditions, these were insufficient grounds to bring a suit for sexual harassment under federal law.

Although the case against Clinton was dismissed, his victory was short-lived. The Jones lawsuit led to the revelations about a scandal in the White House and ultimately to his impeachment. Although he was acquitted by the Senate, his presidency was marred by the long series of events stemming from Jones's lawsuit.

For more information: Mezey, Susan Gluck. *Elusive Equality: Women's Rights, Public Policy, and the Law.* Boulder, Colo.: Lynne Rienner, 2003.

—Susan Gluck Mezey

Cohens v. Virginia, 19 U.S. 264 (1821)

The 1820 case of the *Cohens v. Virginia* is a case that solidified the position of the Supreme Court to oversee issues concerning the states and the actions of individuals in those states. The case was precipitated when the Cohen brothers were found to be selling Washington, D.C., lottery tickets in Virginia, where the selling of any lottery tickets was prohibited at the time. The Commonwealth's position was that state law was enforceable on individuals of another state (or the District), and that the Cohens should pay a fine of $100 (or about $25,000 today). The court upheld the Virginia court's decision regarding the Cohen finding and aggressively addressed the issues argued by the Commonwealth's attorney in support of Virginia's contentions and the arguments provided by the defense attorney, since both parties agreed on the facts of the case.

The Cohen defense in the case focused on three arguments; first, that the state of Virginia has no authority over lawful actions within the District of Columbia. Second, that "no writ of error lies from this court to a state court," meaning that the Supreme Court has taken issue with the State Court, and third, that the Supreme Court had no jurisdiction over that state court, because no constitutional or federal law had been violated.

Chief Justice MARSHALL emphasized the point that the first two arguments were extremely important and the Supreme Court opinion would have far-reaching impact. The CHIEF JUSTICE clearly articulated that the questions of authority over interstate issues were not specifically delineated, and that there might be the possibility of as many differing opinions as there were states in the Union. The case appears to be have been accepted by the Supreme Court in order to address the issues of state authority within the context of the Constitution and the structure of the republic and the Supreme Court.

The Court offered the opinion that although there was no specific language in the second section of the third article of the Constitution regarding this type of conflict, the language implied that arguments between the states were within the scope of the Supreme Court mandate. The jurisdiction of the Supreme Court does depend upon the characters of the parties; the Court understood this to mean "[A] controversy between two or more states, between a State and citizens of another State" and "between a State and foreign States, citizens or subjects." This interpretation clearly dispenses with the argument regarding the first and third arguments presented by the Cohen defense.

The review of the argument regarding the restriction of the lottery sale prohibition in one State was evaluated against the lawful sale within another political jurisdiction. Because the lottery, in this case, was not authorized by Congress, as a national effort, the corporate intent of the lottery organization must operate within the structure of not only the laws of district but may be restricted in another state. Additionally, the court differentiated between those actions that would be the obligations of all citizens, such as the construction and maintenance of public buildings rather than a lottery that would be used to raise funds for other purposes.

The value of the *Cohen* decision is that the Supreme Court defined their role to interpret the intent of the framers of the Constitution and spoke to the issue that the Constitution is a living document, within the minds of the people, and that only with the positive actions of the public, can the Constitution remain viable. In this case the court also provided a variety of examples in order to place a frame of reference for potential areas of jurisdiction subject only to the Supreme Court, those issues where concurrent jurisdiction with a state court system exists, and those areas where use of the Supreme Court should not be involved. The Court went further, by placing some boundaries on the interpretation of the 1803 *MARBURY V. MADISON* case without reversing the opinion or the reasoning in that case. In *Marbury*, the court systems aids in the definition of congressional authority to delegate to agencies within the scope of checks and balances. Further, the *Marbury* case established the need for the judiciary to limit the incremental expansion of agency authority through case law.

The opinion of the Court also discussed the Eleventh Amendment to the Constitution which, although protecting a state, still allowed suit to be brought against a state by a plaintiff. The defense motions regarding the question of the Supreme Court's jurisdiction were denied.

Grounded in the Constitution, the Eleventh Amendment, and the *Marbury* case, the Supreme Court clearly defined the need and obligation to oversee conflicts that arise across state lines and the scope of Supreme Court authority. In articulating that authority, and the boundaries, the Cohen case formed the foundation for future cases dealing with individuals in conflict with states.

The opinion in the case of *Cohens v. Virginia* provides the reader not only with the finding of facts but more important, conclusions of law, demonstrating the continued maturation of the United States of America while wrestling with the conflicts that arise within a democratic republic.

For more information: Friedman, Lawrence M. *A History of American Law.* New York: Simon and Schuster, 1973.
—Kevin G. Pearce

Cohen v. California, 403 U.S. 15 (1971)

The Court in *Cohen v. California* held that a state may not make the "simple public display" of offensive words a criminal offense. Without a more compelling and specific reason, such speech, even though offensive to many, is protected by the First Amendment.

Paul Robert Cohen was convicted under a California law prohibiting "maliciously and willfully disturbing the peace or quiet of any neighborhood or person . . . by . . . offensive conduct" because he wore a jacket with the words "Fuck the Draft" on it while in the Los Angeles County Courthouse. Cohen testified that he wore the slogan on his jacket to express his opposition to the draft and the Vietnam War. Aside from wearing his jacket, Cohen engaged in no unusual act and made no loud or threatening noise.

Justice HARLAN began the opinion of the Court with the observation that "at first blush" this case seems "too inconsequential to find its way into our books." He then noted that "the issue it presents is of no small constitutional significance" since Cohen was convicted solely on his speech and not on any other identifiable conduct.

While speech is protected, the Court noted that this does not give "absolute protection to every individual to speak whenever or wherever he pleases, or to use any form of address in any circumstances that he chooses." However, none of the exceptions to the general rule of protection were present in the *Cohen* case. California could not claim that the restriction was legitimate based on the state's authority to restrict the "time, manner, and place" of public speech; Cohen was tried under a general law "applicable throughout the State" rather than a specific law identifying the limitations. Restrictions regarding the "place" of speech must be spelled out and not generalized.

Even though Cohen's message or speech was a "vulgar allusion" to the Selective Service System, it did not fall under the "States' broader power to prohibit obscene expression" because to be obscene, an expression, however crude, must be, "in some significant way, erotic." [*Roth v. United States*, 354 U.S. 476 (1957).] Cohen's message did not fall under the other "justifying circumstances of so-called 'FIGHTING WORDS'" because Cohen's message was individualized, it did not take the form of personal insult, and it was clearly not "directed to the person of the hearer." Finally, the conviction could not be upheld on grounds of privacy. There is no generalized privacy right in a public location such as the Los Angeles County Courthouse; individuals objecting to Cohen's message "could effectively avoid further bombardment of their sensibilities simply by averting their eyes."

Absent these justifications for placing restrictions on speech, the question became could California "acting as guardians of public morality . . . remove this offensive word from the public vocabulary?" Harlan responded is that it could not. Citing the case upholding the right of high school students to peaceably protest the Vietnam War, *TINKER ET AL. V. DES MOINES INDEPENDENT SCHOOL DISTRICT*, 393 U.S. 503, 508 (1969), Harlan reiterated that an "undifferentiated fear or apprehension . . . is not enough to overcome the right to freedom of expression." The right to engage in public discussion without unreasonable governmental interference is essential to our political system, which can only flourish in open debate. While this may produce some speech that is distasteful to some, this is a matter of individual style and taste, matters left largely to the individual. The Court noted that "while the particular four-letter word . . . here is perhaps more distasteful than most others of its genre, it is nevertheless often true that one man's vulgarity is another's lyric."

Justice Harlan added that speech serves not only to convey "relatively precise, detached explication," but also to convey "inexpressible emotions" and that "words are often chosen as much for their emotive as their cognitive force." Indeed, the more important element may often be the emotive element of the message. One of the "prerogatives of American CITIZENSHIP is the right to criticize public men and measures—and that means not only informed and responsible criticism but the freedom to speak foolishly and without moderation."

Finally, Harlan warned of the danger of allowing the State to forbid certain words "as a convenient guise for banning the expression of unpopular views." The Court refused to allow such a risk.

For more information: Sunstein, Cass. *Democracy and the Problem of Free Speech.* New York: Free Press, 1995.

—Alex Aichinger
—Charles Howard

Coker v. Georgia, 433 U.S. 484 (1977)

In *Coker v. Georgia,* the Court held that the death penalty was a grossly disproportionate punishment when imposed for the crime of raping an adult woman and thus violated the cruel and unusual punishment clause of the Eighth Amendment.

The defendant in *Coker* was already serving various prison sentences for murder, rape, kidnapping, and aggravated assault when he escaped from prison. He broke into the home of Alan and Elnita Carver, locked Mr. Carver in the bathroom, threatened Mrs. Carver with a knife, and raped her. Afterward, he drove away in the couple's car taking Mrs. Carver with him. Mr. Carver was able to free himself and notified the police, who apprehended the defendant. Coker was convicted of rape and, at a separate sentencing hearing, the jury sentenced him to death by electrocution.

Justice WHITE, joined by Justices STEWART, BLACKMUN, and STEVENS, authored the Court's opinion. Justices BRENNAN and MARSHALL wrote separate concurring opinions maintaining that the death penalty was an unconstitutional punishment in all cases. Justice White began by arguing that CAPITAL PUNISHMENT was not an invariably cruel and unusual punishment. He further contended that the Eighth Amendment precluded more than just barbaric

punishments, but punishments that were excessive as well. A punishment that made no measurable contribution to acceptable goals of punishment and therefore amounted to nothing more than the purposeless and needless imposition of pain and suffering or a punishment that was grossly disproportionate to the severity of the crime would be considered excessive.

In determining whether Coker's sentence was prohibited under the Eighth Amendment, White looked first to the judgments of state legislatures and the behavior of juries. He noted that at no time in the previous 50 years had a majority of states authorized capital punishment for rape. White also observed that after the death penalty laws of all states were invalidated following *FURMAN V. GEORGIA,* 408 U.S. 238 (1972), none of the states that had previously imposed death as a punishment for rape chose to make rape a capital felony. Moreover, he pointed out that Georgia was currently the only state in which the death penalty could be imposed upon a defendant convicted of raping an adult woman. Turning to the behavior of juries, White noted that Georgia juries rarely imposed the death penalty on convicted rapists who did not kill anyone in the course of committing rape.

White therefore determined that the judgments of legislatures and juries indicated that death for raping an adult woman was unconstitutional. However, he contended that in the end, the Court must use its own judgment in determining the constitutionality of the punishment in question. He explained that although rape was a serious crime deserving of severe punishment, it did not compare with murder in terms of moral depravity or harm to the victim and the public. He reasoned that for the murder victim, life was over, but for the rape victim, although life may not be nearly as pleasant as before, it was not over and normally not beyond repair.

Justice POWELL concurred in the judgment and dissented in part, arguing that the Court's opinion was unnecessarily broad and that for cases of aggravated rape, the death penalty would not always be unconstitutional.

Chief Justice BURGER, joined by Justice REHNQUIST, dissented. He maintained that a rapist violated the victim's privacy and personal integrity and caused serious physical and psychological harm. The victim's life and health were irreparably affected so that it was impossible to measure the resulting harm. Burger wrote that rape was not merely a physical attack; it destroyed the human personality. He accused the Court of taking too little account of the profound suffering experienced by the rape victim and her family.

For more information: Friedman, Lawrence M. *Crime and Punishment in American History.* New York: Basic Books, 1993.

—Jen DeMichael

Colegrove v. Green, 328 U.S. 549 (1946)

In *Colegrove v. Green,* the Court upheld the decision of an Illinois district court and dismissed a suit that claimed the populations of the congressional districts of Illinois were unequal and therefore unconstitutional.

In Illinois, the districts had been drawn based on population figures from the census of 1900 but had not been updated since. By 1946 the population of these districts ranged from approximately 112,000 to 914,000, yet each district received one representative in Congress despite the variation in populations. Kenneth Colegrove, a professor of political science at Northwestern University, Kenneth Sears, a professor of law at the University of Chicago, and Peter Chamales, a Chicago lawyer, brought the suit against Illinois Governor Dwight H. Green and other state officials to order the redrawing of Illinois congressional districts.

In the plurality opinion, Justice FRANKFURTER, joined by Justices Reed and BURTON, found the issue of legislative apportionment to be beyond the jurisdiction of the Court. Frankfurter reasoned that the obligation to fairly apportion congressional districts rested squarely with Congress since the Constitution specified that "Representatives, shall be prescribed in each State by the Legislature thereof; but the Congress may at any time by Law make or alter such Regulations . . ." (Article I, Section 4). The plurality opinion reasoned that the suit could be dismissed under *Wood v. Broom,* 287 U.S. 1 (1932), which found that relevant districting laws did not specify any requirements of equality, but the opinion instead based the decision on issues of jurisdiction. In a concurring opinion, Justice RUTLEDGE found that the Court did have jurisdiction under *Smiley v. Holm,* 285 U.S. 355 (1932), although he agreed that the complaint should be dismissed for "want of equity" because the proposed remedy of the petitioners for the upcoming election to elect at-large members of Congress would result in less equal representation than the current apportionment scheme.

In disposing of the case for the above reasons, the Court did not consider the charges of discrimination made by the petitioners in regard to the violation of rights under the EQUAL PROTECTION CLAUSE of the Fourteenth Amendment to the Constitution, which in part states that "No state shall make or enforce any law which shall abridge the privileges or immunities of citizens of the United States; nor shall any state . . . deny to any person within its jurisdiction the equal protection of the laws" (Amendment 14, Section 1). The petitioners argued that the rights afforded under the equal protection clause of the Constitution were violated by the state of Illinois because of the legislatively instituted reduced effectiveness of voters in underrepresented congressional districts.

Colegrove is notable because it established a long-standing PRECEDENT of courts not entering matters of legislative reapportionment. The famous declaration of Justice Frankfurter in the plurality opinion that "Courts ought not to enter this political thicket" was generally followed until *BAKER V. CARR,* 369 U.S. 186 (1963), when the Supreme Court intervened by directing equal representation among legislative districts and eventually establishing the principle of one man, one vote.

For more information: McKay, Robert B. *Reapportionment; The Law and Politics of Equal Representation.* New York: Twentieth Century Fund, 1965.

—Andrew Reeves

Collector v. Day, 78 U.S. 113 (1870)

In *Collector v. Day,* the Supreme Court held that the government is constitutionally prohibited from taxing the salaries of judges under the reserved powers clause of the Tenth Amendment.

In 1864 Congress passed an INCOME TAX on salaries in excess of $1,000. Buffington, a tax collector for the internal revenue service, imposed a tax of $61.50 on the salary of Massachusetts state justice J. M. Day between the years of 1866 and 1867. Justice Day paid the tax levied against him but under protest, and he filed suit against the government on the question of whether the United States can levy a tax against the income of a person who receives a salary as a judicial officer of a state.

Justice Nelson delivered the opinion for a 7-1 court majority, ruling that it is unlawful for the United States to tax the salary of a state judge. The main reasoning for this decision was that a judge is an instrument used to carry out the legitimate powers granted state governments through the Constitution. He relies on the PRECEDENT set forth in *McCULLOCH V. MARYLAND,* 17 U.S. 316 (1819), in which the Court ruled that if it is within the powers of the government to tax one means of execution of power then it may tax all others at will. While the states and federal government reserve the right to concurrently tax and execute power, and the states, through the Tenth Amendment, have the power to tax the means used in execution of power, it is held by the Court that allowing such activity would unduly interfere with or possibly prohibit the government's ability to execute its powers. Justice Nelson also cites *Dobbins v. The Commissioners of Erie,* 41 U.S. 435 (1842), in which it was established that states could not tax the salaries of a U.S. government officer. The Court contends that there is no express constitutional prohibition on the federal government taxing the means by which states carry out their powers and, likewise, there is no prohibition on the states levying taxes on the means used by the federal government. However it is necessary for mutual self-preservation to refrain from such activities in the spirit of the Constitution. The opinion of the Court states that the instrumentalities used by the states to carry out their reserved powers are not subject to taxation by the federal government.

Justice BRADLEY dissented on the grounds that officers of the government are still citizens of the United States and therefore subject to the same taxation as everyone else. He believes that the issue of states taxing the federal government and subsequently interfering with its functions is wholly different from the general government taxing the instrumentalities of the state. He also contends that the Court has established a vague precedent as to which state functions are protected from taxation and which are not, since states use myriad means to carry out their powers.

Collector v. Day is now primarily of historical interest, since the Sixteenth Amendment, proposed in 1909 and passed in 1913, states unambiguously that "The Congress shall have power to lay and collect taxes on incomes, from whatever source derived, without apportionment among the several States and without regard to any census or enumeration."

For more information: Weismann, Steven. *The Great Tax War from Lincoln to T.R. to Wilson: How the Income Tax Transformed America.* New York: Simon and Schuster, 2002.

—Benjamin Niehaus

Colorado Republican Federal Campaign Committee et al. v. Federal Election Commission, 518 U.S. 604 (1997)

This is the first of two decisions emanating from Colorado and involving challenges to the Federal Election Campaign Act (FECA). Maintaining that political spending was tantamount to POLITICAL SPEECH, the Supreme Court ruled that "independent expenditures" made by political parties could not rationally be subjected to the same restrictions as "coordinated expenditures" because the former did not embody the same threat of corruption posed by the latter.

The Colorado Federal Election Campaign Committee purchased radio advertisements in which it attacked Tim Wirth—whom, they expected, was likely to be the Democratic Party's nominee for Senate in 1986. At the time they purchased the attack ads, the Republican Party had not nominated its senatorial candidate. It therefore argued that the attack ads did not count toward the "coordinated expenditure" limitation provision of FECA.

Key to the court's decision was a core definitional question: Did the purchase of the attack ads constitute a "coordinated expenditure" or an "independent expenditure"? The FEC argued that since the advertisements purchased

by the Republican Party were aimed at the Democratic Party's eventual senatorial nominee, the expenditures were, for all intents and purposes, "coordinated" with the Republican Senate campaign, even though the party had not yet selected its own nominee. The Republican Party responded that this was an independent expenditure by a political party and therefore not subject to the same restrictions imposed on PACs by the FECA.

Insofar as the court acknowledged that "coordinated expenditures" could appear to have a corrupting influence on a candidate, it conceded that Congress had sufficient justification to impose limits on them in the same spirit that it limited other types of spending that essentially took the form of a contribution to a candidate. However, the Court argued that Congress could not justify limiting independent expenditures because (1) they did not take the form of *quid pro quo* corruption and (2) because such expenditures were key methods of conveying the party's ideas.

> A political party's independent expression not only reflects its members' views about the philosophical and governmental matters that bind them together, it also seeks to convince others to join those members in a practical democratic task, the task of creating a government that voters can instruct and hold responsible for subsequent success or failure. The independent expression of a political party's views is "core" First Amendment activity no less than is the independent expression of individuals, candidates, or other political committees (615–616).

Insofar as independent expenditures constitute a vital aspect of political parties' core First Amendment speech rights, the Court ruled that Congress would have to demonstrate a compelling interest in restricting such expenditures. Since independent expenditures were not made directly to a candidate, the Court ruled that there was not a sufficient risk of corruption to justify their restriction.

In his concurrence, Justice KENNEDY raised an important related issue. He argued (1) that there was no difference between a party's expenditures and contributions, (2) that the Court should not have distinguished between the two, and (3) that, therefore, neither should be subject to restrictions because both sorts of expenditures constituted speech by the party. The Court did not address this issue until *Federal Election Commission v. Colorado Republican Federal Campaign Committee,* 533 U.S. 431—"Colorado II" (2001).

For more information: Hasen, Richard L. *The Supreme Court and Election Law.* New York: New York University Press, 2003.

—Mark Rush

comity

Comity is the courtesy one jurisdiction gives by enforcing the laws of another jurisdiction. Comity is granted out of respect, deference, or friendship, rather than as an obligation. In American constitutional law, comity has arisen in two ways. First, in the modern context comity is usually an issue that involves the federal courts' willingness (or unwillingness) to rule on a state law in the absence of a decision by a state court on the same issue.

During the antebellum period the status of slaves brought to free states raised particularly troublesome comity questions. Before 1830, courts in Louisiana, Kentucky, Mississippi, and Missouri gave comity to free state and emancipated slaves who had lived or temporarily lived in a non-slaveholding jurisdiction. However, the trend was against comity as symbolized in DRED SCOTT V. SANDFORD, 60 U.S. 393 (1857), in which the Supreme Court held that slave states were under no obligation to grant comity to free slave laws, but the Court was ambiguous about whether or not northern states were obligated to grant comity to southern laws regulating slavery. In Mitchell v. Wells, 37 Miss 235,282 (1859), Mississippi's highest court refused to acknowledge the freedom of a slave whose owner had taken her to Ohio, where he legally manumitted her. In Lemmon v. The People, 20 NY 562 (1860), New York's highest court upheld the free status of slaves brought to New York City by a traveler who was merely changing ships for a direct boat to Louisiana.

Interstate comity conflicts have also arisen regarding divorce laws. Despite claims that a divorce proceeding was an "act or judicial proceeding" that all other states were obligated to enforce under the Constitution's "Full Faith and Credit" provision found in Article VI, various states have refused to recognize divorces granted under laws more lenient than their own. However, in most areas of law, interstate comity has worked smoothly. For example, states usually allow visitors to drive cars with driver's licenses from other states, usually recognize marriages and adoptions of other states, and often grant professional licenses as a matter of reciprocity and comity.

The second concept of comity has also led to the modern doctrine of "ABSTENTION," which stems from the notion that the state and federal courts are equally obligated to enforce the U.S. Constitution. Justice Sandra Day O'CONNOR writes in Brockett v. Spokane Arcades, Inc., 472 U.S. 491 (1985), that federal courts should abstain from reaching a decision on federal issues until a state court has addressed the state questions.

Similarly, on grounds of comity pursuant to federal law, the Supreme Court has generally refused to allow federal courts to intervene in pending cases in state courts absent a showing of bad faith harassment. As is stated in YOUNGER V. HARRIS, 401 U.S. 37 (1971), comity is a proper respect for state courts and recognition that the entire country is made up of a union of separate state governments and a continuance of the belief that the national government will fare best if the states and their respective institutions are left free to perform their separate functions in their separate ways.

For more information: Hazard, Geoffrey C., Jr., and Michele Tartuffo. *American Civil Procedure: An Introduction.* New Haven, Conn.: Yale University Press, 1993.
—William W. Riggs

commercial speech

Commercial speech refers to the right of corporations to exercise First Amendment free speech rights.

In its First Amendment free speech cases, the Supreme Court has recognized a variety of speech protected by the Constitution. These include POLITICAL SPEECH, SYMBOLIC SPEECH, religious speech, and commercial speech. Commercial speech was first recognized in 1975 and became one of the fastest growing issues before the Court.

In 1980 the Court established a commercial speech standard in *Central Hudson v. New York Public Service Commission.* New York had banned advertising by electric utilities in order to promote energy conservation. In *Central Hudson*, the Court created a new standard to be used in all commercial speech cases. The first part requires that any speech not be misleading or advertise illegal products or services. The government had to have a substantial interest in limiting commercial speech. The law must advance that substantial interest, and the law must not limit more speech than is necessary. Using the test in *Central Hudson*, the Court found that the ban on utility advertising was too broad because it prevented advertising that promoted conservation.

With the *Central Hudson* test in hand, the justices began using it against bans on advertising for the liquor and gambling industries. In *Rubin v. Coors* (1995), Coors Brewing Company challenged a 1935 regulation prohibiting brewers from advertising the alcohol content of their high alcohol beers. The ban was to prevent strength wars in which brewers increased the alcohol content to attract consumers. The Court found that preventing strength wars was not a substantial interest of the state and that the ban on advertising alcohol content did not advance the desire to prevent strength wars. For that reason the federal regulation was struck down as unconstitutional.

In *Liquormart 44 v. Rhode Island* (1996), the Supreme Court considered a state law that prohibited the advertising of prices for alcohol. Rhode Island said its substantial interest was limiting alcohol abuse by preventing stores from competing on price and making alcohol consumption less expensive. Once again the Court did not agree that the ban on advertising advanced the interest in reducing alcohol abuse, finding no connection between alcohol prices and the amount of abuse of that product. The state law did not pass the *Central Hudson* test and was declared unconstitutional.

Commercial speech protections were also invoked against bans on advertisements for state-sponsored lotteries and casino gambling. Part of the 1934 Communications Act and subsequent amendments to the law banned television and radio advertising of lotteries, casino gambling, or other games of chance. States that ran their own lotteries were exempt from the ban. Edge Broadcasting owned a radio station in North Carolina that served a large listening audience in neighboring Virginia. Edge sought to run ads for the Virginia lottery at that station but was prohibited by federal law because the radio station was located in a non-lottery state, North Carolina. Edge sued the federal government, arguing that the ban on advertising was a violation of its commercial speech rights. In *Edge Broadcasting v. United States,* the Supreme Court disagreed.

In his Court opinion, Justice WHITE found the federal government had a substantial interest in protecting non-lottery states and their citizens from advertisements. Congress had narrowed the law to only ban advertising in the non-lottery states, thus tailoring the law to that interest. Congress could make the choice of favoring non-lottery states over lottery states without violating the Constitution.

A different issue arose about casino advertising in *Greater New Orleans Broadcasting v. United States* (1999). Greater New Orleans also involved the 1934 law banning all casino advertising, even in states with casinos unless they were run directly by the state. A group of broadcasters in Louisiana sought to advertise the privately run casinos in the state but were forbidden by the law and challenged it as a violation of commercial speech rights. In this case the Court agreed, striking down the ban.

The justices recognized that the federal government had an interest in limiting the social cost of gambling by limiting advertising but found that the ban had so many exemptions that it did not meet that interest. Congress also had the interest in protecting states without casinos from a barrage of advertising, but in this case Louisiana had casinos and hence little interest in limiting their advertisement. For those reasons the ban on in-state casino advertising was struck down.

For more information: Baldwin, Jo-Jo. "No Longer That Crazy Aunt in the Basement, Commercial Speech Joins the Family." *University of Arkansas Little Rock Law Journal* 20, no. 163 (1996); Costello, Sean. "Strange Brew: The State of Commercial Speech Jurisprudence." *Case Western*

Reserve Law Journal 47, no. 681 (1997); Skilken, Melissa. "This Ban's for You: *44 Liquormart v. Rhode Island.*" *University of Cincinnati Law Review* 65, no. 1387 (1997).

—Douglas Clouatre

communists, rights of

From the formation of the Communist Party of the United States in 1919 to the mid-1950s, the Supreme Court ruled on numerous questions regarding the CIVIL RIGHTS of American communists.

In the early years there was confusion over differences between socialism and communism. Socialism is a political system that advocates social reform for a more equal distribution of property and labor, with community or government control of major means of production and distribution. Socialist parties generally support small businesses and democratic government but strive for an egalitarian society by promoting government aid and social programs. Communism is a system developed by Karl Marx in which there is no private property or social class divisions. In this system, socialism is viewed as merely an intermediate stage between capitalism and communism. Many communists believed that the violent overthrow of government was necessary to achieve their goal of a communist society.

There had been socialist and reform parties prior to 1919, but the formation of the Communist Party of the United States started a new conservative backlash. In this reaction all persons with socialist leanings were suspected of communist sympathies; indeed, a communist could be anyone who went against the status quo. The Palmer Raids led by Woodrow Wilson's attorney general, A. Mitchell Palmer, launched the Red Scare of 1919–20. These raids and prosecution of large numbers of suspected communists were met with criticism for Palmer's infringement of CIVIL LIBERTIES, including the detention of thousands of citizens without charge. The rest of the 1920s was relatively calm with few prosecutions and little growth for the Communist Party. The Great Depression, beginning in 1929, stimulated a revival of communist activity and anticommunist sentiment and persecution. In this second wave, states—many with criminal syndicalism laws already on the books—prosecuted suspected communists, including labor union organizers and strikers. The federal government did not participate because a 1924 law restricted the FBI's ability to investigate political activities and because federal courts demanded better evidence of illegal activity. For example, the Supreme Court ruled in the 1937 case *DeJonge v. Oregon* that Oregon's criminal syndicalism law infringed upon the rights of communists to free speech and peaceable assembly.

In 1938 the House of Representatives established a committee, commonly known as the Dies Committee, to investigate foreign propaganda and activity in the United States; it remained active until 1945. The Alien Registration Act, more commonly known as the Smith Act, was passed in 1940, making it illegal to knowingly or willfully advocate subversion and to organize or be a member of a society that advocated or taught subversion. However, during World War II the Soviet Union was allied with the United States, so the committee focused on investigating Nazi activities and the Smith Act did not initially affect communists. In January of 1945, however, the House Un-American Activities Committee (HUAC) was established as a permanent successor to the Dies Committee. Anticommunist sentiment resurfaced and escalated.

In July 1945 the FBI was granted wide-ranging powers to wiretap anyone suspected of subversion without providing proof that suspects posed a national security threat. In October, J. Edgar Hoover, the director of the FBI, warned of the threat from American communists in a speech to the International Association of Police Chiefs. His speech was followed in May 1946 by Winston Churchill's famous "Iron Curtain" speech, in which Churchill warned of the impeding threat of communism and the Soviet Union's goal of world domination. Churchill's speech marked the beginning of the Cold War. Communists were now officially public enemies. A year later President Harry Truman issued Executive Order 9835 to root out government employees who were disloyal. Review boards were to determine loyalty, and defendants were denied public trials. Tribunals operated on the principle of guilty until proven innocent.

HUAC began investigating in Hollywood, California, accusing the motion picture industry of producing procommunist propaganda. In the fall of 1949 the Soviet Union tested its first atomic bomb and China became a Communist country. In 1950, Alger Hiss, a former adviser to Franklin Roosevelt and president of the Carnegie Endowment for International Peace, was found guilty of passing information to the Soviets in the 1930s. The same year the Internal Security Act of 1950, also known as the McCarran Act, became law. It required compulsory registration of communist organizations and disclosure of their member lists. The year 1950 also marked the beginning of the Korean War and the McCarthy Era.

Although HUAC was still very active when Joseph McCarthy took over as chairman of the Senate Permanent Subcommittee on Investigations, a new era of infringement on civil liberties began. The Supreme Court generally supported the policies of the day. In *Garner v. City of Los Angeles Board of Public Works,* the Court ruled that communities could fire employees who did not sign a loyalty pledge such as that required by Truman's executive order. The most historic case was *DENNIS V. UNITED STATES,* in

which the Court ruled that the conspiracy provision of the Smith Act is constitutional and that conspiracies present a "clear and present danger."

Stalin died in 1953, the Korean War ended the same year and with it the McCarthy Era. In 1954 a new Communist Control Act banned the Communist Party, but it was not enforced. By the late 1950s the Supreme Court had changed its stance. In 1957 the Court in legislative standing distinguished between preparedness for subversion and advocacy of subversion. The ruling declared the conspiracy provision of the Smith Act void. In 1961, in companion cases, *Scales v. United States* and *Noto v. United States,* the Court ruled that the membership clause of Smith Act also violated the First Amendment. These three cases effectively dismantled the Smith Act. Finally, in *Albertson v. Subversive Activities Control Board* (1965), the Supreme Court ruled that the McCarran Act violated the Fifth Amendment because registration led to self-incrimination. Ultimately the Court found that the rights of communists are the same as everyone else's.

For more information: Fried, Albert, ed. *McCarthyism: The Great American Red Scare.* New York: Oxford University Press, 1997; ———. *Communism in America: A History in Documents.* New York: Columbia University Press, 1997.

—Mariya Chernyavskaya

commutation

Although the word *commutation* does not appear in the text of the Constitution, the Supreme Court has interpreted the pardoning power of Article II, Section 2 to include the power to commute criminal sentences (*Armstrong v. United States,* 73 U.S. 766, 1871).

In theory, a commutation involves a simple reduction in the severity of a sentence. Were such reductions simply a matter of years, days, or dollars, commutations would hardly have ever presented complex legal issues for the federal courts.

The Supreme Court has also granted presidents the power to attach "conditions" to commutations (*Ex Parte Wells,* 59 U.S. 307, 1865) resulting in a wild variety of questionable practices. Presidential "conditions" have included joining the navy, avoiding alcohol or individuals with bad reputations, forsaking firearms, leaving the United States "forever," or going to North Carolina. Such conditions allow critics to suggest the president has improperly usurped both the judgment of courts and the power of the legislature to determine the extent of criminal punishments. James R. Hoffa appeared to have a legitimate First Amendment challenge to a presidential condition when his disappearance rendered his case MOOT. Richard Nixon conditioned Hoffa's commutation on future noninvolvement in union activities (*Hoffa v. Saxbe*, 378 F. Supp.1221, D.D.C.,1974).

In other instances, the motives behind commutations have been more transparent and, in some instances, disturbing. Presidents have granted commutations to squelch publicity and remove potential "martyr" status from outspoken critics, political opponents, and even attempted assassins. Supporters of female suffrage learned commutations of the sentences they had received for public protests simultaneously eliminated any hope for legal resolution on voting rights in the appellate process. In the case of "Super Bandit" Gerald Chapman, Calvin Coolidge commuted a federal prison sentence in order to allow for the application of a state sentence—Chapman's hanging for murder (*Chapman v. Scott,* 10 F.2d 156, D.Conn., 1925).

In 1927 the Supreme Court was asked to consider whether the commutation of a death sentence to "life in prison," against the will of the recipient, was in fact a "reduction" in the severity of his sentence (*Biddle v. Perovich,* 274 U.S. 480). Similarly, in 1974, the Court was asked to consider whether the commutation of a death sentence to life in prison without any possibility of parole was in fact a "reduction" in the severity of sentence (*Schick v. Reed,* 419 U.S. 256). In both instances the Court answered in the affirmative, but the intensity of the dissent in the latter case and the qualified nature of its majority opinion may very well have signaled the nearness of the end of unbridled discretion in the power of the president to commute sentences.

For more information: Krent, Harold J. "Conditioning the President's Conditional Pardon Power." *California Law Review* 89 (2001): 665–1,720.

—P. S. Ruckman, Jr.

compelling state interest

Compelling state interest, or "compelling governmental interest," as it is sometimes called, is a standard or test courts use to judge whether laws are constitutional when they limit or intrude upon some fundamental right.

The courts use three different standards by which to measure the constitutionality of legislation. The most common is the "RATIONAL BASIS" test. Legislators only have to show that they had a reasonable purpose in passing the contested law. A second level is the intermediate review of legislation that limits or intrudes on rights that are considered important but not compelling. To pass constitutional muster in this area legislators must prove that they have an important interest and have used appropriate means. Laws considered intermediate are those that make distinctions based on sex or gender, ILLEGAL ALIENS, and illegitimate children.

The third level is the so-called SUSPECT CLASSIFICATION standard. This includes legislation based on race, RELIGION, nationality, ethnic background, residency, and privacy. When laws distinguish people on any of these bases, legislators must prove that they have a compelling state interest in so legislating and have used the least restrictive means. Two things happen when laws touch upon suspect classifications. The courts will utilize what is called "heightened judicial scrutiny," or "STRICT SCRUTINY," and the burden of proof of constitutionality shifts from those who challenge the law to those who defend it.

The roots of the compelling state interest standard lie in a theory of CONSTITUTIONAL INTERPRETATION called the Preferred Freedoms doctrine first enunciated by Chief Justice Harlan Fiske STONE in an obscure footnote in a minor case, UNITED STATES V. CAROLENE PRODUCTS, 304 U.S. 144 (1938). In that footnote Justice Stone, building on statements by Justices Oliver Wendell HOLMES and Benjamin CARDOZO, stated that some constitutional rights, particularly those protected by the First Amendment, are so fundamental to a free society that they deserve an especially high degree of judicial protection. This footnote signaled the Court's shift in interest from economic issues to CIVIL RIGHTS, a shift that reached its zenith during the WARREN Court years.

The suspect classification concept, requiring a compelling state interest and least restrictive means, is a judicially created legal principle. It can be expected to change as society and the justices on the Supreme Court change. Perhaps age will become a suspect classification as baby boomers reach retirement age; perhaps sexual orientation will become a suspect class as well. Poverty and educational funding differences are possible candidates to be declared suspect (and therefore subject to heightened judicial scrutiny and the compelling state interest standard), but so far the courts have refused to accord them that status. Currently both are considered under the rational basis standard. As a general principle the Supreme Court has declared suspect only those classes of people who constitute "discrete and insular minorities" who are politically powerless and have little possibility of redressing their grievances through normal political processes.

For more information: Epstein, Lee, and Thomas G. Walker. *Constitutional Law for a Changing America: Rights, Liberties and Justice.* 4th ed. Washington, D.C.: CQ Press, 2001; Pritchett, Herman C. "Preferred Freedoms Doctrine." In *The Oxford Companion to the Supreme Court of the United States,* ed. Kermit L. Hall. New York: Oxford University Press, 1992.

—Paul J. Weber

Complete Auto Transit v. Brady, 430 U.S. 274 (1977)

In *Complete Auto Transit v. Brady,* the Supreme Court articulated the rules to be used by states for apportioning taxation on businesses that operate in several states. In crafting these rules the Court upheld a state law against commerce clause claims that it did not use a tax formula that fairly assessed a company's business in the state.

Many states impose an INCOME TAX on businesses that are either incorporated or do businesses within their borders. Yet many businesses operate in several states, and that means that all of these states could make a claim to tax. However, were all of these states to tax businesses, for example, on the entire income that they make while operating nationwide or worldwide, the result would be double or multiple taxation of the same income. Such taxation might not only hurt the business but it might also violate the U.S. Constitution's commerce clause, which prohibits states from interfering with INTERSTATE COMMERCE. The issue then is how companies operating in several states can be taxed by multiple states.

In *Complete Auto Transit v. Brady,* the Supreme Court had to rule on whether a state of Mississippi law that taxed a business violated the commerce clause. In ruling that it did not, Justice BLACKMUN wrote for the Court, stating that a state tax would be upheld if it met four criteria: (1) There must be a substantial nexus between the state and the company doing business; (2) the tax is fairly apportioned; (3) the tax cannot discriminate against interstate commerce; and (4) the tax must be related to the services provided by the state.

Thus, for example, if a business is incorporated in a state or actually has a store or other physical presence in the state, there is a nexus. On the other hand, if there is no physical presence and the only sales are by mail or over the Internet, there is less but not necessarily no nexus. Instead, one may have to look to see if the company purposively directed marketing toward the state.

Second, for a tax to be fairly proportioned, it must reflect the percentage of business or income the company derives from that state. Thus, if 10 percent of the company's income comes from sales to New York, that state may be able to tax this 10 percent. Or if an airline has 5 percent of its flights going into and out of Missouri, that state may be able to tax 5 percent of the company's income.

Third, the tax cannot discriminate against interstate commerce. By that, it cannot impose excessive burdens on a business or favor in state as opposed to out of states companies. Finally, for a tax to be proportionate to services provided, a state could tax to recoup the costs of regulation or inspection it must provide to the business.

Overall, the four-part *Complete Auto Transit v. Brady* rule is an important test that allows states to tax businesses that operate across the country. While the test was created before the rise of the Internet, it remains an important tool for taxing businesses, even though some critics contend that it has not caught up with the reality of interstate commerce and a world where many businesses have no presence in a state except through the Web.

For more information: Schultz, David. "State Tax Commuters: Classifications and Estimates." *15 State Tax Notes,* 355 (1998).

—David Schultz

Congress and the Supreme Court

The Supreme Court's jurisdiction, or authorization to hear arguments and render a decision in a particular case, is established partly by the U.S. Code and partly by various sections of the U.S. Constitution.

Congress cannot alter the U.S. Supreme Court's ORIGINAL JURISDICTION, or the situations in which that court is authorized to conduct a regular federal court trial that includes: arguments by both the plaintiff's and defendant's lawyers; presentation of evidence; deliberations; and judgment. It is interesting to note that in most years, the U.S. Supreme Court hears fewer than five cases over which it has original jurisdiction. The U.S. Supreme Court's original jurisdiction is classified as either "exclusive" or "nonexclusive."

The U.S. Supreme Court has original, exclusive jurisdiction, meaning that it is the only court that has authority to conduct a trial over all controversies between or among two or more states. The U.S. Supreme Court has original, nonexclusive jurisdiction over cases to which a foreign official is a party, all cases where one state sues the citizens of another state or non-U.S. citizens, and all cases to which the United States and a state are parties. Since the U.S. Supreme Court has nonexclusive jurisdiction in these situations, at least one other court is authorized to conduct a trial in that situation. The other court(s) must accept the case if the U.S. Supreme Court refuses a petition by the parties to be heard in that court.

In cases over which the U.S. Supreme Court has original jurisdiction, the parties cannot APPEAL the judgment in the case, because there is no higher court to hear an appeal.

Since Congress has the power to enact legislation that changes the U.S. Code, Congress has authority to alter the U.S. Supreme Court's appellate jurisdiction. As set forth in 28 U.S.C. §§1251–1259, the high court has jurisdiction over appeals from a state's highest court when it has found that a U.S. statute is unconstitutional, or a state statute is unconstitutional, or a state law violates federal laws or TREATIES. The high court has authority to take an appeal from a U.S. District Court, from which appeals are usually

United States Capitol building in Washington, D.C. *(Library of Congress)*

made to the U.S. COURT OF APPEALS, when the District Court has ruled that a U.S. statute is unconstitutional.

Congress has used its power to determine appellate jurisdiction to demonstrate its dissatisfaction with certain rulings. Additionally, since it is very difficult to amend the Constitution via the route set forth in that document, Congress has, on a few occasions, attempted to change constitutional law by circumventing the procedural rules for amendments.

In *Ex parte McCardle,* 74 U.S. 506 (1869), William McCardle was arrested by federal authorities for writing and publishing editorials that criticized Reconstruction. McCardle filed a habeas corpus petition, asking the court to determine whether he was being deprived of his constitutional rights as a result of his incarceration. This request was denied, on the ground that the Reconstruction Acts under which he was arrested were unconstitutional. McCardle appealed to the Supreme Court under an 1867

congressional statute that conferred jurisdiction on appeal to the High Court. After the Supreme Court heard arguments in the case, but prior to its announcing a decision, Congress withdrew the law that gave jurisdiction to the high court.

At that point, McCardle asked the Supreme Court if it was legal and constitutional for Congress to withdraw previously granted jurisdiction. The Court validated congressional withdrawal of the Court's jurisdiction but noted that the statute that repealed future jurisdiction did not affect jurisdiction previously exercised. In *Ex parte McCardle,* Congress eroded the Supreme Court's appellate jurisdiction more than any other case since.

During the Great Depression the Roosevelt administration had serious clashes with the U.S. Supreme Court. After President Roosevelt introduced his unprecedented and unusual New Deal legislative program, the high court found several key pieces of New Deal legislation, all of which were intended to break the cycle of depression and unemployment, to be unconstitutional as violations of the commerce power. The administration was so determined to effectuate their legislation that they attempted to pack the court with Roosevelt appointees who would not try to invalidate laws that originated in the president's office. After the Court reversed its previous decisions about invalidity of New Deal legislation, the president withdrew his COURT-PACKING PLAN. However, the Roosevelt administration continued to take a very authoritarian stance that in any other era would have been found to be executive branch seizure of powers intended for the other branches of government.

During World War II, the Court clashed again with Congress and the executive branch. The Emergency Price Control Act of 1942, established to prevent wartime inflation in items that were scarce at home, appointed a very powerful administrator to set and enforce price controls. *Yakus v. United States*, 321 U.S. 414 (1942), involved a merchant who violated the act's price control measures and claimed, as a defense, that the act was unconstitutional because it: (1) prohibited JUDICIAL REVIEW of measures established by the administrator, hence denied due process of law to an individual who questioned those measures; (2) granted the administrator powers that were intended to be reserved for Congress; (3) violated the Sixth and Seventh Amendments to the Constitution by preventing an individual accused of a crime pursuant to regulations created by the administrator a fair trial; and (4) included administrative review measures that precluded judicial review of prices established under the act, and therefore violated the Constitution as legislative interference with the judicial branch of government.

The Supreme Court's majority held that Congress and the administrator had complied with all necessary constitutional restrictions, that the defendant pursued a course that left him without STANDING to question the act or the administrator's authority. Although two justices published a very strong dissent, the majority of the Supreme Court was clearly prepared to allow erosion of their appellate power. Perhaps the justices were worried that criticism of the act would result in another Court-packing scheme or were convinced that in wartime, it was necessary to bend to the will of the executive and legislative branches in ways that the high court would not allow in peacetime.

McCardle was cited approvingly in a McCarthy era case, *Bruner v. United States*, 343 U.S. 112 (1952), that found that repeal of a law that previously conferred jurisdiction did not retroactively affect jurisdiction that was exercised while the law was in effect.

In *Felker v. Turpin*, 116 S. Ct. 2333 (1996), the dispute focused on a habeas corpus petition, which is a prisoner's request that a court determine whether his incarceration is depriving him of his constitutional rights. A 1996 Act of Congress gave U.S. Courts of Appeals a "gate-keeping" function over the filing of second or successive habeas corpus petitions, 28 U.S.C. §2244(b). The result of this law was denial of the Supreme Court's power to hear appeals from denials of second or successive habeas petitions. Upholding the limitation, which was nearly identical to the congressional action at issue in *McCardle*, the high court held that its jurisdiction to hear appellate cases had been denied, but that the statute did not annul the Court's jurisdiction to hear habeas corpus petitions filed as original matters in the Supreme Court.

The Illegal Immigration Reform and Immigrant Responsibility Act of 1996 stripped federal courts of jurisdiction over Immigration and Naturalization Service (INS) decisions on whether and to whom to grant asylum. Effectively, when INS refuses to grant asylum to an individual, a federal court can no longer review that decision.

Two additional examples of Congress wresting jurisdiction from the Supreme Court are the Prison Litigation Reform Act of 1996, 18 U.S.C. §3626, which restricts the "remedies that a judge can provide in civil litigation relating to prison conditions"; and the Antiterrorism and Effective Death Penalty Act of 1996, 22 U.S.C. §2349-aa (10), which limits the number of habeas corpus petitions that a state prisoner is allowed to file in federal courts, in addition to other limits on federal court authority related to such petitions.

For more information: Gunther, Gerald. "Congressional Power to Curtail Federal Court Jurisdiction: An Opinionated Guide to the Ongoing Debate." *Stanford Law Review* 36 (1984): 895, 910.

—Beth S. Swartz

constitutional interpretation

Constitutional interpretation is a function performed by all three branches of government whereby the actors analyze the meaning of the nation's supreme law in an attempt to apply its basic principles to individual cases and controversies. The Supreme Court, as the only nonelected branch of government, plays a unique role in this process.

The Court interprets the Constitution in order to determine how specific disputes ought to be resolved in light of the guiding principles of the Constitution by which Americans must live. Constitutional interpretation requires thoughtful deliberation on the part of the justices and their law clerks, who work diligently to ascertain the original intentions of the framers and apply those principles, given the evolution of American legal standards and jurisprudence and in light of the changing social circumstances of the nation, to current disputes.

Given the Constitution creates general principles and rules, its words are necessarily vague and imprecise. This vagueness has made the Constitution robust and its principles applicable throughout the changing circumstances of history, while at the same time making interpretation of the document a much more complex endeavor. Changes in society and law can make constitutional interpretation an especially difficult task for the Supreme Court and one of the most important functions the institution serves.

There are different philosophies and approaches to constitutional interpretation. Oftentimes, an individual's nomination and confirmation to the Supreme Court, especially during the 20th century, has been influenced by and concerned with his or her judicial philosophy of constitutional interpretation. One philosophy of constitutional interpretation is "strict construction." A strict constructionist believes in an interpretation of the Constitution in narrow terms.

Strict constructionists understand the Constitution to contain restraints and powers specifically addressed, but they do not read the document to contain expansive, liberal rights and restrictions. They read the Constitution "literally." Strict constructionists view the Tenth Amendment, which reserves to the states the powers not granted to the federal government by the Constitution, as justification for a narrow reading of the document. Justices Felix FRANKFURTER and Antonin SCALIA are representative of the strict constructionist camp, as are founders such as Thomas Jefferson.

A loose constructionist, on the other hand, interprets the Constitution liberally, favoring an expansive interpretation of the literal words of the document. Loose constructionists look to the Constitution as a living document and interpret the document to contain many more concepts than may be found in its literal meaning. Loose constructionists read the NECESSARY AND PROPER CLAUSE of the Constitution, Article I, Section 8, clause 18, to justify an expansive, liberal understanding of the powers granted to the federal government by the Constitution. Justices Earl WARREN and Ruth Bader GINSBURG are representative of loose constructionists, as are founders such as Alexander Hamilton.

Another philosophical split among theories on constitutional interpretation is between originalists and instrumentalists. Originalists believe the Constitution should only be interpreted as the framers would have understood it, claiming the document should be construed in light of the circumstances of the times in which it was ratified. Instrumentalists, on the other hand, seek to interpret the Constitution as though it were ratified in modern times, owing to the fact that current interpretations of the document affect modern circumstances. Originalists believe such an interpretation works against the vision the framers had for the nation.

Throughout our nation's history, dramatic political and legal battles have been fought over the Court's interpretations of the Constitution. Almost every major social dilemma and legal controversy has, at one point, been influenced by an interpretation of the Constitution by the Supreme Court. The Court can serve as a vital participant in the process of constitutional interpretation, because "politically accountable" participants of the process may often fear upholding the rights and responsibilities enshrined in the document, for fear of retaliation by the majority at the ballot box.

One of the first major public controversies was decided by the Supreme Court in the early years of the nation in a case called *MCCULLOCH V. MARYLAND,* 4 Wheaton 316 (1819). There, the Court was asked to decide whether the language of Article I gives Congress the power to charter a national bank. While such a power is not specifically granted by the Constitution, the Court concluded the language of the document, specifically the necessary and proper clause, juxtaposed with the intentions of the framers deduced thereby, implied a power to create a bank. A more narrow reading of the Constitution might have yielded a different conclusion, namely that the federal government may not charter a national bank. Such a holding might have had a significant impact in the course of history, affecting the powers of the federal government in a variety of areas.

Constitutional dilemmas concerning race relations and CIVIL RIGHTS have come before the Court on numerous occasions, and the Court has, in turn, had to interpret the Constitution in order to "find" the answers to these controversies. In *PLESSY V. FERGUSON,* 163 U.S. 537 (1896), the Court read the Fourteenth Amendment to allow segregation of the races, as long as the separate facilities were equal. However, over the nearly 60 subsequent years, that principle was slowly eroded by an evolving jurisprudence of civil rights that recognized the impossibility of separate equality, culminating in the Court's conclusion in *BROWN V. BOARD OF EDUCATION,* 347 U.S. 483 (1954), that the doctrine of separate but equal cannot be justified in the realm of public education. The Court thereby effectively, though not explicitly, overruled its long-standing interpretation of the Fourteenth Amendment. This example of constitutional interpretation demonstrates how evolving legal standards and changing social circumstances can play an important role in the outcome of an effort to interpret the meaning of the supreme law.

In *LOCHNER V. NEW YORK,* 198 U.S. 45 (1905), the Supreme Court, in the midst of major changes in the economic system and circumstances of the nation, namely industrialization, interpreted the Constitution to grant all citizens a right to contract. The justices read the Constitution to require minimal governmental regulation of an individual's right to contract his or her labor to an employer. The decision, which has been widely criticized, is an example of the Court interpreting the Constitution by using what it understood to be the framers' original intentions without considering the wider, less "legal," social circumstances of the controversy at hand. In interpreting the Constitution, the Court used the language and history of the document to "create" a new right, one with constitutional weight.

Later in the 20th century, during a time of heightened national fear and turmoil, the Court found itself interpreting the Constitution in order to square the need for patriotism and national security with the rights guaranteed each individual by the BILL OF RIGHTS in general, and the First Amendment in particular. In *West Virginia Board of Education v. Barnette,* 319 U.S. 624 (1943), the Court overruled its recent decision in *Minersville School District v. Gobitis* (1940) and concluded the First Amendment does not require individuals to salute the American flag over legitimate religious objections. Owing to the heightened sense of patriotism during World War II, this case is an example of the role the Court can play in constitutional interpretation, in stark contrast to the legislature's inability to act, for fear of possible retaliation by the majority at the ballot box.

Interpretation of the Constitution is a task in which all three branches of government participate, but one in which the Court plays a unique role. The Court's position as the paramount legal institution gives the body an important power to direct the course of American jurisprudence as well as resolve important controversies in American society. The Court, in 1803, declared that "[i]t is emphatically the province and duty of the judicial department to say what the law is." Again, in the wake of *Brown,* facing a constitutional crisis in Arkansas, the Court reaffirmed its role as the final arbiter of constitutional disputes in *COOPER V. AARON,* 358 U.S. 1 (1958). Different philosophies of constitutional interpretation have become a source of political contention, with conservatives often favoring strict construction and liberals preferring a more loose construction. Thus, judicial nominations have often been wrought with debates over judicial philosophy concerning constitutional interpretation.

For more information: Levy, Leonard W. *Original Intent and the Framers' Constitution.* Chicago: Ivan R. Dee, 2000; Shaman, Jeffrey M. *Constitutional Interpretation: Illusion and Reality.* Westport, Conn.: Greenwood Press, 2000; Whittington, Keith. *Constitutional Interpretation.* Lawrence: University of Kansas Press, 1999.

—Tom Clark

Continental TV v. GTE Sylvania, 433 U.S. 36 (1977)

In this case the Supreme Court held that in order to find that a manufacturer's restrictions on retailers is a violation of the Sherman Antitrust Act, a court had to show that the restrictions unreasonably restrained and suppressed competition between brands.

Continental TV v. GTE Sylvania was a complex antitrust dispute between Sylvania, a TV manufacturer, and Continental TV, one of its retail distributors. In order to increase its sales Sylvania instituted a new policy that restricted retailers to whom it had sold TVs so that they could sell only from the locations where they were franchised. But Sylvania did not limit itself from putting new franchises nearby. In this case Sylvania franchised a new store within a mile of Continental TV's San Francisco outlet. Continental owners protested to no avail. Continental then proposed opening a new store in Sacramento, but Sylvania concluded that it had sufficient outlets there and refused to give a new franchise. Continental then unilaterally began moving Sylvania TVs and other merchandise from its San Jose, California, warehouse to a retail location it had leased in Sacramento. In retaliation Sylvania terminated all of Continental TV's franchises.

Continental then sued, arguing that Sylvania's "vertical control" violated Section 1 of the Sherman Antitrust Act by prohibiting the sale of Sylvania products from other than specified locations. A jury at the district court level convicted Sylvania of restraint of trade in violation of antitrust laws. The Ninth Circuit COURT OF APPEALS reversed this on a divided vote, and the Supreme Court accepted the case on APPEAL.

Justice POWELL wrote the majority opinion, joined by Chief Justice BURGER and Justices STEWART, BLACKMUN, and STEVENS. Justice WHITE concurred and Justice BRENNAN dissented, joined by Justice MARSHALL. Justice REHNQUIST did not participate in the case.

The key question for the majority was whether the Court should follow the PRECEDENT of *United States v. Arnold Schwinn and Company* (1967). In that case the Court had ruled that once a manufacturer had sold its products to a retailer and no longer retained title, dominion, or risk over the product, it could not restrict the area where the retailer sold the product. If the manufacturer did restrict the retailers this was a per se violation of the Sherman Antitrust Act. However the *Schwinn* ruling had been the subject of continuous controversy and confusion, and in this case the Court overruled it.

The majority reasoned that vertical restrictions such as those present in both the *Schwinn* and the *Sylvania* cases had some value in limiting destructive intra-brand competition but could promote inter-brand rivalry and thus did not violate antitrust laws. Therefore, in place of the per se rule upheld in *Schwinn* to regulate vertical restrictions, the Court proposed returning to the so-called rule of reason that had controlled antitrust cases prior to that case.

Justice White concurred in the result but wanted to distinguish rather than overrule *Schwinn.* For him a critical difference is that Schwinn, a bicycle manufacturer, had a commanding share of the market, and restrictions in that case had the result of restricting where customers could buy the products. Sylvania, on the other hand, had a miniscule market share, and the vertical restrictions had no measurable impact on customers' ability to purchase TVs.

Justice Brennan dissented in a brief opinion, joined by Justice Marshall. He argued that the per se rule of *Schwinn* is good clear law and should have been retained.

For more information: Grimes, Warren S. "GTE Sylvania and the Future of Vertical Restraint Laws." *Antitrust* (Fall 2002). Publication of the American Bar Association Anti-Trust Division.

—Paul J. Weber

contraceptives

Many states, as well as the federal government, have passed laws regulating contraceptives, with such policies usually justified as protecting public health and morality. These laws have frequently been challenged in court, as unwarranted restrictions on personal liberty. The Supreme Court's ruling on contraceptives grew out of several cases. In MEYER V. NEBRASKA, 262 U.S. 390 (1923), the Supreme Court found that the Fourteenth Amendment to the Constitution guaranteed that every individual was surrounded with a zone of privacy, and that the federal and state governments were prohibited from interfering with matters that fell within that zone.

Four years later, the Supreme Court dealt with *BUCK V. BELL*, 274 U.S. 200 (1927), a case that involved procreation, a right that would seem to exist within the "zone of privacy" established in *Meyer*. However, in *Buck*, the Court upheld a state law that enabled a mental hospital administrator to decide that the state's best interests were served by involuntary sterilization of a "feebleminded" individual. Although the compelling interest of the state overruled the need to protect the feebleminded individual's Fourteenth Amendment rights, those rights might also be served because sterilizing these "imbeciles" or "unfit individuals" constituted kindness to them. If they had the power to reason, they would choose to be sterilized so they could not bear degenerate offspring whose criminal behavior would destine them to death row, or "feebleminded" children whose lack of intelligence would eventually cause them to starve to death. The state law should be upheld because the state's interest in sterilization of hospital inmates overrode the need to protect feebleminded individuals' CIVIL RIGHTS. The state established its compelling interest in sterilization of the feebleminded by demonstrating that accomplishment of this procedure would eventually reduce state expenses through reduction in jail and mental hospital populations.

In its 1942 decision in the case of *SKINNER V. OKLAHOMA*, 316 U.S. 535 (1942), the Supreme Court demonstrated that its reasoning regarding the zone of privacy, Fourteenth Amendment rights, procreation, and contraception had evolved significantly during the 15 years since its *Buck* decision. The Supreme Court in *Skinner* found that a state law providing for involuntary sterilization of "habitual criminals" was unconstitutional. The justices reasoned that sterilization would cause a habitual criminal irreparable injury by permanently preventing the individual from exercising the constitutionally guaranteed right of procreation. While in *Buck* the Court found that the interests of a state could override those of a feebleminded individual, in *Skinner* the Court held that there was no state interest so compelling that it would override protection of rights, such as that of procreation, guaranteed by the Fourteenth Amendment.

As recently as the 1960s, some states invoked their POLICE POWERS to outlaw the distribution and/or use of contraception. On several occasions, plaintiffs brought cases challenging such laws all the way to the Supreme Court, only to be dismissed for lack of STANDING (*Tileston v. Ullman*, 318 U.S. 44, 1943) or lack of a live controversy. Eventually, efforts to test contraception bans bore fruit in the landmark case *GRISWOLD V. CONNECTICUT*, 381 U.S. 479 (1965). In addition to striking down a state law forbidding the sale and use of contraceptive devices, the Supreme Court also enunciated the right to PRIVACY that has been so important in other contexts (e.g., *ROE V. WADE*, 410 U.S. 113, 1973, and subsequent abortion cases, and *LAWRENCE V. TEXAS*, 2003, dealing with sodomy laws). The majority opinion focused on privacy within marriage and ruled that the state could not outlaw contraceptives for married couples. Seven years after *Griswold*, the Court broadened the right to privacy by overturning a state's attempt to outlaw contraceptives for unmarried persons in *EISENSTADT V. BAIRD*, 405 U.S. 438 (1972).

In *CAREY V. POPULATION SERVICES INTERNATIONAL*, 431 U.S. 678 (1977), the Supreme Court further expanded its protection of contraceptive freedom by striking down three challenged provisions of a New York statute: that minors under 16 could not legally obtain contraceptives, that adults could only purchase contraceptives from a licensed pharmacist, and that no person could display or advertise contraceptives. The case specifically addressed nonmedical contraceptive devices that require no prescriptions. The majority characterized the requirement for a licensed pharmacist to sell over-the-counter products as a burdensome restriction on protected individual liberties without a compelling state interest justifying it. Furthermore, the absolute ban on sales to minors was deemed unacceptable, with a plurality of the justices extending the right to privacy to young people. The display and advertising restrictions fell on First Amendment grounds.

Another case involving contraception and the First Amendment was soon to follow. In *Bolger v. Youngs Drugs*

Prods. Corp., 463 U.S. 60 (1983), the Court overturned a federal law against unsolicited mail advertisements for contraceptives. While the mailings in question were commercial, they also included public health information on venereal disease and family planning, which opened up arguments for even higher levels of constitutional protection. Even though the Court opted to rule based on the qualified protections afforded COMMERCIAL SPEECH, a majority still found that the mailings warranted First Amendment protection.

The flip side of a right to use contraceptives is the freedom not to use them. Until recently, the only practical way to compel contraception was to order individuals to undergo sterilization procedures, something which states have sometimes done as part of their police powers. As noted above in *Buck v. Bell,* the Court considered whether a state could forcibly sterilize people with hereditary forms of mental deficiencies (such as insanity and imbecility) if they are patients in public institutions. A majority ruled that this use of state power was justified. Writing for the Court, Justice HOLMES argued that society often demands the sacrifice of the lives of its best citizens and could therefore demand a lesser sacrifice (sterilization) of those "who already sap the strength of the State." The Court rejected arguments that the state's failure to extend this power to similarly situated people outside the institutions violated the EQUAL PROTECTION CLAUSE.

Fifteen years later, when another forced sterilization case came before the bench, the Court ruled quite differently but did not reverse *Buck.* In *Skinner v. the State of Oklahoma ex rel. Williamson,* 316 U.S. 535 (1942), the Court overturned a state policy to perform surgical sterilizations on some repeat felons (those convicted of crimes involving moral turpitude) in the prison population. The Court's opinion explicitly refers to procreation as a basic civil right. The majority, disturbed by this penalty's applicability to armed robbers but not to embezzlers, based its decision on the equal protection clause, although Chief Justice STONE concurred on due process grounds.

For more information: Cruz, David B. "'The Sexual Freedom Cases?' Contraception, Abortion, Abstinence and the Constitution." *Harv. C.R.-C.L. L. Rev.* 35 (Summer 2000): 299.

—Elizabeth Ellen Gordon
—Beth S. Swartz

Cooley v. Board of Wardens, 53 U.S. 299 (1851)

In *Cooley v. Board of Wardens,* the Supreme Court held that a Pennsylvania law requiring ships entering the port of Philadelphia to take on a pilot, although a regulation of INTERSTATE COMMERCE, was not contrary to the commerce clause. The Board of Wardens had brought suit against Cooley to recover statutory penalties for failing to take on a pilot. In his APPEAL, Cooley had challenged the Pennsylvania law as a violation of that clause of the Constitution which gives Congress the power to regulate interstate commerce.

The plaintiff's argument was based on the position that the delegation of the commerce power to Congress was an exclusive one, leaving the states with no authority to regulate this subject. Since *GIBBONS V. OGDEN,* 22 U.S. 1 (1824), had established that the regulation of navigation was the regulation of commerce, a finding that the commerce power was exclusive would have meant that Cooley was correct in his contention that the Pennsylvania law was in violation of the commerce clause. Although Chief Justice MARSHALL had defined the commerce power broadly in *Gibbons,* he had stopped short of concluding that this delegation of power was broad enough to completely disable the states from regulating the subject.

The Constitution does not contain any language that expressly prohibits the states from regulating interstate commerce. However, the argument that the grant of the commerce power was by its very nature exclusive was a compelling one. After all, problems created by a multiplicity of state regulations and taxes on interstate commerce had been a major reason for the calling of the convention that drafted the new Constitution in the first place. However, as a practical matter, an arrangement in which the states were completely barred from regulating any aspect of commerce did not seem workable. Indeed, the first Congress had apparently recognized this when it provided in 1789 that pilots on all waterways in the United States were to be regulated by existing state laws, and by "such laws as the States may respectively hereafter enact . . . until further legislative provision shall be made by Congress." (Act of August 7, 1789, ch 9, 1 Stat. 154)

This federal statute, which was passed in the earliest days of the Republic, was a significant factor in Justice Curtis's opinion for the Court in the *Cooley* case. He observed that, since the grant of the commerce power to Congress was a constitutional one, Congress could not delegate this power back to the states by ordinary legislation. If the law was constitutional, it was because the states retained some power to regulate commerce under the Constitution. Hence, the Court found itself required to render a decision on the question of the commerce power's exclusiveness.

Curtis acknowledged the diversities of opinion that existed on this subject. He attributed these to the fact that the commerce power extended to a variety of subjects, some of these imperatively demand[ed] a single uniform rule, while others, like the regulation of pilots, required the diversity that could best be provided by state or local legislation. Any workable interpretation of the commerce power would have to accommodate this diversity. The solution developed by Curtis has come to be known as the doctrine of SELECTED EXCLUSIVENESS. Although the delegation of the commerce power to Congress makes federal regulation of interstate commerce supreme, it is not always exclusive. In some areas, such as the regulation of pilots, Curtis held that state regulation was permissible, and, in fact, desirable, due to "the superior fitness . . . of different systems of regulation, drawn from local knowledge and experience, and conformed to local wants." On the other hand, some subjects of the commerce power were of such a nature as to require exclusive legislation by Congress. With respect to these subjects, the doctrine of selected exclusiveness holds that the commerce power is exclusive. Moreover, even in those areas of interstate commerce where local legislation may be desirable, state regulation can only exist when Congress has left these areas unregulated.

The *Cooley* decision remains one of the Court's most significant commerce clause decisions. Not only did it clarify the constitutional status of state laws affecting interstate but it also clarified the role of the Court in this area. Under the doctrine of selected exclusiveness, the question of whether state laws affecting interstate commerce fall within the area of permissible local legislation is essentially a constitutional one. Consequently, it is the responsibility of the Court to determine when such state legislation is permitted, and when it interferes with the free flow of commerce that the commerce clause was designed to protect.

For more information: Corwin, Edward S. *The Commerce Power versus States Rights.* Princeton, N.J.: Princeton University Press, 1936; Frankfurter, Felix. *The Commerce Clause Under Marshall, Taney and Waite.* Chicago: Quadrangle, 1964.

—Justin Halpern

Cooper v. Aaron, 358 U.S. 1 (1958)

Cooper v. Aaron forcefully asserted the power of the judicial branch, declaring the Supreme Court the "ultimate interpreter" of the Constitution. It did so by emphatically affirming the Court's decision in BROWN V. BOARD OF EDUCATION OF TOPEKA, 347 U.S. 483 (1954), that racial segregation in public education was a violation of the EQUAL PROTECTION CLAUSE of the Fourteenth Amendment and by unequivocally denouncing the refusal of certain Southern politicians to abide by that decision. As the first major post-*Brown* challenge to desegregation, *Cooper* stirred strong reactions among the justices, six of whom remained from *Brown.* The opinion of the Court was not only unanimous but also, for the only time in history, signed by all nine justices. The decision, which was originally penned predominantly by Justice William BRENNAN, had two main thrusts: First, there could be no delay in implementing desegregation; and second, the Supreme Court was supreme in interpreting the Constitution.

Cooper arose in September 1957 after the governor of Arkansas, Orval Faubus, halted the integration of the Little Rock school system the day before it was scheduled to begin. Faubus ordered the Arkansas National Guard to prevent the entry of nine African-American students—the so-called Little Rock Nine—into Central High School in Little Rock. He was trumped three weeks later when, following a lower court opinion that the governor's reasons for defiance were unpersuasive, President Dwight D. Eisenhower grudgingly sent armed military personnel to enforce *Brown.* Although the African-American students did attend school, their experiences were wrought with racial antagonism. Hoping to avoid similar tension in September 1958, the school board petitioned for, and received from a federal district court, a delay in implementing desegregation plans. The NAACP appealed the case, and the Supreme Court scheduled oral arguments for a special August session (the Court normally begins each term in October) before the commencement of the new academic year.

The Court's decision in Cooper is notable for its directness—both in validating the constitutional concept of "equal justice under law" and in declaring judicial prerogative to say what the law is. First, the Court flatly rejected educational tranquillity as a justification for denying African-American children their constitutional right not to be discriminated against in school. Any delay in desegregation, the justices determined, violated the ideals "embodied and emphasized" in the Fourteenth Amendment. Second, relying upon the supremacy clause of Article VI as well as Chief Justice John MARSHALL's opinion in MARBURY V. MADISON, 5 U.S. 137 (1803), the Court stressed the "basic principle that the federal judiciary is supreme in the exposition of the law of the Constitution." This meant not only that the Court's decision in Brown was final but also that all officers of government—regardless of branch and level—were bound to obey it. "No state legislator or executive or judicial official," the Court famously said, "can war against the Constitution without violating his undertaking to support it."

The aftershocks of *Cooper* were profound. On one level, the case exacerbated lingering indignation among Southerners who felt the Court had intruded in their affairs by striking down segregation in *Brown. Cooper* was an indication that the Court meant business and that it would not be circumvented by dilatory techniques or state defiance. On another level, however, *Cooper* also reasserted judicial independence (or, perhaps, judicial supremacy) in the most forceful way possible. The Court's claim to near exclusivity in determining constitutional meaning implicates not only issues of FEDERALISM but also those of SEPARATION OF POWERS. For this reason, the merits of the Court's opinion in *Cooper*—though praised for ardently upholding *Brown*—are debated and questioned even today.

For more information: Farber, Daniel A. "The Supreme Court and the Rule of Law: *Cooper v. Aaron* Revisited." *University of Illinois Law Review* (1983): 387.

—Justin Crowe

Coppage v. Kansas, 23 U.S. 1 (1915)

In *Coppage v. Kansas,* the Court held that Kansas had violated the due process clause of the Fourteenth Amendment by prohibiting employers from refusing to employ persons who were members of labor unions. Kansas had passed legislation banning "yellow dog" contracts—agreements that prohibited employees from joining labor unions. Plaintiff Coppage had fired employee Hedges when he refused to terminate his union membership, and the Kansas Supreme Court had upheld a local court's conviction of Coppage.

In writing the majority opinion, Justice Pitney argued that such agreements did not contain any coercive element. Regarding the contract between Hedges and Coppage, "there is nothing to show that Hedges was subjected to the least pressure or influence, or that he was not a free agent, in all respects competent, and at liberty to choose what was best from the standpoint of his own interests." In other words, since Hedges was not forced or tricked into not signing the agreement, and was fully aware of the consequences of his refusal to sign it, the state has no legitimate role to play in exerting its influence in this private arrangement.

Pitney cited *Adair v. U.S.,* 208 U.S. 161 (1908), quoting that "[t]he right of a person to sell his labor upon such terms as he deems proper is, in its essence, the same as the right of the purchaser of labor to prescribe the condition upon which he will accept such labor from the person offering to sell it." Each party in any contract of labor has the right to bargain over conditions such as wage, hours, and conditions. To Pitney, membership in a labor union is simply another condition open to negotiation, and if Coppage wanted to terminate Hedges' employment because he would not sign the aforementioned agreement, he was well within his rights as a contracting party to do so.

Central to Pitney's decision is a notion of the "equality of right between employer and employee." Echoing the ascendant laissez-faire views of the day, Pitney asserted that the rights of personal liberty and private property included the "right to make contracts for the acquisition of property." Pitney made no apologies for the position of power that most employers held over their employees. Instead, such inequalities were to be expected. "And, since it is self-evident that, unless all things are held in common, some persons must have more property than others, it is from the nature of things impossible to uphold freedom of contract and the right of private property without at the same time recognizing as legitimate those inequalities of fortune that are the necessary result of the exercise of those rights." Given these natural inequalities, it is folly to think contracting parties necessarily will be bargaining from equal STANDING. Absent coercion, though, any state interference is "repugnant to the 'due process' clause of the Fourteenth Amendment, and therefore void." Building on *Adair* and LOCHNER V. NEW YORK, 198 U.S. 45 (1905), Pitney endorsed the SUBSTANTIVE DUE PROCESS perspective that was so prevalent during this era in the Court's history.

In his dissent, Justice HOLMES presented a narrower reading of the due process clause. He claimed he could find nothing in the Constitution to prevent the enactment of the Kansas legislation. While presenting no personal opinion about the wisdom of labor union membership, Holmes claimed that a reasonable man could certainly believe that such membership was necessary to securing a fair contract. Such a belief, right or wrong, "may be enforced by law in order to establish the quality of position between the parties in which LIBERTY OF CONTRACT begins." This concern for quality of position motivated Holmes in much the same manner here as it did in *Adair* and *Lochner.* He ended his opinion by reiterating his belief that all three cases should be overruled.

For more information: Gillman, Howard. *The Constitution Besieged: The Rise and Demise of Lochner Era Police Power.* Durham, N.C.: Duke University Press, 1993.

—Christopher Stangl

corporate speech

Corporate speech is protected under the First Amendment as a freedom of speech, acknowledging the right of corporations alongside consumers and independents to free expression within certain legal limits.

Speech in pursuit of economic self-interest is a subset of the First Amendment cases. The lesser status of COMMERCIAL SPEECH was generally regarded as less worthy than political or opinion expression as well as the informative function of the press. The United States Supreme Court has generally avoided regulation of content, and historically, commercial speech was generally not accorded First Amendment protection. However, the Court extended its oversight into this area in the 1970s.

The initial case bringing commercial speech within the province of the First Amendment was *Virginia State Board of Pharmacy v. Virginia Citizens Consumer Council,* 425

U.S. 748 (1976). The majority of the Court ruled that a regulation prohibiting pharmacists from advertising prices was unconstitutional. Advertising is one of the few areas in which nonobscene content may be regulated.

Commercial speech in relation to the protection of the First Amendment was next considered by the Court in *Young v. American Mini Theatres, Inc.,* 427 U.S. 50 (1976). This case involved a Detroit ZONING ordinance that limited the right to show certain "adult" movies within a certain number of feet of each other in order to allow development of certain blighted areas. The Court upheld the limitations but stopped short of out-and-out repression of X-rated entertainment.

A variety of other speech restrictions were litigated generally defining the limits of the protection to be accorded advertisements. *Central Hudson Gas and Electric Corp. v. Public Service Commission,* 447 U.S. 100 (1980), involved an attempt by the New York State Public Utilities Commission to stop a regulated monopoly from advertising rates and services that would have an effect on all consumers, not just those using the advertised program.

Since providing electric and gas utilities is lawful, the U.S. Supreme Court found that the First Amendment applied in this case and to advertising in general as long as no deception is attempted or intended. However, because the advertiser knows more about the product than the consumer, the government has an interest in regulating content.

The Supreme Court writing in *Central Hudson* developed a four-part test to determine whether the speech may be regulated. First, the Court must decide whether the speech is within the bounds of the First Amendment. Second, for commercial speech to be protected, it must be lawful and not misleading. Third, the government interest must be substantial. Finally, regulations must be very closely written in order to regulate only what the government has a legitimate interest in regulating.

In 1996 the Supreme Court refined the rules laid out in *Central Hudson* in a case known as *44 Liquormart v. Rhode Island,* 517 U.S. 484. In that case, the state of Rhode Island prohibited all advertising of prices by liquor stores. The stated reason was to promote temperance in alcohol consumption. The case was heard on the basis of a challenge to the ban on price advertising. The Court ruled that when a state entirely prohibits publication of truthful, non-misleading commercial messages for reasons unrelated to preservation of the fair bargaining process, a judge may look to a wider application of the First Amendment than simple regulation of commercial speech.

In January of 2003, the Court decided to hear a case that involved not only advertising about a corporation but also whether a corporate entity had the right to speak publicly about issues affecting its business and be afforded the full panoply of First Amendment protection. Marc Kasky had sued Nike, Inc., under a California statute allowing any individual to sue a company if he or she believes that the company is engaging in unfair trade practices, anywhere in the world. The suit concerned the company's press releases about working conditions in some of Nike's overseas manufacturing plants. These reports were in response to statements by Kasky about Nike's business practices in these overseas facilities.

Nike had defended on the basis that it was entitled to the full benefits of the First Amendment. The California Supreme Court held that Nike's statements were ordinary commercial speech and as such subject to the California law. Briefs were filed and preparations were made for argument before the Court. Then, without warning, in June of 2003, the Court announced that the case should be dismissed as certiorari having been improvidently granted [*Nike, Inc. v. Kasky,* 123 S.Ct. 2554 (2003)].

For more information: Shiffrin, Steven H. *The First Amendment, Democracy, and Romance.* Cambridge, Mass.: Harvard University Press, 1990.

—Stanley M. Morris
—Rebecca Singer

Court of Appeals, U.S.

The federal judiciary is a three-tiered system, consisting of 94 U.S. District Courts in the entry-level tier, 13 U.S. Courts of Appeals in the middle tier, and one U.S. Supreme Court, standing alone in the top tier.

Twelve of the U.S. Courts of Appeals, each of which is located in one of the 12 judicial circuits distributed geographically throughout the United States, hear appeals from cases decided in the 94 U.S. District Courts located within the 12 circuits. To be heard in the U.S. Court of Appeals, an APPEAL from a U.S. District Court's decision must be filed in the appellate court for the judicial circuit in which the trial court was located. The 13th appellate court, the U.S. Court of Appeals for the Federal Circuit, is located in the nation's capital and has nationwide jurisdiction over specialized cases, including those dealing with patent, trademark, copyright, and international trade matters. Currently, the U.S. Court of Appeals employs 179 judges, with each circuit employing at least the statutorily mandated minimum of three judges. An appeal from a decision in a U.S. District Court located within court circuits one through 12 must be filed in the U.S. Court of Appeals within the U.S. District Court's circuit. Together, the U.S. Courts of Appeals annually review a total of approximately 50,000 appeals from U.S. District Court decisions.

Trials in the Courts of Appeals are usually conducted before a three-judge panel. Occasionally, in a highly important or controversial lawsuit, all of a circuit's judges hear the case. During a U.S. Court of Appeals trial, the judges are interested only in hearing each party's argument; the parties are not expected to recall witnesses or present previously examined evidence to the judges. Usually, the appellant (U.S. Court of Appeals terminology for the party making the appeal; analogous to a trial court plaintiff) alleges that the lower court failed to properly apply the law to the facts of the case, or that the law used in the trial court was unconstitutional or void because of conflict with a federal law. The respondent (party who prevailed in U.S. District Court; analogous to a trial court defendant) usually responds with a claim that the law was both valid and properly applied.

A party who is dissatisfied with the U.S. Court of Appeals' decision in his case would petition to appeal to the highest federal court, the U.S. Supreme Court.

A party who disagrees with the U.S. Court of Appeals decision on his/her case does not have the *right* to have his case heard before the U.S. Supreme Court. Instead, a party who hopes to present an appeal to the high court must provide the Supreme Court justices with a petition in a specific, statutorily mandated format, stating the reasons why the case and the U.S. Court of Appeals' decision therein deserves to be considered by the U.S. Supreme Court. The nine justices receive thousands of these petitions annually but exercise their power to choose the cases they find most important so that they can consider, whatever they decide, a reasonable number of cases. In practice, the high court typically hears 150 to 200 cases annually. The present-day FEDERAL COURT SYSTEM resembles, but is not identical to, the judiciary established by the first Congress' passage of the JUDICIARY ACT OF 1789. That legislation established the U.S. District Courts and U.S. Circuit Courts as trial courts and provided the Supreme Court with jurisdiction over any and all appeals from either of the lower courts and authority to serve as the "court of last resort," from which no appeal was possible.

In the 25 years following the Civil War, the Supreme Court justices began to fall far behind schedule in the attendance at circuit courts. Additionally, westward expansion of the nation, growing population, and complex, war-related lawsuits contributed to a growing caseload in all of the federal courts. The Supreme Court fell several years behind schedule, the crowded dockets in the circuit and district courts prevented the judges from holding court in all of the districts within their jurisdiction, and district judges often presided alone in the circuit courts while also trying to manage the heavy caseload of the U.S. District Courts.

Finally, in 1891, Congress passed the Evarts Act, which aimed to make the entire federal judiciary more efficient and also to reduce the Supreme Court justices' workload to a manageable level. This legislation effectively abolished the requirement that the justices "ride the circuit" and also sharply limited the categories of cases that the Supreme Court was required to hear on appeal. The effectiveness of the Evarts Act in reducing the workload of the high court was demonstrated almost immediately after the bill's enactment, since the number of new cases before the high court dropped from 275 in 1890 to 123 in 1892.

Perhaps most important, the Evarts Act created a more efficient judiciary by establishing the U.S. Courts of Appeals, the first federal courts designed exclusively to hear appeals from trial courts. The Evarts Act established nine Courts of Appeals, one for each of the nine judicial circuits in existence at that time. The new courts were to be staffed by the existing circuit court judges plus a new judge in each circuit. The Circuit and U.S. District Court judges were also authorized to sit on three-judge U.S. Court of Appeals panels. This act also granted the Supreme Court limited authority to decide which cases it would hear. And finally, although the Evarts Act retained the requirement that the Supreme Court justices "ride the circuit," in reality, the justices ceased any attempt to comply with this requirement.

Later congressional action expanded the size and number, as well as the jurisdiction, of the Courts of Appeals. By the 1920s, each of these courts had at least three judges, and the number of judicial circuits was increased from nine to 11. In the 1930s Congress added to the workload of these courts by giving them jurisdiction over appeals from decisions of federal regulatory agencies. And much later, in the 1980s, Congress combined the jurisdictions of the U.S. Court of Claims with those of the U.S. Court of Customs and Patent Appeals to create the U.S. Court of Appeals for the Federal Circuit.

U.S. Court of Appeals judges, like all other federal judges, are appointed for life and can be removed from office only through impeachment that results in congressional conviction for treason, bribery, or other heinous act. Second, Congress cannot reduce judges' compensation for as long as they serve on any federal court. These provisions, both of which are included in the Constitution, were originally intended to prevent elected officials who are susceptible to political pressure, such as the president and Congress, from exerting similar pressure on a federal judge by reducing his/her salary to less than a living wage, or by altogether eliminating his/her salary. To date, these constitutional provisions have proved to be quite effective in maintaining an honest judiciary.

The Courts of Appeals have become an integral part in a three-tiered FEDERAL COURT SYSTEM. Their clearly defined jurisdiction and role have helped to create a federal judiciary that dispenses justice quickly and efficiently while helping the judiciary to maintain its constitutional mandate to act in a fair and equitable manner.

For more information: Administrative Office of the United States Courts. "U.S. Courts of Appeals." United States Courts: Federal Judiciary. Available online. URL: http://www.uscourts.gov/courtsofappeals.html. Downloaded May 12, 2004; Apex Learning. "Foundations of American Government" and "Structure of the Federal Courts." Beyond Books.com (2003). Available online. URL: http://www.beyondbooks.com/gov91/9b.asp. Downloaded May 12, 2004.

—Beth S. Swartz

court-packing plan

President Franklin D. Roosevelt's 1937 proposal to add additional justices to the Supreme Court—dubbed the "court-packing plan"—aimed to create a majority on the high court favorable to New Deal programs. Ultimately, Congress rejected the controversial plan, eroding Roosevelt's 1936 election mandate and effectively stalling the New Deal.

By 1937 the nine Supreme Court justices were split on the administration's social and economic reforms. Three were firm supporters: Louis BRANDEIS, Benjamin CARDOZO, and Harlan Fiske STONE. Four justices were consistently anti-New Deal: Pierce Butler, James McReynolds, George SUTHERLAND, and Willis VAN DEVANTER. Chief Justice Charles Evans HUGHES and associate justice Owen Roberts were swing voters. On "Black Monday," 27 May 1935, the Supreme Court delivered three unanimous decisions which struck down centerpiece New Deal programs, including the National Industrial Recovery Act. Over the next year, the Court also invalidated the Railroad Retirement Act and the Agricultural Adjustment Act, confronting the administration with the prospect of a judicial rollback of the New Deal that might impair national recovery. One noted jurist wrote, "If the Constitution, as interpreted by the Court, prevents the proper solution of our social and economic problems, should we do something to the Constitution to meet the difficulty, or should we do something to the Supreme Court?" President Roosevelt, using the mandate from his historic 1936 election, clearly thought he could succeed in the latter course.

FDR's congressional allies introduced the Judicial Reorganization bill in February 1937. Among the plan's provisions was a proposal to add one Supreme Court justice for every member older than 70 years, with a cap of six additional justices. The Constitution is ambiguous on the number of justices who should be on the Supreme Court, but, historically, the size had ranged from six to 10. President Roosevelt claimed that the plan would ease the workload on the Court's aging justices, none of whom were his appointees. His underlying motive, however, was to tilt the Court in favor of New Deal legislation.

A tidal wave of public protest and editorial outcry swamped the court-packing plan. Critics charged the president with subverting the Constitution and destroying the independence of the judiciary. Even Democratic Party support was tepid. When the bill's Senate floor leader, Joe

Discouraged by the Supreme Court's rejection of key New Deal measures—and emboldened by his landslide reelection in 1936—President Franklin D. Roosevelt made a controversial move to add political allies to the Court bench. Claiming that he had to "save the Constitution from the Court and the Court from itself," Roosevelt announced a plan for the reorganization of the federal judiciary (1937), in which he proposed an additional justice for each existing justice aged 70 or over. The surprised man with Roosevelt in this cartoon is Harold Ickes, Roosevelt's secretary of the interior and leader of the Public Works Administration; the cartoon indicates that even some of Roosevelt's fellow New Dealers found his reorganization plan objectionable. In what would prove to be his greatest defeat in his four terms as president, Roosevelt's bill was voted down in Congress. Cartoon by Walter Berryman *(Library of Congress)*

Robinson, died unexpectedly, the plan stalled. What public enthusiasm existed waned when the Court in the spring of 1937—with Hughes and Roberts voting with the majority—upheld two key New Deal laws: the Wagner Labor Relations Act and the Social Security Act. Journalists dubbed the episode "the switch in time that saved nine." FDR backpedaled, agreeing to a compromise plan to make one additional appointment for every justice 75 years or older, but in July the Senate rejected the plan handily, 70 to 20. A month later, Congress passed the Judicial Procedure Reform Act which had stripped out FDR's most controversial proposals, including the increase in the numbers of federal justices.

Retirements and deaths on the Supreme Court soon allowed Roosevelt to appoint several justices whom he found more ideologically suitable. But the court-packing plan had a high political cost, uniting FDR's critics and eroding his support in Congress. In the 1938 midterm elections, Democrats retained their majority but lost almost 80 seats in Congress. A new coalition of Republicans and conservative Democrats, forged to oppose the court-packing plan and determined to stall further New Deal programs, controlled Congress for the next 20 years.

For more information: Leuchtenburg, William. "The Origins of Franklin D. Roosevelt's 'Court-Packing Plan.'" *Supreme Court Review* (1966): 347–400; Nelson, Michael. "The President and the Court: Reinterpreting the Court-Packing Episode of 1937." *Political Science Quarterly* 103, no. 2 (1988): 267–293.

—Matt Wasniewski

Coyle v. Smith, 21 U.S. 559 (1911)

In *Coyle v. Smith,* the Court ruled that the power to admit new states into the Union extends only to their admission on an equal footing with other states. The Court affirmed Oklahoma's right to move its state capital, even though Congress had stipulated as a condition of statehood that no such removal should take place.

Oklahoma was formally invited into the Union by the Enabling Act of 1906, in which the Republican-dominated Congress required that the capital of Oklahoma "shall temporarily be at the city of Guthrie, and shall not be changed there from previous to" 1913. Further, Congress required that Oklahoma's Constitutional Convention "by ordinance irrevocable, accept the terms and conditions of this act." The convention passed an "ordinance irrevocable," accepting the conditions imposed by Congress, which was ratified alongside the state's constitution by the people of the territory.

The territorial capital of Guthrie was widely resented because it represented a Republican stronghold in an overwhelmingly Democratic state. In 1910 voters passed a referendum authorizing removal of the capital to Oklahoma City, assuming such a move would wait until after 1913. Oklahomans awoke the day after passage to find that Governor Charles Haskell had hung a hand-painted sign over the clerk's desk at a hotel in Oklahoma City reading "Governor's Office."

A group of large property interests petitioned the Court on the grounds that moving the state capital prior to 1913 had violated the terms of the Enabling Act of 1906. Article IV, Section 3 of the U.S. Constitution gives Congress the authority to admit new states into the Union. The issue before the Court was this: had Congress exceeded its authority when it attempted to prohibit Oklahoma from moving its state capital? Speaking for the Court, Justice Lurton wrote that the power to admit new states is "not to admit political organizations which are less or greater, or different in dignity or power," from the original 13 states. The Court thus rejected the argument that the Enabling Act of 1906 could prohibit Oklahoma from moving its state capital because doing so would mean that Congress could exercise certain powers over new states which it could not exercise over the original 13. Quoting from *Escanaba Co. v. Chicago,* 107 U.S. 678 (1882), the Court reiterated the Enabling Act "ceased to have any operative force [in the new state], except as voluntarily adopted by her."

"Has Oklahoma been admitted upon an equal footing with the original states?" asked Justice Lurton. "If she has, she by virtue of her jurisdictional sovereignty . . . may determine for her own people the proper location of the local seat of government. She is not equal in power to them if she cannot."

Justices McKenna and HOLMES dissented without comment.

For more information: Scales, James R., and Danney Goble. *Oklahoma Politics: A History.* Norman: University of Oklahoma Press, 1982.

—Christopher J. Wright

Coy v. Iowa, 487 U.S. 1012 (1988)

In *Coy v. Iowa,* the Court held that the defendant's right to physically face witnesses was an essential part of the Sixth Amendment confrontation clause, and that this right of confrontation included both the defendant's ability to see the witnesses testify against him and the witnesses' ability to see the defendant. In 1985 Iowa enacted a law allowing the judge in a child sexual abuse case to order the defendant removed from the courtroom while a child victim testified or to permit the victim to testify behind a screen or mirror. In this case a screen was provided which allowed the defendant to see the victims and observe their demeanor but blocked their view of him. The two girl victims testified about the sexual abuse and were subject to "unrestricted cross-examination." Coy was convicted of two counts of lascivious acts with a child. The Court accepted the case for review after the Supreme Court of Iowa ruled that the procedures did not violate Coy's rights under the Sixth and Fourteenth Amendments. Forty-one states joined amicus curiae briefs urging the Court to affirm the Iowa decision.

The main issue in this case was the meaning of the Sixth Amendment's confrontation clause. Writing for the Court in a 6-2 decision, Justice Antonin SCALIA stated that the clause "guarantees the defendant a face-to-face meeting with witnesses appearing before the trier of fact." Quoting from Justice HARLAN's concurring opinion in *California v. Green*, 399 U.S. 149 (1970), Justice Scalia emphasized that the "right to 'confront' the witness" and "meet face to face all those who appear and give evidence" was "the irreducible literal meaning" of the confrontation clause. Justice BLACKMUN and Chief Justice REHNQUIST dissented, arguing that since witnesses are not required to look at the defendant, the only issue was whether the confrontation clause requires a physical setting that allows witnesses the opportunity to look at the defendant. The majority opinion held that it does, arguing that although a witness is not compelled to "fix his eyes upon the defendant" and "may studiously look elsewhere," the judge or jury "will draw its own conclusion" from this.

Justice Scalia argued that "there is something deep in human nature" that regards face-to-face confrontation as essential, concluding: "It is always more difficult to tell a lie about a person 'to his face' than 'behind his back.'" The dissenters maintained that the essence of the confrontation clause has always been cross-examination, not confrontation. They cited Wigmore's classic treatise on evidence, which concluded that confrontation was provided "to allow for cross-examination," and that the common law did not recognize a separate right to confrontation "as distinguished from cross-examination."

The majority opinion acknowledged that the rights found in the confrontation clause are not absolute, and that exceptions may be recognized if those rights come into conflict with important public policy interests. Justice Scalia concluded that although the need to protect victims of sexual abuse from the trauma of courtroom testimony might justify an exception to the face-to-face confrontation requirement, it must be supported by "individualized findings that these particular witnesses needed special protection." In her concurring opinion Justice O'CONNOR, joined by Justice WHITE, stated that the right of confrontation is not absolute but only a "preference" that may be overcome if necessary to support an important public policy. Noting that many states had adopted special arrangements to protect victims of child sexual abuse, she asserted that "the protection of child witnesses is, in my view and in the view of a substantial majority of the States, just such a policy." Justice O'Connor agreed that the "generalized legislative finding" presented by Iowa in this case was inadequate to justify an exception. However, if a court made a case-specific decision to shield a child victim during testimony, the confrontation clause could yield to the "compelling state interest of protecting child witnesses." In applying this decision, some state courts struck down laws that did not guarantee face-to-face confrontation, while others upheld special arrangements in child sexual abuse cases as appropriate exceptions to the general right of confrontation. This issue was resolved in *Maryland v. Craig*, 497 U.S. 836 (1990). Justice O'Connor, writing for a five-member majority that included the concurring and dissenting justices in *Coy v. Iowa* (1988), held that the Sixth Amendment confrontation clause expresses a constitutional preference for face-to-face confrontation and not an absolute requirement. Even though Maryland's use of one-way television meant that the testifying child could not see the defendant, the procedure was permissible if based on an individualized finding of necessity.

For more information: Finkelman, Byrgen, ed. *Child Abuse: A Multidisciplinary Survey; Victim as Witness: Legal and Psychological Issues*, Vol. 8. New York: Garland, 1995; Marsil, Dorothy F., Jean Montoya, David Ross, and Louise Graham. "Children as Victims and Witnesses in the Criminal Trial Process: Child Witness Policy: Law Interfacing With Social Science." *Law and Contemporary Problems* 65 (2002): 209–241; McGough, Lucy S. *Child Witnesses: Fragile Voices in the American Legal System.* New Haven, Conn.: Yale University Press, 1994.

—Barbara J. Hayler
—Christopher Stangl

Craig v. Boren, 429 U.S. 190 (1976)

Craig v. Boren established a new constitutional test for laws that distinguished between men and women. The United States Supreme Court ruled that the EQUAL PROTECTION CLAUSE of the Constitution's Fourteenth Amendment prevented states from making gender distinctions unless the states were furthering important government policy and the gender distinction was substantially related to that policy.

Curtis Craig, then under 21, and Carolyn Whitener, a liquor storeowner, sued the governor of Oklahoma, David Boren, in 1976. They challenged an Oklahoma law that forbid men ages 18–21 from purchasing "nonintoxicating" 3.2 percent beer. Women 18–21 could legally drink it. Craig and Whitener argued the law violated the Fourteenth Amendment's equal protection clause: "[nor] shall any State . . . deny to any person within its jurisdiction the equal protection of the laws." Oklahoma defended the law by demonstrating that young men caused more traffic accidents than women. Young men were more likely to drive drunk than were women of the same age. A higher drinking age for men thus served to prevent traffic accidents.

Justice William BRENNAN, writing for a 7-2 majority of the U.S. Supreme Court, declared the Oklahoma drinking age statute unconstitutional. He further ruled that gender-discriminatory laws were permitted only if they bore a substantial connection to an important government objective, not just a rational relationship to legitimate government interest that had earlier been applied to gender discrimination cases. While conceding that the Oklahoma law furthered public safety, he argued that "archaic and overbroad generalizations" about the behavior of young males and females did not support using gender as a proxy for who is likely to be driving drunk. Oklahoma's goal of reducing drunk driving could be met by a gender-neutral law.

Justice William REHNQUIST, joined by Chief Justice Warren BURGER, dissented. They feared that the newly created INTERMEDIATE SCRUTINY test was too vague to be workable and that it would permit the prejudices of judges to usurp the legitimate decisions of legislators. Nor were they convinced that males suffered such a history of systematic discrimination that they deserved special protection under the Constitution.

The intermediate scrutiny test developed in *Craig v. Boren* holds gender classifications to a more searching inquiry than other social and economic legislation that receives only RATIONAL BASIS scrutiny. Rational basis scrutiny only requires a challenged law to be reasonable and to be "rationally related" to a legitimate government interest.

Unlike the STRICT SCRUTINY test applied to race and ethnicity, which obliges the state to demonstrate a compelling governmental interest and to show that the means used to accomplish that interest are least intrusive on individual rights, the intermediate scrutiny test reflects the view that there may be legitimate justification for treating women and men differently, where this is rarely true in the case of race.

For more information: Cushman, Clare, ed. *Supreme Court Decisions and Women's Rights: Milestones to Equality.* Washington, D.C.: CQ Press, 2001.

—Timothy J. O'Neill

cross burning

The practice of cross burning originated in the 14th century as a means for Scottish tribes to signal each other. In the United States, however, cross burning is inextricably joined with the history of the Ku Klux Klan. The Klan of the 19th century—starting after the Civil War and disappearing by the end of Reconstruction in 1877—did not practice cross burning; but the Klan of the 20th century, revived in 1905, became strongly associated with cross burning.

From the inception of the "second" Klan, cross burnings have been used to communicate both threats of violence and messages of common philosophy. The first known incident in the United States occurred in 1913 when a Georgia mob celebrated the lynching of Leo Frank. This "gigantic" burning cross on Stone Mountain was visible throughout much of Atlanta. One month later the second known cross burning took place during a Klan initiation ceremony on Stone Mountain where a 40-foot cross burned while the members took their oaths of loyalty.

The 20th century Klan's philosophy did not differ much from that of the previous century, with violence and intimidation being an integral part of their modus operandi. Throughout its history the Klan has used cross burning as a means of intimidation and a threat of looming violence.

During the 1930s and 1940s the Klan burned crosses in front of synagogues and churches, proposed housing projects where blacks were likely to reside, and union halls. A series of cross burnings in the late 1940s prompted Virginia to enact its first version of the cross-burning statute in 1952. Today, 13 states and the District of Columbia have prohibitions against cross burning.

Provoked by the CIVIL RIGHTS Movement and the progress made by blacks in the legislatures and the courts, the Klan launched a new wave of violence in the 1950s and 1960s. Members of the Klan burned crosses on the lawns of those associated with the civil rights movement and used a variety of forms of violence toward blacks as well as whites who were viewed as sympathetic to the civil rights movement.

A burning cross has remained a symbol of the Ku Klux Klan as it can be found in much of the Klan's literature, and burning crosses often are the climax of a Klan rally or initiation. Essentially, a burning cross has continued to be a symbol of the Klan and its ideology.

At the end of the 1960s the U.S. Supreme Court fashioned a test that was significantly more protective of dangerous speech, such as cross burning, than the previous "clear and present danger" test used in previous cases. In *Brandenburg v. Ohio*, 395 U.S. 444 (1969), the Court, in a per curiam opinion, employed a test allowing government to punish the advocacy of illegal action only if the advocacy was directed to inciting or producing imminent lawless action and was likely to incite or produce such action. By requiring empirical evidence of imminent harm, the "Brandenburg Test" protects the advocacy of lawlessness except in unusual instances.

During the late 1980s and early 1990s the country experienced a rash of cross burnings. The city of St. Paul, Minnesota, had enacted a hate crime statute known as the Bias-Motivated Crime Ordinance (1989), which, among other things, made it a misdemeanor for anyone to place "on public or private property, a symbol, object, appellation, characterization or graffiti, including but not limited to, a burning cross or Nazi swastika, which one knows or has reasonable grounds to know arouses anger, alarm or resentment in others on the basis of race, color, creed, RELIGION or gender. . . ." Several teenagers allegedly burned a cross inside the fenced yard of a black family that lived across the street from the house where they were staying. R.A.V.'s (one of the teenagers) counsel in the trial court had successfully moved to have the case dismissed on the ground that the St. Paul ordinance was substantially overbroad and impermissibly content-based, thus an unconstitutional limit on freedom of speech as guaranteed under the First Amendment.

The Minnesota Supreme Court reversed the trial judge and held the ordinance to be an appropriate means of achieving a government interest. An unusually fractious Supreme Court nevertheless delivered a nine-to-zero decision striking down the St. Paul ordinance.

Justice Antonin SCALIA writing for the Court condemned the St. Paul ordinance as being wholly incompatible with the First Amendment as it aimed to silence speech on the basis of its content. The opinion noted that the ordinance singled out for limitation only speech that communicated a message of racial, gender, or religious intolerance. Other justices wrote that the ordinance was "overbroad," that is, it could be used to limit speech or expression that would otherwise deserve constitutional protection.

In 1952 the Virginia General Assembly enacted a law to ban cross burning on another person's property without permission. In 1968 the ban was expanded to cover any public place. In 1975 language was again added deeming cross burning as carrying the intent to intimidate. On August 22, 1998, Ku Klux Klan leader Barry Elton Black led a demonstration on private property in Carroll County, Virginia. The rally, which drew about 30 people, included burning a cross more than 25 feet tall. The cross was visible to nearby homeowners and motorists for three-quarters of a mile along a state highway.

At the end of the rally Black was arrested by the sheriff for violating Virginia's law prohibiting cross burning.

Black was convicted in June 1999 by an all-white jury after which the American Civil Liberties Union drew national attention when it hired an African-American lawyer to defend Black. The attorney, David P. Baugh, said the law violated the right to free speech, no matter how distasteful that speech might be.

The Virginia Appeals Court upheld the conviction while the state's supreme court, in a four-to-three decision in November 2001, found the state law prohibiting cross burnings unconstitutional and threw out the conviction of Black and those in a companion case. In May 2002 the U.S. Supreme Court granted certiorari and in April 2003 handed down its decision reversing the Virginia Supreme Court and concluding that cross burning that intends to intimidate is not a form of expression protected by constitutional free-speech rights. In the opinion, written by Justice Sandra Day O'CONNOR, the Court distinguished Virginia's statute from the Minnesota law in *R.A.V. v. City of St. Paul* (1992) in that Virginia's law dealt only with cross burning that intended to intimidate and did not single out for reproach only that speech directed toward one of the specified disfavored topics. The Court did invalidate the part of the Virginia law that created a prima facie assumption that cross burning intends to intimidate.

A majority of the Court in *Black* seemed to consider cross burning, with its distinct history in this country, as more severe than hate speech that has recently been protected by the Court. In adopting new statutes, states must be cautious not to criminalize any or all acts that may appear to be threatening as those may well be struck down by this Court.

For more information: *Black v. Commonwealth of Virginia,* Va. Supt.Ct., 262 Va. 764 (2001); *Brandenburg v. Ohio,* 395 U.S. 444 (1969); *R.A.V. v. City of St. Paul, Minnesota,* 505 U.S. 377 (1992); *Virginia v. Black,* 538 U.S. 343 (2003).

—Mark Alcorn

Cruzan v. Director, Missouri Department of Health, 497 U.S. 261 (1990)

In *Cruzan v. Director, Missouri Department of Health,* the United States Supreme Court held that an individual had a constitutional right to refuse medical treatment but upheld the state of Missouri's requirement that clear and convincing evidence of that intent must be presented before that right could be exercised. In the absence of that evidence, the state of Missouri has the right to overrule parents and family to maintain medical treatment.

The case arose from a tragic car accident that left Nancy Cruzan in a persistent vegetative state. Surgeons attempted to preserve her life by implanting a feeding tube in her stomach. After it became clear that Cruzan had virtually no chance of recovery, her parents—as co-guardians—asked a Missouri court to end artificial feeding procedures. Upon finding that Cruzan had severe brain and bodily injuries and would never recover and had in a previous conversation expressed that she would not want to continue living in such a state, the court ordered the removal of the tube.

The state of Missouri challenged the ruling, claiming in part that Cruzan's previous conversation, which was with her housemate, was unreliable for the purpose of determining her intent and that no person could terminate medical treatment for an incompetent person without a living will or clear convincing evidence of the incompetent person's intent. A divided Missouri Supreme Court agreed with the state, and Cruzan's parents appealed to the U.S. Supreme Court.

The U.S. Supreme Court ruled in favor of the state of Missouri, with Chief Justice REHNQUIST writing for a 6-3 majority. The Court concluded that a competent person has a constitutional right to refuse unwanted medical treatment. However, the Court noted in the case of an incompetent person, the state had the right to require heightened evidence of intent so as to protect the interests of an individual from abuse of guardians or even family members, as well as to support the state's own institutional interests in the lives of its citizens. The Court found that a state may place a high burden of proof on those seeking to terminate an incompetent individual's life-sustaining treatment.

Writing in dissent, Justice BRENNAN observed that upholding the Missouri Supreme Court would require that Nancy Cruzan be kept alive in an irreversible vegetative state for perhaps 30 years, against the wishes of her family and guardian. Brennan argued that the standard applied by the Court was an infringement on Nancy Cruzan's RIGHT TO DIE with dignity. While the case was decided against the parents' right to terminate the life-support equipment, the Court did expressly establish that a competent individual had a right to refuse medical treatment. This has led some litigants to argue that the case is supportive of a constitutional right to assisted suicide. However, the U.S. Supreme Court rejected that argument seven years later in *Washington v. Glucksberg*, 521 U.S. 702 (1997).

Despite the U.S. Supreme Court decision, Nancy Cruzan was not forced to remain on life support for much longer. More evidence of her wish to terminate life support was discovered, meeting the burden required by Missouri. The feeding tube was removed, and she died shortly after on December 26, 1990.

For more information: Ball, Howard. *The Supreme Court and the Intimate Lives of Americans: Birth, Sex, Marriage, Childrearing, and Death.* New York: New York University Press, 2002; Colby, William H. *Long Goodbye: The Deaths of Nancy Cruzan.* Carlsbad, Calif.: Hay House, 2002; Fireside, Bryna J. *Cruzan v. Missouri: The Right to Die Case.* Berkeley Heights, N.J.: Enslow, 2003; Woodman, Sue. *Last Rights: The Struggle Over the Right to Die.* Boulder, Colo.: Perseus, 2001.

—Kevin M. Wagner

curator, office of the

The office of the curator was created in 1974 to provide professional supervision over the artifacts and memorabilia retained by the Supreme Court. According to the curator's office, its mission is to "preserve and record the history of the Supreme Court; preserve the building and its architectural features; develop, administer, and preserve the collection of the Court; create historical exhibits; conduct tours; provide a photographer to record historic events; and assist justices and Court personnel with historical and illustrative materials." (As explained in the Office of the Curator Docent Program Application, available at www.supremecourtus.gov.)

The curator's office maintains the Court's collection of antique furnishings, archives (of documents, videos, photographs, and cartoons), memorabilia, and artwork. The curator's staff also conducts research about the Court and answers information requests from the justices, the public, and scholars.

In addition to its curatorial responsibilities, the office designs educational programs for the more than one million visitors who come to the Court each year (as of 2003). The office staffs an information desk on the ground floor of the SUPREME COURT BUILDING in order to answer questions about the function, history, and architecture of the Court and about ongoing exhibits. In the theater that is located near the information desk, the curator's office shows a continuously running 23-minute film about the history and role of the Court. The staff creates rotating exhibits (on display on the ground floor) about the history of the Court, often showcasing pieces from its collection. In 1994 the curator installed a permanent exhibit on the architecture and construction of the Supreme Court building. The curator's staff also delivers public lectures in the courtroom, explaining the history and operation of the Court as well as the architectural features of the building. These 20-minute lectures are delivered every hour, Monday through Friday, when the Court is not in session. (See the Supreme

Court's Web site, www.supremecourtus.gov for the calendar.) In addition, the staff conducts private tours of the Court for guests of the justices, academic groups, and foreign dignitaries. The tours typically include the courtroom lecture, the east and west conference rooms, the elliptical staircases, the library, and an introduction to the exhibits created by the curator's office.

The first curator was Catherine Hetos Skefos, who served as curator before the office was officially created (1973–76). She was succeeded by Gail Galloway, the curator in 1976–2001. The current curator of the Court is Catherine Fitts.

For more information: Supreme Court of the United States. Available online. URL: http://www.supremecourt us.gov. Downloaded May 12, 2004; Supreme Court Historical Society. Available online. URL: http://www.supreme courthistory.org. Downloaded May 12, 2004.

—Judithanne Scourfield McLauchlan, Ph.D.

D

Dartmouth College v. Woodward, 4 Wheaton 518 (1819)

This 1819 Supreme Court case, *Dartmouth College v. Woodward,* denied the right of a state legislature to alter the charter of a private college without its consent. The case has come to be recognized as one of the most important early Supreme Court cases dealing with property rights.

Dartmouth had received its royal charter in 1769. The grant was to last "forever." It vested control of the college in a self-perpetuating board of trustees. Yet the college had violated its charter; it was supposed to be a school for Native Americans. In 1770 the board of trustees had drawn a line of separation between the college and the Indian Charity School.

In 1779 the first president was succeeded by his son, John Wheelock, who lacked tact and had difficulties with the trustees on personal, sectarian, and political grounds. The Wheelock faction were Presbyterian Republicans whereas the board were Congregationalist Federalists. In 1815 the trustees removed Wheelock. (William Woodward, the college secretary, Wheelock's nephew and ally, whose name is associated with the case, was also chief justice of the county Court of Common Pleas.) Wheelock sought aid from the Jeffersonian Republicans. In 1816 the Republicans carried New Hampshire, electing the governor, William Plumer, an ex-Federalist, and a majority of the legislature.

In 1816 the legislature enacted a modification of the charter. It tried to make the school the state university, enlarged the board of trustees, and subjected its acts to veto by overseers appointed by the governor. The ousted trustees with their sympathetic professors and students continued to operate as the college off campus. They brought suit saying the legislation violated both the New Hampshire and U.S. Constitutions. The state court ruled that the college was a public corporation and that its charter was subject to amendment by the state legislature.

Daniel Webster, a Dartmouth alumnus, was attorney for the trustees before the U.S. Supreme Court. Webster participated in more than 150 Supreme Court cases over a period of 38 years. His cocounsel was Joseph Hopkinson, author of "Hail Columbia!" and defender of Justice Samuel CHASE in the latter's impeachment trial before the U.S. Senate. Representing the State was William Wirt, President Monroe's attorney general, who could not give the case the attention it required, and two Congressmen, John Holmes and Salmon Hale. (The latter considered the former mediocre.)

Webster's performance was memorable, especially his peroration: "It is, sir, as I have said, a small college—and yet there are those who love it. . . ." Webster later lobbied the Court by sending revised copies of his arguments to his friend, Justice Joseph STORY, for distribution among "such of the judges as you feel proper." He also sent a copy to New York's Chancellor James Kent, who also had influence with some on the Supreme Court.

Chief Justice MARSHALL held that the college was a private corporation, that its charter constituted a contract, and that the New Hampshire legislature had impaired the obligations of that contract contrary to the U.S. Constitution. (There is no similar restriction in the Constitution against the federal government's impairing the obligations of a contract. The framers had in mind state interferences for the benefit of insolvent debtors.)

Earlier Marshall had prevented the legislature of Georgia from rescinding the corrupt Yazoo land sales. The *Dartmouth* PRECEDENT benefited expansion of business enterprise in the fields of railroad construction, insurance, commerce, and industry. But should such immunity leave corporations free to act against the public interest?

In 1837 a later Supreme Court, under Chief Justice TANEY, without challenging the basic principle of *Dartmouth,* ruled in the Charles River Bridge case that a legislative charter must be construed narrowly and a corporation could claim no implied rights beyond the specific terms of a grant. Webster had argued unsuccessfully for the original franchisee (the Charles River Bridge owners).

For more information: Bartlett, Irving H. *Daniel Webster*. New York: W. W. Norton, 1978; Baxter, Maurice G. *Daniel Webster and the Supreme Court*. Amherst: University of Massachusetts Press, 1966; Remini, Robert V. *Daniel Webster: The Man and His Time*. New York and London: W. W. Norton, 1997.

—Martin Gruberg

Daubert v. Merrell-Dow Pharmaceuticals, 509 U.S. 579 (1993)

In 1993 the Supreme Court's *Daubert v. Merrell-Dow Pharmaceuticals* laid out the standard for the admission of expert testimony in federal court. The Court ruled that federal judges must act as "gatekeepers" and assess the quality of expert testimony.

Courts face a seemingly intractable problem when faced with expert testimony. On the one hand, wholesale admission of experts risks inaccurate decisions and encourages the submission of dubious testimony. On the other hand, given that the trial process needed the experts in the first place, how could judges assess their quality? How could courts navigate between these two dangers?

Prior to *Daubert*, courts had largely applied one of two approaches. The first approach set the bar for admissibility fairly low, trusting the jury to sort out the experts. The second method relied on a 1923 PRECEDENT excluding polygraph results, *Frye v. U.S.* (293 U.S. 1013, 1923), which ruled that only evidence "generally accepted" within the relevant scientific field should be admitted. Both solutions had problems: the former put too much trust in the jury, while the latter did not explain how general acceptance was to be measured or what counted as the "relevant scientific field."

The Daubert family sued Merrell-Dow on the grounds that their product, Bendectin, a drug for morning sickness, had caused birth defects. Here the primary issue was causation: could expert testimony show that Bendectin was responsible for the alleged harm? The Federal District and Appellate courts ruled that under *Frye*, the family's expert testimony should be excluded because their methods were not "generally accepted" among epidemiologists. The Dauberts appealed, arguing that the Federal Rules of Evidence had liberalized the standards for expert testimony and effectively overruled *Frye*.

The Supreme Court ruled that the Federal Rules of Evidence superseded *Frye* and remanded the decision. However, the Court also interpreted the Federal Rules of Evidence as creating an affirmative obligation for judges to scrutinize scientific testimony in order to determine on its legal reliability (or scientific validity) and its helpfulness to the jury. The Court abandoned the narrower test in *Frye*, instead relying on judicial discretion and acknowledging the flexibility such a broad standard required. However, the Court did offer four examples to serve as guideposts: (1) Was the theory testable? (2) Had the theory been peer-reviewed? (3) Had an error rate been established? (4) Was the theory generally accepted? While these standards remain suggestions, their frequent use by lower courts has created an unofficial test for admissibility.

Justice REHNQUIST dissented. In short, he was unsure that the federal judiciary possessed the expertise necessary to carry out the Court's "gatekeeper" requirement.

The *Daubert* ruling has since been supplemented by two cases: *G.E. v. Joiner* (522 U.S. 136, 1997) ruled that appellate courts should be very deferential in reviewing a *Daubert* determination, while *Kumho v. Carmichael* (526 U.S. 137, 1999) ruled that *Daubert* applied to the admission of all expert testimony, not just "scientific" experts (as opposed to technical ones).

The *Daubert* ruling has led to abundant legal and academic commentary on the interaction between law and science, and the capacity and desire of federal courts to carry out their newly mandated role as gatekeeper.

For more information: *Cardozo Law Review* 15 (Special issue 1994): Entire issue; Faigman, David L. *Legal Alchemy: The Use and Misuse of Science in the Law*. New York: W.H. Freeman and Co., 1999; Jassanoff, Shelia. *Science at the Bar*. Cambridge, Mass.: Harvard University Press, 1995.

declaratory judgment

Declaratory judgment refers to one authorized by 28 U.S.C. 2201 and 2202 in which a court decides the parties' rights or status.

A party usually brings a declaratory judgment action in order to determine the meaning or legality of a contract or statute or to define the powers and duties of governmental agencies. A declaratory judgment removes uncertainty before an actual loss and reduces the number of potential lawsuits. It may substitute for an existing remedy. A court may declare a status, the presence or absence of any right, obligation, power, liability, privilege, or immunity or any fact upon which those depend. Two well-known Supreme Court cases, BROWN V. BOARD OF EDUCATION OF TOPEKA, 347 U.S. 483 (1952), and ROE V. WADE, 410 U.S. 113 (1973), brought judicial declarations that state practices and statutes were unconstitutional.

The texts of 28 U.S.C. sections 2201 and 2202 and Federal Rule of Civil Procedure 57 specify the procedure for declaratory judgment actions in the federal courts. Rule 57 expressly permits a jury trial, provides the existence of an adequate legal remedy, does not prevent a declaratory judgment, and authorizes a court to speedily decide an action for declaratory relief. A declaratory judgment is especially appropriate when it will end a disagreement arising from undisputed facts.

28 U.S.C. 2201(a) provides in part:
In cases of actual controversy, . . . any court of the United States, . . . may declare the rights and other legal relations of any interested party seeking such declaration, whether or not further relief is or could be sought. A declaration shall have the force and effect of a final judgment or decree and shall be reviewable.

Rule 57 provides in part:
The procedure for obtaining a declaratory judgment . . . shall be in accordance with these rules, and the right to trial by jury may be demanded. . . . The existence of another adequate remedy does not preclude a judgment for declaratory relief in cases where it is appropriate.

A party must satisfy three requirements in order to maintain a declaratory judgment action. First, it must show a justiciable controversy in which the complaint presents a real, substantial, and existing dispute and does not merely request an advisory opinion based upon a hypothetical or speculative situation. Second, it must assert a practical interest, that is, some substantial right, status, or other legal relation that the defendant has some power to influence. A practical interest involves a monetary or personal interest directly in issue or at risk. Third, it must present a question ripe or ready for court decision. A court may only exercise its jurisdiction in response to a complaint, or request, for declaratory judgment if it finds facts presenting issues appropriate and ready for determination. The complaint's demand for relief must precisely state the relief sought.

The plaintiff does not necessarily bear the burden of proof in a declaratory judgment action. The burden of proof rests with the party who would have borne it had the parties sought other relief. For instance, the insured bears the burden of proving coverage in a declaratory action on an insurance policy, but the insurance company bears the burden of proving a policy exclusion.

Most states have adopted the Uniform Declaratory Judgments Act, which provides for declaratory relief in state courts.

For more information: 28 U.S.C. 2201, 2202; *Federal Rule of Civil Procedure 57*; *Black's Law Dictionary.* 7th ed. St. Paul, Minn.: West, 1999.

—Patrick K. Roberts

Dennis v. United States, 341 U.S. 494 (1951)

Dennis v. U.S. upheld the convictions for conspiracy of the 11 leaders of the U.S. Communist Party under the 1940 Smith Act (making it a crime to advocate or organize the overthrow of the U.S. government through force and violence).

Because of illness, William Z. Foster, national chairman of the CPUSA, was not tried. Eugene Dennis was secretary general and actual operating head of the party. Other defendants included the editor of the *Daily Worker*, the party's newspaper, some state chairmen, and other national board members. Testifying against them were some ex-Communists and FBI undercover agents.

The 1948 trial was a nine-month marathon. It took nine weeks after the trial opened before the hearing of evidence got under way. Defense attorneys raised interminable legal objections. Before the trial was over, half the defendants and many of their attorneys were cited for contempt. The jury found all the defendants guilty as charged.

The Supreme Court upheld the convictions in a 6-2 decision. (Justice Tom CLARK, who, as attorney general, had brought the indictment in the case, did not participate.) Chief Justice VINSON wrote the opinion for the Court, holding that individual rights had to be limited when there is a clear and present danger to the security of society. He reiterated COURT OF APPEALS Chief Judge Learned Hand's formula: whether the gravity of the evil, discounted by its improbability, justified an invasion of free speech necessary to avoid the danger.

Justices FRANKFURTER and JACKSON wrote concurring opinions. Frankfurter, as usual, deferred to a legislative judgment of appropriateness. He and Jackson emphasized the charge of conspiracy and said it is not a protected right.

Dissenting were Justices BLACK and DOUGLAS. They trivialized the charges against the defendants, arguing that they were not charged with any overt acts designed to overthrow the government. No evidence, they argued, had been introduced at the trial that the defendants had been engaged in seditious conduct. The evidence dealt with what was said at meetings and the Marxist-Leninist doctrine taught from books.

The *Dennis* case occurred at the height of the cold war. In the 1950s, after the Korean War ended and Stalin died, the WARREN Court in the *Yates* case (*Yates v. U.S.*, 354 U.S. 298, 1957), involving second- and third-level CPUSA leaders, distinguished between advocacy of abstract doctrine and advocacy directed at promoting unlawful action.

For more information: Barth, Alan. *Prophets with Honor: Great Dissents and Great Dissenters on the Supreme Court.* New York: Vintage Books, 1975; Bollinger, Lee. *The Tolerant Society: Freedom of Speech and Extremist Speech in America.* New York: Oxford University Press, 1986.

—Martin Gruberg

Department of Justice

The U.S. Department of Justice is an executive department of the U.S. government, headed by the attorney general of the U.S. (AG). The JUDICIARY ACT OF 1789 established the AG as a member of the president's cabinet and as the chief legal officer of the federal government. In 1870 Congress established the Department of Justice (DOJ), placed the AG at its helm, and created the position of solicitor general to assist the AG in representing governmental agencies in litigation before the U.S. Supreme Court. Today, the DOJ functions as if it were a law firm capable of providing any and all necessary legal services to the federal government and all of its component pieces.

While the DOJ is too large for the AG to be intimately acquainted with the current details of every individual's or office's daily work, he or she still oversees the administration of the original function of the DOJ, which is representing the United States in court. On request, the AG also gives legal advice and opinions to the president and the heads of the executive departments.

The DOJ staff is allocated to several different bureaus and offices. The Federal Bureau of Investigation, which is the U.S. government's lead law enforcement agency and is principally concerned with detection and prevention of crime, reports directly to the attorney general.

The associate attorney general is the principal supervisor of the criminal division of DOJ, which is responsible for enforcing approximately 900 federal criminal laws; the Immigration and Naturalization Service, which enforces naturalization, immigration, and alien laws; the Bureau of Prisons; the Civil Division, which represents the government in civil lawsuits arising from the commercial and governmental activities of federal agencies; and the U.S. Marshal's Service.

The deputy attorney general heads the Antitrust Division, which is responsible for enforcement of all federal ANTITRUST LAWS; the CIVIL RIGHTS Division, which enforces antidiscrimination laws; the Tax Division; and the Office of Justice Assistance.

The Drug Enforcement Agency is a department of the DOJ, and its head reports directly to the AG. Other offices within the DOJ that report directly to the AG are the offices of Legal Policy; Legal Counsel; Professional Responsibility; and Intelligence Policy and Review.

In terms of the DOJ's relationship with the U.S. Supreme Court, the direct link between the two agencies is the solicitor general. Whenever disputes arise between or among government offices, agencies, bureaus, or other subdivisions, or between/among one of these groups and an outside agency, and the problems persist long enough to reach the Supreme Court, the solicitor general conducts their litigation.

During a typical one-year Supreme Court term, the solicitor general's office handles approximately 2,500 cases before the Supreme Court, files 30 petitions for writs of certiorari, and participates in ORAL ARGUMENT in 75 per-

cent of the cases the Court hears on the merits. During that same one-year period, the solicitor general is also typically responsible for deciding whether to authorize APPEAL or to appear as an intervenor or friend of the court in more than 2,000 cases, covering subjects as varied as the activities of the entire U.S. government.

The solicitor general determines the cases in which Supreme Court review will be sought by the government and decides on the position the government will take before the Court. With the assistance of a large staff of attorneys, the solicitor general's office prepares the petitions, briefs, and other documents the government must file during its Supreme Court litigation. Government cases that reach the high court are always argued by the solicitor general himself or by a staff attorney, picked especially for the case at hand.

The solicitor general participates in a wide variety of cases before the Supreme Court. In 2003 (1) the solicitor general's office represented the Federal Election Commission when the National Rifle Association appealed a decision of a D.C. District Court panel that found unconstitutional funding limitations and disclosure requirements pertaining to "electioneering communications" in the Bipartisan Campaign Financing Law, 116 Stat. 81, Case 02-1675; (2) the solicitor general participated in an environmental quality case, *02-1343 Engine Manufacturers' Association v. South Coast Air Quality*, as a friend of the court, speaking on behalf of an environmental air quality district, 540 U.S. (2003); and (3) in Case No. 02-1016, *Lee M. Till v. SCS Credit Corp.*, 124 U.S. §1951 (2004), the solicitor general nominated a deputy to participate in oral argument as a friend of the court in a case involving fraudulent and deceptive practices in auto financing.

Clearly, during any presidential administration, the solicitor general has a position of enormous responsibility that presents constant intellectual challenges. Although the solicitor general always advocates the position of the federal government, his knowledge must have enormous breadth because of the staggering variety of matters in which the government is involved. Although the attorney general is the titular head of the DOJ, one should never underestimate the legal talent required of the solicitor general.

Today, solicitors general have few administrative duties and are basically free to concentrate on the "interest of the United States" with respect to litigation. However, that concept is perpetually elusive; discerning just what position the interest of the United States supports is always a challenge. Solicitors general are sworn to maintain fidelity to the rule of law and to uphold the principle that the United States will win its point whenever justice is done its citizens in the courts.

For more information: Department of Justice. "Department of Justice Offices and Functions." United States

Department of Justice (2003). Available online. URL: http://www.usdoj.gov/index.html. Downloaded May 12, 2004; Waxman, Seth P., solicitor general. "Presenting the Case of the United States As It Should Be: The Solicitor General in Historical Context." Supreme Court Historical Society (1998). Available online. URL: http://www.usdoj.gov/osg/aboutosg/sgarticle.html. Downloaded May 12, 2004.

—Beth S. Swartz

Deshaney v. Winnebago County Social Services Department, 489 U.S. 189 (1989)

The Supreme Court held in *Deshaney v. Winnebago County Social Services Department* that Winnebago County Social Services' failure to provide Joshua Deshaney, a minor, with adequate protection against his father's violence did not violate Joshua's substantive rights under due process.

Joshua Deshaney was beaten repeatedly by his father, with whom he lived. After several complaints of suspected child abuse from local hospital staff and others, county social services took steps to protect Joshua but failed to remove him from the custody of his father. At four years of age, Joshua was again beaten by his father, this time leaving him permanently brain damaged and severely retarded. Acting on Joshua's behalf, his mother argued that the state, through its social services agency, had assumed a "special relationship" with Joshua through "word and deed" and was obligated to protect him in these circumstances. Failing to do so was an abuse of government power and deprived him of this liberty interest in freedom from unjustified intrusions on personal security. It therefore violated his SUB-STANTIVE DUE PROCESS rights. Their argument relied strongly on *Youngberg v. Romeo,* 457 U.S. 307 (1982)—a child confined by the state has the right to reasonably safe conditions—and *Estelle v. Gamble,* 429 U.S. 97 (1976)—deliberate indifference to a state prisoner's serious illness or injury is unconstitutional.

Justice REHNQUIST, writing for the Court, held that the purpose of the due process clause is to forbid the state itself from depriving an individual of life, liberty, and property without due process of law. It does not, however, ensure that the state protect individuals from invasion by private actors. *Youngberg v. Romeo* does not apply, since Joshua was not in state custody at the time of his injury. The fact that he had been in temporary custody at one time does not make the state responsible forever. The state's duty to protect occurs when the state limits an individual's freedom to act on his own behalf, not from its knowledge of his situation or the intent to help him. Although the state must protect his due process rights, it is not required to provide those particular governmental aids necessary to realize those rights, a state is not required to fund a medi-

cally necessary abortion even though it falls within a woman's protected freedom of choice. The state, therefore, had no constitutional duty to protect Joshua. The Court, however, suggested that this case could be a matter for Wisconsin state law to decide.

Justice BRENNAN wrote a dissenting opinion: Rather than arguing that the state failed to act, petitioners would have been wiser to argue that the state deprived Joshua of his freedom to act on his own behalf. Restraint is not necessarily an action but may also be interpreted as a refusal to act when the state is the only protection available. Left in the care of his abuser, Joshua was unable to report for or defend himself, and the state cannot be innocent of the resulting harm.

For more information: Kearney, Mary Kate. "*DeSheney's* Legacy in Foster Care and Public School Settings." *Washburn Law Journal* (March 2002): 41–42. Available online. URL: http://washburnlaw.edu/wlj/41-2/articles/kear.pdf. Downloaded May 12, 2004.

—Karen Aichinger

Dickerson v. United States, 530 U.S. 428 (2000)

In *Dickerson v. United States,* the Court held that *MIRANDA V. ARIZONA,* 384 U.S. 436 (1966), expressed a constitutional rule that could not be overturned by statute law, and that the principles set forth in *Miranda* and elaborated in subsequent cases "govern the admissibility of statements made during custodial interrogation in both state and federal courts." During custodial interrogation by FBI agents, Charles Thomas Dickerson implicated himself in several bank robberies and was subsequently indicted on federal charges. In response to a motion to suppress his statement, the trial judge ruled that Dickerson's statement was inadmissible because he had not received the required *Miranda* warnings. The government appealed to the COURT OF APPEALS for the Fourth Circuit.

The Fourth Circuit panel decided to hear arguments on the status and continuing validity of the *Miranda* decision. A provision of the Omnibus Crime Control and Safe Streets Act of 1968, found in Title 18, § 3501 of the U.S. Code, stated that a confession "shall be admissible in evidence if it is voluntarily given." [*U.S. v. Dickerson,* 166 F.3d 667, 671 (1999).] Section 3501 was an attempt to overrule the *Miranda* decision as it applied in federal courts and return to a "voluntariness" standard. Although the federal prosecutors had initially raised the question of § 3501's applicability, the government declined to make this argument on APPEAL. The Justice Department took the position that § 3501 was unconstitutional and specifically directed federal prosecutors not to rely on it when litigating the admissibility of statements.

The Washington Legal Foundation and the Safe Streets Coalition petitioned, as they had in previous cases involving § 3501 claims, for permission to file an amicus curiae BRIEF. The Court of Appeals granted this motion and also authorized the amici to use some of the government's ORAL ARGUMENT time. Paul Cassell, a long-time opponent of the *Miranda* ruling, argued the amici case. Judge Karen Williams, writing for the court, was highly critical of the Justice Department's failure to defend the law but asserted that even so, the issue was properly before the panel. She then concluded that *Miranda* was a judicially created procedural rule, not a constitutional requirement, and that § 3501 therefore overruled it.

The decision of the Fourth Circuit panel was immediately controversial. The Federalist Society recommended that Judge Williams receive the "judicial courage award" for her decision. In contrast, the House Democratic leadership claimed that striking down *Miranda* would create "an unfortunate and chaotic situation in which both effective law enforcement, and Americans' confidence in their CIVIL LIBERTIES, would suffer" [Brief Amicus Curiae of the House Democratic Leadership in Support of Petitioner, p. 4]. Twenty-three separate amicus curiae briefs were filed with the Court, 17 supporting the Fourth Circuit decision and 6 urging the Court to reverse that decision and affirm the constitutional status of *Miranda*. The status of Paul Cassell as Court-appointed amicus was also continued.

Chief Justice William REHNQUIST authored the majority opinion in the 7-2 decision. It was surprisingly brief, only 13 pages long. There was only one other opinion, a dissent written by Justice SCALIA and joined by Justice THOMAS. Justice Rehnquist agreed with the appellate court that the issue was whether *Miranda* was based on the Court's supervisory authority over the federal courts, which Congress could modify or set aside, or was a constitutional rule based on the Court's authority to interpret and apply the Constitution. He held that *Miranda* was a constitutional decision and could not be overruled by an act of Congress.

The appellate court had supported its decision with references to Supreme Court decisions describing the Miranda warnings as "prophylactic" [*New York v. Quarles*, 467 U.S. 649, 653 (1984)] and "not themselves rights protected by the Constitution" [*Michigan v. Tucker*, 417 U.S. 433, 444 (1974)]. Both these opinions had been written by then-Associate Justice Rehnquist. He stated that although "language in some of our opinions . . . supports the view" taken by the appellate court, the Court's application of *Miranda* to cases arising in state courts, where the Court has only constitutional authority, confirmed its constitutional basis [*Dickerson v. U.S.*, 530 U.S. 428, 438].

Justice Rehnquist briefly explored the possibility that the Court itself might overrule the *Miranda* decision but concluded that the principles of STARE DECISIS "weigh heavily against overruling it," whether or not individual justices agreed with the original decision [*Dickerson v. U.S.*, 530 U.S. 428, 443]. He noted that *Miranda* "has become embedded in routine police practice," and that law enforcement practices had long since adjusted to its requirements.

Although *Miranda* left open the possibility that Congress or the states might develop alternatives to the prescribed warnings, such alternatives must be "equally as effective in preventing coerced confessions" [*Dickerson v. U.S.*, 530 U.S. 428, 441]. Section 3501, which authorized judges to determine voluntariness based on the totality of the circumstances and did not require suspects to be informed of their rights under the Fifth Amendment, fell short of this "constitutional minimum."

Dickerson v. U.S. was a compromise opinion upholding the validity of both *Miranda* and its progeny, a total of more than 60 cases presenting sometimes contradictory or confusing rulings. It did not clarify or reassert the "bright-line" rule that *Miranda* originally set forth, but it did repudiate past attempts to undermine its constitutional status.

For more information: Kamisar, Yale. "*Miranda* Thirty-Five Years Later: A Close Look at the Majority and Dissenting Opinions in *Dickerson*." *Arizona State Law Journal* 33 (2001): 387–425; Leo, Richard A., and George C. Thomas III, eds. "The *Miranda* Debate: Law, Justice, and Policing." Boston: Northeastern University Press, 1998; Symposium. "Miranda After Dickerson: The Future of Confession Law." *Michigan Law Review* 99 (2001): 879.

—Barbara J. Hayler

dicta

Intertwined with the legal holding or rule in a Supreme Court opinion one can often find commentary and conjecture by the author, which legal scholars and analysts refer to as *dicta*. Dicta are passages that do not carry the weight of law but help to elucidate what the opinion's author thought about the issue and what his or her intentions were in crafting the rule or holding in the case. Important passages of dicta can serve lawyers who are trying to ascertain how a rule will or should be interpreted, but they can also be sources of extreme controversy. Because they do not have precedential value, dicta can often serve to muddy the already murky waters of major controversies or unsettled areas of law.

It is important to understand the difference between dicta and elements of the opinion that serve to explain the legal holding or rule of the decision. Most of a Supreme Court opinion is concerned with justifying the legal holding. The author will cite previous case law, principles of the common law, statutes, legal treatises, and other sources of legal authority. The justice will then apply what has been unearthed from those sources of legal authority to the case at bar. Finally, the opinion will explain why that application commands the result reached by the Court in the instant controversy.

Passages of dicta, however, go further. They express conjecture or speculation about the future. A justice may speculate as to how the ruling in the current case will apply in other circumstances. Dicta may comment on what motivated the case to come before the Supreme Court or what the author anticipates will be the popular reception of the ruling. Justices may also use dicta to express personal or ideological opinion that cannot properly be incorporated into a legal argument. Most important, however, dicta allow the reader of an opinion to gain some insight into the crafting of an opinion by learning something more than what legal factors influenced the decision.

The power of dicta is a matter of concern and controversy. Many scholars debate the appropriateness of citing dicta when trying to apply an opinion to a new case. It is well accepted that dicta do not carry the weight of law, but that does not mean that such passages do not have insightful value for legal arguments. Lawyers and legal scholars alike can use dicta in powerful ways to understand what the Court has done and what it will do in the future. While dicta can be useful and insightful, their value should not be overstated. The most important part of a Supreme Court opinion is the legal argument and principle announced. For therein lies the point of law that matters and will most directly influence the legal system.

For more information: Baum, Lawrence. *The Supreme Court.* Washington, D.C.: CQ Press, 1998; Carter, Lief. *Reason in Law.* Boston: Little, Brown, 1979.

—Tom Clark

die, right to

The right to die is recently protected and qualified under the U.S. Constitution.

In the 20th century, controversy over the right to die became almost as controversial as the right to life, which formed the core of the antiabortion argument. Supporters of the right to die argue that individuals have the right to die with dignity and that it is wrong to use medical technology to keep a person alive who is in a vegetative state or who chooses to die before major illnesses, such as cancer, destroy the quality of life. Opponents of the right to die insist that the sanctity of life requires medical technology be used as long as the life force is present and contend that any attempt to hasten death is murder.

In 1776 the authors of the Declaration of Independence established the right of citizens of this new country to "life, liberty, and the pursuit of happiness," understanding that a person's life is his/her most precious commodity. In 1787 the UNITED STATES CONSTITUTION incorporated that classical liberal theory and gave it the force of law. Medical technology in the more than two centuries since the Declaration of Independence has added a new twist to the question of guaranteeing life. Courts and legislatures have frequently been asked to determine whether or not the individual has a constitutional "right to die" as well as a constitutional right to live.

The New Jersey courts were asked to consider the right-to-die question in 1976 when 22-year-old Karen Ann Quinlan was placed on life support after a drug overdose. Because Quinlan had never regained consciousness and was classified as brain-dead, the New Jersey Supreme Court approved the removal of a respirator at the request of her family. However, years of court battles ensued before the respirator was removed, and Quinlan lived for several more years without the respirator. The *Quinlan* case began a nationwide debate on the right to die. In 1987 the New Jersey Supreme Court acted to further expand the right of terminally ill individuals to choose death over life in three separate cases.

In 1990 the Supreme Court established the PRECEDENT on the right-to-die issue when it was asked to determine in *CRUZAN V. DIRECTOR, MISSOURI DEPARTMENT OF HEALTH,* 497 U.S. 261, whether or not the parents of a young woman left in a vegetative state had the right to allow her to die naturally by removing all life support; or if the state had a compelling reason to sustain her life, even through artificial means. In line with her reported wishes, the parents of Nancy Beth Cruzan wished to have her removed from sustaining life support.

Cruzan had been unconscious since she was involved in a 1983 automobile accident at the age of 26 and had spent several years in a state-run health care facility being kept alive through hydration and a feeding tube. The nursing home refused to remove the hydration and feeding tube, and the Cruzans turned to the courts. During the trial, a friend testified that Nancy Cruzan had told her that she would not want to live a "half-life." After a judge agreed with the Cruzans, the nursing home appealed to the Missouri Supreme Court who upheld their claim that life support should be continued because Nancy Cruzan was neither legally brain-dead nor terminally ill. The United States Supreme Court agreed to hear the case.

Through a 5-4 decision, the Court determined that a competent person has a "liberty interest" under the due process clause of the Fourteenth Amendment to refuse medical treatment. However, in the absence of "clear and convincing evidence" that an incompetent person wished to forgo life support, the state's interest in sustaining life was more compelling and was not in violation of the U.S. Constitution. In the opinion of the Court, close family members do not inherit the "liberty interest" when a patient becomes incompetent, and the burden remained on the incapacitated person's family to prove that the patient would have refused life support. In cases where the incompetent person's wishes had not been made known either through a living will or durable power of attorney, a state court or legislature could establish rules governing the right to die.

States were free, according to the *Cruzan* decision, to choose to allow either the continuation or termination of life support. In a subsequent trial, Missouri accepted additional testimony from Cruzan's friends about her wishes not to be on life support as "clear and compelling" evidence of her intentions, and life support was removed. Nancy Cruzan died 12 days later. In 1991 the Patient Self-Determination Act required medical facilities to inform incoming Medicare and Medicaid patients of their rights to make informed decisions about their own care, including the right to refuse medical treatment, and the right to execute a living will or a durable power of attorney. Most doctors recommend that medical personnel discuss "do not resuscitate orders" with terminally ill patients and their families.

In light of the *Cruzan* decision and in view of various state decisions on the right to die, states have generally accepted a common-law right of individuals to refuse life-sustaining treatment and acknowledged the constitutional right of a "liberty interest" in avoiding unwanted medical treatment. In the wake of a number of newsworthy "assisted suicides," courts and legislatures have also been asked to determine if the right to die includes allowing terminally patients to seek medical assistance in ending their lives.

In 1989 in Michigan, Dr. Jack Kevorkian, often called "Dr. Death," created a "suicide machine" to help terminally ill patients end their lives "with dignity" at a time of their own choosing. On June 4, 1990, Dr. Kevorkian used his machine for the first time to assist a 54-year-old with Alzheimer's to end her life. Throughout the decade, Kevorkian continued to help more than a hundred patients exercise their right to choose to die. When Michigan's first ban on assisted suicides was deemed unconstitutional, the Michigan legislature substituted a second act, and Michigan voters later affirmed their actions. Kevorkian was later sentenced to prison.

The Supreme Court rejected challenges to laws banning assisted suicides in New York and Washington in 1997. In *VACCO V. QUILL,* 521 U.S. 793, several New York physicians and three terminally ill patients sued New York State for violating their Fourteenth Amendment rights by a ban on assisted suicides. Similarly, in *Washington v. Glucks-*

berg, 521 U.S. 702 (1997), four physicians, three terminally ill patients, and a nonprofit counseling group based their challenge to Washington's law on the grounds that the ban placed as "undue burden" (as established by *PLANNED PARENTHOOD OF SOUTHEASTERN PENNSYLVANIA V. CASEY,* 505 U.S. 833) on their "liberty interests" guaranteed by the due process clause of the Fourteenth Amendment. In the absence of federal law on the issue, decisions will continue to be made on a state-by-state basis.

For more information: Logue, Barbara J. *Last Rights: Death Control and the Elderly in America.* New York: Lexington Books, 1993; Woodman, Sue. *Last Rights: The Struggle over the Right to Die.* New York and London: Plenum Trade, 1998.

—Elizabeth Purdy

disability rights

The Americans with Disabilities Act (ADA), enacted on July 26, 1990, is the nation's most far-reaching attempt to combat discrimination on the basis of disabilities. The ADA emerged out of the disability rights movement of the 1970s and 1980s, modeled on the experience of African Americans and women, two other historically oppressed groups in the United States.

The first comprehensive disability rights law in the United States was the 1973 Rehabilitation Act which prohibited discrimination on the basis of disability in programs receiving federal financial aid, such as public schools, government-funded hospitals, and public transportation systems. Two years after the passage of the Rehabilitation Act, Congress enacted the 1975 Education of All Handicapped Children Act (EAHCA), later renamed the Individuals with Disabilities Education Act (IDEA). This law required public school systems to provide a "free, appropriate education" to children with disabilities. During the 1980s, disability rights laws, such as the Air Carriers Access Act of 1986 and the Fair Housing Amendments of 1988, were also enacted.

Congress modeled the ADA on the 1964 CIVIL RIGHTS ACT as well as the 1973 Rehabilitation Act. At the signing ceremony on the White House lawn, President George Bush promised that the law provided people with disabilities "with a powerful expansion of protections in their basic CIVIL RIGHTS." And on its one-year anniversary, he called it "one of the most comprehensive civil rights bills in the history of this country."

The ADA prohibits discrimination against individuals on the basis of their disability, which is defined as a physical or mental impairment that substantially limits one or more of the major life activities. The law is wide-ranging, guaranteeing rights in employment (Title I), in the delivery of state and local government services and programs, including public transportation (Title II), in public accommodations (Title III), and in telecommunications (Title IV).

At the time of its passage, Congress estimated that there were at least 43 million people with disabilities in the United States and that this number would increase as the population aged. To help secure the civil rights of people with disabilities, Congress allowed individuals complaining of discrimination to sue private businesses as well as state and local governments; most ADA suits are filed in the federal courts and, in the majority of cases, the courts have ruled in favor of the defendant.

Title I is intended to prevent employers from discriminating against a qualified individual with a disability who, with or without a reasonable accommodation, can perform the essential functions of a job. When an employee or job applicant requests an accommodation, the employer must provide it unless it would impose an undue hardship.

On June 22, 1999, the Supreme Court decided three companion cases that limited the scope of protection available under the ADA. In *Sutton v. United Air Lines*, 527 U.S. 471 (1999); *Murphy v. United Parcel Service*, 527 U.S. 516 (1999); and *Albertsons, Inc. v. Kirkingburg*, 527 U.S. 555 (1999); the Court said that people whose impairments such as severe myopia (nearsightedness) or hypertension (high blood pressure) are being corrected by wearing eyeglasses or taking medication are not considered disabled under the ADA even if employers fire them or refuse to hire them on the basis of these conditions. The Court said that if Congress had intended to include such individuals within the protection of the law, it would not have identified only 43 million people as disabled.

Another important decision, *TOYOTA MOTORS V. WILLIAMS*, 584 U.S. 184 (2002), established a standard for determining if a person is substantially limited in a major life activity. The Court ruled that the woman who brought the suit, a factory worker, was not substantially limited in the major life activity of performing manual work because, although she could not perform the tasks required in her factory job, she could bathe and brush her teeth and do household chores in her home.

Because the Supreme Court decisions meant that individuals such as these were not entitled to sue under the ADA, the courts are not able to judge if they are victims of discrimination. Disability rights advocates insist that these rulings are contrary to the legislative history of the ADA as well as to government regulations. They argue that the Supreme Court has removed the protection of the ADA from a large number of individuals who were considered disabled by members of Congress when they passed the law in 1990.

Title II mandates that state and local governments provide people with disabilities an equal opportunity to receive or participate in services, programs, or activities. The law applies to myriad institutions such as state and county prisons, schools, voter registration facilities and polling places, government-funded mental hospitals, and ZONING boards. Because most state and local government programs receive federal financial assistance, they had already been covered by the 1973 Rehabilitation Act, but Title II includes a wider range of state and local government agencies and programs than were covered by the Rehabilitation Act. Government regulations require a public entity to make reasonable modifications in its programs and services unless the modifications would fundamentally alter the programs or impose an undue burden on the public entity.

In 1998 the Supreme Court decided *Pennsylvania Department of Corrections v. Yeskey*, 524 U.S. 206 (1998), a case brought by a man who was denied admission to boot camp because of his hypertension. The Court ruled that the ADA applied to correctional facilities, such as state prisons, rejecting the state's argument that it was not applicable because prisons and jails do not constitute services, programs, or activities.

In *Olmstead v. L.C.*, 527 U.S. 581 (1999), the Supreme Court underscored the ADA's protection of persons with mental disabilities. The case was brought by two women who were confined to a psychiatric unit of a state hospital even though they could be cared for in a community-based living program. The Court ruled that states that institutionalize such individuals unnecessarily violate the ADA's mandate to place them in the least restrictive setting.

Title III prohibits discrimination in public accommodations, encompassing privately owned businesses such as hotels and restaurants, day care centers, bowling alleys, golf courses, theaters, grocery stores, and shopping centers, to name just a few. The law requires business owners to make reasonable modifications in their policies and practices to allow people with disabilities to have access to their goods and services unless the modifications would fundamentally alter the nature of their business.

The first important Title III ruling by the Supreme Court was *Bragdon v. Abbott*, 524 U.S. 624 (1998), involving a dentist who refused to treat a woman with asymptomatic HIV in his office. She said that her disease prevented her from having children and the Court agreed that she was disabled because her HIV status substantially limited the major life activity of reproduction.

In another Title III case, *PGA TOUR V. MARTIN*, 532 U.S. 661 (2001), the Supreme Court decided that a professional golfer with a disability should be allowed to ride a golf cart during tournament play because permitting him to ride the course was a reasonable modification that did not fundamentally alter the game.

Most people agree that the ADA has been responsible for instituting major changes in the lives of people with disabilities as well as the rest of the society. However, following the lead of the Supreme Court, the federal courts have not greatly contributed to furthering the disability rights guarantees established by Congress in the ADA.

For more information: Blanck, Peter David, ed. *Employment, Disability, and the Americans with Disabilities Act: Issues in Law, Public Policy, and Research.* Evanston, Ill.: Northwestern University Press, 2000; Francis, Leslie Pickering, and Anita Silvers, eds. *Americans with Disabilities: Exploring Implications of the Law for Individuals and Institutions.* New York: Routledge, 2000.

—Susan Gluck Mezey

docket

The docket is a comprehensive list of all cases in which petitioners request that their case be heard before the Supreme Court during a given term. Cases come to the Court through either original or appellate jurisdiction. Under ORIGINAL JURISDICTION, the Court hears cases from ambassadors, public ministers, or the U.S. government. Parties that lose at the U.S. COURT OF APPEALS or the State Supreme Court appeal to the U.S. Supreme Court as a final arbiter. Paying a $300 filing fee, the aforementioned parties file petitions requesting that their case be heard. The petitioner's case is then given a number and officially placed on the docket.

Officially, the docket is defined as a comprehensive list of the legal cases to be heard by a court. The media and court scholars however, commonly refer to the docket as the cases the Supreme Court has decided to grant review and will render decisions, though technically the docket is much broader in scope since it encompasses all requests that are filed. Between October and late June 2003, approximately 7,000 requests were filed and placed on the docket. Historically the number of cases on the docket has grown over time. Initially the Supreme Court docket was very small with only a few petitioners requesting that their cases be heard. While 1,460 requests comprised the docket in 1945, by 1960 the number of requests increased more than 55 percent to 2,313 cases. An expanding docket coincides with the increasingly litigious nature of U.S. society.

Clerks, recent law school graduates, summarize the major points of each case that appears on the docket. Summaries are then circulated to the justices for review. Convening in conference, usually held on Fridays, justices review the summaries to determine whether the Court should grant certiorari. For cases they deem to be particularly important, justices often review the entire case rather than relying on the summary. Approximately 130 requests from the docket are reviewed on a weekly basis during conference. Four justices—on rare occasions three justices—must vote affirmatively for a case to proceed to plenary review and possibly ORAL ARGUMENT. This list of accepted cases, according to journalists and Supreme Court scholars, is often referred to as the docket. The number of accepted cases has fluctuated, peaking in the mid 1980s at 160 cases and declining in the late 1980s, with written decisions being rendered on approximately 80 cases in 2002.

The docket acts a barometer of the Court's interests. Until 1937, the Court heard cases that involved federal attempts to regulate the economic issues of states, ruling in favor of states. This changed however, with decisions that favored the federal government after 1937. The Court gave federal government significant latitude and expanded domain on issues pertaining to the economy and military. Under an activist Court the docket, in the 1950s through the 1970s, emphasized CIVIL RIGHTS in education, employment, voting, school desegregation, and equal protection for women. By the 1980s, the Court's docket and subsequent decisions illustrated the importance of states right. Cases that addressed CIVIL LIBERTIES, the environment, and the death penalty have been placed on the docket during the 1990s through 2003.

Today, the Court has an automated docket system that tracks all cases. It contains information about cases, that are pending and cases that have been decided upon. The status of cases for the current term and the prior term can be determined through this automated system. Using the automated system, individuals can conduct searches for cases by using the Supreme Court docket number, a lower court docket number, the case name, or a keyword search.

For more information: Hazard, Geoffrey C., Jr., and Michele Tartuffo. *American Civil Procedure: An Introduction.* New Haven, Conn.: Yale University Press, 1993.

—Antoinette Pole

dormant commerce clause

The dormant commerce clause, also sometimes referred to as the dormant power of the commerce clause, refers to the protection from state regulation that is provided to INTERSTATE COMMERCE by the Constitution's commerce clause. State regulations and taxes on interstate commerce under the Articles of Confederation were the primary reason for the Constitution's delegation of power to regulate "commerce among the states" to Congress (Article I, Section 8, clause 3). However, the question of whether this delegation excluded the possibility of any state regulation is not directly addressed by the Constitution.

This question was raised in *GIBBONS V. OGDEN*, 22 U.S. 1 (1824), the first case involving the commerce clause to come before the Supreme Court. After Ogden, who enjoyed a steamship monopoly granted by the state of New York, obtained a injunction from a state court barring him from operating in New York waters, Gibbons appealed to the Supreme Court, citing the commerce clause. Gibbons reasoned that his operation of a steamship between New Jersey and New York was interstate commerce, and the Constitution's grant of this power to Congress prevented the states from regulating it. In his opinion, Chief Justice John MARSHALL agreed that interstate navigation was interstate commerce, and he indicated some sympathy for Gibbons's argument that the power was intended to be exclusive. However, Marshall ultimately avoided making a ruling on the question of the commerce power's exclusiveness by deciding the case on narrower grounds. Since Gibbons was operating under the authority of a license issued under the federal Coasting Act (1789), the CHIEF JUSTICE concluded that the New York monopoly was in conflict with a federal law. Therefore, the New York law was invalid on grounds of national supremacy.

Notwithstanding the sympathy he showed for the concept of a federally exclusive commerce power in *Gibbons,* just five years later the Marshall Court issued a decision which suggested that, in the absence of federal regulation, the states did have the power to regulate some aspects of interstate commerce. In *Wilson v. Blackbird Marsh Creek Company,* 27 U.S. 245 (1829), the Court considered the constitutionality of a Delaware law that authorized the construction of a dam across a navigable stream for the purpose of protecting the health and improving the value of property for nearby inhabitants. In his opinion, Marshall recognized that the outcome would have been different if Congress had passed any law bearing on the subject. However, he concluded that such a measure was not "repugnant to the power to regulate commerce in its dormant state[.]" Hence, although Marshall's tenure as chief justice is generally associated with an expansive approach to interpreting the powers of the national government, this decision did leave the door open to some state regulation of those areas of interstate commerce that had not been regulated by Congress.

This issue was addressed more explicitly and at greater length in *COOLEY V. BOARD OF WARDENS,* 53 U.S. 299 (1851). This case involved a Pennsylvania law, which levied a fine on vessels that entered the Port of Philadelphia without taking on a pilot. Regulation of the use of pilots was clearly regulation of navigation. Under the PRECEDENT set by Marshall in *Gibbons,* the regulation of interstate navigation was the regulation of interstate commerce. However, Congress had not passed any legislation directly regulating the use of pilots. It had provided in 1789 that pilots were to be regulated by state laws, both those in existence at the time, and those that might be enacted later. In his opinion for the Court, Justice Curtis observed that if the commerce power was exclusive, Congress could not return it to the states by ordinary legislation. This act could only be consti-

tutional if the states retained some power to regulate interstate commerce under the Constitution.

Hence, in order to resolve the case, Curtis was led to confront the question of whether the states retained any power to regulate interstate commerce, a "question . . . never . . . decided by this court[.]" His answer was sensible, and yet at the same time complex. Due to its scope, the commerce power extended to "many, . . . exceedingly various subjects, quite unlike in their nature[.]" Some of these subjects, according to Curtis, were "in their nature national . . . [and] require exclusive legislation by Congress." On the other hand, others, such as the regulation of pilots, could, in the absence of federal regulation, be regulated by the states.

The result of these early commerce clause decisions was the emergence of the concept of the dormant commerce clause. Unlike some of Congress's other delegated powers, the power to regulate interstate commerce is not exclusive. In the absence of federal regulation, some areas may be regulated by the states. However, not all unregulated areas of interstate commerce are open to state regulation. The dormant commerce clause protects some aspects of interstate commerce, even where Congress has not acted. The responsibility for determining the scope of the protection afforded by the dormant commerce clause, and the extent of permissible state regulation of interstate commerce, has ultimately resided with the Supreme Court.

The case of *Southern Pacific Co. v. Arizona,* 325 U.S. 761 (1945), presents an excellent illustration of the type of constitutional analysis used by the Court in order to determine the extent of permissible state regulation. In the interest of public safety, Arizona had enacted a law limiting the length of trains to 14 passenger cars and 70 freight cars. When the state brought suit against the railroad for operating trains in excess of these limits, the railroad argued that the Arizona law violated the commerce clause. In his opinion for the Court, Justice STONE acknowledged that the delegation of the commerce power to Congress "does not exclude all state power of regulation." However, he also pointed out that, even in the absence of federal legislation, "the commerce clause . . . affords some protection from state legislation inimical to the national commerce[.]"

Hence, to determine the constitutionality of the Arizona statute, the Court was placed in the position of being an "arbiter of the competing demands of state and national interests." As is often the case when it is called upon to reconcile competing constitutional claims, the Court resorted to a balancing test. In this case, the state's use of its police power to promote public safety had to be balanced against the national interest in the free flow of commerce. The Court found that the Arizona length requirement substantially increased the railroad's operating costs. On the other hand, the Court agreed with the trial court's finding that the "law had no reasonable relation to safety[.]" In the light of these findings, the Court concluded that the Arizona law violated the commerce clause, because "the state interest is outweighed by the interest of the nation in an adequate, economical and efficient railway transportation service[.]"

As was noted in *Cooley v. Board of Wardens,* the scope of the commerce power is broad, covering many different subjects. Therefore, disputes involving the constitutionality of state regulations of interstate commerce occur in industries other than transportation. An interesting example is the case of *Hunt v. Washington Apple Advertising Commission,* 432 U.S. 333 (1977).

A North Carolina statute had required that containers of apples shipped into the state be identified under the U.S. Department of Agriculture grading system or be labeled as ungraded. Growers from the state of Washington, which had its own nationally recognized grading system, challenged the statute. Despite the obvious burden that was created for producers shipping apples from Washington, North Carolina maintained that the statute was "a valid exercise of [its] inherent POLICE POWERS designed to protect its citizenry from fraud and deception in the marketing of apples[.]" Although reasonable exercises of the state police power may create burdens for interstate commerce without coming into conflict with the dormant commerce clause, the invocation of the police power cannot be a mere pretext.

In this case, the Court found it implausible that barring the use of the nationally recognized Washington grading system in the state would help protect North Carolina consumers. However, it was clear that North Carolina growers would benefit from the elimination of the competitive advantage afforded to Washington's growers by their state's reputation for quality. As a result, the Court affirmed the U.S. District Court's holding that the North Carolina statute was unconstitutional. In fact, in view of these findings it seems likely that this statute embodied the kind of discrimination against interstate commerce that the commerce clause was designed to prevent in the first place.

A recent case with important implications for the thriving area of internet commerce is *Quill Corp. v. North Dakota,* 504 U.S. 298 (1992). Here the Court found that a vendor that conducted its business through the mail, without a physical presence in state, could not be subject to the state sales tax, referring to this as "a discrete realm of commercial activity that is free from interstate taxation." Hence, barring further federal legislation on the subject, it seems likely that state efforts to tax e-commerce may also be prevented by the dormant commerce clause.

The Supreme Court's adjudication of disputes involving the dormant commerce power has placed it in the position of enforcing the constitutionally mandated protection for interstate commerce, while at the same time upholding reasonable exercises of the state police power that may affect that commerce. When state exercises of this power are reasonable, and the burden on interstate commerce is not excessive, a state law may be determined to fall within the zone of permissible state regulation. However, the dormant commerce clause prevents enactments that substantially burden interstate commerce, and this is still more the case when they manifest an intention to promote a state's own economy by discriminating against the products of other states.

For more information: Benson, Paul R. *The Supreme Court and the Commerce Clause, 1937–1970.* New York: Dunellen Publishing, 1970; Corwin, Edward S. *The Commerce Power versus States Rights.* Princeton, N.J.: Princeton University Press, 1936; Draper, Lewis. *The Federal Power over Interstate Commerce and Its Effect on State Action.* Philadelphia: University of Pennsylvania Press, 1892; Frankfurter, Felix. *The Commerce Clause Under Marshall, Taney and Waite.* Chicago: Quadrangle, 1964.

—Justin Halpern

double jeopardy

The double jeopardy clause of the Fifth Amendment ("nor shall any person be subject for the same offense to be twice put in jeopardy of life or limb") protects criminal defendants from multiple trials on the same charges and multiple punishments for the same offense.

The double jeopardy doctrine developed under English law, as a way of protecting the individual from the state's power to harass and intimidate through the threat or practice of continuous prosecution. The Fifth Amendment unambiguously protects the acquitted defendant whom the state seeks to retry until a conviction is secured. However, there are situations in which an individual may be tried more than once for the same alleged actions. A defendant may be tried in multiple court systems (state and federal, or several states) on charges arising out of the same incident (e.g., Terry Nichols's federal conviction did not bar Oklahoma from convicting him in August 2004 for his role in the Oklahoma City bombing). Also, a defendant may be subject to both criminal and civil proceedings based on the same incident (e.g., O. J. Simpson's acquittal on murder charges was followed by a finding of civil liability for those same deaths.) Additionally, new trials awarded at a defendant's request are not considered to violate the double jeopardy clause (e.g., Clarence Gideon's successful APPEAL led the Supreme Court to order a retrial with the assistance of counsel).

In *Benton v. Maryland,* 395 U.S. 784 (1969), the Supreme Court extended the protection against double jeopardy to include defendants in state courts. *Benton* reversed *PALKO V. CONNECTICUT,* 302 U.S. 319 (1937), in which the majority rejected arguments that the double jeopardy clause should be incorporated as part of due process.

The double jeopardy clause offers defendants some protection from additional "punishments" imposed by the government after criminal conviction and sentencing. For example, imposing exorbitant drug taxes on individuals convicted of drug offenses has been considered punitive and therefore a double jeopardy violation (*Department of Revenue of Mont. v. Kurth Ranch*, 511 U.S. 767, 1994). However, some kinds of civil forfeiture of property following drug convictions have been allowed because the Court did not consider them punitive (*U.S. v. Usery*, 518 U.S. 267, 1996). Similarly, the Court has ruled that civil confinement of sexually violent predators following incarceration is not a double jeopardy violation (*Kansas v. Hendricks*, 521 U.S. 346, 1997).

A convicted offender facing a new trial enjoys certain protections against stiffer penalties imposed in a subsequent conviction. In *North Carolina v. Pearce*, 395 U.S. 711 (1969), the Court held that a judge could not impose a harsher sentence following a retrial than that which was imposed on the original conviction. Jury sentencing in subsequent trials has proved to be a more complex issue. The Court has ruled that, once convicted of a capital crime but sentenced to a punishment less than execution, a defendant could not be sentenced to death on subsequent trials (*Bullington v. Missouri*, 451 U.S. 430, 1981; *Arizona v. Rumsey*, 467 U.S. 203, 1984). However, in *Sattazahn v. Pennsylvania*, 537 U.S. 101 (2003), the Court pronounced that a jury may impose a death sentence in a new trial, even though a previous sentencing jury's deadlock led to a default life prison sentence. The distinguishing feature of these cases is how closely the jury decision in the penalty phase resembles an acquittal.

For more information: Thomas, George C. III. *Double Jeopardy: The History, the Law.* New York: New York University Press, 1998.

—Elizabeth Ellen Gordon

Douglas, William Orville (1898–1980) *Supreme Court justice*

Serving 36 years and seven months on the United States Supreme Court—longer than any other person in history—William O. Douglas will be remembered as a liberal activist judge whose reputation as a devoted civil libertarian is surpassed only by his love for the environment.

Douglas was born in Maine, Minnesota, and grew up in a financially challenged situation in or near Yakima, Washington. His father, a Presbyterian minister, died when Douglas was six. Graduating from Whitman College in Walla Walla, Washington, Douglas went on to law school at Columbia University. In August 1923, after his first year in law school, he married his first of four wives, Mildred Riddle, in La Grande, Oregon. After the wedding the couple moved to New York and Mildred found a teaching job to help him complete law school.

Despite graduating near the top of his class, Douglas's less than two years practicing law on Wall Street were unhappy and he returned to Columbia, this time on its faculty. When a faculty rift developed over the selection of the law school's new dean, he moved to Yale Law. During his tenure (1929–34) he developed expertise in both corporate law and finance. While in New Haven he came to recognize, with some influence from the school of legal realism, legal doctrines as devices that could be manipulated for social good.

Douglas left Yale for Washington during President Franklin D. Roosevelt's first term in the White House. In 1936 Douglas was appointed to the newly created Securities and Exchange Commission and in 1937 was elevated to its chairmanship.

With the resignation of Louis D. BRANDEIS from the Supreme Court in 1939, Douglas's supporters lobbied President Roosevelt seeking to secure the appointment for Douglas. The president was looking for a Westerner to fill Brandeis's seat and considered Douglas part-Westerner. Helping the cause was a press conference by Republican Senator William Borah of Idaho, the new ranking member of the Senate Committee on the Judiciary, in which he proclaimed Douglas to be "one of the West's finest and brightest sons."

President Roosevelt nominated Douglas on March 20, 1939, and he was confirmed 62-4 on April 4, 1939. On the day he was confirmed he was 40-years old and the youngest appointee to the Court since Joseph STORY in 1811.

While Douglas came to the Court with expertise in finance and corporate law, the decisions of the Court for which he wrote the majority opinions that are considered to be significant are primarily those in which he defended the rights of the individual.

He wrote for a unanimous Court in SKINNER V. OKLAHOMA, 316 U.S. 535 (1942), in striking down the Oklahoma Criminal Sterilization Act, holding that the right to have offspring was a fundamental right.

During World War II there were cases in which Douglas sided with the government versus the individual. In *Hirabayashyi* (1943) and *Korematsu* (1944) he was in the majority siding against Japanese Americans who had violated curfews and relocation orders aimed at only that ethnic group.

In three voting rights cases Douglas wrote two opinions protecting the rights of suffrage for minorities, and in one he upheld the power of the state. In *Lassiter v. Northhampton County Board of Elections*, 360 U.S. 45 (1959), he wrote for a unanimous Court holding that states have broad powers to determine the conditions of suffrage and that if a literacy test was applied to voters of all races it was not discriminatory. Four years later Douglas wrote the majority opinion for the Court and found that Georgia's system for primary elections for statewide and congressional offices based on county units discriminated against urban areas and was, therefore unconstitutional. This decision, *GRAY V. SANDERS*, 372 U.S. 368 (1963)—in which the Court held that the conception of political liberty throughout the history of the United States could be only one thing, i.e., ONE PERSON, ONE VOTE—was a significant bridge between *Baker v. Carr*, 369 U.S. 186 (1962), and the legislative apportionment cases of 1964. The third case, a challenge to a $1.50 annual poll tax as a precondition for voting in Virginia was based on the Twenty-fourth Amendment making poll taxes unconstitutional. The Court in *HARPER V. VIRGINIA STATE BOARD OF ELECTIONS*, 383 U.S. 663 (1966), argued that the political franchise is a fundamental right that cannot be denied because of lack of wealth, property, or economic status.

Douglas wrote two significant opinions in defense of the protection against self-incrimination as provided by the Fifth Amendment. In *Ullman v. United States*, 350 U.S. 422 (1956), he wrote a vigorous dissent arguing the need to protect other rights as well as self-incrimination under the Fifth Amendment. The majority held that the immunity being offered to a witness to testify in front of a federal grand jury during a Communist Party investigation was constitutionally sufficient under the Fifth Amendment if it kept a person from being jailed. Writing for the majority in *Griffin v. California*, 380 U.S. 609 (1965), Douglas asserted that prosecutors and judges cannot comment adversely on a defendant's failure to testify in a criminal proceeding because the defendant pays a price for invoking a constitutional right.

Perhaps the best known opinion of Douglas is *GRISWOLD V. CONNECTICUT*, 381 U.S. 479 (1965), in which the Court established the right to PRIVACY upon which the majority opinion in *ROE V. WADE*, 410 U.S. 113 (1973), is based. In his opinion Douglas wrote "there are specific guarantees in the BILL OF RIGHTS that have penumbras, formed by emanations from those guarantees that help give them life and substance. . . . Various guarantees create zones of privacy."

At the end of December 1974 Douglas suffered a stroke from which he never fully recovered. He was absent for much of the remainder of the October 1974 term but did return for the start of the next. On November 12, 1975, he submitted a letter of retirement to President Gerald R. Ford, who, ironically, was behind one of the four impeachment attempts discussed or actually launched against Douglas during his tenure on the bench.

During the more than 36 years that Douglas was on the Court he wrote 1,306 opinions—including 550 for the

Justice William O. Douglas *(United States Supreme Court)*

majority and 583 in dissent (not including separate commentary). During the 1940s he was mentioned several times as a potential vice presidential candidate, and in 1948 he pondered a dark horse run for the Democrat nomination for president. He will also be remembered for his unending advocacy for the powerless—which is somewhat of a paradox considering his reputation for the manner in which he treated his staff and members of his own family as well as his four wives—and his ends-oriented approach to deciding how to vote in conference and how to write his opinions. He died on January 19, 1980, just over four years after leaving the Court.

For more information: Abraham, Henry. *Justice, Presidents, and Senators: A History of the U.S. Supreme Court, Appointments from Washington to Clinton.* 4th ed. Lanham, Md.: Rowman and Littlefield, 1999; *Gray v. Sanders,* 372 U.S. 368 (1963); *Griffin v. California,* 380 U.S. 609 (1965); *Griswold v. Connecticut,* 381 U.S. 479 (1965); *Lassiter v. Northampton County Board of Elections,* 360 U.S. 45 (1959); Murphy, Bruce Allen. *Wild Bill: The Legend and Life of William O. Douglas.* New York: Random House, 2003; *Skinner v. Oklahoma,* 316 U.S. 535 (1942); *Ullman v. United States,* 350 U.S. 422 (1956);

Wasby, Stephen L., ed. *He Shall Not Pass This Way Again.* Pittsburgh, Pa.: University of Pittsburgh Press, 1990.

—Mark Alcorn

Dred Scott v. Sandford, 60 U.S. 393 (1857)

In *Dred Scott v. Sandford,* 60 U.S. 393 (1857), the Court held that Congress had no power to prohibit slavery in the territories of the United States. Chief Justice Roger B. TANEY, in a 7 to 2 decision, ruled that the due process clause of the Fifth Amendment protected the right of an owner to take his slave into territories held by the United States in trust for all Americans, Southerners and Northerners.

Through its decision, the Court attempted to end the most bitter controversy then dividing the country—whether slavery would be confined to the states where it then existed or would expand into the West. The Court, however, failed miserably in its object. Antislavery settlers in Kansas Territory ignored the decision and continued to drive out slave-owning migrants from Missouri and other slave states. President James Buchanan, like Taney a Democrat, who had been informed in advance by a justice as to how the Court would decide the case, supported the Court's decision. His request to Congress to admit Kansas as a slave state, however, only succeeded in alienating many members of his own party.

The Republican Party was founded in 1854 to oppose the extension of slavery to the territories. The party called for resistance to Taney's constitutional ruling. Abraham Lincoln, the Republican candidate, was elected to the presidency in 1860. Eleven Southern states reacted by seceding from the Union. The *Dred Scott* decision, then, was one of the events that precipitated the Civil War.

Through its holding in *Dred Scott,* the Court suffered a self-inflicted wound. The Court lost much of the public's respect. Republicans, who controlled both Congress and the presidency during the Civil War and Reconstruction (1865–77), further weakened the Court by altering the number of justices three times between 1863 and 1869. In the years following *Dred Scott,* the Supreme Court reached its lowest ebb since the early years of the republic.

Dred Scott was born a slave in Virginia. His owner moved to St. Louis and sold him to a doctor in the U.S. Army, John Emerson. In 1834 Emerson took Scott with him when he was transferred to Illinois, a state that had entered the union as a free state under the terms of the Northwest Ordinance of 1787. In 1836 Scott accompanied Dr. Emerson to Ft. Snelling, located in the portion of Louisiana Territory from which Congress had banned slavery in the Missouri Compromise of 1820. Emerson and Scott returned to Missouri in 1838. In 1854 Scott sued for his freedom in the U.S. District Court in St. Louis.

Article III of the U.S. Constitution grants to the federal courts jurisdiction over suits between citizens of different states. Scott, as a citizen of Missouri, sued his owner, John F. A. Sandford, a citizen of New York. Sandford, Emerson's brother-in-law, had inherited Scott. Sandford argued that blacks could never be citizens of the United States and therefore could never sue in federal court. Federal judge Robert Wells decided that Scott was still a slave even though he had lived in the free state of Illinois and the free territory of Louisiana. Scott then appealed to the U.S. Supreme Court. The Court heard arguments in the case in the spring of 1856 but then asked for rearguments in order to postpone a decision until after the presidential election of 1856, won by Buchanan. For the first time in the Court's history, each of the nine justices wrote an opinion in the same case, making it difficult to ascertain what the majority's position was on the important issues before it.

Taney agreed with the defendant's CONSTITUTIONAL INTERPRETATION that black persons of African descent were not and never could be citizens of the United States. America, said Taney, was a country of white men founded by white men for white men. Blacks were forcibly brought first to British North America and then to the United States after independence for the sole purpose of serving as slaves. Taney alleged that the dominant opinion at the time of the Constitution's ratification in 1788 was that blacks had no rights which white men were bound to respect.

By ruling that Scott was not a citizen, Taney could have ended his opinion there, for the Court had no jurisdiction to hear a suit between a noncitizen and a citizen. He was determined, however, to resolve the slavery controversy once and for all. He went on to rule that each state had the power to decide for itself whether residence in free territory made a slave forever free. Most importantly, he held that Congress could not exclude slavery from the western territories.

Taney's use of the language "nor shall any person be deprived of life, liberty or property without due process of law" to strike down an act of Congress was the first application of the doctrine of SUBSTANTIVE DUE PROCESS. Between 1895 and 1936, conservative justices employed the doctrine to declare unconstitutional efforts by Congress to regulate economic activity, such as manufacturing, oil production, mining, and agriculture. From 1937 onward, liberal justices found numerous state laws infringing on the freedoms of the criminally accused and other vulnerable groups in American society in violation of the due process clause of the Fourteenth Amendment. Under the substantive, as opposed to the procedural, interpretation, the due process clauses of the Fifth and Fourteenth Amendments do not simply require fair trials, they demand just laws.

Congress and the state legislatures overturned the Court's decision by means of the Thirteenth, Fourteenth, and Fifteenth Amendments, ratified between 1865 and 1870. The Thirteenth abolished slavery not only in the territories but also in the states. The Fourteenth made blacks citizens of both their state and the United States. The Fifteenth made blacks full members of the American political community by guaranteeing them the right to vote in state and federal elections.

For more information: Fehrenbacher, Don E. *The Dred Scott Case: Its Significance in American Law and Politics.* New York: Oxford University Press, 2001; Finkelman, Paul. Dred Scott v. Sandford: *A Brief History with Documents.* New York: Palgrave, 1997.

—Kenneth Holland

drug testing

The Supreme Court has considered the permissibility of mandatory and random drug testing in several different contexts, developing specific criteria for such an evaluation particular to each context.

The evaluation of drug testing has developed around Fourth Amendment jurisprudence, as the Court has considered drug testing a special breed of search and seizure. Generally, the protections of the Fourth Amendment extend to the administration of drug testing. However, in certain contexts, the Court has found sufficient justification for the relaxation of those requirements. For example, the Court has concluded that different standards ought to be invoked for determining the permissibility of mandatory drug testing in a public school than ought to be used for determining the constitutionality of mandated drug testing in an employment setting. Yet still different standards must be met to require drug testing in the area of government-supported health care. The evaluation of drug testing has been affected by Fourth Amendment jurisprudence in general and has had specific repercussions for other areas of law and policy, especially the war on drugs.

The Supreme Court has ruled the setting of a public school is significantly different from others. Indeed, the Court's rulings with respect to drug testing in schools have rendered public schools one of the areas of public authority least subject to the requirements of the Fourth Amendment. In the seminal case in this area, NEW JERSEY V. T.L.O., 468 U.S. 325 (1985), the Court concluded that the need for effective disciplinary procedures in schools requires some easement of the normal requirements imposed on public authorities by the Fourth Amendment. "The warrant requirement, in particular, is unsuited to the school environment. . . ." The Supreme Court thus held that requiring a warrant to conduct certain types of searches, including drug tests, would inure to the detriment of the need for swift and effective discipline in a public school. In *T.L.O.* the justices further noted the "probable cause" requirement "is not an irreducible requirement of a valid search." "Rather, the legality of a search of a student should depend simply on the reasonableness, under all the circumstances, of the search."

Later, in *Veronia School District 47J v. Acton,* 515 U.S. 646 (1995), the Supreme Court extending its holding from *T.L.O.* to uphold a program requiring mandatory drug testing of school athletes. Juxtaposing the principles enunciated in *T.L.O.* with respect to the nature of the relationship between school authorities and schoolchildren with those discussed in *Skinner v. Railway Labor Executives' Assn.,* 489 U.S. 602 (1989) (see below), the Court found sufficient state interest in deterring drug use among school athletes to permit uniform, mandatory drug testing of participants in extracurricular activities.

With the context of certain employment settings, the Supreme Court has allowed for the easement of Fourth Amendment requirements with respect to drug testing. Specifically, the Court has ruled that certain occupations or industries inherently have special circumstances that justify a lesser level of Fourth Amendment protection. For example, there is a justifiable reason for allowing a liberal imposition of mandatory drug testing on railroad workers because of the safety concerns inherent in their duties. Similarly, U.S. Customs officials seeking certain positions, because of the security issues implicit in their job functions, may be subjected to random drug testing with a lower level of suspicion than others. However, the Supreme Court has refused to extend these relaxations of the Fourth Amendment to some other types of employees. For example, candidates for public office may not be required to pass a drug test.

In *Skinner v. Railway Labor Executives' Assn.,* the Supreme Court considered whether a federal governmental requirement that blood and urine tests of employees in certain positions be conducted after any railway accident. The regulation was passed in light of evidence that alcohol and drug abuse among persons in those positions may often contribute to such accidents. The Supreme Court held such a requirement reasonable on several grounds. First, the government clearly presented a "special need" in requiring persons in safety-sensitive positions to submit to testing when an accident occurs. Second, because the regulations narrowly and specifically defined the circumstances under which an individual must submit to a toxicology testing, there was no need to apply a warrant requirement. Finally, the Court found no need to impose a requirement of individualized suspicion, because the regulations, again, were found to be narrowly tailored to persons who ought reasonably to expect less privacy, owing to the safety-sensitivity of their job positions.

The same year, in *Treasury Employees v. Von Raab,* 489 U.S. 656 (1989), the Supreme Court upheld the mandatory drug testing of Customs officials seeking promotion or transfer to a position that met one of three criteria: (1) "direct involvement in drug interdiction"; (2) the responsibility for carrying a firearm; or (3) the handling of "'classified' material." For reasons similar to those deduced in *Skinner*, the Court found a compelling government interest in requiring these drug tests and again allowed for an easement of Fourth Amendment protections.

However, in *Chandler v. Miller*, 520 U.S. 305 (1997), the Supreme Court refused to extend such a relaxation to a requirement that candidates for public office submit to and pass a drug test. The Court distinguished *Veronia, Skinner*, and *Von Raab*, holding that the Georgia statute was not designed to narrowly target persons who may be involved in illicit drug use and was not a credible means for deterring illicit drug use. The suspicionless tests, in the Court's view, were simply an effort on the part of the State to project a certain image.

In 2001 the Court handed down a seminal opinion in *Ferguson v. Charleston*, 532 U.S. 67 (2001). There, a local hospital was engaged in the practice of performing drug screening on urine collected from pregnant mothers and, if the results revealed evidence of cocaine use, turning that evidence over to law enforcement officials. Such a practice was held to violate the Fourth Amendment. The Court declined to extend the relaxations allowed in *Veronia, Skinner*, and *Von Raab* and chose to apply the holding from *Chandler*. The Court concluded that the actual purpose served by the policy was wholly distinguishable from the purpose of crime control, which would, perhaps, justify the policy.

Thus, over many years of consideration, the Court has developed criteria for the evaluation of mandatory and random drug testing procedures. When pursuing a legitimate and compelling state interest, under certain circumstances, there can be a diminished expectation to privacy and therefore diminished Fourth Amendment protections. However, absent a genuine nexus between the actual purpose and function of the drug testing policy and the purported governmental interest, the regular requirements of the Fourth Amendment will apply.

For more information: Lawler, Jennifer. *Drug Testing in Schools: A Pro/Con Issue.* Berkeley Heights, N.J.: Enslow, 2000; Persico, Deborah A. Veronia School District v. Acton: *Drug Testing in Schools.* Berkeley Heights, N.J.: Enslow, 1999; Potter, Beverly A., and J. Sebastian Orfali. *Drug Testing at Work: A Guide for Employers.* Oakland, Calif.: Ronin, 1998.

—Tom Clark

E

EEOC v. Arabian American Oil Co., 499 US 244 (1991)

In *EEOC v. Arabian American Oil Co.*, the Supreme Court held that TITLE VII OF THE CIVIL RIGHTS ACT OF 1964 did not apply "extraterritorially to regulate the employment practices of United States firms that employ American citizens abroad."

The background of the case concerned a naturalized U.S. citizen who was born in Lebanon and worked for the Arabian American Oil Company (Aaramco) in Saudi Arabia. The plaintiff (a Mr. Boureslan) was fired by Aaramco. He subsequently filed a complaint with the EQUAL EMPLOYMENT OPPORTUNITY COMMISSION (EEOC) claiming discrimination because of his race, RELIGION, and national origin and sued in District Court. The EEOC joined the case in support of Mr. Boureslan, but the case was dismissed. This ruling was also affirmed by the U.S. COURT OF APPEALS for the Fifth Circuit. The case was then appealed to the U.S. Supreme Court.

After hearing arguments in the case, the Supreme Court ruled against the EEOC and Mr. Boureslan. The main concept in the 6-3 ruling was that the court found no "clear evidence" of congressional intent to extend Title VII protection to any American employed abroad. The Supreme Court went on to state that the case "falls short of demonstrating the clearly expressed affirmative congressional intent that is required to overcome the well-established presumption against statutory extraterritoriality."

In delivering the majority opinion of the Court, Chief Justice REHNQUIST (1972–present) wrote, "It is a long-standing principle of American law that legislation of Congress, unless a contrary intent appears, is meant to apply only within the territorial jurisdiction of the United States." [*Foley Bros. v. Filardo* 336 U.S. 281 (1949).]

In other words, absent an explicit law passed by the Congress of the United States, or in this case, a lack of a clear definition of what an "employee" actually is, the decision eliminates most CIVIL RIGHTS protections for U.S. citizens working outside the borders of the United States. The applicable law then becomes that of the foreign country the employee is working in if one exists. Chief Justice Rehnquist reinforced this thought when he wrote, "While Title VII consistently speaks in terms of 'States' and state proceedings, it fails even to mention foreign nations or foreign proceedings."

However, after the ruling by the Supreme Court was published, Congress acted swiftly to amend the meaning of what an employee is when it passed the Civil Rights Act of 1991. Specifically, Congress redefined what a covered employee is by stating, "With respect to employment in a foreign country, such term includes an individual who is a citizen of the United States."

Because of the now explicit language added by Congress in 1991, Title VII of the Civil Rights Act clearly applies to all U.S. citizens employed by a U.S. employer abroad. However, it does not apply to non-U.S. citizens working for U.S. employers abroad.

For more information: Custred, Harry Glynn, A. Janell Anderson, and M. Ali Raza. *The Ups and Downs of Affirmative Action Preferences*. Wesport, Conn.: Praeger, 1999.

—John P. Carobine

Eisenstadt v. Baird, 405 U.S. 438 (1972)

In *Eisenstadt v. Baird*, the Supreme Court guaranteed the right of access to birth control for single people that had been granted to married people in *GRISWOLD V. CONNECTICUT*, 381 U.S. 479, in 1965.

The plaintiff, William Baird, had given a lecture on birth control to students at Boston University in 1969. At the end of his lecture, he gave a female student a package of Emko vaginal foam at her request. Baird was arrested under Massachusetts law, which stated that anyone who illegally distributed CONTRACEPTIVES to unmarried persons could be charged with a felony and be sentenced for up to five years in prison.

The decision in *Eisenstadt* overturned the Massachusetts law that prohibited anyone other than physicians and pharmacists from providing birth control in any form. Even physicians and pharmacists were not allowed to distribute contraceptives to unmarried persons. The law allowed public health agencies, registered nurses, and hospital-run maternity health clinics to tell married people where to legally obtain contraceptives. An additional exception was granted to those who sought to use contraceptives to prevent the spread of venereal disease.

The Massachusetts Supreme Judicial Court explained the purpose of the Massachusetts law in *Commonwealth v. Allison*, 227 Mass. 57, 62, 116 N.E. 265, 448 266 in 1917: "to protect purity, to preserve chastity, to encourage continence and self restraint, to defend the sanctity of the home, and thus to engender in the State and nation a virile and virtuous race of men and women." Massachusetts argued that banning the distribution of birth control drugs, medicines, instruments, and articles to unmarried persons served as a deterrent to premarital sex.

Under Massachusetts law, a single person could be charged with a misdemeanor and fined $30 or sentenced to three months in jail for having sex. The U.S. Supreme Court contended that it "would be plainly unreasonable to assume that Massachusetts has prescribed pregnancy and the birth of an unwanted child as punishment for fornication." An additional point of interest in the Massachusetts law was that it equated the distribution of birth control with performing or advertising illegal abortions, which was also punishable by five years in prison.

The state of Massachusetts argued before the Supreme Court that William Baird had no STANDING to challenge the Massachusetts law because he was neither a physician nor a pharmacist, nor was he a single person who been denied access to birth control. Citing *Griswold,* the Court asserted that the standards of standing were relaxed in certain cases and granted Baird standing in his challenge of the Massachusetts law. The Court then determined that allowing only married persons to obtain contraceptives was a denial of the equal protection guaranteed under the Fourteenth Amendment. Writing for the plurality in *Eisenstadt,* Justice BRENNAN contended that "it is the right of individuals, married or single, to be free from government interference into matters so fundamentally affecting a person as the decision whether to bear or beget a child." The Supreme Court also rejected the argument that states had a reasonable interest in regulating the distribution of contraceptives on the grounds that they might present a potential health hazard.

For more information: *"Eisenstadt v. Baird,"* on Douglas Butler, "Abortion: Medicine, Ethics, and Law" CD-ROM, 1997; Lindgren, J. Ralph, and Nadine Taub. *The Law of Sex Discrimination.* Minneapolis and St. Paul: West, 1993.

—Elizabeth Purdy

Ellsworth, Oliver (1745–1807) *chief justice of the United States*

Oliver Ellsworth, born to a prominent Connecticut family in 1745, would serve in a number of significant capacities during the nation's founding period prior to his appointment as the third CHIEF JUSTICE of the U.S. Supreme Court in 1796.

After two years at Yale, Ellsworth transferred to the University of New Jersey (later Princeton University) where he studied for the ministry before switching to law and graduating in 1766. Admitted to the Connecticut state bar in 1771, Ellsworth struggled to build his legal practice, often supporting himself through farming and woodchopping while walking the 20 miles between the capital in Hartford and his home in Windsor because he was too poor to afford a horse. By 1775, however, he was one of the most successful attorneys in Hartford.

By the mid-1770s, Ellsworth had become active in politics and the independence movement, serving as a delegate to the Connecticut General Assembly that met following the Battle of Lexington, and as a Connecticut delegate to the Continental Congress from 1776 through the end of the Revolutionary War in 1783. He became a judge of the Connecticut Supreme Court in 1785, and in 1787 he was selected as a delegate to the Constitutional Convention in Philadelphia, where he would be credited with introducing the phrase "United States" and would help to craft the Great Compromise on legislative apportionment that would rescue the convention from deadlock and ultimately produce the U.S. Constitution. Elected in 1789 to represent Connecticut in the U.S. Senate, Ellsworth supported Alexander Hamilton's economic policies and the Jay Treaty and was responsible for the development of the JUDICIARY ACT OF 1789, establishing the basic framework for the federal judiciary that survives to this day.

President Washington appointed Ellsworth to serve as chief justice of the United States Supreme Court in 1796, a position he would hold for the next three years. As chief justice, Ellsworth would champion expanding the authority of the federal courts and the extension of common law procedures to issues of equity and admiralty law. However, illness and his simultaneous appointment as commissioner to France in 1799 and 1800 limited his effectiveness on the Court, although he was somewhat successful in limiting the issuance of seriatim opinions, separate opinions by each

Chief Justice Oliver Ellsworth *(United States Supreme Court)*

justice, in favor of per curiam opinions in which the court issued decisions as a whole.

Plagued by ill health and preoccupied with negotiating a cessation of the Quasi-War with France, Ellsworth resigned the chief justiceship in 1800 and retired to Connecticut the following year. In his later years, Ellsworth would write a newspaper column dispensing farming advice while serving on the governor's council and, briefly, as chief justice of the Connecticut Supreme Court prior to his death in 1807.

For more information: Casto, William R. *The Supreme Court in the Early Republic: The Chief Justiceships of John Jay and Oliver Ellsworth.* Columbia: University of South Carolina Press, 1995; ————. *Oliver Ellsworth and the Creation of the Federal Republic.* New York: Second Circuit Committee on History and Commemorative Events, 1997.
—William D. Baker

eminent domain

Eminent domain, or "condemnation," is the legal process by which a public agency, or a private entity that has been granted quasi-public authority for a specific, limited purpose, is empowered to purchase private property in exchange for "just compensation" in order to dedicate the property to or utilize the property for a "public use" as defined by a state or federal constitution, statute, or ordinance.

Private entities that may be granted the power of eminent domain include but are not limited to utility companies, railroads, and redevelopment corporations.

"Just compensation" is the "fair market value" of the property plus any expenses the owner must incur in order to transfer the property's title to the government entity that is the new owner. The "fair market value" is the price the owner would have received for the parcel of land and any improvements that exist thereon, such as buildings, sewers, gas lines, or electrical or cable media wiring, if he/she had not been compelled to sell the property to the government entity, but had instead, on his/her own initiative, sold the property using the real estate sales methods that are standard or generally accepted in the area. The entity taking title by eminent domain must cover the previous property owner's expenses related to the condemnation, including but not limited to moving expenses, purchase of similar property, real estate agent and/or brokers' fees, attorney's fees, and various state and local taxes and bank fees incidental to real estate purchase, sale, and financing agreements.

The U.S. and state constitutions allow a government or quasi-governmental agency to exercise its power of eminent domain only (1) as a last resort, after the government entity has been unable to purchase the land through good faith negotiation with the owner, and (2) by initiating an eminent domain petition or proceeding in the appropriate local court. In the U.S. Constitution, the government's authority to exercise eminent domain is rooted in the Fifth Amendment: No person shall . . . be deprived of . . . property, without due process of law . . . nor shall private property be taken for public use without just compensation.

From the beginning of the United States, the state courts recognized the existence of circumstances that necessitated a state or local government entity's exercise of the power of eminent domain. However, the U.S. Supreme Court did not officially recognize that the federal government might also need to exercise eminent domain until its decision in *Kohl v. United States*, 91 U.S. 367 (1876). In *Kohl,* the majority of the Supreme Court agreed that the federal government has authority, which cannot be changed by any state law or constitutional provision, to exercise eminent domain when it is necessary for a public purpose established by federal law or the U.S. Constitution. When it needs land within the borders of a state for a public purpose, the federal government can initiate eminent domain proceedings (1) in a state court, if the state consents to those proceedings; or (2) in a federal court, regardless of any action taken by the state in regard to that property.

In *Kohl*, the Supreme Court clarified that a state government that exercised eminent domain was required to pay the owner of the seized property "fair compensation," in a manner and amount similar to the amount that would be offered to the owner if a private party purchased the land, or if the federal government exercised eminent domain over the property.

The Supreme Court has used the Fifth Amendment's undefined term *public use* as an opportunity to keep the concept of eminent domain dynamic and adaptable to the ever-changing needs and demands of government. Early in U.S. history, public use of land implied utilization for transportation or supplying water. During the early 20th century, the federal government began to exercise eminent domain to establish public parks, to preserve places of historic interest, and to promote general beautification of the countryside.

In the mid-20th century, the Supreme Court again broadened the apparent meaning of *public use* in its landmark decision in BERMAN V. PARKER, 348 U.S. 26 (1954), to include urban renewal projects, destruction of slums, erection of low-cost housing in place of deteriorated housing, and the general improvement of both the aesthetic and economic value of property. The Supreme Court noted in *Berman* that it would be a mistake to attempt to ascertain a concrete meaning for the term *public use*. Instead, in *Berman*, the majority agreed that *public use* should not be subject to a concrete definition. Instead, it must encompass the general public welfare, which is a dynamic concept that recognizes that the actions that a government might take to promote public safety, health, morality, peace, law, and order cannot be completely described at any instant in time.

During the course of U.S. history, it is clear that the Supreme Court has intentionally broadened the scope of *public use* for which a state or federal government or its entity can exercise eminent domain. Although the concept of eminent domain predates U.S. history, and the language of the Fifth Amendment is more than 200 years old, the Supreme Court's interpretation of *public use* and the reasons for exercise of eminent domain have kept the constitutional concepts dynamic and applicable to real life situations despite dramatic changes in U.S. culture.

For more information: American Planning Association. Available online. URL: http://www.planning.org. Downloaded May 12, 2004; Klop, Jeremy R. *Eminent Domain.* Charlottesville: University of North Carolina Press, 1998; Sinnitt and Sinnitt. "Eminent Domain." Findlaw for Legal Professionals. Available online. URL: http://library.lp.findlaw.com/articles/file/00512/008398. Downloaded May 12, 2004.

—Beth S. Swartz

Employment Division, Department of Human Resources of Oregon v. Smith, 495 U.S. 872 (1990)

Employment Division v. Smith asked if the religious use of a hallucinogenic drug is protected by the First Amendment's free exercise of RELIGION clause. The Supreme Court said it was not and further altered free exercise doctrine by saying states need not justify general laws if they restrict religious freedom.

Alfred Smith and Galen Black were drug abuse counselors when they were dismissed for using peyote, a drug often used in Native American religious worship. Both men brought suit not against the private clinic, as it was agreed the clinic had the ability to dismiss for such reasons, but instead sued Oregon for refusing to give the unemployment compensation because they were dismissed for religiously based actions. Oregon claimed that being dismissed because of "misconduct" related to work prevented the petitioners from receiving compensation. The Oregon Supreme Court disagreed, stating that the free exercise clause of the First Amendment protected the actions of the petitioners from unjustified regulation by the state.

On certiorari, the U.S. Supreme Court found in favor of the Employment Division in a 6-3 decision. Justice SCALIA wrote for the majority that "generally applicable, religion-neutral criminal laws" do not need to be justified in court for each person claiming a religious exemption. "[D]emocratic government must be preferred to a system in which each conscience is a law unto itself." Scalia justified this shift in Court policy by distinguishing this ruling from previous "hybrid situations," in which freedom of religion was joined by another protection to make the scrutiny against the state stricter. Freedoms of religion and speech in CANTWELL V. CONNECTICUT, 310 U.S. 296 (1940), and the freedom of religion with PARENTAL RIGHTS in WISCONSIN V. YODER, 406 U.S. 205 (1972), are two examples of these hybrid cases.

The decision stands out because it arguably overturned 20th century free exercise jurisprudence, returning to the standard set in REYNOLDS V. U.S., 98 U.S. 145 (1879). In *Reynolds*, religious beliefs are fully protected by the Constitution, but religious actions can be regulated just as any other behavior can be, as long as the state presents a RATIONAL BASIS for doing so. The departure from this belief/action doctrine came with *Sherbert v. Verner*, 374 U.S. 398 (1963), as the Court held that states must show a compelling interest when restricting a religious act, whether intentional or not, and that the law is the least restrictive way to achieve the goal.

Justice O'CONNOR, joined in part by the three dissenters, wrote an opinion concurring with the result that unemployment compensation need not be paid, but defending the free exercise jurisprudence as it had evolved since *Reynolds*. Religious behavior, like religious belief, must "at least be presumptively protected by the Free Exercise Clause"; governments, to be constitutional, must pass the compelling interest test when restricting religious acts, even if the law meant no harm to religious actors.

Three years after *Smith,* the U.S. Congress attempted to reinstate the *Sherbert/Verner* compelling state interest test for free exercise cases when it passed the Religious Freedom Restoration Act, but the Court struck down the law in *City of Boerne v. Flores,* 521 U.S. 507 (1997), because it attempted to interpret what case law should be—breaching the Constitution's SEPARATION OF POWERS and FEDERALISM where interpretation is solely the job of the courts.

For more information: Fisher, Louis. *Religious Liberty in America: Political Safeguards.* Lawrence: University Press of Kansas, 2002; Long, Carolyn N. *Religious Freedom and Indians Rights: The Case of Oregon v. Smith.* Lawrence: University Press of Kansas, 2000.

—David Claborn

Engel v. Vitale, 370 U.S. 421 (1962)

Engel v. Vitale, or the Regents' Prayer Case, was the first of the SCHOOL PRAYER cases. In it, the Supreme Court declared the public composition and recitation of a nondenominational prayer to be an unconstitutional breach of the First Amendment's establishment of religion clause.

The cases predating *Engel* were *McCollum v. Board of Education,* 333 U.S. 203 (1948) and ZORACH V. CLAUSON, 343 U.S. 306 (1952), where "released-time" religious instruction was declared unconstitutional if on public school grounds but allowed if off campus. In *Engel,* the New York Board of Regents crafted the following nondenominational prayer: "Almighty God, we acknowledge our dependence upon Thee, and we beg Thy blessings upon us, our parents, our teachers and our Country" and recommended it to its public school districts throughout the state. The Union Free School District in Hyde Park accepted and made it a daily policy to recite the prayer, allowing students to remain silent or leave the classroom if they desired. The parents of 10 students, including Steven Engel, along with the ACLU brought suit against the school board's president William Vitale claiming he violated their rights to live free of an established RELIGION. The Regents' Prayer survived the New York trial court, New York appeals court, and the Federal COURT OF APPEALS because those courts claimed there were sufficient protections for students unwilling to participate in the prayer.

The Supreme Court disagreed. Justice Hugo BLACK wrote for the 6-1 majority, "[t]here can, of course, be no doubt" that reciting the prayer "is a religious activity. . . . There can be no doubt that New York's state prayer program officially establishes the religious beliefs embodied in the Regents' prayer." "Neither the fact that the prayer may be denominationally neutral nor the fact that its observance on the part of the student is voluntary can serve to free it from the limitations of the Establishment Clause." So whether the school policy coerced anyone into religious activity was not a factor for the Court, as it had been in previous cases. Instead the Regents' Prayer violated the very principle of disestablishment. "[A] union of government and religion tends to destroy government and to degrade religion," Justice Black wrote.

Justice Potter STEWART was the lone dissenter, listing off all the activities that are solemnized by invocations to God, such as the opening of court sessions, daily congressional prayers, and at the inaugurations of presidents, on coins and in the Pledge of Allegiance. Stewart wrote the ruling denied schoolchildren "the opportunity of sharing in the spiritual heritage of Nation." Justices FRANKFURTER and White recused themselves from the decision.

The public reaction to *Engel* was largely hostile, at least partly due to the misunderstanding that it was simply PRAYER IN SCHOOL that was being prohibited, rather than the public construction and administration of prayer. This difference between these two was complicated by Justice DOUGLAS's concurrence where he wrote, "Our system at the federal and state levels is presently honeycombed with such [religious] financing. . . . I think it is an unconstitutional undertaking whatever form it takes." This essentially called Justice Stewart's "spiritual heritage of the Nation" unconstitutional.

For more information: Schultz, David. "Church State Relations and the First Amendment." In *Law and Politics: Unanswered Questions,* edited by David Schultz. New York: Peter Lang, 1994

—David Claborn

Equal Employment Opportunity Commission

With a budget of $2.25 million, and approximately 100 employees located at its central headquarters in Washington, D.C., the U.S. Equal Employment Opportunity Commission (EEOC) emerged in May of 1965 to oversee the implementation of TITLE VII OF THE CIVIL RIGHTS ACT OF 1964.

Though the EEOC began with the enforcement of federal equal employment opportunity (EEO) laws aimed at ending workforce discrimination based on race, sex, color, RELIGION, and national origin, increases in the breadth and scope of EEO policy have led to expansions in the number of protected classes covered by EEO law. For instance, in addition to implementing Title VII mandates aimed at protecting racial and ethnic minorities, women, and the religious beliefs of employees, the EEOC has also been charged with enforcing federal EEO laws aimed at protecting men and women who perform substantially equal work in the same establishment from sex-based wage discrimination (1963 Equal Pay Act); individuals 40 years and over (1967 Age Discrimination in Employment Act); qualified individuals with disabilities in the private sector, state, and local government (Title I & Title V of the 1990 Americans with Disabilities Act); and qualified individuals with disabilities in the federal government (Sections 501 & 505 of the 1973 Rehabilitation Act).

Through the 1991 Civil Rights Act, the EEOC has also gained the ability to provide monetary damages in cases of intentional employment discrimination. As a result of the expansion of EEO laws, the EEOC is now charged with coordinating all federal EEO regulations, practices, and policies; interpreting employment discrimination laws and monitoring federal sector employment discrimination programs; providing funding and support to state and local Fair Employment Practices Agencies (FEPAs); and sponsoring outreach and technical assistance programs (EEOC, www.eeoc.gov).

If an individual believes an employer, labor union, or employment agency has discriminated against them because of their race, color, sex, religion, national origin, age, or disability, either when applying for a job or during the course of their employment, that person has the right to file a discrimination charge. Charges can be filed either by mail, telephone, or in person, to either the EEOC or a local EEOC agency, within 180 days of the alleged discriminatory act. Charge are classified as either Category A (given priority investigative and settlement efforts due to early recognition of discrimination); Category B (requiring further investigation to determine if violation occurred); or Category C (immediately closed due to insufficient evident or because of jurisdictional factors).

If the EEOC determines "reasonable cause" to the alleged charge, the commission recommends the Alternative Dispute Resolution (ADR). If both parties volunteer to participate in this alternative to the traditional investigative or litigation process, a mediation session is scheduled and conducted by a trained and experienced mediator. If mediation is unsuccessful, the commission may bring suit in federal court. However, a Right-to-Sue-Notice is issued to the charging party if the EEOC determines that there is "no reasonable cause" to the allegation. This allows the individual to file action in court without the EEOC's involvement.

For more information: U.S. Commission on Civil Rights. Available online. URL: http://www.usccr.gov. Downloaded May 12, 2004; U.S. Equal Employment Opportunity Commission. Available online. URL: http://www.eeoc.gov. Downloaded May 12, 2004.

—Mitzi Ramos

equal protection clause

The equal protection clause is one of the primary clauses in the Constitution used to protect the equal rights of individuals regardless of their race, gender, ancestry, or national origin.

The equal protection clause is contained within Section I of the Fourteenth Amendment to the Constitution of the United States and reads, "nor shall any State . . . deny to any person within its jurisdiction the equal protection of the laws." The Amendment was ratified in 1868, in the wake of the Civil War.

The historical circumstance that brought about its enactment was the continued subordination of African Americans by the former Confederate states. Adding a guarantee of equal protection to the Constitution was intended to grant the newly freed slaves the same CITIZENSHIP rights as white Americans. Yet, the framers of the amendment constructed the language of the clause so broadly that it can be interpreted as espousing a general norm of equality that is broader than the historical circumstances surrounding the amendment's ratification.

In the years immediately following the ratification of the Fourteenth Amendment, the Supreme Court's rulings actually limited the scope of the equal protection clause and legitimated racial segregation. In the SLAUGHTER-HOUSE CASES, 83 U.S. (16 Wall.) 36 (1873), the Court narrowly read the equal protection clause to apply only to state laws that discriminated against former slaves. And in PLESSY V. FERGUSON, 163 U.S. 537 (1896), the Court sanctioned racial segregation by upholding "separate but equal" facilities for blacks and whites on railway passenger cars.

The 20th century brought more stringent enforcement and broader application of equal protection guarantees. The origins of the modern Court's analysis of equal protection claims can be traced to Justice's Harlan F. STONE's "footnote four" in UNITED STATES V. CAROLENE PRODUCTS CO., 304 U.S. 144 (1938). Justice Stone stated that the Court would no longer give legislation regulating economic activity heightened scrutiny, as had been the Court's practice during the Lochner era in the first decades of the 20th century. Rather, the Court would judge economic regulations merely by whether they rested upon a "RATIONAL BASIS." He went on to add that legislation prejudicial against "discrete and insular minorities" would be subject to "a more searching judicial inquiry."

It was not until the mid-20th century and the WARREN Court that the emerging "two-tiered" approach to equal protection claims became solidified in constitutional doctrine. Under this approach, the Court gives the highest scrutiny to "SUSPECT CLASSIFICATIONS," such as race. Therefore, if a law treats individuals differently based on their race, it must pass the "STRICT SCRUTINY test." Under this test, the legislation will be upheld only if there is a "COMPELLING STATE INTEREST" for the racial differentiation. The test makes it very difficult for this type of legislation to pass constitutional muster. Also, it was not until the Warren Court that laws permitting racial segregation were struck down. For example, in the landmark ruling BROWN V. BOARD OF EDUCATION, 347 U.S. 483 (1954), the Court, holding that "the doctrine of 'separate but equal' has no place," found that racial segregation in education violates the equal protection clause.

Cases involving "AFFIRMATIVE ACTION" programs, even though they are intended to benefit and not to harm racial minorities, are also subject to strict scrutiny. This standard was established by Justice Sandra Day O'CONNOR in CITY OF RICHMOND V. J. A. CROSON, 488 U.S. 469 (1989), and it replaced a lower standard of scrutiny for affirmative action programs that had been used since REGENTS OF THE UNIVERSITY OF CALIFORNIA V. BAKKE, 438 U.S. 265 (1978). O'Connor's opinion also stated that only narrowly tailored affirmative action programs that remedy actual past discrimination would be upheld.

When reviewing economic regulations and legislation making distinctions based upon "nonsuspect" classifications, such as sexual orientation, age, ALIENAGE, and indigency, the Court employs the lowest standard of scrutiny, known as minimal scrutiny, which relies on the "rational basis test." This test asks whether there is a rational or reasonable basis for the legislation. It is relatively easy for economic regulations and legislation that treats individuals differently based on any of these nonsuspect categories to be upheld under this standard. For example, since the end of the *Lochner* era, the Court has struck down economic regulations in only two cases, ALLEGHENY PITTSBURGH COAL CO. V. COUNTY COMMISSION, 488 U.S. 336 (1989), and *Morey v. Doud*, 354 U.S. 459 (1957). However, recent rulings have indicated that the Court may be applying the rational basis test more strictly. For example, in ROMER V. EVANS, 517 U.S. 620 (1996), the Court struck down Colorado's Amendment 2, which prohibited special protections for homosexuals, using the rational basis test.

The Burger Court invented a third standard of JUDICIAL REVIEW for evaluating equal protection claims. This standard is known as "exacting scrutiny" and falls in between strict and minimal scrutiny. This middle tier applies to the "quasi-suspect" categories of gender and illegitimacy. The exacting scrutiny test asks whether there is a substantial relationship between the means and ends of the legislation.

Under this test, sometimes legislation is upheld, but other times it is struck down. The Court developed this test, as applicable to gender, in CRAIG V. BOREN, 429 U.S. 190 (1976). And in UNITED STATES V. VIRGINIA, 518 U.S. 515 (1996), which required the formerly all-male Virginia Military Institute to admit women, Justice Ruth Bader Ginsberg strengthened the exacting scrutiny test. She reasoned that an "exceedingly persuasive justification" must be demonstrated for laws that make gender-based distinctions.

Since the Fourteenth Amendment's passage, the Supreme Court has faced the problem of how to apply the principle of equality before the law. In particular, the different tiers of scrutiny that the Court has constructed to evaluate equal protection claims have been criticized. The Court has encountered problems with consistency in determining which classes of individuals are considered suspect. Also, the Court's definition of equal protection rights in terms of membership in groups based on immutable characteristics has been controversial. Despite these criticisms, the Supreme Court's rulings have, through the years, increasingly advanced the norm of equality in the laws of the country and have extended equal protection to a broader range of citizens.

For more information: Perry, Michael. *We the People: The Fourteenth Amendment and the Supreme Court.* New York: Oxford University Press, 1999.

—Jill Abraham

Equal Rights Amendment

The Equal Rights Amendment (ERA), which provided for the legal equality of the sexes, first was introduced in Congress in 1923 on the 75th anniversary of the 1848 Seneca Falls women's rights convention. ERA grew out of the achievement of woman suffrage with the passage of the 19th Amendment in 1920. Its principal author, Alice Paul, and other feminists believed that legal, social, and economic equality must complement political equality before—as the ERA declared, "men and women shall have equal rights throughout the United States and in every place subject to its jurisdiction."

ERA proved contentious from the beginning, sparking conflicts across party and economic lines. A powerful combination of prominent women opponents and labor activists objected, arguing that if ERA were enacted it would undermine important legislation that extended protections to women in the workplace. In 1940 the Republican Party platform formally endorsed ERA, but, for years, despite pleas from numerous sponsors in Congress, opponents kept ERA bottled up in the House Judiciary Committee refusing to let the measure reach the floor for a vote. Public interest waned.

An influx of young feminists in politics during the 1960s revived efforts to pass ERA. In arguing for a constitutional amendment, many of these women contrasted the progress of the postwar CIVIL RIGHTS movement with a century of Supreme Court decisions that circumscribed women's rights. In the early 1870s, the high court failed to extend to women many of the protections it had afforded to recently freed male slaves under the EQUAL PROTECTION CLAUSE of the 14th Amendment. In *BRADWELL V. ILLINOIS*, 16 Wall., 83 U.S. (1873), the justices refused to apply equal protection to nullify a state regulation that denied law licenses to women. Two years later, in *Minor v. Happersett*, 21 Wall., 88 U.S. (1875), the Supreme Court also decided that those protections could not be invoked to topple state laws that prevented women from voting. The court held similar positions on women participating on juries and acting as estate executors. In the following century, it did little to redress gender inequities. In *Goesaert v. Cleary*, 335 U.S. 464 (1948), for example, the court decided in favor of restrictions that kept women from tending bar. In *Hoyt v. Florida*, 368 U.S. 57 (1961), the justices upheld a state law that blocked women from jury duty.

U.S. Representative Martha Griffiths of Michigan, a trained lawyer, was determined to change the Supreme Court's pattern of paternalism toward women. Griffiths originally had believed judicial rulings would gradually extend economic and social protections to women. But by the mid-1960s she, along with other women in Congress, had grown disillusioned. Griffiths believed a constitutional amendment was the only recourse to reverse a history of judicial decisions which, she argued, denied that women were "'persons' within the meaning of the Constitution."

The wording of the Equal Rights Amendment was altered so that it became less a vehicle for change than an affirmation of existing rights: "equal rights under the law shall not be abridged or denied . . . on account of sex." Using a special parliamentary device called a discharge petition, Griffiths released the amendment from the Judiciary Committee for debate on the House floor. In August 1970 ERA passed the House overwhelmingly. In 1972 the Senate approved and it was signed into law. The legislation required ratification by two-thirds (38) of the states within a seven-year period. Thirty states quickly approved, but an antifeminist movement, spearheaded by conservative activist Phyllis Schlafly, successfully blocked full ratification despite a congressionally approved extension to 1982.

Even though the ERA failed to become law, its legacy helped to liberalize later Supreme Court decisions, especially as the Court began to extend the equal protection clause to women in the 1970s. In *Reed v. Reed*, 404 U.S. 71 (1971), shortly after ERA had passed the House, the justices cited the 14th Amendment in reversing a state law that prevented women from acting as estate administrators. That decision overturned a century of PRECEDENT. Other important cases soon followed. In *Taylor v. Louisiana*, 419 U.S. 522 (1975), the court rejected the precedent it first had set in *Strauder v. West Virginia*, 100 U.S. 303 (1880), prohibiting women from serving on juries. In the 1980s, arguing that because women had been systematically denied employment in the past based on their gender, the Supreme Court began extending AFFIRMATIVE ACTION protections to women in the workplace.

In *JOHNSON V. TRANSPORTATION AGENCY OF SANTA CLARA COUNTY*, 480 U.S. 616 (1987), the Court supported a voluntary affirmative action plan that provided women better job promotion opportunities. While the three decades since ERA passed Congress have marked a sea change in the role women play in business, politics, and society, proponents still insist that a constitutional amendment is required to ensure full gender equality.

For more information: Hoff-Wilson, Joan. *Rights of Passage: The Past and the Future of the ERA*. Bloomington: Indiana University Press, 1986.

—Matthew Wasniewski

Erie Railroad Co. v. Tompkins, 304 U.S. 64 (1938)

In *Erie Railroad Co. v. Tompkins*, the Supreme Court reversed the longstanding rule of *SWIFT V. TYSON*, 41 U.S. (16 Pet.) 1 (1842), and held that in cases based on diversity jurisdiction federal courts must follow state common law. An important original justification for creating a separate FEDERAL COURT SYSTEM was the need for an authoritative way to resolve the inevitable disputes between citizens of different states. New Yorkers did not necessarily trust Pennsylvania courts to treat them fairly, and the distrust was mutual. So the new federal courts were given "diversity jurisdiction"—the authority to hear disputes between individuals from different states.

Tompkins, a resident of Pennsylvania, brought his lawsuit against Erie Railroad Company, which was based in New York, in federal court in New York under diversity jurisdiction. Tompkins had been injured in Pennsylvania while walking along a path next to the railroad tracks in the middle of the night. When a freight train passed by the path, Tompkins was struck on the head by what he described as "a black object that looked like a door," knocked to the ground, and the wheels of the train ran over his right arm. [*Tompkins v. Erie*, 90 F.2d 603, 604 (1937).] He sued the Erie Railroad Company, the owner of the property adjacent to the railroad tracks, seeking compensation for his injuries.

Personal injury or tort claims are generally governed by state common law, principles developed by state court judges to resolve legal disputes, rather than statutes passed by legislatures. Erie Railroad argued that under Pennsylvania common law Tompkins should be considered a trespasser and the railroad was only liable for any "willful and wanton" injuries it caused. Under New York common law and that of most other states, because the railroad path had been used for a long time with no objection from the railroad, the company was responsible for any injuries negligently caused to a person on the "permissive path."

The Supreme Court previously held in *Swift v. Tyson*, 41 U.S. (1842), that while federal courts were required to follow state statutes in diversity cases they were not required to follow state common law. In accordance with *Swift*, the lower court in *Erie* rejected the railroad's Pennsylvania common law argument and a jury awarded Tompkins $30,000 in damages for negligence.

In framing the question on APPEAL as whether "the federal court was free to disregard the alleged rule of the Pennsylvania common law," the Supreme Court set the stage for reversing *Swift v. Tyson*. Criticism of the rule in *Swift* had grown stronger after the Supreme Court's decision in *Black & White Taxicab Co. v. Brown & Yellow Taxicab Co.*, 276 U.S. 518 (1928). In that case, Brown & Yellow Taxicab, a Kentucky-based company, reincorporated in Tennessee in order to obtain an exclusive contract with a Kentucky-based railroad company. Under Kentucky common law the contract would have been void. The Supreme Court, relying on *Swift*, enforced the contract over the vigorous dissent of Justice Oliver Wendell HOLMES.

Justice Louis BRANDEIS, writing for the Court in *Erie Railroad Co. v. Tompkins*, stated that time had shown both the "political and social" defects of the *Swift* ruling and that "the benefits expected to accrue from the rule did not accrue." Brandeis was particularly troubled by the "injustice and confusion" under *Swift* that allowed parties to strategically manipulate their choice of federal or state court in order to gain an advantage under the applicable laws. It was this type of calculated "forum shopping" that troubled many about the *Black & White Taxicab* case.

Ultimately, Brandeis concluded that not only was *Swift* an erroneous interpretation of the JUDICIARY ACT OF 1789 but it was "'an unconstitutional assumption of powers by the courts of the United States which no lapse of time or respectable array of opinion should make us hesitate to correct.'" (quoting Justice Holmes's dissent in *Black & White Taxicab Co. v. Brown & Yellow Taxicab Co.*)

While *Erie* determined that federal courts must follow state common law in diversity cases, the exact basis for the unconstitutionality of *Swift*, especially as it impacted the constitutionality of Federal Rules of Civil Procedure enacted in the same year, became a subject of much continued debate.

For more information: Ely, John Hart. "The Irrepressible Myth of Erie." *Harvard Law Review* 87 (1974): 693; Freyer, Tony. *Harmony and Dissonance: The Swift and Erie Cases in American Federalism.* New York: New York University Press, 1981; Purcell, Edward A. *Brandeis and the Progressive Constitution: Erie, the Judicial Power, and the Politics of Federal Courts in the Twentieth Century.* New Haven, Conn.: Yale University Press, 2000.

—Lori A. Johnson

Escobedo v. Illinois, 378 U.S. 478, 84 S. Ct. 1758 (1964)

The *Escobedo v. Illinois* decision by the Supreme Court was an important case because it set the basis for considering when a person held in custody and interrogated by the police is entitled to speak to his lawyer, and whether or not he can remain silent so as not to incriminate himself.

This case formed the basis with the MIRANDA V. ARIZONA case in 1966 for the establishment of the custodial person's rights. In the *Escobedo* case, the police took Danny Escobedo into custody in regards to his brother's murder. During his custody, he repeatedly asked to see his lawyer. In addition to the aforementioned, Escobedo's lawyer was at the police station making similar requests to see his client. The police admitted that they knew of the requests but refused to allow Danny and his lawyer to meet. At no time was Danny made aware of his right to remain silent during the interrogative process. Subsequently to these rights denials, Danny made incriminating remarks and then confessed to the crime.

All persons taken into custody in suspicion of committing a crime have the right to counsel and the right to not become a witness against himself. These rights were established within the Constitution, and it is clearly understood that the Supreme Court thought that by allowing a prisoner to retain these rights the Court was not setting a new standard, but rather enforcing previously enumerated rights. Danny offered that if he had an opportunity to talk to his lawyer he never would have confessed to the crime and that he was significantly denied his freedom to consult with his lawyer. Therefore, the Court believed that the circumstances surrounding the *Escobedo* case warranted a notice to be established to a suspect prior to interrogating a subject during an investigation.

The *Miranda* case set the final pieces in place, and the law enforcement community believed that the warning would hamper their abilities to conduct their investigations and get confessions, but those fears proved baseless. Despite these restrictions, cases are regularly solved during the interrogation process without the use of physical intimidation or denial of rights. Modern police forces often make the explication that a person was read his rights be listed in the narrative of the case report, a procedural duty for the officer. Thus when the officer signs his name to the report the officer is swearing that he did in fact read the person his rights. At other times the rights to counsel and to remain silent may need to be refreshed during a long interrogation process, and it is the responsibility of the officer to make sure that the subject wants to continue answering questions.

The court threw out the *Escobedo* case because the confession was obtained by denying Danny of his rights. This case is also known within the legal field as the pre-indictment confession case because Escobedo had not officially been charged prior to the interrogation. Although the *Miranda* case took the spotlight away from the *Escobedo* case, the *Escobedo* case still stands as the major turning point for the way in which police departments allowed interrogations to be conducted. Irrespective of the fact that the public more readily knows the *Miranda* case than the *Escobedo* case, the latter case established two of the most important rights for a person being taken into custody in the belief that he had committed a crime. We hear these important rights often on television shows when our favorite detective arrests the perpetrator of the crime. Most do not realize that these two phrases "You have the right to remain silent, you have the right to an attorney . . ." were not the result of some intelligent writer, but rather an intelligent lawyer arguing for his client's rights.

For more information: *Escobedo v. Illinois*, 378 U.S. 478, 84 S. Ct. 1758 (1964); *Miranda v. Arizona*, 384 U.S. 436 (1966).

—Ernest Alexander Gomez

establishment clause of the Constitution

The establishment clause of the Constitution forbids the national and state governments from creating, or appearing to create, an official RELIGION.

In the very first words of the BILL OF RIGHTS comes the ambiguous establishment clause, "Congress shall make no law respecting an establishment of religion." The establishment clause played almost no role in Supreme Court decision making until well into the 20th century, but since 1947, with the INCORPORATION of the establishment clause in EVERSON V. BOARD OF EDUCATION, 330 U.S. 1 (1947), the development of church and state doctrine has been a focal point of controversy and Court activity.

At the framing of the Constitution, the clause was originally proposed with the clearer phrasing "Congress shall make no law establishing religion." Only after a compromise with the House of Representatives did the "respecting an establishment of religion" become the final phrasing. And the difference matters.

People often think of the establishment clause (or better, disestablishment or nonestablishment clause) as the separation of church and state. However, that does not come from the Constitution as much as from a letter Thomas Jefferson wrote to a Baptist church explaining his view that there should be a "wall of separation" between church and state. Jefferson's view was in the minority among those voting on the first 10 amendments to the new Constitution. For the other founding fathers, the clause simply stated that the nation would not have a denominational affiliation, for that was left up to the states. And indeed, several states were officially aligned with a specific denomination well into the 1800s when the practice withered away politically rather than legally.

The Court's official understanding of the proper role of church and state is spelled out in LEMON V. KURTZMAN, 403 U.S. 602 (1971). The *Lemon* test took the neutrality standard that had evolved over the previous two decades: that laws (a) must have a secular purpose, and (b) must not advance or inhibit religion; and added a third prong, (c) laws must avoid excessive entanglement between the church and state.

Confusion over the *Lemon* test is widespread because several examples can be given which seem to conflict. For instance, public schools cannot recite prayers, but state legislatures can; nativity scenes violate the Constitution, unless there is a Christmas tree nearby to dilute the religiousness; and religious instruction during the school day is not allowed by the Constitution, unless it occurs outside of the physical school building.

The confusing nature of these rulings is not a factor of the test as much as it is of a Court that has not settled on how strictly to apply the *Lemon* test. When the Supreme Court applies the test strictly in one case, the result can be almost contradictory to the case in which it decides to apply the test with less rigor. Not having a prescribed level of scrutiny is common, though. The confusion then is directed not at the test but at the inability of public schools and city governments to know when the Supreme Court will find an action unconstitutional and when it will not.

Generally, this question of how strictly to apply the *Lemon* test differentiates two schools of understanding the establishment clause: separationists and accommodationists. Separationists are more likely to use the phrase *wall of separation between church and state*, and they believe it should be kept "high and impregnable" in Justice BLACK's words in *Everson*. Separationists apply *Lemon* strictly when an establishment issue arises. Accommodationists, on the other hand, read the establishment clause as prohibiting Congress from declaring a national religion or preferring one to another, but laws do not have to be shorn of morality and history to be declared constitutional. They apply *Lemon* only selectively because "[w]e are a religious people whose institutions presuppose a Supreme Being" as Justice DOU-GLAS wrote in *ZORACH V. CLAUSON*, 343 U.S. 306 (1952).

Despite the appearance of both camps in case law, the Court has shown a pattern to its establishment decisions. Two types of questions come up: (a) is there a governmental endorsement of the religion, or (b) is there material aid flowing from state to church?

The first set of examples come from public school cases, since they are often the scenes for establishment questions. Regarding a governmental endorsement of religion, if students are younger than high school, the Court is likely to apply the *Lemon* test with more rigor. Public SCHOOL PRAYER is an unconstitutional breach of the establishment clause— *Engel v. Vitale*, 370 U.S. 421 (1962), *LEE V. WEISMAN*, 505 U.S. 577 (1992), *SANTA FE INDEPENDENT SCHOOL DISTRICT V. DOE*, 530 U.S. 290 (2000). As students grow older than middle school age, the Court grows more lenient in applying *Lemon*. This is because "secondary school students are mature enough and are likely to understand that a school does not endorse or support" an establishment of religion when the distinction becomes more complicated. [*Westside Community Schools v. Mergens*, 496 U.S. 226 (1990).]

In the second of the two questions about aid flowing from state to church, this tendency to include age as a factor holds true as well. When the school is an elementary through high school, the Court more often uses *Lemon* to strike state laws as unconstitutional. In *Meek v. Pittenger*, 421 U.S. 349 (1975), the Court stated that public-financed services such as guidance counseling and instructional materials given to private schools is an establishment problem. When the students of the religious school are older, the chances of the policy being stricken decrease. So, for example, a blind college student receiving public scholarships to become a minister is not an establishment violation. [*Witters v. Washington Department of Services for the Blind*, 474 U.S. 481 (1986).]

To add more nuance to the matter, when the Court detects a hint of free exercise in essentially establishment questions, it tends to defer to free exercise and apply *Lemon* more loosely. More specifically, if students or their parents receive aid that then makes its way to a religious institution via their individual choices, the Court is less likely to apply the *Lemon* test strictly, or at all. All of the following have been upheld: tax benefits mainly for parents of parochial school students in *MUELLER V. ALLEN*, 463 U.S. 388 (1983), computers and instructional materials to religious school in *MITCHELL V. HELMS*, 500 U.S. 793 (2000), and state assistance for a deaf student attending a religious school in *ZOBREST V. CATALINA FOOTHILLS SCHOOL DISTRICT*, 509 U.S. 1 (1993). Vouchers are the bellwether for this type of establishment case, and they were specifically upheld in Cleveland's voucher plan in *Zelman v. Simmons-Harris*, 122 S. Ct. 2460 (2002).

Outside of the education cases, establishment questions appear to have the pattern of questions of direct governmental aid and governmental endorsement. The issue of tax dollars flowing through, or into, religious institutions became concrete with the 1996 charitable choice provision in the welfare reform law. "Pervasively sectarian" faith-based organizations were prohibited from providing welfare services before 1996 because it would be an entanglement of church and state. The charitable choice provision declared that faith-based providers do not make an entanglement, and further that state governments must not consider a group's religious identity when considering their fitness to be a provider. The mechanism faith-based groups will use when providing job training and child care is the aforementioned voucher, declared constitutional in *Zelman*.

On the question of governmental endorsement of religion in noneducational scenarios, the Supreme Court has been comparatively more lenient in allowing suspect policies to stand. When religious symbols are part of an environment that suggests no denominational preference, such as a nativity scene among other secular Christmas symbols, the Court has allowed the practice. (*LYNCH V. DONNELLY*, 465 U.S. 668 [1984]; *Allegheny County v. ACLU*, 492 U.S. 573 [1989], where a Jewish Menorah next to a Christmas tree is not violative, but a Nativity scene by itself in a public building is.)

If following this line of reasoning was not confusing enough, a recent change is blurring what has historically been an establishment question altogether. Public institutions will often open their buildings to civic groups for meetings but will not allow the same access to Bible clubs and worship. The reasoning is usually that the government wanted to avoid entanglement between church and state, but the Supreme Court has ruled this too strict form of separatism is instead discriminating against people because they are religious, and it is unconstitutional. So for instance, when the University of Missouri and school districts in New York and Nebraska refused to allow Christian groups to use campus buildings that secular groups used, the Supreme Court found this a violation of the religious free speech rights, rather than either of the religion clauses in the First Amendment: *Widmar v. Vincent*, 454 U.S. 263 (1981), *LAMB'S CHAPEL V. CENTER MORICHES SCHOOL DISTRICT*, 508 U.S. 384 (1993), and *Board of Education of the Westside Community Schools v. Mergens*, 496 U.S. 226 (1990), respectively. This discrimination regarding access to public buildings applies also to tax dollars.

So in *ROSENBERGER V. UNIVERSITY OF VIRGINIA*, 515 U.S. 819 (1995), when the University of Virginia funds student group costs such as newspaper printings, evangelical newspapers cannot be disregarded because they are religious. In other words, it is unconstitutional to stop public money from flowing into religious groups if the decision to disperse the money considered one's religion. These cases show a Supreme Court prioritizing establishment concerns lower than the rights of the religious when those rights are framed as an individual's free speech rights. Because religious groups have noticed this shift in the Court, long gone are the days of defending religious tradition as necessary to policy or institutions with a Supreme Being inherent within.

Considering all of the above, it is not surprising that the future direction of establishment cases and even the existence of the *Lemon* test seem ripe for a change. Few constitutional scholars turn down the chance to take a swipe at establishment doctrine when given the chance, and rarely are parties even going to agree a case is rightly deemed an establishment question. Forecasting this change is risky business, but a good guess will have to consider future justices on the Supreme Court and the balance of their competing visions for the church/state relationship.

For more information: Curry, Thomas J. *Farewell to Christendom: The Future of Church and State in America.* New York: Oxford University Press, 2001; Levy, Leonard. *The Establishment Clause: Religion and the First Amendment.* Chapel Hill: University of North Carolina Press, 1994; Monsma, Stephen V. *When Sacred and Secular Mix: Religious Nonprofit Organizations and Public Money.* Lanham, Md.: Rowman and Littlefield, 1996.

—David Claborn

Everson v. Board of Education, 330 U.S. 1 (1947)

In *Everson v. Board of Education*, the Court introduced the now-familiar doctrine that "The First Amendment has erected a wall between church and state. That wall must be kept high and impregnable." Despite this language of a strict separation between church and state, the Court upheld the constitutionality of a New Jersey statute that permitted a school district to reimburse parents who sent their children to public and certain private schools, including Catholic schools. This ruling introduced an ambiguity into subsequent interpretations of the establishment clause. It provided grounds for arguments that demand a strict separation of RELIGION from public life (strict separationism) and for arguments that simply demand that government be neutral toward religion and not prefer one religion over another (non-preferentialism).

Arch Everson, a New Jersey taxpayer, brought the suit, making two arguments about the constitutionality of the statute. First, he made the legal argument that the statute violated his Fourteenth Amendment right not to be deprived of property except by due process of law—in other words he argued that it was unconstitutional for the state to tax him to provide for a program that furthered the private benefit of certain citizens rather than the public

interest. Second, he argued that the statute violated the First Amendment's ban on laws "respecting the establishment of religion" because it allowed government funds to help reimburse the cost of religious education.

Justice Hugo BLACK, who authored the majority opinion, denied Everson's first argument—the argument from due process. Black held that it was not a violation of a taxpayer's due process rights if a group he disagreed with benefited personally from legislation designed by the state to advance a public interest. He argued: "The fact that a state law, passed to satisfy a public need, coincides with the personal desires of the individuals most directly affected is certainly an inadequate reason for us to say that a legislature has erroneously appraised the public need." While the Court had from time to time invalidated state statutes designed to advance certain public interests, Black observed that it was unquestionably in the public interest to ensure that students were able to obtain a secular education.

Thus, the important question became whether the busing program—which indirectly supported the religious education obtained in Catholic schools—violated the First Amendment's establishment clause. Despite Black's aforementioned language about a "high and impregnable" wall of separation between church and state, the Court held that the New Jersey statute was not in violation of the First Amendment. Because the Court had previously ruled in *PIERCE V. SOCIETY OF THE SISTERS*, 26 U.S. 510 (1925), that parents are permitted to send children to religious schools instead of public schools if those religious schools meet secular educational standards imposed by the state, Black argued that religious schooling could legitimately be said to fulfill the public interest of providing students a secular education.

Further, the majority argued that it was within New Jersey's constitutional power to authorize broad public benefits like busing without consideration of the recipients' religious beliefs; after all, no one could question the propriety of allowing state-paid police and fire departments to protect all children whether students at secular or religious schools. The First Amendment, Black concluded, "requires the state to be a neutral in its relations with groups of religious believers and nonbelievers; it does not require the state to be their adversary."

Justices JACKSON and RUTLEDGE authored dissenting opinions. The theme of both dissents was that the Court's decision did not follow through on the logic of a wall of separation between church and state. Jackson's argument emphasized that American public schools are based on "the premise that secular education can be isolated from all religious teaching, so that the school can inculcate all needed temporal knowledge and also maintain a strict and lofty neutrality as to religion." The Catholic school, Jackson noted in contrast (and perhaps under the influence of a fear of Catholicism that was pervasive in heavily Protestant America mid-20th century), "is the rock on which the whole structure [i.e., the Catholic Church] rests, and to render tax aid to its Church school is indistinguishable to me from rendering the same aid to the Church itself."

Further, Jackson's dissent relied on an expanded definition of "establishment of religion." More than simply prohibiting support of an official state or national church (like the state-supported Church of England that was an important cause of tension between the American colonies and their mother country), Jackson took this clause to require a complete isolation of religion from public life. "It was intended not only to keep the states' hands out of religion, but to keep religion's hands off the state, and, above all, to keep bitter religious controversy out of public life by denying to every denomination any advantage from getting control of public policy or the public purse."

Rutledge's dissent, which relied on an extensive analysis of pre-constitutional Virginia's debate about religious liberty, particularly through James Madison's "Memorial and Remonstrance Against Religious Assessments" and Thomas Jefferson's "Virginia Bill for Establishing Religious Freedom," echoed Jackson's. Interpreting the First Amendment in light of these documents, Rutledge concluded: "The Amendment's purpose was not to strike merely at the official establishment of a single sect, creed or religion, outlawing only a formal relation such as had prevailed in England and some of the colonies. . . . It was to create a complete and permanent separation of the spheres of religious activity and civil authority by comprehensively forbidding every form of public aid or support for religion."

Rutledge presented the separation of church from state as a gradual process, advances of which had been won and protected by the Court's intervention. He argued that at that time "the only serious surviving threat to maintaining that complete and permanent separation of religion and civil power which the First Amendment commands is through the use of the taxing power to support religion, religious establishments, or establishments having a religious foundation, whatever their form or special religious function." In Rutledge's mind the New Jersey program clearly used the taxing power, and though the program did not establish direct legal support for Catholic schools it had the impermissible effect of supporting these schools. In Rutledge's dissent, this effective support of religious schooling should have invalidated the New Jersey program.

The Court's doctrine of a "wall of separation," introduced in *Everson v. Board of Education*, was both controversial and ambiguous then, and it continues to be today. Nevertheless, it established the boundaries within which debates on the establishment clause are still conducted.

For more information: Levy, Leonard W. *The Establishment Clause*. Chapel Hill: University of North Carolina Press, 1994.

—Jason Ross

Ewing v. California, 538 U.S. 11 (2003)

In *Ewing v. California*, the United States Supreme Court upheld a California law that sentenced an individual to 25 years to life for the stealing of three golf clubs worth $399. This ruling upheld what has come to be known as "three strikes and you're out" laws.

Crime rates in the United States rose significantly in the early 1990s. In response, many states passed mandatory minimum sentences for individuals who were repeat felony offenders. One type of mandatory minimum law came to be known as the "three strikes" law, under which a person who commits a second felony receives an enhanced punishment for the second offense, while one who commits a third offense gets an even larger punishment, perhaps even life imprisonment.

Since 1993, 26 states and the federal government have enacted some variation of a three strikes law. In California the three strikes law was passed in 1993 as a result of the abduction and murder of Polly Klass by Richard Davis, a repeat felon. The California three strikes law is similar to those found in other states, and it included provisions for those convicted of a second or third felony.

In *Ewing v. California*, Gary Ewing was on parole after serving a nine-year prison term for first-degree robbery. He already had numerous run-ins with the law, for robbery and burglary. Ewing entered the pro shop at a golf course, stole three clubs valued at $399 each, for a total theft of $1,197, and later was caught and charged for grand theft. Ewing asked the trial judge to treat the grand theft like a misdemeanor and not a felony, and he also asked the judge to ignore his previous convictions, all with the purpose of avoiding sentencing under the three strikes law. The judge refused, counted the grand theft as a felony, and also counted the four prior felony convictions. Because he had at least two felonies, the judge sentenced Ewing to jail for 25 years to life. A California Appeals Court affirmed the sentence, the state supreme court declined to review, and the case was accepted for review by the United States Supreme Court.

Ewing argued that his sentence of 25 years to life violated the Eighth Amendment's cruel and unusual punishment clause in that it was disproportionate to the crime. Relying upon *Solem v. Helm*, 463 U.S. 277, 279 (1983), where the Court held that the Eighth Amendment prohibited "a life sentence without possibility of parole for a seventh nonviolent felony," Ewing contended that a possible life sentence for the stealing of three golf clubs worth less than $400 each was unconstitutional. Justice O'CONNOR, writing for a split majority in a 5-4 opinion, rejected that argument.

First, the Court did acknowledge that the Eighth Amendment does contain a narrow proportionality principle that applies to noncapital murder cases. However, the Court said that it would only strike sentences if they were grossly disproportionate to the crime. Citing *Rummel v. Estelle,* 445 U.S. 263 (1980), where the Court held that it did not violate the Eighth Amendment for a state to sentence a three-time offender to life in prison with the possibility of parole, the O'Connor majority in *Ewing* contended that enhanced sentences under recidivist statutes like the California three strikes law, aimed at deterring and incapacitating repeat offenders, served an important state interest and were therefore constitutional. Moreover, the Court noted, while there might be serious questions regarding how effective the three strikes laws were in deterring criminals, questions about effectiveness and the types of punishments enacted were matters of legislative discretion and not issues for the judiciary to address.

Justice O'Connor was joined by Justices REHNQUIST and KENNEDY. Justice SCALIA wrote a concurrence arguing that the Eighth Amendment only banned certain modes of punishment. Justice THOMAS issued a concurrence arguing that the Eighth Amendment contained no proportionality requirement. In dissent, Justices STEVENS and BREYER contended that the Eighth Amendment does in fact contain a proportionality requirement and that Gary Ewing's sentence was unconstitutional.

Ewing v. California is an important case because it effectively shrank the scope of JUDICIAL REVIEW for certain types of sentences, giving Congress and state legislatures significant ability to enact tough and lengthy punishments.

For more information: Austin, James. *"Three Strikes and You're Out": The Implementation and Impact of Strike Laws.* Washington, D.C.: U.S. Department of Justice, Office of Justice Programs; National Institute of Justice, 1999; Marshall, Patrick. "Three-Strikes Laws." *CQ Researcher* 12 (18, May 10, 2002): 417–432; Schultz, David. "No Joy in Mudville Tonight: Impact of 'Three Strike' Laws on State and Federal Corrections Policy, Resources, and Crime Control" *Cornell Journal of Law and Public Policy* 9 (2000): 557; Vitiello, Michael. "Three Strikes: Can We Return to Rationality?" *Journal of Criminal Law and Criminology* 87 (1997): 395–481; Zimring, Frank E., et al. *Punishment and Democracy: 3 Strikes and You're Out in California.* New York: Oxford University Press, 2001.

—David Schultz

exclusionary rule

The exclusionary rule provides that evidence obtained by police officers in violation of the Fourth Amendment guarantee against unreasonable searches and seizures is not admissible in a criminal trial to prove guilt. The primary purpose of the exclusionary rule is to deter police misconduct. While some proponents argue that the rule emanates from the Constitution, the Supreme Court has indicated it is merely a judicially created remedy for violations of the Fourth Amendment.

Application of the exclusionary rule may lead to the exclusion of evidence and the acquittal of persons who committed heinous crimes. Consequently, the exclusionary rule has been the subject of intense debate. Proponents argue it is the only effective means of protecting individual rights from police misconduct, while critics decry the exclusion from trial of relevant evidence.

The Supreme Court first addressed the exclusionary rule in *WEEKS V. UNITED STATES,* 232 U.S. 383 (1914), ruling that evidence illegally obtained by federal law enforcement officers was not admissible in a federal criminal trial. Because the *Weeks* decision applied only to the federal government, state police officers were free to seize evidence illegally without fear of exclusion in state criminal proceedings. Additionally, evidence seized illegally by state police could be turned over to federal law enforcement officers for use in federal prosecutions because federal officers were not directly involved in the illegal seizure. This was known as the "silver platter doctrine."

In 1949, in *Wolf v. Colorado,* 338 U.S. 25 (1949), the Supreme Court applied the Fourth Amendment to the states, incorporating it into the due process clause of the Fourteenth Amendment. However, the Court refused to mandate the remedy of the exclusionary rule. Finally, in 1961, in *MAPP V. OHIO,* 367 U.S. 643 (1961), the Court took the step it failed to take in *Wolf* and explicitly applied the remedy of the exclusionary rule to the states.

Decisions since *Mapp* have created several exceptions to the exclusionary rule. In 1984 the Court held in *Massachusetts v. Sheppard,* 468 U.S. 981 (1984), that evidence obtained by the police acting in good faith on a SEARCH WARRANT issued by a judge, that is ultimately found to be invalid, may nonetheless be admitted at trial. The Court stressed that the primary rationale for the exclusionary rule—deterrence of police misconduct—did not warrant exclusion of evidence obtained by police who act reasonably and in good faith reliance upon the actions of a judge. By "good faith" the Court meant the police are unaware that the warrant is invalid. In *Illinois v. Krull,* 480 U.S. 340 (1987), the Court extended the good faith exception to the exclusionary rule to instances where the police act in reliance on a statute that is later declared unconstitutional.

In *Arizona v. Evans*, 514 U.S. 1 (1995), the Court refused to apply the exclusionary rule to evidence seized by a police officer who acted in reliance on a computer entry, made by a court clerk, which was later found to be in error.

The Court has been reluctant to extend the reach of the exclusionary rule to proceedings other than the criminal trial. The Court has consistently refused to apply the exclusionary rule to evidence seized by private parties, if they are not acting in concert with, or at the behest of, the police. The rule does not apply to evidence presented to the grand jury. The rule is inapplicable in both civil tax assessment proceedings and civil deportation proceedings. The exclusionary rule does not apply to parole revocation hearings.

The Court has also been reluctant to apply the exclusionary rule to aspects of the criminal trial that are not directly related to the determination of guilt. Thus illegally obtained evidence may be used to impeach a defendant's testimony, or to determine the appropriate sentence for a convicted defendant.

The exclusionary rule has aroused much debate since its application to the states in 1961. Application of the rule may result in the loss of relevant evidence, which frustrates effective prosecution of wrongdoers. Using evidence seized in violation of the Constitution, on the other hand, impairs the integrity of the entire judicial process. Without a means of enforcing the Fourth Amendment's prohibition on unreasonable searches and seizures, the amendment is reduced to a "form of words" as police have little incentive to act lawfully. While courts and commentators have suggested there are alternate means of enforcing the Fourth Amendment, such as civil suits for damages, criminal prosecutions of police engaged in illegal activity, and administrative sanctions, the Supreme Court concluded in *Mapp* that these alternate means of enforcing the Fourth Amendment were ineffectual.

Despite heavy criticism, the exclusionary rule remains in place, although its application has been limited and exceptions created. So long as the rule exists, it will serve as the primary legal constraint on unlawful searches and seizures. It will also continue to result in the freeing of some "guilty" people. It is both the reward and the price we pay for living under a government of limited powers.

For more information: Amar, Akhil Reed. *The Constitution and Criminal Procedure*. New Haven, Conn.: Yale University Press, 1997; Cole, David. *No Equal Justice*. New York: New Press, 1999; Decker, John F. *Revolution to the Right: Criminal Procedure Jurisprudence During the Burger-Rehnquist Court Era*. New York: Garland, 1992; *Arizona v. Evans*, 514 U.S. 1 (1995); *Illinois v. Krull*, 480 U.S. 340 (1987); *Mapp v. Ohio*, 367 U.S. 643 (1961); *Massachusetts v. Sheppard*, 468 U.S. 981 (1984); *Nix v.

Williams, 467 U.S. 431 (1984); *Weeks v. United States*, 232 U.S. 383 (1914); *Wolf v. Colorado*, 338 U.S. 25 (1949).

—Craig Hemmens

executive privilege

Executive privilege is the president's authority to keep secret certain documents and communications generated by the executive branch. This authority allows the president to withhold information from Congress, the courts, and the general public where appropriate, but whether a particular communication or piece of information is privileged is often a matter of dispute.

When the president uses executive privilege to challenge a court-issued subpoena, the reviewing courts have the last word as to whether the material must be turned over. Those courts will ordinarily review the materials in secret (*in camera*) to determine whether the nature of the material is sufficiently sensitive to justify the president's use of the privilege. Where the President invokes executive privilege to deny information to Congress, however, the courts will generally not play a role. Instead, the amount of information to be disclosed depends on political bargaining between the president and Congress, with the ultimate resolution depending on whether the president wants to risk political criticism for being overly secretive and whether the Congress wants to risk political criticism for being overly intrusive into the internal affairs of the president.

Nowhere in the Constitution is there mentioned the words *executive privilege*. Yet, in *United States v. Nixon*, 418 U.S. 683, 708 (1974), the Supreme Court held that "[t]he privilege is fundamental to the operation of Government and inextricably rooted in the SEPARATION OF POWERS under the Constitution." *Nixon* was not the first case to recognize prerogatives of the president to withhold information (and presidents since Washington have withheld information from Congress), but it was the first case to use "executive privilege" and to attach the concept explicitly to the Constitution.

Famously, Chief Justice John MARSHALL, riding circuit and hearing Aaron Burr's treason trial, ruled that President Jefferson must release information that could be of help to Burr in his defense. Chief Justice Marshall issued the subpoena to the president (who complied, though maintaining that his compliance was voluntary), but the CHIEF JUSTICE was especially deferential to the responsibilities of the president. He cautioned future courts that though it may occasionally be necessary to require the president to produce information, "[i]n no case of this kind would a court be required to proceed against the president as against an ordinary individual."

In *Nixon*, the Supreme Court approved of an executive privilege protecting confidential communications and the secrecy of internal executive branch deliberations, reasoning that "those who expect public dissemination of their remarks may well temper candor with a concern for appearances and for their own interests to the detriment of the decision-making process." For a president to receive honest advice exploring policy options that may be unpopular, it is necessary that presidential advisers know that their advice will not appear in the next day's newspapers, congressional hearings, or courtrooms. Because disclosures even years after a given conversation could hamper the free flow of advice, the Supreme Court has held that executive privilege may be asserted by a former president for those conversations occurring during his presidency.

Keeping in mind that the privilege is designed to ensure that the president is able to perform his responsibilities properly, the District of Columbia Circuit has formulated the "ultimate question" of executive privilege inquiries as whether denying the privilege "will impede the president's ability to perform his constitutional duty" or hamper the "effective functioning of the presidency." The other branches of government have their responsibilities, too, and the Supreme Court has held that executive privilege claims—at least those in response to judicial proceedings—must be balanced against the harm that would be done by keeping the information secret. In *Nixon* itself, the Court concluded that "the demonstrated, specific need for evidence in a pending criminal trial" trumped the president's "generalized interest in confidentiality." Where the president's claims are less "generalized" ("In this meeting the president discussed options available to promote the Mid-east peace process."), or when the judiciary's need for the information is less "specific" ("We need the tapes to determine whether any adviser advocated illegal action at any time."), the result may be different.

The Supreme Court, therefore, has taken a pragmatic approach to executive privilege controversies, seeking to avoid, where possible, interference with the president's duties. Where, however, the duties of the judicial branch come in conflict with an executive offering little reason for being uncooperative, then the needs of the courts will prevail. To invoke Chief Justice Marshall's words, "[i]n no case . . . would a court be required to proceed against the president as against an ordinary individual," but in most circumstances the court must proceed in some way, giving due regard for the constitutional authority and duties of the executive.

Sometimes that due regard requires courts to protect the deliberations and communications of subordinate officials in the executive branch, in which the president was not personally involved. Presidential advisers who must brief the president often prepare memoranda analyzing data and making recommendations that may not reach the president for any number of reasons. These memoranda reflect the executive branch decision-making process but reflect the *president's* decision-making process only by inference.

If all documents prepared by subordinates were to fall within the deliberative process privilege, potentially every piece of information in the executive branch could be kept secret, thereby eviscerating such "government in the sunshine" initiatives as the Freedom of Information Act. On the other hand, if the only information subject to the privilege is that in which the president has personal involvement, subordinate officials would still fear public criticism for unpopular recommendations, and the purposes of executive privilege would not be completely fulfilled.

The question then becomes where to draw the line. Which subordinate officials should receive the benefit of executive privilege is a question as yet unanswered by the Supreme Court. D.C. Circuit case law has indicated, however, that the deliberative process branch of executive privilege applies to those officials who are "operational[ly] proximat[e]" to the president, *Ass'n of Am. Physicians & Surgeons, Inc. v. Clinton*, 997 F.2d 898, 910 (D.C. Cir. 1993), but not officials in the executive branch departments. This distinction allows officials close to the president to advise him without fear of exposure, but denies officials in the departments the same protection.

To a certain extent, then, an adviser's title (as presidential adviser or as a member of a department's staff) may affect the confidentiality of his recommendations. The courts have not yet been presented with a privilege claim for deliberation occurring within an executive *department*, however, and it is possible that such an exertion of privilege would be sustained if the information would reveal the executive branch decision-making process.

Although executive privilege is typically equated with protecting executive branch communications and deliberations, it is worth noting that there are other elements of executive privilege as well. The president has the authority to protect state and military secrets, the identity of, and information given by, informers, and information gathered in preliminary investigations that may unfairly stigmatize individuals if prematurely disclosed.

For more information: Berger, Raoul. *Executive Privilege: A Constitutional Myth.* Cambridge, Mass.: Harvard University Press, 1974; Breckenridge, Adam C. *The Executive Privilege: Presidential Control over Information.* Lincoln: University of Nebraska Press, 1974; Cox, Archibald. *Executive Privilege. U. Pa. L. Rev.* 122 (1974): 1,383; Rozell, Mark J. *Executive Privilege: Presidential Power, Secrecy, and Accountability.* 2nd ed. Lawrence: University of Kansas Press, 2002.

—Michael Richard Dimino, Sr.

Ex parte Milligan, 71 U.S. 2 (1866)

In *Ex parte Milligan* the Supreme Court struck down President Lincoln's power to authorize military trials of suspected Confederate sympathizers. The Court confronted wartime interests and a Radical Republican Congress in issuing its decision limiting the president's WAR POWERS.

During the Civil War President Lincoln granted his military commanders broad powers to arrest civilians and to try them in military courts. In 1864 Lambdin Milligan was arrested in Indiana and convicted by a military commission of supporting the Confederacy. He was sentenced to be hanged on May 19, 1865. Milligan sought a writ of habeas corpus claiming the military commission did not have the authority to try him. In March 1866 the Supreme Court heard arguments in an atmosphere highly charged with pressure from the Radical Republican Congress and a perceived lack of legitimacy after the Court's *Dred Scott* decision.

Justice Davis delivered the opinion for a divided Court voiding the military commission's verdict and sentence. He asserted that the case presented the gravest question ever addressed by the Court "for it is the birthright of every American citizen when charged with a crime, to be tried and punished according to the law." "By the protection of the law human rights are secured," Justice Davis wrote, "withdraw that protection and they are at the mercy of wicked rulers, or the clamor of an excited people." The Constitution expressly requires that those charged with crimes are entitled to be tried by a jury in a court of law. Even Congress could not have created the commission that tried Milligan.

Military courts cannot legally operate in a state where civilian authorities are fully functioning. Placing civilian matters under military control "destroys every guarantee of the Constitution, and effectually renders the 'military independent of and superior to the civil power.'" The Court pointed out that Indiana was never part of the rebellion and that Milligan could have been tried in the federal court which was in session shortly after the commission trial. It held that the "constitution is a law for rulers and people, equally in war and in peace, and covers with the shield of its protection all classes of men, at all times, and under all circumstances." Therefore, because the military commission trial violated express provisions of the Constitution, Milligan's conviction and sentence were overturned. Justice Davis acknowledged the danger to the union presented by the Civil War but asserted that a "country, preserved at the sacrifice of all the cardinal principles of liberty, is not worth the cost of preservation."

Chief Justice Salmon CHASE delivered an opinion in which four justices concurred in part and dissented in part. These justices agreed that the commission that tried Milligan was unconstitutional but argued that, in war, Congress can make the determination that some areas are in such public danger as to require military tribunals.

For more information: O'Brien, David. *Constitutional Law and Politics: Volume 1.* 5th ed. New York: W. W. Norton, 2003.

—Jeffrey Davis

Ex parte Young, 209 U.S. 123 (1908)

In *Ex parte Young,* the Supreme Court held that the Eleventh Amendment to the UNITED STATES CONSTITUTION does not bar lawsuits that seek injunctive relief against state officials from being brought in federal courts. The case arose out of laws passed by the state of Minnesota fixing railroad rates for travel and shipping within the state. Shareholders of the railroads considered the rates too low and an unjust taking of their property in violation of the due process rights granted by the Fourteenth Amendment to the U.S. Constitution. The shareholders brought suit in federal court against the state's attorney general, Edward Young, asking the court to enjoin him from enforcing the railroad rate laws. The attorney general moved to have the case dismissed, asserting that the federal court had no jurisdiction because the Eleventh Amendment prohibits bringing lawsuits against states in federal court.

The Supreme Court ruled that the federal court did have jurisdiction over the state attorney general. The Supreme Court reasoned that since a state cannot permit one of its officials to violate the Constitution, if the attorney general were to "use . . . the name of the state to enforce an unconstitutional act," he would not be acting with the authority of the state. The attorney general then could not enjoy the protection given to states by the Eleventh Amendment, but, instead, would be "subjected in his person to the consequences of his individual conduct" in federal court.

To reach this conclusion, the Supreme Court also had to rule that the state railroad laws violated the Fourteenth Amendment's due process clause. The Court found that the railroads were effectively denied the ability to challenge the rate laws in a state forum. While the railroad technically could have violated the rate-setting laws and then challenged the constitutionality of the laws as part of its defense to prosecution, the Supreme Court noted that severe penalties attached to the laws made this an unlikely option. The fines were so enormous and imprisonment so severe that they intimidated any company from violating the laws to challenge their validity. The Court found that access to the federal courts was therefore necessary to ensure the protection of the railroad's federal rights.

The Court also ruled that, in protecting federal rights, federal courts may issue injunctions against state officials.

Federal courts should use their injunctive power sparingly, however, and issue injunctions only "in a case reasonably free from doubt."

The decision of *Ex parte Young* limiting Eleventh Amendment SOVEREIGN IMMUNITY protection to the state itself and not to state officials has been called a "fiction" by both commentators and the Supreme Court. They note that this rule is not based on consistent reasoning. On the one hand, the Fourteenth Amendment can only be violated by a state, so the attorney general must have been deemed to have been acting on behalf of the state for there to have been a violation to remedy. On the other hand, the attorney general was deemed not to have been acting on behalf of the state because, if he had been, the Eleventh Amendment would not have permitted the federal court to retain jurisdiction over him.

In the years since *Ex parte Young* was decided, the Supreme Court has sought to maintain the protection of the Eleventh Amendment by restricting the applicability of the *Ex parte Young* decision. In *Edelman v. Jordan,* 415 U.S. 651 (1974), the Supreme Court ruled that the *Ex parte Young* rule could only be used to secure a state official's *future* compliance with the law; it could not be used to give relief for a state official's *past* actions. Then, in *Pennhurst State School & Hospital v. Halderman,* 465 U.S. 89 (1984), the Supreme Court ruled that the *Ex parte Young* rule only applies when a state official is accused of violating *federal* law. When a state official is accused of violating *state* law, the Eleventh Amendment prohibits the official from being sued in federal court. Finally, in *Seminole Tribe v. Florida,* 517 U.S. 44 (1996), the Supreme Court recognized that Congress may pass certain laws that provide for specific, limited remedies upon their violation. In such situations, the broader relief given under *Ex parte Young* is not available.

For more information: Brant, Joanne C. "The Ascent of Sovereign Immunity." *Iowa L. Rev.* 83 (1998): 767; Tribe, Lawrence H. *American Constitutional Law.* 2nd ed. Foundation Press, 1988.

—Amy M. Henson

ex post facto law

An ex post facto law is law that makes certain actions illegal after these acts have already been completed. This concept is significant because there is an ex post facto protection that is defined within the Constitution.

The protection can be understood to be that no legislative body may pass any retroactive laws at the state or the federal level. Legislative restrictions are delineated in the Constitution in Article I, Section 9 and Section 10 (federal government and the states respectively). The aforementioned provisions only apply to the criminal statutes in each state and nationally. Nonetheless, some civil laws can be deemed a violation of the due process clause of the Fourteenth Amendment to the Constitution. Further, the restrictions only apply to the legislative bodies but not to the judiciary. Therefore, the justices of the Supreme Court and local judges and or magistrates may make judicial rulings that can stand as ex post facto decisions that then may become laws.

Criminalizing a behavior retroactively is considered an unfair application of law. There are really three main areas within the law where this concept may be better elaborated. The first area where this ex post facto law could be problematic is if an act done by a citizen was innocent at the time of act completion and later was classified as a crime and anyone who had done the act was now guilty. This concept of making an act a crime is retributive, and this sort of law could serve political purposes. The removal of a person's freedom without consideration is not something that is allowed for in the Constitution and goes against the very base of our legal system. Another area where the ex post facto concept would be troublesome is when an act that is against the law and has a lesser penalty assigned to the crime is then retroactively assigned a higher penalty so that when the act was committed it originally had a different penalty value. This could extend a person's time incarcerated, might have altered the decision-making process of the jury, and creates an atmosphere where a person was not represented properly within the law. This also could be utilized for political purposes and/or group retaliation by the courts.

Therefore, unless a compelling reason exists for the court to provide for society, this retroactive penalty is not a valid idea. The final area where an ex post facto law may be difficult is in terms of any rules or law pertaining to evidence that alters what can be presented as evidence against someone, which, if it were allowed, would then make it easier to convict someone of a crime. This application of the law is also deemed an unfair practice, in the sense that changing the rules in order to convict someone speaks of conviction without proper equality.

There actually was a belief once that the idea of an ex post facto law included both criminal and civil statutes. The direction of the ex post facto restriction changed in the case of *CALDER V. BULL* (1798). The Supreme Court, when considering the ex post facto restriction, decided that the restriction should stand as a criminal-statute-only distinction and limited whether or not it could be utilized in a civil proceeding as a decision-making rationale.

A brief example may help in understanding the ideas expressed in regards to the ex post facto restrictions. For example, if a person commits an act that he thinks is innocent, say that a person named "A" likes to juggle sharp objects in a park. Now let us believe that two days later on a Monday, the Supreme Court stated in a unanimous decision that any use of sharp objects in the parks was prohibited. The decision by the court has a penalty assigned to it of up to six months in jail and a fine. In addition, based upon the need to protect persons who frequent the parks, the action is criminally retroactive for one month. This decision stands and thus, the juggler named "A" is liable for criminal behavior if he had juggled sharp objects in the last month in a park. This law could not stand if the Congress had passed the same law, because the Congress cannot make a criminally retroactive law. So, in regards to protecting society, the Supreme Court may look at many opinions, get many briefs arguing certain points, and then make a decision that impacts a few persons for the betterment of the entire society. This ability by one branch to not allow the other to have complete control is indicative of the checks and balances system that supports the Supreme Court. If we allowed congressional officials to make laws retroactively, then the power of the Supreme Court would be diminished and the rule of law would be less effective. The benefits to society are important factors for the Supreme Court to consider, and no decision by the high court is done lightly without measuring the overall impact upon society, but when the needs of our society are seen to be paramount to the needs of a few persons, then the decision in respect to criminal matters is more often than not made in favor of society.

In 2003 the Supreme Court overturned a decision in favor of a California ex post facto criminal law in the *Stogner v. California* case. The case involved some alleged actions by Mr. Stogner that were considered to be criminal and thus he was charged with a retroactive new law. The defense for Mr. Stogner argued that the law could not apply to his actions because it was criminalizing actions where the statute of limitations had expired. The Supreme Court majority (case decided 5 to 4) believed that statute was "unfairly retroactive as applied to Stogner" and they concluded "that a law enacted after expiration of a previously applicable limitations period violates the ex post facto clause when it is applied to revive a previously time-barred prosecution."

This determination of whether an ex post facto law is appropriate for society depends on who is attempting to be protected, and in essence, the Supreme Court must consider who is to be impacted with a decision, the overall public good, and many other issues. The overall public safety often carries with it a greater weight, but it must be balanced in terms of the individual rights of persons that are enumerated within the Constitution. Sometimes when laws are enacted and the public response is unknown and only estimated, therefore, when the Court considers multiple factors the decision is often more equitable for society as a whole but each decision must apply to actions in the present. The Court often tries to get it right the first time so there is less of a need for laws that reach backward. Either way that a law is established it must fit into the protections that the Constitution allows for society.

For more information: *Bankers Trust v. Blodgett*, 260 U.S. 647, 652 (1966); *CALDER V. BULL*, U.S. (3 Dall.) 386, 390 (1798); *U.S. v. Powers*, 307 U.S. 214 (1939).

—Ernest Alexander Gomez

F

Fairness Doctrine

Because of the perceived scarcity of the airwaves, the federal government sought to make sure that all opinions were broadcast, calling it the Fairness Doctrine. The early years of the radio air waves were indeed a time of scarcity. Everyone with a transmitter wished to have their signal on the air and heard in as many receivers as possible. Some regulation would be needed to stop what would otherwise be unintelligible gibberish coming out of the speaker. For this purpose, the Federal Communication Commission (FCC) was created by the 1934 Communications Act.

In attempting to better serve what was perceived as the "public interest," the FCC created what became known as the Fairness Doctrine, sometimes called the "equal time rule." This rule required that if an advocate of one public position or set of ideas was broadcast, the opposing view was to be given equal time. Supposedly this treatment was supposed to produce fair and balanced use of the broadcast spectrum.

This requirement was never a law passed by Congress and signed by a president or ruled upon by the courts. It was simply the policy of the FCC and enforced by the commission since broadcast licenses were not private property but were held as a mere license to be used for the "public convenience, interest or necessity." The "public convenience and necessity" rule had been a part of the law since the beginning of the FCC, but the Fairness Doctrine was not crafted until 1949.

The policy was changed only after technology improved to the point that the FCC's jurisdiction over cable television and broadcast licenses increased from 108 in 1948 to more than 2,000 a few years later. The constitutionality of the Fairness Doctrine was challenged in 1969 on First Amendment grounds. The Court upheld the rule in *RED LION BROADCASTING v. FCC*, 395 U.S. 367 (1969), but cautioned that if the policy should ever restrain free speech it would declare the policy unconstitutional.

For more information: Tribe, Laurence H. *American Constitutional Law.* Mineola, N.Y.: Foundation Press, 1988.

—Stanley M. Morris

Federal Communications Commission v. Pacifica Foundation, 438 U.S. 726 (1978)

In *Federal Communications Commission v. Pacifica Foundation,* the Supreme Court ruled in a 5-4 decision that of all forms of communication, broadcasting has the most limited First Amendment protection. At the heart of *FCC v. Pacifica* is a controversial 12-minute satirical monologue by George Carlin entitled "Seven Dirty Words You Can't Say on Television" (later renamed "Filthy Words"), which was first aired on Tuesday, October 30, 1973, around 2:00 in the afternoon by New York's WBIA radio station (owned by Pacifica Radio Foundation).

During an airing of "Filthy Words," a father was driving with his young son. Upon hearing the broadcast, he filed a complaint with the FCC. He noted that although he understood that Carlin's record was being sold for private use, he could not understand why Pacifica was broadcasting "Filthy Words" over the air. In turn, the FCC forwarded the complaint directly to the Pacifica Foundation for comment. According to Pacifica, the monologue had been played during a show about contemporary society's attitudes toward language; the station had noted that the broadcast would contain "sensitive language which might be regarded as offensive to some," and the station was not aware of any other complaints about the broadcast.

Having examined the evidence, the FCC issued a declaratory order granting the complaint on February 21, 1975. The commission noted that even though Pacifica could be subject to administrative sanctions (56 F.C.C. 2d 94, 99), formal sanctions would not be imposed. However, in the event of subsequent complaints, the commission would be forced to decide whether it would utilize any of the available sanctions authorized by Congress.

In addition to this ruling, in the memorandum opinion, the FCC noted its intent to clarify the standard employed to consider the escalating number of complaints concerning indecent radio broadcasts. The FCC also advanced several reasons for treating this type of speech so differently from other forms of expression. As explained by the FCC, the power to regulate indecent broadcasts comes directly from two statutes: statute 18 U.S.C. 1464 (1976 ed), which prohibits the use of "obscene, indecent, or profane language by means of radio communications"; and statute 47 U.S.C. 303 (g), which requires the commission to "encourage the larger and more effective use of radio in the public interest."

Upon examining the language of Carlin's monologue to this statutory backdrop, the FCC found that certain words did indeed depict sexual and excretory activities in a way partially offensive, and that these broadcasts were being aired in the early afternoon when children were undoubtedly in the audience. Consequently, because of the indecent language in Carlin's monologue, it would no longer be aired during the day but during a time of day when children would not be exposed.

The Pacifica Foundation appealed the FCC's ruling to the U.S. COURT OF APPEALS for the District of Columbia Circuit. In a 2-1 decision, the Court of Appeals reversed the commission's ruling. Though Judge Leventhal supported the FCC's ruling, Judge Tamm disagreed by noting that the commission had gone overboard with its ruling, and Judge Bazelon also concurred by noting that the application of censorship was inappropriate. The FCC appealed this decision to the United States Supreme Court.

The Supreme Court justices were charged with determining whether JUDICIAL REVIEW was appropriate; whether the FCC ruling was a form of censorship forbidden by statute 326; whether the broadcast was indecent as defined by statute 1464; and whether the ruling violated the First Amendment. In a 5-4 decision, the justices found that George Carlin's "Filthy Words" monologue was worthy of First Amendment protection because it was indecent rather than obscene.

Nevertheless, even though the print media could not be sanctioned for publishing Carlin's monologue, a broadcaster could be held responsible because of the radio's pervasive presence in terms of its ability to invade the privacy of a home and in being easily accessible to children. However, instead of banning Carlin's monologue, the Court chose to regulate the material by ruling that it could be broadcast at a time when children are expected to be asleep. This ruling further reinforced the standard that of all forms of communication, broadcasting has the most limited First Amendment protection because of its pervasive nature.

For more information: Federal Communications Commission. Available online. URL: http://www.fcc.gov/. Downloaded May 12, 2004; Legal Information Institute. Cornell Law School. Available online. URL: http://www.law.cornell.edu/. Downloaded May 12, 2004; Pacifica Radio Foundation. Available online. URL: http://www.pacifica.org/. Downloaded May 12, 2004.

—Mitzi Ramos

federal court system

The federal judiciary is a three-tiered system, consisting of 94 U.S. District Courts in the entry-level tier, 13 U.S. Courts of Appeals in the middle tier, and one U.S. Supreme Court, standing alone in the top tier.

The 94 U.S. District Courts are the federal judiciary's trial courts, or courts of general jurisdiction. Together, these courts hear and decide approximately 900,000 cases annually. Each U.S. District Court is located in one of the 94 judicial districts that are geographically distributed throughout the U.S. They are called entry-level courts because they are the federal courts in which lawsuits are initiated. The parties to a specific dispute both appear in District Court, and their attorneys explain the disagreement to the fact finder who decides which party's argument shall prevail and establishes an equitable remedy, usually a sum that the losing party must pay to the prevailing party, to end the dispute.

If one of the parties disagrees or is dissatisfied with the District Court's decision of his case, that party may APPEAL to one of the 13 U.S. Courts of Appeals. Twelve of these courts, which together contain all of the 94 judicial districts, are located in the 12 judicial circuits, which are distributed geographically throughout the United States, while the 13th appellate court, the U.S. COURT OF APPEALS for the Federal Circuit, has nationwide jurisdiction over specialized cases, such as patent, trademark, copyright, and international trade laws. Currently, there are 179 U.S. Court of Appeals judges, with each circuit employing at least the statutorily mandated minimum of three judges. An appeal from a decision in a District Court located within court circuits one through 12 must be filed in the Court of Appeals within the District Court's circuit. Together, the U.S. Courts of Appeals annually review a total of approximately 50,000 appeals from U.S. District Court decisions.

A trial in a U.S. Court of Appeals is not a reenactment of the parties' U.S. District Court trial. Whereas a District Court trial is usually heard by one judge, a Court of Appeals trial is usually conducted before a three-judge panel. Occasionally, in a highly important or controversial lawsuit, all of a circuit's judges hear the case. Also, in a U.S. Court of Appeals trial, the parties' District Court witnesses are not

Federal court system chart

recalled, and their evidence is not re-presented. The appellate court judges hear each party's argument. Usually, the appellant (U.S. Court of Appeals terminology for the party making the appeal; analogous to a trial court plaintiff) alleges that the lower court failed to properly apply the law to the facts of the case. The respondent (party who prevailed in District Court; analogous to a trial court defendant) usually responds with a claim that the law was properly applied.

If a party to a Court of Appeals case were dissatisfied with its decision, the next step would be an appeal to the highest-level court in the federal court system, the U.S. Supreme Court. While there are several differences between this court and the other federal courts, the most important difference is that a party who disagrees with the

U.S. Court of Appeals decision on his/her case does not have the *right* to have his case heard before the high court (U.S. Supreme Court).

Instead, each party who would like to present an appeal to the high court must provide the justices with a petition in a specific, statutorily mandated format, stating the reasons why the case and the Court of Appeals' decision therein deserves to be considered by the U.S. Supreme Court. From the thousands of correctly formatted petitions the high court receives each year, the nine justices have the power to choose the cases they will hear that year and reject the remainder. They generally choose between 150 and 200 cases, but this number may vary widely from year to year, because no particular number of cases is mandated by statute.

The following types of cases are among those that may be chosen by the high court: (1) cases that require resolution of an unprecedented issue of federal law or of constitutionality, when the Justices agree that a U.S. Supreme Court PRECEDENT would help prevent or resolve future lawsuits; or (2) a question of whether a state law violates a federal law or the U.S. Constitution.

As in the Courts of Appeals, a trial in the Supreme Court is not a replay of the District or Court of Appeals trial of the case. The high court is most interested in the validity and constitutionality of U.S. and state laws. Unlike the other courts, the Supreme Court may accept or may even request opinions and information from experts in matters similar to a case before them, or from other sources whose opinions and information may provide insight that will assist the high court in reaching a fair and equitable decision. Also, except in unusual circumstances, Supreme Court cases are heard by all of the nine justices. If at least five of them can agree on a decision, their opinions prevail in the case. However, unlike the lower courts, the opinions of any or all of the four justices who disagreed from the majority may be published, in addition to the majority's opinion.

The present-day federal court system resembles, but is not identical to, the judiciary established by the first Congress's passage of the JUDICIARY ACT OF 1789. This historic piece of legislation established the U.S. District Courts and U.S. Circuit Courts as trial courts, and the Supreme Court to hear any and all appeals from either of the lower courts and to serve as the "court of last resort," from which no appeal was possible.

The 1789 Act was cognizant of the fact that travel was very difficult as well as too costly for many individuals. To ensure that even an individual without the means to travel could have his day in court, the 1789 Act required that that each Supreme Court justice visits each Circuit Court twice annually. Soon after the passage of this act, it became clear that the country's climate and lack of roads made the travel itself problematic, particularly for the older justices. Later, while the increasing availability of railroad routes and improvements to public routes made travel less arduous, the increasing population and concomitant increase in the number of lawsuits initiated in District Court resulted in crowded court schedules.

The justices began to find that they could not hear and decide each case in a given circuit within the time constraints created by their two-visits-per-year schedule. "Riding the circuit" became an exercise in frustration, with an increasing backlog of cases in each circuit. Eventually, the 1789 law's mandate that the Supreme Court hear any and all appeals from lower court cases resulted in a workload that all of the justices agreed was unmanageable. Finally, Congress passed the Judiciary Act of 1891, also known as the Evarts Act, which aimed to reduce the justices' workload to a manageable level. The Evarts Act abolished the mandate that the justices "ride the circuit" and also sharply limited the categories of cases that the Supreme Court would hear on appeal. The effectiveness of the Evarts Act was demonstrated almost immediately after its enactment, since the number of new cases before the high court dropped from 275 in 1890 to 123 in 1892.

Although the U.S. court system was not created until the passage of the Judiciary Act of 1789, the colonies all had court systems in place prior to the American Revolution. The colonial courts later became the state courts that are still functional today. The federal courts were never intended to supplant these systems, but rather to provide the appropriate forum for cases that could not be decided under state law. Currently, most states' court systems are three-tiered, hence very similar in structure to the federal system.

The function of each level in the state systems is also analogous to the comparable function in the U.S. courts, with one major exception: while decisions of the U.S. Supreme Court cannot be appealed, decisions of the top state courts can, in some instances, be appealed to the U.S. Supreme Court. If a case before the highest state court requires interpretation of state law, the highest state court is considered to be the ultimate authority, and this case *cannot* be appealed to the Supreme Court. However, if a state law is involved in a decision of a state's highest court, and a party questions whether the state law violated a federal law or the U.S. Constitution, the case may be accepted on appeal to the U.S. Supreme Court. There is no similar, further opportunity for appeal after the U.S. Supreme Court has rendered a decision.

From a 21st-century perspective, it is abundantly clear that corruption within the federal courts, which have the power to strike down laws, uphold baseless convictions, interfere with the operation of the legislative and executive branches of government, and inflict innumerable other inequities on the American public, could be tragic. Fortunately, the U.S. Constitution contains two provisions that have been quite effective in keeping the federal judiciary fair and honest. First, all federal judges are appointed for life, and they can be removed from office only through impeachment that results in congressional conviction for treason, bribery, or other heinous act.

Second, Congress cannot reduce judges' compensation for as long as they serve on any federal court. Clearly, these provisions were originally intended to prevent elected officials who are susceptible to political pressure, such as the president and Congress, from exerting that type of pressure on a federal judge by reducing his/her salary to less than a living wage, or by altogether eliminating his/her salary.

Since population and lifestyle continue to evolve and change in the United States, the federal court system will never be perfectly equipped to handle every possible legal situation. However, as long as it continues to be as effective as it has been for the last 200+ years, the federal court system will remain the most equitable judiciary on Earth. Instead of classifying it as "somewhat out-of-date," it would be more accurate to classify the federal court system as a perpetual "work-in-progress."

For more information: Apex Learning. "Foundations of American Government" and "Structure of the Federal Courts." Beyond Books (2003). Available online. URL: http://www.beyondbooks.com/gov91/9b.asp. Downloaded May 12, 2004; Minnesota Legislative Reference Library. "U.S. Supreme Court—A Brief History." Minnesota Legislative Reference Library (2000). Available online. URL: http://www.leg.state.mn.us/lrl/links/legal.asp. Downloaded May 12, 2004.

—Beth S. Swartz

Federal Election Commission v. Colorado Republican Federal Campaign Committee, 533 U.S. 431 (2001)

In this case, the Supreme Court ruled that "coordinated" campaign expenditures made by political parties could be subject to close restrictions under the Federal Election Campaign Act (FECA). In an earlier case (*Colorado I*), the Court had distinguished coordinated and independent expenditures made by political parties. It ruled that the latter posed no threat of corruption and therefore could not be subject to strict regulations. In this case, however, the Court ruled that coordinated expenditures did necessitate close regulation and control.

The Republican Party of Colorado challenged the constitutionality of the limitations placed on "coordinated expenditures" by the Federal Election Campaign Act. In *Colorado I*, the court had ruled that independent expenditures by political parties were tantamount to protected POLITICAL SPEECH. While the court acknowledged that all speech is subject to reasonable regulations, Congress could not justify restricting political speech in the form of independent expenditures. The court reasoned that since independent expenditures were not coordinated with any particular candidate's campaign, they presented no real threat of corruption of elected officials. In *Colorado I*, the court had contrasted coordinated and independent expenditures. Insofar as coordinated spending served essentially the same purpose as a contribution to a particular candidate, the court ruled that coordinated spending could be restricted to prevent parties from using such expenditures to get around the FECA limitations on actual contributions.

In *Colorado II*, the Republican Party returned to challenge this distinction, arguing that coordinated expendi-

tures were as much a part of a political party's expressive role as independent expenditures. Accordingly, the Republican Party argued that restrictions on coordinated expenditures imposed by the FECA ought to be declared unconstitutional.

As the court noted, FECA defines a "contribution" broadly—both in formal as well as functional terms. The definition includes "expenditures made by any person in cooperation, consultation, to concert with, or at the request or suggestion of, a candidate, his authorized political committees or their agents." The question in this case was whether a party's coordinated election expenditures on behalf of one of its candidates should be treated (and therefore subject to the same restrictions and limitations) as coordinated expenditures made by PACs.

The Court wrestled with two key issues. First, the expressive aspect of coordinated expenditures notwithstanding, the Court had to decide whether the appearance or threat of corruption posed by such expenditures was sufficiently palpable to justify congressional regulation. Second, the Court had to decide whether coordinated expenditures by political parties were any different from similar expenditures made by PACs or other players in the electoral process.

In *Buckley v. Valeo* (1976), the Court had acknowledged that coordinated expenditures could be equated to outright contributions to candidates. Therefore, it sustained Congress's regulation of such expenditures because it acknowledged that unlimited coordinated expenditures could be used to circumvent the FECA "through prearranged or coordinated expenditures amounting to disguised contributions" (424 U.S. 1, 47).

In *Colorado II*, the Court ruled that coordinated expenditures by a political party could be subjected to the same restrictions imposed on other groups for two reasons. First, such expenditures by a political party could have the same corrupting impact as expenditures by any other political group. Second, the Court noted that if parties were free to make unlimited coordinated expenditures, they would essentially become conduits through which PACs and other groups could funnel campaign contributions to particular candidates. In so doing parties would become the corrupting link that the FECA sought to break between candidates and political groups:

> Coordinated spending by a party should be limited not only because it is like a party contribution, but for a further reason. A party's right to make unlimited expenditures coordinated with a candidate would induce individual and other nonparty contributors to give to the party in order to finance coordinated spending for a favored candidate beyond the contribution limits binding on them. . . . Individuals and nonparty groups who

have reached the limit of direct contributions to a candidate give to a party with the understanding that the contribution to the party will produce increased party spending for the candidate's benefit. The Government argues that if coordinated spending were unlimited, circumvention would increase: because coordinated spending is as effective as direct contributions in supporting a candidate, an increased opportunity for coordinated spending would aggravate the use of a party to funnel money to a candidate from individuals and nonparty groups, who would thus bypass the contribution limits that *Buckley* upheld (533 U.S. 431, 446).

Perhaps the most remarkable aspect of *Colorado Republican II* was the Supreme Court's dismissal of the role of the political party. In *Colorado I,* the Court had urged that independent spending was indeed part of a political party's speech and a means by which a party could convey its message.

In *Colorado II,* the same Court dismissed the party as merely a conduit through which other interested actors funnel campaign funds in order to influence candidates:

whether they like it or not, [parties] act as agents for spending on behalf of those who seek to produce obligated officeholders. It is this party role, which functionally unites parties with other self-interested political actors, that the Party Expenditure Provision targets. This party role, accordingly, provides good reason to view limits on coordinated spending by parties through the same lens applied to such spending by donors, like PACs, that can use parties as conduits for contributions meant to place candidates under obligation (533 U.S. 452).

Thus, as Justice THOMAS noted in dissent, the court drew two conclusions: "coordinated expenditures [by political parties] are no different from contributions, and political parties are no different from individuals and political committees" (467). Adhering to this vision, the Court renders parties unable to claim that they have a special relationship with their nominees. Accordingly, the court's vision of the party-candidate relationship suggests that a nominee can somehow be corrupted by the party organization whose nomination he or she seeks. While this may seem counterintuitive, to the extent that this vision does animate the Court's jurisprudence it allows the Court to regard contributions and coordinated expenditures by political parties in the same corrupting light that it regards similar financial contributions by other interest groups.

Thus, *Colorado II* allows Congress to drive a wedge between party organizations and their nominees. While this is justified on the basis of preventing the appearance of corruption, it raises important questions concerning the relationship between candidates and the party organizations whose support they seek.

Colorado I and *II* left campaign finance law in an odd state. Independent expenditures by political parties were not subject to the same limitations imposed on their coordinated expenditures. This difference of treatment could be regarded as sensible to the extent that one could argue that a coordinated expenditure could serve the same purpose of a bribe whereas an independent expenditure did not. However, from a practical standpoint, independent expenditures can be used to influence a candidate in virtually the same way that coordinated expenditures can. The only real difference is that coordinated expenditures may have the appearance, potentially, of involving quid pro quo influence, whereas the impact of independent expenditures would seem more attenuated.

For more information: Hasen, Richard L. *The Supreme Court and Election Law.* New York: New York University Press, 2003.

—Mark Rush

Federal Election Commission v. Massachusetts Citizens for Life, Inc., 479 U.S. 238 (1986)

In *Federal Election Commission v. Massachusetts Citizens for Life, Inc.,* the Court held that laws which prohibit corporations from making expenditures to influence elections cannot be constitutionally applied to a class of ideological nonprofit corporations.

Massachusetts Citizens for Life (MCFL) is a grassroots nonprofit advocacy corporation that opposes abortion and euthanasia. The Federal Election Campaign Act forbids "expenditures" by corporations "for the purpose of influencing any election for federal office" [2 U.S.C. § 441b]. *Buckley v. Valeo,* 424 U.S. 1 (1976), previously limited that provision to "express advocacy," meaning advocacy that urged votes for or against specific candidates with language such as "vote for," "elect," "Smith for Congress," or similar terms. The Federal Election Commission claimed that MCFL had violated the Federal Election Campaign Act by distributing tens of thousands of copies of a newsletter that urged voters to "Vote Pro-Life" and listed whether candidates had taken the "pro-life" position on three issues. MCFL argued that the newsletter was not express advocacy, that it fell within a statutory exemption for news media, and that the ban on corporate expenditures on express advocacy could not be constitutionally applied to nonprofit advocacy groups. The Supreme Court unanimously rejected the first two contentions but agreed with the third by a 5-4 vote.

Justice BRENNAN wrote the principal opinion, which was the opinion of the Court except for one section where he wrote for a plurality of four. After dealing with the statutory issues, Justice Brennan turned to the constitutional issues. His opinion, in a section joined by Justices MARSHALL, POWELL, and SCALIA, described the requirements placed on corporations that wish to make political expenditures in federal elections: they must limit their spending to money from a "separate segregated fund," often described as a political action committee ("PAC"). A nonprofit corporation's PAC can only accept contributions from members of the nonprofit and must comply with substantial disclosure requirements. Contributions to PACs are also limited in size. The Court concluded that the PAC requirement burdened MCFL's ability to speak. The plurality emphasized the risk that small organizations with limited resources would choose to not engage in POLITICAL SPEECH rather than comply with the requirements imposed on PACs. Justice O'CONNOR's concurrence, which provided the fifth vote for the Court's decision, relied instead on the additional requirements of organizational structures and the limitation to soliciting contributions from members.

Having concluded that the law burdened MCFL's speech, the Court turned to the question of whether a COMPELLING STATE INTEREST justified the restriction. The majority acknowledged the long-standing regulation of corporate political activity, citing concerns about the "corrosive influence of concentrated corporate wealth." [*MCFL,* 479 U.S. at 257.] Justice Brennan reasoned that the resources of a corporation do not depend on the support for its political positions in the same way that the resources of an advocacy organization or a political campaign do, and that corporations should not be able to leverage commercial success into political power. However, he reasoned that groups like MCFL do not represent a similar sort of danger, because its resources were not based on its success in the marketplace. Because all contributions to MCFL are based on support for its viewpoints, Justice Brennan concluded that it ought to be able to engage in speech as if it were an unincorporated association, while complying with only the disclosure limitations that apply to unincorporated associations.

The majority stressed three features of MCFL that were "essential to [the] holding"—*MCFL,* 479 U.S. at 263–264. MCFL "was formed for the express purpose of promoting political ideas, and cannot engage in business activities." Second, it has no shareholders or others who have an economic incentive to associate with it even if they disagree with its political positions. Finally, MCFL was not established by a business corporation or labor union and has a policy against accepting corporate or union contributions, thus foreclosing any danger of its use as a conduit for corporations or unions to circumvent the restrictions on political expenditures. Chief Justice REHNQUIST wrote a dissent, joined by Justices WHITE, BLACKMUN, and STEVENS, in which he argued that the Court should have deferred to Congress's judgment about the need to regulate corporate political activity.

Lower courts have taken divergent views on the scope of *MCFL.* Several of the federal courts of appeals have applied *MCFL* to organizations that accept small amounts of corporate or union money. The Supreme Court has not yet ruled on whether those rulings were correct, although it has implied in several subsequent decisions that the "essential" features of *MCFL* should be interpreted literally. In *FEC v. Beaumont,* 539 U.S. 146 (2003), the Court rejected an interpretation that would have allowed *MCFL* organizations to make contributions to candidate's campaigns as well as independent expenditures.

For more information: Winkler, Adam. "Beyond Bellotti." *Loy. L.A. L. Rev.* 32 (November 1998): 133.
—Adam H. Morse

federalism

A constitutional system of government that separates power between the national and subnational (typically referred to as states, provinces, or republics) levels of government. Both levels have their own respective institutions, actors, and procedures to govern the citizenry. Both levels also reign within their individual spheres of power, but a change to the constitution must include the backing and consensus of both to be considered legitimate.

Federal systems are markedly different than either unitary systems, where constitutional authority is vested in the national government and subnational and local governments derive their authority from the national government, or confederations where subnational governments hold constitutional authority and the national government is thus the more passive of the two levels. Examples of states that have adopted the federal model include Australia, Brazil, Canada, Germany, India, Mexico, Pakistan, Switzerland, the United States, and Venezuela. This is in contrast to Great Britain and France, for example, which have unitary systems, and the European Union (EU), which is a confederation.

In the United States, the Articles of Confederation (1781–1789) preceded the federal system of government. However, financial struggles, currency problems, and civil disorder were but a few of the numerous obstacles plaguing the Articles. Debate at the Constitutional Convention of 1787 deliberated the shortcomings of the fragmented and highly decentralized confederation but also expressed apprehension for adopting the type of centralized authority exhibited by the British monarchy. The founding fathers consequently advocated a federal system, with a strong and independent national government that was balanced by separated institutions and checks and balances among the executive, legislative, and judicial branches. While the word *federal* does not appear in the body of the U.S. Constitution, the Tenth Amendment provides the foundation for American federalism. It vests constitutional power in the national government, with all other powers not specifically mentioned or prohibited by the Constitution being reserved for the states or the people. This is reinforced by the NECESSARY AND PROPER CLAUSE found in Article I, Section 8 of the Constitution, which gives Congress the power "to make all laws which shall be necessary and proper for carrying into execution" its delegated powers, and the national supremacy clause, found in Article VI of the Constitution, which declares the constitution and laws of the national government "the supreme law of the land."

Political scientists have traced the evolution of the American federal system through several phases. The initial phase immediately following the ratification of the Constitution was one characterized as *dual federalism*. During this period, from 1787 until approximately 1932, there was a functional separation between the powers of the national government and the states. The national government mostly contained itself to enumerated powers specifically mentioned in the Constitution (i.e., national defense, tariffs, foreign affairs, etc.) while states focused on policy realms and the reserved powers inherent to their particular spheres of attention (i.e., education, criminal justice, etc.). The Anti-Federalists challenged the authority of the national government early in this phase. However, the Supreme Court, under Chief Justice John MARSHALL (1801–35), upheld the power of the national government in *MCCULLOCH V. MARYLAND* (1819) and *GIBBONS V. OGDEN* (1824). The Civil War likewise jeopardized the vitality of the union, but states managed to maintain their stature after the consolidation of the North and South, and during the Reconstruction Era with the Thirteenth, Fourteenth, and Fifteenth Amendments to the Constitution. After two world wars, and a Great Depression that persisted into the 1930s, dual federalism evolved into what has been termed *cooperative federalism*. During this phase from 1933 through 1963, states welcomed assistance from the federal government through President Franklin D. Roosevelt's New Deal program and various public works projects. Grants and outlays in funding from the national government to the states provided relief from high unemployment rates and a depressed economy.

Political scientists further characterize this evolution as a transformation from layered cake to marble cake federalism, where the functions of the national government and state governments changed from neat layers to a merging of policy responsibilities. State and local governments competed for grants-in-aid for service and infrastructure projects as the post-World War II baby boom era created greater demand for government spending. Cooperative federalism evolved into *centralized federalism* (sometimes also referred to as *creative federalism*) from 1964 until 1979. President Lyndon B. Johnson's Great Society established the federal government as the safeguard of underprivileged Americans in a program designed to stamp out poverty. New grant-in-aid programs, based on eligibility requirements, formulae, and commitments by state and local governments to match federal funds, created a "carrot and stick" environment of competition. The subsequent phase of NEW FEDERALISM, which began in 1980, expanded what was referred to as the "devolution revolution." The Nixon administration first instigated the trend to return responsibilities to the states during the early 1970s by utilizing large block grants and revenue sharing. President Ronald Reagan and his ideologically conservative supporters later advocated a reduction in social programs.

Reagan decreased the amount of federal aid to state and local governments and convinced Congress to consolidate several categorical grants into block grants with fewer use restrictions. This "Reagan Revolution" was the most discernible return of power back to the states since the pre-New Deal era, but it was not without controversy. The number of unfunded mandates, federal directives (i.e., environmental standards) that require the compliance of state and local governments but offer no moneys to assist, dramatically increased. This burdened budgets and forced states and localities to reconsider their spending practices in light of the added costs, most of which were not offset by higher revenues.

The Clinton administration's new federalism of the 1990s maintained the trend toward devolving power to the states, but the national government served as a guide and proponent to help states find solutions to their problems. The decision rendered by the Supreme Court in *U.S. v. Lopez*, 514 U.S. 549 (1995), is a recent example that indicates the Court's willingness to place limitations on the powers of Congress, and thus the national government.

The 20th century of American federalism, in particular, was indicative of a complex system of intergovernmental relations. Contemporary governance is fragmented across the nation with one national government, 50 state governments, and more than 87,000 local governments consisting of counties, municipalities, townships, school districts, or special districts. This arrangement has dispersed political power, increased opportunities for participation, and improved efficiency by assigning specific governmental activities to various levels (i.e., the national government controls defense policy, state governments regulate commerce within their boundaries, and local governments maintain police and fire services). But critics argue that it has also resulted in a lack of accountability, muddled policy making, and inconsistent governance across the nation. The division of power between levels of government was a fundamental principle of the Constitution and will continue to evolve in future eras.

For more information: Dye, Thomas R. *American Federalism: Competition Among Governments.* Lexington, Mass.: Lexington Books, 1990; Elazar, Daniel. *American Federalism: A View From the States.* New York: Harper and Row, 1984; Peterson, Paul E. *The Price of Federalism.* Washington, D.C.: Brookings Institution, 1995; Riker, William H. *Federalism: Origin, Operations, Significance.* Boston: Little, Brown, 1964; Wright, Deil S. *Understanding Intergovernmental Relations.* Pacific Grove, Calif.: Brooks/Cole Publishing Company, 1988.

—Daniel Baracskay

Ferguson v. Skrupa, 372 U.S. 726 (1963)

In *Ferguson v. Skrupa*, the Court unanimously upheld Kansas's statute making it a misdemeanor to operate a business of debt adjustment except as part of the lawful practice of law. This case is significant for its deference to legislatures concerning economic policy and for the majority opinion's definitive rejection of SUBSTANTIVE DUE PROCESS. Frank Skrupa, doing business as "Credit Advisors," challenged the Kansas law as a violation of the due process clause of the Fourteenth Amendment. Skrupa claimed that his business was "useful and desirable," and not "inherently immoral or dangerous." The state could regulate the practice of this profession, but it violated his rights by absolutely banning nonlawyers from engaging in it. Although several other states had similar laws, Kansas courts agreed with Skrupa.

The Supreme Court reversed. In a brief opinion written by Justice BLACK, the Court emphasized its deference to the legislature in economic matters. Citing *LOCHNER V. NEW YORK,* 198 U.S. 45 (1905), and *ADKINS V. CHILDREN'S HOSPITAL* 264 U.S. 525 (1923), among other cases, Black emphasizes that substantive due process has been "discarded." Rather, "we have returned to the original constitutional proposition that courts do not substitute their social and economic beliefs for the judgments of legislative bodies, who are elected to pass laws."

Drawing from Justice Oliver Wendell HOLMES's dissent in *Lochner,* Black cites the "vague contours" of due process to determine that the state legislature "was free to decide for itself that legislation was needed to deal with the business of debt adjusting." "Whether the legislature takes for its textbook Adam Smith, Herbert Spencer, Lord Keynes, or some other is no concern of ours," Black writes. To draw constitutional lines between "prohibitory" and "regulatory" economic legislation would return to the days of *Lochner* and make the Supreme Court a "superlegislature." "The Kansas debt adjusting statute may be wise or unwise," he writes. "But relief, if any be needed, lies not

with us but with the body constituted to pass laws for the State of Kansas." Black rejected Skrupa's equal protection challenge by stating that the law did not constitute "invidious discrimination," citing *Williamson v. Lee Optical,* 348 U.S. 483 (1955). Clients of debt adjusters may need legal advice concerning BANKRUPTCY proceedings, "advice which a nonlawyer may not legally give him." Thus "if the State of Kansas wants to limit debt adjusting to lawyers," Black concludes, "the EQUAL PROTECTION CLAUSE does not forbid it."

Justice HARLAN did not join Black's opinion for the Court. He issued a one-sentence opinion concurring in the judgment "on the ground that this state measure bears a rational relation to a constitutionally permissible objective." He also cited *Williamson.* Harlan's short opinion in *Ferguson* reflected his disagreement with the majority's wholesale rejection of substantive due process—an objection he had expressed in *POE V. ULLMAN,* 367 U.S. 497, 522 (1961), at 539-545, and would later reiterate in his separate concurring opinion in *GRISWOLD V. CONNECTICUT,* 318 U.S. 479 (1965), at 499. *Ferguson v. Skrupa* epitomizes the Court's deference in areas of economic policy after 1937. This case was considered to be the "death knell" for substantive due process generally until its revival two years later in *Griswold.* Black would reject this revival and the resulting RIGHT TO PRIVACY, citing *Ferguson;* Justice STEWART would only later come to accept it.

For more information: Hetherington, John. "State Economic Regulation and Substantive Due Process of Law." *Northwestern University Law Review* 58 (1958): 13, 226; Macedo, Stephen. *The New Right v. The Constitution.* Washington, D.C.: The Cato Institute, 1987.

—Frank J. Colucci

fighting words

"Fighting words" is the term given by the United States Supreme Court to a type of speech that is not protected by the free speech clause of the First Amendment to the U.S. Constitution: personal insults or other statements by a speaker directed at a listener that are likely to cause that listener to react violently against the speaker. This issue first arose before the Supreme Court in the case of *Chaplinsky v. New Hampshire,* 315 U.S. 568 (1942).

In *Chaplinsky,* a man named Chaplinsky who was on a public street in New Hampshire called a police officer "a God-damned racketeer" and "a damned fascist." Chaplinsky was arrested and convicted for violating a New Hampshire law that prohibited the use of "any offensive, derisive or annoying word to any other person who is lawfully in the street." He appealed his conviction to the U.S. Supreme Court.

The Supreme Court said there are certain types of speech which were never intended to be protected as free speech. One of these types of speech are "fighting words," which the Court defined as "words which by their very utterance inflict injury or tend to incite an immediate breach of the peace" or as the Court also phrased it, "such words, as ordinary men know, are likely to cause a fight." Stated simply, they are words (typically insults) likely to provoke a person to fight. The Court explained that this type of speech is not protected as free speech because the public interest in maintaining public safety and order far outweighs any slight value such words might have in communicating ideas.

The Court also went on to explain that to determine whether words are "fighting words," one must determine if "men of common intelligence" would understand that the words would be likely to cause the "average" person to fight. Thus, a person could not be punished for giving only a relatively mild insult to a person with a high degree of emotional sensitivity who then responds violently, because most people would agree that a mild insult would not cause the "average" person to react violently.

The Supreme Court in a later case, COHEN v. California, 403 U.S. 15 (1971), clarified that to be considered "fighting words," the words must be directed at a particular person or group. Therefore, words simply shouted out in public or worn on clothing, even if considered vulgar and generally offensive, would not be "fighting words" unless they were directed at a particular person.

The Supreme Court also later explained, in the case of TEXAS v. JOHNSON, 491 U.S. 397 (1989), that even conduct considered highly offensive in general, such as burning the U.S. flag in public, is not a fighting word unless it is meant as "a direct personal insult" toward a particular person watching.

Although the "fighting words" doctrine remains valid law today, the Supreme Court has never upheld another conviction for fighting words in any case to come before it. In addition, the doctrine has been heavily criticized by scholars, lawyers and judges, among other reasons for offering justification or even encouragement of violent behavior. Critics argue that the rule is obsolete and is a leftover legal relic from an earlier time when social norms required that men fight to defend their "honor" if insulted. A better alternative, critics suggest, is to expect people to learn to peacefully ignore hurtful words, rather than have the law declare that they are expected to react violently. Nevertheless, despite doubts about the continued survival of the doctrine, many lower courts continue to uphold the doctrine. In practice, a large percentage of modern convictions occur as a result of people being stopped, questioned, or held in custody by police officers, who after being insulted by the persons with whom they are dealing, then charge the person

with violating whatever local law prohibits speech that could be considered "fighting words."

For more information: Volokh, Eugene. *The First Amendment: Problems, Cases and Policy Arguments.* New York: Foundation Press, 2001.

—Rick Swanson

First English Lutheran Church v. County of Los Angeles, 482 U.S. 304 (1987)

In *First English Lutheran Church v. County of Los Angeles,* the Supreme Court held that a landowner can be compensated for a temporary regulatory taking of property under the just compensation clause of the Fifth Amendment. In 1957 the First English Lutheran Church purchased 21 acres of land located in a canyon along the banks of a creek that is the natural drainage channel for a watershed area. On that land the church built Lutherglen, a retreat center and recreational area for handicapped children. In 1977 a fire destroyed 3,860 acres of land in the watershed, creating a serious flood hazard where the property was located. Soon thereafter, in February 1978, a large storm came and the runoff from the rains flooded the church's land and destroyed all of Lutherglen's buildings. In reaction to this natural disaster, the County of Los Angeles adopted an ordinance prohibiting the construction or reconstruction of any buildings or structures within the designated flood-protection area. Lutherglen was included in this designated area.

A month later, the First English Lutheran Church filed suit in a California court claiming that the ordinance denied them all use of Lutherglen. They sought to recover damages in inverse condemnation for the loss of use of their property. Inverse condemnation occurs when the government has taken private property through regulation rather than through condemnation, and thus the state should pay the property owner.

The Fifth and Fourteenth Amendments had the most relevance to this case. The Fifth Amendment says private property shall not be taken for public use without just compensation. The Fourteenth Amendment says a LAND USE regulation must advance a legitimate state interest, and the state must show that a less restrictive regulatory alternative is not available, thus making the Fifth Amendment applicable to states.

In a 6-3 decision, Chief Justice REHNQUIST delivered the opinion of the Court with Justices BRENNAN, WHITE, MARSHALL, POWELL, and SCALIA. Rehnquist argued that landowners are able to receive compensation for "temporary" regulatory taking. Even though the land was not put to "public use," the church was unable to use its land because of the government regulation. The Court cites many cases in which the government temporarily took property for use during World War II with no question that monetary compensation would be required for such use. In *San Diego Gas & Electric Co. v. San Diego*, 450 U.S. 657 (1986), Justice Brennan writes, "Nothing in the Just Compensation Clause suggests that 'takings' must be permanent and irrevocable." It held that "where the government's activities have already worked a taking of all use of property, no subsequent action by the government can relieve it of the duty to provide compensation for the period during which a taking was effective." Temporary takings that deny property owners all use of their property are not different in kind from permanent takings.

Justices STEVENS, BLACKMUN, and O'CONNOR dissented and argued that the type of regulatory program in this case cannot be considered a taking under the U.S. Constitution. In the case of regulations being created to protect health and safety, the government entity need not provide compensation. The majority opinion distorts PRECEDENT in regards to regulatory takings when it makes no distinction between permanent and temporary regulatory takings. Justice Stevens believed "a regulatory program that adversely affects property values does not constitute a taking unless it destroys a major portion of the property's value. The church should have exhausted state remedies to invalidate the ordinance in question before bringing the issue to the Supreme Court." Finally, the Court is incorrect in concluding that it is the TAKINGS CLAUSE and not the due process clause, which is the primary constraint on the use of unfair or improper government decision-making.

The dissenters feared that the Court's ruling would result in a litigation explosion, and that land planners and local officials would hesitate to take action on important issues for fear of being held liable for damage actions. This could be most detrimental if necessary regulations were not made when issues of health and safety arose.

For more information: Walston, Roderick E. "The Constitution and Property: Due Process, Regulatory Takings, and Judicial Takings." *Utah Law Review* 379 (2001).

—Jason Walker
—Martin Dupuis

first Monday in October

Federal law (28 U.S.C.§ 2) sets the opening of the U.S. Supreme Court term on the first Monday in October. This was not always the case. Prior to 1917, the start date of the Court's sessions changed a number of times. When the Court met for the first time in 1790, it was in February and a second session was convened in August. In 1873 Congress set the meeting day as the second Monday in October and

then moved it to the first Monday in 1917 as the Court's DOCKET grew. Although the start date has not changed for many years, Congress retains the power by law to select a different start for the Court's session.

The significance of the first Monday has undergone two procedural changes in recent decades. Until 1975, when the first Monday in October arrived, the Court did not convene in public session; rather, that was the date on which the justices began closed-door deliberations to review hundreds of petitions that had accumulated during the summer to decide which ones deserved ORAL ARGUMENT and decision and which ones should simply be denied. But in October 1975, the Court changed its practice and met for the closed-door conference during the week prior to the first Monday. The first Monday in October then became the first day on the bench for oral arguments for the nine justices.

In another procedural change, the Court now technically remains in session during its summer recess that usually spans July, August, and September. Prior to 1979, the Court formally adjourned in late June or early July and ended that term of Court. Any emergency business that required the full Court's attention during adjournment required that a special session be convened. Now the Court holds a yearlong session, which does not end until the day before the first Monday in October.

The opening of the Court term has been memorialized in popular culture through a play and a movie, both entitled *First Monday in October*. The play about the Court, written by playwrights Jerome Lawrence and Robert E. Lee, was performed on Broadway in 1978, starring Henry Fonda and Jane Alexander. The movie, adapted from the play and directed by Ronald Neame, premiered in 1981 and starred Walter Matthau and Jill Clayburgh. The plot featured the arrival of the first woman justice on the Court, an idea that was fictional when the movie opened but that soon became reality when Justice Sandra Day O'CONNOR was appointed to the Court by President Ronald Reagan later the same year.

For more information: Witt, Elder, ed. *The Supreme Court A to Z: A Ready Reference Encyclopedia*. Washington, D.C.: CQ Press, 1994.

—Stephen Wermiel

flag burning

Flag burning was an emotional and politically charged debate in the late 1980s and early 1990s. Two Supreme Court decisions forced lawmakers to vote on a constitutional amendment to prohibit flag burning. The amendment, narrowly defeated, would have been the first successful effort to amend the First Amendment.

The first important case was TEXAS V. JOHNSON, the controversial Supreme Court decision that overturned the conviction of an outspoken political activist and self-styled communist who had burned an American flag as a part of a protest at the 1984 Republican Convention.

The case began at the 1984 Republican National Convention in Dallas, Texas. Gregory Lee Johnson and a number of other protesters staged a series of demonstrations and "die-ins" to protest the Reagan administration's policies on nuclear arms and Central America. During one demonstration a fellow protester handed Johnson a flag that had been taken from in front of a local bank. Johnson doused the flag with lighter fluid and set it on fire. Johnson and 18 other demonstrators were arrested and Johnson was charged under a Texas statute for desecration of a venerated object. He was found guilty and sentenced to one-year imprisonment and a $2,000 fine.

The Texas Court of Criminal Appeals reversed Johnson's conviction by a five to four decision. The Supreme Court agreed to hear the case and oral arguments were set for March 21, 1989. Noted litigator William Kunstler represented Johnson before the Court. On June 21, 1989, the Supreme Court handed down a five to four decision that upheld the Texas court's reversal of Johnson's conviction.

In Justice Brennen's majority opinion he stressed that Johnson's act was clearly one of POLITICAL SPEECH and that no evidence of a breach of peace was present. He stated, "We are tempted to say, in fact, that the flag's deservedly cherished place in our community will be strengthened, not weakened, by our holding today." Justices MARSHALL, BLACKMUN, SCALIA, and KENNEDY, who wrote a concurring opinion, joined Brennen.

Chief Justice REHNQUIST, joined by Justices Byron WHITE and Sandra Day O'CONNOR filed a long and emotional dissent in which he recited flag history and quoted extensively from poems praising the flag. Justice STEVENS also dissented, arguing that Texas had not prosecuted Johnson for the content of his message, only his means.

Public and political reaction to the decision was vitriolic and emotional. Nine days after the decision was released President George Bush made a speech in front of the Iwo Jima Memorial endorsing a constitutional amendment to outlaw flag desecration. Many members of Congress also supported the amendment. Supporters of the flag amendment said that the flag was a symbol of national unity and allowing its desecration dishonored veterans. Opponents of the flag amendment supported freedom of speech and argued that an amendment would lead to a weakened Constitution.

The Congress ended the original debate by passing the Flag Protection Act of 1989. In June of 1990 the Supreme Court in the case UNITED STATES V. EICHMAN declared the federal law unconstitutional. The vote was five to four along exactly the same lines as the previous case.

On June 26, 1990, the U.S. Senate defeated a constitutional amendment that would have overturned the two decisions and outlawed flag burning. The vote was hotly debated, and many political commentators believed that voting against the amendment would lead to political attacks by opposition candidates. Other commentators believed that President George Bush would use the issue to polarize voters in his reelection campaign.

After the initial vote the flag burning issue dropped from the nation's political radar, and it played no role in subsequent elections. The case remains an important one for SYMBOLIC SPEECH and served as a catalyst for a national debate on the meaning of the First Amendment.

For more information: Goldstein, Robert. *Flag Burning and Free Speech.* Lawrence: University Press of Kansas, 2000; Howard, Charles. "A Lonely Place of Honor: A Rhetorical Analysis of the Movement to Amend the Constitution to Prevent Flag Burning." Ph.D. dissertation, University of Kansas, 1992.

—Charles C. Howard

flag salute

America's most common form of paying respect to a national emblem or symbol, the flag salute, started as part of a nationwide public school observance in 1892 honoring the 400th anniversary of Columbus's discovery of America. Immediately it became popular and was widely used in schools in every state. By 1935, 24 states had statutes requiring instruction in flag respect; nine specifically required that the flag-salute ceremony be conducted regularly in all public schools. None explicitly demanded pupils participate in the ceremony as it was, at the time, inconceivable that anyone might refuse.

As early as 1918, Mennonites, among others, refused the salute and pledge and, for the most part, school officials chose to grant exemptions. This indulgence continued until the Jehovah's Witnesses objected in the 1930s and 1940s.

The Witnesses were decidedly unpopular in the 1930s and 1940s consequent to their peculiar views, methods of aggressive proselytizing, and repeated and severe condemnations of other religions. Many local governments sought to curb the Witnesses with anti-peddling ordinances, usually successfully challenged in court. For example, in *Lovell v. Griffin,* 303 U.S. 444 (1938), the high court struck down a local permit ordinance granting blanket discretion to the licensing authority, and in *Schneider v. Irvington,* 308 U.S. 147 (1939), the Court held that pamphleteering on the public streets could not be prohibited altogether, even for the ostensible purpose of preventing littering.

In the mid-1930s a Witnesses leader endorsed nonsaluting and sparked a wave of refusals just as the flag salute became an issue again with war raging in Europe. School officials reacted with disciplinary action. In Pennsylvania and Massachusetts alone there were more than 200 Jehovah's Witness children expelled from school. In most instances these children still faced compulsory education laws, meaning that they had to enroll in private schools or be liable to prosecution.

The best hope for the Witnesses was litigation in the courts. They brought suits in six states to compel readmission of their children and lost each time. On four occasions in the 1930s the Supreme Court refused petitions for certiorari from these rulings. Finally, in April 1940 the Court heard a Jehovah's Witness readmission case.

Walter Gobitis had brought suit before a federal district judge in Philadelphia for an injunction compelling the readmission of his two expelled children to the Minersville, Pennsylvania, public schools. The district court held that the compulsory flag salute violated the religious freedom clause when enforced against the Jehovah's Witnesses, and the circuit court of appeals affirmed this decision. The school board appealed to the Supreme Court, which, to the surprise of many, reversed the district and appeals courts. The Court, in *Minersville v. Gobitis*, 310 U.S. 586 (1940)—with Justice Felix FRANKFURTER writing for an 8–1 Court with Justice Harlan Fiske STONE dissenting—held that a child could constitutionally be expelled from public school for refusing to participate in the daily ceremony, even though this violates the child's religious beliefs. The Court's position was that only felt necessities of society could compel the free exercise provision to be overridden.

Within two years *Gobitis* was under fire from all sides. The decision had ushered in a bad period for the Jehovah's Witnesses with a great deal of violence being directed at them. In one week the DEPARTMENT OF JUSTICE received reports of hundreds of physical assaults on Jehovah's Witnesses by citizens and public officials. As the violence grew, so did unfavorable reaction to *Gobitis*. Further complicating the situation was congressional passage of a joint resolution codifying the rules of flag etiquette.

In *Jones v. Opelika*, 316 U.S. 584 (1942), in a dissenting opinion Justices Hugo BLACK, William O. DOUGLAS, and Frank MURPHY, along with Stone, wrote that they believed that *Gobitis* was wrongly decided.

The Jehovah's Witnesses filed a class-action lawsuit in Charleston, West Virginia, in August 1942, and the case was heard by a three-judge panel. Walter Barnette's children, and others, had been expelled from school for insubordination, could not afford private schooling, and faced potential fines or imprisonment for failing to adhere to compulsory

education laws. The three-judge panel decided unanimously in favor of the children, who were readmitted to school promptly. The case, *West Virginia v. Barnette*, 319 U.S. 624 (1943), reached the Supreme Court in March 1943, and the decision was announced on June 14 (Flag Day), 1943, upholding the lower court's ruling.

Justice Robert H. JACKSON wrote one of the more eloquent opinions in Court history deciding the case on free speech grounds rather than freedom of RELIGION. The Court held that the government could not compel citizens to express beliefs without violating freedom of speech and regardless of whether the objections to saluting the flag were religiously based or not. This freedom had to be respected. At the end of his opinion Jackson wrote "If there is any fixed star in our constitutional constellation, it is that no official, high or petty, can prescribe what shall be orthodoxy in politics, nationalism, religion, or other matters of opinion or force citizens to confess by word or act their faith therein."

The pledge gained the potential for even more controversy in 1954 when—in an attempt to distinguish the United States from "godless" communism—Congress added the words "under God." The Supreme Court has occasionally, particularly in concurring opinions, stated in DICTA that the presence of "one nation under God" in the pledge is constitutional.

A future Court opinion may change what, in some situations, is permissible, e.g., such as teachers leading school children in the pledge; what is unlikely to change is people being compelled to salute the flag.

For more information: Manwaring, David R. "Freedom of Conscience: The Flag-Salute Case." In *The Third Branch of Government: 8 Cases in Constitutional Politics*, ed. C. Herman Prichett and Alan F. Westin, 20–49. New York: Harcourt, Brace & World, 1963; *Lovell v. Griffin*, 303 U.S. 444 (1938); *Minersville v. Gobitis*, 310 U.S. 586 (1940); *Schneider v. Irvington*, 308 U.S. 147 (1939); *West Virginia v. Barnette*, 319 U.S. 624 (1943).

—Mark Alcorn

Flast v. Cohen, 392 U.S. 83 (1968)

Flast v. Cohen expanded the concept of STANDING to sue by allowing taxpayers, under certain circumstances, to challenge the constitutionality of federal programs in court.

In *FROTHINGHAM V. MELLON*, 262 U.S. 447 (1923), the U.S. Supreme Court held that simply being a federal taxpayer did not give one standing to legally challenge a federal program. Frothingham brought suit against a program that provided federal funds to the states for the welfare of mothers and infants. She argued that the program took her property (i.e., tax money) without due process of law. Justice

George SUTHERLAND's opinion for a unanimous Court concluded that Frothingham's interest in the case as a taxpayer was so minute that there was no personal injury to her. Thus, since she could show no real stake or interest in the outcome of the case, she did not have standing to bring the suit so the Court could not rule on the constitutionality of the program.

In *Flast*, a federal program providing funds to parochial schools for textbooks and other materials was challenged as violating the First Amendment free exercise and establishment clauses. Like Frothingham, Flast's only claim for standing to sue was that she was a taxpayer and that her taxes were, in whatever minor and remote way, used to finance the program. Unlike Frothingham, however, the Supreme Court held that Flast had standing to sue and could, thus, proceed with her case.

In an 8 to 1 decision, the opinion by Chief Justice Earl WARREN explained that *Frothingham* was not an absolute bar against TAXPAYER SUITS. Instead, taxpayers would have standing to sue if they met a two-part test. First, the program would have had to be enacted under Congress's power to tax and spend as enumerated in Article I, Section 8 of the Constitution. Second, the program would have to be alleged to violate a specific constitutional limitation on that power to tax and spend. Although both Frothingham and Flast had met the first part of the test, only Flast met the second. Frothingham had challenged the maternity and infants program on general notions of appropriate federal power while Flast's challenge was based on provisions in the Constitution (i.e., the religion clauses) that specifically limited how the federal government could spend taxpayer money. The Court left for another day whether constitutional provisions other than the RELIGION clauses might be of this type.

The decision in *Flast* was consistent with other decisions by the Warren Court making it easier for individual rights claims to be heard in the federal courts. The BURGER and REHNQUIST courts, however, have refused to extend the *Flast* ruling. For example, in *U.S. v. Richardson*, 418 U.S. 166 (1974), the Court held that a taxpayer did not have standing to sue in a case involving covert expenditures by the Central Intelligence Agency (CIA) because the challenge was based on the statement and account clause of Article I, Section 9 and, thus, did not meet the second part of the *Flast* test. Similarly, in *Valley Forge College v. Americans United for Separation of Church and State*, 454 U.S. 464 (1982), the Court concluded that a transfer of federal property to a religious college did not meet the first part of the *Flast* test since the transfer was based not on Congress's Article I, Section 8 power to tax and spend but on the Article IV, Section 3 property clause, which grants Congress the power to dispose of property belonging to the United States.

The two-pronged *Flast* test, therefore, continues to allow standing to sue to taxpayers only in those cases in which a program is challenged as violating the religion clause's specific limitations on congressional power to tax and spend.

For more information: O'Brien, David M. *Constitutional Law and Politics, Volume One: Struggles for Power and Governmental Accountability.* 5th ed. New York: W. W. Norton, 2003.

—Michael W. Bowers

Fletcher v. Peck, 6 Cranch 10 U.S. 87 (1810)

In *Fletcher v. Peck*, the Supreme Court upheld a land sale by the state of Georgia even though the sale occurred as a result of fraud. In the process, the decision here was important both for the Court's protection of property rights and because the decision involved one of the major land scandals in the 19th century.

In the early days after the American Revolution, the various states tried to devise new ways of governing. Some of these ways were not new but were rather the old ways of land fraud. In 1795 the state of Georgia issued a grant of five million acres of land, called the Yazoo, named after the river and a native tribal name, to James Gunn by way of a bill passed by the legislature. Gunn then sold a portion of the lands to John Peck, a citizen of Massachusetts, who in turn further subdivided, selling 15,000 acres to Robert Fletcher, a citizen of New Hampshire. Peck had presented to Fletcher a warranty deed. Unfortunately for the sale, the Georgia legislature had in 1796 passed a new bill that purported to rescind the 1795 grant to Gunn and others, who, it had been discovered, had been thoroughly bribed to deliver up the original grant.

Fletcher sued Peck to recover his money from the sale. Peck had, from all that was known in the law at that time, transferred a void deed to Fletcher, even though he was not one of the original perpetrators. At the time, it was clear that it was not possible for a citizen of one state to sue a state if he was not a citizen of that state. The states had, almost contemporaneously, enacted the Eleventh Amendment explicitly prohibiting that action. This amendment was the result of a similar action between a South Carolinian and the state of Georgia.

It was plain that, under the Constitution, the federal courts had jurisdiction to hear the action, as between the parties, Fletcher and Peck, being citizens of different states. What was not plain, at that time, was whether the federal courts could act to enforce so blatant an action, which was in reality based upon a fraudulent act of the Georgia legislature. What was needed was a way for the Georgia legislature to be held to account for its actions in helping initiate the sale of five million acres of land to speculators.

Justice John MARSHALL studied Article 1, § 10, Cl.1, of the new Constitution which stated in part, "No State shall . . . pass any BILL OF ATTAINDER, EX POST FACTO LAW, or *Law impairing the Obligation of Contracts. . . .*" *The problem became one of how to construe the first act of the Georgia legislature in such a way as to not violate the letter of the Eleventh Amendment and yet allow Fletcher his conclusive verdict to obtain the return of the money paid to Peck.*

Marshall had found a way to reach what he perceived as the correct solution to the vicissitudes of the Georgia legislature. He considered the nature of a land grant or deed and determined a deed, and by implication a legislative grant, to be a completed act at the time of the first conveyance and not subject to being revoked without assent of the grantee. An additional aspect was that he had found a way to declare that the Supreme Court could review actions of the states.

For more information: Finkelman, Paul, & Melvin I. Urofsky. *A March of Liberty: A Constitutional History of the United States, Volume one: From the Founding to 1890.* 2nd ed. New York and Oxford: Oxford University Press, 2002; Magrath, C. Peter. *Yazoo: The Case of* Fletcher v. Peck. New York: W. W. Norton, 1967; Schwartz, Bernard. *A History of the Supreme Court.* New York: Oxford University Press, 1993.

—Tracey L. Gladstone-Sovell
—Stanley M. Morris

Florida v. Bostick, 501 U.S. 429 (1991)

In *Florida v. Bostick,* the Supreme Court ruled that the state of Florida did not violate the Fourth Amendment rights of Terrance Bostick when a voluntary search of his suitcase yielded a stash of illegal drugs. Justice O'CONNOR delivered the Court's opinion and was joined by Justices REHNQUIST, WHITE, SCALIA, KENNEDY, and SOUTER. Justice MARSHALL filed a dissenting opinion and was joined by Justices BLACKMUN and STEVENS.

The Fourth Amendment of the Constitution stipulates that "the right of the people to be secure in their persons, houses, papers, and effects, against unreasonable searches and seizures, shall not be violated, and no Warrants shall issue, but upon probable cause, supported by Oath or affirmation, and particularly describing the place to be searched, and the persons or things to be seized." This right, however, has never been understood to be absolute, and the Supreme Court has recognized several exceptions to the Fourth Amendment's warrant requirement. One of these exceptions occurs when individuals allow law enforcement officials to conduct *consensual* searches of persons or property.

During the "war on drugs" in the 1980s, the Broward County sheriff's department began a practice of randomly boarding buses and asking passengers for permission to search their belongings. Terrance Bostick was a passenger on one of these buses and was asked by two officers for his consent to search his luggage. Though being told he had the right to refuse to give his consent, Bostick granted the officers permission, upon which they discovered a quantity of cocaine in his bag. Bostick was then arrested and charged with drug trafficking.

At a pretrial hearing, Bostick argued that the drugs had been seized in violation of the Fourth Amendment, a claim that was denied by the trial court. While an appellate court upheld the trial court's ruling, the Fourth Amendment question was considered important enough that it was certified to the Florida State Supreme Court. There the court found that "an impermissible seizure result[s] when police mount a drug search on buses during scheduled stops and question boarded passengers without articulable reasons for doing so, thereby obtaining consent to search the passengers' luggage." Thus the practice of "working the buses" to combat the trafficking of illegal drugs is unconstitutional. Based on this finding, the state of Florida appealed to the United States Supreme Court.

Justice O'Connor began her opinion by pointing out that the Court has repeatedly authorized the police to "approach individuals at random . . . in public places to ask them questions and to request consent to search their luggage, so long as a reasonable person would understand that he or she could refuse to cooperate." The question for the Court, then, was whether this rule applied in the context of passengers on a bus. For O'Connor, there was little doubt that no seizure had taken place. The Court had authorized similar encounters in airports and had argued that "even when officers have no basis for suspecting a particular individual, they may generally ask questions of that individual, ask to examine the individual's identification, and request consent to search his or her luggage." Surely the fact that Bostick was on a bus does not remove this situation from the overall thrust of these rulings.

Justice O'Connor next took up Bostick's argument that being in the "cramped" space of a bus makes a police encounter far more intimidating. With only one exit from the bus, and the police officers blocking that exit by standing in the aisle, a reasonable person would conclude that they were not "free to leave" and were thus "seized" in the meaning of the Fourth Amendment. O'Connor, however, disagreed. While such a person might indeed feel confined on a bus, that consequence is a result of his own choices, not police action. In addition, O'Connor reflected, "Bostick was a passenger on a bus that was scheduled to depart. He would not have felt free to leave the bus even if the police had not been present."

Finally, Bostick also argued that the search was unconstitutional because no reasonable person would have freely consented to being searched by the police when he knew that his luggage contained illegal drugs. This violates the "reasonable person" standard of the Court's Fourth Amendment rulings. According to O'Connor, though, Bostick was relying on a flawed reading of the reasonable person standard. The reasonable person test assumes that such a person is innocent. Hence "the fact that the [respondent] knew the search was likely to turn up contraband is, of course, irrelevant; the potential intrusiveness of the officers' conduct must be judged from the viewpoint of an innocent person in [his] position."

In a heated dissenting opinion, Justice Marshall accused the majority of doing great violence to the Fourth Amendment. The practice of "working the buses," according to Marshall, "bears all of the indicia of coercion and unjustified intrusion associated with a [violation of] the Fourth Amendment." While the government certainly has a strong interest in thwarting the spread of illegal drugs in society, that interest may not come at the price of individual CIVIL LIBERTIES. Moreover, "withholding this particular weapon from the government's drug war arsenal would hardly leave the police without any means of combating the use of buses as instrumentalities of the drug trade . . . [and] there is no reason to expect that [buses would become] law enforcement-free zones."

For more information: Greenhalgh, William W., ed. *The Fourth Amendment Handbook: A Chronological Survey of Supreme Court Decisions.* 2nd ed. Chicago: ABA Publishing, 2002; Lasson, Nelson B. *The History and Development of the Fourth Amendment to the United States Constitution.* Baltimore: Johns Hopkins University Press, 1937.

—Eric C. Sands

Food and Drug Administration v. Brown & Williamson Tobacco Corp., 529 U.S. 120 (2000)

In *FDA v. Brown & Williamson Tobacco Corp.,* the plaintiff was actually a group of cigarette manufacturers, retailers, and advertisers who had united for the purposes of suing the FDA in federal court. The group's complaint stated that the FDA had no statutory authority to regulate tobacco products because tobacco manufacturers did not claim that smoking was in any way therapeutic or beneficial.

The FDA's new rules and regulations could not take effect without congressional approval of a set of regulations that would establish new standards for governing (1) accessibility of cigarettes for children and adolescents; (2) the amount of time youngsters would be exposed to promotion and advertisement of tobacco products; and (3) utilization of new, stringent health warnings in tobacco products' advertisements and packaging.

In order for the FDA's new rules and regulations to take effect, Congress had to approve of them. Congress held hearings to give its members an opportunity to learn more about the new rules and regulations. At one such event, the FDA had presented to Congress factual evidence showing that in the United States, tobacco use was directly responsible for more than 400,000 deaths annually. While adult smokers accounted for most of these deaths, FDA exhibited information showing that most adult smokers became tobacco addicts when they were less than 18 years old. The FDA asserted that enforcement of its proposed regulations would reduce minors' use of tobacco products by establishing limits on youngsters' exposure to television and print advertisements for these products and by requiring stronger warnings on product packaging and advertisements. If fewer teenagers started smoking, fewer adults would be addicted to tobacco, and the incidence of tobacco-related death and disease in future generations would be reduced. The district court decided in favor of the FDA, finding that that there was ample statutory authority for FDA's regulation of tobacco products.

The FDA claimed that the Food, Drug, and Cosmetic Act (FDCA), 21 U.S.C. § 301 *et seq.,* which granted FDA power to regulate drugs, also implied that the FDA was authorized to (1) create and enforce rules and regulations regarding the sale, advertising, and promotion of tobacco products, because all tobacco products contain nicotine, an organic substance that is usually classified as a drug; and (2) regulate "devices," a term that could be construed to include cigarettes, cigars, and tobacco sold for smoking in pipes or chewing, since each of these tobacco products or methods of using tobacco was, in essence, a specialized tool intended solely for the purpose of delivering nicotine to the human body.

Dissatisfied with this outcome, the tobacco manufacturers appealed the decision to the U.S. COURT OF APPEALS for the Fourth Circuit, *FDA v. Brown and Williamson Tobacco Corp.,* 153 F.3d 155 (1998), where once again they lost the case. The plaintiff, who had already prepared a petition to have this case heard by the high court, filed it immediately.

The appellate court found that FDA's interpretation of the FDCA was inconsistent with evidence showing that prior to 1995, the FDA repeatedly asserted that it lacked jurisdiction over tobacco products. Additionally, the Court of Appeals found that several long-standing provisions of the FDCA itself prohibited the FDA from becoming involved in regulating tobacco products. Hence, the appellate court reversed the district court's decision, finding that the FDA could not regulate tobacco products because Congress had never passed a law granting FDA that power.

Dissatisfied with the appellate court's verdict, FDA appealed to the U.S. Supreme Court. That court's decision, *FDA v. Brown and Williamson Tobacco Corp.*, first noted precedents established in prior case law that required courts to use common sense when reading laws. After finding that Congress had passed tobacco-specific laws such as the first package-labeling law long after the FDCA became law, the court held that the existence of the post-FDCA laws regarding cigarette warnings must be interpreted as evidence that Congress did not intend to grant FDA jurisdiction over tobacco products.

The court noted that the FDCA requires that FDA take responsibility for insuring that every product under its jurisdiction is demonstrably safe and effective for its intended use. Since tobacco is inherently dangerous when used as intended, FDA would be in violation of the FDCA if it regulated marketing of tobacco products. The court then held that Congress could not have intended to create this nonsensical situation.

No matter how important, conspicuous, and controversial an issue may be, an administrative agency's power to regulate in the public interest must always be grounded in a valid grant of authority from Congress. Courts have no authority to decide to extend a statute's scope beyond the point where Congress indicated it would end. Hence, the Supreme Court held that Congress, which is bound to protect commerce and the national economy, had passed laws that created a well-structured regulatory scheme for tobacco products and related matters. Any tobacco safety regulations created by the FDA would be redundant and would not be utilized, since Congress was the only branch of government responsible for regulating tobacco products.

For more information: American Public Health Association. "FDA: Regulation of Tobacco Products." APHA Factsheets (October 2002). Available online. URL: http://www.apha.org/legislative/factsheets/FDA_tobacco.htm. Downloaded May 13, 2004; Slud, Martha. "Supreme Court: Tobacco Scores a Victory." *CNN Money* (March 2000). Available online. URL: http://money.cnn.com/2000/03/21/companies/tobacco_fda. Downloaded May 13, 2004.

—Beth S. Swartz

Forsyth County v. Nationalist Movement, 112 S. Ct. 2395 (1992)

In *Forsyth County v. Nationalist Movement,* the Supreme Court struck down a requirement that a group pay a special fee to hold a march. The decision in this case represented a major protection for free speech and assembly. Under the First Amendment's free speech clause, the Supreme Court has recognized that government could restrict the time, place, or manner of speech. One of those restrictions was to require

permits of those planning to use public spaces including roads, parks, and sidewalks for protests. The permit requirements gave local governments time to prepare for any problems, close off roads, and provide protection for protesters.

Forsyth County, Georgia, 30 miles north of Atlanta, had been home to several protests by white supremacy groups based in the county. After one particularly violent episode, the county board passed a new ordinance requiring that anyone seeking to conduct a march on county grounds pay a fee for the issuance of a permit. The county administrator would determine the size of the fee though it could never exceed $1,000. The fee was created to reimburse costs for planning security and other arrangements for marches.

The Nationalist Movement sought to march in Forsyth County and sought a permit from the county. They were assessed a $100 fee for administrative purposes. The group refused to pay and sued. They charged that the fee was based on the content of their speech and intended to prevent them from marching in Forsyth County because their views were disliked by the government. They appealed to the Supreme Court.

Five justices agreed with these charges. Writing for the majority, Justice BLACKMUN argued that the county administrator determined the level of the fee he charged based on the content of the group's speech. Speech that was deemed controversial required higher fees for administrative purposes and placed a burden on the speakers. Justice Blackmun found that the $100 fee was 20 times larger than the $5 fee charged a Girl Scout troop that applied for a permit. A motorcycle racing group was charged $25 for a permit to conduct a race on county roads. The different fees charged could only be explained by the content of the speech of these different groups.

Blackmun also ruled the discretion given the county administrator for charging the fee. The administrator was given no guidelines by the county for determining how much a group should be charged. This would allow the administrator to abuse his position by charging more to groups he disfavored. Any charges must be tied to specific guidelines that do not make decisions based on the content of speech.

The Forsyth County decision placed states and localities in a difficult position. In upholding the right of individuals to protest in a PUBLIC FORUM, the government must provide security and services. The Forsyth County decision required specific rules that might not always be appropriate for all local governments.

For more information: Crump, David. "Camouflaged Incitement." *Georgia Law Review* 1 (1993): 29; Yackle, Larry. "Parading Ourselves." *Boston University Law Review* 73 (1992): 791.

—Douglas Clouatre

Fortas, Abe (1910–1982) *Supreme Court justice*

Abe Fortas was appointed by President Lyndon Johnson in 1965 to serve on the U.S. Supreme Court, where he remained until 1969.

Abe Fortas was more renowned for his pre-Court activities than for the few years he served on the Supreme Court. Fortas was a protégé of William O. DOUGLAS at Yale Law School, where he edited the law review, graduated second in his class, and taught for a few years as assistant professor. A liberal Democrat, he was brought to Washington by Douglas to work at the new Securities and Exchange Commission. He served as undersecretary of the Interior (1942–46; he was one of the youngest undersecretaries in history) and then founded a prominent District of Columbia law firm (Arnold, Fortas and Porter), which represented such major corporations as Coca Cola and Philip Morris.

In 1948 Fortas successfully represented Lyndon Johnson in a challenge to the latter's nomination for U.S. Senator. From that time on (including during his time on the Supreme Court), Fortas was a close advisor to LBJ.

During the cold war Fortas's firm defended more than a hundred persons accused of disloyalty (including Owen Lattimore and Lillian Hellman). In 1954 in the case of *Durham v. U.S.* (214 F.2d 862), he helped broaden the definition of legal insanity. He persuaded a federal COURT OF APPEALS that the 19th century McNaghten test for insanity in criminal cases should be updated in the light of modern psychiatric insights. (Fortas was a trustee of the William Alanson White Psychiatric Foundation and a frequent contributor to psychiatric journals.)

In 1962 Fortas was selected by the Supreme Court to represent Clarence Earl Gideon, an indigent Florida inmate, who appealed his conviction because of denial of counsel. Fortas's victory in *GIDEON V. WAINWRIGHT*, 372 U.S. 335 (1963), a unanimous decision, established that states must provide legal representation for those who lack the means to hire attorneys.

In 1965 President Johnson nominated a reluctant Fortas to the Supreme Court. (Earlier LBJ had tried unsuccessfully to get Fortas to replace Robert Kennedy as attorney general. Fortas and his wife, attorney Carolyn Agger, enjoyed a rich lifestyle; he felt it would be a sacrifice to take a government job.) On the Court Fortas joined with William O. Douglas in liberal decisions against censorship, RACIAL DISCRIMINATION, restrictions on the rights of political dissenters, and violations of church-state separation; they disagreed in cases dealing with government regulation of business.

Fortas's opinion in *IN RE GAULT*, 387 U.S. 1 (1966), gave juvenile defendants many of the constitutional protections provided adults. He also spoke for the Court in *Epperson v. Arkansas*, 393 U.S. 97 (1968), striking down Arkansas' anti-evolution statute, and *TINKER V. DES MOINES SCHOOL DISTRICT*, 383 U.S. 503 (1968), allowing schoolchildren to engage in symbolic protest of the Vietnam War.

Fortas's credo was that "the courts may be the principal guardians of the liberties of the people. They are not the chief administrators of its economic destiny."

In 1968 he was nominated by President Johnson to succeed Earl WARREN as CHIEF JUSTICE. Republicans and conservative Democrats filibustered against the liberal ally of LBJ. (Republicans, expecting to win the 1968 presidential election, wanted Nixon to nominate the next chief justice.) It was discovered that Fortas had advised Johnson regarding CIVIL RIGHTS and student opposition to the Vietnam War. He had even helped LBJ craft his 1966 State of the Union address. Fortas withdrew from consideration.

In 1969 he became the first associate justice to resign under pressure of public criticism and possible impeachment. He had received an annual fee from a foundation controlled by Louis Wolfson, who was being investigated for violation of federal securities laws.

For more information: Kalman, Laura. *Abe Fortas: A Biography.* New Haven, Conn., and London: Yale University Press, 1990; Murphy, Bruce Allen. *Fortas: The Rise and Ruin of a Supreme Court Justice.* New York: William Morrow, 1988; Shogan, Robert. *A Question of Judgment: The Fortas Case and the Struggle for the Supreme Court.* Indianapolis, Ind., and New York: Bobbs-Merrill, 1972.

—Martin Gruberg

Frankfurter, Felix (1882–1965) *Supreme Court justice*

Felix Frankfurter (b. Vienna, Austria, November 15, 1882; d. Washington, D.C., February 21, 1965) was appointed by President Franklin Roosevelt in 1939 to the Supreme Court, where he served until 1962.

Felix Frankfurter was 12 years old when he saw America for the first time. He came to New York in 1894 with his mother Emma and his five siblings to meet his father Leopold, who had emigrated in 1882 in order to build a new life for his family. This new home must have seemed a world away from the Austria they had left behind. Leopold Frankfurter had studied to be a rabbi in a family tradition that reached back three centuries. Here in New York, he worked selling furs on Manhattan's East Side. He inculcated in his children the love of learning and diligent study which his parents had inculcated in him. His son Felix embodied this intellectual excitement early on.

Felix Frankfurter enrolled in Public School 25 immediately upon his arrival in New York. The young pupil spoke German, Hungarian, Yiddish, and Hebrew, but he quickly learned English and adapted well to American customs. He graduated from City College, City University of New York, then renowned as the "Poor Man's Harvard." His early experiences with public education would deeply influence his later work as an associate justice of the Supreme Court. Notwithstanding his humble origins, Frankfurter began his studies at Harvard Law School in 1903, distinguishing himself as one of its finest students. One of Frankfurter's professors recommended his pupil to the U.S. Attorney General for the Southern District of New York, Henry L. Stimson, who hired him as an assistant in Theodore Roosevelt's trust-busting campaign. This marked the beginning of Felix Frankfurter's long career in public service and his lifelong commitment to progressive causes and the protection of CIVIL RIGHTS.

During World War I Frankfurter took a leave of absence from his position as professor of law at Harvard to work for the Department of Labor in Washington, D.C. There he undertook investigations of the trial of Tom Mooney and the Bisbee Deportations. Mooney had been tried and convicted for his alleged participation in a bombing at the San Francisco Preparedness Day Parade. Frankfurter recommended a reassessment of the trial, as its fairness was highly questionable. With regard to the Bisbee incident, Frankfurter had to investigate the forced migration of striking copper miners from Colorado to Arizona by an angry mob. The incident drew international attention. Frankfurter recommended that the government hold to account those responsible for driving the miners out. These recommendations inspired angry responses from the president and sparked much public debate. During his time in Washington, Frankfurter met Marian Denman, to whom he was wed in 1919 by Judge Benjamin CARDOZO. After World War I, Frankfurter returned to Harvard, but he never lost touch with events and people in Washington. He was a trusted adviser to President Franklin Delano Roosevelt, and he recommended many of his students (a.k.a the "hot dogs") for positions in the New Deal administration.

Frankfurter did not shy away from controversy where justice was concerned. After his return to Harvard he wrote an article criticizing the notorious Sacco-Vanzetti case in which two radicals were sentenced to death for a murder committed after a factory robbery in Braintree, Massachusetts. The case was rife with procedural irregularities, and it seemed likely that the pair had been prosecuted because they were foreigners and radicals. Notwithstanding the threats of many Harvard alumni to withdraw their contributions and pressure for his immediate resignation, Frankfurter stood by his position. He went on to participate in the Scopes trial, in which he supported the right to teach evolution in public schools, to help found the ACLU, and to advise the NAACP on legal issues. When Frankfurter was nominated to the Supreme Court in 1939, many of these causes became flashpoints in the nomination debates. In addition to the fact that he had championed such causes,

Justice Felix Frankfurter *(United States Supreme Court)*

his Jewish faith and immigrant origins sparked opposition. However, Frankfurter unapologetically defended himself and was elected to the Court by a unanimous vote.

A number of the cases Frankfurter heard involved public education and RELIGION. In *Illinois ex rel. McCollum v. Board of Education,* 333 U.S. 203 (1948), Frankfurter concurred in the Court's decision to invalidate a policy that allowed public facilities to give religious instruction to public school children on a voluntary basis on the grounds that the policy violated the separation of church and state. He also decided a number of cases that involved attempts to exclude blacks from the political process. In *Terry v. Adams,* 345 U.S. 461 (1953), the Court held that the "Jaybird Party" (a Texas political organization) and the Democratic Party had unconstitutionally deprived blacks of their votes by selecting Democratic candidates on the basis of a preprimary in which only whites voted. In *Gomillion v. Lightfoot,* 364 U.S. 339 (1960), the Court intervened for the first time in a question of local redistricting. The boundaries of Tuskegee, Alabama, had been redrawn to exclude almost all its black voters, and Justice Frankfurter opposed eloquently in his opinion in the case.

Frankfurter's tenure on the Supreme Court coincided with World War II, an event that posed many challenges to

CIVIL LIBERTIES within the United States. Frankfurter supported the Court's decision in *KOREMATSU V. UNITED STATES,* 323 U.S. 214 (1944), which upheld the legality of the internment camps to which many Japanese-Americans were relocated under executive wartime powers. In *Minersville School District v. Gobitis,* 310 U.S. 586 (1940), the Court upheld a Pennsylvania school district's requirement that all children salute the flag daily, notwithstanding their religious objections. Frankfurter noted the importance of religious freedom but stated that "to affirm that the freedom to follow conscience has itself no limits in the life of a society would deny that very plurality of principles which, as a matter of history, underlies the protection of religious toleration. . . . Our present task then . . . is to reconcile two rights in order to prevent either from destroying the other."

In these cases, as in many others, Frankfurter tried to balance individual liberty with the needs of a secure and united society. He attempted to do this through reasonable interpretation of the Constitution. This judicial task was often undertaken under difficult circumstances, including world war abroad and socialist and communist threats at home. Frankfurter's legal thought was characterized throughout by a sensitivity to protecting the rights of minorities, awareness of the need to preserve the security of the state as a whole, and careful attention to historical developments in legal and constitutional doctrine in the United States.

For more information: Mendelson, Ed Wallace. *Felix Frankfurter: The Judge.* New York: Reynal and Company, 1964; Thomas, Helen Shirley. *Felix Frankfurter: Scholar on the Bench.* Baltimore: John Hopkins University Press, 1960.
—Tara Helfman

freedom of assembly and association

Freedom of assembly and association refer to two rights the First Amendment guarantees. The First Amendment of the U.S. Constitution prohibits the federal government from interfering with an individual's right to (1) hold and practice religious or other deeply personal beliefs; (2) choose those with whom he or she meets, gathers, socializes, or attends meetings or events of any sort; provided such gathering is peaceful; and (3) express his or her thoughts, verbally or in writing; or (4) contact the government, either directly or through the press, to complain, without risk of reprisal, about some governmental mal-, mis-, or nonfeasance and to ask the government to correct this problem.

For more than 60 years after the enactment of the BILL OF RIGHTS, the Supreme Court interpreted its provisions literally, finding them applicable only to the federal government. However, in 1873, soon after Congress passed the post-Civil War Fourteenth Amendment, the Supreme Court was faced with the question of whether Congress intended the new amendment to extend the rights the First Amendment protected from federal interference to protect those rights from state interference. In the *Slaughter-House Cases,* 83 U.S. 36 (1873), only a minority of the Supreme Court found the rights protected from state interference. Finally, more than 40 years later, the Supreme Court held, in the case of *Bunting v. Oregon,* 243 U.S. 426 (1917), that the due process clause of the Fourteenth Amendment prohibited states from interfering with rights guaranteed by the First Amendment.

Since the middle of the 20th century, the Supreme Court has focused on free speech or free expression as the core concept of the entire Bill of Rights and has held that legislation cannot infringe upon free speech even if there was a RATIONAL BASIS for adopting the law [*West Virginia Board of Education v. Barnette,* 319 U.S. 624 (1943)]. Subsequently, the Supreme Court clarified this opinion by finding that it is more important for a government to protect personal rights guaranteed in the Bill of Rights than to protect economic interests. Additionally, a government cannot regulate the content of a speech unless it has substantial justification, such as a threat of imminent violence or probability that members of the general public may be endangered [*Kovacs v. Cooper,* 336 U.S. 77 (1949)].

Since its decision in *Edwards v. South Carolina,* 372 U.S. 229 (1963), the Supreme Court has extended its concept of expression protected by the First Amendment to include use of a medium other than speech to communicate a message. An example of such "constructive speech" is a civil protest, march, or other form of assembly that uses public areas, such as streets and parks, in a peaceful and lawful manner to inform the public about a particular topic or belief.

When a group associates in this manner, a government cannot require disclosure or registration of its membership unless the government's interest in this information is so compelling that it justifies interference with constitutional rights. Additionally, a government cannot justify denial of a public benefit based on an individual's current or past membership or participation in a particular group.

The right to petition the government for a redress of grievances guarantees people the right to initiate a lawsuit or administrative action to request that a government remedy a specific mal-, mis-, or nonfeasance. If many individuals join in such a petition, the right of assembly is involved in conjunction with the right to petition.

For more information: *Encarta Encyclopedia.* "Civil Rights." Microsoft MSN (2003); Legal Information Institute. "Bill of Rights: An Overview of the First Amendment." Cornell University (2002). Available online. URL: http://www.law.cornell.edu/topics/first_amendment.html. Downloaded May 13, 2004.
—Beth S. Swartz

Frontiero v. Richardson, 411 U.S. 677 (1973)

In *Frontiero v. Richardson,* the Supreme Court held the policy of the U.S. military requiring female members of the armed services to prove the dependency of their spouses, while male personnel were automatically entitled to benefits for their spouses, unconstitutional as a violation of the Fifth Amendment due process provision.

Sharron Frontiero, a lieutenant in the U.S. Air Force, applied for dependent benefits, an increased housing allowance, and medical benefits for her husband. Her application was denied on the grounds that she failed to prove that she provided more than half of her husband's support. Male members of the military were provided benefits automatically upon application without any inquiry into how much support they provided for their wives. Frontiero's claim had two parts. On the one hand, she argued that the requirement that servicewomen demonstrate the extent of their spousal support while servicemen had no such burden of proof was procedural discrimination. In addition, a military man received benefits for his spouse regardless of her personal wealth or income. A military woman and her husband would be denied the benefits if his earnings were more than 50 percent of their income. Thus the law also had a disparate impact on women and men. That difference constituted a form of SEX DISCRIMINATION.

Eight members of the Court agreed that the policy was discriminatory and unconstitutional. Only Justice REHNQUIST differed from the conclusion of the majority. Among the eight justices, however, only four held that laws that discriminated on the basis of sex should be subjected to the most rigorous constitutional standard, STRICT SCRUTINY. That standard requires the government to demonstrate that any discrimination serves a COMPELLING STATE INTEREST and that the means the law uses are narrowly tailored to achieve that purpose. Had the Court agreed to subject sex discrimination to strict scrutiny, it would be extremely difficult for any laws that made distinctions between men and women to meet the constitutional test.

The four justices who argued for strict scrutiny used some of the strongest language ever employed by the court when discussing gender inequality. Citing the nation's long and unfortunate history of sex discrimination, they noted that laws that classify people by sex "often have the effect of invidiously relegating the entire class of females to inferior legal status without regard to the capabilities of the individual members." Such legislation put women "not on a pedestal, but in a cage."

The three members of the Court who concurred in the result explained that they preferred to leave the matter of scrutiny to the political process. At the time of the ruling, Congress had passed the EQUAL RIGHTS AMENDMENT (ERA) to the Constitution and the states were in the process of considering ratification. Had three-fourths of the states approved the amendment, it would have had the effect of requiring strict scrutiny for any legal distinction based on sex. As the requisite 37 states never ratified the ERA, the constitutional status of sex discrimination remains problematical.

The ruling in *Frontiero* did, however, have the effect of prohibiting such policies as differences in Social Security benefits based on sex. Like the military benefits at issue, Social Security payments had been allotted on the assumption that men were the primary breadwinners and that women were the dependent spouses.

For more information: Hoff, Joan. *Law, Gender, and Injustice: A Legal History of U.S. Women.* New York: New York University Press, 1991.

—Mary Welek Atwell

Frothingham v. Mellon, 262 U.S. 447 (1923)

In *Frothingham v. Mellon,* the Supreme Court ruled that only a person who has a legitimate or real legal dispute can bring a case to the federal courts.

The case and controversy clause of Article III of the Constitution requires that federal courts hear and decide only cases and controversies put before them. One requirement of the clause is that a litigant has STANDING, that they demonstrate that they have suffered some direct injury. The standing requirement has been used to limit the ability of taxpayers to challenge the spending decisions of government. Because of the large amount of revenue collected by the federal government and subsequently spent by Congress, the direct effect of any program on any single taxpayer would be so small that it would prevent them from proving any injury to their interests.

Frothingham v. Mellon represented the first case in which the Supreme Court considered whether a federal taxpayer could challenge a congressional decision to spend government money in a certain way. Under Article I, Congress is granted the power to spend money for the general welfare. In 1921 Congress passed the Maternity Act, providing money to states to improve the maternal services provided women and their children. Frothingham, a federal taxpayer, challenged the law as a federal invasion of the power of the states to provide for their citizens' health, safety, and welfare. She asked the federal courts to stop Congress from spending money on this project.

The Court refused. Writing for all of the justices, Justice SUTHERLAND ruled that Frothingham did not have proper standing to sue. Frothingham was one of millions of taxpayers who have their money spent by Congress. Because of this she had been unable to show that she had suffered a specific and direct injury from the Maternity Act. Instead her tax dollars represented only a small portion of all the money spent by the federal government. Any damage done to her would be minute and collective. Because this would be true of most TAXPAYER SUITS it would nearly impossible for an individual to show a direct and specific harm from congressional spending.

The *Frothingham* decision eliminated the opportunity for most taxpayer suits. The justices rightly feared that if they opened up the Court to such challenges, the justices would be faced with a barrage of cases challenging the many thousands of spending decisions made by Congress. This would transfer many spending decisions from the peoples' elected representatives to unelected judges. Justice Sutherland and the Court preferred to defer to the judgment of Congress when deciding the proper method for spending federal money.

Frothingham remained good law until the late 1960s when the WARREN Court decided in *FLAST V. COHEN* (1968) that taxpayers could sue the government if revenues were spent in an unconstitutional manner. This broadened the reach of the federal courts in overseeing Congress's spending power.

For more information: Epstein, Richard. "Standing in Law and Equity: A Defense of Citizen and Taxpayer Suits." *The Green Bag* 6 (2002): 17; Staudt, Nancy. "Taxpayers in Court." *Emory Law Journal* 52 (Spring 2003): 771.

—Douglas Clouatre

Fuller, Melville Weston (1833–1910) *chief justice of the United States*

Melville Weston Fuller was appointed by President Cleveland in 1888 to be CHIEF JUSTICE of the United States, serving until 1910. His tenure on the Court was famous for its support of economic rights.

Fuller was born on February 11, 1833, in Augusta, Maine, to a prominent New England family. Following his parents' divorce, he was raised in the home of his maternal grandfather, a chief justice of the Maine Supreme Court. Having graduated from Bowdoin College in 1853, Fuller read law, briefly attended the Harvard University School of Law, and was admitted to the Maine bar, making him the first U.S. Supreme Court Chief Justice to have had any significant formal legal training.

Fuller left Maine for Chicago in the late 1850s, where he was a prominent Democrat and supporter of Senator Stephen Douglas. After a brief stint in politics as a delegate to the 1861 Illinois Constitutional Convention and a term in the Illinois House of Representatives, Fuller married the daughter of a prominent Chicago banker and

devoted himself full-time to his lucrative legal practice and real estate concerns. During his decades in private practice, Fuller distinguished himself as a corporate attorney specializing in appellate work and appearing frequently before the U.S. Supreme Court. On the death of Chief Justice Morrison WAITE in 1888, President Grover Cleveland appointed Fuller to serve as chief justice, in part in an unsuccessful attempt to secure Illinois's electoral votes in that fall's presidential election.

Although Fuller was a competent administrator over the course of his 22 years at the court's helm, he was not known for his judicial leadership nor for the depth of his legal reasoning as the court struggled to deal with the legal repercussions of the U.S. transformation into an industrial nation. The author of 840 majority opinions, Fuller was a frequent champion of property rights, contractual agreements, and corporate interests, drafting majority opinions limiting the authority of states to regulate imported goods in 1890's *Leisy v. Hardin* and invalidating the federal INCOME TAX in 1895's *POLLOCK V. FARMERS LOAN & TRUST CO.* In 1895's *UNITED STATES V. E. C. KNIGHT CO.*, Fuller's majority opinion narrowly interpreted the Constitution's commerce clause in exempting the sugar trust from regulation under the Sherman Antitrust Act.

Fuller was generally unsympathetic to the CIVIL RIGHTS claims of plaintiffs, maintaining in his dissent in 1898's *United States v. Wong Kim Ark* that the children of Chinese immigrants were not American citizens and dissenting against the application of constitutional protections to newly acquired island territories in 1901's *Downes v. Bidwell*. The Fuller Court also issued landmark rulings affirming "separate but equal" accommodations in 1896's *PLESSY V. FERGUSON*, limiting governmental interference in contracts in 1905's *LOCHNER V. NEW YORK*, and establishing that compensation for private property appropriated for public use was subject to due process provisions of the Fourteenth Amendment in 1897's *Chicago, Burlington & Quincy Railroad Company v. Chicago*.

As chief justice, Fuller worked to maintain a consensual and collegial working relationship among the various justices with whom he served, curtailing the drafting of dissenting opinions and initiating the tradition of the justices shaking hands with one another prior to their morning conferences. Fuller died in office on July 4, 1910, and was buried in Chicago's Graceland Cemetery.

For more information: Ely, James W., Jr. *The Chief Justiceship of Melville W. Fuller, 1888–1910.* Columbia: University of South Carolina Press, 1995; ———. *The Fuller Court: Justices, Rulings, and Legacy.* Santa Barbara, Calif.: ABC-CLIO, 2003.

—William D. Baker

Fullilove v. Klutznick, 448 U.S. 448 (1980)

In *Fullilove v. Klutznick,* the Supreme Court upheld an AFFIRMATIVE ACTION program for federal contractors.

The case began when H. Earl Fullilove and other contractors filed suit claiming they had been economically harmed by the minority business enterprise (MBE) provision of the Public Works Employment Act of 1977. This act required that at least 10 percent of federal funds granted for local public works programs had to be used to obtain services or supplies from businesses owned by minority group members. Fullilove filed suit against Secretary of Commerce Richard M. Klutznick, the program administrator, as well as the State and City of New York, claiming that the act violated Title VI of the CIVIL RIGHTS ACT OF 1964, the EQUAL PROTECTION CLAUSE of the Fourteenth Amendment, and the Equal Protection component of the due process clause of the Fifth Amendment. The District Court and the U.S. COURT OF APPEALS upheld the provision as a remedy for past ethnic and RACIAL DISCRIMINATION. The United States Supreme Court affirmed this decision, adding that "even under the most exacting standard of review the MBE provision passes constitutional muster. . . ."

Chief Justice BURGER wrote for the majority, joined by Justices WHITE and POWELL. Justices MARSHALL, BRENNAN, and BLACKMUN concurred. The majority opinion states that the limited use of racial and ethnic criteria in the minority business provision was not in violation of Title VI of the Civil Rights Act of 1964 or the equal protection clauses because it was substantially related to achieving a congressionally authorized goal of enhancing minority business opportunities and overcoming the results of past discrimination. The Court reasoned that Congress was justified in granting the minority business enterprise provisions under the spending power but could also have done so under the commerce clause. The Court further held that Congress did not have to act "in a wholly 'color-blind' fashion." The majority's opinion affirmed the authority of Congress to license limited used of racial and ethnic criteria in granting public contracts. The opinion also highlighted the importance of deferring to Congress on issues dealing with equal opportunity legislation.

Justices STEWART and REHNQUIST dissented, declaring that the minority business enterprise provision of the Public Works Employment Act amounts to reverse discrimination because it denied certain business owners the opportunity to benefit from government contracts due to the business owners' class or ethnicity. They reasoned that denial of benefits on such grounds is not compatible with equal protection under the law. Justice STEVENS also dissented, arguing that Congress failed to govern impartially, as required by the Fifth Amendment. He reasoned that Congress had not demonstrated the justification for making a legal distinction in the preference for minority business owners because members of this class did not share relevant characteristics.

This was a difficult case that produced five different opinions, no one of which had more than three justices in agreement. However six justices did agree that affirmative action is permissible to overcome the results of past discrimination. This conclusion was undermined nine years later in CITY OF RICHMOND V. J. A. CROSON CO., 488 U.S. 469 (1989), when another six-person majority declared a Richmond, Virginia, set-aside program unconstitutional. For all practical purposes *Fullilove* was overruled in GRUTTER V. BOLLINGER, when Justice O'CONNOR, writing for a 5-4 majority, explicitly rejected past discrimination as a basis for affirmative action programs.

For more information: Teaching American History. *"Fullilove v. Klutznick."* Ashbrook Center for Public Affairs. Available online. URL: http://teachingamericanhistory.org/library/index.asp?document=91. Downloaded May 13, 2004; The OYEZ Project. *"Fullilove v. Klutznick."* Supreme Court Multimedia. Available online. URL: http://www.oyez.org/oyez/resource/case/130. Downloaded May 13, 2004.

—Colleen Hagan

fundamental rights

Fundamental rights are those rights that the Supreme Court has held are implicitly protected by the U.S. Constitution. These rights include the right to marry, to travel from state to state, to vote in state elections, and a RIGHT TO PRIVACY that is broad enough to cover access to CONTRACEPTIVES and, perhaps most controversially, abortion.

Unlike such rights as freedom of RELIGION, freedom of speech, and the right to a jury trial, fundamental rights are not explicitly mentioned in the text of the Constitution. Therefore, some critics argue that the Supreme Court, which is not democratically elected or accountable to the public, should not create rights that are not directly supported by the constitutional text. These critics argue that issues such as abortion and access to contraception should be decided by the people or by elected officials accountable to the people. Others counter that the framers of the Constitution could not put every fundamental right into writing, and that if the Court did not protect rights that do not explicitly appear in the Constitution, then the government could deprive us of such things as the right to get married or could even tell people who do not own property that they could not vote in state elections.

The Supreme Court itself has often seemed confused about where fundamental rights come from. The Court has sometimes said that fundamental rights can be implied from the entire Constitution. At other times, Supreme Court justices have suggested that they come from the

NINTH AMENDMENT, which says, "The enumeration in the Constitution, of certain rights, shall not be construed to deny or disparage others retained by the people." At yet other times, the Court has argued that fundamental rights come from the parts of the Fourteenth Amendment that protect due process of laws and the equal protection of the laws.

The Court has also struggled with how to decide what rights are fundamental. The Court has generally relied upon vague phrases to explain what rights are fundamental. It has said that those rights "implicit in ordered liberty" are fundamental and that the Court uses its "reasoned judgment" to decide what those rights are. This vagueness, coupled with the fact that some fundamental rights, especially abortion, are extremely controversial, has put these rights at the center of many national debates. Political figures often call upon the president to nominate justices who will interpret the text of the Constitution more narrowly and not protect implicit rights. Others counter that the rights protected by the Court as fundamental are among the most important to a free and equal society. This is an important area of debate with no easy answers that will doubtless continue for a long time and will be a central concern each time that the president has an opportunity to nominate a new Supreme Court justice.

For more information: Gerstmann, Evan. *Same-Sex Marriage and the Constitution.* Cambridge: Cambridge University Press, 2004; Scalia, Antonin. *A Matter of Interpretation.* Princeton, N.J.: Princeton University Press, 1997.

—Evan Gerstmann

Furman v. Georgia, 408 U.S. 238 (1972)

In *Furman v. Georgia,* the U.S. Supreme Court ruled that Georgia's capital sentencing process was arbitrary and capricious in violation of the Eighth Amendment's prohibition against cruel and unusual punishment. This ruling effectively produced a moratorium on death sentences across the United States. Even though the court struck down the Georgia law by a vote of 5-4, nine separate opinions were issued in the ruling with justices in the five-member majority split over the rationale behind the ruling.

Justices MARSHALL and BRENNAN, who were staunch opponents of the death penalty, held Georgia's law to be a per se violation of the Eighth Amendment simply because the law allowed for the possibility of a death sentence. One justice cited the wanton and freakish imposition of the death sentence, while the other two justices in the majority thought the jury had too much unguided discretion in deciding the death sentence.

This decision also relied upon social SCIENTIFIC EVIDENCE that suggested the Georgia system was producing a discriminatory pattern of sentencing mostly minority defendants to death, when that option was available to them. The ruling resulted in more than 600 death row prisoners being resentenced across the nation. States responded to the Furman ruling by temporarily halting their pursuit of death sentences and revising their death penalty sentencing statutes. Some states created mandatory death sentences to reduce the discretion placed in the jury's hands, while other states provided juries with more guidance during the sentencing process.

For more information: Bedau, Hugo Adam, ed. *The Death Penalty in America.* Oxford: Oxford University Press, 1997.

—Patricia E. Campie

G

Garcia v. San Antonio Metropolitan Transit Authority, 469 U.S. 528 (1985)

Garcia v. San Antonio Metropolitan Transit Authority upheld the regulation of state employees under the federal Fair Labor Standards Act as a valid exercise of Congress's commerce clause power. The decision reversed the Court's holding in NATIONAL LEAGUE OF CITIES V. USERY, 426 U.S. 833 (1976), which exempted "traditional governmental functions" of states from federal regulation.

The San Antonio Metropolitan Transit Authority (SAMTA) argued that as a state agency undertaking local government activities it qualified for an exemption from the minimum wage and overtime requirements of the federal act. A transit employee named Joe Garcia sought the protection of the federal legislation and challenged the exemption. The Federal District Court of Western Texas exempted SAMTA, citing *National League of Cities* in support. The Supreme Court reversed the Texas ruling.

Garcia is also a landmark in the jurisprudence of FEDERALISM. The constitution divides governing between the states and the federal government. The Supreme Court is called on to serve as the umpire of disputes between governments over the scope of their powers. During the New Deal presidency of Franklin Roosevelt, the Supreme Court found many of the administration's efforts to regulate the national economy unconstitutional on federalism grounds. The Court eventually became more sympathetic to national regulation and oversaw an expansion of federal activity largely under the auspices of Congress's commerce power. A wide ranging commerce power gave Congress the ability to legislate in many areas traditionally assumed to be the sphere of the states. Congress went one step further and began to regulate the states in their employment activities. *Garcia* was the zenith of the Supreme Court's permissibility with the commerce clause and federal regulation of state activities. Recent years have seen the Court reinvigorate limits on the commerce power in cases such as *United States v. Lopez,* 115 S. Ct. 1624 (1995), and revive state immunity in cases such as *Alden v. Maine,* 527 U.S. 706 (1999).

Given the exemption that states could receive from federal labor standards, under *National League of Cities,* the states were understandably keen to ensure that a broad definition of such functions was formulated by the courts. Writing for the majority in *Garcia,* Justice BLACKMUN found that the search for such a core of traditional responsibility conducted in the interim between *National League of Cities* and *Garcia* had been unfruitful. Of the 15 lower court decisions Blackmun cited as relevant, five had exempted states or their agencies and 10 had not. Regardless of the results, Blackmun wrote, it was "difficult, if not impossible, to identify an organizing principle that places each of the cases in the first group on one side of a line and each of the cases in the second group on the other side."

Justice Blackmun's opinion in *Garcia* is the embodiment of a "functionalist" approach to federalism. Federalism, he argued, requires flexibility more than it requires formalism or rigidity of categories. For a federation to endure and for the units in a federation to flourish, he claimed, they must be allowed to experiment and work outside the bounds of rigid structures. A judiciary patrolling the border between federal and state power is ultimately hostile to such practices. Blackmun encouraged the judiciary to thin out its patrols and allow governments to blur the lines.

The big question was how the courts were to provide flexibility for evolving federal arrangements yet avoid judicial subjectivity. Blackmun argued that it could not be done, and that subjectivity was inevitable. Thus, questions that had once received judicial resolution were better served by political processes. The majority claimed that state interests are protected through the institutions of national government, namely, the electoral college and the Senate. "The principal and basic limit on the federal commerce power is that inherent in all congressional action— the built in restraints that our system provides through

State participation in federal governmental action." Since one house of Congress is made up of the nominal representatives of the states, such representation should ensure that federalism is respected. According to the court's ruling in *Garcia*, if the federal legislation at hand made it through the national political process, that meant that state cautions had been observed. It therefore became unnecessary for the court to consider state sovereignty or any other limit that might be argued to overrule congressional action. This perspective has come under increasing fire in the late 1990s and in the beginning of the 21st century.

For more information: Howard, A. E. Dick. "*Garcia:* Of Federalism and Constitutional Values." *Publius: The Journal of Federalism* 16 (Summer 1986): 17–31.

—Gerald Baier

gay and lesbian rights (same-sex discrimination)

Same-sex discrimination occurs when individuals of homosexual or bisexual orientation are given less rights or are arbitrarily treated differently in the law in comparison to those who are heterosexual.

The gay and lesbian rights campaign tries to overcome discrimination and achieve a status not significantly or substantially different from heterosexual identity. The United States Supreme Court has issued several opinions regarding the rights of gays and lesbians since 1986, with the votes and opinions of the various justices representing the different views in what Justice SCALIA and others call the "cultural war" over this issue.

All five of the Supreme Court's gay rights rulings have examined state laws under the Fourteenth Amendment. In particular, there are two important clauses, the due process clause, guaranteeing the law will not deprive individuals of rights to liberty, including those expressed in the First Amendment, and the EQUAL PROTECTION CLAUSE, guaranteeing a right to equal protection of the laws. Each of these clauses has a unique history in the Court's use of JUDICIAL REVIEW.

BOWERS V. HARDWICK, 478 U.S. 186 (1986), held, 5-4, that the due process clause guarantees of liberty did not give the Court legal authority to invalidate Georgia's statute making sodomy (oral or anal sex) a felony as enforceable on private premises against adult consenting homosexuals. The Court argued that the state interest had a RATIONAL BASIS in the expressed majority will for a traditional culture of morality and law. In other words, the Court denied that homosexual sodomy must exist as fundamental right.

Hurley v. Irish-American Gay and Lesbian Group of Greater Boston, 515 U.S. 557 (1995), was about an organization of war veterans' exclusion of a gay pride banner in a city-permitted street march to celebrate St. Patrick's Day

and Massachusetts's law forbidding sexual orientation discrimination in public places. The Court unanimously held the state interest was not sufficiently compelling to override private individuals and members of a private organization guaranteed the right to free speech and free association by the due process clause and First Amendment. This meant the state's antidiscrimination policy could not mandate integration of a gay pride message with the content of a separate and unrelated private message expressed in public.

ROMER V. EVANS, 517 U.S. 620 (1996), was about Amendment 2 in Colorado's constitution. A majority of voters statewide approved its language targeting individuals with a gay, lesbian, or bisexual orientation for a deprivation of local guarantees of CIVIL RIGHTS. The Court held, 6-3, that the equal protection clause invalidated the same-sex discrimination in this state action.

Boy Scouts of America v. Dale, 530 U.S. 640 (2000), is similar to *Hurley*, at least on a superficial level. Dale, an Eagle Scout and scoutmaster, and a student at Rutgers University, joined and led its gay and lesbian organization in expressing a message of gay-friendly counseling for teens in the community, a fact covered by a local newspaper. When BSA executives learned of it, they excluded Dale from membership in the organization, expressing an interpretation of the Boy Scout creed that one must be "morally straight" could not include someone with an openly expressed gay identity.

Dale sued the BSA, relying on a New Jersey statute similar to the one in Massachusetts and the federal equal protection clause. The Court divided, 5-4, over the material relevance of the legal authority in *Hurley* to the facts in *BSA*. The dissenters said *Hurley* did not control the Court because Dale did not seek to express his gay identity message as part of his Eagle Scout role. *BSA* has an ambiguous status as a landmark decision. It is **not** a landmark, if one agrees *Hurley* properly controlled the Court. It **is** a landmark if one agrees with the dissenters that the fact-pattern in *BSA* was sufficiently different from *Hurley* not to control the judgment of the Court.

In *LAWRENCE V. TEXAS*, 539 U.S. 558, No. 02-102 (2002), the Supreme Court held, 6-3, that homosexual sodomy cannot be made a misdemeanor in state law under federal constitutional rights guaranteed in the Fourteenth Amendment. The Court's judgment directly invalidated a state interest with express language targeting homosexual sodomy rather than sodomy per se as criminal conduct. It also is a landmark decision because the majority opinion expressed the logic that the due process clause authorized the Court to invalidate police intrusion against sodomy per se made criminal conduct by a state on any individual's private premises with another consenting adult. In doing so, it overruled *Bowers*. It stopped short of saying homosexual sodomy is a fundamental right.

Gay rights protesters demonstrate for the right to obtain a marriage license. *(Tim Boyle/Newsmakers)*

After overturning *Bowers* in *Lawrence*, the relevant Court precedents about same-sex discrimination are *Hurley, Romer, BSA,* and *Lawrence*. Justice Scalia's dissenting opinion in *Lawrence* expressed the fear that now no standard exists by which to uphold the rational basis of any law enforcement interest deriving from an expressed majority will that morally disapproves of who the sexual partner might be on the private premises of an adult individual. In particular, the next most logical step in the campaign for gay and lesbian rights would be ending the military's policy of excluding openly gay and lesbian members of the services, and invalidating state bans on same-sex marriage.

Even before *Lawrence*, the supreme courts of several states considered the problematic nature of denying same-sex marriage permits. In *Baker v. State*, 744 A.2d 864 (Vt. 1999), the Vermont Supreme Court, in a unanimous vote, held that a liberal legal culture, expressed in the state's constitution of equal benefits for all persons, meant that some form of legal same-sex civil union was required in the state. The ruling opinion directed statewide elected lawmakers to equalize state marriage benefits without same-sex discrimination. The legislative process complied by enacting the state benefit of a legal civil union for its gay and lesbian residents (2000).

In the 1990s, the Supreme Court of Hawaii held that its constitutional provision against discrimination because of gender, and a federal declared fundamental right to marry, made the state interest in denying marriage permits to same-sex couples constitutionally suspect. However, conservative resistance in the population was sufficient to pass a counter referendum vote so that only the state legislature could define a legal marriage.

The thorniest remaining problem in the long cultural war in the United States about constitutional rights and their impact on the lives of gays and lesbians is a discovery of the best standard in a rule of law doctrine about same-sex discrimination.

For more information: Eskridge, William N., Jr. *Gay Law: Challenging the Apartheid of the Closet.* Cambridge, Mass.: Harvard University Press, 1999; Murdoch, Joyce, and Deb Price. *Courting Justice: Gay Men and Lesbians v. the Supreme Court.* New York: Basic Books, 2001; Olyan, Saul B., and Martha C. Nussbaum, eds. *Sexual Orientation and Human Rights in American Religious Discourse.* New York: Oxford University Press, 1998; Strasser, Mark. *Legally Wed: Same-Sex Marriage and the Constitution.* New York: Cornell University Press, 1997.

—Sharon G. Whitney

Geduldig v. Aiello, 417 U.S. 484 (1974)

In *Geduldig v. Aiello,* the Supreme Court held that California's disability insurance system, in excluding pregnancy as a disability, was not creating SEXUAL DISCRIMINATION that violated the EQUAL PROTECTION CLAUSE of the Fourteenth Amendment. The disability insurance program provided private employees up to 26 weeks of benefits for injury and illness that temporarily disabled them from working. Employees contributed 1 percent of their wages, to a maximum of $85 annually, and the money was placed in a special trust fund within the state treasury. Section 2626 of the Unemployment Insurance Code provided for a definition of disability, which included mental or physical illness and mental or physical injury, and explicitly excluded pregnancy as a qualifying disability.

The appellants in the case were four women, three of whom had experienced complications due to pregnancy. The fourth woman, Jacqueline Jamarillo, experienced a normal pregnancy. In 1973 the California State Court of Appeals construed the code as including pregnancy complications as qualifying disabilities, thus excluding only normal pregnancy. The state legislature amended section 2626 to include those conditions resulting from an abnormal pregnancy. The normal pregnancy of Jaramillo, therefore, was the issue in *Geduldig.* The state argued that the disability fund was totally self-supporting, drawing its money only from employee contributions. In the years prior to the litigation, it had paid out between 90 percent and 103 percent of its revenue in benefits. The state was committed to maintaining the 1 percent contribution rate so as to avoid a burden on low-income workers. To add normal pregnancy as a qualifying disability would exceed the budget of the insurance program and render it insolvent.

The Court noted that these were policy determinations. The essential issue for the Court was whether these policy considerations violated the equal protection clause. The Court found that they did not. It found that the state had a legitimate interest in maintaining its disability program as self-supporting. The state had a legitimate interest in keeping benefit payments at an adequate level for the disabilities it did cover, rather than covering more disabilities less adequately. Furthermore, the state had a legitimate interest in keeping employee contributions low.

The Court did not find evidence of invidious discrimination, saying, "while it is true that only women can become pregnant, it does not follow that every legislative classification concerning pregnancy is a sex-based classification" like those discriminations based on sex identified in *Reed v. Reed,* 404 U.S. 71 (1971), and *FRONTIERO V. RICHARDSON,* 411 U.S. 677 (1973). Rather than categorizing citizens into classes based on sex, California's disability insurance program classified workers into two groups: "Pregnant women and nonpregnant persons," with women occupying spaces in both groups.

The dissent was written by Justice BRENNAN, who was joined by Justices DOUGLAS and MARSHALL. The dissent found that there was sex discrimination; while not all women are pregnant at any moment in time, pregnancy is a condition that is linked to gender. "By singling out for less favorable treatment a gender-linked disability peculiar to women," the state created a sex-based double standard. Male-specific disabilities were covered, but female-specific conditions, namely, pregnancy, were not. The dissent relied on *Reed* and *Frontiero* to invoke a higher standard of scrutiny for the sex discrimination that it identified. The dissent complained that in not applying the higher level of scrutiny of *Reed* and *Frontiero* the Court was returning to an earlier period of invidious sex-based classifications, such as those upheld in *MULLER V. OREGON,* 208 U.S. 412 (1908), *Goesaert v. Cleary,* 335 U.S. 464 (1948), and *Hoyt v. Florida,* 368 U.S. 57 (1961).

The Supreme Court would agree upon an intermediate level of scrutiny for sex discrimination in *CRAIG V. BOREN,* 429 U.S. 190 (1976). In 1978 Congress passed the Pregnancy Discrimination Act, which amended TITLE VII OF THE CIVIL RIGHTS ACT OF 1964 to include discrimination of a pregnant employee as sex discrimination.

For more information: Siegel, Reva. "She the People: The Nineteenth Amendment, Sex Equality, Federalism, and the Family," *Harvard Law Review* 115 (February 2002): 947–1,046.

—Kathleen S. Sullivan

Gibbons v. Ogden, 22 U.S.1 (1824)

Gibbons v. Ogden was decided by Chief Justice John MARSHALL on March 2, 1824. It was the first opportunity the Supreme Court had to interpret the commerce clause of Article I, Section 8 of the Constitution. This clause gives Congress the power to regulate commerce with other nations, between states, and with Native-American tribes. The case emerged from a conflict between two different sources of commercial regulation: the state of New York and the federal government.

Aaron Ogden held an exclusive license to operate steamboats from New York to parts of New Jersey through a monopoly established by the New York State Legislature. However, when Thomas Gibbons began running his steamboat along Ogden's route, Ogden sued him. Gibbons argued that his boats were licensed under a 1793 Act of Congress regulating ships employed in the coastal trade and fisheries. He claimed that since this was a federal law, his licenses were valid and the New York State monopoly could not exclude him from navigating in the area. The New York State courts found for Ogden and so Gibbons appealed to the Supreme Court.

Chief Justice Marshall found for Gibbons. He stated that the Constitution vests the power to regulate international and INTERSTATE COMMERCE in Congress exclusively, and that the states could not encroach on this power. States could only pass laws governing commerce within their own boundaries, so long as those laws did not affect interstate or international commerce. Marshall's interpretation of the federal government's regulatory power was very expansive, leaving the door open for Congress to pass almost any law governing interstate and foreign commerce provided that it did not conflict with any other constitutional provisions.

Since the decision was handed down, Congress has used its regulatory power not only to regulate commerce directly but to establish government agencies such as the Drug Enforcement Administration (DEA) and even to fight hate crimes (e.g., Church Arson Prevention Act of 1996, Title 18 U.S.C. Section 246).

For more information: Schwartz, Bernard. *A History of the Supreme Court.* New York: Oxford University Press, 1993.

—Tara Helfman

Gideon v. Wainwright, 372 U.S. 335 (1963)

Gideon v. Wainwright is the landmark United States Supreme Court decision which established an indigent defendant's right to appointed counsel in state criminal trials.

The case came to the Supreme Court's attention when Clarence Earl Gideon submitted a hand-printed petition from prison requesting the Court hear his case. Gideon had been charged with and convicted of breaking and entering into a Panama City, Florida, poolroom and stealing a pint of wine and coins from a cigarette machine. At his trial he asked the judge to appoint counsel for him because he could not afford to hire an attorney. When doing so, Gideon asserted, "The Supreme Court says I'm entitled to be represented by counsel." Nevertheless, the trial judge denied his request; and Gideon defended himself. He was found guilty. Gideon's APPEAL to the Florida Supreme Court, contending that he had been unconstitutionally denied his right to counsel at trial, likewise was rejected.

Gideon was incorrect about the United States Supreme Court's right to counsel doctrine. It had not ruled that the Sixth Amendment's "Assistance of Counsel" guarantee requires appointment of counsel for indigent defendants in state trials. Rather, it had ruled that the Sixth Amendment requires appointment of counsel for all indigent federal felony defendants. The Sixth Amendment, according to the Court, did not apply to the states; and, therefore, there was not a general right to appointed counsel in state criminal trials. Indigent state defendants had a right to appointed counsel only in cases which could subject

defendants to the death penalty or cases involving "special circumstances." "Special circumstances" included a defendant's illiteracy, ignorance, youth, or mental illness; the complexity of the charges; or the behavior of the prosecutor or trial judge. Gideon's case did not meet the "special circumstances" rule, nor did he even suggest it did.

Gideon may have been wrong about settled Supreme Court doctrine, but his timing could not have been more right. The "special circumstances" rule had been heavily criticized. Moreover, it did not fit the current Supreme Court's philosophy supporting equality in the criminal justice process. Chief Justice Earl WARREN even had instructed his law clerks to watch out for a case on appeal that could serve as a vehicle for overturning the "special circumstances" rule. Gideon's case became that vehicle, and the Supreme Court appointed the very able attorney and future Supreme Court justice Abe FORTAS to represent Gideon.

The Supreme Court found for Gideon, overturning the "special circumstances" rule. Justice BLACK, writing for the Court, concluded:

> [R]eason and reflection require us to recognize that in our adversary system of justice, any person haled into court, who is too poor to hire a lawyer, cannot be assured a fair trial unless counsel is provided for him. This seems to us an obvious truth.

The Sixth Amendment, the Court found, applies to the states. An indigent state defendant has a right to appointed counsel.

The Court's decision did not address the scope of this right, whether it applies to indigent state defendants charged with all types of crimes or only with felonies. Later decisions would address that question. Nevertheless, the Court's decision loomed large not only for Gideon but for the workings of the criminal justice system. Gideon was retried, with appointed counsel, and found not guilty; and public defender offices are now part of the legal landscape.

For more information: Lewis, Anthony. *Gideon's Trumpet.* New York: Random House, 1964.

—Georgia Wralstad Ulmschneider

Ginsburg, Ruth Bader (1933–) *Supreme Court justice*

Ruth Bader Ginsburg has had a dynamic professional life as a scholar, a lawyer, a judge, and currently as a United States Supreme Court justice since she was appointed to that body by President Clinton in 1993. Her career can best be understood as having two dichotomous segments. First, she has been an activist scholar and practicing attorney whose career focused on obtaining constitutional equality for women. Second, she has served as a federal jurist who believes clearly in the rule of law and the binding nature of PRECEDENT.

Ruth Bader Ginsburg graduated in 1959 from Columbia Law School where she tied for the first seat in her class. She greatly desired to serve as a law clerk for Supreme Court Justice Felix FRANKFURTER, but he was not prepared to hire a woman as a clerk. So in 1963 she became a law professor at Rutgers University. It was in 1971, when Ginsburg's students asked her to teach a seminar on Women and Law, that she became fascinated with the possibilities that the law holds for guaranteeing gender equality.

The same year Professor Ginsburg was named the first tenured woman at Columbia Law School and became the general counsel of the American Civil Liberties Union's Women's Rights Project. Over the next eight years, building on the work of such women as Pauli Murray, Ginsburg crafted a legal approach that would transform the status of women under the Constitution. For these activities many know her as the "Thurgood MARSHALL of the women's movement." The strategy began with her filing the petitioner's BRIEF in the landmark case of *Reed v. Reed,* 404 U.S. 71 (1971). This case represented the first time in American history that the Supreme Court found a gender-based classification unconstitutional. Her reasoning in this brief would form the foundation for the six cases in favor of gender equity that she would argue before the Supreme Court. As Professor Ginsburg has said, "After that 1971 decision, and until 1980, the year I became a U.S. COURT OF APPEALS judge, the business of ridding the statute books of laws that discriminate on the basis of sex consumed most of my days."

Her first argument before the Court was the landmark case of *FRONTIERO V. RICHARDSON,* 411 U.S. 677 (1973), in which the Court decided that the armed services could not award married men different spousal benefits than married female military personnel. No other member of the current Supreme Court has argued a case before the Court. In addition to the famous brief in *Reed,* she participated in writing eight other briefs to the Court, as well as 15 amicus curiae (friend of the court) briefs. In all of these cases, the lawyer Ginsburg argued that legislation distinguishing between men and women, even to protect women, is based on stereotypes and should be held to the most rigorous scrutiny by the Court. She believed that the EQUAL PROTECTION CLAUSE of the Constitution guaranteed the legal equality and sameness of citizens despite gender differences.

In 1980 President Jimmy Carter named Ruth Bader Ginsburg to the Federal Appellate Court in Washington, D.C. Her philosophy as a judge was quite different from her perspective as an activist lawyer. Justice Ginsburg articulates the values of JUDICIAL RESTRAINT or the belief that

Justice Ruth Bader Ginsburg *(United States Supreme Court)*

the law should be interpreted as narrowly as possible by the courts and that broad policy changes should come from elected legislatures. She embraces the norm of collegiality, arguing that appellate judges should exercise discretion and write dissents as sparingly as possible in order to increase the legitimacy of the courts. Ginsburg also advocates incrementalism, asserting that law evolves and changes, but slowly; previous court decisions or precedents need to be respected and reconsidered sparingly. Because of her cautious philosophy as well as her important constitutional legacy, President Bill Clinton appointed her to the Supreme Court in 1993. The Senate confirmed her with an impressive 96-3 vote for approval.

In her years on the Court, she has disappointed political liberals with her temperate judicial philosophy and annoyed conservatives with her support of individual CIVIL LIBERTIES and CIVIL RIGHTS. Her majority opinion in the *UNITED STATES V. VIRGINIA,* 518 U.S. 515 (1996), case has been her most controversial decision to date. In this case the Court examined the male-only admissions policy of the Virginia Military Institute (VMI); Justice Ginsburg determined that the state must show "exceedingly persuasive justification" in order to treat women differently from men, in this case by excluding women from VMI. This is a more stringent requirement for the state than previous precedent required, and it provides a stronger constitutional protection against gender discrimination. Many scholars note that the Court's decision in *VMI* is the fulfillment of her work as an attorney in the 1970s.

For more information: Kerber, Linda K. *No Constitutional Right to be Ladies: Women and the Obligations of Citizenship.* New York: Hill and Wang, 1998; Morris, Melanie K. "Ruth Bader Ginsburg and Gender Equality: A Reassessment of her Contribution." *Cardozo Women's Law Journal* 9 (2002): 1–25; Yarbrough, Tinsley E. *The Rehnquist Court and the Constitution.* Oxford: Oxford University Press, 2000.

—Michelle Donaldson Deardorff

Gitlow v. New York, 268 U.S. 652 (1925)

The Supreme Court's decision in *Gitlow v. New York* incorporated the First Amendment's freedoms of speech and press to the states.

During the early 20th century, the fear of communism was rampant in the United States. In light of this fear, many states, including New York, created commissions that investigated communist activity. Benjamin Gitlow was arrested as a result of raids carried out by the state of New York's commission. Gitlow was charged with distributing subversive material, the *Left Wing Manifesto,* under criminal anarchy laws. Gitlow's attorneys argued that the state of New York had violated Gitlow's freedom of speech. The defense failed, and Gitlow appealed his case.

The Supreme Court ruled, in a 7-2 decision penned by Justice Edward Sanford, that the state law would be upheld. More important for the future of CIVIL LIBERTIES, however, the Court also incorporated the First Amendment's protection of the freedoms of speech and press to the states. INCORPORATION limits states from impinging upon an individual's right of freedom of speech, no longer limiting the protections of the BILL OF RIGHTS to the federal government. According to the Court, "we may and do assume that freedom of speech and of the press . . . are among the fundamental personal rights and 'liberties' protected by the due process clause of the Fourteenth Amendment against impairment by the States."

However, the Court argued that there is a fundamental dichotomy between an individual's belief and action taken pursuant to that belief. Specifically, "the statute does not penalize the utterance or publication of abstract 'doctrine' . . . having no quality of incitement to any concrete action." Instead, "What it [New York's statute] prohibits is language advocating, advising, or teaching the overthrow of

organized government by unlawful means." The Supreme Court also argued that it should assume the validity of the statute rather than provide for the rights of individuals first. Justice Oliver Wendell HOLMES, in his dissenting opinion, argued that the proposed dichotomy between belief and action was false, and that "Every idea is an incitement," and took the majority, and especially Sanford, to task for failing to apply the correct test to determine the constitutionality of Gitlow's action.

Although the Supreme Court had previously incorporated a portion of the Bill of Rights to the states, the TAKINGS CLAUSE of the Fifth Amendment in *Chicago, Burlington and Quincy Railroad Co. v. Chicago,* 166 U.S. 226 (1897), *Gitlow* was the first case in which the "traditional" rights and liberties were incorporated to the states. This case was the watershed for the incorporation of the freedoms of RELIGION, the rights of a jury trial, right to counsel, and many other of the protections that are widely regarded as the rights required to protect democracy. Moreover, *Gitlow* foresaw a major change in the Supreme Court's case DOCKET, made evident in Justice Harlan STONE's famous footnote four in *UNITED STATES V. CAROLENE PRODUCTS,* 304 U.S. 144 (1938), in which he argued that the Supreme Court would assume the responsibility for the protection of minority rights and the liberties of politically unpopular dissenters.

For more information: Epstein, Lee, and Thomas G. Walker. *Constitutional Law for a Changing America: Rights, Liberties, and Justice.* 4th ed. Washington, D.C.: CQ Press, 2001; Irons, Peter. *A People's History of the Supreme Court.* New York: Penguin, 1999.

—Tobias T. Gibson

Goldwater v. Carter, 444 U.S. 996 (1979)

In *Goldwater v. Carter,* the Supreme Court (acting without ORAL ARGUMENT) dismissed a complaint filed by Senator Barry Goldwater pertaining to the termination of a defense treaty between the United States and Taiwan. In conjunction with formal recognition of the People's Republic of China in Peking, on December 15, 1978, President Jimmy Carter terminated a defense treaty with Taiwan (termination was necessary out of respect to the Chinese belief of the "One China" policy). According to the terms of the treaty termination was possible by either party, provided they give the other country one year's notice. Senator Barry Goldwater sued President Carter claiming that termination of a treaty required legislative approval. By the time the case reached the Supreme Court, the one-year notice had almost expired. Therefore, the Court issued its decision without listening to oral argument.

Unfortunately, the Supreme Court could not articulate a single opinion offering clear guidance regarding termination of TREATIES. Part of the difficulty involved a congressional resolution on treaty termination. Justice POWELL stated in a concurring opinion, "Although the Senate has considered a resolution declaring that Senate approval is necessary for the termination of any mutual defense treaty, no final vote has been taken on the resolution" (444 U.S. at 999). Therefore, according to Justice Powell, "the Judicial Branch should not decide issues affecting the allocation of power between the President and Congress until the political branches reach a constitutional impasse. Otherwise, we would encourage small groups or even individual Members of Congress to seek judicial resolution of issues before the normal political process has the opportunity to resolve the conflict" (444 U.S. at 998).

In a separate concurring opinion, Justice REHNQUIST determined that the case should be dismissed because the issues represented a nonjusticiable political question. "While the Constitution is express as to the manner in which the Senate shall participate in the ratification of a treaty, it is silent as to that body's participation in the abrogation of a treaty" (444 U.S. at 1003). Rehnquist continued by stating, "in light of the absence of any constitutional provision governing the termination of a treaty, and the fact that different termination procedures may be appropriate for different treaties, the instant case in my view must surely be controlled by political standards" (444 U.S. at 1003).

Three justices, BLACKMUN, BRENNAN, and WHITE, dissented from the Court's dismissal of Goldwater's claim. Writing on behalf of himself and Justice White, Justice Blackmun indicated that presidential power to terminate a treaty is such a substantial issue that the Court should not render a decision until after it has heard oral arguments. Writing a separate dissenting opinion, Justice Brennan concluded, "Abrogation of the defense treaty with Taiwan was a necessary incident to Executive recognition of the Peking Government, because the defense treaty was predicated upon the now abandoned view that the Taiwan Government was the only political authority in China. Our cases firmly establish that the Constitution commits to the President alone the power to recognize, and withdraw recognition from, foreign regimes" (444 U.S. at 1007). Therefore, since the Constitution confers recognition of sovereignty to the executive branch, the president possessed the authority to terminate a treaty without the consent of the Senate.

For more information: Adler, David Gray, and Larry N. George, eds. *The Constitution and the Conduct of American Foreign Policy.* Lawrence: University of Kansas Press, 1996; Bellia, Patricia L. "Executive Power in Youngstown's Shadows." *Constitutional Commentary* 19 (2002): 87.

—Kirk A. Randazzo

Good News Club v. Milford Central School District, 533 U.S. 98 (2001)

In *Good News Club v. Milford Central School District*, the Supreme Court ruled that if a school district allows outside activities, it cannot discriminate against any viewpoints, particularly those promoting RELIGION.

The case began in the small upstate New York community of Milford when an evangelical pastor and his wife asked the local schools for permission to operate an after-school bible and hymn-singing club for children ages six through 12. The applicants, Stephen and Darleen Fournier, were district residents who qualified in all respects to oversee an after-school activity on school grounds. The school district did open its doors to after-school activities by groups having an educational, artistic, social, civic, or recreational focus. The school objected to the Good News Club on the grounds that the national Christian evangelical program for children was what its advertising said it was and that religious organizations were not within the description of programs acceptable to the school district.

Pastor Fournier and his wife sued the Milford School District in the U.S. District Court for the Northern District of New York under *42 U.S.C. § 1983*, the CIVIL RIGHTS ACT as well as the First and Fourteenth Amendments of the UNITED STATES CONSTITUTION on behalf of the Club. The school district asked for a preliminary injunction to win an initial ruling that might determine the outcome of the case. The Court ruled in favor of the school district stating in particular that the club was "decidedly religious in nature, and not merely a discussion of secular matters from a religious perspective," which was permitted. The plaintiffs, the club, appealed to the United States COURT OF APPEALS for the Second Circuit, which upheld the order from the district court.

The club appealed to the United States Supreme Court, which reversed the lower courts, ruling that the actions of the school district did not take place in a viewpoint neutral manner, and therefore the regulations of the school board violated the First Amendment of the U.S. Constitution.

Both sides of the controversy had created a "limited public forum." In a limited PUBLIC FORUM, the governmental body, whether it be a federal, state, or local department, may not reject speech on the basis of it being from a particular viewpoint, in this case, evangelical Christianity. There were several rulings prior to the release of this case that supported the ruling, particularly *ROSENBERGER V. RECTOR AND VISITORS OF UNIV. OF VIRGINIA*, 515 U.S. 819 (1995). Referring to that case, Justice THOMAS, writing for the majority, wrote, " . . . we held that a university's refusal to fund a student publication because the publication addressed issues from a religious perspective violated the Free Speech Clause." The opinion of the Supreme Court also relied upon another prior ruling in *LAMB'S CHAPEL V. CENTER MORICHES SCHOOL DIST.*, 508 U.S. 384 (1993). In analogizing between the hymn book and stickers of the Good News Club, the majority opinion was that, "Like the church in *Lamb's Chapel*, the club seeks to address a subject otherwise permitted under the rule, the teaching of morals and character, from a religious standpoint." The dissent among other things pointed out that there was possibility of confusion between school activities and club activities because the club started immediately after school.

—Stanley M. Morris

Goss v. Lopez, 419 U.S. 565 (1975)

The Supreme Court acknowledged that minors possess specific due process rights that are generally to be provided prior to a school suspension in *Goss v. Lopez.* Following a period of student demonstrations in several Columbus, Ohio, public high schools in February and March 1971, nine students were suspended for up to 10 days as a result of their roles in the unrest. Several students claimed that they were not involved in the demonstrations and yet were punished without the opportunity to defend themselves or, at a minimum, present their side of the dispute to school officials.

Ohio law provided free public education to children from age six to 21 and, while not legally mandated to do so, once that right has been granted to Ohio children, a state may not arbitrarily deprive any person of life, liberty, or property without due process of law. The court found that children possess a property interest in obtaining a public education and that this entails due process rights. That is, these children were found to have the right to claim a free education, and this entitlement carried with it subsequent due process claims more extensive than those granted them by the challenged state law.

Parents of the suspended children filed a CLASS ACTION lawsuit against the Columbus Board of Education and public school administrators, alleging that the due process clause of the Fourteenth Amendment guarantees both notice and a hearing. The Ohio law required school officials to notify parents within 24 hours of a suspension and inform the parents of the reasons supporting the suspension, but granted no other due process rights. The district court agreed with the parents and found the Ohio law unconstitutional. The Supreme Court, in a 5-4 decision, affirmed the decision.

In writing for the majority, Justice WHITE found that due process requires that students be provided with oral or written notice of the charges, an opportunity to defend oneself, and, should the charges be denied by the child, a hearing where school administrators may discuss evidence they possess and allow the child to present his or her version of events. Further, he wrote that because the conse-

quences of a suspension could have serious implications for a student and that student's educational opportunities in the future, due process rights serve to protect the minor. "If sustained and recorded, those charges could seriously damage the students' standing with their fellow pupils and their teachers as well as interfere with later opportunities for higher education ad employment."

The majority cited the influential case *TINKER V. DES MOINES SCHOOL DISTRICT,* 393 U.S. 503 (1969), where public high school students were allowed to wear black armbands to protest the U.S. role in Vietnam. Justice White agreed with the outcome in *Tinker,* noting that, as in that case, high school students in this case do not "shed their constitutional rights" at the door of the public high school.

Attempting to balance the rights of minors and those of school administrators, Justice White stopped short of mandating hearings in all circumstances given that it may be too expensive and too burdensome for schools. He noted that emergency circumstances would justify school administrators making suspension decisions without holding hearings until a later date. However, he added that "requiring effective notice and informal hearing permitting the student to give his version of the events will provide a meaningful hedge against erroneous action."

In their dissent, Justice POWELL and three other justices find that short-term suspensions will rarely, if ever, impact the student's educational future and noted that all nine minors named in the class action lawsuit finished the semester without any significant decline in academic performance. Justice Powell also noted that school administrators should be granted the authority to exercise discretion in determining which student should be suspended in order to maintain order in the public schools.

For more information: Elias, Jack A. *Due Process and Higher Education: A Systematic Approach to Fair Decision Making.* San Francisco, Calif.: Jossey-Bass, 2000.

—Susan Zinner

Gratz v. Bollinger, 539 U.S. 244 (2003)

Decided the same day as *GRUTTER V. BOLLINGER,* that upheld the University of Michigan law school's AFFIRMATIVE ACTION admissions policy, the *Gratz* ruling declared the university's undergraduate admissions policy unconstitutional. Jennifer Gratz and Patrick Hamacher, two white students, applied for admission to the University of Michigan's College of Literature, Science and the Arts. Both had credentials in the "qualified" range but were rejected. They sued, alleging that the university's use of racial preferences violates the EQUAL PROTECTION CLAUSE of the Fourteenth Amendment, Title VI of the CIVIL RIGHTS ACT OF 1964, and 42 U.S.C. °1981.

Writing for a 6-3 majority that included Justices O'CONNOR, SCALIA, KENNEDY, and THOMAS, Chief Justice REHNQUIST ruled first that the petitioners had been injured and therefore had proper STANDING to sue, and second, that the way the university used race as a factor in undergraduate admissions was not narrowly tailored to achieve its goal of diversity. Therefore it violated the equal protection clause, Title VI, and 42 U.S.C. °1981.

The University of Michigan employed a "selection index" to help its admissions office rank several thousand applicants each year. The index was based on a 150-point scale. Up to 80 points for G.P.A., 12 points for standardized test scores, eight points for a strong high school curriculum, and three points for an outstanding essay. Other categories included in-state residency (10 pts.), alumni relationship (4 pts.), outstanding leadership (5 pts.), coming from an under-represented county (6 pts.), overcoming adversities such as poverty (5 pts.), special talents such as sports ability (20 pts.), and a "miscellaneous" category in which members of three minority groups, African-American, Hispanic, and Native American were automatically given an extra 20 points. Since under the university's guidelines, achieving 100 points is tantamount to automatic admission, the selected minorities are given one-fifth of the points needed for admission.

The Court ruled that this index does not provide the individualized consideration required under Justice POWELL's opinion in *REGENTS OF THE UNIVERSITY OF CALIFORNIA V. BAKKE* (1978). The scheme is not saved by admission counselors' ability to "flag" cases for special consideration, since that leaves the large majority of applicants with only perfunctory review. Finally, while the university may have a compelling interest in diversity, the cost and inconvenience of individualized consideration does not override the need for a narrowly tailored remedy.

Justices O'Connor, Thomas, and BREYER concurred in the judgment but wrote separate opinions. Justice STEVENS dissented, arguing that petitioners Gratz and Hamacher did not have standing to sue, a position rejected by the majority. Justice SOUTER also dissented, pointing out that an applicant can only be rejected because his combined qualifications do not outweigh those of other applicants. Race is only a "plus" factor, not in itself a deciding one. Justice GINSBURG noted that race is a continuing problem in America that universities must help solve. Michigan's honest, open affirmative action program is preferable to achieving the same goal "through winks, nods and disguises."

Gratz is important primarily as a companion to *Grutter v. Bollinger*. It illustrates what is not a constitutionally acceptable use of affirmative action.

For more information: Ezorsky, Gertrude. *Racism and Justice.* Ithaca, N.Y.: Cornell University Press, 1991.

—Paul J. Weber

Gravel v. United States, 408 U.S. 606 (1972)

In *Gravel v. United States*, the Supreme Court in a 5-4 vote with BRENNAN, DOUGLAS, MARSHALL, and STEWART dissenting held that the speech and debate clause privilege of the Constitution applies to congressmen and their aides in the performance of their duties but does not extend beyond that.

The Constitution authorizes the Senate and the House of Representatives to discipline its members. However, Article I, Section 6 of the Constitution, referred to as the speech and debate clause, also provides safeguards for its members against harassment and intimidation. This privilege of membership has its roots in British practice. The English Parliament in its historical struggles with the British Crown, asserted that its members were immune from arrest during its sessions, and the English Bill of Rights of 1689 embodies this guarantee. In the American Constitution, without the protection of the speech and debate clause, a U.S. president could order the arrest or otherwise intimidate members of Congress in opposition to administration goals and policies. The speech and debate clause provision ensures the integrity of the legislative process through the independence of the individual legislator during the performance of their legislative duties and serves to reinforce the SEPARATION OF POWERS among the government's three branches.

Interpretation of the language of Article I, Section 6 has generally centered on a definition of what is legitimate legislative activity and generated two kinds of constitutional questions: what is protected and who is protected within the speech and debate clause? *Gravel v. United States* addressed both what and who was to be protected.

On June 29, 1971, Senator Mike Gravel, Dem. Alaska, held a public meeting of the Subcommittee on Buildings and Grounds of which he was the chair. Before the hearing began, Gravel made a statement regarding the Vietnam War and then read portions of a classified government document entitled *History of the United States Decision-Making Process on Vietnam Policy*, now known as the *Pentagon Papers*, which provided details of U.S. involvement in the war. Senator Gravel proceeded to introduce the document into the committee's record and arranged for possible republication of the document. There were also media reports that a member of Gravel's staff, Dr. Leonard Rodberg, had spoken with a second publisher regarding possible republication of the classified documents. A grand jury was convened to investigate whether or not any criminal violations had occurred concerning the handling of classified materials. Dr. Rodberg was subpoenaed to testify. Senator Gravel moved to quash the subpoena as a violation of the speech and debate clause because ordering the aide to testify was tantamount to having the senator testify, which according to senator Gravel would violate the speech and debate clause. The district court denied the motion by Senator Gravel but limited the questioning of Senator Gravel's aide. The COURT OF APPEALS affirmed the motion's denial but modified the protective order in ruling that congressional aides and other persons may not be questioned regarding legislative acts and were within the scope of the congressional privilege intended by the speech and debate clause, thereby foreclosing further inquiry by the grand jury. The government petitioned for certiorari to the Supreme Court challenging the ruling of the Court of Appeals.

The Supreme Court answered the question of what is protected by the speech and debate clause by upholding the right of a grand jury to inquire into the circumstances under which a member obtained classified government documents and arranged for their private republication. The court reasoned that the speech and debate clause recognizes speech, voting, and other legislative acts to be immune from liability, however, the speech and debate clause does not extend immunity to either senator or aide to violate an otherwise valid criminal law in preparing or implementing legislative acts.

The Supreme Court's decision in the *Gravel* case not only answered what was protected under the speech and debate clause but also explicitly answered who was protected under the speech and debate clause by fully bringing congressional staff as well as congressional members under the speech and debate clause's protection. In recognizing the expanding role of staff, the court acknowledged that the rapidly changing technology necessary in the performance of legislative duties makes the day-to-day work of congressional aides equivalent to being an alter ego of the congressional member. Not to recognize congressional staff accordingly would significantly diminish the intended effect of the speech and debate clause.

Gravel v. United States illustrated that legislative acts are not all-encompassing. The heart of the speech and debate clause is speech or debate in either House. In this case, the private publication arrangements by Senator Gravel were not part and parcel of the legislative process.

For more information: Kalven, Harry, Jr. *A Worthy Tradition: Freedom of Speech in America.* New York: Harper and Row, 1988.

—William W. Riggs

Gray v. Sanders, 372 U.S. 368 (1963)

Gray v. Sanders, was a landmark case in which Georgia's county-unit primary voting system was declared unconstitutional. It is known as the "ONE PERSON, ONE VOTE" case.

For decades, the Supreme Court declined to enter the political thicket of redistricting. It consistently held that apportionment was a matter of politics and not law. Before the 1961–62 apportionment, population disparities among state legislative constituencies ranged as high as 987 to 1. In 1962, however, in *Baker v. Carr,* 369 U.S. 186 (1962), the Supreme Court held that the courts did indeed have jurisdiction over redistricting issues.

In 1962 a Georgia voter sued to restrain the state from using the county-unit system as a basis for counting votes in a Democratic primary election for the nomination of a U.S. senator and statewide officers. Such primary elections were governed by a Georgia statute, which allocated a certain number of unit-votes to each county. The least populous county had two units, and the most populous county, being 309 times more populous then the smallest one, gave one resident in Echols County an influence in the nomination of candidates equivalent to 99 residents of Fulton County.

The state denied that the county-unit system would be unconstitutional and alleged that it was designed "to achieve a reasonable balance as between urban and rural electoral power." The state also tried to rely on the similarity of the Georgia's county-based system for electing members to the presidential elections' Electoral College during presidential elections.

> The Court called analogies to the electoral college inapposite. The Court realized and expressed the opinion that, although each voter has one vote, the county-unit system weights the rural vote more heavily than the urban vote. [372 U.S. 368, 379]. The Court then "pulled" the principle of equal vote weight from the Constitution by comparing urban Georgia voters with African Americans and women.

The Fifteenth Amendment prohibits a state from denying or abridging a Negro's right to vote. The Nineteenth Amendment does the same for women. If a state in a statewide election weighted the male vote more heavily than the female vote or the white vote more heavily than the Negro vote, none could successfully contend that that discrimination was allowable. How then can one person be given twice or 10 times the voting power of another person in a statewide election merely because he lives in a rural area or because he lives in the smallest rural county? The Court held that "The EQUAL PROTECTION CLAUSE requires that, once a geographical unit for which a representative is to be chosen is designated, all who participate in the election must have an equal vote—whatever their race; whatever their sex; whatever their occupation; whatever their income and wherever their home may be in that geographical unit" [372 U.S. 379–380]. The decision is marked by an often quoted passage by Justice DOUGLAS saying that "[t]he conception of political equality from the Declaration of

Independence, to Lincoln's Gettysburg Address, to the Fifteenth, Seventeenth, and Nineteenth Amendments can mean only one thing—one person, one vote." [372 U.S. 368, 381].

Commentators note that, although the Court treated their result as self-evident and stated that similar reasoning "underlies many of our decisions," this was the first case concerning voting strength and, in fact, *Gray* was actually unprecedented. As Hasen puts it, "the Court majority simply made up this political equality rule out of whole cloth." (*Hasen, p. 22*).

The "one person one vote" principle was followed in a series of Supreme Court cases on weighted voting. In these cases the principle was extended to all levels of government and was further defined. In *Westberry v. Sanders*, 376 U.S. 1 (1964), the Court struck down the election of members of Congress from unequally populated districts. In *REYNOLDS v. SIMS*, 377 U.S. 533 (1964), the Court applied the equal protection clause to invalidate unequally weighted voting in state legislative elections, and in *Avery v. Midland County*, 390 U.S. 474 (1968), the principle of equally weighted votes was extended to local elections.

Soon after these decisions the Court defined different standards for congressional districts on one hand and state and local elections' districts on the other. In state and local districting plans, population disparities under 10 percent generally require no justification from the state and even 89 percent deviation has been upheld for preserving county borders (see *Guffney v. Cummings*, 412 U.S. 772 [1973], and *Brown v. Thompson*, 462 U.S. 835 [1983]).On the other hand, among congressional districts within a particular state, exact mathematical equality is required. This was confirmed in *Karcher v. Daggett*, 462 U.S. 725 (1983), when a deviation of even less than 1 percent from population equality was not sustained due to the lack of a proof of a good-faith effort to achieve mathematically exact apportionment. Some authors see insistence on precise equality of district population especially curious in light of the fact that distribution of 435 seats among the 50 states inevitably entails more than 70 percent deviations among districts of different states (see, for example, Baker, Gordon E. *Whatever Happened to the Reapportionment Revolution in the U.S.* In *Electoral Laws and Their Political Consequences*, New York: Agathon Press, 1986, 257–276, 275–276), edited by Bernard Grofman and Arend Lijphart.

For more information: Hasen, Richard L. *The Supreme Court and Election Law: Judging Equality from* Baker v. Carr *to* Bush v. Gore. New York and London: New York University Press, 2003; Lowenstein, Daniel Hays, and Richard L. Hasen. *Election Law: Cases and Materials*. 2nd ed. Durham, N.C.: Carolina Academic Press, 2001.

—Jurij Toplak

Green v. County School Board of New Kent County, Virginia, 391 U.S. 430 (1968)

In *Green v. County School Board of New Kent County, Virginia*, the Supreme Court ruled that allowing black and white students the freedom to choose their schools did not satisfy a school board's obligation to desegregate its historically segregated school system.

In a unanimous decision written by Justice William J. BRENNAN, Jr., the Court rejected the school choice plan adopted in 1965 by the school district outside of Richmond, Virginia, finding that the plan was unlikely to achieve any real progress toward desegregating a school system that had maintained separate black and white schools under Virginia laws dating back more than half a century. The Court said that after three years of operation, the freedom of choice plan still had 85 percent of black students attending an all-black school.

The decision was significant in a number of important ways. Coming 14 years after the ruling in *BROWN V. BOARD OF EDUCATION*, 347 U.S. 483 (1954), the *Green* decision clearly showed the Supreme Court's frustration that more progress had not been made toward school desegregation. Whereas in *Brown II*, the Court called for progress with "all deliberate speed" [*Brown v. Board of Education*, 349 U.S. 294, 301 (1955)] in *Green* the Court said the delays that had resulted were "no longer tolerable." The Court said, with apparent impatience, "The burden on a school board today is to come forward with a plan that promises realistically to work, and promises realistically to work now."

The decision also continued the Court's unusual effort, begun by Chief Justice Earl WARREN in *Brown*, to have all school desegregation cases decided by unanimous vote.

Green was also of great significance because the Court identified the six areas of school operations in which identification on the basis of race contributed to discrimination and the creation of separate systems for whites and blacks. The six areas, which came to be known in subsequent rulings as the "*Green* factors," were student assignment, faculty, staff, transportation, extracurricular activities, and facilities. The Court found that "racial identification" extended "to every facet of school operations." The message to federal courts from this finding suggested that desegregation had to be achieved in each of these six areas of school operation for there to be meaningful desegregation.

The force of the *Green* factors was blunted some years later when the Supreme Court ruled in *Freeman v. Pitts*, 503 U.S. 467 (1992), that effective desegregation could be achieved factor by factor and did not have to occur all at one time to satisfy the Constitution. Justice Anthony M. KENNEDY wrote that a federal court could relinquish supervision of some aspects of a school system where there has been compliance with a desegregation order while retaining control over other aspects in which compliance has not yet been achieved.

For more information: Douglas, Davison M. *Reading, Writing & Race: The Desegregation of the Charlotte Schools.* Chapel Hill: University of North Carolina Press, 1995; Greenberg, Jack. *Crusaders in the Courts: How a Dedicated Band of Lawyers Fought for the Civil Rights Revolution.* New York: Basic Books, 1995.

—Stephen Wermiel

Gregg v. Georgia, 428 U.S. 153 (1976)

In *Gregg v. Georgia*, the U.S. Supreme Court upheld the constitutionality of Georgia's redesigned capital sentencing process. Four years earlier, the court had struck down Georgia's process for sentencing defendants to death.

In *Gregg*, Georgia presented a two-stage process for trying and sentencing defendants accused of a capital offense. This process involved an initial conviction phase where the jury was asked to determine guilt, followed by a second phase where the jury determined the sentencing penalty. During the penalty phase, the jury was also given guidelines on determining the death sentence. If they found at least one aggravating factor, out of 10 factors defined by statute to make the crime more despicable, the death sentence was warranted. Two factors listed as being aggravating were the depravity of the act and the motive of financial gain. The Georgia law also provided for expedited appellate review of all death penalty sentences so that immediate oversight would be available to ensure that the process was well regulated. In all, five states had their death penalty statutes reviewed at the same time Georgia's statute was reviewed in *Gregg*. Of these, Georgia, Florida, and Texas laws were upheld, while Louisiana and North Carolina laws were struck down due to those states having mandatory death sentence provisions.

The *Gregg* decision was reached by a 7-2 majority, with Justices MARSHALL and BRENNAN the lone dissenters, finding any law upholding the use of the death penalty as a per se violation of the Eighth Amendment's ban on cruel and unusual punishment. Writing for the majority, Justice STEWART found that the Georgia sentencing scheme provided enough guidance and information for jurors to reach their decision with little risk of an arbitrary or capricious result. In addressing the concern that the death penalty itself violated the Constitution's prohibition against cruel and unusual punishment, Stewart wrote that while deterrence had long been a goal of CAPITAL PUNISHMENT practices, no consistent empirical evidence had been produced to either support or refute the deterrent effect. In the absence of deterrence, however, he found that retribution was still a goal of capital punishment. He noted that a large majority of U.S. citizens found the death penalty both a necessary and appropriate punishment. In upholding the constitutionality of capital punishment's retributive function Stewart wrote "moral outrage is not a forbidden objective nor one inconsistent with our respect for the dignity of men." Since *Gregg*, the Court's rationale justifying the use of the death penalty has remained rooted in the goal of retribution, even though the processes of sentencing and review continue to be challenged.

For more information: Bohm, Robert M. *The Death Penalty in America. Current Research.* Cincinnati, Ohio: Anderson, 1991.

—Patricia E. Campie

Griggs v. Duke Power, 401 US 424 (1971)

The *Griggs v. Duke Power* case is viewed as a landmark Supreme Court case and the most significant decision in regards to employment discrimination under the responsibilities enumerated within TITLE VII OF THE CIVIL RIGHTS ACT OF 1964. The decision resulted in the establishing of new definitions of what discriminatory employment practices could be. Most notably, the case established that there did not need to be any intent by a company to deny employment to certain protected members within society, but rather, if the process accomplished the same effect—that then was a violation.

Some black workers at the Duke Power Dan River Steam Station in North Carolina believed they had been the victims of discriminatory employment and promotion practices and subsequently brought this case to court. Duke Power had historically discriminated against the black employees as far as which jobs they could do and which promotions they could be allowed to take. In 1965 Duke Power stopped this outright practice and then established certain requirements for promotion, which included a high school degree, and other testing in order to be considered for other positions within the company. The alleged intent by Duke was not to continue discrimination practices, but inadvertently the end result was the same. Blacks, because of previous discriminatory practices, were not afforded the same access to education as whites were afforded in the years leading up to 1965. Since a larger proportion of blacks were excluded with these new standards, the Supreme Court thought that "practices, procedures, or tests neutral on their face, and even neutral in terms of intent, cannot be maintained if they operate to 'freeze' the status quo of prior discriminatory employment practices." This circumstance of excluding persons through an evaluative measure is known as disparate impact, and no company can engage in such endeavors.

The original intent of the Title VII regulations in relation to the *Griggs* decision was to place the burden of proof upon the company to prove that they did not engage in such practices or that the practices were necessary in order to conduct their business. The burden of proof in disparate impact cases has evolved many times over the years, but then the burden was shifted from the employer to the plaintiff claiming the unfair treatment. Pursuant to this interpretation, the burden shifted again until it was the duty of the plaintiff to identify through direct evidence that the disparate impact was based upon improper or illegal procedures.

The *Griggs* case is believed by some to be one of the most controversial cases in employment law. In terms of the overall restrictions toward employers, the subsequent case law history has fluctuated between strong regulation and loose interpretation. Irrespective of the intent, in order to evaluate a person for a job, the tests given or the evaluation practices must measure the skills of the applicant to the tasks associated with the job. This understanding is because of the *Griggs* case, which to this day is still a standard for protection for underrepresented persons in the labor force.

For more information: Tompkins, Jonathan. *Human Resource Management in Government.* New York: Harper-Collins College, 1995.

—Ernest Alexander Gomez

Griswold v. Connecticut, 381 U.S. 479 (1965)

In *Griswold v. Connecticut,* the Supreme Court upheld access to birth control for married couples and articulated the right of individual privacy for the first time. The argument over access to birth control was an old argument in the United States, harking back to the late 1880s with the passage of the Comstock Law, which identified birth control materials as "obscene" and prevented their being transported through the U.S. mail. Doctors, nurses, and women's clinic workers were not allowed to inform women about birth control until Margaret Sanger (1879–1966) devoted her life to a sustained campaign to legalize birth control.

Asking the courts to intervene when states denied access to birth control was complicated by the issues of STANDING and RIPENESS. In the past, medical personnel and birth control advocates had been denied the right to sue because they had no substantial personal interest and had suffered no damage from such laws. By the time a case made its tedious journey through the legal system, it was no longer consider "ripe" (relevant).

In the absence of successful challenges, laws that prevented access to birth control remained on the books but were rarely enforced. In 1943, in *Tileston v. Ullman,* 318 U.S. 44, which involved Connecticut's ban on birth control drugs and devices, the Supreme Court denied standing to Dr. Tileston who was banned from giving birth control advice to his patients even when their lives were at risk from pregnancy. In 1961, when two married women were denied access to birth control devices and challenged the Connecticut law in *POE V. ULLMAN,* 367 U.S. 556, the Court concluded that the case was not "ripe" because it had never been enforced. A group of Connecticut birth control advocates, headed by Estelle Griswold, the widow of a Yale University president, set out to win the right to challenge the law by opening a Planned Parenthood clinic in New Haven. By previous arrangement, police arrested Estelle Griswold and Dr. C. Lee Buxton, an internationally known gynecologist and Yale University professor, and charged them with "aiding and abetting" individuals to circumvent the existing law. Both were found guilty and fined $100.

In a move that surprised the nation and angered judicial purists, the Supreme Court decided in a 7-2 decision in *Griswold v. Connecticut* that access to birth control was protected by an inherent right to privacy within the context of the institution of marriage. Judicial purists were outraged at what they saw as the Supreme Court's attempt to reinstate SUBSTANTIVE DUE PROCESS, the practice by which the Court essentially made law rather than interpreting it. The right to privacy was not stated anywhere in the U.S. Constitution, although many legal scholars argued that the right was inherent in the BILL OF RIGHTS, particularly in the NINTH AMENDMENT, which stated that "the enumeration in the Constitution, of certain rights, shall not be construed to deny or disparage others retained by the people."

Some scholars insisted that the right to privacy had been integrated into the language of the entire U.S. Constitution. The basis for many of these claims could be traced to what became known as the BRANDEIS brief, written by lawyers Louis D. BRANDEIS (who would later serve on the Supreme Court from 1916 to 1939) and Samuel Warren for the *Harvard Law Review,* in which they presented a classical liberal argument that the right to privacy should evolve from the right of the "inviolate personality," which dictated that individuals should be left alone to pursue their own happiness.

Before *Griswold,* the Supreme Court had accepted the right to privacy only in the circumstances of libel, which protected individuals from being the subject of untrue and malicious written statements, and the Fourth Amendment's guarantee of protection from unreasonable searches and seizures. Despite the 7-2 majority, the fact that the justices wrote six separate opinions is evidence that the justices were divided on the legal grounds for accepting the right to privacy. Writing for the majority, Justice POWELL stated that "guarantees in the Bill of Rights have penumbras, formed by emanations from those guarantees that help give them life and substance," and maintained that the Constitution contains "various guarantees" that "create zones of privacy."

Within the context of *Griswold,* Justice BLACK concluded that the Court was dealing with "a right of privacy older than the Bill of Rights—older than our political parties, older than our school system. Marriage is a coming together for better or for worse, hopefully enduring, and intimate to the degree of being sacred. It is an association that promotes a way of life, not causes; a harmony in living, not political faiths; a bilateral loyalty, not commercial or social projects. Yet it is an association for as noble a purpose as any involved in our prior decisions." This right to privacy articulated in *Griswold* served as the PRECEDENT for the privacy argument in ROE V. WADE in 1973.

For more information: Grossman, Joel B., and Richard S. Wells. *Constitutional Law and Judicial Policymaking.* New York and London: Longman, 1988; O'Brien, David M. *Constitutional Law and Politics, Volume II: Civil Rights and Civil Liberties.* New York: W. W. Norton, 1991.

—Elizabeth Purdy

Grove City College v. Bell, 465 U.S. 555 (1984)

Grove City College v. Bell held that even indirect federal support of a college was sufficient to trigger CIVIL RIGHTS protections; it further held that such support could be compartmentalized into specific programs. This case marked an important, though temporary, reversal for civil rights and the movement for women's equality. *Grove* also represents a rare congressional reversal of a Court decision, as within four years of the 1984 decision the Congress had overridden a presidential veto to reinstate the full impact of TITLE IX.

Title IX of the Education Act ensured that there was no sexual discrimination in colleges and universities that accepted federal aid. Title IX, for example, requires that colleges and universities offer an equal number of athletic scholarships to men and women.

Grove City College is a small, private, and coeducational liberal arts college in Western Pennsylvania. The college rejected state and federal funding, but its students did receive grants from the federal government in the form of financial aid. The U.S. Department of Education held that this constituted federal aid (indirectly) and required Grove City to abide by the terms of Title IX. The college resisted, arguing that the financial aid was assistance to the students, rather than the college. As Justice POWELL pointed out in his concurring message, there was never any hint that Grove City had violated Title IX, just that they refused to certify that they were in compliance.

Grove City can be broken into two legal questions. The "indirect support" question was whether financial aid to the college's students constituted a form of indirect aid to the college. The "compartmentalization" question was whether the college needed to certify its Title IX compliance on an institutional basis or whether it could simply certify that the specific program receiving federal assistance was in compliance.

Byron WHITE, in the opinion of the Court, held that such indirect assistance did in fact constitute federal aid and therefore mandated that the college make arrangements for nondiscrimination in tuition-supported areas. However, White also held that the program was responsible for the certification, not the college. This provided an opportunity for colleges and universities to compartmentalize their federal funding. For example, accept funds for research funding but reject equality in athletic scholarships.

William BRENNAN's dissent struck at exactly that provision, which is but a paragraph in White's decision. Brennan argued that White " . . . completely disregards the broad remedial purposes of Title IX that consistently have controlled our prior interpretations of this civil rights statute." The short paragraph allowing compartmentalization of funding sanctions was deemed a major blow to women's and civil rights.

The reaction to *Grove City* was swift. Women's rights and civil rights groups mobilized to restore the broad application of sanctions for refusing to comply with Title IX. These groups immediately organized a strong lobbying effort in Congress to overturn *Grove City.* Clearly, if universities could compartmentalize programs they could discriminate in areas where federal funding was not a question, for example in athletics. In 1988 Congress passed the Civil Rights Restoration Act over the veto of Ronald Reagan, restoring the broad sanctions for violation of Title IX.

Grove City is an interesting decision on a couple of points. First, it must be remembered that the outcome was overwhelmingly against Grove City College and supported the position of women's rights groups. The one paragraph that allowed institutions to compartmentalize their programs and engage in selective discrimination was the problem. Second, from the perspective of judicial decision-making, *Grove City* is a fascinating case study. White's compartmentalization argument is clearly a departure from case law on the subject. It was an uncharacteristically activist reading of the law. The reaction to the compartmentalization section of the decision could not have come as a surprise, given the dissent. Why was it such a small part of the decision? Did White think that he could get away with such a substantial change to Title IX because Reagan would veto any legislation attempting to overturn *Grove City?* As a judicial decision, *Grove City* is somewhat of an enigma for those attempting to understand how the court makes decisions in relation to other branches of government.

The reaction to *Grove City* was fierce from both the left and the right. Conservatives, many of whom consider Title IX an affront to the independence of the network of conservative colleges and in some cases consider it contrary to biblical teachings, chafe that the indirect support argument was accepted. Liberals reacted swiftly and successfully against the compartmentalization argument.

For more information: Cohen, Greta L., ed. *Women in Sport: Issues and Controversies.* Newbury Park, Calif.: Sage, 1993.

—Tim Hundsdorfer

Grutter v. Bollinger 539 U.S. 306 (2003)

In the summer of 2003 the United States Supreme Court's decision of *Grutter v. Bollinger* was issued, making it its most important ruling on AFFIRMATIVE ACTION since its 1978 case, REGENTS OF THE UNIVERSITY OF CALIFORNIA V. BAKKE. In *Grutter v. Bollinger,* the court upheld the constitutionality of affirmative action, but with some important qualifications. Barbara Grutter, a white Michigan woman, applied to the University of Michigan law school. She had a grade point average of 3.8 and a law school admissions test score of 161. She was denied admission and sued the university, alleging that the law school had accepted less qualified minority applicants. That is discrimination, she argued, and violates the Fourteenth Amendment EQUAL PROTECTION CLAUSE, Title VI of the CIVIL RIGHTS ACT OF 1964, and federal law prohibiting racial preferences.

Writing for a 5-4 majority that included Justices STEVENS, SOUTER, GINSBURG, and BREYER, Justice Sandra Day O'CONNOR held that the law school's admission policy is constitutional because it is a narrowly tailored use of race as only one of several factors in an admissions process designed to create a student body diverse enough to create a critical mass of minorities. The majority followed the PRECEDENT set in *Bakke* upholding the use of race as a valid consideration in admissions as long as there is no numerical or percentage "quota" of minority students. The Court ruled that the use of race to help achieve a diverse student body is a compelling interest of the university, but because it is a public, tax-supported school, it is subject to STRICT SCRUTINY by the courts. Strict scrutiny means that courts examine the intent and sincerity of the policy and whether the means used are narrowly tailored to meet the objectives. The Court also declared that neither remedying past discrimination nor achieving racial balance is a constitutionally acceptable ground for affirmative action. Instead, the majority insisted on a more individualized consideration of the credentials of each applicant, including not only academic credentials but how they might add to the diversity of the student body. Finally, the court observed that affirmative action should end in about 25 years.

Justice Ginsburg concurred to emphasize that the Court's decision accords with international understanding of the purpose of affirmative action as stated in the International Convention on the Elimination of All Forms of Racial Discrimination (ratified by the United States in 1994), and the Convention on the Elimination of All Forms of Discrimination against Women (1979). She also supported the intention to "sunset" affirmative action over the next generation.

Four justices (REHNQUIST, SCALIA, THOMAS, and KENNEDY) dissented, arguing that affirmative action is unconstitutional. Justice Thomas's dissent asserts that the Constitution abhors classifications based on race because these harm all citizens, including those they intend to help. He also observes that Michigan has no compelling interest in having a law school at all, to say nothing of an elite law school, and that using race is an illusory solution, because it does nothing for those too poor or uneducated to participate in elite higher education. He makes the interesting observation that only 16 percent of the law school's graduates stay in Michigan.

Grutter is considered a very important case for several reasons. First, two influential groups, a retired military officer association and a number of Fortune 500 business executives, wrote "friend-of-the-court" briefs supporting affirmative action. The majority opinion cited these briefs several times. Second, although the 2002–2003 Supreme Court was generally considered a conservative court, this decision, along with *Lawrence v. Texas,* striking down an antisodomy statute, showed that the Court is not insensitive to changes in politics and cultural values. Finally, in the case the Court rejected evidence of past discrimination as a basis for affirmative action, insisting that it can only be used to promote diversity.

For more information: Ezorsky, Gertrude. *Racism and Justice.* Ithaca, N.Y.: Cornell University Press, 1991.

—Paul J. Weber

H

Haig v. Agee, 453 U.S. 280 (1981)

In *Haig v. Agee,* the Supreme Court overturned a lower court decision declaring unconstitutional the revocation of a passport by the secretary of state. Philip Agee, an American citizen residing in West Germany, had worked for the Central Intelligence Agency (CIA) from 1957 to 1968. During his employment with the CIA, Agee held key positions in a division responsible for the gathering of covert intelligence in foreign countries. In 1974, at a press conference in London, Agee announced his intent "to expose CIA officers and agents and to take the measures necessary to drive them out of the countries where they are operating" (453 U.S. at 283). Since that public statement Agee traveled abroad extensively, consulting sources in local diplomatic circles and exposing undercover operatives. In response to these actions, U.S. Secretary of State Alexander Haig revoked Agee's passport in 1979.

Agee immediately brought suit against the secretary claiming that Congress had not delegated authority to revoke a passport, and that the revocation—prior to a hearing—violated his Fifth Amendment right to PROCEDURAL DUE PROCESS, and his liberty interest in a right to travel, as well as a First Amendment right to criticize the government. At trial, the federal district court agreed with Agee that revocation exceeded the secretary's authority as stipulated in the Passport Act of 1926, and ordered the secretary to reinstate Agee's passport. A divided panel of the Courts of Appeals affirmed this decision.

Writing for a 7-2 majority of the Court (MARSHALL and BRENNAN dissenting), Chief Justice BURGER overturned the lower court's decision. In his opinion, Burger indicated the Passport Act does not explicitly confer the power of revocation upon the secretary nor does it expressly authorize denial of passports. However, "it is beyond dispute that the secretary has the power to deny a passport for reasons not specified in the statutes" (453 U.S. at 290). Citing the Court's decision in *Kent v. Dulles,* 357 U.S. 116 (1958), Burger acknowledge the executive's authority to deny pass-

ports to individuals participating in illegal activities. Additionally, in *Zemel v. Rusk,* 381 U.S. 1 (1965), the Court held that the secretary of state could restrict travel to Cuba if such travel posed a risk to national security. These precedents indicate that the secretary of state possesses authority beyond the explicit text of particular statutes and that this authority includes revocation of passports.

Chief Justice Burger then addressed the constitutional claims argued by Agee and concluded they were without merit. "Revocation of a passport undeniably curtails travel, but the freedom to travel abroad with a 'letter of introduction' in the form of a passport issued by the sovereign [country] is subordinate to national security and foreign policy considerations; as such, it is subject to reasonable governmental regulation" (453 U.S. at 306). Agee's actions not only jeopardized the security of the United States but also endangered the interests of other countries, thereby damaging foreign relations. As such, the concerns of national security outweigh Agee's individual constitutional challenges.

For more information: Bellia, Patricia L. "Executive Power in Youngstown's Shadows." *Constitutional Commentary* 19 (2002): 87; Roth, Brad R. "The First Amendment in the Foreign Affairs Realm: 'Domesticating' the Restrictions on Citizen Participation." *Temple Political and Civil Rights Law Review* 2 (1993): 255.

—Kirk A. Randazzo

Hammer v. Dagenhart, 247 U.S. 251 (1918)

In *Hammer v. Dagenhart,* the Court declared a federal law intended to limit the use of child labor unconstitutional. The Child Labor Act of 1915 was designed to prevent the use of child labor by restricting the interstate shipment of products produced by child labor. The Court held that this was an unconstitutional use of the commerce power.

Writing for the Court, Justice Day rejected the government's position that the legislation was necessary to prevent those states which permitted child labor from enjoying an unfair advantage over other states. According to Day's interpretation of the Constitution, there were limits on the purposes for which Congress could use the commerce power. For a variety of reasons, some states might enjoy an economic advantage, and the commerce power was not intended to give Congress a general authority to equalize such conditions.

The dual federalist philosophy that dominated the Court during this period held that the Tenth Amendment prevented Congress from using its powers for the purpose of regulating matters that were reserved to the states. According to Justice Day, the Constitution's delegation of legislative powers to Congress was not intended to destroy the local power always existing and carefully reserved to the states in the Tenth Amendment to the Constitution. This local power, according to Justice Day, included police regulations relating to the trade and affairs of the states.

Hence, although the act in question was on its face a regulation of commerce, the Court found that upholding it would sanction an invasion by the federal power of the control of a matter purely local in its character. Applying the act's prohibition on the interstate shipment of goods produced by child labor would have the effect of extending Congress's regulatory power to a subject that was reserved to the states. Consequently, the Court concluded that the act transcended the authority delegated to Congress over commerce.

The fact that it resulted in the invalidation of a law designed to prevent the abuse of child labor made the *Hammer* decision very controversial. Many felt that the Court was sacrificing society's interest in preventing the exploitation of children on the altar of dual FEDERALISM. In his defense of the decision, Justice Day stressed the Court's overriding concern with preserving the fundamentals of the federal system. In his opinion, "allowing this type of federal regulation of local matters would threaten the power of the states over local matters . . . and thus our system of government [would] be practically destroyed."

The narrow conception of the commerce power advanced by the Court in *Hammer* was rejected by the Court some 23 years later in UNITED STATES V. DARBY, 312 U.S. 100 (1941). Like the Child Labor Act, the Fair Labor Standards Act of 1938 prohibited the interstate shipment of goods produced in violation of its provisions concerning wages and hours, and child labor. However, in this case, the Court overruled the *Hammer* PRECEDENT. Writing for the Court, Justice Day emphasized that the motive or purpose of congressional regulations of commerce were not proper subjects for judicial scrutiny, and regulations such as the ones in the Fair Labor Standards Act were within the PLENARY POWER conferred on Congress by the commerce clause.

For more information: Benson, Paul R. *The Supreme Court and the Commerce Clause, 1937–1970.* New York: Dunellen Publishing, 1970; Corwin, Edward S. *The Commerce Power versus States Rights.* Princeton, N.J.: Princeton University Press, 1936.

—Justin Halpern

J. W. Hampton, Jr., & Co. v. United States, 276 U.S. 394 (1928)

J. W. Hampton, Jr., & Co. v. United States upheld congressional authority to delegate legislative power to the executive branch and upheld the use of tariffs to protect industries within the United States. Section 315 of the Tariff Act, which became law on September 21, 1922, included a "flexible tariff provision." This statute gave the president the power to raise rates on tariffs to higher rates than those assigned by the Tariff Act itself. Section 315 (a) stated, when the president determines:

> . . . that the duties fixed in this act do not equalize the said differences in costs of production in the United States and the principal competing country he shall, by such investigation, ascertain said differences and determine and proclaim the changes in classifications or increases or decreases in any rate of duty provided in this act.

On May 19, 1924, President Calvin Coolidge used this provision, concluding that the tariff on barium dioxide imported from Germany should be raised from four cents per pound to six cents per pound.

J. W. Hampton, Jr., & Co. imported barium oxide into New York, whereupon the collector of customs levied a six cents per pound dutiable rate on the company. When charged the tariff, the company made two distinct claims. First, the Tariff Act unconstitutionally delegates legislative power to the president, because Article 1, Section 8 of the Constitution declares that only "the Congress shall have power to lay and collect taxes, duties, imposts and excises." Second, the Tariff Act in itself is unconstitutional, because the Constitution gives Congress the power to lay taxes to raise revenue, not to protect industries within the United States.

The United States Supreme Court decided *J. W. Hampton, Jr., & Co. v. United States,* 276 U.S. 394 (1928), on April 9, 1928, by a vote of 9 to 0; Chief Justice William Howard TAFT delivered the opinion of the Court. Chief Justice Taft began his opinion in regards to the first claim that Section 315 violated the Constitution by illegally delegating legislative powers to the president. First Taft explained that the intent of Congress is "perfectly clear and perfectly intelligible." Congress admitted that they themselves may not have enacted tariffs strong enough to protect American industries, so once the statute is enacted, the executive branch must determine when the levels of tariffs are insufficient. Since the president is chief executive, he was given the power.

Second, although the Constitution clearly defines the government in terms of three branches, the three branches of government are coordinated parts of one government; all working together, and at times, duties will overlap.

Third, Taft described congressional authority over INTERSTATE COMMERCE and how Congress had delegated powers to the INTERSTATE COMMERCE COMMISSION, an executive agency. Taft explained,

> The same principle that permits Congress to exercise its rate-making power in interstate commerce by declaring the rule which shall prevail in the legislative fixing of rates . . . justifies a similar provision for the fixing of customs duties on imported merchandise. If Congress shall lay down by legislative act an intelligible principle to which the person or body authorized to fix such rates is directed to conform, such legislative action is not a forbidden delegation of legislative power.

Known as the "Hampton Intelligible Principle" doctrine, this has become a major PRECEDENT in administrative law.

Justice Taft did not give much credence to the second claim concerning Congress unconstitutionally laying taxes to protect industries, rather than to collect revenue. He cited historical precedence dating back to the first revenue act, passed on July 4, 1779, where Congress included in its reason for taxing imports "protection of manufacturers."

This case became widely known for two reasons. First, the "intelligible principle" guideline, written for the Court on behalf of Chief Justice Taft, gave this case a defining role in administrative law. Second, although several protective tariffs had already been used during U.S. history, this case was the first time the Supreme Court took up the issue.

For more information: Epstein, Lee, and Thomas G. Walker. *Constitutional Law for a Changing America: Institutional Powers and Constraints.* 2nd ed. Washington, D.C.: CQ Press, 1995; Nowak, John, Ronald D. Rotunda, and J. Nelson Young. *Handbook on Constitutional Law.* St. Paul, Minn.: West, 1978.

—Jewerl Maxwell

Harlan, John Marshall (1899–1971) *Supreme Court justice*

John Marshall Harlan II was an associate justice of the United States Supreme Court, serving on it from 1955 to 1971. Born into a family of civic-minded lawyers, Harlan seemed almost destined for a life of public service. Harlan's

Justice John Marshall Harlan *(Library of Congress)*

great-grandfather was a member of Congress and a state attorney general. His father was a Republican lawyer-activist in Chicago and an alderman. His grandfather was the distinguished Justice John Marshall Harlan who served on the United States Supreme Court from 1877 to 1911.

Educated in his younger years at boarding schools in Canada and New York state, he attended Princeton University from 1916 to 1920. While at Princeton he won a prestigious Rhodes Scholarship to Oxford University. There Harlan studied jurisprudence. Following his stint at Oxford, Harlan returned to the United States and continued to pursue his interest in law. He joined the prestigious law firm Root, Clark, Buckner and Howland; enrolled in New York Law School; and was admitted to the bar in 1925.

Befriended by the firm's very able trial lawyer Emory Buckner, Harlan, too, became a well-known, very skilled litigator, specializing in corporate and antitrust matters. Buckner also mentored Harlan in his public service career. Harlan was Buckner's chief assistant when Buckner became a U.S. attorney in 1925, heading up the unit that enforced Prohibition. Then, when Buckner was appointed a special attorney of New York in 1928, Harlan became his assistant. In 1930 Harlan returned to Root, Clark, Buckner and Howland, becoming a partner in 1931. Harlan's celebrated private practice was interrupted twice more. First, in World War II he served as the chief of the operational analysis section of the Eighth Air Force, the section charged with improving bombing accuracy over Germany. Second, in 1951 he became chief counsel for Governor Thomas Dewey's New York State Crime Commission, a post that placed him in contact with Dewey's then aide Herbert Brownell.

It was Harlan's association with Brownell, coupled with his Republican background and stellar legal career, that made him such an attractive judicial candidate to President Eisenhower. In 1954, upon the recommendation of his attorney general, Herbert Brownell, Eisenhower nominated Harlan to replace Justice Robert H. JACKSON on the U.S. Supreme Court. Harlan's confirmation by the Senate was delayed briefly by conservative and southern senators to express their unhappiness with the WARREN Court, specifically its school desegregation decision. Moreover, conservative and southern senators ironically attacked Harlan as an "ultraliberal" and as a judicial activist.

During his tenure on the Court, Harlan, unlike the majority of his fellow justices, eschewed JUDICIAL ACTIVISM. Rather, he, like his mentor on the Court Felix FRANKFURTER, was a strong advocate for judicial restraint. He believed that the Court should play a limited role in promoting social and political reform. The Court, according to Harlan, should defer to the decisions of the elected branches of the federal and state governments. His advocacy of judicial restraint was fueled by his respect for the principles of SEPARATION OF POWERS and FEDERALISM, as was apparent in his dissent in *Baker v. Carr,* 369 U.S. 186 (1962), the landmark decision which held that state reapportionment cases could be heard by federal courts. His restrained approach was also apparent in his *MIRANDA V. ARIZONA,* 384 U.S. 436 (1966), dissent in which he attacked the restrictions placed on police interrogations.

While he was considered a conservative, Justice Harlan, nevertheless, would not hesitate to vote with his more liberal activist colleagues when he deemed it appropriate. In *COHEN V. CALIFORNIA,* 403 U.S. 15 (1971), he wrote the opinion for the Court holding that wearing a jacket in a courthouse with an anti-draft expletive emblazoned on it is protected by the First Amendment free speech guarantee. Harlan approached each case individually, meticulously, and with attention to detail. "Judicial craftsmanship" was his watchword.

For more information: "Mr. Justice Harlan: A Symposium," *Harvard Law Review* 85 (December 1971): 369–391; Yarbrough, Tinsley L. *John Marshall Harlan: Great Dissenter of the Warren Court.* Oxford: Oxford University Press, 1992.

—Georgia Wralstad Ulmschneider

Harmelin v. Michigan, 501 U.S. 957 (1991)

In *Harmelin v. Michigan,* the Court considered whether the cruel and unusual punishment clause of the Eighth Amendment prohibited a sentence of life imprisonment without parole that was imposed under a statute making that sentence mandatory for any defendant convicted of possession of more than 650 grams of cocaine. The Court held that such a sentence was constitutional.

On May 12, 1986, law enforcement officers stopped Ronald Harmelin, a 46-year-old unemployed Air Force veteran with no prior felony convictions, for running a red light. They subsequently found 672.5 grams of cocaine in the trunk of his car. A 1978 Michigan law mandated a sentence of life imprisonment without the possibility of parole for those convicted of possession of more than 650 grams of cocaine.

Prior to *Harmelin,* the Court addressed the concept of proportionality under the Eighth Amendment in four noteworthy noncapital cases. In *Weems v. United States,* 217 U.S. 349 (1910), the Court held that a term of 12 to 15 years of imprisonment plus the termination of individual rights, such as the right to PRIVACY, violated the cruel and unusual punishment clause. Seventy years later in *Rummel v. Estelle,* 445 U.S. 263 (1980), the Court held that a sentence of life imprisonment with the possibility of parole was not disproportionate when applied in the case of a man convicted under the Texas habitual offender statute of three nonviolent felonies.

Two years later in *Hutto v. Davis,* 454 U.S. 370 (1982), the Court held that the Eighth Amendment did not preclude a 40-year prison sentence for possessing and distributing approximately nine ounces of marijuana. Finally, in *Solem v. Helm,* 463 U.S. 277 (1983), the Court held that a sentence of life imprisonment without the possibility of parole that had been imposed on a habitual offender convicted of seven nonviolent felonies in South Dakota was significantly disproportionate and therefore violated the cruel and unusual punishment clause. The Court distinguished this case from *Rummel* because, unlike the defendant in *Rummel,* who was eligible for parole, the defendant in *Helm* in all likelihood would have spent the rest of his life in prison.

In *Harmelin,* a five-to-four majority rejected the defendant's Eighth Amendment challenge to a life-without-parole sentence. However the majority split as to its reasoning. Justice SCALIA, joined by Chief Justice REHNQUIST, took the position that the Eighth Amendment did not contain a proportionality requirement that applied to prison sentences. Justice Scalia acknowledged that the Eighth Amendment arguably contained a proportionality requirement that could sometimes be applied in capital cases. He argued, however, that the framers of the Constitution were concerned about inhumane or torturous kinds of punishments, but not about the relationship between the length of incarceration and the crime or crimes of which a defendant had been convicted.

In an opinion concurring in part and concurring in the judgment, Justice KENNEDY, joined by Justices SOUTER and O'CONNOR, expressed disagreement with the Scalia-Rehnquist view that the Eighth Amendment contained no proportionality principle that applied to prison sentences. Justice Kennedy contended that there was such a principle, but that it was a very narrow one that forbids only extraordinarily long prison sentences that are grossly disproportionate to the crimes. Justice Kennedy asserted that Ronald Harmelin's life-without-parole sentence did not fall into this category, primarily because the possession of such a large quantity of cocaine was an extremely serious offense that could easily have led to drug-related violence.

All five justices who made up the majority agreed that the mandatory nature of the sentence in and of itself did not violate the Eighth Amendment. Justice Scalia argued that nothing in the text or history of the Eighth Amendment entitled noncapital defendants to individualized sentencing under which factors such as the defendant's lack of a criminal record and his amenability to rehabilitation could be considered as mitigating factors. Justice Kennedy opined that the Court might be justified in striking down mandatory prison sentences under truly exceptional circumstances. He concluded, however, that Harmelin's case did not fall within this category.

Justice WHITE, joined by Justices BLACKMUN, MARSHALL, and STEVENS, issued a dissenting opinion that objected to both Justice Scalia's and Justice Kennedy's approaches to Eighth Amendment proportionality jurisprudence. Justice White stressed that the Court's prior decisions made it clear that grossly disproportionate prison sentences were forbidden by the Eighth Amendment. It was also significant, according to Justice White, that the Michigan law under which Harmelin was sentenced was the harshest such law in the country and that arguably more serious offenders in Michigan—second-degree murderers, rapists, and armed robbers—received shorter sentences than did Ronald Harmelin. These factors, Justice White concluded, left no doubt that Harmelin's sentence was unconstitutionally disproportionate.

Harmelin v. Michigan is a significant decision in Eighth Amendment history. Although only two justices took the position that the Eighth Amendment contains no proportionality principle applicable to lengthy terms of imprisonment, the majority opinion ensures that successful proportionality challenges will be exceedingly rare.

The *Harmelin* decision was cited heavily in two 2003 decisions upholding prison sentences imposed under California's "three-strikes" law. In EWING V. CALIFORNIA, 583 U.S. 11 (2003), the Court upheld a 25-year sentence imposed on a man whose third strike was stealing three golf clubs valued at $1,197. In *Lockyer v. Andrade,* 583 U.S. 63 (2003), the Court affirmed a 50-year sentence imposed on a man whose third strike was shoplifting videotapes worth approximately $150.

For more information: Haas, Kenneth C. "Excessive Sentences." In *Encyclopedia of American Prisons,* edited by Marilyn D. McShane and Frank P. Williams III, 427–436. New York: Garland, 1996; Hackney, G. D. "A Trunk Full of Trouble: *Harmelin v. Michigan." Harvard Civil Rights-Civil Liberties Law Review* 27:1 (1992): 262–280.

—Kenneth C. Haas
—Rosalyn S. Sutherland
—Ryan Donaghy

harmless error

Procedural errors that do not affect the final outcome of a court case are called harmless errors. *Chapman v. California,* 386 U.S. 18 (1967), is one of the earlier cases of the 20th century that explores this doctrine. This case, as well as others that gather support from this doctrine, help define errors that are constitutional in nature and involve rights basic to the trial and that could never be harmless as subject to the harmless error doctrine. *Chapman v. California, Delaware v. Van Arsdall,* and ARIZONA V. FULMINANTE each help to explain this legal doctrine.

Petitioners Ruth Elizabeth Chapman and Thomas LeRoy Teale were convicted by the state of California for robbing, kidnapping and murdering a bartender. Under California statute, the Constitution explains that in a criminal case the witnesses' testimony, or unwillingness to testify, can be commented on by the court and counsel. Throughout the trial, the prosecution repeatedly brought to the attention of the Court the unwillingness of both Chapman and Teale to testify, inferring their guilt numerous times based on those actions. Justice Hugo BLACK delivered the opinion of the Court, explaining after applying the harmless-error doctrine that the error was not harmless and violated the petitioners' Fifth Amendment rights to self-incrimination. California's harmless-error provision, which the state of California failed to prescribe to, includes the following three conditions:

a. This Court has jurisdiction to formulate a harmless-error rule that will protect a defendant's federal right under the Fifth and Fourteenth Amendments to be free from state penalties for not testifying in his criminal trial.
b. Before a constitutional error can be held to be harmless the court must be able to declare its belief that it was harmless beyond a reasonable doubt.
c. The state in this case did not demonstrate beyond a reasonable doubt that the prosecutor's repetitive comments

to the jury and the trial court's instruction concerning the petitioners' failure to testify did not contribute to their convictions.

Delaware v. Van Arsdall, 475 U.S. 673, 681 (1986), is another case where examination of the harmless-error doctrine helped to determine the decision. In the case, the respondent was charged with the murder of a woman. However, the Delaware court refused to allow cross-examination by the defense counsel regarding an agreement that was made by a witness and the prosecution. After the respondent was convicted, the Delaware Supreme Court reversed the decision, explaining that restricting the defense's cross-examination was a violation of the confrontation clause of the Sixth Amendment. The Court refused to consider whether the prior ruling was subject to harmless error beyond a reasonable doubt.

The Court held in this case that the ruling was, indeed, subject to the harmless error doctrine because of the government's failure to prove beyond a reasonable doubt that the error was harmless. Furthermore, the Court explained that the following factors should be taken into account, even if the violation of the confrontation clause had been made: the importance of the witness's testimony, if the testimony was cumulative, the presence corroborating testimony on material points, the extent of cross-examination otherwise permitted, and the overall strength of the prosecution's case. Chief Justice REHNQUIST, giving the opinion for the court, stated that by rebuffing the state's effort to show that the error did not contribute to the verdict, the court found the ruling unconvincing.

Arizona v. Fulminante, 499 U.S. 279 (1991), is a more recent court case involving the doctrine. In the case Oreste Fulminante was charged for the murder of his 11-year-old stepdaughter, after admitting evidence that his confession was coerced. The confession came while he was in prison, and to a man named Anthony Sarivola, who claimed Fulminante's life was in danger if he did not confess to the crime. Agreeing with the Arizona Supreme Court that the confession was, in fact, coerced, the underlying problem in this particular case revolves around the use of coercion as a base for measuring whether harmless error was involved. In cases prior to *Arizona v. Fulminante* the use of coerced confessions was not necessarily applicable to the harmless-error analysis, and *Chapman* even recognizes coerced confessions as those that can never be treated as harmless-error. This case actually broadens the scope of the harmless-error doctrine, applying it to confessions that were once seen as inadmissible.

Harmless-error doctrine has been used in many different channels in the court system and has seen an expansion over the years, often not in favor of the rights of the prosecuted. Each of the cases presents an interesting account of this doctrine's use and its shaping in the past few decades.

For more information: Bentele, Ursula, and Eve Cary. *Appellate Advocacy: Principles and Practice.* Cincinnati, Ohio: Anderson Publishing, 1998; Traynor, Roger J. *The Riddle of Harmless Error.* Columbus: Ohio State University Press, 1970.

Harper v. Virginia State Board of Elections, 383 U.S. 663 (1966)

In *Harper v. Virginia State Board of Elections,* the Court held that the imposition of a poll tax by a state as a condition of voting violates the EQUAL PROTECTION CLAUSE of the Fourteenth Amendment. The Virginia Constitution had required the legislature of that state to levy a poll tax of $1.50 on all residents age 21 or older and conditioned the right to vote on payment of the tax. Residents of Virginia challenged these provisions, but the district court dismissed their complaint, relying on an earlier Supreme Court case, *Breedlove v. Suttles,* 302 U.S. 277 (1937), in which a similar tax had been upheld. Because the Twenty-fourth Amendment, had, in the meantime, outlawed poll taxes in federal elections, *Harper* concerned only their use in state elections.

The Fourteenth Amendment directs that "[n]o State shall . . . deny to any person within its jurisdiction the equal protection of the laws." Justice DOUGLAS, writing for the Court, explained that legal classifications that restrain the exercise of FUNDAMENTAL RIGHTS must, under well-established PRECEDENT interpreting the Fourteenth Amendment, be closely scrutinized. Because the right to vote was the "preservative of all rights" [*YICK WO V. HOPKINS,* 118 U.S. 356 (1886)], strict analysis by the Court was in order whenever any infringement of it was alleged. Accordingly, the Court had, in the past, upheld state laws imposing reasonable residence restrictions on the right to vote [*Pope v. Williams,* 193 U.S. 621 (1904)] but had rejected laws that prohibited members of the armed forces from voting [*Carrington v. Rash,* 380 U.S. 89 (1965)], as well as distinctions based on the homesite or occupation of the prospective voter.

On this basis, the Court concluded that a state may not use wealth or the payment of a fee to distinguish between those who may and those who may not vote in elections. The Court reasoned that although a state has an interest in fixing voter qualifications, neither the affluence of the voter nor the payment of a fee has any relation to the ability of an individual to "participate intelligently in the electoral process." Thus, the imposition of a poll tax constituted "invidious" discrimination and violated the equal protection clause.

The Court rejected the contention that the poll tax was no different from any other fee required by the state for a variety of licenses, such as a driver's license. The right to vote, unlike a license to drive, was a fundamental right, and the interest of the state was limited to that of prescribing proper qualifications for those who may vote. The Court likened the poll tax, which distinguished potential voters on the basis of wealth, to classifications based on race. Like race, wealth was a "capricious or irrelevant factor" in determining the qualifications of voters [*Harper,* 383 U.S. at 668]. Additionally, the Court explicitly overruled the holding of *Breedlove,* in which a Georgia statute imposing a poll tax of one dollar was upheld against an equal protection claim. The Court declared that because accepted notions of equality and equal treatment vary over time, the equal protection clause will necessarily be interpreted differently in different eras. As an illustration of this, the Court cited *BROWN V. BOARD OF EDUCATION,* 347 U.S. 483 (1954), which had reexamined and reversed the rule of "separate but equal" adopted 58 years earlier in *PLESSY V. FERGUSON,* 163 U.S. 537 (1896).

Justice BLACK and Justice HARLAN, the latter joined by Justice STEWART, dissented. Justice Black asserted that the poll tax served the state policies of raising revenue and of confining the right to vote to those who took an interest in promoting the welfare of the state. Because the poll tax furthered these interests, it was not "irrational," "arbitrary," or "invidious" and consequently did not violate the equal protection clause. Justice Black accused the majority of effectively amending the Constitution to implement a preferred governmental policy. According to Justice Harlan, the tendency of a poll tax to promote civic responsibility and the view that people with property have a greater stake in public affairs were at least rational bases supporting the constitutionality of such a tax. The equal protection clause, Justice Harlan concluded, did not "rigidly impose upon America an ideology of unrestrained egalitarianism."

For more information: Hasen, Richard L. *The Supreme Court and Election Law.* New York: New York University Press, 2003.

—Andy V. Bardos
—Nicole M. James
—Kevin G. Pearce

Harris v. Forklift Systems, Inc., 510 U.S. 17 (1993)

In *Harris v. Forklift Systems, Inc,* the Supreme Court held that SEXUAL HARASSMENT occurs when a reasonable person would describe the work environment as hostile or abusive. The victim need not demonstrate specific psychological harm.

Teresa Harris was a manger at Forklift Systems, an equipment rental company where she was the only woman in a position of authority. The company's president, Charles Hardy, targeted her for an ongoing barrage of unwanted sexual comments and behaviors. He belittled her intelligence as a woman, suggested that she accompany him to a motel to work out business issues, and made comments about her clothing. He also asked Harris and other female employees to retrieve coins from his front pants pockets and to get down on the floor to pick up money he threw there. When Harris complained to Hardy, he claimed to be surprised that she was offended by his "joking" and promised to stop. Later, however, in front of other employees and customers he accused Harris of exchanging sex for a business contract. At that point, Harris left the company and brought suit under the CIVIL RIGHTS ACT OF 1964 for sexual harassment, claiming that Hardy's behavior had created a hostile work environment.

The lower courts denied Harris's claim because she did not suffer a specific injury but the Supreme Court disagreed. They found that unlawful discrimination under the Civil Rights Act, including sexual harassment, included "the entire spectrum of disparate treatment of men and women" in employment. In a workplace "permeated with discriminatory intimidation, ridicule, and insult" where conditions create a hostile environment, a violation occurs. They held that a hostile environment was one in which a "reasonable person" would find severe and pervasive abuse.

In writing the opinion of the Court, Justice Sandra Day O'CONNOR noted that the harassing conduct did not need to cause a "nervous breakdown" but only to be serious enough to detract from the employee's job performance. In determining when behavior had crossed the line into a hostile environment, the Court suggested considering the frequency, severity, threatening, or humiliating qualities of the conduct. The ruling clearly intended to place the burden of defining sexual harassment on conduct that a reasonable person would find hostile, not on the measurable effects on the victim.

Justice Ruth Bader Ginsberg, the other woman on the Court, wrote a concurring opinion in which she argued that discriminatory conduct, in the form of sexual harassment, occurred when working conditions were so altered as to "make it more difficult to do the job."

Harris v. Forklift Systems raises the question of defining the "reasonable person" who gets to decide when behavior creates a hostile environment. Will a reasonable man have a different standard than a reasonable woman? While Hardy thought his conduct was just "joking," most women would probably agree with Harris that it was abusive. Some scholars have argued that in determining reasonableness, the courts should consider the reasonable "person" to be the same sex as the victim. If the target of harassment is female, the reasonable person standard would reflect the expectations of a woman who expected to be treated with respect in the workplace.

For more information: Forell, Caroline A., and Donna M. Matthews. *A Law of Her Own: The Reasonable Woman as a Measure of Man.* New York: New York University Press, 2000.

—Mary Welek Atwell

Harris v. McRae, 448 U.S. 297 (1980)

In *Harris v. McRae,* the United States Supreme Court upheld the Hyde Amendment to Title XIX of the Social Security Act, which banned the use of Medicaid funds for abortions. The Hyde Amendment was first introduced in the House of Representatives by Henry Hyde (Rep.-Ill.) and in the Senate by Jesse Helms (Rep.-N.C.) in 1976 as an amendment to an appropriations bill for the Departments of Labor and Health, Education, and Welfare (now Health and Human Services). The Hyde Amendment stated that: "None of the funding contained in the Act shall be used to perform abortions except when the life of the mother would be endangered if the pregnancy were carried to term." The amendment was designed to reduce the impact of *ROE V. WADE,* 410 U.S. 113 (1973), which had guaranteed a constitutional right to an abortion. Congress reaffirmed the Hyde Amendment each year during the appropriations process.

Cora McRae, an indigent pregnant woman, had gone to a New York Planned Parenthood clinic to arrange for a doctor-recommended abortion. Because of the Hyde Amendment, Medicaid refused to pay for the abortion because McRae's life was not in danger. McRae and four other women from Connecticut and Minnesota challenged the Hyde Amendment on behalf of all indigent pregnant women. The ages of the five women ranged from 15 to 25. Two were suffering from pregnancy-related depression and one had been diagnosed with phlebitis. The women argued that the Hyde Amendment violated the due process clause of the Fifth Amendment.

The five women were joined in their suit by the Women's Division of the Board of Global Ministries of the United Methodist Church, whose membership included women who had also been denied public funding for medically necessary abortions. The Women's Division insisted that it was being bound by religious beliefs in which they did not share in clear violation of the freedom of exercise and establishment clauses of the First Amendment. In a companion suit filed by the New York City Health and Hospital Corporation, the largest provider of abortions to indigent pregnant women in New York City, six physicians claimed that their ability to provide adequate health services had been compromised by the Hyde Amendment. The

pro-choice advocates argued that states should be forced to treat abortions as part of women's health services and pointed out that the Hyde Amendment ignored legitimate medical emergencies such as when the fetus was already dead or in cases of rape and incest.

On the antiabortion side of the issue, Secretary Patricia R. Harris of the Department of Health and Human Services, who had been charged with implementation of Medicaid funds by the U.S. government, was joined by antiabortionist Isabella Pernicone, who had been given legal status as guardian *ad litem* for all unborn fetuses, and by Henry Hyde and Jesse Helms who allegedly represented all taxpayers.

In *Harris v. McRae,* Justice STEWART, writing for the majority, maintained that states were not bound to pay for abortions despite the Hyde Amendment. Neither did the "funding restrictions of the Hyde Amendment . . . impinge on the 'liberty' protected by the due process clause of the Fifth Amendment." Even though the Court stood by *Roe v. Wade,* Justice STEVENS argued that "it does not follow that a woman's freedom of choice carries with it a constitutional entitlement to the financial resources to avail herself of the full range of protected choices."

The Court gave scant consideration to the claim that the Hyde Amendment violated religious freedom, deciding that all appellees lacked STANDING to challenge on those grounds. Justices MARSHALL and Stevens joined Justice BRENNAN in a strong dissent to the majority view, arguing that the "State's interest in protecting the potential life of the fetus cannot justify the exclusion of financially and medically needy women from the benefits to which they would otherwise be entitled solely because the treatment that a doctor has concluded is medically necessary involves an abortion."

After a number of variations in the Hyde Amendment since its inception in 1976, Congress has generally allowed exceptions in cases of rape and incest and when a mother's life or health is at risk. Most states also continue to deny funding for abortions for their poorest women. Hawaii, New York, and Washington treat abortion as part of general health services for women. Fourteen additional states provide nondiscriminatory public funding: Alaska, California, Connecticut, Idaho, Illinois, Massachusetts, Minnesota, Montana, New Jersey, New Mexico, Oregon, Texas, Vermont, and West Virginia. Mississippi and South Dakota publicly fund abortions only to save a mother's life, and the remaining states abide by current Medicaid law as specified by the Hyde Amendment.

For more information: "*Harris v. McRae*" on Douglas Butler, "Abortion: Medicine, Ethics, and Law" CD-ROM, 1997; Milbauer, Barbara. *The Law Giveth: Legal Aspects of the Abortion Controversy.* New York: Atheneum, 1983.

—Elizabeth Purdy

Hawaii Housing Authority v. Midkiff, 467 U.S. 229 (1984)

In *Hawaii Housing Authority v. Midkiff*, the Court upheld the sweeping provisions of the Land Reform Act of 1967 enacted by the Hawaii legislature, finding it to be within the scope of the "public use" requirement of the Fifth and Fourteenth Amendments. In writing the Court's decision, Justice O'CONNOR reaffirmed and clarified the principles outlined in BERMAN V. PARKER, 348 U.S. 26 (1954), which involved an urban renewal plan enacted by Congress for the District of Columbia and the sale of condemned property to private interests.

In the 1960s, the Hawaii legislature held hearings on land ownership in the state and discovered that "while the state and federal governments owned almost 49 percent of the state's land, another 47 percent was in the hands of only 72 private landowners." The legislature determined that this highly concentrated land ownership was responsible for inflated land and home prices and injured "the public tranquility and welfare." To correct this perceived social evil, the legislature enacted the Land Reform Act of 1967, which provided for state condemnation of large tracts of land and resale of individual lots to the individuals already leasing those lots. The landowners challenged the law as an unconstitutional "taking" of private land not for a public purpose and, therefore, in violation of the Fifth and Fourteenth Amendments. They argued that because the land was sold to private individuals, the "public use" provision of the Fifth Amendment was not satisfied.

Justice O'Connor cites *Berman v. Parker*, 348 U.S. 26 (1954), as the "starting point for our analysis of the act's constitutionality." The *Berman* decision dealt with the definition of "public use" in cases involving the use of EMINENT DOMAIN. The definition presented in *Berman* is a broad one: "We deal, in other words, with what traditionally has been known as the police power. An attempt to define its reach or trace its outer limits is fruitless, for each case must turn on its own facts." As the police power is essentially legislative power, the definition of public use is essentially a legislative function, subject, of course, to specific constitutional limitations. As the *Berman* case states, "The definition is essentially the product of legislative determinations addressed to the purposes of government. . . ." *Berman* concludes that once the public use has been legislatively affirmed, "the power of eminent domain is merely the means to the end. . . ." Justice O'Connor concludes the discussion of public use with the observation that "The 'public use' requirement is thus coterminous with the scope of a sovereign's police power." In effect, once a "public use" purpose has been determined, how the public use will be achieved is also within the state's power.

Based on her discussion of *Berman*, O'Connor notes, "we have no trouble concluding that the Hawaii Act is constitutional." The Hawaii legislature determined that the existing concentration of land ownership led to "perceived social and economic evils," and the state's decision to regulate on behalf of the public welfare "is a classic exercise of a State's POLICE POWERS."

Addressing the concern that the law may not "be successful in achieving its intended goals," the Court declared that the wisdom of legislation of this sort is not the Court's concern. "When the legislature's purpose is legitimate and its means are not irrational," questions as to the wisdom of otherwise constitutional legislation addressing social and economic ills are to be answered in the political, not judicial, arena. The Court reemphasizes this point when it declares "it is only the taking's purpose, and not its mechanics, that must pass scrutiny under the public use clause."

Finally, the Court addresses the fact that the beneficiaries of the law are private individuals and concludes that this "does not condemn that taking as having only a private purpose." To emphasize this point, O'Connor cites *Rindge Co. v. Los Angeles*, 262 U.S. 700 (1923), which upheld use of eminent domain to obtain land for highways: "It is not essential that the entire community, nor even any considerable portion . . . directly enjoy or participate in any improvement in order [for it] to constitute a public use." O'Connor concludes with the observation that the Land Reform Act was enacted "not to benefit a particular class of identifiable individuals but to attack certain perceived evils of concentrated property ownership in Hawaii—a legitimate public purpose."

For more information: Haar, Charles, and Jerold Kayden. *Landmark Justice: The Influence of William J. Brennan on America's Communities*. Washington, D.C.: Preservation Press, 1989.

—Alex Aichinger

Hazelwood School District v. Kuhlmeier, 484 U.S. 260 (1988)

The Supreme Court ruled in *Hazelwood School District v. Kuhlmeier* that school officials may censor a high school newspaper or other forms of student expression that are part of the curriculum or that may be seen as speaking for the school. The high court said that as long as the steps school authorities take to restrict school-sponsored expression are reasonably related to legitimate pedagogical concerns, their actions will not violate the First Amendment guarantee of freedom of speech.

The *Hazelwood* case involved the decision of a high school principal near St. Louis, Missouri, to delete two articles from the high school newspaper, the *Spectrum,* which was produced as part of a journalism class. Just prior to publication, the principal pulled an article on teenage pregnancy at the school because he felt that students who were not named would still be identifiable, and he killed a story on divorce because he felt parents should have been asked to consent to the publication and should have been allowed to comment in the article.

In a 6-3 decision, Justice Byron R. WHITE said the issue was not whether the student speech had to be tolerated by the school, but rather whether it had to be promoted by the school. In this way, the Court said the case differed from two earlier rulings: TINKER V. DES MOINES INDEPENDENT SCHOOL DISTRICT, 393 U.S. 503 (1969), in which the Court said student speech was protected as long as it did not substantially disrupt school operations; and *Bethel School District v. Fraser,* 478 U.S. 675 (1986), in which the Court said school officials had the authority to restrict student speech that was vulgar and inappropriate for a student audience. In *Hazelwood* the speech was neither disruptive nor vulgar.

However, the Court said the newspaper could be regulated because it was part of the curriculum over which the school was entitled to maintain control and was also seen by the community as part of the voice or message of the school. The Court also concluded that the student newspaper was not a PUBLIC FORUM open to a broad exchange of views on any subject.

The decision prompted a strong dissent by Justice William J. BRENNAN, Jr., who said the Court's opinion approves brutal censorship and denudes high school students of much of the First Amendment protection that *Tinker* itself prescribed.

The Court's ruling in *Hazelwood* involved only a high school newspaper. Subsequent rulings by lower federal courts have applied the decision to regulate the content of other school activities, from the content of bulletin boards to the selection of plays to be performed by students to material in the yearbook. The decision has also influenced rulings on controversial advertising in school newspapers.

For more information: Raskin, Jamin B. *We the Students: Supreme Court Decisions for and about Students.* 2nd ed. Washington, D.C.: CQ Press, 2003.

—Stephen Wermiel

Heart of Atlanta Motel v. United States, 379 U.S. 241 (1965)

Heart of Atlanta Motel v. U.S. is a landmark CIVIL RIGHTS case in the area of public accommodations.

On July 2, 1964, Congress passed the 1964 CIVIL RIGHTS ACT. Title II of the law forbade private acts of racial segregation in areas of public accommodation such as hotels, motels, and restaurants. Whether Congress has the authority to prohibit private RACIAL DISCRIMINATION in places of public accommodations was a debated issue at the time.

The Civil Rights Act of 1875 had declared that racial discrimination in public accommodations was to be the law of the land. However, in the *Civil Rights Cases of 1883* the Supreme Court had declared the Civil Rights Act of 1875 unconstitutional. The legal basis for the Civil Rights Act of 1875 was the Fourteenth Amendment. For the 1964 Civil Rights Act it was the commerce clause (Article I, Section 8).

Two hours after President Lyndon Johnson signed the 1964 Civil Rights Act into law, Moreton Rolleston, an attorney, and a major investor in the Heart of Atlanta Motel in Atlanta, Georgia, filed suit seeking to invalidate the law. The motel could not claim that it was not operating in INTERSTATE COMMERCE. It was located two blocks from an interstate exit and about a mile from the junction of three interstate highways. In addition both a Georgia state road and a U.S. highway ran by its front door. Also most of its customers were from out of town and a large number were from other states.

Rolleston, representing the motel, claimed that the *Civil Rights Cases* had already settled the issue of the constitutionality of such legislation. The Court rejected his argument that using the commerce clause as the basis of the act was an unconstitutional expansion of the commerce clause.

Katzenback v. McClung, 379 U.S. 294 (1964), was the companion case to the *Heart of Atlanta Motel* case. The case focused on Ollie's BBQ Restaurant in Birmingham, Alabama. The Federal Bureau of Investigation watched the restaurant for weeks and found that only occasionally would an out-of-state motorist visit the restaurant. Ollie McClung's restaurant was located in a neighborhood and was not near any state or federal highways. Investigation of its business records showed that all supplies were purchased locally.

Ollie's BBQ was not engaged in interstate commerce in any direct way. However, the Court ruled, as it had in a number of cases in previous decades, that Congress had the power to regulate not only the mainstream of commerce but the tributaries, and even the watershed of commerce [cf. WICKARD V. FILBURN, 317 U.S. 111 (1942)]. Consequently the commerce clause could be applied to virtually all public accommodations.

For more information: Cortner, Richard C. *Civil Rights and Public Accommodations: The Heart of Atlanta Motel and McClung Cases.* Lawrence: University Press of Kansas, 2001; Schwartz, Bernard, ed. *Statutory History of the United States: Civil Rights,* Part 1. New York: Chelsea House, 1970.

—A. J. L. Waskey

Herrera v. Collins, 113 S.Ct. 853 (1993)

In *Herrera v. Collins*, the U.S. Supreme Court held that a claim of ACTUAL INNOCENCE was not cause for a new hearing if the statute of limitations on such hearings has already expired, unless clear and convincing evidence existed where no reasonable juror could have initially found the defendant eligible for the death penalty.

Appellant Herrera had provided the Court with affidavits affirming his innocence, polygraphs that demonstrated his honesty, and eyewitnesses who recanted their testimony, including a judge who affirmed Herrera's innocence. Under a recent Texas law, however, Herrera's evidence was disallowed because it had been produced after the maximum 30-day post-conviction period had expired. The Court reviewed the Herrera petition just days before Herrera's scheduled execution and found that he was not entitled to a federal hearing on his claims of actual innocence. This opinion denying Herrera's request for a new hearing was written by Chief Justice William REHNQUIST.

Rehnquist's rationale for denying Herrera's petition was rooted in earlier PRECEDENT from *McClesky v. Zant*, 499 U.S. 467 (1991), where the Court held that all legal arguments must be presented at the defendant's first APPEAL. In response to Rehnquist's opinion, Justice BLACKMUN wrote a dissent, with Justices STEVENS and SOUTER concurring. Blackmun argued that since Texas law did not, at that time, provide any procedure by which the petitioner could introduce a claim of ACTUAL INNOCENCE, the only recourse was to bring a habeas petition in federal court. And, he argued, the standard for relief on the merits of an actual innocence claim "must be higher than the threshold standard for merely reaching that claim . . . that had been procedurally defaulted or is successive or abusive." In addition, Blackmun voiced confusion over the logic from the majority, which impugned the petitioner's evidence on the grounds that its credibility had never been tested when that problem existed because the habeas petition had been denied. The dissent concludes by lamenting that the Court's decision to allow executions of persons who demonstrate viable claims of actual innocence amounts to nothing more than "simple murder."

For more information: Baird, Robert, and Stuart Rosenbaum. *Punishment and the Death Penalty: The Current Debate.* Amherst, N.Y.: Prometheus, 1995.

—Patricia E. Campie

Hodgson et al. v. Minnesota et al., 497 U.S. 417 (1990)

Hodgson et al. v. Minnesota et. al. struck down a Minnesota statute that banned any abortion from being performed on an unemancipated minor until at least 48 hours after a physician gave written notice of the intended procedure to both the minor's parents.

The notice the physician had to give was mandatory unless the minor's physician concluded that an immediate abortion must be performed in order to save the life of the minor, the parents authorized the abortion in writing before the required notice was sent to them, or if the minor claimed she was a victim of parental neglect or abuse. In the latter instance a notice of her statement had to be given to the proper authorities. There was a "judicial bypass" provision in the statute which declared that any judge could authorize the abortion if they found that the minor was mature and capable of giving consent or if not informing the parents would be in the minor's best interest. Two obstetrics and gynecology physicians, four clinics that performed abortions, six pregnant minors, and a mother of a pregnant minor filed suit against the state of Minnesota. They argued that the statute violated the due process and EQUAL PROTECTION CLAUSES of the U.S. Constitution. The district court held that with judicial bypass provision the statute passed constitutional muster but that absent bypass, it was unconstitutional.

This Supreme Court case is unusual in that there is no majority opinion. Rather, shifting coalitions of concurring and dissenting opinions fashioned a rule. Justice STEVENS announced the judgment of the Court. A majority of justices agreed that the 48-hour rule is a reasonable exercise of a state's legitimate and strong interest in the welfare of its young citizens. That interest extends to a minor's decision to have an abortion. Parents have an interest in controlling the upbringing of their children that may rise to the level of protected liberty interest. The family also has a right to PRIVACY in its upbringing of children that is constitutionally protected from undue state intervention.

Based on the above principles, four justices, Stevens, MARSHALL, BRENNAN, and BLACKMUN, agreed with parental notification of a planned abortion, but not with the both parents provision without the possibility of judicial bypass. The two parents requirement is especially harmful if the parents are separated, or if it is a situation in which family violence is a problem. Stevens argued that this requirement did not further any state interest in protecting pregnant minors or family integrity.

Justice O'CONNOR objected that the two-parent notification with a judicial bypass provision is constitutional because interference in family affairs does not exist if the minor can use the bypass provision to keep from notifying one or both parents. She provided the crucial fifth vote for a majority rule that a state requirement of 48-hour prior notification to one parent of a minor's intent to have an abortion, with a provision for a judicial bypass, is constitutional.

Justices KENNEDY, REHNQUIST, WHITE, and SCALIA argued that the statute was constitutional, with or without a judicial bypass provision.

For more information: Legal Information Institute: Supreme Court Collection. *"Hodgson v. Minnesota."* Cornell University Law School. Available online. URL: http://supct.law.cornell.edu/supct/html/88-1125.ZO.html. Downloaded May 13, 2004.

—Wendy Groce

Hoke v. United States, 227 U.S. 308 (1913)

In *Hoke v. United States,* the Supreme Court held up as constitutional a law passed by Congress to prohibit the interstate transportation of women for immoral purposes. This was known as the Mann Act. The suit was brought by one Effie Hoke who had been convicted under the law on the charge that she did entice a woman to cross interstate boundaries for the purpose of prostitution.

The issue in this case was whether the law in question violated the interstate commerce clause of the U.S. Constitution. Writing for a unanimous Supreme Court, Justice McKenna ruled that it did not. Attorneys for the plaintiff had argued that the law was unconstitutional, first because it restricted people's ability to move freely across state borders, and second that the POLICE POWERS assumed by Congress in this law went beyond the powers granted to it under the interstate commerce clause. The powers to regulate the morals of a population are known as police powers and are generally reserved to the states. Justice McKenna said that Congress is free to regulate INTERSTATE COMMERCE even if that commerce involves moving people across state borders. Although the power to regulate the morals of the population is given to the states only, trafficking in women for purposes of prostitution does involve commerce and may be regulated by Congress without overstepping its role under the interstate commerce clause. Justice McKenna used *Gloucester Ferry Co. v. Pennsylvania,* 114 U.S. 196 (1885), as a PRECEDENT. In that case the Court ruled that Congress has the power to regulate interstate commerce even if the means used exhibit some of the qualities of state police powers.

The ruling in this case was significant because it asserted that Congress does have police powers if the activity being regulated is involved in interstate commerce. Because police powers had previously been considered exclusive state powers, this ruling represented a large increase in the reach of Congress. This case became a precedent in later congressional efforts to outlaw RACIAL DISCRIMINATION in activities that are interstate in nature.

For more information: Schultz, David. *Property, Power, and American Democracy.* New Brunswick, N.J.: Transaction Press, 1992.

—Blane Parrent

Holmes, Oliver Wendell, Jr. (1841–1935) *Supreme Court justice*

Oliver Wendell Holmes, Jr. (b. Boston, Mass., March 8, 1841; d. Washington, D.C., March 6. 1935), was appointed to the Supreme Court in 1902 by President Theodore Roosevelt. He served as an associate justice for 30 years until January 1932.

In an autobiographical sketch, the young Oliver Wendell Holmes, Jr., identified himself as part of a "long pedigree of Olivers and Wendells" that had resided in Boston. His immediate family was exceptionally talented. Oliver Wendell Holmes, Sr., was a Paris-educated physician who taught at Harvard Medical School. Dr. Holmes was also a dazzling raconteur and popular author of light verse. Mrs. Holmes, nee Amelia Jackson Lee, was the bright and affectionate daughter of a prominent Boston judge. Their son demonstrated keen affinities for literature, art, philosophy, and classical languages, pursuing these studies at Harvard College. Upon graduating in 1861, he took up an officer's commission to serve in the 4th Infantry Battalion. At the time he wrote, "If I survive the war I expect to study law as my profession or at least for a starting point."

Having fought in many of the major battles of the Civil War and having been gravely injured three times, Oliver Wendell Holmes, Jr., survived to enroll in Harvard Law School in 1864. In 1867 Holmes was admitted to the bar and started a three-year apprenticeship at a Boston law firm. He quickly distinguished himself in the legal profession. In 1870, when he was only 29, Holmes was hired as a lecturer in constitutional law at Harvard Law School and was appointed editor of the *American Law Journal.* Two years later he married Fanny Dixwell, whom he had known from childhood. Upon her death in 1929, Holmes wrote to their longtime friend, English historian Sir Frederick Pollock, "for sixty years she made life poetry for me."

Holmes's early work sharpened his analytical skills and expanded his knowledge of case law and legal literature. His vast knowledge of American law was tempered by the dominant philosophies of the day, most notably the theory of social Darwinism as articulated by Herbert Spencer. Like biological Darwinism, social Darwinism viewed life as a struggle to exist in which only those best fittest for the struggle survived. Within the context of social Darwinism, though, this capacity for survival extended not only to living organisms but also to institutions and practices.

Justice Oliver Wendell Holmes, Jr. *(Library of Congress)*

However, Holmes did not shy away from challenging prevailing social and legal theories. He disagreed with utilitarian reformers who believed that the common law should be replaced by a body of clearly codified, logically organized rules. They believed that systematizing the law along almost mathematical lines would lead to greater consistency in the judicial process. Holmes viewed the law as something more organic. In one of the greatest works of American legal scholarship, *The Common Law* (1881), Holmes wrote that in the common law judges do not make decisions by mechanically following PRECEDENT. Instead, legal practice and traditions are formed by "able and experienced men" who administer the law in accordance with "instinctive preferences and inarticulate convictions" consistent with public policy. If public policy changes with the succession of a new class of legislators, legal practice changes also. In this way, Holmes challenged the static and consistent body of law envisioned by the utilitarians with an evolutionary view in which "the law is always approaching, and never reaching consistency. . . . It will become entirely consistent only when it ceases to grow."

Shortly after the publication of *The Common Law*, Holmes was appointed to the Supreme Judicial Court of Massachusetts. He became chief justice of that court in 1899. During his two decades on the bench, Holmes wrote more than 1,000 opinions, of which those on constitutional issues are most notable. In the 1896 case of *Vegelahn v. Guntner*, Holmes wrote a dissenting opinion which supported the right of workers to organize and strike against their employers as a legitimate and effective means of bargaining over wages. In his advisory opinion on the question of whether a Massachusetts act granting suffrage to women in town and city elections was constitutional if approved by popular referendum, Holmes wrote that although "the [Massachusetts] Constitution establishes a representative Government, not a pure democracy," it did not prohibit the legislature from appealing to direct consent on laws affecting local issues.

It was in his 30 years as an associate justice of the United States Supreme Court (1902–32) that Holmes made his greatest impact on American law. In *Schenk v. U.S.*, 249 U.S. 47 (1919), Holmes formulated the *clear and present danger* doctrine with respect to the question of free speech and the World War I Sedition Act. Writing for the Court, he stated that the test of whether speech fell outside First Amendment protection would be "whether the words are used in such circumstances and are of such a nature as to create a clear and present danger that they will bring about the substantive evils that Congress has a right to prevent." Holmes disagreed with the Court's denial of CITIZENSHIP to a Hungarian immigrant on the grounds that she was a pacifist. He wrote that "if there is any principle of the Constitution that more imperatively calls for attachment than any other it is the principle of free thought—not free thought for those who agree with us but freedom for the thought that we hate."

In his dissenting opinion in *Frank v. Mangum*, 237 U.S. 309 (1915), and in his opinion for the majority in *Moore v. Dempsey*, 261 U.S. 86 (1923), Holmes squarely confronted the problem of the "judicial lynching" of blacks and Jews in the South by hostile courts. In *Frank*, he exhorted a divided court, "it is our duty . . . to declare lynch law as little valid when practiced by a regularly drawn jury as when administered by one elected by a mob intent on death."

Holmes's personal commitment to Social darwinism had a profound impact on the decisions he made in court. In *BUCK V. BELL*, 274 U.S. 200 (1927), a decision for which he is often criticized, Holmes upheld a Virginia law that implicitly authorized the forced sterilization of epileptics and the mentally ill. He argued that the government could justly sterilize those who "sap[ped] the strength" of society in the pursuit of a better citizenry. He most famously noted, "[t]hree generations of imbeciles are enough." However, in an earlier case, Holmes seemed more willing to subordinate his social Darwinist beliefs to constitutional requirements. In *LOCHNER V. NEW YORK*, 198 U.S. 45 (1905), Holmes dissented with the Court's ruling invalidating a

New York law establishing a 10-hour workday for bakery workers, writing, "The Fourteenth Amendment does not enact Mr. Spencer's *Social Statistics.*"

During his 30 years of service on the Supreme Court, Holmes wrote 873 opinions, making him the most prolific judge in the Court's history. In the process, he earned the reputation of being a champion of liberal causes and an advocate for the advancement of legal science. While some judges preferred to base their opinions on general principles of common law, Holmes believed that it was the responsibility of the judge to be as precise about the law as possible. He encouraged members of the Court to base their opinions on particular statutes rather than on vague principles of law. He also encouraged the Court to interpret the Constitution progressively—not to be bound by what may have been true at the time the Constitution was ratified, but to try to apply its fundamental principles to contemporary problems. In Holmes' free speech and CIVIL RIGHTS cases, we can see this approach to CONSTITUTIONAL INTERPRETATION at work.

Oliver Wendell Holmes, Jr., retired from the Supreme Court in 1932 at the age of 90. He died four years later, two days before his 94th birthday.

For more information: Holmes, Oliver Wendell, Jr. *The Common Law.* New York: Dover Publications, 1991; Lerner, Max. *The Mind and Faith of Justice Holmes: His Speeches, Letters and Judicial Opinions.* New York: Halcyon House, 1943.

—Tara Helfman

Home Building and Loan Association v. Blaisdell, 290 U.S. 398 (1934)

Home Building and Loan Association v. Blaisdell upheld a 1933 Minnesota statute that, as the rising unemployment of the Great Depression caused large numbers of people to face losing their homes, allowed debtors to apply to a district court judge to temporarily forestall property foreclosures. While assessments of the effect of national crises on CONSTITUTIONAL INTERPRETATION tend to focus on the military powers of the executive, *Home Building and Loan v. Blaisdell* demonstrates that national crises are potentially relevant to legislative economic powers as well. *Blaisdell* contains an exchange of classic positions on the flexibility of interpretive principles, as well as foreshadowing a major shift in Supreme Court jurisprudence with respect to legislative powers.

The central legal question of the case was whether the Minnesota statute violated the "contract clause" in Article I, Section 10 of the Constitution, which states that no state may pass a law "impairing the Obligation of Contracts." (Due process and equal protection claims were also made by the appellant but were considered insubstantial by both the majority and dissenting opinions.) As both opinions agreed, the Minnesota law raised questions that were directly relevant to the primary reason the contract clause was adopted: to prevent states from relieving debtors of their obligations to creditors.

From the originalist position represented in the dissenting opinion of Justice George SUTHERLAND, the identification of the underlying purpose of the contract clause is to essentially settle the matter, compelling the conclusion that the statute was invalid. To the dissenters, the crisis created by the Great Depression was irrelevant: "[t]he Minnesota statute either impairs the obligation of contracts or it does not. If it does not, the occasion to which it relates becomes immaterial, since then the passage of the statute is the exercise of a normal, unrestricted, state power and requires no special occasion to render it effective. If it does, the emergency no more furnishes a proper occasion for its exercise than if the emergency were non-existent." Indeed, the contract clause was enacted with crises in mind: legislatures were particularly likely to relieve debtors during severe economic downturns. Because the statutory grace period for foreclosures denied the agreed-upon remedy available the creditors, to the dissenters the law represented a clear impairment of a private contract and was therefore constitutionally impermissible, irrespective of the policy justifications of the Minnesota legislature. "If the provisions of the Constitution be not upheld when they pinch as well as when they comfort," concluded Sutherland, "they may as well be abandoned."

The majority opinion of Chief Justice Charles Evans HUGHES, in upholding the law, advocated a more flexible standard of interpretation. To the majority, the argument that the meaning of constitutional texts should be limited to how the framers would have applied them to problems of their time "carries its own refutation." While national crises could not permit ignoring the text of the Constitution— "[e]mergency does create power . . . or diminish the restrictions imposed upon power granted or reserved"—they may be considered when interpreting ambiguous constitutional provisions. While there could be little doubt in this case that the underlying mortgage agreements represented a contract, whether a law that suspended foreclosures without *relieving* debt was an "impairment" of contracts was, contrary to the arguments of the dissenters, not a self-evident proposition. The restriction on the state's POLICE POWERS represented by the contract clause is not "an absolute one and is not to be read with literal exactness like a mathematical formula." In light of the ambiguities of the text and considering the context of the Minnesota legislation, the majority concluded that it was a reasonable exercise of the state's police powers. Explicitly invoking his predecessor's opinion in *MCCULLOCH V. MARYLAND,* Chief Justice Hughes argued in response to the dissenters that a constitution could not be construed narrowly in the manner of an ordinary statute. Under the majority's interpretive standard, the legislation was (irrespective of its merits as public policy) within the legitimate powers of state governments.

In addition to providing eloquent examples of two crucial schools of American constitutional interpretation and the increased deference generally shown to political branches during times of crisis, *Home Building and Loan v. Blaisdell* is also significant because of its timing. While it is traditionally thought that there was a clear shift in the Supreme Court's jurisprudence with respect to the legislative power to regulate the economy following FDR's 1936 landslide victory (and his subsequent threat to expand the Court due to its perceived recalcitrance), the reality is significantly more complex. As Chief Justice Hughes noted in this 1934 opinion, "there has been a growing appreciation of public needs and of the necessity of finding ground for a rational compromise between individual rights and public welfare." The Supreme Court's reconsideration of the doctrines of the *Lochner* era was well under way before the Supreme Court began more systematically upholding New Deal legislation in 1937.

For more information: Ackerman, Bruce. *Private Property and the Constitution.* New Haven, Conn.: Yale University Press, 1978; Cushman, Barry. *Rethinking the New Deal Court: The Structure of a Constitutional Revolution.* New York: Oxford University Press, 1998.

—Scott Lemieux

H. P. Hood & Sons v. DuMond, 336 U.S. 525 (1949)

In *H. P. Hood & Sons v. DuMond,* the Supreme Court held that states may not deny facilities for the acquirement and shipment of milk in INTERSTATE COMMERCE for the protection or benefit of local economic interests.

H. P. Hood & Sons, a Massachusetts-based company, owned two plants in New York where it bought milk from local farmers and prepared it to be shipped to distributors in Massachusetts. The controversy arose when Hood applied to the Massachusetts commissioner of agriculture for a license to operate an additional plant in Greenwich, New York. Under the authority of New York state law, the commissioner denied Hood's application on grounds that a new plant would foster destructive competition among milk buyers and producers and would be contrary to the public interest of the citizens of New York. The commissioner found no evidence that producers lacked buyers or that producers might receive a higher price for their milk. The commissioner did find, however, that a new plant would increase costs for existing buyers in Greenwich and decrease the milk supply in New York markets.

Writing for the Court majority, Justice JACKSON ruled that the business under which Hood operated was inherently that of interstate commerce, and the actions of the commissioner must be judged against the precedents and history that surrounded the interpretation of the commerce clause. Although the Court has recognized the authority of states to regulate, specifically, the milk market, the importance of the commerce clause and the ills that it seeks to prevent cannot be ignored. *Milk Control Board v. Eisenberg Farm Products,* 306 U.S. 346, 350, 530 (1939), was a similar case that involved the regulation of both the interstate and intrastate milk industry.

The Court, however, found that the Eisenberg case involved interstate activity only incidentally and not necessarily and, thus, could be distinguished from the *Hood* case. Instead, the Court relied on *Baldwin v. GAF Seelig, Inc.,* 294 U.S. 511 (1935), in which it was argued that a state activity affecting interstate commerce was struck down by the Court because of its economic purpose. The Court found that the intentions and effects of *Hood* were no different than those of *Baldwin* and, accordingly, should be struck down. The Court found that the federal government has the sole ability and authority to regulate the economic effects of interstate commerce on the individual states.

Justice BLACK, joined by Justice MURPHY, dissented. He argued that state and federal interests should be balanced to determine an action's conformity with the commerce clause. The dissenting justices distinguished *Baldwin* from *Hood* because *Baldwin* involved discrimination against interstate suppliers and blocking milk from a particular state. *Hood* involved no such discrimination or desired effect. The justices found *Eisenberg* to be applicable because both cases involved economic interests and potential, but not proved, limitations upon interstate commerce as a whole. The justices argued that Congress and its authorities have long cooperated with state and local authorities regarding such matters. The majority's decision, they argued, left a wide area of vulnerability whereby destructive business practices could become immune to local regulation and would be dealt with less effectively by the federal government.

Justice FRANKFURTER, joined by Justice RUTLEDGE, also dissented from the opinion, advocating a balancing test so that states could act to curb destructive business practices in the absence of congressional action. Agreeing with the majority that *Hood* involved the withholding of instruments of interstate commerce for the purpose of local needs, the justices left open the question of whether the commerce clause prohibited state regulation for such purposes. Instead, the outcome should be based upon a balancing of state and federal interests. Therefore, the case should have been remanded to the Supreme Court of New York so that the interests of the state could be clarified.

In this opinion the Court relies upon an absolute standard of commerce clause interpretation. Rather than weighing the interests of the state against those of the federal government, the Court rules all state regulation of interstate commerce for economic reasons violates the commerce clause. The effectiveness of state regulations and practices of cooperation between state and local authorities are irrelevant according to this standard.

For more information: *Baldwin v. GAF Seelig, Inc.,* 294 U.S. 511 (1935); *H. P. Hood & Sons v. DuMond,* 336 U.S. 525 (1949); *Milk Control Board v. Eisenberg Farm Products,* 306 U.S. 346, 350, 530 (1939).

—Tim Harper

Hughes, Charles Evans (1862–1948) *chief justice of the United States*

Charles Evans Hughes was CHIEF JUSTICE of the United States from 1930 to 1941, appointed by President Herbert Hoover, as well as an associate justice from 1910 to 1916, appointed by President William Howard TAFT.

Born in Glens Falls, New York, on April 11, 1862, Hughes was a child prodigy, entering college at 14, graduating first in his law school class at Columbia, and being admitted to practice law in New York at 22. Stern and studious but fair and eloquent, he quickly established himself as a preeminent corporate lawyer in New York City and rapidly advanced in his career. Exhaustion led Hughes to a teaching position at Cornell Law School, where he enjoyed the scholar's life with his wife and children.

Encouraged to return to law practice, Hughes went back to corporate practice in New York and reestablished himself as the leader of the corporate bar. Riding this reputation and success investigating corporate monopolies led to election as Republican governor of New York in 1906, where he served as a reformer in the public interest until 1910. The combination of his progressive public service and leadership at the bar made Hughes a logical choice for the Supreme Court when he was nominated as associate justice in 1910 by President Taft, who was not unmindful of Hughes's potential as a competitor for the presidency in 1912. Hughes enjoyed his service on the Court, where he developed a close relationship with the legendary Justice Oliver Wendell HOLMES. He was prolific, frequently writing the Court's opinions and often commanding the support of his colleagues.

With Hughes's reputation enhanced by his service on the Court, the presidency loomed as an approachable goal, and he resigned in 1916 to run against Woodrow Wilson. The election was quite close but Wilson proved victorious. Hughes's public career, however, was not over, and he served the nation as secretary of state under Harding and Coolidge, promoting American responsibilities on the world stage, as well as other important posts.

In 1930 he was nominated by President Hoover to succeed William Howard Taft as chief justice, who had encouraged Hughes's appointment. Although fabulously qualified, Hughes's nomination was not without its critics, whose concerns ranged from his corporate law connections with the financial establishment to his age at 68 to his previous resignation from the Court to seek political office. Nonetheless, Hughes was confirmed by a comfortable margin in the Senate and went on to preside over the Court with intelligence, grace, and wisdom, as well as a towering presence that embodied the public perception of a fine judge.

He led the Court through the turbulent New Deal era, when President Franklin D. Roosevelt's ambitious progressive program for the nation faced constitutional challenges in the courts. Initially opposed to the panoply of New Deal legislation as contrary to the theories of laissez-faire economics that underlay prevailing constitutional doctrine, the Hughes Court faced the president's wrath, which manifested itself in the Court Packing Bill, legislation designed to give Roosevelt several new appointments to the Supreme Court. While the nation debated this proposal, Hughes vehemently opposed the president's plan while leading his

Chief Justice Charles Evans Hughes *(Library of Congress)*

Court to uphold key New Deal legislation in what came to be known as "the switch in time that saved nine." In this transition, the Supreme Court adopted new approaches to constitutional doctrine, which led to a focus on civil rights and liberties for most of the rest of the century.

Hughes is especially well known for authoring seminal decisions protecting freedom of expression, such as *Stromberg v. California*, 283 U.S. 359 (1931), and *Near v. Minnesota*, 283 U.S. 697 (1931), and supporting the rights of defendants, such as in the Scottsboro Boys cases, *Powell v. Alabama*, 287 U.S. 45 (1932). He served with great distinction until 1941, when he resigned at 80 years of age. Hughes died in 1948. Hughes's prodigious capacity for political and intellectual leadership permitted him to serve his country and make contributions that continue to be felt. He is rated as one of the greatest chief justices and is a remarkable American.

For more information: Abraham, Henry J. *Justices, Presidents and Senators*. revised ed. Lanham, Md.: Rowman and Littlefield, 1999; Pussey, Merlo. *Charles Evans Hughes*. 2 vols. New York: Macmillan, 1951.

—Luke Bierman

Humphrey's Executor v. United States, 295 U.S. 602 (1935)

In *Humphrey's Executor v. United States*, the Court upheld Congress's power to limit presidential removal power in agencies with legislative and judicial functions, granting Congress the final say regarding agency members.

William E. Humphrey had been nominated by President Herbert Hoover to serve on the Federal Trade Commission. Humphrey was confirmed by the Senate and began serving his term. Hoover lost the 1932 election and shortly after taking office, President Franklin Roosevelt asked Humphrey to resign because Roosevelt believed Humphrey's conservative views could hinder the positive effects of Roosevelt's New Deal programs. Humphrey refused to resign, so President Roosevelt determined to use presidential removal power that had been upheld in *Myers v. United States*, 272 U.S. 52 (1926). The FTC Act stated that commissioners could only be removed by the president for "inefficiency, neglect of duty, or malfeasance of office," whereas this situation was clearly policy driven.

Nine years earlier, former president and then CHIEF JUSTICE William Howard TAFT delivered the opinion of the Court in *Myers v. U.S.* (1926). Taft wrote that the President:

> . . . in the absence of any express limitation respecting removals, that as his selection of administrative officials is essential to the execution of laws by him, so must be

his power of removing those whom he cannot continue to be responsible. It was urged that the natural meaning of the term *executive power* granted the president included the appointment and removal of executive subordinates.

Chief Justice Taft's opinion struck down an 1876 statute which denied the president unrestricted removal power of first-class postmasters, in effect affirming the president's power of removal included members of independent regulatory commissions.

President Roosevelt believed *Myers v. U.S.* justified his removal of Humphrey. Shortly after his removal, Humphrey died. However, the executor of Humphrey's estate felt President Roosevelt acted inappropriately and determined to recover Humphrey's lost salary.

Humphrey's Executor v. United States was decided on May 27, 1935, by a vote of 9 to 0; Justice George SUTHERLAND delivered the opinion of the Court. The Court focused on two main questions in this case. First, did the Federal Trade Commission Act limit President Roosevelt's removal of commissioners? Second, if the FTC Act did limit such powers, was this constitutional?

Justice Sutherland believed the first question was rather easy to answer. In his opinion, the Congress clearly limited the president's power to remove FTC commissioners. Sutherland wrote, "The commission is to be nonpartisan; and it must, from the very nature of its duties, act with impartiality. It is charged with the enforcement of no policy except the policy of the law. Its duties are neither political nor executive, but predominantly quasi judicial and quasi legislative."

In the second question, the Court found that such limitation of presidential removal power by the FTC Act was indeed constitutional because of the "quasi judicial" and "quasi legislative" aspects mentioned above. Sutherland explained that *Myers v. U.S.* was a different scenario because that case was "confined to purely executive officers." On the other hand:

> The Federal Trade Commission is an administrative body created by Congress to carry into effect legislative policies embodied in the statute in accordance with the legislative standard therein prescribed, and to perform other specified duties as a legislative or as a judicial aid. Such a body cannot in any proper sense be characterized as an arm or an eye of the executive. Its duties are performed without executive leave and, in the contemplation of the statute, must be free from executive control.

The key significance in this case is the Court's ruling that some agencies are purely executive, while other agencies fall outside of executive control.

For more information: Hall, Kermit L. *The Oxford Companion to the Supreme Court of the United States.* New York: Oxford University Press, 1992; O'Brien, David M. *Constitutional Law and Politics, Volume One: Struggles for Power and Governmental Accountability.* 5th ed. New York: W. W. Norton, 2003.

—Jewerl Maxwell

Hurtado v. California, 110 U.S. 516 (1884)

In *Hurtado v. California,* the Supreme Court upheld Joseph Hurtado's murder conviction, denying the plaintiff's claim that California's failure to charge him with the crime through a grand jury indictment was a denial of due process of law. Under the procedures created by the Constitution and Penal Code of the state of California, charges had been brought against Hurtado through a process of information, whereby the committing magistrate determined whether there was sufficient cause to order that a defendant be held to answer for a crime on the basis of his examination of documentary evidence, including witness testimony contained in written depositions. Hurtado's attorney had argued that the due process clause of the Fourteenth Amendment made it necessary for the states to use the process of grand jury indictment, which is required for the federal courts by the Fifth Amendment.

The use of grand jury indictment for serious crimes was required under English common law, and it was argued on Hurtado's behalf that the concept of due process of law embraced those procedures, such as grand jury indictment, which had become established practice under common law. In support of this position, the plaintiff's counsel cited the Court's decision in *Murray v. Hoboken Land Improvement Company,* 59 U.S. 372 (1855). In this case, the Court had held that the use of a distress warrant issued by the Treasury against a delinquent collector was due process, because such summary methods had been common practice under common law. In his opinion for the Court in *Hurtado,* Justice Matthews maintained that this was not a correct interpretation of the *Murray* decision, and that, while the existence of a practice under common law was sufficient to establish it as due process, existence under common law was not necessary to establish that a practice was consistent with the due process clause.

Matthews observed that to make existence under common law a necessary criterion for due process would be to deny every quality of the law but its age, and to render it incapable of progress or improvement [*Hurtado v. California*]. Instead, he argues that due process refers to the law of the land in each state. Consequently, legal proceedings conducted pursuant to the enactments of a state's legislative body would normally be considered due process of law under the Fourteenth Amendment. However, the due process clause does place some limits on legislative power. According to Matthews, it had to be exercised within the limits of those fundamental principles of liberty and justice that lie at the base of all our civil and political institutions. In this case, the Court concluded that the process mandated by California law safeguarded the substantial interests of the prisoner and could not be considered inconsistent with due process of law.

The *Hurtado* PRECEDENT has not been reversed. Unlike many of the other provisions of the BILL OF RIGHTS, the Fifth Amendment's grand jury requirement still does not apply to the states. Nevertheless, the case is not without significance for subsequent developments. In later decades, the Court concluded that although grand jury indictment may not be required by the due process clause, the fundamental principles of liberty and justice at the base of our civil and political institutions do include most of the other provisions of the Bill of Rights. Hence, the reasoning contained in this decision helped establish the foundation for the process of incorporating the Bill of Rights into the Fourteenth Amendment's due process clause.

For more information: Cortner, Richard C. *The Supreme Court and the Second Bill of Rights: The Fourteenth Amendment and the Nationalization of Civil Liberties.* Madison: University of Wisconsin Press, 1981; Curtis, Michael Kent. *No State Shall Abridge: The Fourteenth Amendment and the Bill of Rights.* Durham, N.C.: Duke University Press, 1990.

—Justin Halpern
—Kendal Waite

Hustler Magazine v. Falwell, 485 U.S. 46 (1988)

In *Hustler Magazine v. Falwell,* the Supreme Court, on certiorari, reversed the preceding decision of the U.S. COURT OF APPEALS for the Fourth Circuit. The previous court upheld the ruling of an earlier decision, NEW YORK TIMES CO. V. SULLIVAN, 376 U.S. 254 (1964), 11 L Ed 2d 686, 84 S Ct 710, which had held that, under the First Amendment, "defendants may be held liable for defamation of public figures only if the defamatory falsehood was published with 'actual malice'[.]" Attorneys for *Hustler Magazine* argued that the actual malice standard must be satisfied prior to Jerry Falwell recovering damages for emotional distress. The Supreme Court rejected the use of the case since there was no proof that the fictional statement was produced with actual malice.

The Supreme Court held that "the free speech guaranties of the First Amendment prohibit public figures and public officials from recovering for the tort of intentional infliction of emotional distress by reason of the publication of a caricature . . . unless it is shown that the publication contains a false statement of fact which was made with actual malice[.]" Therefore, the minister, Jerry Falwell, could not receive compensation for intentional infliction of emotional distress due to the fact that he is considered a public figure. Furthermore, according to the lower courts' findings and the Supreme Court's acceptance of these findings, the advertisement parody published by *Hustler Magazine* demonstrated no proof that actual facts were being described. Despite the negative consequences, the advertisement parody was a published opinion that is protected under the First Amendment of the Constitution. Although there is an interest to protect public figures and public officials from emotional distress, one may not be denied First Amendment rights to accomplish this goal.

Hustler Magazine v. Falwell is a case that may be considered worthy of notice. The case "presents us with a novel question involving First Amendment limitations upon a state's authority to protect its citizens from intentional infliction of emotional distress." Although there is no question that the publication of the advertisement parody caused Jerry Falwell emotional distress and would be viewed as repulsive to a majority of those who witnessed the parody, the primary concern is whether the one affected may receive compensation.

The respondent suggests that the protection of public figures from emotional distress is in the interest of the state and that this alone is enough to deny First Amendment protection concerning speech. However, the Supreme Court disagreed. "At the heart of the First Amendment is the recognition of the fundamental importance of the free flow of ideas and opinions on matters of public interest and concern. 'The . . . freedom to speak one's mind is not only an aspect of individual liberty—and thus a good unto itself—but also is essential to the common quest for truth and the vitality of society as a whole'." The First Amendment continues to remain of vital importance to individuals' ability to express their thoughts and ideas.

For more information: Smolla, Rodney A. *Jerry Falwell v. Larry Flynt: The First Amendment on Trial.* New York: St. Martin's Press, 1988.

—Leila Kawar

I

illegal aliens

The U.S. Supreme Court has addressed the rights of non-nationals who are present in the country unlawfully in a variety of contexts, including cases dealing with due process protections, access to government benefits, and labor rights. Despite the plentiful jurisprudence in this area, "illegal aliens" is a term that rarely appears defined, and when it does, as in 8 U.S.C. 1365(b) (referring to aliens who were unlawfully in the United States at the time they committed a felony) and 29 C.F.R. 500.20(n) (referring to aliens without employment authorization), it is generally in a context-driven and inconsistent manner.

Foreign aliens, meaning individuals who are not citizens or nationals of the United States, may be present in the country illegally because they crossed the border undetected or because they violated the conditions of their admission, for example by overstaying their visas or by failing to file change of address forms, or by committing ordinary crimes. Although the terms *illegal immigrants* and *illegal aliens* are often used interchangeably, they differ slightly in meaning since not all aliens are immigrants—aliens who can prove that they fall into one of the statutorily enumerated categories of temporary visitors (for example, holders of student, business, or tourist visas) are technically not immigrants.

Prior to 1996, aliens were allowed different due process rights depending on whether they had entered the country illegally or were "on the threshold" of initial unlawful entry. Excludable aliens, meaning those who were apprehended while attempting to unlawfully enter the country, could not assert a liberty interest under the Constitution to be admitted into the United States or to be released from detention (*Shaughnessy v. Mezei*, 345 U.S. 206 [1953]). The Supreme Court did, however, extend them the protections of the Fifth Amendment (*Wong Wing v. U.S.*, 163 U.S. 228, 238 [1896], *Jean v. Nelson*, 472 U.S. 846, 858–82 [1985]) and all arriving aliens were guaranteed the right to a fair hearing and to district court review if they sought asylum in the United States (*McNary v. Haitian Refugee Center, Inc.*, 498 U.S. 479 [1991]).

By contrast, those who were determined to have fully entered the country had access to greater legal protections. In 1996 Congress passed a law, the Illegal Immigrant Responsibility and Immigration Reform Act (IIRIRA), which removed the distinction between excludable and deportable aliens. A major unresolved question is whether this will imply a change in either of their constitutional rights (*Kurzban*, 2000).

The general tendency of the Supreme Court has been to protect the due process rights of aliens once they are inside the United States. Aliens also have access to First Amendment rights (*Accardi v. Shaughnessy*, 347 U.S. 260 [1954]). Although illegal aliens are subject to removal if they are apprehended, the Court has struck down some state laws that discriminate against them. For example, it has enforced equal protection rights for undocumented schoolchildren in the provision of public education. By contrast, it upheld a provision of the California Labor Code that prohibited an employer from knowingly employing aliens if they were not entitled to lawful residence in the United States (*De Canas v. Bica*, 424 U.S. 351 [1976]). The Court's decisions regarding the constitutionality of state laws dealing with immigrants have been influenced by changes in federal immigration policy.

In the early 1980s, the Court ruled that affording undocumented workers the protection of U.S. labor laws promoted the purposes of both labor and the immigration laws (*Sure-Tan, Inc. v. NLRB*, 467 U.S. 883 [1984]), but it recently interpreted new federal legislation prohibiting employers from knowingly hiring unauthorized workers to hold that undocumented immigrant workers are not entitled to back pay (*Hoffman Plastic Compounds, Inc. v. National Labor Relations Board*, 535 U.S. 137 [2002]).

While it has on occasion moved to protect aliens from discrimination in state law, the Supreme Court has consistently allowed the federal government to selectively enforce immigration law, permitting the government to discriminate against aliens in ways that would not be permisible against U.S. citizens (*Seven Star, Inc. v. U. S.*, 873 F.2d 225 [9th Cir.], *cert. denied*, 493 U.S. 893 [1989]; see also *Reno v. American Arab Anti-Discrimination Comm.*, 119 S. Ct. 936 [1999], *no jurisdiction*, 525 U.S. 471 [2000]). In these cases, the Court has maintained that immigration policies pertain exclusively to the political branches of the government in order to justify its reluctance to subject federal measures related to immigration to substantial JUDICIAL REVIEW.

Certainly, federal policies relating to immigrants have become more punitive since the mid-1980s, despite the fact that enforcement remains drastically underfunded. In general, the Supreme Court has been reluctant to preempt the congressional PLENARY POWER over immigration policy in order to provide the approximately seven million illegal aliens who now live and work within U.S. borders with the same constitutional rights enjoyed by U.S. citizens.

For more information: Aleinikoff, T. Alex. "Citizens, Aliens, Membership and the Constitution." *Constitutional Commentary* 7:9 (1990); Kurzban, Ira J. *Kurzban's Immigration Law Sourcebook.* 7th ed. Washington, D.C.: American Immigration Law Foundation, 2000.

income tax

Taxes have always been contentious, often times raising legal issues before the Supreme Court.

"No taxation without representation" was a battle cry that helped persuade colonists to rebel against Britain. But taxes are necessary if government is to provide services that citizens demand. In the early days of the American republic taxes on imports was the source of most government revenue. This proved inadequate in times of emergency.

The income tax was first imposed as a Civil War tax in 1862 and lasted only 10 years. However, in 1894 Congress imposed a new income tax of 2 percent on individual and business income. Several companies sued, including one called *Farmers Loan & Trust Company*. They claimed income taxes violated the federal constitution. Indeed, income taxes did raise important constitutional issues. First, is an income tax a direct tax or an indirect tax? The distinction was critical, since the Constitution mandates that direct taxes have to be apportioned among the states in proportion to the census, that is the number of people, not their income or wealth. If an income tax were deemed a direct tax, it would be unconstitutional since it is not apportioned by population. Second, even if an income tax were considered an indirect tax, it still needed to be uniform and fulfill a variety of other constitutional requirements. Eventually the uniformity requirement was interpreted to apply only to geographic uniformity and was not held to require that a tax be uniform as applied to people of differing income levels.

The controversy surrounding federal income taxes raged throughout the 19th century. In 1895 the Supreme Court decided POLLOCK V. FARMERS LOAN AND TRUST CO., 157 U.S. 429 (1895). It declared the income tax law of 1894 unconstitutional. A tax on incomes derived from property, the Court declared, is a direct tax that Congress, under terms of Article I, sections 2 and 9 of the Constitution, can only apportion among the states according to population. The Court then held a second set of hearings regarding *Pollock* and produced a 5 to 4 decision striking down the income tax on the grounds that it is a direct tax.

Confusion on whether an income tax was or was not a direct tax continued even after *Pollock*, as did political pressure to pass an income tax to provide the government adequate revenues. The Court gave evidence of awareness of the dangerous consequences to national solvency by taking refuge in redefinitions of direct tax and excise taxation. In a series of cases from 1899 to 1902, the Court held the following taxes to have been levied merely upon one of the incidents of ownership and hence, to be excises: a tax which involved affixing revenue stamps to memoranda evidencing the sale of merchandise on commodity exchanges, inheritance taxes, and a war revenue tax upon tobacco on which the imposed excise tax had already been paid and which was held by the manufacturer for resale. In *Flint v. Stone Tracy Co.*, 220 U.S. 107 (1911), the Court even upheld a tax on the income of corporations as an indirect tax on the privilege of doing business in the corporate form. In 1902 Congress proposed a constitutional amendment to clear up the confusion and make clear its intent to establish an income tax.

Finally, in 1913, states ratified the Sixteenth Amendment, which reads: "Congress shall have power to lay and collect taxes on incomes, from whatever source derived, without apportionment among the several States, and without regard to any census or enumeration." Income taxes since that time have become much more complex and certainly take a greater percentage of income than in 1913. Not surprisingly, they remain highly contentious.

For more information: *Knowlton v. Moore*, 178 U.S. 41 (1900); *Nicole v. Ames*, 173 U.S. 509 (1899); *Patton v. Brady*, 184 U.S. 608 (1902); Seidman, J. S. *Seidman's Legislative History of Federal Income Tax Law, 1938–1861.* Clark, N.J.: Lawbook Exchange, 2003.

—Charlsey T. Baumeier

incorporation

Incorporation is the process through which the Supreme Court used the due process guarantee of the Fourteenth

Amendment to make key clauses in the BILL OF RIGHTS applicable to the states.

Before the Fourteenth Amendment was ratified in 1868, the prevailing sentiment was that states had total authority in all areas not specifically granted to the national government. The Bill of Rights, the first eight amendments to the U.S. Constitution, was interpreted to restrain the national government from infringing on the CIVIL LIBERTIES of the people. States were free to create and enforce any law that did not specifically encroach on federal authority. The Supreme Court used JUDICIAL REVIEW to change this interpretation by a process called selective incorporation.

Chief Justice John MARSHALL, in BARRON V. BALTIMORE, 32 U.S. 243 (1833), writing for a unanimous bench, set an early PRECEDENT that the Bill of Rights was meant to restrain only the power of the general government and did not protect citizens from the power of their own states. Barron v. Baltimore remained the controlling precedent for 35 years.

The incorporation process would not have been possible without ratification of the Fourteenth Amendment in 1868. After the Civil War ended in 1865, the Thirteenth, Fourteenth and Fifteenth Amendments were passed to end slavery, secure the Union, and ensure legal equality for blacks. Some advocates of equal treatment believed the "privileges and immunities" clause of the Fourteenth Amendment nationalized the Bill of Rights. That clause reads, "No state shall make or enforce any law which shall abridge the privileges or immunities of citizens of the United States." It was not to be.

In Butchers' Benevolent Association v. Crescent City Livestock Landing and Slaughterhouse Company, 83 U.S. 36 (1873), commonly called "The SLAUGHTER-HOUSE CASES," Justice Samuel F. Miller, writing for a five-justice majority, destroyed all chances of incorporation by use of the privileges and immunities clause. He argued that incorporation would "radically change the whole theory of the relations of the State and Federal governments to each other and of both these governments to the people." and the Fourteenth Amendment was not intended to do that. The privileges and immunities clause was rendered useless as a tool for incorporation.

Advocates of making the Bill of Rights applicable to the states turned to the due process clause of the Fourteenth Amendment. HURTADO V. CALIFORNIA, 110 U.S. 516 (1884), was the first opportunity for the Supreme Court to consider incorporating the Bill of Rights by using the due process clause. While this attempt failed, it did open the door. Justice Mathews, writing for the majority, stated "It is not supposed that these [state] legislative powers are absolute and despotic. . . . Arbitrary power, enforcing its edicts to the injury of the persons and property of its subjects, is not law." If this phrase weakened the prece-dent that states are immune from the Bill of Rights, the dissent of Justice HARLAN (I), laid the foundation for incorporation. He observed, "There are principles of liberty and justice laying at the foundation of our civil and political institutions that no state can violate." He then stated, "[D]ue process of law protects the fundamental principles of liberty and justice." Hurtado is significant because Justice Harlan establishes the notion that principles of liberty and justice are natural rights guaranteed to all people and that must be protected at all levels of government.

In Chicago, Burlington and Quincy Railroad v. Chicago (1897), the Court ruled, "states must abide by the Fifth Amendment's commands regarding public use of private property." Justice Harlan, an advocate of total incorporation of the Bill of Rights, wrote in the majority opinion for the Court that a state violated the Fourteenth Amendment due process clause when it did not give adequate payment for private property seized by the state. For the first time the Supreme Court incorporated a clause from the Bill of Rights using the Fourteenth Amendment.

A subsequent case heard by the Supreme Court in regards to incorporation opened the door to selective incorporation. In Twining v. New Jersey, 211 U.S. 78 (1908), the Court established three guidelines for the process of selective incorporation. The first principle is that some provisions of the Bill of Rights may protect citizens from the states by the due process clause of the Fourteenth Amendment. The second principle is that the civil liberties embodied by the first eight amendments of the Constitution are "fundamental and inalienable rights" and finally, that the Court would not incorporate the entire Bill of Rights. Rather it would consider incorporation on a case-by-case basis.

Gitlow v. New York, 268 U.S. 652 (1925), is cited as the groundbreaking decision that began the era of selective incorporation. The First Amendment right to free speech was incorporated. Justice Sanford's opinion for the majority stated "the freedom of speech and press, protected by the First Amendment from abridgment by Congress—are among the fundamental personal rights and 'Liberties' protected by the due process clause of the Fourteenth Amendment." In Near v. Minnesota, 283 U.S. 697 (1931), the Court made its first decision upholding freedom of the press. Chief Justice Charles Evan HUGHES writing for the majority stated "[I]t is no longer open to doubt that liberty and press are safeguarded by the due process clause of the Fourteenth Amendment from invasion by the states." Chief Justice Hughes used similar language in Stromberg v. California, 283 U.S. 359, 368 (1931), where he found that "It has been determined the conception of liberty under the due process clause of the Fourteenth Amendment embraces the right of free speech." The Supreme Court of the United States had embraced the idea of incorporation.

During the next 25 years the Supreme Court would use the doctrine of selective incorporation to apply most of the clauses of the first eight amendments to the states. The clauses not incorporated are: the SECOND AMENDMENT right to bear arms, the Third Amendment right against quartering soldiers, the Fifth Amendment right to a grand jury hearing [at the state level], the Seventh Amendment right to a trial by jury in a civil case, and the Eighth Amendment right against excessive bail. These clauses have not been incorporated for various reasons. They may not meet the test of being a fundamental right, or the unincorporated clauses may simply not have come before the Court in the form of a federal question.

The Supreme Court used an incremental process to bring states under the Bill of Rights. It gradually moved away from an accepted "states rights" doctrine that was prevalent during the Civil War to a cautious but progressive stance applying constitutional protections of life, liberty, and property to the states. The process of incorporation illustrates that the Constitution is a living document flexible enough to protect citizens' rights from government abuse at all levels.

For more information: Epstein, Lee, and Thomas G. Walker. *Constitutional Law for a Changing America: Rights, Liberties and Justice.* 5th ed. Washington, D.C.: Congressional Quarterly Press, 2004; Herbele, Klaus H. "From *Gitlow to Near:* Judicial 'Amendment' by Absent Minded Incrementalism." *The Journal of Politics.* Vol. 34, no. 2 (May 1972): 458–483; Fairman, Charles, Leonard Levy, and Stanley Morrison. *The Fourteenth Amendment and the Bill of Rights: The Incorporation Theory.* Introduction by Leonard Levy. New York: Da Capo, 1970.

—Robert Charles

Indian rights

From the early years of the new republic, the Supreme Court has played a large role in defining the status and rights of Native Americans, particularly in recognizing the sovereignty of Indian tribes. The rights and status of Indian tribes and individual Native Americans have occupied a large part of the Supreme Court's attention throughout its history and continue to be one of the issue areas to produce the most Supreme Court opinions. While the Court has always been a staunch supporter of the sovereignty of Indian tribes, individual decisions concerning specific government policies have generally been very deferential to the Congress and have tended to follow the political trends within the other branches of government.

Historical Background

Native Americans (also referred to as American Indians, Indians, indigenous peoples, or First Nations) are the communities who lived on the North American continent prior to the arrival of European explorers and settlers, and their modern-day descendants. At the time of the arrival of Europeans, there was a great deal of diversity among Native American communities, which continues to this day. These communities were typically tribally organized hunter-gatherer societies, although many tribes also engaged in substantial agriculture and a widespread trade network existed across the continent. Many tribes were organized into large nations or federations, including most famously the Iroquois Confederation of the northeast. During the colonial period and through the Revolutionary War, various Indian tribes were frequent and valued allies of the English, the French, and the colonists. Indian tribes were generally treated as foreign nations in these alliances and in the conclusion of TREATIES that governed borders and the sale of land to serve the growing population of colonists.

Today, Native Americans comprise less than 1 percent of the population of the United States and are concentrated in the Upper Midwest, the Northwest, the Southwest, and the states of Oklahoma and Alaska. There are currently more than 550 federally recognized tribal entities (more than 200 of which are Native Alaskan villages) in addition to tribal communities that continue to seek official recognition, all with their own distinct cultures, histories, and languages. Most recognized tribes are organized on reservations that typically represent a mere fraction of their historical lands and within which they are able to exercise an amount of sovereign self-governance, as will be discussed in more depth below. Many individual Native Americans, while maintaining ties to their tribes, have moved off of the reservations in search of employment or educational opportunities. While the Navajo of the Southwest, the whaling Makah of Washington State, and the Seminole of Florida may have little in common culturally, they are all governed by the same body of Federal Indian Law that has provided a constant flow of issues for the consideration of the United States Supreme Court.

Role of the Supreme Court in Defining the Status of Indian Tribes

The United States Supreme Court has taken a very active role in defining and explaining the relationship between the U.S. government and the Indian tribes, beginning from the very early years of the Court's existence, particularly under the influence of Chief Justice John MARSHALL. The three decisions announced in *Johnson v. M'Intosh,* 21 U.S. 543 (1823), *Cherokee Nation v. Georgia,* 30 U.S. 1 (1832), and *Worcester v. Georgia,* 31 U.S. 515 (1832), collectively form the early core of federal Indian law. In these three cases, the Supreme Court established several important doctrines protecting the rights and independent status of the Indian tribes that, while frequently defied by the Congress and the president for many years, have gained renewed importance in defining contemporary debates about the federal government's policy toward the Indian tribes.

Decided in 1823, *Johnson v. M'Intosh* represents one of the earliest statements of the Supreme Court regarding the rights and status of the Indian tribes, particularly as regards land. This case concerned a land dispute between two non-Indians who claimed to have the right to a piece of property. Both parties traced their claim to a purported grant of land by the Indian tribe that had previously controlled the area. In order to settle this dispute, the Court held that Indian tribes hold "aboriginal title" to land, which contains all of the use rights that would be of value to any landowner but that can only be sold or otherwise alienated to the federal government. This doctrine has continued to be invoked by tribes attempting to reclaim land taken by state governments or private individuals as recently as *Rosebud Sioux Tribe v. Kneip*, 430 U.S. 584 (1977), and numerous cases decided in the lower courts.

The "Cherokee Cases," *Cherokee Nation v. Georgia*, decided in 1831, and *Worcester v. Georgia*, decided in 1832, famously define the status of Indian tribes as "domestic dependent nations"—a term that has confused legal scholars and policy-makers ever since. As "domestic dependent nations," Indian tribes are considered to possess the necessary sovereignty for self-government but to have no powers of international relations. Both of these cases arose from the same ongoing conflict between the state of Georgia and the Cherokee Nation concerning the right of the Cherokees to govern themselves within their own territory and to maintain possession of their lands. The Court declined to rule on the conflict in *Cherokee Nation* because Marshall ruled that, as citizens of a "dependent domestic nation," the Cherokees did not have the right to sue their own state (Georgia) in federal courts. Samuel Worcester deliberately had himself arrested in order to bring the conflict itself before the Court, at which time the Court ruled that a state government could not legally disturb an Indian tribe's rights as sovereign or their rights to Indian lands. These holdings continue to form the core of Federal Indian Law even though the Cherokees were ultimately removed from their lands with the approval of President Jackson, in violation of the Court's orders.

Until Congress abolished the power to make treaties with the Indian tribes in 1873, a series of treaties were made that governed relations between the United States and the Indian tribes. These treaties, made between Indian tribes and the federal government (or the British Crown in the colonial years), generally extinguished the land rights of the tribe to a particular area of land in exchange for various guarantees of protection, money, or rights (e.g., the right to fish in traditional areas). The Supreme Court has repeatedly been asked to apply, interpret, or enforce the provisions of these treaties, including the recent dispute over the fishing rights of several tribes in Washington state in *Washington v. Washington State Commercial Passenger Fishing Vessel Assn.*, 433 U.S. 658 (1979). The Supreme Court has repeatedly ruled that these treaties are, like any other treaties, the "supreme law of the land" (U.S. Constitution, Article VI). Congress can, however, abrogate these treaties as long as they state their intention to do so explicitly.

The rights guaranteed to the tribes in these treaties, while respected and enforced as the highest law of the land by the Supreme Court, in fact have had only limited influence because of the Court's adoption of the doctrine of PLENARY POWER. In *Cherokee Nation v. Hitchcock*, 187 U.S. 294 (1902), the Court ruled that the Constitution's grant of authority to the Congress "to regulate commerce . . . with the Indian tribes" (Article I, section 8) meant that the Congress had blanket authority to govern the Indian tribes in whatever manner they saw fit. This blanket authority was so extensive that the Court did not object to the efforts of the Congress to terminate all programs for Indian tribes and indeed terminate the special status of Indian tribes as tribes during the "termination" period of the 1950s. Ultimately, the termination policy was reversed in the early 1970s through congressional action only after a period of political organization and activism within the Native American community.

The Supreme Court and Native American Sovereignty

As discussed above, the Supreme Court considers Indian tribes as "dependent domestic nations." As a consequence, tribes are generally considered sovereign for the purposes of self-government within "Indian country." Indian country refers to land that is held in trust by the federal government for an Indian tribe or an individual Native American, which includes the vast majority of land on reservations or trust lands allotted to individual Native Americans. In *Alaska v. Native Village of Venetie*, 522 U.S. 520 (1998), however, the Supreme Court held that the 213 federally recognized Alaska Native villages which are governed by the Alaska Native Claims Settlement Act of 1971 do not reside in "Indian Country" because the settlement act extinguished aboriginal title to the state of Alaska. Similarly, the benefits of sovereignty apply only to those tribes that enjoy federal recognition. While the Court has repeatedly limited the extension of tribal jurisdiction over nonmembers, they have continued to support tribal SOVEREIGN IMMUNITY, which protects tribal governments (in much the same way as a state or local government is protected) from most kinds of lawsuits.

One of the most widely publicized and controversial aspects of sovereignty is the presence of casino gambling on many reservations. The Supreme Court ruled in *California v. Cabazon Band of Mission Indians,* 480 U.S. 202 (1987), that state laws regulating gambling could not apply to Indian tribes operating in Indian Country, although outright criminal prohibitions could. Because so many states allows at least some forms of gambling, such as state lotteries or charity bingo, this decision essentially legalized casino gambling on Indian reservations. In response to concerns over this decision, the Congress passed the Indian Gaming Regulatory Act of 1990, which required tribes to form agreements with state governments before operating full-scale casino gambling. These compacts have been made in a variety of states, including California, New York, and Michigan, although the majority of tribes do not currently operate casinos because they often consider it to be economically inefficient given the remote location of the reservation, or because the tribe itself is concerned about possible negative consequences in their communities.

The Supreme Court and Native American Civil Rights

In general, Native Americans enjoy all of the same CIVIL RIGHTS guarantees against the federal government and against state governments that are enjoyed by all citizens of the United States. As such, all of the Supreme Court's rulings regarding the right to vote, freedom of speech, all of the procedural guarantees in criminal law issues, and all of the other areas in which the Court has been active apply equally to Native American individuals. However, many civil rights issues are colored by tribal sovereignty when one of the parties involved is a tribal government. The Supreme Court has frequently been asked to weigh in on the rights of individuals against tribes. As tribes have become more active in governmental and economic spheres since the 1970s, these types of conflicts have increased, paralleling the growth in jurisdictional conflicts discussed above.

The number of these cases grew substantially just before and after the passage of the Indian Civil Rights Act of 1968. During the 1950s, the Court heard several cases of conflicts between the actions of tribes as local governments and the constitutional rights of local members. Following passage of the Indian Civil Rights Act of 1968, the Court took a firm stance that the sovereign rights of tribes vis-à-vis their members trump the individual constitutional rights of those members. The paramount case in this line was *Santa Clara Pueblo v. Martinez,* 436 U.S. 49 (1978), in which the Court upheld a tribal rule that limited tribal membership to children whose *fathers* had been tribal members. Although this rule clearly discriminates on the basis of sex to a degree that would be unacceptable in any state government action, the Court let it stand in order to protect the right of tribes to determine their own membership.

AFFIRMATIVE ACTION or preferential hiring is one notable area in which the Supreme Court's rulings have diverged widely between Native Americans and non-Native Americans. While racially based hiring preferences and other preferential policies grouped together under the term *affirmative action* have been disfavored by the Court in the 1980s and 1990s, those rulings do not apply to preferential hiring in the Bureau of Indian Affairs. In *Morton v. Mancari,* 417 U.S. 535 (1974), the Court ruled that preferential hiring and promotion policies within the Bureau of Indian Affairs are not RACIAL DISCRIMINATION. This policy provides a hiring preference for Native Americans who are enrolled members of a federally recognized tribe and who have at least one-quarter Indian blood. The court upheld this policy because the preference is based on the *political status* of being an Indian, and the policy supports the ability of the Native Americans to support in their own sovereign self-governance.

Free exercise of Native American religious practices has been another controversial area of civil rights law in which the Supreme Court has been involved, but the Court has supported restrictions. The Court refused to exclude Native Americans who used peyote as a part of religious ceremonies from a generally applicable antinarcotics law that made use of peyote criminal and conditioned state employment on passing drug tests that included peyote in *Employment Division, Department of Human Resources v. Smith,* 490 U.S. 1045 (1989). In this decision, the Court determined that criminal laws of general applicability would control, even if they conflicted with the free exercise of RELIGION by Native Americans (or any other people). Similarly, the Court has refused to exempt Native Americans from the prohibition of killing or possessing bald eagles and other protected species in *United States v. Dion,* 476 U.S. 734 (1986), despite treaty provisions guaranteeing the right to use parts of the sacred bald eagle to certain tribes.

For more information: Deloria, Vine, and Clifford M. Lytle. *American Indians, American Justice.* Austin: University of Texas Press, 1983; Washburn, Wilcomb E. *Red Man's Land, White Man's Law.* 2nd ed. Norman: University of Oklahoma Press, 1995; Wilkins, David E. *American Indian Sovereignty and the United States Supreme Court: The Masking of Justice.* Austin: University of Texas Press, 1997.

—Rachel Bowen

inherent powers

"Inherent powers" are powers neither expressed nor clearly implied by the constitutional text. Instead they derive from the sheer fact of national sovereignty or the core functions of a governmental body. Some hold that such unenumerated powers have no place in our system. As Madison put it, "[P]owers inherent, implied, or expedient, are obviously the creatures of ambition; because the care expended in defining powers would otherwise have been superfluous." Others hold that "the Constitution is not a suicide pact"; thus, it must not be read to deny to government any power that is truly essential.

The Supreme Court's contribution to the debate has been episodic and sometimes short-sighted. A few inherent powers have been conceded to courts themselves or to Congress, e.g., powers to hold recalcitrant witnesses in contempt. The most significant issues, however, have concerned broad claims of inherent presidential powers. In Madison's terms, the executive has been the most ambitious branch. Pressured by wars and other emergencies, courts have sometimes acquiesced.

Two seminal cases expanding presidential power beyond the specific grants of the Constitution and laws were IN RE NEAGLE, 135 U.S. 1 (1890), and IN RE DEBS, 158 U.S. 564 (1895). Notably, these politically charged decisions also augmented the security and power of the judicial branch itself. *Neagle* held that the president had power to assign a U.S. marshal to protect a philandering Supreme Court justice. In *Debs*, the president sought to enjoin a railroad strike, avowedly to protect INTERSTATE COMMERCE. Despite the state governor's objections and congressional silence, the Court upheld the action.

The most sweeping claims of inherent presidential powers have arisen in the national security domain. The Constitution assigns to the president the "executive power," the "commander-in-chief," and the treaty-making powers. Over the years, the Supreme Court has generously interpreted these clauses, while presidents progressively expanded their claims to preeminence in national defense and foreign affairs. Today they claim substantial powers to act unilaterally in time of war or emergency. Moreover, their announcement of an emergency is hard to challenge.

The original understanding of the commander-in-chief clause focused on the need for civilian control of the military. Presidential actions by themselves could not determine whether the nation was in a state of war or peace [*Fleming v. Page*, 50 U.S. 603 (1850)]. Yet in the PRIZE CASES, 67 U.S. 635 (1863), the Court accepted belated congressional approval in place of a prior declaration of war.

In the diplomatic realm, the Court has acknowledged presidential powers to recognize foreign governments, employ secret overseas agents, gather and control information, terminate TREATIES, and negotiate "executive agreements" without Senate ratification. Yet the Court may restrain presidents if their action clearly usurps legislative power, and especially where it impinges on fundamental personal rights.

If the president has leeway before Congress acts, once Congress does act the president is bound. Congress has powers to declare war, to appropriate funds, to establish an army and navy, and to regulate both foreign commerce and military justice. It also has powers to organize and oversee the executive and judicial branches, to appoint and remove officers, and to obtain necessary information as "grand inquest of the nation."

The leading case on Congress's power to limit the president's actions as commander-in-chief is the Steel Seizure Case, YOUNGSTOWN SHEET & TUBE CO. V. SAWYER, 343 U.S. 579 (1952). When steelworkers went on strike during the Korean War, President Truman, persuaded that a prolonged strike would jeopardize the war effort, ordered the secretary of commerce to seize and operate the mills. Since no statute authorized the seizure, the government relied upon the president's powers as chief executive and commander-in-chief. Despite the *In re Debs* PRECEDENT, the Court held that only Congress could authorize such a seizure of property. In a concurring opinion which has come to be regarded as definitive, Justice JACKSON stressed the fact that Congress had laid down specific procedures, not followed by the president, for dealing with labor disputes. (He also showed that *United States v. Curtiss-Wright Corp.*, 299 U.S. 304 [1936], often cited as recognizing extremely broad, inherent presidential powers, "involved, not the question of the President's power to act without congressional authority, but the question of his right to act under and in accord with an Act of Congress.")

The ability of Congress to limit the president's actions or even to reverse them extends to diplomatic activities as well. In *La Abra Silver Mining Co. v. United States*, 175 U.S. 423 (1899), the Court held that Congress could intervene in a diplomatic process and could abrogate completed treaties at any time.

There is *no* precedent invalidating a congressional regulation of the president's military or diplomatic activities. Yet questions arise in connection with executive claims that Congress has in fact granted or delegated its power to the president. The Court has shown sympathy to such claims, not insisting that the congressional sanction be timely, specific, and clear. Congressional authorization can be retroactive; it can be found in the appropriation of funds to carry out an activity, or the authorization or funding of a general program under which, to the knowledge of Congress, the activity was carried on.

In several cases where personal rights were implicated, the Court interpreted delegations more narrowly, taking the view that "the clearest language would be necessary to satisfy us that Congress intended that the power given by these acts should be so exercised."

More recent decisions, however, have shown more solicitude for executive power than for personal rights. Increasingly, it seems, judicial deference to the "political branches" means deference to the Imperial Presidency. Neither Congress nor the Court can effectively check actions of which they are unaware. Scrutiny is awkward when one is persuaded that information is properly withheld. Yet on occasion the Court has found ways to review classified information and judge independently the issue before them.

The Court's hesitancy to enforce firm limitations in the national security domain stems in part from the "political questions" doctrine—that some issues, not resolvable by legal reasoning or judicial order, must be left to the "political branches." Thus, as an alternative to reviewing a presidential action, the Court will sometimes decline to decide the merits of the case. Yet the Court has never held that all cases potentially affecting national security are nonjusticiable. Many such cases have been adjudicated on the merits, especially where personal rights were at stake.

Even when persuaded that the asserted state interest justifies curtailing personal rights, the Court has insisted that the policy be narrowly drawn so that its impact does not exceed what is essential.

An area in which the Court has exercised especially great restraint involves the rights of aliens to enter or remain in the United States. The Court has held that the government has inherent power to exclude aliens, and that deportation need involve very few procedural safeguards. Others who can expect only limited protection from the courts include prisoners of war [*Hirota v. MacArthur*, 338 U.S. 197 (1948)] and, perhaps, the "unlawful combatant" category deployed in the current war on terrorism. As of 2003, many CIVIL LIBERTIES aspects of the war on terrorism remain to be argued, in and outside the courts.

It is clear in principle that actions taken in the name of national security are fully subject to constitutional limitations. In HOME BUILDING AND LOAN ASSOCIATION V. BLAISDELL, 290 U.S. 398 (1934), the Court stated, "The Constitution was adopted in a period of grave emergency. Its grants of power to the Federal Government and its limitations of the power of the States were determined in the light of emergency and they are not altered by emergency. . . . [E]ven the war power does not remove constitutional limitations safeguarding essential liberties." There has never been a decision to the contrary.

The Supreme Court declared unconstitutional the legislative veto, the power of one or both houses of Congress to reject a presidential or bureaucratic action, in *Immigration and Naturalization Service v. Chadha*, 462 U.S. 919 (1983). This decision invalidated more congressional acts than the Court had done in its entire history.

Jagdish Chadha was a man without a country. He came to the United States on a British passport, even though he was an East Asian born in Kenya. When his student visa to the United States expired, both Kenya and Britain refused his return. The Immigration and Naturalization Service

(INS) nonetheless ordered Chadha deported. He appealed under a special provision of the Immigration and Nationality Act granting the attorney general the power to suspend deportation when deportation would impose an extreme hardship on the individual. The law also authorized either house of the U.S. Congress to veto the attorney general's decision. This was one of the 295 veto provisions that had been inserted in 200 different statutes since 1932. The U.S. House of Representatives passed a resolution vetoing the attorney general's decision, alleging that there was no hardship. The INS joined with Chadha when he appealed to the federal courts, arguing that the legislative veto contained in the act was a violation of the Constitution's SEPARATION OF POWERS.

Chief Justice Warren BURGER, writing for the majority, held that a legislative veto was unconstitutional under Article I, section 7 of the Constitution. The Constitution requires that all legislation be approved by both houses of Congress and be presented to the president for his approval. The resolution to veto the attorney general's action had only been passed by the House of Representatives. Congress must abide by the attorney general's delegated authority until Congress explicitly revokes it. While admitting that this constitutional scheme of divided legislative power is "clumsy, inefficient, even unworkable," Burger asserted, "we have not yet found a better way to preserve freedom than by making the exercise of power subject to the carefully crafted restraints spelled out in the Constitution."

Justices Byron WHITE and William REHNQUIST dissented, objecting to the majority's formalistic approach to the separation of powers. According to White, courts are obliged to accommodate the Constitution to the necessities of modern government. Congress transferred lawmaking powers to the president, bureaucracy, and independent regulatory agencies in order to ensure that jobs are accomplished. It sought to retain control over delegated power through congressional oversight and the legislative veto. The only alternative was for Congress to abdicate its lawmaking function and accept that representative bodies have no role in contemporary government.

Some observers feared that *Chadha* would cause a governmental train wreck in which unelected bureaucrats would assume greater control over government. Others hoped that the decision would put Congress on notice not to legislate "fuzzy" laws. The *Chadha* decision caused neither. Congress now writes provisions in statutes requiring the bureaucracy to ask its approval on controversial issues such as weapon sales to foreign nations. An "informal" veto requiring prior congressional approval of agency actions is now common. The question of how to make the bureaucracy accountable to Congress is very much alive.

For more information: Craig, Barbara. *Chadha: The Story of an Epic Constitutional Struggle.* Berkeley: University of California Press, 1988.

—Timothy J. O'Neill

In re Debs, 158 U.S. 564 (1895)

In the case *In re Debs,* the Supreme Court of the United States unanimously upheld the authority of the federal government (i.e., the president) to use force to end, and prevent any furtherance of, a railroad strike.

In Chicago, in May 1894, a dispute over better wages and working conditions arose between the Pullman Palace Car Company and its employees. When the (railroad) car company rejected their demands, workers went on strike. An association known as the American Railway Union (ARU), led by a future leader of the Socialist Party— Eugene V. Debs—joined the workers in a boycott against the car company.

On July 2, 1894, a district attorney of Illinois, Thomas E. Milchrist, and the U.S. attorney general, Richard Olney, filed a bill of complaint in the Circuit Court of the United States. The bill asserted that the railroads were engaged in INTERSTATE COMMERCE and transportation of the mails. It then charged that Debs was one of the officers of the ARU who conspired with employees of the car company to strike against the railroads in Chicago; and that he proceeded to obstruct railroad service and to wage further strikes among employees of other railroads. After the complaint was filed, President Grover Cleveland had the attorney general secure an injunction ordering all members of the strike to refrain from interfering with the services of the railroads. After the injunction, a federal grand jury issued an indictment charging Debs and others with conspiracy.

To protect the railroads, President Cleveland sent federal troops to Chicago. The Constitution gave him that power, however only upon request of the state legislature, or when it was not in session, the governor of that state. President Cleveland had sent the troops to Chicago without any such request.

On December 14, 1894, Debs was found guilty of contempt for defying the injunction. While imprisoned Debs petitioned the Supreme Court, disputing the injunction. He argued that the president lacked the authority to secure the order without explicit authorization from Congress. Clarence Darrow, who later became famous for defending John Scopes in the "Monkey Trial," represented Debs in the Supreme Court.

The Supreme Court addressed two issues: (1) whether the obstruction of interstate commerce and the transportation of the mails authorized a direct interference by the federal government without a request from the governor; and (2) whether that authority, if it exists, gave the government the power to enforce the injunction. The Court answered both issues in the affirmative and denied Debs' petition for relief.

For more information: Ginger, Ray. *Eugene V. Debs: A Biography.* New York: Collier Books, 1962.

—Matthew R. Doyle
—Carrie A. Schneider

In re Gault, 387 U.S. 1 (1967)

The inception of the modern juvenile justice system began in 1967 with the United States Supreme Court decision in *In re Gault.* In an 8-1 decision, the U.S. Supreme Court found the Arizona Juvenile Code violated the due process clause of the Fourteenth Amendment since it denied juveniles several PROCEDURAL DUE PROCESS rights. The decision had a tremendous impact on the juvenile justice process creating a framework that still exists today. Prior to 1967 the focus of the system was ensuring the social welfare of the juvenile. The system focused on the child's right to custody and not on the child's right to liberty.

Fifteen-year-old Gerald Gault had been found delinquent by the Juvenile Court of Gila County, Arizona for making lewd telephone calls to a neighbor. At the time the prank calls were made, Gerald was on probation for being present when another boy stole a wallet. As punishment for making the prank calls, Gerald was sentenced to the State Industrial School until the age of 21, a period of six years. Gerald Gault had been denied adequate written notice of charges, the right to counsel, the privilege against self-incrimination, and the right to confront and to cross-examine witnesses.

Justice FORTAS delivered the Supreme Court's opinion. The juvenile justice system was created in order to protect children from the harsh realities of the adult criminal justice system. It was an attempt by states to protect, care for, and rehabilitate juveniles. Fortas pointed out that the results of the system had not been entirely acceptable. Since Gerald Gault was 15 years old at the time of his offense he was denied procedural safeguards and subsequently sentenced to the State Industrial School for a period of up to six years. If he had been over the age of 18, he would not have been tried in juvenile court and would have been entitled to rights under the Constitution. The law he violated was a misdemeanor. As an adult, he would have received a $5 to $50 fine or been incarcerated for up to two months. Since he was a minor he was denied procedural rights guaranteed to adults and subsequently sentenced to a period of incarceration of up to six years. Children were often left without both the procedural safeguards guaranteed to adults and rehabilitative treatment. Since a gap existed between the benevolent intent and the practice in reality, procedural safeguards are required. The Fourteenth Amendment and the BILL OF RIGHTS are not only for adults. Children have the right to liberty.

The emphasis on procedural rights dominated the juvenile justice system for two decades. During the 1980s the view began to change. A rapid increase in juvenile crime occurred between 1985 and the mid-1990s. Since then juvenile crime has decreased. During this time the focus moved away from ensuring the fairness of the system to focusing on the offenses committed. The media increased its coverage of juvenile crime. State legislatures reexamined their statutes and began to emphasize deterrence and punishment. Today juveniles are often waived to adult court.

For more information: Berkheiser, Mary. "The Fiction of Juvenile Right to Counsel: Waiver in the Juvenile Courts." *Florida Law Review* 54 (September 2002): 577–686; Miller, Frank W., et al. *The Juvenile Justice Process: Cases and Materials.* 4th ed. New York: Foundation Press, 2000.

—Benjamin Steiner

In re Neagle, 135 U.S. 1 (1890)

In re Neagle held that a U.S. marshal is immune from state criminal prosecution when the officer is acting to prevent a breach of the peace of the United States.

In re Neagle was argued on March 4 and 5, 1890, and decided April 14, 1890, by a vote of 6 to 2. The facts in the case involve a violent story of romance, betrayal, and violent death out of the Old West.

Both David S. Terry and Stephen J. Field had gone to California following the 1849 gold strike. There they both became justices of the California Supreme Court. In the years that followed Terry became chief justice of the California Supreme Court. In 1859 Terry killed Senator David Broderick in a duel. Shortly afterward Terry left California and joined the Confederate Army. Field, remaining in California, was deeply grieved by Broderick's death and ever after hostile toward Terry. In 1863 President Lincoln appointed Field to the United States Supreme Court.

In 1880 Sarah Althea Hill met Senator William Sharon, king of the Comstock Lode. Senator Sharon was then 60 years of age, very wealthy and a widower with a taste for young women. In a complicated romance Althea became the "rose of Sharon" with a monthly stipend. The complication arose from Althea's claim that Sharon had "married" her without benefit of clergy under California law (section 75), which at that time permitted a couple to marry if both signed a written declaration of marriage and then cohabitated. Their secret marriage was made public over a year later when they parted.

In 1883 with Terry as her attorney Althea sued for divorce with her "marriage document" as evidence. The California court granted her a divorce and a monthly alimony. However, Sharon resorted to the federal courts with the claim that the document was a forgery. Eventually Justice Field became involved because as a Supreme Court justice he was also required to "ride circuit" in the circuit that included California.

In 1885 Althea appeared in Field's court with Terry as her attorney. The case eventually went against them and she was ordered to surrender the "marriage" document as a forgery. However, before the decision Sharon died. Althea then married Terry.

By 1888 they had lost to Sharon's children in both California and federal courts. They swore to get Field for his role in the case in letters to California newspapers. In response to the threats the attorney General advised appointing a marshal to protect Field. Marshal David Neagle was assigned the duty.

On August 14, 1889, Field and Neagle were traveling on circuit and had stopped to eat breakfast in a café in Lathrop, California. Terry and Althea entered and made further threats. Terry then slapped the seated Field twice while Neagle ordered him to stop. Terry then reached for his pocket and was shot dead by Neagle. Terry however was unarmed. Althea, throwing herself on his body in hysterics, tried to rouse a lynch mob against Neagle and Field. Both were then arrested, but Field was ordered released by the governor of California. Field then secured a federal writ of habeas corpus for Neagle from Judge Lorenzo Sawyer, who had participated with Field in the decision invalidating Mrs. Terry's marriage, in order to get him out of California where popular regard for the Terrys could have had fatal consequences.

Justice Samuel F. Miller issued the opinion of the Court. Justice L. Q. C. Lamar and Chief Justice Melville FULLER joined in dissent. Justice Stephen J. Field did not participate. The issue was whether a federal court could preempt the operation of California law by making a determination that Terry's death was justifiable homicide. At this time federal law was understood to mean a statute. Did "law" mean acts done under the authority of the United States? The majority decided yes, but the dissenters condemned this as a federal invasion of California's state rights.

For more information: Buchanan, A. Russell. *David S. Terry of California: Dueling Judge.* San Marino, Calif.: Huntington Library, 1956; Field, Stephen J. *Personal Reminiscences of Early Days in California.* New York: Da Capo Press, 1968; McCracken, Brooks W. "Althea and the Judges." *American Heritage* vol. xviii, no. 4 (June 1967): 60–79; Wagstaff, A. E., ed. *The Life of David S. Terry: Presenting an Authentic, Impartial and Vivid History of His*

Eventful Life & Tragic Death. New York: Augustus M. Kelly, 1971.

—A. J. L. Waskey

intermediate scrutiny

When a law classifies or treats people differently based on quasi-suspect categories, like gender or illegitimacy, and the constitutionality of that law is challenged, the standard of JUDICIAL REVIEW used is intermediate scrutiny. (In contrast, race is considered a "suspect" classification, which requires the highest level of review, or STRICT SCRUTINY.)

Gender is considered quasi-suspect perhaps because historically legislative classifications based on gender have evolved less out of a desire to discriminate against women and more out of a desire to "protect" them—no matter how misguided this desire may have been. In addition, gender classifications do not meet the "discrete and insular minority" requirement of a SUSPECT CLASSIFICATION, meaning that judicial protection is given to those groups who are regular losers in the political struggle due to widespread prejudice against them.

Intermediate scrutiny (also called "exacting scrutiny," "heightened scrutiny," or the strict rationality test) requires that the challenged statute be substantially related to an important state interest in order for it to be upheld. For example, a law distinguishing between legitimate and illegitimate children in the award of state welfare benefits was held to be unconstitutional because the Supreme Court did not find a substantial relationship between the differential treatment and the government's interest in the regulation of welfare payments [*New Jersey Welfare Rights Organization v. Cahill,* 411 U.S. 619 (1973)].

Previously, under the WARREN Court, review was limited either to strict scrutiny, the highest level of judicial review and the most difficult for a statute to survive, or the RATIONAL BASIS test, a very low level of review. As a mechanism to review cases of nonracial discrimination and to allow for the opportunity for statutes to survive judicial review (meaning a statute is held to be constitutional), the BURGER Court (1969–86) developed intermediate scrutiny.

The Burger Court honed intermediate scrutiny over several years. In *Reed v. Reed,* 404 U.S. 71 (1971), the Court overturned an Idaho statute giving preference to males over females in certain proceedings. While the Court did not address whether gender was a suspect class (when a law categorizes or treats people differently based on characteristics that historically have been used for purposes of discrimination, like race, it is "suspect"), it did signal that gender-based classifications would be taken seriously.

It was in 1976 that the Court settled on intermediate scrutiny as the level of judicial review for gender-based classifications, which it deemed quasi-suspect. In *CRAIG V.*

BOREN, 429 U.S. 190, an Oklahoma statute restricting the sale of nonintoxicating beer to males under the age of 21 and females under the age of 18 was overturned because the gender classification failed to serve an important governmental objective and was not substantially related to achievement of those objective (today, this is the standard that quasi-suspect classifications must meet to survive intermediate scrutiny).

Intermediate scrutiny has been applied to situations involving both female and male plaintiffs. In *MISSISSIPPI UNIVERSITY FOR WOMEN V. HOGAN,* 458 U.S. 718 (1982), the Court struck down the women-only policy of Mississippi University's (a state school) nursing school, holding that the single-sex admission policy could only survive judicial review if it compensated for discrimination against women in the field of nursing, not just generally in education or employment. This case fine-tuned intermediate-level scrutiny by articulating that the requisite important governmental purpose must be substantially related to an actual purpose of the legislation, not a hypothesized purpose after the fact.

More recently, the Court struck Virginia's creation of a separate all-female military institute as a response to a lower court's finding that the state's all male Virginia Military Institute (VMI) violated the EQUAL PROTECTION CLAUSE [*U.S. V. VIRGINIA,* 116 S.Ct. 2264 (1996)].

While statutes reviewed under strict scrutiny are often overturned, some gender-based classifications survive intermediate scrutiny. For example, in *MICHAEL M. V. SUPERIOR COURT OF SONOMA COUNTY,* 450 U.S. 464 (1981), the Court upheld a California statute criminalizing the act of sexual intercourse with a minor female (statutory rape), finding that the intent of the statute (to discourage such conduct) was substantially related to the criminalization of the act.

In spite of the Court's intention to clearly define the distinction between intermediate and strict scrutiny, and nonracial and RACIAL DISCRIMINATION, sometimes the lines between the categories are blurred. One notable example involves Justice POWELL's opinion in *REGENTS OF THE UNIVERSITY OF CALIFORNIA V. BAKKE,* 438 U.S. 265 (1978), holding that racial quotas are impermissible but AFFIRMATIVE ACTION programs are not. He applied intermediate scrutiny, looking for a substantial relationship between the state's interest in diversity and the use of racial quotas. Historically, strict scrutiny, which requires that a classification be related to a "pressing public necessity," is used where race is involved.

For more information: O'Brien, David M. *Constitutional Law and Politics.* Vol. 2, *Civil Rights and Civil Liberties.* 3rd ed. New York: W. W. Norton, 1997.

—Deirdre O'Sullivan

International Society for Krishna Consciousness, Inc. v. Lee, 505 U.S. 672 (1992)

In *International Society for Krishna Consciousness v. Lee,* the United States Supreme Court held that airport terminals operated by public agencies are not public forums and that reasonable regulations prohibiting solicitation in such terminals do not violate the First Amendment. In reaching these conclusions, the court recognized that governmental agencies acting as proprietors of property, as opposed to acting in their official capacities, may regulate access to public property without infringing upon the right of citizens to free speech.

The International Society for Krishna Consciousness, Inc., is a not-for-profit religious corporation whose members perform a religious ritual that involves soliciting donations in public places. The Krishnas filed a lawsuit seeking to enjoin Walter Lee, the police superintendent of the Port Authority of New York and New Jersey, from enforcing the Port Authority's prohibition of repetitive solicitation inside airport terminals. In their lawsuit, the Krishnas argued that the ban on solicitation violated their right to freedom of speech because the airport terminals are public forums where speech could not be restricted. They also argued that, even if the terminals were not public forums, the ban on solicitation was invalid because it was an unreasonable policy.

The Krishnas' case presented the Supreme Court with an opportunity to apply the forum-based analysis it had previously adopted to evaluate restrictions on speech on government-owned property. Under that analysis, restrictions placed on speech in traditional public forums or designated public forums would survive scrutiny under the First Amendment only if they were narrowly tailored to serve a compelling government interest. Restrictions placed on speech on all other government property would survive scrutiny as long as they were reasonably related to a legitimate government interest. Applying this analysis to the Krishnas' contentions, the Court rejected them both.

First, the Court rejected the contention that airport terminals were either traditional or designated public forums. The Court concluded that, when viewed in the proper historical context, airport terminals were recent developments. As such, there was no tradition of public discourse inside airport terminals on which the Krishnas could rely. Next, the Court concluded that the Port Authority's acquiescence in some instances of solicitation did not amount to an intentional designation of the terminals as arenas for public discourse. On the contrary, it was clear to the Court that the Port Authority considered providing efficient transportation to be the designated purpose of the airport terminals.

Furthermore, the Court rejected the contention that all transportation terminals are public forums. The court noted that most other transportation terminals, particularly bus stations and train stations, were historically privately owned, rather than publicly owned. Moreover, the Court rejected the notion that a general rule could be adopted for all transportation terminals. Instead, the Court concluded that new types of terminals developed in the future should be considered individually to determine whether they are public forums.

Second, the Court rejected the contention that the prohibition of solicitation inside the airport terminals was unreasonable. The Court concluded that the Port Authority had a legitimate interest in prohibiting solicitation, which was viewed as potentially disruptive to the airport terminals. The Court concluded that solicitation could inconvenience travelers or cause them to suffer duress. Most important, the Court concluded that the prohibition was reasonable because the Krishnas were allowed to solicit donations from airport patrons on the sidewalk outside the airport terminal.

In a companion case, *Lee v. International Society for Krishna Consciousness, Inc.,* 505 U.S. 830 (1992), the Supreme Court held that the Port Authority's ban on the distribution of literature was unconstitutional under the Fourth Amendment. The primary reason for this ruling was the Court's finding that passing out leaflets or pamphlets is less intrusive than soliciting donations and, therefore, less burdensome on the airport's patrons.

For more information: Acosta, R. Alexander. "Revealing the Inadequacy of the Public Forum Doctrine: *International Society for Krishna Consciousness, Inc. v. Lee,* 112 S.Ct. 2701 (1992)." *Harvard Journal of Law and Public Policy* 16 (1993): 269–279; Newberry, Gary E. "Constitutional Law: *International Society for Krishna Consciousness, Inc. v. Lee:* Is the Public Forum a Closed Category?" *Oklahoma Law Review* 46 (1993): 155–174.

—Mark A. Fulks

International Union, UAW v. Johnson Controls, 499 U.S. 187 (1991)

In *International Union, UAW v. Johnson Controls,* the Supreme Court held that an employer was not permitted to bar a woman of childbearing age from working in a job in which she was exposed to material that might harm her unborn child.

During the late 1970s, as women began to move into industrial jobs in greater number, many employers refused to allow them to work in areas where toxic materials, such as lead, were used; in some cases, they were permitted to work in such areas if they were able to prove they were infertile. Women began challenging these policies, known as fetal protection policies, claiming they violated TITLE

VII OF THE CIVIL RIGHTS ACT OF 1964, the section of the law prohibiting employment discrimination on the basis of sex, among other things. The employers argued that they were justified in excluding childbearing women from potentially hazardous jobs, such as battery making, for two reasons: first, because only men and infertile women could successfully perform the jobs (known as the "business necessity" defense); and second, because it was "reasonably necessary for the normal operation" of the business to limit such jobs to men and infertile women (known as the "bona fide occupational qualification" or "bfoq" defense).

Beginning in the early 1980s, the federal courts were asked to rule on the question of whether fetal protection policies violated Title VII. In deciding these cases, the courts balanced the company's stated concern for the health of the fetus (as well as its fear of a lawsuit if the fetus were harmed) against the right of the woman to decide where she should work.

Johnson Controls manufactured car batteries, a job that exposed employees to lead. In 1982 it adopted a policy that excluded all fertile women of childbearing age from high lead exposure positions. The United Auto Workers (UAW) sued on behalf of the employees, arguing that lead could be transmitted through both parents, that most women workers do not get pregnant, and that the company was obligated to control the risk of fetal harm in the workplace.

The Seventh Circuit COURT OF APPEALS ruled in the company's favor because it believed that the company's interest in avoiding the risk of birth defects outweighed the woman's right to self-determination in the workplace. Two years later, the Supreme Court reversed the lower court. Speaking for a unanimous Court, Justice Harry BLACKMUN stated that the company's policy was discriminatory because it allowed fertile men, but not fertile women, to choose whether to work in jobs that exposed them to lead. Rejecting the company's argument that concern for fetal safety was an "essential element of battery making," Blackmun declared that the company's interest in the potential health of the woman's child did not justify the job restrictions. Ultimately, the company could not satisfy the Court that fertile women were less capable than men or infertile women of working safely and effectively in producing batteries. Although a victory for working women, while vindicating their right to assume responsibility for the health of their children, the Court did not address the issue of the employer's responsibility for ensuring a safe workplace for parents as well as their children.

For more information: Mezey, Susan Gluck. *Elusive Equality: Women's Rights, Public Policy, and the Law.* Boulder, Colo.: Lynne Rienner, 2003.

—Susan Gluck Mezey

Internet and censorship

With the invention of the Internet in 1995, coined the "information superhighway," the Supreme Court rendered its first decision related to the Internet just two years after its inception. The Court has addressed the intersection of the Internet and free speech, copyright, and due process. In addition to determining the constitutionality of various issues, the Court has been forced to define the Internet, illustrated in *Reno v. American Civil Liberties Union,* 521 U.S. 844 (1997). Justices grappled with whether the Internet was akin to broadcast media like radio and television, which have been highly regulated, or whether the Internet acted more like print media such as newspapers and magazines in which more latitude has been given. Historically, the government has not placed heavy regulations on the Internet, unlike the cable industry. Instead, the Court has treated the Internet more like print media and in many instances akin to private telephone conversations with emphasis on preserving new telecommunications technologies—curtailing government regulation, until its most recent decision in *U.S. v. American Library Association,* 02-36 (2003).

Reviewed by the Supreme Court in 1997, 2002, and 2003, justices determined the constitutionality of three acts that seek to protect minors from the potentially harmful affects of the Internet. In *Reno v. American Civil Liberties Union,* 521 U.S. 844 (1997), the Supreme Court ruled that the Communication Decency Act (CDA) of 1996 was unconstitutional. The CDA prohibited the transmission of obscene, indecent, or offensive messages to individuals under 18 years of age. Transmission of obscene, indecent, or offensive materials through the Internet to minors could result in a $250,000 fine and up to two years in prison. While the CDA was designed to protect minors, the Supreme Court ruled that the law simultaneously prevented adults from receiving information guaranteed to them under the First Amendment. The act essentially suppressed information that adults had a constitutional right to receive and disseminate. Fundamental to determining the constitutionality of the CDA was defining the Internet. According to Justice John Paul STEVENS, "encouraging free expression in a democratic society is more important than the unproven benefits of censorship."

Since the CDA was deemed unconstitutional, the Children's Online Privacy Protection Act (COPPA) was passed in 1998 to protect children's privacy. The act prohibits online retailers from obtaining personal information from children under 12 without parental consent. Personal information includes a home address, mailing address, e-mail address, etc. Though the third circuit court ruled COPPA unconstitutional, the Supreme Court retracted the lower court's decision. In *Ashcroft v. American Civil Liberties Union,* 535 U.S. 564 (2002), the Court ruled that relying only on "community standards" was insufficient reason for finding COPPA unconstitutional. Despite overturning the lower court ruling, the Court prevented the federal government from enacting COPPA until the lower court further reexamined COPPA.

A third attempt to protect children, the Children's Internet Protection Act of 2000 requires federally funded libraries to install Internet filters to block pornography from all computers that provide Internet access. Filtering software however is often overzealous in its attempt to block undesirable sites. In May 2000 a panel of three federal district court judges declared the Children's Internet Protection Act of 2000 unconstitutional as it infringed upon the First Amendment guarantee of free speech.

In *U.S. v. American Library Association,* 02-36 (2003), the Supreme Court overturned the lower court's decision, ruling that filtering materials to prevent children from viewing pornography is not unconstitutional. The First Amendment protects sexually explicit material, but it does not protect obscenity and child pornography. Unlike previous acts, the Children's Internet Protection Act does not charge anyone with a crime; rather it prevents libraries from receiving federal funds if they do not comply with the law, hence making it constitutionally defensible.

In *New York Times Co. v. Tasini,* 533 U.S. 483 (2001), and *Eldred v. Ashcroft,* 537 U.S. 186 (2003), the Court has also examined the constitutionality of copyright laws as they apply to the Internet. Jonathan Tasini, president of the National Writers Union, sued the New York Times Company, contending that publishing companies were not paying authors for work published in two online databases. A federal district court ruled in favor of the publishers, though this was overturned by the second circuit COURT OF APPEALS. Unhappy with the reversal, the publishers appealed to the Supreme Court.

In *Eldred v. Ashcroft,* 537 U.S. 186 (2003), the Supreme Court found that the print and electronic publishers had indeed infringed upon the copyrights of freelance authors and that publishers must obtain authorization from authors in order to publish materials through online databases. In a second case that involved copyrights, the lead plaintiff, Eric Eldred of Eldritch Press, in conjunction with other nonprofit Internet publishers, filed a claimed against the United States arguing that Congress's reauthorization of copyright law unfairly favored creators and corporations by extending copyrights to 70 years after an artist's death and 95 years for work owned by corporations. The Court ruled against the plaintiffs, asserting that the extension of the Copyright Extension Act (CTEA) (1998) by Congress falls within its authority and it is not unconstitutional.

Not only has the Court reviewed free speech and copyright issues, but it also examined whether information about convicted sex offenders could be published on the Internet, in addition to requiring offenders to register with the Department of Public Safety under Megan's Law. The second circuit court of appeals ruled that the publication of a sex offender's name over the Internet would deprive the registrant of liberty, as well as violating the due process clause. On March 5, 2003, in *SMITH ET AL. V. DOE ET AL.* and *Connecticut Department of Public Safety et al. v. Doe* the Supreme Court upheld the right of states to publish the name and photo of a sex offender on the Internet. States are not required to assess whether the sex offender poses a potential threat to the community after the individual completes his prison sentence. According to the Court, publishing information on the Internet is only intended to inform the public and it does not create an additional punishment, therefore it is not unconstitutional.

A 1967 Supreme Court decision, reaffirmed in 1992, found that states could not require retailers to collect sales taxes on goods coming into the state unless the retailer had a physical presence or tie to the state. Initially, this impacted mail-order companies, and more recently Internet companies, which are not required to collect and pay sales and use taxes unless they are physically located in the state. Some argue that this has created a loophole for online retailers. Further protecting online retailers was the passage of the Internet Tax Freedom Act of 1998, which prohibited states and localities from passing any new or special taxes on Internet commerce transactions.

While the Court has rendered several decisions related to the Internet, certiorari has been denied in several cases including *Lunney v. Prodigy Services Company,* 99-1430, and a California case involving the *DVD Copy Control Association.* The Supreme Court in *Lunney* upheld a New York court of appeals decision. A New York youth, Lunney, was victimized when an impostor opened Internet accounts using his name and sent threatening messages. Lunney sued Prodigy Services Company—the Internet service provider. The lower court found that ISPs are not legally and financially liable for e-mail communications or bulletin board messages that defame another user.

For more information: Kalven, Harry, Jr. *A Worthy Tradition: Freedom of Speech in America.* New York: Harper and Row, 1988; Krause, Jason. "Can Anyone Stop Internet Porn?" *American Bar Association Journal* (September 2002): 58.

—Antoinette Pole

Internet and the Worldwide Web

The Internet and the Web are relatively new forms of communication and commerce that raise numerous constitutional and legal issues under the First Amendment and the commerce clause.

In 2000, the first year in which the U.S. Census Bureau measured e-commerce separately from more conventional retail sales, the total of all Internet sales exceeded $20 billion, most of which came from business-to-business transactions. By 2002, total Internet sales had almost doubled, to nearly $40 billion. This staggering sales increase is even more impressive when one considers that the oldest of these high-profile Internet businesses is only approximately 10 years old. Prior to the mid-1990s, it was impossible to do the sort of fast-paced, high-volume business necessary to contribute to the Internet businesses' bottom line, since the software and hardware necessary for using the Internet efficiently were not developed until the early 1990s. It is unquestionable that in a very brief period of time, Internet companies have carved out a distinct sector in both national and international economy.

To the federal and state government that are dependent on funds collected through sales taxes, Internet businesses are problematic. While a majority of traditional mail-order businesses have routinely ignored sales tax laws, total mail-order sales were, until recently, so minimal that it was not worthwhile for state tax departments to track down and prosecute violators. This situation became more complicated with the passage, and subsequent extension of, the Internet Tax Freedom Act, which prohibits collection of both sales tax on Internet transactions and use tax on Internet service. The combined result of this act's prohibition on tax collections and the recent huge increase in Internet sales has been a widespread shortfall in tax-supported state departments administering such matters as education, health and child care, and prisons. To date, the Supreme Court has offered no suggestions or solutions for this problem.

For an Internet business, a domain name has the relative importance of a conventional business's name, address, telephone number, advertising logo, and trademark combined. Just as a bricks-and-mortar business could not remain viable if its name, display windows, and advertisements were concealed by those of another business, an Internet business cannot remain viable without its unique domain name. Alternatively, from a different perspective, tampering with an Internet business's domain name is equivalent to theft of a person's identity. To oversee the domain name industry, Congress created the Internet Corporation for Assigned Names and Numbers (ICANN) and appointed individuals with Internet expertise to act as arbitrators in the event of disputes over domain names.

Originally, Congress allowed a company called Network Solutions, Inc. (now called Verisign), to have a monopoly over domain name registration service. A 1998 Supreme Court decision, *Thomas v. Network Solutions, Inc.*, 1998 U.S. Dist. LEXIS 14696 (D.D.C. 1998), ended this monopoly. Since January 1, 2000, other companies have been allowed to become domain name registrars and to compete with NSI/Verisign for clients. Despite the cessation of their monopoly, NSI/Verisign is still by far the largest provider of domain registration.

Until very recently, a domain name registrar was immune from lawsuits related to mismanagement of its Internet service. This PRECEDENT changed on June 13, 2003, when the U.S. Supreme Court refused to accept certiorari from a lower court's decision and thereby established a new precedent of requiring domain name registrars to be held accountable for their mismanagement of crucial public resources such as the Internet [*Kremen v. NSI*, Case No. 01-15899 (U.S. Court of Appeals, 9th Cir.), 2003].

Another unforeseen, Internet-related legal issue arose when public libraries began to offer Internet-based research services to their patrons. Congress passed a law, the Children's Internet Protection Act, or *CIPA*, 47 U.S.C. §254(h), that requires libraries that receive federal assistance for Internet access to install software that blocks obscene or pornographic images. The American Library Association (ALA) argued that by preventing reading and viewing some types of information, CIPA violated the guarantee of free speech found in the First Amendment to the U.S. Constitution. The U.S. Supreme Court disagreed with the ALA. Citing the federal government's authority to attach conditions to the receipt of federal funds, the high court decided that the federal government had not overstepped its bounds by filtering the content of Internet information received at libraries. The Supreme Court found that in light of the dynamic nature of the Internet, the government's actions were entirely reasonable [*United States v. American Library Association, Inc.*, U.S. Supreme Court Case #02-361 (June 2003)].

The U.S. Supreme Court has dealt with the problem of "spam," or unsolicited, unwanted e-mail, by upholding the validity of a state's tough antispam law. In *State of Washington v. Heckel*, 24 P.3d 404 (Supreme Court State of Washington, June 7, 2001), *cert. denied*, 122 S.Ct. 467 (2001), the Washington state supreme court decided that the state law's prohibition on commercial e-mail with deceptive subject lines and return addresses was constitutional. By requiring that individuals refrain from using intentionally misleading subject lines and incorrect return addresses, the Washington law does not place an excessive burden on commerce but instead facilitates commerce by eliminating fraud and deception. By denying certiorari in the *Heckel* case, the U.S. Supreme Court upheld the validity of the state's tough antispam law and established a high court precedent strongly disfavoring those who perpetrate spamming on others.

For more information: American Library Association. "The Children's Internet Protection Act (CIPA)." CIPA and

Libraries (December 2003). Available online. URL: http://www.ala.org/cipa. Downloaded May 14, 2004; Soares, Christine. "Are Domain Names Property? The Sex.com Controversy." *Duke Law and Technology Review.* Available online. URL: http://www.law.duke.edu/journals/dltr/articles/2001dltr0032.html. Downloaded May 14, 2004; Sweig, Michael. "In the Law and On the Net: A Compilation." The U.S. Supreme Court (2002). Available online. URL: http://ecl.flashcommerce.com/l. Downloaded May 14, 2004.

—Beth S. Swartz

Internet taxation

Internet taxation refers to the taxing of sales and purchases made over the Web. Such taxation raises legal questions about when and whether states have the authority to tax Internet activities without violating the commerce clause.

There are two vexing tax issues related to the Internet. First, as the total of Internet purchases has risen substantially during each of the past seven years, sales tax has become an increasingly controversial topic. Second, and independent of the sales tax issue, is the matter of access tax. If such taxes become law, each monthly bill from an Internet service provider (ISP) will include taxes similar to those charged by local and long distance telephone services for use of their electronic networks, in addition to the ISP's fees for utilizing their connection to the Internet.

The Sales Tax Issue

Nearly every individual who has taken advantage of the convenience of "click and charge" online shopping has probably also considered the lack of sales tax on Internet transactions as an additional reason to shop online. However, the concept of the Internet as a tax-free shopping zone is at odds with the experience of a smaller group of individuals. Why are some Internet transactions subject to sales tax while others are immune to these fees?

In general, the relationship between the locations of the customer and the merchant determines whether one party or the other is obligated to pay sales tax. If a customer lives in a state in which an Internet merchant has a store, warehouse, office, phone answering service, or even a parking lot, a nexus, or geographical connection, exists between the customer and the merchant [*Quill v. North Dakota*, 504 U.S. 298 (1992)]. When a nexus exists, the merchant is responsible for collecting sales tax from the customer and forwarding that sum to the appropriate taxing authority.

Since the Internet can create virtual offices, some businesses have decentralized to the point where orders can be taken in one state and filled in one of several others in which the business has warehouses or from which the business drop-ships merchandise. These new business structures have created situations in which a merchant must pay sales tax without having direct contact with the customer. For instance, if a customer telephones a company that has executive offices out of state but a nationwide order-taking facility in the customer's state, the merchant is responsible for sales tax even if the chosen merchandise is shipped to the purchaser from a third state.

If a merchant is responsible for collecting sales tax from a buyer, and fails to do so with a taxable transaction, the purchaser is then required to forward the appropriate sum to the taxing authority. In this case, the tax is called a "use" tax rather than a sales tax, and the only difference between a "use" tax and a "sales" tax is the identity of the person who sends the money to the taxing authority. Use taxes were originally created as a backup plan, to be sure that the state collected its appropriate share on every taxable transaction. Previously, most states have avoided strict enforcement of use taxes on small purchases, since the amounts collected would not justify the enforcement costs. However, in order to make up for sales tax that is not collected from Internet transactions, some states have recently increased their efforts to collect use taxes.

Many larger retailers with local storefronts can sell their products tax free over the Internet because they have established separate legal subsidiaries to handle Internet business. For example, the Barnes & Noble Web site is not the same company as the store of the same name at the local shopping mall. If the online Barnes & Noble does not actually have a physical presence in your state, such as business offices or a warehouse, no sales tax is charged for online purchases. State governments may call a halt to this practice of establishing a separate legal entity principally to avoid sales taxes, since this practice has recently raised increasingly noisy protest from conventional retailers whose customers must still pay sales tax.

The sales tax/nexus issue becomes more complicated when a company's online and off-line entities experience some customer interaction. For example, a situation might exist in which a consumer buys tax-free golf clubs from Wal-Mart.com and is allowed to return them to the local Wal-Mart store for store credit. When the consumer uses this credit to buy a more expensive item, should this item be tax-free to the extent that the selling price of the golf clubs was tax-free? To date, there are no court precedents that determine whether such entities are legally independent of each other.

Many state governments are dependent on sales tax revenue, which totals about $150 billion annually for the entire United States, or approximately one-third of all state revenues. With the exception of Alaska, Delaware, Montana, New Hampshire, and Oregon, which have no sales taxes, the states use moneys collected as sales tax to fund essential services such as schools, police, roads, and prisons. In 2003 the federal government estimates that unpaid sales tax from online transactions will be approximately $11 billion.

In 2002 state governments organized to fight back. Under a state-led initiative known as the Streamlined Sales and Use Tax Agreement (SSUTA), 40 states and the District of Columbia have pledged to simplify their sales tax codes and facilitate tax collection. Currently, compliance with SSUTA is voluntary. However, a portion of SSUTA provides that upon ratification by 10 states representing a minimum of 20 percent of the U.S. population, the organization will lobby Congress for federal legislation to the same effect as the currently voluntary plan. In preparation for congressional action, several national retailers have already entered negotiations with member states, seeking amnesty in return for future collection of sales tax. Since a majority of the states are pushing SSUTA forward, it is likely that higher priority will be given to collection of sales and use taxes in the near future.

The Access Tax Issue

In 1998 Congress passed the Internet Tax Freedom Act (ITFA), which established a three-year moratorium on taxing Internet access services at the state or local level. "Internet access service" is defined as any service that allows users to obtain information, e-mail, or other online services and includes small Internet service providers (ISPs), large information portals such as Yahoo and other Web sites and companies that provide connectivity and information, such as AOL. When ITFA was originally enacted, homes and offices with Internet access service paid an average of approximately $25 per month, mostly for fees such as AOL. In December 2001 President Bush signed a two-year extension of the IFTA.

With the most recent extension of IFTA about to expire, Congress may deem all forms of Internet access, including cable and DSL, tax-free. With the Internet apparently on the road to becoming the medium of choice for voice transmission, a service that was formerly the exclusive province of local telephone companies, the companies themselves are confused, and state governments are clearly displeased, because they could lose billions in local taxes on telephone service. Tax moratorium proponents mention the "digital divide" that keeps lower income households off line and conclude that lower taxes would help these households afford essential e-communication connections. However, this "divide" has little basis in fact. Lower income people are off line because they cannot make the initial outlay necessary to purchase PCs, not because of the cost of the monthly service.

The extension of the IFTA passed in the House before the members left for their December 2003 holiday break but was tabled in the Senate. While in 2004 the Senate did follow the House and eventually extend the tax moratorium,

it is important to consider that funding for scientific research will become nonexistent if income sources like federal taxes on telephone service are eliminated. Without significant government support, the Internet itself would have never happened. While it makes no sense to smother the Internet with taxes, the federal government should assess the impact on scientific research before eliminating sources of funding.

For more information: Nolo Law for All. "Internet Law." Law Center (2004). Available online. URL: http://www. nolo.com/lawcenter/auntie/index.cfm/catID/ 2535B59D-F306-49ED-89E6921E069ABD0E. Downloaded May 14, 2004.

—Beth S. Swartz

interstate commerce

Interstate commerce refers to commerce or trade that crosses state lines or occurs in more than one state. Who can regulate interstate commerce and how has been a subject of significant debate in the Supreme Court since the writing of the Constitution.

The U.S. Supreme Court has been faced with the task of interpreting the U.S. Constitution's commerce clause, which is contained in Article I, Section 8 and reads: "Congress shall have power . . . to regulate commerce . . . among the several states . . ." many times throughout its history. Typically, significantly changes in the high court's definition or assessment of the impact of a frequently used constitutional phrase evolve over several decades. Hence, it is noteworthy that the high court's definition of the commerce clause and assessment of its impact has changed many times since the ratification of the U.S. Constitution.

During the first third of the 19th century, the Supreme Court's decisions consistently reflected Chief Justice John MARSHALL's interpretation of the commerce clause. At that time, the states had not yet fully adjusted to the concept of a strong federal government, and Congress was frequently unsure of the appropriate federal–state allocation of power. Hence, whenever a new federal law overlapped with a preexisting state law, Congress was reluctant to allow federal law to preempt state law. Justice Marshall tried to prevent Congress from wasting its time on this question, at least with respect to commercial affairs. His opinion in *GIBBONS v. OGDEN*, 9 Wheat. 1 (1824), clearly provided the federal government with regulatory authority over all business activities that involved more than one state.

When Chief Justice TANEY was at the helm of the high court, from 1837 to 1864, the justices were divided on the meaning of the commerce clause. In an 1847 opinion known as the *License Cases*, 5 How. 504 (1847), the U.S. Supreme Court held that state law, rather than federal law, should regulate the sale of liquor imported from abroad. However, two years later, in the *Passenger Cases,* 7 How. 283 (1849), the same court reverted to John Marshall's interpretation of interstate commerce and found that a state law that taxed foreigners arriving at state ports represented an unconstitutional exercise of authority that properly belonged to the federal government.

After the Civil War (1861–65), interstate commerce issues became entwined with interpretation of the equal protection and due process clauses of the Fourteenth Amendment, and in the process, John Marshall's concept of federal PREEMPTION of state laws related to commerce gave way to a far more restricted view. In the *Sugar Trust Case,* 156 U.S. 1 (1895), a sugar refinery owner established a monopoly by purchasing stock in all of his competitors' companies. The Supreme Court held that the Sherman Antitrust Act, which provided penalties for such monopolistic behavior, was inapplicable to the refinery owner. State law prevailed because the questioned business dealings pertained only to manufacturing within one state's borders, and not to selling or transporting the manufactured product. Federal law would apply only if the product was later sold out of state.

The PRECEDENT established by the U.S. Supreme Court's separation of "manufacturing" and "commerce" encouraged the state governments to adopt a laissez-faire economic policy. Adherents to this doctrine believed that federal interference with or intervention in economic matters, or federal government's imposition of statutory limits on corporate power would place private property rights at risk and might disrupt the social and economic status quo. The precedent established by the *Sugar Trust Case* restricted the usefulness of the Sherman Act by defining interstate commerce in a way that nearly eliminated the possibility of federal preemption of state laws regulating commerce. Hence, as a result of the *Sugar Trust Case* decision, for many years thereafter, federal laws were unable to regulate growth of businesses or prevent development of monopolies.

In 1911 the Supreme Court decided two landmark cases, *STANDARD OIL CO. v. U.S.,* 221 U.S. 1 (1911), and *U.S. v. American Tobacco Co.,* 221 U.S. 106 (1911), known as the *Trust Cases.* In those cases, the high court found that Standard Oil and American Tobacco, both of which were huge monopolies, had violated the Sherman Act by unreasonably restraining trade. Unfortunately, the precedent set by these cases greatly restricted the scope of the Sherman Act, because by inference, reasonable restraint of trade was legal.

Eventually, the limitations on the federal government's ability to regulate interstate commerce contributed to the 1929 stock market crash that triggered the Great Depression. In 1932, after FDR was elected president, his top priority was effectuation of his New Deal, which was basically a legislative program calling for an end to laissez-faire economics in order to allow the nation to recover from the depression. While Congress was immediately amenable to this plan, the Supreme Court was not. In fact, exhibiting arrogance and an attitude of judicial supremacy, the high court found that two key pieces of New Deal legislation, the National Industrial Recovery Act and the Agricultural Adjustment Act, were unconstitutional because the laws attempted to control matters beyond the reach of the federal government's commerce power [*U.S. v. SCHECHTER POULTRY CORP.,* 295 U.S. 495 (1935), and *U.S. v. BUTLER,* 297 U.S. 1 (1936)].

FDR responded by introducing a piece of legislation that would have allowed him to appoint six additional Supreme Court justices, thereby providing a sufficient number of allies to weight the high court's vote in favor of New Deal legislation. Although FDR's court-packing plan died in the Senate Judiciary Committee, FDR's introduction of the bill into Congress proved to be a wake-up call for the Supreme Court. Beginning in 1937, the high court upheld every New Deal law presented to it.

The Court upheld the constitutionality of many pieces of New Deal legislation in 1937, including the National Labor Relations Act (NLRA), which was tested before the Supreme Court in *NATIONAL LABOR RELATIONS BOARD V. JONES & LAUGHLIN STEEL CORP.,* 301 U.S. 1 (1937). The NLRA was applicable to businesses involved in manufacturing as well as those involved in sale and transport of tangible goods, hence to vote in favor of its constitutionality was in direct opposition to the precedent set in the high court's recent cases that had declared New Deal legislation with similar, direct involvement in businesses to be unconstitutional. The Supreme Court's only explanation of the contradiction was, "These cases are not controlling here [,]" [301 U.S. 1 at page 41]. By the end of that year, the high court had relied on the commerce power provided in the Constitution to uphold the federal government's authority to regulate the nation's entire economy. For the remainder of Justice HUGHES's tenure as CHIEF JUSTICE, the U.S. Supreme Court practiced its newly adopted policy of JUDICIAL RESTRAINT, trusting that the Congress had enough collective intelligence to enact laws that did not violate the Constitution or conflict with other federal or state laws.

The 1964 CIVIL RIGHTS ACT, which has been upheld by the Supreme Court despite many challenges, utilizes the commerce power as the basis for prohibitions against discrimination on the basis of race, RELIGION, color, or national origin. For many years after the 1964 act became law, the Supreme Court appeared willing to stretch the commerce clause to cover a wide variety of situations, some of which involve discrimination, and some of which do not. However, this trend now appears to be a thing of the past. In the last decade, federal statutes that involve matters as diverse as gun control on school property, and civil remedies for sex crimes, have attempted to derive authority for their existence from the commerce clause. The Supreme Court has become increasingly hesitant to stretch the commerce clause to provide authority for such specific and rarely used legislation. In *U.S. v. Lopez,* 514 U.S. 549 (1995), and later, in *U.S. v. MORRISON,* 529 U.S. 598 (2000), which noted precedents established in *Lopez,* the Supreme Court declared that the federal government is not in the business of tailoring laws to fit a few convenient test situations. In striking down the laws in both *Lopez* and *Morrison,* the Supreme Court noted that the situations covered by those voided statutes could be rewritten into local or state law.

Hence, although the U.S. Supreme Court was willing in the past to stretch the Constitution's commerce clause to provide authorization for Congress to pass a vast array of laws, the Court is apparently not willing to be as lenient in the future.

For more information: du Pont, Pete. "Government Control Thyself." Washington Times Online (September 17, 1999). Available online. URL: http://www.ncpa.org/oped/dupont/dup83199.html; Legal Information Institute. "Limitations on Reach of Federal Commerce Power." Cornell University School of Law (2003). Available online. URL: http://supct.law.cornell. edu/supct/index.html. Downloaded May 14, 2004.

—Beth S. Swartz

Interstate Commerce Commission

The Interstate Commerce Commission (ICC) was established in 1887 by the Interstate Commerce Act to regulate certain carriers involved in transportation among states. The ICC was the United States's first regulatory agency, and it was created due to escalating public complaints in the 1880s about deceptive railroad practices and rates.

In the last half of the 19th century monopolistic trusts were in control of huge sectors of the national economy, hurting small businesses and consumers. The empires that controlled the railroad were able to exert enormous control over agriculture and other industries that relied heavily on the rail system. This allowed enormous prosperity for a few, but caused dreadful social problems. Additionally, in 1886 the Supreme Court ruled that states could not regulate interstate railroads. Only the federal government could do that. The following year Congress created the Interstate Commerce Commission. It originally consisted of five members but over the years was increased to seven, then nine, and finally, in 1920, capped at 11 members. Members served a six-year term and were appointed by the president but could not be dismissed by the president. The ICC elected its own chairperson, unlike most other regulatory agencies. For a long time the ICC's usefulness was limited by the Congress's failure to give it enforcement power and by the vague language of the Supreme Court's interpretation of its power.

When it first came into existence, the Interstate Commerce Commission only regulated railroads. Its main purpose was to guarantee that rates were not used to stifle competition. Starting with the Hepburn Act in 1906, however, the ICC's power gradually expanded to all common carriers such as buses, trucks, barges, and freight forwarders. Its power also increased because of the Supreme Court's expanding interpretations of the interstate commerce clause in Article I of the U.S. Constitution. One important milestone in the expansion of ICC power was the Transportation Act of 1920 by which the government returned railroads to private companies after World War I. This law changed the ICC's role from approving railroad rates to setting them. The ICC also gained the power to organize mergers, decide suitable profit levels, and manage labor disputes that affected INTERSTATE COMMERCE. In the 1950s the ICC enforced Court-mandated desegregation of railroad cars.

From 1910 until 1934, when the Federal Communications Commission was created, the ICC also regulated telegraph, telephone, and cable communication. The commission's days were numbered, however. In 1966 its regulatory powers were taken over by the Department of Transportation. During the 1980s President Reagan tried many times to abolish the ICC, claiming that deregulation had made it unnecessary. His proposals were refused by Congress, but the ICC's powers over rates and routes in trucking and railroads were truncated in 1980 by the Staggers Rail Act and the Motor Carriers Act. The agency's control over interstate trucking was discarded altogether in 1994. Finally in 1995 this once powerful agency was closed down. Its few remaining roles were reassigned to the new National Surface Transportation Board.

For more information: Stone, Richard D. *The Interstate Commerce Commission and the Railroad Industry: A History of Regulatory Policy.* New York: Praeger, 1991.

—Wendy Groce

J

Jackson, Robert (1892–1954) *Supreme Court justice*
Robert H. Jackson (February 13, 1892–October 9, 1954) led an active life on and off the Supreme Court. (He was appointed by Franklin Roosevelt and served on the Court from 1941 to 1954.) Jackson became an attorney after only one year of law school and little college plus clerking in a lawyer's office. He was mainly self-educated but had a superb style in expressing himself.

Governor Franklin Roosevelt appointed Jackson to a commission to study New York state's judicial system. Jackson went from being special counsel to the Securities and Exchange Commission (1936), to assistant attorney general (1936–37), to solicitor general (1938–40), to attorney general (1940), to Supreme Court justice (1941).

Jackson was a key player in the court-packing fight, strongly advocating the judicial reorganization bill. Justice BRANDEIS said that Jackson ought to be made solicitor general for life. Jackson made an unsuccessful bid for governor of New York in 1938. He had been mentioned for president and hoped to be appointed CHIEF JUSTICE in 1941 when HUGHES retired. Instead, at only 49, he became associate justice.

As justice, Jackson was a believer in the limits of judicial power. He opposed JUDICIAL ACTIVISM from the left as well as the right. Like FRANKFURTER, he was deferential to national and state legislative branches. He championed the federal commerce power and opposed state interferences with INTERSTATE COMMERCE. In *Edwards v. California*, 314 U.S. 160 (1941), he held that California could not bar indigent migrants from entering the state. He upheld the relocation of Japanese persons during World War II and postwar actions against Communist subversion. Yet he declared unconstitutional Truman's seizure of the steel mills (*YOUNGSTOWN SHEET AND TUBE CO. V. SAWYER*, 343 U.S. 579). Jackson attacked secrecy where there should be disclosure and publicity where there should be privacy.

Jackson often voted with Frankfurter. However, they were in sharp disagreement in the FLAG SALUTE case, *West Virginia State Board of Education v. Barnette*, 319 U.S. 624 (1943). Jackson believed in a high wall of separation between church and state. He dissented in *EVERSON V. BOARD OF Education*, 330 U.S. 1 (1947), and *Zorach v. Clauson*, 343 U.S. 306 (1952), and was in the majority in *McCollum v. Board of Education*, 333 U.S. 203 (1948).

Jackson served as chief prosecutor for the United States at the Nuremberg trials of Nazi war criminals (1945–46). He dominated the trial but this became a liability. The international judges were irritated at what they saw as his erratic behavior and high-handedness. His year and a half absence from the Supreme Court handicapped that tribunal. However, his experiences at Nuremberg influenced how he regarded obnoxious speech. He championed the responsibility of governments for the maintenance of public order, even against verbal aggression. He dissented in *TERMINIELLO V. CHICAGO*, 337 U.S. 1 (1949). Jackson stated: "There is danger that, if the Court does not temper its doctrinaire logic with a little practical wisdom, it will convert the constitutional BILL OF RIGHTS into a suicide pact."

Jackson was disappointed at being passed over in favor of Fred VINSON for the Chief Justiceship. His feud with Justice BLACK probably eliminated him from consideration when Harlan STONE died. Jackson blamed Black for his not getting the appointment and accused Black of judicial impropriety in not disqualifying himself in certain cases. He regarded his opponents on the Court as judges "drunk with power."

Jackson suffered a heart attack in the spring of 1954. His doctors told him that continuing his normal activity risked death at any time. He nonetheless returned to work, participating in the *Brown* school desegregation case (*BROWN V. BOARD OF EDUCATION*, 347 U.S. 483). In the last months of his life he prepared his Godkin Lectures for Harvard, *The Supreme Court in the American System of Government*, but died before delivering them.

For more information: Desmond, Charles S., Paul A. Freund, Potter Stewart, and Lord Shawcross. *Mr. Justice*

Jackson: Four Lectures in His Honor. New York and London: Columbia University Press, 1969; Gerhart, Eugene C. *America's Advocate: Robert H. Jackson.* Indianapolis, Ind.: Bobbs-Merrill, 1958; ———. *Robert H. Jackson: Lawyer's Judge.* Albany, N.Y.: Q Corp., 1961; Kornstein, Daniel. *Thinking Under Fire: Great Courtroom Lawyers and Their Impact on American History.* New York: Dodd, Mead, 1987; White, G. Edward. *American Judicial Tradition.* New York: Oxford University Press, 1976.

—Martin Gruberg

Jay, John (1745–1829) *first chief justice of the United States*

John Jay was the first CHIEF JUSTICE of the United States, nominated by first President George Washington and confirmed by the Senate in 1789 after the new government under the Constitution became effective. He served until 1795 when he resigned to become governor of New York upon election to that position.

Jay was born in New York City in 1745, the descendant of French Huguenots who had moved to England before emigrating to British America. He graduated from King's College (now Columbia University) in 1764 and was admitted to the bar in 1768. He became a very successful and prominent lawyer in New York City, marrying into the influential Livingston family. He opposed independence before the Revolution but was not supportive of British restrictions on trade and liberties. Increasingly recognized as a leader of the colonial movement for independence, Jay was a delegate to the First and Second Continental Congresses before returning to New York where he was the primary drafter and proponent of the influential New York State Constitution of 1777.

Jay was recognized for his legal and political skills by being appointed to serve as the first chief justice of New York under its new Constitution. Jay served only briefly in this position, becoming the president of the Continental Congress in 1778. He was sent to Spain as minister plenipotentiary but was unable to gain formal recognition for the new country. Jay was designated with John Adams and Benjamin Franklin to negotiate the Treaty of Paris to secure independence from and peace with Great Britain in 1783. Congress under the Articles of Confederation appointed Jay as secretary of foreign affairs, but his capacity for achievement was muted by the rivalries and inefficiencies of the governmental structure. This experience led him to become a forceful advocate for a strong central government, capable of conducting more effective foreign affairs.

Jay is recognized as one of the three authors of *The Federalist Papers,* along with Alexander Hamilton and John Madison, and the five papers he contributed (nos.

Chief Justice John Jay *(Library of Congress)*

2–5 and 64) focus on international relations under the Constitution. His legal and political acumen and support for the constitutional structure earned him appointment by President George Washington as the first chief justice of the United States. He became disillusioned with the Supreme Court, however, concluding that it was impotent, with little real power or authority. Thus, notwithstanding his responsibilities to the Court, he agreed to a diplomatic mission to England that led in 1794 to Jay's Treaty, which sought to resolve disputes from the conclusion of the war and over commerce and navigation. While on this mission, Jay was elected governor of New York and he resigned from the Supreme Court to return to New York, where he served from 1795 to 1801. He declined John Adams's offer to return to the Supreme Court as chief justice in 1801 and retired to his estate, where he spent the remaining years of his life as a farmer and active abolitionist. He died in 1829.

For more information: Abraham, Henry J. *Justices, Presidents and Senators.* Rev. ed. Lanham: Rowman and Littlefield, 1999; Morris, Richard. *John Jay, the Nation and the Court.* Boston: Boston University Press, 1967.

—Luke Bierman

J.E.B. v. Alabama, 511 U.S. 127 (1994)

In *J.E.B. v. Alabama*, the Supreme Court ruled that "PEREMPTORY CHALLENGES"—challenges that allow parties to exclude jurors without giving a reason—used to exclude jurors solely on the basis of gender violated the EQUAL PROTECTION CLAUSE of the Fourteenth Amendment to the U.S. Constitution. The state of Alabama, acting on behalf of an unwed mother, brought suit against J.E.B. for paternity and child support. During jury selection, Alabama used nine of its 10 peremptory challenges to remove male jurors, while J.E.B. used nine of his 10 peremptory challenges to remove female jurors. Because the original jury pool had consisted of more females than males, the resulting jury selected was comprised of all female jurors. J.E.B. objected to Alabama's peremptory challenges on the ground that they were used to eliminate jurors solely because they were male. J.E.B. argued that the Supreme Court's reasoning in *BATSON V. KENTUCKY*, 476 U.S. 79 (1986), which held that peremptory strikes based solely on race violated the equal protection clause, extended to prohibit intentional discrimination in jury selection based solely on gender. The Supreme Court agreed.

Writing for the majority of the Court, Justice BLACKMUN ruled that "[a]s with race, the core guarantee of equal protection, ensuring citizens that their State will not discriminate, would be meaningless" were the Court to allow the exclusion of jurors on the basis of assumptions that arise solely from the juror's gender [*J.E.B. v. Alabama*, 511 U.S. 127, 146 (1994)].

Justice Blackmun began his opinion by recounting the history of discriminatory treatment of women, particularly with respect to jury service. The Court believed that this history of SEXUAL DISCRIMINATION warranted "heightened scrutiny" of state actions based solely on gender [*J.E.B. v. Alabama*, 511 U.S. 127, 136 (1994)]. In reviewing Alabama's gender-based peremptory challenges, the Court determined that they failed to meet the heightened level of scrutiny because "discrimination on the basis of gender in jury selection" does nothing to further "the State's legitimate interest in achieving a fair and impartial trial" [*J.E.B. v. Alabama*, 511 U.S. 127, 136 (1994)].

The Court rejected Alabama's argument that striking males from the jury was justified by the perception that males might be more sympathetic to a man alleged to be a father out-of-wedlock, while women might be more sympathetic to a single mother. "We shall not accept as a defense to gender-based peremptory challenges the very stereotypes the law condemns," Justice Blackmun wrote. The Court reasoned that "[w]hen state actors exercise peremptory challenges in reliance on gender stereotypes, they ratify and reinforce prejudicial views of the relative abilities of men and women" [*J.E.B. v. Alabama*, 511 U.S. 127, 140 (1994)]. The Court ruled that "[a]ll persons, when granted the opportunity to serve on a jury, have the right not to be excluded summarily because of discriminatory and stereotypical presumptions that reflect and reinforce patterns of historical discrimination" [*J.E.B. v. Alabama*, 511 U.S. 127, 141–42 (1994)].

Justice Blackmun took care to note that the Court's decision did not eliminate all peremptory challenges. "Parties may still remove jurors whom they feel might be less acceptable than others on the panel; gender simply may not serve as a proxy for bias" [*J.E.B. v. Alabama*, 511 U.S. 127, 143 (1994)]. Thus, peremptory challenges based on characteristics that are disproportionately associated with one gender are permissible. The Court used the example that striking all jurors who have military experience is not unconstitutional, even though it will disproportionately affect men. A party alleging gender discrimination must make an initial showing that the party using the strike intentionally discriminated on the basis of gender. The party using the strike must then explain the basis for the strike. So long as the reason given for the strike is something other than gender, and the judge finds the reason credible, the strike will stand.

Several justices, however, expressed concern about the additional restraints that this case placed on peremptory challenges. Justice O'CONNOR, writing in concurrence, complained that the decision forced lawyers to articulate their "hunches and educated guesses," which are "often inarticulable" [*J.E.B. v. Alabama*, 511 U.S. 127, 148 (1994), (Connor, J., concurring)]. While she ultimately concluded that eliminating gender discrimination was worth the price, Justice O'Connor would have limited the decision to peremptory challenges by government attorneys only, not by private parties or criminal defendants. Justice SCALIA, in a dissenting opinion joined by Chief Justice REHNQUIST and Justice THOMAS, also lamented that the peremptory challenge system "loses its whole character when . . . 'reasons' for strikes must be given" [*J.E.B. v. Alabama*, 511 U.S. 127, 162 (1994), (Scalia, J., dissenting)]. Justice Scalia believed that the majority's holding was based on political correctness, lacked common sense, and was contrary to the Court's reasoning in past jury selection cases.

For more information: Coebergh, Bastian K. "The United States Supreme Court on Gender-Based Peremptory Jury Challenges." *Land & Water L. Rev.* 31 (1996): 195; Howie, Brian A. "A Remedy Without a Wrong: J.E.B. and the Extension of Batson to Sex-Based Peremptory Challenges." *Wash. & Lee L. Rev.* 52 (1995): 1,725.

—Amy M. Henson

Jehovah's Witnesses and the Supreme Court

The Supreme Court's rulings in the Jehovah's Witnesses cases resulted in some of the most important contributions to the protection of free speech and RELIGION. More than any other religious group, the Jehovah's Witnesses have used the American judicial system to advance constitutional rights for all Americans.

Charles Taze Russell established this missionary movement (Jehovah's Witnesses reject the title of a church) in 1872, although the name Jehovah's Witnesses was not adopted until 1931. The movement preaches that Jesus Christ has invisibly returned to earth and at the end of a thousand-year reign, the wicked will be annihilated. They attack orthodox Christianity as corrupt. Their "witnessing" to God causes them to attack the concentration of power in government, corporations, and churches.

During the 1930s and 1940s Witnesses descended on small neighborhoods, moving door-to-door and aggressively insisting that their message be heard. They paraded down public streets without a permit and drove sound trucks through quiet towns proclaiming their message at a high volume. They picketed Catholic churches on Sunday mornings with signs proclaiming, "Religion is a Snare and a Racket."

Their aggressive proselytizing caused angry confrontations with local authorities. Almost 19,000 Witnesses were arrested, and there were 2,000 reported cases of mob violence against them. During World War II the Witnesses were seen as unpatriotic because they refused to serve in the military. The Jehovah's Witnesses created their own legal department and fought a sustained campaign of litigation to assert their right to freely exercise their beliefs. They won more than 150 suits in state supreme courts and more than 30 decisions in the U.S. Supreme Court.

In CANTWELL V. CONNECTICUT, 310 U.S. 296 (1940), Jesse Cantwell and his two sons were arrested for soliciting money without first obtaining a license. The Court overturned the conviction, finding that the local official's authority to determine whether the solicitations were based on a genuine religious claim placed an unconstitutional restraint on free religious belief. The Cantwells had also stopped two Catholics and, with their permission, played a phonograph record that insulted the Catholic Church. The Cantwells were convicted of disturbing the peace. The Supreme Court also overturned this conviction, holding that suppressing religious views that merely annoyed listeners violated the free speech clause of the First Amendment.

Cantwell was the first case in which the Court held that the free exercise of religion clause of the First Amendment applied to the states through the Fourteenth Amendment's due process clause. Prior to *Cantwell,* the Court had held that the Constitution's First Amendment applied only to the national government, not to the states.

There followed a series of cases where the Court offered conflicting decisions. It upheld a nondiscriminatory licensing fee to sellers of religious books and pamphlets in *Jones v. City of Opelika,* 316 U.S. 584 (1942), but later struck down such fees (*Jones v. City of Opelika II,* 319 U.S. 103 [1943]). It declared unconstitutional a city ordinance prohibiting door-to-door solicitations for religious causes (*Murdock v. Commonwealth of Pennsylvania,* 319 U.S. 105 [1943]) but upheld a state child labor law punishing the guardian of a nine-year-old child who sold religious publications after normal work hours (*Prince v. Massachusetts,* 321 U.S. 158 [1944]).

In *Minersville School District v. Gobitis,* 310 U.S. 586 (1940), the Court upheld a state law suspending seventh grader Lillian and fifth grader William Gobitis. The students refused to salute the flag or pledge allegiance, believing that the flag was a graven image and that the Bible forbids worshipping an idol. An 8-1 majority ruled that the government's interest in nurturing patriotism was sufficient to sustain the law. Following the decision, Jehovah's Witnesses children were expelled from school for refusing to salute the flag in 31 states. Three years later a 6-3 majority reversed itself and struck down the compulsory FLAG SALUTE as a violation of freedom of speech in *West Virginia State Board of Education v. Barnette,* 319 U.S. 624 (1943).

More recent Supreme Court cases have used Jehovah's Witnesses' complaints to overturn state laws. In *Wooley v. Maynard,* 430 U.S. 705 (1977), the Court struck down a New Hampshire law requiring that the state's motto, "Live Free or Die," be displayed on automobile license plates. The law infringed on a Jehovah's Witness's right not to be coerced to display a state-approved belief. In 2002 the Supreme Court ruled that local governments could not require Jehovah's Witnesses to register before embarking on door-to-door proselytizing (*WATCHTOWER V. VILLAGE OF STRATTON,* 122 S. Ct. 2080).

For more information: Manwaring, David R. *Render Unto Caesar.* Chicago: University of Chicago Press, 1962.
—Timothy J. O'Neill

Jim Crow laws

Jim Crow laws refer to the series of laws and state constitutional provisions that made racial segregation a legal and ubiquitous part of life in the Southern United States during the last decades of the 19th century and first half of the 20th.

One impetus for Jim Crow laws began in the 1870s with a series of court decisions. The most sweeping decision was made by the Supreme Court in 1883 when it struck down the Civil Rights Act of 1875, stating that the Constitution did not protect against discrimination by private business or individuals, but only from discrimination by the government. As a result, Southern states began adopting laws to segregate African Americans and whites and limited the activities of African Americans. A series of court cases followed, the most notable being the SLAUGHTER-HOUSE CASES, *United States v. Reese* (1876), and *United States v. Cruikshank* (1875). These cases culminated with *PLESSY V. FERGUSON* in 1896; here the Supreme Court ruled that "separate but equal" facilities could be provided for African Americans even under the terms of the Fourteenth Amendment. Southern states began to further restrict the access of African Americans by creating "whites only" or "colored" water fountains, restrooms, restaurants, motel accommodations and even by limiting entrances at libraries, courthouses, and movie theaters. These separate accommodations did not by any stretch of the imagination meet the constitutional provision of "equal."

However they continued to multiply and flourish. States began adopting literacy tests, poll taxes, and grandfather clauses to limit the voting power of African Americans. Aggression at polling places and threats of violence also limited the number of African Americans who voted. Segregation laws further legalized the idea of white supremacy by banning interracial marriages, dating, and even any mixing of the two races in areas such as sports competitions. Among the many effects of Jim Crow laws was to further weaken the economic power and freedom African Americans possessed. Banks were often extensions of the Jim Crow enforcers, refusing to give loans to African Americans and thus making it nearly impossible for African Americans to purchase and own property. Thus, most African Americans were forced to eke out a living in rural areas as sharecroppers, indebted to their former masters. Many fled north in search of jobs and to escape life under brutal and demeaning Jim Crow laws.

For nearly a century the federal government did little to assist African Americans. Some found ways to cope on their own. Towns such as Mound Bayou, an all-African-American community, popped up in the south as a way to escape segregation and violence. Organizations such as the Niagara Movement, which advocated vigilant protest, and movements such as the "Tuskegee Machine," which advocated education in trade fields as a means of achieving equality over time, sprang up as means to deal with the inequality. No organization had quite the lasting effect as the National Association of Colored People (NAACP). The NAACP advocated use of courts as a way of overturning unconstitutional segregation laws. At its inception the NAACP concentrated on fighting lynching that was occurring with alarming regularity and was widespread even in states like Kentucky that had not joined the Confederacy in the Civil War. The next focus of the NAACP was fighting for the CIVIL LIBERTIES of African Americans. In the 1930s their attention turned to fighting school segregation and, as an extension, the constitutionality of "separate but equal." African Americans used a variety of methods to cope such as legal challenges, public awareness campaigns, and self-help through the formation of their own schools, music and literature, and religious institutions.

The CIVIL RIGHTS ACT OF 1964 and the VOTING RIGHTS ACT OF 1965 ended decades of Jim Crow laws and segregation. Today the legacies of slavery and more than a century of segregation after the abolishment of slavery still shape our country. Years of unequal access have left a disproportionately low number of African Americans owning their own homes, earning college degrees, and achieving economic security. On the other hand, enormous strides have been made and Jim Crow laws have been relegated to the dustbin of history.

For more information: Dailey, Jane, Glenda Elizabeth Gilmore, and Bryant Simon. *Jumpin' Jim Crow: Southern Politics from Civil War to Civil Rights.* Princeton, N.J.: Princeton University Press, 2000; Lively, Donald E. *The Constitution and Race.* New York: Praeger, 1992.

—Lindsay B. Zoeller

Johnson v. Transportation Agency of Santa Clara County, 480 U.S. 616 (1987)

In *Johnson v. Transportation Agency of Santa Clara County*, the Court ruled 6-3 that voluntary AFFIRMATIVE ACTION plans used to remedy imbalances between the male and female employees in traditionally male jobs were legal under the provisions of TITLE VII OF THE CIVIL RIGHTS ACT OF 1964. The case uses the framework established in *UNITED STEELWORKERS OF AMERICA V. WEBER*, 433 U.S. 193 (1979), to gauge the legality of the affirmative action plans and applies the framework to SEX DISCRIMINATION claims. *Johnson* extends the logic of *Weber*, a case dealing with race-based affirmative action in a private company, to sex-based affirmative action in a public company.

In 1979 Diana Joyce worked for the Santa Clara Transportation Agency as a road maintenance worker. Joyce had worked as a maintenance worker for five years, filling in occasionally as a road dispatcher when such a position became available. Road dispatchers were highly paid skilled crafts workers and in 1979, not one of the 238 skilled workers was a woman. Joyce, along with Paul Johnson, applied for the road dispatcher's position. Paul Johnson had worked for the agency for three years longer than Joyce but had only served two years compared to Joyce's five years on the road maintenance crew. Still, Johnson had temporarily served as road dispatcher for three months and had served as a road dispatcher in a previous position. Both Johnson and Joyce, along with seven other candidates, were considered "well qualified" for the position. Both Johnson and Joyce were then interviewed and given scores between 70 and 80. Johnson received the second highest interview score of 75 while Joyce received a 73. The candidates were then interviewed again by a three-person board, which recommended that Johnson receive the position. The county's affirmative action office, however, suggested to the director of the Transportation Agency that Joyce be selected. Joyce was given the road dispatcher's job and Johnson sued, arguing that he had been discriminated against because of his sex in violation of Title VII of the Civil Rights Act of 1964.

Justice BRENNAN, joined in opinion by Justices MARSHALL, BLACKMUN, POWELL, and STEVENS, found the affirmative action plan's use of sex as one factor in a promotion decision consistent with Title VII's purpose of eliminating the effects of employment discrimination and consistent with the guidelines established in *Weber*. Specifically, the Court said the affirmative action plan was moderate and flexible and did not impose strict quotas. Moreover, the plan did not create set-asides but instead required that men and women compete together for possible jobs. Finally, the plan was intended to be a temporary remedy and did not unduly infringe on the rights of those not benefiting from the plan. The fact that *Weber* dealt with a private company and *Johnson* with a public company was not a relevant factor to the majority.

Although joining the case outcome, Justices Stevens and O'CONNOR wrote concurring opinions. Justice Stevens expressed the opinion that affirmative action plans were legal even absent a finding of past discrimination, while Justice O'Connor felt that evidence of past discrimination was a necessary element of such policies. In *Johnson*, O'Connor felt that the lack of women in skilled positions was sufficient to justify the affirmative action program.

In dissent, Justice WHITE noted that statistically imbalances were not sufficient to justify affirmative action policies. Rather, Justice White noted that without a finding of intentional or systematic discrimination, affirmative action policies were wrongly implemented. Justice SCALIA, joined by both Justices White and REHNQUIST, also expressed extreme dissatisfaction with the majority's ruling in a dissenting opinion. Scalia accused the majority of going beyond the mandates of Title VII by attempting to achieve a statistical balance between men and women in jobs even without a finding of discrimination. Scalia contended that the imbalance between men and women in traditionally male jobs was not because of discrimination but because women did not want or were not qualified for these jobs. Moreover, Scalia held that the manual laborers in question here were the least likely to have benefited from discrimi-

nation in the past and thus suffer unfairly from the Court's ruling. Scalia accused the majority of converting Title VII "from a guarantee that race or sex will *not* be the basis for employment determinations, to a guarantee that it *will* (Scalia, dissenting, *Johnson v. Transportation Agency of Santa Clara County*, 480 U.S. 664, 1987. Italics in original).

Johnson is the Court's only decision to date dealing with sex-based affirmative action plans, inspired 40 amicus curiae (friend of the court) briefs, and stands as a landmark ruling.

For more information: Urofsky, Melvin. *Affirmative Action on Trial.* Lawrence: University of Kansas Press, 1997.
—Andrea Hunt

judicial activism and restraint

Judicial activism and judicial restraint are opposing philosophies that refer to the behavior of judges, traditionally to justices of the Supreme Court. Both have two key elements: how judges function within the American political system and how judges interpret the Constitution. Thus, judicial activism and judicial restraint simultaneously operate on two levels—one concerning the Court's relation to the other branches of government, the other concerning the Court's engagement with the Constitution itself.

The first level focuses on judges as political officers; it concerns the Court's role as a "countermajoritarian" (against the majority) institution. This refers to how the judiciary figures in the SEPARATION OF POWERS. We can identify political, or countermajoritarian, activism and restraint by several measures. Simplest among these measures is the willingness to use the power of JUDICIAL REVIEW to nullify legislative enactments, whether congressional laws or town ordinances. Other indicators include the treatment of "political questions," the changing size of Court's DOCKET, the reach of application of individual decisions, and whether the Court second-guesses the judgment of the elected branches on policy matters or defers to those branches of government in curing popular ills. Together, these facets constitute an expanded version of what Alexander M. Bickel called the "countermajoritarian difficulty"—the problem of an undemocratic branch wielding substantial power in a polity rooted in democratic principles.

Countermajoritarian activism envisions a significant role for judges in the justification and legitimation of legislative enactments. It sees no reason why the judiciary should necessarily yield to the legislature or executive, and it declines to subjugate the judiciary's role in the lawmaking process to a mere rubber-stamping of congressional action. Furthermore, countermajoritarian activism displays a willingness—an eagerness even—to settle disputes *between* branches and *within* branches. It is perfectly comfortable establishing policy rather than merely setting guidelines for other actors' policies, and it may elect to tackle a particular issue even when an opportunity for other branches and lower courts to act is still reserved. Conversely, countermajoritarian restraint wishes to let the democratic process run its course—without judicial interference. It defers to the judgment of Congress and nullifies legislative acts only when they explicitly violate a clear constitutional provision. In addition, countermajoritarian restraint desires to distance the Court from "political questions" that might implicate it in a power struggle with one or more governmental branches; it prefers to let elected officials resolve matters of public policy.

The second level focuses on judges as legal officers; it concerns the Court's role as an "interpretive" institution. This refers to the method and tools judges use when reading the Constitution. As with countermajoritarian activism/restraint, we can identify legal, or interpretive, activism and restraint by several measures. First and foremost, there is the method of interpretation used to explicate both constitutional powers and rights. Generally conceived in terms of "strict construction" versus "loose construction," interpretive method includes the degree of breadth in reading constitutional provisions, the practice of looking to extra-constitutional materials in decision-making, the weight given to factors such as language and legislative intent, and the relevance of morality and justice in law. Other factors include the role of PRECEDENT (STARE DECISIS), the creation of new constitutional tests or doctrines, and the extent to which formerly unsettled judicial expectations and issues of general legal principle are resolved.

Interpretive activism favors a broad and expansive reading of constitutional rights and powers. It supports looking beyond the actual text of provisions and statutes to incorporate individual values and moral beliefs in weighing constitutional claims, and it views CONSTITUTIONAL INTERPRETATION as a "constructive" enterprise—one designed to make the law the best it can possibly be. Furthermore, interpretive activism refuses to consider the Court bound by the decisions of earlier courts or even by its own decisions. It views the law as alive and seeks to foster constitutional evolution of the document's provisions to the changing nature of American society and American government. Interpretive restraint, on the other hand, supports a more restricted reading of constitutional provisions. It emphasizes the document's actual words as the only legitimate basis for adjudicating constitutional claims and expresses hesitance at the use of extra-constitutional sources. Finally, interpretive restraint sees great value in "interpretive stability." It is hesitant not only to overrule an earlier decision explicitly but also to weaken one substantially, fearing that insufficient respect for the principles of stare decisis will threaten the credibility of the Court.

Historically, activism has been viewed strictly as a liberal endeavor—a contention that has lost validity in the current political climate. Today, activism and restraint—whether countermajoritarian or interpretive—can each be either liberal or conservative, either Democratic or Republican. Over the course of the 20th century alone, in fact, both liberal and conservative Courts have been activist. Some commentators trace the beginning of activism to the early 1900s, when the Court began striking down legislation it thought economically unwise with a justification known as SUBSTANTIVE DUE PROCESS. This process, which began in *LOCHNER V. NEW YORK*, 198 U.S. 45 (1903), and ended three decades later in *WEST COAST HOTEL V. PARRISH*, 300 U.S. 379 (1937), marked a period of both countermajoritarian and interpretive activism by a conservative Court. On the former, the Court was frequently and aggressively striking down economic legislation (especially during the New Deal) and thus substituting its economic judgment for that of Congress; on the latter, it was reading into the Constitution a laissez-faire economic philosophy that was unsupported by textual evidence.

Those who deny that activism began with the *Lochner* Court believe that the true beginning of activism was the liberal WARREN Court of the 1950s and 1960s. Much like the *Lochner*-era Court before it, the Warren Court practiced both countermajoritarian and interpretive activism. Comprised of men who recognized the often-inequitable nature of the political system and were devotees to the "fix-it" ideology of the New Deal, the Warren Court made egalitarianism the bulwark of its activism. This jurisprudential goal was made a reality in two ways: the assertion (and expansion) of judicial power and the codification of previously nonexisting rights. The former is evident in the Court's entrance into formerly "political" realms such as legislative apportionment in *Baker v. Carr*, 369 U.S. 186 (1962); the latter is manifested, among other places, in the Court's wholesale creation of a RIGHT TO PRIVACY in *GRISWOLD V. CONNECTICUT*, 381 U.S. 479 (1965). In the process, the Court both nullified a striking number of federal and state laws as well as enhanced the role of the judiciary in overseeing—and, to some extent, crafting—public policy regarding issues such as CIVIL RIGHTS and rights of the accused. It is primarily for these reasons that the Warren Court is often regarded as the prototypical "activist" Court.

Recently, the REHNQUIST Court has embraced a type of neoconservative activism in an attempt to gradually scale back particular aspects of the liberal Warren Court revolution. In the area of FEDERALISM especially, the Court has both aggressively displayed the judicial power and "creatively" interpreted the Constitution. The two techniques, in fact, are often used in tandem in order to reconstruct what the Rehnquist Court believes is the proper balance between local and national power. Thus, the Court has used the power of judicial review to strike down numerous statutes that it considered an encroachment upon the autonomy and immunity of the states as designed by the Tenth and Eleventh Amendments.

In *United States v. Lopez*, 514 U.S. 549 (1995), for instance, the Court struck down the Gun Free School Zones Act; similarly, in *Printz v. United States,* 521 U.S. 898 (1997), with the Brady Handgun Violence Protection Act. More recently, the Court nullified the Age Discrimination in Employment Act in KIMEL V. BOARD OF REGENTS, 528 U.S. 62 (2000), and the VIOLENCE AGAINST WOMEN ACT in UNITED STATES V. MORRISON, 529 U.S. 598 (2000). In each instance, the Court has invalidated popularly driven policy aims expressed through democratic means; in each instance, the Court has used tradition and history to derive new meaning from established constitutional provisions.

Traditionally, activism has been viewed as dangerous and restraint as prudent. Nonetheless, there is normative support for, and accompanying critique of, each philosophy. Proponents of activism assert the need for the Court to fulfill its obligation to penetrate the full depths of constitutional meaning. In order to do so, they reason, the Court must be prepared both to encounter the political branches and to search for the true "spirit" of the law. They view restraint as a convenient excuse to shirk this responsibility and a practical method of reestablishing the Court as a timid or passive institution. Conversely, proponents of restraint emphasize fidelity to the principles of separation of powers and republican government. They stress leaving lawmaking to the democratically elected branches and urge fidelity to the actual words of the Constitution. Activism, they contend, not only aggrandizes legislative and executive power for the judiciary but also disregards the "letter of the law" in search of what nine unelected officials believe is the correct result.

Whatever the normative evaluation of activism or of restraint, there is a growing belief that the terms themselves are of limited utility in contemporary constitutional discourse. Part of the problem is that scholars have been unable to agree on precisely what constitutes activism or restraint, part is that activism and restraint have all too often been utilized as political rhetoric rather than legal reality, and yet another part is preconceived connotations about the vices of activism and the virtues of restraint. Regardless, as judicial behavior becomes more complex and constitutional jurisprudence more varied, the terms *judicial activism* and *judicial restraint* will continue to create more confusion than illumination. After nearly a century of use, it is possible that the concepts may have finally worn out their welcomes.

For more information: Bickel, Alexander M. *The Least Dangerous Branch.* New Haven, Conn.: Yale University Press, 1986; Bork, Robert H. *The Tempting of America.* New York: Free Press, 1990; Dworkin, Ronald. *Taking Rights Seriously.* London: Duckworth, 1977.

—Justin Crowe

judicial review

Judicial review is the power of the courts to declare laws unconstitutional. Judicial review, perhaps the most important source of judicial power in the United States, is the unique function of the judiciary whereby it decides the constitutionality of acts by the other two branches of government. Judicial review serves to empower the courts, as the judiciary cannot enforce its decisions through funding or administrative exercises. That is, the courts have neither the purse nor the sword to enforce their rulings. Judicial review is the judiciary's major "check and balance" against the legislative and executive branches of government. Because judicial review is such an important part of the judiciary's role in American government, it is ironic that the Constitution of the United States does not grant this power to the courts. Rather, careful and deliberate legal craftsmanship has allowed the judiciary, ever since the time of Chief Justice John MARSHALL, to create this important power for itself, which, by and large, the other branches of government have recognized as a legitimate function of the courts. However, judicial review presents theoretical problems for a democratic society and has been the source of much academic debate. Nonetheless, judicial review is an important element of the role of the courts in American democracy.

Efforts to justify the exercise of judicial review have been made since the nation's founding. In the late 18th century, individuals such as James Iredell, Alexander Hamilton, and James Wilson wrote publicly to convince the American people to accept the judiciary they had designed. Most notably, in *The Federalist* #78, Alexander Hamilton advocated judicial review on the grounds that the Constitution represents boundaries that legislators may not cross, and the courts can best protect those boundaries. If the legislature breaks the rules of the Constitution, the people can be sure the courts, through judicial review, will reign in such excesses.

However, what has come to be recognized as the most important justification of judicial review is the Court's opinion, by Chief Justice John Marshall, in MARBURY V. MADISON, 1 Cranch 137 (1803). In *Marbury*, the Court considered whether Congress could legislatively expand the Court's constitutionally-defined ORIGINAL JURISDICTION. The Court concluded Congress could not do so, holding for the first time an act of Congress void as in violation of the Constitution. The CHIEF JUSTICE noted the Court's original jurisdiction was detailed in the Constitution and could not, therefore, be altered by an Act of Congress. Relying on the supremacy clause of the Constitution, the Court noted that no act of the legislature may contradict the Constitution, thereby planting the seeds of what would develop into the most important power of the judiciary.

The Court did not, however, use this new power to rule a piece of federal legislation unconstitutional again until

1957, when, in the case of *Scott v. Sandford*, 19 Howard 393 (1857), it held that Congress could not prohibit slavery in some territories. While the controversial decision did have some impact on the Court's public image, the power of judicial review survived the episode. As the 19th century drew to a close, the Court became increasingly concerned with economic policy and used the power of judicial review to overturn federal and state laws affecting the economy. In the early 20th century, the Court handed down its infamous opinion in *LOCHNER V. NEW YORK*, 198 U.S. 45 (1905).

In *Lochner*, the Court held New York's regulation of bakers' hours to violate the Constitution because such would violate a "freedom to contract." The Court used judicial review to create a new right—to read a freedom *into* the Constitution. This function of judicial review has subsequently been nicknamed "lochnerizing." During the 1930s, the Court continued to use judicial review to strike down important pieces of FDR's New Deal. Later in the 20th century, the focus of judicial review shifted to the protection of CIVIL LIBERTIES and allowed the Court to promote legislation to protect the rights of the criminally accused as well as racial minorities and women.

The development of judicial review has spawned a heated academic debate concerning the role of an unelected, life-tenured judiciary in a democracy. There is a concern among scholars as to how an independent, and therefore by design unaccountable, judiciary can legitimately review the actions of branches of government that are elected by the people and are, consequently, representative of the will of the majority. One common explanation is that American democracy is "liberal democracy." That is, our government is one of limited powers. It follows that there must be some way to check the potential excesses of the majority. While Congress passes laws by a majority rule, the BILL OF RIGHTS, for example, sets important limits on what laws Congress may enact. Being unaccountable, the judiciary is, in theory, more apt to stand up for the rights of the minority when the majority may choose to violate them. No matter how one justifies judicial review, the practice has become unequivocally accepted by the legal community and the American people.

While it may present problems for democratic theory, the institution of judicial review provides an important check to balance the exercise of majority will in the United States and serves as the most important source of federal judicial power.

For more information: Bickel, Alexander. *The Least Dangerous Branch.* New Haven, Conn.: Yale University Press, 1962; Ely, John Hart. *Democracy and Distrust.* Cambridge, Mass.: Harvard University Press, 1980; Whittington, Keith. *Constitutional Construction.* Cambridge, Mass.: Harvard University Press, 1999.

—Tom Clark

Judiciary Act of 1789

Enacted on September 24, 1789, the Judiciary Act of 1789 is one of the most important pieces of legislation Congress ever passed. The act performed three functions. First, it clarified Article III of the UNITED STATES CONSTITUTION by creating a hierarchical FEDERAL COURT SYSTEM. Second, it declared the Supreme Court the final court to decide issues of federal law. Finally, it triggered *MARBURY V. MADISON*, 5 U.S. 137 (1803), an immensely important case that declared the Court's authority to review congressional acts.

Constitutional Clarification

The act added depth to Article III of the Constitution. However impressive the Constitution was as an overall governing scheme at the time, sections of it intentionally lacked clarity. For example, Article III simply declared that federal judicial power would be vested in a Supreme Court and "in such inferior Courts as Congress may from time to time ordain and establish." The framers wrote Article III broadly so Congress could create and, from time to time, alter the makeup of the judiciary. Fulfilling its obligations, the First Congress clarified Article III and gave voice to constitutional silence by creating a hierarchical federal court system comprised of 13 district courts, three circuit courts, and, of course, the United States Supreme Court.

Every state plus Kentucky and Maine, which were then parts of Virginia and Massachusetts, received a federal district court and district court judge. These district courts were not powerful trial courts like today's district courts. The district courts could hear only certain minor cases, like admiralty and maritime cases. While some opponents of the act feared the creation of federal district courts, their fears were allayed somewhat since the federal district courts' boundaries were the same as the states' political borders, their jurisdiction was limited, and each district judge had to reside in the district for which he was appointed.

The act also created three federal circuit courts that would act as the primary federal trial courts. Composed of the eastern, middle, and southern circuits, these three circuit courts had ORIGINAL JURISDICTION over the vast majority of federal legal issues, as well as some appellate powers to review district court decisions. Each circuit court tribunal consisted of two U.S. Supreme Court justices and the district judge of the district in which they sat. When a district judge's case was on appeal, however, he could not sit on the circuit court and review his own decision.

The Supreme Court justices "rode circuit" twice a year when they traveled to and presided over these circuit court cases. Most justices despised riding circuit since the full Supreme Court could overturn individual justices' circuit riding decisions and because it forced them to travel long distances on horseback over primitive roads and often through bad weather. Notwithstanding a very brief time during the first Jefferson administration, Congress did not abolish circuit riding until 1891.

The act also granted these new federal circuit courts "diversity jurisdiction." Diversity jurisdiction allowed federal courts to hear disputes between citizens of different states or between a state (or its citizens) and a foreigner that turned on state law. The amount in controversy, however, had to exceed $500. Additionally, one of the parties in the controversy had to live in the state over which the district court presided. The circuit courts received diversity jurisdiction because Congress believed that state courts might apply state law in a manner that would discriminate against out-of-state litigants.

Note, however, that the act did not grant federal courts "federal question" jurisdiction. Federal question jurisdiction, unlike diversity jurisdiction, is a kind of original jurisdiction that provides federal trial courts with the authority to hear disputes turning on federal law. Congress did not grant "federal question" jurisdiction until 1875. Up until 1875, unless a federal court heard a case under its diversity jurisdiction that involved issues of both state and federal law, or an APPEAL made it to the U.S. Supreme Court, state courts interpreted and applied federal law, when applicable, to disputes.

The act, as it addressed the United States Supreme Court, called for six justices. This number was significant because it established two justices to ride on each of the three circuits. Of the six justices, one served as CHIEF JUSTICE and the other five as associate justices. The act further declared that the Court should hold two sessions annually (in August and February) at the seat of government. Parties could appeal cases to the Supreme Court from the circuit court only if the amount in controversy exceeded $2,000. Finally, as described below, the act empowered the Court to review certain state court decisions.

The Final Court to Decide Issues of Federal Law

Section 25 of the act allowed litigants to appeal to the U.S. Supreme Court those state supreme court decisions that: (1) involved issues of the validity of a federal law or treaty; (2) upheld a state law that a party challenged as violating federal law, federal TREATIES, or the U.S. Constitution; or (3) interpreted any clause of the U.S. Constitution, a federal treaty, or a federal statute. Section 25—which contained no amount-in-controversy minimum—supplemented the Constitution's supremacy clause, which held the Constitution and all federal laws made thereunder were the supreme law of the land, notwithstanding any contrary state laws. Section 25 fostered the Supreme Court's preeminence over all courts because it made the Court the final and sovereign judicial forum over matters concerning federal law. The Court used section 25 as a tool in numerous cases to review state court decisions and pronounce Supreme Court dominance.

Marbury v. Madison and Judicial Review

Finally, it must be noted that section 13 of the act, which granted the Court power to issue writs of mandamus in certain circumstances, gave rise to *Marbury v. Madison*. *Marbury* is an important case because it established the Court's power to review congressional acts. Pursuant to section 13, William Marbury asked the Court to issue a writ of mandamus ordering President Jefferson to deliver Marbury's commission as justice of the peace. The Court, however, held that section 13, the basis for Marbury's cause of action, unconstitutionally expanded the Court's original jurisdiction. Congress, it said, only could legislate the Court's appellate jurisdiction, not its original jurisdiction. Thus, the Court ruled that section 13 was unconstitutional and established its authority to review congressional acts.

Conclusion

The Judiciary Act of 1789 performed three functions. It clarified Article III of the Constitution by creating a hierarchical judicial system, made the U.S. Supreme Court the final appellate court on matters concerning federal law, and gave rise to *Marbury v. Madison*. For these reasons, the act is landmark legislation.

For more information: Bourguignon, Henry J. "The Federal Key to the Judiciary Act of 1789." *South Carolina Law Review* 46 (1995): 647–702; Currie, David P. *The Constitution in Congress: The Federalist Period: 1789–1801*. Chicago: University of Chicago Press, 1997; Marcus, Maeva. *Origins of the Federal Judiciary: Essays on the Judiciary Act of 1789*. New York: Oxford University Press, 1992.

—Ryan J. Owens

jury size and voting

The U.S. Constitution, at Article III, Section 2 (The trial of all crimes, . . . shall be by jury. . . .) and the BILL OF RIGHTS, in Amendments VI (right to a jury in a criminal trial) and VII (juries in civil trials), demonstrate the importance the framers of the Constitution placed on the venerable British concept of trial by jury.

First utilized in England in the mid-14th century, by 1789, when the U.S. judiciary was established, juries were an essential element of the British court system. Then, as now, the British system required 12 jurors on every panel and a unanimous vote of the panel to effect a decision in a case. However, if there was ever a logical reason for these requirements, it is now lost in history. Although both the Constitution and Bill of Rights mention the right to a jury trial, neither document established a jury's correct size or the vote necessary for a decision. Since the Constitution's ratification occurred about 400 years after the British established their traditions for jury size and vote, the framers may have presumed that in the absence of instructions to the contrary, individual U.S. courts would follow the 12-member-jury/unanimous-vote tradition unless Congress or the Supreme Court established new parameters.

For more than 100 years after the Constitution was ratified, the U.S. courts followed the British tradition with regard to both jury size and voting. Then came the case of *Thompson v. Utah,* 20 U.S. 343 (1898), a case that questioned the constitutionality of a Utah law, enacted subsequent to a public referendum, that mandated eight-member juries. The Court ruled that the framers intended that "jury" as used in the Sixth Amendment should mean a panel of at least 12 individuals, since the rule of "innocent until proven guilty" mandates that a criminal defendant have the benefit of the diversity of opinions inherent in a larger group. Despite the public's belief that an eight-member jury could dispense justice as well as a 12-member panel, the Utah law was found unconstitutional, and criminal convictions made by an eight-member jury impaneled under that law were found void.

The *Thompson* ruling remained unchallenged until 1970, when in another jury size case, *Williams v. Florida,* 399 U.S. 78 (1970), the U.S. Supreme Court turned its back on *Thompson* and held that the 12-juror PRECEDENT was a historical accident—a matter totally unrelated to the function of a jury. Since neither the Constitution nor the Bill of Rights specified the size of a jury, the Supreme Court held that a state law could establish a jury size of as few as six individuals, which was the minimum necessary to represent a cross-section of the community and participate in meaningful group deliberations; or as large as 12 or more jurors. However, to insure that an innocent individual would not be deprived of rights due to a jury error, the Court mandated that a jury of fewer than 12 members be allowed to make decisions only by unanimous vote.

After spending three-quarters of a century hearing cases that dealt with variations on the "number of jurors" theme, the vote of the jurors was the pivotal matter in *Apodaca v. Oregon,* 406 U.S. 404 (1972), and a companion case, *Johnson v. Louisiana,* 406 U.S. 356 (1972). In both *Apodaca* and *Johnson,* state laws required 12 jurors per panel. However, in *Apodaca,* a decision could be made on the basis of the votes of at least 80 percent (10, 11, or all 12) of the jurors on the panel, while in *Johnson,* the minimum vote required to make a decision was at least 75 percent (nine, 10, 11, or all of the 12) of the jurors on the panel. After stating that there was no evidence that the framers intended to "enshrine unanimity," the Supreme Court noted that the jury was not intended to block conviction.

Instead, the jury's purpose was to protect an individual from governmental oppression by interposing a layer of common sense between the government and individual.

Finally, the Supreme Court held that if the judge's instructions clearly informed the jury that an inaccurate vote could deprive an innocent man of his freedom, a vote of 75 percent of a jury fulfilled its purpose and would result in a valid verdict. To continue to use court resources after achieving that vote, in order to seek unanimity, was wasteful and unnecessary.

When the Constitution and Bill of Rights were written, 400 years of precedent in the British courts had established that their juries have exactly 12 members and that valid jury decisions be based on a unanimous vote. While the true intentions of the framers remain unknown, their wording of Article III of the Constitution and Amendments Six and Seven of the Bill of Rights was broad enough to allow the American courts to break with the British tradition without running afoul of the Constitution. While the evolution of a distinct set of jury precedents for the U.S. court system was slow to start, the Supreme Court's precedents have now provided latitude in both number of jurors, which can now vary from six to 12, and necessary vote for a valid decision, which can now vary from 75 percent to unanimous, depending on the size of the jury panel.

For more information: Cardona, George. "Jury Size and Unanimity." UCLA School of Law (2001). Available online. URL: http://www.law.ucla.edu/students/academicinfo/coursepages/s2001/503f/unanweb. Downloaded May 14, 2004; Hunter, Margo. "Improving the Jury System: Nonunanimous Verdicts." PLRI U.C. Hastings School of Law (1996). Available online. URL: http://w3.uchastings.edu/plri/spr96tex/juryuna.html. Downloaded May 14, 2004.

—Beth S. Swartz

justiciability

Justiciability refers to the ability of an individual to bring an issue before a court of law. Article III, Section 2 of the U.S. Constitution sets up the power of the judiciary, stating that it extends only to "cases and controversies." This means that courts are only able to hear issues in an adversarial context and resolve them through the judicial process. From this constitutional principle, the doctrines of justiciability have been created to further delineate the boundaries of justiciable issues. The doctrines consist of six basic standards.

First, no court shall give an advisory opinion. An advisory opinion is essentially a hypothetical question brought before the court for advice. For instance, the president may wish to request that the Supreme Court look into the constitutionality of a piece of legislation before he signs it.

Because the bill is not yet law, it does not yet actually exist as a CASE OR CONTROVERSY in need of review. This doctrine keeps the judiciary out of the realm of politics.

Next, a person who sues must have STANDING. This requires that the plaintiff have an actual injury traceable to an infraction and have a substantial likelihood to be resolved by the court. Plaintiffs cannot simply have an interest in resolving a dispute that does not specifically injure them; they may not sue in another's interest. The exception to this is when a guardian files suit for a minor.

Third, the controversy must not be MOOT. Once an issue has been settled by the two parties, it may not come before a court. An issue also cannot be resolved by a court if the defendant or plaintiff has died. The exceptions to this requirement refer to issues which are capable of repetition and yet might evade review. An example of this has been abortion litigation. A woman's pregnancy will normally come to full term before the judicial process is completed. Because of her ability to become pregnant again the issue can be brought before a court.

Fourth, a controversy must be ripe for review. An individual cannot file a suit based on something that is merely likely to occur but must have already taken place. Nor is a court likely to take a case in some new area, such as a technological innovation, until there is some degree of certainty it can make a wise decision. The issue must be ready for review. This prevents courts from making premature judgments.

Fifth, courts may not hand down decisions on political questions. A political question is an issue that may be constitutional in nature, but would be better handled by another branch of government. This refers to jurisdiction, because the courts cannot look at issues that are constitutionally delegated to another branch of government. This standard, again, keeps the courts independent and above politics.

Finally, individuals may not file collusive or "friendly" suits. These are suits in which the two sides either want the same outcome or have no adversity between them. Individuals must show real adversity or injury in order to bring an issue before a court.

For more information: Hazard, Geoffrey C., Jr., and Michele Tartuff. *American Civil Procedure: An Introduction.* New Haven, Conn.: Yale University Press, 1993.

—Kate Hanratty

juvenile death penalty

The juvenile death penalty is the imposition of CAPITAL PUNISHMENT upon offenders who were under the age of 18 when they committed the crime. Whether youths should be treated the same as adults for purposes of punishment by death is very controversial. Juveniles have been treated differently from adults since the common law period, when it was recognized that juveniles were not as mentally or emotionally developed as adults and thus should be judged differently. This led to the development of the infancy defense, which held that youths under the age of 14 were presumed incompetent and thus not criminally liable for their misdeeds, and eventually to the creation of the juvenile court system in the early part of the 20th century.

While there has been a consistent effort over time to recognize the reduced liability of juveniles, there has also been a steady effort to hold the most serious juvenile offenders accountable for their actions. This has taken several forms, including allowing juveniles charged with serious crimes to be transferred to criminal court. Another form has been the imposition of the death penalty. Approximately 365 juvenile offenders have been executed in America. Twenty-one juvenile offenders have been executed since the Supreme Court upheld the constitutionality of the death penalty in 1976. Of the 40 states that currently allow the death penalty, 18 have a minimum age of 18, five have a minimum age of 17, and 17 have a minimum age of 16.

The Supreme Court has determined that some (but not all) juveniles may be given the death penalty. In *Thompson v. Oklahoma*, 487 U.S. 815 (1988), the Supreme Court, applying the "evolving standards of decency" test, held that it was unconstitutional to execute juveniles who committed their crime at age 15 or younger. The Court noted that a national review of state legislation showed "complete or near unanimity among all 50 states . . . in treating a person under 16 as a minor" and that this showed that "the normal 15-year-old is not prepared to assume the full responsibilities of an adult."

The following year, in *Stanford v. Kentucky*, 492 U.S. 361 (1989), the Supreme Court held that the "evolving standards of decency" test did not bar the execution of juveniles who were either 16 or 17 when they committed their crime. The Court noted that a majority of states that allowed the imposition of the death penalty allowed 16-year-olds to be executed. This demonstrated to the Court that there was no national consensus against executing 16-year-olds, unlike the consensus that existed against executing 15-year-olds.

The rate at which juvenile death sentences have been handed out has remained constant at about 2 percent of all death penalty sentences. This rate has remained constant in the face of both increases and decreases in juvenile violence and homicide rates, which suggests its imposition is not related to the incidence of homicide. More than two-thirds of the juveniles executed have been African American. This suggests that race may play a factor in the sentencing decision. Of the 139 juvenile death sentences that have been resolved since 1976 (either by reversal or execution), 118, or 85 percent, have been reversed on APPEAL. This suggests that the imposition of the juvenile death penalty is often improperly decided.

While there now exists a clear demarcation regarding who may be executed, the debate over the appropriateness of executing young offenders rages on. Opponents of the juvenile death penalty continue to argue that younger offenders are both less culpable and more amenable to rehabilitation, thus making them poor candidates for capital punishment. Supporters of the death penalty for juveniles stress the importance of providing a punishment that "fits the crime." In *Patterson v. Texas*, 536 U.S. 984 (2002), three Supreme Court justices took the relatively unusual step of dissenting from a denial of certiorari in a case involving an application for a stay of execution of a juvenile death sentence. The dissenting justices argued that the Court should reconsider its ruling in *Stanford v. Kentucky*. While this argument was unsuccessful, it highlights the growing trend toward abolition or at least restriction of the juvenile death penalty. Several state legislatures have recently raised the minimum age for death penalty eligibility to 18, and several state courts have interpreted their own constitutions to limit the applicability of the death penalty to persons under 18. It remains to be seen whether a societal consensus in favor of abolishing the juvenile death penalty will develop.

For more information: Bureau of Justice Statistics. *Capital Punishment 1999.* Washington, D.C.: Bureau of Justice Statistics, 2001; Gardner, Martin R. *Understanding Juvenile Law.* New York: Matthew Bender, 1997; *Patterson v. Texas*, 536 U.S. 984, 123 S. Ct. 24, 153 L.E.2d 2887 (2002); *Stanford v. Kentucky*, 492 U.S. 361, 109 S. Ct. 2969, 106 L.E.2d 306 (1989); Streib, Victor. *Death Penalty in a Nutshell.* St. Paul, Minn.: West, 2002; *Thompson v. Oklahoma*, 487 U.S. 815, 108 S. Ct. 2687, 101 L.E.2d 702 (1988).

—Craig Hemmens

juvenile rights

Juvenile rights are those rights afforded youth who come to the attention of law enforcement and the juvenile court. Juvenile rights, although often the same, are distinguished from the rights guaranteed adult criminal defendants because of the distinct differences between the juvenile and adult criminal court.

History

Historically, juveniles were not afforded any of the procedural rights guaranteed adult defendants. Under English common law the king was granted the power of being "father of his country." Accordingly, under the doctrine of *parens patriae* (Latin for father of his country), the king was able to intervene in the life of an unruly youth and act in the best interest of the child. The development of the juvenile justice system in the United States largely mirrored England's. During the early 1800s America became increasingly urbanized. Early American cities were unprepared for this development, giving rise to a substantial population of urban poor, many of whom were juveniles.

Accordingly, a rise in crime committed by young people transpired. However, juveniles between the ages of seven and 14 were still afforded protection, as they were deemed less culpable for their actions than adults. "Juvenile delinquency" was officially defined in 1818. In 1825 New York State opened the House of Refuge, which was the first reformatory utilized to house juvenile delinquents. Juveniles were sent to these institutions for delinquent and status offenses under laws based on *parens patriae,* which essentially allowed the courts to act in the best interests of the child.

An early challenge to this procedure was *Ex parte Crouse,* 4 P.S.C. 9 (1838), where a father challenged his daughter, who had been placed in a house of refuge for a status offense, had been imprisoned without a jury trial. However, the Pennsylvania Supreme Court upheld the doctrine of *parens patriae* thereby allowing the imprisonment of juveniles who were deemed beyond parental control.

In 1899 Illinois established the first juvenile court. Although there were several challenges in the state courts, the now separate juvenile court continued to operate under *parens patriae,* which did not afford juveniles any specific procedural rights. This continued up until the 1950s and '60s when the United States Supreme Court began incorporating the BILL OF RIGHTS to the states for criminal matters. The Court's expanded application began to influence the juvenile justice systems in several states.

Supreme Court Decisions

During this era of procedural change the Supreme Court began to consider juvenile issues and grant juveniles some of the same rights guaranteed adults. In *Haley v. Ohio*, 332 U.S. 596 (1948), the Court held that the due process clause of the Fourteenth Amendment applies to the police in obtaining juvenile admissions or confessions. Accordingly, in *Gallegos v. Colorado*, 370 U.S. 49 (1962), the Court held that prolonged periods of isolation of a juvenile by the police may result in confessions that are deemed involuntarily obtained and in violation of the juvenile's due process rights.

Even though the Court acted on behalf of juveniles in deciding *Haley* and *Gallegos*, it was not until 1966 that it heard a challenge on juvenile court procedure. In *Kent v. United States,* 383 U.S. 541 (1966), the Court held that a transfer of a jurisdiction in a juvenile hearing is a "critically important" stage in the judicial process. In holding this way the Court afforded juvenile defendants due process protections, specifically the right to a hearing, in a transfer proceeding. The *Kent* case marked the beginning of the due process movement in the juvenile court. In IN RE GAULT, 387 U.S. 1 (1967), the Court held that the due process clause of the Fourteenth Amendment applies to proceedings in state juvenile courts to adjudicate a juvenile delinquent. Essentially, the Court afforded juveniles substantially the same rights as adults in adjudicatory proceedings. Those rights included timely notice of specific issues, notification of the right to counsel and the appointment of counsel if the family cannot afford an attorney, protection against self-incrimination, and sworn testimony subject to cross-examination.

In *In re Winship*, 397 U.S. 358 (1970), the Court held that an adjudication must be based upon the same burden as a criminal conviction, reasonable doubt. However, the Court has not afforded juveniles all the procedural rights guaranteed adults. In *McKiever v. Pennsylvania*, 403 U.S. 528 (1971), the Court held that the Sixth Amendment does not require trial by jury in juvenile delinquency proceedings. After *McKiever*, the Court returned to affording juveniles rights. In *Davis v. Alaska*, 415 U.S. 308 (1974), the Court held that juveniles have the right to examine another minor's confidential record in order to effectively cross-examine any juvenile that testifies against them.

In *Breed v. Jones*, 421 U.S. 519 (1975), the Court held that a juvenile who has undergone adjudication proceedings in juvenile court cannot be tried on the same charge as an adult in a criminal court because to do so would constitute DOUBLE JEOPARDY. After the *Breed* case the Court began to favor societal protection over safeguarding juvenile rights. In *Fare v. Michael C.*, 442 U.S. 707 (1979), the Court held that the request by a juvenile probationer during police questioning to see his probation officer, after having received Miranda warnings by the police, is not equivalent to asking for a lawyer and therefore is not considered an assertion of the right to remain silent.

In *Smith v. Daily Mail Publishing Company*, 443 U.S. 97 (1979), the Court held a West Virginia law making it a crime to publish the names of alleged juvenile delinquents violated the First Amendment. In *Schall v. Martin*, 467 U.S. 253 (1984), the Court allowed that pretrial detention of accused juvenile delinquents without bail did not violate due process. In NEW JERSEY V. T.L.O., 468 U.S. 1214 (1984), the Court held that for a search to be valid, public school officials need only reasonable grounds to suspect that the search will produce evidence that the student has violated either the law or the rules of the school.

Supreme Court cases reflect a transformation that occurred in the juvenile justice system during the same period the cases were decided. As juveniles were afforded more rights, and official procedures were established, the once informal juvenile court was transformed into a formal court of law. In view of this difference, it is evident that the Supreme Court has had considerable influence over juvenile rights.

For more information: Binder, Arnold, Gilbert Geis, and Dickson Bruce. *Juvenile Delinquency: Historical, Cultural and Legal Perspectives*, 3rd ed. Cincinnati, Ohio: Anderson, 2001; Hemmens, Craig, Benjamin Steiner, and David Mueller. *Criminal Justice Casebriefs: Significant Cases in Juvenile Justice.* Los Angeles: Roxbury, 2003.

—Benjamin Steiner

K

Katzenbach v. Morgan, 384 U.S. 641 (1966)

The United States Supreme Court decision in *Katzenbach v. Morgan*, 384 U.S. 641 (1966), held that by the authority of Section 5 of the Fourteenth Amendment, congressional power overrides state law in the area of voting rights. In New York, state law required that voters be able to read and write English. However, in passing the federal VOTING RIGHTS ACT of 1965, Congress expressly stated that voters who were educated in Puerto Rico schools and who had reached the sixth grade could not be denied the right to vote, even if they did not speak English. The U.S. Supreme Court, through Associate Justice William BRENNAN's opinion, held that Congress did have the power, under the Fourteenth Amendment guarantee of equal protection of the laws, to enforce legislation against the states in protecting voting rights.

The state of New York required that individuals wishing to register to vote had to complete a form, in English, regarding their residency, CITIZENSHIP, and other questions. In writing the 1965 Voting Rights Act, U.S. Representative Emanuel Cellar, a Puerto Rican and chair of the House Judiciary Subcommittee that wrote the overall legislation, included a section within the bill that held that persons who had completed the sixth grade in a public, or accredited private, school in Puerto Rico could not be denied the right to vote. Thousands of immigrants from Puerto Rico had moved to New York City, and before the 1965 Voting Rights Act, they had been denied the right to vote based on their inability to speak English. In challenging this section of the Voting Rights Act, voters in New York believed that the right of the states to determine registration requirements of prospective voters should outweigh federal legislation.

In his opinion, Justice Brennan held that the section of the Voting Rights Act in question was appropriate under the Fourteenth Amendment's Section 5, which reads that "The Congress shall have power to enforce, by appropriate legislation, the provisions of this article." Justice Brennan held that the Fourteenth Amendment's Section 5 was a "positive grant of legislative power authorizing Congress to exercise its discretion in determining whether and what legislation is needed to secure the guarantees of the Fourteenth Amendment," most notably the right to equal protection under the law. As was written into the 1965 Voting Rights Act, Puerto Ricans were protected to secure "perfect equality of CIVIL RIGHTS and equal protection of the laws."

Subsequent cases following *Morgan* have tested a number of areas, most notably amendments to the original Voting Rights Act of 1965. In 1970 Congress passed a number of amendments, most notably the prohibition of federal and state governments denying the right to vote to 18-year-olds. In the case *Oregon v. Mitchell,* 400 U.S. 112 (1970), the U.S. Supreme Court rejected the power of the federal government to enforce the 18-year-old voting provision on state governments, thus prompting the passage of the Twenty-sixth Amendment. The Court, in a majority opinion written by Associate Justice Hugo BLACK, held that the Fourteenth Amendment's Section 5 did not enable Congress to write laws that were broader in scope than the Fourteenth Amendment was originally designed to address. However, four dissenters argued that under *Morgan,* the Court had to accept Congress's more expansive reading of the Fourteenth Amendment's power to regulate voting requirements by the states.

For more information: Friedman, Lawrence M. *A History of American Law.* New York: Simon and Schuster, 1973.

—J. Michael Bitzer

Katz v. United States, 389 U.S. 347 (1967)

The *Katz v. United States* case altered the understanding of what actually makes a search valid within the prescriptions of the Fourth Amendment. This decision expanded the restrictions upon the law enforcement community and set a PRECEDENT for electronic surveillance. The Supreme

Court's ruling affirmed that Mr. Katz's Constitutional rights were violated by the FBI's intrusion into an area where Mr. Katz rightly believed he had privacy protections.

The Federal Bureau of Investigation believed that Mr. Katz was transmitting betting information across state lines, thereby making the act a federal criminal violation. They placed an electronic listening device outside of the booth that he would use in advance of his arrival at the booth. In court, the government introduced the tapes of the information that Mr. Katz made and he was convicted. The argument by the defense was that there was an intrusion into an area that Mr. Katz believed to be safe from government intrusion.

The lower courts did not agree and offered that there had not been any physical intrusion by the government and therefore the conviction would stand. When the case reached the Supreme Court it was overturned and a new way to view what constituted an illegal search was established by using a two-prong test. The Fourth Amendment would be violated if the government intruded upon an area where a person did have a right to expect privacy. The other part of the test was whether or not the place where the person believed he had a right to PRIVACY was also a place where a reasonable person would expect privacy. These two premises when taken together make the barrier that precludes the government from searching this area to gather evidence against a person. Think of the area to be searched not as a physical location but rather a place where the person believes that they have privacy. Because of the advent of technology, there are more places where a person may expect privacy, such as in locked electronic files that are placed within a computer.

Technology developments have raised a lot of questions as to in what circumstances do people believe that they have privacy. Some of the questions being asked in courts may involve music piracy and whether or not a person has a right to retrieve songs from friends over the Internet.

The term *search* developed an expanded definition over the years after the Katz case, and the areas where a person has held a constitutional right to be safe from illegal government intrusion have diminished in response to terrorism threats. The need to protect society against infrastructure damage, whether that is in the form of electronic communication or in terms of physical places to be searched, has to be balanced against the rights of individual persons.

Many have argued that the Katz decision was too vague and thus allowed criminals an opportunity to argue the privacy issue in every case where a search had been conducted. More recently others have offered that the new powers given to the police in order to battle terrorists have given law enforcement agencies too many citizen invasive rights. The latter argument utilizes the Katz decision as a basis for protecting the freedoms of people from the impact of these new POLICE POWERS. Whichever argument is followed, the Katz decision was a landmark and it appears that the justices considered future challenges because the decision was strong but pliable enough to accommodate the needs of the future circumstances.

For more information: *California v. Ciraolo,* 476 U.S. 227 (1986); *Smith v. Maryland,* 442 U.S. 735 (1979).

—Ernest Alexander Gomez

Kennedy, Anthony M. (1936–) *Supreme Court justice*

Anthony M. Kennedy was appointed to the United States Supreme Court by President Reagan in 1987. Like the justice he replaced, Lewis POWELL, Kennedy is a moderate centrist. He once acknowledged that "It's easier to be a REHNQUIST or a Scalia than a Kennedy." Because of his moderation, he was twice passed over by President Reagan in favor of two ideologues, Robert Bork and Douglas Ginsburg. When their nominations aborted, Kennedy seemed a safe choice.

The son of a Sacramento, California, lawyer-lobbyist and an activist in civic causes (Earl Warren was a family friend), Kennedy attended Stanford University and Harvard Law School. He took over his father's practice when his father died unexpectedly. He taught Constitutional Law at the McGeorge School of Law at the University of the Pacific (1965–87) and continued to teach summer classes in Constitutional Law at the University of Salzburg, under the auspices of the McGeorge School. He was appointed to the U.S. COURT OF APPEALS in 1975, and he joined the Supreme Court in 1987.

Kennedy frequently votes with the Court's conservatives (Rehnquist, SCALIA, and THOMAS) and is often paired with O'CONNOR. (Like O'Connor, he often writes concurring opinions even when he joins the majority opinion.) He has voted to nullify AFFIRMATIVE ACTION, ABORTION RIGHTS, and other liberal policies but has sided with the more liberal members in cases dealing with religious freedom, speech and expression, and discrimination.

Kennedy voted to uphold the right to burn the American flag as a political protest in *TEXAS V. JOHNSON,* 491 U.S. 397 (1989), and to bar states from imposing term limits on members of Congress but also joined 5-4 rulings that made it harder for states to draw voting districts intended to boost the political influence of minorities. He authored an opinion that threw out a Colorado measure that barred laws protecting homosexuals from discrimination; he stated that a state could not "deem a class of persons a stranger to its laws" in *ROMER V. EVANS,* 517 U.S. 620 (1996), but four years later Kennedy provided the fifth vote to allow the Boy Scouts to bar homosexuals from serving as troop leaders in

Boy Scouts of America v. Dale, 530 U.S. 640 (2000). He has voted to establish judicial limits on congressional actions based on the commerce clause.

Kennedy is a advocate of JUDICIAL RESTRAINT. In 1992 O'Connor, SOUTER, and Kennedy in *PLANNED PARENTHOOD V. CASEY*, 505 U.S. 833, stated that overturning *ROE V. WADE*, 410 U.S. 113 (1973), would do "profound and unnecessary damage to the Court's legitimacy." Yet Kennedy sided with the dissenters in *Sternberg v. Carhart*, 530 U.S. 914 (2000), when the Court narrowly struck down laws banning so-called "partial birth" abortions. In *MADSEN V. WOMEN'S HEALTH CENTER, INC.*, 512 U.S. 753 (1994), and *Hill v. Colorado*, 530 U.S. 703 (2000), he was in dissent in holding that states should not be able to prohibit the "unpopular speech" of protesters outside abortion clinics.

Kennedy authored the 1992 ruling that school-initiated prayers at public high school graduation ceremonies were an unconstitutional government establishment of RELIGION in *LEE V. WEISMAN*, 505 U.S. 572, and reaffirmed that position in *SANTA FE INDEPENDENT SCHOOL DISTRICT V. DOE*, 530 U.S. 290 (2000), but a few years later in another 5-4 case decided that public school teachers could offer remedial help at church-run schools. In *ROSENBERGER V. UNIVERSITY OF VIRGINIA*, 515 U.S. 819 (1995), he held that public schools could provide monetary and other support to campus religious groups as long as the support is allocated on a neutral basis. Kennedy wrote the majority opinion in *BOERNE V. FLORES* 521 U.S. 507 (1997), that struck down the Religious Freedom Restoration Act, which sought to protect the free exercise of religion.

Kennedy wrote the opinion in *Ashcroft v. Free Speech Coalition*, 122 S. Ct. 1389 (2002), striking down a federal law banning virtual child pornography.

Kennedy was the author of the five-justice opinion in *BUSH V. GORE*, 531 U.S. 98 (2000). He was not being consistent with his usual adherence to STARE DECISIS. Jeffrey Rosen in *The New Republic* alleged that Kennedy was lobbying to be appointed CHIEF JUSTICE by Bush to succeed William Rehnquist.

The majority's opinion was murky. It found the recount unconstitutional, mostly because there was no guidance as to what the Florida legislature meant in requiring ballot counters to discern "the clear intent of the voter." However, when the Supreme Court first was presented with the case, it deemed unworthy of consideration the "clear intent" argument. The majority emphasized that its consideration was "limited to the present circumstances" (i.e., that the case constituted no PRECEDENT).

In 2003 Kennedy told Congress at a hearing on the Supreme Court's budget that too many people were behind bars in America and that prison terms were often too long.

He criticized the proliferation of "mandatory minimum" sentences.

For more information: Gillman, Howard. *The Votes That Counted: How the Court Decided the 2000 Presidential Election*. Chicago: University of Chicago Press, 2001; Noonan, John T., Jr. *Narrowing the Nation's Power: The Supreme Court Sides with the States*. Berkeley: University of California Press, 2002; Rosen, Jeffrey. "The Agonizer." *New Yorker*, Nov. 11, 1996, pp. 82–90; Yalof, David Alistair. *Pursuit of Justices: Presidential Politics and the Selection of Supreme Court Nominees*. Chicago and London: University of Chicago Press, 1999; Yarbrough, Tinsley. *The Rehnquist Court and the Constitution*. New York: Oxford University Press, 2000.

—Martin Gruberg

Kimel v. Board of Regents, 528 U.S. 62 (2000)

In *Kimel v. Board of Regents*, the Supreme Court ruled that the Eleventh Amendment bars states from being sued by private individuals for violations of the Federal Age Discrimination Act.

The Eleventh Amendment to the Constitution forbids individuals from suing state governments in federal courts. This SOVEREIGN IMMUNITY from lawsuits was intended to protect states from being controlled by federal judges. The amendment was ratified in 1798 to overrule the Court's decision in *CHISHOLM V. GEORGIA* (1795) that allowed such suits. The Eleventh Amendment's ban on suits was weakened by the passage of the Fourteenth Amendment, which allowed Congress to pass laws to prevent states from denying due process to their citizens. It also gives individuals the power to sue state government in federal court.

The Eleventh Amendment had been ignored and rarely used by the Court during much of the 20th century but was revived during the 1990s. The case of *Kimel v. Board of Regents* (1998) saw the justices grappling with the tension between the Eleventh and the Fourteenth Amendments.

The Kimel decision dealt with the 1975 Federal Age Discrimination Act. Under the act private employers and state and local governments were forbidden from using age for hiring, firing, or promoting employees over the age of 50. Kimel was a librarian at Florida State University who claimed the state of Florida had discriminated against him on the basis of his age and sued the state in federal court. The state of Florida claimed sovereign immunity from suit, using the Eleventh Amendment to support their argument.

The justices agreed with the state. In a five to four decision, they ruled the state was immune from any suits involving the Age Discrimination Act. Writing for the majority, Justice KENNEDY found that Congress had explicitly overridden the state's sovereign immunity, claiming AGE DISCRIMINATION was a violation of the Fourteenth Amendment's due process clause. The key question for the Court was whether age discrimination was forbidden under that amendment. They found that it was not.

According to the majority, age discrimination was not the same as race discrimination. Under Court doctrine, race was considered a SUSPECT CLASSIFICATION, one that involved a discrete and insular minority with a history of governmental and societal discrimination against them. The justices had explicitly refused to make age a suspect classification in *Massachusetts v. Murgia* (1976), because those over 50 were not a small and insulated minority and there was no proof of rampant societal and governmental discrimination against those over 50.

The justices ruled that the Fourteenth Amendment's due process clause protected discrete and insular minorities from state discrimination. If such a minority group had its rights violated by the state government, Congress could step in and override sovereign immunity by passing a law banning such state discrimination, but because age was not a suspect classification, Congress could not pass a law under the Fourteenth Amendment overriding sovereign immunity. Instead Kimel would have to depend upon state law and state courts to hear his age discrimination claim.

For more information: McCafferty, Evelyn. "Age Discrimination and Sovereign Immunity." *Alabama Law Review* 52, no. 3 (Spring 2001): 1,057; Neugebauer, Gregory. *"Kimel v. Board of Regents."* Duquesne University Law Review 39 (2000): 242.

—Douglas Clouatre

Korematsu v. United States, 323 U.S. 214 (1944)

The United States Supreme Court held that loyal citizens of Japanese ancestry could be relocated to detention camps during World War II solely on the basis of their race in *Korematsu v. United States.* Ironically, while upholding one of the most dramatic restrictions on personal liberty ever imposed on Americans, the Court also established the constitutional doctrine protecting racial and ethnic minorities.

The Japanese attack on Pearl Harbor on December 7, 1941, unleashed near hysteria. The fear of an imminent Japanese invasion prompted President Franklin D. Roosevelt to authorize the relocation of 112,000 people of Japanese ancestry living on the West Coast to mass internment camps in the Western desert. Approximately 70,000 of them were American citizens. No internee received a trial or hearing. Similar relocation orders were issued in Canada.

This 1942 photograph shows the Mochida family awaiting the evacuation bus to an internment camp. *(National Archives)*

Fred Toyosaburo Korematsu, born in America of Japanese parents, twice tried to enlist in the army but failed the medical exam. He refused to report for relocation, in part because he did not want to be separated from his girlfriend. He was otherwise a law-abiding citizen. Military police arrested him for failing to report for relocation.

Korematsu argued that the relocation program violated his CIVIL RIGHTS. It was not required by national security because there was no reasonable fear that he would commit sabotage or espionage during the war. The order discriminated against Japanese Americans purely on the basis of race and therefore deprived him of his liberty and property "without due process of law," a violation of the Fifth Amendment to the United States Constitution.

The federal government argued that military necessity and national security required relocating Japanese Americans. It was impossible to hold a hearing for each individual.

The Supreme Court, which had only recently begun to play a strong role in the defense of minority rights, was reluctant to overturn an administrative measure considered militarily necessary. Justice Hugo BLACK, writing for the majority, recognized that only the "gravest imminent danger to the public safety constitutionally justified" exclusion. Black rejected Korematsu's claim that he was discriminated against purely because of his race. Korematsu's conviction was upheld.

Ironically, Justice Black's decision also laid the foundation for future attacks on racially discriminatory laws. He wrote, "[A]ll legal restrictions which curtail the civil rights of a single racial group are immediately suspect" and are "subject to the most rigid scrutiny." This language would be key to the Court's campaign to end racial segregation in America during the 1950s and 1960s.

Justice Frank MURPHY dissented. He agreed that exclusion would be constitutional if there was an "immediate, imminent and impending" danger to the public, but the exclusion order was issued almost a year after the attack on Pearl Harbor. No imminent danger was pending. Murphy bluntly called the order the "legalization of racism." Justice Robert H. JACKSON, also dissenting, pointed out that no such treatment had been imposed on white citizens from Germany or Italy, whose homelands were also at war with the United States. Justice Owen J. Roberts dissented on similar grounds.

In 1983 Congress released a study condemning the forced relocation as unjustified by military necessity. The War Department had misrepresented or deliberately suppressed evidence that would have exonerated Japanese Americans from suspicions of espionage. In 1988 President Ronald Reagan signed legislation formally apologizing to Japanese Americans who had been held in detention camps. The act paid $20,000 to each survivor. The Presidential Medal of Freedom, the nation's highest civilian award, was awarded to Fred Korematsu in 1998.

For more information: Irons, Peter. *Justice at War.* New York: Oxford University Press, 1983.

—Timothy J. O'Neill

L

labor union rights

The roots of labor union rights in the United States can be traced to the case of *Commonwealth v. Hunt,* 45 U.S. Mass (1842), in which the Massachusetts Supreme Court ruled that labor unions were not illegal conspiracies. This ruling was in contrast to a ruling by the New York State Supreme Court in 1835 that had ruled that a shoemaker's union in Geneva, New York, was illegal because the union was guilty of "a statutory offence because such practice was injurious to trade and commerce." Also in 1842, both Connecticut and Massachusetts passed laws prohibiting children from working more than 10 hours per day. By 1845 Pennsylvania had also passed a law barring the employment of anyone under 12 years of age for commercial occupations. New Hampshire took the idea of a limited workday one step farther with the legal adoption of the 10-hour day for all workers in 1847. By 1868 the federal government passed an eight-hour workday applying to laborers, mechanics, and workmen employed by the government.

By the latter 19th century the federal government was much more involved in the relations between workers and private businesses. In 1888 the first federal labor relations law was passed though it only applied to railroad companies. The next year Congress passed the Erdman Act, which provided for mediation and voluntary arbitration on the railroads.

In the early 20th century the U.S. Supreme Court's rulings in four cases seemed to mark a step by the federal government to limit the power of unions. In the case of *Lochner v. New York,* 198 U.S. 145 (1905), the Court declared a New York maximum hour law unconstitutional under the due process clause of the Fourteenth Amendment. In *Muller v. Oregon,* 208 U.S. 412 (1908), the Court ruled that female maximum hour laws were constitutional because of differences in a woman's "physical structure." In *U.S. v. Adair,* 208 U.S. 161 (1908), the Court ruled that section 10 of the Erdman Act forbidding a person from being fired for belonging to a union was unconstitutional. Finally, in 1911, the Court upheld an injunction ordering the AFL to eliminate the Bucks Stove and Range Company from its "unfair" list in *Gompers v. Bucks Stove and Range Company,* 221 U.S. 418.

Nineteen-fourteen is a year of mixed gains and losses for labor unions in terms of rights granted by the federal government. In 1914 Congress passed the Clayton Act, part of which limits the use of injunctions in labor disputes. However, in the same year in Ludlow, Colorado, national guardsmen attacked a tent colony of striking miners, literally setting a large number of miners and their families on fire. Following the Ludlow massacre President Wilson appointed the Colorado Coal Commission to investigate the attack as well as labor conditions in the mines. Shortly after the Ludlow massacre some strides were made in expanding labor union rights with the passage of the Lafollette Seamen's Act in 1915 regulating the working conditions of seamen. Also, in 1916, a nationwide railroad worker strike was adverted with passage of the Adamson Act granting the limiting of workdays to eight hours.

Bolstered by the Clayton, Lafollette Seamen's, and Adamson Acts, unions continued to push for new rights in the 1920s. Union momentum culminated in passage of the Railway Labor Act (1926) and the Hayes-Cooper Act (1929). The Railway Labor Act required employers to bargain collectively and prohibited them from discriminating against employees who wanted to join a union. The act also provided for voluntary arbitration and mediation in labor disputes. The Hayes-Cooper Act approved the regulation of shipping prison labor goods in INTERSTATE COMMERCE. The only major block to an expansion of union rights in the 1920s was the Supreme Court's ruling against the Journeymen Stone Cutters in the case of *Bedford Cut Stone Company v. Journeymen Stone Cutters' Association, et al.,* 275 U.S. 37 (1927). In *Bedford* the Court ruled against the journeymen's attempt to prevent the purchase of nonunion cut stone holding that the action was an illegal restraint of free trade.

During the Great Depression labor unions continued to expand their rights mainly through new acts of Congress.

Congress provided for the payment of prevailing wages to employees of contractors and subcontractors working on public construction with the Davis-Bacon Act (1931). Federal injunctions were prohibited in labor disputes with the Anti-Injunction Act (1932). The Wagner Act (1935) established the right of workers to organize and elect their own leaders for collective bargaining. Wagner also established the first national labor policy protecting workers' right to organize.

Later, the Wagner Act was upheld and declared constitutional by the Supreme Court in the case of NLRB V. JONES & LAUGHLIN STEEL CORPORATION, 301 U.S. 1 (1937). The Public Contracts Act, passed in 1936, was probably the most comprehensive declaration of labor rights up to that time establishing labor standards including overtime pay, child labor provisions, minimum wages, and safety standards on all federal contract jobs.

The 1940s and 1950s saw labor gain new rights along with new restrictions placed on certain labor union practices. In *Apex Hosiery Company v. Leader*, 310 U.S. 469 (1940), the Supreme Court ruled that a sit-down strike is not an illegal restraint of trade under the Sherman Antitrust Act. However, the Taft-Hartley Act (1947) restricted union activities and permitted states to pass "right-to-work" laws. Labor union rights were also curbed with passage of the Landrum-Griffin Act in 1959 that regulated the internal affairs of unions in order to lessen corruption.

The 1960s and 1970s was an era in which rights were not gained so much for labor unions per se as they were for all American public and private employees. THE CIVIL RIGHTS ACT OF 1964 prohibits discrimination by any employer on the basis of race, color, RELIGION, sex, or national origin. The Age Discrimination in Employment Act of 1967 made it illegal to discriminate in hiring or firing anyone between 40 and 65 on the basis of age. Finally, in 1974 the Employee Retirement Income Security Act established the regulation of pension funds by Congress.

Acts passed by Congress in the 1960s and 1970s have shaped and galvanized many of the rights shared by both union and nonunion laborers in the United States today. Perhaps the greatest legacy of labor unions is the American government and public expectations of minimum standards for all employees.

For more information: Fillippelli, Ronald L. *Labor in the USA: A History.* New York: Alfred A. Knopf, 1984; Foner, Philip S. *Women and the American Labor Movement: From Colonial Times to the Eve of World War I.* New York: Free Press, 1979; ———. *We, the Other People: Alternative Declarations of Independence by Labor Groups, Farmers, Woman's Rights Advocates, Socialists, and Blacks, 1829–1975.* Chicago: University of Illinois Press, 1976; Green, Janet Wells. *From Forge to Fast Food: A History of*

Child Labor in New York State. New York: Council for Citizenship Education, 1995.

—Scott M. Brown

Lamb's Chapel v. Center Moriches School District, 508 U.S. 393 (1993)

The United States Supreme Court unanimously ruled that a New York school district violated the First Amendment rights of religious groups by prohibiting them from use of school facilities after hours in *Lamb's Chapel v. Center Moriches School District.* First Amendment issues were often presented before the Court, so when reviewing, the Court had many precedents to consider.

New York state law allowed access to school facilities after school hours to local groups. There were 10 situations where local groups had such access, and the school board was allowed to select usage based on these situations. The law prohibited use of school amenities for religious purposes. The Center Moriches school board allowed social, civic, recreational, and political groups access to facilities but denied religious groups access.

Lamb's Chapel, a nondenominational evangelical church, asked the school board for permission to use the Center Moriches auditorium in 1988. The group wished to show a six-part film entitled "Turn Your Heart Toward Home" regarding parenting and family issues after school. The school board denied Lamb's Chapel use of the facility because of the religious beliefs of the organization.

Suit was filed in New York courts by Lamb's Chapel against the school district claiming a violation of their First Amendment rights of free speech and assembly, free exercise of RELIGION, establishment of religion, and the EQUAL PROTECTION CLAUSE of the Fourteenth Amendment. The district and appeals court rejected the church's arguments and ruled in favor of the school board. Lamb's Chapel then appealed to the U.S. Supreme Court who agreed to hear the case, and oral arguments were presented in February 1993.

The REHNQUIST Court unanimously ruled in favor of Lamb's Chapel on June 7, 1993. Justice Byron WHITE delivered the opinion of the court along with two concurring opinions. Justice Kennedy delivered one and Justice SCALIA joined by Justice THOMAS provided another concurring opinion. According to Justice White, the denial of the church's request violated the church's right to free speech because the denial was based solely on the perspective of the film. The New York law did not prohibit a film about parenting and family issues. The denial of the showing was based solely on the perspective of the group that wished to show it.

Center Moriches school board claimed that allowing Lamb's Chapel use of the facilities would violate the ESTAB-LISHMENT CLAUSE of the First Amendment. However, the

Supreme Court decided it did not violate the clause since the film would not have been shown during school hours and other groups were allowed to use school buildings after hours, so it would not seem like the school board was endorsing any particular religion.

PRECEDENT established by *LEMON V. KURTZMAN,* 403 U.S. 602 (1971), created a test for issues regarding the establishment clause of the First Amendment. The three-pronged test created a set of guidelines for reviewing government legislation and regulations with regards to First Amendment issues. First, the legislation and regulations must have a secular purpose. Second, the laws must have a primary effect that neither advances nor restrains religion. Finally, the laws must not foster an excessive governmental entanglement of religion.

The *Lemon* test was applied to *Lamb's Chapel* by Justice White, leading him to the conclusion that the church's right to free exercise and free speech should not be infringed upon since there was not deemed to be the establishment of a religion. Justice White reasoned that "challenged governmental action has a secular purpose, does not have the principal or primary effect of advancing or inhibiting religion, and does not foster an excessive entanglement with religion" in his opinion.

Justices Kennedy, Scalia, and Thomas presented concurring opinions because they did not agree with the standard of the three-prong test presented in *Lemon.* However, since the majority did agree with the standard, the *Lemon* test remained the approach to use when considering establishment issues. In addition, *Lamb's Chapel* determined that the circumstances behind the usage of school facilities by religious organizations were essential when evaluating usage. The viewpoint presented rather than the group presenting it became the most significant issue. A message could not be discriminated against solely on the basis of its messenger.

The precedents established in *Lamb's Chapel* were reaffirmed during the 1995 term by cases such as *ROSENBERGER V. RECTOR AND VISITORS OF THE UNIVERSITY OF VIRGINIA,* 515 U.S. 819 (1995), and *Capitol Square Review and Advisory Board v. Pinette,* 515 U.S. 753 (1995).

For more information: Hoekstra, Valerie J., and Jeffery A. Segal. "The Shepherding of Local Public Opinion: The Supreme Court and Lamb's Chapel." *The Journal of Politics* 58, no. 4 (1996): 1,079–1,102; O'Brien, David M. *Supreme Court Watch 1995.* New York: W. W. Norton, 1996.

—Carol Walker

land use

Land use planning, which involves creation and maintenance of an efficient infrastructure for a population in a manner that ensures a sense of unity and preserves natural systems to the greatest extent possible, is fundamental to the long-term sustainability of a community.

Land use is not the same as ZONING. Land use deals with the impact of development on natural resources regardless of location relative to population density; hence, land use may have impact on urban, suburban, or rural real estate. Additionally, land use is often subject to regulation by federal rather than local government, since it may involve interstate waterways or other geographical features. Zoning is concerned with maintaining a certain mixture of residential, business, and industrial property use in cities and suburbs. In order to enact zoning regulations or laws, the state in which the community is located must pass legislation that enables local governments to enact zoning laws and rules.

Zoning and land use laws and regulations must pass the challenge presented by the Fifth Amendment's "takings" clause, which prohibits government from taking private property without just compensation. Additionally, these laws and regulations must comply with the Fourteenth Amendment, which prohibits taking an individual's property without due process of law. These provisions clearly mandate that every level of government respect and protect the rights of property owners. Hence, federal, state, and local governments must attempt to balance strict respect for private property owners against the goal of restricting certain types of land use in order to protect the long-term welfare of the entire population.

In *LUCAS V. SOUTH CAROLINA COASTAL COUNCIL,* 505 U.S. 1003 (1992), the U.S. Supreme Court decided that regulations that denied the property owner all "economically viable use of his land" constituted one of the discrete categories of regulatory deprivation that required compensation without the usual case-specific inquiry into whether the land use advanced a compelling public interest. Hence, if a law has the same effect as physically taking a parcel of land and forbidding the owner to use it for his own benefit, it is practical and economically sensible to compensate the property owner.

In *Dolan v. City of Tigard,* 512 U.S. 374 (1994), the plaintiff applied for a city construction permit to expand her store and pave her parking lot. The city agreed to grant her permit on the condition that she dedicate part of her land for: (1) a greenway along a nearby creek to help alleviate runoff from the pavement; and (2) a pedestrian/bicycle path to relieve traffic congestion from the city's growing business district. The landowner sued the city, claiming that attaching conditions to her construction permit violated the Fifth Amendment's "takings" clause, as applied through the Fourteenth Amendment's due process clause.

The Supreme Court held that the city had failed to present conclusive evidence that the walkway/bicycle path would reduce traffic congestion and therefore could not require Dolan to give up her property as a condition of the permit. In addition, the city failed to explain why a public greenway was necessary, when plaintiff was willing to allow a private one. The requirements for the permit were: (1) inequitable, because they were not adequately connected to a legitimate state interest; and (2) unjustified when considered in relation to the benefit they would provide for the city.

The land involved in *Palazzolo v. Rhode Island Coastal Resources Management Council*, 533 U.S. 606 (2001), was in a coastal salt marsh that had been protected by a state wetlands statute since 1971. The state law allowed only minimal development on such land. In 1978 the plaintiff purchased two parcels within the protected area, with the intention of filling the marshland and creating a beach club. After the plaintiff's repeated applications for development permits were denied, he filed an inverse condemnation action in Rhode Island Superior Court.

Palazzolo asserted that the state law deprived him of all economically beneficial use of this property and therefore affected him as if the property had been taken without compensation. Hence, plaintiff claimed that the state's wetlands regulations violated the Fifth and Fourteenth Amendments to the U.S. Constitution. The trial court ruled against Palazzolo, finding that: (1) he had no right to challenge the regulations that predated his purchase of the property; and (2) he could not claim he was denied all economically beneficial use of his property, since there was undisputed evidence that one of the two parcels had at least $200,000 development value.

The U.S. Supreme Court held that acquisition of title after the effective date of the regulations did not bar the takings claims, and that there was compensation due to the plaintiff pursuant to the takings claim. However, Palazzolo failed to establish a deprivation of all economic value, because one of the parcels was worth at least $200,000 as the potential site of a residence.

Since each of the preceding cases found that a landowner was owed compensation for a governmental "taking," it is reasonable to say that from 1992 until 2001, the U.S. Supreme Court appeared to be willing to gradually expand the protection of private-property rights against government regulation.

However, that trend was apparently not only ended but also reversed in 2002 in *Tahoe Sierra Preservation Council v. Tahoe Regional Planning Agency*, 122 S. Ct. 1465 (2002). The Tahoe Regional Planning Agency was created jointly by the states of Nevada and California. Both states feared that additional development near the lake would reduce water quality and cause permanent environmental damage, and agreed that it would be better if one administrative agency rather than two had authority to deal with problems affecting the entire lake basin. In order to develop a comprehensive land use plan for the lake and its surrounding area, the agency suspended all development on or near the lake for 32 months. Real estate owners sued, claiming that the moratorium constituted a "taking." While the federal district court agreed with the landowners, the COURT OF APPEALS reversed their decision, finding that no "taking" had occurred.

The U.S. Supreme Court agreed with the Court of Appeals' conclusion, holding that the moratorium did not constitute a "taking" of the landowners' property. The high court held that to decide whether a "taking" had occurred, it was necessary to consider landowners' expectations, actual impact, public interest, and reasons for the suspension of development.

The reason for the moratorium was development of a plan that would allow all the lake to maintain its beauty into perpetuity, thereby protecting its present and future economic value, and benefiting all lake-region property owners. Additionally, the moratorium itself was brief in comparison to the expected economic life of the proposed developments. Finally, the Supreme Court concluded that to adopt a rule requiring compensation for every brief deprivation of property usage would impose unreasonable financial obligations upon governments, since landowners could claim they were due compensation for even the normal delays involved in processing land use applications.

While the Supreme Court's ruling appears narrow, it nonetheless marks a significant change from the recent direction of "takings" cases. Instead of taking the logical step of creating a new PRECEDENT to clarify the meaning of "taking," in *Tahoe*, the Supreme Court resurrected the venerable "Penn Central test" (*PENN CENTRAL TRANSPORTATION CO. V. NYC*, 438 U.S. 104 [1978]), that must be performed on a case-by-case basis and requires answers to three questions: (1) the effect of the regulation on the landowner; (2) landowner's reasonable, investment-backed expectations; and (3) character of the government's action. These questions are so broad that they make the outcome of takings cases unpredictable and increase the likelihood that the precedent set by this case is likely to have a broad effect. It could signal that property-rights protection is running out of gas. If anything, it will embolden bureaucratic agencies to resist property-rights challenges to their edicts.

Finally, it should be noted that Justice STEVENS's opinion takes repeated notice of the "essential" nature of local land-use controls, including moratoria. Although he was correct in noting that requiring local governments to compensate the victims of their regulation would turn development prohibitions into a "luxury few governments could afford," in fact, it is very rarely necessary to use multiyear prohibitions on all land use to protect the environment. Additionally, the need to enact local land-use controls to protect our environment concerns does not excuse the government from having to pay for what it takes. In *Tahoe*, no one questioned the government's aims but the tools it chooses to use.

For more information: Adler, Jonathan H. "Property Damage." National Review (May 1, 2002). Available online. URL: http://www.nationalreview.com/adler/adler050102.asp. Downloaded May 14, 2004; Smart Communities Network. "Sustainable Land Use." Energy Efficiency and Renewable Energy Network—U.S. Department of Energy (2003). Available online. URL: http://www.sustainable.doe.gov/landuse/luintro.shtml. Downloaded May 14, 2004; Volokh, Alexander. *"Tahoe-Sierra Preservation Council, Inc. v. Tahoe Regional Planning Agency,* 122 S. Ct. 1465 (2002)." *Harvard Law Review* 16 (2002): 200.

—Beth S. Swartz

Lawrence v. Texas, 539 U.S. 558 (2003)

Lawrence v. Texas is a gay rights case that overruled *BOWERS V. HARDWICK*, 478 U.S. 186 (1986). It reversed a constitutional law that made it a crime to engage in same-sex sodomy. In fact, the majority opinion from the Supreme Court of the United States swept away all existing statutes that made it a crime for two consenting adult persons on private premises to engage in sodomy.

Justice Anthony KENNEDY wrote the U.S. Supreme Court's majority opinion. Justices John Paul STEVENS, David SOUTER, Ruth Bader GINSBURG, and Steven BREYER joined it. It cited evidence that invalidated *Bowers* and said antisodomy statutes applied to consenting adults on private premises violates a person's liberty in the due process clause of the U.S. Constitution's Fourteenth Amendment. Justice Sandra Day O'CONNOR voted with the majority against Texas, but her concurring opinion said it was unnecessary to overrule *Bowers* and that it was sufficient to overrule statutes that targeted homosexuals as a class because they violate the EQUAL PROTECTION CLAUSE in the Fourteenth Amendment. Justice Antonin SCALIA wrote a dissenting opinion, joined by Chief Justice William H. REHNQUIST and Justice Clarence THOMAS. They adhere to *Bowers* because its logic upholds statutes with a RATIONAL BASIS in public morality and because a strict construction of the U.S. Constitution permits that kind of discrimination. Justice Thomas's separate dissent said such statutes are an unworthy way to expend valuable enforcement resources. If he were a legislator, he would vote to repeal them because they are "uncommonly silly."

Houston police responded to a reported weapons disturbance in Lawrence's apartment but saw him and his homosexual partner engaged in sodomy, a misdemeanor, and arrested them. They pleaded no contest to their prosecution, but alleged that the statute violated their Four-teenth Amendment rights guaranteed by the due process and equal protection clauses, and under a similar equal protection provision of the Texas constitution. They lost their case in the Texas court system. On APPEAL to the Court, it considered three questions: (1) whether the Texas statute violates the equal protection clause of the Fourteenth Amendment; (2) whether the criminal convictions based on the statute violate the liberty and privacy protected by the due process clause of the Fourteenth Amendment; and (3) whether *Bowers* should be overruled.

Kennedy's analysis of *Bowers* admitted the moral/religious tradition of disapproval against homosexuality but asserted that a person's privacy was more fundamental and complex in the traditional legal culture of Western civilization and the United States than what the *Bowers* Court acknowledged. He relied on two kinds of evidence available in 1986 not acknowledged by the *Bowers* Court. Most unusual, he cited as legal authority a 1981 decision by the European Court of Human Rights granting a right of privacy for a gay person against Northern Ireland, a decision that bound, as well, all member nations of the Council of Europe through the European Convention on Human Rights. Less controversial, he noted that early American statutes banned all non-procreative sex, even between married individuals. Their enforcement was apparently more against rapists, pedophiles, and bestiality, etc. True, in 1986, about half of the states had antisodomy statutes, but it was not until the 1970s that states began specifically to discriminate against homosexual sodomy.

Kennedy admitted O'Connor's equal protection logic had merit against Texas and the other three states criminalizing homosexual sodomy. He concluded it might be too narrow to stop more states from criminalizing partner-neutral sodomy. O'Connor wrote that was not a practical conclusion. It was more practical to conclude a movement in the states would invalidate all partner-neutral antisodomy bans.

Scholars who have studied Justice Scalia's opinions know his dissents have a sharp rhetorical style and particular philosophical vision. This vision is evident in his *Lawrence* dissent, where he elevates majority will over individuals' noneconomic rights. He argues that *Lawrence* sides with a homosexual agenda in a cultural war against existing disapproval of homosexuality.

Landmark constitutional law decisions prime political campaigns to control law and courts. If contemporary political theorists left and right see things correctly, then the impact of *Lawrence* is a day soon without antihomosexual laws. Congressional Republicans propose a constitutional amendment to ban gay marriage. Presidential candidates will debate whose judicial temperament is a model for the next Supreme Court vacancy. Scholars of law and courts analyze individual justices' votes and written opinions to try to predict future outcomes. In 5-4 decisions, O'Connor has the most pivotal fifth votes, making her the strategic center. Kennedy's opinions outflank her on the left in divided pro-gay rights decisions. In *Eisenstadt,* Justice Potter STEWART adhered to *Griswold,* despite the dissenting words there that Thomas quotes, so if he is Thomas's model, the next pro-gay rights decision might be 7-2.

For more information: Murdoch, Joyce, and Deb Price. *Courting Justice: Gay Men and Lesbians v. the Supreme Court.* New York: Basic Books, 2001; Richards, David A. J. *Identity and the Case for Gay Rights.* Chicago: University of Chicago Press, 1999; Scalia, Antonin. *A Matter of Interpretation: Federal Courts and the Law.* Princeton, N.J.: Princeton University Press, 1997; Schultz, David A., and Christopher A. Smith. *The Jurisprudential Vision of Justice Antonin Scalia.* Lanham, Md.: Rowman and Littlefield, 1996.

—Sharon G. Whitney
—Philip A. Dynia

lawyer advertising

In 1977 the United States Supreme Court decided a landmark case, *Bates v. State Bar of Arizona,* 433 U.S. 350 (1977), that legalized conventional advertising for attorneys nationwide and marked the beginning of a new category and explosive growth in legal advertising in the United States. Since 1977 legal advertising has become one of the largest in the $13.6 billion U.S. Yellow Pages industry. Most lawyers in private practice today use U.S. Yellow Pages advertising. This is in stark contrast to a few decades ago, when lawyer advertising was uncommon and strongly discouraged by bar associations across the country.

In *Bates,* the Supreme Court held that a bar association's prohibition against lawyer advertising was a violation of the First Amendment right of free speech. At the time, very few lawyers advertised their services, due to long-standing tradition and professional codes of conduct that viewed lawyer advertising as detrimental to the profession's honor and prestige. Since the ruling, however, advertising by lawyers has become acceptable to the legal profession as well as the general public. Additionally, legal advertising is branching out from the yellow pages genre and is now fairly common on Internet, television, and radio, and in print media.

California Dental Association v. Federal Trade Commission, Case No. 97-1625 (May 24, 1999), the U.S. Supreme Court's latest pronouncement on advertising by professionals, found the majority and dissenting opinions differing with respect to an antitrust challenge to restrictions on dentists' advertising, but failing to deal with First Amendment issues, and forgetting to clarify matters that have been obscure for too long. Instead, *California Dental Association v. Federal Trade Commission* asks whether a dental society's rules against misleading advertising that prevented dentists from advertising price discounts and service quality violated ANTITRUST LAWS.

The Federal Trade Commission concluded that the California Dental Association's guidelines that intended to restrict truthful, nondeceptive advertising about fees and quality of service violated §5 of the Federal Trade Commission Act, 15 U.S.C. §45. The Ninth Circuit upheld that FTC ruling, but the Supreme Court's review resulted in a remand for further review by the Ninth Circuit.

Because the majority of the Supreme Court dealt with whether the FTC should have used a rule of reason approach, most of the opinion discussed whether the FTC should have used "rule of reason" analysis instead of a "quick look" approach and failed to resolve the matter of whether the association's advertising restraints violated antitrust laws.

However, the majority opinion includes some analysis about professional advertising that will be of interest to all professionals. The Court majority offered this view:

"In a market for professional services, in which advertising is relatively rare and the comparability of service packages not easily established, difficulties in quantification of services or monitoring by individual patients or clients, partly because of the specialized knowledge required to evaluate the services, and partly because of the difficulty in determining whether, and the degree to which, an outcome is attributable to the quality of services (like a poor job of tooth-filling) or to something else (like a very tough walnut)."

Consumers are bombarded with advertising messages of all sorts. Dealing with advertising in all forms has become a crucial survival skill for the times. Many consumers, patients (and lawyers' clients) would welcome much more truthful, nondeceptive information than they currently receive about price and service quality as they are selecting professionals with whom to work.

Some might wish that the professions could find better ways to work in cooperation with consumer and client groups to let information flow more freely. Indeed, in the absence of comparative information available at or before the point of selection of a professional, how is a patient (or client) going to be confident he or she has made a carefully reasoned choice?

The "common view" mentioned in the Supreme Court's majority opinion—that "the lay public is incapable of adequately evaluating the quality of medical services" (or other professional services, for that matter)—is not nearly so "common" as it once was.

For more information: Pritchard, LaVerne. "First Look at U.S. Supreme Court's Latest Case on Professionals' Advertising: *California Dental Association v. Federal Trade Commission,* No. 97-1625." Pritchard Law Webs. Available online. URL: http://www.priweb.com/legalethics3.htm.

—Beth S. Swartz

Lee v. Weisman, 505 U.S. 577 (1992)

In *Lee v. Weisman,* the Supreme Court of the United States held that nonsectarian prayers performed at voluntary public school graduations are unconstitutional. Robert E. Lee, the principal of Nathan Bishop Middle School in Providence, Rhode Island, invited Rabbi Gutterman to give the invocation and benediction for the school's graduation exercises. It had become customary for the school district to invite local clergy to solemnize the voluntary ceremony, which is held on school grounds. Principal Lee gave the rabbi a pamphlet which gave guidance for writing public prayers at civic ceremonies and advised him to keep the prayers nonsectarian.

At the graduation, the rabbi gave an invocation saying, in part: "God of the free, Hope of the Brave: . . . For the destiny of America, we thank You . . . Amen." The rabbi closed the ceremony giving a benediction which said in part: "O God, we are grateful to You for having endowed us with the capacity for learning . . . We give thanks to You, Lord, for keeping us alive, sustaining us, and allowing us to reach this special, happy, occasion. Amen." Daniel Weisman, whose daughter was in the graduation ceremony, filed suit to prevent such prayers at future graduations. The federal district court ruled the school district's practice unconstitutional and the COURT OF APPEALS upheld the district court's decision. Principal Lee and the school district appealed the decision to the Supreme Court of the United States.

The Supreme Court, in a divided five to four decision, held that the school's practice violated the First Amendment's ESTABLISHMENT CLAUSE that forbids excessive government involvement in RELIGION. First, the school's involvement in the prayer was too extensive. It decided that an invocation and benediction be given, it chose the rabbi to deliver the prayers, and it directed the content of the prayers by providing the rabbi with the prayer guide pamphlet and advising him to keep the prayers nonsectarian. Second, graduating students experienced subtle coercive pressure to either participate in the prayers or remain respectfully silent during the prayers. There was no way to either avoid participating or avoid the appearance of participating. The majority asserted that the state must not put a student dissenter in the position of either participating in the prayer or protesting. And finally, the majority argued that the fact that the ceremony was voluntary did not eliminate the inherent coercion. Participating in school graduation is one of life's most significant occasions and thus, in practicality, it is not voluntary.

Four justices dissented from the majority opinion and challenged its reasoning. The dissenting justices argued that the majority opinion was wrong and destroyed an important American tradition. Public schools had been allowing nonsectarian prayers to God at public ceremonies for years. Moreover, they argued that the majority's claim of coercion did not make sense and was not scientifically grounded. Coercion only exists when acts are "backed by threat of penalty." Lastly, the dissenters claimed the majority opinion was "only a jurisprudential disaster and not a practical one." They stated that all the schools needed to do to comply with the majority opinion is to announce that "while all are asked to rise for the invocation and benediction, none is compelled to join in them, nor will be assumed, by rising, to have done so."

For more information: Epstein, Lee, and Thomas G. Walker. *Constitutional Law for a Changing America: Rights, Liberties, and Justice.* 4th ed. Washington, D.C.: CQ Press, 2001.

—Keith Rollin Eakins

Legal Services Corporation v. Velazquez, 531 U.S. 533 (2001)

In *Legal Services Corporation v. Velazquez,* the United States Supreme Court ruled that a law barring a federally funded legal services corporation from challenging the then existing welfare laws was a violation of its First Amendment free speech rights. This decision was an important limitation upon the ability of the government to restrict the free speech rights of individuals and organizations, even if the government provides money to the latter.

The free speech clause of the First Amendment is supposed to prevent the government from limiting the ability of the people to speak their minds or express their own views on a wide range of issues. However, the Supreme Court has recognized that not all forms of communication are considered "speech" under the First Amendment, such as obscenity. There are also situations where the government can place some limits on either the time, manner, or place where speech is expressed, such as restriction on the use of loudspeakers or megaphones at night in parks. However, there is some question regarding whether the government can limit the individual right to free speech if government funds are involved.

In *Rust v. Sullivan*, 500 U.S. 173 (1991), the Supreme Court upheld a rule restricting the ability of doctors employed by federally funded family planning clinics from counseling or discussing abortion with their patients. In that case the Court stated that there was no viewpoint discrimination in prohibiting discussion of abortion because the government had a right to create the clinics and then define the limits regarding how the money is used. Specifically, it had a right to say that its money could not be used for abortions or even counseling patients on abortion. Thus, *Rust* appeared to mean that the government could place limits on how its money is used, even if it appeared to restrict what physicians said to their patients.

Using *Rust v. Sullivan* as a PRECEDENT, when Congress passed the 1996 Omnibus Consolidated Rescissions and Appropriations Act, this law contained a new provision that made it illegal for a federally funded legal service corporation to challenge the constitutionality or legality of any federal or state welfare law. Lawyers representing the New York City Legal Services Corporation grantees challenged the restriction in federal district court as a form of viewpoint discrimination under the First Amendment and the court struck down the law. The second circuit COURT OF APPEALS agreed and issued an injunction preventing enforcement of the law. The case was appealed to the Supreme Court, which upheld the lower court ruling.

Writing for the Court, Justice Kennedy sought to distinguish this case from *Rust v. Sullivan*. He argued that in *Rust* the concern of the Court was to be sure that in situations when the government is using public funds and it seeks to communicate its own message by using private actors or persons, it may place some limits on these individuals to ensure that the government's message is not "garbled" or "distorted." In effect, the government may spend its own money to convey its own message, and it is not a form of viewpoint discrimination to then limit the speech of the speaker.

However, Kennedy saw the limits on the legal services corporation in a different light. Besides contending that a limit on lawyers' free speech rights might make it more difficult for them to provide an adequate and fair defense, he also argued that this limit on free speech rights might impede the ability of the courts to find the truth that occurs by way of attorneys aggressively advocating for their clients. Most important, Kennedy and the Court asserted that unlike *Rust*, where government funds were being used to articulate its message, this was not the case in *Velazquez*. Here the speech on the part of the attorneys was clearly private, and there was little chance that the comments or arguments by them would distort or garble any views held by the government. In effect, these federally funded legal service corporation attorneys were not private actors being hired to communicate the viewpoint of the government. They were instead private individuals expressing their own views to represent their clients. The government had no ability to use its funding power to restrict the First Amendment rights of these individuals.

Legal Services Corporation v. Velazquez is an important First Amendment free speech case. It stands for the proposition that simply receiving public money does not necessarily entitle the government to limit private persons in their ability to express their own personal views. It is unclear, however, whether *Rust v. Sullivan* is still a valid ruling in light of *Velazquez*. While the Supreme Court did try to distinguish doctors counseling patients in federally funded clinics and lawyers representing clients in federally funded legal service clinics, some would argue that there is no real difference and that therefore the distinction between the two is insignificant, thereby questioning whether *Rust* is still good law.

For more information: Kramer, Daniel C. *The Price of Rights: The Courts, Government Largess, and Fundamental Liberties.* New York: Peter Lang, 2003.

—David Schultz

legislative standing

"Standing to sue," according to *Black's Law Dictionary*, means that a party has sufficient stake in an otherwise justiciable controversy to obtain judicial resolution of that controversy. In discussing "legislative standing," this entry will focus on the standing of legislators and, in particular, of members of Congress in the federal courts.

In the 1970s members of Congress began to use the courts, rather than the political process, to attempt to resolve disputes with the executive branch. The dramatic increase in congressional lawsuits was directly related to the dramatic increase in executive power. Although this rise in executive power occurred largely because of express delegations from Congress and with tacit congressional approval, Congress began to respond to this challenge by designing innovative techniques for controlling the executive branch and executive agencies (e.g., the creation of the Congressional Budget Office, the legislative veto, and the submission of amicus curiae briefs).

Most congressional suits have been dismissed by the federal courts, either because Congress had alleged no injury in fact and, therefore, lacked standing to sue or because the issues involved were held to be nonjusticiable "political questions." One of the difficulties with legislators' suits is the subject matter of the suits themselves. Consider some of the suits filed by members of Congress during those early cases in the 1970s. Members challenged the constitutionality of the Vietnam War, e.g., *Mitchell v. Laird,*

488 F. 2d. 611 (D.C. Cir. 1973); the legality of ending economic sanctions against Rhodesia, *Diggs v. Shultz,* 470 F. 2d. 461 (D.C. Cir. 1973); the validity of a "pocket veto," *Kennedy v. Sampson,* 364 F. Supp. 1075 (D.D.C. 1973); the authority of the executive branch to withhold information relating to the nuclear tests at Amchitka Island, Alaska, *Environmental Protection Agency v. Mink,* 410 U.S. 73 (1973); the legality of firing Watergate Special Prosecutor Cox by Acting Attorney General BORK, *Nader v. Bork,* 366 F. Supp. 104 (D.D.C. 1973); granting the House of Representatives the right to vote on the cession of the Panama Canal, *Edwards v. Carter,* 436 U.S. 907 (1978); and continuing the effect of mutual defense treaty with Taiwan despite presidential action terminating it, GOLDWATER V. CARTER, 444 U.S. 996 (1979). These sorts of issues tend to be avoided by the federal courts as non-justiciable "political questions," and federal courts have imposed more rigorous standing requirements in order to avoid hearing these legislative lawsuits. [See *Baker v. Carr,* 369 U.S. 186 (1962), for more about the "political questions" doctrine.]

Legislators do have standing to claim they have been deprived of something to which they are personally entitled. For example, in *Powell v. McCormack,* 396 U.S. 486 (1969), the Supreme Court allowed review of a congressman's claim based on lost salary resulting from his unlawful exclusion from Congress.

However, in the leading case concerning legislative standing, *Raines v. Byrd,* 421 U.S. 811 (1997), the Court took a formalistic approach and substantially restricted the ability of members of Congress to seek redress of grievances in the federal courts. In this case, Senator Byrd and five other members of Congress brought suit, alleging that the Line Item Veto Act violated Article I of the Constitution. The Court held that the members of Congress did not have a sufficient personal stake in the dispute and had not alleged a sufficiently concrete injury to have established standing under Article III. The Court held that an "especially rigorous" standing requirement is needed "when reaching the merits of the dispute would force [a constitutional decision in an inter-branch conflict]" and that an "institutional injury," such as the alleged diminution of voting power alone is insufficient to confer standing and that the federal judiciary should not intervene in suits involving congressional plaintiffs if other collegial remedies, such as legislative repeal or suspension, have not yet been exhausted.

Raines created two systems of standing, one for non-legislative plaintiffs, and a stricter one for members of Congress who are precluded from establishing standing on the basis of the more lenient injury test. Critics of the *Raines* decision claim that the Court's drastic limitation of congressional standing through the personal injury requirement will invite the very phenomenon that it sought to avoid—the erosion of our system of checks and balances.

However, the denial of standing in *Raines* does not foreclose all congressional standing. For example, if Congress passed a law forbidding first-term members from voting on appropriations bills or any member from voting on projects in his or her own district, the Court suggested that such members might have standing on the ground that their vote was nullified or denied in a discriminatory manner. In *Raines,* the Court held that challenges by members "solely because they are members of Congress" would lack sufficient grounds for standing.

For more information: Alexander, James I. "Note and Comment: No Place to Stand: The Supreme Court's Refusal to Address the Merits of Congressional Members' Line-Item Veto Challenge in *Raines v. Byrd.*" *Journal of Law & Policy* 6 (1998): 653–698; Black, Henry Campbell. *Black's Law Dictionary.* St. Paul, Minn.: West, 1990; Blank, Adam L. "Casenote: Raines v. Byrd: A Death Knell for the Congressional Suit?" *Mercer Law Review* 49 (Winter 1998): 609–624; Devins, Neal, and Michael A. Fitts. "The Triumph of Timing: *Raines v. Byrd* and the Modern Supreme Court's Attempt to Control Constitutional Confrontations." *Georgetown Law Journal* 86 (November 1997): 351–375; McGowan, Carl. "Congressmen in Court: The New Plaintiffs." *Georgia Law Review* 15, no. 2 (Winter 1981): 241–267; Meyer, Carlin. "Imbalance of Powers: Can Congressional Lawsuits Serve as Counterweight?" *University of Pittsburgh Law Review* 54 (Fall 1992): 63–128; "Note: Standing to Sue for Members of Congress." *Yale Law Journal* 83 (July 1974): 1,665–1,688; "Note: Congressional Access to the Federal Courts." *Harvard Law Review* 90 (1977): 1,632–1,655; "Note: Standing in the Way of Separation of Powers: The Consequences of *Raines v. Byrd.*" *Harvard Law Review* 112 (May 1999): 1,741–1,758; Scalia, Antonin. "The Doctrine of Standing as an Essential Element of the Separation of Powers." *Suffolk University Law Review* XVII (1983): 882–899; Scourfield, Judithanne V. "Congressional Participation as *Amicus Curiae* before the U.S. Supreme Court during the Warren, Burger, and Rehnquist Courts (October Terms 1,953–1,997)." PhD dissertation, Rutgers University, 2003; Sullivan, Kathleen M., and Gerald Gunther. *Constitutional Law.* 14th ed. New York: Foundation Press, 2001; Weiner, David J. "The New Law of Legislative Standing," *Stanford Law Review* 54 (October 2001): 205–234.

—Judithanne Scourfield McLauchlan

Lemon v. Kurtzman, 403 U.S. 602 (1971)

Lemon v. Kurtzman declared unconstitutional state financial assistance to church-related elementary and secondary schools. From this case came the *"Lemon"* test, which has been subsequently applied to similar questions addressing the entanglement of church and state when government aid was provided to religious schools.

Lemon v. Kurtzman was a consolidation of two separate lower court cases. The first lower court case involved a Rhode Island statute, *R.I. Pen. Laws Ann. 16-51-1 et seq.* (Supp. 1970), authorizing the state to pay a supplement (up to 15 percent of salary) to teachers of nonpublic schools who taught secular subjects in those schools. The statute's purpose was to address the finding that the quality of education in nonpublic schools was at risk due to the rapidly rising salaries needed to attract and retain competent teachers in those schools. The other lower court case involved a Pennsylvania statute, *Pa. Stat. Ann., Tit. 24, ss 5601–5609* (Supp. 1971). This statute authorized the state to directly reimburse nonpublic schools for actual expenditures related to teachers' salaries, textbooks, and instructional materials for the teaching of secular subjects in those schools. The stated purpose of the statute was to address the perceived crisis in nonpublic schools due to rapidly rising expenses. Plaintiffs challenged these statutes authorizing government involvement with religious schools, claiming they were contrary to the establishment clause of the First Amendment to the United States Constitution. That amendment states "Congress shall make no law respecting an establishment of religion. . . ."

The analysis used by Chief Justice BURGER in this case has come to be known as the *Lemon* Test. This three-prong analysis requires a consideration of the following: (1) The statute must have a secular legislative purpose; (2) The principal or primary effect of the statute must be one that neither advances nor inhibits RELIGION; (3) The statute must not foster an excessive government entanglement with religion.

In applying this analysis to the Rhode Island statute, the court found excessive government entanglement in two areas—the need for state government monitoring of church school teachers' classroom conduct necessary under the statute, and state government review of church school financial records to determine the amount of money spent on secular v. religious education. The Pennsylvania statute suffered from the same problems, magnified by the provision concerning direct payment to the religious schools. Both state statutes, therefore, failed the third prong of the *Lemon* Test. The statutes were ruled unconstitutional.

The *Lemon* Test has stood for more than 30 years. In the 1980s and 1990s the Court in some cases began to blur the distinction between the second prong concerning whether the primary effect of the statute advances religion and the third prong concerning whether the statute fosters an excessive government entanglement with religion. [See *Agostini v. Felton*, 521 U.S. 203 (1997)]. However, the *Lemon* test has not been overruled and remains an integral part of the analysis in these cases.

For more information: David A. Schultz. "Church and State Relations and the First Amendment." In *Law and Politics: Unanswered Questions*, edited by David A. Schultz. New York: Peter Lang, 1994, 235–236.

—Scott Childs

liberty of contract

Liberty of contract was a legal doctrine constructed by the Supreme Court in the 19th century that placed limits on the ability of the government to regulate working conditions.

As the United States industrialized during the 19th century, state governments began passing regulations of business and labor. These included minimum wage laws, maximum working hour laws, and work safety regulations. These laws came under attack before the Supreme Court as violations of the Fourteenth Amendment's due process clause. This clause prohibited taking life, liberty, or property without due process. The Court considered whether the liberty portion of the clause included the right to contract out for work.

In *ALLGEYER V. LOUISIANA* (1897), a unanimous Court defined a new liberty of contract. Speaking for the Court, Justice Rufus Peckham struck down a Louisiana law prohibiting out-of-state marine insurance. In making the ruling, Peckham defined the liberty to contract as freedom to enjoy one's faculties, to live and work as they wish, to pursue any livelihood, and to enter into any contracts essential for their life. Such a broad reading of liberty would place the Court in opposition to many state laws regulating economic life.

Yet the liberty of contract was not an absolute right. The next year in *Holden v. Hardy* (1898) the Court upheld a Utah law regulating the working hours and wages of miners. The seven-member majority found that mining was dangerous work and that the state regulation of it was protecting the health, safety, and welfare of its citizens. In such cases, the liberty of contract could be restrained by state law.

The health, safety, and welfare exception to liberty of contract was narrowed in *LOCHNER V. NEW YORK* (1905). In *Lochner*, five justices struck down a New York law limiting working hours and regulating working conditions of bakers. Justice Peckham wrote the decision, finding that baking was not a dangerous occupation, unlike mining, and that the law was benefiting special interests rather than the overall health, safety, and welfare of the people of New York.

Lochner was undermined three years later by the decision in *MULLER V. OREGON* (1908). In *Muller*, the Court unanimously upheld an Oregon law limiting working hours for women in the laundry business. The decision found that the liberty of contract did not extend to women because their gender made them weaker and more vulnerable and that the state had to step in to protect them and their maternal function of caring for children.

Fifteen years later the same issue of special laws protecting women in the workplace came before the Court. In *ADKINS V. CHILDRENS HOSPITAL* (1923), the Washington, D.C., government set maximum working hours and a minimum wage for women. Unlike in *Muller,* the Court struck down this law. According to Justice SUTHERLAND, the Nineteenth Amendment had granted women the right to vote and had given them political power. With that power they no longer required the special protection of the government as found in wage and working hours laws. The law was only special interest legislation protecting women, rather than protecting the community's health, safety, and welfare. It violated the women's rights to liberty to contract.

As the 1920s advanced, liberty to contract became a less popular tool for the Court in striking down state and federal legislation. It was not until the 1930s and the New Deal that states began passing more restrictive laws on prices, wages, and working conditions and the justices revived liberty of contract. In *Morehead v. Tipaldo* (1936), the Court struck down a New York State law setting a minimum wage for women. In the decision, Justice Butler ruled the law was similar to the one struck down in *ADKINS* and violated the right of women and their employers to contract out for wages.

Liberty to contract came under direct attack in 1936 as Franklin Roosevelt offered a Court reform plan that would have packed the Court with his supporters. The Court responded by opposing the president's plan but also by reconsidering its dedication to the liberty of contract. In *WEST COAST HOTEL V. PARRISH* (1937), five justices upheld a Washington State minimum wage law. In his opinion, Chief Justices HUGHES stated that he could not find the liberty of contract anywhere in the Constitution and that as far as he was concerned it did not exist and could not be used in future cases. Parrish was the end of the liberty to contract. While litigants in future cases would use it to challenge state laws, the Court never again used that liberty as a basis for ruling a law unconstitutional.

For more information: Ely, James. *The Chief Justiceship of Melville W. Fuller.* Columbia: University of South Carolina Press, 1995; Gillman, Howard. *The Constitution Besieged.* Durham, N.C.: Duke University Press, 1993; Paul, Ellen, and Howard Dickman, eds. *Liberty, Property and Government.* New York: State University of New York Press, 1989.

—Douglas Clouatre

lie detector tests

Lie detector tests are devices that are used to render diagnostic opinions of the veracity of an individual. Such devices include polygraphs, voice stress analyzers, and psychological stress evaluators. The utilization of lie detector tests and their results is strictly regulated by federal, state, and local laws, particularly in the courtroom and in the employment arena.

The evolution of the law regarding the admissibility of polygraph evidence began with the seminal case of *Frye v. United States,* 293 F. 1013 (D.C. Cir. 1923). Frye appealed his murder conviction on the grounds that the trial court had erroneously excluded defense evidence of a systolic blood pressure deception test, a precursor of the modern polygraph. The appellate court grappled with the question of when novel SCIENTIFIC EVIDENCE moves from the experimental to the established and concluded that such evidence must have gained general acceptance in the particular field in which it belongs. The *Frye* court held that the systolic blood pressure deception test had not gained sufficient acceptance in the psychological and physiological communities and upheld the lower court's inadmissibility ruling.

For 70 years following *Frye,* the general acceptance in the scientific community standard led to a per se rule of inadmissibility for polygraph evidence in a majority of jurisdictions, although some courts allowed the evidence if both parties stipulated to its use, and a very few jurisdictions, most notably New Mexico, rejected the exclusionary trend. However, in 1993 the U.S. Supreme Court altered the standard for evaluating the admissibility of expert scientific testimony. In *DAUBERT V. MERRELL-DOW PHARMACEUTICALS, Inc.,* 509 U.S. 579 (1993), the Court held that the restrictive *Frye* test was trumped by the Federal Rules of Evidence, particularly Rule 702, which allows expert testimony if it is based on specialized knowledge and will assist the trier of fact. The mere fact that the opinion of the scientific community may be divided is not an automatic bar to admission; more important factors include the underlying theory or technique's ability to be tested, the known rate of error, the history of peer review and publication, the level of acceptance in the scientific community, and the existence of standards for determining acceptable use.

Nevertheless, in spite of the acknowledgment by some federal courts that a reevaluation of the admissibility of polygraphs was called for, the majority of post-*Daubert* opinions expressed significant reluctance to change their exclusionary positions, preferring to rely on the fundamental principle that the jury is the lie detector.

In 1998 the U.S. Supreme Court gave some support to the exclusionary jurisdictions when it upheld a per se ban on polygraph evidence in military courts. In *United States v. Sheffer,* 523 U.S. 303 (1998), a plurality of the Court rejected the argument that the EXCLUSIONARY RULE was prohibited by the Sixth Amendment right of the accused to present evidence. However, four justices found the rule unwise and indicated that a later case involving different circumstances might compel another result. In the meantime, however, the trend of lower court decisions has been to exclude polygraph evidence, although lie detector results are frequently used by law enforcement, prosecutors, and other government officials in various decision-making stages, such as determinations of probable cause for arrests.

In contrast to the legal uncertainty of polygraph use in the courtroom, lie detectors have a comparatively clearly defined status in the employment arena due to the 1988 passage of the Employee Polygraph Protection Act (EPPA), 29, U.S.C. Sections 2001, *et seq.* The act makes it unlawful for any employer engaged in or affecting commerce to use lie detector tests on employees or prospective employees or to discharge, discipline, or deny employment or promotions based on the results of any such test. However, the exceptions to the prohibitions are critical. The EPPA does not apply to any governmental entity, and, in fact, government agencies such as the U.S. Department of Defense, the Central Intelligence Agency, and local police departments routinely depend on polygraph testing of employees. Furthermore, private employers are permitted to request an employee to submit to a polygraph as part of an ongoing investigation involving economic loss or injury to the employer's business. Additionally, employers engaged in security services or in the manufacture or distribution of controlled substances may use polygraph tests. However, these private employers may not take an adverse action against an employee or prospective employee if the results of the polygraph test are the sole basis for the action. The requirement that there be additional supporting evidence underscores the law's continuing attempts to balance the benefits of polygraphic science against the potential dangers of overdependence.

For more information: Bradley, Robert C. *Science, Technology, and Criminal Justice.* New York: Peter Lang, 2004.

Lochner v. New York, 198 U.S. 45 (1905)

Lochner v. New York is one of the most well known decisions rendered by the Supreme Court, normally being viewed as a high point in the assertion of the Court's willingness to exercise SUBSTANTIVE DUE PROCESS and a primary example of the LIBERTY OF CONTRACT doctrine.

The case involved a challenge to a New York state law that prohibited bakery employees from working more than 10 hours per day or 60 hours per week. Lochner owned a bakery in Utica, New York, and was prosecuted for violating the bakery law, in terms of having employees work more than 60 hours a week. Lochner availed himself of the courts to challenge the validity of the law. In 1905 the United States Supreme Court heard the case.

Justice Rufus Peckham wrote the majority opinion in a case that featured stirring dissents and a closely divided court (a 5-4 decision). The majority followed the ALL-GEYER V. LOUISIANA, 165 U.S. 578 (1897), decision. Justice Peckham begins by noting that liberty of contract is protected by the Fourteenth Amendment, in that individuals have the right to purchase or sell labor without undue interference. In this instance, the state has abrogated the liberty, asserting that its decision is based on the state's POLICE POWERS, the authority relating to "the safety, morals, and general welfare of the public." Peckham and the majority carried out a balancing test—weighing the liberty of contract versus the state's police power. In the end, they believed that the balance must be decided in favor of liberty of contract.

First, according to Peckham, the law appears to try to directly regulate one industry, and there is no reason to single out bakeries as opposed to other industries. Second, Peckham notes that the state alleges that its legitimate interest is the health and welfare of the public; hence, laws designed to make the populace healthier are a valid exercise of the police power. The majority opinion concludes as to this point that it is not clear that there is, in fact, a direct relation between the law and the health of employees to justify the law being upheld.

Justice John Marshall HARLAN (with whom Justices WHITE and Day concurred) dissented, contending that the state had properly exercised its police power to protect the physical well-being of those working in bakeries. He goes on to claim: "Whether or not this be wise legislation, it is not the province of the court to inquire." Justice Oliver Wendell HOLMES also dissented, observing that the majority opinion is underlain by a particular economic theory, social Darwinism. Holmes goes on to state that the Court should not be in the business of supporting one social theory over another. In a famous statement, he asserts that: "The Fourteenth Amendment does not enact Mr. Herbert Spencer's Social Statics."

Lochner is an important case, in that it marks a key point in the evolution of the Court's support of the market against government regulation. The majority opinion is normally interpreted as one of the classic examples of substantive due process in operation. From the time of this decision into the 1930s, the Supreme Court struck down a number of laws under the logic of substantive due process.

For more information: Friedman, Lawrence M. *A History of American Law.* New York: Simon and Schuster, 1973; Schwartz, Bernard. *A History of the Supreme Court.* New York: Oxford University Press, 1993.

—Steven A. Peterson

Locke v. Davey, 540 U.S. 712 (2004)

Locke v. Davey stated that public scholarships can exclude devotional religious studies without violating the First Amendment's free exercise of RELIGION clause.

Washington State offers its lower income, higher achieving residents the Promise Scholarship, which Joshua Davey was awarded in 1999. Davey chose to go to a college affiliated with his Assembly of God denomination, Northwest College. He chose a double major in pastoral ministries and business, at which point the college informed Davey his choice of major would sacrifice his state scholarship, according to state constitutional law. Davey brought suit, arguing the free exercise, establishment, and free speech clauses of the Constitution do not allow laws to discriminate against students because of their choice of a religious major. The Federal COURT OF APPEALS for the ninth circuit agreed, saying the state singled out the religious for unfavorable treatment and that this exclusion was not narrowly tailored enough to pass the COMPELLING STATE INTEREST test.

Chief Justice REHNQUIST wrote for the 7-2 majority overturning the ninth circuit that the case represents a conundrum. The First Amendment states that Congress cannot "establish a religion" nor can it "prohibit the free exercise" of religion. "These two clauses are frequently in tension," Rehnquist stated. "In other words, there are some actions permitted by the ESTABLISHMENT CLAUSE but not required by the free exercise clause." On the one hand, recent religion cases have shown that when public funds and religious training mix, it is not a violation of the establishment clause if the mix came about because of an "independent and private choice of the recipient." [See *Zelman v. Simmons-Harris,* 536 U.S. 639 (2002); ZOBREST V. CATALINA FOOTHILLS SCHOOL DIST., 509 U.S. 1 (1993)]. The question in *Davey* is not whether states can provide the funding, but can states "deny them such funding without violating the free exercise clause."

If the Court accepted Davey's point that the scholarship applicants were in a PUBLIC FORUM, then Washington would have to satisfy the strictest level of scrutiny in justifying the discrimination against religious students. "But the Promise Scholarship Program is not a forum for speech. The purpose of the Promise Scholarship Program is to assist students from low- and middle-income families with the cost of postsecondary education, not to 'encourage a diversity of views from private speakers.' . . . Our cases dealing with speech forums are simply inapplicable," said Rehnquist, quoting *U.S. v. American Library Assn., Inc.,* 539 U.S. 194 (2003). "The state is merely choosing not to fund a distinct category of instruction." Since the case is not a question of the equal protection of those acting on their religion, the Court asked Washington to show simply a rational basis for its decision, which it did in pointing to the state constitution's ban on funding religious training.

Justice SCALIA's fiery dissent accuses the decision of failing to protect a religious minority—the religiously devout, as opposed to those who hold a "tepid, civic version of faith." After arguing against the majority's reasons for doing this, Scalia writes, "No, the interest with which the Court defers is not fear of an Establishment Clause violation, budget constraint, avoidance of endorsement, or substantive neutrality—none of these. It is a pure philosophical preference: the State's opinion that it would violate taxpayers' freedom of conscience *not* to discriminate against candidates for the ministry." Washington "created a generally available public benefit" and then "carved out a solitary course of study for exclusion: theology."

Locke is interesting in part because it apparently limits how far the Christian Free Speech strategy can go. In previous cases before the Court, Virginia, New York, and Nebraska, as well as other states, shied away from mixing public money and property with its religious usage, until the Court called it discrimination, where Evangelical college student group newspapers must be considered for funding if all other student groups are. *LAMB'S CHAPEL V. CENTER MORICHES SCHOOL DISTRICT,* 508 U.S. 384 (1993), and *Board of Education of the Westside Community Schools v. Mergens,* 496 U.S. 226 (1990), ruled that when public buildings are opened to public groups, religious groups must not be excluded. So states hoping to keep church and state separate may end up violating the free exercise clause, but as *Locke* shows, not always.

For more information: Brown, Stephen P. *Trumping Religion: The New Christian Right, the Free Speech Clause, and the Courts.* Tuscaloosa: University of Alabama Press, 2002.

—David Claborn

Loving v. Virginia, 388 U.S. 1 (1967)

In *Loving v. Virginia,* the Supreme Court ruled that Virginia's prohibition of interracial marriages violated the EQUAL PROTECTION CLAUSE of the Fourteenth Amendment. In this case the WARREN Court extended its equal protection doctrine to strike down one element of RACIAL DISCRIMINATION in the social framework of many U.S. states.

Two Virginia residents, Mildred Jeter, an African-American woman, and Richard Loving, a Caucasian man, were married in Washington, D.C., in June 1968. Upon returning to Virginia they were indicted for violating that state's law prohibiting interracial marriage. The Lovings pled guilty and were sentenced to one year in prison. This sentence was suspended on the condition that the Lovings leave the state for 25 years. In the opinion issuing this sentence the trial judge asserted, "[t]he fact that [God] separated the races shows that he did not intend for the races to mix" (388 U.S. at 3).

Chief Justice Earl Warren delivered the opinion for the unanimous Supreme Court striking down the Virginia laws prohibiting and voiding interracial marriage. While marriage is traditionally within the state's area of control, that control cannot contravene express constitutional prohibitions such as the equal protection clause of the Fourteenth Amendment. Virginia argued that, because the statute punishes members of each race equally, it is not based upon a racial classification and the Court should employ the RATIONAL BASIS test when considering its validity. The Court rejected this argument. It pointed to the Virginia Supreme Court's opinions upholding the laws in order "'to preserve the racial integrity of its citizens,' and to prevent . . . 'a mongrel breed of citizens,' and 'the obliteration of racial pride'" (388 U.S. at 7, quoting *Naim v. Naim,* 197 Va. 80, 87 S.E.2d 749 [1955]). It concluded, therefore, that "equal application does not immunize the statute from the very heavy burden of justification which the Fourteenth Amendment has traditionally required of state statutes drawn according to race" (388 U.S. at 9). It employed the STRICT SCRUTINY test and found that there "is patently no legitimate overriding purpose independent of invidious racial discrimination which justifies this classification" (388 U.S. at 11).

The Court also held that Virginia's laws violate the due process clause of the Fourteenth Amendment. "The freedom to marry," the Court asserts, "has long been recognized as one of the vital personal rights essential to the orderly pursuit of happiness by free men" (388 U.S. at 12). Virginia's laws unconstitutionally interfered with the exercise of that right. Chief Justice Warren wrote that to "deny this fundamental freedom on so unsupportable a basis as the racial classifications embodied in these statutes, classifications so directly subversive of the principle of equality at the heart of the Fourteenth Amendment, is surely to deprive all the State's citizens of liberty without due process of law" (388 U.S. at 12).

For more information: O'Brien, David. *Constitutional Law and Politics: Volume 2.* 5th ed. New York: W. W. Norton, 2003.

—Jeffrey Davis

Lucas v. South Carolina Coastal Council, 505 U.S. 1003 (1992)

In *Lucas v. South Carolina Coastal Council,* the U.S. Supreme Court held that a law that deprives a landowner of all economically viable use of his land violates the last clause of the Fifth Amendment. This clause, the TAKINGS CLAUSE, prohibits the taking of private property for a public use without just compensation. *Lucas* addressed whether a law designed to protect public safety and property can prohibit a landowner from developing his property, without the government having to compensate the landowner for lost development rights.

In 1986 David Lucas purchased two of the last four undeveloped oceanfront lots in a development on Isle of Palms, South Carolina, for $975,000. Mr. Lucas intended to build single family homes on the lots, which would have been allowed under the existing ZONING regulations. The shoreline in this area was notoriously unstable, with all or a part of the lots underwater for half of the past 40 years. In 1988 South Carolina adopted the Beachfront Management Act (BMA) to protect the beach/dune system that serves as a storm barrier to dissipate wave energy and stabilize the shoreline. The BMA established a minimum setback from the ocean for new development and authorized no variances or exceptions. The setback requirement prevented Mr. Lucas from building any homes on the lots. Mr. Lucas sued the South Carolina Coastal Council (SCCC), the state agency that administered the BMA, alleging that the setback requirement violated the takings clause. The trial court awarded Mr. Lucas $1.2 million, but the South Carolina Supreme Court reversed the trial court's decision.

The U.S. Supreme Court, in a 6-2 decision (one justice filed a statement) written by Justice SCALIA, ruled that when a law denies a landowner all economically beneficial use of his property, the law violates the takings clause and a court does not need to examine the public purpose behind the law. The Court did recognize a narrow exception: when the contested law prohibits an activity that a state's property and nuisance law already prohibited, the regulation does not violate the takings clause since state law already forbids the landowner from engaging in the activity. When the Court examined the BMA's setback restriction, it found that the restrictions deprived Mr. Lucas of all the economically beneficial use of his property. The U.S. Supreme Court remanded the case to the South Carolina courts to determine if the narrow state property and nuisance law exception applied, and Mr. Lucas was prohibited from building on the lots before the BMA was enacted. The lower court eventually determined it did not and found for Mr. Lucas.

Justice Scalia's opinion states that regulations that are so restrictive that they render property valueless and violate the takings clause are relatively rare. However, in recent years the Supreme Court has adjudicated a number of cases that, taken as a group, have significantly increased protection for private property rights.

For more information: Callies, David L., ed. *After Lucas: Land Use Regulation and the Taking of Property without Compensation.* Chicago: Section of Urban, State, and Local Government Law, American Bar Association, 1993.

—Robert W. Malmsheimer

Lujan v. Defenders of Wildlife, 504 U.S. 555 (1992)

In *Lujan v. Defenders of Wildlife,* the Supreme Court held that Congress cannot statutorily eliminate the constitutional requirement that in order to maintain STANDING a person must have suffered a concrete injury.

Article III of the U.S. Constitution requires that there be an actual CASE OR CONTROVERSY in any action brought before the courts. Part of the case or controversy requirement is that a person must have standing; that is, they must have suffered, or can prove they will suffer, a direct and personal injury caused by some unlawful government action, and that the courts are capable of redressing that injury.

The Defenders of Wildlife, an environmental group, along with other groups, sued the secretary of the Interior to enjoin an administrative regulation that exempted government-funded projects in foreign nations from compliance with the Endangered Species Act (ESA). The group sued under a provision of the ESA that authorized "any person" to sue to prevent a government action that may be likely to jeopardize endangered species.

To satisfy the standing requirement the groups alleged that group members had traveled to Egypt and Sri Lanka to observe endangered species and intended to return to both countries to continue observing the species, and that the members would suffer harm as a result of U.S. projects in the areas that were likely to endanger or threaten the species.

In its opinion the court made several holdings on the standing issue. Among its holdings were that an organization cannot maintain standing based on a claim that any person visits or uses an ecosystem that has been or may be affected by government activity. That an organization cannot maintain standing based on a claim that any person has an interest in studying a threatened or endangered species anywhere in the world and as such has standing. That an organization cannot maintain standing based on a claim that any person with a professional interest in threatened or endangered species alleges standing. And finally, that an organization cannot maintain standing based solely on the citizen suit provision of the ESA absent a showing of an actual injury.

Specifically addressing the citizen suit provision of the ESA, the court stated that allowing Congress "to convert the undifferentiated public interest in executive officers' compliance with the law into an 'individual right' vindicable in the

courts is to permit Congress to transfer from the president to the courts the chief executive's most important constitutional duty, to 'take care that the laws be faithfully executed.'" In short, the Court held that it could not allow Congress to unilaterally strip the president of the constitutional power of executing the law through the executive agencies.

Despite these holdings, the Court did not strike down the citizen suit provision of the ESA itself as unconstitutional but merely held that in order to proceed under the provision, an organization or person must show some real and actual injury.

For more information: Lockhart, William B., et al. *The American Constitution—Cases, Comments, Questions.* 8th ed. St. Paul, Minn.: West, 1996.

—John L. Roberts

Lynch v. Donnelly, 465 U.S. 668 (1984)

In *Lynch* the Court held that, regardless of its religious significance, the City of Pawtucket, Rhode Island, had not violated the ESTABLISHMENT CLAUSE by including a crèche, or nativity scene, in its annual Christmas display.

For more than 40 years the City of Pawtucket had an annual Christmas display in a park owned by a nonprofit organization and located in the heart of the city's shopping district. The display included—along with the crèche—a Santa Claus house, candy-striped poles, reindeer pulling Santa's sleigh, a Christmas tree, a clown, and a teddy bear. The American Civil Liberties Union (ACLU) and others argued that the city was promoting religious beliefs and challenged the city's actions in Court. The U.S. COURT OF APPEALS for the First Circuit upheld the district court's order enjoining the city from including the crèche in the display.

The Supreme Court—in a 5-4 decision with Chief Justice Warren E. BURGER writing the opinion and Justice Sandra Day O'CONNOR providing the crucial fifth vote—reversed the decisions of the lower courts. The Court held that whatever the benefit to one faith or RELIGION or to all RELIGIONS, it was inconsequential. Burger's opinion stated that the display of the crèche was no more an advancement or endorsement of religion than the congressional and executive recognition of the origins of Christmas itself as "Christ's Mass," or the exhibition of hundreds of religious paintings in government-supported museums.

The opinion noted that Thomas Jefferson's concept of a "wall of separation between church and state" was a useful metaphor, but it was not practical. The Court held that the Constitution does not require complete separation of church and state; but that it does require accommodation and forbids hostility toward any religion. He cited the fact that the first Congress, in the same week it approved the establishment clause in the BILL OF RIGHTS, enacted legislation providing for paid chaplains for both houses of Congress.

Four pages of Burger's 20-page opinion explained the historical religious traditions of the United States. He wrote that the history of this country is filled with official acknowledgment of the role religion plays in American life as well as the history of accommodation of all faiths and forms of religious expression combined with hostility toward none. He supports this conclusion by citing several presidents and their Thanksgiving proclamations, executive orders, and other official announcements of presidents and of the Congress that have pronounced both Christmas and Thanksgiving national holidays in religious terms, the use of the national motto *In God We Trust,* and that the National Gallery of Art had long exhibited masterpieces with religious messages depictions of the birth of Christ, the Crucifixion, and the Resurrection. The display of the crèche, according to the Court, was not an endorsement or advancement of religion anymore than the actions of government mentioned in those four pages, and there certainly was not an excessive entanglement between religion and government.

Justice O'Connor, in a concurring opinion, took the stance that the establishment clause forbids a government endorsement of religion, which differs greatly from the *Lemon* test's "advancement" prong that forbids statutes from advancing or inhibiting religion. In other words, the Court seemed, in *Lynch,* to be backing away from the three-prong test established in LEMON V. KURTZMAN (1971), and moving toward a more relaxed standard. The Court also stated that the Constitution mandated accommodation, not just tolerance, of all religions and forbids hostility, thereby signifying, in general, a reduction in the separation of church and state.

For more information: Dorsen, Norman, and Thomas Viles. "The *Lynch* and *Allegheny* Religious Symbol Cases." In *Religion and American Law,* edited by Paul Finkelman. New York: Garland, 2000; Ingber, Stanley. *"Lynch v. Donnelly."* In *The Oxford Guide to Supreme Court Decisions,* edited by Kermit Hall. New York: Oxford University Press, 1999.

—Mark Alcorn

Madsen v. Women's Health Center, Inc., 512 U.S. 753 (1994)

In *Madsen v. Women's Health Clinic*, the Supreme Court upheld a 1993 Florida injunction that provided a 36-foot "buffer zone" between antiabortion protesters and individuals who wished to enter family-planning clinics on the grounds that the state of Florida had a significant interest in protecting the rights of women to seek legal health services. The idea of the "buffer zone" was that antiabortion protesters were required to stay far enough away from staff and clients entering the family-planning clinics that the protesters could not interfere with access to the clinics. Before the "buffer zone" was instituted, protesters frequently buttonholed individuals entering the clinics to physically prevent them from entering. It was also common practice to shout at those entering clinics and call them names and generally harass them to the point that they would give up trying to receive family-planning services. Another common tactic was to enter the clinics' parking lots and take down license numbers that were then traced to allow the harassment to continue at the homes of both staff and clients. It was hoped that the "buffer zones" would keep the protesters far enough away from the clinics so that these kinds of activities would cease and access to the clinics would be unimpeded.

In 1993 in BRAY V. ALEXANDRIA WOMEN'S HEALTH CLINIC, 506 U.S. 263, the Court upheld an unlimited right to legal protests at clinics that performed abortions. That decision was followed by the shooting death of Dr. David Gunn by an antiabortionist at a clinic in Pensacola, Florida. In *Madsen*, the Aware Woman Center for Choice of Melbourne, Florida, along with several other clinics, had sought an injunction to keep antiabortionists from interfering with free access to the clinic and to keep them from physically harming or harassing anyone who entered the clinic. The Florida court issued the injunction only after an earlier permanent order to ban protesters from blocking access to the clinic and from physically manhandling individuals entering and leaving the clinic had failed to prevent the harassment.

As many as 400 protesters arrived at the clinic several times a week. The clinic building had been attacked with butyric acid, and antiabortionists jammed the locks with glue to prevent entry into the clinic. Antiabortionists also frequently stalked clinic staff and checked license plates on cars in the parking lot to gain access to information that allowed them to threaten and harass clinic staff and patients at their homes. Harassing the children and neighbors of clinic staff was also common practice. Judy Madsen, Ed Martin, Shirley Hobbs, and others who were regular protesters at the clinic sought to overturn the injunction, arguing that it violated their right to free speech.

In a 6-3 decision that was affirmed in part and reversed in part, Chief Justice REHNQUIST declared that the injunction that banned protesters from crossing the buffer zone around the clinic and its driveway and which limited noise restrictions did not violate the First Amendment rights of abortion protesters. According to the Court, the restrictions were not content-based or viewpoint-based because injunctive remedy could have been made available to anyone else suffering from similar harassment for some other reason.

The Court rejected the buffer zone as applied to the private property on either side of the clinic. The noise restrictions included in the injunction were designed to prevent antiabortionists outside the clinic from singing, chanting, whistling, shouting, yelling, using bullhorns, auto horns, or sound amplification equipment, or from making other excessive noises that disturbed the patients inside the clinic. The Court determined, however, that a 300-foot buffer zone, which had been established to protect clients and staff from being verbally harassed, could burden speech more than was necessary to serve government interests. The buffer zone had been extended to 300 feet by a Florida judge after the 30-foot buffer zone did not stop the intrusive actions of the protesters. The Court also held that the clinic could not prevent the protesters from displaying signs expressing their antiabortion sentiments.

For more information: *"Madsen v. Women's Health Clinic,"* on Douglas Butler, "Abortion: Medicine, Ethics, and Law" CD-ROM, 1997; Peck, Robert S., and L. Anita Richardson. "Abortion Protests." *ABA Journal* (May 1994): 48.

—Elizabeth Purdy

Mapp v. Ohio, (367 U.S. 643 (1961)

In *Mapp v. Ohio,* a majority of the U.S. Supreme Court held that as a matter of due process, evidence obtained by an unlawful search and seizure in violation of the Fourth Amendment could not be used against a defendant in a state court. The decision overruled a previous decision that limited the constitutional applicability of the EXCLUSIONARY RULE only to criminal federal prosecutions but not to states' ones [*Wolf v. Colorado,* 338 U.S. 25 (1949)], and led the way to the application of most of the protections that are guaranteed under the BILL OF RIGHTS binding on the states.

Dolloree Mapp, the appellant, was arrested, tried, and convicted for holding obscene material in violation of Ohio's state laws. The liable material was unlawfully seized during a search of Mapp's residence for another person, regarding a bombing. The search was conducted without a warrant, after the police forcibly entered and handcuffed the appellant. Both Ohio's COURT OF APPEALS and the Supreme Court of Ohio affirmed the conviction, citing the permissibility of evidence obtained by an unlawful search and seizure under the *Wolf* ruling. Mapp appealed to the U.S. Supreme Court.

Although the proceedings focused on the federal question of whether the Ohio statute violated the First Amendment's right to freedom of thought and expression and the due process clause under the Fourteenth Amendment, the Court's opinion eventually revolved around the applicability of the exclusionary rule to states' conduct that was only briefly mentioned in an amicus curiae submitted by the ACLU.

In its opinion, written by Justice CLARK and concurred by Justices WARREN, BLACK, DOUGLAS, and BRENNAN, the Court annexed the exclusionary rule (applied in the context of federal prosecutions in 1914, WEEKS V. U.S., 232 U.S. 398) to the Fourth Amendment's right to PRIVACY and incorporated it into the due process clause of the Fourteenth Amendment.

Thus, the Court reversed *Wolf's* decision that separated the exclusionary rule and the right to privacy, applying the exclusionary rule as binding upon all states.

Justice Black concurred in a separate opinion, applying the exclusionary rule on the basis of the "close interrelationship" between the Fourth Amendment's prohibitions against unreasonable search and seizure and the Fifth Amendment's prohibition against imposed self-incrimination.

The dissenting opinion, written by Justice HARLAN and joined by Justices FRANKFURTER and Whittaker, and to an extent also by Justice STEWART, held that the case did not require reexamination of the *Wolf* decision but should have focused on the constitutionality of the Ohio law, concluding that the case was sound.

The ruling has been criticized for excluding evidence from the Court, hindering the police in performing its duties, and possibly absolving a guilty defendant based on a "technicality," overburdening the society while preserving the Fourth Amendment's rights of the defendant. Thus, subsequent cases attempted to narrow the scope of *Mapp's* decision, particularly its inapplicability while questioning witnesses [*Alderman v. United States,* 394 U.S. 165 (1969); *United States v. Calandra,* 414 U.S. 338 (1974)], and when the police misconduct was in "good faith" [*UNITED STATES v. LEON,* 468 U.S. 897, 926 (1984); *Massachusetts v. Sheppard,* 468 U.S. 981, 990-91 (1984)].

For more information: Friedman, Lawrence, M. *Crime and Punishment in American History.* New York: Basic Books, 1993.

—Maya Sabatello

Marbury v. Madison, 1 Cranch (5 U.S.) 37 (1803)

The Supreme Court decision rendered in *Marbury v. Madison* created the doctrine of JUDICIAL REVIEW, establishing the Court's power to interpret the constitutionality of laws passed by Congress. Written by Chief Justice John MARSHALL, the opinion set a PRECEDENT that prevails to modern times that the Court may nullify legislation that contravenes the U.S. Constitution.

Marbury v. Madison had its origins in the power shift from the Federalist presidential administration of John Adams to the ascendant Jeffersonian-Republican faction in the federal government. Shortly after losing the election of 1800 to Thomas Jefferson, President Adams appointed a slate of nominees to federal judiciary posts. He hoped to stack the judiciary with Federalists to negate Jeffersonian-Republican dominance in the executive and its majority in Congress.

Adams named Secretary of State John Marshall CHIEF JUSTICE of the United States and made 200 additional judicial appointments in his last month in office—including more than 40 new justices of the peace for the District of Columbia. Many of Adams's so-called midnight judges and other appointments were presented to the Senate on March 2 and confirmed on March 3. On the last day of his administration Adams frantically signed commissions while outgoing Secretary of State Marshall sealed them for delivery. In the rush, several were set aside and undelivered, including that of William Marbury, whom the Senate had confirmed as a justice of the peace.

After President Jefferson's inauguration on March 4, 1801, Marbury requested that the new secretary of state, James Madison, deliver his commission. When Madison refused, Marbury and several other nominees requested that the Supreme Court issue a writ of mandamus to compel Madison to carry out his official duties by delivering the commissions. Marbury insisted that Madison had no discretionary power in this instance and must fulfill his responsibilities. To bolster his case, Marbury cited Section 13 of the 1789 Judicial Act which empowered the Supreme Court to issue such a writ. By ignoring the proceedings—believing the Supreme Court could not exert its will on the president or Congress—Jefferson and Madison confronted Marshall with a dilemma. For, if the Court found in favor of Marbury and issued a writ of mandamus, Madison might very well disregard it. That outcome could provoke a constitutional crisis and, more important for Federalist jurists, weaken their authority. Marshall hoped to avoid such a scenario at all costs.

In a unanimous, 5-to-0 decision, Marshall wrote the Court's opinion. The chief justice agreed that Marbury and the other plaintiffs were due their commissions. In doing so, however, he injected questions distinct from Marbury's: Could the Supreme Court determine the case at all? Did it have the power to issue a writ of mandamus? Marshall had read Article III of the Constitution, which established the courts, and compared it with the text of Section 13 of the 1789 Judiciary Act. He determined that the act violated the intent of the Constitution that, in fact, Article III did not support the legislation. He reasoned, therefore, that the Supreme Court was not empowered to issue a writ of mandamus and denied Marbury's request. He also declared the Judiciary Act's provision to be nullified. In doing so, he boldly set forth a new function for the Court. "It is emphatically the province and duty of the judicial department to say what the law is," Marshall wrote, ". . . a law repugnant to the constitution is void . . . courts as well as other departments are bound by that instrument."

Marshall did not pull this concept out of thin air. It origins lay in 17th-century British and colonial American courts whose jurists surmised that a legislative act that violated "natural law" could be declared invalid. Much of Marshall's argument was drawn from Alexander Hamilton's *Federalist No. 78*, which posited that courts could "declare all acts contrary to the manifest tenor of the Constitution void." Finally, Marshall worked from associate justice Samuel CHASE's earlier opinion in *CALDER V. BULL*, 3 Dall. (3 U.S.) 386 (1798), which reasoned that natural law—in Chase's view the foundation of the Constitution—placed limitations on legislative actions.

Not until the *DRED SCOTT V. SANDFORD* case in 1857 did the Court nullify another act of Congress—in that case

declaring the 1820 Missouri Compromise unconstitutional. But Marshall's landmark opinion in *Marbury v. Madison* amplified the role of the judiciary branch in the system of checks and balances. From 1803 forward the Supreme Court has been the final arbiter of the constitutionality of laws passed by Congress.

For more information: Clinton, Robert. *Marbury v. Madison and Judicial Review.* Lawrence: University Press of Kansas, 1989; Corwin, Edwin. *John Marshall and the Constitution: A Chronicle of the Supreme Court.* New Haven, Conn.: Yale University Press, 1919.

—Matthew Wasniewski

marriage, right to

The U.S. Supreme Court recognizes a fundamental right to marriage under the equal protection clause of the Fourteenth Amendment to the Constitution. With exceptions, states and the federal government are not allowed to substantially interfere with the decision of a man and a woman to marry. [*Zablocki v. Redhail*, 434 U.S. 374 (1978).]

The right to marriage is really a right to obtain official government recognition of a couple's personal relationship. Contemporary constitutional doctrine holds that, with exceptions, the dynamics of one's personal relationships are mostly a matter of private right. Similarly, people and religious institutions have full discretion to approve or reject various types of relationships consistent with their beliefs. The issue of the right to marry arises when two people ask for governmental recognition of their partnership. Government recognition symbolizes general social approval of a relationship. In addition, couples who are officially married are entitled to special government benefits and privileges (among other things, tax breaks, health-care and social welfare benefits, inheritance privileges, and alimony and division of property if the relationship breaks down). Right of marriage cases, therefore, revolve around the question of when governments may constitutionally *withhold* their official acknowledgment of a relationship.

In the Supreme Court's first major decision regarding marriage, *REYNOLDS V. UNITED STATES*, 98 U.S. 145 (1879), the Court affirmed the constitutionality of a federal antibigamy statute as enforced against polygamous Mormons. It is likely that the contemporary Supreme Court would affirm this 19th-century decision, specifically the part of the decision regarding state-recognized bigamy and polygamy (as opposed to the right of individuals to enter into private, multi-partner relationships). The right to marriage, therefore, may be assumed to apply only to two-person relationships.

Supreme Court opinions throughout the 20th century paid homage to the sacred nature of the marital relationship and the offensiveness of state attempts to overregulate that relationship. They did not, however, specifically or authoritatively describe the scope of a right to marry. In 1967 the Court struck down a Virginia law prohibiting interracial marriage as unconstitutional under the equal protection clause of the Fourteenth Amendment in LOV-ING V. VIRGINIA, 388 U.S. 1 (1967). The Court's decision implicitly placed a high value on marriage as an exercise of personal autonomy, but its analysis focused on the constitutionality of governmental RACIAL DISCRIMINATION (of which a ban on interracial marriage was a specific instance).

Zablocki v. Redhail was the first Court decision to explicitly recognize that entering into marriage was a constitutional right and that government regulations that posed a direct and substantial obstacle to the exercise of that right would be subject to the STRICT SCRUTINY of the Court (which in practice means that the law in question is almost always unconstitutional). The state law that was struck down in the case prevented a person failing to pay child support from marrying unless that person paid all owed child support and showed that the supported child was not receiving welfare and would not do so in the future. The opinion of the Court, written by Justice MARSHALL, noted that earlier Court cases recognized a constitutional right to PRIVACY in making decisions about various aspects of family life. Marriage is the foundation of American family life; the right of privacy, therefore, logically includes decision making about entering into marriage.

The Court emphasized that most government regulations of people who are married are likely to be constitutional. The kind of laws that are subject to more searching scrutiny are those that directly and significantly interfere with one's ability to *enter into* a marital relationship. For example, the Supreme Court, in *Turner v. Safley,* 482 U.S. 78 (1987), unanimously held unconstitutional a prison regulation that made it very difficult for inmates to become married.

Furthermore, the right to marry does not imply that *any* type of personal relationship must be officially recognized by federal and state governments as marriage. The *Reynolds* case, for example, allows for the prohibition of bigamy and polygamy. In addition, by force of greater logic, a person in a relationship that involves illegal conduct (incest, bestiality, relationships between adults and minors) cannot assert a right to have that relationship labeled marriage.

The Supreme Court has not ruled whether same-sex couples have a constitutional right to be married. *LAWRENCE V. TEXAS,* No. 02-102, 123 S.Ct. 2472 (2003), held that consensual sexual acts between adults of the same sex are constitutionally protected behavior. The Court, however, expressly declined to comment on what the decision implied regarding the constitutional status of same-sex marriages.

Currently more than 35 states explicitly define marriage as a relationship between a man and a woman. The Vermont and Hawaii Supreme Courts have held that state prohibitions on same-sex marriages violate their respective state constitutions. [*Baker v. Vermont,* 170 Vt. 194, 744 A.2d 864 (Vt. 1999); *Baehr v. Lewin,* 74 Haw. 530, 852 P.2d 44 (Haw. 1993).] The state of Hawaii amended its constitution to overturn the decision of its Supreme Court. Vermont enacted a civil union law that extends the legal benefits of marriage to same-sex partners yet avoids calling same-sex unions marriages.

Some politicians and scholars suggest that if just one state recognizes same-sex unions, all 50 states will be forced to accept them. This prediction rests on the fact that states have traditionally honored marriage licenses issued by other states. In addition, some see the Constitution's full faith and credit clause, Article IV, Section 1 as requiring states to honor out-of-state marriage licenses: full faith and credit shall be given in each state to the public acts, records, and judicial proceedings of every other state.

In response to this concern, the federal government passed the Defense of Marriage Act, P.L. 104-199, 110 Stat. 2419 (Sept. 21, 1996). The act states that, for the purposes of receiving federal benefits, the terms *marriage* and *spouse* refer only to relationships between a man and a woman. The act also authorizes states to refuse to honor same-sex marriage licenses issued by other states. It is unclear whether the full faith and credit clause actually requires a state to honor an out-of-state marriage license. It is also unclear whether the federal government has the constitutional authority to nullify the full faith and credit clause through legislation.

For more information: Chauncey, George. "Why Marriage?" *The History Shaping Today's Debate Over Gay Equality.* New York: Basic Books, 2004.

—James Daniel Fisher

Marshal, office of the

The Marshal is probably best known for gaveling the court to order and "crying" (announcing the arrival of) the Court with this phrase: "Oyez! Oyez! Oyez! All persons having business before the Honorable, the Supreme Court of the United States, are admonished to draw near and give their attention, for the Court is now sitting. God save the United States and this Honorable Court." The Marshal attends all sessions of the Court and manages all aspects of the courtroom, including seating, security, recording of the proceedings, and keeping counsel to strict time limits by controlling the white and red warning lights that are on the lectern.

Following tradition, both the Marshal and the Clerk of the Court (who sit at either end of the bench) wear formal cutaway suits to the courtroom when the Court is sitting.

The position was created by the Judiciary Act of 1867, which gave the Court the authority to appoint a marshal, to remove him, and to set his compensation. As provided for in the JUDICIARY ACT OF 1789, prior to 1867, the Marshal's duties were performed either by the Clerk or by the Marshal of the judicial district in which the Court was located. From 1801 to 1867, for example, the 12 men who served as marshals for the District of Columbia also served informally as marshal of the Supreme Court.

The Marshal could be described as the Court's chief operating officer, as its general manager, its paymaster, and its chief security officer. Indeed, nearly half of the Court's 400 employees report to the Marshal. The Marshal is responsible for overseeing the operations of the SUPREME COURT BUILDING, including security, space management, maintenance and cleaning, renovation, property and supplies, procurement and contracting, telecommunications, parking, managing the motor pool, and coordinating most events at the Court. From the original duty of maintaining order in the courtroom, the Marshal's responsibility now includes overseeing the Supreme Court's police force.

The Marshal is responsible for coordinating most ceremonies at the Court, including the investiture of new justices, and he is also responsible for arranging special events, such as the reception of foreign dignitaries. In addition, the Marshal is responsible for escorting the justices to formal functions outside the Court.

Moreover, the Marshal is responsible for financial matters, including the disbursement of payroll and the payment of the Court's bills as a treasury disbursing officer.

Initially, the Marshal was directed "to serve and execute all process and orders issues by the Court or a member thereof." A noteworthy exercise of this responsibility occurred during the tenure of Marshal Frank Key Green (1915–38), when Green served a subpoena on business tycoon J. Pierpont Morgan, Jr. Government officials were trying to reclaim Martha Washington's will, which Morgan's father allegedly had stolen. After receiving the subpoena, Morgan returned the will. Today the job of officially serving papers (usually disbarment orders) is delegated to the clerk's office.

For more information: Biskupic, Joan, and Elder Witt. *Guide to the U.S. Supreme Court.* Vol. II. 3rd ed. Washington, D.C.: Congressional Quarterly Press, 1997; Federal Judicial Center. "United States Marshals." Judicial Administration and Organization. Available online. URL: http://www.fjc.gov. Downloaded May 17, 2004; Judiciary Act of

Chief Justice John Marshall *(United States Supreme Court)*

1867, 14 Stat. 433; Supreme Court Historical Society. Available online. URL: http://www.supremecourthistory.org. Downloaded May 17, 2004; Supreme Court of the United States. Available online. URL: http://www.supremecourtus.gov. Downloaded May 17, 2004; U.S. National Archives and Records Administration. "Guide to the Records of the Supreme Court of the United States." Research Room. Available online. URL: http://www.archives.gov/research_room/federal_records_guide/supreme_court_of_united_states_rg267.html. Downloaded May 17, 2004.

—Judithanne Scourfield McLauchlan

Marshall, John (1755–1835) *chief justice of the United States*

John Marshall (b. Prince William County [now Fauquier County], Virginia, September 24, 1755; d. Philadelphia, Pennsylvania, July 6, 1835) was appointed to the Supreme Court by President John Adams in 1801. He served as CHIEF JUSTICE until 1835, becoming one of the greatest figures in the judicial history of the United States.

John Marshall was the first of 15 children born to Thomas and Mary Marshall. He received much of his early education in their Virginia home. Indeed, it was under his father's instruction that Marshall received much of his military training. Marshall fought with distinction in Washington's army, advancing to captain-lieutenant in 1776 and to captain after serving at Valley Forge and Monmouth. While visiting his father in Yorktown, John Marshall met Mary Ambler, the daughter of the Virginia state councillor. Determined to marry her, John announced his intention to become a lawyer, a profession sufficiently respectable to secure the consent of Mary's family. He began preparing for the bar by attending law lectures at the College of William and Mary in the spring of 1780. After only a few months at the college (and as little as six weeks of classes), Captain John Marshall was admitted to the Virginia bar on August 28, 1780.

Marshall distinguished himself as a capable lawyer in his early days of legal practice. A contemporary source described his skill as an orator: "No matter what the question; though 10 times more knotty than the gnarled oak, the lightning of heaven is not more rapid nor more restless, than his astonishing penetration." This skill would serve Marshall well when, in 1782, he was elected for the first of three terms in the Virginia House of Delegates. Among his colleagues there were Thomas Jefferson, Patrick Henry, and Richard Henry Lee. Although well-liked and widely respected by his fellow delegates, John Marshall shared the opinion of many outside observers in considering the body volatile and quarrelsome. Nevertheless, he served it ably, emerging as one of the leading proponents of the Nationalist cause. When Virginia convened its constitutional convention in 1788, Marshall emerged as one of the leading advocates of ratification.

Marshall moved into national politics at the encouragement of George Washington. In 1799 he ran for Congress as a Federalist and won by a narrow majority in the intensely pro-Jeffersonian district of Richmond. In Congress Marshall earned a reputation for his moderate and conciliatory nature and was appointed secretary of state. His service in that capacity was brief but memorable, as he laid the foundations for the landmark case, MARBURY V. MADISON (1 *Cranch* 137 [1803]). Before John Adams left office in 1801, he filled all open offices in the federal courts with Federalists, much to the chagrin of his successor, Thomas Jefferson. William Marbury was nominated and confirmed as a justice of the peace for the District of Columbia, but the retiring secretary of state, John Marshall, failed to deliver his confirmation. Marbury sought a writ of mandamus from the Supreme Court commanding the new secretary of state, James Madison, to deliver the commission. It was as chief justice of the Supreme Court that Marshall revisited the final days of the Adams presidency and

struck a victory for the Federalist cause. Not only did he order that Marbury's commission be recognized; not only did he stigmatize the Jeffersonians as a violators of the law; but he affirmed the legal supremacy of the Constitution and established the legitimacy of JUDICIAL REVIEW.

In COHENS V. VIRGINIA, 6 *Wheaton* 264 (1821), the Court had to address a challenge by Virginia to the right of the Supreme Court to review decisions by state courts regarding questions of federal law. Although the Court upheld the state law in question, Marshall used this opportunity to advance a number of arguments in favor of the supremacy of the federal judiciary. He explained that the Constitution was a creation of the people, not of the states— that "[I]t is the creature of their will, and lives only by their will. But this supreme and irresistible power to make or unmake resides only in the whole body of the people; not in any subdivision of them." Consequently, judges had to interpret the Constitution for the benefit of the people as a whole, and not for the exclusive benefit of the states.

Marshall had expressed similar views in McCULLOCH V. MARYLAND, 4 *Wheaton* 316 (1819). Here he stated "that the government of the Union, though limited in its powers, is supreme within its sphere of action." In this case, the Court had to determine the constitutionality of the Second National Bank of the United States. Marshall wrote that even though the Constitution did not explicitly authorize Congress to incorporate a national bank, the Constitution enabled it to enact such laws as were "necessary and proper" for the execution of the powers granted to it. In the case of the national bank, Congress had passed a law "necessary and proper" for the exercise of its power over the sword and the purse.

In FLETCHER V. PECK, 6 Cranch 87 (1810), and DARTMOUTH COLLEGE V. WOODWARD, 4 Wheaton 518 (1819), Marshall gave construction to the contract clause of the Constitution. In *Fletcher*, the Court declared a state law unconstitutional for the first time. In question was a 1796 Georgia law repealing an act selling land to private speculators. Marshall based this decision on the contract clause, which prohibited states from passing laws that impaired contractual obligations. Similarly, Marshall defended the corporate charter of Dartmouth College from an attempt by the New Hampshire legislature to alter its governing board, notwithstanding the provisions of the college's 1769 charter.

In *Gibbons v. Ogden*, 9 Wheaton 1 (1824), Marshall construed the commerce clause of the Constitution as including not only the exchange of goods but the transit of persons and even new vehicles such as steamboats across state lines. This favored a broad scope for the regulatory powers of Congress. In *Brown v. Maryland*, 12 Wheaton 419 (1827), Marshall formulated the "original package doctrine," namely, that as long as goods introduced into a state by foreign trade remain in the hands of the importer and in their original packaging, they cannot be taxed by the state. During his 34 years on the Supreme Court, Marshall did a great deal to define the nature of the Court as an institution. As the first chief justice to convene a session in Washington, D.C., he settled the Court into its new home and into its new position within American life. In addition, he insisted that the justices issue only one opinion for the Court in delivering their judgments so as to make the Court speak with unity, authority, and certainty. Above all, Marshall struggled to realize the Federalists' vision of America. He defended the primacy of the federal government over states' rights by arguing that the *people*, not the states, were sovereign. The Constitution, he argued, expressed the will of the people. However, Marshall's tendency to interpret the Constitution broadly irked Jeffersonians, who favored a more rigid, state-centered interpretation. Through expansive interpretation, Marshall defined more precisely the executive, legislative, and judicial powers enumerated in the Constitution. He did so at the expense of the states, which he consistently subordinated to the power of the federal government. In this manner the man who presided over the Supreme Court's first term in Washington, D.C., ensured that its foundations in FEDERALISM were strong.

For more information: Schwartz, Bernard. *A History of the Supreme Court.* New York: Oxford University Press, 1993.
—Tara Helfman

Marshall, Secretary of Labor, et al. v. Barlow's, Inc., 76 U.S. 1143 (1978)

Marshall, Secretary of Labor, et al. v. Barlow's, Inc., established limits against warrantless searches in a business's nonpublic work areas.

On September 11, 1975, Ferrol G. "Bill" Barlow, president and general manager of Barlow's, Inc., refused an OSHA inspector the ability to search employee areas of his business without a warrant. Mr. Barlow called upon the Fourth Amendment of the UNITED STATES CONSTITUTION as his reason for refusing the inspector. The secretary of Labor, relying on Section 8 of the Occupational Safety and Health Act of 1970 giving the secretary power to search the work area of any employment facility within the act's jurisdiction, requested that the United States district court for the District of Idaho issue an order compelling Mr. Barlow to allow the inspection to take place. This was issued and Mr. Barlow again refused inspection.

Barlow took the case before the district court and won with the conclusion that the Fourth Amendment did not allow for warrantless searches. The three-judge court also ruled that Section 8 of the act was unconstitutional and entered an injunction against any such searches and seizures pursuant to the act. The secretary then appealed the ruling to the United States Supreme Court, which agreed to take the case.

The Court decided against the secretary on the grounds that the Fourth Amendment protects both commercial buildings and private homes under the warrant clause, which states ". . . *and no Warrants shall issue, but upon probable cause, supported by Oath or affirmation, and particularly describing the place to be searched, and the persons or things to be seized.*" To have a "general warrant" would be in direct contention with the amendment, which was largely based on the "colonists' experience with the writs of assistance . . . that granted sweeping power to customs officials and other agents of the King to search at large for smuggled goods" *United States v. Chadwick*, 433 U.S. 1, 7–8 (1977).

The secretary argued that the Court had made exceptions in the past, citing *United States v. Biswell*, 406 U.S. 311, 316 (1972), and *Colonnade Catering Corp. v. United States*, 397 U.S. 72, 74, 77 (1970). Mr. Justice WHITE delivered the opinion of the Court, explaining that some industries had a long-standing relationship with the government, and it was understood that constant supervision was necessary. *Colonnade* dealt with liquor and *Biswell* with firearms. Justice White also cited *Almeida-Sanchez v. United States*, 413 U.S. 266, 271 (1973), remarking "a central difference between those cases [*Colonnade* and *Biswell*] and this one is that businessmen engaged in such federally licensed and regulated enterprises accept the burdens . . ., whereas the petitioner here was not engaged in any regulated or licensed business," as was the case with Barlow's, Inc., an electrical and plumbing installation business.

Mr. Justice STEVENS presented his dissenting opinion arguing that the federal statute determined by Congress in the "interest of the public and the health of the nation's workforce" were more important than the interests of ". . . a businessman . . . in preventing a Government inspector from viewing those areas of his premises which relate to the subject matter of the regulation" (Carter, 2000).

For more information: Carter, Lief, and Christine Harrington. *Administrative Law and Politics, Cases and Comments.* New York: Addison Wesley Longman, 2000.

Marshall, Thurgood (1908–1993) *Supreme Court justice*

Thurgood Marshall was a giant figure in the U.S. CIVIL RIGHTS movement and was the first African American on the U.S. Supreme Court, serving as an associate from 1967 to 1991.

To say that Thurgood Marshall was the first African American on the U.S. Supreme Court is trite. Marshall was so much more than that. He was a brilliant legal strategist, keystone of the drive to end segregation, and a constitutional scholar of such skill that of 112 decisions written for the appellate court, none were ever reversed. Thurgood Marshall was born to a railroad porter and a teacher in Baltimore, Maryland, in 1908.

After a principal made him memorize the Constitution as a punishment, Marshall commented: "I learned it backward and forward." Marshall worked summers and through his freshman year at Lincoln College in order to make the tuition payments and repay a family debt for his brother's tuition.

Marshall graduated with honors and sought to attend law school at the University of Maryland Law School in Baltimore. It was close to home and the tuition was very low. Numerous lawyers he sought help from in Baltimore dissuaded him however—the University of Maryland had rarely accepted black applicants. Marshall never applied.

Instead, Marshall attended Howard University's law program, and while it initially had a very low reputation, he was in the first class of a rebuilt program that would come to be highly regarded. Marshall impressed the faculty and was given a position in the school's law library. He graduated at the head of that new class; only six remained out of 36 that began the program.

Marshall did not have an easy time finding a position out of law school. A brief experience in private practice left him in debt and with a new realization that he would get into public advocacy. Marshall took a position with the National Association for the Advancement of Colored People (NAACP) and toured the South working to break down barriers of segregation in the courts. He did not engage in civil disobedience. His chosen battleground was in the courts and his weapon was the law. He would become the NAACP's greatest litigator.

Given Marshall's long tenure on the Court, it is perhaps surprising that the case for which he will be remembered was not one in which he rendered a decision or a dissent, but one which he argued. Marshall did much more than argue *Brown v. Board of Education*, 347 U.S. 483 (1954), however; he *orchestrated* it. The case, which eventually ended racial segregation in the U.S., was a case that Thurgood Marshall built from the ground up.

Marshall's greatest legal talent was as a strategist. Rather than attack the problem of segregated education head on, he planned a methodical attack, not only the landmark cases, but also the keystone cases upon which the landmarks would be built. He carefully chose the right cases, the right question of law and the right litigants. By building precedents of less controversial cases, Marshall eroded the legal ground upon which segregation relied, and he was often criticized for his careful approach.

The victory over segregation brought attention and in 1961 John F. Kennedy made Marshall a bench appoint-

Justice Thurgood Marshall *(United States Supreme Court)*

ment to the federal appeals court. After a bitter battle in the Senate, Marshall later received a full appointment. He was selected in 1965 by Lyndon Johnson to be the first black solicitor general in U.S. history. After only a year, Marshall would be elevated to the Supreme Court by Johnson. This historic appointment came at a crucial time, elevating Marshall to the status of a black legal icon representing the law-abiding, hard-working, educated possibilities of black Americans.

Marshall was far more prolific in dissent than as an author of opinions. He was the final liberal appointment on the Court for many years. Following Johnson's appointment of Marshall, Nixon would make key selections that shifted the Court considerably to the right. Marshall was a solid, if unobtrusive member of the liberal bloc of justices. In his early career, his only decision of note was *Amalgamated Food Employees Union v. Logan Valley Plaza*, 391 U.S. 308 (1968), in which the Court affirmed the right of employees to peacefully picket on private property. Later, Marshall would go on to write a number of important dissents, a reflection of his status of a liberal judge on a conservative court. Among his more important dissents are *CITY OF RICHMOND V. CROSON*, 488 U.S. 469 (1989), and *SAN ANTONIO V. RODRIGUEZ*, 411 U.S. 1 (1973).

By 1969 Nixon had completed the conservative transformation of the Court with the appointments of BURGER and BLACKMUN. Later appointments of REHNQUIST and POWELL led to a pronounced shift of the character of the Court. Marshall now found himself as the most liberal member of an increasingly conservative Supreme Court, especially on issues such as the death penalty. Marshall became the author of biting dissents that he feared harmed his position with his colleagues. Marshall wrote 937 dissents during his career on the Court.

An example of Marshall's scathing writing style comes from his concurrence from REGENTS OF THE UNIVERSITY OF CALIFORNIA V. BAKKE, 438 U.S. 265 (1978): "For it must be remembered that, during most of the past 200 years, the Constitution as interpreted by this Court did not prohibit the most ingenious and pervasive forms of discrimination against the Negro. Now, when a state acts to remedy the effects of that legacy of discrimination, I cannot believe that this same Constitution stands as a barrier."

The ascendancy of William Rehnquist to Chief Justice in 1986 pushed Marshall even further from the inner circle of the Court. The retirement of BRENNAN, in 1990, sealed Marshall's career. In failing health, struggling against an unfavorable majority and merely hanging on until someone more favorable could appoint a replacement, Marshall lashed out at Bush's choice to succeed Brennan. The tension on the Court during the next session became unbearable and Marshall decided to retire in 1991. His health deteriorated further and he died a few days following Bill Clinton's inauguration in 1993, where he was supposed to swear in the vice president.

Marshall's legacy will always be tied to *Brown,* as the first black Supreme Court justice and as a liberal activist. Randall Bland critiques Marshall's contribution as lacking in judicial scholarship, though gives him high marks for advocacy. Marshall was certainly a giant figure in the history of the U.S. Supreme Court, not only as the first black member, but also as the greatest advocate on behalf of African Americans both before and upon the Court.

For more information: Bland, Randall. *Justice Thurgood Marshall: Crusader for Liberalism.* Bethesda, Md.: Academica Press, 2001; Williams, Juan. *Thurgood Marshall: American Revolutionary.* New York: Random House, 1998.
—Tim Hundsdorfer
—Charlotte Worstall

Martin v. Hunter's Lessee, 14 U.S. 304 (1816)

In *Martin v. Hunter's Lessee,* the Court upheld the constitutionality of Section 25 of the JUDICIARY ACT OF 1789 ruling that the Court had the power to review state judgments that rested on federal law. In this case that power extended to reversing the judgment of the Virginia Court of Appeals on a dispute regarding ownership of certain property in Virginia.

Denny Martin inherited the disputed property in 1781 from his uncle, Lord Fairfax, a British subject. Virginia, however, claimed to have confiscated the land because it belonged to a British loyalist. In 1789 Virginia granted some of the Fairfax lands to David Hunter. Martin sued. He argued that the land had not been taken by Virginia until after 1783; therefore, the land was protected under the 1783 Treaty of Peace with Great Britain, which prohibited such confiscations. The district court ruled in favor of Martin.

The Virginia Court of Appeals did not hear the case until 1810. In the interim period, negotiations had taken place in which a group that included future Chief Justice John MARSHALL arranged to buy the land from Martin. However, the Virginia Court of Appeals reversed the district court and ruled in favor of Hunter. The case was then heard by the Supreme Court in *Fairfax's Devisee v. Hunter's Lessee,* 11 U.S. 603 (1813). The Court reversed the Virginia Court of Appeals and mandated that the state court enter judgment for Martin. In 1815 the Virginia Court of Appeals issued a decision refusing to comply with the Supreme Court's mandate.

Virginia argued that the Constitution did not extend the appellate power of the federal courts to final state court rulings; therefore Section 25 of the Judiciary Act of 1789 was unconstitutional in extending such appellate power to the federal courts. Additionally they argued that if it was important that a controversy be heard in federal court then it could be removed from the state system into the federal system earlier, before a final state court ruling.

Justice Joseph STORY wrote the *Martin v. Hunter's Lessee* opinion for a unanimous Supreme Court (absent Marshall due to his personal interests in the case) rejecting Virginia's arguments. Story focuses on Article III of the Constitution, which defines judicial power as extending to "all cases." Story reasons: "It is the *case,* then, and not the *court,* that gives the jurisdiction." Cases in state court that involve federal laws and the Constitution are subject to the Supreme Court's appellate jurisdiction. There is no expressed limit in the Constitution that prevents such review just because the suit took place in state courts.

Story also focuses on the Court's previously established ability to review state executive and legislative action for constitutionality. There is no further danger to state sovereignty from a similar power over state judicial action. Indeed, Story reasons, it is necessary for there to be an "absolute right of decision, in the last resort." Final appellate jurisdiction in the Supreme Court upholds the supremacy of federal law (Article VI of the Constitution) and provides for "uniformity of decisions throughout the whole United States."

The Court also dismisses Virginia's removal argument. Story first points out that no such right of removal is specified in the Constitution. Additionally he reasons that "if the right of removal from state courts exists before judgment, because it is included in the appellate power, it must, for the same reason, exist after judgment." So it will not matter if the state ruling was "final" or not; the Supreme Court will still have appellate jurisdiction.

Finally Story turns to history. Such appellate jurisdiction was recognized during the creation of the Constitution. Additionally it has been recognized in numerous cases since that time, and "no state tribunal has ever breathed a judicial doubt on the subject, or declined to obey the mandate of the Supreme Court, until the present occasion."

This case is noteworthy for its reinforcement of the power of the Court's appellate power over state court decisions. It also ties closely to the continuing controversy between federal and state power that would ultimately be fought over in the Civil War. These issues of state and federal power would be revisited in a number of important Court cases, including a very similar controversy in COHENS V. VIRGINIA, 19 U.S. 264 (1821), that challenged the Court's power to review state criminal judgments.

For more information: Levy, Leonard W. *Seasoned Judgments: The American Constitutions, Rights, and History.* New Brunswick, N.J.: Transaction Publishers, 1995; McKay, Robert B. *An American Constitutional Law Reader.* New York: Oceana Publications, 1958.

—Matthew A. Johnson

Masson v. New Yorker, 111 S. Ct. 2419 (1991)

In *Masson v. New Yorker,* the Supreme Court ruled that a reporter who deliberately altered quotes from an interview may be liable for libel. The *Masson* case thus represents an important ruling on the First Amendment rights of reporters and the media.

The Supreme Court since the 1960s has been involved in redefining the legal term of libel. The British Common Law had allowed comment on public events and figures, including criticism, as long as it was true or not done with malice. In 1964 the U.S. Supreme Court, in the case of NEW YORK TIMES V. SULLIVAN, rewrote libel law for the states requiring that any libel suit by a public figure or public official could not be won unless it was shown that the media had acted with actual malice. A series of cases following the Sullivan decision further defined the new libel law. One of those, *Masson v. New Yorker* (1991), saw the Court determine that the paraphrasing of direct quotes was protected from libel law if the paraphrases did not change the meaning of the quote.

Gregory Masson, a prominent psychologist involved with the Sigmund Freud Archives, was interviewed by a reporter from the *New Yorker* magazine. In writing her story, the author, Janet Malcolm, paraphrased several quotes from Masson which he later said were untrue. The interview was published in the *New Yorker* magazine and a subsequent book. Masson sued the magazine for libel, claiming statements about him being an "intellectual gigolo" and comments about the Freud Archives defamed him and were untrue.

Under the Supreme Court's definition of libel, Masson was considered a public figure, someone who sought out the media and had access to it. In order to win a libel suit as a public figure, Masson would have to proved that the magazine and Malcolm acted with actual malice or a reckless disregard for the truth. Masson claimed that by paraphrasing parts of the interview and putting those paraphrases in quotation marks, Malcolm had deliberately and inaccurately reported what he had said and placed him in a bad light.

Masson's suit was dismissed by the trial judge, and he appealed all the way to the Supreme Court. In *Masson v. New Yorker,* the justices produced a muddied ruling. Writing for seven members of the court, Justice Kennedy stated that the press could change the actual words of the quotation, in order to remove extraneous or irrelevant comments, as long as it did not change the meaning of the quote. According to Kennedy, this would allow writers to paraphrase in order to meet space requirements of a story and make the story more interesting to readers.

Masson, though, won the right to a trial on the issue of whether the quotes in the Malcolm piece were libelous to him. Masson went back to court and in 1994 he lost a court ruling that found that he had not been libeled by Malcolm's paraphrasing of his words.

For more information: Kaltenbach, Richard. "Fabricated Quotes and the Actual Malice Standard." *Catholic University Law Review* 41 (1992): 745; Lessner, Jonathan. "Masson v. New Yorker Magazine." *University of Miami Law Review* 45 (1990): 159; Pavlik, Michael. "Masson v. New Yorker." Case Western Reserve Law Review 40 (1990): 875.

—Douglas Clouatre

Mathews v. Eldridge, 424 U.S. 319 (1976)

In *Mathews v. Eldridge,* the Court held that the due process clause of the Fifth Amendment does not require an evidentiary hearing prior to the termination of disability benefits. It is regarded as the case with which the Supreme Court called a halt to the explosion of administrative due process set in motion six years earlier by *Goldberg v. Kelly,* 397 U.S. 254 (1970). It is also the case in which the Court advanced a methodology for determining administrative due process interests, and a vocabulary with which to consider those interests. The language and techniques expressed in *Mathews v. Eldridge* evolved from earlier administrative due process decisions and drew on the similar language and techniques of the administrative search cases. With these tools, administrative due process matured and was no longer but a poor relation of criminal due process.

The rationale the Court developed to accompany and shape the legalization of the administrative state is characterized as an "interest-balancing" approach. Justice POW-ELL, writing for a 6-2 majority, put the new technique succinctly:

> [I]dentification of the specific dictates of due process generally requires consideration of three distinct factors: First, the private interest that will be affected by the official action; second, the risk of an erroneous deprivation of such interests through the procedures used, and the probable value, if any, of additional or substitute procedural safeguards; and finally, the Government's interest, including the function involved and the fiscal and administrative burdens that the additional or substitute procedural requirement would entail.

As important as the three-step method the court devised—determine the private interest, determine if that interest is met by existing procedures, and balance that interest against the governmental interest in summary procedures—was the example it provided in applying that method to the termination of disability benefits. Of particular interest is the Court's assessment of the government's interest. Looking back at *Goldberg v. Kelly*, which also recommended weighing governmental and individual interests, we find an important distinction between the public or government interest as defined and applied in *Mathews* as compared with that in *Goldberg*. *Goldberg*, following the tradition of criminal justice jurisprudence, gave consideration to a governmental interest in protecting FUNDAMENTAL RIGHTS to individual dignity: "[I]mportant governmental interests are promoted by affording recipients a pre-termination evidentiary hearing. From its founding the Nation's basic commitment has been to foster the dignity and well-being of all persons within its borders."

Thus, when the due process calculus was made in *Goldberg v. Kelly*, there were governmental interests to be weighed on both sides of the scale: "The interest of the eligible recipient in uninterrupted receipt of public assistance, coupled with the State's interest that his payments not be erroneously terminated, clearly outweighs the State's competing concern to prevent any increase in its fiscal an administrative burdens."

In *Mathews*, the governmental interest was represented exclusively in terms of the financial and administrative burden of providing increased protection. Although the Court stated that "[f]inancial cost alone is not a controlling weight," no other state interest was articulated. Indeed, a closer look at the structure of the *Mathews* due process methodology reveals that there is no place on the scale for a public interest in protecting the interest of the individual. The latter interest is characterized as "private" and assumed to be in opposition to public or societal interests.

The interest-balancing approach of *Mathews v. Eldridge* has been criticized for leading to the decline of administrative due process into a valueless cost-benefit analysis. The Court recognized, as have its critics, that there is a problem of fit between a rights approach and an administrative system, and it attempted to resolve that problem. The goals it promoted, while perhaps insufficient, may be fair and reasonable ones in the realm of administrative [versus criminal law] regimes.

Criticism of the absence of "values" in the *Mathews* calculus of interests followed promptly among scholars of administrative justice. In fact, several critiques of the "valueless" direction of administrative due process preceded the *Mathews* decision. Whether their efforts to enhance the rights strategy of administrative due process with an injection of values can work to protect the individual in the regulatory state remains to be seen. In fact, the whole approach of interest balancing even in administrative due process has been questioned: "This reliance upon 'weight,' which is a useful approach for dealing with bananas, leaves something to be desired where factors such as those in *Mathews* are concerned." Another commentator suggested, "The interest balancing methodology seems to contradict the basic libertarian presuppositions of the text [the Bill of Rights] that it would implement." Others challenge the entire "rights strategy" in the control of administrative power.

The due process methodology established in *Mathews* effectively severed the connection of administrative due process to the methodology of criminal due process. Although this consequence of *Mathews* is not often acknowledged, it had an enormous impact on the direction of procedural rights in the criminal process.

For more information: Mashaw, Jerry L. *Due Process in the Administrative State.* New Haven, Conn.: Yale University Press, 1985; Rubin, Edward L. "Due Process and the Administrative State." *California Law Review* 72 (1984): 1,044–1,179.

—Rosann Greenspan

McCleskey v. Kemp, 481 U.S. 279 (1987)

In *McCleskey v. Kemp*, the Supreme Court held that no matter how convincing broad statistical evidence might be, only evidence of racial bias in a specific case would show a violation of due process in that case.

The case began as a simple murder case. Warren McCleskey and three friends tried to rob a furniture store in Atlanta, Georgia. Unknown to them, the store was equipped with a silent alarm system that alerted police. As an officer walked into the store, he was shot and killed. During the ensuing trial one of the accomplices identified McCleskey as the triggerman. McCleskey was African American; the officer white. A jury of 11 whites and one African American found McCleskey guilty and recommended the death penalty.

The Legal Defense Fund of the NAACP saw this case as an opportunity to show the racism prevalent in the criminal justice system and, just possibly, persuade the Supreme Court to rule that the death penalty is unconstitutional. They introduced into evidence a recently completed statistical study of the death penalty in Georgia. Called "The Baldus Study," this research examined 2,484 murder cases in the state of Georgia over the period from 1973 to 1979. The authors showed significant differences in the sentencing of African Americans and whites. For instance, it showed that (a) if their victims were white, African-American defendants were 4.3 times as likely to receive the death penalty than if their victims were black; (b) of the 128 cases in which the death penalty was imposed, 108 involved white victims; (c) when the alleged murderer was black and the victim white, prosecutors sought the death penalty 70 percent of the time. If both the alleged murderer and victim were white, prosecutors sought the death penalty in only 32 percent of the cases. The authors concluded that this was irrefutable evidence of disparate treatment, violating the EQUAL PROTECTION CLAUSE of the Fourteenth Amendment. They also argued that this differential treatment violated the due process clause and the "Cruel and Unusual" phrase of the Eighth Amendment.

Writing for a 5-4 majority of the Supreme Court, Justice POWELL argued that even if the Baldus Study is statistically valid research (and he does not challenge the findings), it does not prove that RACIAL DISCRIMINATION was present in McCleskey's trial. In any death penalty case, a defendant must prove that "the decision-makers in *his* case acted with discriminatory purpose." McCleskey offered no such proof. Justice Powell added that under Georgia's sentencing procedures the jury focuses on the particular nature of the crime that was committed and the particular characteristics of the individual defendant, and therefore it meets the criteria for constitutionality. Jury discretion can benefit the criminal defendant when the jury chooses to be lenient, but it is not required to do so. Finally, Powell states that McCleskey's arguments are best made before a legislature that can change its death penalty statutes, not before a court that can only enforce the law.

Justices BRENNAN, MARSHALL, BLACKMUN, and STEVENS dissented. Brennan wrote that "6 of every 11 defendants convicted of killing a white person would not have received the death penalty if their victims had been black," and that in cases comparable to McCleskey's, "20 of every 34 would not have been sentenced to die if their victims had been black." Blackmun adds that "disparate enforcement of criminal sanctions destroys the appearance of justice, and thereby casts doubt on the integrity of the judicial process." Justice Stevens points out that there are certain categories of extremely serious crimes for which the death penalty is imposed without regard to race. He urges Georgia to narrow its death-eligible categories to these crimes and thereby rid itself of even the appearance of racial bias.

For more information: Baldus, David, George Woodruff, and Charles Pulaski. *Equal Justice and the Death Penalty.* Boston: Northeastern University Press, 1990; Epstein, Lee, and Thomas G. Walker. *Constitutional Law for a Changing America: Rights, Liberties and Justice.* 4th ed. Washington, D.C.: CQ Press, 2001.

—Paul J. Weber

McConnell v. Federal Election Commission, 549 U.S. 93 (2003)

In *McConnell v. Federal Election Commission,* the United States Supreme Court upheld the major campaign finance reform provisions of the McCain-Feingold Act. This law imposed new limits on how money may be used by individuals and some groups to influence elections.

As a result of campaign spending and fund-raising abuses by Richard Nixon surrounding the 1972 presidential election (commonly referred to as Watergate), Congress passed the Federal Election Campaign Act (FECA) in 1974. FECA sought to impose both spending and contribution limits upon candidates who ran for federal offices, including the House, Senate, and the presidency.

Yet in *Buckley v. Valeo,* 424 U.S. 1 (1976), the Supreme Court struck down the expenditure limits as an unconstitutional violation of the First Amendment free speech clause. The Court ruled that the use of money for political purposes could only be regulated if it tended to corrupt or lead to the appearance of corruption, and that while campaign contributions could corrupt the political process, expenditures could not and therefore the latter could not be limited.

In addition, in that opinion, the Court made a distinction between two different types of advertising or speech: express and issue advocacy. If advertisements clearly used candidates' names in their advertising and urged their election or defeat, such advertising would be considered express advocacy. Yet if there was no explicit urging of a candidate's election or defeat, or the use of what came to be known as the magic words, then the advertising would be considered issue advertising. The significance of this distinction is that while the Court held that some groups, such as labor unions and corporations, could be barred from engaging in express advocacy without violating the First Amendment, limits on spending by individuals and groups to engage in issue advocacy would be unconstitutional.

As a result of *Buckley* decision, especially the distinction between express and issue advocacy, and a Federal Election Commission ruling that permitted unions and corporations to donate unlimited amounts of money to political parties to help the latter do party building, voter education, and get out the vote activities, several holes appeared in FECA. Money given for these purposes came to be known as soft money donations. Individuals wishing to circumvent the contribution limits imposed by FECA began either to make unlimited soft money donations to the parties, or spent money for what came to be called shame issue advocacy ads where candidates were attached or endorsed but no explicit urging of their election or defeat was made. By the early 1990s, so much money was spent on issue advocacy and soft money donations that FECA was all but ineffective in limiting campaign contributions.

Senators John McCain (Rep.-Ariz.) and Russell Feingold (Dem.-Wis.), and Representatives Christopher Shays (Rep.-Conn.) and Martin Meehan (Dem.-Mass.), sought to amend FECA to ban soft money contributions to political parties and to place some limits on issue advocacy. After several years of efforts, they passed the Bipartisan Campaign Finance Reform Act (BCRA) in 2002. BCRA, among other things, banned soft money contributions to political parties and made it a presumption that any ads run within either 60 days of a general election, or 30 days of a primary, were express advocacy. BCRA also imposed new disclosure requirements, it limited the ability of federal candidates to raise soft money for state parties, and it prevented state parties from seeking to influence federal elections.

BCRA was immediately challenged in the federal courts by a host of groups, including the National Rifle Association, the American Civil Liberties Union, the Chamber of Commerce of the United States, the AFL-CIO, and Senator Mitch McConnell. Their arguments were that the soft money and express advocacy regulations violated their First Amendment free speech rights. Senator McConnell and the groups also claimed that the new disclosure rules were unconstitutional and that the new limits on state parties violated the First Amendment.

In 2003 a special three-judge panel struck down several of the BCRA provisions in an incomprehensible 1,638-page opinion. The Supreme Court took the case on expedited APPEAL, took the unusual opportunity to hold oral arguments for an entire day on September 8, 2003, and then on December 10, by a 5-4 vote, upheld both the soft money ban and the new express advocacy rule, as well as the other major provisions of BCRA.

Both Justices STEVENS and O'Connor wrote for the majority. Using the *Buckley v. Valeo* PRECEDENT as the basis of its decision, the Court stated that it would subject contribution limits to less exact scrutiny than it would apply to expenditure limits such that the former would be upheld so long as there was evidence that they corrupted or tended to corrupt the electoral process. The Court noted the extensive evidence of corruption that had been provided in the record, including testimony from lobbyists, interest groups, and legislators regarding the impact soft money had on campaigns. Second, the Court upheld the new express advocacy rule, indicating both that the distinction between issue and express advocacy they had articulated in *Buckley* was not a constitutional rule and that the evidence regarding ads since 1976 was that few ads ever actually used the magic words.

Overall, *McConnell v. Federal Election Commission* was heralded by its supporters as an important decision affirming the ability of Congress to regulate money in politics. It rejected the idea advocated by Senator McConnell and others that money was equivalent to speech and that therefore campaign finance regulations were unconstitutional.

For more information: Malbin, Michael, ed. *Life After Reform: When the Bipartisan Campaign Reform Act Meets Politics.* Lanham, Md.: Rowman and Littlefield, 2003; Schultz, David. *Money, Politics, and Campaign Finance Reform Law in the States.* Durham, N.C.: Carolina Academic Press, 2002.

—David Schultz
—Rochelle Miller

McCulloch v. Maryland, 4 Wheat. (17 U.S.) 316 (1819)

In *McCulloch v. Maryland*, the Court set the PRECEDENT for a broad interpretation of the Constitution's NECESSARY AND PROPER CLAUSE and determined the distribution of powers between the states and the federal government. This case, surrounded by controversy and heated arguments, was the first Supreme Court case to give the Court the ability to draw the line between states' rights and the federal government.

McCulloch v. Maryland centered around James McCulloch, head cashier of the Baltimore Bank, and his refusal to pay a tax imposed by the Maryland state legislature. By resorting to a loose interpretation of the Constitution, John MARSHALL was able to justify Congress's authority to create the bank in question. In his decision, Marshall stated that "although the power to charter a corporation is not a specifically enumerated power, there is nothing in the Constitution that excludes it." This decision states that anything not specifically forbidden to the federal

First Bank of the United States *(New York Public Library)*

government is now considered to be a power of that government. By adopting this attitude regarding constitutional rights, the Court has greatly increased the power of the federal government, giving it the advantage over states' rights in most cases.

Once the issue of creating the bank was resolved, the Court moved on to the issue "whether the state of Maryland may, without violating the Constitution, tax a branch of the Bank of the United States." Marshall's decision on this question relates directly to the states' ability to undermine the federal government through taxation of all other federal agencies. If the states were allowed to tax agencies of the federal government, those agencies would lose all enforcement abilities and eventually dissolve. By not allowing the taxation of the bank, the Court ensures that agencies such as the mail, the mint, patents, and federal courts are safe from state interference, therefore allowing the federal government to be completely independent from the states themselves.

After the decision of the Court was delivered, many critics began to voice their dissent. The most controversial aspect of the case was the strong endorsement of a broad interpretation of the power of the federal government. James Madison, who as president signed the bank into creation, felt the ruling would create a breakdown in the SEPARATION OF POWERS and specifically give too much power to Congress to govern the nation. Despite the criticisms, the benefits of a broad CONSTITUTIONAL INTERPRETATION can still be seen today. This broad interpretation of the Constitution gave the federal government the power to create programs to benefit society. These programs include the building of roads, canals, and bridges, and also the creation of many educational, scientific, and literary institutions throughout the nation. The New Deal and the Welfare State

were created with a broad constitutional interpretation in mind. *McCulloch v. Maryland* also paved the way for various other social, scientific, and educational programs in place today.

For more information: Gunther, Gerald, ed. *John Marshall's Defense of McCulloch v. Maryland.* Stanford, Calif.: Stanford University Press, 1969; Presser, Stephen B. "Marbury, McCulloch, Gore & Bush." *The John Marshall Law Review* 33 no. 4 (Summer 2003): 1,157–1,163.

McIntyre v. Ohio, 514 U.S. 334 (1995)

In *McIntyre v. Ohio,* the United States Supreme Court struck down an Ohio law that prohibited the distribution of ANONYMOUS POLITICAL SPEECH. The case was an important defense of individual speech rights under the First Amendment, but it also left open many questions regarding what type of disclosure can be mandated in political campaigns.

In *Buckley v. Valeo,* 424 U.S. 1 (1976), the Supreme Court upheld disclosure requirements in the 1974 amendments to the Federal Election Campaign Act. These provisions required candidates, political parties, and political organizations to disclose expenditures and the names, addresses, and occupations of all contributors above $200. In defending these requirements, the Court ruled that disclosure was necessary to prevent corruption or its appearance or to otherwise give the public and the government the ability to review the financial information of candidates or political organizations in order to detect corruption and make sure that applicable regulations are being followed. *Buckley* seemed to stand for the proposition that disclosure in the context of political or political campaigns was constitutional.

In *McIntyre,* at issue was a state law that made anonymous POLITICAL SPEECH illegal. The state required that all political speech, such as leaflets or commercials, contain some information regarding who produced it. Margaret Levy opposed a school levy that was on the ballot and she then produced a leaflet urging voters to oppose it also. She distributed the leaflet even though her name did not appear on it. She was charged and fined by the Ohio Elections Commission with a violation of the state law barring anonymous political speech. A county court reversed the fine, a state court of appeals reinstated the fine, and then the Ohio Supreme Court affirmed, arguing that the law banning anonymous political speech did not violate the First Amendment because the need to police false and misleading political claims that might come with anonymous speech outweighed the concerns of the First Amendment. The case was taken to the Supreme Court and they struck the law down as unconstitutional.

In writing for the Court, Justice STEVENS first began by noting that there was a long tradition in supporting anonymous speech. This right grew out of the literary realm with works by George Eliot, Charles Dickens, and even William Shakespeare often appearing anonymously or under a pen name. This right has also had a political tradition with pamphlets, with, for example, the authors of the *Federalist Papers* (Alexander Hamilton, James Madison, and John JAY) publishing under the name Publius. Thus, Stevens contended that anonymous political speech was part of a long tradition in the United States and individuals had a right to express their political views without indicating their identity.

Stevens distinguished the type of disclosure in *Buckley* from that found in the Ohio law. In *Buckley,* the disclosure governed candidate elections and not issue referenda as the Ohio law did. Second, the law upheld in *Buckley* was aimed at preventing corruption that could occur or transpire when money is given to candidates. Here, there were no candidates to corrupt. Finally, the interest in preventing false or fraudulent political speech was not necessarily served by requiring disclosure; other means were available to do that. Overall, Justice Stevens and the Court ruled that any goals that the Ohio law contained were overwhelmed by the important First Amendment free speech rights of the speaker to remain anonymous.

As a result of *McIntyre v. Ohio,* many state and local laws mandating the identity of the speaker were declared invalid. Yet what remains unclear as a result of the case is when disclosure is permitted. Does *McIntyre* stand for the proposition that disclosure is only permitted in cases where it involves candidates and not referenda or issues? Or is the case limited to situations that involve individuals distributing leaflets, and not political parties, organizations, or groups? The recently decided *MCCONNELL V. FEDERAL ELECTION COMMISSION* (2003) upheld disclosure requirements under the McCain-Feingold law, but it did little to clarify how its ruling could be reconciled with *McIntyre v. Ohio.*

For more information: Hasen, Richard L. *The Supreme Court and Election Law.* New York: New York University Press, 2003.

—David Schultz

Meritor Savings Bank v. Vinson, 477 U.S. 57 (1986)

In *Meritor Savings Bank v. Vinson,* the Supreme Court held that hostile environment SEXUAL HARASSMENT was a form of SEXUAL DISCRIMINATION. Actions that interfered with one's work performance need not have tangible or economic effects on the victim in order to support a claim of sexual harassment.

Mechell Vinson, an employee at the Meritor Savings Bank for four years, claimed that her supervisor had constantly subjected her to sexual harassment by demanding sexual favors, fondling her in front of others, exposing himself, following her into the women's restroom, and even raping her on several occasions. Sidney Taylor, the supervisor, denied the allegations. The bank denied any knowledge of Taylor's behavior and argued further that Vinson had not suffered any tangible loss and that therefore no violation of her right to be free from sex discrimination had occurred.

The Court upheld Vinson's claim on the grounds that the CIVIL RIGHTS ACT OF 1964 prohibiting sex discrimination was not limited to actions that had a tangible or economic effect, but that discrimination extended to the general "conditions of employment," including unwelcome sexual advances. Even if the harassing behavior had no direct economic effect, such as an increase or decrease in salary, the law forbade conduct that unreasonably interfered with an individual's work or created "an intimidating, hostile, or offensive working environment." Thus the Court clarified that sexual harassment involved not just quid pro quo, where a supervisor demands sexual favors in exchange for a benefit or threatens financial consequences if the favors are denied. After *Vinson* it was also clear that a hostile environment, based on discriminatory sexual behavior, was prohibited just as was harassment based on race, RELIGION, or national origin.

The Court attempted to define the point at which unpleasant conduct crosses the threshold and becomes actionable as sexual harassment. It must be "sufficiently severe or pervasive to alter the conditions of employment and create an abusive working environment." They also explained that even if, as a lower court had found, Vinson's conduct was "voluntary," such a finding was not relevant to a sexual harassment claim. The correct inquiry, the Court ruled, is not whether the victim acquiesced in sexual activity, but whether she had indicated that the advances were unwelcome. In other words, the focus in sexual harassment is on the actions of the harasser, usually a person in a position of power over the victim.

In *Vinson,* the Court did not settle the question of employer liability for sexual harassment, although they found the Meritor Savings Bank's general nondiscriminatory statement and complaint procedure inadequate. By requiring an employee to bring a complaint first to a supervisor, it provided no mechanism for claims such as Vinson's when the supervisor was the harasser. The issue of liability would be addressed in future cases, including *Faragher v. City of Boca Raton,* 524 U.S. 775 (1998).

For more information: MacKinnon, Catherine A. *Sex Equality.* New York: Foundation, 2001; Rundblad, Georgeanne. "Gender, Power, and Sexual Harassment." In *The Criminal Justice System and Women,* edited by Barbara Raffel Price and Natalie J. Sokoloff. New York: McGraw-Hill, 2003.

—Mary Welek Atwell

Metro Broadcasting Inc. v. Federal Communications Commission, 497 U.S. 547 (1990)

The Supreme Court's ruling in *Metro Broadcasting Inc. v. FCC* was a milestone in the legal battle over the constitutionality of government AFFIRMATIVE ACTION programs. The Court upheld a federal plan that gave minority-owned companies preference in the competition for some radio and television broadcast licenses.

The case involved two separate policies adopted in 1978 by the Federal Communications Commission (FCC). For new broadcast licenses, the FCC said it would consider minority ownership as one among numerous factors. For existing licenses, the FCC said broadcasters whose continued ownership might be in question could transfer their rights to minority-owned companies and avoid a competition for the license.

By a 5-4 vote, the Supreme Court, in an opinion by Justice William J. BRENNAN Jr., upheld both FCC policies under the Constitution's guarantee of equal protection of the laws that the Court has said is implicit in the Fifth Amendment due process clause. The Court said the policies were not an improper use of race and did not violate the rights of nonminority companies.

When *Metro Broadcasting* was decided, two critical constitutional questions were unresolved despite several earlier Supreme Court decisions. One question was how closely the courts should scrutinize the federal government's reasons for using affirmative action or how much deference should be given to the objectives of Congress and federal agencies. A second question was what government justifications were acceptable for considering race in decision-making. In *Metro Broadcasting,* the Supreme Court answered both questions, but at least one of the answers was not the final word.

By a 5-4 vote, the Supreme Court said that federal affirmative action programs should not be subjected to the Court's most skeptical and searching scrutiny. The Court said federal affirmative action could be measured by what is known as INTERMEDIATE SCRUTINY, meaning the program must be substantially related to an important governmental objective. This part of the decision was overruled five years later, also by a 5-4 vote, in ADARAND CONSTRUC-

TORS, INC., V. PENA, 515 U.S. 200 (1995). The Court established that the highest level of scrutiny should be used to examine all government programs taking race into account, whether at the federal, state, or local level.

As to the second issue, in *Metro Broadcasting* the Supreme Court said that the goal of achieving diversity in broadcast programming through diversity of ownership was a legitimate one that justified the use of race as a factor in licensing. That aspect of the ruling has not been specifically overruled, although critics have argued that the rationale of programming diversity would not satisfy the higher standard of scrutiny imposed by the subsequent *ADARAND* ruling.

For more information: Baynes, Leonard M. "Life After *Adarand*: What Happened to the Metro Broadcasting Diversity Rationale for Affirmative Action in Telecommunications Ownership?" *University of Michigan Journal of Law Reform* 33 (2000): 87; Curry, George E., ed. *The Affirmative Action Debate.* Reading, Mass.: Addison-Wesley, 1996.

—Stephen Wermiel

Meyer v. Nebraska, 262 U.S. 390 (1923)

In *Meyer v. Nebraska,* the issue is whether a Nebraska act (Laws 1919, c. 249) violates the Fourteenth Amendment of the U.S. Constitution. The information against Meyer charged that he, while an instructor at Zion Parochial School in Nebraska, taught the subject of reading, in the German language, to 10-year-old Raymond Parport. The charges were based on an act related to the teaching of foreign languages in the state of Nebraska approved April 9, 1919, and is as follows:

Section I—No person, individually or as a teacher, shall, in any private denominational, parochial or public school, teach any subject to any person in any language other than the English language.

Section II—Languages, other than the English language, may be taught as languages only after the pupil has successfully attained and passed the eighth grade as evidenced by a certificate of graduation issued by the county superintendent of the county in which the child resides.

Section III—Any person who violates any of the provisions of this act shall be deemed guilty of a misdemeanor and upon conviction, shall be subjected to a fine of not less than twenty-five dollars ($25), no more than one hundred dollars ($100) or be confined to the county jail for any period not exceeding 30 days for each offense.

Section IV—Whereas, any emergency exists, this act shall be in force from and after its passage and approval.

The Nebraska Supreme Court (107 Ned. 657) upheld the conviction of Meyer. Its reasoning for upholding the conviction—the offense charged and established against

Meyer was direct and intentional teaching of the German language as a distinct subject to a pupil who had not passed the eighth grade in a parochial school. Keep in mind that a pupil does not normally enter the eighth grade until the age of 12. The Nebraska Supreme Court held that the act forbidding the German language . . . in a parochial school was a valid exercise of POLICE POWERS, that the act came within the police powers of the state (*State v. Bartles*, 191 Iowa 1060, 181 N.W. 508, and *Pohl v. State*, 102 Ohio St. 474, 132 N.E. 20), and that the act did not conflict with the Fourteenth Amendment of the U.S. Constitution.

Per Nebraska's Supreme Court, the purpose of the act was that the English language should be and become the mother language of all children reared in Nebraska and that the so-called dead languages are not in the spirit or the purpose of the act. The intention of the act was to require that the education of all children in the state be conducted in the English language and that children should not be taught any other language in schools until they had grown into the language and it had become a part of them.

The basis for Meyer's APPEAL is that the Nebraska act, as constructed and applied, infringes the liberty guaranteed him by the due process clause of the Fourteenth Amendment, which states:

> No state . . . shall deprive any person of life, liberty or property without due process of the law.

The due process clause doctrine establishes that liberty may not be interfered with under the guise of protecting the public interest by legislative action, which is arbitrary or without reasonable relation to some purpose within the competency of the state to effect. What constitutes proper exercise of police power is not final or conclusive, as determined by the legislature, but is subject to supervision by the courts.

The U.S. Supreme Court did not attempt to define liberty in the *Meyer v. Nebraska* ruling but denoted the rights of the individual. Meyer's right to teach are within the liberty of the Fourteenth Amendment and in a 7-2 decision by the U.S. Supreme Court, the Nebraska act (Laws 1919, c. 249) was ruled unconstitutional. The judgment was reversed and the cause remanded for further proceedings not inconsistent with this opinion. Any legislature that could impose restrictions on the people of the state without doing violence to the letter and spirit of the Constitution will hardly be affirmed. State regulations of liberty must be related, reasonably, to proper state objectives. The state may do much but the individual has certain rights, which must be respected.

For more information: *Meyer v. Nebraska*, 262 U.S. 390 (1923); United States Constitution. Amend. XIV, Section 1.

Available online. URL: http://www.ourdocuments.gov/doc.php?flash=true&doc=43&page=transcript. Downloaded May 17, 2004.

—Terrie D. Williams

Miami Herald Publishing Co. v. Tornillo, 418 U.S. 241 (1974)

In *Miami Herald Publishing Co. v. Tornillo*, the United States Supreme Court held that Florida's "right of reply" statute violates the First Amendment's guarantee of freedom of the press as applied to the states through the Fourteenth Amendment's due process clause. In 1913 Florida enacted a "right-to-reply law," which stipulated that if a candidate for nomination or election is criticized by a newspaper concerning either his personal character or official record, the candidate has the right to demand that the newspaper print, free of cost, any reply that the candidate wishes to make to the newspaper's charges. In September of 1972, the *Miami Herald* published a set of disparaging editorials concerning Pat Tornillo's candidacy for the Florida House of Representatives. When the *Miami Herald* refused to print his response, Tornillo brought suit against the paper. The paper in turn argued that the statute on its face violates the guarantees of a free press.

The Court unanimously rejected the state's argument that a "right to reply" statute is needed to ensure an accessible, fair, accurate, and accountable press. Chief Justice BURGER, writing for the majority, agreed that "a responsible press is an undoubtedly desirable goal," but concluded that "press responsibility is not mandated by the Constitution and like many other virtues it cannot be legislated." [*Miami Herald v. Tornillo*, 418 U.S. 241 (1974)] Instead, the Court accepted the paper's claim that the Florida statute violated its right to free press by, in effect, regulating the content of the newspaper.

Extending earlier decisions in *Associated Press v. United States*, 326 U.S. 1 (1945), BRANZBURG V. HAYES, 408 U.S. 665 (1972), and *Columbia Broadcasting System, Inc. v. Democratic National Committee*, 412 U.S. 94 (1973), the Court maintained that the core question in this case was not whether the paper was being prevented from saying whatever it wished but rather whether the paper was being "compelled" to publish that which "'reason' tells them should not be published." [*Associated Press v. United States*] The Court then held that the statute acted as a "command" in the same sense as a statute that forbids the publication of certain matters, because "it exacts a penalty on the basis of the content of a newspaper," that of the cost to the newspaper to print the mandated reply. The Court argued that a government-enforced right of access would inherently "'[dampen] the vigor and [limit] the variety of public debate.'" [*Miami Herald v. Tornillo*]

Furthermore, the Court held that the statute was unconstitutional because of "its intrusion into the function of editors." [*Miami Herald v. Tornillo*] The Court argued that the determination of what content, views, and materials will go into each paper comprises the exercise of editorial judgment, which is at the core of the First Amendment guarantee of a "free" press.

This case is also noteworthy because of Justice White's concurrence which condemned the Court for its decision on a companion case handed down the same day, *Gertz v. Welch* [418 U.S. 323 (1974)]. The Court in *Gertz* greatly curtailed the ability of private individuals to win libel suits against the press or obtain damages, and White used his concurrence to state that the Court's decision in *Gertz* "trivializes and denigrates the interest in reputation by removing virtually all the protection the law has always afforded." [*Miami Herald v. Tornillo*] Drawing a parallel between the two decisions, White agreed that the First Amendment prohibits the government from dictating what the press prints but refused to conclude that it also prohibited protections against and remedies for libel.

Overall, the Court's decision in *Miami Herald* reflects the Court's ongoing commitment to protecting the print media against government regulation of content and its belief that there is not a companion "right of access." However, it should be noted that the Court has not extended such protection to broadcasters. For example, in direct contrast to the Court's decision in *Miami Herald*, the Court determined in RED LION BROADCASTING CO. V. FCC, 395 U.S. 367 (1969), that broadcasters must give free air time to victims of their criticism.

For more information: Barron, Jerome A. *Freedom of the Press for Whom? The Right of Access to the Mass Media.* Bloomington: Indiana University Press, 1973; Bezanson, Randall P. *How Free Can the Press Be?* Champaign: University of Illinois Press, 2003; Schmidt, Benno C. *Freedom of the Press v. Public Access.* New York: Praeger, 1976.

—Amy Steigerwalt

Michael H. et al. v. Gerald D., 491 U.S. 110 (1989)

The Supreme Court affirmed decisions by California courts that the father of a child conceived in an adulterous relationship did not experience any due process violations when he was denied visitation rights normally granted to biological fathers in *Michael H. et al. v. Gerald D.*

The mother of the child, Carole D., entered into an affair with Michael H. several years after marrying Gerald

D. She gave birth to a daughter, Victoria, in 1981 and, as required by California law, her husband was listed as the father on the birth certificate. Carole D. confided to Michael H., however, that she believed that he was the biological father of the child. For the next several years, Carole D. lived not only with Michael H. and Gerald D. at different times but also lived with a third man. During this time, Michael H. publicly acknowledged Victoria as his child.

The California statute stated that the child of a married woman living with her husband who is not sterile or impotent will be acknowledged as the de facto father of the child. Further, this presumption can be challenged only if a motion is made for a blood test within two years of the date of the child's birth by the child's mother or by her husband. A 1981 blood test determined that it was more than 98 percent certain that Michael H. was the biological father of the child, yet this determination was made without the mother having requested this information via a motion in a California court. When Michael H. challenged the law, both the Superior Court and the California Court of Appeal, Second District, determined that he had no right to be granted visitation rights. The Supreme Court of California declined to review the case and the U.S. Supreme Court affirmed.

Michael H. alleged that his liberty interest, protected by the due process clause of the Fourteenth Amendment, in establishing and maintaining a relationship with Victoria were violated since he was denied a hearing in which he could assert these rights. Victoria, represented by a guardian *ad litem*, alleged that her due process rights were denied when she was not allowed to maintain a relationship with Michael H.

Justice SCALIA (1982–   ), in a 6-3 decision, wrote for a divided majority. He found that Michael H. was, in effect, seeking acknowledgement by the state of California that he was the true father of Victoria. Justice Scalia noted that such a finding could endanger the special status of the family given that "California law, like nature itself, makes no provision for dual fatherhood." The claims made by Victoria, according to Justice Scalia, are even weaker than those of Michael H. "(F)or whatever the merits of the guardian *ad litem*'s belief that such an arrangement can be of great psychological benefit to a child, the claim that a State must recognize multiple fatherhood has no support in the history or traditions of this country." The court also cited the public policy argument that irreparable harm may be done to a marriage if a biological father were to be granted visitation rights of his putative child.

In a strongly worded dissent, Justice BRENNAN (1956–90) and two other justices found that the majority's reliance on the concept of tradition, including traditional notions of the familial unit, are not sufficient to protect the due process rights of Michael H. Noting that cases such as

Griswold v. Connecticut, 381 U.S. 479 (1965), and *EISEN-STADT V. BAIRD,* 405 U.S. 438 (1972), which allowed CON-TRACEPTIVES to be distributed to married and unmarried individuals and in *Vitek v. Jones,* 445 U.S. 480 (1980), which found that an individual could not be arbitrarily moved from a prison to a psychiatric facility, were not rights traditionally protected by the due process clause of the Fourteenth Amendment,

Justice Brennan wrote that to find otherwise would offend our societal notions of justice and fairness. Justice Brennan found that "(i)t is a bad day for due process when the State's interest in terminating a parent-child relationship is reason to conclude that that relationship is not part of the "liberty" protected by the Fourteenth Amendment. Also, the interests of Michael H. in this case trump those of the state, according to Justice Brennan.

For more information: Rein, Stewart. *Betrayal of the Child: A Father's Guide to Family Courts, Divorce, Custody and Children's Rights.* Twin Lakes, Wis.: Lotus Press, 2001.
—Susan Zinner

Michael M. v. Superior Court of Sonoma County, 450 U.S. 464 (1981)

In *Michael M. v. Superior Court of Sonoma County,* the United States Supreme Court held that gender-specific statutory rape laws did not violate the EQUAL PROTECTION CLAUSE and were constitutional. At the time of this case, California's statutory rape law criminalized sexual intercourse by a male with a female under 18 who was not his wife—prosecuting only males and protecting only females.

Justice REHNQUIST wrote for the majority that California had a compelling interest in preventing the "tragic human costs of illegitimate teenage pregnancies" and that gender-specific statutory rape laws would serve as a legitimate means to deter teenage pregnancies. Therefore, they were constitutional. The majority reasoned that females should feel deterred from a (heterosexual) sexual encounter by fear of getting pregnant, and a law punishing only males would "'equalize' the deterrents on the sexes."

The plaintiff's lawyer had argued that the statute was overinclusive because it also applied to (heterosexual) sex between people using CONTRACEPTIVES, or sex with a female who could not get pregnant. But Justice STEWART's concurrence dismissed this idea as fostering defenses which would be "difficult if not impossible" to prove.

Justice BLACKMUN's concurrence noted the incongruity that while underage females have privacy rights after they are pregnant (i.e., whether to choose to have an abortion), they do not have these same rights to engage in sex in the first place. His characterization of the sexual activity

between Michael M. and Sharon got more attention. Sharon had testified that Michael punched her in the face two or three times, causing bruises. "I said, 'No,' and I was trying to get up and he hit me back down on the bench and then I just said to myself, 'Forget it,' and I let him do what he wanted to do. . . ." Yet Blackmun wrote:

> Sharon appears not to have been an unwilling participant in at least the initial stages of the intimacies. . . . [Michael's] and Sharon's nonacquaintance with each other before the incident; their drinking; their withdrawal from the others of the group; their foreplay, in which she willingly participated and seems to have encouraged; and the closeness of their ages (a difference of only one year and 18 days) are factors that should make this case an unattractive one to prosecute at all . . . (483–485).

In other words, Blackmun did not see this as the forcible rape case that it was. Feminists and legal theorists were quite alarmed at his interpretation (as well as at the majority's reason for upholding the gender-specific nature of the law), but to charge statutory rape, neither force nor nonconsent have to be proven—one only has to prove that the act occurred with an underage person. Hence, Michael could be charged with statutory rape.

In dissent, Justice BRENNAN wrote that pregnancy prevention was certainly not the historical purpose behind statutory rape laws; the laws were intended to protect female "virtue," and state-level court decisions in California from 1895 to 1978 had acknowledged that. He also found that California did not meet the "burden of proving that there are fewer teenage pregnancies under its gender-based statutory rape law than there would be if the law were gender-neutral." Justice STEVENS in a separate dissent expressed support for the protective nature of statutory rape laws, although he found both parties "equally guilty" and he characterized the majority's idea about "[equalizing] the deterrents on the sexes" as "fanciful." In short, the dissenters were more concerned with punishing teens equally rather than with gendered stereotypes, or with possible violations of equal protection and the right to PRIVACY.

Although the Court had struck down numerous gender-specific laws in the decade before this case, they found gender-specific statutory rape laws to be constitutional. Here, the majority sustained California's stated purpose of preventing pregnancy without acknowledging that sexual intercourse does not necessarily lead to pregnancy. This case left the legal door open for laws that treated males and females differently to be declared constitutional, if they could be linked to physical differences such as females' ability to get pregnant and/or give birth.

For more information: Andre-Clark, Alice Susan. "Note: Whither Statutory Rape Laws: Of Michael M., the Fourteenth Amendment, and Protecting Women from Sexual Aggression." *Southern California Law Review* 65 (1992): 1,933–1,673; Cocca, Carolyn. *Jailbait: The Politics of Statutory Rape Laws in the United States.* Albany: State University of New York Press, 2004; McCollum, James. "Case Development: Constitutional Law—Statutory Rape—Gender-Based Classification Regarding Statutory Rape Law Is Not Violative of the Equal Protection Clause of the Fourteenth Amendment: *Michael M. v. Superior Court.*" *Howard Law Journal* 25 (1982): 341–365.

—Carolyn E. Cocca

Michigan v. Long, 463 U.S. 1032 (1983)

Michigan v. Long holds that the supreme court of a state must make a plain statement that its decision expanding an individual's rights rests on independent and adequate state grounds in order to avoid JUDICIAL REVIEW by the U.S. Supreme Court. *Long* was decided 6-3, with Justice Sandra Day O'CONNOR writing the majority opinion. Justice BLACKMUN wrote a concurring opinion, and Justices BRENNAN, MARSHALL, and STEVENS were in dissent.

In *Long,* the Supreme Court of Michigan gave a pro-defendant opinion on the reasonableness of a police search and seizure of an automobile. It held that the police failed to adhere to both federal and state grounds for an individual's right to a reasonable search and seizure. O'Connor's majority opinion said that the police did not violate the federal right to a reasonable search and seizure, and reversed Michigan on that basis.

The controversy is over how to approach a presumption that justices of the 50 state supreme courts exercise an independent and competent interpretation of governmental law enforcement powers and individual rights. According to the dissenters, the institutional tradition of the U.S. Supreme Court was to exercise judicial review only if the lower court constricted an individual's right, not if it expanded it. O'Connor's opinion held if the lower court ambiguously intermixes state grounds with a prior interpretation the U.S. Supreme Court gave for a parallel federal constitutional right, then the highest court might exercise its judicial review powers.

Some scholars claim *Long* empowers the Court to actively curb a progressive expansion of individual rights in state courts. Others claim it enables a uniform development of state constitutional rights for individuals.

For more information: Solimine, Michael E., and James L. Walker. *Respecting State Courts: The Inevitability of Judicial Federalism.* Westport, Conn.: Greenwood Press, 1999.

Miller v. Johnson, 515 U.S. 900 (1995)

In *Miller v. Johnson,* a five-member majority of the Court declared that redistricting is presumptively unconstitutional when race has served as the "predominant factor" in the drawing of the district lines.

Such plans, also known as "racial gerrymanders," are subject to STRICT SCRUTINY by the Court. They are constitutionally acceptable only if the Court determines that the plan is narrowly tailored to serve a COMPELLING STATE INTEREST. Strict scrutiny is sometimes called "strict in theory, fatal in fact." Plans subject to strict scrutiny are almost always declared unconstitutional.

Applying the "predominant factor," the court struck down the Eleventh Congressional District in Georgia, one of only two districts (out of 11) in Georgia that had a majority of black voters. (At the time, Georgia had a population that was 27 percent black.) The plan was then sent back to the Georgia legislature to redraw. The legislature subsequently deadlocked, and the district court drew its own plan. The district court's plan drew only one majority-black district.

Although the legislature appealed, the Supreme Court upheld the lower court plan in *Abrams v. Johnson,* 521 U.S. 74 (1997). The Supreme Court affirmed the district court's conclusion that it would be impossible for two majority-black districts to be created without allowing race to "predominate over other traditional and neutral districting principles" [87].

The majority opinion in *Miller* clearly identifies the essential problem as predominant racial intent. Using this reasoning, a district does not have to be ugly (or more precisely, to violate "traditional districting principle") to violate the Constitution. Its appearance is merely circumstantial evidence of the intent of the designer. "Shape is relevant not because bizarreness is a necessary element of the constitutional wrong or a threshold requirement of proof, but because it may be persuasive circumstantial evidence that race for its own sake, and not other districting principles, was the legislature's dominant and controlling rationale in drawing its district lines" [913]. This theory is in *Shaw v. Hunt,* 515 U.S. 900 (1996), decided the following year. REHNQUIST, writing for the Court, states: "The plaintiff bears the burden of proving the race-based motive and may do so either through 'circumstantial evidence of a district's shape and demographics' or through 'more direct evidence going to legislative purpose'" [904].

Unusually, Justice O'CONNOR wrote a concurrence in addition to joining in the majority opinion in *Miller.* In it she states that "To invoke strict scrutiny, a plaintiff must show that the State has relied on race in substantial disregard of customary and traditional districting practices." On its face, O'Connor's concurrence seems to assert a somewhat different principle. This alternative principle is also stated in her earlier plurality opinion in *SHAW V. RENO,* 509

U.S. 630 (1993), and the later plurality opinion in *Bush v. Vera*, 517 U.S. 952 (1996).

In both of these cases, O'Connor's plurality opinions seem to assert that violation of traditional principles is an integral part of the problem, and not just circumstantial evidence of intent. "Put differently, we believe that reapportionment is one area in which appearances do matter. A reapportionment plan that includes in one district individuals who belong to the same race, but who are otherwise widely separated by geographical and political boundaries, and who may have little in common with one another but the color of their skin, bears an uncomfortable resemblance to political apartheid. It reinforces the perception that members of the same racial group—regardless of their age, education, economic status, or the community in which they live—think alike, share the same political interests, and will prefer the same candidates at the polls. We have rejected such perceptions elsewhere as impermissible racial stereotype" [647, emphasis added]. And "Significant deviations from traditional districting principles, such as the bizarre shape and noncompactness demonstrated by the districts here, cause Constitutional harm *insofar as they convey the message* that political identity is, or should be, predominantly racial. For example, the bizarre shaping of Districts 18 and 29, cutting across preexisting precinct lines and other natural or traditional divisions, *is not merely evidentially significant; it is part of the Constitutional problem*" [980–981, emphasis added].

Leaving aside the apparent conflict among these decisions, there remains significant uncertainty about how to apply this new predominant intent standard. For example, suppose that:

- A redistricting plan is approved by a legislature by a majority vote. Of that voting majority, more than half of the legislators vote for the plan for purely nonracial reasons. However, a small coalition of legislators makes racial motivation a top priority, and, without their additional votes, the plan could not have passed.
- The first priority of everyone in the legislature voting on the plan is to maximize the chance of keeping their own seat, but everyone's second priority is to maximize the number of majority-white seats.
- The first priority of everyone in the legislature is to ensure at least one majority-black seat, but once ensured they prefer maximizing their chance of capturing the most seats for their party to any other goal, including additional majority-minority seats.
- The original authors of a redistricting plan design it entirely with the motivation of maximizing the number of majority-white seats. The legislature who authorizes the plan, while aware of the original motivation and

impact, vote for the plan entirely because it satisfies other goals.

Even if we could look into the heads of each legislator, and know their exact motivations, it is not clear which of these situations is "predominantly motivated by race." No PRECEDENT or well-established legal theory yet exists to distinguish among these cases.

Despite its ambiguities, *Miller* and the other recent racial gerrymandering cases are important because they have had a dramatic effect on the way districts are drawn in the United States. Many experts believe that these cases have led to significant changes in the racial and partisan composition of the U.S. Congress.

For more information: Issacharoff, Samuel, Pamela S. Karlan, Richard H. Pildes, and Lloyd J. Mercer. *The Law of Democracy: Legal Structure of the Political Process.* 2nd ed. Westbury, N.Y.: Foundation Press, 2001; Kousser, J. Morgan. *Colorblind Injustice: Minority Voting Rights and the Undoing of the Second Reconstruction.* Chapel Hill: University of North Carolina Press, 1999.

—Micah Altman

Milliken v. Bradley, 418 U.S. 717 (1974)

Milliken v. Bradley is an important case focusing on the EQUAL PROTECTION CLAUSE as applied to remedies for RACIAL DISCRIMINATION in public schools. The majority held that interdistrict remedies were not constitutional absent a finding that the discrimination in one district affected segregation in other districts.

The facts of the case revolved around decisions by the municipal government of Detroit and the Michigan state government that led to segregated schools in Detroit. The trial court found that state and city officials had made decisions that produced racial segregation in the public schools. The trial court further concluded that desegregation efforts could not be successful if these were limited to the city boundaries. Hence, an order was issued that included Detroit and 53 surrounding school districts in a desegregation plan. The case went to the United States Supreme Court, where the ruling of the district court was reversed.

Chief Justice Warren BURGER wrote the majority opinion for a sharply divided Court, with his opinion being supported by five justices with four justices dissenting. Burger began by noting that cross-district remedies might be appropriate under certain circumstances: "Boundary lines may be bridged where there has been a constitutional violation calling for interdistrict relief, but the notion that school district lines may be casually ignored or treated as a mere administrative convenience is contrary to the history of public education in our country."

He goes on to say that cross-district remedies only make sense if there have been violations of equal protection across districts. Burger said: "Before the boundaries of separate and autonomous school districts may be set aside by consolidating the separate units for remedial purposes or by imposing a cross-district remedy, it must first be shown that there has been a constitutional violation within one district that produces a significant segregative effect in another district." In the final analysis, according to Burger, "To approve the remedy ordered . . . would impose on the outlying districts, not shown to have committed any constitutional violation, a wholly impermissible remedy based on a standard not hinted at [in] any holding of this Court."

Justice MARSHALL's dissent argued that the majority opinion was "a giant step backwards." He contended that the Court's decision, in essence, allowed state decisions supporting segregation to go unchallenged and unremedied. In his view, "it becomes the duty of the State to eliminate root and branch all vestiges of racial discrimination and to achieve the greatest possible degree of actual desegregation."

Justice WHITE also authored a dissent. He stated:

The core of my disagreement is that deliberate acts of segregation and their consequences will go unremedied. . . . The result is that [Michigan], the entity at which the 14th Amendment is directed, has successfully insulated itself from its duty to provide effective desegregation remedies by vesting sufficient power over to public schools in its local school districts.

This is an important case, in that the Supreme Court noted that there were limits to developing remedies to address de jure segregation in public schools. The case serves as an indication that the Supreme Court was backing away from an activist role in attacking de jure segregation.

For more information: Strickman, Leonard. "School Desegregation at the Crossroads." *Nw. U. L. Review* 70 (1975): 725.

—Steven A. Peterson

Minnesota v. Cloverleaf Creamery Company, 449 U.S. 456 (1981)

In *Minnesota v. Cloverleaf Creamery Company,* the United States Supreme Court reversed a Minnesota Supreme Court decision that had found a Minnesota law prohibiting plastic milk containers violated the EQUAL PROTECTION CLAUSE of the Fourteenth Amendment of the U.S. Constitution. In the process, the Supreme Court reaffirmed that "when a state court reviews state legislation challenged as violative of the Fourteenth Amendment, it is not free to impose greater restriction as a matter of federal constitutional law than [the United States Supreme Court] has imposed."

The Minnesota legislature, acting with the support of Minnesota's pollution control agency and other environmental agencies, passed a law prohibiting the use of plastic nonreturnable milk containers. Proponents of the law argued that "It would promote resource conservation, ease solid waste disposal problems, and conserve energy." Opponents of the act "presenting empirical evidence, argued that the act would not promote the goals asserted by the proponents."

Opponents of the act sued in Minnesota District Court and the district court found that, based on evidence, the legislature had no RATIONAL BASIS for the law under the equal protection clause and the law interfered with INTERSTATE COMMERCE. The Minnesota Supreme Court affirmed the district court on the equal protection argument and did not address the commerce clause argument. The Minnesota Supreme Court held that the act promoted the state interests but found that "the evidence conclusively demonstrates that the discrimination against plastic nonrefillables is not rationally related to the act's objections." Justice BRENNAN, writing for the majority stated that "[i]t is not the function of the courts to substitute their evaluation of legislative facts for that of the Legislature." In effect, a court must determine whether a legislature, when passing an act, had a rational basis from the legislature's view. A court is not to impose its own view of rationality on a law.

The Court also held that states are limited by the commerce clause even when addressing areas of legitimate local concern. If state laws are disguised to hide an unconstitutional intent, i.e, economic protectionism, the Supreme Court applies a per se rule of invalidity. The Court may also strike down an evenhanded statute imposing incidental burdens on interstate commerce if the burdens imposed on commerce exceed the claimed local benefits. Justice Brennan, for the Court, determined that the Minnesota statute did not discriminate between interstate and intrastate commerce, and "the burden imposed on interstate commerce by the statute [was] relatively minor." In fact, several of the milk-producing companies challenging the law were Minnesota companies. The Court noted that while the district court did find evidence that the law was intended to help certain businesses and industries in Minnesota, the actual purpose was to benefit the environment and conserve energy. In that respect, the law treated in-state and out-of-state businesses evenly without significant burdens on interstate commerce.

As Justice STEVENS pointed out in his dissent, the Cloverleaf Creamery Company case appears unique because the Supreme Court reversed a state supreme court ruling on a state law issue. Nonetheless, as Justice Brennan showed, the Minnesota Supreme Court relied heavily on the U.S. Constitution's Fourteenth Amendment equal protection clause. Therefore, the majority found the Minnesota Supreme Court overstepped its bounds.

For more information: Chemerinsky, Erwin. *Constitutional Law.* Gaithersburg, Md.: Aspen Law and Business, 2001.

—Erick-Woods Erickson

minors, rights of

Minors, or children under 18, have limited rights under the Constitution and the laws of the country.

Under parental control, minors have rights only to basic necessities. Very young children are not held accountable for their choices or actions; their parents are responsible for them. As children grow older their rights and responsibilities grow as well. As they mature into adolescence and into adulthood their protection and support transitions from parents or legal guardians to the state. Over time, the Supreme Court has increasingly granted some rights enjoyed by adults to minors. However, as children develop into adolescence and their cognitive abilities increase, so does their legal accountability. No longer does the law assume they do not understand the consequences of their actions.

Until the age of majority, the law restricts minors' rights in various ways. The age of majority in most states is 18. However, in Alabama, Nebraska, and Wyoming it is 19, and in Mississippi it is 21. Until that time, minors do not have the right to vote in local elections, view or participate in any type of pornography, purchase tobacco or liquor products, gamble, enter into legally binding contracts, consent to medical care, marry, or enlist in the armed forces or work at most jobs without parental consent. They may not manage their property without a guardian of the estate. The law considers minors under parental control until they reach the age of majority.

Parents are required to provide their children with adequate care, including shelter, food, clothing, education, and medical care. Parents cannot kick their minor children out of the house unless they are deemed out of control, in which case they become wards of the state. Minors are also protected from abuse and neglect by their parents and other caretakers. If they are abused the state may remove them and put them in foster care or some other safe environment.

The Constitution does not mention minors or their rights. However, the BILL OF RIGHTS and the Fourteenth Amendment have been interpreted as providing minors with rights with restrictions. Parents and schools legally regulate minors' activities in utilizing these rights. Under the First Amendment parents and schools may supervise freedom of expression. A parent can dress their children in whatever manner they deem appropriate. School's may establish dress codes. Parents and schools may also censor the speech of minors, including in school newspapers. Parents and teachers may prohibit profanity in the home and classroom. Freedom to express and practice RELIGION and of assembly are also rights limited by parents and schools.

Regarding the SECOND AMENDMENT, federal law prohibits the sale of handguns to anyone under the age of 21, and of rifles and shotguns to anyone under the age of 18. States and cities also regulate the right to bear arms. In most states, a minor can legally carry a gun but must have written parental consent. However, even with written permission, the minor may not carry a gun into a place where it is prohibited, such as school. Furthermore, a minor cannot legally purchase a gun or ammunition but may receive them as gifts.

Fourth Amendment search and seizure rights apply to minors usually in the same manner as with adults. Probable cause must exist before a search can be conducted, and the search must be reasonable. Any evidence obtained in an illegal search is inadmissible in court. The due process clause of the Fourteenth Amendment guarantees that this applies to state governments as well.

The Fifth Amendment's right against self-incrimination applies to minors. When taken into custody a minor has the right to remain silent. To waive this right, however, a minor's competence must be judged according to his or her age, level of maturity, and past record with the police.

The Sixth Amendment guarantees the right to counsel to minors whether in juvenile or adult court. When a minor is brought before a juvenile court, the Seventh Amendment's right to a jury trial is not guaranteed; however, some states have granted this right to minors— Alaska, Colorado, Michigan, New Mexico, Texas, and Wyoming.

The Eighth Amendment protects minors against cruel and unusual punishment. However, in states with the death penalty, minors tried as adults are not protected against this type of punishment. As with adults, sentencing minors to death is not defined as cruel and unusual punishment.

The Fourteenth Amendment grants due process and equal protection rights, but these are limited when applied to minors. Along with TITLE VII OF THE CIVIL RIGHTS ACT OF 1964, the Fourteenth Amendment protects against state-sponsored discrimination on the basis of age, sex, and race. Nevertheless, the law discriminates in certain situations. Minors may not purchase tobacco or liquor products. States and cities require girls to wear tops in public. Students may be bussed against their will to correct racial imbalance. These are all examples of how law might discriminate against minors based on their age.

For more information: Hempelman, Kathleen A. *Teen Legal Rights.* Rev. ed. Westport and London: Greenwood

Press, 2000; Rosenheim, Margaret K., Franklin Zimring, David S. Tanenhaus, and Bernadine Dohrn, eds. *A Century of Juvenile Justice.* Chicago and London: University of Chicago Press, 2002.

—Matthew R. Doyle

Miranda v. Arizona, 384 US 436 (1966)

The cases that ultimately led to the 5-4 decision in favor of *Miranda* mostly involved a defendant who was in police custody, was denied his right to counsel, and was at some point questioned by the police or a prosecuting attorney. Justice WARREN delivered the opinion for the Court and thus began the historical turning point in law enforcement practices and criminal rights standards in modern times.

The interrogations were typically conducted in a room that was outside of normal access by the public or the defense attorneys. None of the defendants were given a full warning of their rights at the beginning of the custody process. In every one of the underlying cases the police or the prosecuting attorneys were able to elicit oral admissions. In three cases, signed statements were developed as well. All of this evidence was considered admissible at their trials and resulted in convictions of the defendants.

The Court's mandate was established to protect and preserve the rights of the accused while in police custody in locations outside of the public eye. The warnings apply only to those situations where someone is within police custody, is being interrogated for suspicion of committing a crime, and is basically deprived of their freedom in a significant way. These Fifth Amendment protections exclude undercover officers and others posing as normal citizens and not as overt law enforcement officers or agents for the government.

Therefore after the *Miranda* decision, the prosecution could not use any statements made by the defendant, irrespective of whether they were exculpatory or inculpatory, that had been derived from the police questioning. The results of the questioning were restricted to the time starting after a suspect had been taken into custody—deprived of his freedom of action in any significant way—and were established to safeguard the Fifth Amendment's elaborated privilege protecting people from self-incrimination. Most of the support came from the opinion that someone within police custody could be coerced into incriminating themselves.

The precursor decision came in *ESCOBEDO V. ILLINOIS* (1964), which defined the need for the Court to establish legal protections in order to make the process of police interrogations a more evenhanded event. In that case the defendant engaged in conversation with another defendant without properly being informed that he had the "right to remain silent." Escobedo's lawyer was also not allowed to see his client. The court decided that the information obtained by the police in that case was inadmissible due to the violation of Escobedo's Sixth and Fourteenth Amendment rights.

The *Miranda* violations of the Fifth Amendment privileges made the following tenets necessary for law enforcement officers: the subject of the arrest / custody must—prior to the conducting of any interrogation—be made aware in a clear manner that he has the right to remain silent, and that anything he says will be used against him in court. The person in custody must also be made aware of the fact that he has the right to consult with counsel and even to have that lawyer available to him and present when engaged in custody during most law enforcement proceedings and especially during any interrogation. Of special note is that if the subject in custody does not have the financial means available to him, then the court will appoint a public defender for the person in order to allow the person in custody a fair trial. In addition, the subject that is being questioned by the police can at any time stop the questioning.

The *Miranda* decision was one of the most controversial cases in the history of the American legal system. The Warren Court's decision was expanded shortly after *Miranda* in *Mathis v. United States* (1968) and in *Orozco v. Texas* (1969). The repercussions of the *Miranda* decision have been reduced as the courts have since narrowed the impact in *New York v. Quarles* (1984) and in *Oregon v. Elstad* (1985). The later court decisions have afforded the law enforcement community more leeway in protecting themselves in emergent circumstances, but the decision stills stands as a revolutionary CIVIL LIBERTIES rallying point.

The federal and law enforcement communities mostly utilize and abide by the decision in their actions with many agencies such as the Chicago Police Department, making it a department-wide common inclusion in case reporting and arrest procedures. Challengers to *Miranda* were debunked when Justice REHNQUIST offered that the decision should stand and that it existed as a constitutional rule that could not be overturned through an act of Congress. Almost 40 years after the *Miranda* decision, the protections allowed still are impacting the court.

For more information: Friedman, Lawrence M. *Crime and Punishment in American History.* New York: Basic Books, 1993.

—Ernest Alexander Gomez

Mississippi University for Women v. Hogan, 458 U.S. 718 (1982)

In *Mississippi University for Women v. Hogan*, the United States Supreme Court decided that a state's operation of a single-sex nursing school violated the U.S. Constitution.

In 1884 Mississippi established the oldest state-run, all-female college in the United States. The college, known today as Mississippi University for Women (MUW), opened a School of Nursing in 1971. The nursing program was open only to women.

Joe Hogan, who lived and worked near MUW, applied for admission. Otherwise qualified, he was not allowed to enroll in the bachelor's degree program because of his sex. School officials told him that he was welcome to audit courses, however, and they alerted him to two state-run nursing programs open to men but located at some distance from MUW.

Hogan claimed denying him entry to the bachelor's degree program at MUW violated the Fourteenth Amendment to the Constitution, which says, "No state shall . . . deny to any person within its jurisdiction the equal protection of the laws."

Six years earlier, in CRAIG V. BOREN, 429 U.S. 190 (1976), the U.S. Supreme Court established the principle that when a state discriminates on the basis of gender, it violates the EQUAL PROTECTION CLAUSE unless it can show that its gender classifications serve important governmental objectives and . . . [are] substantially related to the achievement of those objectives.

Writing for the Court in the present case, Justice Sandra Day O'CONNOR declared that the standard had to be applied free of gender stereotypes, and that if the purpose of the policy was to preserve traditional, inaccurate assumptions about the proper roles of men and women, the policy was illegitimate.

Mississippi asserted that its objective was not to reinforce the character of nursing as a women's profession, but to compensate women for years of workplace discrimination. Furthermore, the state declared, the policy was necessary to protect women by eliminating the potentially domineering presence of men in the classroom.

Justice O'Connor noted that compensatory discrimination may be justified in certain cases, but only when the members of the gender being protected actually suffer a disadvantage related to the classification. In the case of nursing, doors had never been closed to women; on the contrary, women were vastly overrepresented in the profession. She concluded that the actual objective underlying the classification was the perpetuation of a gender stereotype.

The second question was whether gender segregation was substantially related to the state's desire to forestall male domination in the classroom. The Court found that MUW's policy of allowing men in the classroom as auditors and as enrollees in continuing education courses fatally undermined that claim. The Court held that gender-segregated state schools were unconstitutional if their purpose was to perpetuate an outmoded stereotype.

Andrew Johnson *(Library of Congress)*

In dissent, Justice POWELL argued that the purpose of the MUW program was not to perpetuate a gender stereotype, but to offer an additional choice to Mississippi's women, who had the opportunity to attend two other coeducational nursing schools, if they chose, and he argued that Hogan's claimed harm, the need to travel to attend a bachelor's program, was constitutionally trivial.

For more information: *United States v. Virginia*, 518 U.S. 515 (1996).

—William H. Coogan

Mississippi v. Johnson, 71 U.S. 475 (1867)

In *Mississippi v. Johnson,* the Court denied injunctive relief to halt enforcement of the Reconstruction Acts to the state of Mississippi. The case is an important one regarding the power of the Supreme Court in relation to the president of the United States.

The Reconstruction Acts, passed over the veto of President Andrew Johnson, required the appointment of generals, with the requisite military force to carry out orders, in five military districts covering the states that seceded from the Union at the beginning of the Civil War. This military command was to enforce the rights of all persons in the district and to suppress insurrection and disorder. These military commanders had the authority to try, at the discretion of the military commander, all those committing criminal acts or disturbing the peace. These proceedings could occur in either local civil tribunals or through military tribunals, regardless of whether or not the civil courts were open and functioning at the time of trial.

Furthermore, the Reconstruction Acts gave final approval of the reconstituted state governments, and whether to admit their duly elected representatives to Congress, to the federal government. Until the state governments were so approved, any government operating in the state was to be considered provisional and subject to the military authority put in place by the Reconstruction Acts. Finally, the acts set out specific requirements for the registration of voters and the contents of the state constitutions for the reconstructed South.

Mississippi asserted that the Court had the power to issue an injunction based on a distinction between the president's enforcement of executive duties, involving political issues, and the duties of his office which involved no discretion, called "ministerial duties" by the parties. Counsel for Mississippi argued that the appointment of generals was a ministerial duty which the Court could legally enjoin. This argument was based on the famous case *MARBURY V. MADISON,* 5 U.S. 137 (1803), in which Chief Justice John MARSHALL, by a writ of mandamus (an order from the Court requiring specific action not subject to discretion), required President Jefferson to issue the commission of Marbury, who had been appointed a justice of the peace by a previous administration. Thus, the argument was that if the Court could force action with respect to a ministerial duty in *Marbury,* then it could restrain action with respect to such a duty in the instant case. Johnson, believing despite his veto that the issuance of an injunction in this case would set a dangerous PRECEDENT, sent his attorney general to argue against Mississippi.

Salmon P. CHASE, writing for a unanimous Court, held that the obligation of the president to appoint commanders under the Reconstruction Acts was closer to an executive duty and refused to grant Mississippi an injunction. Chase said that "the exercise of powers to see that the law is faithfully executed" was an executive duty not amenable to an injunction issuing from the Supreme Court. This assertion was supported by the fact that the Court had never before entertained a bill for injunction of executive presidential action in any case, despite numerous opportunities to do so.

Concerns over the SEPARATION OF POWERS underlie the decision in *Mississippi v. Johnson.* The Court held that it did not have the authority to restrain the actions of either the president or of Congress, although Chase opined that it did have the authority to hear cases once action had been taken. Furthermore, any attempt to enjoin the actions of either branch would quickly lead to ridiculous results. For instance, had the Court issued an injunction in this case, Chase speculated, it would be impossible, should the president refuse to obey, for the Court to enforce its order. Yet, even if the president did obey an injunction from the Court, that would bring him into conflict with the Congress that originally passed the Reconstruction Acts. This would in turn require the Court to enjoin any impeachment proceedings against the president in the Senate which were likely to follow. Such a situation would create a constitutional quagmire, which the Court was keen to avoid.

Finally, the Court held that it did not matter whether the bill seeking injunction was aimed at Andrew Johnson as president or at him as a citizen of the United States, for any relief sought against his actions would be relief sought against actions of the president.

For more information: Du Bois, W. E. B. *Black Reconstruction in America 1860–1880.* Cleveland, Ohio: World, 1964; McPherson, James M. *Ordeal by Fire: The Civil War and Reconstruction.* New York: Alfred A. Knopf, 1982.

—Banks Miller

Missouri v. Holland, 252 U.S. 416 (1920)

Missouri v. Holland, U.S. Game Warden, was an important case in the development of the INHERENT POWERS of the government of the United States in foreign affairs.

Missouri is located on one of the great migratory flyways. Every year the blue October skies hold vast flocks of birds flying south for the winter. Waterfowl, especially geese and ducks, flying in their V-shaped wedge formations, honking their calls to each other, silhouette the sky with skein after skein stretching as far as the eye can see.

By the early 1900s, the state of Missouri, like all American states, had established hunting regulations to allow the hunting of migratory birds. However, conservationists were very concerned that overhunting would cause many species to become extinct as had recently happened to the passenger pigeon. In response to conservationist concerns, Congress passed a law in 1913 to regulate the hunting of migratory birds. Two federal district courts declared the law to regulate the hunting of migratory birds based on the commerce clause to be unconstitutional because there is nothing expressed or implied in the Constitution to authorize the regulation. The cases were not appealed.

On July 3, 1918, Congress passed the Migratory Bird Treaty Act as legislation to implement the Migratory Bird Treaty of December 8, 1916, with Great Britain acting on behalf of Canada. Missouri sued to stop Ray P. Holland, a federal game warden, from enforcing the law. Missouri argued that the law and hence the treaty were not authorized by the Constitution; that the treaty infringed upon Missouri powers, reserved to it by the Tenth Amendment; and that once the birds entered Missouri air space they became the property of the state of Missouri.

The case was argued before the Supreme Court on March 2, 1920, and decided on April 19, 1920, by a seven to two vote. Justice Oliver HOLMES delivered the opinion for the Court, and Justices Willis VAN DEVANTER and Mahlon Pitney dissented.

Holmes, in a short, cryptic opinion, concluded that the government of the United States did, in foreign affairs, have the authority "under the Constitution" to make TREATIES and to implement them under the NECESSARY AND PROPER CLAUSE, Article I, Section 8. He also concluded all treaties are the law of the land (Article VI) so the claims of Missouri could not limit the treaty-making power of the federal government. Justice Holmes also dismissed Missouri claim to a property interest in migrating birds by noting that they were wild and the property of no one.

This case created a new federal power, and along with it fears that the treaty power would be used to take away liberties. In 1953 Senator John Bricker (Rep.-Ohio) proposed the "Bricker Amendment" to overturn the case. The proposed amendment failed but renewed calls for repealing *Missouri v. Holland* still occur.

For more information: Lofgren, Charles A. "*Missouri v. Holland* in Historical Perspective." *Supreme Court Review* (1975): 77–122.

—A. J. K. Waskey

Mistretta v. United States, 488 U.S. 361 (1989)

In *Mistretta v. United States,* the Supreme Court upheld the constitutionality of Congress's law that created a commission and gave it the power to make sentencing guidelines.

Congress passed the Sentencing Reform Act of 1984 out of concerns that federal judges were giving similarly situated convicted criminals widely different sentences. For example, one federal district court judge might sentence a person convicted of possession of drugs to one year of probation, while a judge in another part of the country (or the judge in the courtroom right down the hall) might hand down a sentence of 10 years. This could be true even if the amount of drugs possessed was the same, and the backgrounds of the criminal defendants were similar. For most of the 20th century, Congress and many criminal justice professionals thought that it was good for judges to have this wide discretion. Congress thus set up a system of indeterminate sentences. Although Congress specified penalties for each crime, Congress also gave sentencing judges

wide discretion to determine how long a convicted defendant should spend in prison. For many crimes, judges also had the discretion to sentence an offender to supervised freedom (probation) instead of time in prison, or even to impose a sentence of just a fine. The philosophy behind this wide discretion is that judges are in the best position to determine what sentence would be needed to rehabilitate each individual offender.

Dissatisfaction with wide sentencing disparities by federal judges came at a time when Congress and many criminal justice professionals had decided that rehabilitation of offenders was not working. Many criminals were committing more crimes after leaving prison or probation. It thus became more important for sentences for crimes to serve as punishment for the offender. The criminal justice system should punish persons that commit crimes in order to keep them off the streets, in order to deter others from committing crimes, and to express society's disgust with the criminal conduct. Under this philosophy, sentences should vary with the seriousness of the crime but should not vary a great deal between offenders who commit the same crime. (Certain background factors of the offender are important to sentencing, however, especially the offender's prior criminal record.)

The Sentencing Reform Act of 1984 created a seven-member group of professionals called the U.S. Sentencing Commission and gave it the job of developing "guidelines" for federal judges to follow in imposing sentences. Congress provided that the Sentencing Commission would be made up of at least three federal judges and would be located in the judicial branch. The Sentencing Commission set forth specific penalties for each crime based on factors such as the seriousness of each crime, and specific categories of offenders based on factors such as the offender's prior record. In sentencing an offender, a trial judge must categorize each offender and then choose from a fairly narrow range of sentences. A judge who imposes a sentence outside the guidelines will probably be reversed by the COURT OF APPEALS.

John Mistretta was convicted of possessing and selling cocaine and was sentenced to 18 months in jail and a fine by a federal judge acting under the guidelines. Mistretta challenged his sentence on the grounds that the Sentencing Reform Act of 1984 was unconstitutional because it violates principles of SEPARATION OF POWERS. Congress, as established in the Constitution as the legislative branch of government, is supposed to create laws. This function is not be performed by the other two branches of government. In writing sentencing guidelines, Mistretta argued, the Sentencing Commission is in fact legislating. Congress has delegated too much of its legislative authority to the Sentencing Commission, a body located in the judicial branch of government. District courts ruled that the guidelines were unconstitutional and that judges need not follow them. The Supreme Court accepted Mistretta's APPEAL in order to settle the confusion.

In deciding that the Sentencing Reform Act was constitutional, the Court reasoned that Congress can delegate some of its legislative responsibilities to other branches as long as it sets forth specific and detailed guidance for them to follow. Here, Congress had given the Sentencing Commission very specific guidelines to follow in developing sentences. Furthermore, sometimes one must expect Congress to seek assistance from expert bodies outside of Congress. In developing sentencing guidelines, Congress needed assistance from experts in the judicial branch. The Court explained, "[d]eveloping proportionate penalties for hundreds of different crimes by a virtually limitless array of offenders is precisely the sort of intricate, labor-intensive task for which delegation to an expert body is especially appropriate" [488 U.S. 379]. One Justice, Justice SCALIA, agreed with Mistretta that the Sentencing Reform Act violated separation of powers and filed a dissenting opinion.

For more information: Epstein, Lee, and Thomas G. Walker. *Constitutional Law for a Changing America: Institutional Powers and Constraints.* 5th ed. Washington, D.C.: CQ Press, 2004.

—Karen Swenson

Mitchell v. Helms, 530 U.S. 793 (2000)

Mitchell v. Helms overturned a ruling that barred Louisiana school districts from distributing federal educational funds to parochial schools. The convoluted 15-year court battle over the educational program in question reflected a considerable amount of change in and confusion about the Court's ESTABLISHMENT CLAUSE jurisprudence, but the decision itself is a landmark in the REHNQUIST Court's attempt to reshape establishment clause doctrine.

The case was initially filed as *Helms v. Cody* in Louisiana in 1985 as a challenge to certain applications of Chapter 2 of the federal Education Consolidation and Improvement Act of 1981. This law provides federal funds to school districts which then disburse funds to individual schools, including parochial schools, to finance purchase of educational materials like textbooks and library resources. After five years of hearings and deliberations, the court ruled that the provision of federal funds to parochial schools under Chapter 2 was unconstitutional, and four years later (in 1994) the judge in the case permanently barred these federal funds from going to parochial schools. Shortly thereafter this judge retired and a new judge (relying on the logic of several of the establishment clause decisions the Rehnquist Court issued in the 12 years since *Helms v. Cody* had been filed) reversed his predecessor's

ruling and permitted the provision of federal funds to parochial schools under Chapter 2.

Those who opposed distribution of these federal funds to parochial schools appealed the reversal, but while the case was at the U.S. COURT OF APPEALS, the Supreme Court issued yet another significant ruling, *Agostini v. Felton,* 521 U.S. 203 (1997), which overruled two prior Supreme Court decisions (*Aguilar v. Felton,* 473 U.S. 402 [1985], in its entirety and *School Dist. of Grand Rapids v. Ball,* 473 U.S. 373 [1985], in part). Because of these and other changes in the Court's establishment clause doctrine, the Court of Appeals struggled to discern a clear principle in the Supreme Court's jurisprudence on which it could decide the APPEAL. In reversing the decision that the Court of Appeals ultimately reached, the Supreme Court provided a clear principle in *Mitchell v. Helms.*

The principle, asserted vigorously by Justice THOMAS in his plurality opinion, was that of neutrality. Thomas's principle would allow government programs that were offered broadly to citizens or groups without consideration of recipients' RELIGION and would not invalidate programs that permitted government funds to flow to religious entities by the private choices of individuals.

Following this principle, Thomas rejected at least three strategies previously employed by the Court for judging the acceptability of government programs under the establishment clause. First, Thomas argued that the notion of private individual choice bound up in the neutrality principle superseded language of "direct" or "indirect" aid to religion; so long as aid passes from government to religious entities through the choices of individual beneficiaries, this aid is constitutionally acceptable. In addition, the neutrality principle made irrelevant the objection that government aid cannot be put to religious use. "The issue is not divertibility of aid but rather whether the aid has an impermissible content. Where the aid would be suitable for use in a public school, it is also suitable for use in any private school." Finally, Thomas rejected the argument that government aid cannot go to "pervasively sectarian" institutions. This concern is irrelevant if a program is neutrally constructed and, in Thomas's mind, the term *sectarian* reflects the "shameful pedigree" of anti-Catholic sentiment that emerged in America in the late 19th century. "This doctrine," Thomas concluded, "born of bigotry, should be buried now."

Justice O'CONNOR concurred with Thomas's holding in the *Mitchell* case and with his overruling of two previous Supreme Court rulings, *Meek v. Pittenger,* 421 U.S. 349 (1975), and *Wolman v. Walter,* 433 U.S. 229 (1977), that had invalidated programs similar to the one *Mitchell* upheld, but she reached these conclusions on different principles than did Justice Thomas. O'Connor objected that "the plurality's treatment of neutrality comes close to assigning that factor singular importance in the future adjudication of establishment clause challenges to government school-aid programs." Thomas's articulation of such a strong principle of neutrality went even beyond the revisions made to the Court's establishment clause framework in *Agostini*, and its rejection of much of the language that had been used in establishment clause cases put the status of many of those cases in question. For these reasons O'Connor authored her concurrence on the more nuanced but more complicated principles set forth in *Agostini*.

In dissent, Justice SOUTER lamented that the plurality decision (and to a lesser degree the concurring opinion) misunderstood or misrepresented the tradition of establishment clause jurisprudence, and the tradition of the clause itself; Souter presented a long restatement of his understanding of this tradition. It seems clear, however, that the ground on which debate about the establishment clause is conducted has shifted from the strict separation of religion and public life that Justice Souter supports to an approach that demands that government treat religious organizations and individuals equally with respect to their nonreligious counterparts.

For more information: Lupu, Ira C. "Government Messages and Government Money: Santa Fe, *Mitchell v. Helms*, and the Arc of the Establishment Clause." *Wm and Mary L. Rev.* 42 (2001): 771.

—Jason Ross

Mobile v. Bolden, 446 U.S. 55 (1980)

In *Mobile v. Bolden*, the Supreme Court upheld the at-large election of commissioners adopted by the city in 1911 against challenges that such a system violated the EQUAL PROTECTION CLAUSE of the Fourteenth Amendment, the Fifteenth Amendment, and Section 2 of the 1965 VOTING RIGHTS ACT.

While the Supreme Court voted 6-3 to allow Mobile, Alabama, to continue electing its three commissioners on an at-large basis, the decision itself was rather fractured. The case was originally argued during the Court's 1978–79 term and then reargued during its 1979–80 term before being decided on April 22, 1980. Justice Potter STEWART wrote the plurality opinion for the four members of the Court who argued the electoral system in place lacked the "discriminatory motivation" required for a Fifteenth Amendment violation and the "purposeful discrimination" needed to run counter to the equal protection clause of the Fourteenth Amendment [*Mobile v. Bolden*, 446 U.S. 55, 61–68 (1980)].

Additionally, Justice Stewart (with Chief Justice Warren BURGER and Justices Lewis POWELL and William REHNQUIST in tow) noted that the statutory claim of a Voting Rights Act violation had little value. In the Court's judgment,

the 1965 law simply reiterated the prohibitions contained in the Fifteenth Amendment and did not have any effect protecting minority voting that differed from the protections contained in the amendment itself [*Mobile v. Bolden*]. That question of motivation would provide the backdrop for changes introduced in the Voting Rights Act in the wake of the Mobile opinion.

Citing *Gomillion v. Lightfoot*, 364 U.S. 339 (1960), and other precedents, Justice Stewart argued that in order to support the findings of the district court and the COURT OF APPEALS that the at-large commission system violated the Fourteenth and Fifteenth Amendments discriminatory intent and motivation would have to exist. Yet, the previous courts found that African-American voters in the city could "register and vote without hindrance" [*Mobile v. Bolden*]. Under such circumstances, according to the Court, the discovery of constitutional violations, by the trial and appellate courts, was in error.

Stewart also rejected the points made by Justice Thurgood MARSHALL in dissent, referring to Justice Marshall's arguments as political theory rather than law—theory that would turn the Court into a "super-legislature" protecting certain groups from electoral defeat [*Mobile v. Bolden*].

In a brief concurring opinion, Justice Harry BLACKMUN noted that the district court failed to consider more moderate alternatives to forcing a mayor/single-member district council system on the city, thereby providing relief "not commensurate with the sound exercise of judicial discretion" [*Mobile v. Bolden*]. Justice John Paul STEVENS's concurrence agreed that there was no constitutional right to have proportional representation for racial minorities; but he declined to focus on the motivation of decision-makers, arguing that this would put the Court into "the political thicket" deciding endless litigation over every multimember district system in existence [*Mobile v. Bolden*].

The three dissenting justices (William BRENNAN, Byron WHITE, and Thurgood Marshall) each wrote separately with Justice Marshall providing the most extensive comments. In Justice Marshall's view, there was no need to show discriminatory intent in matters involving minority-vote dilution. Following the logic of *White v. Regester*, 412 U.S. 755 (1973), the dissent notes that the right to vote is a fundamental right subject to the strict-scrutiny review standard [*Mobile v. Bolden*]. All that is thus needed to invalidate multimember district systems is a showing of discriminatory impact. The right to vote is more than "the right to cast meaningless ballots" [*Mobile v. Bolden*].

While blacks (referred to as Negroes in the decision) constituted more than 35 percent of the city's population, none had ever been elected to the commission in the racially polarized city with its long history of official discrimination. This is all the proof needed to show that the dilution of minority votes has occurred.

Following this decision, the 1982 extension of the Voting Rights Act amended Section 2 to consider the effect of actions on minority voters, rather than on the intent of the action. Faced with these circumstances, the city then adopted a mayor/single-member district system of government despite its victory in support of the commission form in *Mobile v. Bolden.*

For more information: Davidson, Chandler, ed. *Minority Vote Dilution.* Washington, D.C.: Howard University Press, 1984; Grofman, Bernard, Lisa Handley, and Richard Niemi. *Minority Representation and the Quest for Voting Equality.* New York: Cambridge University Press, 1992.

—Norman Provizer

moot

When a legal dispute is resolved such that there is no longer an actual controversy, a case is considered to be moot. In other words, when a case becomes "hypothetical," it is moot. Mootness is one of a number of reasons why the Supreme Court may refuse to hear a case.

The Constitution mandates that the Court can only hear actual cases and controversies, and mootness serves to limit the Court's DOCKET as a technical requirement. Often times, the Court has used mootness as a means of avoiding politically controversial cases. Unfortunately, mootness has at times prevented the Court from hearing important cases, due to the nature of the dispute. Most notably, the abortion issue could not make it to the Court for many years, because by the time a case could be appealed, the instant case became moot. Furthermore, whether a case is moot is not necessarily an objective standard. Mootness is necessarily related to the technical requirement of STANDING, because it requires that the parties involved actually be affected by the outcome of the case.

In 1997 the Court refused to hear the case of *Arizonans for Official English v. Arizona* on the grounds it presented a moot question. In that case, a woman challenged a requirement that only English be spoken at the workplace. However, by the time the case reached the Supreme Court, she had resigned from her position. The Court therefore considered the issue moot and declined to render a decision.

In 1999 the Supreme Court dismissed as moot a case it had already scheduled for ORAL ARGUMENT. The case, *United States v. Weatherhead,* 528 U.S. 1042 (1999), involved the Freedom of Information Act (FOIA). Sally Croft was facing federal criminal charges in Oregon and had requested a letter from British authorities expressing the view that she could not receive a fair trial in Oregon. The U.S. government refused to declassify the letter on national security grounds. However, before the Court could hear oral argument, the government reversed its position, declassified the letter, and rendered the case moot.

Aside from being a technical requirement, the justices may use mootness for political ends. Mootness can be used to avoid politically "dangerous" cases the justices do not think it prudent for the Court to address. Notably, mootness was used, for a long time, to avoid rendering abortion decisions. Given that pregnancy lasts only nine months, it would be very difficult for a woman to initiate a lawsuit that makes it to the Supreme Court before the end of her pregnancy. Given that her pregnancy will necessarily be over by the time the court hears her APPEAL, it becomes very easy for the Court to declare the controversy moot. Thus the great difficulty in getting an abortion case to be heard by the Supreme Court until *ROE V. WADE.* Mootness is a technical requirement for getting a case heard by the Supreme Court. It is related to standing and requires a case not be "hypothetical." By not hearing cases that have already been settled, the Court restricts itself to actual cases and controversies. Furthermore, mootness can serve as an important political tool for the justices.

For more information: Baum, Lawrence. *The Supreme Court.* Washington, D.C.: CQ Press, 1998; Dickson, Del. *The Supreme Court in Conference.* New York: Oxford University Press, 2001.

—Tom Clark

Morrison v. Olson, 487 U.S. 654 (1988)

In *Morrison v. Olson,* the Supreme Court upheld the independent counsel provisions of the Ethics in Government Act of 1978. The act allowed for the appointment of an independent counsel to investigate potential infringement of federal laws or statutes by high ranking executive officials.

The Ethics in Government Act of 1978 was a result of the involvement of senior Nixon officials in the Watergate scandal. Several members of the administration were found to be involved in the burglary at the Watergate Office Complex in Washington, D.C.

Title VI of the Ethics in Government Act of 1978 initiated a procedure where an independent counsel could be appointed when the attorney general receives evidence of wrongdoing by an executive official. The attorney general must determine that the evidence is "sufficient to constitute grounds to investigate whether any person [covered by the act] may have violated any federal criminal law."

Morrison v. Olson was a result of an investigation by the House Judiciary Committee concerning the Environmental Protection Agency (EPA). Upon reviewing evidence, the House Judiciary Committee believed that Olson, an employee of the attorney general's office, had given false testimony at an early investigation concerning the EPA. Moreover, the House Judiciary Committee believed that other members of Olson's office withheld important documents and therefore obstructed the Judiciary Committee's investigation.

The Special Division, the special court crafted in the Ethics in Government Act, appointed an independent counsel (Morrison) to investigate to see if Olson's testimony was false and/or if he had thwarted the case by any other means. When Independent Counsel Morrison was successful in obtaining subpoenas from a grand jury, Olson appealed in federal district court, where he argued the independent counsel statute was unconstitutional, and the investigation should cease. The district court upheld the constitutionality of the statute but was overturned by the COURT OF APPEALS.

Morrison v. Olson was decided on June 27, 1988, by a vote of 7-1; Chief Justice REHNQUIST delivered the opinion of the Court, Justice SCALIA dissented, and Justice Kennedy did not participate.

The opinion of the Court relied on three main points. First, the independent counsel statute did not violate the appointments clause of the Constitution (Article II, Section 2, clause 2) because the Court considered the independent counsel to be an "inferior officer." Second, the powers allocated to the Special Division did not violate Article III of the Constitution. Rehnquist wrote, "Congress' power under the Clause to vest the 'Appointment' of inferior officers in the courts may, in certain circumstances, allow Congress to give the courts some discretion in defining the nature and scope of the appointed official's authority." Third, the statute did not violate SEPARATION OF POWERS, because it did not impermissibly interfere with the functions of the executive branch.

Morrison v. Olson has also been widely cited because of Justice Scalia's scathing dissent. Scalia argued that the independent counsel was a clear violation of the doctrine of separation of powers and, "Without a secure structure of separated powers, our BILL OF RIGHTS would be worthless." Scalia argued that Congress had usurped executive authority because the independent counsel was not an "inferior officer."

The significance of this case is the Court's acceptance of the independent counsel statute and the allowance for limitations on removal of officers carrying out executive responsibilities.

For more information: Hall, Kermit L. *The Oxford Companion to the Supreme Court of the United States.* New York: Oxford University Press, 1992.

—Jewerl Maxwell

Mueller v. Allen, 463 U.S. 388 (1983)

In *Mueller v. Allen,* the Supreme Court upheld a Minnesota statute allowing parents of schoolchildren to take state INCOME TAX deductions of up to $700 for certain education expenditures.

A group of Minnesota citizens sued the state's commissioner of revenue, arguing that a tax deduction for parents of children attending religious primary and secondary schools violated the ESTABLISHMENT CLAUSE of the First Amendment to the Constitution. The Federal District Court granted SUMMARY JUDGMENT for the state, a judgment that was affirmed by the Minnesota court of appeals. Surprising many, the Supreme Court upheld the constitutionality of the tax deduction in a 5-4 decision.

Writing for a majority that included Chief Justice BURGER and Justices WHITE, POWELL, and O'CONNOR, Justice REHNQUIST acknowledged that the Court has historically chosen to walk a fine line in its application of the establishment clause rather than simply striking down all laws which serve to aid religious establishments. In deciding the constitutionality of such cases, Rehnquist based his decision on the *LEMON V. KURTZMAN,* 403 U.S. 602 (1971), PRECEDENT with its three-part test: "First, the statute must have a secular legislative purpose; second, its principal or primary effect must be one that neither advances nor inhibits RELIGION; finally, the statute must not foster 'an excessive government entanglement' with religion."

In addressing the first test, Rehnquist argued that the statute is clearly secular in nature and is intended to promote education in a general sense, a goal of primary importance to the welfare of the state. He recognized that the Courts have lauded the value of private education, both in its function to educate as well as taking some of the burden of education from the shoulders of the state. With regards to the second test, Rehnquist asserted that since the deduction is available to all parents and is only one among many statutes allowing tax deductions, it offers no specific advantage to parents of children attending sectarian schools. Rehnquist went further to argue that even if it did, benefiting parents of schoolchildren at sectarian schools is wholly different from advancing the institutions as such. Finally, with regards to the third test, Rehnquist found that the only entanglement that the government must incur is to insure that no tax relief is granted for the purchase of textbooks of a religious nature.

Justice MARSHALL, joined by Justices BRENNAN, BLACKMUN, and STEVENS, penned a vigorous dissent. In it, Marshall asserted that contrary to the belief of the majority, the secular intent of the statute is wholly inadequate in proving its constitutionality. Marshall argued that since students attending public schools typically incur none of the expenses named as deductible by the statute, the law constitutes a de facto monetary reward to parents who choose to send their children to private schools—which in Minnesota are overwhelmingly religious. Finally, he observed that secular textbooks, when used in a religious school, are inherently utilized to further the goal of promoting religion. Therefore if states are going to extend tax relief it must only be applicable for books which are also utilized in the public schools.

For more information: O'Brien, David. *Constitutional Law and Politics: Civil Rights and Civil Liberties.* 5th ed. New York: W. W. Norton, 2003.

—Jacob Fowles

Muller v. Oregon, 208 U.S. 412 (1908)

In *Muller v. Oregon,* the Supreme Court unanimously ruled that Oregon's statute limiting the amount of hours a woman could work in a single day was constitutional. Oregon did not permit women employed in any mechanical establishment, factory, or laundry to work more than 10 hours in a single day. Curt Muller, an owner of a laundry business, was convicted for requiring one of his female employees to work more than the statutory maximum allowed. When the Supreme Court of Oregon upheld his conviction, he appealed the case to the United States Supreme Court.

Muller claimed that the Oregon law treated similarly situated persons differently, thereby constituting class legislation in violation of the Fourteenth Amendment's EQUAL PROTECTION CLAUSE. He also claimed that the state had overstepped its bounds by passing such a law. In addition, Muller relied on a recently decided case to claim that the Oregon law violated his federal constitutional right to contract. The right to contract was established by the U.S. Supreme Court just three years earlier in LOCHNER V. NEW YORK, 198 U.S. 45 (1905). While that case also called into question the constitutionality of legislation that placed a cap on the number of hours that an employee may work, the Court ruled that such a limitation was constitutionally impermissible.

According to the Court, *Muller* warranted a different decision from that in *Lochner* simply because the Oregon legislation at issue in *Muller* applied only to women. The Court reasoned that women were significantly different from men, thereby justifying differential treatment. The Court stated that a woman's "physical structure and the performance of her maternal functions" rendered her less capable than a man of meeting her own basic needs (208 U.S. 411, 421). The Court expressed its concern that long hours at work may have detrimental effects on a woman's health, especially on her ability to produce "vigorous offspring" (ibid.). In fact, the Court framed women's health as a matter of public interest, "in order to preserve the strength and vigor of the race" (ibid.). The Court relied on a BRIEF submitted by Louis D. BRANDEIS on behalf of Oregon to support its reasoning about the differences between men and women. This brief has come to be known as the BRANDEIS BRIEF. It included a vast amount of material gathered from the fields of medicine and psychology as well as statistical data all pointing to the conclusion that not only were women significantly different from men, but they were in need of precisely the kind of protective legislation that Oregon had enacted.

Muller is regarded as one of the key cases demonstrating the Court's reluctance to recognize sex-based discrimination as unconstitutional before its landmark decision in *Reed v. Reed,* 404 U.S. 71 (1971). *Muller* illustrates a broader issue as well, which is the extent to which there are differences between men and women and the degree to which these differences justify differential treatment in a legal order that is committed to equal protection.

For more information: Novkov, Julie. *Constituting Workers, Protecting Women: Gender, Law, and Labor in the Progressive Era and New Deal Years.* Ann Arbor: University of Michigan Press, 2001.

—Susan M. Dennehy

Munn v. Illinois, 94 U.S. 113 (1876)

In *Munn v. Illinois,* the Court affirmed that the state's police power in regulating certain uses of private property was not in violation of the due process clause of the Fourteenth Amendment. Specifically, the Court held that the Illinois legislature was within its authority in regulating grain storage rates at Chicago warehouses (known as elevators). The Illinois legislature recently had set rates for any grain storage operator doing business in any city with a population of more than 100,000 residents. The practical effect of this legislation was to target the elevators operating in Chicago (the only city meeting the criteria) where a virtual monopoly of firms was gouging farmers by colluding to fix rates. While such a law was popular with the burgeoning Grange movement, the elevator operators claimed that it represented a violation of the Fourteenth Amendment due process clause and infringed on the commerce power of Congress.

In his majority opinion, Chief Justice WAITE upheld the statute and traced the police power back to the Magna Carta. He claimed that the founding of the United States changed "the form, but not the substance" of our government and formulated a notion of state authority based on this claim. To Waite state power was equal to that enjoyed by Parliament save for those powers delegated to the federal government of the United States and those reserved to the people.

More specifically, Waite held that the state of Illinois neither infringed on Congress's commerce authority—he deemed any effect on INTERSTATE COMMERCE "incidental"—nor did it deprive the elevator owner of his property. As Waite declared, when "one devotes his property to a use in which the public has an interest, he, in effect, grants to the public an interest in that use, and must submit to be controlled by the public for the common good, to the extent of the interest he has thus created." The virtual monopoly of elevator operators made the public interest in this case evident, and Waite inferred from the general power to regulate the use of property the specific right of the Illinois legislature to set a maximum rate. Waite clearly acted with an eye toward the real-world conditions surrounding the case. However, in deferring to the legislature he also made clear his preference for a limited judicial role. Treating the elevator operators' claims of abuse as a political question, he stated flatly that "[f]or protection against abuses by legislatures the people must resort to the polls, not to the courts."

Dissenting, Justice Field (joined by Justice Strong) pushed the majority's public interest argument to its logical extreme. Field maintained that "there is hardly an enterprise or business engaging the attention and labor of any considerable portion of the community, in which the public has not an interest." Field then concluded that the Court's decision only serves "to destroy, for all useful purposes, the efficacy of the constitution guaranty [of a right to private property]." To Field, the value of property was in its use. Title and possession of property is of little value if the state can mandate aspects of usage.

Field does not try to draw a line defining what role police power does have, and he does not articulate any types of usage that would call for regulation. However, he does not see any misuse of property in the present case that would call for state interference. While Field was on the losing side, his robust reading of the due process clause foreshadowed the SUBSTANTIVE DUE PROCESS view—and the subsequent activist turn—of the Court, most notably in LOCHNER V. NEW YORK, 198 U.S. 45 (1905).

For more information: Currie, David P. *The Constitution in the Supreme Court: The First Hundred Years, 1789–1888.* Chicago: University of Chicago Press, 1986.

—Christopher Stangl

Justice Frank Murphy *(United States Supreme Court)*

Murphy, Frank (1890–1949) *Supreme Court justice*
Frank Murphy was appointed by Franklin Roosevelt to the Supreme Court in 1940 and served until 1949. Murphy was judge on the Recorder Court, the city's highest criminal court, from 1924 till 1930. He presided fairly over the Sweet trial, one of the major CIVIL LIBERTIES cases of the day. Clarence Darrow had been hired by the NAACP to defend 11 Negroes against charges of murder during a race riot. (Later Murphy became a board member of the NAACP.)

In 1930 Murphy became Detroit's mayor. He organized the U.S. Conference of Mayors and became its first president. In 1935–36 he was the last governor general of the Philippines and the first high commissioner. Murphy was elected governor of Michigan in 1936. He refused to use troops to evict sit-down automobile plant strikers in 1937. He was for law and order but did not want to go down in history as "Bloody Murphy." This led to his defeat for reelection in 1938.

President Franklin Roosevelt named him attorney general in 1939. Insiders thought that Murphy would be moving on to the War Department, with Robert JACKSON replacing him at Justice. (Jackson was a New Yorker and there were already too many New Yorkers in the FDR cabinet.) However, Murphy was a pacifist and neo-isolationist, not a good fit in the War Department in 1940. As attorney general Murphy crusaded against political corruption and established what became the Civil Rights Division.

He was appointed to the Supreme Court in 1940, succeeding Pierce Butler, a fellow Catholic. (On Murphy's death, when President Truman appointed a Protestant, Cardinal Spellman of NYC complained.) Murphy had long been away from the law before becoming attorney general and justice. On the Court he allied with BLACK and DOUGLAS. Like Black and Douglas, Murphy reversed his position in the FLAG SALUTE controversy from *Gobitis* (*Minersville School District v. Gobitis*, 310 U.S. 586, 1940) to *Barnette* (*West Virginia State Board of Education v. Barnette*, 319 U.S. 624, 1943). He championed civil liberties in behalf of racial and religious minorities, political dissenters, and criminal defendants ("tempering justice with Murphy," it was said).

Murphy wanted to serve in World War II. He continued to badger the White House for missions abroad until Roosevelt's death. (If Murphy wished to leave the Court for another post after 1945, it was not likely since Truman held against the former attorney general the prosecution of Boss Pendergast of Kansas City, Mo.)

Murphy retreated from a dissent to a concurrence in the Japanese curfew case (*Hirabayashi v. U.S.*, 320 U.S. 81, 1943) but dissented in the detention camp case (*KOREMATSU v. U.S.*, 323 U.S. 214, 1944). He championed Indian claims.

Murphy sought to impose judicial checks on the growth of militarism. He dissented in the Court's denial of the habeas corpus petition of General Yamashita (*In re Yamashita*, 327 U.S. 1, 1946). General MacArthur had lobbied the military tribunal to hold Yamashita responsible for Philippine atrocities, even though the evidence was slight as to his culpability. The U.S. Army trumped the Geneva Convention and the Articles of War.

Murphy dissented in *Wolf v. Colorado*, 338 U.S. 25 (1949), in which the Court upheld state use of illegally seized evidence. Many of Murphy's dissents later became law. However, posterity has remembered him as a symbol of militant partisanship in politics and law. He was ever a crusader, a consistent libertarian.

For more information: Fine, Sidney. *Frank Murphy: The Detroit Years.* Ann Arbor: University of Michigan Press, 1975; ———. *Frank Murphy: The New Deal Years.* Chicago and London: University of Chicago Press, 1979; ———. *Frank Murphy: The Washington Years.* Ann Arbor: University of Michigan Press, 1984; Howard, J. Woodford, Jr. *Mr. Justice Murphy: A Political Biography.* Princeton, N.J.: University of Princeton Press, 1968.

—Martin Gruberg

music censorship

Music censorship refers to the practice of limiting music available for public consumption based on content that is perceived as offensive. Censorship of music can include the deletion of musical content and recently by restrictions on to whom it can be legally sold. The American public generally regards music as a social commentary equal in value to newsprint or news broadcast and equally subject to censorship and freedom of expression regulations.

Censorship of music has generally sought to ban lyrics in four areas: sexual content, violence, obscene language, and drug abuse. Not surprisingly, battle lines have been drawn across the political spectrum. Conservatives believe it is the responsibility of government to restrict materials that are offensive and not acceptable for mass consumption. On the left are First Amendment fundamentalists who believe that any and all restrictions placed on music are a violation of freedom of speech. The common argument made for censorship is that music affects the norms and attitudes of society, and that offensive material leads to a society where offensive behavior is deemed acceptable. Further, proponents of censorship argue that music rife with violence and sexual innuendo leads to a society that is more violent and sexually prurient. On the opposite end of the spectrum, free-speech proponents argue that music reflects the feelings and opinions of the society. Most Americans fall in between and believe it is the responsibility of government to support freedom of speech in music but that protections end when musical material is overtly offensive. But how to draw that line?

It is generally assumed that music censorship began with rock 'n' roll. However musical censorship began in the United States as early as the Puritans who banned the use of musical instruments in their religious ceremonies. Restrictions were placed on the general public beginning in 1912 when the Massachusetts legislature made dancing the tango a misdemeanor. The multiplication of censorship efforts began along side the rise of rock 'n' roll. Though that music was innocent by today's standards, many parents reacted negatively to the new style of music that drew heavily on African-American musical tradition in a racially tense time. The easiest way to react was to seek a widespread ban on the music.

Material suitable for radio and television differs from what is legal to produce and sell. The Federal Communications Commission (FCC) is charged with regulating television and radio broadcasting. Their power is foggy, however, due to two conflicting codes under which the FCC operates. The first code states that the FCC does not have the right to interfere with the right of free speech. The second code states that the FCC has the power to fine those who broadcast obscene, indecent, and profane language on the radio. Despite the confusion raised by these conflicting codes, a series of court cases has supported government's ability to limit what radio and TV stations can broadcast. The most prominent case was the *FCC V. PACI-FICA FOUNDATION* (1978), which denied the FCC the ability to censor material prior to its broadcast but allowed it to punish those who air inappropriate content.

A more recent development in the censorship and regulation of music controversy occurred with the Parents Music Resource Center (PMRC). Founded by Tipper Gore in 1985 in response to offensive lyrics found in an album purchased by one of her children, the PMRC was concerned with the rise of lyrics promoting sex, drug use, violence, and the occult in rock music. The PMRC asserted that such lyrics were having an unhealthy effect on impressionable youth. Further, they argued, parents are unable to effectively regulate what their children listen to because of lack of information or warning.

The group's influence was immediate and substantial. Five months after PMRC's founding, the Senate held hearings on musical content. Efforts by the PMRC led the music industry to voluntarily place labels warning of the content of music on the record, lest they be faced with governmental action. Proponents argued that labels would alert consumers and parents to offensive material; giving them a better opportunity to know what they or their children were purchasing and thereby allowing parents some ability to regulate the music their children listened to. First Amendment purists argued that the warning labels dampen artists' ability to express themselves and amount to censorship of musical freedom. On the other hand, proponents of warning labels argue that labels allow artists greater artistic freedom because consumers will not be shocked by what they hear on an album.

The debate surrounding censorship of music grows as the scope to which the public is surrounded by music grows, and the material used by musical artists expands.

For more information: Barnet, Richard D., and Larry L. Burris. *Controversies of the Music Industry.* London: Greenwood Press, 2001; Cloonan, Martin, and Reebee Garofalo, ed. *Policing Pop.* Philadelphia, Pa.: Temple University Press, 2003; Nuzum, Eric. *Parental Advisory: Music Censorship in America.* New York: Perennial, 2001.

—Lindsay B. Zoeller

Muskrat v. United States, 219 U.S. 346 (1911)

In *Muskrat v. United States*, the Supreme Court reversed and dismissed the claims of David Muskrat that challenged the constitutionality of a series of congressional restrictions imposed on land owned by Cherokees. In so doing, the court enunciated the principle that federal judicial power was limited to actual cases and controversies.

In this opinion the Court put words to a tradition that had guided its decision-making for more than a century, but one that had never before been clearly stated. Namely: that it would not hear friendly suits, nor issue hypothetical opinions, nor address any questions beyond those contained in real cases or controversies.

The *Muskrat* case has its origin in a long list of disputes that grew out of the complexities of Indian TREATIES and the congressional struggle at the turn of the 19th to the 20th century to address them. The General Allotment Act of 1887 pronounced a new federal Indian policy: former tribal lands were to be subdivided, then individually bought and sold. This initiated a complex process wherein Indian claims to land titles became a critical element in determining federal allotments, tribal boundaries, treaty provisions, corporate and personal ownership.

Subsequent congressional legislation, in order to clarify the factual questions that arose as well as remediate the bureaucratic inadequacies that a multitude of these disputes revealed, often would invite suits against the government. The legislation specified that these cases were to be tried in federal Courts of Claims to determine the details and resolve the differences in these matters, and that such decisions could be reviewed by the Supreme Court.

Muskrat v. United States bears all of these characteristics. It was born of a 1907 statute wherein Muskrat and others were individually named and authorized to bring suit in the Court of Claims "to determine the validity of any acts of Congress" [*Muskrat v.* 219 U.S. 346, 360 (1911)] that since 1902 had regulated Cherokee lands. The legislation instructed the attorney general to represent the federal government in the case, and the U.S. Treasury to pay the lawyers' fees for the attorneys who represented Muskrat and Cherokee citizens. Muskrat's suit was, in short, orchestrated, planned, and paid for by Congress.

In delivering the opinion for a unanimous (7-0) Court, Justice Day highlighted the lack of genuine adversarial interests that existed between the Cherokees and the United States, the transparent objective to garner Supreme Court approval for the "doubtful character" of congressional legislation in these matters, and the unofficial practice of the Court only to hear actual cases and controversies. Faced with an unabashed congressional invitation to render an advisory opinion here, Day declared, "Is such a determination within the judicial power conferred by the Constitution? We think it is not."

Day's opinion traced the development of this tradition to Washington's presidency, when the administration and Congress asked for the justices' advice and counsel on a wide range of issues from treaty matters with France and Britain to settling Revolutionary War pensions for widows and orphans. In correspondence, Chief Justice JAY and his associates declined to assist on the grounds that such action would violate the unique power that was vested only in the judiciary by Article III of the Constitution.

Declaring that this was neither a case nor a controversy and, as such, fell outside its constitutional jurisdiction, Justice Day laid the foundation for the gradual development of the modern Court's limitation of congressional attempts to place issues before the Court. The holdings of *Muskrat* were reaffirmed in *Aetna Life Insurance Co. v. Haworth*, 300 U.S. 227 (1937), and further sharpened in *LUJAN V. DEFENDERS OF WILDLIFE*, 504 U.S. 555 (1997), that said it is the Court, not the Congress, that ultimately determines what is a true CASE OR CONTROVERSY.

In dismissing *Muskrat* for lack of jurisdiction, the Court for the first time and in an official decision, pointedly and clearly proclaimed that its function and power must remain limited to exercising the judicial power. Namely, adjudicating lawsuits between authentic litigants where genuine interests were at stake.

For more information: Casto, William R. "The Early Supreme Court Justices' Most Significant Opinion." *Ohio Northern University Law Review* 29 (2002): 173; Kannan, Phillip M. "Advisory Opinions by Federal Courts." *University of Richmond Law Review* 32 (1998–99): 769.

—George Peery
—Eric C. Sands

N

National Association for the Advancement of Colored People v. Alabama, 357 U.S. 449 (1958)

In *NAACP v. Alabama*, Justice HARLAN, writing for the Supreme Court, ruled that the state of Alabama violated the due process clause of the Fourteenth Amendment by requiring the state chapter of the NAACP to disclose its membership list as a condition of doing business in Alabama. In so holding, the Court ruled that the freedom of association is "an inseparable aspect of the 'liberty' assured by the due process clause of the Fourteenth Amendment. . . ."

The NAACP opened an office in Alabama without complying with a state law requiring businesses to register with the state. The state of Alabama filed suit to compel the NAACP to comply with the law or close its operations in Alabama. While releasing most of the information requested, the NAACP refused to supply its membership lists to the state of Alabama and was held in contempt and fined $100,000. The NAACP appealed this action to the U.S. Supreme Court.

Citing the fact that past disclosure of its membership led to economic reprisal and physical threats to its members, the NAACP argued that disclosing the membership lists would "abridge the rights of its rank-and-file members to engage in lawful association in support of their common beliefs."

Alabama's argument for disclosure relied on the Supreme Court's decision in *Bryant v. Zimmerman*, 278 U.S. 63 (1928), which upheld a similar New York statute requiring disclosure of the membership lists of the Ku Klux Klan. As for threats and violence faced by members of the NAACP in the past, Alabama noted that this was the result of individual action and not state action.

In deciding for the NAACP, Justice Harlan noted that "group association" often enhances the effective "advocacy of public and private points of view, particularly controversial ones. . . ." Any statute that has the effect of curtailing this association is "subject to closest scrutiny" and can be justified only if the state can demonstrate a compelling interest in disclosure.

The Court dismissed the *Bryant* case with the observation that the Klan had a history of "unlawful intimidation and violence," and this created the COMPELLING STATE INTEREST in disclosure. The NAACP, on the other hand, was dedicated to nonviolence and CIVIL RIGHTS. As for the second argument that past violence against revealed members of the NAACP was directed at them by private citizens and not the state of Alabama, the Court noted that the "crucial factor is the interplay of governmental and private action, for it is only after the initial exertion of state power represented by the production order that private action takes hold."

In concluding, Justice Harlan noted the "vital relationship between freedom to associate and privacy in one's association." This relationship becomes of utmost importance when the privacy of association is "indispensable to preservation of freedom of association, particularly where a group espouses dissident beliefs." What the state of Alabama cannot do directly, it cannot do indirectly; it cannot require the membership of the NAACP and directly punish those on the list, nor can it make the membership a matter of public knowledge and wait for the "manifests of public hostility" by citizens of Alabama.

For more information: Gutman, Amy, ed. *Freedom of Association.* Princeton, N.J.: Princeton University Press, 1989.

—Alex Aichinger

National Labor Relations Board (NLRB) v. Jones & Laughlin Steel Corporation, 301 U.S. 1 (1937)

In *National Labor Relations Board v. Jones & Laughlin Steel Corporation,* the Supreme Court upheld the right of Congress to establish a National Labor Relations Board under its power to regulate INTERSTATE COMMERCE. The

This cartoon of September 1937 depicts the angry Congress of Industrial Organizations leader John L. Lewis after the Supreme Court's ruling in *National Labor Relations Board v. Jones & Laughlin Steel Corporation.* *(Library of Congress)*

National Labor Relations Board was created by the National Labor Relations Act, also known as the Wagner Act, in 1935. The purpose of the act was to protect employees' right to organize and join labor unions. The NLRB was granted to power to hear complaints of unjust labor practices and enforce corrective measures. The reasoning behind the act was the thought that labor unrest and strikes cause interruptions to interstate commerce, which Congress had a right to prevent.

Jones & Laughlin was one of the largest steel producers in the nation. Numerous grievances were filed against the company's plant in Aliquippa, Pennsylvania, including discriminating against workers who wanted to join a labor union. The NLRB ordered the company to reinstate 10 workers who had been fired due to their involvement in a labor union. The company refused stating that its steel production facilities were engaged in manufacturing actions that are purely intrastate activities and thus outside the power of Congress. Lower courts ruled in favor of Jones & Laughlin so the NLRB appealed to the Supreme Court.

Chief Justice HUGHES delivered the opinion of the Court for a five-person majority that included Justices BRANDEIS, CARDOZO, Roberts, and STONE. His opinion first addressed the scope of the Wagner Act. The Court found that the act was within the sphere of constitutionally granted congressional authority. The act expressly states the jurisdiction of the NLRB, which includes any action of unfair labor practices affecting commerce. It goes even further to explain the term *commerce,* which in this case is interstate and foreign commerce. Acts of labor that might be construed as local in nature are not immune to NLRB supervision. It is labor's effect upon commerce that is the criterion, not where the labor itself is performed.

Second, the Court attended to the unfair labor practices in question. The CHIEF JUSTICE acknowledged that any single employee is helpless in dealings with an employer, and therefore a union is essential in order to put employees on the same level as the employer when it comes to negotiations. Next the Court tackled the application of the act to employees engaged in production. The movement of iron ore, coal, and limestone constitutes a "stream" or "flow" of commerce, and any problems along the way would cripple the whole process and therefore substantially affect interstate commerce. Although actions may seem to be intrastate in character, they might have such an impact on interstate activity that their control is essential as well.

The last thing addressed by the Court was the effects of unfair labor practice in the respondent's venture. Industrial war or labor unrest would paralyze interstate commerce, and in the Court's view the right of employees to organize and choose their representatives is indispensable to industrial peace. Therefore, based on the close relationship of manufacturing and interstate commerce, the Court had no doubt that it is well within Congress's constitutional authority to defend the rights of employees to self-organization and their right to choose representatives for collective bargaining. The lower court's decision was reversed.

Justice McReynolds delivered a blistering dissent for himself and Justices Butler, SUTHERLAND, and VAN DEVANTER. He reiterated the more classic view that in a business such as Jones & Laughlin Steel there could be two distinct movements in interstate transportation. The first brings raw material to the plant and ends there, while the second moves their products to other states. In *Schechter Poultry Corp. v. United States,* 295 U.S. 495 (1935), the Court ruled that the commerce clause did not include commodities which had come to rest after interstate commerce. In addition, in *Carter v. Carter Coal Co.,* 298 U.S. 238 (1936), the Court ruled that Congress lacked the authority to police labor relations in respect to commodities before interstate commerce had begun. Justice McReynolds believed that the NLRB's powers are far too sweeping because industrial strife is not close enough to interstate commerce. He added that the Wagner Act is an infringement of employers' right to contract with whom they want.

NLRB v. Jones & Laughlin is important in that it signaled a shift in the Supreme Court toward allowing Congress greater authority to regulate commerce. It was one of the first cases to support New Deal legislation. The

Court's willingness to allow Congress to take actions to establish labor peace and industrial practices took the steam out of President Roosevelt's COURT-PACKING PLAN.

For more information: Epstein, Lee, and Thomas G. Walker. *Constitutional Law for a Changing America.* 4th ed. Washington, D.C.: CQ Press, 2001; The OYEZ Project. "*NLRB v. Jones and Laughlin Steel Corp.*, 301 U.S. 1 (1937)." U.S. Supreme Court Multimedia. Available online. URL: http://www.oyez.org/oyez/resource/case/283. Downloaded May 17, 2004.

National League of Cities v. Usery, 426 U.S. 833 (1976)

National League of Cities v. Usery was the first decision to rule unconstitutional congressional exercise of the commerce power since the New Deal. At issue in *National League of Cities* was the permissible scope of the federal Fair Labour Standards Act, which had been amended to include employment standards for state and local government workers. The majority opinion of the court was written by then associate justice William REHNQUIST. The decision spells out a vision of FEDERALISM much at odds with the post-New Deal consensus on the Court. In that regard it is a precursor to the federalism controversies that preoccupied the Court in the late 1990s and beyond.

Justice Rehnquist's opinion centers on the concept of state sovereignty and how it is to be best protected by the Constitution and the courts. Rehnquist acknowledged in his decision that the commerce power is wide ranging, subject only to the limits prescribed by the Constitution. He further accepted that those limits are generally understood to be the guarantees of individual rights provided by the Constitution. Rehnquist's innovation was to interpret the federal nature of the Constitution as a comparable restraint upon congressional action. He argued that the sovereignty of the states acts as an affirmative limit on the scope of the commerce clause.

The majority claimed that in much the same way as the right to a fair trial or the right to due process limits the applicability of the commerce power on individuals or corporations, state sovereignty should limit the scope of the commerce power as it applies to the states. Justice Rehnquist did not provide a great deal of evidence to suggest that state sovereignty was something that the Constitution's authors explicitly sought to protect. He relied instead upon the habit of the Court to respect state sovereignty in the past. This was particularly true when Congress had attempted to regulate the states as states.

Much of the commerce clause expansion that typified the post–New Deal certainly offended what might be labeled state sovereignty, but generally by means of preempting or overruling what was traditionally state jurisdiction. Commerce clause regulation by Congress frequently filled in areas and activities previously undertaken by the states or presumed to be within the ambit of the states. The commerce power had much less frequently been used by Congress to actually regulate the states in the conduct of their own activities. By trying to set wage and overtime rates for local government employees, Congress was setting out to regulate the states as employers. The federal government argued that its regulation of states and local governments as employers was no more abusive of state jurisdiction than the preemption of state authority more typical of commerce clause expansion.

Given that state employees represented a high proportion of the workforce, efforts to control prices and wages would be stymied if they could not apply to state employees as well as those in the private sector. Rehnquist rejected this argument, claiming that the Court had "repeatedly recognized that there are attributes of sovereignty attaching to every state government which may not be impaired by Congress, not because Congress may lack an affirmative grant of legislative authority to reach the matter, but because the Constitution prohibits it from exercising the authority in that manner." In other words, the commerce power may very well allow Congress to make laws regulating employment, but it does not permit Congress to tell the states how to conduct their own affairs.

What qualified as the undeniable attributes of state sovereignty is left somewhat vague by the majority. Rehnquist did suggest that "traditional state functions" needed to be left untouched by Congress. At a minimum, Rehnquist believed that the hiring and remuneration of state employees was an "undoubted attribute of state sovereignty."

National League of Cities was a stunner. The court had not overruled an attempt at commerce regulation by Congress in nearly 40 years prior. Rehnquist's credentials as an advocate of state autonomy were firmly cemented by his opinion. Rehnquist's doctrinal innovation would, however, prove to be short-lived. Limitations on Congress based on state sovereignty may have challenged conventional wisdom, but they did not in turn become conventional wisdom. After an attempt to flesh out a standard of traditional state functions in *Hodel v. Virginia Surface Mining and Reclamation Association*, 452 U.S. 264 (1981), the Court overturned *National League of Cities* in GARCIA V. SAN ANTONIO METROPOLITAN TRANSIT AUTHORITY, 469 U.S. 528 (1985), nine years later.

For more information: Powell, Jeff. "The Compleat Jeffersonian: Justice Rehnquist and Federalism." *Yale Law Journal* 91 (1982): 1,317–1,370.

—Gerald Baier

National Organization for Women v. Scheidler, 510 U.S. 249 (1994)

In *National Organization for Women v. Scheidler*, a unanimous Supreme Court upheld the right of the National Organization for Women (NOW), the Delaware Women's Health Organization, Inc. (DWHO), and the Summit Women's Health Organization, Inc. (SWHO) to use the RACKETEER INFLUENCED AND CORRUPT ORGANIZATIONS ACT (RICO) to prohibit the physically and emotionally damaging actions of antiabortion protesters outside of family-planning clinics that perform abortions. The RICO chapter of the Organized Crime Control Act of 1970 was originally directed at mafia-type activities, which banned organized groups from engaging in economic extortion by "force, violence, or fear."

The activities outside family-planning clinics that led to the Supreme Court action included violence, barricades of clinic entrances, forcible entry, intimidation, and other less forceful methods aimed at preventing access to abortions. In addition to Joseph Scheidler, John Patrick Ryan, Randall A. Terry, Andrew Scholberg, Conrad Wojnar, Timothy Murphy, Monica Migliorino, Vital-Med Laboratories, Inc., Pro-Life Action League, Inc. (PLAL), Pro-Life Direct Action League, Inc. (PDAL), Operation Rescue, and Project Life were named in NOW's suit, which charged the antiabortionists with engaging in a national conspiracy of racketeering activity that used violence and intimidation to shut down abortion clinics and prevent access to legal abortions, which was guaranteed under *ROE V. WADE*, 410 U.S. 113 (1973), and repeatedly upheld by the Supreme Court, and to prevent the physicians and clinic staff from engaging in a lawful business. Punishment under RICO included imprisonment of up to 20 years and PUNITIVE DAMAGES. NOW's strategy was to make intrusive antiabortion protest so financially costly that it would deter the protesters from interfering with access to constitutionally protected abortions.

Lawyers for the antiabortionists argued that the NOW had no STANDING in the case and that the clinics claimed no injury. They also insisted that RICO was intended to prevent illegal economic activity and should not be used to place bans on actions protected by the First Amendment. The Court granted NOW standing, which gave them the right to bring the suit. The Court contended that "Respondents (were) wrong . . . in asserting that the complaint alleges no "injury" to DWHO and SWHO "fairly traceable to the defendant's allegedly unlawful conduct."

The Court declared, "RICO does not require proof that either the racketeering enterprise or the predicate acts of racketeering in 1962(c) were motivated by an economic purpose." The Court based its decision in part on the congressional preface to RICO, which explained that the RICO was intended to target racketeering activity that drained billions of dollars from the American economy. Chief Justice Rehnquist, writing for the Court, maintained that while the antiabortionists might "not benefit the protesters financially, . . . they still may drain money from the economy by harming businesses such as the clinics."

Many legal scholars and court watchers reacted to the decision with dismay and contended that the Court was setting a dangerous PRECEDENT by using RICO for political purposes. It was also argued that the Court's actions were unnecessary since Congress had solved the problem of violence at family-planning clinics with the Freedom of Access to Clinic Entrances Act of 1994, which protected the constitutional right to exercise freedom of choice with the force of the federal government.

For more information: *"National Organization for Women, et al., v. Scheidler, et al.,"* on Douglas Butler, "Abortion: Medicine, Ethics, and Law" CD-ROM, 1997; Vitiello, Michael. "Has the Court Really Turned RICO Upside Down?: An Examination of *NOW v. Scheidler." The Journal of Criminal Law and Criminology* 85 (1995): 1,223–1,257.

—Elizabeth Purdy

Nebbia v. New York, 291 U.S. 502 (1934)

In its ruling in *Nebbia v. New York*, the U.S. Supreme Court began shifting its focus from protecting an individual's right to contract, in terms of economic liberty, to a perspective that allowed government regulation of the economy.

From the 1890s to the 1932 election of Franklin D. Roosevelt, the U.S. Supreme Court put forth the constitutional principle that individuals enjoyed a protected right to economic liberty, otherwise known as economic SUBSTANTIVE DUE PROCESS. Within this judicial adaptation of laissez-faire economics, individuals had the right to economic contract without governmental interference, particularly from laws dealing with minimum wage, maximum hours worked, and regulations regarding working conditions.

This idea was most notably affirmed in the U.S. Supreme Court decision of *Lochner v. New York*, 198 U.S. 45 (1905), in which a New York law limited a workweek for bread bakery employees at 60 hours. The Court struck down a bakery maximum hours law as violating the constitutional "right to purchase or to sell labor" between employers and employees. Yet the Court did affirm some regulatory state power imposing maximum hours for women in *MULLER V. OREGON*, 208 U.S. 412 (1908), and a 10-hour workday for factory workers in *Bunting v. Oregon*, 243 U.S. 426 (1917). In 1934 the Court's *Nebbia* decision signaled that the idea of economic substantive due process was nearing its end as a judicial doctrine.

Following the stock market crash of 1929 and the onset of the Great Depression, state governments enacted regulatory measures to correct the economic conditions facing the United States in the early 1930s. One such measure was New York's creation of a milk control board, which established minimum and maximum prices for consumers. The reasoning behind the control board was to ensure the survival of a billion-dollar industry within the state, as well as public health and safety issues. The board established a price of nine cents per quart of milk, but Leo Nebbia sold two quarts of milk, with a five-cent loaf of bread, for a total of eighteen cents. The board charged Nebbia with violating the price order and convicted him. Nebbia challenged the board's authority under the due process clause of the U.S. Constitution's Fourteenth Amendment, arguing that the state was violating his right to conduct business by fixing the price of milk.

The U.S. Supreme Court acknowledged that while an individual has the right to "exercise exclusive domain over property and freely to contract about his affairs," the state has the power to "regulate the use of property and the conduct of business." The Court sided with New York in determining that the "legislature might reasonably consider further regulation and control desirable for protection of the industry and the consuming public." Under Associate Justice Owen J. Robert's majority opinion, the Court held that if "the laws passed are seen to have a reasonable relation to a proper legislative purpose, and are neither arbitrary nor discriminatory, the requirements of due process are satisfied."

However, the Court failed to heed its own opinion in subsequent cases. Two years after the *Nebbia* decision, in *Morehead v. New York ex rel. Tipaldo* (1936), the U.S. Supreme Court struck down New York's minimum wage law for women. Two months following the controversial *Morehead* decision, in which both Democrats and Republicans denounced the Court, President Roosevelt announced his "court-packing" plan. Within the midst of the president's attempt to reshape the court to accept government regulatory power over the economy, the Supreme Court handed down WEST COAST HOTEL CO. V. PARRISH, 300 U.S. 379 (1937), dealing with a state minimum wage law for women. In *West Coast Hotel*, Chief Justice HUGHES's majority opinion acknowledged that the "Constitution does not speak of freedom of contract," and that "regulation which is reasonable in relation to its subject and is adopted in the interests of the community is due process." In light of the *West Coast Hotel* decision, some scholars have contended that the "switch in time that saved nine" and ultimately doomed FDR's COURT-PACKING PLAN is compatible with the deferential decision in *Nebbia*.

For more information: Gillman, Howard. *The Constitution Besieged: The Rise and Demise of Lochner Era Police*

Powers Jurisprudence. Durham, N.C.: Duke University Press, 1993; Kens, Paul. *Lochner v. New York: Economic Regulation on Trial.* Lawrence: University Press of Kansas, 1998.

—J. Michael Bitzer

Nebraska Press Association v. Stuart, 427 U.S. 539 (1976)

In *Nebraska Press Association v. Stuart,* the United States Supreme Court was confronted by the issue of whether a state trial court could impose prior restraints upon members of the news media in their coverage of a highly publicized criminal trial and held that the trial court's "gag order" violated the First Amendment's free press clause.

In October 1975, police in a small Nebraska town discovered the bodies of six persons murdered in their home. A suspect was arrested the next morning, and the case attracted widespread news coverage.

The county court judge entered a restrictive order due to concerns that the media coverage would make it difficult or impossible to provide a fair trial. The order required members of the media to follow certain guidelines in covering the case. After the defendant was bound over for trial in a district court, the Nebraska Press Association intervened and requested that the county court's order be set aside. The district judge entered his own, less restrictive, order that would apply only until the jury was seated and which covered only five specific subjects considered prejudicial to the defendant. This order also required the media to follow press guidelines.

On appeal, the state supreme court balanced the presumption that a PRIOR RESTRAINT on publication is invalid under the First Amendment against the rights of a criminal defendant to a fair trial under the Sixth and Fourteenth Amendments. While limiting further the district court's order, it still held that the district court was justified in enforcing it. Nebraska Press Association sought and was granted review by the U.S. Supreme Court.

The Supreme Court first considered whether the issue was MOOT, given that the pretrial gag order had expired when the jury was impaneled. Applying an exception to the general jurisdictional requirement that it decide only "actual" controversies, the Court found that the dispute was "capable of repetition, yet evading review." It then proceeded to consider the prior restraint issue.

The Court began by citing earlier highly publicized trials in American history, including the trials of Aaron Burr and Bruno Hauptmann (the Lindbergh kidnapping), as examples of other situations in which trial rights and freedom of the press had come into conflict. This was nothing new, the Court said, although the speed of communications in the modern world has made the problem greater. The

Court questioned whether a gag order on media within a trial court's jurisdiction would even be effective in a trial that drew coverage from media outside its jurisdiction.

The Court refused to accept the petitioner's invitation to give freedom of the press preeminence over fair trial rights. There was no indication that the framers intended one right to take precedence over another. In this case it was unnecessary to do so. The Court had previously reversed convictions in cases where a trial court had failed to insulate jurors from prejudicial publicity, as in *Sheppard v. Maxwell,* 384 U.S. 333 (1966). The Court had not previously considered the constitutionality of prior restraint of publication for the purpose of preserving a fair trial, but it had held against such prior restraint in other areas. For example, it held in *Near v. Minnesota ex rel. Olson,* 283 U.S. 697 (1931), that a state could not prevent publication of allegedly malicious articles. Likewise, in *New York Times v. United States,* 403 U.S. 713 (1971), the Court dissolved a federal court injunction against publication of the Pentagon Papers, notwithstanding a national security claim by the government.

In this case, the Court found little in the record to show that the trial court had taken steps to ensure a fair trial short of banning media coverage. Moreover, it was unclear that the order would have protected the defendant's rights in any event. Therefore, the Court held that the order violated the First Amendment and reversed the state supreme court's ruling.

This case is important because it considers two of the most important rights guaranteed by the U.S. Constitution. It recognizes the importance of an accused criminal defendant's right to trial by an impartial jury. However, it refuses to accept an infringement upon the freedom of the press in a case where other means were available to preserve the defendant's trial rights. High-profile criminal trials have taken place throughout our history and continue to this day. This case provides guidance to trial judges as they seek to administer justice without violating other important rights.

For more information: Hudon, Edward V. "Freedom of the Press versus Fair Trial: The Remedy Lies with the Courts." *Val. U. L. Rev.* 1 (1966): 8.

—Paul D. Stanko

necessary and proper clause

It is a core principle that the Constitution enumerates the powers of government and limits government to the exercise of the powers enumerated. The most detailed enumeration is of the powers of Congress, yet Article I, Section 8 concludes with the provision that Congress may make all laws necessary and proper to the exercise of the powers before granted.

When anti-federalists protested that this clause was an additional grant of such sweeping power that it negated the principle of limited government, federalists insisted that, on the contrary, it merely stated a truism. The idea of the clause was implicit in any workable system of enumerated powers and granted no additional power whatsoever.

Debate resumed after ratification when it was proposed to establish a national bank. Proponents claimed this was necessary and proper to the enumerated powers to tax and to borrow funds; opponents disagreed. Did "necessary and proper" mean indispensable, convenient, or something between? The bank law was passed and its constitutionality was later upheld by the Court. In *McCullough v. Maryland,* 17 U.S. 316 (1819), Chief Justice MARSHALL rejected the narrow, "indispensable" reading and declared: "To employ the means necessary to an end, is generally understood as employing any means calculated to produce the end. . . . Let the end be legitimate, let it be within the scope of the constitution, and all means which are appropriate, which are plainly adapted to that end, which are not prohibited, but consist with the letter and spirit of the constitution, are constitutional. . . . [T]o inquire into the degree of its necessity, would be to pass the line which circumscribes the judicial department, and to tread on legislative ground."

Although Marshall reserved the possibility of intervening in a case where the legislature acted on the mere pretext of pursuing a warranted purpose, this decision effectively abdicated judicial enforcement of the necessary and proper clause as a limit on congressional power. For Marshall, the Constitution placed limits on the ends government might pursue, not—unless expressly prohibited—on the means it might employ.

The actual impact of this decision of course depends on how broadly the enumerated powers themselves are understood. Perhaps because of the difficulty of amending the Constitution under Article V, the courts have declined to strictly employ canons of construction like *expressio unius est exclusio alterius* (to mention one thing excludes the rest). Otherwise an amendment would be needed in order to establish an air force in addition to an army and navy, and the only federal crimes would be those expressly listed, such as counterfeiting, piracy, treason, and military offenses.

In addition, the economic and constitutional crisis of the 1930s yielded an interpretation of the INTERSTATE COMMERCE clause so broad as to permit a vast expansion of federal regulatory and spending programs, with sweeping delegations of congressional power to administrative agencies.

Aside from the BILL OF RIGHTS and a handful of recent commerce clause and Eleventh Amendment cases, the limits on national power have become hard to discern, and the chief beneficiary of the kind of flexibility intended by the necessary and proper clause is not Congress but the executive branch.

For more information: Barnett, Randy E. "The Original Meaning of the Necessary and Proper Clause." *U. of Pennsylvania Journal of Constitutional Law*, 6 (October 2003); McCloskey, Robert G. *The American Supreme Court.* 3rd ed. Chicago: University of Chicago Press, 2000.

—Daniel N. Hoffman

New Deal constitutionality

The election of Franklin Roosevelt as president in 1932 marked a dramatic shift in federal government policy. Starting in 1933, Roosevelt initiated a series of bills later called the New Deal. These laws made the federal government responsible for the economic well-being of the nation. The New Deal vastly expanded the power of the federal government and was looked at suspiciously by those who favored more limited government. This included the United States Supreme Court. Through a series of court cases, the New Deal was tested for its constitutionality, with the justices striking down several laws between 1933 and 1936.

One of the first laws considered by the justices involved Roosevelt's decision to remove the United States from the gold standard. In the gold clause cases, holders of government bonds, who were guaranteed payment in gold but were paid in dollars that were worth less, sued the federal government. They contended that their property had been taken. They wanted the Court to order the federal government to pay their debts in gold but the Court refused.

In a 5 to 4 decision, Justice HUGHES ruled that the president had the power to take the country off of the gold standard. It was a major victory for the Roosevelt administration in its efforts to control the country's finances. New Deal opponents saw it as a crushing defeat. One of those opponents was Justice James Clark McReynolds, who dissented in the case by declaring that the Constitution was gone and comparing Roosevelt's actions to Nero.

The gold clause cases were only the beginning. In 1935 the Court heard challenges to the National Industrial Recovery Act (NIRA) and the National Recovery Administration (NRA). The NIRA was the centerpiece of the New Deal. It granted the president the power to set wages and prices in most industries and to limit the supply of commodities such as oil. The NIRA was intended to raise wages and prices to end the deflation of the Great Depression. The president and his appointees at the NRA were involved in the most minute decisions on trade including regulations of the chicken industry. Purchasers of live chickens were required to close their eyes when reaching into coops to choose which animals they would buy. This was done to prevent them from selecting the healthiest chickens.

The Schechter brothers were charged with violating this particular segment of the NRA and were fined under the law. They appealed their fine all the way to the Supreme Court and in *Schechter v. United States*, a unanimous Court struck down the NIRA as exceeding presidential power. Congress had unconstitutionally given its commerce power to the president. He had unconstitutionally used that power to regulate purely local commerce. Under the Constitution only Congress could regulate commerce and it had to be commerce between or among the states.

The Court also struck at the NIRA and its attempt to limit oil production and transportation. The president was given the power to prohibit oil shipments that would create oversupply and lower the price. In *Panama Refining v. Ryan* (1935), the Supreme Court struck down this portion of the NIRA as the over-delegation of congressional power to the president. The president was making laws without any standards provided by Congress. This made the president the legislative and executive power and was forbidden under the constitutional theory of the SEPARATION OF POWERS.

The Court's overturning of the NIRA angered many people, though not the Roosevelt administration, which was having great difficulty in making the program work properly. They were less pleased with the Court's decision in UNITED STATES V. BUTLER (1936). *Butler* was a challenge to the 1933 Agricultural Adjustment Act (AAA). The AAA paid farmers to produce fewer crops and raise the price of their commodities. The money for these subsidies came from taxes on processors of such commodities as wheat, corn, and cotton. Butler was one of these and refused to pay the tax. He challenged the AAA as an improper use of Congress's taxing power. He argued that Congress could not tax to redistribute wealth from one group, processors, to another group, farmers. In a 6 to 3 decision, the Court agreed with Butler

Writing for the majority, Justice Roberts stated that Congress's taxing power was limited to providing revenue for the government, not as part of a regulation that redistributed money to favored groups in society. The AAA was not trying to raise revenue with its tax and was declared unconstitutional.

The striking down of the AAA created a greater furor within the Roosevelt administration, which feared the Supreme Court would strike down the Social Security Act and the National Labor Relations Act, both coming to the justices in 1937. Upon his reelection in 1936, Roosevelt proposed a Court "reform" plan intended to add six members to the Court, all Roosevelt appointees and probable supporters. Congress rejected this threat to the Court's independence, but Roosevelt's threat did appear to silence some justices who were critical of the New Deal. In a series of decisions, the justices changed course, upholding several New Deal laws.

In *NLRB v. Jones & McLaughlin* (1937), the Court ruled Congress had broad commerce power to regulate wages and labor practices throughout the country. This was a contradiction of past cases that had ruled Congress did not have that power under the commerce clause. In *Steward Machine Co. v. Davis* (1937), the Court upheld the Social Security Act and the taxing process in which social security payments were financed. *Davis* contradicted the Court's ruling in *Butler* about the power of Congress to tax in order to redistribute money.

After these 1937 decisions, the constitutionality of the New Deal was never successfully challenged before the Supreme Court. A series of justices, seven of the nine, retired or died and were replaced by Roosevelt supporters.

For more information: Cushman, Barry. *Rethinking the New Deal Court.* New York: Oxford University Press, 1998; Maidment, Richard. *The Judicial Response to the New Deal.* Manchester, N.Y.: Manchester University Press, 1991; White, G. Edward. *The Constitution and the New Deal.* Cambridge, Mass.: Harvard University Press, 2000.

—Douglas Clouatre

new federalism

The Supreme Court's "new federalism" jurisprudence since 1986 has expanded state sovereignty at the expense of Congress's policymaking and enforcement authority, primarily through its interpretation of the INTERSTATE COMMERCE clause and the Eleventh and Fourteenth Amendments. In deciding these cases, the Court reversed almost 60 years of decisions allowing the federal government to regulate the conduct of private individuals under the interstate commerce clause. Moreover, by expanding the scope of the Eleventh Amendment, the Court allowed states to escape the consequences of their actions in violating federal CIVIL RIGHTS laws. This trend of limiting commerce authority and reinvigorating state SOVEREIGN IMMUNITY has caused concern that Congress's power to regulate private behavior and guarantee civil rights is being eroded by the Court.

Interstate Commerce Clause

Article I, Section 8 of the U.S. Constitution gives Congress the authority to regulate commerce among the states. Known as the interstate commerce clause, this has long been interpreted by the courts to allow Congress a great deal of leeway in determining the type of conduct to regulate, such as setting limits on wages and hours, prohibiting RACIAL DISCRIMINATION in places of public accommodation, and regulating the banking industry.

In 1995 the Court began to reconsider well-established principles that had been in place for almost 60 years in *United States v. Lopez*, 514 U.S. 549 (1995). In *Lopez*, the Court ruled that the Gun-Free School Zones Act, a portion of the 1990 crime bill that banned the possession of firearms within 1,000 feet of a school, was unconstitutional. The majority said that the law exceeded Congress's authority under the interstate commerce clause because the possession of weapons in schools was not sufficiently related to interstate commerce.

In *UNITED STATES V. MORRISON*, 529 U.S. 598 (2000), the Court again struck a federal law, this time a portion of the 1994 VIOLENCE AGAINST WOMEN ACT (VAWA). The Court ruled that the portion of the law that allowed victims of gender-motivated violence to file civil actions against their attackers in federal court was unconstitutional. Unlike *Lopez,* in which the Court said that Congress had not shown a sufficient link between guns at schools and interstate commerce, in *Morrison,* Congress had held extensive hearings on the effects of rape and domestic violence on women's employment opportunities and other aspects of interstate commerce. Nevertheless, the Court ruled that Congress had not demonstrated a sufficient link between gender-based violence and interstate commerce.

The Eleventh Amendment

The Eleventh Amendment, ratified in 1798, bars a private individual from suing a state in federal court without its consent. Based on the principle of state sovereignty, the amendment provides states with immunity from suits in which people ask for monetary damages; the amendment does not apply to individuals who seek injunctive relief (court orders) requiring the state to do something or refrain from doing something.

In 1996 the Court's new federalism jurisprudence influenced its decision on Congress's power to deny states immunity. In *Seminole Tribe of Florida v. Florida*, 517 U.S. 441 (1996), the Court held that the Indian Gaming Regulatory Act of 1988, which authorized suits by Native Americans against states, was unconstitutional because Congress lacked the authority to abrogate the state's immunity from suit under the Indian interstate commerce clause.

Three cases decided in 1999 were further indications that the Court's "new federalism" jurisprudence was enhancing the state's autonomy. In *Florida Prepaid Postsecondary Education Expense Board v. College Savings Bank*, 527 U.S. 627 (1999), and *College Savings Bank v. Florida Prepaid Postsecondary Education Expense Board*, 527 U.S. 666 (1999), the Court decided that private individuals cannot sue state entities for false advertising or trademark and patent infringement. The key decision in this trilogy, *Alden v. Maine*, 527 U.S. 706 (1999), arose from a dispute between state employees and the state of Maine over wages and hours. In this case, the Court barred private suits for money damage against state governments in state, as well as federal, courts, ruling that if the Eleventh Amendment blocks parties from suing states in federal court, it blocks them in state court as well.

The Fourteenth Amendment

The Fourteenth Amendment was ratified in 1868 to prohibit states from denying equal rights and due process of law; Section 5 of the amendment allows Congress to enact laws to enforce its guarantees. The Court has held that, under some circumstances, Section 5 gives Congress the power to abrogate (remove) a state's Eleventh Amendment immunity from suit. Indeed, following its ruling in *Seminole Tribe,* Congress was only permitted to abrogate state immunity when enacting laws to uphold equal rights or due process under the authority of Section 5.

In *BOERNE V. FLORES,* 521 U.S. 507 (1997), the Court further limited Congress's power to pass laws allowing individuals to sue states for monetary damages. The Court ruled that such laws were unconstitutional unless there was sufficient evidence that states had been guilty of unconstitutional actions and the laws did not increase the state's legal obligation to the individuals involved. Described by the Court as the "congruence and proportionality" test, this became the standard for determining whether a congressional statute enacted under Section 5 had lawfully abrogated state immunity. If the law in question was within Congress's authority to enact it under Section 5, states could be sued for monetary damages. If the law was not within Congress's authority under Section 5, states retained their Eleventh Amendment immunity from suit for such damages.

Beginning in 2000, the Court decided several cases in which state employees filed suit against the states for whom they worked, accusing them of violating the 1967 Age Discrimination in Employment Act (ADEA), the 1990 Americans with Disabilities Act (ADA), and the 1993 Family and Medical Leave Act (FMLA), respectively. In each case, the initial question the Court was asked to address was whether the employees could sue the state government for money damages or if the state was immune from such suits because Congress lacked the authority under Section 5 to take away its immunity.

In the first case, *KIMEL V. FLORIDA,* 528 U.S. 62 (2000), the Court decided that Congress did not have the authority to allow individuals to sue states for money damages under the ADEA. A year later in *Garrett v. University of Alabama at Birmingham,* 531 U.S. 356 (2001), a case involving the ban on employment discrimination on the basis of disability, the Court similarly ruled that Congress did not have the authority to revoke the state's Eleventh Amendment immunity in ADA suits brought by private individuals. In both cases, the Court said there was insuffi-

cient evidence that the states were guilty of discrimination against older workers or people with disabilities to justify the law that authorized the suits. Moreover, the Court indicated, these laws were trying to force the states to take actions beyond their constitutional requirements. In other words, the Court believed that the laws authorizing employees to sue states for damages under these laws were not "congruent and proportional" to the states' conduct.

In May 2003, in a case involving an employee who sued the state under the FMLA, the Court seemed to reverse course by deciding in favor of the employee. In *Nevada Department of Human Resources v. Hibbs,* 123 S.Ct. 1972 (2003), the Court ruled that because the FMLA was intended to prohibit gender discrimination, it fell within Congress's authority to enact laws guaranteeing equal rights under Section 5. Although many people applauded this decision, they believed it unfair that individuals were permitted to sue states for money damages in FMLA cases, but not in cases involving charges of discrimination on the basis of age or disability.

When considering the past decade of "new federalism" decisions, by deciding these cases in favor of states' rights and expanding state immunity from suit, the Court has dramatically reduced Congress's authority to make public policy regulating gun possession, Native American gaming, violence against women, and age and disability discrimination, as well as patent infringement and false advertising.

For more information: Nagel, Robert F. *The Implosion of American Federalism.* New York: Oxford University Press, 2001; Noonan, John T., Jr. *Narrowing the Nation's Power.* Berkeley: University of California Press, 2002.

—Susan Gluck Mezey

New Jersey v. T.L.O., 429 U.S. 325 (1985)

In *New Jersey v. T.L.O.,* the Supreme Court ruled that the Fourth Amendment prohibition on unreasonable searches and seizures does indeed apply to searches of students and/or their belongings in public schools. While the Court determined the search to be valid, this case stands for the principle that school officials do not stand in loco parentis, or in the place of parents, at least with respect to STUDENT SEARCHES.

Parents are uniquely positioned vis-à-vis their children. Of the many rights that parents have, one is the right to monitor their children's possessions and to confiscate anything they disapprove of. This right arises out of a parent's duty to rear and care for their children. Those who stand in loco parentis usually possess the rights and obligations that parents possess. School officials have long been considered to be in loco parentis because children spend much time in their care and custody. Rather than confer on school officials all the protections usually granted to parents, the Court decided that school officials are state agents who must meet certain standards before searching students or their belongings.

Student's interests must be balanced against the school's interests. Students have an interest in maintaining their privacy, while schools have an interest in maintaining order and a learning environment. Each of these interests deserves a level of respect. Ordinarily the Fourth Amendment requires that a search be conducted only after an official obtains a warrant or, at the very least, after an official has determined that there is probable cause (meaning that there is reason to believe that the individual to be searched has committed a crime or is likely to commit a crime). The Court ruled that neither a warrant nor probable cause were necessary in order to justify a student search. Such a requirement is too cumbersome because school officials must have flexibility in order to identify disruptive behavior immediately and to dispel it as quickly as possible.

The only requirement is that the search be reasonable. A reasonable search meets two criteria: (1) the search was justified at its inception (rather than after the fact in light of what was found), and (2) the scope of the search was reasonably related to the circumstances that gave rise to the initial justification for the search.

Three justices dissented in part of this decision. Justices BRENNAN and MARSHALL agreed that the warrant requirement is too cumbersome for school officials but maintained that probable cause should be present in order to justify a student search. Justice STEVENS focused his dissent on the narrow issue of whether the EXCLUSIONARY RULE should apply to student searches, which the majority did not address.

The result is that school officials have been given much wider latitude in conducting a search than is usually given to officials by the Fourth Amendment. At the same time, the Court imposed some restrictions because it was not willing to go so far as to give school officials unlimited power vis-à-vis students with respect to searches.

For more information: Dise, John H. *Searches of Students, Lockers, and Automobiles.* Detroit, Mich.: Educational Risk, Inc., 1994; Hinchey, Patricia H. *Student Rights: A Reference Handbook.* Santa Barbara, Calif.: ABC-CLIO, 2001.
—Susan M. Dennehy

New State Ice Company v. Liebmann, 285 U.S. 262 (1932)

In *New State Ice Company v. Liebmann*, the Court held that the ability to operate an ice business was a private concern protected by the Constitution and not a "public business" which the state could restrict.

The *New State Ice Company,* licensed by the Corporation Commission of Oklahoma to manufacture, sell, and distribute ice within Oklahoma City, brought suit against Liebmann to prevent him from operating an ice business without first obtaining a license from the commission, as required by an act of the 1925 Oklahoma legislature. The act declared the making and selling of ice to be a "public business" restricted by the state commission and requiring proof of necessity in the community.

Liebmann contended that denying him the right to operate a private ice business, a "common calling," deprived him of liberty and property in violation of the due process clause. Writing for the Court, Justice SUTHERLAND declared that all businesses are regulated, but the question before the Court is "whether the [ice] business is so charged with a public use as to justify the particular restriction. . . ." Sutherland refers to the cotton gin (*Frost v. Corporation Commission,* 278 U.S. 515, 1929) and grist mills as businesses with a true public interest. Such businesses were regarded as industries of "vital concern to the general public," necessary to the existence of the communities they served, and justifying government limitations to protect the public.

Sutherland argued, although a necessity, making ice is an ordinary business that does not affect the prosperity of the entire state. Ice is no more necessary than food, clothing, or shelter—none of which are regulated as a public use. Gas, electricity, and refrigerators had become available in the home, and the consumer was no longer at the mercy of the ice company. According to Sutherland, the New State Ice Company was attempting to use the Court to prevent business competition and maintain a monopoly, since their argument was not based on public safety issues; i.e., state control to ensure the conditions of manufacture and distribution and purity of the product, or to prevent extortion.

Sutherland concludes that states may experiment with legislation, but the Constitution protects certain essential liberties that the state cannot legislate against. "The opportunity to apply one's labor and skill in an ordinary occupation with proper regard for all reasonable regulations" is one of those liberties.

Justice BRANDEIS wrote a noteworthy dissent upholding a state's right to regulate business and defending the general principle that the Constitution can accommodate new situations and conditions that may alter the definition of public necessity and justify new regulation. Public necessity is an adaptation to the "machine age," intended to protect the community by preventing waste and duplication. This concept is not static, and whether a public utility is required for the welfare of the community is a decision for legislators familiar with local conditions. It is not the Court's place to judge the wisdom or foolishness of state policy. The function of the Court is "only to determine the reasonableness of the Legislature's belief in the existence of evils and in the effectiveness of the remedy provided."

Brandeis then reviewed Oklahoma's history to justify ice production as a monopoly. Competition among Oklahoma's ice plants has often resulted in higher prices and poor or no service. Consequently, most ice companies now operate as state-regulated monopolies, ensuring affordable prices, equitable distribution, accurate weights, sanitary practices, and good service. Ice is a necessity of life for the home, industry, and agriculture. A refrigerator "is still an article of relative luxury," and the law must protect individuals of limited or no means.

Given these facts, to hold the act unreasonable and void would mean the Court was improperly functioning as a "super-legislature." All businesses are regulated in some manner, but when constant, detailed supervision is warranted, the business is commonly identified as a "public" one, even though privately owned. The state's reasonable regulation of any business to protect the public is not limited by the due process clause.

Certifying a business as a public convenience is a "recent social-economic invention," through which the state controls or terminates it for the public interest. This legislative power "seems indispensable in our ever-changing society."

Finally, Brandeis warned that current conditions—the depression, unemployment, falling prices, and rising economic losses—were thought to be partially due to courts limiting new methods. "It is one of the happy incidents of the federal system that a single courageous state may . . . serve as a laboratory, and try novel social and economic experiments without risk to the rest of the country." The Court must be careful not to stifle the states' experiments.

For more information: Urofsky, Melvin I. *Louis D. Brandeis and the Progressive Tradition.* Boston: Little, Brown, 1981.

—Karen Aichinger

New York Times Co. v. Sullivan, 376 U.S. 254 (1964)

New York Times Co. v. Sullivan afforded the Supreme Court the opportunity to craft the most vigorous affirmation of the freedom of the press in the history of American constitutional law.

A full-page advertisement published in March 1960 and funded by supporters of Dr. Martin Luther King, Jr., alleged widespread violence and abuse by police in Alabama and prompted Respondent Sullivan, the Montgomery, Alabama, police commissioner, to sue the *New York Times* for libel and defamation of character.

In the lower state courts, Sullivan won judgment and was awarded $500,000 by a jury, because Alabama libel law required only that the individual prove injury to reputation,

but also because there were some minor factual errors in the advertisement. (Dr. King had been arrested four, not seven, times, for example.)

Writing for a unanimous Supreme Court, Justice William BRENNAN reversed the lower court and, in the name of the First Amendment, effectively inverted much of the traditional legal understanding of libel. To give the press some "breathing room" and to avoid the "chilling" of expression, investigation, and inquiry that are essential in our system of democracy, Brennan devised a new federal constitutional standard that put the onus on a public official to prove that a reported story or allegation was false, that it did actual damage to one's reputation, and that the news outfit acted with "actual malice" or "reckless disregard" for the truth. (Importantly, "known lies" still did not garner constitutional protection, as the Court made clear in another case decided on the same day.)

What the *Sullivan* case did therefore was enable the media to report on stories of public consequence and involving public officials without fear of a civil suit brought in retaliation for criticism or for the occasional (unwitting) factual error. In essence, Brennan explained, the issues in this case should be considered "against the background of a profound national commitment to the principle that debate on public issues should be uninhibited, robust, and wide open, and that it may well include vehement, caustic, and sometimes unpleasantly sharp attacks on government and public officials."

The *timing* of this decision was critical, especially because civil and voting rights issues were increasingly gaining national attention in the early 1960s. Had the Supreme Court not carved out such extensive protections for the press, it seems safe to assume that media scrutiny of southern officials would have been considerably more cautious, even muted. Indeed, without the "teeth" that the *Sullivan* decision gave to the First Amendment, it is unclear exactly what degree of denunciation of public officials would be allowable. From criticism of the president's moral reasoning (or occasional moral lapses) to the fascination with various Hollywood starlets' new romances and weight-control programs, our attention is constantly focused on public figures. What *Sullivan* wrought then is a system that affords the media—from the *New York Times* to the *National Enquirer*—the editorial license and discretion to report on such individuals and events so long as they do not reproduce that which they *know* to be false.

For more information: Kalven, Harry. "The New York Times Case: A Note on 'The Central Meaning of the First Amendment.'" *The Supreme Court Review* (1964); Lewis, Anthony, ed. *Make No Law: The Sullivan Case and the First Amendment.* New York: Random House, 1991.

—Brian K. Pinaire

New York v. Ferber, 458 U.S. 747 (1982)

In *New York v. Ferber,* the Supreme Court declared constitutionally valid a 1977 New York statute prohibiting the intentional promotion of sexual performances by minors. Times Square bookstore proprietor Paul Ferber was arrested and convicted for selling to an undercover police officer two videos featuring autoerotic acts by boys under 16 years of age and therefore minors under New York law. Ferber's conviction was affirmed by the appellate division of the New York Supreme Court. Later, however, the New York Court of Appeals reversed, holding that the statute was both under-inclusive and overbroad in violation of the First Amendment's free speech guarantees. The state appealed to the Supreme Court.

The Supreme Court's decision in *Ferber* was unanimous, with the majority opinion written by Byron WHITE upholding the statute and concurring opinions issued by Sandra Day O'CONNOR, William BRENNAN, and John Paul STEVENS. The key question in the case was whether the state had a compelling interest to regulate the promotion and distribution of child pornography even when the material fell short of the legal definition of obscenity. While the Court had created a standard for unprotected obscenity in *Miller v. California,* 413 U.S. 15 (1973), New York argued that the harm done by dissemination of child pornography justified greater regulatory latitude. While offering a review of the Court's obscenity rulings and reluctance to limit expression, Justice White's majority opinion identified *Ferber* as the Court's "first examination of a statute directed at and limited to depictions of sexual activity involving children."

To address the state's authority to restrict the distribution and promotion of child pornography, Justice White offered several reasons that the "States are entitled to greater leeway in the regulation of pornographic depictions of children" even absent obscenity. First, the Court found a COMPELLING STATE INTEREST in preventing "sexual exploitation and abuse of children" and declared that task to be a "government objective of surpassing importance." Second, Justice White's opinion stated that films and photographs depicting child sexual activity are tied to sexual abuse by circulating a lasting record of minors' participation in sexual conduct, and their distribution encourages production of works depicting child sex acts. Third, the Court ruled it permissible for the state to restrict the advertising and selling of such materials as a means of shrinking their market.

The Court also noted that the intrinsic value of performances of child sexual conduct is either minimal or nonexistent. Finally, the majority concluded that this result is not inconsistent with the Court's past rulings, as the evil the statute regulated outweighed any expressive interests. Furthermore, the material in question was such a threat to chil-

dren as not to be afforded First Amendment protections. The majority indicated that its ruling rendered child pornography a class of regulated speech apart from obscenity. The state may prohibit film and video productions harmful to actual minors but may not ban literary, scientific, or artistic depictions of child sexual conduct in which no minor children are harmed or involved in its creation.

The Court rejected the New York Court of Appeals finding that the statute was under-inclusive, declaring it constitutionally appropriate for New York to single out child pornography as a category of expression worthy of regulation. The majority also rejected the lower court's claim that the statute was unconstitutionally overbroad because it potentially restricted materials of medical, artistic, or educational value. Instead, the Court ruled that the benefits garnered from the regulation of child pornography dwarfed the potential harm to legitimate activities. It is this failure to allow exceptions for activities of value that is discussed most thoroughly in the concurring opinions of Justices O'Connor, Brennan, and Stevens, with the latter two expressing the most sympathy for Ferber's claims. However, neither justice found sufficient grounds to dissent from the Court's ruling.

The decision in *Ferber* was extended to possession of child pornography eight years later in *Osborne v. Ohio,* 495 U.S. 103 (1990), in which a divided Supreme Court ruled *Ferber* applicable to state efforts to regulate possession. The significance of *Ferber* as PRECEDENT is also evident given the Court's decision in *Ashcroft v. Free Speech Coalition,* 535 U.S. 234 (2002), which overturned sections of the Child Pornography Prevention Act of 1996 banning virtual depictions of sexual acts involving minors. To the extent that the statutes prohibited material that brought no direct harm to actual children as specified in *Ferber,* they did not pass constitutional muster.

For more information: Dwyer, Susan. *The Problem of Pornography.* Belmont, Calif.: Wadsworth Publishing Company, 1995; Hixson, Richard F. *Pornography and the Justices: The Supreme Court and the Intractible Obscenity Problem.* Carbondale and Edwardsville: Southern Illinois University Press, 1996.

—Richard L. Vining, Jr.

New York v. United States, 505 U.S. 144 (1992)

In *New York v. United States,* the Supreme Court struck down provisions in congressional legislation designed to force the states to develop facilities for the disposal of low-level nuclear waste. In doing so, the case rejuvenated the concept of state immunity from regulation by Congress and revived the spirits of states rights supporters. The effect of the case on the balance of power between state and federal legislatures in the constitution was modest, but the case did signal a desire by the Court to protect state interests over the promotion of national priorities as defined by Congress and carried out through the commerce clause.

On the urging of the National Governors Association, Congress passed legislation in 1985 requiring States to develop low-level radioactive waste disposal facilities. To discourage the temptation to ship the waste to less populous states, the States were required to take responsibility for their own waste and to build, either by themselves or in cooperation with other states, facilities for its disposal. Those states that did not comply with the legislation or were tardy in setting up their facilities faced a sliding scale of sanctions and penalties. States that failed to develop facilities by the deadline were required to assume ownership of the waste, which made the state, not the producer, responsible for its storage or disposal.

For the most part the legislation and the strategy were successful. Forty-nine states either built facilities or participated in regional schemes to dispose of the waste. New York State had done neither and was the sole state facing the "take title" clause. New York and the reluctant counties it proposed as sites for a facility applied to the Supreme Court for relief. They did not challenge Congress's ability to regulate the field of radioactive waste. There was an evident element of interstate traffic in radioactive waste that both parties conceded Congress was entitled to oversee as commerce. The entire field of radioactive waste was also open to Congress through the supremacy clause. What the appellants did challenge was the ability of Congress to enlist the states, through both positive and negative incentives, as agencies of its policy. The Court was not asked to decide any jurisdictional issues, simply whether Congress had the authority to compel the states into such action.

The Court upheld the core of the legislation as a legitimate exercise of the commerce power and of the federal spending power; it took issue only with the "take title" provisions. The Tenth Amendment was invoked as a possible limit on the manner in which Congress exercised its powers. Most Tenth Amendment cases, as Justice O'CONNOR noted in her majority decision, turn on whether or not states could be regulated under the commerce clause by laws that were generally applied to private citizens and organizations. In this case, the law was purposely designed to operate directly on the states alone. The burdens were placed directly on the shoulders of the states and only indirectly did the law regulate the actual producers.

The Court disapproved of the structuring of the "take title" provisions. O'Connor cynically noted that the states had the "choice" of accepting title to the waste or disposing of it according to Congress's wishes. The federal government argued that the states implied their consent by requesting that Congress pass the legislation in the first place. The majority responded that it was not the states' privilege to give up their sovereignty, even by negotiation. State sovereignty, it claimed, is not solely about protecting the states. Rather FEDERALISM, and the division of authority inherent in it, was designed for the protection of individuals. Therefore, reasoned the majority, exercises in cooperative federalism had to adhere to the rules of sovereignty. Otherwise accountability was lost. To avoid such a vacuum, the court ruled that congressional direction of the states, as in the take title provisions, was not permitted.

For more information: Adler, Matthew D., and Seth F. Kreimer. "The New Etiquette of Federalism: New York, Printz, and Yeskey." *Supreme Court Review* (1998): 71.

—Gerald Baier

1983 lawsuits

1983 lawsuits refers to cases arising under 42 U.S.C. 1983. That statute authorizes a state or federal court to grant civil relief to a victim of a state or local official or other person acting under color of law who violates a federally protected right. Well-known cases litigated under Section 1983 that reached the Supreme Court include *BROWN V. BOARD OF EDUCATION OF TOPEKA*, 347 U.S. 483 (1952), and *ROE V. WADE*, 410 U.S. 113 (1973).

Section 1983 developed from the Civil Rights Act of 1871, a reconstruction era CIVIL RIGHTS statute, also known as the Ku Klux Klan Act. The 1871 act represented a federal response to Klan activities denying former slaves their civil rights.

The current version of 42 U.S.C. 1983 grants redress to individuals and provides:

> Every person who, under color of any statute, ordinance, regulation, custom, or usage of any State or Territory of the District of Columbia subjects, or causes to be subjected, any . . . person . . . to the deprivation of any rights, privileges, or immunities secured by the Constitution and laws, shall be liable to the party injured in an action at law, suit in equity, or other proper proceeding for redress. . . .

While Section 1983 expressly authorizes actions only against those acting under color of state law, the Supreme Court in *Bivens v. Six Unknown Named Agents of Federal Bureau of Narcotics,* 403 U.S. 388 (1971), authorized similar relief in cases of violations of federally protected rights by federal agents.

Section 1983 remained largely unused for almost one hundred years. Civil rights claims brought under Section

1983 now represent a rapidly growing source of civil litigation. These arise in a variety of factual situations, extending from LAND USE issues to conflicts with law enforcement personnel. Many 1983 plaintiffs claim police misconduct. Plaintiffs may bring claims under Section 1983 in either state or federal court, but federal, rather than state, law applies.

The statute, itself, specifies the elements a plaintiff must prove in order to gain relief under the statute: (1) a person, (2) under color, or pretense, of any statute, ordinance, regulation, custom, or usage, (3) subjects another person to (4) a violation of federally protected rights. Proof of these elements entitles the plaintiff to several types of relief. These include an injunction that the defendant stop the offending activity, a DECLARATORY JUDGMENT of illegality or unconstitutionality, or monetary damages to compensate and punish. A person may sue both individuals and governmental entities because of civil rights violations. A plaintiff who presents a claim against a government must also prove that the government, itself, was the "moving force" behind the deprivation.

Plaintiff may not sue a governmental entity based solely on the conduct of an employee but must base the suit on a statute, regulation, custom, policy, or usage that deprived the individual of rights. The entity may be liable when the alleged unconstitutional action demonstrates a policy, ordinance, regulation, or decision of the body's officers or an official with final policy authority.

1983 cases involve many different situations. Some involve claims the entity failed to properly train its employees. Jail condition cases represent the largest number of civil rights claims. Typically, the prisoner files these claims pro se, on his own behalf, and not through an attorney. These take many forms, ranging from allegations about prison conditions to failure to provide appropriate medical care. Some plaintiffs allege law enforcement used excessive force in arresting or controlling the prisoner. Others allege law enforcement failed to protect them from other prisoners or physical harm. Still others allege denial of access to the courts by failing to provide adequate law libraries or assistance from legally trained persons.

Damages recoverable in claims brought under 42 U.S.C. 1983 include: (1) nominal damages, merely because of the violation, (2) actual damages, which compensate for harm actually sustained as a result, such as medical expenses, (3) PUNITIVE DAMAGES, intended to deter defendant and others from like conduct, and (4) attorneys' fees for prosecuting the civil action.

Plaintiff may recover punitive damages against individual defendants when the plaintiff shows the defendant's conduct involves reckless or callous indifference to the federally protected rights of others. However, a plaintiff may not recover punitive damages against a governmental entity.

1983 defendants possess two related immunity defenses, absolute immunity and qualified immunity. Both comprise affirmative defenses which defendant must prove.

Absolute judicial immunity applies to conduct closely associated with the judicial phase of the criminal process, including prosecutors while functioning as a part of the judicial process. Judicial immunity applies only to adjudicative acts, but not to administrative, legislative, or executive functions these officials may perform. Qualified immunity may be available for those functions. Thus, a judge may not have absolute judicial immunity for terminating a bailiff or clerk but may have qualified immunity. Additionally, judicial immunity will not apply where the judge takes action in the absence of jurisdiction.

Qualified immunity protects governmental officials such as police officers, school board members, hospital administrators, prison officials, and judicial officials for discretionary acts outside the judicial or quasi-judicial area. These can only be liable for violations of clearly settled law, which a defendant, absent extraordinary circumstances, would know. The judge must decide the existence of clearly settled law and whether the defendant acted reasonably with regard to that law. A jury must decide any disputed facts.

For more information: 42 U.S.C. 1983; Nahmod, Sheldon H. *Civil Rights and Liberties Litigation.* 4th ed. St. Paul, Minn.: West, 2001; Schwartz, Martin A., et al., eds. *Section 1983 Litigation.* New York: Wesley, 1997; Smolla, Rodney A. *Federal Civil Rights Acts.* 3rd ed. St. Paul, Minn.: West, 2001.

—Patrick K. Roberts

Ninth Amendment

The Ninth Amendment to the UNITED STATES CONSTITUTION reads: "The enumeration in the Constitution, of certain rights, shall not be construed to deny or disparage others retained by the people." This particular constitutional amendment, largely forgotten since its addition to our founding document in 1791, is largely the product of the work and vision of James Madison, who, in early June 1789, introduced in the House of Representatives the controversial subject of a declaration or BILL OF RIGHTS to be added to the original Constitution. Influenced by a variety of sources, including several state constitutions and declarations of rights, such as the Virginia Declaration of Rights of 1776, Madison argued that the Ninth Amendment, especially in the hands of an independent federal judiciary, would both protect individual liberties and limit governmental powers.

From 1791, when the Bill of Rights became part of the Constitution, until 1965, when the United States Supreme Court handed down its ruling in the case of

GRISWOLD V. CONNECTICUT, this "retained rights" provision of the Constitution lay dormant, often viewed (more by scholars than jurists) as either a truism (ours is a government of limited powers) or a dead letter (the clause was too open-ended to be worth anything in constitutional litigation). And this kind of treatment of the Ninth was at the hands of those scholars who had not forgotten its very existence.

The Supreme Court essentially resurrected the Ninth Amendment in 1965 when, in the *Griswold* case from Connecticut, it struck down a 1879 Connecticut law that banned the use of and any advice on how to use CONTRACEPTIVES (*Griswold v. Connecticut*, 381 U.S. 479 [1965]). By a 7 to 2 vote, the Court ruled that the Connecticut statute violated the fundamental right to marital privacy, a right, according to Justice William O. DOUGLAS, older than the Bill of Rights itself. Conceding that such a right was nowhere specifically written in the Constitution, Douglas argued that the Ninth Amendment, at least as a rule of construction, pointed the way to the existence of fundamental, UNENUMERATED RIGHTS as worthy of protection as FUNDAMENTAL RIGHTS written in the text of the Constitution.

Even more than Douglas did Justice Arthur Goldberg rely on the Ninth Amendment in his concurring opinion in *Griswold*, an opinion joined by Chief Justice Earl WARREN and Justice William BRENNAN. Focusing on "the language and history of the Ninth Amendment," Goldberg vigorously advanced the thesis that the Ninth Amendment was neither a truism nor a dead letter and therefore should be taken seriously by anyone in the necessary conversation about the nature and extent of fundamental, unenumerated rights in our constitutional democracy.

Following its rebirth in *Griswold*, the Ninth Amendment would come to occupy a fairly prominent place in the debate concerning personal freedom, especially reproductive autonomy, as in the *Roe* decision of 1973. This open-ended clause of the Constitution, reflecting as it does Madison's concern with the appropriate fit between individual liberty and governmental power, is forgotten no more.

For more information: Barnett, Randy, ed. *The Rights Retained by the People.* Fairfax, Va.: George Mason University Press, 1989; Black, Charles, Jr. *A New Birth of Freedom: Human Rights Named and Unnamed.* New York: Grosset/Putnam, 1997; Shaw, Stephen K. *The Ninth Amendment: Preservation of the Constitutional Mind.* New York: Garland, 1990.

—Stephen K. Shaw

nude dancing

Forms of striptease or "burlesque" have been around since the 1930s. Contemporary "gentleman's clubs" offer an atmosphere of provocative topless and nude dancing, alcohol, and music. Unlike the 1930s, which offered more "tease" than "strip," modern clubs leave nothing to the imagination.

While some communities see this industry as a benefit for tourism and convention business, many others have attempted to eliminate the establishments through a series of laws and regulations. Many of these regulations have been challenged as violations of the First Amendment. The Supreme Court has given local communities wide latitude in regulating this activity through a variety of measures including ZONING, liquor licensing, and outright bans.

In *California v. LaRue* (1972), the Supreme Court ruled that a state law that denied liquor licenses to establishments that offered nude dancing was constitutional. The Court's ruling however focused on the Twenty-first Amendment rather than First Amendment considerations. Other cases during the 1970s and 1980s hinted that nude dancing could be protected by the First Amendment but did not explicitly state the boundaries.

In *BARNES V. GLEN THEATRE* (1991), the Court ruled that nude dancing was expressive. Chief Justice REHNQUIST in the majority opinion stated that nude dancing was "within the outer perimeters of the First Amendment, although only marginally so." The majority then moved on to uphold the state's zoning regulations stating that the intent of the law was not aimed at the erotic message but was a general prohibition against public indecency. The Court's ruling was a 5 to 4 decision with a fractured majority, which left many people confused as to the state of the law.

Justice SOUTER, in a concurring opinion, suggested that the secondary effects of crime and sexual assaults that might be related to nude dancing should justify its regulation. Justice WHITE and three other dissenters argued that the Indiana statute was prohibiting expressive conduct and that nudity was essentially related to the message of the dance.

In the case of *Pap's A.M. v. City of Erie* (2000), the Court reaffirmed that nude dancing had symbolic meaning but this time ruled that laws banning nude dancing entirely could be upheld because of the negative "secondary-effects" that accrue to areas with adult entertainment establishments, such as crime, prostitution, and drug use. They did not require cities to prove that these effects were present or that they were affected by restricting nude dancing.

This decision was again split and hotly contested, with two concurring opinions within the seven-person majority. Justice Souter again concurred saying he wanted more proof on whether the secondary effects were impacted by the ban. Justice STEVENS dissented, arguing that the total ban was over broad and that zoning laws were a less restrictive means to achieve the same results. Justice SCALIA concurred with the majority but ridiculed its reasoning, arguing that the community had the right to uphold morals as long as specific messages were not targeted.

For more information: Manuto, Ron, and Sean Patrick O'Rourke. "Dances with Wolves: Nudity, Morality and the Speech/Conduct Doctrine." *Free Speech Yearbook* 32 (1994): 86–109; McBride, Michael. "*Pap's A.M. v. City of Erie:* The Wrong Route to the Right Decision." *Akron Law Review* 34 (2000).

—Charles C. Howard

O'Connor, Sandra Day (1930–) *Supreme Court justice*

Sandra Day O'Connor became the U.S. Supreme Court's 102nd justice and first female member in September of 1981. She was born on March 26, 1930, in El Paso, Texas, to Harry A. Day and Ada Mae Wilkey Day. O'Connor established her educational roots at Stanford University, where she majored in economics and received her B.A. graduating magna cum laude in 1950. She then attended Stanford Law School, where she ranked third of 102 students, served as editor for the *Stanford Law Review*, was inducted to Order of the Coif, and eventually received her LL.B. two years later in 1952. Upon completing her education, she married fellow law student John Jay O'Connor III and settled in Phoenix, Arizona.

O'Connor has had a distinguished career practicing law, which began in 1952 when she served as deputy county attorney of San Mateo County, California, while her husband finished his final year of law school. Upon obtaining his law degree, John O'Connor was offered the opportunity to work in Frankfurt, West Germany, in the Judge Advocate General's Corps of the United States Army. During this period, Sandra Day O'Connor joined her husband in West Germany and worked as a Civil Quartermaster Corps attorney specializing in contracts. In 1957 the O'Connors returned to the United States and settled in Maryvale, Arizona. Sandra Day O'Connor worked part-time in her private law practice and became active in civic affairs. She served on the Maricopa County Board of Adjustments & Appeals and the Government's Committee on Marriage & Family; she worked as an administrator for the Arizona State Hospital; and she volunteered her time at the Salvation Army and impoverished schools. O'Connor also became involved in the Republican Party where she served as district chair.

By 1965 O'Connor was ready to enter public office and was elected assistant attorney general of Arizona. Because of her growing civic, legal, and overall career record, in 1969 Governor Jack Williams appointed O'Connor to the Arizona State Senate. Running as a Republican, she was quite successful in her 1970 and 1972 reelection campaigns. Because of her excellence as a legislator, in 1972 O'Connor became the first woman to be given the post of majority leader. As a legislator, O'Connor's voting record reflected moderate to conservative views. While she favored limited government spending, the death penalty, and some select feminist views, O'Connor also supported the EQUAL RIGHTS AMENDMENT, property rights for women, and, on average, seemed to favor a woman's right to have an abortion. During her time as Arizona's assistant attorney general and senator, O'Connor continued her civic involvement by serving as chairman for the Maricopa County Juvenile Detention Home Visiting Board, the Maricopa County Bar Association Lawyer Referral Services, and the Arizona Supreme Court Committee to Reorganize the Lower Courts. O'Connor also shared her time by participating in the Arizona State Personnel Commission, the National Defense Advisory Committee on Women in the Services, the Arizona Criminal Code Commission, and the State Bar of Arizona Committees on Legal Aide, Public Relations, Lower Court Reorganization, and Continuing Legal Education.

In 1975 O'Connor decided to pursue a career change and successfully ran in an election for the post of justice on the Maricopa County Superior Court. During her time on the bench, O'Connor continued her political activism by serving as alternative delegate to the 1972 Republican National Convention, cochairing Richard M. Nixon's reelection committee in Arizona, and in 1976, backing Ronald Reagan for the Republic nomination for president (which eventually went to Gerald Ford). She also continued her civic involvement by becoming chairman of the Maricopa County Superior Court Judges' Training and Education Committee; board member and secretary for the Arizona Academy; president and Board of Trustee member for the Heard Museum; and member of the Arizona Board of Achievement and the Phoenix Historical Society Board of Directors.

Justice Sandra Day O'Connor *(United States Supreme Court)*

In 1979 O'Connor's judicial career continued to prosper through an appointment to the Arizona Court of Appeals. Though she was initially regarded as competent but undistinguished, she quickly gained recognition (both nationally and in the legal circle) by attending a judicial conference in England with Chief Justice Warren BURGER; participating in programs on FEDERALISM and the state courts, and sharing her judicial philosophy; and, by publishing her conference remarks in an article for the *William and Mary Law Review* (Summer 1981 issue). During the period, O'Connor also participated in the Anglo-American Exchange and became vice chairman of the Arizona Select Law Enforcement Review. She also served as vice president of Soroptimist Club of Phoenix; advisory board member and vice president for the National Conference of Christians and Jews in Maricopa County; and member of the Board of Visitors for Arizona State University Law School, the Liaison Committee on Medical Education, and the Stanford University Board of Trustees.

To help fill the vacancy left by newly retired Justice Potter Stewart, President Ronald Reagan nominated O'Connor to serve as an associate justice of the Supreme Court in July 1981. This nomination was due in part to a campaign promise to nominate a female Supreme Court justice, and to offset criticisms regarding Reagan's opposition to the 1980 Equal Rights Amendments. With Senate confirmation obtained on September 21, 1981, O'Connor took her seat on September 25, 1981.

During her first year as associate justice, O'Connor made it clear she was conservative by joining Burger and REHNQUIST on 62 of 84 opinions. She not only watched out for the rights of states but she also sought to curb excessive appeals. By her second year on the Supreme Court, feminist and pro-choice activists became leery with O'Connor's conservative stance on certain key issues. For instance, even though she split from conservatives by favoring the elimination of pension plans that failed to offer women equity with men, she refused to allow her decision to become retroactive. O'Connor also supported the minority view to uphold local laws which curbed the access of women to abortions. This caused much concern in light of the fact that the Supreme Court had already ruled to legalize abortions. Nevertheless, regardless of her controversial positions on issues, O'Connor continued her civil participation by becoming a member of the National Board of the Smithsonian Association; a position maintained to this day.

Although O'Connor was initially a strong conservative, by the late 1980s she became more of a centrist in light of a sharply divided Court between conservatives and liberals. To many, this move toward the middle exhibited her growing political independence; especially in light of her swing vote on issues of AFFIRMATIVE ACTION, the death penalty, and abortion. For instance, in terms of her most notable opinions, O'Connor endorsed affirmative action for minorities if "narrowly tailored" to correct a demonstrated wrong but ruled that government programs setting aside a fixed percentage of public contracts for minority businesses violated the EQUAL PROTECTION CLAUSE in *CITY OF RICHMOND V. J. A. CROSON CO.*, 488 U.S. 469 (1989). In *PLANNED PARENTHOOD OF SOUTHEASTERN PENNSYLVANIA V. CASEY*, 505 U.S. 833 (1992), O'Connor criticized the constitutional foundation for the Court's original 1973 recognition of the right to abortion yet declined to overturn the ruling. O'Connor has also sought to limit the instruction of the federal courts on state power, and to limit the federal judicial power with respect to the legislative and executive branches. Today, Sandra Day O'Connor has become a role model for Americans regardless of age and gender.

For more information: First Gov—The U.S. Government's Official Web Portal. Available online. URL: http://www.firstgov.gov. Downloaded May 17, 2004; U.S. National Archives and Records Administration. Available online. URL: http://www.archives.gov. Downloaded May 17, 2004; United States Supreme Court. "The Justices of the Supreme Court: Sandra Day O'Connor." Supreme Court Historical Society (2003). Available online. URL: http://www.supremecourtus.gov/about/biographies current.pdf. Downloaded May 17, 2004.

—Mitzi Ramos

O'Hare Truck Service, Inc. v. City of Northlake, 518 U.S. 712 (1996)

In the case of *O'Hare Truck Service, Inc. v. City of Northlake,* the Supreme Court extended the protections against retaliation for political party affiliation it had provided for public employees to independent government contractors. The First Amendment protections for freedom of speech and freedom of association provided the basis for the decision. This case was decided at the same time that the Court handed down its decision in *County Commissioners, Wabaunsee County, Kansas, v. Umbehr,* 518 U.S. 668 (1996).

Like many cities, the city of Northlake, Illinois, maintained a list of qualified towing companies who would respond to police requests whenever they needed to have a vehicle towed. Typically, they would run through the list on a rotational basis giving all the qualified towers opportunities to earn towing fees. Typically, any responsible towing company (i.e., one that is capable, financially solvent, and provides good service) could be on the list. O'Hare Truck Service, owned by John Gratzianna, was one of the companies on the list. In 1993 the mayor of Northlake, Reid Paxson, approached Gratzianna to request support for his upcoming reelection campaign. Mr. Gratzianna not only declined to make a contribution but he actively supported Mr. Paxson's opponent. Shortly afterward, O'Hare Truck Service was removed from the "approved" list of towing services for the City of Northlake. O'Hare Truck Service sued alleging that its First Amendment rights had been violated.

The Supreme Court majority (in the 7-2 decision) made clear that they viewed this case as one in a line of cases prohibiting governments from using political criteria to make decisions about eligibility or qualification for doing most types of government work. The three most important precedents cited by the Court in this case were *Elrod v. Burns,* 427 U.S. 347 (1976), which said that a county sheriff could not dismiss a deputy because he belonged to a different political party; *Branti v. Finkel,* 445 U.S. 507 (1980), which said that if a government wanted to apply a political party litmus test as a reason for removing someone from a particular job, the government must "demonstrate that party affiliation is an appropriate requirement for the effective performance of the public office involved"; and, finally, *Rutan v. Republican Party of Illinois,* 497 U.S. 62 (1990), which said that a political party litmus test could not be used as a criterion in deciding who to hire for a reg-

ular government job. It is interesting to note, that like the *O'Hare Truck* case, *Elrod* and *Rutan* were also cases from Illinois, a state with a long tradition of using patronage in making decisions about hiring and firing public employees. The Supreme Court saw only minor differences between hiring an employee and hiring a company that would hire employees to do work the government wanted done. From this perspective, there was no reason to treat independent contractors any differently from employees when it came to protecting their freedom of speech and the right to support any political party they liked. The dissent in this case, by Justices Antonin SCALIA and Clarence THOMAS, was actually included as part of their dissent in *County Commissioners, Wabaunsee County v. Umbehr.* Political patronage, they passionately argued, has a long tradition in the United States and has been practiced since the founding of the country. The laws of Northlake and Illinois allowed the city to base its decisions about who to contract with on whatever criteria it chose, including political support and, to the dissenters, that is a choice for the citizens and elected officials of Northlake to make, not the Supreme Court. While the majority agreed that the local government did retain the freedom to terminate contracts "at will" (if that language is included in the contract), "at will" could not be used as an excuse to "coerce" political support from a contractor. Scalia and Thomas contend that the Court should anticipate a flood of cases where any contractor having a government contract terminated or losing a competition for a new contract will cry "political retaliation."

For more information: Janota, Laura, and Marilyn Doubek. "Despite Ruling, Patronage Still Lives." *Daily Herald* (Arlington Heights, Ill.), October 8, 1998, p. 1.

—Charles W. Gossett

Olim v. Wakinekona, 461 U.S. 238 (1983)

In *Olim v. Wakinekona,* the court addressed two questions: "Do state prison administrators have the authority to transfer prisoners to out-of-state prisons?" and "Does the interstate transfer of a prisoner deprive the inmate of a liberty interest protected by the due process clause of the Fourteenth Amendment?" The Court held that states do have the power—via state statute (and, it should be noted, congressionally approved and state codified interstate corrections compacts)—to transfer inmates to prisons in other states even when, as here, "the transfer involves long distances and an open ocean crossing [. . .]." Additionally, the Court held that confinement in such cases does not implicate a liberty interest protected by the due process clause of the Fourteenth Amendment because: (1) such transfers are "within the normal limits or range of custody which the conviction has authorized the state to impose," and (2) because Hawaiian regulations "place no substantive limitations on official discretion" and the "regulations governing prison transfers do not create a substantive liberty interest protected by the due process clause."

In addition to inmate Wakinekona's complaint (based on Hawaii's administrative Rule IV requiring an impartial hearing) that his PROCEDURAL DUE PROCESS rights had been violated due to a biased disciplinary hearing by prison administrators, it is also argued that his transfer to a California prison was a violation of his SUBSTANTIVE DUE PROCESS rights due to the severity and hardship of such a transfer. Simply, in this case the Court was concerned with whether the interstate transfer of Wakinekona constituted a sufficiently "grievous loss" to trigger the protection of *procedural* due process. In addition to establishing a state's right to transfer prison inmates to jurisdictions outside of an inmate's home state—and thus, further dismissing an inmate's expectation that he will be incarcerated in proximity to his home or place of conviction (*Meachum v. Fano,* 427 U.S. 215 [1976]; *Montayne v. Haymes,* 427 U.S. 236, [1976])—the Court held that the interstate transfer of an inmate does not trigger *procedural* due process protections because it does not constitute an extraordinary form of punishment.

However, not all of the justices believed the interstate transfer of inmates to be consistent with the intent of the U.S. Constitution. Dissenting in *Olim v. Wakinekona,* Justice MARSHALL, joined by Justices Brennen and STEVENS, asserts that interstate prison transfers violate an inmate's liberty interests because the transfer is significantly punitive. They write:

> There can be little doubt that the transfer of Wakinekona from a Hawaiian prison to a prison in California represents a substantive qualitative change in the conditions of his confinement. In addition to being incarcerated, which is the ordinary consequence of a criminal conviction and sentence, Wakinekona has in effect been banished from his home, a punishment historically considered to be among the severest.

In *Olim v. Wakinekona,* Justice Marshall is vehement in his opposition to the practice of "legal banishment" and consistently advocated for the protection of inmates' liberty interests throughout his career.

For more information: Gutterman, Melvin. "The Prison Jurisprudence of Justice Thurgood Marshall." *Maryland Law Review* 56 (1997): 1–57; Keyes, J. T. "Banishing Massachusetts Inmates to Texas: Prisoner Liberty Interests and Interstate Transfers after *Sandin v. Conner.*" *New England Journal on Criminal and Civil Confinement* 23 (Summer 1997): 1–46.

—Robert Swan

one person, one vote

The phrase "one person, one vote" describes the principle that every person has the right to an equally weighted vote.

The Supreme Court first articulated this concept in *Gray v. Sanders,* 372 U.S. 368 (1963), when Justice William O. DOUGLAS wrote, "The conception of political equality from the Declaration of Independence, to Lincoln's Gettysburg Address, to the Fifteenth, Seventeenth, and Nineteenth Amendments can mean only one thing—one person, one vote." [372 U.S. at 381.] The *Gray* Court struck down a Georgia law governing vote counting in primary elections to nominate U.S. Senate and statewide office candidates, ruling that a statewide vote counting system that weights some votes more heavily than others is unconstitutional.

In *WESBERRY V. SANDERS,* 376 U.S. 1 (1964), the Court considered a challenge to the unequal apportionment of Georgia's congressional districts. Again the Court applied the "one person, one vote" principle and ruled that, "as nearly as is practicable one man's vote in a congressional election is to be worth as much as another's." [*Wesberry,* 376 U.S. at 7-8.] The *Wesberry* Court quoted James Madison as its source of the "one person, one vote" principle: "If the power is not immediately derived from the people, in proportion to their numbers, we may make a paper confederacy, but that will be all." [376 U.S. at 10.]

Four months after publishing its opinion in *Wesberry,* the Court decided *REYNOLDS V. SIMS,* 377 U.S. 533 (1964). In *Reynolds,* residents of Alabama's largest counties sued the state, claiming that the state's distribution of legislative seats diluted the strength of their votes in violation of the Fourteenth Amendment's EQUAL PROTECTION CLAUSE. The Court detailed its application of the "one person, one vote" principle in *Gray* and *Wesberry* and considered its applicability to state legislative apportionment schemes noting, "Our problem, then, is to ascertain, in the instant cases, whether there are any constitutionally cognizable principles which would justify departures from the basic standard of equality among voters in the apportionment of seats in state legislatures." [*Reynolds,* 377 U.S. at 560.]

The *Reynolds* Court found no reason to depart from the "one person, one vote" principle and struck down Alabama's legislative apportionment scheme as violative of the Fourteenth Amendment's equal protection clause. The Court did not, however, require strict mathematical equality among legislative districts. Instead, according to the Court, "the Equal Protection Clause requires that a State make an honest and good faith effort to construct districts . . .

as nearly of equal population as is practicable." [*Reynolds,* 377 U.S. at 577.]

The Court's tolerance for population deviation among congressional and legislative districts has depended largely on the factual circumstances of the particular reapportionment effort. The Court struck down a New Jersey congressional districting plan in which the population difference between the largest and smallest districts was less than one percent. [See *Karcher v. Daggett,* 462 U.S. 725 (1983).] In the same year, the Court upheld a Wyoming state legislative districting plan with a population differential of 89 percent between the largest and smallest districts. [See *Brown v. Thomson,* 462 U.S. 835 (1983).] Legislators have come to accept the Supreme Court's "one person, one vote" principle, typically creating districts with as near equal population as practicable.

For more information: Lowenstein, Daniel Hays, and Richard L. Hasen. *Election Law.* 3rd ed. Durham, N.C.: Carolina Academic Press, 2004.

—Paul S. Ryan

opinion writing

Opinion writing is the process by which the Court explains and justifies its decisions in individual controversies, using legal craftsmanship to explain the law and the justices' interpretation of it.

The process of writing a judicial opinion is long and has multiple stages. While there is no officially prescribed method for writing an opinion, there are traditions to which the justices have long adhered and a system that has served to streamline the tedious process. The production of sound, coherent, and clear opinions is essential to the legitimacy of the Court, as its opinions are the Court's major method of convincing the people that it is acting in accordance with and not in contravention of the Constitution or the laws of the United States.

Once the justices cast their votes and determine in which direction the Court will rule in a case, the responsibility of who will write the Court's opinion is decided by the CHIEF JUSTICE, if he is in the majority, or, if he is not, by the most senior associate justice in the majority. This power gives senior associate justices and the chief justice, in particular, an important power. The ability to assign the Court's opinion to a particular individual gives the chief justice the opportunity to control the specifics of how the law announced by the Court will be worded. By knowing how certain justices think about the nuances of an individual case, the assigning justice can direct how the language of an opinion will be crafted. Furthermore, in close decisions, an individual justice may use his or her position as a "swing vote" to influence the majority. That is, a swing vote justice may find himself or herself assigned with the majority opinion because the chief justice believes the swing vote justice may leave the majority if the Court's opinion is too far from that justice's preferences.

Many scholars have written extensively on this strategic interplay among justices. Many believe the language of opinions reflects politicking on the bench, and it is often argued that many of the important decisions handed down by the Supreme Court are the product of relentless compromise—the result of a back-and-forth struggle to reach a consensus, or at least a five-justice majority.

Once the responsibility for writing the Court's opinion is assigned, the justice responsible consults with his or her law clerks. The clerks research the law and review the briefs. A clerk will prepare a draft opinion for the justice, providing support, primarily in the form of past opinions, for the Court's decision. The entire process is extremely confidential, and law clerks are careful not to disclose to outsiders how the Court will rule. Once a draft has been prepared, the justice will often circulate the opinion to other justices. The justices will comment on the opinion, and the writing justice's chambers will edit the opinion and prepare a new draft. Other justices may write concurring or dissenting opinions. It is often suggested that a justice may use the threat of a concurring or dissenting opinion in an attempt to shape the language in the majority opinion. Later, a final vote is taken and the majority's opinion is announced by the Court.

For more information: Epstein, Lee, and Jack Knight. *The Choices Justices Make.* Washington, D.C.: CQ Press, 1998; Maltzman, Forrest, James F. Spriggs, Jr., and Paul J. Wahlbeck. *Crafting Law on the Supreme Court.* New York: Cambridge University Press, 2000; Murphy, Walter F. *Elements of Judicial Strategy.* Chicago: University of Chicago Press, 1964.

—Tom Clark

oral argument

Oral arguments are part of the U.S. Supreme Court's decision-making process and a standard feature of American appellate practice.

After submitting written briefs, lawyers for the parties in a case (and sometimes third parties) make oral presentations before the justices of the U.S. Supreme Court and subject themselves to questioning by the justices. This stage of the Court's process for resolving cases is the "oral argument." The justices use oral arguments when the Court gives "plenary" consideration to a case. In these cases, the Court not only makes a decision in the case but issues a legally binding "opinion of the Court" explaining and justifying the outcome. Oral arguments provide justices a chance to engage in free-flowing debate and questioning with litigants. It is a distinct form of legal deliberation that supplements the other means by which justices work through the legal issues in a case.

Beginning on the FIRST MONDAY IN OCTOBER, the official start of the Supreme Court term, the Court schedules and hears oral arguments in two-week intervals; in other words, the justices hear oral arguments for two weeks, then take a two-week recess. The Court usually stops hearing oral arguments for a given term around mid-April. The Court schedules up to four arguments a day on Mondays, Tuesdays, and Wednesdays (at 10 and 11 A.M., and at 1 and 2 P.M.).

At the beginning of the 19th century, oral arguments were not limited to a set amount of time. Through the 19th and 20th centuries, the Court periodically reduced the standard length of oral arguments. From 1970 to the present, the Supreme Court has granted each party in a case 30 minutes to speak and be questioned. The Court will allow longer arguments in particularly important cases.

The justices as a whole do not sit passively during oral argument. Instead, they are entitled to interrupt a lawyer's presentation at any point and ask questions or make statements. Justices often ask the lawyers hypothetical questions designed to explore the policy implications of a particular argument or position. There is nothing beyond anecdotal evidence to show that oral arguments actually influence the outcome of a case; it is as likely that justices use oral arguments to develop and tighten positions and conclusions already held about a case and its legal issues.

Relative to its influence on justice decision making, oral arguments receive perhaps a disproportionate amount of public attention. Oral arguments are one of the few instances in which the Court acts and deliberates publicly. Journalists and scholars attempt to interpret the behavior of justices at oral argument in order to predict the outcome of cases. This is tricky business, especially as the justices often play devil's advocate with the litigants and may therefore appear skeptical of a position they actually hold.

Oral arguments are held in the courtroom of the SUPREME COURT BUILDING in Washington, D.C. While oral arguments are open to the public and the media, seating is limited. The justices do not allow oral arguments to be broadcast or filmed. The Court instead has recorded and transcribed oral argument proceedings consistently since 1953. Justices have objected to filming or live broadcasts of oral arguments because they worry that doing so will encourage grandstanding among both litigants and justices and affect the overall quality of the arguments. Oral argument transcripts for a current term are available at the Supreme Court's Web site, and transcripts from previous terms are available at the National Archives, the Supreme Court's own library, and at several law-oriented web sites.

For more information: O'Brien, David M. *Storm Center: The Supreme Court in American Politics.* 6th ed. New York: W. W. Norton, 2002.

—James Daniel Fisher

original jurisdiction

Original jurisdiction in the Supreme Court is its right to hear certain types of cases first. Normally, original jurisdiction belongs to trial courts at the lowest level of the judicial system; however, the United States Supreme Court is somewhat unique because it has both original and appellate jurisdiction.

The Constitution of the United States (Article III, Section 2, paragraph 2) says, . . ."In all Cases affecting Ambassadors, other public Ministers and Consuls, and those in which a State shall be Party, the supreme Court shall have original Jurisdiction." Cases involving original jurisdiction usually number only one or two per year if any.

Congress has legislated several times on the original jurisdiction of the Court. The first time was in 1789 when Congress enacted the JUDICIARY ACT OF 1789 organizing the FEDERAL COURT SYSTEM. Section 13 of the Judiciary Act expanded the original jurisdiction of the Supreme Court to cover more types of cases than those listed in the Constitution. In a very famous landmark case, *MARBURY V. MADISON,* 1 Cranch 137 (1803), the Court exercised JUDICIAL REVIEW to declare Section 13 unconstitutional.

The case of *CHISHOLM V. GEORGIA,* 2 Dallas 419 (1793), allowing a plaintiff to sue a state of which he was not a citizen, was so controversial that it led to the adoption of the Eleventh Amendment reducing the original jurisdiction of the Court. The judicial power now "shall not be construed to extend to any suit commenced or prosecuted against one of the United States by citizens of another state, or by citizens or subjects of any foreign state."

The Supreme Court by nature is not a very effective trial court. Consequently, Congress has legislated to provide for original jurisdiction cases in keeping with a request by the Court. Chapter 28 of the United States Code, Section 1251, covers the original jurisdiction of the Court. The act distinguishes between exclusive original jurisdiction and concurrent original jurisdiction.

The Court has exclusive original jurisdiction in cases between two or more states. When a dispute involves two states (usually about property), the Supreme Court exercises both original and exclusive jurisdiction and is the only forum for a decision. If an original jurisdiction action arises, then it proceeds according to Rule 17 of the Supreme Court.

In the three types of concurrent original jurisdiction cases the Supreme Court shares its jurisdiction with lower courts. The concurrent original jurisdiction cases are those between a state and the U.S. government, cases brought by a state against a citizen of another state, and cases involving ambassadors, foreign ministers, or consuls. Normally it appoints a "Master" to supervise a case that is prosecuted at a lower level for matters of fact and law.

For more information: Curtis, Benjamin Robbins, and George Ticknor Curtis. *Jurisdiction, Practice, and Peculiar Jurisprudence of the Courts of the United States.* Littleton, Colo.: F. B. Rothman, 1989; Mullenix, Linda S., Martin H. Redish, and Georgene Vairo. *Understanding Federal Courts and Jurisdiction.* New York: Matthew Bender, 1998.

—A. J. L. Waskey

overbreadth

The overbreadth doctrine is a test applied by the Supreme Court in cases that challenge the constitutionality of laws and policies that seek to regulate forms of speech and expression that are not protected by the First Amendment (e.g., obscenity). A law is unconstitutional according to the overbreadth doctrine if, in the course of regulating unprotected forms of expression, it also infringes upon forms of expression that are protected by the First Amendment.

The overbreadth doctrine has its origins in *Thornhill v. Alabama,* 310 U.S. 88 (1940), which involved a state law that made labor picketing a criminal offense. In his decision for the court, Justice MURPHY wrote that a statute "which does not aim specifically at evils within the allowable area of state control, but on the contrary, sweeps within its ambit other activities that in ordinary circumstances constitute an exercise of freedom of speech or of the press," is an unconstitutional infringement on freedom of speech.

In *Thornhill,* the Court ruled that the statute in question was unconstitutional in its entirety and thus overturned the conviction of Mr. Thornhill. However, the doctrine established by *Thornhill* recognizes that there are portions of some laws that are legitimate exercises of government power, even though other portions of the law infringe upon constitutionally protected speech acts. This condition raises two questions. First, should the entire law be invalidated if only part of it is unconstitutional? Second, if a person is convicted under such a law, should the conviction be overturned if the person's acts themselves were not protected?

The first question was addressed by the Court in *Zwickler v. Koota,* 398 U.S. 241 (1967). In *Zwickler,* the Court argued that the problem with overbroad laws is that they have a "chilling effect" on the exercise of a person's free speech. In other words, by making certain speech acts legal in some circumstances but not in others, people will be afraid to engage in such acts under any circumstances for fear of government reprisal. Consequently, the Court ruled that because of their chilling effect, overbroad laws are by their nature unconstitutional and are invalid in their entirety. However, the Court has also ruled that for statutes to be invalidated, the potential for deterring protected speech must be "real and substantial" and must apply to "PURE SPEECH" as opposed to conduct that can be legitimately curtailed by government. [*Broadrick v. Oklahoma,* 413 U.S. 601 (1973), 615.]

The second question was also addressed by the Court in *Broadrick v. Oklahoma.* In those cases where the statute in question is not invalid in its entirety, convictions for conduct not protected by the First Amendment will not be overturned.

The overbreadth doctrine has been an important judicial tool in protecting First Amendment rights. By facing the possibility that a statute will be overturned if it is overbroad, lawmakers are compelled to guarantee that laws restricting certain forms of speech and expression are "narrowly tailored" so as not to infringe on protected speech.

For more information: Fallon, Richard H. "Making Sense of Overbreadth." *Yale Law Journal* 100 (January 1991): 853; Isserles, Marc E. "Overcoming Overbreadth: Facial Challenges and the Valid Rule Requirement." *American University Law Review* 48 (December 1998): 359; Prentiss, David M. "The First Amendment Overbreadth Doctrine and the Nature of the Judicial Review Power." *New England Law Review* 25 (Spring 1991): 989.

—Steven Jones

overturning Supreme Court decisions

Overturning Supreme Court decisions refers to those constitutional exceptions to the finality with which Supreme Court rulings are ordinarily invested. A Supreme Court decision can be said to be "overturned" when, revisiting either an individual Supreme Court case of the past or revisiting several such cases linked by PRECEDENT or STARE DECISIS, the Court has either overruled the individual case or substituted a substantively new precedent overriding old precedent across cases. Hence, Supreme Court case(s) of the past can be explicitly and directly overruled. Alternatively, an overarching precedent established for a class of cases by the Supreme Court can be reinvented wholesale whether or not every specific case affected through precedent has been explicitly overruled.

These two ways in which Supreme Court decisions are overturned, as opposed to an amendment to the Constitution which could also produce the same effect, could be called directly overturned and indirectly overturned. Directly, a case is first reopened by specific, full citation to the case, then reconsidered, and finally overruled. Indirectly, a new case is heard; there exists in the nature of the case something parallel to, or drawing upon, a precedent already established at the Supreme Court level (perhaps implicitly among the pertinent holdings); and the opinion then issued substantially alters the known precedent.

In the directly overturned case, the original case becomes reopened in light of new evidence or circumstances and a different ruling is thus reached. This sort of reopened Supreme Court Case is explicitly foreseen in such federal rules as Rule 60b of the Federal Rules of Civil Procedure. Statutory opinions of the Supreme Court can also in effect be overturned by Congress through a new statute bearing upon the case previously decided. Such new statutes may themselves become subject to Supreme Court scrutiny.

In the indirect kind of overturn, the fact of overturn may or may not be explicit in the language of the court but becomes obvious upon close reading. Abortion cases heard before the Supreme Court years after the ROE V. WADE precedent are sometimes thought to be, or border on, the indirect class of overturn. For example, WEBSTER V. REPRODUCTIVE HEALTH SERVICES, 492 U.S. 490 (1989), and PLANNED PARENTHOOD V. CASEY, 505 U.S. 833 (1992), have each been thought by some to represent retreats from the core Roe decision. However, in each case, the core holding of Roe, which prefers the interests of the woman in the early stage of pregnancy and permits the interests of the state to intervene only during the most extreme circumstances in the late stage of pregnancy, has remained intact, as of the date of this writing.

In Webster v. Reproductive Health Services, the Court held that none of the challenged provisions of a Missouri state law on abortions were unconstitutional. The Court said that the preamble to the Missouri legislation had not restricted abortions and therefore posed no constitutional question. The Court also held that the due process clause made no mandate for states to enter into the business of abortion, making MOOT an affirmative right to governmental aid to secure constitutional rights. The Court held that no CASE OR CONTROVERSY existed with regard to the counseling provisions of the legislation. Finally, the Court upheld the viability testing requirements, i.e., that the state's interest in protecting nascent life could precede the gestational age of viability. Even in this decision, whose language differs markedly from the Roe ruling, the Court itself explicitly stated that it was not revisiting the core holding in Roe.

In Planned Parenthood v. Casey, the Court again reaffirmed Roe but upheld most of the state's provisions. Although the Court proposed a new precedent to determine the validity of laws regulating abortions, again this precedent did not contradict the core holding of Roe

described above. The new precedent checked whether a state abortion regulation imposes an "undue burden." Justice O'Connor defined this undue burden as a "substantial obstacle in the path of a woman seeking an abortion before the fetus attains viability." Under this new precedent, the only provision to fail the undue-burden test was the requirement for husband notification. None of these holdings could be considered overturn, even indirect overturn.

On the other hand, directly overturned cases occur regularly. The U.S. Senate document Constitution of the United States of America Analysis and Interpretation (Congressional Research Service 2000 supplement) enumerates 219 out of several thousand cases orally argued before the Supreme Court which have been overruled as of June 28, 2000 (5 percent), based on explicit language in the opinions themselves. An example, the 219th overturn, is MITCHELL V. HELMS, S. Ct. 2530 (2000). Based on looser criteria for overturned precedents, many dozens more cases likely have been overturned. These opinions would include those where the Court regarded its new opinion as a clarification or, at most, a "correction." General principles can be overturned to greater or lesser degrees, as in abortion cases, while particular cases can be overruled without necessarily changing general principles, when new facts come to light. Dissents, turnover in membership of the Court, scientific advances, and sociopolitical movements all provide incentives and opportunities for the Court to overturn its own precedents. Stare decisis, on the other hand, inhibits this tendency.

Of the landmark decisions of the Supreme Court from the preceding 100 years, Roe v. Wade, 410 U.S. 113 (1973), constitutes the single decision of the Supreme Court most imminently regarded as a candidate for direct or at least indirect overturn. At present, the Court has largely left the abortion decision in the hands of women and their doctors. To date it has only heard ad hoc and anecdotal claims, and no scientific testimony as to whether, with or without the collaboration of their doctors, individuals can distinguish those pregnancies they would abort from those pregnancies they would not abort, on at least a statistical basis. This question can no longer be considered out of scope of the judicial system and may ultimately produce greater impact on the high court than a federal law on partial birth abortions.

For more information: Epstein, Lee, Jeffrey A. Segal, Harold J. Spaeth, and Thomas G. Walker, et al. *The Supreme Court Compendium: Data, Decisions, and Developments.* 3rd ed. Washington, D.C.: Congressional Quarterly Press, 2002.

—Mark Moran

P

Palko v. Connecticut, 302 U.S. 319 (1937)

In *Palko v. Connecticut*, the Supreme Court affirmed the conviction of Frank Palko on a charge of murder in the first degree, a conviction for which he had been sentenced to death by the state of Connecticut. Palko's initial trial had resulted in a conviction for murder in the second degree. However, the state was able to retry Palko after the Supreme Court of Errors of the State of Connecticut determined that errors of law had been made in the original trial. Lawyers for Palko contended that the Connecticut procedure, which permitted appeals by the state in criminal cases, subjected their client to DOUBLE JEOPARDY in violation of the due process clause of the Fourteenth Amendment. In fact, Palko's attorneys maintained that all of the provisions of the first eight amendments were made applicable to the states by the Fourteenth Amendment.

The argument that the Fourteenth Amendment applied Amendments One to Eight to the states was rejected outright by the Court. In his opinion for the Court, Justice CARDOZO stated that there is no such general rule. He pointed out that the Court had already rejected efforts to apply the Fifth Amendment's grand jury requirement and the right against SELF-INCRIMINATION to the states. Similarly, it had found that the Sixth and Seventh Amendments, guarantees of the right to a jury trial in criminal and civil cases respectively, did not apply to the states.

However, recent Court decisions had also held that the Fourteenth Amendment's due process clause did make some of the other provisions of the BILL OF RIGHTS binding on the states. Specifically, the First Amendment's guarantees of the freedom of speech, of the press, and the right of peaceable assembly, as well as the right to freedom of RELIGION, did apply to the states, because they were implicit in the concept of ordered liberty. Cardozo acknowledged the need for a rationalizing principle, which would enable the Court to make a principled distinction between those provisions of the Bill of Rights which were inherent in due process and those which were not.

According to Cardozo, rights such as the grand jury requirement, the right against self-incrimination, and even the right to trial by jury were valuable but not essential to a scheme of ordered liberty. It was possible, in his opinion, to have a fair and enlightened system of justice without these particular guarantees. On the other hand, those rights that had been applied to the states, such as the First Amendment's guarantees of freedom of thought and speech, were on a different plane of social and moral values. According to Cardozo, these rights were applied to the states because neither liberty nor justice would exist if they were sacrificed. When it came to criminal proceedings, these fundamental principles of due process simply required that persons accused of a crime be given a fair trial. Hence, Cardozo observed that the Court had recently ruled that the defendants in a capital case had been denied due process because they were not properly represented by counsel. However, in this case the Court ruled that Connecticut law's ability to subject Palko to a second trial, after the prosecution had convinced an appellate court that substantial legal errors were made in the first trial, did not violate these fundamental principles of liberty and justice.

This opinion was probably the Court's most significant attempt to articulate a distinction between those clauses from Amendments I–VIII that were inherent in due process and those that were not. For several decades afterward, the Court adhered to the conception of due process advanced by Cardozo and declined to apply specific provisions of the Bill of Rights dealing with the rights of the accused, particularly those contained in the Fifth and Sixth Amendments, to the states. Instead it was maintained that due process simply required basic fairness in criminal proceedings. For example, in *ADAMSON V. CALIFORNIA*, 332 U.S. 46 (1947), the Court declined to apply the Fifth Amendment guarantee against self-incrimination to the states, arguing that it was not necessary to a fair trial. Likewise, in *BETTS V. BRADY*, 316 U.S. 455 (1942), the Court declared that due process only required the appointment of counsel when a court determined that it was necessary to a fair hearing. However, in the long run, this position did not withstand the test of time.

With the notable exception of the Fifth Amendment's grand jury requirement, the 1960s saw the application of most of the Bill of Rights guarantees of the rights of criminal defendants to the states. The ADAMSON decision was reversed by *Malloy v. Hogan*, 378 U.S. 1 (1964), and *Betts v. Brady* was reversed by GIDEON V. WAINWRIGHT, 372 U.S. 335 (1963). Finally, in 1969, in *Benton v. Maryland*, 395 U.S. 784 (1969), the Court ruled that the Fifth Amendment guarantee against double jeopardy also applied to the states, reversing the *Palko* decision.

For more information: Cortner, Richard C. *The Supreme Court and the Second Bill of Rights: The Fourteenth Amendment and the Nationalization of Civil Liberties.* Madison: University of Wisconsin Press, 1981; Curtis, Michael Kent. *No State Shall Abridge: The Fourteenth Amendment and the Bill of Rights.* Durham, N.C.: Duke University Press, 1990.

—Justin Halpern

pardon

Article II, Section 2 of the Constitution provides that the president "shall have power to grant Reprieves and Pardons for Offenses against the United States, except in cases of impeachment." As only hurried, last-minute attention was given to the clause at the convention, the Supreme Court quickly became a critical and frequent interpreter of the nature and scope of the power.

In *U.S. v. Wilson*, 32 U.S. 150 (1833), John MARSHALL suggested the previous practice of British monarchs as the proper standard for interpreting the pardoning power, but without historical reference to clear instances of abuse or eventual restrictions on the power by Parliament. A majority opinion of Justice HOLMES challenged Marshall's view in 1927 (*Biddle v. Perovich*, 274 U.S. 480). Holmes argued that the president's power should instead be considered within the context of republican government, checks and balances, and SEPARATION OF POWERS. For the most part, however, the Supreme Court has allowed presidents to behave as kings in the granting of pardons.

The "pardoning power" has been interpreted to provide for a more general clemency power which includes the power to grant pardons, conditional pardons (*Ex parte Wells*, 59 U.S. 307, 1865), remissions of fines and forfeitures (*The Laura*, 114 U.S. 411, 1885; *Osborn v. United States*, 91 U.S. 474, 1875; *Illinois Central Railroad v. Bosworth*, 133 U.S. 92, 1890), and commutations of sentence (*Armstrong v. United States*, 73 U.S. 766, 1871). The power has also been interpreted to include the ability of presidents to delay the execution of sentences (by respites) and to grant amnesties (or general pardons). The president can grant a PARDON for any (or no) reason at all, at any time, before, during, or after formal prosecution.

Despite Marshall's monarchical standard and later pronouncements that the power is beyond "legislative control" (*Ex parte Garland*, 71 U.S. 333, 1866), presidential practice has been frequently challenged in the federal courts, and scholars continue to debate such issues as possible limitations on the general power, when pardons actually take effect, the eventual impact of pardons, and the conditions in which clemency can be refused by the intended recipient(s). While our nation's history is consistently laced with pardons of politicians, political supporters and hacks, spies and terrorists, wealthy citizens, gangsters and notorious criminals, and entertainers and athletes, presidential behavior has generally received little public scrutiny and no history of pardons has been written. This is all the more amazing given the fact that pardons have also been associated with (if not the central feature of) many of the nation's greatest political scandals (Andrew Johnson's impeachment, Watergate, Iran Contra, Fries' Rebellion, the Whiskey Rebellion, the Whiskey Ring, etc.).

From 1900 to 1993, presidents silently averaged almost 200 acts of clemency per year. In 1972 Richard Nixon set the record for the highest number of individual pardons granted in a single day with 204. Specific and reliable statistics are extremely difficult to obtain on the matter but, today, the general sense is that pardons are typically granted to restore the CIVIL RIGHTS of individuals who have served sentences, been released, and have properly addressed fines and other penalties.

President Gerald Ford issues his controversial pardon of Richard Nixon for his role in Watergate. *(Ford Library)*

For more information: Ruckman, P. S., Jr. "Executive Clemency in the United States: Origins, Development and Analysis (1900–1993)." *Presidential Studies Quarterly* 27 (1997): 251–271.

—P. S. Ruckman, Jr.

parental rights

The Supreme Court has declared that the Constitution protects the right of parents to the care, custody, and control of their children, even though this is not explicitly mentioned anywhere in the Constitution.

The specific rights held by parents include, among other things, the right to make medical and health-care decisions on behalf of their children, to choose the kind of education their children receive, to decide who their children associate with, and whether they can participate in certain activities, etc. The United States Supreme Court has handed down few decisions speaking to the scope and content of parental rights, in large part because the matter has long been regarded as properly located within the domain of state rather than federal power. Parental rights and obligations are usually defined by state legislatures and adjudicated by state courts. While the extent of one's parental rights varies from state to state, it is usually dependent on one's status as the custodial or noncustodial parent, with the former tending to have more rights than the latter.

MEYER V. NEBRASKA, 262 U.S. 390 (1923), and *PIERCE V. SOCIETY OF THE SISTERS*, 268 U.S. 510 (1925), are the first cases in which the Court ruled that the Constitution protects parental rights. In *Meyer*, the Court ruled as unconstitutional a law barring the teaching of a foreign language to a boy who had not yet completed the eighth grade. According to the Court, this law violated the due process clause of the Fourteenth Amendment, which guarantees our right to life, liberty, and due process of law. The Court ruled that the liberty component of this clause encompasses the right of parents to exercise some control over the education of their children. The Court also carefully noted that parental rights entail parental obligations or duties. Parents have the right to control the education of their children because they have the obligation to care for and rear their children.

Parental rights in this form were affirmed two years later in *Pierce*. Oregon required virtually all children eight to 16 years of age to attend public schools, thereby threatening the existence of private schools. Citing *Meyer*, the Court ruled the Oregon law unconstitutional because it infringed the parents' rights to "direct the upbringing and education of children under their control" (268 U.S. 510, 534–535).

About 50 years later the Court was faced with another case testing the scope of parental rights. In *WISCONSIN V.*

YODER, 406 U.S. 205 (1972), the Court decided that Amish parents were constitutionally permitted to withdraw their children from school earlier than state law allowed. Yoder argued that education outside of the Amish community would expose his children to ideas and values that were diametrically opposed and threatening to the foundational values and beliefs of his RELIGION. He claimed that being forced to send his children to a formal high school violated his right to free exercise of religion, guaranteed to him in the First Amendment. Ultimately, six Supreme Court justices agreed with Yoder.

All three of these cases largely involve the education of children, including their religious education. The Court has made clear that parents have certain constitutionally protected rights concerning the education of their children, particularly the right to choose and shape the kind of education that their children receive.

There is another set of cases involving parental rights of a different nature. Collectively, these cases are referred to as "the unwed fatherhood" cases, and they involve the scope of parental rights possessed by fathers who have not married the mothers of their children. There are five of these cases: *Stanley v. Illinois*, 405 U.S. 645 (1972), *Quilloin v. Walcott*, 434 U.S. 246 (1977), *Caban v. Mohammed*, 441 U.S. 380 (1979), *Lehr v. Robertson*, 463 U.S. 248 (1983), and *MICHAEL H. V. GERALD D.*, 491 U.S. 110 (1989).

The first four cases reveal the general pattern that a biological father's parental rights are contingent on whether or not he has established a relationship with his children, such as by providing financial support and by helping to raise them. In *Michael H.*, the Supreme Court refused to invalidate a law that gave legal parenthood to the husband when a child is born to a married woman regardless of any paternity test showing that he is not the biological father and regardless of any relationship established by the biological father with the child.

The Court's most recent case in this area involves a conflict between parental rights and the rights of grandparents.

For more information: Ball, Howard. *The Supreme Court in the Intimate Lives of Americans.* New York: New York University Press, 2002; Buss, Emily. "Adrift in the Middle: Parental Rights after *Troxel v. Granville.*" *The Supreme Court Review* (2001).

—Susan M. Dennehy

Paris Adult Theatre I v. Slaton, 413 U.S. 49 (1973)

In *Paris Adult Theatre I v. Slaton*, the Court held that a Georgia law prohibiting the showing of obscene films in adult movie theatres did not violate the First Amendment. In writing the opinion for the Court, Chief Justice BURGER sent the case back to the Georgia Supreme Court for a rehearing in light of another case decided the same day, *Miller v. California*, 413 U.S. 15 (1973), which provided more clarification for the constitutional definition of obscenity.

Chief Justice Burger began his opinion with a very clear statement on obscenity and the Constitution: "This Court has consistently held that obscene material is not protected by the First Amendment. . . ." [See *Roth v. United States*, 354 U.S. 476 (1957).] The Court then addressed the central argument of the Georgia trial court decision that adult movies were constitutionally protected because they were for the viewing of "consenting adults." While Burger grants that the Court has often recognized the importance of a "state interest in regulating the exposure of obscene material to juveniles and unconsenting adults," it has never declared "these to be the only legitimate state interests permitting regulation of obscene materials." Indeed, the legitimate state interest goes well beyond the traditional idea of specific groups of individuals to include "the interest of the public in the quality of life and the total community environment, the tone of commerce in the great city centers, and, possibly, the public safety itself." The legitimate state interest in regulating obscene material is a broad one and one that is largely a legislative determination.

Addressing the argument that there is no "scientific data which conclusively demonstrate that exposure to obscene material adversely affects men and women or their society," Burger writes that absolute proof of such a connection is unnecessary; it is only necessary to "reasonably determine that such a connection does or might exist." In making such a reasonable determination, the legislature may rely on "belief" rather than on "conclusive evidence or empirical data." If we assume "good books, plays, and art lift the spirit, improve the mind, enrich the human personality, and develop character" without hard empirical evidence, why cannot the opposite assumption be made about what is obscene?

The Court also rejected the argument that consenting adults should be allowed to exercise their "free will" in such matters of taste. While the Constitution does in fact protect exercises of free choice, these are largely confined to matters of "politics, RELIGION, and expression of ideas." Burger noted that unlimited free will "is not allowed in our or any other society."

Similarly, the contention that the RIGHT TO PRIVACY, relied on when the Court struck down state regulation of access to obscenity by consenting adults in their home in *Stanley v. Georgia*, 394 U.S. 557 (1969), was not found to be relevant to this case. The right to privacy which invalidated that state regulation "encompasses and protects the personal intimacies of the home . . ." and was narrowly limited to a person's residence. The right to privacy in *Stanley* does not follow a "distributor or a consumer of obscene material wherever he goes," i.e., into a public theatre. Indeed, Burger noted, "The idea of a 'privacy' right and a place of public accommodation are, in this context, mutually exclusive."

The Court also rejected the claim that the state, by prohibiting the display and distribution of obscene material, is engaging in moral censorship, and attempting to enforce a certain morality. Burger agrees that thought control is not a legitimate interest of the state but maintains that "Preventing unlimited display or distribution of obscene material, which by definition lacks any serious literary, artistic, political, or scientific value as communication, *Miller v. California*, is distinct from a control of reason and the intellect."

Burger concluded his decision with a general statement asserting that conduct that only involves "consenting adults" is, for that reason alone, constitutionally protected. Although the Constitution does establish a "broad range of conditions on the exercise of power by the States," Burger would not expand this general principle "to say that our Constitution incorporates the proposition that conduct involving consenting adults only is always beyond state regulation. . . ." States do, however, maintain a legitimate interest in protecting "a decent society."

For more information: Sunstein, Cass. *Democracy and the Problem of Free Speech.* New York: Free Press, 1995.

—Alex Aichinger

Payne v. Tennessee, 501 U.S. 808 (1991)

In *Payne v. Tennessee*, the Court held that the cruel and unusual punishment clause of the Eighth Amendment does not prohibit the admission of victim-impact evidence in capital-sentencing hearings. By a 6-3 vote, the Court overruled its previous decisions in *Booth v. Maryland*, 482 U.S. 496 (1987), and *South Carolina v. Gathers*, 490 U.S. 805 (1989), both of which declared such evidence to be inadmissible in the penalty phase of capital trials.

Pervis Tyrone Payne was found guilty of murdering Charisse Christopher and her two-year-old daughter, Lacie, and of assaulting Charisse's three-year-old son Nicholas. At the sentencing phase, the prosecution called as a witness Charisse's mother, who described in heartrending fashion how Nicholas cried out almost daily for his dead mother and sister. The prosecutor ended his final argument to the jury by stressing that Nicholas would someday know whether the jurors had provided justice for his family. The jury sentenced Payne to death and the Tennessee Supreme Court affirmed his death sentence. The U.S. Supreme Court heard the case on direct APPEAL.

Payne, citing *Booth v. Maryland* and *South Carolina v. Gathers*, argued that his death sentence should be set aside because his Eighth Amendment rights were violated when testimony was introduced and prosecutorial remarks were made about the victims' personal characteristics and the emotional impact of the murders on the victims' family. In *Booth*, a 5-4 majority, emphasizing that principles of retribution and fairness require juries to focus only on the defendant's prior record and personal responsibility for his crimes, ruled that the use of victim-impact statements exacerbates the risk of arbitrariness and discrimination in capital sentencing and therefore violates the Eighth Amendment's ban on cruel and unusual punishment.

The Court reaffirmed *Booth* in *South Carolina v. Gathers,* another 5-4 decision. In *Gathers,* the Court invalidated a death sentence on the ground that the defendant's Eighth Amendment rights were violated because the prosecutor read to the jury at length from a religious tract found near the victim's body and stressed in his closing argument that the victim's possession of a voter registration card and the religious tract showed that he was both civic-minded and religious. The *Gathers* Court held that the Eighth Amendment requires that a death sentence must be based on the nature of the defendant's actions and his moral blameworthiness for the crime, and not on caprice, emotion, or the personal characteristics of the victim.

In *Payne,* the Court overruled *Booth* and *Gathers,* holding that the victim-impact evidence presented by Charisse's mother and commented upon by the prosecutor did not violate the Eighth Amendment. Chief Justice Rehnquist wrote the majority opinion, which was joined by Justices Kennedy, O'Connor, Scalia, Souter, and White. The chief justice maintained that *Booth* and *Gathers* were premised upon the assumption that a victim's characteristics and evidence of the harm done to his or her family and to other members of the community do not reflect on the defendant's blameworthiness and thus are irrelevant in capital sentencing decisions. According to the majority, however, this assumption was incorrect. The harm caused by a crime has long been a relevant consideration in determining the appropriate punishment. The jury arguably is in a better position to weigh the harm done to the victim and the victim's family when the jurors can hear evidence about the uniqueness of the murder victim and the special loss to the family and the community.

The majority contended that such considerations do not prevent the jury from treating the defendant as a unique human being; they merely permit the jury to appreciate the defendant's blameworthiness in the full context of the crime and its consequences. To the argument that admitting victim-impact evidence would lead to some defendants being executed and others not being executed because of the perceived worthiness or unworthiness of their victims, the majority responded that such evidence is not introduced to show that one victim is more worthy than

another. The goal simply is to enable the jury to consider as much information as possible. *Booth* and *Gathers* misread precedent to require that the individualized consideration of the defendant's culpability be made separate from the harm caused by the defendant. Reversing *Booth* and *Gathers,* the majority claimed, would avert the unfairness and imbalance of a sentencing process that permitted juries to consider the good qualities of defendants and not the good qualities of their victims.

Finally, the majority rejected the argument that overruling *Booth* and *Gathers* would violate stare decisis—the general rule that, absent compelling circumstances, the Court should follow its own past precedents. Chief Justice Rehnquist conceded that stare decisis was the Court's preferred choice. It was not, however, an inflexible doctrine, especially when the Court was reconsidering the vitality of decisions which, like *Booth* and *Gathers,* provoked well-argued dissenting opinions and were decided by the narrowest of margins. The chief justice also asserted that considerations of stare decisis were at their highest in contract and property cases but were considerably less important in constitutional cases such as *Payne,* which focused on evidentiary and procedural rules in criminal cases.

The *Payne* dissenters—Justices Marshall, Blackmun, and Stevens—took the position that the personal qualities that make a victim unique are irrelevant to the defendant's blameworthiness unless he or she was aware of those qualities at the time of the crime. In what was his last opinion before resigning from the Court, Justice Marshall castigated the majority for disregarding the persuasive Eighth Amendment arguments of the *Booth* and *Gathers* majorities and creating an unacceptable risk of arbitrariness and discrimination in capital sentencing. Victim-impact evidence, he argued, tends to distract the jury from its proper consideration of the circumstances of the crime and the character of the defendant. Instead, the jury is likely to focus on such illicit factors as the popularity and status of the victim and the eloquence and poignancy of the testimony offered by the victim's family.

Justice Marshall reserved his harshest criticisms for what he regarded as the *Payne* majority's blithe disregard for the doctrine of stare decisis. He disputed Chief Justice Rehnquist's claim that stare decisis exerts less force in constitutional and criminal law decisions than in those involving economic obligations and entitlements. The Court, he asserted, should not depart from settled precedent without special justifications. He pointed out that the composition of the Court had changed in the four years since *Booth* was decided, but that the law and the facts supporting *Booth* and *Gathers* had not changed. The *Payne* decision, he concluded, would encourage public officials to ignore 5-4 decisions and would also weaken the authority and legitimacy of the Court.

Payne v. Tennessee remains one of the Court's most controversial decisions on CAPITAL PUNISHMENT, the scope of the Eighth Amendment, and the principle of stare decisis. Social-science studies indicate that victim-impact evidence plays a major role in jury decision making in capital cases. Debates concerning both the constitutional and procedural issues raised in *Payne* are certain to continue well into the foreseeable future.

For more information: Padden, Amy L. "Overruling Decisions in the Supreme Court: The Role of a Decision's Vote, Age, and Subject Matter in the Application of Stare Decisis After *Payne v. Tennessee.*" *Georgetown Law Journal* 82, no. 4 (1994): 1,689–1,732; Phillips, Amy K. "Thou Shalt Not Kill Any Nice People: The Problem of Victim Impact Statements in Capital Sentencing." *American Criminal Law Review* 35, no. 1 (1997): 93–118.

—Kenneth C. Haas

Penn Central Transportation Co. v. New York City, 438 U.S. 104 (1978)

In *Penn Central Transportation Co. v. New York City,* the Supreme Court of the United States held that unless government regulations demonstrably alter a property's present value the owner is not entitled to compensation under the TAKINGS CLAUSE of the Fifth Amendment.

Under the Fifth Amendment to the U.S. Constitution, the broad powers of the federal government to take possession of "private property" for "public use" was reaffirmed, provided the authorities offer "just compensation" for the seizure. Underlying this right is the notion that, even with the support of Congress, expenses undertaken for the public good should not be unilaterally imposed upon the individual. When applied to the physical occupation of private land or the seizure of personal property, the application of the Fifth Amendment is relatively straightforward. However, as governments have come to rely upon ever more sophisticated regulatory devices to control the use of privately owned land (e.g., environmental laws, historical preservation statutes, and ZONING regulations), the definition of a government "taking" becomes increasingly less clear. The controversy surrounding *Penn Central Transportation Co. v. New York City* highlights some of the most difficult legal questions arising from governmental regulations.

Relying on statutory authority from the Landmarks Preservation Law of 1965, New York City's Landmarks Preservation Commission was authorized to designate certain historic buildings as "landmarks." Once designated, such "landmarks" were subject to a special series of regulations concerning their alteration, maintenance, and general upkeep. Under the law, any changes to the exterior of the landmark were subject to the prior approval of the city commission.

Two years following the adoption of the preservation commission, New York's Grand Central Terminal was designated a city landmark. Opened in 1913, the Grand Central Terminal came to occupy some of the most valuable real estate in midtown Manhattan. Although the station itself represented a consistent revenue stream for its owner, the Penn Central Transportation Company, the property was not generating revenue consistent with its exceptional location. Under an agreement with UGP Properties, Penn Central proposed two separate plans to build a multistory office building directly above the existing terminal. The Landmark Commission refused to authorize either renovation proposal. Claiming that the building restrictions constituted an unlawful "taking" under the protections afforded it by the Fifth and Fourteenth Amendments, Penn Central filed suit against the city of New York.

In a 6-3 ruling, the Supreme Court argued that, under protection of the Fifth Amendment, Penn Central was not entitled to compensation. Recognizing the difficulty in precisely defining a "taking," the Supreme Court established an ad hoc balancing approach, weighing the economic impact of the government regulation against the invasiveness of the public intrusion.

The economic impact of the regulation on the claimant and, particularly, the extent to which the regulation has interfered with distinct investment-backed expectations are, of course, relevant considerations. So, too, is the character of the governmental action. A "taking" may more readily be found when the interference with property can be characterized as a physical invasion by government than when interference arises from some public program adjusting the benefits and burdens of economic life to promote the common good (*Penn Cent. Transp. Co. v. New York City,* 438 U.S. 104, 124, 1997).

The emphasis on "investment-backed expectations" provides the court with the opportunity to measure the impact of government regulations in terms of an owner's *initial* expectation, rather than basing the claim on some as yet unrealized economic opportunity. In the case of Penn Central, the city regulations had very little impact on the train station's ongoing operations. Relying upon the "investment-backed expectations" standard, the "landmark" designation was of little consequence to Penn Central's bottom-line. When considered in light of the fact that New York City had not physically invaded the Grand Central Terminal, the majority concluded that no "taking" had, in fact, occurred.

In his dissent, Justice REHNQUIST (joined by Chief Justice BURGER and Justice STEVENS) implicitly criticized the majority's reliance on the "investment-backed" distinction. Arguing that a constraint on future profits was, indeed, a burden created for the general benefit of the public at large, the dissenting justices concluded that this was exactly the kind of imposition the takings clause was created to prevent.

The Penn Central ruling is significant because it provides government with a greater degree of flexibility in the regulation of private property. Regulatory costs imposed upon individual property owners could not legally justify public compensation unless the burden can be shown to dramatically interfere with an investor's initial profit expectations.

For more information: Epstein, Lee, and Thomas G. Walker. *Constitutional Law for a Changing America: Institutional Powers and Constraints.* 4th ed. Washington, D.C.: Congressional Quarterly Press, 2001; Hubbard, F. Patrick. "Palazzolo, Lucas, and Penn Central: The Need for Pragmatism, Symbolism, and Ad Hoc Balancing." *Nebraska Law Review* 80 (2001): 465; Walker, Chauncey L., and Scott D. Avitabile. "Regulatory Takings, Historic Preservation and Property Rights Since Penn Central: The Move Toward Greater Protections." *Fordham Environmental Law Journal* 6 (1995): 819.

—Matthew Woessner

Penry v. Lynaugh, 492 US 302 (1989)

In *Penry v. Lynaugh,* the Supreme Court ruled that execution of the mildly mentally retarded is not cruel and unusual punishment under the Eighth Amendment. However, jurors must be instructed to consider the mitigating effects of such a condition before sentencing.

Convicted of the beating, rape, and murder of a woman in Texas, Johnny Paul Penry was sentenced to death. His conviction was appealed on the grounds that executing Penry—who possessed a mental age believed to be approximately six-and-a half, an IQ in the 50s, and a history of repeated childhood abuse—would be cruel and unusual punishment under the Eighth Amendment. Penry's lawyers argued the death penalty could not be constitutionally applied to those who lacked the requisite moral culpability. Counsel further claimed that Penry's sentence was unconstitutional because jurors in the sentencing phase had not been properly instructed to consider his mental retardation and family history as mitigating evidence.

In a 5-4 decision, the Supreme Court held that the execution of the mentally retarded was not a violation of the Eighth Amendment, but nevertheless overturned Penry's sentence on the grounds that he was denied the use of mitigating circumstances during the penalty phase. Although Penry's attorneys presented public opinion poll data demonstrating opposition to executing the mentally retarded, the data were dismissed, as the Court looked instead to legislative trends as the "clearest and most reli-

able objective evidence of contemporary values." Finding that only two states to that date had enacted laws explicitly excluding the mentally retarded from CAPITAL PUNISHMENT, the Court concluded that no national consensus existed, following the "evolving standards of decency that mark a maturing society" doctrine of *Trop v. Dulles,* 356 U.S. 86 (1958). Justice Sandra Day O'CONNOR, writing for the majority, noted, "In our view, the two state statutes prohibiting execution of the mentally retarded, even when added to the 14 states that have rejected capital punishment completely, do not provide sufficient evidence at present of a national consensus." By comparison, O'Connor cited the general consensus at work nationally that drove the banning of executions of the insane (*Ford v. Wainwright*), and establishing a minimum age for eligibility for a capital sentence (*Thompson v. Oklahoma*).

The Court's reluctance to provide a blanket prohibition for executing the mentally retarded further stemmed from O'Connor who wrote, "I cannot . . . conclude that all mentally retarded people of Penry's ability—by virtue of their mental retardation alone, and apart from any individualized consideration of their personal responsibility—inevitably lack the cognitive, volitional, and moral capacity to act with the degree of culpability associated with the death penalty." The varying abilities of those persons classified as "mentally retarded" was so great as to make the entire category of persons placed outside of the penalty unwise, according to the Court. Those suffering from a lesser degree of retardation, and who are shown to be aware of their culpability, are not immune from the ultimate penalty.

Despite O'Connor's holding that mental retardation may not be a blanket exclusion for moral culpability, the Court held that the "sentencing body must be allowed to consider mental retardation as a mitigating circumstance in making the individualized determination whether death is the appropriate punishment in a particular case."

Because the jury in the penalty phase of his trial did not consider both Penry's mental deficiencies as well as the history of abuse that he suffered, the Court overturned the sentence. "In sum, mental retardation is a factor that may well lessen a defendant's culpability for a capital offense. But we cannot conclude today that the Eighth Amendment precludes the execution of any mentally retarded person of Penry's ability convicted of a capital offense simply by virtue of his or her mental retardation alone. So long as sentencers can consider and give effect to mitigating evidence of mental retardation in imposing sentence, an individualized determination whether 'death is the appropriate punishment' can be made in each particular case. While a national consensus against execution of the mentally retarded may someday emerge reflecting the 'evolving standards of decency that mark the progress of a maturing society,' there is insufficient evidence of such a consensus today. . . ."

In the years following *Penry*, a number of states passed legislation banning the execution of the mentally retarded, and subsequently the Supreme Court was asked to reconsider the issue. In *AKINS V. VIRGINIA*, 536 U.S. 304 (2002), the Court found that "much had changed" since 1989. The "consistency of the direction of change," and not simply the additional number of states barring such executions, convinced the Court that significant consensus against executing the mentally retarded had emerged. Thus, the Court in *Atkins* reversed its *Penry* ruling, holding that the execution of the mentally retarded was inconsistent with the Eighth Amendment's prohibition against cruel and unusual punishment.

For more information: Latzer, Barry. *Death Penalty Cases.* Boston: Butterworth-Heineman, 1998; Melusky, Joseph A., and Keith A. Pesto. *Cruel and Unusual Punishment.* Santa Barbara, Calif.: ABC-CLIO, 2003; Palmer, Louis J., Jr. *The Death Penalty: A Citizen's Guide to Understanding Federal and State Law.* Jefferson, N.C.: McFarland, 1998.

—Sharon A. Manna

peremptory challenges

Peremptory challenges are used in both civil and criminal trials to strike potential jurors during voir dire without stating a reason. They are one of the most intriguing remaining bastions of "hunch stereotyping" remaining in the legal system. Proponents and opponents argue their value, but few can disagree that they operate on the basis of guesses by attorneys, sometimes educated, sometimes not. Whether they are important features of our jury system, or condemnable relics that ought to be abandoned, is a theme, perhaps the theme that is at the heart of any discussion of peremptory challenges.

The first step in a criminal or civil jury trial is to pick the jury that will actually hear the case. The process of selecting the jurors from a larger panel of potential jurors is known as the voir dire. The structure of the voir dire differs among the states, and the voir dire is, as are many practices in a particular court system, products of habit, tradition, and custom.

The biggest difference among voir dire is who conducts them. In the federal system, and in some of the states, the judge conducts the voir dire, usually addressing a group of potential jurors. In other states, defense attorneys and prosecutors or plaintiffs' attorneys conduct the voir dire. Sometimes this tracks the "group voir dire" of the federal system, but at other times it takes the form of an individual voir dire. In this circumstance, attorneys for both sides of the dispute question potential jurors one at a time, usually without the other jurors present. This latter practice, of course, allows attorneys to ask tougher and more probing questions, as they do not have to fear antagonizing the other jurors for the other potential jurors are not privy to the questioning.

During the voir dire, attorneys have two kinds of challenges that they make with respect to a juror's inappropriateness to be seated on the actual jury panel. The first kind of challenge is for "cause." In this challenge the attorney is asserting that the juror cannot render an unbiased decision. The questioning, or the juror's own comments indicate that for one reason or another the juror was incapable of judging the evidence objectively and would necessarily favor the arguments or the individuals on one side or another of the dispute.

Some attributes that can lead to a successful challenge for cause include racial prejudice, particular attitudes (favorable or unfavorable) to police officers, assumptions about the guilt of an arrested person ("he must have done something or he would not be a defendant in this court"), friendship with one of the parties to the case, or with one of the attorneys, and other comparable kinds of factors that lead a juror in one direction or another prior to learning the facts of a case. Understandably, attorneys have an unlimited number of challenges for cause, since the presence of biased jurors directly undermines the notion of the "impartial jury." It is important to stress that challenges for cause can only be granted by the judge. If the judge is not persuaded by the lawyer's argument, a challenge for cause is not granted.

Attorneys for both sides have another kind of challenge that they employ to dismiss jurors themselves—the peremptory challenge. This is very, very different than the challenge for cause since it requires no explanation for why the attorney is asking to dismiss a particular juror, though in some instances the attorney may believe he is in fact "correcting" a judge's decision to not grant a challenge for cause. Unlike the challenge for cause, though, attorneys have only a limited number of peremptory challenges.

The exact number of challenges varies both from the federal to the state systems, and within the states. Moreover the number often varies by the gravity of the offense in criminal matters, by the size of the jury, and by the number of codefendants, and typically also varies in the number of peremptory challenges given to the defense and the prosecution. To further complicate "the numbers matter," judges can increase the number of peremptories in particular cases if they deem it important.

Until 1986, peremptory challenges required no explanation, could be used for any reason in a particular case, and but for a very limited exception (a pattern of discrimination across a number of cases, and the burden of proof on the defense to establish this discrimination—see, *Swain v. Alabama*, 380 U.S. 202, 1965) attorneys were free to use their peremptories as they wished. Indeed, it has been said that in the 1950s attorneys in New York used baseball allegiances to decide on the desirability of a particular juror for a case. There were three teams in New York at the time, and if a potential juror indicated he was a Yankee fan, he was struck through the use of a peremptory challenge by the defense; if he was a Dodger fan, he was struck by the prosecution. This left only Giant fans as jurors!

Whether apocryphal or not, the casualness of the selection criteria do indeed track what attorneys routinely do in selecting jurors. They rely on any kind of "hunch" they may have about who would make a better juror—be it someone older or younger, someone more or less educated, someone of one or another religious persuasion, someone taller or shorter, someone with a neat or messy head of hair, etc.

Since 1986, however, two variables, and only these two, are forbidden fruits for justifying a peremptory challenge. In the landmark case BATSON V. KENTUCKY, 476 U.S. 79 (1986), the Supreme Court ruled that race could no longer be used by the prosecutor or the state as the reason for a peremptory challenge. Black jurors, for example, could no longer be challenged simply because an attorney felt a black juror would not favor his or her side; a juror who happened to be black, though, could still be challenged if the basis was not the juror's race. Unlike *Swain,* a pattern of discrimination across a number of cases no longer had to be shown, and the burden of proof was now on the side exercising the peremptory challenges, and not on the side questioning the challenging of minorities. In subsequent cases, the Court extended the prohibition against using race in peremptory challenges to attorneys in civil cases (*Edmonson v. Leesville Concrete Co.,* 500 U.S. 614 [1991]), and to defense attorneys in criminal cases (*Georgia v. McCollum,* 505 U.S. 42 [1992]). Finally, in 1994, the Court reached a similar conclusion about the unconstitutionality of using gender to peremptorarily challenge a juror.

Before turning to the "big question" of the desirability of peremptory challenges, several observations about "peremptoriness in action" are worth making. First, peremptory challenges are perhaps the last arena for stereotyping that the Court continues to systematically accept. The Court allows attorneys to make any kind of assumption (with the exception of those relying on race or gender) about the decision-making proclivities of potential jurors, using in their calculus "hunch" stereotypes related to age, or RELIGION, or, as noted above, many other factors. There is no requirement that the "guesses" be related to any evidence; moreover there is even some evidence that excluded jurors would not have reached a different decision than did the jurors that remained.

Second, the relatively new profession of "jury consultants" specializes, among other things, in helping attorneys exercise peremptory challenges. They maintain that they can provide the kind of informed expertise that allows attorneys to make better peremptory challenges, although there is little evidence to support the claim. Third, though there is not much systematic work on this matter, it is intriguing to speculate on how attorneys self-ration their peremptory challenges. An attorney knows that he or she has only x number of challenges, and that once all are expended, the opportunity to challenge other than for cause is gone. How does an attorney weigh this constraint in the decision on peremptories? The attorney might strongly suspect that the juror is unlikely to favor the argument, but is this juror "less bad" than one who might come along, and thus not worth using one of the limited supply of peremptory challenges? This kind of nuts and bolts examination has been little studied but offers a terrific glimpse into the real world calculi of practicing trial attorneys.

Exploring the ways peremptory challenges are exercised in court, though valuable in providing insights into the "court in action," obscures, or moves to the background, what is the most significant, outstanding question about peremptories—namely, should they still be allowed in the courts at all, or should they simply be abolished? The arguments for elimination of the use of peremptories are many. They begin with the notion that courts should not be complicit in attorneys engaging in stereotyping. This argument became more forceful after the Supreme Court accepted this reasoning with regard to race and gender. The Court concluded that peremptories justified on racial or gender grounds violated the EQUAL PROTECTION CLAUSE of the Fourteenth Amendment and constituted unconstitutional state-supported discrimination. To opponents of peremptory challenges, it simply makes no sense to forbid challenges on these two variables and to allow them on all others. The solution: abolish peremptory challenges and limit challenges to matters of cause.

Justice MARSHALL argued for just such an action in his concurrence in the *Batson* decision. Marshall stated that "the inherent potential of peremptory challenges to distort the jury process by permitting the exclusion of jurors on racial grounds should ideally lead the court to ban them entirely from the criminal justice system" [*Batson,* at 107]. Opponents also stress the lack of public support for peremptory challenges, the ways these challenges demean those excluded and decrease respect for attorneys, and the effect that peremptory challenges have on undermining the laudable goal of a cross-sectional and fair jury. The aim of the peremptory, opponents maintain, is to obtain a jury most likely to favor one's position, and that preference, not fairness, drives the choice to challenge a juror.

There are also those who remain proponents of the peremptory challenge. They point to the long tradition of these challenges in our courts, and the ways the challenges can make trials fairer by doing exactly what they are intended to—i.e., get rid of jurors who are in fact not objective but about whom a causal challenge would be very difficult. Interestingly, in a 1998 survey of trial judges in Wisconsin, the overwhelming number of respondents felt that abolishing the peremptory challenge would have seriously negative effects on the courts. Their support rested on two grounds. First, they felt that from a practical standpoint peremptory challenges saved the courts a substantial amount of time. Rather than to try to develop the grounds to dismiss a potential juror for cause, the peremptory challenge allowed a shortcut for ridding a jury panel of someone genuinely inappropriate for the case. Second, the judges argued that on balance the peremptory challenges did lead to fairer proceedings.

These judges' attitudes have been championed on the current Court by Justice Antonin SCALIA. Scalia has argued on several occasions that the Constitution does not bar lawyers from eliminating jurors on any basis, including race, and that such limits are an obstacle to justice and that they do not necessarily guarantee defendants more racially diverse juries [see *Powers v. Ohio*, 499 U.S. 400 (1991), *Holland v. Illinois*, 493 U.S. 474 (1990), and *Edmonson v. Leesville Concrete Co.*, 500 U.S. 614 (1991)]. The rest of the Court seems to be moving closer to Scalia's camp. In a per curium 7-2 decision, the Court overturned an Eighth Circuit Court ruling and agreed that the Missouri supreme court was correct in upholding a prosecutor's explanation for dismissing a juror because he had long hair [*Purkett v. Elem*, 94-802 (1995)].

The mixed feelings about peremptory challenges were best captured more than 200 years ago by the famous English legal commentator William M. Blackstone. Judge Morris Hoffman in a well-known article pointed out that Blackstone is often quoted for his endorsement of the peremptory challenge as "a provision full of that tenderness and humanity to prisoners, for which our English laws are justly famous." Hoffman goes on to note that immediately prior to this observation Blackstone, apparently harboring a deep-seated ambivalence, characterized the peremptory challenge as "an arbitrary and capricious species of challenge."

The future of the peremptory challenge is unclear. Though the peremptory challenge was always viewed somewhat ambivalently, until *Batson* it was largely unfettered by legal constraints. Since *Batson*, challenges based on race and gender are no longer permissible. Will the Court expand this list or go the whole way and declare peremptory challenges unconstitutional, or perhaps even backtrack and make it more difficult to establish that even race and gender, not to mention other variables, animated a decision to challenge a juror, are important matters for Court consideration? What is clear, though, is that the current situation is not a "stable one," and that *Batson* opened the floodgates for further examination of the nature of challenges in jury selection.

For more information: Brody, David, and John Neiswender. "Judicial Attitudes Towards Jury Reform." *Judicature* 83, no. 6 (May–June 2000): 301–302; Hoffman, Morris. "Peremptory Challenges Should Be Abolished: A Trial Judge's Perspective." *University of Chicago Law Review* 64 (1997): 352–353; Zeisel, Hans, and Shari Diamond. "The Effect of Peremptory Challenges on Jury and Verdict: An Experiment in Federal District Court." *Stanford Law Review* 30 (1978): 491.

—Milton Heumann

Personnel Administrator of Massachusetts et al. v. Feeney, 442 U.S. 256 (1979)

In *Personnel Administrator of Massachusetts et al. v. Feeney*, the Supreme Court held that Massachusetts' Veterans Preference Statute, which gave military veterans preference in hiring for civil service positions, did not violate the EQUAL PROTECTION CLAUSE of the Fourteenth Amendment.

Helen Feeney worked as a Massachusetts state employee for 12 years. She had attempted to enlist in the Women's Auxiliary Army Corps in World War II. She recalled a recruiting officer asking her, "Why does a nice girl like you want to go into service?" She did not enlist because she did not receive the required parental consent from her mother. As a nonveteran, she failed to gain certain positions for which she applied because of the preferences afforded to veterans. Although she performed better than veterans on civil service examinations, veterans were ranked higher than her because of the Veterans' Preference Statute. On one occasion, she received the second highest score on an exam for a job with the Board of Dental Examiners, but she was ranked sixth on the list. On another occasion, she received the third highest test score for an administrative assistant position, but she was ranked 13th. Feeney alleged that the Veterans' Preference Statute violated the equal protection clause of the 14th Amendment because it operated "overwhelmingly" to the advantage of men. The statute did not discriminate on the basis of sex in its language; its language extended to "any person, male or female" who was honorably discharged from the armed services after 90 days of service. The class of citizens from which it drew, however, tended to be male, with more than 98 percent of the veterans in Massachusetts being men at the time of the litigation.

In an opinion authored by Justice STEWART, the Court determined that the Fourteenth Amendment does not preclude any classification by the state. Certain classifications, however, due to their history, raise suspicion of pretext.

"Race is the paradigm" for such classification. The Court had earlier remanded the Massachusetts attorney general's APPEAL of the district court opinion, pending its decision regarding the disparate racial impact of racially neutral laws in WASHINGTON V. DAVIS, 426 U.S. 229. In that case, and in ARLINGTON HEIGHTS V. METROPOLITAN HOUSING DEV. CORP., 429 U.S. 252, the Court determined that a discriminatory effect of a law does not violate the equal protection clause. A statute has only violated the equal protection clause if it can be shown that it had a discriminatory purpose.

To determine whether there was discriminatory purpose in the passage of the Veterans' Preference Statute, the Court conducted a "twofold inquiry." First, it asked whether the classification in the statute was based upon gender. It found that the law classified on the basis of veteran status, and that women are not excluded from serving in the military. Women, therefore, have the opportunity to become veterans. It then asked whether the state of Massachusetts showed discriminatory purpose in its legislation, and it found no gender bias. Acknowledging that women as a group were burdened by the small number of women in the military, the Court refused to consider the question of gender bias in the military, stating "the history of discrimination against women in the military is not on trial in this case."

Justice STEVENS concurred, rejecting the twofold inquiry of the majority opinion. Citing the number of male nonveterans in Massachusetts, he did not find evidence that males as a class were intended to benefit over females as a class.

In his dissent, joined by Justice BRENNAN, Justice MARSHALL identified the presence of discriminatory intent. He found that the statute was neutral in form but that its disparate impact upon women proceeded from a historical exclusion of women from the military. The discriminatory impact of the statute should have been foreseen by legislators. Applying the INTERMEDIATE SCRUTINY test that gender-based discrimination must be related to the achievement of important governmental objectives, he found that the government failed to tie this statute to any of its purported objectives.

For more information: Kerber, Linda. *No Constitutional Right to Be Ladies: Women and the Obligations of Citizenship.* New York: Hill and Wang, 1998.

—Kathleen S. Sullivan

PGA Tour, Inc. v. Casey Martin, 532 U.S. 661 (2001)

In *PGA Tour, Inc. v. Casey Martin*, the Supreme Court ruled that the Americans with Disabilities Act of 1990 (ADA) applied to the Professional Golfers Association (PGA).

In 1997 the PGA, pursuant to the rules of golf, denied golfer Casey Martin the right to use a golf cart in its tournaments. However, Mr. Martin suffers from a Klippel-Trenaunay-Weber Syndrome, a rare blood disorder that inhibits the ability to walk for long periods of time. In response to the PGA's decision, Martin filed suit under Title III of the ADA, which prohibits discrimination against people with disabilities by places of public accommodation. Martin's argument was that golf tournaments organized by the PGA were in fact public accommodations and therefore subject to the rules of the ADA. The PGA countered that a professional golf tournament in which only selected professional golfers may play is not a public area.

The ADA also requires that "reasonable modifications" be made to public accommodations to alleviate the discrimination toward people with disabilities unless that modification "would fundamentally alter the nature" of the goods and services provided. Martin argued that allowing him to use a cart was a reasonable modification that did not alter the fundamental nature of golf. The PGA countered, suggesting that eliminating one of its rules did fundamentally alter the nature of the game.

The court ruled 7-2 in Casey Martin's favor, concluding that golf tournaments are public accommodations and using a cart does not alter the nature of golf. However, in one of the most bizarre decisions ever handed down by the Supreme Court, the justices also ruled that members of the PGA were, in fact, not members of the PGA. Instead, the Court ruled that members of the PGA were actually consumers of the PGA, no different from anyone walking into a grocery store to buy a bottle of milk. The reason the justices adopted such tortured logic was that Title III of the ADA was written to protect consumers at places of business, such as hotels, stores, and offices. The Court needed to establish Martin as a consumer, and the PGA as a "public" store, in order for them to legitimately apply the ADA to Martin's case.

Writing for the majority, Justice STEVENS argued two points. First, because golfers must pay the PGA a $3,000 fee for the opportunity to compete, they are in fact "consumers" of the PGA. Second, because technically, anyone in America could, hypothetically, become a professional golfer, the PGA was a "public accommodation." On a tangential issue, Stevens also argued that the Supreme Court, not the PGA, was in a better position to decide what rules of golf were truly "fundamental" to the game. As such, the Court decided that the golf cart restriction was not part of the "essence of the game" despite the PGA's assertion that it was.

The dissenting justices mockingly derided the majority's logic. Justice SCALIA responded by asking two pointed questions. First, if golfers are consumers of the PGA, does that mean that baseball players are consumers of major league baseball, and basketball players are consumers of the

National Basketball Association? Or, put another way, if the NBA and MLB are public accommodations subject to the ADA, would the NBA have to have a shorter basket for disabled people? Would the National League be required to have a designated hitter to avoid AGE DISCRIMINATION? Justice Scalia also notes that if golfers are consumers of the PGA, then actors trying out for a play are consumers of that play, or anyone applying for a job is actually a consumer of that business. However, the larger question to Justice Scalia was whether the Supreme Court of the United States was the appropriate body to determine the rules of golf. Justice Scalia argued that all sports rules are arbitrary, and it was not for the Supreme Court to tell the PGA, or any other sports organization, what rules they could or could not keep.

The ruling in *PGA v. Casey Martin* has broader implications than simply whether disabled golfers can use a cart. The ruling suggests a severe curtailing of what activities are considered private. In earlier cases, such as *Boy Scouts of America v. Dale*, 530 U.S. 640 (2000), and *California Democratic Party v. Jones*, 530 U.S. 537 (2000), the Court had clearly indicated that certain activities were beyond the regulation of government. The Court typically indicated that certain associations were private and therefore not bound by government rules. However, the PGA case suggests the Court is more willing to allow government to interfere in areas that have traditionally been considered private behavior.

For more information: Krieger, Linda Hamilton. *Backlash Against the ADA: Reinterpreting Disability Rights (Corporealities: Discourses of Disability)*. Ann Arbor: University of Michigan Press, 2003; Pelka, Fred. *The Disability Rights Movement*. Santa Barbara, Calif.: ABC-CLIO, 1997.

—Mathew Manweller

Pierce v. Society of the Sisters, 268 U.S. 510 (1925)

During the 1920s, the United States Supreme Court decided several education cases that provided early support for what would emerge as a constitutional RIGHT TO PRIVACY. The 1925 Supreme Court decision in *Pierce v. Society of the Sisters of the Holy Names of Jesus and Mary*, 268 U.S. 510, is one of those. That case (which combined *Pierce, Governor of Oregon, et al. v. Society of the Sisters* and *Pierce v. Hill Military Academy*) produced a unanimous opinion by Justice James McReynolds that was issued on June 1.

According to McReynolds, the Oregon law in question, requiring all students (with very limited exceptions) between the ages of eight and 16 to attend only public schools, violated the substantive liberty rights contained in the Fourteenth Amendment. Restating the doctrine he expressed two years earlier in *MEYER V. NEBRASKA*, 262 U.S. 390, McReynolds wrote that such action by the state "unreasonably interferes with the liberty of parents and guardians to direct the upbringing and education of children under their control." In this case, he continued, "The fundamental theory of liberty upon which all governments in this Union repose excludes any general power of the state to standardize its children by forcing them to accept instruction from public teachers only. The child is not the mere creature of the state; those who nurture him and direct his destiny have the right, coupled with the high duty, to recognize and prepare him for additional obligations." Because the Society of Sisters provided religious education, there is a tendency to see the opinion's reference to "additional obligations" as connected to religious liberty. Yet, the Hill Military Academy also included in the opinion was not a religious institution. Thus the opinion dealt with secular private education as well as religious school education.

Certainly, the state has considerable power to regulate all schools in reasonable fashion, but in this case, the brief opinion noted that there is nothing in the record indicating that the schools involved "failed to discharge their obligations to patrons, students, or the state." Further, there are no special circumstances or emergencies that would "demand extraordinary measures." Additionally, the decision had to deal with the fact that it was the institutions affected by the Oregon law and not actual parents or guardians of students, subject to the misdemeanor penalty, who brought suit. The law (a 1922 citizen initiative promoted by the Ku Klux Klan among others) was scheduled to go into affect in September 1926. The three-judge district court decision granted a temporary injunction to the two private schools, and the governor of the state, Walter Pierce, appealed.

While McReynolds argued that the schools, as corporations, cannot claim Fourteenth Amendment liberty rights for themselves, he also noted that the businesses are faced with destruction due to the state's unlawful interference with the exercise of liberty rights by those who would choose to send their children to the schools. Therefore, the injunction to prevent such injury was warranted, and, in affirming that judgment, the controversial Justice McReynolds (who would also write the 1927 Supreme Court opinion in another education case, *Farrington v. Tokushiga*, 273 U.S. 284) inched Constitution law closer to a substantive right of privacy and personal autonomy.

For more information: O'Brien, Kenneth B. "Education, Americanization, and the Supreme Court: The 1920s." *American Quarterly* 13 (Summer 1961).

—Norman Provizer

plain view doctrine

The plain view doctrine states that an item within the sight of a police officer who is legally in a position to see the item may be seized without a SEARCH WARRANT, so long as the item is immediately recognizable as contraband or evidence subject to seizure. Plain view is a recognized exception to the warrant requirement of the Fourth Amendment, although a plain view observation technically does not constitute a search, as there is no reasonable expectation of privacy in items left out in the open.

For the plain view doctrine to apply, the police must be "lawfully present." This means the police must have a legal right to be where they are when they observe an item in plain view. This is sometimes referred to as a "valid prior intrusion." Some examples of situations in which a law enforcement officer is lawfully present include a traffic stop or the pursuit of a fleeing suspect.

Under the plain view doctrine, police may seize an item only if it is "immediately apparent" that the item is subject to seizure [*Coolidge v. New Hampshire,* 403 U.S. 443 (1971)]. This means that before an item may be seized, the police must have probable cause that the item is subject to seizure without conducting any further examination of the object. In other words, the officer must be able to tell, by just looking at an item which is out in the open, that the item is seizable. A law enforcement officer cannot move or otherwise manipulate an item to determine if it is seizable. How much an officer could handle an item under the plain view doctrine was at issue in *Arizona v. Hicks,* 480 U.S. 321 (1987). In this case police investigating a shooting entered Hicks's apartment to search for the shooter, possible victims, and weapons. One officer noticed expensive stereo components which seemed out of place in the ramshackle apartment and, suspecting they were stolen, moved the equipment in order to obtain a view of their obscured serial numbers, then read and recorded the serial numbers. After checking with headquarters and learning that the stereo equipment was stolen, the officer seized it. The Supreme Court, per Justice SCALIA, held that the officer's moving of the stereo equipment constituted a search, beyond the scope permissible under the plain view doctrine.

Justice STEWART's opinion in *Coolidge v. New Hampshire* suggested that the discovery of evidence in plain view must be "inadvertent" to satisfy the "immediately apparent" requirement. While lower courts in many states have focused on this language, the Court has since made clear that inadvertence is not necessary. In *Horton v. California,* 496 U.S. 128 (1990), the Court declared that there is no reason to exclude items in plain view just because a police officer has reason to believe he will see them before he actually observes them.

Some courts have expanded the plain view doctrine to the other senses of smell and touch. These courts frequently cite *United States v. Johns,* 469 U.S. 478 (1985), in which the Court suggested that it was "debatable" whether there is a privacy interest in a package "reeking of marijuana." It is unclear whether the Supreme Court currently endorses this expansion of the plain view doctrine.

The plain view doctrine is an important, and logical, exception to the search warrant requirement. It allows police officers to seize evidence without a warrant so long as they are lawfully present and the item seized is clearly subject to seizure. Since the police are lawfully present, requiring them to obtain a warrant before seizing an item that they have seen and know is subject to seizure would unnecessarily complicate the search process without protecting any reasonable expectation of privacy.

For more information: Ferdico, J. N. *Criminal Procedure for the Criminal Justice Professional.* Belmont, Calif.: Wadsworth, 2002; Hemmens, C., J. Worrall, and A. Thompson. *Criminal Justice Case Briefs: Significant Cases in Criminal Procedure.* Los Angeles: Roxbury, 2003; LaFave, W. R., and J. H. Israel. *Criminal Procedure.* St. Paul, Minn.: West, 1998.

—Craig Hemmens

Planned Parenthood of Missouri v. Danforth, 428 U.S. 52 (1976)

In *Planned Parenthood of Missouri v. Danforth,* the Supreme Court ruled on a Missouri abortion law, upholding the provisions that defined fetal viability, required the informed consent of the woman seeking the abortion, and mandated that clinics keep and report records of the procedure. They struck down spousal and parental consent provisions, along with a section prohibiting the use of saline amniocentesis after the first 12 weeks and a requirement that physicians take measures to preserve the life of the fetus or be subject to criminal penalties.

The Missouri case was the first abortion regulation to reach the Supreme Court in the years after *ROE V. WADE,* 410 U.S. 113 (1973). *Roe* had held that the RIGHT TO PRIVACY, implicit in the Constitution, permitted a woman in consultation with her physician to terminate a pregnancy during the first three months. During the later stages of the pregnancy, the state had a stronger interest in protecting the woman's health and preserving fetal life, and therefore, the state's ability to regulate abortions increased. During the latter stages of the pregnancy, once the fetus became viable, the state could prohibit abortions except to protect the life or health of the mother. States with strong "pro-life" constituencies, such as Missouri with a large Roman Catholic population, challenged *Roe* by creating an array of regulations that limited access to abortions.

In *Planned Parenthood v. Danforth,* the Court ruled 6-3 that some of the Missouri rules did not contradict the essential holding in *Roe,* while others unconstitutionally interfered with a woman's right to terminate a pregnancy. The Missouri act defined viability as "that stage of fetal development when the life of the unborn child may be continued indefinitely outside the womb by natural or artificial life-support systems." *Roe* had linked the definition of viability with the third trimester of pregnancy and referred to the point at which a fetus could "potentially live outside the mother's womb, albeit with artificial aid," with the prospect of "meaningful life." The Court did not remark on the statute's use of "unborn child" rather than "fetus" but held that the Missouri definition provided adequate flexibility for physicians to determine viability on a case by case basis.

They also upheld the provision imposing record keeping and reporting requirements on clinics and physicians, as long as reasonable and not unduly burdensome. The Court did not object to requiring a woman's written consent to an abortion, even during the first 12 weeks. They compared it to mandating prior written consent for any other surgical procedure and presumed such a requirement was constitutional. They objected to the third-party consent provisions, however. The Court reasoned that if a state could not interfere with a woman's choice to terminate a pregnancy, the state could not delegate that right to another person—whether a spouse or a parent. They revisited the issue of spousal consent in *Planned Parenthood of Southeastern Pennsylvania v. Casey,* 505 U.S. 833 (1992). In that case, the Court also stuck down a spousal consent provision but based much of their reasoning on the premise that a woman seeking an abortion could face the threat of domestic violence or coercion.

In addition, the Court struck down the provisions that directed physicians' professional decisions. The law prohibited the use of saline amniocentesis after the first trimester, even though it was considered the safest and most widely used procedure. Essentially, as the Court saw it, doctors would be forced to use more dangerous or untested methods, or not to perform the abortion at all. Here the justices found that the state legislature had clearly overstepped its regulatory role. They also objected to the requirement that doctors exercise due diligence to preserve the life and health of the fetus or run the risk of a charge of manslaughter. The law did not specifically distinguish between pre- and post-viability, creating the possibility that physicians could face criminal charges each time they performed an abortion. In recent years, the Court has found similar problems with laws that prohibit "partial birth" abortions. The argument was made in *Stenberg v. Carhart,*

99-830 (2000), that because the Nebraska "partial birth" law was so broadly written, it could have the effect of criminalizing virtually all abortion procedures.

Planned Parenthood v. Danforth was only the first of many cases in which the Supreme Court determined whether states' regulations of abortion were constitutional or whether they violated the principles of *Roe.* As the composition of the Court has changed, they have shown a greater willingness to permit regulations that do not impose an "undue burden" on a woman's right to choose, although many policies have restricted access to abortions even during the first trimester of pregnancy.

For more information: Hoff, Joan. *Law, Gender, and Injustice: A Legal History of U.S. Women.* New York: New York University Press, 1991; Hull, N. E. H., and Peter Charles Hoffer. *Roe v. Wade: The Abortion Rights Controversy in American History.* Lawrence: University Press of Kansas, 2001.

—Mary Welek Atwell

Planned Parenthood of Southeastern Pennsylvania v. Casey, 505 U.S. 833 (1992)

In *Planned Parenthood of Southeastern Pennsylvania v. Casey,* the Supreme Court upheld a woman's constitutional right to obtain an abortion as articulated in *Roe v. Wade,* 410 U.S. 113 (1973), while simultaneously upholding a Pennsylvania law that seriously restricted access to abortions. Citing the doctrine of STARE DECISIS ("let the past decision stand"), the Court stood by Roe's argument that "a woman's decision to terminate her pregnancy is a 'liberty' protected against state interference by the substantive component of the due process clause of the Fourteenth Amendment."

Centrist Justices O'CONNOR, Kennedy, and SOUTER formed an alliance to stand by *Roe,* the landmark abortion case, even though they believed that parts of that 1973 decision were not responsive to medical realities of the 1990s. The conservative bloc of Chief Justice REHNQUIST and Justices WHITE, SCALIA, and THOMAS concurred in upholding the Pennsylvania law but refrained from upholding *Roe.* Justices BLACKMUN and STEVENS, the more liberal members of the Court, filed a separate opinion expressing continued support for *Roe* while dissenting from upholding the legal position of conservative Pennsylvania Governor Robert P. Casey.

Three major elements of Pennsylvania's Abortion Control Act of 1982 as amended in 1988 and 1989 were at issue in *Casey:*

> Informed consent called for a woman seeking an abortion to be provided with information about the dangers of abortion. A minor needed the informed consent of

one parent or judicial bypass in the absence of parental consent.

Spousal consent required married women to notify their husbands before obtaining an abortion except under conditions of medical emergency.

The 24-hour waiting period required a woman to wait 24 hours after expressing her wish to obtain an abortion before the procedure could be performed.

The Supreme Court upheld the provision under *Roe* that provided unlimited access to abortion before viability, rejecting the state's significant interest in a fetus that had no chance of surviving outside the mother's womb. However, the Court accepted the state's right to interfere in abortion decisions after viability had occurred, as long as the law contained exceptions for endangerment of a woman's life or health. The Court also recognized a legitimate state interest in protecting the health of a woman and the fetus from the outset of pregnancy.

Rejecting the "rigid trimester framework" of *Roe v. Wade*, the Supreme Court articulated a new test for determining the fine line between guaranteeing a woman's right to choose and protecting the state's interest in a viable fetus. The "undue burden" test, long advocated by Justice Sandra Day O'Connor, stipulated that no state could place an "undue burden" on a woman's right to choose. The spousal consent provision was considered an "undue burden," while informed consent and a 24-hour waiting period were not.

In response to the complaint that the Philadelphia law limited the ability of medical personnel to care for their patients, the Court replied that the "informed consent provision of Pennsylvania's abortion statute does not prevent a physician from exercising his or her medical judgment." The Court argued that as long as information required by informed consent was "truthful" and "nonmisleading" in explaining the "nature of abortion procedure, about attendant health risks of abortion and of childbirth and about probable gestational age of fetus" it did "not impose undue burden on woman's right to choose to terminate her pregnancy."

Critics of the *Casey* decision claimed that the existence of a 24-hour waiting period automatically placed an "undue burden" on access to abortion for women in certain areas. At the time of the decision, it was estimated that 83 percent of the counties in the United States had no abortion provider. In the wake of antiabortionist violence directed at abortion providers, entire states had been left without access to abortion. A woman who had to travel several hundred miles to obtain an abortion might not be financially able to remain out-of-state for the extended waiting period.

For more information: Lindgren, J. Ralph, and Nadine Taub. *The Law of Sex Discrimination.* Minneapolis and St. Paul: West, 1993; *"Planned Parenthood v. Casey,"* on Douglas Butler, "Abortion: Medicine, Ethics, and Law" CD-ROM, 1997.

—Elizabeth Purdy

"plenary power" doctrine

The "plenary power" doctrine in immigration law is a judicially created rule that purports to limit constitutional and judicial constraints on the substantive decisions of Congress in the exercise of its power to regulate immigration. The immigration power, though not enumerated in the Constitution, has been recognized by the Supreme Court as an exclusively federal power deriving from the inherent sovereignty of the United States under international law and several specific constitutional provisions. In recognizing this broad federal power over immigration, the Supreme Court has asserted that the judiciary must afford considerable deference to Congress's substantive determinations, deeming them largely free from constitutional constraints.

The strength of the doctrine has varied over time. The Supreme Court first recognized the breadth of Congress's power over immigration in *Chae Chan Ping v. United States* (the *Chinese Exclusion Case*), 130 U.S. 581 (1889). In that case, a Chinese laborer who immigrated to the United States in 1875 obtained a certificate authorizing him to reenter the United States after visiting China.

However, in 1888, while he was still in China, Congress repealed the certificate program and invalidated all previously issued certificates. In rejecting his challenge to the 1888 statute, the Court acknowledged Congress's broad authority to exclude noncitizens from the United States, stating that this power is inherent in the sovereignty of the federal government and not subject to constitutional or judicial limitation.

Soon after, in *Fong Yue Ting v. United States*, 149 U.S. 698 (1893), the Court extended this principle beyond exclusion of noncitizens at the border to encompass deportation of noncitizens within U.S. territory. The Court upheld a statute requiring a Chinese noncitizen facing deportation to have a "credible white witness" to refute the government's allegations of deportability, asserting that Congress's power to deport noncitizens is "absolute and unqualified." Since then, the Court has reiterated on numerous occasions that Congress's power over immigration is subject to few constitutional or judicial limits, particularly with respect to "excludable" noncitizens who have not entered the United States. [*E.g., Harisiades v. Shaughnessy,* 342 U.S. 580 (1952); *Mathews v. Diaz,* 426 U.S. 67 (1976).]

However, the Court has never treated Congress's immigration power as literally "plenary" or "absolute and unqualified." Since its decision in *Yamataya v. Fisher,* 189 U.S. 86 (1903), which effectively overruled *Fong Yue Ting* in part, the Court has recognized that deportation procedures must conform with the constitutional requirement of due process, which protects all "persons" within the United States, including noncitizens. The Court has reiterated that conclusion on many occasions since, particularly with respect to "deportable" noncitizens who have entered the United States and lawful permanent residents with established ties to the United States. [*E.g., Bridges v. Wixon,* 326 U.S. 135 (1945); *United States v. Witkovich,* 353 U.S. 194 (1957); *Landon v. Plasencia,* 459 U.S. 21 (1982); ZADVYDAS V. DAVIS, 533 U.S. 678, 693 (2001).] The Court also has invalidated or interpreted immigration statutes to avoid constitutional difficulties where they offend the Constitution's structural principles, such as SEPARATION OF POWERS and the availability of JUDICIAL REVIEW via habeas corpus. Moreover, in cases falling outside the core of Congress's power to regulate admission and expulsion of noncitizens, the Court has been more willing to apply the same constitutional standards and level of scrutiny that apply outside the immigration context. The Court has long closely scrutinized state and local government actions affecting the rights of noncitizens, since the plenary power doctrine applies only to the federal government. [*E.g.,* YICK WO V. HOPKINS, 118 U.S. 356 (1886); *Graham v. Richardson,* 403 U.S. 365 (1971).] Even federal actions have received greater scrutiny to the extent they fall outside the core of Congress's authority over substantive immigration decisions. In *Wong Wing v. United States,* 163 U.S. 228 (1896), for example, the Court invalidated a statutory provision authorizing punishment of Chinese noncitizens unlawfully in the United States by imprisonment at hard labor prior to deportation, concluding that such punishment only could be imposed in a criminal trial subject to constitutional protections that apply to all persons within the United States.

Even for matters more directly implicating Congress's substantive decisions concerning admission and expulsion, as opposed to procedural issues or the rights of noncitizens after entry into the United States, the Court has departed from its earlier, absolutist conception of Congress's power by recognizing at least a "limited judicial responsibility under the Constitution" to scrutinize the reasonableness of Congress's determinations. [*Fiallo v. Bell,* 430 U.S. 787, 793 n.5 (1977).] Recent Supreme Court decisions appear to have continued this trend, applying the same legal standards that would apply outside the immigration context without reference to the plenary power doctrine and, in some cases, embracing rhetoric emphasizing the "important constitutional limitations" that constrain Congress's exercise of the immigration power. [*Nguyen v. INS,* 533 U.S. 53 (2001); *Zadvydas v. Davis,* 533 U.S. 678 (2001); *INS v. St. Cyr,* 533 U.S. 289 (2001).] The trend has been particularly pronounced as to noncitizens who have entered the United States or been admitted with lawful permanent resident status.

However, the continued strength of the plenary power doctrine remains uncertain, especially in the wake of September 11th. In its first major post-September 11th immigration decision, the Court upheld a 1996 statutory provision that mandates detention of certain noncitizens while their deportation hearings are pending. Echoing its earlier pronouncements, the Court asserted that when exercising its immigration power, Congress "may make rules as to aliens that would be unacceptable if applied to citizens." [*Demore v. Kim,* 123 S. Ct. 1708, 1717 (2003).] Several post-September 11th immigration initiatives will likely provide further occasion for the Court to clarify the degree to which Congress's power to regulate immigration is subject to constitutional limitations and judicial scrutiny.

For more information: Legomsky, Stephen H. "Immigration Law and the Principle of Plenary Congressional Power." *S. Ct. Rev.* 1984: 255; Motomura, Hiroshi. "Immigration Law After a Century of Plenary Power: Phantom Constitutional Norms and Statutory Interpretation." *Yale L.J.* 100 (1990): 545; Neuman, Gerald L. *Strangers to the Constitution.* Princeton, N.J.: Princeton University Press, 1996; Spiro, Peter J. "Explaining the End of Plenary Power." *Geo. Immigr. L.J.* 16 (2002): 339.

—Anil Kalhan

Plessy v. Ferguson, 163 U.S. 537 (1896)

In one of the most infamous cases in the history of the Supreme Court, the justices by a 7-1 decision upheld the doctrine of "separate but equal" in *Plessy v. Ferguson.*

The separate but equal doctrine had allowed the state of Louisiana to designate separate facilities in railroad cars for black and white passengers. In its broader implications, the "separate but equal" doctrine allowed states to pass what became known as JIM CROW LAWS and segregate blacks and whites not only in transportation but in other areas such as education, housing, public accommodation, restaurants, entertainment and recreational facilities, drinking fountains, and public waiting rooms. Additionally, the laws allowed states to withhold constitutional protections such as the right to vote and the right to a fair trial. The term *Jim Crow* is believed to have originated in 1830 when a minstrel in blackface performed a parody singing "Jump Jim Crow."

On June 7, 1892, 30-year-old Homer Plessy bought a ticket on an East Louisiana Railway train from New Orleans to Covington, Louisiana, and established himself in the "Whites Only" section of the rail car. Plessy was there to challenge Louisiana's 1890 Act to Promote the Comfort of Passengers, which legalized separation of railway passengers

A drinking fountain on the county courthouse lawn, Halifax, North Carolina, 1938 *(Library of Congress)*

by race. Homer Plessy, who was seven-eighths white and one-eighth black, was specifically chosen for the test case because the state of Louisiana considered him to be black even though genetically he would be considered Caucasian. Plessy was forcibly removed from the train and incarcerated in the local jail. The East Louisiana Railway supported the challenge to the law not on ideological grounds but for the practical reason that separate sections for blacks and whites were more expensive to maintain than single sections.

In the state courts, Albion Tourgee, Homer Plessy's New York lawyer, argued that Louisiana had denied Plessy his property right without due process of law as guaranteed by the Fourteenth Amendment to the U.S. Constitution. This property right, according to Tourgee, was Plessy's "reputation of being white." When the case reached the Supreme Court in 1896, Tourgee also called up the protec-

tions of the Thirteenth Amendment, which abolished slavery, and the Fourteenth Amendment, which also guaranteed equal protection of the laws.

The Supreme Court rejected Tourgee's argument that the contested law violated the Thirteenth Amendment but gave some credence to violations of the Fourteenth Amendment. Ultimately, the Supreme Court upheld the right of Louisiana to establish "separate but equal" facilities. Writing for the majority, Justice Brown admitted that the authors of the Fourteenth Amendment had intended only "to enforce the absolute equality of the two races before the law." In practice, according to Justice Brown, the Fourteenth Amendment "could not have been intended to abolish distinctions based upon color, or to enforce social, as distinguished from political, equality, or a commingling of the two races upon terms unsatisfactory to either."

In his landmark dissent, Justice HARLAN maintained that law in the "state of Louisiana (was) inconsistent with the personal liberty of citizens, white and black, in that state, and hostile to both the spirit and letter of the constitution of the United States." Justice Harlan declared that a system based on the "separate but equal" doctrine was "inconsistent with the guaranty given by the constitution to each state of a republican form of government." However, the decision in *Plessy* would serve as PRECEDENT until the "separate but equal" doctrine was overturned in 1954 in *Brown v. Board of Education*.

For more information: Grossman, Joel B., and Richard S. Wells. *Constitutional Law and Judicial Policymaking.* New York and London: Longman, 1988; Nieman, Donald G. *Promises to Keep: African Americans and the Constitutional Order, 1776 to the Present.* New York and Oxford: Oxford University Press, 1991.

—Elizabeth Purdy

Plyler v. Doe, 457 U.S. 202 (1982)

In *Plyler v. Doe,* the United States Supreme Court struck down a Texas statute that withheld from local school districts any state funds for the education of children who were not "legally admitted" into the United States and that authorized local school districts to deny enrollment in their schools to these children. The Court's 5 to 4 majority decision was written by Justice BRENNAN and based upon the EQUAL PROTECTION CLAUSE of the Fourteenth Amendment.

The case had originally been brought as a CLASS ACTION filed in the U.S. District Court for the Eastern District of Texas on behalf of several school-aged children of Mexican origin complaining of their exclusion from the public schools. By the time the case reached the Supreme Court, similar cases had also been brought in the Southern District of Texas.

The Supreme Court affirmed the decisions of both the district courts and courts of appeals in favor of the plaintiff children. The Court found that illegal entry does not prevent a person from becoming resident for purposes of enrolling his children in public schools [457 U.S. 227 (1982)]. Both the majority and the dissent agreed upon several legal points, namely, that the equal protection clause does apply to undocumented aliens, that ILLEGAL ALIENS do not qualify as a suspect class because their status is the result of voluntary action, and that education is not a fundamental right. The majority and the dissent differed upon the existence of the state's legislative interest justifying the statute. Justice Brennan dismissed the state's claims that the statute was necessary to preserve its limited resources, while the dissent found this to be a plausible claim.

Justice Brennan, writing for the majority, adopted a standard of heightened or INTERMEDIATE SCRUTINY, emphasizing that undocumented children are not responsible for their CITIZENSHIP status as well as the fact that although education is not a fundamental right it does have "a fundamental role in maintaining the fabric of our society" [457 U.S. 221 (1982)] and that illiteracy is an enduring disability which is damaging to both the individual and to society since many of these children will remain permanently within the country. The majority opinion states that denying education to undocumented children would "not comport with fundamental concepts of justice" [457 U.S. 220 (1982)]. Justice Brennan rejected the state's claims that the policy had a putative effect in reducing illegal immigration and that it was in line with federal immigration policies. The dissent, in contrast, applied only a RATIONAL BASIS test in assessing the policy and found that the state's interests in preserving its resources were sufficient to justify the statute. The dissent explicitly rejected the principle of intermediate scrutiny as de facto legislating by the Court.

The case is significant because the Court for the first time extended the constitutional rights held by undocumented aliens to include equal protection rights. Furthermore, because illegal aliens are entitled to equal protection at the level of state law even though they are clearly not treated the same as legally admitted aliens in federal immigration policy, the opinion suggests that the Court may be willing to separate equal protection rights from the longstanding doctrine of federal PREEMPTION of state laws in matters relating to immigration policy.

Justice Brennan's reasoning has been criticized for being result-oriented, and it is not clear that the Court would apply the same protections to illegal immigrant adults as it did to undocumented children. Two subsequent cases, *Martinez v. Bynum,* 461 U.S. 321 (1983), and *Kadrmas v. Dickinson,* 487 U.S. 450 (1988), though not directly related to immigrants, present the Court as much more reluctant to interfere with state laws governing education. In 1994 California's Proposition 187 declared illegal aliens' ineligibility for public services, including public education, in apparent challenge to *Plyler,* but the issue has not yet triggered a Supreme Court decision.

For more information: Olivas, Michael A. "Storytelling out of School." *Hastings Constitutional Law Quarterly* 22 (1995): 1,019; Rubio-Marin, Ruth. *Immigration as a Democratic Challenge.* Cambridge: Cambridge University Press, 2000.

—Leila Kawar

Poe v. Ullman, 367 U.S. 497 (1961)

In *Poe v. Ullman,* the United States Supreme Court dismissed a case about the right of a married couple to use birth control for lack of a justiciable controversy.

A married couple, a married woman, and a doctor challenged a Connecticut law that prohibited the use of CONTRACEPTIVES, even by married couples. The statute also stipulated that any physician distributing information could be charged as an accessory to crime. Both women were married, but due to medical conditions were advised that a pregnancy could be quite harmful and that the use of contraceptives was the safest method to avoid a potentially dangerous pregnancy. The doctor in this case could not legally dispense contraceptives or advise his patients on how to use them because of the Connecticut statute in place. All sued claiming that this law violated their Fourteenth Amendment rights.

The Court dismissed this case because they found that it lacked a real conflict. The majority opinion, written by Justice FRANKFURTER, held that although the law had been in place in Connecticut since 1879, it had been invoked only once, and that was a test case. There was no live controversy. Clearly, he reasoned, the authorities had chosen not to enforce this law, even though it was still on the books. The appellants risked no real danger of being prosecuted under the law since there was a clear tradition of nonenforcement. Therefore, there was no true CASE OR CONTROVERSY, and the Supreme Court lacked authority to decide the case.

Poe v. Ullman is most notable for Justice HARLAN's lengthy and famous dissent. He argued that the Connecticut statute in question is unconstitutional on the grounds that it is an invasion by the state of the privacy of a married couple, including their most intimate relations. Although the RIGHT TO PRIVACY is never mentioned in the Constitution, Harlan finds that it is "embraced" by the right to liberty found in the Fourteenth Amendment and thus should be recognized. He also urged that any law coming into conflict with the liberty or privacy of people should be subject to STRICT SCRUTINY. By this, he meant that any such law would be presumed unconstitutional until the state proved it is necessary and as unintrusive as possible. In his opinion, the Connecticut statute did not pass this test.

Harlan's dissent was used four years later as the basis of the argument to challenge the same Connecticut law. This case, *GRISWOLD V. CONNECTICUT*, 381 U.S. 479 (1965), succeeded in overturning the law. Later, this right was extended to single women as well in *EISENSTADT V. BAIRD*, 405 U.S. 438 (1972). These cases were important because they helped to establish the constitutional right to privacy and paved the way for future decisions respecting privacy and reproductive rights.

—Jamie Goetz

police powers

The "police powers" are the general powers enjoyed by a government to regulate the health, safety, and morals of the people in order to promote the general welfare. These powers were held by the states prior to the ratification of the Constitution and therefore are part of the states' reserved powers. State statutes that criminalize behavior, structure marriage, create public schools, and require vaccinations are all examples of the police powers.

States are empowered to pass whatever statutes they believe will enhance the general welfare unless prohibited from doing so by a specific provision in the U.S. Constitution. The extent to which the federal government enjoys general police powers is a more complex and controversial issue. Because it is a government of delegated powers, exercise of the federal police power must stem directly from one of its enumerated powers, or indirectly from an implied power.

The states' use of the police powers is primarily restricted by two sections of the Constitution: the BILL OF RIGHTS, and Article I, Sections 8 and 10. Because the Bill of Rights has been applied to state governments through the Fourteenth Amendment, state governments are prohibited from violating basic CIVIL LIBERTIES absent a COMPELLING STATE INTEREST. Thus states must tread carefully, for example, in imposing restrictions on First Amendment freedoms or in constructing the process for prosecuting criminals. Should a state statute or practice violate a provision of the Bill of Rights, the burden of proof is on the state that such legislation serves a compelling state interest.

The states' police powers are also limited by Sections 8 and 10 of Article I. Section 10 lists specific areas in which states may not legislate. For example, states may not enter into TREATIES, coin money, or pass bills of attainder. Section 8 confers specific powers on Congress, but states are not forbidden from acting in all of these arenas as well. There exists a realm of concurrent powers in which both Congress and the states can legislate (e.g., taxation), but the police powers of the states must yield to the federal government if federal and state statutes conflict, or if there exists an obvious need for uniformity of laws across the nation.

Congress's use of police powers is ostensibly more circumscribed, having to be rooted in either a specifically delegated power or from an implied power. However, Congress has used its power to regulate INTERSTATE COMMERCE to extend federal authority over a broad range of areas, from CIVIL RIGHTS to environmental protection. From 1937 through the mid-1990s, the Supreme Court upheld most of this legislation, accepting the argument that a vast array of activities affect the flow of commerce between the states and were thus subject to federal authority. A number of the Court's decisions were couched in such broad language that some commentators argue that the federal government had in effect been given general police powers as extensive as those of the states.

However, starting with *United States v. Lopez,* 514 U.S. 549 (1995), the Supreme Court has attempted to restrict Congress's authority under the commerce clause. In striking down a federal statute banning the possession of firearms around schools, the Court argued that upholding such a law would allow the commerce clause to be used as an unlimited grant of federal power. Several subsequent decisions have reinforced this attempt to rein in congressional authority, leaving no doubt that the current Supreme Court sees federal police powers as specific and restricted.

For more information: Berger, Raoul. "Judicial Manipulation of the Commerce Clause." *Tex. L. Rev.* 74 (1996): 695; Choper, Jesse H., and John C. Yoo. "The Scope of the Commerce Clause after Morrison." *Okla. City U. L. Rev.* 25 (2000): 843, 852; Nelson, Grant S. "A Commerce Clause Standard for the New Millennium: 'Yes' to Broad Congressional Control over Commercial Transactions; 'No' to Federal Legislation on Social and Cultural Issues." *Ark. L. Rev.* 55 (2003): 1213.

—Gwyneth I. Williams

political parties, rights of

Political parties enjoy a variety of rights under the Constitution. Political parties of the sort that now influence American politics were not contemplated at the time of the founding, and no direct reference to them appears in the Constitution. In fact, to the extent that they can be equated with interest groups (termed "factions" at that time), the framers attempted to minimize parties' influence on the new government. Nevertheless, the First Amendment explicitly protects the rights of "speech and of the press," along with the "right of the people peaceably to assemble, and to petition the Government for a redress of grievances."

Political parties, as associations of individuals brought together to influence public policy through voting and persuasion, are therefore protected by the First Amendment despite the Constitution's failure to anticipate their development. Exertions of parties' rights, however, often clash with rights of individuals to speak, express themselves, and vote, and the interests of the state in promoting orderly, competitive elections with optimal citizen participation. Because cases adjudicating the rights of parties often raise competing claims between differing interests *within* parties, the Supreme Court's resolution of these claims may depend on its answer to the basic question, "Who is the party?"

The most fundamental right of political parties is the right of self-definition. Determining for itself the qualifications for membership in a party, the party's positions on issues, and the procedure for choosing nominees, not to mention the party's support for the nominees themselves, all impact the party's speech and associational rights under the First Amendment. Nevertheless, adjudication of these claims has not yielded clear results.

Parties, to retain any independent identity, must possess substantial control over the qualifications for membership, and that control is protected by the First Amendment's freedom of expressive association. It is therefore clear that the party may exclude from its membership individuals with whom it has a disagreement, so as to preserve the party's ideological principles. Importantly, though, the Supreme Court has held that where the state grants parties special status in the electoral process, RACIAL DISCRIMINATION is an impermissible motive for denying someone the "right to vote" in the party's primary election, despite the party's generally plenary authority to determine its membership.

Related to party control over its membership is the issue of party control of the nomination process. The Supreme Court has said in DICTA that it is constitutional for states to require parties to nominate candidates by using primary elections, as opposed to caucuses, or vice versa. Nevertheless, states may not determine who may be allowed to vote in those primaries. The Court has struck down states' attempts to require a blanket primary, under which voters cast one ballot for each office in a primary but may vote in the Republican primary for governor, the Democratic primary for attorney general, etc., and has also struck down a state's attempt to require parties to limit participation in primaries to party members.

The Court has thus left to the parties the task of regulating participation in primaries (with the exception of racially discriminatory regulations); it is the decision of the parties whether to "associate" with nonparty members in the primary elections. The fate of the "open primary," under which nonparty members must be allowed to vote in a party's primary, but where the voter is limited to one party's primary, is in doubt. Although *California Democratic Party v. Jones,* 530 US 567 (2000) did not reach the constitutionality of the open primary, much of its language casts doubt on the practice because the system forbids the parties from regulating who may choose the party's nominees.

Under the foregoing examples, the party was exerting rights against state regulation. Occasionally individuals assert First Amendment rights *against parties,* which can succeed only if the Court views the parties as state actors. In *Smith v. Allwright* (1944) and *Terry,* where the Court invalidated party rules barring blacks from participating, the Court treated the party as equivalent to the state and thus held that the party was constitutionally prevented from discriminating on the ground of race. It is clear that parties provide services to the states, notably winnowing the field of candidates such as to make the general election more orderly. In some cases, therefore, party action has been taken to be state action, allowing individuals to raise claims against the parties. It is equally clear, however, that parties are not equivalent to the state in every instance. Were every party action subject to constitutional restrictions, no party would be able to exert the "viewpoint discrimination" necessary to limit its membership to persons who believe in the tenets of the party.

Another crucial, but unsettled, aspect of parties' First Amendment rights is the question whether the party organization can limit access to a primary ballot by one of its members. In claims of this sort, the candidate and his supporters raise First Amendment claims against "the party," which, they argue, is acting as the state in selecting the candidates who will eventually appear on the general election ballot. The crux of these cases, however, is in determining who shall act for the party. Permitting a party to exclude a candidate from the primary ballot allows the party leadership to protect the party membership from itself, in that the leadership has determined that it would be unwise to allow the rank and file to vote for the disfavored candidate. On the other hand, the party leadership is itself accountable to the rank and file, and some decisions about ordering primary elections will always need to be made by the leadership. Thus, the unsettled question is whether party members have a right *vis-à-vis the party* to run in a primary election. The answer depends on whether one equates the party with the state, and whether one equates the individual party member or the party leadership with the party.

The Court has maintained an ideal of the party as a separate entity when it comes to questions of campaign finance. Parties, just like individuals, may make "independent expenditures" promoting political causes during campaigns, and these expenditures are protected against government regulation by the First Amendment. Where its expenditures are "coordinated" with a candidate, however, the expenditures can be treated as "contributions" to that candidate's campaign and therefore limited. Thus, despite the fact that parties' interests virtually always coincide with those of their candidates, the Court has declined to treat parties and candidates as one—either to treat all party spending as coordinated with candidates, or to hold that party expenditures can never be corrupting because the candidates' interests are aligned with their parties'.

For more information: Cain, Bruce E. "Point / Counterpoint: Party Autonomy and Two-Party Electoral Competition." *U. Pa. L. Rev.* 149 (2001): 793; Hasen, Richard L. "Point / Counterpoint: Do the Parties or the People Own the Electoral Process?" *U. Pa. L. Rev.* 149 (2001): 815; Issacharoff, Samuel. "Private Parties with Public Purposes: Political Parties, Associational Freedoms, and Partisan Competition." *Colum. L. Rev.* 101 (2001): 274; Persily,

Nathaniel, and Bruce E. Cain. "The Legal Status of Political Parties: A Reassessment of Competing Paradigms." *Colum. L. Rev.* 100 (2000): 775.

—Michael Richard Dimino, Sr.

political question doctrine

Under Article III of the Constitution, the federal courts have the power to decide all cases and controversies. This clause requires that before a judge becomes involved in a case, there must exist a dispute between two litigants that the courts have the tools and expertise to handle. Some cases, according to the Courts, are best left to the other branches including decisions about war and peace and about the internal procedures of each branch. These issues have been deemed political questions and the courts have refused to rule on them.

The political question doctrine is based on the SEPARATION OF POWERS and the view that the political branches, Congress, and the president, are granted the power to make important decisions for the nation. It was officially recognized by the Court in the case of *Luther v. Borden* (1849). The case centered on the 1842 Dorr Rebellion in Rhode Island. Thomas Dorr led a rebellion against the Rhode Island government and attempted to overthrow it. Dorr was arrested and a series of court cases followed. Luther, one of Dorr's supporters, had his house searched by Borden, a militiaman for the Rhode Island government. Luther claimed that Borden did not represent a proper government and that his search of Luther's house was a trespass. His case went through the court system as he pushed the judges to declare the Rhode Island government void under the guaranty clause. Lower judges declined to make a ruling, and he appealed to the Supreme Court.

The justices also refused. Speaking for eight members, Chief Justice TANEY ruled that the question about what government was the proper one for Rhode Island was a political question best left to the political branches. According to Taney, the guaranty clause required a republican form of government for each state and gave Congress the power to use military means to ensure that such a government existed. When writing the clause, the framers had realized that quick action might be required and that Courts were too deliberate as shown by the fact the rebellion had occurred in 1842 and the decision was being issued in 1849. For these reasons, the decision was deemed a political question that would best be solved by Congress.

Taney's ruling was based on the most unusual of circumstances—a rebellion attempting to overthrow a state government. His decision in *Luther,* while settling that case, provided only limited guidance for future cases. The political question doctrine could be invoked by other courts when faced with a difficult decision they did not want to make. Justices realize that decisions that impinge on the internal procedures of the other branches might be seen as interference in the decision making of those branches. The Supreme Court has also come to recognize that the Constitution cedes purely political decisions to those branches directly responsible to the people.

One area where the courts had refused to become involved was challenges to legislative reapportionment or the drawing of district lines. In *Colgrove v. Green* (1946), the Court had ruled that the decision to redraw lines for the Illinois state legislature was a political question that could not be decided by the Court. The majority warned against the justices becoming involved in the reapportionment process, which was termed a "political thicket" by the majority.

Colgrove, though, barely lasted 15 years. In BAKER V. CARR (1962), the Court ignored the *Colgrove* decision and ruled that the reapportionment of the Tennessee legislature was not a political question. Writing for six justices, Justice William BRENNAN ruled that reapportionment involved the EQUAL PROTECTION CLAUSE rather than the guaranty clause. The justices had ample tools for using the equal protection clause to determine whether a voting district discriminated against voters. In addition, Brennan argued that legislative reapportionment was not delegated to a particular branch such as Congress or the president so that the Court would not be violating the separation of powers.

The result of *Baker* was that the Supreme Court became deeply involved with the legislative reapportionment debate and settling disputes among the political parties. The *Baker* decision also weakened the political question doctrine by establishing weaker guidelines for allowing the courts to intervene. Warnings from dissenters in *Baker* that the Court was becoming entangled in political issues were borne out by the flurry of reapportionment cases that followed *Baker*. Suddenly the drawing of district lines and the arrangement of voters in those districts were no longer a political decision but rather a legal one.

Yet it was invoked several times by the Supreme Court and lower courts when faced with challenges to the congressional war power in both the Vietnam War and the First Persian Gulf War (1991). In a series of cases the courts either refused to hear challenges to the constitutionality of the war or ruled such questions were best left to the political branches.

In 1993 the Court extended the doctrine to include questions of the internal workings of the other branches. In *Nixon v. United States*, the justices considered whether an impeached federal judge could challenge the use of a Senate committee to collect facts for the full Senate when trying him for impeachment. Nixon claimed that under Article I, the full Senate was to try him or conduct a trial with witnesses and testimony. When a Senate committee did that instead and the Senate voted to remove him, he appealed.

The Supreme Court ruled that the question of how to conduct an impeachment trial was left to the Senate. The Constitution set up certain requirements, including a two-thirds vote, and those were the only ones restricting the Senate's procedure. The courts could not and would not tell senators how to use that power.

The political question doctrine continues to be invoked by the Court when faced with decisions the justices feel they are not properly equipped to handle. The doctrine is a method of limiting the power of the judiciary over issues best handled by the political branches of government.

For more information: Franck, Thomas. *Political Questions/Judicial Answers*. Princeton N.J.: Princeton University Press, 1992; McCormack, Wayne. "The Political Question Doctrine." *University of Detroit Mercy Law Review* 70: 793; Strum, Philippa. *The Supreme Court and Political Questions*. Tuscaloosa: University of Alabama Press, 1978.

—Douglas Clouatre

political speech

Political speech refers to communication about government and politics that is protected under the First Amendment.

The First Amendment's protection against abridgment of "the freedom of speech" is most vigorous when the abridged speech is political, that is, when "it involves 'interactive communication concerning political change.'" Such communication can range from a candidate debate to public demonstrations and protests, the placing of a newspaper advertisement, and an infinite number of other ways of conveying a message about governmental affairs. The Court has recognized that ensuring open public debate on public policy was the principal motivation for the First Amendment and for that reason has held political speech worthy of special attention. Severe restrictions of First Amendment rights in the political context trigger STRICT SCRUTINY, while more moderate restrictions trigger less exacting review.

To say that political speech is generously guarded by the First Amendment is not, however, to say that it may not be regulated. Often there are weighty interests encouraging the suppression of political speech, and occasionally those interests have resulted in the Court upholding speech restrictions. One such interest is simply the running of orderly, fair elections; the Court has recognized that "there must be a substantial regulation of elections if they are to be fair and honest and if some sort of order, rather than chaos, is to accompany the democratic processes."

As an example of a viewpoint-neutral regulation upheld by the Court, an ordinance banning electioneering within 100 feet of polling places is constitutional (assuming it is applied evenly to adherents of all political views), even if the area in the regulation encompasses sidewalks, streets, and other places often used as places for political persuasion. The Court has reasoned that such regulations inhibit speech, but only as much as necessary to protect voters from intimidation. Absent the "intimidation" justification, however, states may not broadly prohibit electioneering on election day.

Ordinarily, the Court has been protective of the rights of individuals to debate policy and of the rights of candidates to conduct campaigns. Citizens have the right to distribute anonymous political literature.

Also, candidates have the right to urge voters to place them in office, even if in doing so the candidates happen accidentally to mislead the public. As the Court has said, "the constitutional guarantee [of free speech] has its fullest and most urgent application precisely to the conduct of campaigns for political office." [*Roy*, 401 U.S. at 272.] Judicial candidates, too, have the right to announce to the public their views on disputed issues, in the hope that they will gain the approval of the voters, but it is unclear whether judicial candidate promises of conduct in office are protected to the extent that *Brown* protected the promises of legislative candidates.

Campaign financing is another area where the usually potent guarantees of the First Amendment have faltered in the face of the Court's belief that combating "corruption and the appearance of corruption" justifies restrictions on speech. Beginning with *Buckley v. Valeo*, 424 U.S. 1 (1976) (per curiam), and continuing through *Nixon v. Shrink Mo. Gov't PAC*, 528 U.S. 377 (2000), the Court has drawn a distinction between the protections given to political expenditures and political contributions. Expenditures enable the speaker to communicate a message to the voting public. (After all, political speech could be suppressed easily if the government could ban the spending of money to promote political causes by, for example, printing flyers, buying speakers and a microphone, buying television advertisements, etc.) Thus, as long as that speech focuses on an "issue" and does not explicitly call for the election or defeat of a candidate, independent expenditures may not be limited.

Where, however, an expenditure is coordinated with a candidate's campaign, or where the donor seeks to give money directly to the campaign so that the candidate can spend the money to promote his candidacy, then some regulations are permitted. The Court has held that contributions pose the risk that candidates, once in office, will seek to satisfy the wishes of donors, neglecting the needs of voters who did not give monetary support to the candidate's campaign. This "corruption," the Court held, justifies restrictions that limit the amount individuals may contribute to a campaign.

Where there is no such risk of "corruption," however, there is no need to limit contributions, and consequently such limitations are unconstitutional. This has led to the invalidation of restrictions on expenditures in elections on initiatives and referenda, and on independent spending in candidate elections by "ideological corporations," that is, those corporations that are designed to promote a particular set of policies rather than for profit making. The Court has permitted governments to prohibit political spending by for-profit corporations in candidate elections, however, holding that such spending distorts the marketplace of ideas in two related ways.

First, the Court has noted that contributions by for-profit corporations consist of money that was given to the corporations for reasons entirely apart from their political advocacy. Second, the advantages of doing business as a corporation (including perpetual life and limited liability for shareholders) allow corporations to amass money and produce advertising in amounts "hav[ing] little or no correlation to the public's support for the corporation's political ideas." Thus, fear of the influence of corporate money, as well as fear of "quid-pro-quo corruption" have induced the Court to tolerate some substantial limitations on political speech. Voting per se is not protected by the First Amendment and is not "speech" or "expressive conduct." For that reason, voters have no right to cast a ballot for Donald Duck as a means of registering a protest against the political system or the candidates running under that system, and states have no obligation to provide for write-in voting. In the words of the Court, "the function of the election process is 'to winnow out and finally reject all but the chosen candidates,' . . . not to provide a means of giving vent to 'short-range political goals, pique, or personal quarrels.'" While more speech than purely political discussion is protected by the First Amendment, the rigor with which the First Amendment will be applied in a given case may depend on the type of speech at issue. It thus becomes necessary to classify speech as political or something else, in order to apply the appropriate level of judicial scrutiny to a regulation restricting the speech, and occasionally this can be a difficult distinction to make.

In most cases, it is relatively easy to differentiate political speech from other types of communication. A sign advertising a sale on groceries is commercial speech; research published in the *Journal of the American Medical Association* is scientific; a sign requesting the reader to vote for a candidate is political. What of the company that wishes to make a statement about its labor policies (political), and in the process convince consumers to buy its product (commercial)? The Supreme Court recently agreed to hear such a challenge, but dismissed the case without deciding whether such speech should be considered political (and protected strenuously) or commercial (and deserving of less protection).

For more information: Dimino, Michael R. "Pay No Attention to That Man Behind the Robe: Judicial Elections, the First Amendment, and Judges as Politicians." *Yale L.* 21 and *Pol'y Rev.* 301 (2003); Meiklejohn, Alexander. *Free Speech and its Relation to Self-Government.* New York: Harper, 1948; Schauer, Frederick, and Richard H. Pildes. "Electoral Exceptionalism and the First Amendment." *Tex. L. Rev.* 77 (1999): 1,803; Symposium. "The Federal Election Laws, Campaign Finance, Free Speech, Soft Money, Hard Choices." *Ariz. St. L.J.* 34 (2002): 1,017–1,216.

—Michael Richard Dimino, Sr.

Pollock v. Farmer's Loan & Trust, 157 U.S. 429 (1895)

The United States Supreme Court examined and then invalidated an INCOME TAX that was passed by Congress in 1894 in *Pollock v. Farmer's Loan & Trust.*

Congress had imposed a personal income tax on income from real estate and other personal property investments, such as stocks and bonds. The Court held that this act violated Article I, Section 9 of the U.S. Constitution, since individual states were granted the power to impose direct taxation. Direct taxes imposed by the federal government were to be apportioned among the states based on their congressional representation.

Congress had imposed a 2 percent tax on personal income in excess of $4,000 with the Tariff Act of 1894. This tax affected about 2 percent of the U.S. population at that time. Charles Pollock, a stockholder in a New York bank, brought the suit to the Court to prevent the bank from paying the tax. The FULLER Supreme Court heard the case a few months later with only eight justices present. Justice Howell E. Jackson was incapacitated due to tuberculosis and unable to participate in the hearing.

Pollock claimed that the tax was invalid because a tax on income from land was the same as a tax on land itself. He also argued that the tax failed to meet the Constitution's uniformity test. The Court's initial decision was split four-to-four. Pollock's attorney requested that the case be reheard because the initial decision did not answer the questions presented. After being reheard, the full Court decided in a five-to-four decision to strike down the tax in favor of Pollock's arguments. Justice Melville FULLER authored the opinion of the Court.

The decision rendered in *Pollock* sparked much political debate. Critics slammed the Court's opinion for ignoring a previous PRECEDENT. The Court's 1796 decision, for example, had upheld a carriage tax. The 1881 decision in *Springer v. United States,* 102 U.S. 586, had allowed a federal income tax on personal income during the Civil War and several years after.

Support for a federal income tax increased in the late 19th century in the political arena because of the depression of 1893 and industrialization. Many politicians, including members of the Democratic Party and progressive Republicans, criticized the decision rendered in *Pollock.* Presidential candidate William Jennings Bryan bashed the ruling in his "Cross of Gold" speech during the 1896 Democratic national convention. Yet, with the defeat of Bryan and the return of economic prosperity, it seemed that the decision in *Pollock* would stand.

Perhaps due to the controversy the decision sparked, the Court did not refer to *Pollock* in future taxation cases. Subsequent rulings upheld taxes on inheritances, tobacco, stock sales, and commodity exchange sales. However, the debate over taxes did not end with these decisions.

A tariff bill introduced in Congress in 1909 sparked more debates and prompted Democrats in Congress to propose the adoption of new income tax laws. With the support of President William Howard TAFT, Senator Nelson Aldridge of Rhode Island introduced a constitutional amendment to permanently impose a federal income tax. This amendment attempted to overturn the *Pollock* decision of the Supreme Court. Amendments had only overturned previous Supreme Court decisions in two instances: with the ratification of the Eleventh Amendment (lawsuits against states) in 1795 and the Fourteenth Amendment (CIVIL RIGHTS) in 1868.

Congress reversed the decision rendered in *Pollock* with the ratification of the Sixteenth Amendment in 1912. This amendment allowed Congress to impose tax on "income from whatever source derived." Subsequent rulings of the Supreme Court later questioned the *Pollock* decision. Chief Justice WHITE in *Stanton v. Baltic Mining Company,* 240 U.S. 103 (1916), determined that the Sixteenth Amendment conferred no new powers of taxation on the federal government. Instead, it prohibited the use of a "mistaken theory" provided by *Pollock.*

The adoption of the Sixteenth Amendment was the first amendment passed since Reconstruction. The federal government would not have been provided with the financial base for its great expansion had Congress not overturned the decision in *Pollock.* If the *Pollock* decision had survived, the United States would be a very different place to live today.

For more information: Ely, James W., Jr. *The Fuller Court: Justices, Rulings, and Legacy.* Denver: ABC-CLIO,

2003; Westin, Alan Furman. "The Populist Movement and the Campaign of 1896." *The Journal of Politics* 15, 1 (1953): 3–41; Witt, Elder. *The Supreme Court.* Washington, D.C.: Congressional Quarterly, 1994.

—Carol Walker

pornography and obscenity

The issue of obscenity has been one of the most problematic areas of law confronting the Supreme Court of the United States in modern times due to the varying opinions among the justices. If a work of pornography is deemed obscene by the Court, it receives no protection under the First Amendment and governments may legally ban it. Yet the Court's chief difficulty has been coming up with an agreed upon definition of what makes something "obscene." It is a challenging task for those on the Court who seek to regulate obscenity so as not to chill the expression of artists, authors, scientists, and others who enrich the culture of American life.

Obscenity Prior to the 1950s: The Restrictive Hicklin Test

Up until the 1950s, the Court adhered to a broad definition of obscenity called the *Hicklin* test. Taken from a British case, *Regina v. Hicklin,* L.R. 3 Q.B. 360 (1868), it left a vast amount of expression unprotected by the First Amendment. Under the definition, a work was deemed obscene if any part of the material had a tendency "to deprave or corrupt those whose minds are open to such immoral influences, and into whose hands a publication of this sort may fall." In judging whether materials were obscene, the Court did not have to consider the social value of the items or assess the value of the work as a whole. In other words, a single sexually explicit passage in an entire book or other work could cause the entire work to be declared obscene. Moreover, if the material was found likely to fall into the hands of children it could be banned. The effect of this rule was the prohibition of a vast number of works that contained any sexual content.

In the 1930s, however, some of the lower federal courts began to liberalize the strict *Hicklin* test. In the case of *United States v. One Book Entitled "Ulysses" by James Joyce,* 5 Fed. Supp. 182 (1933), a federal district court judge decided to allow the importation and sale of Joyce's book into the United States. In his decision, which was affirmed by the COURT OF APPEALS, Judge John M. Woolsey rejected the *Hicklin* test in favor of focusing on the literary value of the entire work and its effect on an average person. Emboldened by such liberal decisions and the

Supreme Court's refusal to weigh in on the controversial issue, the pornography industry thrived by the 1950s.

The End of the Hicklin Test: Roth v. United States (1957)

In 1957 the Supreme Court chose to end its silence and officially bury the *Hicklin* test. In *Roth v. United States,* 354 U.S. 476 (1957), the Court, in a 6-3 decision, declared the *Hicklin* standard unconstitutional because its effect was to ban material legitimately treating sex. The Court then held that the proper test for obscenity is "whether to the average person, applying contemporary community standards, the dominant theme of the material, taken as a whole, appeals to the prurient interest." In other words, *Roth* required that the effect of the work must be considered *as a whole* upon the *average person* in the community.

While the new *Roth* standard was decidedly a more narrow interpretation of obscenity, it left a few questions unanswered. First, what did it mean by "contemporary community standards"? Should the standards be viewed in light of the country as a whole, the state, or the town? Second, what did it mean to consider the "dominant theme of the material taken as a whole"? In *Jacobellis v. Ohio,* 378 U.S. 184 (1964), the Court provided some guidance. Justice BRENNAN, writing for the Court in *Jacobellis,* stated that the contemporary community standards to be applied were national, not local. Furthermore, Justice Brennan asserted that for a work to be adjudged obscene, it must be "utterly without redeeming social value." Remarkably, in less than 10 years, the test of obscenity had radically changed from one allowing for the banning of materials containing *any* treatment of sex to one tolerant of works that were predominantly sexual.

The Court Retreats from the Permissive Roth Test: Miller v. California (1973)

Roth and *Jacobellis* were decided by a Court comprised of a majority of justices possessing permissive views on the issue of obscenity. Led by its charismatic Chief Justice Earl WARREN, the Warren Court reversed nearly every obscenity conviction case it considered, but with the election in 1968 of President Richard Nixon, who ran for president promising to reverse the liberal obscenity decisions of the Warren Court, things would soon change. Five months after taking office, Nixon was fortunate enough to be able to replace progressive firebrand Warren, who was retiring, with Warren BURGER, a solid conservative, as CHIEF JUSTICE. Nixon later appointed three more justices, dramatically transforming the Court from a decidedly liberal to a decidedly conservative body in a few short years.

The first major obscenity case tackled by the Burger Court was the notorious *Miller v. California,* 413 U.S. 15 (1973). Marvin Miller was a seller of adult materials who, attempting to increase sales, mass-mailed pamphlets featuring couples with their genitals exposed engaging in sex acts. After an unsuspecting mother and son received the pamphlet and complained to the police, Miller was convicted by the state of California for mailing unsolicited sexually explicit material. The Burger Court upheld Miller's conviction and changed the *Roth* and *Jacobellis* standards for judging obscenity in two significant ways. First, the Court held that contemporary community standards were to be defined by the local rather than national community. Second, in order for sexually oriented works to be protected, they must have "serious literary, artistic, political, or scientific value." This requirement was less protective than the *Jacobellis* standard, which protected all sexually oriented works unless they were "utterly without redeeming social value." After *Miller,* local governments were able to fashion obscenity laws according to the values of the community, and prosecutors were much more confident in seeking obscenity convictions. The Burger Court proved to be an ally of law enforcement by upholding convictions in most of the obscenity cases it decided. The *Miller* standard for obscenity is still valid law today.

Child Pornography: A Stricter Standard

In *NEW YORK V. FERBER,* 458 U.S. 747 (1982), the Court unanimously upheld a New York law criminalizing the distribution of all materials depicting children under 16 engaged in sexual conduct. Ferber, a bookstore owner convicted under the statute, challenged its constitutionality because it banned even materials that were not obscene under the *Miller* standard. The Court ruled that the *Miller* standard did not apply to child pornography statutes because states have a compelling interest in safeguarding the physical and psychological well-being of children, who can become victims in the production of child pornography.

Internet Pornography: Reno v. ACLU (1997)

The Communications Decency Act of 1996 (CDA) was passed by Congress to protect minors from harmful material on the Internet. The CDA criminalized intentional transmissions of "obscene or indecent" messages that depict or describe "sexual or excretory activities or organs" to anyone under 18 years of age. A number of parties filed suit, challenging the constitutionality of the CDA. In *Reno v. ACLU,* 521 U.S. 844 (1997), the Court in a 7-2 decision held that the act failed the *Miller* test and violated the First Amendment. First, the terms *indecent* and *patently offensive* encompass large amounts of nonpornographic material with serious social value. Second, the CDA would burden legitimate adult communication because of exposure to

criminal liability if children somehow accessed their messages. While the present Court, led by the conservative Chief Justice William H. REHNQUIST, tends to tilt in a conservative direction in obscenity cases, a majority of the justices realized that reducing public discourse on the Internet to the level of what is acceptable to children is not consistent with maintaining vigorous First Amendment rights in a free society.

For more information: Epstein, Lee, and Thomas G. Walker. *Constitutional Law For a Changing America: Rights, Liberties, and Justice.* 4th ed. Washington D.C.: CQ Press, 2001; Hixon, Richard F. *Pornography and the Justices: The Supreme Court and the Intractable Obscenity Problem.* Carbondale: Southern Illinois University Press, 1996.

—Keith Rollin Eakins

Powell, Lewis F., Jr. (1907–1998) *Supreme Court justice*

Lewis F. Powell, Jr. (September 19, 1907–August 25, 1998) was known as a centrist balancer on the Supreme Court. He was appointed by Richard Nixon at 64, one of the oldest appointees to the Court; yet he served 16 years (1971–87). He was Virginia's first Court member since Reconstruction.

Powell graduated first in his class at Washington & Lee Law School and then went on to Harvard Law. He became president of the American Bar Association, the American Bar Foundation, and the American College of Trial Lawyers. (He championed federally financed legal services for the poor.)

Powell was chairman of the Richmond, Virginia, school board, supervising the peaceful integration of the city's public schools. He was later a member of the state board of education.

Powell was the only Democrat among Nixon's Supreme Court appointees. He wrote thorough and thoughtful opinions, often on the side of JUDICIAL RESTRAINT (perhaps the influence of his Harvard professor, Felix FRANKFURTER). He was a conservative on matters of crime and law enforcement. Powell dissented in *FURMAN V. GEORGIA,* 408 U.S. 238 (1972), arguing that the death penalty was not a "cruel and unusual punishment."

Powell was a social moderate. In more than 30 RELIGION cases decided while he was on the Court, he was in the majority nearly every time. He took a strict separationist view of the establishment clause.

ROE V. WADE, 410 U.S. 113 (1973), was first argued before Powell's appointment. It was reargued on his insistence that it was his duty to participate. He followed BLACKMUN's position. Powell authored three 1983 decisions which reaffirmed *Roe* (*Akron v. Akron Center for Reproductive Health*, 462 U.S. 416; *Planned Parenthood Association of Kansas City, MO, v. Ashcroft*, 462 U.S. 476; and *Simopoulis v. Virginia*, 462 U.S. 506).

His role as swing justice was demonstrated in the AFFIRMATIVE ACTION case of *REGENTS OF THE UNIVERSITY OF CALIFORNIA V. BAKKE*, 438 U.S. 365 (1978). He sided with the four justices who struck down the U. Cal.-Davis formula of minority set-asides but then joined the other camp in upholding other means of promoting diversity.

In *Lloyd v. Tanner*, 407 U.S. 551 (1972), 5-4, he sided with the property rights of a private shopping center over the rights of those who wished to distribute leaflets. In the 1972 cases of *Apodaca v. Oregon*, 406 U.S. 404, and *Johnson v. Louisiana*, 406 U.S. 356, Powell allowed states to depart from unanimous jury verdicts. In *BOWERS V. HARDWICK*, 478 U.S. 68 (1986) Powell was in the five-member majority that upheld Georgia's sodomy law but later he announced he had erred in voting as he had (just as he later expressed regret for supporting CAPITAL PUNISHMENT).

His involvement with schools was called on in several education cases. He was the author of a 5-4 decision in *SAN ANTONIO INDEPENDENT SCHOOL DISTRICT V. RODRIGUEZ*, 411 U.S. 1 (1973), refusing to craft a new fundamental right under equal protection to equalized educational funding. However, in *PLYLER V. DOE*, 462 U.S. 725 (1982), he required Texas to give a free public education to the children of ILLEGAL ALIENS. In *GOSS V. LOPEZ*, 419 U.S. 565 (1975), another 5-4 decision, Powell dissented in opposing the Court's invalidating an Ohio statute permitting up to 10 days' suspension for a student without notice or hearing. He didn't think brief suspensions were a constitutional matter.

Powell was the author of a unanimous decision, *Board of Directors of Rotary International v. Rotary Club of Duarte*, 481 U.S. 537 (1987), stating that the Constitution did not protect SEX DISCRIMINATION by most all-male clubs.

For more information: Londynski, Jacob W. "Justice Lewis F. Powell, Jr.: Balance Wheel of the Court." In *The Burger Court: Political and Judicial Profiles*, edited by Charles M. Lamb and Stephen C. Halpern. Urbana and Chicago: University of Illinois Press, 1991.

—Martin Gruberg

prayer in school

The First Amendment to the Constitution states "Congress shall make no law respecting an establishment of RELIGION, or prohibiting the free exercise thereof." The ESTABLISHMENT CLAUSE here points toward a principle of the separation of government from religion; neither should involve itself with the other. This clause deals with the separation of church and state; and of all the areas in which church and state come into conflict, there is likely no area that is as charged with emotion as the issue of SCHOOL PRAYER.

Throughout much of the country's history, most public schools have been involved in or related to a great variety of events and activities that express or reflect religion, e.g., distribution of Bibles, teaching about religion, holding devotional services, and most prevalent of all, prayer in school.

As immigration added to the nation's religious diversity, the Protestant orientation of public school religious instruction increasingly came under scrutiny. There was not, however, an immediate avenue for relief.

The Supreme Court held in *BARRON V. BALTIMORE*, 32 U.S. 243 (1833), that guarantees of the BILL OF RIGHTS did not limit state or local governments. Furthermore, early interpretations of the establishment clause were focused on government not favoring one religion over another rather than just government support of religion in general. It was not until *Gitlow v. New York*, 268 U.S. 652 (1925), that the Court made any portion of the First Amendment applicable to the states through the due process clause of the Fourteenth Amendment.

Not until *Everson v. Board of Education of Ewing Township, New Jersey*, 330 U.S. 1 (1947), did the Court apply the establishment clause to the states. In *Everson*, the Court ruled unconstitutional bus fare reimbursement for parents of children attending private religious schools. The complaints against the Protestant orientation were greatly strengthened by the Court's INCORPORATION of the establishment clause.

Into the 1960s the Bible was read regularly in most public schools in the South and East. In other schools, students recited state-written prayers. There were Separationist groups who believed these practices violated the establishment clause and should be stopped. Their initial suit was successful as they challenged a New York requirement that teachers lead public school children each morning in reciting a prayer written by the state's Board of Regents. Justice Hugo L. BLACK wrote the opinion, in *Engel v. Vitale*, 370 U.S. 421 (1962), for an 8 to 1 Court holding that the 22-word nondenominational prayer written for students in public schools was unconstitutional on establishment clause grounds. The Court's rationale was that school children, who are young and impressionable, should not have teachers and other authority figures leading them in prayers. Prayers in school deserved heightened scrutiny as opposed to, for example, legislative prayers. The public's response to the decision in *Engel* was quick and quite negative with the volume of mail to the Court exceeding that of any other case.

On the last day of the October 1962 term, the Court handed down its decision in *Abington School District v. Schempp* and *Murray v. Curlett*, 374 U.S. 203 (1963), finding that the reading of the Lord's Prayer and Bible verses in public schools represented an unconstitutional establishment of religion, even though students had the option of excusing themselves from participation.

The public outrage over the Court's decisions in *Engel* and *Abington School District* led Congress to consider nearly 150 proposals to overturn the decisions through a constitutional amendment. In 1966 and 1971 simple majorities of Congress passed versions of a prayer-in-school amendment, falling short of the requirement of a two-thirds vote in both houses in order to send amendment proposals to the states.

It would be nearly two decades until the Court would hear another school prayer case, but in the interim there were several cases decided by the Court that would have an impact on the school prayer cases of the 1980s and 1990s.

LEMON V. KURTZMAN, 403 U.S. 602 (1971), was one of three companion cases involving public assistance for salaries and textbooks to private schools, some of which were religious. The significance of the 8-0 decision ruling the assistance unconstitutional was the three-prong test the opinion by Chief Justice Warren BURGER set forth. The "Lemon Test" established criteria to assess legislation: the statute must have a secular legislative purpose; its principal or primary effect must be one that neither advances nor inhibits religion; and the statute must not foster an excessive government entanglement with religion. In *Lemon*, the statutes in question failed two of the three criteria.

Throughout the 1980s there were attempts by members of Congress and state legislatures to introduce legislation intending to bring prayer into the schools using "moments of silence" or such other means. The catalyst for this nationwide push was *Stone v. Graham*, 449 U.S. 39 (1980), wherein the Supreme Court ruled unconstitutional a Kentucky law requiring the posting of the Ten Commandments in classrooms. The Alabama legislature passed a law requiring that each school day begin with a moment of "silent mediation or voluntary prayer." A student's parent sued claiming the law violated the establishment clause and Court agreed, in *WALLACE V. JAFFREE*, 472 U.S. 38 (1985), that the law was instituted for a religious purpose, thus unconstitutional.

In addition to *Stone*, another Court decision in the 1980s prompting legislation was *Widmar v. Vincent*, 454

Football players at Odessa High School in Odessa, Texas, pray in their locker room. *(Joe Raedle/Newsmakers)*

U.S. 263 (1981). The University of Missouri at Kansas City had decreed that its facilities could not be used by student groups "for purposes of religious worship or religious teaching." The Court struck down Missouri's prohibition of the use of state university buildings for "religious worship," holding that the establishment clause does not require state universities to limit access to their facilities by religious organizations.

Three years after the *Widmar* decision, Congress passed the Equal Access Act which extended the analysis from *Widmar* to public secondary schools. This act was upheld in *Board of Education of the Westside Community Schools v. Mergens,* 496 U.S. 226 (1990), with Justice Sandra Day O'CONNOR writing for an 8 to 1 Court that it was permissible for a student group to form a Christian club to read and discuss the Bible, share Christian fellowship, and pray together in the public school building. This decision permitted religious activities to take place in public schools though the Court noted that it was important that the activity be student-led and initiated in order to avoid excessive entanglement.

Thirty years after *Engel*, the Court ruled in *LEE v. WEISMAN,* 505 U.S. 577 (1992), that invocations and benedictions at public school graduation ceremonies supervised by school authorities violated the earlier rulings preventing school-sponsored prayer. *Weisman* is significant in that it extended the prohibition of school prayer to graduation ceremonies, and the Court also rejected the chance to overturn the "Lemon Test."

The Court further extended its ban on prayer at school in *Sante Fe Independent School District v. Doe,* 530 U.S. 290 (2000). The Sante Fe school district had a practice in which students voluntarily chose to have a public, student-led prayer before football games. The Court, with the opinion written by Justice John Paul STEVENS, held that the prayer—despite its voluntary nature—violated the separation of church and state. Too many people, such as the players, bands, and cheerleaders, were required to be at the games, and one could not assume that they all voluntarily agreed to participate in the prayer.

The attitude of the current Supreme Court is that prayer in school, be it actual prayer or moments of silence, in situations where the students feel compelled to be present is a violation of the establishment clause. Moreover, the three-prong "Lemon-Test" is still in place and used to determine the constitutionality of statutes.

For more information: Epstein, Lee, and Thomas G. Walker. *Constitutional Law for a Changing America: Rights, Liberties, and Justice.* Washington, D.C.: Congressional Quarterly Press, 1998; Finkelman, Paul, ed. *Religion and American Law: An Encyclopedia.* New York: Garland, 2000; Smith, Rodney K. *Public Prayer and the Constitution: A Case Study in Constitutional Interpretation.*

Wilmington, Del.: Scholarly Resources, 1987; Urofsky, Melvin, and Paul Finkelman. *March of Liberty: A Constitutional History of the United States.* New York: Oxford University Press, 2002.

—Mark Alcorn

precedent

Precedents are decisions or courses of conduct previously derived by a court or other legal body that serve to guide that court or body in making future decisions. In court, a precedent serves two purposes. First, a precedent gives a party to a lawsuit a general understanding as to how the law will be applied to the party's facts and issues in dispute. Second, a precedent serves as a guide to and restraint on a judge directing the judge to base decisions on previous cases dealing with the same or similar issues and facts, instead of newly deciding each case.

> [T]he use of precedent [is] an indispensable foundation upon which to decide what is the law and its application to individual cases. It provides at least some degree of certainty upon which individuals can rely in the conduct of their affairs, as well as the basis for orderly development of legal rules. [See *Canada Packers, Ltd. v. Atchison, Topeka and Santa Fe Railway Co.,* 385 U.S. 182, 185 (1966).]

The use of judicial precedents is characteristic of Anglo-American law and a distinct difference compared to civil law derived from the French Empire and the earlier Roman Empire, in which legal precedents were not commonly used.

The use of precedent is strongly tied to the judicial policy of STARE DECISIS, which requires courts to uphold, apply, and maintain settled law and legal concepts through the use of precedent. Both precedents and stare decisis ensure stability and consistency in the judicial process. Court reliance on a precedent, however, does not mean that the law will not change. Over a course of time and the interaction between changing laws and changing socioeconomic views, those decisions that served as reliable precedents may be modified or replaced.

For more information: *Black's Law Dictionary.* 6th ed. St Paul, Minn.: West, 1990.

—Erick-Woods Erickson

preemption

Preemption is the displacement of state law by federal laws or regulations. The supremacy clause of Article VI of the UNITED STATES CONSTITUTION provides that: "This

Constitution, and the Laws of the United States which shall be made in Pursuance thereof; and all TREATIES made, or which shall be made, under the Authority of the United States, shall be the Supreme Law of the Land; and the Judges in every State shall be bound thereby, any Thing in the Constitution or Laws of any State to the Contrary notwithstanding." Pursuant to this clause, federal laws or regulations can override state law in three ways: (1) express preemption; (2) field (or implied) preemption; and (3) conflict preemption. [*Pacific Gas & Electric Co. v. State Energy Resources Conservation & Development Comm'n*, 461 U.S. 190, 203–204 (1983).] Regardless of the type of preemption at issue, a court's analysis turns on the purpose of Congress.

The first—express preemption—exists where a federal statute explicitly provides for the displacement of state law. Thus, for example, where a federal law expressly prohibits the imposition of any additional or different requirements than those set out under the federal law, any such requirements under state law would be expressly preempted. As a result, they would have no further force or effect.

The second—field preemption—occurs where the scheme of federal regulation is so comprehensive that one can reasonably infer that Congress left no room for supplemental state regulation. Because field preemption is so sweeping, courts do not readily find it. The more comprehensive a federal statutory or regulatory scheme is, however, the more likely it is to displace any state regulations in that field, regardless of whether they conflict with the federal scheme. Moreover, to the extent that a particular area is viewed as being "national" in concern, field preemption may be more readily inferred.

The third—conflict preemption—exists either where there is an actual conflict between federal and state law or where the state law "stands as an obstacle to the accomplishment and execution of the full purposes and objectives of Congress." [*Hines v. Davidowitz*, 312 U.S. 52, 67 (1941).] Thus, for example, under the third category, courts may find that a state law is preempted if it effectively discourages conduct that a federal law specifically encourages. [See, e.g., *Nash v. Florida Industrial Comm'n*, 389 U.S. 235, 239 (1967), invalidating a state unemployment compensation law to the extent that it denied benefits to applicants because they had filed unfair labor practice charges with the NLRB.]

For more information: Tribe, Laurence H. *American Constitutional Law.* 2nd ed. Mineola, N.Y.: Foundation Press, 1989.

—Anne M. Voigts

Pregnancy Discrimination Act of 1978

The Pregnancy Discrimination Act of 1978 (PDA) amended TITLE VII OF THE CIVIL RIGHTS ACT OF 1964 in order to provide legal protections for pregnant women in their workplaces.

Unlike many European countries, prior to the PDA there was no federal law in the United States that provided clear guidelines to employers as to the legal treatment of pregnant employees in the workplace; instead, each state generated their own regulations. Such employment protections are still necessary. In recent years, more than 4,000 cases of pregnancy discrimination have been brought to the EQUAL EMPLOYMENT OPPORTUNITY COMMISSION and the states' Fair Employment Practices Agencies.

Congress passed the PDA after the Supreme Court decision of *General Electric Company v. Gilbert*, 429 U.S. 125 (1976). In this case, an employee benefit program denied women pregnancy benefits although male employees were covered for a large number of temporary disabilities. The Court stated that the plan discriminated against pregnant workers but not against women; therefore, it did not violate the requirements of Title VII, which only protected against gender discrimination. If pregnancy discrimination is not SEX DISCRIMINATION, Title VII provided no statutory protection for pregnant workers.

The PDA states that any discrimination on the basis of pregnancy, childbirth, and any related condition is sex discrimination. Courts and employers can no longer argue that pregnancy discrimination differentiates between the pregnant and the nonpregnant, in order to avoid violating the statutory protection against gender discrimination. Consequentially, employers who have disability programs for their employees cannot exclude pregnancy from the covered disabilities. The PDA did not, however, address neutral employment requirements that do not discriminate between men and women but have a disparate impact on pregnant employees.

Newport News Shipbuilding and Dry Dock Co. v. EEOC, 462 U.S. 669 (1983), is considered by some scholars to be the completion of Title VII coverage for pregnant workers. It is ironic that this was a case brought by male workers whose dependents did not receive the same benefits as female employees, because males did not have similar pregnancy disability benefits for their spouses. According to *Newport News*, the PDA requires that employers treat pregnancy-related disabilities as equivalent to nonpregnancy-related disabilities.

In 1987 the Supreme Court in *California Federal Savings and Loan v. Guerra*, 479 U.S. 272 (1987), found that Title VII of the Civil Rights Act of 1964, as amended by the PDA, does not overturn a state statute that requires employers to provide pregnancy leave and guarantee continued employment after the pregnancy. Title VII thus prevents states from discriminating against pregnant women; but it does not forbid states from providing additional legal protections. In the same year, the Supreme Court in *Wim-*

berly v. Labor and Industrial Relations Commission, 479 U.S. 511 (1987), found that the PDA does not force states to give preferential treatment to women because of pregnancy but allows states to treat them the same as temporarily disabled employees.

As currently interpreted by the Supreme Court, pregnancy discrimination (excluding fetal protection) is prevented by the PDA. It is the right of the states, however, to determine the extent to which they will expand these rights. However, while lower federal courts have decided such pregnancy-related issues as employer coverage of infertility treatments, breast-feeding in the workplace, and postnatal complications, the Supreme Court has not yet decided whether the PDA protects these "pregnancy-related" issues.

For more information: Deardorff, Michelle D. "Legitimated Inequality: Constitutional Implications of the United States Pregnancy Discrimination Act of 1978." 1 *Studia Politica: Romanian Political Science Review* 1, no. 4 (2001): 1,103–1,130. Greenberg, Judith G. "The Pregnancy Discrimination Act: Legitimating Discrimination against Pregnant Women in the Workforce." *Maine Law Review* 50 (1998): 225.

—Michelle Donaldson Deardorff

prior restraint

In constitutional terms, a prior restraint is simply any scheme that allows officials to prohibit speech before it actually takes place. Historically, this was often done through the imposition of licensing or other administrative preclearance schemes, though more recent prior restraints include injunctions under the same rubric.

Under the First Amendment, the imposition of such prepublication restraints are particularly disfavored. As the Supreme Court has observed, "[a]ny system of prior restraint of expression comes to this Court bearing a heavy presumption against its constitutional validity." [*Bantam Books, Inc. v. Sullivan,* 372 U.S. 58, 70 (1963).] That presumption, however, is not absolute, though constitutionally permissible systems of prior restraint are decided exceptions to the general rule of unconstitutionality. In *Near v. Minnesota,* 283 U.S. 697 (1931), Chief Justice HUGHES suggested three categories of exceptions: (1) where justified by national security concerns in time of war; (2) where obscene publications were at issue; and (3) where incitements to violence or revolution were involved. In current practice, prior restraints in the form of injunctions in copyright infringement and trade secret cases are also granted on occasion.

Despite these exceptions, the classic example of a prior restraint (and the courts' typical reaction to it) is set out in the Pentagon Papers case, *New York Times Co. v. United States,* 403 U.S. 713 (1971), in which the United States sought a court order prohibiting the *New York Times* and the *Washington Post* from publishing the contents of a classified study on the Vietnam policy. Although the government asserted that the publication of that study would jeopardize national security, the Court held that the government had not met the heavy burden necessary to justify such a restraint. Over time, the prior restraint doctrine has been applied in a range of different contexts. In part because of this, both courts and legal commentators have at times questioned the logic of the prior restraint doctrine's focus on timing and its continuing validity as an independent doctrine.

For more information: Blasi, Vincent. "Toward a Theory of Prior Restraint: The Central Linkage." *Minn. L. Rev.* 66 (1981): 11; Emerson, Thomas I. "The Doctrine of Prior Restraint." *Law & Contemp. Probs.* 20 (1955): 648; Jeffries, John. "Rethinking Prior Restraint." *Yale L. J.* 92 (1983): 409; Redish, Martin. "The Proper Role of the Prior Restraint Doctrine in First Amendment Theory." *Va. L. Rev.* 70 (1984): 53.

—Anne M. Voigts

prisoners, rights of

Prisoners' rights have many aspects, including prison conditions, access to courts, and CIVIL LIBERTIES. Although the federal district courts have been home to most of the action in regards to prisoners' rights, the Supreme Court has always set the tone. Until 1964, the Court gave no real avenue through which inmates could access the federal courts, but between 1964 and 1987 the Supreme Court made many important decisions regarding how states were to treat their incarcerated citizens. Recently, the Court seems to have reverted back to the so-called hands-off approach of the pre-'64 era, with assists from both Congress and the executive branch helping them along.

A 1964 unanimous per curium opinion was the first time that the Supreme Court recognized a prisoner's right to sue for violations of his constitutional rights [*Cooper v. Pate,* 378 U.S. 546 (1964)]. During the early part of this period, the Court tended to leave decisions on prison conditions to the lower courts, focusing instead on civil liberties.

The Court's first full opinion of such a matter came a few years later in *Johnson v. Avery,* 393 U.S. 483 (1969), where the Court upheld the right of an inmate "writ-writer" to act as a lawyer for other inmates if a state did not provide other access to legal help. The Court continued to uphold a prisoner's constitutional rights allowing a Buddhist inmate access to the prison chapel [*Cruz v. Beto,* 405 U.S. 319 (1972)], preventing prison officials from censoring outgoing mail [*Procunier v. Martinez,* 416 U.S. 396 (1974)], granting due process rights in administrative actions [*Wolf v. McDonnell,* 418 U.S. 539 (1974)], and limiting the use of punitive segregation cells to 30 days [*Hutto v. Finney,* 437 U.S. 678 (1978)].

The tide began to turn in *Bell v. Wolfish,* 441 U.S. 520 (1979), when the court upheld the use of double celling to deal with overcrowding, limited prisoner's access to outside books and other packages, allowed prison officials to search cells without inmates observing, and permitted strip searches after contact visits. The real change came after *Turner v. Shafley,* 41 Cr.L. 3239 (1987). In a case about inmates corresponding with other inmates, the Court held that the needs of the prison administration superceded that of an individual prisoner's constitutional rights and that any prison regulation that was reasonably related to a legitimate penological interest would be upheld. Hereafter, the Court would employ the RATIONAL BASIS test to determine the constitutionality of prison rules.

About this time, the Court also began to limit how the lower courts dealt with prison conditions. By 1984, 24 percent of the nation's prisons were under some form of federal court rule including at least one in 43 different states. In *Wilson v. Seiter,* 501 U.S. 294 (1991), the Court held that in order to prove that general conditions of confinement were in violation of the Eighth Amendment, the inmate needed to show deliberate indifference on the part of prison administrators and prove that they acted wantonly in allowing the conditions to persist. This ended consistent rulings by the lower courts that a showing of totality of adverse conditions was all that was needed.

The Prison Litigation Reform Act of 1995 and the Anti-Terrorism and Effective Death Penalty Act of 1995 have limited the Court's potential involvement in inmate litigation. The PLRA limits inmates' access to courts generally but also limits judicial involvement in prison administration. In *U.S. v. French,* 000 U.S. 99-224 (2000), the Court held that the act did not violate SEPARATION OF POWERS and that courts could be forced to respond to state requests for the lifting of supervision. The AEDPA makes it more difficult for prisoners to gain habeas corpus relief in federal courts by limiting the federal courts' ability to overturn state rulings.

For the time being, it would seem that all three branches of government have decided to limit prisoners' access to federal courts, and the Supreme Court itself has essentially removed itself from the issue. If prison populations continue to grow and sentences continue to lengthen, problems may arise that require the Court to step back into the fold. For now, it seems, a prisoner's only real option for relief resides in the state courts.

For more information: Anderson, James, and Laronistine Dyson. *Legal Rights of Prisoners: Cases and Comments.* Lanham, Md.: United Press of America, 2001; Cripe, C. A. *Legal Aspects of Corrections Management.* Gaithersburg, Md.: Aspen Publication, 1997; DiIulio, John J., Jr., ed. *Courts, Corrections and the Constitution.* New York: Oxford University Press, 1990; Fliter, John. *Prisoner's Rights: The Supreme Court and Evolving Standards of Decency.* Westport, Conn.: Greenwood Press, 2001; Mushlin, Michael, and Donald Kramer, eds. *Rights of Prisoners.* 3rd ed. St. Paul, Minn.: Thomson West, 2002; Palmer, John. *Constitutional Rights of Prisoners.* 7th ed. Cincinnati, Ohio: Anderson, 2003; Smith, C. E. *Law and Contemporary Corrections.* Belmont, Calif.: Wadsworth Publishing, 2000.

—Eric J. Williams

privacy, right to

The right to privacy is the quintessential modern right. Often characterized simply as "the right to be let alone," analysis of the nature and extent of one's right to privacy has figured prominently in political debate, scholarly writings, and judicial decisions; nonetheless, the precise source and contour of this fundamental constitutional right remain elusive.

In 1890 two Boston attorneys, Samuel D. Warren and Louis D. BRANDEIS, wrote what still stands as the most influential essay on privacy and arguably the most famous law review article ever published. "The Right to Privacy" argued that the law needed to adapt to social changes, primarily technological ones, that were undermining one's "right to be let alone," which Warren and Brandeis broadened by the concept of "an inviolate personality." They argued that preventing unwarranted intrusion into one's personal life was essential given increases in social and technological complexity.

In 1928 Brandeis, now a justice of the United States Supreme Court, having been appointed to the Court by President Woodrow Wilson in 1916, authored one of the most influential dissents in the history of the Court in the case of *Olmstead v. United States,* 277 U.S. 438 (1928). In *Olmstead,* the Court, by a vote of 5 to 4, ruled that governmental WIRETAPPING of telephone conversations did not violate the Fourth Amendment's protection against unreasonable searches and seizures since no physical intrusion of the home occurred; moreover, in the opinion of Chief Justice William Howard TAFT, telephone conversations were not tangible property that could be seized improperly.

In his dissent, which reads like the words of a prophet, Brandeis countered, "The progress of science in furnishing the government with means of espionage is not likely to stop with wiretapping. Ways may some day be developed by which the government, without removing papers from secret drawers, can reproduce them in court. . . . Can it be that the Constitution affords no protection against such invasions of individual security?" (277 U.S. 438, 474). Brandeis's warning went unheeded in *Olmstead;* however, four decades later, in KATZ V. UNITED STATES, 389 U.S. 347 (1967), the Court overruled Olmstead and essentially adopted Brandeis's point of view.

The seminal ruling on privacy occurred two years before *Katz* in GRISWOLD V. CONNECTICUT, 381 U.S. 479 (1965), where the Court discovered a right to "marital privacy," a right considered older than the BILL OF RIGHTS itself in the opinion of Justice William O. DOUGLAS. Douglas found constitutional sanction for privacy and personal autonomy in the marital relationship in several amendments—First, Third, Fourth, Fifth, Ninth, and Fourteenth. *Griswold* became the pivotal PRECEDENT for the Court's extension of privacy in the next decade, particularly in the form of intellectual and associational freedom and reproductive autonomy in the cases of *Stanley v. Georgia,* 394 U.S. 557 (1969), EISENSTADT V. BAIRD, 405 U.S. 438 (1972), and ROE V. WADE, 410 U.S. 113 (1973).

The Supreme Court's discovery and conception of the fundamental, constitutional right to privacy, especially beyond the confines of the Fourth and Fifth Amendments and related criminal justice concerns, signaled a new and often controversial era in the debate over the nature and extent of fundamental UNENUMERATED RIGHTS. What the Court has done in its development of the modern right to privacy is to advance a jurisprudence of individual liberty and personal autonomy that is based strongly on the Court's understanding of inherent human dignity, as witnessed in the 2003 decision in LAWRENCE V. TEXAS, where the Court overruled its controversial 1986 decision in the Georgia antisodomy case of BOWERS V. HARDWICK, 478 U.S. 186 (1986). The Court conceives of privacy as not simply an area of one's life where one seeks to avoid the unwanted gaze of the government or society; more important is the fact that the Court recognizes that in private, intimate associations one seeks to define oneself with dignity.

For more information: Garrow, David J. *Liberty and Sexuality: The Right to Privacy and the Making of* Roe v. Wade. New York: Macmillan, 1994; Rosen, Jeffrey. *The Unwanted Gaze.* New York: Vintage Books, 2001.

—Stephen K. Shaw
—Christina Wampler

Prize Cases, 2 Black 635, 17 L.Ed. 459 (1862)

In the *Prize Cases,* the Supreme Court upheld President Lincoln's power to blockade Southern ports before Congress declared hostilities or authorized the action. In the case the Court held that the president has WAR POWERS to defend the nation even without a congressional declaration of war.

Four ships named the *Amy Warwick,* the *Crenshaw,* the *Hiawatha,* and the *Brilliante* were captured by the U.S. Navy as they made for Southern ports after the outbreak of the Civil War. The ships were seized pursuant to President Lincoln's April 1861 order blockading Southern ports. Although seven Southern states seceded in March 1861, Congress did not declare hostilities or approve the blockade until late summer. The ships' owners challenged the seizure claiming that President Lincoln had exceeded his executive authority. Justice Robert Grier wrote the opinion for a divided Court holding that the Constitution and acts of Congress had authorized the president to act.

Justice Grier acknowledged that the law of nations requires that a war exist before blockades may be employed. Article I of the Constitution grants the power to declare war to Congress alone. Under the Constitution the president "has no power to initiate or declare war against a foreign nation or domestic state." However, in 1795 and in 1807 Congress had authorized the president to "use the military and navy forces of the United States in case of invasion by foreign nations, and to suppress insurrection against the government of a State or the United States." While the Constitution only allows Congress to initiate war, the president's duty to see that the laws are faithfully executed requires him to defend the nation when it is attacked.

The question remaining, therefore, was whether the Southern insurrection arose to the level of a war such that it would justify instituting a naval blockade. The Court defined war as the "state in which a nation prosecutes its right by force," but it held that a war need not always be between independent sovereign states. Insurrections may, at times, rise to the level of war. If an insurgent force declares its independence from the sovereign or holds property in hostility to the sovereign a war exists, according to the Court. Justice Grier writes that even when a war is not declared, the Court is bound to take judicial notice of a civil war "when the regular course of justice is interrupted by revolt."

Four justices dissented from the Court's decision in an opinion written by Justice Nelson. The dissenters argued that because a rebellion took place in Massachusetts during the Constitutional Convention the framers understood the danger and expressly empowered Congress to respond to that danger. Justice Nelson argues that the reading of the 1795 and 1807 laws to grant the president war powers was "simply a monstrous exaggeration." According to the dissent the president has no power "to declare war or to recognize its existence within the meaning of the law of nations."

For more information: O'Brien, David. *Constitutional Law and Politics: Volume 1.* 5th ed. W. W. Norton: New York, 2003.

—Jeffrey Davis

procedural due process

Procedural due process is concerned with providing fair and impartial processes. It focuses on the way in which laws are applied, ensuring that the process of implementing policy will not be irregular, arbitrary, or unreasonable.

The concept of due process of law is established through both the Fifth and Fourteenth Amendments. The Fifth Amendment states that no person shall be "deprived of life, liberty, or property, without due process of law" and the Fourteenth Amendment reinforces this stating: "nor shall any State deprive any person of life, liberty, or property, without due process of law; nor deny to any person within its jurisdiction the equal protection of the law." The courts generally distinguish between two types of due process, procedural and substantive. SUBSTANTIVE DUE PROCESS refers to the constitutionality of the law or policy itself. The more conventional understanding of due process, however, refers to procedural regularity or fairness and is specifically identified as procedural due process. The accepted understanding of due process is that the Constitution does not prevent the government from taking away "life, liberty, or property" but does guarantee a fundamental fairness in the way in which the government acts to deprive a citizen of these things.

Procedural due process requires that the affected person receive all the process that is due to them. As such, due process is understood to deal in degrees of protection, meaning that the government is generally expected to employ more extensive procedures when it seeks to impose the death penalty than when it is imposing a lesser punishment. This variation exists because how much process is due depends on several factors. These factors may include the importance of the affected interest (such as life v. property), the risk of an erroneous decision, and the cost of the procedures to be used. Regardless of what level of process the government is expected to employ, the key factor remains the constitutionality by which governmental policy is implemented.

Procedural due process is now considered applicable to both national and state governments. This was not always the case, however. Until the late 20th century the Court held the due process clause as only a general guarantee of procedural fairness at the state level of the legal process. Under early rulings of the Court, such as in HURTADO V. CALIFORNIA, ADAMSON V. CALIFORNIA, and ROCHIN V. CALIFORNIA, the BILL OF RIGHTS only limited the national government while states were merely required to uphold a fundamental fairness on a case by case basis, designated as the "fundamental fairness standard."

The shift in the application of the Bill of Rights to both state and federal government came through the single dissenter in the original *Hurtado* case, Justice John HARLAN, Sr. Justice Harlan's reading of the due process clause put forth the idea that there should be a total INCORPORATION of the personal liberties guaranteed in the first eight amendments into the Fourteenth Amendment. This would make the due process clause applicable to the states as well as the federal government. Justice Hugo BLACK later took up this idea, which came to be known as total incorporation. Although Justice Black was not able to persuade a majority to uphold the idea of total incorporation, his advancement of the idea led to the strategy of selective incorporation.

Selective incorporation states that selective clauses of the Bill of Rights are to be held binding for the states as they are required by fundamental fairness. Although the Court began the groundwork for the development of selective incorporation in early cases such as *Wolf v. Colorado,* in 1949, it was not until the 1960s that the Court fully embraced the idea of federalizing the state criminal procedure through the selective incorporation of the Bill of Rights. *MAPP V. OHIO*, in 1961, marked the beginning of this process. After this ruling, which overturned *Wolf v. Colorado* by applying the EXCLUSIONARY RULE to states, the Court overturned several more cases. These rulings made additional provision of the Bill of Rights necessary to fundamental fairness and therefore incorporated into due process, limiting the states along with the federal government. The idea of selective incorporation now provides the primary mechanism for which the courts have applied most of the guarantees in the Bill of the Rights to the states as well as the national government.

Due process is also generally accepted as applying to both civil and criminal trials. In a civil case the defendant faces possible deprivation of wealth through a money judgment or loss of personal liberty through an injunctive decree. This entitles defendants in civil trials to procedural due process essentials such as a fair and orderly hearing before an unbiased judge. Criminal trials are also guaranteed the procedural fairness, as defendants face loss of liberty or even life. The due process clause has proved less significant in determining the procedures required in criminal cases than civil cases, however, because the Constitution contains a number of provisions explicitly designed to limit the powers of the government in criminal procedure.

For more information: Orth, John. *Due Process of Law: A Brief History.* Lawrence: University Press of Kansas, 2003; Rotunda, Ronald D. *Treatise on Constitutional Law: Substance and Procedure.* 3rd ed. Vol. III. St. Paul, Minn.: West Group, 1999.

public forum

The U.S. Supreme Court has declared that the free speech clause of the First Amendment to the U.S. Constitution includes a "public forum doctrine," which allows people to use public property for free speech activities. This doctrine has its origin in the historical fact that before the existence of modern mass media, citizens would meet and engage in public discussion on the streets, sidewalks, and park-like areas of town squares. People would read the latest news posted on a wall or in a newspaper, share other news by word-of-mouth, and debate the issues involved in the news.

According to the public forum doctrine, all government-owned (public-owned) property can be divided into three types. First, a "traditional public forum" is government property that has historically been used for public gatherings and discussions. The Supreme Court regularly lists parks, streets, and sidewalks as public forums. Although the Court has never declared that those are the only types of government property that are traditional public forums, the Court has never declared that any other government property meets the definition of a traditional public forum. In other words, whether other types of property can be considered a traditional public forum is an open question.

The second type of government property is a "designated public forum." This occurs when government intentionally sets aside some type of government property for use as a public forum. For example, a bulletin board, a room, or an atrium might be designated for use by the public as a forum.

The third and final type of government property is all other government property; that is, property that is neither a traditional public forum nor a designated public forum is simply not a public forum. For example, office space in government buildings is not a public forum while in use by government workers; neither are courtrooms or legislative assemblies while in session, as well as public school classrooms during classtime. As another example, in the Court's most recent public forum case titled INTERNATIONAL SOCIETY FOR KRISHNA CONSCIOUSNESS (ISKCON) v. LEE, 505 U.S. 672 (1992), the Court declared that publicly owned airport terminals are not public forums.

Under the public forum doctrine, the type of speech regulations the First Amendment allows to regulate government property depends on whether the property is a traditional or designated public forum, or is not a public forum. If a speech regulation involves a traditional public forum, the government must show a "compelling" justification for any limits placed on free speech activities within that forum.

Also, the government may not discriminate on the basis of the subject matter of the speech or the viewpoint of the speaker. As a practical matter, this means few restrictions may be placed on speech in a traditional public forum, other than regulations to maintain public safety and order, known as "time, place, and manner" restrictions. For example, a person driving a car at 3:00 A.M. in a residential neighborhood using an electronic megaphone to ask people to support a particular presidential candidate is using a

public street, but the government may nevertheless prohibit even POLITICAL SPEECH done in this manner and at this time and place.

If the government designates property to be used as a public forum, the government again must show a "compelling" reason for limiting free speech and may enact time, place, and manner restrictions. In addition, the government may enact regulations to preserve the nature of the forum, even including limiting the subject matter of the speech if necessary, but government still may not discriminate against any single viewpoint among the topics it allows for discussion. For example, if government creates a bulletin board for use as a public forum, a regulation can restrict the size and number of flyers any one person or group may post but may not prohibit only Democrats or only pro-environment groups from posting flyers. Or, if a public school district generally opens a classroom for meetings by after-school student groups, the school district may restrict the number of people that may be in the room according to the fire code, but the government may not prohibit only a religious group or only a gay rights group from using the room. However, if government sponsors a public debate on the death penalty, the government may prohibit a person from speaking who wants to discuss abortion and taxes, because that is not the designated purpose of the forum.

Finally, in government property that is not a public forum, the government can enact any restrictions on speech as long as those restrictions are "reasonable." Generally this means that government acting as a property manager may restrict any speech activities that are incompatible with the government property functioning as its primary use. In other words, government has broad leeway to regulate property that is not a public forum for its intended use as something *other than* a forum for public discussion.

The Court's most recent description of the public forum doctrine in *ISKCON* has led many commentators as well as the dissenting justices in the *ISKCON* case to criticize the Court's narrowing of the definition of traditional public forums to seemingly include nothing other than parks, streets, and sidewalks.

Critics argue that in a modern era where town squares increasingly no longer either exist or serve as a primary meeting place for public discussion, other types of government property (such as airport terminals or government-leased shopping malls) must be recognized as "traditional" public forums to be used by people to directly confront a mass audience in person. Otherwise, only those individuals or groups who can afford the use of the mass media will be able to communicate their ideas directly to a large audience, a concept that runs contrary to the basic purpose of the free speech clause: promoting robust public discourse. For this reason, several state supreme courts have interpreted the free speech provisions of their respective state

Constitutions as creating state public forum doctrines more protective of free speech than the federal public forum doctrine. For example, a few state supreme courts have decided that even some *privately-owned* property within their states, such as large indoor shopping malls, are public forums to a limited degree.

For more information: Volokh, Eugene. *The First Amendment: Problems, Cases and Policy Arguments.* New York: Foundation Press, 2001.

—Rick A. Swanson

public trial

In the United States, the right of a defendant to have a public trial is guaranteed by the Sixth Amendment to the Constitution. It states that: "the accused shall enjoy the right to a speedy and public trial. . . ."

The right to a public trial is fundamental to the judicial system for a number of reasons, namely, it acts as a safeguard against any attempts to employ our judicial system as a vessel of persecution. It publicly ensures that the defendant is given a fair, accurate, and unbiased trial. Further, it discourages the practice of perjury, any misconduct on part of the participants, i.e., impartiality of judges or flagrantly unjust behavior on the part of the prosecution, etc., and guarantees that decisions are not based on secret bias or partiality. Many argue that it also provides a therapeutic value to the community, which is needed after certain types of criminal offenses.

The use of public trials is not original to the birth of the United States but has its roots in English common law. General distrust of secret trials dates back to the Spanish Inquisition, the English Court of State Chamber, and the monarchy's overuse and abuse of the "lettre de cachet." It was widely felt that the use of secret trials was a threat to personal liberty, and that they led to the possibility of abuse of power by the judiciary.

In the United States, the right to public trial first appeared in a state constitution in 1776. The right to a public trial became guaranteed with the adoption of the BILL OF RIGHTS and subsequently the Sixth Amendment in 1791. Today almost all states require that a trial be public by constitution, statute, or judicial decision. The right is protected by the due process clause and is so universal in the United States that the Supreme Court has not many cases dealing with the issue.

The Sixth Amendment provides a right guaranteed to protect the defendant. It may be waived if strict conditions are met. The trial may be closed to the public if the defendant can give evidence that a public trial would compromise the integrity, impartiality, or fairness of the trial. The prosecution can also move that a case be closed to the public if they are able to meet the same strict requirements. In *Waller v. Georgia* (1984), the Court ruled that the Sixth Amendment rights of the defendant were compromised by closing the seven days of proceedings to protect two hours of testimony protecting the identity of people whose phone conversations were recorded. Thus, public access to trials is rarely waived.

Recently, the growth in press coverage of court cases has caused the balance between First and Sixth Amendment rights to be under constant scrutiny. The First Amendment protects the access to a trial by the public and the press. However, arguments are made that the increasing press coverage of trials is affecting the integrity of trials and leading to decisions that are more political and less judicial. For example, the O. J. Simpson trial was the most watched event in history; together with the rise in court television programming many questions regarding the defendant's rights to a fair and impartial trial have been raised. Opponents of broadcasting trials claim it is contaminating the jury pool, setting unrealistic court settings as the expected norm, and making decisions that are based on sensation rather than judicial principles. However, proponents argue that it raises the public's confidence in the judicial process, it puts confidence in the judicial system, and it makes the understanding of the justice system more accessible.

For more information: Heller, Francis H. *The Sixth Amendment to the Constitution of the United States.* New York: Greenwood Press, 1969; Stuckey, Gilbert B. *Procedures in the Justice System.* New York: Macmillan, 1991.

—Lindsay B. Zoeller

punitive damages

Punitive damages occur as a result of someone committing a tort against another. A tort is committed when a private individual or public entity breaches a legal duty which results in harm to another individual. In most circumstances, a tort claim is filed when someone intentionally injures another person, or, through negligence, allows someone to be harmed (physically, emotionally, or financially). When such events occur, individuals file a tort claim by suing for compensation.

The American tort system allows individuals to sue for two separate types of damages. Plaintiffs can sue for compensatory damages (sometimes referred to as actual damages) and sometimes sue for additional punitive damages (sometimes referred to as exemplary damages). Compensatory damages compensate victims for losses that can be readily proven, such as property damage, hospital bills, and pain and suffering. Punitive damages are awards given in excess of compensatory damages. They are intended to punish individuals and businesses that act negligently, and therefore they serve as a deterrent against future misconduct.

It is generally accepted by legal and political communities that victims of torts deserve to be fully compensated by the liable party through compensatory damages. However, there is less of a consensus about the merits of punitive damages. Punitive damages are more controversial because they compensate individuals beyond the actual damages incurred.

Before the 1970s, punitive damages were only awarded for "intentional torts." These were torts where the defendant intentionally harmed another individual. Eventually, the courts lowered the standard to "gross negligence." Under this standard, plaintiffs did not have to prove a tort was intentionally committed; they only had to show that defendants acted without regard for others. In the 1970s the courts also made it easier for someone to sue for punitive damages by liberalizing STANDING requirements. Standing is a legal term describing whether a person even has a right to bring a case to court. When these two legal standards were lowered, the number of tort filings began to increase. Although a variety of studies have shown that punitive damage awards are still rare, the sizes of the damage awards are growing significantly.

Punitive damages have a legitimate function. They are designed to protect consumers from the harmful effects of negligent individuals and businesses. By maintaining sufficiently large punitive damage awards, individuals and businesses consider the costs of building products or taking actions that may harm others. Therefore, punitive damages are not only intended to punish intentional and negligent behavior but they also act as a deterrent against future deviant behavior.

Unfortunately, the increase in punitive damage awards has also created a host of negative secondary effects. Broadly categorized, large punitive damages create an incentive for individuals to sue wealthy defendants, such as corporations, hospitals, and insurance companies, in hopes of winning large legal judgments. The threat of large punitive damages also scares people away from engaging in specific behaviors that are beneficial to society.

Large punitive damages create a "lottery mentality" toward lawsuits. Because of the contingency fee system (a system where lawyers are not paid unless they win in court), clients can seek punitive damages where the probability of success is very low. Because there are no costs to the plaintiffs, there is little reason not to file a lawsuit that has a little chance of succeeding. However, the allure of a huge settlement attracts plaintiffs, despite the low probability of winning.

Large punitive damages also create an "in terrorem" effect. The possibility of massive punitive damage awards scares defendants into paying out-of-court settlements. Many businesses adopt the rationale that it is better to pay a relatively small damage settlement, even if the facts of the case do not indicate culpability, than to take the risk of paying out a massive court-ordered settlement. The end result is that many defendants are paying damages in cases where they were not negligent.

Large punitive damage awards also hurt consumers. When large punitive damages are paid by corporations, doctors, and businesses, those costs are passed along to consumers. If a car company must pay large damages, it will raise the price of cars to recoup the losses. When a doctor is sued for malpractice, he must pay higher insurance premiums. In turn, the doctor must charge his patients more to pay for the insurance.

In addition to paying higher prices for goods and services, consumers also suffer a loss of available products on the market. Anecdotal evidence suggests that products such as warning devices for Jacuzzis, vaccines, ambulance services, waste cleanup, and sports safety devices have been removed from the market due to the fear of litigation costs.

Large punitive damage awards also deter innovation. A study of the American pharmaceutical industry reveals that after some high profile CLASS ACTION lawsuits the number of companies doing contraception research fell from eight to two. Furthermore, many research companies have abandoned clinical trials of AIDS vaccines due to the fear of litigation.

Because punitive damages most commonly fall upon the producers of products, doctors, or insurance companies which protect corporations and hospitals, allied in favor of tort reforms is a coalition of small business, industry, medical, insurance, and corporate interests. In opposition to tort reform measures have been consumer activists and trial lawyers. Consumer activists firmly believe the only way to rein in corporations that produce dangerous products is to threaten them with massive punitive damage awards.

Trial lawyers oppose tort reforms because punitive damages are a source of their income. A limitation of punitive damages will directly limit the amount of income a plaintiff lawyer can earn. Politically, the Republican Party has been more sympathetic to the interests in support of tort reform and therefore most often responsible for introducing tort reform legislation. In general, the Democratic Party has been more sympathetic to the consumer protection and trial lawyer groups opposed to tort reform.

By a wide margin, the most popular way to limit the impact of punitive damages has been to cap, or limit, the size of punitive damage awards. Fourteen states have enacted laws that limit the amount of punitive damages a jury may award—usually about $500,000 or three times the compensatory damages.

The federal courts have also become involved in punitive damages policy. Congress has never enacted comprehensive punitive damage limits. However, in a landmark 1996 case, *BMW of North America, Inc. v. Gore,* 116 S. Ct. 1589, the United States Supreme Court ruled that "grossly excessive" punitive damage awards violate the due process clause. In the Gore case, Dr. Ira Gore purchased a new BMW automobile and later discovered the car had been repainted without his knowledge. He sued. The jury awarded $4,000 in compensatory damages and $4 million in punitive damages. The Court noted that in a fair legal system all potential defendants should know what possible punishments may be imposed. Continuing, they argued that large damage awards were arbitrary and amounted to an unconstitutional seizure of property. In the future, the Court required that all courts consider three criteria when awarding damages—the "reprehensibility" of the defendant's conduct, the ratio between compensatory and punitive damages, and what existing statutory penalties would be imposed for similar misconduct.

More recently, the court affirmed its decision in *BMW v. Gore.* In *State Farm Mutual Automobile Insurance Co. v. Campbell* (Case 538 U.S. 408 [2003]), the court rejected a $145 million punitive damage award that was added to a $1 million actual damage award. The court argued that a punitive damage award 145 times larger than the compensatory damage award violated the principles set forth in *BMW v. Gore.* However, in the *State Farm* case, the Court went further by noting that trial courts should not allow juries to know the wealth of the defendant. In many cases, juries levy larger damages against wealthier defendants. The Court suggested that punitive damages should not be a function of the wealth of the defendant.

For more information: Daniels, Stephen, and Joanne Martin. *Civil Juries and the Politics of Tort Reform.* Evanston, Ill.: Northwestern University Press, 1995; Posner, Richard. *Economic Analysis of Law.* Boston: Little, Brown, 1973.

—Mathew Manweller

pure speech

Pure speech is a type of expression that takes the form of the written or spoken word. It does not include any kind of expressive actions.

Pure speech includes verbal expression such as speeches and public addresses, as well as published forms of communication, such as books, editorials, pamphlets, and letters. When drafting the BILL OF RIGHTS, James Madison was particularly concerned with this type of speech. He was especially interested in making sure that political and social protests, which in those days usually took the form of speeches and publications, were protected. This is why political and social speech is customarily granted more protection under the First Amendment than other types of speech, such as COMMERCIAL SPEECH, obscenity, or libel.

Pure speech is different from another popular form of expression now protected under the First Amendment, SYMBOLIC SPEECH. While pure speech pertains to words, symbolic speech is different in that it communicates through actions. Symbolic speech includes any conduct or imagery used with the intent of expressing some belief or viewpoint. One important case in defining the level of protection that pure speech is given actually dealt with the issue of symbolic speech. In *TINKER V. DES MOINES,* 393 U.S. 503 (1969), five high school students participated in a Vietnam War protest by wearing black armbands to school. They were suspended. They and their parents sued on the grounds that the armbands were a form of symbolic speech. They argued that the school denied them their First Amendment right to free speech by not allowing symbolic armbands that caused no disruption of any kind. The Court majority ruled that the students' suspensions did violate their right to free expression.

Writing for a majority, Justice FORTAS observed that, "Our problem involves direct, primary First Amendment rights akin to "pure speech." This case is important for recognizing the elevated protection given to pure speech. By saying that the students' act of symbolic speech—wearing armbands—was a type of expression that is akin to pure speech and therefore needed to be protected, the Court is recognizing that pure speech is the fundamental First Amendment right that must be guaranteed above other forms of expression.

A more controversial form of symbolic conduct is FLAG BURNING. The Supreme Court has repeatedly held, in cases such as *TEXAS V. JOHNSON,* 491 U.S. 397 (1989), and then later in *UNITED STATES V. EICHMAN,* 496 U.S. 310 (1990), that people have a constitutional right to express themselves by desecrating the American flag. Pure speech, however, is generally more protected than symbolic speech because the founders viewed pure speech as the most critical form of expression, and most needing protection.

Another form of speech differentiated from pure speech is commercial speech, commonly known as advertising. Its main purpose is not to relay a political or social message but rather to sell whatever product or service it is advertising. Although courts have acknowledged that this type of speech is protected under the First Amendment, they have generally allowed more regulation by the government in this area than to other types of speech, like pure speech, for a variety of reasons. This type of expression is intricately related to the area of commerce and so is an area over which governments have constitutional authority to regulate. Governments have a substantial interest in regulating commercial speech to protect consumers against deceptive or false advertisements. Therefore commercial speech is not accorded the same high standard of protection under the First Amendment as is pure speech.

New issues keep this area of law interesting. For example, in *DVD Copy Control Association Inc. v. Andrew Bunner,* No. 03 C.D.O.S. 7684, a 2003 case, the California Supreme Court ruled that Web sites posting certain types of computer code to reveal trade secrets do not enjoy pure speech protection under the First Amendment. The Court held that because this issue deals with commerce speech, restrictions can be placed on what is permitted to be posted on Web sites.

For more information: Epstein, Lee, and Thomas G. Walker. *Constitutional Law for a Changing America: Rights, Liberties, and Justice.* 4th ed. Washington, D.C.: CQ Press, 2001; First Amendment Center. Available online. URL: http://www.firstamendmentcenter.org. Downloaded November 22, 2003; Lafferty, Shannon. "A Win for Computer Code Protection; Trade Secrets Trump the First Amendment, a State High Court Rules." *National Law Journal* 200 (September 2003): 12; Lambert, Adam S. "Campus Law." *Association for the Promotion of Campus Activities* (August 2001). Available online. URL: http://www.apca.com/082001.html#pure_speech>. Downloaded May 18, 2004.

—Jamie Goetz

R

racial discrimination

Racial discrimination occurs when unequal or unfair treatment is provided to a person or group of people on the basis of their race.

Under the Fourteenth Amendment of the U.S. Constitution, such discrimination is unconstitutional when engaged in by the federal government or by a state, or by an individual or organization on behalf of a state (e.g.: by the police). Instances of private racial discrimination (racial discrimination by a private employer, for example) are dealt with separately, under TITLE VII OF THE CIVIL RIGHTS ACT OF 1964. The Supreme Court has addressed issues of racial discrimination on a number of occasions, including in the areas of education, housing, and employment.

The Supreme Court plays an important role in protecting against instances of racial discrimination engaged in by governmental actors (both state and federal). The Supreme Court analyzes such incidents of racial discrimination using the due process clause of the Fifth Amendment and the EQUAL PROTECTION CLAUSE of the Fourteenth Amendment. The Fifth Amendment applies to the federal government and states in part that ". . . no person shall . . . be deprived of life, liberty, or property, without due process of law. . . ." The equal protection clause of the Fourteenth Amendment applies to the states, and provides that ". . . [n]o state shall . . . deny to any person within its jurisdiction the equal protection of the laws." Both the Thirteenth Amendment (prohibiting slavery) and the Fifteenth Amendment (prohibiting discrimination in the right to vote) have also played key roles in restraining governmental discrimination.

Under the equal protection clause, the primary means by which racial discrimination is constrained by the Supreme Court, developed legal doctrine provides that instances of racial discrimination by the government can only be permitted if the government is able to meet the STRICT SCRUTINY test, developed by the Court in KOREMATSU V. UNITED STATES, 323 U.S. 214 (1944). Strict scrutiny provides that discrimination on the basis of race is unconstitutional unless there is an overwhelming governmental reason (a "compelling" reason, in legal terms) for such discrimination.

The Court began to explicitly treat instances of classification based on race as "suspect" classifications requiring the strict scrutiny referenced above during the mid-20th century. In *Korematsu,* the Supreme Court was asked to determine the constitutionality of an executive order issued by President Roosevelt, preventing persons of Japanese ancestry from certain West Coast areas. While the Supreme Court upheld the order, Justice BLACK, writing for the majority, noted that "[a]ll legal restrictions which curtail the CIVIL RIGHTS of a single racial group are immediately suspect . . . [C]ourts must subject them to the most rigid scrutiny."

Historically, the Supreme Court has permitted instances of racial discrimination. The Supreme Court in *PLESSY V. FERGUSON,* 163 U.S. 537 (1896), for example, addressed the issue of racial discrimination occurring in the form of racial segregation (forced physical separation of races) and articulated the now MOOT principle of separate but equal. In this case, the Supreme Court upheld a Louisiana statute which made it illegal for African Americans to ride in the same train car as whites. Despite a strident dissent in which Justice HARLAN stated that "[o]ur Constitution is color-blind," the Court's decision in *Plessy* confirmed that racial discrimination in the form of segregation was permissible if based on the established customs and traditions of the people of the state.

The doctrine of separate but equal established in *Plessy* was ultimately overruled by the Court in its famous decision *BROWN V. BOARD OF EDUCATION,* 347 U.S. 483 (1954). In this case the Court faced the issue of racial discrimination in the form of racial segregation in education. The Court considered whether a state law that required segregation in public schools solely on the basis of race was unconstitutional, even where tangible factors may be equal between segregated schools. Looking at the effect of segregation on public education, the Court determined that separate was not equal, and that the impact of a segregated education would impact children for life. *Brown* did not end racial discrimination, however. In the aftermath of *Brown,* many states and local communities used every means available to avoid desegregating public schools. Racial discrimination continued (and does to this day) in other areas, including employment and housing.

Issues of racial discrimination continue to come before the Supreme Court, including those within the context of education. AFFIRMATIVE ACTION has been one of the more divisive racial discrimination issues facing the contemporary Supreme Court. First coined by President Johnson in Executive Order 11246, requiring federal contractors to take "affirmative action" to ensure that no employers were discriminated against in hiring or during the course of their employment on the basis of race, affirmative action programs have been instituted around the country in an effort to compensate for a history of racial discrimination.

Most recently, in *GRATZ V. BOLLINGER,* the Supreme Court confronted an affirmative action admissions policy to the undergraduate program and the law school at the University of Michigan. The Court in this instance ruled that the undergraduate admissions program violated the equal protection clause of the Fourteenth Amendment, while the law school admissions policy was permissible. Although the details of the Court's decision in this matter are beyond the scope of this encyclopedic entry, it is generally important to note that the Court continues to confront issues of racial discrimination, and that the Court and the country itself continue to be divided over the issue of appropriate contemporary treatment of instances where individuals are treated differently on the basis of race.

For more information: Davis, Abraham L., and Barbara Luck Graham. *The Supreme Court, Race and Civil Rights.* Thousand Oaks, Calif.: Sage, 1995.

—Amy P. Wilson

Racketeer Influenced and Corrupt Organizations Act (RICO)

The Racketeer Influenced and Corrupt Organizations Act, widely known as RICO, was enacted into law as TITLE IX of the Organized Crime Act of 1970. RICO was enacted to address the problems of organized crime, although the law has been applied more broadly.

RICO came out of hearings headed by Arkansas Senator John L. McClellan, highlighting the difficulties that law enforcement agencies faced trying to prosecute organized crime organizations. RICO is a far-reaching statute. It prohibits *investing* in racketeering activities, *acquiring* or maintaining an interest in such an enterprise by means of racketeering activity, using a pattern of racketeering activity to *conduct* an enterprise, and *conspiring* to do any of those three things. The statute defines a pattern of racketeering activity as the commission of at least two listed "predicate acts" within a 10-year period. The predicate acts include various federal crimes such as fraud and money laundering. Notably, the list also includes mail and wire fraud. Those acts largely account for the expansive and contested uses of RICO. The statute provides substantial criminal penalties, up to 20 years in prison for each count. The statute also provides powerful civil penalties, including forfeiture of property and private rights of action for treble damages and attorneys's fees.

RICO contains unusually broad language, particularly concerning "racketeering." As three dissenting members of Congress pointed out in 1970: "In a criminal statute where the term 'organized crime' is an operative definition, it is not defined." The reach of the statute has been controversial ever since. Critics argue that RICO has been applied far afield from its original intent. Supporters of the statute, including a former Senate staff member who drafted the bill, maintain that it was always intended to reach beyond the images of the Mafia that mark the legislative history.

RICO has been used successfully against organized crime. Leaders of major crime families in New England, Philadelphia, and Kansas City received life sentences in RICO prosecutions. The DEPARTMENT OF JUSTICE used RICO to take control of the Fulton Fish Market in New York City and to force organizational reforms in the Teamsters Union.

RICO has also become a powerful tool in white-collar cases that have nothing to do with traditional organized crime. That expansion is epitomized by federal prosecutor Rudolph Giuliani's controversial criminal RICO complaint against the brokerage firm Drexel Burnam in 1989. Insurers and other major financial institutions have also been subject to RICO complaints. Old-style machine politicians have been successfully prosecuted under RICO. So have law enforcement officials; the corrupt dealings between the FBI and the Irish mob in Boston resulted in a successful RICO prosecution.

Important Supreme Court Decisions

U.S. v. Turkette (1981). The first important test of the criminal provisions in RICO involved the extent to which the statute federalized state crime. The defendant in a RICO prosecution for drug dealing argued that RICO was intended solely to protect legitimate business enterprises from infiltration by racketeers and therefore should not be read to make a federal crime out of an association which performs *only* illegal acts (but which has not attempted to infiltrate a legitimate enterprise). In an 8-1 decision, the

Supreme Court ruled that the term *enterprise* encompassed both legitimate and illegitimate enterprises and that neither the language nor the legislative history of the act limits its application to legitimate enterprises. The implication of this interpretation was significant for the balance between federal and state law enforcement. The Court reviewed various objections to this "federalization" of state crime in the legislative history of RICO and ruled that Congress knowingly adopted a law that "would entail prosecutions involving acts of racketeering that are also crimes under state law."

Sedima v. Imrex, Co. (1985). The first important test of the civil RICO provisions came in a joint pair of cases that tested how closely RICO is tied to traditional concepts of organized crime. The civil remedies available under RICO are modeled after federal ANTITRUST LAW. These powerful provisions—treble damages and attorneys' fees—did not become popular for almost 10 years after the act became law, when it became clear that RICO extended far beyond organized crime. The plaintiff in *Sedima* claimed injuries from an overbilling scheme and RICO jurisdiction by virtue of mail and wire fraud. The lower courts sought to limit civil RICO claims to cases with "RICO-type injury," reasoning that otherwise defendants would be unfairly "stigmatized with the appellation 'racketeer'" and that punitive-like damages would be available without the protections of criminal law. The 5-4 majority in *Sedima*, however, concluded that the fact that RICO is used against respected businesses is "hardly a sufficient reason for assuming that the provision is being misconstrued." The majority court concluded that the fact that RICO has been applied in situations not expressly anticipated by Congress "does not demonstrate ambiguity. It demonstrates breadth."

Scheidler v. National Organization for Women, Inc. (2003). One of the most controversial uses of the RICO involved civil claims against antiabortion groups that were seeking to shut down legal abortion clinics. A lawsuit by the National Organization for Women (NOW) against Operation Rescue and several named activists claimed that they were trying to close clinics in violation of federal extortion laws. The case made it to the U.S. Supreme Court in 1994 on the question whether "enterprise" or "racketeering activity" had to have an overriding economic motive. NOW prevailed in a unanimous decision that alarmed many civil libertarians but which was, on its face, restricted to statutory interpretation. NOW also prevailed at a subsequent jury trial. The case eventually made it back to the U.S. Supreme Court.

In *Scheidler v. NOW* (2003), the Court ruled that participants in alleged conspiracy to shut down abortion clinics had not "obtained" property—from clinics, clinic staffs, or women seeking clinics' services—as required for extortion under the Hobbs Act. By an 8-1 vote, the justices agreed that whatever tactics Joseph Scheidler, Operation Rescue, and the Pro-Life Action League used against clinics, they did not fit the definition of extortion in the Hobbs Act, which requires "the obtaining of property" of someone else under threat of force. Even if they succeeded in closing a clinic, the court reasoned, the protesters would not "obtain" the property. In a solo dissent, Justice STEVENS criticized the majority's "dramatic retreat" from earlier positions, arguing that the narrow interpretation will benefit only "professional criminals."

Recent Developments

RICO continues to be used in novel and controversial ways. Under President Clinton, the Department of Justice filed a criminal RICO complaint against the tobacco industry, alleging a four-decade-long conspiracy to intentionally deceive the American public by denying that smoking caused disease. The complaint survived a motion to dismiss and, to the surprise of many, was continued by the Department of Justice under President Bush.

On the legislative front, there have been no significant changes in the structure of the RICO statute since it was first adopted in 1970. Various activities have been added to the list of "predicate acts" (e.g., trafficking in counterfeit goods, 1996; activities related to child pornography, 1988). Perhaps the most significant addition came through the USA PATRIOT Act of 2001, which added terroristic activities. In the first major use of this provision, federal prosecutors in Florida charged a professor and seven coconspirators on charges of providing financial support to the Palestinian Islamic Jihad. The indictment relies on RICO to charge the alleged terrorist financiers.

For more information: Levi, Michael. *Fraud: Organization, Motivation and Control.* 2 vols. Brookfield, Vt.: Ashgate, 1999; *National Organization for Women, Inc. v. Scheidler,* 510 U.S. 249 (1994); *Scheidler v. National Organization for Women, Inc.,* 537 U.S. 393 (2003); *Sedima v. Imrex. Co.,* 473 U.S. 479 (1985); *U.S. v. Turkette,* 452 U.S. 576 (1981).

—Ross E. Cheit

Ragsdale et al. v. Wolverine World Wide, Inc., 535 U.S. 81 (2002)

In *Ragsdale et al. v. Wolverine World Wide, Inc.,* the Supreme Court held that employees who have not been informed that a previous absence would be counted as family medical leave, are not required to receive more than 12 weeks of leave under the Family and Medical Leave Act of 1993. The case upheld the Eighth Circuit COURT OF APPEALS decision that a Labor Department regulation requiring an employer to grant an additional 12 weeks of leave to an employee who has not been informed that a previous absence would be counted as part of the 12 weeks of leave guaranteed by the FMLA of 1993 is invalid.

The Court's decision protects employers who offer more generous leave policies by requiring employees to prove actual harm caused by the employer's not informing the employee an absence will count as FMLA leave.

FMLA, enacted in 1993, provides for a minimum of 12 weeks of unpaid leave per year for eligible employees under certain circumstances including: "(1) the birth of the employee's son or daughter, and to care for the newborn child; (2) the placement with the employee of a son or daughter for adoption or foster care, and to care for the newly placed child; (3) to care for the employee's spouse, son, daughter, or parent with a serious health condition; and, (4) because of a serious health condition that makes the employee unable to perform one or more of the essential functions of his or her job." [29 CFR § 825.200(a)].

Wolverine World Wide, Inc., had employed Tracy Ragsdale for a year when she became ill. Under Wolverine's leave policy, she was granted 30 weeks of medical leave in 1996. Unable to return to work after 30 weeks, Ragsdale requested an additional 12 weeks of leave under the Family Medical Leave Act. She filed suit claiming that under Section 825.700(a) of Title 29 of the Code of Federal Regulations, she was entitled to 12 additional weeks of leave because Wolverine had not notified her that the first 30-week leave would be counted against her FMLA entitlement.

The Court reviewed the particular regulation used by the Department of Labor, which states: "If an employee takes paid or unpaid leave and the employer does not designate the leave as FMLA leave, the leave taken does not count against an employee's FMLA entitlement." [29 CFR § 825.700(a)]

In a split 5-4 decision, the Court ruled that 29 CFR § 825.700(a) fails to take into account the provisions provided by Congress in the FMLA itself. Within the act, Congress provides that an employee can successfully sue an employer under the FMLA if the employee demonstrates: (a) the employer violated the FMLA; (b) the employee suffered harm; and (c) the harm suffered by the employee was caused by the employer's violation of the act. If all three are proved, then the courts can customize the relief to fit the harm suffered by the employee.

Although 29 CFR § 825.700(a) supports Ragsdale's claim, the Court ruled that the regulation is contrary to the act and beyond the authority of the secretary of labor. In Ragsdale's case, the Department of Labor adopted additional and inconsistent remedies to the act's own provisions. Specifically, the DOL regulation failed to take into account whether Ragsdale suffered harm as a result of Wolverine's lack of notification, and whether any penalty would be appropriate under the specific facts and circumstances. By

having a more generous leave policy provided to her, the Court ruled Ragsdale had not been harmed by Wolverine's lack of notification that the 30 weeks provided by the company would count against the 12-week minimum required by the FMLA.

While the majority opinion focused on not penalizing an employer that provides leave in addition to the 12-week minimum but fails to notify the employee, the dissenting opinion focused on the portion of the act that requires notification to employees and employee notification to her employer. [29 CFR § 825.300 (a) and 29 CFR § 825.301(b)(1)]. In her dissent, Justice O'CONNOR cites that the individualized notification, as required by the DOL, may be the first time an employee learns that the leave is protected by the FMLA.

Justice Kennedy delivered the opinion of the Court joined by Chief Justice REHNQUIST; and Justices STEVENS, SCALIA, and THOMAS. Justice O'Connor, joined by Justices SOUTER, GINSBURG, and BREYER, filed a dissenting opinion.

For more information: Aalberts, Robert J., and Lorne H. Seidman. "Employee Notice Requirements Under the Family and Medical Leave Act: Are They Manageable?" *Pepperdine Law Review* 24 (1997): 1,209; Department of Labor, Code of Federal Regulations, Title 29, Chapter V, Part 825; Rigler, Jane. "Analysis and Understanding of the Family and Medical Leave Act of 1993." *Case Western Reserve* Journal of International Law 45 (1995): 457.

—Wendy Escoffier

rape and the death penalty

The Supreme Court's CAPITAL PUNISHMENT jurisprudence includes a general principle of proportionality between the crime and the punishment. The Court has found that the death penalty is a disproportionate punishment prohibited under the Eighth Amendment when imposed upon an offender who rapes an adult but does not kill the victim in the course of the rape. However, the Court has failed to answer the question of whether the Eighth Amendment permits the imposition of capital punishment on a non-killer convicted of the rape of a minor.

In *FURMAN v. GEORGIA,* 408 U.S. 238 (1972), the Court invalidated all then-existing death penalty laws, finding that lack of written guidelines in sentencing led to arbitrary, capricious, and discriminatory sentences in violation of the Eighth Amendment's cruel and unusual punishment clause. The *Furman* Court did not decide that the death penalty per se was cruel and unusual. Only four years later, in *GREGG v. GEORGIA,* 438 U.S. 153 (1976), the Court made it clear that death was not always an unconstitutional punishment when imposed for the crime of murder. The *Gregg* Court also declared that the Eighth Amendment barred both barbaric and excessive punishments. A punishment was considered excessive if it: (1) made no measurable contribution to acceptable goals of punishment and so was nothing more than the purposeless and needless imposition of pain and suffering; or (2) was grossly disproportionate to the severity of the crime. The Court also observed that capital punishment had a long history of acceptance in the United States and also in England. The Court noted that since *Furman,* 35 states had enacted new laws providing death as a punishment for at least some crimes that led to murder. The Court further found that the actions of juries in imposing the death penalty were compatible with the legislative judgments indicating that capital punishment was still necessary in appropriate cases. However, the *Gregg* Court specifically reserved the question of whether death would be a disproportionate punishment when imposed for crimes other than murder.

One year after *Gregg,* in *COKER V. GEORGIA,* 433 U.S. 584 (1977), the Court declared that death was a grossly disproportionate punishment when imposed for the crime of raping an adult woman and therefore violated the cruel and unusual punishment clause of the Eighth Amendment.

Justice WHITE, joined by Justices STEWART, BLACKMUN and STEVENS, wrote for the Court. Justices BRENNAN and MARSHALL added concurring opinions noting their opposition to capital punishment in all cases. Justice White began by observing that a majority of the states had not authorized the death penalty for rape at any time in the last 50 years. He explained that in 1925, 18 states as well as the District of Columbia and the federal government provided death as a punishment for the rape of an adult woman, but that in 1971 the number had dropped to 16 states plus the federal government.

Moreover, after *Furman,* of those 16 states that had originally authorized death as a punishment for rape, only Florida, North Carolina, and Georgia made rape a capital offense when reviving their death penalty statutes. However, the laws of North Carolina and Florida were later invalidated because they made the death penalty mandatory. This left Georgia as the only state that authorized death for raping an adult woman. White therefore concluded that although the state legislatures had not unanimously repudiated death as a punishment for rape, recent legislative trends indicated that death was no longer regarded as an appropriate punishment for the rape of an adult woman.

White then considered the behavior of juries. He pointed out that out of all the rape convictions in Georgia since 1973, the Georgia Supreme Court had reviewed 63 rape cases and of those only six cases involved a death sentence. Moreover, one of these six capital sentences was set aside leaving only five convicted rapists currently under sentence in Georgia. White conceded that two other states,

Florida and Mississippi, currently provided the death penalty for rape, but only when the victim was a child.

Although the judgments of legislatures and juries pointed to the conclusion that the Eighth Amendment prohibited the imposition of the death penalty as a punishment for raping an adult woman, White argued that in the end, the Court must use its own judgment in considering the constitutionality of the punishment in question. White stressed that rape was a reprehensible and violent crime. However, it was different from murder in that, by definition, rape did not involve the unjustified taking of human life. A rape victim's life was not over, and usually it was not beyond repair, but for the murder victim, life was over.

Justice POWELL authored an opinion concurring in the judgment and dissenting in part. He contended that the Court's opinion should have been limited to the facts of the case at hand and that death might be an appropriate punishment in cases of aggravated rape.

In a dissenting opinion, Chief Justice BURGER, joined by Justice REHNQUIST, criticized the Court for failing to fully appreciate the profound suffering the crime of rape imposed upon victims and their families. He maintained that a rapist violated both the victim's privacy and personal integrity and also inflicted serious psychological and physical harm. Moreover, he asserted that rape was not simply a physical attack. Burger stressed that the crime of rape destroyed the human personality and gravely affected the victim for the rest of her life.

The Court in *Coker* left unanswered the question of whether death would be an unconstitutional punishment when imposed upon a defendant convicted of raping a child. The Louisiana Supreme Court held that the death penalty was not an excessive punishment for the rape of a child under the age of 12 in *State v. Wilson,* 685 So. 2d 1063 (La. 1996). The state court distinguished *Coker* contending that the *Coker* Court was careful to refer only to the rape of an adult woman in its opinion. The case was appealed to the United States Supreme Court in 1997, but the Court declined to hear the case. At that time Louisiana was the only state that authorized capital punishment for child rape. However, Georgia has since enacted its own bill providing death as a punishment for an offender convicted of raping a child.

For more information: Friedman, Lawrence M. *Crime and Punishment in American History.* New York: Basic Books, 1993.

—Jen DeMichael

rational basis

The rational basis test is the lowest level of scrutiny that the Supreme Court applies to constitutional issues. In nearly every case where it is applied, the Court rejects the constitutional challenge to a law or governmental action. How this "minimal scrutiny" standard came to be so important illustrates the limited power of the Supreme Court, how it decides cases, and the changed attitudes about the importance of individual rights and FEDERALISM. The rational basis test is one of the hidden keys to understanding the Supreme Court. The phrase rarely appears in news coverage, but when, and how seriously, the Court applies it can determine the outcome of cases.

The classic statement of the rational basis test can be found in the 1938 case, UNITED STATES V. CAROLENE PRODUCTS, 304 U.S. 144, when the Court, in an opinion by Justice Harlan F. STONE, said that "regulation affecting ordinary commercial transactions is not to be pronounced unconstitutional unless in the light of the facts made known or generally assumed it is of such a character as to preclude the assumption that it rests upon some rational basis within the knowledge and experience of the legislators." This statement represented a tacit recognition of the new role of the Supreme Court in American politics, which had changed dramatically the previous year. It would now defer to Congress, the president, and even the states regarding issues of economic regulation, setting a pattern that it would largely follow up to the present day.

It is easy, but misleading, to see the Supreme Court as the most powerful institution in American politics. At least since the famous MARBURY V. MADISON case, the Court has taken on the power to declare unconstitutional actions of the Congress, president, and other parts of the government. This might seem to make the Court superior to the Congress or the president, but as Alexander Hamilton pointed out in *Federalist* 78, the Court has neither the "purse" nor the "sword." That is, the justices do not control government budgets or armies, so they really have no way to enforce their will unless Congress, the president, the states, and the public recognize the authority of the Court.

The New Deal era most dramatically showed the practical limits on the Court's authority, and the rational basis test was the result. The Court had struck down several pieces of sweeping legislation that Congress had enacted to combat the economic crisis, and in response President Roosevelt proposed what came to be called a "court packing" plan. He proposed creating a new seat on the Court, filled by a nominee of his choosing, for every sitting justice over the age of 70, so that a new Court majority would likely approve the laws he wanted. The proposal became MOOT when the Court, apparently having gotten the message, began in 1937 to approve every law regulating the economy, abandoning its old LIBERTY OF CONTRACT doctrine and loosening limits on federal regulation of activities that might otherwise be controlled by the states.

A year later, in *Carolene Products,* the Court formalized its new position. Henceforth, economic regulation would only have to pass the lenient rational basis requirement that it further a legitimate governmental interest, and as long as the justices could conceive of a reason that might support the legislation, the Court would approve it. This minimal standard of scrutiny is sometimes called the any conceivable rational basis test, to emphasize how lenient it is. For the next four decades the Court upheld one piece of legislation after another under this standard.

If that were the whole story, the Supreme Court would not have had much to do after 1937 and would not be the prominent and often controversial institution it is today. *Carolene Products* also contained the now-famous footnote 4, in which the Court speculated that there might be other circumstances—such as when the government discriminates against minorities, restricts voting rights, or violates specific prohibitions of the Constitution—when something more than minimal scrutiny would be appropriate. This footnote foreshadowed the double standard employed by the Court for the rest of the century, whereby infringements of rights deemed by the Court to be fundamental would be subject to very STRICT SCRUTINY, as would any governmental SUSPECT CLASSIFICATIONS, such as RACIAL DISCRIMINATION. In those areas, the Court has continued to make many important rulings, even while it stayed away from economic regulation by using the often perfunctory rational basis test. Although some prominent critics have emerged in recent years, this double standard distinguishing personal from economic liberties has been widely supported by legal scholars.

Although the Court is still highly likely to side with the government, application of the rational basis test has become less predictable as the composition of the Court has shifted and new issues have come before it. In *Moore v. East Cleveland,* 431 U.S. 494 (1977), the Court struck down a ZONING ordinance that defined single-family in such a way as to prohibit a child from living with his grandmother. Even though zoning would usually be considered economic regulation, subject only to minimal scrutiny, the interference with family living arrangements raised privacy concerns. Justice POWELL wrote in his opinion of that "this Court must examine carefully the importance of the governmental interests," rather than simply assume a legitimate purpose. In another case, CLEBURNE V. CLEBURNE LIVING CENTER, the Court declined to recognize mental retardation as a suspect classification, which would trigger strict scrutiny, and evaluated an ordinance that required neighborhood approval for a group home under the rational basis test. Instead of routine approval, the Court declared the requirement to be irrational and struck it down. This new approach by the Court is sometimes called "rational basis with teeth," as the Court's "bark" under the rational basis test is occasionally backed up by the "bite" of invalidation.

This reinvigorated test of rationality reflects the general tendency of the Court in recent decades to shy away from formulaic application of either strict scrutiny—under which the governmental action is usually invalidated—or minimal scrutiny. To make it more confusing, the Court has developed "mid-level" scrutiny, which is the least predictable of all. Varying standards in particular cases may produce more finely tuned results but lessen predictability and provoke criticism that the Court is again thrusting itself into political matters.

Federalism and sexual preference are two areas where the recent "bite" of the Court has been particularly sharp and controversial. In 1937 the Court abandoned its stricter interpretation of the commerce clause, which had limited federal involvement in areas the Court had deemed reserved to the states, and began upholding, under the rational basis test, any federal regulatory initiative. That changed dramatically in 1995, when the Court invalidated a federal law because the regulated activity (carrying guns near schools) did not substantially effect INTERSTATE COMMERCE. [*United States v. Lopez,* 514 U.S. 549.] Substantial is a keyword of mid-level scrutiny, so it appeared that the Court was at least raising the rational-basis standard, and both this shift of emphasis, and the resulting striking down of federal regulation, are hotly debated today.

In *ROMER V. EVANS,* 517 U.S. 1146 (1996), the Court struck down a state constitutional amendment that sought to prevent sexual preference from being a protected category under state or local antidiscrimination laws. Although the Court declined to make sexual preference a "suspect classification" that would trigger strict scrutiny, it found that the amendment failed even the rational basis test. Similarly, in *LAWRENCE V. TEXAS* (2003), the Court did not declare homosexual sodomy to be a fundamental right but nonetheless struck down a state prohibition as failing to serve any legitimate interest, the minimal requirement under the rational basis test.

This willingness of the Court to declare governmental actions irrational shows the continual erosion of the sharp double standard heralded by *Carolene Products.* Future cases will show whether the Court will continue to raise the rational basis standard or revert to sharper distinctions and more predictable outcomes, and whether its new approach will be accepted by scholars and the public as providing more nuanced justice, or criticized as being too unpredictable and intrusive on the political process.

For more information: Tribe, Laurence H. *American Constitutional Law.* New York: Foundation Press, 2000.

—Dennis Coyle

reapportionment and redistricting

"Reapportionment" and "redistricting" are terms with similar, but not identical meanings referring to the geographic distribution of political representation. Reapportionment is the process by which legislative representation is distributed among states. Redistricting, by comparison, is the process of drawing new legislative district boundaries.

Following each decennial census, Congress reapportions the 435 seats of the House of Representatives among the 50 states according to population. State legislatures then redistrict their states, creating or eliminating districts gained or lost in congressional reapportionment and adjusting legislative districts for changes in population. Despite the slight difference in the meanings of these two terms, they are often used interchangeably.

Legislative redistricting has long been used by state legislators as a tool to retain political power. Incumbent legislators are responsible for drawing district boundaries. Creating "safe" districts in which legislators will face little competition is typically the primary objective. Prior to the 1960s, legislators throughout the South often refused to redraw legislative districts despite growing and shifting populations. This resulted in dramatic underrepresentation for people of color living in urban areas.

This tactic was employed for decades, with courts unwilling to stop it. This changed when the Supreme Court issued its landmark decision in *BAKER V. CARR,* 369 U.S. 186 (1962). Residents of five Tennessee counties challenged a 1901 Tennessee apportionment law on constitutional grounds. The district court dismissed the claim on the ground that it involved a political question over which the court had no jurisdiction. The Supreme Court reversed the district court on APPEAL, ruling that federal courts do have jurisdiction over constitutional claims challenging legislative apportionment and redistricting plans.

Baker made it clear that legal challenges to legislative districting plans should not be dismissed by district courts under the "political question" doctrine. This ruling cleared the way for other voting rights lawsuits. Over the next two years, the Supreme Court firmly established the principle of "ONE PERSON, ONE VOTE" with its decisions in *GRAY V. SANDERS, WESBERRY V. SANDERS,* and *REYNOLDS V. SIMS.*

In *Gray v. Sanders,* 372 U.S. 368 (1963), and *Wesberry v. Sanders,* 376 U.S. 1 (1964), the Court applied the "one person, one vote" principle and struck down Georgia laws that weighted some votes more heavily than others in federal congressional elections. Four months after publishing its opinion in *Wesberry,* the Court decided *Reynolds v. Sims,* 377 U.S. 533 (1964), striking down Alabama's legislative apportionment scheme as violative of the EQUAL PROTECTION CLAUSE. *Reynolds* extended the "one person, one vote" principle to state legislative offices. In explaining why reapportionment and redistricting must be based primarily on population, the Court reasoned, "Legislators represent people, not trees or acres. Legislators are elected by voters, not farms or cities or economic interests."

At the time *Reynolds* was decided, the CIVIL RIGHTS movement was in full swing. A primary goal of civil rights activists was to secure effective voting rights for people of color in the Deep South. One year after the Supreme Court's decision in *Reynolds v. Sims*, Congress enacted the VOTING RIGHTS ACT (VRA) of 1965. The VRA prohibits election procedures which deny or dilute the right to vote on account of race. A VRA violation can be established by showing that members of a community of color have less opportunity than other members of the electorate to elect representatives of their choice. The VRA does not, however, establish a right to have members of a community of color elected in numbers equal to their proportion in the population.

The VRA inspired a flood of lawsuits challenging racially discriminatory election laws, including redistricting and reapportionment laws. The remedy most often sought by plaintiffs in race-based redistricting lawsuits was the creation of majority-minority districts (i.e., districts containing a voting majority of the racial minority group that brought the lawsuit).

In *THORNBURG V. GINGLES*, 478 U.S. 163 (1986), the Supreme Court authorized the creation of majority-minority districts as a remedy in VRA vote dilution cases under certain circumstances set forth in the opinion. In their efforts to create majority-minority districts, legislatures sometimes abandoned the traditional redistricting criteria of compactness and contiguity. The resulting oddly shaped districts attracted the attention of the Supreme Court in 1993.

In *SHAW V. RENO*, 509 U.S. 630 (1993), the Court considered a challenge to a long, snakelike majority-minority congressional district in North Carolina. Republican plaintiffs argued that the district in question was so extremely irregular on its face that it could be viewed only as an unconstitutional effort to segregate the races for purposes of voting. Unlike earlier voting rights lawsuits seeking to increase the political representation of communities of color, the plaintiffs in *Shaw* attacked the creation of a majority-black district.

The *Shaw* Court announced that plaintiffs may sue state legislatures for drawing district boundaries on the basis of race in violation of the equal protection clause of the Fourteenth Amendment. The Court reasoned that such "racial gerrymandering" resulted in stigmatic harm (by reinforcing the stereotype that members of the same racial group think and vote alike) and representational harm (by encouraging elected officials from such districts to represent only the members of their racial group rather that the district as a whole) to society at large.

The Court's 1993 decision in *Shaw* marked a turning point in the effective use of majority-minority districts as a

remedy in VRA claims. The Court elaborated on "racial gerrymandering" in *MILLER V. JOHNSON*, 515 U.S. 900 (1995), and *Bush v. Vera*, 517 U.S. 952 (1996) (plurality opinion), ruling that race may be considered by legislatures in drawing district boundaries but that race may not be a "predominant" factor in the redistricting process. To prove the predominance of race as a redistricting factor, a plaintiff need only demonstrate that the challenged district "subordinated [to race] traditional race-neutral districting principles," such as "compactness, contiguity, and respect for political subdivisions or communities defined by actual shared interests."

The Court's *Shaw* decision leaves public officials responsible for reapportionment and redistricting in a difficult position. The VRA demands that race be taken into account when drawing district boundaries, while the Supreme Court has prohibited the use of race as a predominant factor.

For more information: Lowenstein, Daniel Hays, and Richard L. Hasen. *Election Law*. Raleigh, N.C.: Carolina Academic Press, 2004.

—Paul S. Ryan

Red Lion Broadcasting v. FCC, 395 U.S. 367 (1969)

In *Red Lion Broadcasting v. Federal Communications Commission*, the Supreme Court upheld against First Amendment challenge the FCC's FAIRNESS DOCTRINE, which required broadcasters to present coverage of all sides of controversial public issues. The case provides the constitutional justification for greater government regulation of broadcast media.

Red Lion owned WGBC, a Pennsylvania radio station that broadcast a 15-minute program by Rev. Billy James Hargis. During a 1964 show, Hargis discussed a book titled *Goldwater—Extremist of the Right*. Hargis stated that the book's author, Fred Cook, had worked for a Communist publication, been fired from a newspaper for making false charges about city officials, and defended Alger Hiss. Upon hearing of the broadcast, Cook demanded free reply time on the station under the "personal attack" provision of the fairness doctrine. An FCC investigation found that Cook had been personally attacked and that Red Lion refused to provide a transcript of Hargis's program or provide Cook free air time to reply. The D.C. circuit upheld the FCC decision, and Red Lion appealed. The Supreme Court consolidated *Red Lion* with a Seventh Circuit case (*U.S. v. Radio Television News Directors Association*) that struck the recently revised "right to reply" provisions of the personal attack and political editorializing rules as violations of freedom of speech and press.

The Court upheld the FCC restrictions by an 8-0 vote, Justice DOUGLAS not participating. Justice WHITE's opinion for the Court upheld the fairness doctrine based on the unique nature of broadcast media. Unlike print, the number of broadcasters is limited by the public radio spectrum, and not all who want to use broadcast media can have access. To avoid cacophony, the federal government must allocate these scarce frequencies through temporary licenses. All who desire broadcast licenses cannot receive them, and "it is the right of the viewers and listeners, not the right of the broadcaster, which is paramount."

Those who possess these scarce, temporary licenses to use the public airways enjoy them not as owners but as "the fruit of a preferred position conferred by the government." Striking the fairness doctrine would in practice grant licensees a government-conferred monopoly to exclude the views of others. As White writes, "there is no sanctuary in the First Amendment for unlimited private censorship in a medium not open to all."

Broadcasters argued that the fairness doctrine would result in self-censorship. Stations—in order to avoid equal time rules—would eliminate all coverage of controversial public issues. White, however, found this possibility "at best speculative." Further, because radio frequencies are public and serve the entire community, the First Amendment allows government to compel licensees "to give suitable time and attention to matters of great public concern." As White concludes, "in view of the scarcity of broadcast frequencies, the Government's role in allocating those frequencies, and the legitimate claims of those without governmental assistance to gain access to those frequencies for expression of their views, we hold the regulations and ruling at issue here are both authorized by statute and constitutional."

Although the FCC repealed the fairness doctrine in 1987, *Red Lion* continues to provide a justification for increased government regulation of broadcast media based on its unique characteristics. Compare this case with *MIAMI HERALD V. TORNILLO*, 418 U.S. 241 (1974), where the Court unanimously struck Florida's rule allowing those personally attacked by newspapers to have a "right to reply."

Red Lion also provides support for the Court's ruling in *FCC V. PACIFICA*, 438 U.S. 726 (1978), which upheld regulations banning indecent but nonobscene broadcasts. More recently, *Red Lion* has guided how the courts should treat claims of access to and government regulation of new media. [See especially *Turner Broadcasting System I v. FCC*, 512 U.S. 622 (1994), and *Turner Broadcasting System v. FCC II*, 520 U.S. 180 (1997), (cable television), and *Reno v. American Civil Liberties Union*, 521 U.S. 844 (Internet).]

For more information: Donohue, Hugh. *The Battle to Control Broadcast News: Who Owns the First Amendment?* Cambridge, Mass.: MIT Press, 1989; Krattenmaker, Thomas, and Lucas Powe. *Regulating Broadcast Programming*. Washington, D.C.: American Enterprise Institute, 1994.

—Frank J. Colucci

Regents of the University of California v. Bakke, 438 U.S. 265 (1978)

Regents of the University of California v. Bakke was an important Supreme Court case that upheld the use of affirmative action within schools and academic institutions.

Bakke was argued before the Supreme Court in October 1977 and decided in June 1978, by a vote of 5 to 4. The case reached the Supreme Court of the United States on APPEAL from the Supreme Court of California by WRIT OF CERTIORARI. Allan Bakke was a white male who applied to the Davis Medical College at the University of California in 1973 and 1974. Even though he was a highly qualified applicant, Bakke was refused admission both times. He sued the University for admission on the grounds that the medical school's dual track admissions policy denied him equal protection under the Fourteenth Amendment and was a violation of Title VI of the CIVIL RIGHTS ACT OF 1964, which prohibited federally funded programs and activities from discriminating against anyone on the basis of race, color, or national origin.

Davis Medical College admitted only 100 students each year through its dual-track admissions program. Under the regular admissions procedure, five admissions committee members rated applicants on a scale of 1 to 100 on the basis of their overall grade point average, grade point average in science courses, scores on the Medical College Admissions Test (MCAT), extracurricular activities, and other biographical information. As a result, the highest rating a student could obtain was 500. A separate procedure was administered for designated minority applicants, i.e., African Americans, Chicanos, Asians, or Native Americans, in order to give them credit for overcoming "disadvantage." The separate admissions procedure entailed the same rating process; however, minority applicants did not have to meet the same 2.5 minimum GPA requirement as other applicants. A certain number of places were set aside each year at the medical school for minority applicants. In the years Bakke applied, 16 places were reserved for designated minorities.

Justice POWELL wrote the opinion for a deeply divided court. Four justices ruled in favor of Bakke while another four found the admissions program constitutional. Powell was located somewhere in the middle. He found the medical school's quota unconstitutional as a violation of the Fourteenth Amendment's EQUAL PROTECTION CLAUSE. Powell explained that by permitting designated minorities to apply for all 100 open seats while permitting all other applicants to apply for only 84, the medical school was denying an entire group opportunities on the basis of race and ethnicity. He continued by saying that the equal protection clause could not mean one thing when applied to one person and another thing when applied to a person of another race. For this reason, the admissions policy was also a violation of Title VI. Powell wrote, "The clock of our liberties . . . cannot be turned back to 1868. . . . It is far too late to argue that the guarantee of equal protection to *all* persons permits the recognition of special wards entitled to a degree of protection greater than that accorded to others." On these grounds, he rejected the Regents' argument that the Court ought to apply a limited interpretation to the Fourteenth Amendment.

Powell next elaborated on what has become one of the most famous and contentious aspects of the opinion: whether race might lawfully be used as a consideration in university admissions processes. Powell concluded that diversity in higher education was a COMPELLING STATE INTEREST, and that universities might consider race as one element in a range of admissions considerations in order to cultivate a heterogeneous student body. Although the University of California's admissions policy pursued this goal unconstitutionally, the goal of diversity was, in and of itself, constitutional. Powell cited the approach used at Harvard University as a model of the lawful pursuit of a diverse student body. Under this program, race or ethnicity might be used as a "plus" between two otherwise equally competitive applicants. Above all, though, Powell maintained that diversity constituted a compelling state interest insofar as a diverse student body can be conducive to a free, open, and representative exchange of ideas.

In the end, the Court ordered Davis Medical College to admit Bakke since he was more qualified than any of the minority applicants for whom places had been set aside. However, the overall message of the Court to universities was that they might continue to take into account race and ethnicity in their admissions decisions. The Supreme Court has revisited *Bakke* on numerous occasions, most notably in the recent *GRUTTER V. BOLLINGER*, 123 S.Ct. 2325 (2003), case. In *Grutter*, the Supreme Court again upheld the legitimacy of diversity-based admissions criteria in higher education, this time within the context of the University of Michigan Law School's admissions policy.

For more information: Skrentny, John David. *The Minority Rights Revolution.* New York: Belknap Press, 2002.
—Tara Helfman

Rehnquist, William Hubbs (1924–   ) *chief justice of the Supreme Court*

William Hubbs Rehnquist was appointed to the Supreme Court by Richard Nixon in 1972 and was nominated to be the nation's 16th chief justice by Ronald Reagan in 1986. Chief Justice Rehnquist has been a consistent voice of conservatism and JUDICIAL RESTRAINT on the Court.

Born into a middle-class and staunchly Republican household in Milwaukee, Wisconsin, on October 1, 1924, Rehnquist served in the Army Air Corps in North Africa in World War II. Following the war, Rehnquist enrolled at Stanford University on the GI Bill, where he graduated Phi Beta Kappa with a B.A. and M.A. in political science in 1948, followed by a masters in government from Harvard University two years later. In 1950 Rehnquist enrolled in Stanford Law School, where one of his professors described him as "the outstanding student of his law school generation." He graduated first in his class two years later, two positions above Sandra Day, who would later serve with Rehnquist on the Supreme Court.

Following a clerkship with Supreme Court Justice Robert JACKSON, Rehnquist married Natalie Cornell, with

Chief Justice William Rehnquist *(Library of Congress)*

whom he would have three children, and took a position with a law firm in Phoenix, Arizona. In the years that followed, Rehnquist was active in Republican party politics and a vocal opponent of school desegregation and CIVIL RIGHTS legislation. In 1969 President Nixon appointed Rehnquist assistant attorney general for the Justice Department's Office of Legal Counsel. Just two years later, Nixon nominated Rehnquist to replace retiring justice John Marshall HARLAN on the U.S. Supreme Court, a position he assumed following Senate confirmation on January 7, 1972.

In the years that followed, Rehnquist, beginning with his landmark majority opinion in 1975's *NATIONAL LEAGUE OF CITIES V. USERY*, carved out a role for himself as one of the most consistently conservative voices on the Court on issues concerning states rights and the limits of federal authority. Despite the presence of three other Republican appointees, his was often the sole dissenting vote in resisting what he saw as inappropriate JUDICIAL ACTIVISM in cases such as *ROE V. WADE* (1973), *United States Steel Workers of America v. Weber* (1979), and *Richmond v. J. A. Croson Co.* (1989). Rehnquist was also adamant in his opposition to the expansion of the Fourteenth Amendment's EQUAL PROTECTION CLAUSE to include such nonracial issues as the rights of women, children, and minorities, and he has consistently supported the death penalty and the interests of law enforcement in disputes concerning rights of those accused of crimes.

By the time Rehnquist was tapped by President Reagan to replace retiring Chief Justice Warren BURGER in 1986, the court was undergoing a noticeable shift to the right, a trend that has continued during Rehnquist's tenure as CHIEF JUSTICE. Today, along with justices Antonin SCALIA and Clarence THOMAS, Rehnquist anchors the court's conservative wing. As chief justice, Rehnquist has proved willing, on at least some issues, to modify his own positions for the purposes of arriving at consensus or increasing the size of a majority, even siding with more liberal justices on occasion.

In addition to his responsibilities as chief justice, Rehnquist has written two books on Supreme Court history, *The Supreme Court: How It Was, How It Is* (1988) and *Grand Inquests: The Historic Impeachments of Justice Samuel Chase and President Andrew Johnson* (1992), the latter of which likely served him well when he presided over the impeachment of President Bill Clinton in 1999.

For more information: Davis, Sue. *Justice Rehnquist and the Constitution: The Quest for a New Federalism.* Princeton, N.J.: Princeton University Press, 1998; Maltz, Earl M., ed. *Rehnquist Justice: Understanding the Court Dynamic.* Lawrence: University Press of Kansas, 2003; Schwartz, Herman. *The Rehnquist Court: Judicial Activism on the Right.* New York: Hill and Wang, 2002.

—William D. Baker

religion

The UNITED STATES CONSTITUTION contains several clauses that deal with religious liberty and the relationship between government and religion.

Article VI of the U.S. Constitution states, "but no religious Test shall be required as a Qualification to any Office or public Trust under the United States." The First Amendment states, "Congress shall make no law respecting the establishment of religion, or prohibiting the free exercise thereof." These two references are the only treatments of religion in the Constitution. In 1791 the First Amendment was interpreted to be a restriction primarily on the Congress. Several states, such as Massachusetts, had an official religion, and this practice was allowed. By 1833 all states dispensed with the government-sponsored religion. The section of the First Amendment that deals with religion is often interpreted as having two prongs. The first prong is disestablishment. In short this means that there is no official religion of the state as exists in Great Britain with the Church of England. The second prong is freedom of exercise. This freedom is much more difficult to negotiate because the actions of religious groups or individuals are often in conflict with other responsibilities of the state.

The first case dealing with the free exercise of religion to reach the Supreme Court was *REYNOLDS V. U.S.*, 98 U.S. 145 (1879). In this case, a male Mormon (Church of Jesus Christ of Latter-Day Saints) from Utah had been charged with violating a law prohibiting bigamy. He appealed based on the fact that bigamy was an accepted practice in his church. Chief Justice WAITE delivered the opinion of the court that it was legitimate for Congress to outlaw bigamy and this consideration was not overruled based on the free exercise clause. In this opinion, the Court drew a distinction between government restricting religious belief as opposed to outlawing religious practice. In Justice Waite's opinion he quoted a letter which Thomas Jefferson wrote to the Danbury Baptist Association in 1802, in which Jefferson used the phrase, "building a wall of separation between church and state."

The first disestablishment clause to reach the high court was *Bradfield v. Roberts*, 145 U.S. 291 (1899). In this case Congress had appropriated monies for building an expansion to a hospital in the District of Columbia. The hospital was open to the public but run by an order of Roman Catholic nuns. A citizen of the district sued claiming that this appropriation violated the disestablishment of religion. The Court disagreed, stating that the hospital provided a public service and was not violating disestablishment simply because it was operated by religious adherents.

These two cases helped lay an outline of principles for interpreting the First Amendment, but for the most part the Supreme Court did not hear many cases concerning religious establishment and practice before the mid-1940s.

Up until this time most matters of religion and government were handled at the state level. In 1940 the case CANTWELL v. CONNECTICUT, 310 U.S. 296 (1940), displayed the Court's increased willingness to participate in matters of church/state controversy.

In the *Cantwell* case three ministers of the Jehovah's Witnesses were convicted in New Haven, Connecticut, for violating a local ordinance requiring them to get a municipal permit before accepting any contributions, collected door to door, for their religious organization. The local ordinance allowed the municipal authorities to use their judgment to determine the legitimacy of the religious motivation of those seeking a permit. The Witnesses were convicted of soliciting without a permit. On APPEAL the Witnesses claimed that the due process clause of the Fourteenth Amendment (now being interpreted to apply to the states as well as the national government) applied in this case and that the municipal ordinance in New Haven denied them their freedom of speech and freedom of religious expression. The Court agreed, opening the door for further cases of church/state conflict to be decided by appealing to the Supreme Court.

Following *Cantwell*, a good number of church/state cases came before the Court. They can be categorized as dealing with: government intervention in church controversies; free exercise of minority religions; free exercise and conscientious objection to war; religious expression in the public schools; government aid to religious institutions; and religious displays on public property. There are also a number of miscellaneous cases such as dealing with the existence of legislative chaplains.

A clear legal principle that has emerged from cases involving government intervention in church property is that the Court will always side with the highest church authority, e.g., Presbyterian Church in the *United States v. Mary Elizabeth Blue Hull Memorial Presbyterian Church*, 399 U.S. 440 (1970); *Serbian Eastern Orthodox Diocese for the United States of America and Canada v. Milivojevich*, 426 U.S. 696 (1976); and *Jones v. Wolf*, 443 U.S. 595 (1979). In all of these cases there was an intrachurch conflict dealing with actions taken by the church hierarchy and those who opposed the hierarchy. In all of these cases the Court respected church sovereignty by finding for the highest religious authority.

Two cases that have come before the Supreme Court have been particularly influential in organizing thought concerning the Court's treatment of cases involving church and state. The first is LEMON V. KURTZMAN, 403 U.S. 602 (1971). The case dealt with state aid to church-related elementary and secondary schools in Rhode Island and Pennsylvania. Chief Justice BURGER delivered the opinion of the Court and in it he advocated three principles for the Court to use when examining cases of church/state conflict.

Burger wrote that when state action touching on the religion clauses is challenged, for a challenged law to stand it must (a) have a secular purpose, (b) have a primary effect of neither advancing nor inhibiting religion, and (c) foster no excessive entanglement between church and state. This test, often called the *Lemon Test,* has been likened to a *strict neutrality* standard for determining the constitutionality of church/state relations.

One case where the Court used the criteria presented in the opinion of *Lemon v. Kurtzman* was in the case WALLACE V. JAFFREE, 472 U.S. 38 (1985). In this case the constitutionality of three Alabama statutes was challenged. These statutes authorized a one-minute period of silence in all public schools at the beginning of each school day "for meditation or voluntary prayer." Justice Stevens delivered the opinion of the Court and claimed that two of the three statutes were unconstitutional because they contained no secular purpose and that its actual purpose was a state endorsement of religion.

Another case heard by the Court that involved prayer in public schools is LEE V. WEISMAN, 505 U.S. 577 (1992). In this case the principal at Nathan Bishop Middle School in Providence, Rhode Island, followed a tradition of inviting local clergy to participate in the school's graduation ceremony. The father of a student objected to the practice and took the matter to court. Justice Kennedy wrote the opinion for the Court and declared that the school's practice violated the second part of the three-pronged *Lemon Test.* In other words, the school's invitation of local clergy to the graduation ceremony failed to "have a primary effect that neither advances nor inhibits religion." The use of the *Lemon Test* when examining the propriety of prayer in the public schools has been one of the more controversial aspects of Supreme Court decisions concerning church/state relations.

Another proposed standard is the *accommodationist* standard. This standard is more favorable to various religions because the assumption is that there are many linkages between religion and government and that these actions are only to be curtailed when there is a COMPELLING STATE INTEREST for government restrictions.

An example of a case where these principles came into conflict is *Employment Division v. Smith*, 494 U.S. 872 (1990). In this case two men in Oregon were fired from their jobs because they ingested peyote as part of a ceremony for the Native American Church of which both were members. Both men applied for unemployment but were denied because they were fired for misconduct, i.e., ingesting a controlled substance. The Court found for the state of Oregon because the Court agreed that the law against possessing a controlled substance did serve a secular purpose and was neutrally applied across all religions. Therefore in this case the Court used the strict neutrality principle to decide the case. If the Court had used the accommodationist standard it is questionable if the outcome of the case would have been the same. It is likely that future decisions on church/state matters will continue to display the tension between the principles of strict neutrality and accomodationism.

For more information: Choper, Jesse, Richard Fallon, Yale Kamisar, and Steven Shiffrin. *Constitutional Law: Cases-Comments-Questions.* 9th ed. St. Paul, Minn.: West Group, 2001; Fowler, Robert, and Alan Hertzke. *Religion and Politics in America: Faith, Culture, and Strategic Choices.* Boulder, Colo.: Westview Press, 1995; Miller, Robert, and Ronald Flowers. *Toward Benevolent Neutrality: Church, State, and the Supreme Court.* Waco, Tex.: Baylor University Press, 1992; Wald, Kenneth. *Religion and Politics in the United States.* 4th ed. Lanham, Md.: Rowman and Littlefield, 2003; Witte, John. *Religion and the American Constitutional Experiment: Essential Rights and Liberties.* Boulder, Colo.: Westview Press, 2000.

—Adam Kradel

religion, public displays of

A key quality of the relationship between religions and the government in the United States is that there is no establishment of RELIGION.

The First Amendment to the Constitution states that, "Congress shall make no law respecting the establishment of religion." The plain meaning of the words is that there is no single religion picked out as the official religion of the United States in the same way that Sweden has the Church of Sweden.

One question that arises from disestablishment is whether it is legitimate for agents of the government to overtly recognize religious holidays. This is questionable because it is possible that large religions, such as Christianity or Judaism, could become de facto established if adherence to such a faith was seen as being promoted by government officials.

Before 1983 the Supreme Court avoided this controversy by simply refusing to hear cases dealing with such matters. The Court decided to address the matter in the case of LYNCH V. DONNELLY, 465 U.S. 668. The case dealt with controversy over an elaborate 400,000-square-foot display in the town of Pawtucket, Rhode Island. The display was traditionally erected during the Christmas holiday season. It included a nativity set depicting Jesus of Nazareth as a baby and various other New Testament figures. The scene also included a Santa Claus, a Santa Claus house, reindeer pulling Santa's sleigh, a banner proclaiming "Season's Greetings," candy-striped poles, and a Christmas tree. Various members of the Pawtucket community and the Rhode Island affiliate of the ACLU filed suit claiming that the display violated the disestablishment of religion.

Chief Justice BURGER wrote the opinion for the majority and upheld the constitutionality of the display. Burger wrote that rather than "mechanically invalidating all government statutes that confer benefits or give special recognition to religion in general or to one faith—as an absolute approach would dictate—the Court has scrutinized challenged legislation or official conduct to determine whether, in reality, it establishes a religion or religious faith." He continued to propose a standard of, "would a reasonable person feel excluded" by a particular display. In *Lynch v. Donnelly,* the court found that the display in Pawtucket was sufficiently diverse in its collection of characters, i.e., New Testament characters, reindeer, and elves, that a reasonable non-Christian would not feel excluded.

Lynch v. Donnelly acted as a precursor to the case ALLEGHENY COUNTY V. ACLU Greater Pittsburgh Chapter, 492 U.S. 573 (1989). Here the case concerned two recurring holiday displays located in downtown Pittsburgh. The first was a nativity set placed on the staircase of the Allegheny County Courthouse and the second was a Chanukah menorah placed just outside the City-County Building next to a Christmas tree and a sign saluting liberty. The Court found that the nativity set violated the disestablishment of religion because it was a Christian symbol placed by itself on public property. The Court ruled that the menorah, which is a symbol of the Jewish holiday season of Chanukah, did not violate the ESTABLISHMENT CLAUSE because alongside the menorah were two secular seasonal symbols.

It may seem odd that a nativity set placed by itself is unconstitutional but a nativity set placed alongside a number of secular holiday decorations would be considered constitutional. It is evident, however, that the two different configurations do communicate two distinct messages. One establishes a religious symbol on its own. The other displays a multitude of symbols. When speaking of the nativity set display, Justice BLACKMUN in the majority opinion for *Allegheny County v. ACLU of Pittsburgh* said, "Here, Allegheny has transgressed this line. It has chosen to celebrate Christmas in a way that has the effect of endorsing a patently Christian message." When referring to the menorah, Blackmun said, "The necessary result of placing a menorah next to a Christmas tree is to create an 'overall holiday setting.'"

Using the logic from *Allegheny,* in 1995 the court ruled that the Ku Klux Klan could not be prohibited from erecting a plain white cross in a state-owned town square. The reason for this was that the square also contained a Christmas tree and a menorah, and therefore the display was in accordance with the ruling in *Allegheny v. ACLU of Pittsburgh.*

For someone to use the aforementioned cases to determine where and when a religious display can occur on public property is difficult. The *Allegheny* case has at times been called the "Reindeer Ruling" because of the necessity for secular figures to accompany religious symbols in government decorations. One thing that is certain is that exclusively religious symbols standing on their own do not pass constitutional muster. In 2003 the chief justice of the Alabama supreme court created considerable controversy by refusing to remove a display of the Judeo-Christian 10 Commandments from the Alabama Judicial Building. Other courts have included displays of the 10 Commandments along with other scenes of the history of the law, but in Alabama the 10 Commandments stood alone. On August 20, 2003, the U.S. Supreme Court refused to hear the case, and on August 27 the Alabama justice had the display removed.

For more information: Miller, Robert, and Ronald Flowers. *Toward Benevolent Neutrality: Church, State, and the Supreme Court.* Waco, Tex.: Baylor University Press, 1992.
—Adam Kradel

Renton v. Playtime Theaters, 475 U.S. 41 (1986)

In *Renton v. Playtime Theaters*, the Supreme Court held that a ZONING ordinance that regulates the time, place, and manner of locating adult theaters without considering the content of the movies they show, does not violate the First and Fourteenth Amendments.

In May 1980, the mayor of Renton, Washington, suggested that the city council enact zoning legislation to deal with adult entertainment uses. At that time, there were no adult entertainment businesses in the city. The city's planning and development committee held public hearings, reviewed the experiences of Seattle and other cities, and received a report from the city attorney's office advising about the developments in other cities.

In April 1981 the city council enacted an ordinance prohibiting any "adult motion picture theater" from locating within 1,000 feet of any residential zone, single- or multiple-family dwelling, church, or park, and within one mile of any school. The term *adult motion picture theater* was defined as an enclosed building used for presenting motion picture films, video cassettes, cable television, or any other such visual media, distinguished or characterized by an emphasis on matter depicting, describing, or relating to specified sexual activities or specified anatomical areas for observation by patrons. In early 1982, Playtime Theaters acquired two existing theaters in Renton intending to use them to exhibit feature-length adult films. The theaters were located within areas proscribed by the ordinance.

When the plaintiffs filed the lawsuit, the city council amended the ordinance in several respects, adding a statement of reasons for its enactment and reducing the minimum distance from any school to 1,000 feet. The lawsuit filed by Playtime Theaters argued that the Renton city ordinance violated the First and Fourteenth Amendments. The district court ruled in favor of Renton, but the COURT OF APPEALS reversed and remanded the case for reconsideration. Justice REHNQUIST wrote the majority opinion for the Court, joined by Chief Justice BURGER and Justices O'CONNOR, Rowell, STEVENS, and WHITE.

Justice BLACKMUN concurred but wrote no opinion. Justice Rehnquist wrote that the ordinance is a valid governmental response to serious problems created by adult theaters and satisfies the dictates of the First Amendment. He cites *Young v. American Mini-Theatres, Inc.*, 427 U.S. 50 (1976), as the controlling PRECEDENT. Since the ordinance does not ban adult theaters altogether, it is properly analyzed as a time, place, and manner regulation. It is content-neutral and designed to serve a substantial governmental interest without unreasonably limiting alternative avenues of communication. The city council's predominant concerns were with the secondary effects of adult theaters on the surrounding community, not with the content of adult films themselves. The ordinance by its terms is designed to prevent crime, protect the city's retail trade, maintain property values, and generally protect and preserve the quality of the city's neighborhoods, commercial districts, and the general quality of urban life. If the city had been concerned with restricting the message purveyed by adult theaters, Rehnquist argued, it would have tried to close them or restrict their number rather than circumscribe their choice of locations. Further, the ordinance was not "under-inclusive" for failing to regulate other kinds of adult businesses, since there was no evidence that, at the time the ordinance was enacted, any other adult business was located in, or even contemplated moving into, Renton. The fact that Renton chose first to address the potential problems created by one particular kind of adult business in no way suggests that the city had singled out adult theaters for discriminatory treatment. Also, the ordinance allowed for reasonable alternative avenues of communication. The ordinance left about 520 acres of land area open to adult theater sites.

Justice BRENNAN dissented, joined by Justice MARSHALL. While they agree that the majority used the right "time, place, and manner" First Amendment test, they argue that the test was misused and actually only a cover for outlawing a particular kind of speech, i.e., adult entertainment. The theaters were zoned only on the basis of the content of the movies they would show, therefore this was not a content-neutral ordinance and should have been overturned.

For more information: Dairys, David., ed. *The Politics of Law: a Progressive Critique.* 3rd ed. New York: Basic Books, 1998.

—Amy Oliver

Republican Party of Minnesota v. White, 536 U.S. 765 (2002)

In *Republican Party of Minnesota v. White,* 536 U.S. 765 (2002) 247 F.3d 854, the Supreme Court struck down a section of the Minnesota judicial code of conduct set forth by the Minnesota Supreme Court because it violated the First Amendment protection of free speech.

Many states select their judges through elections by the public so the state will provide certain guidelines to guarantee that the judges remain impartial and independent. One of the most important aspects of this code of conduct is the "announce clause" where the judges or judicial candidates are stopped from making statements that would announce their views on most disputed legal or political issues.

Minnesota had one of the more restrictive "announce clauses," and candidates for the Minnesota Supreme Court, led by Gregory Wersal, filed suit in order to have this clause overturned. These candidates argued that the clause was a violation of the First Amendment protection of freedom of speech and kept the candidates from running a meaningful campaign for office. The state of Minnesota countered with the arguments that the state has a compelling right to, and must, preserve both the state judiciary's impartiality and the public's perception of impartiality in the judiciary.

In a close decision, the Supreme Court rejected the reasoning of the state of Minnesota and reversed the lower court's decision in the process. Freedom of speech has long been considered one of the most important and essential rights protected in the BILL OF RIGHTS of the Constitution. It was also one of the first rights to be applied to the states through the due process clause of the Fourteenth Amendment, dating back to *GITLOW V. NEW YORK,* 268 U.S. 652 (1925). First Amendment freedom of speech cases also always face the highest level of scrutiny where the law must serve a COMPELLING STATE INTEREST [*Republican Party of Minnesota v. White,* 536 U.S. 765, 8-9 (2002) 247 F.3d 854] to not have the law struck down as unconstitutional.

Justice Antonin SCALIA, writing for the Court, decided that the state of Minnesota failed to meet this standard in the minds of the majority of the Supreme Court because the code of conduct, as it was written, did not promote the lack of bias against either party in a lawsuit. The law instead stopped speech regarding particular issues or views on legal issues, and to pursue this objective would be both basically impossible as well as undesirable in the minds of the justices.

The Minnesota state constitution requires judicial elections so the announce clause would place an improper restriction on the freedom of speech because the public would have a right to know the viewpoints of the candidates on major issues to vote properly. The candidates must also have protection for this kind of speech because POLITICAL SPEECH forms the core of First Amendment freedoms and the candidates must have the right to completely participate in the electoral process if their selection as judges depends on it.

The four dissenters, led by Justice Ruth Bader GINSBURG, argued that the state of Minnesota did meet the level of scrutiny necessary for the judicial code of conduct to be declared constitutional. The judiciary maintains a very important role in upholding the law while being both impartial and independent of either the other two branches of government or the parties that come before the court to have their disputes settled. Judges can never be tied to certain constituencies or owe their position to the support of certain interest groups.

This role is much more important than how the judges gained their offices, so the fact that many states have elections to choose their judges does not change the relationship judges must have to the law or the Constitution. The other two branches do not have to meet this high standard, and these restrictions of the freedom of speech for judicial candidates are necessary in the minds of the dissenters. There must be a balance maintained between the candidates' free speech rights and the interest of the state to guarantee an impartial judiciary.

The state of Minnesota has reasonably created this balance in several ways, while still allowing the public to choose its judiciary, by making sure the elections are nonpartisan and having a code of conduct that guarantees that candidates always respect the high standards that come with being a member of the legal profession. The proper methods for selecting judges are being debated more often with every passing day in the chambers of government. The states will look for a definitive answer from the courts and especially the United States Supreme Court. This case was a landmark one in many ways because it was the first of its kind, but it will certainly not be the last.

For more information: Epstein, Lee, and Thomas Walker. *Constitutional Law for a Changing America: Rights, Liberties and Justice.* 4th ed. Washington, D.C.: CQ Press, 2001; Hilden, Julie. "Can the First Amendment Rights of Candidates for Elected Judgeships Be Curtailed? The U.S. Supreme Court Scrutinizes a State Judicial Conduct Code." FindLaw. Available online. URL: http://www.findlaw.com. Downloaded March 21, 2002.

—Billy Monroe

Reynolds v. Sims, 377 U.S. 533 (1964)

In *Reynolds v. Sims,* the U.S. Supreme Court ruled that states must respect the ONE PERSON, ONE VOTE principle when reapportioning and redistricting state legislative representation. Chief Justice Earl WARREN wrote the majority opinion for the Court at the height of the CIVIL RIGHTS movement. Residents of Alabama's largest counties sued the state, claiming that the state's distribution of legislative seats violated the state and federal constitutions.

The state had established the boundaries of its legislative districts in the early 1900s and had not adjusted them since. Residents of the state's largest counties argued that uneven population growth over the course of 60 years, combined with the state's failure to redistribute legislative representation, had diluted the strength of their votes in violation of the EQUAL PROTECTION CLAUSE of the Fourteenth Amendment.

At the time the lawsuit was initiated, approximately 25 percent of Alabama's total population lived in legislative districts which could elect a majority of the state's legislators. Bullock County, for example, with a 1960 population of 13,462, was allocated two seats in the state house of representatives. Mobile County, with a population of 314,301, was given only three seats. Jefferson County, the most populous county in the state with 634,864 residents, was allocated seven seats.

The federal district court had ruled that Alabama violated the equal protection rights of individuals living in the state's most populous counties by denying them equal representation. The district court relied on the Supreme Court's 1962 landmark decision in *BAKER V. CARR,* 369 U.S. 186 (1962), which authorized lower courts to consider Fourteenth Amendment challenges to legislative apportionment schemes.

The Supreme Court affirmed the decision of the district court, ruling that Alabama's apportionment scheme violated the equal protection rights of voters living in the state's more populous legislative districts. The Court imparted national significance on its decision, noting that Alabama's unconstitutional legislative apportionment is "illustrative and symptomatic of the seriousness of this problem in a number of the States." [*Reynolds,* 377 U.S. at 555.]

The Court reasoned that "the right of suffrage can be denied by a debasement or dilution of the weight of a citizen's vote just as effectively as by wholly prohibiting the free exercise of the franchise." [*Reynolds,* 377 U.S. at 555.] The Court continued,

> It would appear extraordinary to suggest that a State could be constitutionally permitted to enact a law providing that certain of the State's voters could vote two, five, or 10 times for their legislative representatives, while voters living elsewhere could vote only once. . . . Of course, the effect of state legislative districting schemes which give the same number of representatives to unequal numbers of constituents is identical. [*Reynolds,* 377 U.S. at 564.]

Reynolds is often cited as the Supreme Court decision establishing the principle of "one person, one vote." In fact, the Court had articulated this principle in earlier opinions. These earlier decisions had applied the "one person, one vote" principle in the context of federal elections and had relied on constitutional provisions other than the Fourteenth Amendment.

Reynolds is significant for its unequivocal pronouncement that the equal protection clause of the Fourteenth Amendment requires states to respect the "one person, one vote" principle when reapportioning and redistricting state legislative representation.

For more information: Lowenstein, Daniel Hays, and Richard L. Hasen. *Election Law.* Durham, N.C.: Carolina Academic Press, 2004.

—Paul S. Ryan

Reynolds v. United States, 98 U.S. 145 (1878)

In *Reynolds v. United States,* the U.S. Supreme Court upheld the conviction of George Reynolds for practicing polygamy in the territories against a claim of religious freedom. It marked the first time in which the meaning of the First Amendment's free exercise of RELIGION guarantee was fully addressed by the high Court. The issue arose in 1874 when Reynolds, a ranking member of the Church of Jesus Christ of Latter-day Saints, commonly called the Mormon Church, was indicted for bigamy, convicted, and sentenced to two years at hard labor. In appealing to the Supreme Court, he argued that as an accepted doctrine of his church, "it was the duty of male members . . . to practice polygamy," and that this duty was called for by different sources which the members thought to be of divine origin.

In upholding the Morrill Act of 1862, which forbade and punished polygamy practiced in the territories, a unanimous Court, speaking through Chief Justice Morrison R. WAITE, read the First Amendment as saying that "Congress was deprived of all legislative power over mere opinion, but was left free to reach actions which were in violation of social duties or subversive of good order." Waite reviewed the traditional condemnation of multiple marriages in modern Western society and cited studies suggesting that "polygamy leads to the patriarchal principle, which, when applied to large communities, fetters the people in stationary despotism, while that principle cannot long exist in connection with monogamy." He concluded: "Laws are made for the government of actions, and while they cannot interfere with mere religious belief and opinions, they may with practices."

In justifying the dichotomy between religious thought, or belief, which is guaranteed absolutely, and religious action, which is not, the CHIEF JUSTICE imagined other, extreme religious practices which were well beyond the protective shield of the Constitution's free exercise shield: "Suppose one believed that human sacrifices were a necessary part of religious worship, would it be seriously contended that the civil government under which he lived could not interfere to prevent a sacrifice? Or if a wife religiously believed it was her duty to burn herself upon the funeral pile of her dead husband, would it be beyond the power of the civil government to prevent her carrying her belief into practice? . . Can a man excuse his practices to the contrary because of his religious belief? To permit this would be to make the professed doctrines of religious belief superior to the law of the land, and in effect to permit every citizen to become a law unto himself." Thus, it was early established by the Court that the free exercise guarantee, while absolutely protecting religious thought, would generate a balancing test regarding activities carried out in the name of religion.

Interestingly, the Court's decision against polygamy had very little effect on the Utah Mormons, and the political battle against the practice continued. President Chester A. Arthur in 1881 called plural marriages an "odious crime"; James G. Blaine warned against such "abominations disguised as religious practices"; and the Edmunds Law of 1882 put teeth into laws against polygamy. Under it, hundreds of Mormons were arrested, fined, and jailed. The Edmunds-Tucker Law of 1887 was even more stringent. In 1890, Wilford Woodruff, president of the Mormon Church, in defeat, formally renounced the practice, and with the exception of deviant offshoots of the church, plural marriages faded into history.

Although the early test of polygamy, like the hypothetical examples suggested by Chief Justice Waite, was an easy one given the hostile climate of public opinion toward the practice at the time, others less compelling would later challenge and divide the Court.

Such an issue was presented in EMPLOYMENT DIVISION, DEPARTMENT OF HUMAN RESOURCES OF OREGON V. SMITH, 494 U.S. 872 (1990). There, the free exercise clause was tested against a state law which included the use of peyote, as a prohibited mind-altering drug, resulting in Oregon's denial of unemployment benefits to persons who had been dismissed from their jobs because of their religiously inspired consumption of the drug as a sacrament.

Justice Antonin SCALIA, for a sharply divided five-to-four majority, noted, "We have never held that an individual's religious beliefs excuse him from compliance with an otherwise valid law prohibiting conduct that the State is free to regulate. On the contrary, the record of more than a century of our free exercise jurisprudence contradicts that proposition. . . . We first had occasion to assert that principle in *Reynolds v. United States.*"

So it is that the Reynolds Court's decision to measure the seemingly absolute message of the Constitution's free exercise of religion guarantee against the perceived needs of society, as encoded into law, continues, with the weight of public opinion, then as now, the determining factor.

For more information: Gordon, Sarah B. *The Mormon Question: Polygamy and Constitutional Conflict in Nineteenth-Century America.* Chapel Hill: University of North Carolina Press, 2001; Magrath, C. Peter. "Chief Justice Waite and the 'Twin Relic': *Reynolds v. United States.*" *Vanderbilt Law Review* 18 (1965): 507; Noonan, John T., Jr., and Edward M. Gaffney, Jr. *Religious Freedom: History, Cases, and Other Materials on the Interaction of Religion and Government.* New York: Foundation Press, 2001.

—Kenneth F. Mott

Richardson v. McKnight, 521 U.S. 399 (1997)

Richardson v. McKnight held that prison guards employed by private firms are not entitled to a qualified immunity from suit by prisoners charging a violation. Qualified immunity, as established in *Harlow v. Fitzgerald,* 457 U.S. 800 (1982), means that government officials performing their duties are protected from civil suit liability so long as they do not violate established legal rights that a sensible person would have known.

Richardson v. McKnight began when two prison guards bound Mr. McKnight, a prisoner at Tennessee's South Central Correctional Center, too tightly. Mr. McKnight claimed that by binding him so tightly, the guards had violated his constitutional rights. When Mr. McKnight brought suit against the guards, they claimed that they were entitled to qualified immunity from suit and the case should be dismissed. The district court noted that the Tennessee prison system had begun privatizing their guard services and that both guards involved were employed by private firms. Considering that private firms employed the guards, the district court held that the guards are not entitled to qualified immunity from suits, as are their governmental counterparts. The United States Supreme Court affirmed this decision.

Justice BREYER wrote the opinion, joined by Justices STEVENS, O'CONNOR, SOUTER, and GINSBURG. The justices relied heavily upon *Wyatt v. Cole,* 504 U.S. 158 (1992), to support their decision. *Wyatt v. Cole* established the principle that not all private defendants are entitled to qualified immunity, emphasizing the history and purposes underlying the request for immunity. Following this idea, the majority opinion states that history does not support the tradition of providing immunity to private prison guards. The opinion also supports the view that merely performing a governmental function does not qualify a private individual for immunity. This is especially applicable to persons who are not directly under governmental direction and supervision. When these precedents were applied to McKnight, the Court ruled against the prison guards.

Justice SCALIA dissented, supported by Justices Kennedy, THOMAS, and Chief Justice REHNQUIST. The justices relied on the *Procunier v. Navarette,* 434 U.S. 555 (1978), PRECEDENT. This case held that both supervisory and subordinate state prison officials are entitled to qualified immunity. The dissenters were dissatisfied that the majority would refuse to allow the guards qualified immunity because they were employed by a private agency, despite their performing the same function as state-employed guards. According to the dissent, history does not reject qualified immunity for private guards. It only lacks a court case where qualified immunity was granted to a private guard. Believing there should be no distinction between the public and private sector when performing indistinguishable duties, the four justices dissented.

For more information: Rosenbloom, David. *Administrative Law for Public Managers.* Boulder, Colo.: Westview Press, 2003; Rosenbloom, David, and Kravchuk, Robert. *Public Administration: Understanding Management, Politics, and Law in the Public Sector.* 5th ed. Ohio: McGraw-Hill, 2002; *Harlow v. Fitzgerald,* 457 U.S. 800 (1982); *Richardson v. McKnight,* 521 U.S. 399 (1997).

—Jaeryl Covington
—Eric C. Sands

RICO   See RACKETEER INFLUENCED AND CORRUPT ORGANIZATIONS ACT.

RICO and abortion

The Racketeer Influenced and Corrupt Organizations Act (RICO) [18 U.S.C.A. §§1961–1968] laws, a powerful tool against the scourge of organized crime, has since gained a secondary use, that of creating criminal and civil claims of action against antiabortion protesters and blockaders. While the scope of RICO's power in this application has since been curtailed by the Supreme Court, a recent statute, the Freedom of Access to Clinic Entrances Act [18 U.S.C.A §248 (FACE)] has taken the place of this tactic.

RICO was passed in 1970 to create criminal and civil liability for participating in what is commonly known as organized crime. RICO creates three main offenses: (1) using illegal income, that which is derived from racketeering activity or collection of unlawful debt, to acquire, establish, or operate an enterprise; (2) the acquisition or maintenance of an interest in or control of an enterprise; (3) the use of an enterprise to racketeer or collect unlawful debts. The Act makes it a crime to conspire in violating any of the three main provisions of the act [18 USCA §1962(a)-(d)]. In addition to criminal penalties, RICO has a civil enforcement provision which allows one citizen to sue another for damage done to a business or property through a RICO violation [18 USCA §1964(c)].

The act provides a lengthy definition of what constitutes racketeering activity. It includes the threat to commit and the performance of crimes from murder to extortion, as well as crimes relating to drugs, gambling, fraud, witness intimidation, and theft (to name a few), which affect INTERSTATE COMMERCE [18 USCA §1961(1)]. The definition of racketeering in RICO also incorporates violations of federal laws such as the Hobbs Act [18 USCA §1951], another federal statute aimed against organized crime. The purpose of RICO is to end the practice of racketeering itself, and thus it can be enforced against persons involved in both legitimate and illegitimate businesses; the important element in any RICO litigation is proving racketeering. Notably, there is no limitation in the language of the act narrowing it to apply only to traditional notions of "organized crime." This is exhibited by the lack of the phrase *organized crime* anywhere in the statute and by a reading of the legislative history.

As a result of the broad interpretation of RICO, it began to be applied in a previously unexpected context, against antiabortion protesters. The application was first recognized in 1989 by the Third Circuit COURT OF APPEALS in *Northeast Women's Center, Inc. v. McMonagle,* 888 F.2d 1342. Clinics offering reproductive services, doctors, employees, and patients of these clinics, and local governments have all sought remedies under RICO. Most claims assert a civil violation of §1962(c), the use of an enterprise to racketeer. To win a case under this section of RICO, four elements must be proved. The plaintiff must establish that the defendant antiabortion protester(s) (1) is an enterprise, (2) that the defendant runs or participates in running (3) through a pattern (4) of racketeering activity. An enterprise can be comprised of any individual or group of associated individuals. No profit-seeking motive is required to establish an enterprise. A pattern is generally defined as two or more acts within 10 years of each other.

The exact racketeering activity, or "predicate act," most often complained of in the cases against antiabortion activists is extortion, which is defined by the Hobbs Act or state law. The Hobbs Act defines extortion as obtaining property through the wrongful use of threatened or actual force. For the purposes of RICO, "property" is interpreted to include intangible rights such as the right to conduct a business, the right to seek medical services, and the right for physicians and clinicians to perform their jobs.

Plaintiffs encountered varying degrees of success in winning cases against antiabortion protesters. However, the application of RICO to acts by antiabortion protesters as extortion was effectively curtailed by the Supreme Court's decision in *Scheidler v. National Organization for Women, Inc.*, 537 U.S. 39 (2003). The Supreme Court held that the activities described, an alleged conspiracy to shut down abortion clinics through blockades, aggressive picketing, and pamphleteering, did not meet the definition of extortion as defined by the Hobbs Act. The Court highlighted the fact that the definition of extortion requires that property be obtained. The Supreme Court found that the protesters did not obtain or attempt to obtain property from either the women seeking abortions or the clinics providing abortions. The acts the antiabortion activists performed were akin to coercion, generally defined to be the use of force or threat of force to restrict another's freedom of action, which was not included in the Hobbs Act or RICO.

While this decision was seen as a victory for pro-life activists, antiabortion protesters are not free to resume the same activities for which they were prosecuted under RICO. In 1994 Congress passed FACE, a law designed to stop aggressive clinic blockades. FACE grants strong civil and criminal penalties, comparable to those of RICO, including money damages and jail time.

The most prominent application of the RICO laws as applied to antiabortion protesters can be traced through the Supreme Court decision in *National Organization for Women, Inc. v. Scheidler*, 510 U.S. 239 (1994), and the decision on the case's APPEAL after remand *Scheidler v. National Organization for Women, Inc.*, 537 U.S. 393 (2003).

For more information: Kemper, Kurtis A. "Civil Liability of Antiabortion Protestors under Racketeer Influenced and Corrupt Organizations Act (RICO) in Light of *Scheidler v. National Organization for Women, Inc.*" In *American Law Reports*.

—Amy-Marie Culver

Ring v. Arizona, 536 U.S. 584 (2002)

In *Ring v. Arizona*, the Supreme Court held that in capital murder cases, the jury and not the judge must determine whether the presence or absence of aggravating factors merits the imposition of the death penalty. This is an important Sixth Amendment case that affects how the death penalty may be imposed as a punishment.

The basic rules regarding how the death penalty is imposed today in the United States were outlined in GREGG V. GEORGIA, 428 U.S. 153 (1976). In that case Georgia had a death penalty statute that provided for guided discretion when the jury was to make a decision regarding what penalty to impose in a capital murder case. Once a person had been convicted of murder, there would then be a second hearing or trial to determine the penalty. Juries would have to weigh a list of statutorily defined aggravating and mitigating factors against one another to decide whether execution was an appropriate penalty. Aggravating factors could include the heinousness of the crime, for example, while mitigating factors might be the upbringing of the defendant. If the jury decided that the aggravating factors outweighed the mitigating ones, they could impose the death penalty. Finally, the state law provided for automatic review of all death sentences. The Supreme Court upheld this procedure and ruled that it was neither a violation of the Eighth Amendment's cruel and unusual punishment prohibition nor of the Fourteenth Amendment's due process clause. As a result of *Gregg*, states had been using the two-stage process in death penalty cases since 1976.

In addition to *Gregg*, two other cases influenced the process regarding how sentencing in death penalty cases would be applied. In *Walton v. Arizona*, 497 U.S. 639 (1990), the Supreme Court had ruled that aggravating factors were not considered elements of a crime but instead were merely sentencing considerations. While in *Apprendi v. New Jersey*, 530 U.S. 466 (2000), the Court ruled that a judge in a jury trial could not double a sentence on a person convicted of a crime because to do so would violate the right to a trial by jury because a jury must determine beyond a reasonable doubt every element of a crime the accused was charged with violating. To allow for a doubling of a sentence, in this case, because of the presence of a "racial animus," let a judge and not a jury decide an additional fact.

In *Ring*, the jury had deadlocked on whether the defendant Timothy Ring was guilty of premeditated murder but found him guilty of felony murder. Under state law, an individual found guilty of felony murder could not be sentenced to death unless there was a separate hearing where the judge weighed mitigating and aggravating factors and found at least one of the latter and none of the former that justified lenience. The trial judge found two aggravating factors present in the Ring case and sentenced the defendant to death. Ring appealed to the Arizona Supreme Court claiming that his Sixth Amendment right to a trial by jury was violated. The Court upheld his conviction and the case was appealed to the United States Supreme Court which reversed.

Writing for the Court, Justice GINSBURG agreed with Ring that his Sixth Amendment rights had been violated. The Court first noted that *Walton* and *Apprendi* were in conflict. She argued that a basic tenet of American law was that in situations where judges presided over jury trials, it was up to the latter to determine the facts of a case and whether the prosecution had proved all of the elements of the crime as defined by statute. Thus, whereas *Walton* had allowed for a scenario to decide whether specific facts were present and warranted the death penalty, *Apprendi* suggested that judges did not have this authority in jury trials to determine facts.

The Court in *Ring* explicitly overruled *Walton* and stated that in jury trials, juries and not judges must determine whether aggravating factors exist and how they fit into the determination of a punishment. In effect, *Ring* stated that at least in the context of the death penalty, apparent sentencing factors such as aggravating factors are factual matters left for a jury to decide. Thus, since the Sixth Amendment guaranteed a person a right to a trial by jury, leaving it up to a judge to decide these matters violated Ring's rights.

Ring v. Arizona was a controversial death penalty decision. Many see it as an important protection of individual rights, whereas others saw the case as throwing confusion into the law. This confusion was whether other individuals sentenced to death before *Ring* could ask for a new trial or punishment hearing if the judge had determined whether aggravating factors existed and merited execution.

For more information: Bedau, Hugo Adams. *The Death Penalty in America: Current Controversies.* New York: Oxford University Press, 1997.

—David Schultz

ripeness

Ripeness is a judicial concept meaning a court case is nonjusticiable, that is, it cannot be heard in a court if the controversy is premature for review.

A case is premature for review when extrajudicial or lower court remedies have not been exhausted, or the problem has not yet actually occurred. *International Longshoreman's Union v. Boyd* (1954) is a good example of the latter. In 1952 Congress passed a law mandating that all aliens seeking admission into the United States from Alaska be "examined" as if they were entering from a foreign country. Believing that the law might affect seasonal American laborers working temporarily in Alaska, the longshoremen's union challenged the law in court. The Court ruled that because the statute had not been put into place and its effects had not yet happened, there were no grounds for a lawsuit. If the Court were to rule on no more than a possible wrong in the statute it would be giving an advisory opinion. A ruling to determine the constitutionality of legislation before any effect is experienced is far too remote and far too abstract for the proper exercise of the judicial function.

Ripeness comes under Article III of the United States Constitution. Article III states that "The judicial power shall extend to all cases in law and Equity, arising under this constitution. . . ." The "case" requirement of Article III has always been held to require an actual controversy that is of such a nature that it can be resolved with some finality in a court of law. A determination of ripeness requires a court to balance the fitness of the issues for judicial decision, the hardship to the parties caused by withholding court consideration, and the potential for setting poor precedents. A court must specifically determine how much the parties will be harmed if the court does not make a decision.

The Court has held that if the only harm is legal costs, it will not risk settling an issue prematurely. Another consideration the Court has expressed is that a premature ruling on a statute, policy, or issue could dramatically hinder an agency or government from improving upon the legislation so that the basis for controversy is removed. Finally, the Court looks at whether Congress has provided for preimplementation JUDICIAL REVIEW of an issue to determine if the case is ripe for judicial review or not.

Ripeness has been called one of the "Canons of Judicial Restraint" that, along with the concepts of advisory opinions, MOOT cases, friendly suits, and STANDING, have been used by the courts to limit the cases coming before them to actual cases and controversies.

For more information: Beers, Roger. "Ripeness in Environmental Litigation." Environmental Litigation Files (2000). Available online. URL: http://www.rbeerslaw.com/ripeness.html. Downloaded May 18, 2004; http://www.fedsoc.org/Publications/practicegroupnewsletters/administrativelaw/ripeness-adminv2i3.html

—Amy Oliver

Rochin v. California, 342 U.S. 165 (1952)

In *Rochin v. California,* otherwise known as the Stomach Pumping case, the Court established the "Shocks-the-Conscience" rule.

The Rochin case began on July 1, 1949, when three deputy sheriffs of California's Los Angeles County, acting on information that Antonio Rochin was selling narcotics, went to the two-story house where Rochin lived with his mother, common-law wife, brothers, and sisters. Finding an outside door open, they entered the house and ascended the stairs to the second floor to find the door to Rochin's bedroom locked. They forced open the door to find Rochin inside, half-dressed and sitting on the side of the bed. The deputies spotted two capsules on the nightstand beside the bed and asked, "Whose stuff is this?

Rochin grabbed the two capsules and put them into his mouth. The officers jumped on Rochin and attempted to retrieve the capsules. When force did not work, they hand-cuffed Rochin and took him to a nearby hospital. He was strapped to a gurney. The officers ordered a doctor to put a tube into Rochin's stomach to administer an emetic solution. The emetic worked, for Rochin vomited up the two capsules that were seized as evidence. Laboratory analysis revealed that they contained morphine.

Rochin was tried in the Superior Court of Los Angeles County, sitting without a jury, on the charge of possessing "a preparation of morphine" in violation of the California Health and Safety Code. The two capsules, the chief evidence against him, were admitted over his objection. The facts of the violent manner in which the capsules had been obtained were testified to openly by one of the deputies. Rochin was convicted and was sentenced to 60 days' imprisonment.

Rochin appealed to the district court of appeal for the second appellate district of the state of California, which upheld the conviction despite finding that the officers had committed several crimes—breaking and entering, assault and battery, and torturing and false imprisonment. Rochin petitioned the supreme court of California for a hearing. It was denied, but two justices dissented from the denial. One of the dissenting justices wrote that a conviction gained by physical evidence from the body of the accused person by physical abuse is as invalid as an oral confession obtained by torture.

The United States Supreme Court granted Rochin's petition for certiorari because a serious question was raised about the limitations that the due process clause of the Fourteenth Amendment places on the conduct of criminal proceedings by the states. Rochin's case was argued on October 16, 1951, and decided on January 2, 1952, in an 8-0 decision.

Justice Felix FRANKFURTER, writing for the Court, noted that it was very aware that criminal law was a state responsibility, and that nearly all the criminal cases in the United States are state cases. However, the Court was responsible for reviewing the "due process" of state actions. He then went on to deal with the main issue in the case, which was whether the police procedure forcing Rochin to vomit violated the due process clause of the Fourteenth Amendment.

Frankfurter held that while the behavior of the Los Angeles County deputy sheriffs was not specifically prohibited in the Constitution, it was conduct that violated the due process clause in a manner that "shocked the conscience of civilized decency." To allow the conviction to stand would allow brutality to act under color of law. Rochin's conviction was reversed.

In 1952 the Supreme Court was still viewing the BILL OF RIGHTS as applying to the federal government. Only those parts of the Bill of Rights that were of a "scheme of

ordered liberty" were applicable to the states. Frankfurter's interpretation of the due process clause protected those personal immunities that are implicit in the concept of ordered liberty. Justices Hugo BLACK and William O. DOUGLAS argued in a concurring opinion for incorporating the Fifth Amendment through the Fourteenth. Black also criticized Frankfurter for using a subject natural law approach.

Some students of the Court believe that "Shock the Conscience Test" is now useless. Others point out that the *Rochin* decision was made on the basis of the Fourteenth Amendment alone, which suggests there are rights independent of the Bill of Rights.

For more information: Warden, Lew M., Jr. "Notes and Recent Decisions: Constitutional Law: Due Process under the Fourteenth Amendment: Protection Against Physical Mistreatment: Admissibility of Evidence." *California Law Review* 40, no. 2 (June 1952): 311–317.

—A. J. L. Waskey

Roe v. Wade, 410 U.S. 113 (1973)

In 1973 the United States Supreme Court issued a landmark decision in *Roe v. Wade* that guaranteed a woman a constitutional right to obtain an abortion. Since it was decided, *Roe v. Wade* has been one of the most controversial decisions the Court ever issued.

Roe built on the opinion in GRISWOLD V. CONNECTICUT, 381 U.S. 479 (1965), which had articulated a right to PRIVACY for the first time. The Court first heard arguments in *Roe* in 1971 with two vacant positions on the Court due to the death of Republican John M. HARLAN and the retirement of Democrat Hugo L. BLACK. Chief Justice BURGER was uncomfortable with deciding a case of this magnitude with an incomplete court and wanted to wait until nominees Democrat Louis POWELL and Republican William REHNQUIST were added to the Court.

The Court then reheard arguments the following year and issued a decision on January 22, 1973. The challenge concerned a Texas law that had criminalized abortions. The Court granted STANDING to Jane Roe but denied that status to a physician convicted of performing two illegal abortions in Texas. The Does, a married couple who were challenging the law on a hypothetical basis, had been denied standing by a federal district court. The Supreme Court suspended the qualification of RIPENESS on the grounds that even though Jane Roe had already delivered her baby by the time the case was decided, "the normal 266-day human gestation period is so short that (a) pregnancy (would always come) to term before the usual appellate process (was) complete."

"Jane Roe" was actually Norma McCorvey, a Texan who had allegedly become pregnant in 1970 while working with a carnival in Augusta, Georgia. McCorvey already had one child who was being raised by her mother in Texas. Initially, McCorvey claimed that she was raped because Texas law would have allowed her to claim an exemption from Texas's strict abortion law, but she later backed down on that claim.

After McCorvey was denied an abortion, her case was taken by two young Texas lawyers who had been waiting for a test case to challenge the law. Sarah Weddington and Linda Coffee developed their challenge on every ground they could imagine would have any weight with the Supreme Court, including the due process clause of the Fifth Amendment, the equal protection clause of the Fourteenth Amendment, and the individual rights guarantee of the NINTH AMENDMENT.

During her original argument before the Court, members of the Court directed Weddington toward the privacy argument. Privacy, thus, became the grounds on which the Court based their belief that the "right of privacy, whether it be founded in the Fourteenth Amendment's concept of personal liberty and restrictions upon state action, as we feel it is, or, as the District Court determined, in the Ninth

Amendment's reservation of rights to the people, is broad enough to encompass a woman's decision whether or not to terminate her pregnancy."

Roe v. Wade reached the Supreme Court at a time when social awareness had been raised about the experience of forcing a woman to give birth to a fetus that was already known to be severely deformed. As far back as 1945, Alan Guttmacher had developed the idea of therapeutic abortions, and they had become common practice at hospitals throughout the country. The issue of therapeutic abortions took on new meaning for Americans in 1962 when Sherri Finkbine, a mother of four and the host of a local children's television show in Phoenix, Arizona, learned that thalidomide, the mild tranquilizer she had taken after her husband brought it home from Europe, was likely to cause extensive birth defects in the child she was carrying.

More than 10,000 seriously deformed babies had been born to mothers in West Germany who had taken the drug in the first few weeks of pregnancy, and similar incidents were reported in large numbers in England, Canada, and Australia. Because of the publicity in her case, Finkbine eventually obtained an abortion in Europe. Four years

Thousands of antiabortion protesters gather outside the White House before the start of the rally in Washington, D.C., on the anniversary of *Roe v. Wade*. *(Jamal Wilson/Getty)*

later, during an outbreak of German measles (rubella) in San Francisco, more married women than single women were seeking abortions because of evidence that at least 90 percent of women who were infected with the virus would give birth to deformed babies.

Within this social environment and the legal environment established by *Griswold* in 1965, the Supreme Court made its decision in *Roe.* Drawing on his expertise in medical law, Justice Harry BLACKMUN spoke for the majority of the Court, declaring that "state criminal abortion laws, like those involved here, that except from criminality only a life-saving procedure on the mother's behalf without regard to the stage of her pregnancy and other interests involved violate the Due Process Clause of the Fourteenth Amendment, which protects against state action the right to privacy, including a woman's qualified right to terminate her pregnancy."

Because the Court acknowledged the state's legitimate and interest in protecting both a pregnant woman and her unborn fetus, Blackmun developed a trimester system to determine the "compelling" point at which the state's right to protect the fetus should be allowed to override the right of the pregnant woman to control her own body. During the first trimester (one to three months), "the abortion decision and its effectuation must be left to the medical judgment of the pregnant woman's attending physician." From the end of the first trimester to the point of viability (identified as 24 weeks), a state might exercise its right to interfere in an abortion decision. From the sixth month to birth, "the State, in promoting its interest in the potentiality of human life, may, if it chooses, regulate, and even proscribe, abortion except where necessary, in appropriate medical judgment, for the preservation of the life or health of the mother."

Some states immediately responded by passing restrictive legislation to challenge *Roe* in the courts; and from 1973 onward, antiabortion forces lobbied for a constitutional amendment to abolish abortion. With the elections of Ronald Reagan in 1980 and George Bush in 1988, abortion became a major focus of federal legislation and policies, and views on abortion became the litmus test for nomination to the Supreme Court. Despite all the efforts toward overturning *Roe,* the conservative-controlled Court reaffirmed *Roe* in PLANNED PARENTHOOD OF SOUTHEASTERN PENNSYLVANIA V. CASEY, 505 U.S. 833 (1992). Two decades after *Roe,* Norma McCorvey declared that she had joined the antiabortionists in fighting to overturn *Roe.* However, the case was never about "Roe" as a person; it was always about pregnant women as a class.

For more information: Faux, Marian. *Roe v. Wade: The Untold Story of the Landmark Supreme Court Decision That Made Abortion Legal.* New York: New American Library, 1988; Reagan, Leslie J. *When Abortion Was a Crime: Women, Medicine, and Law in the United States.* Berkeley: University of California Press, 1997; "Roe v. Wade," on Douglas Butler, "Abortion: Medicine, Ethics, and Law" CD-ROM, 1997.

—Elizabeth Purdy

Romer v. Evans, 517 U.S. 620 (1996)

In *Romer v. Evans,* a 6-3 vote of the justices for the Supreme Court of the United States declared unconstitutional a state law that denied certain rights to homosexuals.

In *Romer,* the Court agreed that Amendment 2 of Colorado's constitution violated the EQUAL PROTECTION CLAUSE of the Fourteenth Amendment to the U.S. Constitution because its language was evidence of no other state interest than an expressed animosity toward a narrow class, homosexually oriented persons, for a broad and general discrimination in Colorado's political culture, and to "so deem a class of persons a stranger to its laws" a state cannot do. Justice Kennedy wrote the opinion for the majority of the Court. Justice SCALIA wrote a strong dissent, joined by Chief Justice REHNQUIST and Justice THOMAS.

After certain metropolitan city councils in Colorado passed ordinances granting antidiscrimination protections to gays, lesbians, and bisexuals, a statewide majority of voters in 1992 ratified a citizens' initiative on the ballot that amended the Colorado constitution to ban such governmental guarantees for gays, lesbians, and bisexuals without first ratifying a constitutional amendment to that effect. Amendment 2 prompted Evans and members of the city councils to seek a court injunction against its enforcement, claiming it violated the Fourteenth Amendment to the U.S. Constitution in its provision that a state action not deny any person of the right to equal protection of the laws. Roy Romer, then governor, represented the state's interest under the U.S. Constitution with two claims. One asserted individuals' private expressive CIVIL LIBERTIES under the First Amendment, including the right of religious expression against homosexuality. The other asserted the public's limited resources in affording nondiscrimination extended to other classes of political minorities under the equal protection clause of the Fourteenth Amendment, specifically racial and ethnic minorities of color. The litigants first presented their claims in the state's own court system, with its results going against the Second Amendment.

From the dissenters' point of view, the analysis is as follows. Given that gays, lesbians, and bisexuals are a unique political minority, concentrated in major metropolitan areas more than elsewhere, there is no constitutional reason why a broader majority rule cannot deny them political power there, declaring that the struggle for expanding CIVIL RIGHTS to them must occur at a statewide level of public policymaking. To hold contrary presents two problems. First, it ignores relevant judicial precedents upholding moral preferences of a voting majority in the political culture against the consensual sexual conduct of certain political minorities.

For example, in the 19th century, the Court upheld acts of Congress against adherents of bigamy or polygamy in the Church of Jesus Christ of Latter-day Saints (Mormons). More recently, it upheld a Georgia felony statute against homosexual sodomy, in *Bowers v. Hardwick*, 478 U.S. 186 (1986). Second, the *Romer* majority takes sides in a cultural war waged by political liberals in elite academic institutions who accept these diverse private consensual sexual preferences of a political minority as morally equal to a normal variation of orthodox heterosexual conduct.

According to the majority opinion, the historical weight of relevant federal precedents in the equal protection of the laws is that it "neither knows nor tolerates classes among citizens," citing Justice HARLAN's lone dissent in *PLESSY V. FERGUSON*, 163 U.S. 537 (1896), upholding Louisiana's interest in a legal code of separation by racial color in public accommodations. In other words, the Court concluded that Amendment 2 had no RATIONAL BASIS and was like discrimination in society and law which blacks historically faced.

For more information: Bansford, Stephen. *Gay Politics vs. Colorado and America: The Inside Story of Amendment 2.* Cascade, Colo.: Sardis Press, 1994; Keen, Lisa, and Suzanne B. Goldberg. *Strangers to the Law: Gay People on Trial.* Ann Arbor: University of Michigan Press, 1998.

—Sharon G. Whitney

Rosenberger v. Rector and Visitors of the Univ. of Virginia, 515 U.S. 819 (1995)

In *Rosenberger v. Rector and Visitors of the Univ. of Virginia*, the Court held that a public university's refusal to pay the printing costs of a Christian student magazine—while paying the printing costs of other student journals—constitutes viewpoint discrimination in violation of the First Amendment and is not mandated by the ESTABLISHMENT CLAUSE of the same amendment.

The *Rosenberger* Court was confronted with a conflict between two key First Amendment principles. It is well-established that the government may not favor any type of private speech on the basis of viewpoint; however, it is equally well-established that the government may not favor one RELIGION over another under the establishment clause. In *Rosenberger*, the University of Virginia (a state institution) refused to pay a Christian magazine's printing costs from the university's general student activity fund (SAF) for fear of violating the establishment clause. Ultimately, in a 5-4 decision, the Court concluded that the

university's refusal to pay the newspaper's printing costs constituted impermissible viewpoint discrimination under the First Amendment and further concluded that the university's payment of the newspaper's printing costs would not violate the establishment clause.

A wide variety of extracurricular student organizations exist on the university's hallowed "grounds," from a cappella singing groups to newspapers and magazines. Some of these organizations may receive money from the university's SAF; however, before any student organization is eligible to apply for reimbursement of certain expenses from the SAF, it must first become a contracted independent organization (CIO). Generally speaking, any student group willing to disclaim university approval of its activities can become a CIO.

Certain CIOs, including "student news" groups, are eligible to seek reimbursement of certain expenses from the SAF. The SAF is a fund that receives its money from a mandatory fee charged to each student each semester ($14 per semester in 1991). The student council, subject to review by a faculty body, has the initial authority to distribute funds and does so based on factors including the size of the CIO, its financial self-sufficiency, and the university-wide benefit of its activities. "Religious activities" were specifically excluded from receiving SAF funding under the 1991 SAF guidelines.

Fifteen CIOs received SAF funding during the 1990–91 school year as "student news" groups. The SAF directly paid the private contractors that had provided services to the CIOs (in the case of news journals, usually printing presses) rather than providing money directly to the students. Ronald Rosenberger's student organization, Wide Awake Productions (WAP), qualified as a CIO in 1990.

WAP published a magazine entitled *Wide Awake: A Christian Perspective at the University of Virginia*. After being granted CIO status, WAP requested that the printing costs for its magazine be paid through the SAF, as printing costs for other student-run publications were. The student council denied the request under the SAF guideline prohibiting the funding of "religious activities." WAP subsequently filed suit, alleging that the university's refusal to authorize payment of its printing costs on the basis of its religious viewpoint constituted impermissible viewpoint discrimination under the First Amendment. The university prevailed in the trial court and in the U.S. COURT OF APPEALS for the Fourth Circuit, and WAP appealed to the Supreme Court.

The Supreme Court, in a 5-4 opinion written by Justice Kennedy and, interestingly, joined by the other so-called conservative justices (REHNQUIST, O'CONNOR, SCALIA, and THOMAS), ruled for WAP. The Court, applying a limited purpose PUBLIC FORUM analysis similar to that in *LAMB'S CHAPEL V. CENTER MORICHES SCHOOL DIST.*, 508 U.S. 384

(1993), first held that the university's decision to withhold SAF funding from WAP did constitute impermissible viewpoint discrimination under the First Amendment. The university argued that the Court's holding in *Widmar v. Vincent,* 454 U.S. 263 (1981), gave it the right to make necessary academic judgments in allocating SAF funds. However, the Court distinguished *Widmar* on the grounds that *Widmar* involved a proper statement of the law only when the *government* is the speaker, i.e., when a university determines the content of the education it provides. In *Rosenberger,* by contrast, the speakers at issue were private speakers, seeking access to a forum created by the university. Since the government had created a "metaphysical" limited purpose public forum in the SAF, the government could not subsequently limit access to the SAF on the basis of CIOs' viewpoints. The university argued that the SAF guideline simply excluded CIOs on the basis of *content,* rather than viewpoint, which would have merited less constitutional scrutiny. However, the Court held that the guideline by its terms disfavored student journals with religious viewpoints.

The Court then held that no establishment clause violation would occur if the university provided SAF funds to WAP, because the program at issue was sufficiently neutral toward religion. The government did not create the SAF to advance religion; rather, the SAF was created to open a forum for speech and to support certain student organizations. Additionally, the Court noted that that student journals, as CIOs, were specifically required to disclose that they did not speak for the university. Since vital speech principles were at stake—the Court noted that the guideline could well be applied to deny funding of essays by hypothetical student contributors named Plato, Spinoza, and Descartes—and since the SAF was neutral toward religion and did not constitute a tax because it was collected only from students rather than the public-at-large, the Court reversed the Fourth Circuit and held that the university could not discriminate on the basis of viewpoint.

For more information: Oliver, A. Louise. "Tearing Down the Wall: *Rosenberger v. Rector of the University of Virginia.*" *Harv. J. L. & Pub. Pol'y* 19 (1996): 587; Stolz, John S. "Casenote: Rosenberger v. Rector and Visitors of the University of Virginia." *Seton Hall Const. L. J.* 7 (1997): 1,047.

—Joshua M. Dickman

Rostker v. Goldberg, 453 U.S. 57 (1981)

In *Rostker v. Goldberg,* the Supreme Court decided that registering men, but not women, for a military draft did not violate the Constitution.

In 1980 Congress held lengthy hearings on whether to require women to register for the draft. When it declined to

do so, several men filed suit, arguing that the male-only draft policy violated the equal protection principle protected by the due process clause of the constitution.

In the decades leading up to the *Rostker* case, the U.S. Supreme Court had ruled many laws aimed at preserving archaic gender stereotypes unconstitutional. In *Reed v. Reed,* 404 U.S. 71 (1971), the Court found that men could not be presumed more capable than women to act as executors of an estate. In *FRONTIERO V. RICHARDSON,* 411 U.S. 677 (1973), the Court ruled that military benefits for dependent spouses had to be distributed without regard to gender.

In *CRAIG V. BOREN,* 429 U.S. 190 (1976), a case that overruled an Oklahoma law allowing women, but not men, to purchase liquor at the age of 18, the justices established a standard that would make it particularly difficult for laws treating men and women differently to pass constitutional muster. It said that any such legislation had to be "substantially related to . . . important government objectives." Following that decision, the Court determined, in *Orr v. Orr,* 440 U.S. 268 (1979), that eligibility for alimony payments in the aftermath of a divorce could not be restricted to women.

The *Rostker* decision was different. Writing for the Court's majority, Justice REHNQUIST observed that Congress's decision to register males alone was due great deference from the judiciary for two reasons. First, the Constitution explicitly granted to Congress the authority to raise and regulate the armed forces, and second, the Court's military expertise was too limited to allow it to second-guess the legislative branch.

That point made, the Court considered whether, despite its reluctance to question Congress's military judgment, the constitutional violation was so glaring that the policy had to be overturned. The majority asserted that the equal protection provisions of the Constitution prevent discrimination only between individuals in similar situations. Were women and men similarly situated? Congress had decided that men alone were suitable for combat duty. Since the purpose of a draft was to raise combat troops, women and men were in different circumstances. The court concluded that the male only registration policy did not violate the Constitution.

In *Rostker* and in another case validating a California law that imposed criminal penalties for statutory rape on men alone (*MICHAEL M. V. SUPERIOR COURT,* 450 U.S. 464 [1981]), the majority effectively determined that when there were any relevant physical differences between the sexes, government policies treating men and women differently did not have to pass the constitutional hurdle erected by *Craig v. Boren.* After *Rostker,* most suits against SEX DISCRIMINATION practices were based on claims that the policies violated provisions of statutes, such as the CIVIL RIGHTS ACT OF 1964, and not on the Constitution.

For more information: Mezey, Susan Gluck. *In Pursuit of Equality: Women, Public Policy, and the Federal Courts.* New York: St. Martin's Press, 1992.

—William H. Coogan
—Richard Flannery

rule of four

The "rule of four" is an informal rule used by justices of the Supreme Court to help determine which cases they should accept for review.

The Court receives several thousand requests for review a year, but it has almost complete discretion to decide which cases to accept or reject. Most often, lawyers appealing a case to the Supreme Court submit a petition for a WRIT OF CERTIORARI (or, a "cert." petition); this is a request that the Court take action to rectify an error of judgment by another court. The rule of four states that the Court will review a case ("grant cert.") if four of the nine justices vote to hear the case.

The rule of four is intended to ensure that cases accepted for review are both important and of interest to a critical mass of justices. At the same time, by requiring the vote of only four justices, the rule is designed to prevent some majority of justices from rigidly controlling the composition of the Court's DOCKET.

The rule of four was developed after the passage of the Judiciary Act of 1925, which made Court review of most cases discretionary. Along with the Court's increased discretion came the Court's development of a rule for determining which cases to accept.

From the several thousand cases that come to the Court every year, the CHIEF JUSTICE, with advice from other justices, develops a relatively short list of cases that are serious candidates for review (the "discuss list"). Cases that do not make the discuss list are automatically rejected for review; in other words, the cert. petition is denied. On most Fridays during the Supreme Court's term (and on Thursdays late in the term), the justices meet in conference and, among other business, vote to grant or deny cert. to cases on the discuss list. This is when the justices use the rule of four.

Sometimes justices will vote to "join three." A reflection of some indecision or relative indifference, a join three vote indicates that a justice, otherwise inclined to reject review, will vote to hear a case if three other justices do so.

Scholar H. W. Perry, Jr., reports that if exactly four justices vote to grant cert., the chief justice can request that the case be discussed again at a later conference ("relisted"). This practice is intended to assist in docket control; with additional consideration, one of the four justices voting for cert. may change his or her mind.

For more information: O'Brien, David M. *Storm Center: The Supreme Court in American Politics.* 6th ed. New York: W. W. Norton, 2002; Perry, H. W., Jr. *Deciding to Decide: Agenda Setting in the United States Supreme Court.* Cambridge, Mass.: Harvard University Press, 1991.

—James Daniel Fisher

Rust v. Sullivan, 500 U.S. 173 (1991)

In *Rust v. Sullivan*, in a 5-4 decision, the Supreme Court upheld a so-called gag rule that prevented women's health clinic workers that received funds through Title X of the Public Health Service Act from mentioning the word *abortion* in counseling pregnant patients. The decision was a triumph for the Reagan and Bush administrations who had steadily sought to erode access to abortion.

In 1970 Congress established Title X to channel appropriations for family-planning, research, education, and health services. Family-planning counseling at Title X clinics had historically been allowed to offer a full range of options for pregnant women, which included abortion counseling along with pregnancy services and information on adoption. On several occasions, Congress had refused to exclude abortion counseling from the range of services offered at Title X clinics. Bypassing congressional action in 1988, Ronald Reagan executively authorized the Department of Health and Human Services to establish a policy that required Title X counselors to respond to a request for information about abortion with "this project does not consider abortion an appropriate method of family planning and therefore does not counsel or refer for abortion." The counselor was then required to refer the patient only to those "providers that promote the welfare of mother and unborn child."

Angry reactions to the decisions came from a variety of groups. Pro-choice advocates were angry at the limitations on exercising a legal right. The medical profession accused the Supreme Court of interfering with their First Amendment rights of free speech to provide comprehensive health counseling to their patients and to practice medicine to the best of their abilities. CIVIL RIGHTS advocates were outraged because the decision only affected poor women who depended on government funds and who were disproportionately black and Hispanic. Title X subsidized clinics that provided low-cost health care to around five million poor women. Many of Title X's clients were pregnant teenagers with high rates of infant mortality and a myriad of health problems.

Justice Harry BLACKMUN, author of the decision in *ROE V. WADE,* angrily charged his brethren on the Court with "viewpoint-based suppression of speech" and criticized them for allowing the government to obliterate "the freedom to choose as surely as if it had banned abortions outright." Congress reacted to the Court's decision in *Rust* with the Wyden-Porter bill that reaffirmed the original intention of Title X services by a vote of 73-25 in the Senate and 272-156 in the House of Representatives. On November 19, 1992, George Bush vetoed the legislation, and the veto was narrowly sustained. Many clinics around the country, included the Planned Parenthood clinic in the Bronx in New York, where the plaintiff Dr. Irving Rust acted as medical director, rejected Title X funding rather than give up the right to offer their patients a full range of family-planning options.

One of Bill Clinton's first actions as president was to rescind the gag rule upheld in *Rust v. Sullivan.* Clinton told the secretary of Health and Human Services to develop new guidelines for discussing abortions at clinics that received Title X funds, and Congress later enacted the guidelines into federal law.

For more information: Dellinger, Walter. "Gag Me with a Rule." *New Republic,* January 6, 1992, 14–16; "*Rust v. Sullivan,*" on Douglas Butler, "Abortion: Medicine, Ethics, and Law" CD-ROM, 1997.

—Elizabeth Purdy

Rutledge, John (1739–1800) *Supreme Court justice*
John Rutledge was appointed to the Supreme Court in 1789 by President George Washington and he served until 1795. Rutledge was an associate justice of the U.S. Supreme Court from 1789 until 1791, and CHIEF JUSTICE for a brief period during 1795.

John Rutledge was born near Charleston, South Carolina, in 1739. One of several children of an Irish immigrant couple, Rutledge was educated at home by his father, who was both a physician and an Anglican priest, until he was a teenager. Later, he traveled to England to study law and in 1760 was admitted to practice law there. Immediately thereafter, Rutledge returned to Charleston to begin his legal career. In 1763 Rutledge married Elizabeth Grimke, with whom he eventually had 10 children. During the 1760s, Rutledge established an excellent reputation in the legal community and built a very lucrative practice. He also invested in real estate and quickly became a major landowner and slaveholder.

In 1761 Rutledge was elected to the South Carolina provincial assembly, a position that he was to hold until 1776. He simultaneously served as temporary provincial attorney general for 10 months in 1764. In 1765, the year when the British Stamp Act created serious unrest in the colonies, Rutledge became very active in the self-government movement.

The state of South Carolina sent Rutledge to the First and Second Continental Congresses in 1774 and 1775, respectively. Unlike his younger brother, Edward Rutledge, who rose to prominence in national politics and became a signatory of the Declaration of Independence, John Rutledge's focus during 1776 was on state politics. He was elected president of the lower house of the South Carolina provincial legislature, and in that leadership position he helped to draft a state constitution and reorganize the state government. He resigned this post in 1778 due to a disagreement with political opponents' revisions to the state constitution. Despite this political strife, the people of South Carolina elected Rutledge governor in 1779.

By May of 1780, despite a valiant effort by the state militia, the British had invaded and seized control of South Carolina and also confiscated Rutledge's property and imprisoned him. After escaping from prison in 1781, he joined General Nathaniel Greene's group of Continental Army recruits and fought in their successful campaign to wrest South Carolina from British control.

Later in 1781, Rutledge participated in reestablishment of South Carolina's government and was appointed governor *pro temps.* Due to discomfort in that role, he resigned from that office in January 1782 and immediately accepted a seat in the lower house of the state legislature. During 1782–83, in addition to working as a legislator, Rutledge was also a delegate to the Continental Congress.

In 1784, after serving very briefly as a judge in the South Carolina chancery court, Rutledge was again elected to the lower house of the state legislature and continued to serve in that position until 1790.

Rutledge was one of the most influential delegates at the 1787 Constitutional Convention, acting as chairman of the Committee of Detail, serving on five other committees, and frequently addressing the assembled delegates and advocating the interests of the plantation-owning slave-holders of the South. It is ironic that he was the mouthpiece of these major landholders, because Rutledge's dedication to his political endeavors throughout the 1780s allowed him neither time nor energy to reestablish his vast plantations and therefore prevented him from recouping the financial losses he suffered as a result of the Revolutionary War.

In 1789, after he had served as a member of the Presidential Electoral College, the Senate quickly confirmed Rutledge as one of President George Washington's appointees to the position of associate justice of the U.S. Supreme Court. Although Rutledge resigned from that post in 1791 in order to become chief justice of the South Carolina Supreme Court, he remained active in national politics. During his tenure there, he was an outspoken critic of Jay's Treaty, a June 1795 accord that required the British to relinquish control of their western outposts, assessed monetary penalties for British seizure of American ships, and gave the United States limited trading privileges with the British-held West Indies.

Late in 1795, while the U.S. Senate was not in session, President George Washington appointed Rutledge as chief justice of the U.S. Supreme Court. Believing that Senate confirmation of this appointment would be virtually automatic, the president asked Rutledge to preside over one term of the U.S. Supreme Court before the Senate reconvened. Unfortunately, the Senate refused to confirm him as chief justice, stating that their decision was based on his opposition to Jay's Treaty. However, it is possible that the Senate's true reason for refusing Rutledge's confirmation was the intermittent mental illness from which he had suffered since his wife's death in 1792. Immediately after the Senate announced its decision, Rutledge's long and illustri-ous public career abruptly ground to a halt. Little is known about his life between that time and his death in 1800. He was interred at St. Michael's Episcopal Church in Charleston.

For more information: *The Supreme Court of the United States—Its Beginnings and Its Justices, 1790–1991.* Commission on the Bicentennial of the United States Constitution, 1992; United States National Archives and Records Administration. "America's Founding Fathers: Biographical Index." National Archives Experience (2003). Available online. URL: http://www.archives.gov/national_archives_experience/constitution_founding_fathers.html. Downloaded May 18, 2004.

—Beth S. Swartz

S

Saenz v. Roe, 526 U.S. 489 (1999)

In *Saenz v. Roe*, the Supreme Court struck down a state durational residency requirement on the amount of money a new resident could receive in welfare benefits. The case represented an important Fourteenth Amendment decision reaffirming the right of interstate travel, and the case also placed a limit on the ability of states to discriminate against people emigrating into their state.

In *SHAPIRO V. THOMPSON*, 394 U.S. 618 (1969), the Supreme Court had struck down laws in Washington, D.C., and in several states that had imposed one-year residency requirements before newcomers to a state could collect welfare benefits. Even though there is little evidence to support this belief, residency requirements were imposed on the assumption that poor people would migrate to states with high welfare benefits and therefore add to the tax burden. In *Shapiro*, the Court found these residency requirements discriminatory, a violation of the Fourteenth Amendment's EQUAL PROTECTION CLAUSE, and also a violation of the First Amendment right to interstate travel.

Shapiro was decided by the WARREN Court and authored by liberal William BRENNAN. Some critics of the decision contended that the case was no longer good law or that were the Supreme Court to review residency requirements again it would uphold them. In 1992 California enacted a one-year residency requirement for welfare benefits that stated that persons would collect the level of welfare they would have received in the former state if they had resided in California for less than one year.

However, in 1992, three California residents challenged the California law and a district court judge enjoined the law which was affirmed by the COURT OF APPEALS. The Supreme Court took the case and was unable to reach a decision but nonetheless halted enforcement of the law.

Then in 1996 Congress passed a new welfare law that authorized states to impose residency requirements such as the one in California. The state then announced that it would now enforce the 1992 law, and in 1997 two new residents to California challenged the residency requirements and the 1996 federal law authorizing them.

Writing for the Court, Justice STEVENS struck down both the California residency requirements and the 1996 federal law authorizing them. In his decision the justice reaffirmed *Shapiro v. Thompson* as good law, thereby dispelling the notion that the Supreme Court had changed its mind. While acknowledging that the word *travel* or the right to interstate travel is nowhere clearly written in the Constitution, Stevens contended that this right is a "firmly embedded" right all of us enjoy. This right includes the right to travel across state borders and not be treated as an unwelcome alien. To do that would be a violation of the equal protection clause.

More surprising, citing Article IV, section 2 of the Constitution, Stevens noted that this clause guaranteed to each citizen of a state all of the "privileges and immunities" enjoyed by citizens in the other states. In other words, he saw the right to interstate travel as a basic privilege and immunity guaranteed by the Constitution and that to improve residency requirements upon immigrants moving from one state to another would be denying some the rights enjoyed by others. This APPEAL to the privileges and immunities clause was considered a surprise because the Supreme Court had not used it to decide a case since the 19th century and most legal scholars thought that decisions such as the *SLAUGHTER-HOUSE CASES*, 83 U.S. 36 (1873), had killed off this clause as a tool to protect rights.

Overall, *Saenz v. Doe* was an important case reaffirming the right of citizens to travel about freely in the United States, even if it meant that they would be collecting benefits from the new states they moved to.

For more information: Maher, Kevin. "Like a Phoenix from the Ashes: *Saenz v. Roe*, the Right to Travel, and the Resurrection of the Privileges or Immunities Clause of the Fourteenth Amendment." *Texas Tech Law Review* 33 (2001): 105.

—David Schultz

San Antonio Independent School District v. Rodriguez, 411 U.S. 1 (1973)

In *San Antonio Independent School District v. Rodriguez,* the Supreme Court upheld the Texas school financing system. In doing so, the Court held that poor people are not a suspect class and education is not a fundamental right. This is a complex case involving issues of equal protection and due process.

Texas, like most states, partly relies on local property taxes to finance its schools. This type of funding system results in schools in poor areas not receiving as much funding as schools in wealthy areas. To illustrate: In the late 1960s, Edgewood Independent School District, the poorest district in San Antonio, spent $356 per student. In contrast, Alamo Heights, the wealthiest district, spent $594.

In the areas of equal protection and due process, the Court presumes the state action in question is valid unless given a reason to presume otherwise. Two reasons to presume otherwise are if either a suspect class or a fundamental right is involved.

In *Rodriguez,* the Court held that poor people are not a suspect class. A class is suspect if the class is "saddled with such disabilities, or subjected to such a history of purposeful unequal treatment, or relegated to such a position of political powerlessness as to command extraordinary protection from the majoritarian political process." Race is an example of a suspect class. The Court held that poor people are not a suspect class, and, as such, the Court had no reason to presume the school finance system was invalid.

Even if no suspect class is involved, if a fundamental right is involved, the Court may presume the school financing system is invalid. The Supreme Court in *Rodriguez* held that education is not a fundamental right under the due process clause of the Fourteenth Amendment. The importance of the activity is not determinative of whether the activity is fundamental for equal protection purposes. Rather, to be fundamental the right must be "explicitly or implicitly guaranteed by the Constitution." Nowhere in the Constitution is the right to education explicitly guaranteed. Although one could argue the Constitution implicitly guarantees the right to education, the Court rejected this contention.

Since the Court held that poor people are not a suspect class and education is not a fundamental right, the Court presumed the state action was constitutional. The financing system would be struck down only if there was not a rational relationship between the means and the end. The Court concluded that partially relying on local taxes to fund schools was rationally related to the purpose of local control. Consequently, the Court held that the Texas school financing system was constitutional.

The treatment of education was slightly altered in the subsequent case *Plyler v. Doe,* 457 U.S. 202 (1982), in which the Court held that states could not completely deny public education to a particular class of children.

For more information: Nowak, J. E., and R. D. Rotunda. *Constitutional Law.* St. Paul, Minn.: West Group, 2000.
—Daniel J. Singel

Santa Clara County v. Southern Pacific Railroad, 118 U.S. 394 (1886)

The *Santa Clara County v. Southern Pacific Railroad* ruling established the PRECEDENT that corporations hold the same rights as individual people do under the U.S Constitution.

The ruling extended the Fourteenth Amendment's EQUAL PROTECTION CLAUSE to corporations. That clause says that no state shall "deprive any person of life, liberty, or property, without due process of law; nor deny to any person within its jurisdiction the equal protection of the laws." The Fourteenth Amendment was passed to ensure equal rights for former slaves after the Civil War.

Corporations have successfully used the *Santa Clara* case to claim many further rights, including freedom of speech in the campaign finance arena, freedom of privacy in battling corporate disclosure, and other equal protection claims.

The case itself dealt with the fairly mundane topic of the proper taxation of fence posts on land held by the Southern Pacific Railroad. The Court upheld a lower court's ruling that the state had incorrectly included the value of the fence posts in its property tax assessment of land owned by the railroad.

The opinion never actually stated that corporations deserved the same constitutional protections as people do. In fact, the opinion explicitly says that the lower court should have ruled on the tax issues without reaching the question of corporate personhood:

> [the] court below might have given judgment in each case for the defendant upon the ground that the assessment, which was the foundation of the action, included property of material value which the state board was without jurisdiction to assess, and the tax levied upon which cannot, from the record, be separated from that imposed upon other property embraced in the same assessment. As the judgment can be sustained upon this ground, it is not necessary to consider any other questions raised by the pleadings and the facts found by the court. *Santa Clara County v. Southern Pacific Railroad,* 118 U.S. 394, 417 (1886).

However, prior to oral arguments (or by some accounts prior to the reading of the opinion), Chief Justice Waite is reported to have said "The Court does not wish to hear argument on the question whether the provision of the

Fourteenth Amendment to the Constitution, which forbids a State to deny any person in its jurisdiction the equal protection of the law, applies to corporations. We are all of the opinion that it does."

The clerk who wrote the headnotes, J. C. Bancroft Davis, wrote Waite prior to publishing the opinion to confirm if this quote accurately captured what Waite said. Waite replied that "I think your mem. in the California Rail Road tax cases expresses with sufficient accuracy what was said before the arguments began. I leave it with you to determine whether anything need be said about it in the report inasmuch as we avoided meeting the Constitutional question in the decision."

Davis then published the headnotes to say "the defendant Corporations are persons within the intent of the clause in section 1 of the Fourteenth Amendment to the Constitution of the United States, which forbids a State to deny to any person within its jurisdiction the equal protection of the laws."

The *Santa Clara* ruling capped a decades-long effort by corporate America to win such protection. Corporations were not mentioned in the Constitution and were originally not considered to be persons. Rather, they were thought of as artificial persons—creations of the government, subject to strict charters outlining their authorities and subject to strict regulation in ways that individuals were not.

Four similar cases where corporations had asserted Fourteenth Amendment rights (94 U.S. 155, 94 U.S. 164, 94 U.S. 179, 94 U.S. 180 [1877]) had previously been rebuffed by the Supreme Court. In these cases, the Court ruled without ever reaching the question of whether the corporation was a person.

It was highly unusual for the Court to issue a ruling with such monumental implications without any explanation for the ruling in the written opinion. If indeed the Court did mean to declare that corporations did have the rights of persons, why would Chief Justice Waite leave it up to the discretion of a clerk to decide whether or not to include this in the head notes?

These odd circumstances have led some to speculate that railroad interests used long cultivated connections to spin this decision to have their desired effect. J. C. Bancroft Davis, the clerk who wrote the headnotes, had been the president of the Newburgh and New York Railroad. It is possible that he was influenced in how he wrote the headnotes by Justice Field, a longtime supporter of the railroads who wrote a concurring opinion that the Court should have reached the Fourteenth Amendment arguments.

For more information: Hartmann, Thom. *Unequal Protection: The Rise of Corporate Dominance and the Theft of Human Rights.* Emmaus, Pa.: Rodale, 2002.

—Derek Cressman

Santa Fe Independent School District v. Doe, 530 U.S. 290 (2000)

In *Santa Fe Independent School District v. Doe,* the U.S. Supreme Court ruled that a public school district's policy allowing students to pray at high school sporting events violated the ESTABLISHMENT CLAUSE of the U.S. Constitution. While acknowledging the distinction between government-sanctioned speech and private religious expression, the Court rejected by a 6-3 vote the school district's contention that the student prayer was private speech protected by the Constitution's free speech clause.

The decision fits into a line of cases dating to ENGEL V. VITALE, 370 U.S. 421 (1962), in which the Supreme Court has resisted efforts to introduce state-sponsored prayer or other religious expressions in public institutions, especially elementary and secondary schools. The Court relied explicitly on its ruling in LEE V. WEISMAN, 505 U.S. 577 (1992), in rendering its decision against the Santa Fe school district. In *Lee,* the Court rejected the inclusion of clergy-led prayers at public school graduation ceremonies, arguing that such state-sponsored prayers amounted to a constitutionally impermissible form of religious coercion or indoctrination. The Court suggested that Santa Fe's policy, which allowed student-led prayers to be broadcast over public address speakers at high school football games, was analogous to the circumstance in *Lee.* Consequently, the game-day prayers were invalidated, meeting the same fate as religious invocations at graduation ceremonies.

The Santa Fe school district insisted that its policy was not comparable to the situation in *Lee* because the student prayers were purely private speech and therefore not a violation of the establishment clause, which limits only the government's sponsorship of religious expression. The district pointed to the fact that students were selected to lead the prayer through a process of student body elections, not by school administrators or teachers—a mechanism the school district had adopted in response to earlier litigation. The school district also noted that students were not required to attend the sporting events that included the prayers, thereby shielding them from the religious coercion that concerned the Court in *Lee.*

Justice STEVENS, writing for the Court majority, dismissed these claims. For Stevens, the totality of the circumstances surrounding the prayers at football games—they took place during a school-sponsored event, were broadcast over a public address system, and were recited by a student selected through a school-supervised (and designed) election—undermined the school district's claim that the prayers were purely private speech. Indeed, the school-sponsored election process effectively allowed the selection of particular prayers by majority rule, which is tantamount to an impermissible government endorsement of a specific RELIGION. Stevens also countered the district's claims about non-mandatory attendance by noting that some students—cheerleaders, band members, and players themselves—were required to attend the games. Even setting aside these students' mandatory attendance, the district's policy places other students in the unacceptable situation of deciding to attend a game, sometimes under intense social pressure, while being subject to undesirable religious expression.

Chief Justice REHNQUIST's dissent, which was joined by Justices SCALIA and THOMAS, took the majority to task not only for its reasoning in the case but also for the tone of its opinion. He suggested that the tradition of religious expression at public events belies the majority's view that such expressions violate the establishment clause. He also agreed with the district's contention that the prayers were purely private speech and therefore not subject to establishment clause limits. His greatest concern, however, was the "disturbing" tone of the Stevens opinion, which Rehnquist claimed "bristles with hostility to all things religious in public life."

Many conservative groups share Rehnquist's concerns about judicial "hostility" toward religion. The American Center for Law and Justice, for example, represented the Santa Fe school district and has been actively litigating for an expanded role for religious expression in public life since evangelist Pat Robertson established the organization in the early 1990s. Yet despite the efforts of ACLJ and other groups, the Court has remained resistant, and the conspicuous majority votes of Justices Kennedy and O'CONNOR in *Santa Fe* suggest that the "center" of the Court remains skeptical about the introduction of prayer into various aspects of life in public schools.

See also ESTABLISHMENT CLAUSE; *ENGEL V. VITALE.*
—Kevin R. den Dulk

Scalia, Antonin (1936–   ) *Supreme Court justice*

Antonin Scalia was appointed to the Supreme Court in 1986 by President Ronald Reagan. Since his appointment he has earned a reputation as a sharp but conservative member of the Court.

Scalia was born in Trenton, New Jersey, on March 11, 1936, and moved to Queens, New York, at age five. He later studied at Georgetown University, the University of Fribourg (Switzerland), and Harvard Law School. Prior to his appointment to the Court, Justice Scalia spent years in private practice, worked as a law professor specializing in administrative law, and served in the Nixon and Ford administrations as general counsel of the Office of Telecommunications Policy (1971–72), chairman of the Administrative Conference of the United States (1972–74), and assistant attorney general for the Office of Legal Counsel (1974–77).

Justice Antonin Scalia *(United States Supreme Court)*

In 1982 Scalia was nominated and confirmed as a judge on the COURT OF APPEALS for the District of Columbia Circuit. William REHNQUIST's elevation to CHIEF JUSTICE of the United States left open his seat as associate justice, and President Reagan nominated Scalia to fill the position on June 17, 1986; the Senate confirmed the nomination on September 17, 1986; he was commissioned on September 25; and he was sworn in as an associate justice on September 26. Justice Scalia's contribution to the law during his years on the Court has been marked in constitutional law, statutory construction, and legal writing style. He has been a consistent, eloquent advocate for interpreting the Constitution consistent with its original meaning, and for interpreting statutes consistent with their text, rather than by gleaning meaning from legislative history. And he has been forceful in criticizing those who disagree with his interpretive methodologies.

"Originalism" seeks to ascertain and apply to cases the understanding of constitutional provisions at the time of their enactment. Thus, "letters of marque and reprisal," U.S. CONST. Art. I, § 10, cl. 1, mean what they meant in 1789; "cruel and unusual punishments," U.S. CONST. Amend. VIII, mean what they meant in 1791; and "equal protection of the laws," U.S. CONST. Amend. XIV, § 1, means what it meant in 1868. As the justice himself has pithily put it, "the text of the Constitution, and our traditions, say what they say and there is no fiddling with them." Justice Scalia's adherence to originalism has brought him into conflict with supporters of the "living Constitution," who seek to expand on the Constitution's words to bring the document into conformity with modern notions of justice.

In several cases during Justice Scalia's years on the Court, his refusal to expand constitutional rights beyond their original parameters has left him in dissent, while the majority has expanded on old rights and discovered new ones. Although the scope of this article is necessarily limited, a few substantive areas deserve special attention. Particularly notable is his position that the Constitution contains no right to abortion; that decisions regulating ABORTION RIGHTS should be made by the states; and that ROE V. WADE, 410 U.S. 113 (1973), as inconsistent with these ideas, should be overruled.

In PLANNED PARENTHOOD V. CASEY, supra, which replaced Roe's trimester framework with the "undue burden" test, Justice Scalia wrote a separate opinion as notable for its biting rhetoric as for its legal analysis. Characterizing his colleagues as "systematically eliminating checks upon [their] own power," id. at 981, and employing a "verbal shell game," id. at 987, Justice Scalia charged the majority with creating constitutional law out of nothing more than the Court's policy preferences. Instead of relying on value judgments to determine the constitutionality of restrictions on liberty, Justice Scalia has suggested a simple, two-part test: whether the text of the Constitution speaks to the asserted liberty interest, and (if not) whether American traditions permit or forbid such restrictions.

Justice Scalia's use of tradition generally has the predictable effect of denying rights claims, particularly when the right is defined narrowly, as Justice Scalia believes it should be (for example, by defining an alleged right as the right to practice homosexual sodomy, as opposed to the right to engage in close, mutually dependent relationships).

Justice Scalia would respond, however, that it is not the Constitution's job to be protective of all claimed rights, even those of groups and individuals historically disadvantaged by the political process. Instead, the justice views the Constitution as having a limited scope, designed primarily to define the powers and responsibilities of the national government and its component parts. Where the Constitution does not expressly guarantee certain rights, Justice Scalia views it as the job of legislators—not courts—to decide whether the alleged rights are worthy of protection.

Perhaps Justice Scalia's greatest contribution to the law during his service has been his opinion for the Court in *Employment Div., Ore. Dep't of Human Res. v. Smith*, 494 U.S. 872 (1990). That case established that neutral laws of general applicability that have an incidental effect on one's ability to practice his RELIGION do not abridge the free exercise of religion protected by the First Amendment. Oregon prohibited the use of peyote, and Smith smoked the drug as part of an American Indian religious ceremony. Because of the drug use, Smith was fired from his job and applied for unemployment compensation, which was denied because persons fired because of "misconduct" were disqualified from receiving benefits. Smith challenged the denial as violating the Constitution, but the Court, per Justice Scalia, held for Oregon. Because the state's ban on drug use was not directed specifically at the *religious* use of drugs, but rather banned drug use by anybody for any purpose, the statute was generally applicable and therefore constitutional.

Justice Scalia's opinions on the ESTABLISHMENT CLAUSE have had less success persuading his colleagues than has his opinion in *Smith* on the free exercise clause. Consistent with the justice's reliance on originalism as informed by traditions, he would allow more state recognition of religion than is permitted under the Court's current cases. In *LEE V. WEISMAN*, 505 U.S. 577 (1992), for example, Justice Scalia dissented from the Court's striking down a nondenominational graduation prayer at a public high school. Going so far as to call part of the *Weisman* Court's opinion "incoherent" [505 U.S. at 636 (dissenting opinion)], Justice Scalia castigated the majority for invalidating a practice that had been part of American culture since colonial times.

Originalism and reliance on tradition do not yield exclusively conservative outcomes. To be sure, originalism forbids judges from enforcing new rights unknown at the founding and unreflected in American tradition, but where rights are recognized in the Constitution itself, Justice Scalia's originalism requires courts to strike down acts that impinge on those rights. Likewise, Justice Scalia's deference to legislatures and states absent a clear command in the Constitution allows states to adopt liberal laws that the justice would uphold over federal constitutional challenge.

In cases of statutory interpretation, Justice Scalia is a "textualist": The words of the statute, considered in context, are what should inform a judge as to the statute's meaning. Extraneous indications of the legislature's "intent" in enacting a given measure—legislative history, for example—should be ignored, for it is not the legislature's *intention* that governs, but rather the enactment itself that is "law." Justice Scalia has steadfastly refused to rely on legislative history in his opinions and has occasionally denigrated other justices for elevating its importance. Justice Scalia's eschewing of legislative history and his reliance on text, traditions, and original understandings seek to avoid what he views as "the main danger in judicial interpretation": "that the judges will mistake their own predilections for the law." He has sought to limit judicial discretion, so that court decisions, to the extent possible, will reflect law rather than the attitudes of judges. (Commentators, including Smith and Schultz, (1996), have contended that Scalia has been rather hypocritical on this point, and has in fact used his methods to achieve his own policy preferences.) For Justice Scalia, the rule of law requires no less than that judges substantiate their decisions by basing them on law exclusive of personal desire and articulate those decisions through rules that will signify the Court's (and the judge's) willingness to adhere to those rules in future cases.

For more information: Brisbin, Richard A., Jr. *Justice Antonin Scalia and the Conservative Revival.* Baltimore: Johns Hopkins University Press, 1997; Leahy, James E. *Supreme Court Justices Who Voted with the Government.* Jefferson, N.C.: McFarland, 1999; Rossum, Ralph A. "Text and Tradition: The Originalist Jurisprudence of Antonin Scalia." In *Rehnquist Justice: Understanding the Court Dynamic,* edited by Earl M. Maltz, 34–69. Lawrence: University Press of Kansas, 2003; Smith, Christopher E. *Justice Antonin Scalia and the Supreme Court's Conservative Moment.* Westport, Conn.: Praeger, 1993; Smith, Christopher E., and David A. Schultz. *The Jurisprudential Vision of Justice Antonin Scalia.* Lanham, Md.: Rowman and Littlefield, 1996.

—Michael Richard Dimino, Sr.

Schenck v. United States, 249 U.S. 47 (1919)

In *Schenck,* the U.S. Supreme Court first used a time, place, and manner restriction on the exercise of speech under the First Amendment's freedom of expression clause. Justice Oliver Wendell HOLMES wrote the majority opinion. Justice Holmes's opinion created the clear and present danger doctrine used to judge the constitutionality of future abridgements to the First Amendment's free expression clause. Holmes wrote:

> The question in every case is whether the words used are used in such circumstances and are of such nature as to create a clear and present danger that they will bring about the substantive evils that Congress has a right to prevent.

Holmes went on to use the now famous exemplar of falsely screaming "Fire!" in a crowded theater just to exercise one's First Amendment rights even though doing so might result in bodily harm to those fleeing the scene. *Schenck* was decided during America's engagement in the First World War amid the social hysteria and political uncertainty that such times can evoke. Following *Schenck,* the Court used the clear and present danger doctrine to expand restrictions upon free expression, but in later opinions Justice Holmes began to argue against the expansion of his famous opinion

beyond the limited exigent circumstances that he had first described in *Schenck.*

One example of this discontent was evident in *Abrams v. U.S.,* 250 U.S. 616 (1919), where the Court upheld First Amendment restrictions embodied in the Alien and Sedition Acts. In his dissent, Holmes warned against Congress's attempt to "forbid" dissent saying, "the best test of truth is the power of thought to get itself accepted in the competition of the market." As the Court continued to support the clear and present danger rule from *Schenck,* Justices Holmes and BRANDEIS, most notably, showed growing concern that the Court had misinterpreted the limited scope of *Schenck* as a much broader prohibition against general political dissent. In what some called a 360-degree change of heart, Justice Holmes wrote in a 1925 dissent "every idea is an incitement." In this case, *Gitlow v. N.Y.,* 268 U.S. 652 (1925), the clear and present danger doctrine was made more restrictive when Justice FRANKFURTER's opinion held that state laws carry a presumption that First Amendment restrictions are valid as long as they are reasonable means of protecting "attributes of a democracy (that) are threatened by speech." It was not until the 1938 case of *U.S. v. Carolene,* 304 U.S. 144, that the clear and present danger doctrine from *Schenck* began to erode, largely replaced by tests that balanced First Amendment rights against other state interests or by using "less drastic means" to satisfy the state's interest(s). Currently, an "exacting scrutiny" approach is applied to free expression cases before the Court. Under this approach, states "must show that its regulation (of speech) is necessary to serve a COMPELLING STATE INTEREST and that it is narrowly drawn to achieve that end" [*Perry Educational Association v. Perry Local Educational Association,* 460 U.S. 37 (1983) (Justice WHITE for the majority)].

For more information: Hemmer, Joseph, J. *Communication Law: The Supreme Court and the First Amendment.* Lanham, Md.: Austin and Winfield, 2000; Nowak, John E., and Ronald Rotunda. *Constitutional Law.* 4th ed. St. Paul, Minn.: West Group, 1991.

—Patricia E. Campie

Schlup v. Delo, 513 U.S. 298 (1994)

In *Schlup v. Delo,* the Court established the standard of proof for a prisoner to raise concerns that he is "actually innocent" of a crime such that it would be a miscarriage of justice for a federal court not to hear the merits of claims.

Lloyd Schlup was convicted of helping to murder a fellow inmate while he was in a Missouri prison and was sentenced to death. At his trial, Schlup claimed he was not involved in the murder at all, and he introduced a prison video showing that he was actually in the prison cafeteria line around the time that the murder occurred. Schlup was convicted based primarily on testimony by two prison guards that they saw Schlup participate in the murder and on the fact that he could not demonstrate precisely when the murder occurred relative to his appearing in the cafeteria line. Six years after his conviction, Schlup located a sworn statement from the prison official who made the distress call at the time of the attack, confirming that he called for assistance within 15–17 seconds after the attack. The videotape revealed that this call for assistance was broadcast more than 65 seconds after Schlup had already entered the cafeteria line. This appeared to support his claim that the murder occurred more than 40 seconds after Schlup arrived in the cafeteria. In addition, the video showed that a minute and a half after Schlup arrived in the cafeteria, another inmate, who was covered in blood, ran into the cafeteria from the direction of the murder scene.

Schlup attempted to present the evidence that he was actually innocent of the crime in a second federal habeas petition, but the petition was dismissed by the federal court as abusive because it raised issues that could or should have been raised through a proper investigation in the earlier petition. The Eighth Circuit Court of Appeal affirmed, holding that an abusive petition may be excused only if there is cause and prejudice or if the petitioner shows "by clear and convincing evidence that but for a constitutional error, no reasonable juror would have found the petitioner eligible for the death penalty."

In reversing this decision, the Supreme Court held that the standard applied by the Eighth Circuit was too strict. Rather, the Court held that if a capital prisoner could not otherwise show cause and prejudice to excuse his failure to raise constitutional claims in his first federal habeas petition, he was still entitled to a hearing on the merits if he were able to show that refusing to do so would result in a miscarriage of justice. The Court then explained that this miscarriage of justice standard did not require showing clear and convincing evidence of ACTUAL INNOCENCE, but only that "a constitutional violation has probably resulted in the conviction of one who is actually innocent."

For more information: Steiker, Jordan. "Innocence and Federal Habeas." *UCLA L. Rev.* 41 (1993): 303, 377.

—Jeffrey Bleich

Schmerber v. California, 384 U.S. 757 (1966)

In *Schmerber v. California*, the United States Supreme Court held that a forced blood draw from a suspected drunk driver without either a warrant or the consent of the driver did not violate the driver's right against self-incrimination under the Fifth Amendment or his right to be free from unreasonable searches and seizures under the Fourth Amendment. The Court also held that Schmerber's rights to counsel and to due process were not violated by the procedure.

Schmerber was convicted in a municipal court of driving under the influence (DUI). He had been hospitalized after being injured in an automobile accident and was arrested at the hospital. An investigating police officer had a blood sample drawn and analyzed, obtaining incriminating evidence of intoxication. The evidence was used against Schmerber at trial despite his objection that it had been taken from him without his consent and over his refusal to provide the blood sample on the advice of counsel. His conviction was affirmed by the California appellate courts.

Before the Supreme Court, Schmerber argued that the blood draw violated his rights to due process under the Fourteenth Amendment, to the advice of counsel under the Sixth Amendment, to be free from unreasonable searches and seizures under the Fourth Amendment, and against self-incrimination under the Fifth Amendment. The due process and right to counsel claims were rejected offhand. The Court went on to consider the Fourth and Fifth Amendment issues.

The Supreme Court had previously held in *Breithaupt v. Abram,* 352 U.S. 432 (1957), that a blood draw did not violate the Fifth Amendment in a state court prosecution, but that ruling was based upon the fact that the privilege against self-incrimination had not yet been applied to the states. In the interim, the Court had decided *Malloy v. Hogan,* 378 U.S. 1 (1964), applying the privilege to the states through the Fourteenth Amendment. In this case, the Court looked at the merits of Schmerber's claim but still decided against him, holding that the privilege applied only to "testimonial" evidence, such as statements and polygraph examinations. Physical evidence such as blood samples is non-testimonial and therefore not covered by the Fifth Amendment.

Schmerber's Fourth Amendment claim also required the Court to reconsider *Breithaupt v. Abram,* which had rejected a Fourth Amendment claim for the reason that the Court had not yet required the states to exclude evidence obtained in violation of the Fourth Amendment. Since that time, the Court had decided *MAPP V. OHIO,* 367 U.S. 643 (1961), applying the EXCLUSIONARY RULE to the states. This meant that if the blood draw violated Schmerber's right to be free from unreasonable searches and seizures, the evidence could be excluded from evidence at trial. Here again, the Court looked at the merits of Schmerber's claim and found it lacking. The Court held that there was probable cause to believe that Schmerber was intoxicated and that a blood draw would result in relevant evidence. The Court refused to require a warrant in this case because delay would result in destruction of evidence, as the alcohol in Schmerber's bloodstream gradually dissipated. Finally, the Court held that the nature of the search itself was reasonable. The blood draw was done by a trained person in a reasonable manner, creating little if any risk of injury. The Court left open the question of whether a blood draw taken under less favorable circumstances would still be reasonable.

This case is important because it addresses the constitutional rights of persons suspected of drunk driving to refuse to provide evidence of guilt to authorities. By holding that blood tests are not testimonial and are therefore not covered by the privilege against self-incrimination, the Court has prevented these tests from being excluded under the Fifth Amendment. The Fourth Amendment does apply to blood draws, however, while agreeing that such draws are searches under the Fourth Amendment, the Court has held them to be reasonable. Considering the volume of drunk driving cases nationally, *Schmerber* is a landmark decision.

For more information: Kamisar, Yale. "Is the Exclusionary Rule an 'Illogical' or 'Unnatural' Interpretation of the Fourth Amendment?" *Judicature* 62 (April 1978): 66.

—Paul D. Stanko

school prayer

According to the U.S. Supreme Court, organized prayer in the public school setting, whether in the classroom or at a school-sponsored event, is unconstitutional. The only type of prayer that is constitutionally permissible is voluntary prayer by an individual student that is not coercive and does not substantially disrupt the school's educational mission and activities. For example, each student has the right to say a blessing before eating a meal, provided he does this individually, or with others who join him of their own volition. During a meal break or other non-curricular class period, a student can engage in religious activity, alone or with other willing individuals, provided he does not invite unwilling individuals or those unfamiliar with his RELIGION to join him in prayer, or otherwise interfere with other students' rights or well-being or choice of activities.

Based on U.S. Supreme Court precedents, if school officials do not want to risk acting in an unconstitutional fashion, it is imperative that they avoid promoting or encouraging a student's personal prayer. In addition, while students may speak about religious topics with their peers, school officials should intervene if such discussions devolve into religious harassment.

Any group or individual religious activity pursued during a noninstructional period of the school day must actually be student-initiated. Participation or supervision by any school employee might create the appearance of unconstitutional school endorsement or promotion of one religion in preference to another.

The ESTABLISHMENT CLAUSE of the First Amendment to the Constitution forbids state-sponsored prayers in public school settings regardless of the intention of the school officials or administrators, and regardless of any nondenominational intention behind the use or writing of the prayers [*LEE V. WEISMAN*, 505 U.S. 577 (1992)].

Vocal denominational or nondenominational prayers, and ceremonial reading from the Bible, are unconstitutional practices in the public school classroom [*ENGEL V. VITALE*, 370 U.S. 421 (1962); *School District of Abington Township, v. Schempp*, 374 U.S. 203 (1963)]. It is legally irrelevant if the prayer or Bible reading is voluntary, or if students may be excused from the activity or classroom during the prayer. Similarly, student volunteers are prohibited from broadcasting prayers over a school intercom system into the classroom.

In its efforts to prevent even the semblance of support for an organized activity at a public school that might possibly be related to religion, the Supreme Court has even established precedents that cast suspicion on silence. It struck down a statute requiring a moment of silence that students could use for silent prayer or meditation because the high court found the law was enacted for the sole purpose of advancing religion [*WALLACE V. JAFFREE*, 472 U.S. 38 (1985)]. The justices stopped short of deciding whether an enforced moment of silence, regardless of purpose, is ever constitutional in a public school. However, the *Wallace* decision casts doubt on the constitutionality of any organized moment of silence since it appears that the high court would be likely to find that both the purpose and effect of such moments of silence are invariably religion-oriented, with an underlying purpose of advancement of religion.

Supreme Court PRECEDENT, based on a case decided in 2000, established that it is unconstitutional for a school official, including a coach, to initiate or lead a sports team or attendees at a school-sponsored sporting event in prayer [*SANTA FE INDEPENDENT SCHOOL DIST. V. DOE*, 530 U.S. 290 (2000)]. The same decision also prohibited any school official from asking a team member or any other student to initiate or lead a prayer before, during, or after a public school-sponsored athletic activity or event. It is also unconstitutional for a member of the clergy to offer prayers before or after public school athletic activities or events [*Jager v. Douglas County School District*, 862 F.2d 824 (11th Cir.), cert. denied, 490 U.S. 1090 (1989)]. However, whether due to the high court's intention or oversight, it appears that voluntary prayer presented and led by students without official permission or sanction may be constitutional, as long as there is no coercive intent behind the prayer.

Prayers delivered by clergy at official public school graduation ceremonies are unconstitutional [*Lee v. Weisman*, 505 U.S. 577 (1992); *Santa Fe Independent School Dist. v. Doe*, 530 U.S. 290 (2000)], even if the prayer is nondenominational or voluntary. The Supreme Court has not specifically ruled on whether a purely student-initiated non-sectarian graduation prayer is constitutional, and the lower federal courts disagree on the issue. However, when the high court ruled in *Santa Fe* that a district policy allowing student-initiated and student-led prayer before football games was unconstitutional, it effectively ruled out the possibility that any district policy allowing student-initiated and student-led prayers would be permissible at graduation ceremonies.

Moreover, in both *Santa Fe v. Doe* and *Lee v. Weisman,* the Supreme Court expressed particular concern that students could be coerced, through pressure from their peers and others, into praying during school events such as football games and graduation ceremonies. This danger exists regardless of the identity of the person offering the prayer; he or she may be a member of the clergy, or a schoolteacher or administrator, or a student who offers the prayer.

The Court also emphasized in *Weisman* and *Santa Fe* that attendance at major school events like graduation or football games should not be considered "voluntary" even if authorities officially designate it as such. In many school district throughout the United States, special days as diverse as weekly football games and high school graduation are highly significant events that students should be able to attend without fear of religious coercion.

A separate aspect of graduation is sectarian or nonsectarian services that are conducted to honor graduates and are distinct and separate from a school's official graduation ceremonies. If such events are held on school premises but are privately sponsored and do not involve school personnel in any way other than as possible attendees, they can pass constitutional muster even if they include prayers and religious sermons. This quirk exists because of the Supreme Court's decision in *GOOD NEWS CLUB V. MILFORD CENTRAL SCHOOL,* 202 F.3d 502 (2nd Cir. 2000); reversed and remanded, 533 U.S. 98 (2001), which actually lowered the figurative wall of separation between church and state. In that case, the school board attempted to avoid establishment clause problems by allowing the local community to use the school for meetings and other events pertaining to the community's welfare, but expressly prohibited use of school facilities for religious purposes. The high court held that to allow the Good News Club to meet would *not* be an unconstitutional government endorsement of religion, while to exclude the club discriminated against that group because of its viewpoint.

Public school teachers and administrators, in their capacity as private citizens, or on the school premises when they are not in the presence of students, are entitled to the full range of First Amendment rights of freedom of speech and religion. However, teachers hold special status in the school. When students and teachers are in a classroom or assembly, the students are a captive audience and, although they would undoubtedly refute this point, are often extremely impressionable. Students may actually perceive teachers to be government officials and could view religious speech by teachers or other school personnel as a state endorsement of religion. Therefore, it is unconstitutional for teachers to pray with or in the presence of students in school or in their capacities as teachers or representatives of the school. Additionally, to prevent the possibility that anyone might interpret a teacher's action as one that violates the establishment clause, it is constitutional for a school to abridge a teacher's free speech and free-exercise rights in situations where students are present.

The Supreme Court has said that a state's interest in avoiding an establishment clause violation may be so compelling that it justifies abridging an individual's right to free speech that would otherwise protected by the First Amendment [*LAMB'S CHAPEL V. CENTER MORICHES SCHOOL DISTRICT,* 508 U.S. 384 (1993)]. It is also unconstitutional for a teacher to read the Bible in front of students during a daily silent reading period [*Roberts v. Madigan,* 921 F.2d 1047 (10th Cir. 1990), cert. denied, 505 U.S. 1218]. The Supreme Court has upheld the right of legislative bodies to open their sessions with a prayer [*Marsh v. Chambers,* 463 U.S. 783 (1983)]. However, it may be unconstitutional for school boards to start their meetings with prayer, since lower federal courts have found that prayers in a school board meeting are unconstitutional, since such meetings are inextricably involved with a public school system [*Coles v. Cleveland Board of Education,* 171 F.3d 369, U.S. Court of Appeals, Sixth Circuit (1999)].

For more information: Gearan, Anne. "Wall of Separation Lowered—Supreme Court Says Religious Clubs Can Meet at Public School." ABC News (2001). Available online. URL: http://abcnews.go.com/sections/us/DailyNews/supremecourt010611_religion.html. Downloaded May 18, 2004; Longley, Robert. "Public Schools Don't Have a Prayer." U.S. Gov Info/Resources. About.com. Available online. URL: http://usgovinfo.about.com/library/weekly/aa070100a.htm. Downloaded May 18, 2004; Robinson, B. A. "Religion and Prayer in U.S. Public Schools: Introduction, Constitution, and Court Decisions." Ontario Consultants on Religious Tolerance (2003). Available online. URL: http://www.religioustolerance.org/ps_pray.htm. Downloaded May 18, 2004.

—Beth S. Swartz

school vouchers

Tuition vouchers for parochial schools (a kind of government-funded check that can be cashed only at participating schools) have been controversial since 1947 when the United

States Supreme Court first defined the ESTABLISHMENT CLAUSE as requiring strict separation of church and state.

The establishment clause in the First Amendment of the UNITED STATES CONSTITUTION states "Congress shall make no law respecting an establishment of RELIGION, or prohibiting the free exercise thereof. . . ." Voucher programs, which provide public taxes as financial assistance to children attending private or parochial schools, were long considered unconstitutional because they provided tax money for religiously affiliated schools, thus breaking down separation between the state and religion. Courts have changed their rulings over time.

LEMON V. KURTZMAN, 403 U.S. 602 (1971), became the PRECEDENT for cases concerning the constitutionality of programs providing public aid to religiously affiliated institutions. The Supreme Court used *Lemon* to establish a new set of guidelines to test the constitutionality of such programs. This "Lemon Test" established three requirements that a statute must have in order to pass muster: a secular legislative purpose, primary effects that neither advance nor inhibit any religion, and the law must not foster an excessive government entanglement with religion. As long as the program or project did not violate any of the three requirements, then it would be found constitutional in accordance with the *Lemon* precedent.

MUELLER V. ALLEN, 463 U.S. 388 (1983), set a new precedent that somewhat weakened *Lemon*. The Supreme Court decided a Minnesota program authorizing tax deductions for various educational expenses, including tuition, was not a violation of the establishment clause. The Court found the program constitutional because funds were made available to both public and religious schools through the private choice of the beneficiaries. Even though 96 percent of the beneficiaries were parents of children attending parochial schools, the court majority decided that the program did not discriminate and did not imply state approval of any religion.

Three years later the Court decided another case concerning tuition for a blind student attending a Christian College. *Witters v. Washington Department of Services for the Blind*, 474 U.S. 481 (1986), expanded the precedent set in *Mueller.* It maintained that the establishment clause does not prohibit vocational rehabilitation assistance for a disabled student attending private religious schools. A similar case, ZOBREST V. CATALINA FOOTHILLS SCHOOL DISTRICT, 509 U.S. 1 (1993), held that a hearing-impaired student at a Catholic High School could be furnished with a state-funded sign language interpreter.

Almost a decade later, the Supreme Court confronted its first full tuition voucher case. *Zelman v. Simmons-Harris*, 536 U.S. 639 (2002), challenged the voucher system used in Cleveland, known as Ohio's Pilot Project Scholarship Program. The system provided tuition aid for financially challenged or needy students in the Cleveland City School District for the purpose of allowing them to choose between schools. Both religious and nonreligious schools were permitted to participate. Cleveland was the only city covered by this program, primarily because its public school system ranked among the worst performing public school systems in the nation. This program was designed to create competition between schools to stimulate improvement and to give poor families the opportunity to choose better educational institutions for their children.

Because 82 percent of the participating schools were religiously affiliated and 96 percent of the participating students attended religious schools, the system was challenged as a violation of the establishment clause. The Court cited a number of previous cases, including *Lemon v. Kurtzman,* 403 U.S. 602 (1971); *Mueller v. Allen,* 463 U.S. 388 (1983); *Witters v. Washington Department of Services for the Blind,* 474 U.S. 481 (1986); and *Zobrest v. Catalina Foothills School District,* 509 U.S. 1 (1993). *Mueller, Witters,* and *Zobrest* were particularly useful because they established that a neutrally administered government program providing benefits to a wide range of citizens without reference to any religion "is not readily subject to an Establishment Clause challenge." Ohio's Pilot Project Scholarship Program was created for a secular purpose—"providing [non-discriminatory] educational assistance to poor families in a failing public school system." Therefore the Court focused on the question whether or not the program had an effect that either advanced or inhibited religion.

Chief Justice William REHNQUIST, writing the majority opinion for a court divided 5-4, reversed the previous decision made by the Ohio State Supreme Court. In accordance with *Mueller, Witters,* and *Zobrest,* along with the Lemon Test, the Court found that *Zelman v. Simmons-Harris* was constitutional. Any "incidental advancement" of any denomination, wrote Justice Rehnquist, was clearly "attributable to the individual recipient [of the tuition voucher], not to the government," since students were not required to attend religious schools. Because the aid was administered in a neutral fashion and provided beneficiaries with a "genuine choice" between religious and nonreligious schools, the program did not advance or inhibit any particular religion. Nor did the program lead to excessive government entanglement with religion and thus could not be condemned as a violation of the Establishment Clause.

Zelman v. Simmons-Harris is the most authoritative school voucher precedent to date. The rule of law it established is that a "neutral program of private choice, where state aid reaches religious schools solely as a result of the numerous independent decisions of private individuals" carries no implications of government endorsement of religion. However, granted that the decision was 5-4, it is unclear whether this can now be considered settled law.

For more information: Weber, Paul J., and Vincent E. Gabbert. "Tuition Vouchers in the United States: Let the Battles Begin." *Education and the Law* 10, no. 2-3 (1998): 153–163.

—Amber Ruhl

scientific evidence

Scientific evidence is presented at trial by an expert witness concerning technical information that would assist the trier of fact, either the judge or jury, to understand other evidence or decide a fact in dispute in the case. Federal Rules of Evidence 702, 703, 704, 705, 706, and 803(18) govern the admission of scientific evidence.

Courts have long had to determine which scientific evidence was sufficiently reliable to justify admission into evidence and which was speculative and inadmissible. *Frye v. United States,* 293 F. 1013 (D.C. Cir. 1923), a 1923 opinion by the COURT OF APPEALS for the District of Columbia, set forth the sole requirement that admissible scientific evidence must have gained "general acceptance" in the field of study, ". . . courts will . . . admit . . . expert testimony deduced from a well recognized scientific principle or discovery . . . sufficiently established to have gained general acceptance in the particular field in which it belongs."

For 70 years, most state and federal courts followed the "general acceptance" standard, even though the 1975 adoption of the Federal Rules of Evidence seemed to broaden the *Frye* admissibility standard. In 1975 Rule 702 read:

> If scientific, technical, or other specialized knowledge will assist the trier of fact to understand the evidence or determine a fact in issue, a witness qualified as an expert by knowledge, skill, experience, training, education, or otherwise may testify thereto in the form of an opinion or otherwise.

The 1993 U.S. Supreme Court opinion in *DAUBERT V. MERRELL-DOW PHARMACEUTICALS, Inc.,* 509 U.S. 579, 113 S. Ct. 2786, 125 L. Ed. 469 (1993), rejected the one-factor *Frye* test, extended the admissibility of scientific evidence, and held that the Federal Rules of Evidence, rather than *Frye,* applied to admission of scientific evidence in federal court. *Daubert* construed the Federal Rules of Evidence, particularly Rules 702 and 703.

The *Daubert* Court held that the term *scientific* in Rule 702 suggested a grounding in scientific methods and procedures. It also held that "knowledge" suggested more than subjective belief or speculation.

According to *Daubert,* a trial judge plays a "gatekeeper's" role in determining whether testimony meets the reliability and relevance requirements of Rule 702. The trial judge, faced with an offer of expert testimony, must first determine whether the expert proposes to testify to scientific knowledge and whether the evidence will assist the trier of fact to understand or determine a fact in issue. Then the trial judge must assess the scientific validity and reliability of the reasoning or methodology underlying the evidence and whether that reasoning or methodology applies to the case and its facts.

The *Daubert* Court held that Rule 702 requires the trial court to go beyond the exclusive *Frye* standard and consider other factors as well. It suggested the trial court consider at least four factors in determining the admissibility of expert testimony. These include (1) whether the knowledge can be and has been tested; (2) whether the theory or technique has undergone peer review and publication; (3) the error rate and standards for a particular scientific technique; and (4) whether the theory or technique enjoys "general acceptance" in the field.

The Supreme Court revisited admissibility of expert testimony in 1997 in *General Electric Co. v. Joiner,* 522 U.S. 136, 118 S. Ct. 512, and 139 L.Ed. 509, (1997). It held that an appellate court may not reverse a trial court's decision to admit or exclude expert testimony unless it finds the trial court abused its discretion.

A third case, *Kumho Tire Co., Ltd. v. Carmichael,* 526 U.S. 137, 119 S. Ct. 1167, 143 L.Ed. 238 (1999), extended the *Daubert* holding from "scientific" knowledge to include "technical" and/or "specialized" knowledge. The *Kumho Tire* Court emphasized that the *Daubert* factors do not constitute a "definitive checklist or test." The court concluded that a trial court should consider the *Daubert* factors "where they are reasonable measures of the reliability of expert testimony," which the law grants the trial judge wide latitude to determine. *Kumho Tire* makes clear that this deferential "abuse of discretion" standard applies both to the trial court's decision about the method used to test an expert's reliability and the trial court's determination as to whether the expert's testimony is reliable.

Current Federal Rule 702 embodies the holdings of *Daubert* and succeeding cases:

> If scientific, technical, or other specialized knowledge will assist the trier of fact to understand the evidence or to determine a fact in issue, a witness qualified as an expert by knowledge, skill, experience, training, or education, may testify thereto in the form of an opinion or otherwise, if (1) the testimony is based upon sufficient facts or data, (2) the testimony is the product of reliable principles and methods, and (3) the witness has applied the principle and methods reliably to the facts of the case.

Rule 703 specifies the permitted bases of expert opinion testimony. An expert may testify with an opinion or inference from facts known at the hearing. The facts or data need not be admissible in order to admit the opinion or inference if the bases of the expert's testimony are of the type reasonably relied on by experts in the particular field. However, inadmissible facts or data must not be disclosed to the jury unless the court determines that the value in assisting the jury substantially outweighs their detrimental effect.

Rule 704 permits an expert to testify about an issue to be ultimately decided by the trier of fact. However, in criminal cases, no expert witness testifying about the defendant's mental state may give an opinion or inference on whether the defendant possessed the mental state constituting an element of the crime or a defense to it.

Rule 705 allows an expert to testify with an opinion or inference and give reasons for the opinion or inference without first testifying to the underlying facts or data, unless the court requires it. However, cross-examination might require the expert to disclose the underlying facts or data.

Rule 706 permits the court to appoint its own experts.

Rule 803(18) codifies the "learned treatises" exception to the hearsay rule. It authorizes admission of statements in published treatises, periodicals, or pamphlets about history, medicine, science, or art. The court may only admit those statements established as a reliable authority by the testimony of a witness, expert testimony, or judicial notice. Even then, the court may only admit the statements to the extent called to the attention of an expert witness upon cross-examination or relied upon by the expert witness in direct examination. The jury may not see these documents because the court may not receive them as exhibits.

For more information: Federal Judicial Center. *Reference Manual on Scientific Evidence.* 2nd ed. St. Paul, Minn.: West, 2000; Federal Rules of Evidence 702, 703, 705, 706, and 803(18); Graham, Michael H. *Handbook of Federal Evidence.* vol. 2. St. Paul, Minn.: West, 2001.

—Patrick K. Roberts

Scottsboro cases

The Scottsboro cases are commonly known as *Powell v. Alabama,* 287 U.S. 45 (1932), for the Supreme Court case that ultimately overturned the illegal convictions of the nine young black men who were caught up in the extreme prejudice of the American South during the early 1930s at a time when constitutional rights for blacks were ignored. Eight of the nine were found guilty by all-white juries in Alabama and sentenced to death. The ninth, only 13 at the time of the alleged rapes, was sentenced to life in prison. The trials received national attention and served to show the world what passed for justice in Alabama in the 1930s.

The Scottsboro cases began on March 24, 1931, when the young men illegally boarded a train in Chattanooga, Tennessee, and set out on a journey that was scheduled to take them into Alabama and Mississippi. The nine young men were: Clarence Norris, Charlie Weems, Haywood Patterson, Andy Wright, Roy Wright, Willie Robertson, Olen Montgomery, Ozie Powell, and Eugene Williams. Andy and Roy Wright were brothers and both were friends with Patterson and Williams. None of the others even knew each other. The Great Depression had sent a number of similar young men on the road in search of food, jobs, education, or a better life. Clarence Norris would later admit that he thought he might find someone who could teach him how to read.

Decades later Clarence Norris would describe the scene when a group of young white men also illegally boarded the train and tried to push the young black men out of the car. Some of the black men pushed the white men off the train, and in retaliation the young whites fabricated a rape scenario with the cooperation of Ruby Bates and Victoria Price, two young women who were also on the train. When the train pulled into Paint Rock, Alabama, the nine blacks were arrested, and driven 30 miles to the Scottsboro jail. The following day at a hearing, the nine first learned of the rape charges. The young men were justifiably scared. Some were beaten until they told authorities what they wanted to hear. According to Alabama law, all nine could be executed if convicted of rape. Whites in the area stormed the jail, and the National Guard was called in to keep order.

The cases came to trial within two weeks. The chief witnesses contradicted themselves, and later one of the "victims" of the rape admitted to a friend that she had lied. Despite the irregularities evident during the trial, eight of the nine "Scottsboro Boys" were sentenced to death by all-white juries. The Scottsboro trial received enormous publicity, and the Communist Party and the National Association for the Advancement of Colored People (NAACP) fought over who would represent them. The Communist Party won the battle.

Over the course of the next several years, the appeals in the Scottsboro cases resulted in seven retrials and two Supreme Court decisions. The men spent from six to 19 years in jail for a crime that was never committed. In a 7-2 decision in *Powell v. Alabama* in 1932, the Supreme Court overturned all convictions because of inadequate legal representation and ordered them retried.

In *Norris v. Alabama,* 294 U.S. 587, in 1935, the Court again reversed the Alabama court decisions on the grounds that a jury that excluded blacks was not a jury of their peers as guaranteed by the Fifth Amendment. In several subsequent trials all-white juries, allegedly chosen from integrated jury pools, repeatedly convicted the eight men. Alabama ultimately dropped all charges against Roy Wright, Eugene Williams, Willie Robertson, and Olen Montgomery, and Clarence Norris, along with the rest of the men, were pardoned in 1976.

For more information: Goodman, James. *Stories of Scottsboro.* New York: Pantheon, 1994; Kinshasa, Kwando Mbiassi. *The Man from Scottsboro: Clarence Norris and the Infamous 1931 Alabama Rape Trial, in His Own Words.* Jefferson, N.C.: McFarland, 1997.

—Elizabeth Purdy

search warrant

A search warrant is a legal document signed by a judge that contains information sworn to be true by a law enforcement officer. The document allows the government to conduct a lawful search based on current information and is to be done in conjunction with an investigation. The search also has stipulations that require the area to be searched to be a specific place for a specific thing.

The purpose of a search warrant is to search an area for illegal material items or even for a person. The importance of such an endeavor and the approval to invade someone's privacy rights forces the government to verify that the action being done is absolutely necessary for court purposes.

Because each person has constitutional-based rights to be secure in their possessions and privacy, any violation of those rights is of great concern to society. The abilities enumerated to the government and/or the agent for the government are established to force the law enforcement agency to develop probable cause—the high likelihood that the materials to be sought are in fact at a location where the law enforcement officer must go in order to carry out the protection of the public. The standards of proof for these searches is that the information used to describe what is to be searched for is reliable and specific, someone from the law enforcement agency must sign an affidavit (a document where the officer swears that the information is true and correct), and a neutral judge must approve the contents of the information and the location or area to be searched in order to lessen the chance that a person's privacy rights will be violated.

The Fourth Amendment to the Constitution states that only upon probable cause can a warrant be issued that allows the government to make the search. Some searches that are done incident to arrest, that is to say after an arrest is made, are acceptable without a warrant. The dangerous occupation of law enforcement has allowed for certain exemptions of the search warrant rules where an officer may act without a warrant. Allowances for action by the officer are usually very narrowly viewed by the court and must fit into one of the following three categories (they are only guides for decision-making by the judge): actions related to the officer's personal safety, the flight of the offender from prosecution, and the destruction of evidence. Often an officer must provide the following during court in order for his actions to be considered valid during

a warrant-less search: he must articulate his safety concerns, his experience level with similar circumstances, and his observations. Although a search warrant allows the government to search a location for something or someone, the courts have recently begun to recognize that the persons within the location may need to be searched or detained in order to reduce the probability that an officer would get hurt. Yet, the court must also balance the right of the person to be searched to be secure in his/her privacy.

There are many factors to consider when drawing up a search warrant, such as where the information is coming from and whether or not it is reliable. Other considerations for the government agent may include whether the material things or the person to be searched for will be at the place to be searched if the agent took the time necessary to secure the warrant and the judge's signature. The court will allow for emergencies, which are often called exigent circumstances, but this is on a case-by-case basis and many factors must come into play in order for this scenario to be allowed. The court allows for some warrant-less searches to stand because the destruction of evidence or the injury to a government agent is likely to happen.

Still another aspect of a search warrant that has to be considered is the location of the evidence to be searched for. The information provided to the court in the form of an affidavit must describe the exact area to be searched, if possible. For example, if an agent is searching for a million dollars of illegal money bundled together in tape and plastic, and reliable information comes in to the agent as to the money being in a box in an attic, the agent must describe the location and the thing to be searched for. The agent could

Police carrying out a search warrant. *(Monroe County Sheriff's Office)*

not then in the middle of the search of the attic look in a small jewelry box that is hidden in a basement closet on a shelf behind a row of coats. That type of search would not be legal. Yet, if a warrant is written for a person to be searched for in a certain house, the search can be conducted into any place that the person could hide—for the most part.

There are other rules that have been enacted in order to diminish the likelihood that an agent of the government will violate a person's privacy, some of which include how an agent is to announce his presence, the discovery of things that are left out in the plain view for everyone to see, and perhaps the discovery of something not planned for, but still illegal. Sometimes the courts have allowed for the discovery of something illegal that was improperly found, under the argument that the item would have been found despite the fact that the illegal items/evidence were not listed on the warrant. The rules regarding search warrants are sometimes complicated, and the criminal rules managing search warrants have become more restrictive of the government agents in light of privacy rights violations of persons. The opportunity of the government to search a person's private things is not a common occurrence, and the courts view this right very skeptically.

As law enforcement officials have responded to various technologies that made it easier to hide certain items like guns and drugs—so have the criminals transporting and hiding these illegal things. Many search warrants have been thwarted by locations that are difficult to get to and obscure hiding places. In addition, with illegal businesses, like the illegal drug trade, there are persons whose sole job is to notify the sellers of the drugs if the police come around so that the sellers can destroy the evidence before it is seized. This has forced law enforcement officials in the last 30 years to utilize informants more often. Subsequently, the proof needed to make sure that the information is correct has been scrutinized much more in regards to informants.

The balancing of the rights of a person in regard to their privacy and the needs of the government to protect certain evidence and reduce the injury to the government agent during a search warrant has had profound effects upon what may be searched for and when. Once a warrant is issued, the right to search does not exist forever. The warrant will expire and become invalid if it is not successfully served within the accepted time period described by the court. Also, protecting a person from law enforcement abuse is an important concern when a warrant is to be served. Sometimes if a judge feels it is important based on the facts, certain restrictions will be placed upon the times that a warrant can be served. For example, if the place to be searched is a house that has people with children that go to school living in it, the judge may establish that in order to reduce the likelihood of the children getting hurt, the warrant may not be served until after the children are at school.

Despite these allowances, restrictions must be placed upon the actions of the government and its agents in order to reduce the possibility of abuse. Even with these limits the government can, under the normal course of business, perform noncriminal searches of establishments that are regulated by the government, or that the government has a compelling interest in. A good example is searches of meat plants; the government should be allowed to conduct a search of a plant that supplies meat to the public in order to better protect the health of the public.

A search warrant is a limited right to invade someone's privacy in order to secure evidence that would be used in a court of law. There are rules for the warrant, for the process of securing a warrant, and for the delivery of a search warrant, which have been established to create a uniform understanding and to ensure civilian protections. The most common use of a search warrant is in the search for contraband or illegal fruits of criminal activities. There are exceptions to the search warrant allowance in order to protect the public from abuse by the law enforcement powers, but when it comes to the safety of society or of the government agent, some extra protections for those people like police officers are allowed. The citizens' right to be protected against searches that are not reasonable is enumerated within the Constitution and is supported by case law, but it must be understood within the context of societal needs to combat criminal activities within society.

For more information: *Katz v. United States*, 389 U.S. 347 (1967); *Maryland v. Buie*, 494 U.S. 325 (1990); *Terry v. Ohio*, 392 U.S. 1 (1968).

—Ernest Alexander Gomez

Second Amendment

One of the most contentious issues facing someone who would understand the Constitution and opinions of the United States Supreme Court is the subject of firearms and the proper rules concerning their use. The debate about the right to keep and bear arms as set out in the Second Amendment to the U.S. Constitution, which has not been specifically incorporated under the Fourteenth Amendment, has generated an immense amount of heat and not much light. The amendment as written says: "A well regulated Militia, being necessary to the security of a free State, the right of the people to keep and bear Arms, shall not be infringed."

Various analyses of the language of the amendment have arrived at different conclusions. Specifically, one side of the debate holds that the words, "A well regulated Militia. . . ." mean that the founders only meant that the local militia, a predecessor to the National Guard, was to be armed. Others are of the view that the right to possess and use firearms is one of the basic individual rights set out in the U.S. Constitution. There is a limited amount of background represented in the opinions of the Supreme Court, and therefore, this article will consider collateral sources in addition to the opinions of the Court.

The first English statute controlling the conditions of use for weaponry was the Statute of Northampton (1328), which forbade the carrying of arms in the presence of the king unless one were a proper officer to have a weapon in the king's service. This was modified in 1689 by a statute enacted during the reign of William and Mary entitled the Bill of Rights, sec. 7 which stated: "That the subjects which are protestants, may have arms for their defence suitable to their conditions, and as allowed by law." This principle was translated to the United States and assumed fresh vigor as the Second Amendment to the new Constitution.

The impetus to include the Second Amendment came from many state constitutions as exemplified by Article 13 of Pennsylvania's Declaration of Rights passed in 1776, which was a longer version of the amendment. The country was not very old when the debate began and the various opinions were laid out. The issue of whether it was a collective or individual right did not arouse much attention during the 19th century, but in general the consensus was that the right was an individual one. This attitude was based more on a distrust of standing armies than on anything else.

One notable exception to the general laissez-faire attitude toward possession of firearms was the prohibition in Southern states against "mulattoes, Indians and blacks, whether slave or free, from carrying any kind of weapon." In Virginia this ban was instituted in 1640. Antebellum free blacks were subject, even in their homes, to arbitrary search and seizure of firearms. This state of affairs was confirmed by *DRED SCOTT V. SANDFORD*, 60 U.S. (19 How.) 393 (1857), when Chief Justice TANEY wrote that the negro has no rights and is not a citizen, therefore, the government cannot confer upon a noncitizen certain rights. And further: "Nor can Congress deny to the people *the right to keep and bear arms*, nor the right to trial by jury, nor compel any one to be a witness against himself in a criminal proceeding." Slavery was abolished by the Thirteenth Amendment passed in 1865, but the "black codes" enacted in several states under Federal control severely restricted "persons of color" from possessing or owning firearms.

The Civil Rights Act of 1866 did away with any legal distinction between citizens whether white or black. Nevertheless, private parties, such as the Ku Klux Klan, made a practice of disarming blacks. The U.S. Supreme Court ruled in *United States v. Cruikshank*, 92 U.S. 542, 548 (1875), that there was nothing in the federal powers that could stop the practice. This situation persisted until the 20th century, generally through economic regulation,

specifically outlawing anything but the most expensive handguns.

The first restriction on the general populace came with the enactment in 1902 of a general handgun ban in South Carolina, which restricted any pistol sales to all but sheriffs and their deputies. The Sullivan Act in New York City in 1911 sought to restrict gun ownership through a permit system. This act is in force as of this writing. The first nationwide law to restrict firearms was the National Firearms Act of 1934. This law was challenged and became recognized as a case holding to the collective rights view, *U.S. v. Miller*, 307 U.S. 174 (1939). However, the primary ruling in the case was that there was no Second Amendment right for individuals to possess certain military weapons, such as machine guns.

On the subject of the Second Amendment, the Supreme Court has often made comments about it through DICTA, which is a judicial opinion expressed by a judge on points of law that do not necessarily arise in the case being decided and are not involved in it.

In *Poe v. Ullman*, 367 U.S. 497, 523 (1961), a case decided against a marital privacy interest in birth control devices, Justice HARLAN, in his dissent compared the privacy right to other basic individual rights such as the right to keep and bear arms. Harlan's dissent was quoted in *ROE V. WADE*, 410 U.S. 113, 169 (1973), by Justice Potter STEWART in a concurring opinion that makes the same comparison between privacy rights and includes the right to keep and bear arms. On the other hand, Justice DOUGLAS, dissenting in *Adams v. Williams*, 407 U.S. 143, 150 (1972), stated directly that the Second Amendment was to keep the militia alive.

Writing in a concurring opinion in *Printz v. United States*, 521 U.S. 898, 936 (1997), Justice THOMAS rendered the opinion that rather than a restraint on an individual right, the language of the amendment was a restraint on governmental authority. He also expressed the thought that the Supreme Court had never directly ruled on the exact meaning of the Second Amendment.

For more information: Carlson, Andrew. *The Antiquated Right*. New York: Peter Lang, 2002.

—Stanley M. Morris

selected exclusiveness

The concept of selected exclusiveness was developed by the Supreme Court in order to provide a framework for dealing with the vexing question of whether the commerce clause's grant to Congress of the power to regulate commerce among the states is an exclusive grant, which deprives the states of any regulatory power in the area.

Since the problems created by state tariffs and duties on interstate shipments were one of the principal concerns of the framers, a conclusion that this grant was intended to be exclusive would seem reasonable. However, as a practical matter, the Court has found that, in dealing with a subject as broad and varied as INTERSTATE COMMERCE, it is simply not feasible to completely exclude the states' regulatory power from areas that have not been regulated by Congress.

The question of the commerce power's exclusiveness was considered by the Court in *GIBBONS V. OGDEN*, 22 U.S. 1 (1824). In this case, the first involving the commerce clause to come before the Court, it was argued by counsel for the plaintiff that the Constitution's delegation of an exclusive regulatory power over interstate commerce to Congress was incompatible with a steamboat monopoly granted by the state of New York. Although Chief Justice MARSHALL indicated some sympathy for this argument, he ultimately decided the case on narrower grounds. Since Gibbons was operating under the authority of a federal license to engage in the coasting trade, he found that in this case the laws of the state of New York had come into collision with an act of Congress. Hence, the New York statute was rendered invalid by the established principle of national supremacy, and the Court did not have the occasion to decide whether the commerce power was exclusive.

The Court revisited the question of the constitutionality of state regulations of interstate commerce some 26 years later in the case of *COOLEY V. BOARD OF WARDENS*, 53 U.S. 299 (1851). In this case, a Pennsylvania law that levied a fine on vessels that refused to take on a pilot upon entering the Port of Philadelphia was challenged as being contrary to the commerce clause. The Pennsylvania statute was not in conflict with any federal law. In fact, Congress had specifically authorized such state legislation in an act of 1789, which provided that pilots were to be regulated by state laws, both those in existence at the time, and those that might be enacted later (Act of August 7, 1789, ch. 9, 1 Stat. 154).

Justice Curtis, giving the opinion of the Court, reasoned that this provision of the act of 1789 could not be constitutional if the commerce clause prevented the states from legislating on this subject. Hence, in order to decide the case, the Court had to address the question of whether the grant of the commerce power was an exclusive one. Curtis resolved this issue by developing the doctrine of selected exclusiveness. This doctrine is quite complex; however, in Curtis' opinion, this complexity is necessary to accommodate the many diverse subjects that come within the scope of the power to regulate commerce. According to Curtis, some of these subjects "imperatively demand[ed] a single uniform rule," while others "imperatively demand[ed] that diversity, which alone can meet the local necessities of navigation." Obviously, in those areas which

demanded uniform regulation, Congress's power is exclusive. On the other hand, with respect to other subjects, such as the regulation of pilots, state regulation is permissible and, in fact, desirable, due to "the superior fitness . . . of different systems of regulation, drawn from local knowledge and experience, and conformed to local wants." However, although Congress's power to regulate interstate commerce is not always exclusive, it is supreme. Consequently, even in those areas where local legislation is acceptable, it is only permitted in the absence of federal regulation.

For more information: Corwin, Edward S. *The Commerce Power versus States Rights.* Princeton, N.J.: Princeton University Press, 1936; Frankfurter, Felix. *The Commerce Clause Under Marshall, Taney and Waite.* Chicago: Quadrangle, 1964.

—Justin Halpern

Selective Service

Selective Service is an agency of the U.S. government that conducts the registration of males available for a potential military draft. Every male aged 18 to 25, residing in the United States or an American citizen must register with the Selective Service. Conscription, first created in 1863 during the Civil War, was reinstituted by the Selective Service Act of 1917 during the First World War. While there is currently no draft, registration is required under the Military Service Act of 1967.

In the event of an armed conflict, or emergency, Congress may pass legislation enabling the Selective Service to draft registered men to fill the vacancies in the armed services not already filled by voluntary enlistment. The sequence of a potential draft is currently determined by a random lottery and the man's year of birth; starting with those aged 20, then those aged 21, and so forth up to 25-year-olds; 18- and 19-year-olds would be drafted last. Once drafted, men receive physical, mental, and moral evaluations to determine fitness for military service. If approved they have 10 days to file for an exemption, postponement, or deferment of service. After 10 days, they must report to a local Military Entrance Processing Center for induction into the armed forces.

Historically, conscription has been controversial. During the Civil War, a man could get out of service by either presenting a volunteer substitute or by paying $300. That left lower class and poor men most likely to serve. The conscientious objector exemption was not created until the Selective Service Act of 1917 during World War I and was extended only to individuals who were members of pacifist religions. All other objectors were imprisoned, where many died. During the Vietnam War, loopholes in the exemption requirements benefited the upper classes, again leaving the working-class and poor men to fight in the war.

Draft protests were widespread during the Vietnam War. Public resentment against the draft became so predominant that conscription was abolished altogether in 1973. When draft registration was reinstated by President Jimmy Carter in 1980 following the Soviet invasion of Afghanistan, exemptions were made more difficult to obtain. College students, who made up the majority of service exemptions during the Vietnam War, can no longer postpone service until the end of their educational career but only until the end of their current semester or the end of the academic year for seniors. Local draft boards are now required to provide more descriptive representation, showing they are racially and ethnically similar to the community in which they oversee the draft. Finally, conscientious objectors may now claim moral as well as religious objection to war to apply for exemption from military service. This expands the classification to include those not affiliated with pacifist religions but still does not allow exemptions for those who object to a particular war on moral or religious grounds but are not pacifists.

For more information: Military Selective Service Act (50 U.S.C. App. 451 et Seq.); Selective Service System. Available online. URL: http://www.sss.gov. Downloaded May 18, 2004; Shapiro, Peter, ed. *A History of National Service in America.* United States: Center for Political Leadership and Participation, 1994.

—Kate Hanratty

Selective Service Commission v. Minnesota Public Interest Research Group, 468 U.S. 841 (1984)

In *Selective Service Commission v. Minnesota Public Interest Research Group* (MPIRG), the Supreme Court upheld a law that required male students applying for college financial aid to register for the draft. This decision was important because it rejected arguments that the enforcement of the draft laws discriminated against the poor. The case was also important in that it effectively turned colleges into enforcement bodies to ensure that male students comply with the Selective Service Law.

During the Vietnam War the Military Selective Service Act required male citizens between 18 and 26 to register for the military draft. Many individuals were in fact drafted for the war, but individuals who could get into college obtained deferments. This meant, according to some critics, that individuals who came from affluent enough backgrounds could escape the draft by going to college, leaving the poor as the ones who would be drafted and go to Vietnam.

After the war ended, so did the draft and the requirement to register for it. However, in 1980, as a result of the Soviet Union's invasion of Afghanistan, President Carter issued a proclamation ordering males to register for the draft within 30 days of their 18th birthday. In 1984 Congress amended the Higher Education Act of 1965, stipulating that male students would be ineligible for federal college financial assistance unless they could provide proof that they had registered for the draft. Male students would be required, as a condition of receiving financial aid, to provide their college with proof that they had complied with the draft registration law.

Three anonymous individuals challenged the new federal requirement, contending that the law was unconstitutional. They argued that the law requiring proof of compliance with the draft registration law discriminated against the poor, that it was a BILL OF ATTAINDER, and that it violated the Fifth Amendment privilege against self-incrimination. A district court enjoined enforcement of the law and the case was taken by the Supreme Court, which rejected all three arguments.

Writing for the Court, Chief Justice BURGER quickly rejected the bill of attainder claim, arguing that typically bills of attainder name specific individuals who are guilty of a crime. Here, no specific names were issued or mentioned in the law. In addition, the Court looked to see if the registration requirement imposed the traditional types of punishment banned with bills of attainder—(1) was it a legislative punishment; (2) does it further a nonpunitive legislative purpose; and (3) whether the legislative record indicates an intent to punish. The Court did not see any of these purposes with the draft registration and compliance requirements.

Second, Burger rejected claims that the CERTIFICATION of compliance with the draft registration requirement violated the Fifth Amendment. MPIRG had argued that forcing male students to certify that they had complied with the registration requirements was a forced waiver of their privilege against self-incrimination. In effect, they were forced to confess to their noncompliance with the law. Because males are not required to apply for financial aid, they are not being forced to self-incriminate themselves.

In dissent, Justices BRENNAN and MARSHALL stated that the law does violate the Fifth Amendment. Moreover, Marshall also contended that the law violated the EQUAL PROTECTION CLAUSE in that it discriminated against the poor who could not afford to attend college without financial aid. More affluent individuals who could attend college without federal assistance could escape the draft registration requirements simply by not seeking financial aid.

Selective Service Commission v. Minnesota Public Interest Research Group was an important case giving the federal government new powers to enforce the military draft registration requirements. For some it impermissibly made college into a tool of the government to enforce registration, and for others it created a new way for the rich to escape military service.

For more information: Kramer, Daniel C. *The Price of Rights: The Courts, Government Largess, and Fundamental Liberties.* New York: Peter Lang, 2003.

—David Schultz

self-incrimination, right against

The Fifth Amendment of the Constitution enshrines a right against *self-incrimination* by individuals charged with a criminal offense.

Self-incrimination is the compulsory giving of evidence against oneself in a criminal proceeding. This right was also captured by the constitutions of six of the original states and was encouraged by many for inclusion in the federal BILL OF RIGHTS. The colonists had experienced oppression in England, where inquisitorial proceedings by the Star Chamber required those being investigated to testify against themselves.

In the early Republic, this right was considered essential to a fair criminal justice system, though it had a much narrower meaning than it does now. Today, the Court has expanded the protection against self-incrimination and has articulated two main reasons for doing so: first, the right is essential to our accusatorial criminal justice system; and second, it provides protection from governmental intrusion into an individual's privacy. Indeed, Fifth Amendment jurisprudence has often combined with the Fourth Amendment's protections against unreasonable search and seizure to create this protection of privacy. However, the Court has not been able to elucidate a clear and consistent jurisprudential philosophy behind the privilege and has oftentimes left the concept more confused than clarified in the wake of its decisions.

The expression "taking the Fifth" is one with which most Americans are likely familiar. We often encounter it on legal television shows and in fiction books. However, it is important to understand that the Fifth Amendment is not a blanket protection against testifying in a criminal proceeding. The protection is against compulsory incrimination. In *Rogers v. United States,* 340 U.S. 367 (1951), the Court held that a court in a criminal proceeding is charged with determining whether an individual's testimony actually presents a hazard of self-incrimination. Furthermore, the protection against self-incrimination has been held to be an individual right and does not apply to corporations. Therefore, a corporation cannot refuse, for example, to turn over subpoenaed records on Fifth Amendment grounds.

However, since *Boyd v. United States,* 116 U.S. 616 (1886), it has been argued and maintained that, combined with the Fourth Amendment's protections, the privilege may protect an individual from turning over evidence that amounts to compelled testimony.

Additionally, the right has been interpreted by the Court to only bar "testimonial" disclosures. Required participation in a lineup, fingerprinting, modeling clothing, giving handwriting samples, speaking specific words, and giving blood samples do not constitute activities that are protected by the Fifth Amendment.

A basic principle of the right, however, is that it protects compulsory incrimination in any type of proceeding, not just a trial. The Court, in *Counselman v. Hitchcock,* 142 U.S. 547 (1892), thus concluded the right referred to the eventual use of testimony in a criminal case, not the giving of testimony at the actual trial itself. Consequently, the protection applied to grand jury indictments as well as criminal trials. In *Griffin v. California,* 380 U.S. 609 (1965), the Court concluded a prosecutor may not comment to a jury on an individual's refusal to testify in his case, but the Court has also ruled, in *Brown v. Walker,* 161 U.S. 591 (1896), that, once taking the stand, the witness is required to commit full disclosure and cannot raise a Fifth Amendment challenge to cross-examination.

The privilege against self-incrimination is not absolute and can indeed be waived. Specifically, the Court has held that once an individual discloses a fact, that person has waived his or her Fifth Amendment protection from disclosing further details as to that fact. In *Rogers v. United States,* 340 U.S. 367 (1951), the Court held that once Rogers had admitted her connection to the Communist Party, she was not exempt from providing further details as part of her testimony. The Court reasoned that she had already incriminated herself, and further disclosure would not create the hazard of further incrimination.

Finally, it is important to note that the protections of the Fifth Amendment against self-incrimination apply with equal force against the states and the federal government. That is, the privilege has been "incorporated." The Court held in *Malloy v. Hogan,* 378 U.S. 1, 8 (1964), that "[t]he Fourteenth Amendment secures against state invasion the same privilege that the Fifth Amendment guarantees against federal infringement."

The Fifth Amendment's protection from self-incrimination is an important element of our criminal justice system. It provides protection of the accusatorial system of criminal justice from the oppressive inquisitorial methods witnessed by the infamous Star Chamber and ecclesiastical courts of England. Modern Fifth Amendment jurisprudence has endeavored to clarify the principles underlying the privilege, though not always successfully. There have indeed been many back-and-forth decisions that have attempted to explicate a clear doctrine, but those efforts have achieved minimal coherence. It is clear, however, that the right is one the Court has taken seriously and will continue to uphold as a central element of the American criminal justice system.

For more information: Amar, Akhil Reed. *The Bill of Rights.* New Haven, Conn.: Yale University Press, 1998; Garcia, Alfredo. *The Fifth Amendment: A Comprehensive Approach.* Westport, Conn.: Greenwood Press, 2002.

—Tom Clark

Sell v. United States, 539 U.S. 166 (2003)

In *Sell v. United States* (02-5664), the Court was asked to decide if Charles Thomas Sell, a St. Louis dentist charged with Medicaid fraud, should be forced to take psychotropic medications to render him appropriate to stand trial. The Court held that: (1) The Eighth Circuit had jurisdiction to hear the APPEAL to determine the disputed question whether Sell has a legal right to avoid forced medication [*Coopers & Lybrand v. Livesay,* 437 U.S. 463, 468.] (2) The Constitution permits the use of forced antipsychotic drugs to render a mentally ill defendant competent to stand trial on serious criminal charges if the treatment is medically appropriate, if the medication(s) administered will not produce side effects that will effect the fairness of the trial, and if the medication is necessary to further important trial-related interests [*Washington v. Harper,* 494 U.S. 210 (1990) and *Riggins v. Nevada,* 504 U.S. 127 (1992).] (3) The Eighth Circuit erred in approving forced medication solely to render Sell competent to stand trial.

The uniqueness of this case involved setting a PRECEDENT for use of mind-altering medications in order to make a person competent to stand trial for nonviolent crimes. Sell, who was originally arrested for Medicaid fraud, was given bail. However, he went totally out of control in court, yelled, and spit in the face of a judge, causing his bail to be revoked. Sell had a long history of mental illness and a diagnosis of delusional disorder with an underlying schizophrenic process. Previous to his arrest, Sell had called police and complained that a leopard was outside his office attempting to board a bus and wanted the police to shoot him [*ID.,* at 148; Forensic Report, p. 1 (June 20, 1997)]. Sell also made complaints that state officials were trying to kill him; and that God told him to kill FBI agents [*ID.,* at 1]. Sell underwent medical treatment for his psychiatric disorder on several occasions.

In 1998 Sell was indicted for attempting to murder an FBI agent that had arrested him, and a former employee that had planned to testify against him in the fraud case [*ID.,* at 23–29]. This resulted in Sell asking the court to reconsider his competence to stand trial. The magistrate sent Sell to the U.S. Medical Center for Federal Prisoners at Springfield, Missouri, for examination [18 U.S.C. & 4241 (d)]. Two months after admission to the Medical Center, psychiatrists recommended the use of psychotropic medications for treatment of his mental disorder. However, Sell refused to take them. This brought about a petition on behalf of the doctors to administer medication against Sell's will. Sell obtained an outside medical expert who expressed the opinion that Sell suffered only from a delusional disorder, which medications rarely help. Several laypersons that knew Sell also testified that Sell did not suffer from a serious mental disorder [*ID.,* at 147–150].

The reviewing psychiatrist then authorized involuntary administration of psychotropic medications based on his opinion that (1) Sell was mentally ill and dangerous to himself, and (2) to assist Sell in becoming competent to stand trial [*ID.,* at 157]. This was the event that brought about appeals that finally resulted in the Supreme Court hearings. Cases had been established to force psychotropic medication administration when a patient was a danger to himself/herself, and/or others. However, never in the history of the court system had a case been decided in which a person must be forced against his/her will to take mind-altering medication in order to be competent to stand trial.

By the time the Supreme Court became involved with this case, Sell had been incarcerated for five years, been in the open population at the prison, and the only evidence provided to the justices for proof that Sell needed forced medication was that Sell had inappropriately approached a nurse at the Medical Center. He suggested that he was in love with her and was unhappy that she would not have anything to do with him. The nurse redirected Sell and told him his behavior was inappropriate. Sell stated, "I can't help it."

The main consideration in the use of forced medication is the side effects of the given medication. Due to the fact that the patient's thought and cognitive processes are changed, the question was, can a person receive a fair hearing after receiving psychotropic medication? The rules to consider were the First, Fifth, and Sixth Amendments. The Court's decision, rendered on June 16, 2003, was that a person has the right to refuse unwanted psychotropic medication that would be used solely for the purpose of making him/her competent to stand trial.

—Gayle F. Roberts

For more information: Dias, Aaron R. "Just Say Yes: *Sell v. United States* and Inadequate Limitations on the Forced Medication of the Defendants in Order to Render Competence for Trial." *South Carolina Law Review* 55, no. 3 (2004).

separation of powers

Separation of powers is a principle that describes the distribution of power within government between the executive, legislative, and judicial branches. As a point of contrast, the government of Britain fuses the executive and legislative functions in a parliamentary body.

In American government, in addition to each branch having separate and distinct powers, each is constitutionally endowed with powers that, properly speaking, belong to other branches—referred to as the system of "checks and balances." For example, the executive has the power to veto legislation, Congress has the power to control the number and jurisdiction of the courts, the Supreme Court has the power to try federal cases and to interpret the law in those cases, and so forth. Other checks that are exercised over the Court include the appointment process to the Supreme Court by the executive with the consent of the Senate, and the ability of the legislature to impeach judges and propose amendments to overturn decisions of the Court.

This method of distributing power encourages each branch to regulate the other branches (with checks), but at the same time, each branch is constitutionally dependent on other branches. This system of mutual regulation precludes any one branch from dominating and regulates the growth of government in general.

Theoretically, this approach to organizing governmental power is most directly attributed to Montesquieu (1689–1755), who believed that political liberty was compromised when a single group controlled executive, legislative, and judicial power. The founders of the American regime, who had recently escaped a tyrannical monarchy, drew on Montesquieu's principle of separation of powers to create institutional safeguards against executive or legislative tyranny, but this fear of tyranny did not extend to the judicial branch. Rather than fearing its potential power, the founders were concerned with maintaining the *independence* of the judicial branch and safeguarding it against takeover by one of the other branches. In order to insulate the Court from potential attempts at influence by the other branches, the Constitution provides Supreme Court judges with life tenure and protected salaries.

In terms of constitutionally allotted powers, the Supreme Court is the weakest of the three branches. However, over the course of American history, judicial power has steadily expanded to where the Supreme Court is, arguably, close to equal to the other branches. The pivotal step in this progression was Chief Justice John MARSHALL's establishment of the power of JUDICIAL REVIEW in *MARBURY V. MADISON*, 5 U.S. 137 (1803). Judicial review, the power to declare legislation unconstitutional, substantially empowered the Court vis-à-vis the other two branches.

While not specified in the Constitution, judicial review is now firmly entrenched as a legitimate power of the Court.

The ability to review legislation is a considerable power, but it should not be forgotten that the Court's determination is not necessarily final. Within the system of checks and balances, Congress has the power to overrule Supreme Court decisions and to pass amendments to the Constitution.

For more information: Baron de Montesquieu. *The Spirit of the Laws.* Translated by Thomas Nugent. London: G. Bell and Sons, 1914; Rossiter, Clinton, ed. *The Federalist.* New York: Penguin Books, 1999; Rossum, Ralph, and G. Alan Tarr. *American Constitutional Law.* 6th ed. Belmont, Calif.: Wadsworth, 2003.

—Tassili Pender

sexual discrimination

Sexual discrimination is unfair or unequal treatment on the basis of gender. Typically, sexual discrimination occurs when women feel they are denied some benefit or right because of their sex. Men are also sometimes the victims of sexual discrimination, although more rarely. This denial violates both the due process and EQUAL PROTECTION CLAUSEs of the Constitution.

Sex discrimination claims have been brought to the Supreme Court for over a century. In its earliest decisions, the Court often decided these cases in a manner that reinforced traditional gender roles. Beginning in the 1970s, however, the Court began to take a different direction. In a landmark case, *CRAIG V. BOREN*, 429 U.S. 190 (1976), the Supreme Court decided that a law that distinguished between men and women in regards to the legal age of purchasing beer was discriminatory. With this case, a new standard was established to decide sexual discrimination issues. This new test, called "the heightened scrutiny test" requires that all laws with sex as a basis of classification or differentiation must be closely related to an important government purpose. Basically, any law that differentiates between men and women must have a substantial reason for doing so. The Supreme Court has used this standard ever since the 1976 case to decide sexual discrimination controversies.

Even with this new test, some laws based on sex discrimination have been upheld while others were overturned. The laws that the Court has struck down are generally considered "easy" cases, in that they were based on outdated notions of proper roles in society. The field of education provides a good example. The Court has consistently overturned laws that mandate or reinforce sex-segregated education, for lack of substantial reason for doing so. In *UNITED STATES V. VIRGINIA*, 518 U.S. 515 (1996), the United States challenged the state of Virginia because of the male-only admissions policy at the Virginia Military Institute, a public college. The males-only policy was challenged as a violation of the equal protection clause of the Fourteenth Amendment. Virginia Military Institute claimed that its policy was justified because of the rigor and stress that it places on cadets in order to produce "citizen-soldiers." Authorities at the school believed that admitting women would disrupt this intense, militaristic mode of education. The Court found that the state of Virginia did not adequately justify its single sex admissions policy to meet the heightened scrutiny standard. It ordered that women be admitted.

Other controversies in this area are not as simple for the Court to decide. These "difficult" cases are not necessarily based on outdated notions of gender roles but more on physical or real differences between men and women. In *ROSTKER V. GOLDBERG*, 453 U.S. 57 (1981), the Military Selective Service Act was challenged because it required that males register for the draft but not women. The Court found that this distinction based on sex is legal because men and women were not "similarly situated" in regards to the draft. The purpose of draft registration is to lay the groundwork for conscription of individuals who would be deployed in combat positions. Women, however, are excluded from combat roles. Even though the law makes a distinction between men and women, it was upheld because it was necessary to promote an "important governmental interest," the standard established in *Craig v. Boren*.

The area of sexual discrimination is still evolving in the courts. Generally, laws that distinguish between men and women based on old-fashioned notions of gender roles are ruled to be discriminatory and are overturned. Cases that involve physical or other obvious differences between men and women are more difficult for the courts to decide. For the most part, in situations where men and women are not seen to be "similarly situated," laws that distinguish between them are more likely to be upheld.

For more information: Anzalone, Christopher A., ed. *Supreme Court Cases on Gender and Sexual Equality 1787–2001*. Armonk, N.Y.: M. E. Sharpe, 2002; Epstein, Lee, and Thomas G. Walker. *Constitutional Law for a Changing America: Rights, Liberties, and Justice*. 4th ed. Washington, D.C.: CQ Press, 2001.

—Jamie Goetz

sexual harassment

Sexual harassment is defined as a form of SEXUAL DISCRIMINATION prohibited under the CIVIL RIGHTS ACT OF 1964 which makes it illegal to discriminate against an employee with respect to "terms, conditions, or privileges of employment because of such an individual's race, color, RELIGION, sex, or national origin."

The problem of sexual harassment is not new. Unwanted advances and unwelcome sexual contact have been a part of women's experience in the workplace for generations. However, the Supreme Court first identified sexual harassment as a form of discrimination and provided victims with legal remedies in *MERITOR SAVINGS BANK V. VINSON*, 477 U.S. 57 (1986). The Court held in that decision that the Civil Rights Act was intended to abolish a whole range of discriminatory treatment in the workplace and to address behaviors that reinforced gender inequality. They defined two types of harassment that could promote inequities.

Quid pro quo harassment involves the most obvious sort of violation. Here a person with authority, such as a supervisor or employer, makes sexual favors a factor in employment decisions. A female worker may be promised a raise or promotion in exchange for sex, or she may be threatened with firing or demotion if she refuses. Clearly such connections between sexual activities and the conditions of employment constitute a form of discrimination. The second type of harassment defined by the Court is the hostile environment where a worker is exposed to "severe and pervasive" abusive behavior. Although not asked directly for sex, an employee may be forced to endure off-color remarks, offensive pictures, or humiliating "jokes." Such a situation is comparable to exposure to constant and demeaning racial slurs. It makes successful performance of work responsibilities much more difficult and may set female employees up for failure due to the stress of such mistreatment.

In *HARRIS V. FORKLIFT SYSTEMS*, 510 U.S. 17 (1993), the Court held that a hostile environment was one which a "reasonable person" would find abusive. The victim did not need to prove that she had suffered either physical or psychological damage, only that the harassing behavior detracted from her job performance. In using the reasonable person standard to determine the existence of sexual harassment, some have debated whether that person is male or female. It seems clear that often "reasonable men" find behavior acceptable which is offensive to "reasonable women." The relative power of the parties involved, along with gender, seems to play a role in determining reasonableness. It has been suggested that in sexual harassment claims, a reasonable person should be defined as someone the same sex as the victim.

The Supreme Court handed down several important sexual harassment rulings in 1998. In *Oncale v. Sundowner Offshore Services*, 523 U.S. 75, the justices held that a man could be sexually harassed by other men, even if none of them was homosexual. Oncale had been subjected to humiliating, sex-related abuse by his fellow workers on an offshore oil rig apparently because they found him "feminine." The Court ruled that a hostile environment did not need to include sexual desire but could be a general hostility expressed in sexual and derogatory terms.

In the same year, the Court addressed the issue of employer liability for sexual harassment in *Farragher v. City of Boca Raton,* 524 U.S. 775 (1998). They held that employers would be responsible for harassing behavior by employees unless they could demonstrate that they had taken reasonable care to prevent and correct such behavior and that the complaining employee had reasonably failed to take advantage of opportunities to report the abuse. As a result of such decisions, many employers have established required training to inform workers about sexual harassment and have created mechanisms where employees can report troublesome behavior.

The Court has also upheld claims of sexual harassment by students and permitted such victims to seek monetary damages. In *Franklin v. Gwinnett County Public Schools,* 503 U.S. 60 (1992), they ruled that Christine Franklin, a high school student who was subjected to sexual advances and coercive intercourse by a teacher, could sue the school district under TITLE IX of the Education Amendments of 1972. Title IX prohibits excluding, discriminating against, or denying the benefits of education to anyone on the basis of sex. In *Gwinnett,* the Court found that the school district could be held financially responsible for failing to take appropriate action when Franklin complained of the teacher's harassment.

Like many other gender-based offenses, sexual harassment is seldom an isolated act. Typically it is a pattern of behavior, involving repeated and often escalating confrontations. It is most likely to occur where there are unequal power relationships, between supervisors and employees or between professors and students. Studies have shown that in workplaces where women are numerically dominant, quid pro quo harassment is more common. In traditionally masculine jobs, where women are only a small minority, hostile environment discrimination is more pervasive.

Despite court decisions defining and supporting claims of sexual harassment, only a small percentage of victims bring formal complaints. Most apparently believe that their claims will be ignored, that they will be humiliated, or that supervisors will retaliate against them.

For more information: Forell, Caroline, and Donna M. Matthews. *A Law of Her Own: The Reasonable Woman as a Measure of Man.* New York: New York University Press, 2000; Rundblad, Georganne. "Gender, Power, and Sexual Harassment." In *The Criminal Justice System and Women: Offenders, Prisoners, Victims, and Workers,* edited by Barbara Raffel Price and Natalie J. Sokoloff. New York: McGraw-Hill, 2003.

—Mary Welek Atwell

Shapiro, Commissioner of Welfare of Connecticut v. Thompson, 394 U.S. 618 (1969)

In *Shapiro, Commissioner of Welfare of Connecticut v. Thompson,* the Supreme Court ruled that states could not set minimum residency requirement for people to become eligible to receive welfare.

Connecticut, Pennsylvania, and the District of Columbia each passed laws that denied welfare assistance to residents who met all other eligibility requirements but had not resided within the state for at least one year immediately preceding the application for such assistance. Vivian Marie Thompson, a teenager with a one-year-old child, moved from Massachusetts to Connecticut and applied for welfare benefits. She was denied on the grounds that she had not lived in the state for a full year. She sued. Those opposed to the year residency requirement argued that it discriminates, denying equal protection of the laws. Those in favor claim that the requirement deters people from moving to a more generous state to obtain larger benefits. They also argue that a waiting period is needed to protect the welfare programs as a whole, that is, those in need of welfare when they move into a state are likely to become continuing burdens.

The question in this case was whether the state provision violates the EQUAL PROTECTION CLAUSE of the Fourteenth Amendment and the District of Columbia provision violates the due process clause of the Fifth Amendment of the Constitution. Writing for the majority, Justice BRENNAN found that the state and district provisions did violate the Fourteenth and Fifth Amendments, respectively, by infringing on the right to travel freely from state to state. Although not explicitly mentioned, the right to freely travel from one state to another is a basic right under the Constitution. The Court also found that the Social Security Act of 1935 did not, and constitutionally could not, authorize states to impose such requirements for welfare benefits.

The classification of welfare applicants by the states according to whether they had lived in the state for a year in order to be eligible for welfare benefits, argued Brennan, is irrational and violates the equal protection clause. The Social Security Act of 1935 does not allow any plan that restricts the eligibility of welfare recipients based on time of residence in a state, since such a requirement imposes a classification imposing on the constitutional right of welfare applicants to freely travel from state to state. While the Fifth Amendment does not contain an equal protection clause, it does forbid unjustifiable discrimination as a violation of due process.

Justice STEWART concurred to address the dissent of Justice HARLAN. He argued that under the due process and equal protection standards the right to freely travel from one state to another is not a conditional liberty subject to regulation and control.

Chief Justice WARREN, joined by Justices Harlan and Black, dissented. They argued that Congress could exercise its constitutional right by imposing minimal residence requirements in the District of Columbia and by authorizing the states to do the same.

This case is significant in that it supported the right, even of indigents, to travel freely.

For more information: Schwartz, Bernard. *A History of the Supreme Court.* New York: Oxford University Press, 1993.

—R. Nanette Nazaretian

Shaw v. Reno, 509 U.S. 630 (1993)

In *Shaw v. Reno,* the Supreme Court ruled that race-conscious electoral districts could be challenged under the Fourteenth Amendment's EQUAL PROTECTION CLAUSE and that STRICT SCRUTINY was the proper standard to apply.

Under the supervision of the U.S. Justice Department and the authority of the VOTING RIGHTS ACT, North Carolina drew up a U.S. House redistricting plan following the 1990 census that featured two districts with African-American majorities—the 1st and the 12th. In 1992 voters in both of these "majority-minority" districts elected black representatives, North Carolina's first African-American House members since 1901. Distinguishing the newly created 12th district was its particularly bizarre shape: extremely elongated and narrow. In order to connect pockets of black voters in central North Carolina's urban areas, "the I-85 district" followed the interstate and was literally no wider at several points than the highway itself. Several white voters brought a federal suit under the Fourteenth Amendment's equal protection clause, on the claim that the new districts separated voters based on race.

The Supreme Court split 5-4, with conservative Justices O'CONNOR, REHNQUIST, SCALIA, THOMAS, and KENNEDY forming the majority. Heading in a new direction under the equal protection clause, the Court no longer required plaintiffs to demonstrate that racial gerrymandering diluted their voting power or violated the "one voter, one vote" principle. Writing for the Court, Justice O'Connor endorsed the idea that, under strict scrutiny, a state would have to show that race-conscious districts were narrowly tailored to meet a COMPELLING STATE INTEREST. While the usual principles of drawing districts (O'Connor mentions "compactness, contiguity, and respect for political subdivisions") are not constitutionally required, radical departures from these principles could serve as evidence that race was the overriding consideration in districting. According to O'Connor, appearances matter in this area of law: "When a district obviously is created solely to effectuate the perceived common interests of one racial group, elected officials are more likely to believe that their primary obligation is to represent only the members of that group, rather than their constituency as a whole." The Court did not rule on the constitutionality of North Carolina's districting plan but remanded the case for further consideration. When the case came back to the Supreme Court as *Shaw v. Hunt,* 517 U.S. 899 (1996), the Court found North Carolina's districting plan unconstitutional.

In his dissent, Justice WHITE (joined by Justices BLACKMUN and STEVENS) relied on the PRECEDENT case *United Jewish Organizations of Williamsburgh, Inc. v. Carey,* 430 U.S. 144 (1977). Since the plaintiffs in *Shaw,* as members of the white voting majority, could not show that their power in the political process had been stripped from them, they could not make a valid equal protection claim, according to White's analysis. In his dissent, Justice SOUTER argued against applying strict scrutiny to majority-minority districts. As long as individual voters were allowed to "register, vote and be represented," placing some voters in one district does no harm to the rights of other individuals. He argued that "there is no theoretical inconsistency in having two distinct approaches to equal protection analysis, one for cases of electoral districting and one for most other types of state government decisions."

The *Shaw* decision changed the direction of redistricting efforts under the Voting Rights Act. As North Carolina had not been alone in its majority-minority approach, cases from other states followed in *Shaw*'s wake, including *MILLER V. JOHNSON,* 515 U.S. 900 (1995), and *Bush v. Vera,* 517 U.S. 952 (1996), which challenged racially gerrymandered districts in Georgia and Texas, respectively. In both of these cases, the states' districting plans were struck down. The Court's rulings since Shaw have not been entirely consistent, however. In some cases, the Court seemed more receptive to majority-minority districts than in other cases.

For example, in *Hunt v. Cromartie,* 526 U.S. 541 (1999), the Court once again considered North Carolina's 12th District (now redrawn) and concluded that the state had good evidence to show that partisan advantage, rather than race, was the predominant factor in drawing its boundaries. Drawing heavily Democratic districts, even if they happen to be heavily African American (the most reliable Democratic voters), does not trigger strict scrutiny by the courts.

For more information: Coyle, Marcia. "Politics, Law Clash in Racial Redistricting: 'Bizarre' Districts." *National Law Journal,* October 31, 1994; ———. "Where to Draw Line on Race in Redistricting?; High Court Sequel." *National Law Journal,* December 11, 1995.

—Elizabeth Ellen Gordon

Shelley v. Kraemer, 334 U.S. 1 (1948)

Shelley v. Kraemer marked an important point in the Supreme Court's evolution of thinking about constitutional remedies to RACIAL DISCRIMINATION. In this case, the Court ruled racial restrictive covenants a violation of the Fourteenth Amendment's EQUAL PROTECTION CLAUSE.

This case examined the validity of restrictive covenants based on race. For instance, in Missouri, 30 out of 39 property owners signed a 1911 agreement. This agreement (or covenant) restricted ownership of these properties to people of Caucasian descent and excluded African Americans and Asians from acquiring any of these 30 properties. In short, built within the property contracts was a restriction on who could purchase the property. This specific case involved African Americans purchasing some of the 30 properties with the restrictive covenant built in. Other residents sued in the state court system to keep the property from coming into the hands of the African Americans, arguing that the restrictive covenants were valid mechanisms for excluding purchase by persons within definable racial groups. The state courts agreed and enjoined the selling of the properties to the African-American purchasers.

Chief Justice VINSON rendered the majority opinion. He begins by observing that the rights to acquire, enjoy, own, and dispose of property is a fundamental right protected against discrimination by the equal protection clause of the Fourteenth Amendment. Indeed, Vinson notes that the language of the Civil Rights Act of 1866, Section 1 (now 42 U.S. Code Section 1982) explicitly provides for the following: "All citizens of the United States shall have the same right, in every State and Territory, as is enjoyed by white citizens thereof to inherit, purchase, lease, sell, hold, and convey real and personal property."

Vinson goes on to state for the majority that if restrictive covenants are voluntarily adhered to and enforced by private individuals, the Fourteenth Amendment has no applicability, since it is aimed at states' actions that abrogate equal protection. He says, "So long as the purposes of those agreements are effectuated by voluntary adherence to their terms, it would appear clears that there has been no action by the State and the provisions of the [14th] Amendment have not been violated." The key question, then, becomes whether state courts' enforcement of restrictive covenants constitutes "state action." If so, then the equal protection clause has been violated. If not, then there is no violation. Vinson, though, states that the answer to this question is well established. He says: "That the action of state courts and judicial officers is to be regarded as action of the State within the meaning of the 14th Amendment, is a proposition that has long been established by decisions of this Court."

The majority opinion states that some individuals were willing to buy the properties at issue; other individuals were willing to sell their property. Except for the active intervention of a state instrumentality—its courts—the transactions would have proceeded apace. However, the intervention of the courts prevented the voluntary transfer of the property from seller to buyer. Thus it is clear, according to Vinson, that state action had actually occurred. Thus, there was a clear violation of the equal protection clause. Vinson concludes by asserting, "Equal protection of the law is not achieved through indiscriminate imposition of [inequalities]."

This case, then, is important for its definition of the nature of the doctrine of "state action." The reasoning of the majority opinion lays out the extent to which decisions of state instrumentalities, such as courts, that adversely affect constitutional rights of individuals violate the equal protection clause of the Fourteenth Amendment. *Shelley v. Kraemer* is a strong example of how restrictive covenants enforced by courts reflect this logic at work.

For more information: Henkin, Louis. "*Shelley v. Kraemer*: Notes for a Revised Opinion." *University of Pennsylvania Law Review* 110 (1962): 473.

—Steven A. Peterson
—Kylie Peters

Skinner v. Oklahoma, 316 U.S. 535 (1942)

Skinner v. Oklahoma unanimously struck down a policy sanctioning forced sterilization of habitual criminals. Jack Skinner, a man convicted twice for armed robbery and once for stealing chickens, received a vasectomy. Justice William O. DOUGLAS wrote the Court's opinion. It said in part:

> We are dealing here with legislation which involves one of the basic CIVIL RIGHTS of man. Marriage and procreation are fundamental to the very existence and survival of the race. The power to sterilize, if exercised, may have subtle, far reaching and devastating effects. In evil or reckless hands it can cause races or types which are inimical to the dominant group to wither and disappear. There is no redemption for the individual whom the law touches. Any experiment which the State conducts is to his irreparable injury. He is forever deprived of a basic liberty.

There is another crucial aspect to *Skinner.* The policy of forced sterilization made an exception for persons convicted of political crimes or embezzlement, but the state could not show a RATIONAL BASIS for targeting larceny as more likely an inherited tendency than political crimes and embezzlement. Thus, because the ban on the civil right to procreate discriminated without a rational basis against one class of criminal, the Court lifted that ban, on the grounds of a personal right to equal protection of the laws under the Fourteenth Amendment.

Justices Harlan F. STONE and Robert JACKSON wrote separate concurring opinions. Jackson said the state could not discriminate against a group for its biological experiments. Stone said that the state action violated Skinner's constitutional right to due process of law under the Fourteenth Amendment by not holding a hearing first to determine whether a child of his could inherit his criminal traits.

Today we no longer regard eugenics as a valid science for crime prevention, but *BUCK V. BELL,* 274 U.S. 200 (1927), did uphold a Virginia eugenics law as applied to an individual institutionalized in a state mental hospital. In fact, *Skinner* is the first major ruling extending constitutional rights to personal autonomy over the state in claiming a rational basis interest related to sexual reproduction. Later, *LOVING V. VIRGINIA,* 388 U.S. 1 (1967), granted a right to interracial marriage and thus struck down the state interest against miscegenation. *Zablocki v. Redhail,* 434 U.S. 374 (1978), reaffirmed the right to marry in striking down a state action that denied a father who failed to meet his court-ordered child-support obligations permission to remarry. *GRISWOLD V. CONNECTICUT,* 391 U.S. 145 (1965), struck down a ban on contraception, declaring a federal fundamental right of the person to privacy over intimate associations. *ROE V. WADE,* 410 U.S. 113 (1973), laid the basis for a woman's right to choose to terminate a pregnancy. Eventually, in *LAWRENCE V. TEXAS,* 539 U.S. 558 (2003), overruling *BOWERS V. HARDWICK,* 478 U.S. 186 (1986), the RIGHT TO PRIVACY and personal autonomy over intimate associations invalidated a ban on homosexual sodomy in the home.

When the judiciary confronts a governmental restriction on a personal civil right or civil liberty, relying on precedents, how might it draw a principled line regarding its standards of JUDICIAL REVIEW? Put this question, *Skinner,* and its progeny in the context of a claim of a right to same-sex marriage. The fundamental right to personal autonomy over the state interest in regulating marriage and procreation is not a good foundation for affirming same-sex couples have a right to marry. However, given that *Lawrence* and a broad reading of *Skinner* linked a person's right to equal protection of the laws, the judiciary has a valid foundation for lifting a state ban on same-sex marriage, if the state cannot show it has a rational basis in denying that right to same-sex couples.

For more information: O'Brien, David M. *Constitutional Law and Politics.* Vol. 2. 4th ed. New York: W. W. Norton, 2000.

slander and libel

Defamation is a word that can be used to describe both libel and slander. Defamation includes any written or spoken harm to the reputation of any person and/or organization. A written statement or visual depictions of defamation is labeled as *libel. Slander* is described as the verbal, oral, or gestured act of defamation.

In order for libel and slander to be considered defamatory, the statement must have been witnessed by more than the person to whom it was directed. It must have been seen or heard by at least one other person. Also, it is imperative that the statement is blatantly directed to that specific person and can be identified by others to have been referring to that person.

Statements that are considered to be libel and slander are defamatory only if they are false statements; this does not include such items as name-calling, hyperbole, or words that may be taken out of context when in a heated conversation. Defamatory statements are those that harm a person's reputation and are clearly more than insults.

Libel and slander differ from "free speech" in that the freedom of speech allows people to make criticisms and state personal opinions about people and express themselves in such a way. On the other hand, libel and slander are not expressing one's opinion but rather are making false statements and allegations toward another person and presenting them as factual information. As long as personal opinions are not presented as fact then they are not considered to be defamatory statements.

In 1964 the U.S. Supreme Court case, *NEW YORK TIMES COMPANY V. SULLIVAN,* an elected official from Montgomery, Alabama, complained that civil rights activists had committed defamation against him. The Supreme Court ruled that due to the fact that he was a public official, damages could only be collected for libel statements if the false implications were made with "reckless disregard" for the truth.

Due to the ruling made in the *Sullivan* case, the burden of proof in many libel cases was shifted from the defendant to the plaintiff. It is now the responsibility of the plaintiff to prove the falsehood was indeed incorrect and in fact defamatory. In other words they must prove that the falsehood was issued with actual malice. This ruling has since been applied to celebrities and other public figures.

The *Sullivan* case presented a clear victory for the media in that it provided a significant expansion of the protection against libel for the press. With the ruling of the case shifting the burden of proof from the defendant to the plaintiff, it took the pressure off the media and made it more difficult to try. More recently, the Supreme Court has not allowed the expression of opinion to be considered libel or slander, rather they look only at factual misrepresentation.

For more information: O'Neil, Robert M. *The First Amendment and Civil Liability.* Bloomington: Indiana University Press, 2001; Schweber, Howard H. *Speech, Conduct and the First Amendment.* New York: Peter Lang, 2003.

—Osler McCarthy

Slaughter-House Cases, 83 U.S. 36 (1873)

The *Slaughter-House Cases* greatly weakened the privileges and immunities clause of the Fourteenth Amendment. In addition, the dissenters in this case adumbrated the line of doctrine beginning with ALLGEYER V. LOUISIANA, 165 U.S. 578 (1897), and stretching through LOCHNER V. NEW YORK, 198 U.S. 45 (1905), and beyond.

In 1869 Louisiana passed a law chartering a corporation, "The Crescent City Livestock Landing and Slaughter-House Company," and giving it a 25-year monopoly. Competing facilities were ordered closed by the law, although independent butchers could continue to slaughter cattle at rates set by statute. Butchers claimed that their right to "exercise their trade" had been abrogated and that the Thirteenth and Fourteenth Amendments to the Constitution had been violated. In the *Slaughter-House Cases*, the Supreme Court ruled on the issues at stake.

Justice Samuel Miller delivered the majority opinion in the case, which featured a close 5-4 vote. With respect to the Thirteenth Amendment claim, that the monopoly created an "involuntary servitude" in violation of the Thirteenth Amendment, the majority noted simply that this Amendment was designed to end slavery. Since, obviously, slavery was not the issue in this case, that claim automatically failed. After all, "the obvious purpose [of the Thirteenth Amendment] was to forbid all shades and conditions of African slavery." The majority, then, easily disposed of the Thirteenth Amendment claim.

The Fourteenth Amendment claim was largely based on the "privileges and immunities" clause, which stated that "No state shall make or enforce any law which shall abridge the privileges and immunities of citizens of the United States. . . ." Once more the majority notes that the key factor leading to enactment of the Fourteenth Amendment was ". . . the freedom of the slave race, the security and firm establishment of that freedom, and the protection of the newly-made freemen and citizens from the oppressions of those who had formerly exercised unlimited dominion over him." Furthermore, this clause did not create a new set of rights emanating from the national government. According to the majority, the privileges and immunities clause says that any rights given to citizens of a state "shall be the measure of the rights of citizens of other States within your jurisdiction." Thus, this affords no protection to the butchers in New Orleans.

In similar fashion, the "due process" and "equal protection" claims of the plaintiffs were addressed. The majority concluded that "We doubt very much whether any action of a State not directed by way of discrimination against the negroes as a class, or on account of their race, will ever come to be held within the purview of this provision."

The two minority opinions emphasized that privileges and immunities of all citizens of the United States included, according to the dissent authored by Justice Stephen Field, "the right to pursue a lawful employment in a lawful manner. . . ." Justice Joseph BRADLEY, in his dissenting opinion, echoed this view, this time alluding to the due process clause. Bradley notes that "Their right of choice [of employment] is a portion of their liberty; their occupation is their property."

In a sense, both dissenting opinions adumbrated the doctrine of LIBERTY OF CONTRACT, which came to full fruition in *Allgeyer v. Louisiana* and *Lochner v. New York*. The majority opinion essentially eliminated the privileges and immunities clause as a major protection of individual rights of citizens, and it has seldom been used as a major doctrine in subsequent years. The majority's confident view that the Thirteenth and Fourteenth Amendments spoke only to the rights of the former slaves, obviously, has not prevailed historically.

For more information: Schwartz, Bernard. *A History of the Supreme Court.* New York: Oxford University Press, 1993.

—Steven A. Peterson

Smith v. Doe, 538 U.S. 84 (2003)

In *Smith v. Doe*, the Supreme Court ruled that a state law requiring convicted sex felons to register with the department of corrections within 30 days of their release from prison is not a violation of the ex post facto clause of the Constitution. This case upheld legislation that has come to be known as "Megan's Law."

In 1994 Megan Kanka was a seven-year-old New Jersey girl who was sexually assaulted and murdered by a neighbor. This neighbor had previously been convicted of committing sex crimes against children, although no one in Megan's neighborhood knew about that. As a result of this assault, Congress first passed in 1994 a law that called for the mandatory registration of sex offenders who were released from federal prison. While the federal law was called the Jacob Wetterling Crimes Against Children and Sexually Violent Offender Registration Act, and it derived its name from a Minnesota boy who had been abducted but never found, it was referred to as Megan's Law, in reference to Megan Kanka.

By 1996 every state in the country had its own version of a Megan's Law that required both registration by sexual offenders and then community notification of release of such a person into their community. Supporters of Megan's Law contended that registration and community notification would improve public safety, while critics argued that the law would either make it hard for ex-offenders to be released into communities after they had served their sentences, or that the registration constituted an additional punishment after the sentence for the crime had already been served.

In *Smith v. Doe*, at issue was an Alaskan version of Megan's law which was passed in 1994. Here, two individuals, referred to by the Court as John Doe I and John Doe II, were convicted sex offenders who were both released from state prison in 1990 after completing their sentences and rehabilitation. Even though both of them were released from prison before the 1994 Alaskan Megan's law was passed, they were required to register under it. They challenged the registration as a violation of the constitutional ban on EX POST FACTO LAWS. A federal district court rejected their arguments, the Ninth Circuit COURT OF APPEALS reversed, and the United States Supreme Court took certiorari, reversing the Ninth Circuit.

Writing for the Court, Justice Kennedy rejected the claim that the law was ex post facto. To determine whether a law was ex post facto, the Court drew upon its arguments in *Kansas v. Kendricks*, 521 U.S. 346 (1997), where it had upheld laws that required the civil detention of sex offenders after their release from prison. In that case, the Court stated that a critical question to ask about ex post facto laws was whether the legislature intended to punish or create civil proceedings. Drawing upon that rule, the Court in *Smith* contended that it needed to ask first if the statute intended to punish and if it did, then it was ex post facto. If no punishment was intended, but instead it was creating a civil and regulatory process, then the question was whether the overall law was so punitive in purpose or effect that it effectively was punitive and therefore negated the intent to be nonpunitive.

Justice Kennedy found that the Alaskan legislature had intended to create a civil, nonpunitive regulatory system to control convicted sex offenders. Moreover, he also dismissed claims that the registration and notification requirements were so severe that they outweighed the civil and regulatory intent of the Alaskan legislature.

Dissenting Justices STEVENS, SOUTER, and GINSBURG contended that the laws were ex post facto and had a significant stigmatizing effect, and they operated to punish individuals after they had already been released from prison and paid their debts for their crimes. They saw the Alaskan law as making it more difficult for ex-cons to integrate into the community, increasing the chances for recidivism.

As a result of *Smith v. Doe*, Megan's Law can be enforced and sex offenders can be required to register and then have communities notified when they are released. While there is much debate regarding how effective these laws are in deterring sex crimes, or regarding the fairness of these laws to ex-offenders, these laws enjoy broad popular support.

For more information: Lee, Carter Allen. "When Children Prey on Children: A Look at Hawai'i's Version of Megan's Law and Its Application to Juvenile Sex Offenders." *University of Hawaii Law Review* 20 (Fall 1998): 477.
—David Schultz

Souter, David H. (1939–) *Supreme Court justice*
David Souter (born on September 17, 1939), David Hackett Souter became the 105th justice of the Supreme Court on October 9, 1990. He was nominated by President George H. W. Bush to replace William J. BRENNAN, Jr.

Souter was born in Melrose, Massachusetts. He spent his teenage years in the small New Hampshire town of Weare in the home his grandparents left behind on their death, and he graduated in 1957 from Concord High School in the New Hampshire capital. He earned an A.B. degree from Harvard College, spent two years as a Rhodes Scholar at Oxford University, and then received a law degree from Harvard Law School in 1966.

He practiced with a law firm, Orr and Reno, for two years before becoming an assistant attorney general in New Hampshire. In 1971 he became deputy attorney general and in 1976 attorney general, succeeding Warren B. Rudman who later became Souter's leading supporter in the U.S. Senate for confirmation to the Supreme Court. In 1978 he began a five-year tenure on the state superior court bench. In 1983 he was appointed to the New Hampshire Supreme Court by Gov. John H. Sununu, who later, as White House chief of staff, supported the Supreme Court nomination. In May 1990, Souter joined the U.S. COURT OF APPEALS for the First Circuit but served only briefly before moving to the Supreme Court.

The concerns that were raised at Souter's Senate Judiciary Committee hearings in 1990 reflected the fact that he was unknown to both conservative Republican senators and liberal Democratic senators. Commentators called him the "stealth" nominee because he had little or no track record on most of the hot-button constitutional issues of the day, from abortion to the death penalty. Yet he had a reputation as a studious, thoughtful, evenhanded and hardworking lawyer and judge. Each side feared that as a justice he might lean too much toward the other view. He was confirmed by the Senate, 90-9.

As a justice, Souter has been decidedly moderate. According to annual statistical surveys compiled by the *Harvard Law Review*, in his first 10 years on the Court Souter agreed most often with moderate to liberal Justices Ruth Bader GINSBURG and Stephen BREYER, about 84 percent of the time, and least often with the most conservative members, Justices Clarence THOMAS, 59 percent, and Antonin SCALIA, 62 percent. In his first 13 years as a justice, Souter participated in 222 rulings decided by a 5-4 vote; he was on the losing side in 55 percent. What the statistics suggest is that Souter most often finds himself in the moderate wing of the Court that since 1994 has included Justices Ginsburg, Breyer, and John Paul STEVENS.

Souter's most significant majority decision may be his role in the abortion ruling, PLANNED PARENTHOOD OF

Justice David H. Souter *(United States Supreme Court)*

SOUTHEASTERN PENNSYLVANIA V. CASEY, 505 U.S. 833 (1992). He wrote crucial portions of an unusual joint opinion with Justices Sandra Day O'CONNOR and Anthony M. Kennedy that upheld the basic right to abortion established in ROE V. WADE, 410 U.S. 113 (1973).

His most significant other decisions have been in dissenting opinions, where he has emerged as a potent and erudite critic of the conservative majority's efforts to curb the power of Congress in favor of the FEDERALISM interests of the states and of the Court's easing of the separation of church and state. His writing in these cases is marked by two major themes: a respect for PRECEDENT that cautions against overruling established Court doctrines of decades past, and a passion for legal and constitutional history that makes his arguments formidable.

His most important dissents include: ADARAND CON-STRUCTORS, INC. V. PENA, 515 U.S. 200 (1995), in which the majority curtailed AFFIRMATIVE ACTION in federal contracting; *Agostini v. Felton,* 521 U.S. 203 (1997), in which he objected to the majority allowing federal aid to religious schools; *U.S. v. Lopez,* 514 U.S. 549 (1995), in which the majority said Congress improperly passed a law regulating gun possession near schools; SHAW V. RENO, 509 U.S. 630 (1993), in which he challenged the majority's curtailment of using race to draw congressional districts to achieve minority representation; *Missouri v. Jenkins,* 515 U.S. 70 (1995), in which the Court cut back on school desegregation efforts; and ROSENBERGER V. RECTOR AND VISITORS OF UNIV. OF VA., 515 U.S. 819 (1995), in which he objected to the majority's view that protection for freedom of speech required use of public funds to support a religious newspaper.

For more information: Cushman, Clare, ed. *The Supreme Court Justices: Illustrated Biographies, 1789–1993.* Washington, D.C.: Congressional Quarterly, 1995; Urofsky, Melvin I., ed. *The Supreme Court Justices: A Biographical Dictionary.* New York: Garland, 1994.

—Stephen Wermiel

South Carolina v. Baker, 485 U.S. 505 (1988)

In *South Carolina v. Baker,* the Supreme Court upheld Section 310 (b) (1) of the Tax Equity and Fiscal Responsibility Act of 1982 (TEFRA), maintaining that the U.S. Congress had not overstepped its boundaries by requiring purchasers of unregistered (bearer) bonds issued by state and local governments to pay federal INCOME TAX. The decision overruled POLLOCK V. FARMERS' LOAN & TRUST COMPANY, 157 U.S. 429, an 1895 decision that restricted congressional power to tax such bonds. TEFRA was a result of the Reagan administration's attempt to generate income for the national government as a means of bringing the trillion-dollar deficit under control. Supporters of the bill insisted that it was also necessary to curb the practice of using bearer bonds to avoid paying federal income tax on large amounts of money. The Internal Revenue Service (IRS) estimated that the U.S. government had lost approximately $97 billion in 1981 through income tax evasion.

Historically, exempting bonds issued by state and local governments from federal taxes had provided state and local governments with a means of borrowing money to finance various projects. Because of the threat to that ability to generate funds, the state of South Carolina and the National Governors' Association (NGA) sued then Secretary of the Treasury James Baker, insisting that with TEFRA Congress had infringed on state rights of sovereignty by violating the tenets of FEDERALISM granted in the Tenth Amendment of the U.S. Constitution. South Carolina asked the Court to hear the case under its powers of ORIGINAL JURISDICTION, which bypassed all lower courts. The Court then appointed Samuel J. Roberts as special master to conduct evidence and gather evidence on the case. Refusing to accept the argument that the TEFRA violated the sovereign rights of states, Justice William BRENNAN, writing for the majority, contended that South Carolina had failed to prove that it had been "deprived of any right to participate in the national political process or that it was singled out in a way that left it politically isolated and powerless." Brennan cited the Court's 1985 opinion in GARCIA V. SAN ANTONIO METROPOLITAN TRANSIT AUTHORITY, 469 U.S. 528, which required states to look to the political process rather than to the federal courts for redress of grievances against congressional actions.

The Court also rejected South Carolina's claim that TEFRA infringed on the doctrine of intergovernmental tax immunity. In the Court's opinion, those who purchased unregistered bonds had no constitutional right to avoid paying federal income tax on those funds. Nor did states and local governments have a constitutional right to issue bonds that required purchasers to pay lower interest rates than those bonds issued by other parties. Furthermore, the Court rejected the argument put forth by the NGA that TEFRA overstepped the boundaries established by the Court in *FERC v. Mississippi*, 457 U.S. 742 in 1982, which seemed to suggest that the Tenth Amendment limited congressional ability to interfere in the administrative powers of state and local governments.

In her dissent to *South Carolina v. Baker*, Justice Sandra Day O'CONNOR accused her colleagues of overruling "a precedent that it has honored for nearly 100 years" by canceling "the constitutional immunity that traditionally has shielded the interest paid on state and local bonds from federal taxation." O'Connor believed that the Supreme Court should stand by its decision in *Pollock* and insisted that "the Tenth Amendment and principles of federalism inherent in the Constitution prohibit Congress from taxing or threatening to tax the interest paid on state and municipal bonds."

After the *Baker* decision, Congress drastically overhauled federal tax laws, further curtailing the ability of state and local governments to borrow money. Opponents of the *Baker* decision insist that it was part of a pattern by which Congress and the courts have consistently undermined the Tenth Amendment to the United States Constitution. Because of the NECESSARY AND PROPER CLAUSE, Article I, Section I, which provides Congress with the power to enact "all laws which shall be necessary and proper" for exercising its constitutional authority, and Article VI, which established the doctrine of national supremacy, Congress has frequently been allowed to pass legislation in areas that were historically assigned to state governments.

In 1976 in NATIONAL LEAGUE OF CITIES V. USERY, 426 U.S. 833, the Court briefly sided with the states; but by its 1985 decision in *Garcia,* the Court had returned to its support of national supremacy despite Ronald Reagan's promise to return additional powers to state governments. However, during the 1990s, the Court again reversed its position and expressed support for the Tenth Amendment's restrictions on federal power in such cases as *U.S. v. Lopez,*

514 U.S. 549 (1995), in which the Court upheld restrictions on congressional power to regulate INTERSTATE COMMERCE. Several cases in 1997 continued this trend toward limited national government.

For more information: Birnbaum, Jeffrey H., and Alan S. Murray. *Showdown at Gucci Gulch.* New York: Vintage Books, 1987; Bowman, Ann O. M., and Richard C. Kearney. *State and Local Government.* Boston and New York: Houghton Mifflin, 1999; Grossman, Joel B., and Richard S. Wells. *Constitutional Law and Judicial Policymaking.* New York and London: Longman, 1988; Strayer, John A., et al. *State and Local Politics.* New York: St. Martin's, 1994.

—Elizabeth Purdy

South Dakota v. Dole, 483 U.S. 203 (1987)

South Dakota v. Dole upheld Congress's power to attach conditions to federal highway funding to the states in order to promote a national minimum drinking age of 21.

The congressional statute at issue in this case required the secretary of Transportation to withhold a percentage of allocated federal highway funds from states that allowed persons under 21 to purchase and consume alcoholic beverages. South Dakota permitted the sale of beer to persons over 19 years of age and was thus denied federal funds. While Congress is generally understood to possess a general spending power, South Dakota claimed that the statute interfered with the states' power granted under the Twenty-first Amendment to regulate the importation and distribution of liquor.

Chief Justice REHNQUIST, on behalf of the majority, reviewed the established limits to the federal spending power. Four conditions were found to apply. First, congressional spending must be geared to the promotion of the "general welfare." On this count, the judiciary, should be inclined to "defer substantially to the judgment of Congress" on what matters qualify. Second, should Congress seek to condition state behavior through its spending, the conditions for state compliance must be unambiguous. States must have a clear indication of the consequences of their choice.

Third, prior cases established that federal spending may be illegitimate if the conditions imposed are unrelated to the "federal interest" in national programs. In other words, the requirements to receive funding must be reasonably related to the purpose hoped to be achieved by Congress. Finally, other constitutional provisions—such as an amendment—might serve as an "independent bar" to the exercise of the spending power.

The majority found that the first three conditions were easily met by the congressional statute. The goal of deterring drunken driving was seen as suitably national in purpose, the conditions suitably unambiguous, and the requirement that states raise the drinking age to discourage underage drinkers from traveling to neighboring states appeared reasonably related to the achievement of that goal. The only condition that merited much serious justification from the Court was whether or not the Twenty-first Amendment acted as an independent bar to federal spending.

To answer this question Rehnquist clarified the nature of the fourth limitation. The independent bar did not prevent Congress from indirectly achieving what it was not empowered to do directly. Rather it was meant to bar Congress from inducing the states to "engage in activities that would themselves be unconstitutional." For example, states could not be compelled through conditional spending to violate protections against unreasonable search and seizure. That the Twenty-First Amendment envisioned a role for the states in regulating the importation and distribution of alcohol could not alone preclude Congress from policy-making in that field. As long as the other conditions of federal spending were met, Congress was free to offer incentives to the states.

Justice O'CONNOR dissented from the majority on whether there was a reasonable connection between the congressional expenditure and the ostensible national purpose of reducing drunk driving. She found that the law at hand was "far too under- and over-inclusive" to be reasonably related to the expenditure. For O'Connor it strained reason that in order to prevent drunk driving people under 21 had to be barred from purchasing and consuming alcohol. For O'Connor, Congress was entitled to expect safe highways as a condition of the funds that it distributed but could not "impose or change regulations in other areas of the State's social and economic life because of an attenuated or tangential relationship to highway use or safety."

The decision is somewhat peculiar in that Chief Justice Rehnquist takes the unfamiliar role of defending congressional excursions into state territory. Justice O'Connor plays a much more familiar role challenging the strained logic of congressional attempts to broadly regulate in the envelope of its rather narrow constitutional categories. The general spirit of her dissent is replicated by Rehnquist in the Court's overturning of commerce clause regulation of gun-free school zones in *United States v. Lopez*, 514 U.S. 549 (1995). The logic of the case also provides the one potential loophole for Congress in the face of several anti-commandeering Tenth Amendment decisions from the Rehnquist Court. *Printz v. United States*, 521 U.S. 898 (1997), and other cases have established an increased sphere of state immunity from congressional incentives and coercion. Given that *Dole* contemplates a permissible procedure for Congress to compel state behavior, it is likely to serve as a roadmap for future congressional excursions into state policy-making.

For more information: McCoy, Thomas R., and Barry Friedman. "Conditional Spending: Federalism's Trojan Horse." *Supreme Court Review* (1988): 85–127.

—Gerald Baier

sovereign immunity

Sovereign immunity is the protected status for the supreme ruler of a people or country, known as a sovereign, when it comes to lawsuits. This means that states or the federal government generally cannot be sued by individuals without their consent.

The concept of sovereign immunity is based on the centuries-old idea that because a sovereign, historically the king or queen, is the highest authority in the land, it is not possible for any other subordinate authority such as courts to have the power to compel the sovereign to do anything. As far back as the 1200s, it was established in English law that the king could not be sued by name in his own courts. In practice, however, British kings consented to suits through petitions of right and by the 17th century other government officials were able to claim jurisdiction over the crown. The doctrine of sovereign immunity was retained by the fledgling United States despite the lack of a king, resulting in some unusual developments.

In the United States, sovereign immunity appears in four distinct contexts. The United States government itself is a sovereign and therefore immune from lawsuits. However, the federal government has largely waived this immunity. The Federal Tort Claims Act of 1946 renounced sovereign immunity for the federal government over a variety of tort claims. Federal sovereign immunity today largely serves to channel litigation into the appropriate forums rather than substantive protection from liability.

Foreign countries are also considered sovereigns, and the Foreign Sovereign Immunity Act, adopted by Congress in 1976, controls their immunity. The act codifies what had been State Department practice since the 1950s, essentially that foreign sovereigns are immune from lawsuits based on their public acts but are liable for commercial activities such as borrowing money.

Sovereign immunity also plays an important role in the relationship between Native American tribes and state and federal governments. Tribes, legally regarded as separate nations, enjoy many of the same immunities as other sovereigns, although there are limitations. Tribes control their internal governance and are immune from external lawsuits, including suits by states. Congress, however, does retain some authority over the tribes and federal statutes apply to tribes unless specifically exempted.

Under the REHNQUIST Court, though, the most visible aspect of sovereign immunity has involved the states. According to the doctrine of state sovereign immunity, the states of the union retain the status and dignity of sovereigns on equal footing with the federal government. The question of whether states are sovereigns or not goes back to one of the Supreme Court's earliest cases, CHISHOLM V. GEORGIA, 2 U.S. 419 (1793). In *Chisholm*, the Court held that a merchant from a neighboring state could sue Georgia in federal court over an unpaid debt. The reaction to this from many of the states was one of outrage. Facing substantial debt in the wake of the Revolutionary War, the states feared a wave of lawsuits if they were liable in court. In response to the *Chisholm* decision, the Eleventh Amendment was passed by both houses of Congress and ratified by the states.

The Eleventh Amendment provides that "[t]he Judicial power of the United States shall not be construed to extend to any suit in law or equity, commenced or prosecuted against one of the United States by Citizens of another State, or by Citizens or Subjects of any Foreign State." Interpretation of the Eleventh Amendment has been highly contested, but since *Hans v. Louisiana*, 134 U.S. 1 (1890), the dominant understanding by the Court is that the amendment alludes to a general principle of sovereign immunity that extends beyond the strict language of the amendment. As a result of this interpretation, states are protected from lawsuits not only by citizens of other states but by citizens of their own state as well.

Exceptions to state sovereign immunity emerged over the course of the 20th century. In 1908 the Supreme Court ruled in EX PARTE YOUNG, 209 U.S. 123, that state officers such as governors could be sued as individuals if they enforced unconstitutional laws. In *Parden v. Terminal Railway*, 377 U.S. 184 (1964), the Court ruled that states waived their immunity when they participated in INTERSTATE COMMERCE that is regulated by Congress. This doctrine of "implied waiver" did not last long, however. By 1974 Congress needed to expressly waive the states' immunity by legislation, *Edelman v. Jordan*, 415 U.S. 651. Beginning in the 1970s, states received increasing protection from the Court for their right to immunity.

The decision in *Seminole Tribe of Florida v. Florida*, 517 U.S. 44 (1996), brought the quiet doctrine of sovereign immunity back to the forefront of constitutional debate. The Court ruled that Congress could no longer rely on its commerce clause powers to waive a state's immunity, explicitly overturning the earlier case of *Pennsylvania v. Union Gas*, 491 U.S. 1 (1989). In the following years, the Court expanded this reasoning to apply to far-reaching federal legislation including patent law, trademark law, AGE DISCRIMINATION law, federal labor standards, and disabilities discrimination law. The Court has restricted Congress's power to waive the immunity of states to circumstances where it relies exclusively on power from the Fourteenth Amendment. For instance, the Court recently upheld the Family Medical Leave Act in *Nevada Department of Human Resources v. Hibbs*, 123 S. Ct. 1972 (2003), because it was designed to address gender discrimination, an area that the Court has identified as protected by the Fourteenth Amendment. The provisions of the Americans with Disabilities Act applying to states were overturned, however, in *University of Alabama v. Garrett*, 531 U.S. 356 (2001), because the Court determined that people with disabilities are not part of a protected class covered by the Fourteenth Amendment.

For more information: Noonan, John T. *Narrowing the Nation's Power: The Supreme Court Sides with the States*. Berkeley: University of California Press, 2002; Orth, John V. *The Judicial Power of the United States: The Eleventh Amendment in American History*. New York: Oxford University Press, 1987.

—Christopher Shortell

speedy trial

The term *speedy trial* refers to the duty of a court to make sure that a trial attended to in court does not incur any unnecessary delays in coming to a decision. The term can also refer to the right of a person charged with a crime or a tort to an unencumbered or undelayed proceeding, which includes all of the hearings, pretrial motions, and deliberations by the court.

The term *speedy trial* is recognized as a constitutional right granted to the public and delineated in the Sixth Amendment to the Constitution. The importance of this right was established in response to the abuses perpetrated by the English prosecutors. A person may call for a violation of their due process rights if the trial—from start to finish—takes an undue amount of time.

This concept of right to a speedy trial does not refer to a set amount of time, as each case is a different circumstance due to the strength of the case by the prosecution and, perhaps, the strength of the challenge by the defense. The provision to allow for a speedy trial is "an important safeguard to prevent undue and oppressive incarceration prior to trial, to minimize anxiety and concern accompanying public accusation and to limit the possibility that long delay will impair the ability of an accused to defend himself," which was offered by the Court in their opinion in the *U.S. v. Ewell* case in 1966.

A determination for whether or not a trial is speedy must take into consideration the type of crime being addressed and perhaps the legal skill present within the prosecutorial or defense team. This concept of a speedy trial was established in response to the English prosecutorial practices of keeping the accused in prison for prolonged periods of time before commencing the trial process. Many factors may cause a delay, but not all delays impinge upon the rights of the accused in terms of the intrinsic constitutional right to a speedy trial. The speedy trial right has been challenged many times at the Supreme Court level, but at the trial level there have not been many cases where it was determined that a person's rights were found to have been violated. Some decisions may be slow as in the case of *Barker v. Wingo* (1967), where five years had passed between the time the indictment was presented and the trial.

The courts have rejected placing any defined time limits on any type of trial partly owing to a few reasons, one of which can be summarized in that the defense has an obvious opportunity to delay a trial because they are often at a disadvantage versus the prosecution; that is in terms of resources. Despite the aforementioned, the most common test to determine whether a defendant's constitutional rights to a speedy trial have been violated is in the accepted four-pronged test.

The factors for determining if a speedy trial violation occurred include initially the length of the delay that is caused. A year or two may not be a delay—depending on the subject to be addressed. For example, let us say that a person committed a crime and was sentenced to time in a prison for more than a year, but before he was convicted he was out on bond and committed another crime. He gets sentenced and after being in prison, facts lead the prosecutor to want to charge this person with this other crime. The prosecutor may wait however long she needs to— including the entire length of the sentence being served— before bringing charges against the person. The delay concept does not start until the indictment is brought and some prosecutors may wait until they have more evidence against a person such as DNA evidence before starting the process.

Another factor in the determining if a defendant's rights have been violated is the consideration of the reason for the delay. If we follow the previous example, and the reason for the delay after indictment is because the prosecution cannot find their main witness, then they would need to further build their case against the person that is incarcerated. If the judge considers the reason for the delay to be reasonable, then there would be no delay, but if the prosecution filed charges right away and then took 14 years to bring the case to court, because they were incompetent, then the delay argument could be valid if the judge thought so, and there were no extenuating circumstances such as trying to find a witness that had moved away.

The third factor for consideration is if there is a delay prejudicial to the defendant. If we continue on our example, and we find out that there is a delay during the proceedings because the prosecutor knows the defendant does not have enough money to pay his defense lawyer past two months, and the prosecutor delays the trial so that the defendant will lose his lawyer, then the defense has an argument against the prosecution for violation of the right to a speedy trial (among other things). This is just an example and there are no known cases of this ever happening, but it is a good illustration. So if the trial was determined to have lasted too long, and it was determined that the reason for the delay was found to be a ridiculous reason, the judge might then allow for the violation of the defendant's right to a speedy trial to be addressed by the defendant's counsel.

The final factor for considering whether a person's rights have been violated in regards to the speed of trial is whether or not the defendant waived his/her right to a speedy trial. This would be allowed in court if the defendant had some rationale for this. Let us say the defendant knew he was guilty and decided that he needed to harvest his summer crops first, and this was going to be done before going to jail in order to pay his legal fees. The defense attorney may want to establish some negotiation between the prosecutor and the defense attorney in order to mete out a resolution. Therefore, there would be no challenge opportunity if the trial then took a long time to bring to a close. If one were to combine all four of the factors to consider whether a person's right to a speedy trial had been violated, one can see that the judge may have different levels of information available to her when making a decision based upon where a trial is in the process.

The right to a speedy trial is but one of the many available to a defendant and is protected under the Sixth Amendment. The right is also recognized and encapsulated in the Fourteenth Amendment under the due process clause. Historically, there was no time limit on when the prosecution needed to bring their case to court after indictment, and the time when it was brought could be unfair to the defendant— refer to the harvesting of crops example. Would that not be a poor thing if the prosecutor decided to wait until the time when the defendant was to harvest his crops before the charges were brought against the defendant? The defendant would have no right as to when he could go to court and perhaps take a chance of losing his farm based upon allegations that were not yet proved to be true.

In order to avoid this circumstance, the court recognizes a person's right to a speedy and fair trial but balances the time of trial by delegating the individual rules and procedures to the states regarding the methods for improving the time involved with the trial. This being stated, one can see that the state courts have a chance to improve and institute fair procedures in order to make the trial move along faster and in result lessen the burden upon the courts due to the huge amount of cases on the DOCKET. In addition, if a long time passed during the procedures, witnesses may forget what they saw or have their memories clouded. The examples offered may appear extreme, but they illustrate why there is a need to set rules for a speedy trial, and the

Speedy Trial Act of 1974 helped to clarify the rules and rights regarding what is appropriate.

Another circumstance that put a defendant at a disadvantage was the sharing of information, which in the past was not always done. By setting general procedural rules on when information had to be provided, the defendant was guaranteed the best opportunity for his legal team to evaluate the facts against the accused in order to prepare for the trial. If all of the information was shared, then the case could move more quickly because both teams then had a chance to peruse the material and make their arguments before the judge without undue delay. This serves many purposes, but ultimately it follows the rules that each person should be given every opportunity to prove that he is innocent and be presented with the facts so as to not prolong the marring of the defendant's name in a long and drawn out trial. This fundamental right is a way to make the court cases efficient in terms of time and in terms of rights—which is done by giving the defendant the right to a speedy trial.

For more information: *Barker v. Wingo,* 407 U.S. 514, 530 (1972); *Klopfer v. North Carolina,* 386 U.S. 213, 223–224 (1967); Speedy Trial Act of 1974, Pub. L. No. 93-619; Thorpe, F. "The Federal and State Constitutions." H. Doc. No. 357, 59th Congress, 2d Sess. 8, 3813 (1909); *United States v. Ewell,* 383 U.S. 116, 120 (1966).

—Ernest Alexander Gomez

Standard Oil Co. of New Jersey v. United States, 221 U.S. 1 (1911)

In *Standard Oil Co. of New Jersey v. United States,* the Court found that Standard Oil of New Jersey had violated the 1890 Sherman Antitrust Act by accumulating holdings constituting 90 percent of the petroleum industry and engaging in unfair and illegal business practices.

The Court heard the case on appeal from the circuit court for the Eastern District of Missouri, which found that Standard Oil of New Jersey had violated the Sherman Act by conspiring "to restrain the trade and commerce in petroleum . . . and to monopolize the said commerce."

The charges claimed that over a period of 36 years before the claim was brought against Standard in 1906, John D. and William Rockefeller and several other individuals had consolidated their personal stock holdings into a new corporation, Standard Oil of Ohio, which then went about acquiring a vast majority of refineries in Cleveland, Ohio, a major center for U.S. petroleum production. This, in turn, enabled the conglomerate to leverage "preferential shipping rates," which eventually forced competitors to either fold or join the conglomerate by buying stock or otherwise subcontracting with Standard, acting as de facto

appendages of the company. Using this method, Standard eventually purchased refineries throughout the United States, until by 1882 it had attained what the court described as "mastery" over 90 percent of the industry. Standard had also consolidated a hold on the pipeline system of the northeastern United States.

During the period of 1882 to 1889, the circuit court charged, Standard all but forced independent competitors to transfer their stocks and property into Standard corporations in their respective states, issuing trust certificates as payment.

In 1892 the Ohio Supreme Court declared most of Standard Oil of Ohio's holdings illegal, although it considered only the impact Standard's business practices had on INTERSTATE COMMERCE in the period after the establishment of the Sherman Act. Following the ruling, Standard attempted to deflect the Ohio decision by transferring its holdings into the Standard Oil Company of New Jersey, which continued to do business with other Standard companies around the United States and abroad.

The circuit court for the Eastern District of Missouri's original decision found that Standard had received preferential rates from railroad companies, restrained and monopolized pipelines, negotiated contracts with competitors to restrain trade, cut prices to suppress competition, spied on competitors, operated bogus "independent" companies, offered rebates until competition had been entirely eliminated, as well as gained "enormous and unreasonable profits" from the company's unfair practices. In addition to Standard Oil of New Jersey, the court's decree was aimed at 36 domestic companies and one foreign company controlled by Standard's dominant stockholders. The decision ordered the dissolution of the New Jersey company and invoked an injunction against further unfair business practices on Standard's part.

The appellants argued that the acquisitions in question had in fact been made between 1870 and 1882, before passage of the Sherman Act, and that the changes in corporate structure, culminating in the new Standard Oil of New Jersey, complied with the Sherman Act. They argued that the Standard empire did not consist of one monopoly, but several independent corporations. Standard also denied the accusations of conspiring to restrain or monopolize interstate or foreign trade.

The Court affirmed the lower court's decree in an 8-1 decision delivered by Justice WHITE, while clarifying some minor points. The decision called for the dissolution of the New Jersey company and discontinuation of Standard's monopolistic business arrangements with its subsidiaries.

The Court determined that a "rule of reason" must be applied when interpreting the Sherman Antitrust Act and evaluating its provisions to specific cases. While the act did not explicitly define "restraint of trade," Standard's business practices clearly indicated an "intent to drive others from the field and to exclude them from their right to trade, and thus accomplish the mastery which was the end in view." In essence, Standard's business model was not designed to remain competitive, but to remove competition altogether.

Justice HARLAN's concurring decision dissented from the majority on the point of determining what is "unreasonable." In Harlan's opinion, the insertion of "reasonableness" into the interpretation of the Sherman Act constituted an amendment to the act, and therefore was a power beyond the reach of the court.

For more information: Tarbell, Ida. *The History of the Standard Oil Company.* 2 vols. New York: McClure, Phillips, 1904.

—Daniel Skinner

standing

Among the jurisdictional requirements for federal judicial resolution of a case, "standing to sue" is one of the most important.

The standing inquiry that federal courts perform springs from the CASE OR CONTROVERSY requirement of Article III of the U.S. Constitution. While other aspects of the case or controversy requirement focus on the issues in the case, standing turns on who brought the case. Put another way, while the other aspects of the case and controversy requirement look at whether the issues being litigated are properly before the court, the standing inquiry looks at whether the plaintiff is the right person to litigate those issues. Because standing is a jurisdictional issue, a federal court cannot hear a particular case unless the plaintiff establishes standing.

Standing to sue turns on one basic inquiry—namely, whether "a party has a sufficient stake in an otherwise justiciable controversy to obtain judicial resolution of that controversy" [*Sierra Club v. Morton*, 405 U.S. 727, 731 (1972)].

While the standing doctrine incorporates both constitutional requirements and prudential considerations, at an "irreducible minimum," a plaintiff in federal court must demonstrate three things: (1) injury in fact; (2) causation; and (3) redressability [*Valley Forge Christian College v. Americans United for Separation of Church and State*, 454 U.S. 464, 471 (1982)]. More specifically, he must show "'that he personally has suffered some actual or threatened injury as a result of the putatively illegal conduct of the defendant,'" "that the injury 'fairly can be traced to the challenged action,'" and that the injury "'is likely to be redressed by a favorable decision'" *Valley Forge Christian College v. Americans United for Separation of Church and State*, 454 U.S. 464, 471 (1982)].

In practical terms, what this means is that an individual cannot sue in federal court unless there has been actual or threatened harm to him that was caused by the action that is the subject of the suit, and that, if he or she won, would be remedied by relief that the court in question is capable of granting. Thus, as a general matter, one cannot bring a lawsuit to complain of an injury done to someone else. Moreover, generalized grievances or abstract injuries are not sufficient to establish standing. Similarly, even if one has been injured, one cannot bring a lawsuit to challenge an action that did not cause that injury. One also cannot bring suit on the basis of an injury that a judgment in the plaintiff's favor could not remediate.

By enforcing these limits, federal courts seek to ensure that cases are brought by the proper parties, and that, as a result, they have the requisite adversity. That adversity ensures that the issues are fully and aggressively litigated. In so doing, as the Supreme Court observed in *Allen v. Wright* (1984), they help ensure the constitutionally mandated SEPARATION OF POWERS. They ensure that federal courts remain in the business of deciding litigation, not drafting de facto legislation.

For more information: Tribe, Laurence H. *American Constitutional Law.* 2nd ed. Mineola, N.Y.: Foundation Press, 1988; Wright, C., A. Miller, and E. Cooper, 13 *Fed. Prac. & Proc.* Juris. 2d §§ 3531-3531.16

—Anne M. Voigts

stare decisis

Stare decisis is often conceptually described as the circumstance of a court following the previous rulings of a court, if the decision was decided properly and without judicial or procedural error.

The significance of this concept can be recognized through a historical viewpoint in terms of the law, which offers a clear view into how the rule of law has evolved with the complexity of our society.

Stare decisis (Lat.) literally means that one is to stand by the decision which was previously made. This doctrine was originally a common-law term and mostly applied to common-law courts. The stare decisis concept results in a court system that does not move quickly to overturn a decision that was previously decided—unless it is somehow shown within court that there is a major reason to overturn the previous decision. For those of you that like literal Latin, the concept of stare decisis is also known in some writings to be *Stare decisis et non quieta movere;* translated roughly—that one is to stand by things decided and not to disturb the previously decided points. The former style is the accepted method of presentation.

The stare decisis doctrine also encapsulates the concept of setting a legal PRECEDENT. This means the upholding of a court decision by using the previous decision as a guide in coming to a similar decision. In theory this allows for a more consistent approach to addressing cases with similar facts. Therefore, if two people of different races, creeds, and colors commit the same crime, and all of the facts are mostly identical, then the sentences and crime convictions should be the same or very similar. Proponents of stare decisis offer that the law is more uniform then, and because of this it allows for judges and juries to make equitable decisions when pondering guilt, punishment, and action within the court. The stare decisis doctrine has run into challenges because of the opportunity for court members to presuppose the result based upon the similar fact patterns. If this were allowed to propagate then the decision-making process within the legal system may become tainted.

Today a great deal of attention is paid to the administration of justice and whether or not the idea of using a previous case from many years ago as a basis for judging a crime is a fair idea. The courts do allow for hearings, for defense attorney's arguments regarding the specificities of the situation, and for defense or prosecutorial appeal. It can be understood that the courts have remedies to address each person's individual circumstances. Once a decision is made, it stands as law and as a precedent for future cases. As time moves forward, technology often develops faster than law. With this ever-changing situation, we can begin to see that certain laws may become outdated faster than the courts can decide upon the regulation of industries or how to best protect society.

For example, the founders of our Constitution had no idea that we one day would be able to splice genes or transfer words in the form of e-mails over an electronic medium. One critique against stare decisis is whether or not archaic laws that were written a hundred years ago, before certain technology was even invented, should drive modern technological industry law. Such questions regarding precedence within the law are at the root of the challenges against stare decisis.

It should also be noted that the setting of precedence might often be restricted to the individual state court system. Despite these differences among the states, there is one reconciling authority. The Supreme Court decisions have a higher authority versus the state decisions and set the precedence for the rest of the courts throughout the land. The individual states often have unique specificities regarding their own laws, but generally the concepts associated with conduct are quite similar. Subsequently, the setting of precedent in a state case is a rare occurrence. If a decision is reached and then stands without successful challenge, this case decision becomes the standard for other cases that maintain similar fact patterns. In lieu of such information, we should be cognizant that if a case is challenged on the facts, and pursuant to such, the case is overturned because of some good cause—the result then is that

the new case (which the interpretation of facts is based upon) becomes the precedent.

Stare decisis offers a guideline for justices and persons involved with the law to recognize what is accepted and what may be challenged in court based upon the aspects of the case. In criminal cases, the doctrine of stare decisis is a stronger argument, and thus since there is a higher number of criminal cases, the need for stare decisis is greater in that area. The criminal courts have been inundated with a large number of cases because violent actions have risen due to a myriad of problems within society. Therefore, there is a need for a more effective and efficient means of addressing these cases while still giving people their rights. A standard by which to go gives everyone a starting point and lessens the opportunity for new and disparate laws to be established.

In opposition to stare decisis, within the constitutional law area, since there are fewer cases that offer a challenge to the Constitution, stare decisis is a less relevant idea. The rationale for not using the doctrine of stare decisis is that the Constitution was written a couple of hundred years ago in such a way so as to allow the country to grow and alter the interpretation of the law as needed. Therefore, a precedent may be viewed differently over time, and irrespective of opinion, there is always an opportunity for a good lawyer, with knowledge of the law, to challenge a law or a court's interpretation of a law—thereby making the law a living and ever-changing stream of arguments based upon the doctrine of stare decisis.

For more information: Garner, Bryan, ed. *Black's Law Dictionary.* 7th ed. St. Paul, Minn.: West Group, 1999; Gifts, Steven H. *Barron's Law Dictionary.* 4th ed. New York: Barron's Educational, 1996; O'Brien, David, M. *Constitutional Law and Politics,* vol. 2. New York, W. W. Norton, 1991.

—Ernest Alexander Gomez

Stevens, John Paul (1920–) *Supreme Court justice*
John Paul Stevens was appointed to the Supreme Court by President Gerald Ford in 1975.

Stevens was born to a prominent Chicago family on April 10, 1920, and has played a consistently unpredictable role on the Supreme Court since his appointment in 1975. Although a Republican appointee, Stevens has been an increasingly liberal voice as the Court has moved to the right, and he has become known for his independence, his propensity for writing dissenting opinions, his deference toward the legislative branch, and his interest in the particular context of each case considered by the court.

Stevens graduated Phi Beta Kappa from the University of Chicago in 1941 then served in World War II as a naval

Justice John Paul Stevens *(Library of Congress)*

dential candidates in his majority opinion in 1983's ANDER-SON V. CELEBREZZE and pointing out the dangers of vote dilution through the gerrymandering of legislative districts in his concurrence in 1983's *Karcher v. Daggett*. In 1986's BOWSHER V. SYNAR, Stevens wrote a concurring opinion maintaining that a key portion of the Balanced Budget and Emergency Deficit Control Act of 1985 constituted a violation of the Constitution's SEPARATION OF POWERS.

In his decisions, Stevens has demonstrated an interest in the particular contexts from which cases emerge, an affinity for balancing competing values, and a propensity for deference to other political institutions when possible. However, he has had difficulty in convincing other justices to join in his decisions, and he has written more dissenting and concurring opinions than any of his colleagues on the Court. Now the Court's most senior associate justice, Stevens has appeared to become more liberal in recent decades as the Court has moved more and more to the right over the course of the Reagan and Bush presidencies, and he often votes with the Court's more liberal and moderate justices.

For more information: Sickels, Robert Judd. *John Paul Stevens and the Constitution: The Search for Balance.* University Park: Pennsylvania State University Press, 1988.

—William D. Baker

officer on a code breaking team, for which he was awarded the Bronze Star. Following the war, Stevens enrolled at Northwestern University's School of Law where he edited the law review and graduated in 1947 with the highest grades in the law school's history. Stevens clerked with Supreme Court Justice Wiley RUTLEDGE before joining a prominent Chicago law firm and embarking on a successful career as an antitrust attorney. In 1970 President Richard Nixon appointed him to the Seventh Circuit COURT OF APPEALS, where he developed a reputation as an accomplished jurist and legal craftsman.

In the wake of Watergate, President Ford nominated the well-respected, moderate, and noncontroversial Republican Stevens to replace the retiring William O. DOUGLAS on the Supreme Court in 1975. Over the course of his career on the Court, Stevens has established himself as a practical, nonideological, and relatively unpredictable jurist with no apparent consistent judicial philosophy.

For example, although he has generally supported the claims of those alleging gender discrimination, his majority opinion in 1981's ROSTKER V. GOLDBERG upheld the constitutionality of the all-male draft. Stevens has also exhibited a concern for electoral fairness while on the Court, guaranteeing the right of ballot access to third-party presi-

Stewart, Potter (1915–1985) *Supreme Court justice*
Potter Stewart (January 23, 1915–December 7, 1985) was a centrist member of the Supreme Court during his 23 years of service (1958–81). He was appointed by Dwight Eisenhower. Stewart's father was a several-term mayor of Cincinnati and an Ohio Supreme Court justice. The Yale-educated Stewart himself served two terms on the Cincinnati City Council (including as vice mayor) and was appointed by Eisenhower to the U.S. COURT OF APPEALS (1954) and to the Supreme Court (1958).

The Court he joined was evenly divided between the liberal activists (WARREN, BLACK, DOUGLAS, and BRENNAN) and the conservatives (FRANKFURTER, CLARK, HARLAN, and Whittaker). He replaced a fellow Ohioan, Harold BURTON, on the tribunal. With Arthur Goldberg's appointment, the activists were in the majority. However, Nixon's nominees gave Stewart's moderate role more significance.

Stewart placed a high value on adherence to PRECEDENT. Hence he voted with the majority in ROE V. WADE, 410 U.S. 113 (1973), though he had dissented in GRISWOLD V. CONNECTICUT, 381 U.S. 479 (1965). He supported GIDEON V. WAINWRIGHT, 372 U.S. 335 (1963), and judicial scrutiny of legislative districting in *Baker v. Carr*, 369 U.S. 186 (1962), but dissented in ENGEL V. VITALE, 370 U.S. 421 (1962), and MIRANDA V. ARIZONA, 384 U.S. 436 (1966).

As someone who, early on, thought of a career in journalism (he headed Yale's student paper and was offered a job with *Time* after college), Stewart was the Court's most vigorous defender of freedom of the press. He dissented when the Court refused to extend to reporters a protection of their confidential sources. Yet he supported efforts to clamp down on pornography; though he conceded that it was not easy to define what was obscene, he knew it when he saw it (*Jacobellis v. Ohio*, 378 U.S. 197, 1964).

Stewart wrote the majority opinion in *Shelton v. Tucker*, 364 U.S. 479 (1960), holding unconstitutional a state requirement that teachers list all their associations (an effort to weed out civil rights sympathizers), and he authored *Jones v. Mayer*, 392 U.S. 409 (1968), broadly construing provisions of the Civil Rights Act of 1866 to reach private discrimination in housing.

Stewart authored *GREGG V. GEORGIA*, 428 U.S. 185 (1976), allowing CAPITAL PUNISHMENT, though he had condemned in *FURMAN V. GEORGIA*, 408 U.S. 238 (1972), the arbitrary and random imposition of the death sentence.

His opinion in *HARRIS V. McRAE*, 448 U.S. 297 (1980), upheld the Hyde Amendment, excluding abortions from federal Medicaid coverage.

For more information: Yarbrough, Tinsley E. "Justice Potter Stewart: Decisional Patterns in Search of Doctrinal Moorings." In *The Burger Court: Political and Judicial Profiles*, edited by Charles M. Lamb and Stephen C. Halpern. Urbana and Chicago: University of Illinois Press, 1991.

—Martin Gruberg

Stone, Harlan Fiske (1872–1946) *chief justice of the Supreme Court*

Harlan Fiske Stone was appointed to the Supreme Court as an associate justice in 1925 by President Calvin Coolidge and was elevated to CHIEF JUSTICE in 1941 by President Franklin D. Roosevelt, serving in that position until 1946. He is one of only three sitting associate justices to be elevated to chief justice.

Stone was born in Chesterfield, New Hampshire, to a middle-class family who earned their living farming. He earned his bachelor's degree from Amherst College in 1894 and his law degree from Columbia in 1898. Upon graduating from Columbia he taught law at his alma mater and also practiced corporate law on Wall Street. Partly in an attempt to rid himself of the scandals of the previous Warren G. Harding administration, Coolidge appointed him in 1924 as his attorney general.

The following year Coolidge nominated Stone to be an associate justice on the U.S. Supreme Court to fill the vacancy left by retiring Joseph McKenna. The confirmation process was muddied for two reasons. One, western senators were skeptical of Stone due to his Wall Street connections. The second problem was Stone, as attorney general, was seeking an indictment against Democrat Senator Burton K. Wheeler of Montana. Stone, in an attempt to save his nomination and to explain the reasons that caused him to seek the indictment against Senator Wheeler, volunteered to appear before the Committee on the Judiciary—the first nominee ever to do so. Eventually the full Senate confirmed Stone 71-6.

On the Court between 1925 and 1936, his most significant role was dissenting, most often with Louis BRANDEIS and Oliver Wendell HOLMES, Jr., and later, Holmes's replacement, Benjamin CARDOZO.

By the late 1930s many of his dissents were becoming the law of the land. These dissents were based on three premises: he believed that the Constitution gave to the government the appropriate level of power to govern; he insisted that the power to govern had to change to meet changing conditions; and when a matter of constitutional uncertainty arose about the power of government to remedy economic problems, that doubt had always to be resolved in favor of the legislative branch and not the courts.

Two of his best known dissents are in *UNITED STATES V. BUTLER*, 297 U.S. 1 (1936), and *Minersville v. Gobitis*, 310

Justice Harlan Fiske Stone *(United States Supreme Court)*

U.S. 586 (1940). In *Butler,* he showed his judicial philosophy of self-restraint and expressed concern that the majority was reading the Constitution too narrowly. He believed that in an emergency such as the economic depression, courts ought not question the means by which Congress chooses to carry into operation its delegated powers. The power of the courts to declare a statute unconstitutional should examine only the legislative power to enact statutes—not whether the laws establish sound policy.

In *Gobitis,* the eight-member majority held that a Jehovah's Witness child could be expelled from public school for refusing to participate in the daily ceremony of saluting the American flag and pledging allegiance to it. Stone, the lone-dissenter in *Gobitis,* saw his position hold the majority three years later in *West Virginia Board of Education v. Barnette,* 319 U.S. 624 (1943). The reasoning here was slightly different, however, as the Court invoked the free speech clause rather than relying primarily on the religion clause.

Perhaps Stone's greatest contribution to American law came in his majority opinion in UNITED STATES V. CAROLENE PRODUCTS, 304 U.S. 144 (1938), where he proposed in "Footnote Four" the appropriateness of applying different degrees of judicial scrutiny to different types of legislation. In the footnote he suggested that the members of the Court have a duty to subject to more scrutiny legislation that restricts the political processes which can ordinarily be expected to bring about repeal of undesirable legislation and that reflect prejudices against "discrete and insular minorities."

When executive powers collided with CIVIL LIBERTIES during World War II, Stone was sometimes, but not always, a staunch defender of the latter.

There are decisions in which he participated that history will not treat kindly—for instance, *Hirabayshi v. United States,* 320 U.S. 81 (1943), and KOREMATSU V. UNITED STATES, 323 U.S. 214 (1944). In *Korematsu,* the Court, with Stone in the six-member majority, upheld the conviction of Korematsu, an American citizen of Japanese descent, for remaining in a designated military area contrary to Civilian Exclusion Order Number 34, which directed that all persons of Japanese ancestry leave that area. Stone wrote, in *Hirabayshi,* for a unanimous Court in upholding the conviction of an American-born citizen of Japanese ancestry who had intentionally violated a curfew imposed upon West Coast Japanese Americans.

There were important cases in which Stone and his Court advanced the cause of individual rights protection. Stone wrote and voted to advance the cause of individual rights protection more extensively in cases unrelated to the war.

More than any other justice, Stone was responsible for steering the Court over nearly a decade from holding the "white primary" constitutional in *Grovey v. Townsend,* 295 U.S. 45 (1935), to declaring that having one's vote in a primary counted fairly was a federally enforceable right in *U.S. v. Classic,* 313 U.S. 299 (1941), to ruling the "white primary" unconstitutional in *Smith v. Allwright,* 321 U.S. 649 (1944).

Stone is generally considered to be a "great" justice, though not a "great" chief justice. He was not the leader his two predecessors, William Howard TAFT and Charles Evans HUGHES, were. In many ways the chief justiceship was an unhappy ending to an otherwise memorable and stellar career in public life. He was a legal scholar with the ability to narrow the issue in a case, decide and write about only this. This often enabled him to straighten out and clarify a mass of confusing precedents and doctrine so that his opinion could be used in the future as the foundation for other opinions.

He was a fiercely independent, tolerant, courageous judge whose beliefs combined a basic faith in the dignity and worth of the individual with a firm belief in the right and capacity of the people to govern.

For more information: Abraham, Henry. *Justice, Presidents, and Senators: A History of the U.S. Supreme Court, Appointments from Washington to Clinton.* 4th ed. Lanham, Md.: Rowman and Littlefield, 1999; *Hirabayshi v. United States,* 320 U.S. 81 (1943); *Korematsu v. United States,* 323 U.S. 214 (1944); Mason, Alpheus Thomas. *Harlan Fiske Stone: Pillar of the Law.* New York: Viking Press, 1956; *Minersville v. Gobitis,* 310 U.S. 586 (1940); Renstrom, Peter G. *The Stone Court: Justices, Rulings, and Legacy.* Santa Barbara, Calif.: ABC-CLIO, 2001; *Smith v. Allwright,* 321 U.S. 649 (1944); *United States v. Carolene Products,* 304 U.S. 144 (1938); *West Virginia v. Barnette,* 319 U.S. 624 (1943).

—Mark Alcorn

stop and frisk

The "stop and frisk" is the act of a police officer temporarily detaining and questioning a person suspected of criminal activity (the "stop") and, in most cases, subjecting that person to a brief patting-down of his or her outer garments (the "frisk"). An officer may stop a person to confirm or dispel, through questioning, a reasonable suspicion of past, present, or future criminal activity. The frisk ensures an officer's safety by confirming that the person stopped does not possess a weapon. The stop and frisk is constitutional when practiced in accordance with rules developed over several Supreme Court decisions.

Without any legitimate suspicion of criminal activity, a police officer is allowed, like any private citizen, to approach another person, attempt to engage that person in conversation, and even ask permission to search that person and his or her possessions. The approached person, however, has the right to refuse to converse with the officer, deny his or her requests, and walk away. An officer's behavior raises constitutional questions only when the officer attempts to use his or her government authority to engage, question, detain, or search a person or his or her possessions without that person having the discretion to refuse the officer's overtures.

On its face, the Fourth Amendment to the Constitution requires a government officer to have "probable cause" of a crime and a "warrant" (judicial permission to act) before arresting or searching a person and his or her property. The Supreme Court has recognized several exceptions to the probable cause and warrant requirements. A stop and frisk is an exception to both, allowing the police to restrict freedom of movement and be physically intrusive without a warrant and on something less than probable cause. At the same time, the stop and frisk is to be a partial imposition only, something less than a full-blown arrest or search.

In *TERRY V. OHIO*, 392 U.S. 1 (1968), the Supreme Court recognized that, while the stop and frisk did not meet the explicit requirements of the Fourth Amendment, it was a long-standing, valuable investigative tool that could be safely circumscribed. Stop and frisks are often referred to as "*Terry* stops." *Terry v. Ohio* is one of several major criminal procedure decisions of the Supreme Court that uses the Fourth through Sixth Amendments of the Constitution (through the Fourteenth Amendment) to regulate state police and prosecutorial activity. *Terry v. Ohio* and later decisions do limit the scope of police investigative activity; at the same time, they are designed to ensure that police officers have enough authority and flexibility to do their jobs effectively.

Numerous Supreme Court decision have resolved thorny issues related to the constitutionality of the "stop and frisk."

When does an officer have "reasonable suspicion" of criminal activity? Given the variability of human behavior and criminal activity, the Supreme Court's standard for what constitutes a "reasonable suspicion" is highly context-specific. Reasonable suspicion must be based on facts capable of being articulated, which can then be interpreted in light of the officer's investigative experience and the context in which the facts were encountered. An officer's "hunch" or "instinct" by itself is not enough to create a reasonable suspicion.

The presence of several facts together may create a reasonable suspicion where any one of those facts, standing alone, may not. For example, associating with known criminals or hanging around a high-crime area do not by themselves create a legitimate reasonable suspicion of criminal activity [*Sibron v. New York*, 392 U.S. 40 (1968); *Brown v. Texas*, 443 U.S. 47 (1979)]. In addition, the acts of refusing to cooperate with an officer, ignoring an officer, or even running away at the sight of a police officer, by themselves do not create a reasonable suspicion [*Illinois v. Wardlow*,

528 U.S. 119 (2000); *Florida v. Royer*, 460 U.S. 491 (1983)]. The combination of these acts with other suspicious behavior, however, may create, in the right context, reasonable suspicion of criminal activity [*Illinois v. Wardlow*, ibid.].

What is the proper scope of a "stop"? The "stop" of the stop and frisk can become an arrest if an officer is not careful, and the frisk for weapons a full-blown search if an officer is too intrusive. A stop and frisk ends when an officer either dispels his or her suspicion of criminal activity (at which point the person is free to go) or confirms it (at which point the person may be arrested or subjected to a more intrusive search or seizure of property). The detention must last only as long as it takes for the officer, using reasonable means, to investigate his or her suspicions [*United States v. Sharpe*, 470 U.S. 675 (1985)]. An officer may require a person to identify himself or herself, something that, short of a *Terry* stop, people may not be forced to do [*Brown v. Texas*, 443 U.S. 47 (1979)].

When may an officer "frisk," and what is the legitimate scope of that frisk? Technically a frisk is permissible only when an officer has an independent reasonable suspicion that a suspect may possess weapons; in practice, the frisk has been treated as almost automatically justified once reasonable suspicion of criminal activity is established.

The frisk is commonly called a "pat down" search, because an officer is allowed only to pat the outer garments of the suspect's clothing to feel for the presence of items that may be weapons. Groping or reaching into garments (say, rummaging through a suspect's pockets or a backpack) is impermissible. A frisk, in other words, is not a general, open-ended search for evidence. It is justified only as a light search for weapons in order to ensure an officer's safety during the stop.

If an officer, during a proper frisk, incidentally finds evidence of other criminal activity (such as a bag of drugs that falls out of a pocket after being patted), it has been constitutionally discovered; the officer may then act further on that discovery (by, for example, arresting the person) [*Minnesota v. Dickerson*, 508 U.S. 366 (1993)]. If an officer's pat down reveals no weapons or no incidentally discovered evidence of criminal activity, the frisk is over.

When an officer performs a stop and frisk on a driver or passenger of an automobile, the frisk may include those areas of the car's passenger compartment where a weapon could be placed and immediately accessed by the suspect.

The Supreme Court's stop and frisk doctrine, like their jurisprudence on criminal procedure generally, is criticized by different scholars as granting the police either too much or too little investigative authority. In addition, critics charge that the development of stop and frisk doctrine by the Court has been principally motivated by the ideological orientation of a majority of the Court at any given time.

Perhaps it is better to say that *Terry v. Ohio* and its progeny are a good example of constitutional pragmatism.

The rationale for various aspects of stop and frisk doctrine appear grounded more in the justices' (possibly flawed) understanding of the nature of police work than in abstract constitutional theory. These decisions seem to reflect the Court's attempt to strike the best balance between the needs of police officers and the rights of citizens; as the Court's composition has changed, the Court's understanding of the proper balance has changed as well, but not radically.

For more information: Heumann, Milton, and Lance Cassak. *Good Cop, Bad Cop: Racial Profiling and Competing Views of Justice.* New York: Peter Lang, 2003.

—James Daniel Fisher

Story, Joseph (1779–1845) *Supreme Court justice*

Joseph Story was appointed to the Supreme Court by President James Madison in 1811 and he served until his death in 1845.

Frequently included among the lists of the greatest Supreme Court justices, Joseph Story was one of the most important jurists in American history. Born in 1779 in Massachusetts, Story was recognized as an academic prodigy, graduating from Harvard in 1800 and joining the Massachusetts bar in 1801. He earned a reputation as one of the best lawyers in the state but became nationally known with his arguments in FLETCHER V. PECK (1810). In *Fletcher,* Story challenged a Georgia law taking back land that had been sold as part of the Yazoo Land Fraud in which legislators had been bribed. Story was able to convince the Supreme Court that property rights given the owners could not be taken away without violating the contract clause. The Supreme Court accepted his argument and Story won the case.

His success earned him the attention of national political leaders, including James Madison, who appointed him to the Supreme Court in 1811 after three failed attempts to replace the retiring Justice Cushing. Story immediately became the most consistent supporter of Chief Justice John MARSHALL. He approved of Marshall's views that the national government must be stronger than the states and that the Supreme Court and federal law must be supreme to state courts and laws. He received his first opportunity to state those views for the Court in 1816 in the case of MARTIN V. HUNTER'S LESSEE.

In *Martin,* the Virginia Supreme Court refused to accept a U.S. Supreme Court ruling in a land case. The Virginia justices ruled the Supreme Court had no jurisdiction to hear appeals of state supreme court decisions and struck down the 1789 Judiciary Act which gave them that authority. This direct challenge to the Court's authority was answered swiftly by Justice Story. In *Martin,* he ruled that the Constitution made federal law supreme to state law and for that reason made the U.S. Supreme Court supreme to any ruling of a state supreme court. He also provided his view of the founding of the Constitution. According to Story, the Constitution was created by the people rather than the states and the people had given their sovereign powers to the national government. The states could not claim sovereignty in such cases and would have to accept the fact that the national judiciary was supreme.

Story was a strong nationalist who supported a powerful federal government and was suspicious of excessive state power. His opinion in *Martin* placed him squarely with Chief Justice Marshall, and Story joined Marshall's opinions in such important cases as MCCULLOCH V. MARYLAND (1819), *Sturgis v. Crowninshield* (1819), and GIBBONS V. OGDEN (1824). Marshall's domination of the Court and his tendency to write most of the Court's important decisions limited the number of times Story could express his views in an official opinion, but he was active in off Court activities during Marshall's reign.

During the debate over the Missouri Compromise in 1820, Story made a speech in Massachusetts denouncing the idea of allowing slavery to expand to new states such as Missouri. In 1829 he accepted an offer to be a part-time professor at Harvard Law. His seminars were well attended by law students, and his views were spread to new law graduates and had a considerable effect on the development of the law during that time.

In 1833 Story composed his *Commentaries on the Constitution of the United States,* which was an analysis of all the clauses and amendments to the Constitution. His incisive comments on the meanings of vague and uncertain terms in the Constitution provided future lawyers and judges with a guide to how the first generation of Supreme Court justices perceived the meanings of the words in the Constitution. At the same time, Story also participated in the debate over the wisdom and constitutionality of the Bank of the United States, the main political issue of Andrew Jackson's presidency. He distrusted Jackson and was unhappy as the president replaced Marshall-era justices.

Story served some 34 years on the Court, but he was most active in writing opinions during the last 15 years of his term. In 1833 he wrote one of his few dissents to a Marshall opinion in *Cherokee Nation v. Georgia.* The number of his dissents would increase after Marshall died in 1835 and was replaced by Chief Justice Roger TANEY. Taney began a shift on the Court, starting with three major cases decided in 1837. Story dissented in each, including *Charles River Bridge v. Warren Bridge Company,* a decision that appeared to overrule parts of Story's victory in *Fletcher v. Peck.*

Yet while Story frequently found himself in the minority on the Court, he had a considerable impact during the 1840s. He became the Court's spokesman on several slavery related cases. In *U.S. v. Amistad* (1841), Story ruled for the Court that slaves who mutinied and took over the slave ship transporting them to the United States should be sent back to Africa.

In *Prigg v. Pennsylvania* (1842), he upheld a fugitive slave law and required that states return runaway slaves to their owners. The most important decision of this period was in SWIFT V. TYSON (1842). *Swift* dealt with cases where a citizen of one state sued a citizen of another state, with these cases being heard by a federal judge who would apply the proper state law in the case. The question arose to whether a federal judge would be limited by a state court interpretation of a law or if the federal judge could issue his own interpretation. Always suspicious of state courts and judges, Story ruled that federal judges were not bound by the ruling of state courts when they interpreted state law. This allowed federal judges to create their own law when ruling in such cases.

Tyson was his last important decision for the Court. As Story found himself more and more in the minority on most decisions, he considered retirement and planned to leave the Court in 1845, but in September of that year he became ill and died soon after on September 10, 1845.

For more information: Newmyer, R. Kent. *Supreme Court Justice Joseph Story.* Chapel Hill: University of North Carolina Press, 1985; Smith, Jean Edward. *John Marshall.* New York: Henry Holt, 1998; Story, Joseph. *A Familiar Exposition of the Constitution of the United States.* New York: Regnery Press, 1986.

—Douglas Cloutre

strict scrutiny

Strict scrutiny is the highest and most stringent standard used by federal courts to determine the constitutionality of governmental actions. Courts limit the use of strict scrutiny to cases where the government has used SUSPECT CLASSIFICATIONS like race or RELIGION as well as cases where governmental action imposes on FUNDAMENTAL RIGHTS. Under the standard of strict scrutiny, the government bears the burden of showing that its actions satisfy a COMPELLING STATE INTEREST, and that its actions are a necessary means for serving that interest.

The concept of strict scrutiny has its origins in a famous footnote by Justice STONE. Writing for the majority in UNITED STATES V. CAROLENE PRODUCTS CO., 304 U.S. 144 (1938), Justice Stone claims, "There may be narrower scope for operation of the presumption of constitutionality when legislation appears on the face to be within a specific prohibition of the Constitution, such as those of the first ten amendments, which are deemed equally specific when held to be embraced within the Fourteenth."

Later in the footnote, Justice Stone suggests that certain rights, such as the right to vote, peaceably assemble, and the right to free speech are of such importance that potential governmental infringement of those rights may require heightened judicial scrutiny, particularly if the governmental action is aimed at members of religious or racial minority groups.

What qualifies as a suspect classification? The Court has considered suspect any classification based on race, religion, or national origin. In KOREMATSU V. UNITED STATES, 323 U.S. 214 (1944), the Court ruled classification based on Japanese descent was "immediately suspect" and subject to strict scrutiny. The Court has also applied strict scrutiny to redistricting cases, where race was "the predominant factor" in the redrawing of district lines. The Court has been reluctant to expand suspect classification status beyond race, religion, and nationality. For example, in *HARRIS V. MCRAE*, 448 U.S. 297 (1980), the Court ruled that "poverty" did not qualify as a suspect classification, and in *Gregory v. Ashcroft*, 501 U.S. 452 (1991), the Court ruled that "age" was not a suspect classification.

Decisions regarding suspect classification based on gender have been less consistent. Though the Court has ruled government preference or classification based on gender is subject to scrutiny under the EQUAL PROTECTION CLAUSE [*Reed v. Reed*, 404 U.S. 71 (1971), and *CRAIG V. BOREN*, 429 U.S. 190 (1976)], the Court has not applied the strict scrutiny standard to cases involving gender-based classification.

Courts typically view gender as a quasi-suspect classification, subject to scrutiny slightly less strict than classification based on race, religion, or nationality, yet more rigorous than the RATIONAL BASIS standard of ordinary scrutiny. In cases involving gender, the government generally must show an "important" rather than a compelling state interest, and the gender-based classification must be "substantially" related to serving that interest, rather than necessary for serving that interest. The Court has also applied INTERMEDIATE SCRUTINY to cases involving classification based on alien status.

Strict scrutiny also applies to cases where governmental actions infringe upon fundamental rights. The Court has never clearly delineated fundamental rights from other rights, but they are typically understood to include the right of property, the right to vote, the right to free speech, and the right to procreate. Supreme Court rulings since the mid 1970s have consistently ruled privacy as a fundamental right, though not without controversy. SKINNER V. OKLAHOMA, 316 U.S. 535 (1942), is often regarded as the first case to apply strict scrutiny to the issue of fundamental rights.

In *Skinner,* the Court struck down a law mandating surgical sterilization of habitual criminals, ruling it was an unconstitutional exercise of the state's POLICE POWERS. The Court found that the right to procreate was not only a fundamental individual right but also basic to the perpetuation of a race. The Court argued that improper application of the Oklahoma statute could result in "subtle, far reaching and devastating effects. In evil or reckless hands it can cause races or types which are inimical to the dominant group to wither and disappear." The Court has also consistently struck down state laws that either explicitly or implicitly restrict citizens' participation in elections, arguing that the right to vote is fundamental.

The Court has failed to recognize education as a fundamental right and has wavered in its views on freedom of sexual behavior. In SAN ANTONIO INDEPENDENT SCHOOL DISTRICT V. RODRIGUEZ, 411 U.S. 1 (1973), the Court upheld a Texas statute that provided school district funding based on the value of local property taxes. Appellants filed a CLASS ACTION suit on behalf of children in low-income areas, arguing that their fundamental right to education was being impeded by a system that provided them a disproportionately low amount of educational funding. The Court disagreed, ruling that wealth was not a suspect classification, and that education was not a fundamental right.

PLYLER V. DOE, 457 U.S. 202 (1982), challenged the constitutionality of another Texas education statute. In this case, the statute at issue was the Texas Education Code, which allowed districts to deny admission to undocumented children who could not show that they entered the United States legally. The code also denied funding to districts for any undocumented aliens it chose to enroll. As in San Antonio, the Court ruled that education was not a fundamental right. However, the Court, applying the standard of intermediate scrutiny, found that the state's interest in the "preservation of the state's limited resources for the education of its lawful residents," did not justify the use of classification based on undocumented alien status.

When the Court applies strict scrutiny to cases, the government bears the burden of showing that its actions satisfy a compelling state interest, and that its actions are a necessary means for serving that interest. As with the concept of fundamental rights, the Court has never clearly delineated what constitutes a compelling state interest, but several examples exist to illustrate the concept. In Korematsu, the court ruled that the U.S. interest in providing military security justified classification based on Japanese descent. In two recent AFFIRMATIVE ACTION cases, the Court ruled that states have a compelling interest to ensure student body diversity within their universities. However, the Court's assessment of the necessity of classification for securing state interests is less predictable.

For more information: Anderson, Elisabeth S. "Integration, Affirmative Action, and Strict Scrutiny." *New York University Law Review* 77 (2002); Grofman, Bernard. "*Shaw v. Reno* and the Future of Voting Rights." *PS: Political Science and Politics* 28, no. 1. (March 1995): 27–36.

—Michelle D. Christensen

structure of the Supreme Court

There are nine justices of the Supreme Court of the United States. The number of justices is not specified in the U.S. Constitution, which provides only that there shall be "one supreme Court," but is set by legislation.

The JUDICIARY ACT OF 1789, passed after ratification of the Constitution to organize the judicial branch, authorized the Supreme Court to have a CHIEF JUSTICE and five associate justices. Over time, the number of justices has increased or decreased with political objectives and workload demands contributing to the pressures for change. Legislation in 1807, 1837, and 1863 increased the number of justices to seven, then nine, and then 10, respectively, to accommodate the nation's expansion westward, and the justices chosen to fill these new vacancies came from states in the new regions of the country. In the wake of Reconstruction controversies with President Andrew Johnson and continued concern about federal court workload, Congress enacted legislation in 1866 that diminished some of the justices' workload and reduced the number of justices to seven as vacancies occurred but the number of justices never went below eight. In 1869, after President Ulysses S. Grant took office, the number of justices was increased to nine, where it has remained.

These latter episodes suggest that the number of justices is not just a function of organizational need or geographic necessity but of political expediency. Indeed, two other historical events reveal that political dynamics help shape the number of justices of the Supreme Court. In 1801, as the Republicans prepared to take over the executive and legislative branches for the first time after President John Adams lost his reelection bid, the lame duck Federalist Congress enacted the Judiciary Act of 1801, which eliminated some lower court responsibilities of the Supreme Court justices and, with the reduced workload, decreased the size of the Supreme Court by one seat upon the next vacancy, which had the concomitant effect of inhibiting the incoming Republicans' capacity to acquire control over the judiciary. This effort was forestalled when the new Republican Congress quickly repealed the Judiciary Act of 1801, leaving the Supreme Court at its previously authorized size. The desire for enhanced efficiency in the developing federal judiciary ran into partisanship as the size of the Supreme Court and the organization of the federal courts became political bargaining chips.

A far more public controversy over the size of the Supreme Court developed when President Franklin Roosevelt in 1937 proposed adding to the Court an additional justice for each justice over the age of 70, to a total of 15 justices, to ensure that the Supreme Court's workload was being handled timely and efficiently. Roosevelt's frustration with a Court that during his first term consistently rejected his most important New Deal legislation as unconstitutional

American Court Systems Flow Chart

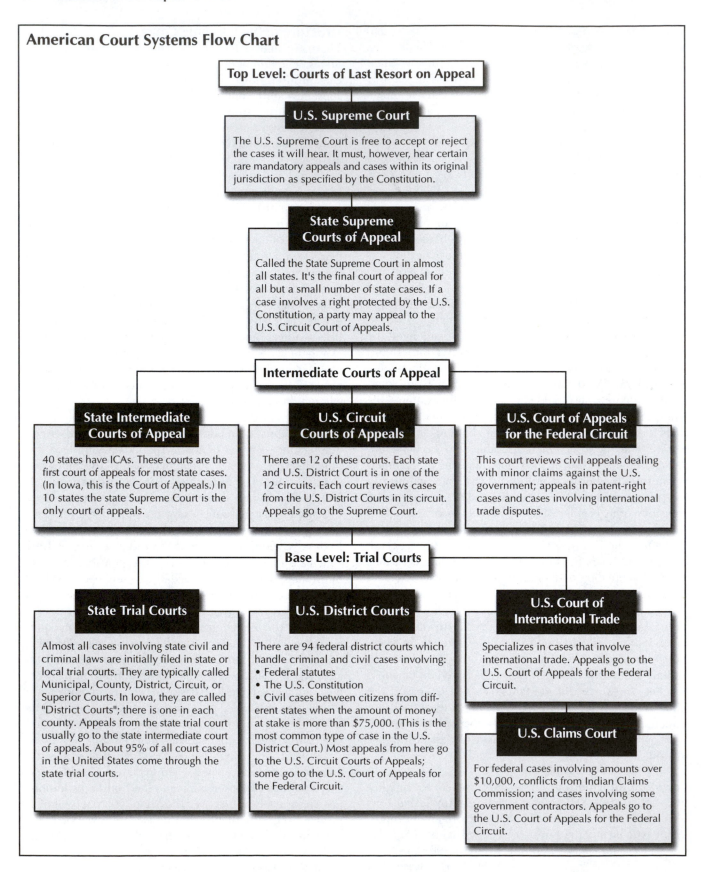

Top Level: Courts of Last Resort on Appeal

U.S. Supreme Court

The U.S. Supreme Court is free to accept or reject the cases it will hear. It must, however, hear certain rare mandatory appeals and cases within its original jurisdiction as specified by the Constitution.

State Supreme Courts of Appeal

Called the State Supreme Court in almost all states. It's the final court of appeal for all but a small number of state cases. If a case involves a right protected by the U.S. Constitution, a party may appeal to the U.S. Circuit Court of Appeals.

Intermediate Courts of Appeal

State Intermediate Courts of Appeal

40 states have ICAs. These courts are the first court of appeals for most state cases. (In Iowa, this is the Court of Appeals.) In 10 states the state Supreme Court is the only court of appeals.

U.S. Circuit Courts of Appeals

There are 12 of these courts. Each state and U.S. District Court is in one of the 12 circuits. Each court reviews cases from the U.S. District Courts in its circuit. Appeals go to the Supreme Court.

U.S. Court of Appeals for the Federal Circuit

This court reviews civil appeals dealing with minor claims against the U.S. government; appeals in patent-right cases and cases involving international trade disputes.

Base Level: Trial Courts

State Trial Courts

Almost all cases involving state civil and criminal laws are initially filed in state or local trial courts. They are typically called Municipal, County, District, Circuit, or Superior Courts. In Iowa, they are called "District Courts"; there is one in each county. Appeals from the state trial court usually go to the state intermediate court of appeals. About 95% of all court cases in the United States come through the state trial courts.

U.S. District Courts

There are 94 federal district courts which handle criminal and civil cases involving:
• Federal statutes
• The U.S. Constitution
• Civil cases between citizens from different states when the amount of money at stake is more than $75,000. (This is the most common type of case in the U.S. District Court.) Most appeals from here go to the U.S. Circuit Courts of Appeals; some go to the U.S. Court of Appeals for the Federal Circuit.

U.S. Court of International Trade

Specializes in cases that involve international trade. Appeals go to the U.S. Court of Appeals for the Federal Circuit.

U.S. Claims Court

For federal cases involving amounts over $10,000, conflicts from Indian Claims Commission; and cases involving some government contractors. Appeals go to the U.S. Court of Appeals for the Federal Circuit.

was apparent to all and this plan would permit the president to appoint immediately five new justices, which would ensure more favorable decisions for the New Deal legislation. Characterized as the court-packing plan, Roosevelt's proposal divided Democrats while the public, bench, and bar found little to like in its blatantly partisan nature, which would alter for the sake of political advantage more than a half century of experience with nine justices.

While the nation debated the court-packing plan and Chief Justice Charles Evans HUGHES made clear that the Court was fully abreast of its responsibilities, the Supreme Court decided a series of cases that upheld key New Deal legislation with at least two justices seeming to change their views on the New Deal legislation and now voting to uphold Roosevelt's proposals. This "switch in time that saved nine," coupled with the resignation of one justice, gave Roosevelt the results he sought so that the defeat of the court-packing plan in the Senate did not deter his goals for the nation. The failure of Roosevelt's court-packing plan, despite his popularity and the Court's reluctance to approve his legislative agenda, reflects the extent to which the number nine has insinuated itself into the national psyche as the appropriate number of justices for the Supreme Court.

A proposal by Chief Justice Warren BURGER to add a tenth justice to administer the federal courts, without any adjudicative responsibilities, received no serious consideration. Notwithstanding political leaders' desire for sympathetic rulings from the Court, alterations to its size seem unlikely as the national expansion has ceased and the Court remains current in its work. After almost 150 years, a Supreme Court of nine justices may have taken on dimensions that transcend constitutional requirement and exist firmly in the lore of American legal, political, and popular culture.

For more information: Abraham, Henry J. *Justices, Presidents and Senators.* Rev. ed. Lanham, Md.: Rowman and Littlefield, 1999.

—Luke Bierman

student activity fees

Mandatory student activity fees have raised constitutional questions. The issue of student activity fees has been twice addressed by the Supreme Court, most recently in BOARD OF REGENTS V. SOUTHWORTH, 529 U.S. 217 (2000).

In *Southworth*, the Supreme Court held that the First Amendment permits a public university to charge students mandatory activity fees that are used to fund programs facilitating extracurricular philosophical, religious, or other student discussions, insofar as there is viewpoint neutrality in the allocation of funds to said organizations.

Although the Court tackled the subject of how public universities should distribute student activity fees in ROSEN-

BERGER V. RECTOR AND VISITORS OF THE UNIVERSITY OF VIRGINIA, 515 U.S. 819 (1995), it had not previously addressed the matter of whether the university could mandate the payment of those fees. In *Rosenberger*, the Court decided that a public university must remain viewpoint neutral in its review and allocation of activity funds to all student organizations, including religious ones, notwithstanding the university's desire to comply with the First Amendment's religious establishment clause. Both cases now provide the framework for how public higher learning institutions are expected to treat mandatory student activity fees.

The Court in *Southworth* ruled against University of Wisconsin students who filed suit against the university alleging that it violated their First Amendment rights by funding student organizations actively engaged in political and ideological activities offensive to their personal beliefs. The students demanded that the university grant them the choice not to fund the offending organizations. The university maintained that the mandatory fees and the speech funded were necessary to meet its educational mission of exposing students to diverse views.

In a unanimous decision, the Court began its *Southworth* analysis by focusing on two closely related precedents: ABOOD V. DETROIT BOARD OF EDUCATION, 431 U.S. 209 (1977), and *Keller v. State Bar of California*, 496 U.S. 1 (1990). Although the Court recognized that the methods of implementing First Amendment provisions used in those cases were inapplicable for the *Southworth* context, the Court found them instructive.

In *ABOOD*, some nonunion teachers protested an agreement reached by the union representing all teachers. As a condition of their employment, this agreement required that all teachers, (union or nonunion), pay a service fee equivalent to union dues. The objecting teachers claimed that the union's use of these fees for POLITICAL SPEECH violated their freedom of association rights guaranteed by the First and Fourteenth Amendments. The Court sided with the teachers and ruled that any objecting teacher could prevent the union's use of that teacher's contribution for political causes unrelated to the union's collective bargaining work. Likewise in *Keller,* the Court held that lawyers admitted to practice in California may be required to be members of a state bar association and provide funds for activities "germane" to the association's policing mission, but they may not be required to fund the association's political activities.

The *Southworth* Court maintained that while it is difficult to determine what is germane in the university context, the objecting students' First Amendment rights must be protected. It then concluded that the university's viewpoint neutrality when allocating funds was sufficient to protect those rights.

For more information: Lilith, Ryiah. *"Board of Regents of the University of Wisconsin v. Southworth."* American University *Journal of Gender, Social Policy, and the Law* 809 (2004).

—Salmon A. Shomade

student newspapers

The student press enjoys certain constitutional protections afforded to other types of publications, although the Court has recognized limitations on these freedoms. Actions by officials in public high schools, colleges, and universities that interfere with student publications can sometimes constitute First Amendment violations.

As a rule, public high school journalists enjoy less constitutional protection than collegiate journalists. In HAZELWOOD SCHOOL DISTRICT V. KUHLMEIER, 484 U.S. 260 (1988), the Supreme Court considered PRIOR RESTRAINT by a high school principal. Page proofs of a student newspaper were routinely submitted to the principal before publication.

In the May 13, 1983, issue, the principal found two articles objectionable on the basis of their content. One article described three students' pregnancy experiences, and the other discussed the impact of divorce on students. The principal removed two entire pages from the issue, thereby removing noncontroversial content as well as the two articles in question. In the resulting legal action, the Court sided with the principal. From the Court's point of view, the fact that the newspaper was published as a journalism class project was extremely important. Because of this curricular connection, the Court did not consider the newspaper to be a PUBLIC FORUM and applied the special circumstances doctrine. Justice WHITE's majority opinion stated: "A school need not tolerate student speech that is inconsistent with its 'basic educational mission,' even though the government could not censor similar speech outside the school."

The Supreme Court explicitly declined to decide whether *Hazelwood* would apply to publications at the collegiate level. (The federal circuit courts have rejected such an extension.) However, the Supreme Court has recognized fairly broad freedoms for college and university journalists before and since *Hazelwood*. In *Papish v. University of Missouri Curators*, 410 U.S. 667 (1973), the Court considered the expulsion of a student who distributed an independent newspaper on the University of Missouri campus. Her expulsion followed the newspaper's publication of a potentially offensive cartoon and headline. While the university maintained that the headline language and cartoon content were obscene, the Supreme Court disagreed. Furthermore, the Court did not feel that the school's actions could be considered legitimate regulation of time, place, or manner of disseminating the newspaper. The Court concluded that the school's disapproval of the publication's nonobscene content

was the only basis for the student's expulsion, and therefore her First Amendment rights had been violated.

More recently, a deeply divided Court ruled in ROSENBERGER V. RECTOR & VISITORS OF THE UNIVERSITY OF VIRGINIA, 515 U.S. 819 (1995), on the issue of a public university funding religious student publications. Under the University of Virginia's regulations, the student organization Wide Awake Productions was fully qualified to be reimbursed for printing costs related to its magazine except for the fact that the publication espoused a religious viewpoint. The Court characterized the university's decision to withhold the funds as impermissible viewpoint discrimination, prohibited by the First Amendment. The four dissenters, basing their arguments on ESTABLISHMENT CLAUSE considerations, maintained that a public university should not fund a publication that was fundamentally an evangelical tool rather than a forum.

For more information: Bryks, Helene. "Comment: A Lesson in School Censorship: *Hazelwood v. Kuhlmeier.*" *Brooklyn L. Rev.* 55 (Winter 1989): 291; Steffan, Brian J. "A First Amendment Focus: Freedom of the Private-University Student Press: A Constitutional Proposal." *J. Marshall L. Rev.* 36 (Fall 2002): 139.

—Elizabeth Ellen Gordon

students, rights of

Students' rights are those certain guarantees that every student is entitled to based on the United States Constitution, BILL OF RIGHTS, and other amendments. These rights include freedom of expression, privacy, fair and equal treatment, equality in education, the right to view school records, religious freedom, and due process. However students' rights often do have the same robust protection that is given to the rights of adults.

Right to free expression for students is derived from the First Amendment to the Constitution that guarantees our right to free expression and free association. As a general principle, government does not have the right to forbid students from saying and writing what they like. Students can form clubs and organizations and take part in rallies and demonstrations. A student has the right to express his or her opinions and beliefs in school if done so in nondisruptive circumstances.

The Supreme Court set an important PRECEDENT in *TINKER V. DES MOINES INDEPENDENT SCHOOL DISTRICT*, 393 U.S. 503 (1969). The Tinker children and others challenged their suspension for wearing black armbands in an antiwar protest. Writing for the majority, Justice FORTAS argued that students in public schools do not leave their First Amendment rights at the schoolhouse door. This is not complete freedom, however. Fortas also wrote that students must express themselves in ways that do not "materially and substantially" disrupt classes or other school activities.

In other cases the Court has upheld as constitutional teacher supervision of STUDENT NEWSPAPERS, including the right to censor objectionable material. Schools may also set up their own codes for students as long as these do not unduly infringe on protected speech and are available and clearly explained to students. These codes may include dress standards, hair length standards, tattoos, and other forms of self-expression. As a general principle codes prohibiting vulgar, indecent, disruptive, and threatening types of expression are constitutional.

Students' right to privacy is grounded in the Fourth Amendment, which prohibits police and other government agents from searching a person and his or her property without "probable cause" to believe that he or she committed a crime, and without having obtained a warrant prior to the search. Students also have the Fifth Amendment right to not talk to police or authority figures and to ask for their parents or a lawyer before they are asked any questions that could put them in danger of incriminating themselves. Again, this right is somewhat more limited than it is for adults. In *NEW JERSEY V. T.L.O*, 469 U.S. 325 (1985), the Supreme Court ruled that school officials, unlike police, may search students without a warrant when they have "reasonable grounds for suspecting that the search will turn up evidence that the student has violated . . . either the law or rules of the school." School officials may not search a large group, or only selected groups of students if they suspect that one person violated a law or school rule. Searches must be specific to suspects. Searches must also be conducted in a reasonable manner based on age and what authorities are looking for. Drug and alcohol tests are considered searches. In a Supreme Court decision, *Vernonia v. Acton,* 515 U.S. 646 (1995), the Court ruled that student athletes can be tested for drugs because athletic programs are voluntary and athletes are role models.

The right of fair treatment for students is found in the Fourteenth Amendment due process clause. Essentially it means that students have the right to be treated according to published rules and standard procedures by authorities such as teachers, school administrators, and police. For example, before he or she can be suspended a student has the right to a hearing to tell his or her side of the story. This right was secured in *Goss v. Lopez,* 419 U.S. 565 (1975). If a student is in fact guilty of something, the punishment cannot be more serious than the misconduct.

Private schools are not held to the same strict standards as public schools since normally parents waive certain rights when they voluntarily put their children in private schools. They must, however, respect students' right to privacy.

Curiously, students have a right to an integrated education, but not to an equal education. Segregated schools were struck down in the landmark case, *Brown v. Board of Education,* 347 U.S. 483 (1954), that declared "separation is inherently unequal." However, in a later case, *San Antonio Independent School District v. Rodriguez,* 411 U.S. 1 (1973), parents in a poor district of San Antonio, Texas, tried to argue that funding of public schools should be equal across the state and not depend on local property taxes that put poor school districts at a strict disadvantage. The Supreme Court refused to mandate equality of funding, even acknowledging that this would continue unequal treatment.

Students' school records must be kept private from the public, although school officials do have the right to release information to officials who "have a legitimate educational interest" in reviewing such records. They must respond to subpoenas for records, but in doing so they must also give notification to parents, except in emergency situations.

Based on the 1974 Family Educational Rights and Privacy Act, also known as the Buckley Amendment, students and their parents have a right to view their own records, including test scores, intelligence quotients, and grades, as well as progress reports, psychological and psychiatric reports, and teacher evaluations. Certain exceptions are made for psychiatric reports and records possessed by counselors, doctors, and social workers that can be withheld from students.

Students retain their freedom of RELIGION even while in school, but this is a complex issue. The ESTABLISHMENT CLAUSE of the First Amendment prohibits government officials (which in this case usually means school administrators and teachers) from encouraging or promoting any or all religions in any way, from leading school prayers or seeming to give approval to any religious activities. Coordinately, the free exercise clause of the First Amendment gives students the right to pray privately or in groups before or after school so long as school personnel do not sponsor such groups. Religious clubs may meet on the same basis as other extracurricular clubs.

Numerous court cases have defined the contours of student rights over the years. While students do not give up their constitutional rights simply because they are students, they are usually treated as minors with all the legal limitations that includes. Students are also limited to some extent because a school is a learning environment, and one student's actions may not infringe upon another student's or disrupt the learning process. It is a continuous challenge to maintain an environment that promotes education and protects students' basic rights.

For more information: American Civil Liberties Union. "Student Rights." Available online. URL: http://www.aclu.org/StudentRights/StudentRightsMain.cfm. Downloaded May 19, 2004.

—Amy Oliver

student searches

School officials may search public school students for drugs or weapons or other evidence of breach of school rules without having probable cause. In *NEW JERSEY V. TLO,* 469 U.S. 325 (1985), the Supreme Court ruled that the Fourth Amendment protection against unreasonable searches and seizures applies in a school setting, but the Court ruled that school searches require neither a warrant nor probable cause as the level of suspicion. Balancing the privacy rights of students against the security needs of administrators, the Court said searches in school may be valid as long as there were reasonable grounds for suspecting that students violated the law or school rules. The *TLO* case involved the search of a student's handbag for cigarettes that turned up evidence of drug possession and dealing. The Supreme Court upheld the search.

The Supreme Court again confronted school searches in the context of DRUG TESTING of students. In *Board of Education of Independent School District No. 92 of Pottawatomie County v. Earls,* 536 U.S. 822 (2002), the Court upheld random drug testing of all students participating in any extracurricular activities. The Court said that given the "special needs" of school administrators in maintaining order and safety in the schools, drug testing could be conducted without any individual suspicion of the students being tested.

The Supreme Court's eased application of Fourth Amendment standards in schools has helped to clear the way for increased use of a variety of security and screening measures, from locker searches to the use of metal detectors at school entrances. The high court has not ruled on these practices, but lower courts have applied the "reasonable suspicion" standard to uphold locker searches and the use of metal detectors. Lower courts have also found that the absence of individual suspicion was not a problem in the use of metal detector screening machines or handheld metal detection devices. The use of metal detectors has been viewed by lower courts much like drug testing, that they are a relatively minor intrusion on a student's privacy rights and that no individual suspicion is necessary for metal detector use. As to locker searches, lower courts have upheld periodic searches of lockers without any individual suspicion; sometimes these searches involve use of drug-sniffing dogs, and at other times they have been described as a periodic sweep to clean out lockers.

Another issue that has not been settled by the Supreme Court is whether individual suspicion is required for the search of a student and that student's belongings, as in the circumstances of the *TLO* case, or whether, as in the drug-testing case, a general concern about safety and enforcement of rules is sufficient to justify the search of individuals.

For more information: Raskin, Jamin B. *We, the Students: Supreme Court Decisions for and about Students.* 2nd ed. Washington, D.C.: CQ Press, 2003.

—Stephen Wermiel

substantive due process

Substantive due process is the concept that the due process clause guarantees individuals certain rights that have *substance.* To understand this idea of *substantive rights,* it is helpful to first understand the better-known concept that the due process clause guarantees *procedural rights.* If you understand what PROCEDURAL DUE PROCESS is, you will understand what substantive due process is *not.* That is a useful beginning at understanding the somewhat vaguer concept of "substantive due process."

As an initial matter, understand that the Constitution actually has two due process clauses. The due process clause of the Fifth Amendment applies to the federal government, while the due process clause of the Fourteenth Amendment was adopted to restrict state governments. Because both contain similar wording, [nor shall any person be deprived] "of life, liberty, or property, without due process of law," this entry will refer to them as if they were one due process clause.

The guarantee of "procedural due process" requires the government, if it chooses to deprive an individual of life, liberty, or property, to use proper procedures. This is consistent with the plain meaning of the words of the due process clause. Procedural due process, for example, requires government to use the procedure of a criminal trial before putting an individual in jail (depriving a person of liberty). A trial with particularly elaborate procedures is required before the government can use the death penalty. Nor can government deprive a person of their money or property without proper notice and a hearing. If government uses proper procedures, however, we certainly expect that these matters are usually part of government's legitimate business.

Substantive due process, in contrast, is a concept that bars government from depriving individuals of liberty in some areas, regardless of the properness of the procedures the government uses. A good example of substantive due process is the Supreme Court's recent decision in *LAWRENCE V. TEXAS,* 123 S. Ct. 2472 (2003). The Court held that the state of Texas cannot make it a crime for consenting adults to have homosexual relations. This is so even if the state legislature uses proper lawmaking procedures to pass this statute, and the criminal justice system uses proper criminal procedures to enforce the law. The Court reasoned that this private behavior is central to liberty and cannot be interfered with by the legislature. Thus, the Texas statute and those similar to it in other states violate the substantive component of the due process clause of the Fourteenth Amendment and cannot stand. Substantive due process, then, allows the courts to examine a law for its substantive validity.

Lawrence v. Texas follows from a line of Supreme Court cases originating in the 1960s striking down state statutes that interfere with personal decisions concerning marriage, procreation, contraception, and family relationships. Another well-known example of a right protected by the substantive component of the due process clause is a woman's right to have an abortion. This right was first recognized by the Court in the famous 1973 case ROE V. WADE, 410 U.S. 113, in which the Court struck down the abortion laws enacted by a majority of states.

In *Lawrence v. Texas,* the Court supported its decision with a quote from PLANNED PARENTHOOD OF SOUTHEASTERN PENNSYLVANIA V. CASEY, 505 U.S. 833 (1992), another one of its abortion cases. The Court explained, "[t]hese matters, involving the most intimate and personal choices a person may make in a lifetime, choices central to personal dignity and autonomy, are central to the liberty protected by the Fourteenth Amendment. At the heart of liberty is the right to define one's own concept of existence, of meaning, of the universe, and of the mystery of human life" [123 S. Ct. at 2481, quoting 505 U.S. at 523].

Substantive due process can be controversial because it gives courts great power to undo acts of the legislature without specific guidance in the Constitution. The due process clause does not explain what it means by "liberty." Sexual relations and abortion are not mentioned in the BILL OF RIGHTS as areas where government cannot interfere. Surprisingly, the Constitution does not even expressly mention a right to PRIVACY.

Most accept that government cannot make unpopular speech a crime, because government is prevented from infringing on our free speech rights by the First Amendment. The Constitution is not so specific about all rights, however. Thus the Court sometimes "locates" rights in the "liberty" portion of the due process clause that are not specifically mentioned. Not just any liberty qualifies for substantive due process protection, of course, only liberties that are "fundamental."

What rights are fundamental and what are not is usually a value judgment that not all justices agree upon at any one time. It is also a value judgment that changes over time. For example, two justices dissented in *Lawrence v. Texas,* which itself reversed a 1986 Court decision that found that the right to engage in homosexual conduct was not a liberty protected by the due process clause. And, several justices seem to favor overruling *Roe v. Wade* because they do not feel that the right to abortion is a fundamental right.

Critics of substantive due process are disturbed that these Court decisions are grounded in little more than the value judgments of the justices. Supporters feel that interpretation of the Constitution in view of contemporary values is a function that the Court is supposed to perform, especially when the language of the Constitution is vague.

During the period of 1905–35, the Court relied on the concept of substantive due process to strike down state and federal laws that regulated the economy. For example, in LOCHNER V. NEW YORK, 198 U.S. 45 (1905), the Court struck down a law of the state of New York setting maximum hours that bakers could work. The Court's rationale was that this law interfered with the economic rights of bakery owners, a right located in the substantive component of the due process clause of the Fourteenth Amendment. This period of the Court's decisions is widely regarded today as wrong. Indeed, the Court reversed trend in 1936 and has since not struck down economic regulations on this basis.

If "procedural due process" is one of the most important principles of CIVIL LIBERTIES, "substantive due process" is one of the most controversial. How will future critics smile on the Court's current treatment of substantive due process? Will the Court's decisions recognizing that "intimate and personal choices" are protected by substantive due process be regarded as great steps forward in civil liberties? Or, like the economic liberty cases, will the Court be discredited with time?

For more information: Gunther, Gerald. *Constitutional Law.* Mineola, N.Y.: Foundation Press, 1991.

—Karen Swenson

summary judgment

Summary judgment refers to the method a trial court uses to decide some or all of the factual issues in a case before trial and avoid trial of those issues. Federal Rule of Civil Procedure 56 governs this pretrial procedure in federal courts. State courts may follow this procedure or a modification of it.

Either the party presenting the claim (usually claimant or plaintiff) or the party defending the claim (usually defendant) may serve a motion for summary judgment in its favor on all or part of the case. The moving party may file supporting affidavits, and the other party may serve opposing affidavits. Both may serve written briefs or suggestions for the court's consideration. The court may hold a hearing. The court will grant judgment if the pleadings, depositions, answers to interrogatories, admissions, and affidavits show that there is no genuine issue about any material fact and that the moving party is entitled to judgment as a matter of law. The moving party has the burden of showing an absence of material fact, which is one so legally significant that it would determine the outcome of the litigation. The court will not grant judgment if it finds a disputed material fact. In making this decision, the court must decide whether the evidence and its reasonable inferences, taken in the light most favorable to the party opposing the motion, clearly show the moving party is entitled to prevail as a matter of law.

The case will proceed to trial if the court finds the case contains a disputed material fact or denies any part of the motion for summary judgment.

Lawyers most frequently use motions for summary judgment in cases that involve interpretation of agreed documents, such as insurance policies, contracts, checks, bills, and notes. In those cases, all parties may recognize the existence of the documents but differ on their meaning. There is, thus, not a dispute over a material fact, but a difference over a matter of law, which only a judge may decide. Summary judgment in those cases may save time and avoid the expense of litigation. Even a partial summary judgment will limit the number of issues and the complexity of trial. Lawyers may also effectively use summary judgment in non-document cases where the parties agree upon the facts but not on their legal effect.

While a motion for summary judgment offers the advantage of saving time and litigation expense and simplifying trial, it also carries with it the double-edged sword of allowing both plaintiff and defendant to see the other's strategy and thought processes. In addition, filing a motion for summary judgment forces the opposing party to become better educated about the case, its facts and issues, and makes a more formidable adversary at trial.

For more information: Federal Rules of Civil Procedure 56.

—Patrick K. Roberts

Supreme Court and foreign policy

The Supreme Court's role in foreign policy is best understood by first reflecting on contemporary perceptions of how such policy is crafted and directed. Such reflection brings the unmistakable conclusion that since at least the presidency of Franklin Delano Roosevelt, foreign policy in the United States has been an executive affair.

Indeed, though the Constitution provides that the president share the treaty power with the Senate and gives the president alone few powers that touch explicitly on foreign affairs, e.g., the power to "receive ambassadors" and his power as commander in chief, the president has nevertheless evolved into the mind and voice of America abroad. In the first decade of the 21st century, continued experience has made it unremarkable for most Americans that the president shapes the country's external relations with few congressional restraints, or that he has several times engaged American troops in combat without congressional approval.

In short, the explicit power of the president in foreign affairs is limited, yet he is unquestionably the key figure shaping the foreign policy of the United States. While this development has several roots, including the acquiescence of Congress itself, it has been aided by the Supreme Court either through explicit ruling or calculated silence. This shift underscores a broader context of *constitutionalism* within which the following discussion must be placed, that is, many expect the Court to police the boundaries of the Constitution's framework, ensuring that the political branches exercise only "agreed power for agreed purposes." In this effort, the Court must either step aside and allow for a political resolution between the contesting branches or interpret the proper location of responsibility for the foreign policy of the nation.

However, a reasonable look at founding sources reveals support for the claims of both those that see Congress as the preeminent force directing foreign policy and those that see the conduct of foreign policy as an exclusively executive affair. In part this reflects ambiguity in the Constitution itself; foreign policy is not explicitly addressed as a single element, yet its signs lay scattered throughout the document: the power to "regulate commerce with foreign nations" is granted to Congress while the executive alone may receive ambassadors; the executive is commander in chief of the armed forces yet must rely on Congress for the monies necessary for their existence. This does not exhaust the possible examples, but it does underscore the lack of clear direction in locating primary responsibility for the conduct of foreign policy. Moreover, the founders themselves were at odds over the proper location of foreign affairs in the Constitution's complex scheme, with James Madison arguing for legislative supremacy and Alexander Hamilton defending the supremacy of the executive.

How has the Supreme Court contributed to the triumph of Hamilton's vision? First we must understand the Court's persistent attitude toward executive control of foreign policy generally, which is nowhere more apparent than in the landmark opinion of Justice SUTHERLAND in *United States v. Curtiss-Wright Export Corporation,* 299 U.S. 304 (1936). The case concerned President Roosevelt's decision, with prior congressional approval, to embargo the sale of military hardware to Bolivia and Paraguay, who were at the time locked in war. The Curtiss-Wright Corporation was profiting from the sale of combat aircraft to Bolivia and had no intention of stopping. They filed suit, arguing in part that Congress's delegation of the power of embargo to the president was unconstitutional. Eventually coming before the Court, the case was decided in the president's favor, with Justice George Sutherland penning a notorious opinion that found in the executive a "very delicate, plenary, and exclusive power . . . as the sole organ of the federal government in the field of international relations—a power which does not require as a basis for its exercise an act of Congress. . . ."

Sutherland could claim he was merely restating the belief of the legendary Chief Justice MARSHALL, who concluded that the president was the "sole organ of the nation in its foreign relations," yet some scholars argue that a substantive change occurred with Sutherland's opinion; the context of Marshall's remark indicates that the president was an organ of communication, not, as Sutherland would have it, the sole author of the country's foreign policy.

The Court has not always embraced the claims made in *Curtiss;* indeed, Justice JACKSON's concurring opinion in *YOUNGSTOWN CO. V. SAWYER,* 343 U.S. 579 (1952), cast much of Sutherland's sweeping claims as *dictum* and having no precedential force. Regardless, Sutherland's opinion continues to have consequences, as it has been invoked by the Court on issues ranging from overseas travel to executive agreements, causing one scholar to note that "the Court has trotted out the sole organ doctrine whenever it has required a rationale to support a constitutionally doubtful presidential action in foreign affairs."

The *Curtiss* PRECEDENT, however, is only one stone in a larger foundation; the Court has also contributed to the domination of the president in foreign affairs through its support of executive agreements. Though they have existed since the presidential terms of General Washington, the use of such agreements has grown tremendously since the presidency of FDR, due in part to the political resources of the president and congressional acquiescence to executive power.

Yet, once again, the Supreme Court's role has been crucial. In *UNITED STATES V. BELMONT,* 301 U.S. 324 (1937), the Court supported FDR's executive agreement on assets concluded unilaterally with the Soviet Union. Once more, Justice Sutherland wrote for the Court, invoking both the presidential power of recognition and the "sole organ" doctrine of *Curtiss* to uphold the president's agreement, which the Court further affirmed in *UNITED STATES V. PINK,* 315 U.S. 203 (1942).

While *Belmont* involved the president's authority in settling international claims, Louis Henkin has cautiously observed that Sutherland's opinion in *Belmont* could likewise provide the president with authority to conclude executive agreements absent congressional authorization in almost any area. Regardless, such agreements have been a primary vehicle for the growth of executive dominance in foreign policy as they are often negotiated without explicit congressional approval, which one critic argues, "subvert[s] the basic constitutional scheme established in Philadelphia." Others, however, see in the growing complexity of international relations the need to defer to those attributes of presidential power—secrecy, dispatch, unity of action—that make foreign policy possible in an increasingly interdependent world.

Yet the absence of Congress's voice can also be, paradoxically, an affirmative source of executive strength. The BURGER Court, in *Dames & Moore v. Regan,* 453 U.S. 654 (1981), upheld President Carter's use of an executive agreement to suspend pending claims against Iran in American courts as part of a deal securing the release of the Tehran hostages. The decision was built partly on the grounds that executive agreements secured without Senate approval had been upheld in earlier cases (e.g. *Pink*); that Congress had not specifically disallowed such action; and that prior congressional enactments, though not specifically addressing the action taken by Carter, nevertheless were of such similar design and scope that their "general tenor" indicated congressional acquiescence in the case at hand. Critics contend, however, that the use of congressional silence or the inferring of a "general tenor" would allow the executive to exercise any legislative power desired so long as Congress does not explicitly rise in protest.

Recently, the Supreme Court has reiterated its support for executive dominance in foreign policy in a decision striking down a California law aimed at providing restitution for Holocaust victims. Justice SOUTER's opinion for the Court in *American Insurance Association et al. v. Garamendi, Insurance Commissioner, State of California,* 123 S. Ct. 2374 (2003), invokes in part *Youngstown* and *Curtiss-Wright* to locate executive responsibility in foreign affairs, and *Dames & Moore* to uphold the president's ability to craft executive agreements "requiring no ratification by the Senate or approval by Congress."

However, the most controversial aspect of the Supreme Court's relationship to foreign policy is its view of the war power; more specifically the controversy lies in the president's seemingly complete capture of this sacred prerogative. Critics cite the Court's refusal to review challenges to the president's use of troops in hostilities, and the application of its "political questions" doctrine in the lower courts, as key factors in the rise of "presidential wars." Indeed, in American conflicts since the Vietnam War, several lawsuits have been brought against presidential use of force absent a declaration of war or in contradiction of procedures outlined in the War Powers Act, yet the trend is dismissal at the lower court level, with judges often finding that the question is political and should thus be left to resolution by Congress and the president wielding the institutional prerogatives assigned by the Constitution. Regardless, presidential dismissal of the War

Powers Act and continued congressional acquiescence in the face of such dismissal makes the trend likely to continue.

The tendency, however, to view foreign policy as merely synonymous with war or executive action should be resisted to gain a clearer picture of the Court's role in the external policies of the United States. Indeed, two areas that have seen recent increased attention are state actions that infringe on foreign policy and suits brought under the Alien Tort Claims Act (ATCA). The former area is often associated with state and local restrictions on commercial activity aimed at "punishing" foreign actors for their support of illiberal political practices, which critics contend is—at the least—a challenge to the Supreme Court's assertion in *Japan Line, LTD. v. County of Los Angeles,* 441 U.S. 434 (1979), that the United States must speak with "one voice" in its external commercial relations. A landmark case in this area, *Crosby v. National Foreign Trade Council,* 530 U.S. 363 (2000), affirmed the critics' view and struck down a Massachusetts law that discriminated against state contract bidders that were "doing business with" the repressive Burmese government, noting in part that the state's law "undermines the President's capacity . . . for effective diplomacy."

The Alien Tort Claims Act, part of the original 1789 Judiciary Act, gives federal court jurisdiction to "any civil action by an alien for a tort only, committed in violation of the law of nations" (28 U.S. Code, sec. 1350). The ATCA has recently been a vehicle for those seeking redress for alleged human rights abuses committed by multinational corporations abroad and has also been used to enter judgments against foreign leaders or other entities outside the borders of the United States. Such judgments could have an impact on the foreign policies of the nation, a point now being underscored by the Bush administration's claim that such suits are undermining the war on terrorism. While these cases have been lodged in the lower courts, they nevertheless highlight the broader scope of the Supreme Court in foreign policy, as a clear ruling by the REHNQUIST Court on the ATCA could either remove this source of presidential consternation or allow it to continue as an unpredictable challenge to his ability to direct foreign relations.

It is important to note that these latter cases arise in part from growing awareness of the effects of globalization in blurring the lines between domestic and foreign policy. Indeed, even Henry Kissinger has asked, after reflecting on globalization and the rumored passing of the traditional notion of state sovereignty, "does America need a foreign policy?" We have seen that the Court has largely deferred to the executive in foreign policy matters, contributing to the dominance of the president in foreign affairs, even as the same Court has often acted to curtail his prerogative domestically. This then underscores an important challenge on the Court's horizon; given the dynamics of globalization, how can the Court maintain the distinction between the executive's domestic face—duly restrained in the conduct of internal policy—and his foreign countenance as the "sole organ" in external affairs?

The Court thus enters the 21st century with a dilemma of its own making. Few would argue that the past century has seen a tremendous growth in the power of the president to shape the external affairs of the United States; the increased use of executive agreements in foreign relations and the frequent use of armed forces in actions just short of declared war are just two areas that distinguish this modern presidency. For the average American it is the president that is himself the embodiment of the nation's foreign affairs. The Supreme Court—and the federal judiciary generally—stand both accused and applauded for this development. For some the Court has neglected its critical role as the fulcrum in a constitutional scale, shifting itself in order to balance the competing ambitions of the political branches; for others, the Court has prudently acknowledged the "decision, activity, secrecy, and dispatch" of the presidential office that makes it ideally suited for the conduct of external relations.

The Supreme Court's role in foreign policy can thus best be characterized over time by pragmatic caution in the face of executive power, justifying its contributions to presidential dominance in foreign policy by underscoring the unique competence of the president in external affairs, his access to intelligence, and his ability to act decisively—without the deliberation that characterizes Congress—in an arena that demands quick decisions and tight control. The Court also recognizes, implicitly, the political benefits of caution and restraint, as its rulings could upset carefully crafted international agreements and power balances.

Lastly, the modern president's role as the "tribune of the people," its guardian and mouthpiece, makes confrontation by the Court an inherently risky business. It may well be that political realities and the need for flexibility by the president make it unwise for the Court to create an unyielding rule regarding the proper location of responsibility in foreign affairs; nevertheless, the Court would do well to reconsider their current doctrine in light of the founders' desire for wisdom and deliberation over mere efficiency and action.

For more information: Adler, David Gray, and Robert George, eds. *The Constitution and the Conduct of American Foreign Policy.* Lawrence: University Press of Kansas, 1996; Carey, George W., and James McClellan, eds. *The Federalist Papers.* Indianapolis: Liberty Fund, 2001; Henkin, Louis. *Foreign Affairs and the United States Constitution.* Oxford: Clarendon Press, 1996; ———. *Constitutionalism, Democracy, and Foreign Affairs.* New York: Columbia University Press, 1990.

—Patrick F. Campbell

Supreme Court and the constitutional amending process

Article V of the U.S. Constitution provides for amendments to be proposed and to be ratified in two ways. Two-thirds of both houses of Congress can propose amendments, or, in a provision never utilized, two-thirds of the states can petition Congress to call a convention for proposing amendments. At congressional specification, either three-fourths of the state legislatures or conventions in three-fourths of the states ratify amendments. Only the Twenty-first Amendment repealing national alcoholic prohibition has been ratified in the latter manner. Article VII specified that the Constitution would not go into effect until ratified by nine of the 13 states, and the amending mechanism poses a similar barrier to further constitutional alterations. Reflecting the importance of the compromise between large and small states at the U.S. Constitutional Convention, Article V continues to specify that states cannot be deprived of their equal suffrage in the U.S. Senate without their consent.

Aware that a wooden amending mechanism could lead to revolution or to a complete constitutional rewrite, like the one that occurred when the current Constitution replaced the Articles of Confederation, the framers did not intend for constitutional change to be impossible. Because they wanted the Constitution to be fundamental law, however, they designed the process to be difficult enough to resist popular whims. The framers appear to have succeeded in both endeavors. The number is somewhat deceptive because most proposals have been redundant, but members of Congress have introduced more than 11.5 thousand amending proposals. Of these, Congress has only proposed 33 by the necessary two-thirds majorities, and the states have ratified only 27 of these. Despite some attempts to revive the EQUAL RIGHTS AMENDMENT, there is general, albeit not complete, consensus that none of the remaining amendments, some of which incorporated specific time limits within their texts, are still pending.

The promise of an early exercise of the amending process in adopting the first 10 amendments, the BILL OF RIGHTS, may well have been responsible for ratification of the Constitution; these amendments continue to be a source of national pride. Subsequent amendments have adjusted judicial jurisdiction (Eleventh) and lifted barriers to voting for African Americans (Fifteenth), women (Nineteenth), individuals who cannot pay poll taxes (Twenty-fourth), and 18 to 21 year olds (Twenty-sixth). Amendments have modernized the electoral college (Twelfth and Twenty-third), validated the national INCOME TAX (Sixteenth), provided for the direct election of senators (Seventeenth), provided for, and repealed, national alcoholic prohibition (the Eighteenth and Twenty-first); changed congressional and presidential inauguration dates (Twentieth); limited presidents to two full terms (Twenty-second);

provided for presidential disability and the selection of new vice presidents (Twenty-fifth), and limited the timing of congressional pay raises (Twenty-seventh). Amendments are often adopted in clusters reflecting movements for national reform. Although many amendments have expanded democracy, amendments can be designed to restore or retain past rights or privileges as well as to create new ones.

Article V is silent about a number of matters involving the amending process. In the nation's early history, the Supreme Court occasionally resolved such issues. Thus, in *Hollingsworth v. Virginia*, 3 U.S. (3 Dall.) 379 (1798), the Court decided that the president's signature was not required to validate a constitutional amendment. In the *National Prohibition Cases*, 253 U.S. 350 (1920), the Court rejected arguments that the Eighteenth Amendment exceeded permissible constitutional authority, a decision it reiterated in *United States v. Sprague*, 282 U.S. 716 (1931).

In *Hawke v. Smith*, 253 U.S. 221 (1920), the Court rejected a state's efforts to predicate ratification of an amendment on a popular referendum. In *Dillon v. Gloss*, 256 U.S. 368 (1921), the Court ruled that Congress could establish a reasonable time limit for ratification of an amendment, in this case seven years. However, in *Coleman v. Miller*, 307 U.S. 433 (1939), the Court indicated that it regarded issues related to the contemporaneousness of ratifications to be political questions for congressional resolution. Thus, in 1992, Congress was left to affirm the belated ratification of the Twenty-seventh Amendment, dealing with the timing of congressional pay raises, even though the original proposal had been made as part of the Bill of Rights in 1789. Similarly, Congress subsequently extended the deadline for the ratification of the proposed Equal Rights Amendment—an action challenged in a U.S. District Court decision in *Idaho v. Freeman*, 529 F. Supp. 1107 (1981), which never reached the Supreme Court because the case was mooted by the amendment's continued failure to be ratified.

Although some states have ratified amendments that they previously rejected, there has been no definitive judicial decision as to whether states may rescind ratification of pending amendments. If *Coleman v. Miller* remains in effect (and some scholars dispute its continuing validity), this decision would presumably be left to Congress. In *Cook v. Gralike*, 531 U.S. 510 (2001), the Supreme Court did decide that a state had no authority to instruct its members of Congress as to how to vote on a pending amendment or to make a notation of the ballot when representatives failed to follow such instructions. Despite some proposals, Congress has never adopted legislation as to how a convention to propose amendments would be organized.

In part because of the difficulty of the amending process, changes in CONSTITUTIONAL INTERPRETATION have been initiated through customs and usages and through congressional and presidential practices. The Supreme Court has also played a major role in constitutional interpretation through its exercise of JUDICIAL REVIEW. Because of this, some major changes in constitutional interpretations (those accompanying the New Deal, for example) have left no mark on the actual constitutional text. Were it not for such changing constitutional interpretations, revolutions or amendments would undoubtedly have to be much more frequent.

Although judicial review enables the Supreme Court to reinterpret the Constitution, constitutional amendments provide a check on this power. In addition to proposing a variety of reforms in the U.S. Supreme Court or the wider judicial system (none of which has been so adopted), members of Congress have frequently introduced amendments that would have reversed Supreme Court decisions on such diverse issues as the constitutionality of child labor, legislative reapportionment, prayer in public schools, abortion, FLAG BURNING, congressional term limits, etc.

On at least four occasions, constitutional amendments have reversed Supreme Court decisions. The Eleventh Amendment reversed the decision in *CHISHOLM V. GEORGIA,* 2 U.S. (2 Dall.) 419 (1793), which had allowed states to be sued by out-of-state citizens. The Fourteenth and Fifteenth Amendments reversed the *Dred Scott Decision,* 60 U.S. (19 How.) 393 (1857), which had declared that blacks were not and could not be U.S. citizens. The Sixteenth Amendment overturned the Court's decision in *POLLOCK V. FARMERS' LOAN & TRUST,* 158 U.S. 601 (1895), declaring the national income tax to be unconstitutional. The Twenty-sixth Amendment reversed a decision in *Oregon v. Mitchell,* 400 U.S. 112 (1970), which had declared that Congress could lower voting ages to 18 in national, but not in state, elections. On other occasions, Court decisions to accept legislation over areas once forbidden, for example, child labor, have made such amendments unnecessary.

Ironically, once amendments become incorporated into the Constitution, they then become subject, like the rest of the document, to judicial interpretations. On occasion, the Court has interpreted amendments more expansively than may have been intended. Thus, the Court has interpreted the Eleventh Amendment to stand for the general principle of state SOVEREIGN IMMUNITY and not simply to prevent suits by out-of-state-citizens.

On other occasions, the Court has interpreted constitutional provisions relatively restrictively. In a series of cases in the aftermath of the ratification of the Thirteenth through Fifteenth Amendments (1865, 1868, 1870), the Court interpreted these amendments fairly narrowly. It thus decided in the *Civil Rights Cases,* 109 U.S. 3 (1883), that the amendments limited only state (as opposed to

Supreme Court building *(Library of Congress)*

private) action; ruled in the *SLAUGHTER-HOUSE CASES,* 83 U.S. (16 Wall.) 36 (1873), that the "privileges and immunities" of U.S. citizens protected by the Fourteenth Amendment were relatively narrow; and eventually even endorsed the doctrine of racial segregation according to the principle of "separate but equal" in *PLESSY V. FERGUSON,* 163 U.S. 537 (1896).

Ironically, since the Supreme Court's decision in *BROWN V. BOARD OF EDUCATION,* 347 U.S. 483 (1954), overturning *PLESSY V. FERGUSON,* the Fourteenth Amendment has become one of the most fruitful sources of judicial decisions, with judicial rulings including issues not only involving race but also gender, age, legitimacy, sexual orientation, etc. The Supreme Court has also relied on the Fourteenth Amendment as the mechanism through which to apply the provisions of the first 10 amendments, which once limited only the national government, to the states.

For more information: Kyvig, David E. *Explicit and Authentic Acts: Amending the U.S. Constitution, 1776–1995.* Lawrence: University Press of Kansas, 1996; Palmer, Kris, ed. *Constitutional Amendments: 1789 to the Present.* Detroit, Mich.: Gale Group, 2000; Vile, John R. *Constitutional Change in the United States: A Comparative Study of the Role of Constitutional Amendments, Judicial Interpretations, and Legislative and Executive Actions.* Westport,

Conn.: Praeger, 1994; ———. *Encyclopedia of Constitutional Amendments, Proposed Amendments, and Amending Issues, 1789–1995.* 2nd ed. Santa Barbara, Calif.: ABC-CLIO, 2003.

—John R. Vile

Supreme Court building

The Supreme Court building is the seat of the court and is located on East Capitol Street adjacent to the Library of Congress and across the street from the Capitol building.

Prior to 1935 the Supreme Court had held its sessions in many different locations. In 1790 when the government first began the Court met on the second floor of the Merchants (Royal) Exchange Building in New York City. When the government moved to Philadelphia the Court met for a time in the Pennsylvania State House (Independence Hall) and later in the City Hall where it shared space with local courts.

When the government moved to Washington, in the District of Columbia, in 1800 the plan of Pierre Charles L'Enfant for the new capital city included a site for the Supreme Court. However, Congress took no action to provide a permanent place for the Court. So it met in a succession of incommodious chambers, shared offices with other courts, and even met for a time in a tavern. By 1809 the Court was housed in a new chamber designed for it in the Capitol but lost it in the War of 1812 when the British burned Washington in 1814. While the Capitol was being rebuilt they met in a rented house, and then returned to the basement of the Capitol building. Late in the 1850s the Court was able to move into the old Senate Chamber where they remained until 1935.

In 1925 former President and then Chief Justice William Howard TAFT began a campaign to have a separate building erected. Construction began in 1932 and was completed in 1935 at a cost of $9,646,000.

The new building was designed by architect Cass Gilbert. The building reflects the Court's place as a coequal branch of the federal government. It is a magnificent Greco-Roman temple in classical Corinthian style designed to match other buildings in the area. The main building material of the "marble palace" is white marble from Georgia and Vermont, cream marble from Alabama, Ivory Vein marble from Alicante, Spain, and Old Convent Vein Siena marble from Liguria, Italy, and some from an African source. The bronze doors weigh six and a half tons each and are covered with carving of symbols of the development of the Western legal tradition. The friezes have sculpted figures of great law givers. Other parts of the building also have sculpted symbols of the law.

By law the Supreme Court building is open to the public from 9 A.M. to 4:30 P.M., Monday through Friday. It is closed on Saturdays, Sundays, and on federal holidays (5 U.S.C. Section 6103). The library is open to members of the Bar of the Court, attorneys for the various federal departments and agencies, and members of Congress.

In the summer of 2003 a five-year, $122,000,000 modernization project to upgrade and replace building systems was begun. The building has not been upgraded since it opened in 1935. In addition, underground parking space for the Court Police Department, a function not needed in 1935, will be created.

For more information: Maroon, Fred J., and Maroon, Suzy. *Supreme Court of the United States.* New York: Thomasson-Grant and Lickle, 1996.

—A. J. L. Waskey

Supreme Court confirmation

Confirmation is the process by which a nominee for a seat on the Court is approved or rejected. The Constitution (Article II, Section 2) states that the president "shall nominate, and by and with the Advice and Consent of the Senate, shall appoint . . . Judges of the Supreme Court." Senate confirmation (or rejection) is thus the other half of a process that begins with the president. All federal judges are subject to these same constitutional requirements, but Supreme Court appointments command the greatest public attention and are far more likely to spark controversy—not surprising given the power and prestige a Supreme Court position currently entails.

The Senate has turned down 26 Supreme Court nominations, either through a negative vote (most common) or by failure to act. This number represents one-sixth of all Supreme Court nominations and is a rate of defeat far higher than any other category of presidential nominations (e.g., cabinet officers, ambassadors). Presidents have been more successful in the 20th century than in the 19th, but that fact may obscure another key element of the current process—since roughly the middle of the 20th century, Supreme Court nominees have received much closer and more intense scrutiny from the Senate. The nominee's qualifications have always been a concern, but with the onset of the WARREN Court (1954–69), the Senate has also been more interested in a nominee's ideology and judicial philosophy. In 1968 President Johnson's nomination of Associate Justice Abe FORTAS to become CHIEF JUSTICE was sidetracked (the Senate refused to vote on the nomination, and eventually the president withdrew it) in part because Fortas was seen to be a liberal activist. In 1987 President Reagan's nomination of Judge Robert BORK was defeated (by a vote of 42-58) because he was perceived as too conservative.

When the president chooses a nominee, the Senate Judiciary Committee will hold hearings. Supporters and opponents will be allowed to testify. Often, interest groups who agree (or disagree) with the perceived philosophy and ideology of the nominee will offer testimony and may also engage in a public relations campaign to persuade senators to their point of view.

Contrary to the practice for the first century and a half, the norm now is that the nominee will also appear before the committee and be questioned by the senators. Nominees typically refuse to discuss cases that might come before them, and in general attempt to be responsive without indicating political or ideological predilections. This is easier if the nominee is a so-called stealth candidate with few public pronouncements and little "paper trail" of speeches and publications that would allow inferences about the nominee's policy preferences. The goal here is to be the exact opposite of Judge Bork, whose (often controversial) views over the years were well established. When hearings are completed, the committee will vote on the nominee and send a recommendation to the full Senate. After a period of public debate, the Senate will vote, with a simple majority needed for confirmation.

One of the enduring questions of CONSTITUTIONAL INTERPRETATION connected with this entire process centers on the issue of the proper roles of president and Senate. There are two schools of thought. One holds that the dominant role is the president's. The responsibility of the Senate is to defer to the president's choice and to confirm the nominee unless clearly unqualified in terms of legal training and ability.

The other school of thought holds that the two branches are coequal in these matters, and that the president typically takes into account factors other than legal qualifications—e.g., judicial philosophy, political ideology, or party affiliation (presidents by and large choose nominees who are of the same party as the president)—and thus individual senators are also free to take these same factors into account in deciding to support or oppose a particular nominee. As noted above, since the late 1960s, while no senator would oppose a nominee solely on the basis of party affiliation, many Senators have not hesitated to vote against nominees they consider outside the mainstream with respect to judicial philosophy or political ideology.

Since the Warren era, it has been obvious that Supreme Court justices have great leeway in how they interpret the Constitution (particularly its more open-ended phrases such as "equal protection" or "due process") and thus ample opportunity to make policy on important issues (e.g., school segregation, reapportionment, prayer in public schools, abortion). Consequently it is not surprising that the confirmation process has become so politicized.

Presidents seek out nominees who share their political philosophy and may even take into account symbolic factors that would have appeal to voters (e.g., President Reagan's pledge to appoint a woman to the Court, President Johnson's choice of the first African American to serve on the Court, President George W. Bush's rumored desire to appoint someone of Hispanic descent). Senators, just as much "political animals" as the president, cannot be blamed for doing likewise. Some presidents have been quite insistent on ideological "purity" (e.g., Reagan, Bush II); others (e.g., Eisenhower, Clinton) less so.

Presidential Supreme Court nominations tend to be more successful if the vacancy comes in the first two years of the president's term. In the last two years in office, the Senate may be less likely to support the president's choice. Thus, some of the opposition to Abe Fortas sprang from the fact that Johnson was a lame-duck president, and Republicans in the Senate expected the next president to be a Republican who could then make his own appointment.

Of course, even more important to presidential success is control of the Senate—if the president's party is in the majority in the Senate, the president's nominee is far more likely to be confirmed. Judge Bork's nomination went to a Senate controlled by the Democrats. Finally, presidents are more likely to succeed with nominees who are perceived as moderate—not too liberal (Fortas) and not too conservative (Bork). George H. W. Bush's choice of David SOUTER and Bill Clinton's choice of Stephen G. BREYER are good examples.

The latter examples raise a final issue: the watershed nature of the Bork nomination and its subsequent effects on the nomination and confirmation process. The liberal interest groups who opposed Bork used his nomination as an occasion for more general political organizing and did the same with George H. W. Bush's nomination of Clarence THOMAS—though Thomas was ultimately confirmed (albeit by the closest Senate vote of any 20th-century nominee). Conservative supporters of Bork, who saw him as a qualified jurist, even if highly ideological and with well-known positions, vowed "payback." Nor was their ire in any way alleviated by the nomination of David Souter—the quintessential stealth candidate—who turned out to be more liberal than many would have imagined.

Thus, Clinton came to the presidency with Senate Republicans willing to use every conceivable parliamentary maneuver to postpone or delay votes on his nominees to the Federal District Courts and the Courts of Appeals. Clinton succeeded with two Supreme Court nominations, largely because they were sitting judges who were considered moderate. George W. Bush came to the presidency with a conscious desire to placate the conservatives in his party by appointing conservative jurists, and Senate

Democrats responded with similar tactics, including in several instances filibusters, a technique rarely used in the past for federal judicial appointments.

In what Professor Mark Tushnet has characterized as "the new constitutional order" with its hallmarks of divided government and highly partisan and ideological divisions in Congress, the nomination to the federal bench of high-profile ideologues is a recipe for disaster. For the foreseeable future, successful Supreme Court nominees will likely be moderate lower federal court judges who can justify controversial decisions by citing their responsibility to follow Supreme Court PRECEDENT.

For more information: Abraham, Henry J. *Justices, Presidents, and Senators: A History of the U.S. Supreme Court Appointments from Washington to Clinton.* Lanham, Md.: Rowman and Littlefield, 1999; O'Brien, David M. *Storm Center: The Supreme Court in American Politics.* 6th ed. New York: W. W. Norton, 2003.

—Philip A. Dynia

suspect classification

When a law categorizes or treats people differently based on characteristics that historically have been used for purposes of discrimination, like race, ALIENAGE, or national origin, this classification is considered "suspect."

An example of a suspect classification is a law that requires African Americans to pass a literacy test in order to vote but makes no such requirement of non–African Americans. It is interesting to note that gender is considered quasi-suspect as opposed to suspect, perhaps because historically legislative classifications based on gender have evolved less out of a desire to discriminate against women and more out of a desire to "protect" them (no matter how misguided this desire may have been). In addition, gender classifications do not meet the "discrete and insular minority" requirement of a suspect classification (or, put another way, judicial protection is given to those groups who are regular losers in the political struggle due to widespread prejudice against them).

In 1944 the Supreme Court articulated the concept of suspect classification. During World War II, individuals of Japanese descent who lived on the West Coast, whether they were citizens of this country or not, were ordered into interment camps. A lawsuit was brought challenging this practice. For the first time the Court clearly stated that legal restrictions curtailing the CIVIL RIGHTS of a single racial group were inherently suspect and subject to the most exacting scrutiny, which could be survived only by the most pressing public necessity [KOREMATSU V. UNITED STATES, 323 U.S. 214]. In this case, the Court considered the war a public necessity. Today, this STRICT SCRUTINY is applied by the Court to determine the constitutionality of a statute that utilizes suspect classifications.

Central to understanding the importance of suspect classification is the status of race in early America. DRED SCOTT V. SANDFORD, 60 U.S. 393 (1857), presents perhaps the most startling portrait of race relations in America. Dred Scott, a slave, contended that he had been freed when his owner took him to live in an area where slavery was outlawed. After his owner's death, Scott sued, only to have the defendant, the owner's brother-in-law, argue that not only was Scott still a slave but he was not a citizen and therefore had no STANDING to sue. The Court agreed, holding that persons descended from African slaves were not citizens of the United States, whether they had been freed or not.

After the Civil War, the Thirteenth (1865), Fourteenth (1868), and Fifteenth Amendments (1870) to the Constitution were ratified. Respectively, these prohibited slavery, contained the EQUAL PROTECTION CLAUSE, and prohibited denying the right to vote based on race. In light of these the Court made some headway in overturning official acts of RACIAL DISCRIMINATION; however, that task was a difficult one that sometimes resulted in decisions that today are viewed with great disdain. One of these was PLESSY V. FERGUSON, 163 U.S. 537 (1896). Plessy argued that a Louisiana law that required "equal but separate" railway cars for members of different races was unconstitutional. The Court upheld the statute, arguing that the equal protection clause applied only to the enforcement of political, not social, equality.

As constitutional jurisprudence in this area has evolved, the Court has made some landmark decisions which have changed the face of this nation and generated much controversy. One of these is BROWN V. BOARD OF EDUCATION, 347 U.S. 483 (1954), where separate education facilities were held to be inherently unequal. Even though we have made headway in the 50 years since then, the concept of suspect classification is still relevant today, particularly in the area of AFFIRMATIVE ACTION.

For more information: Redlich, Norman, John Attanasio, and Joel Goldstein. *Understanding Constitutional Law.* 2nd ed. New York: M. Bender, 1999.

—Deirdre O'Sullivan

Sutherland, George (1862–1942) *Supreme Court justice*

George Sutherland was appointed to the Supreme Court by President Warren Harding in 1922 and served until 1938. As associate justice of the Supreme Court, George Sutherland was the leader of the "Four Horsemen" and an advocate of natural law theory.

George Sutherland was born March 15, 1862, at Buckinghamshire, England. He grew up on the Utah frontier where his Scottish father (Alexander) and English mother (Frances) had gone to practice their new Mormon faith. However, the family soon left the Mormon faith never to return.

At the age of 12 Sutherland began attending Brigham Young Academy. To train for the law he attended the University of Michigan Law School. In 1883 he moved to Salt Lake City where he joined an important law firm. From 1896 until 1900 he served in the territorial legislature, and after statehood as a state senator in the Republican Party. Among the legislation he sponsored were bills for an eight-hour day for miners.

From 1901 until 1903 Sutherland served in the U.S. House of Representatives. In Congress he championed protectionist legislation and tariffs to help Utah's agriculture and industry. From 1905 until 1917 he served in the U.S. Senate. He was defeated for reelection to a third term. He then remained in Washington, D.C., to open a law practice.

President Warren G. Harding appointed Sutherland to the U.S. Supreme Court on September 5, 1922. During his nearly 16 years on the bench he developed a reputation as a conservative, committed to individual liberties and freedom from government control, but with reasonableness.

In economic issues he favored LIBERTY OF CONTRACT. His majority opinion in ADKINS V. CHILDREN'S HOSPITAL, 261 U.S. 525 (1923), declared minimum wage legislation for women unconstitutional because it interfered with a woman's right to contract. However, Sutherland was not opposed to reasonable regulations, such as ZONING, protecting women from mandatory late at night work, or regulating motor vehicles in public.

Sutherland defended CIVIL LIBERTIES as stoutly as he defended property rights. He wrote the decision in the Scottsboro Boys Case, *Powell v. State of Alabama*, 287 U.S. 45 (1932), which overturned the conviction of nine black teenagers for allegedly assaulting two white women, because a criminal defendant in a criminal case has a right to counsel with a reasonable opportunity for consultation.

When President Franklin Roosevelt instituted the New Deal legislative program, Sutherland became the key intellectual opponent. He was able to see that much of the early New Deal program was declared unconstitutional. Sutherland and the Court's other conservatives were branded as the "Four Horsemen."

Despite the failure of President Roosevelt's 1936 post-election "court-packing scheme," Sutherland found himself increasingly isolated. He resigned in 1938, and SUBSTANTIVE DUE PROCESS departed with him and so did an emphasis on natural rights.

Sutherland died at Stockbridge, Massachusetts, July 18, 1942. He was buried at Cedar Hill Cemetery, Washington, D.C.

For more information: Arkes, Hadley. *The Return of George Sutherland: Restoring a Jurisprudence of Natural Rights.* Princeton, N.J.: Princeton University Press, 1997; Paschal, Joel Francis. *Mr. Justice Sutherland: Man Against the State.* Westport, Conn.: Greenwood Press, 1969.

—A. J. L. Waskey

Swann v. Charlotte-Mecklenburg Board of Education, 402 U.S. 1 (1971)

In *Swann v. Charlotte-Mecklenburg Board of Education,* the Court unanimously approved a federal district court's mandated school busing plan as an effort to desegregate the Charlotte-Mecklenburg school system. Following years of litigation, the federal trial court for the Western District of North Carolina ordered the school board to submit a plan for both student and faculty desegregation in its public schools in 1969. After finding the school board's plans unacceptable, the district court appointed an education administration expert, Dr. John Finger, to submit a desegregation plan. Finger's plan redrew school attendance zones and ordered extensive busing to achieve substantially desegregated schools.

In reviewing the desegregation plan in *Swann,* the Supreme Court ruled that BROWN V. BOARD OF EDUCATION II, 349 U.S. 294 (1955), justified the use of "remedial measures" by the district court whenever a constitutional violation had been found. Chief Justice Warren BURGER, writing for the Court, stated that because the school district still contained "vestiges of state-imposed segregation," the district court possessed "broad power to fashion a remedy that will assure a unitary school system." *Swann* found that the district court's mandated bus transportation plan was "within the court's power" to create such a remedy.

Swann is remarkable for its unanimous result in spite of sharp differences of opinion among the nine participating justices. Burger's opinion for the Court underwent extensive editing through six drafts. Justices Hugo BLACK, William DOUGLAS, and Potter STEWART each drafted separate opinions, but all were eventually withdrawn and went unpublished. In its final form, Burger's opinion for the unanimous Court contained numerous compromises on various points, prompting Fifth Circuit Judge Griffin Bell to comment, "It's almost as if there were two sets of views laid side by side."

While *Swann* approved the district court's entire plan for the Charlotte-Mecklenburg school district, the Supreme Court's opinion nevertheless warned that with regard to court-ordered desegregation plans, "it must be recognized that there are limits." Though the Court found that the district court's use of a 71–29 percent white-to-black student ratio for Charlotte-Mecklenburg was permissible as a "starting point" in tailoring desegregation remedies, *Swann* maintained that the imposition of strict racial quotas would be impermissible. Once school boards had performed their "affirmative duty" to desegregate, they could no longer be subject to "further intervention" by district courts without additional findings of state-sponsored discrimination.

Additionally, *Swann* held that the existence of one-race schools was not inherently impermissible, though school officials would nevertheless have the burden of proving that such racial imbalances had not resulted from past discrimination by the school board. Finally, the *Swann* ruling explicitly dodged the question of whether school segregation caused by state discrimination outside the school district warranted a court-mandated remedy. Burger avoided this point of contention among the justices by writing, "This case does not present that question and we therefore do not decide it."

While *Swann* was legally salient in establishing the permissible scope of desegregation orders, the impact of segregation remedies would later be limited by subsequent Burger Court rulings, including MILLIKEN V. BRADLEY, 418 U.S. 717 (1974); *Pasadena v. Spangler*, 427 U.S. 424 (1976); and *Oklahoma City v. Dowell*, 498 U.S. 237 (1992).

For more information: Schwartz, Bernard. *Swann's Way: The School Busing Case and the Supreme Court.* New York: Oxford University Press, 1986; Whitman, Mark. *The Irony of Desegregation Law 1955–1995.* Princeton, N.J.: Markus Wiener, 1998.

—Jowei Chen

Swift and Company v. United States, 196 U.S. 375 (1905)

In *Swift and Company v. United States*, the Court upheld a prosecution under the Sherman Antitrust Act against meat dealers for engaging in monopolistic and anticompetitive practices throughout the country.

The Sherman Antitrust Act of 1890, passed under Congress's commerce clause power, was intended to regulate INTERSTATE COMMERCE. The government argued in *Swift* that the meat dealers were guilty under the act of restraining interstate trade by, among other things, agreeing to fix prices, conspiring with the railroads to get unlawful rates, and refraining from bidding against each other in livestock markets. The distinguishing factor of this case is that each meat dealer was engaged in the alleged practices within his respective state alone. Thus, the dealers argued that each act should be considered individually and, as such, was incapable of directly affecting interstate trade. Justice HOLMES, however, held that "Although the combination alleged embraces restraint and monopoly of trade within a single state, its effect upon commerce among the states is not accidental, secondary, remote, or merely probable." He distinguished this case from *United States v. E.C. Knight Co.*, 156 U.S. 1 (1895), in which a prosecution of similar activities in the sugar industry was overruled, by stating that *Knight* centered around monopolistic production practices. Production, which occurs before transit, does not in itself affect commerce. *Swift*, according to the Court, was a case about monopolistic distribution practices, which the Court had held more directly affect commerce because they involve interstate transit.

Holmes also distinguished this case from *Hopkins v. United States*, 171 U.S. 578 (1898), in which members of the Kansas City Livestock Exchange Association were prosecuted for prohibiting members of the association from buying livestock from any local merchant who was not a member of the exchange. The Court in *Hopkins* held that the transactions engaged in by the merchants were local in nature, even though the livestock would later be sent out-of-state, and therefore not subject to prosecution under the Sherman Act. Justice Holmes distinguished the facts of *Swift* from those of *Hopkins* by noting that in *Hopkins*, "The brokers were not like the defendants before us, themselves the buyers and sellers. They only furnished certain facilities for the sales. Therefore, there again the effects of the combination of brokers upon the commerce was only indirect, and not within the act. Whether the case would have been different if the combination had resulted in exorbitant charges was left open."

In order to further the argument for prosecution of the defendants in this case, Justice Holmes developed the "current of commerce" theory (also referred to as the "stream of commerce" theory). Under this analysis, the activity in question need not have a direct effect on commerce, it merely need be considered "in" commerce or part of the "stream" or "current" of commerce. On this theory Holmes stated: "[C]ommerce among the states is not a technical legal conception, but a practical one, drawn from the course of business. When cattle are sent for sale from a place in one state, with the expectation that they will end their transit, after purchase, in another, and when in effect they do so, with only the interruption necessary to find a purchaser at the stockyards, and when this is a typical, constantly recurring course, the current thus existing is a current of commerce among the states, and the purchase of the cattle is a part and incident of such commerce."

The "current of commerce" theory espoused by Justice Holmes in *Swift* prevailed throughout the 1920s and into the 1930s in commerce clause cases [*Stafford v. Wallace*, 258 U.S. 495 (1922); *Board of Trade of City of Chicago v. Olsen*, 262 U.S. 1 (1923)]. The theory died out, however, under the modern trend of Supreme Court commerce clause analysis, beginning in 1937 in *NLRB* V. JONES & LAUGHLIN STEEL CORP., 301 U.S. 1 (1937). In *Jones & Laughlin*, the Court explicitly rejected the "current of commerce" metaphor, stating that was but one illustration of an instance in which Congress may exercise its regulatory power on interstate commerce. After *Jones & Laughlin*, so long as the regulated activity had a "substantial economic effect" on interstate commerce, it no longer mattered that the activity be "in the current of commerce" as described in *Swift*.

For more information: Adams, Walter, and James W. Brock. *The Bigness Complex: Industry, Labor, and Government in the American Economy.* New York: Pantheon Books, 1986.

—Lauren Hancock

Swift v. Tyson, 41 U.S. (16 Pet.) 1 (1842)

In *Swift v. Tyson*, the Supreme Court declared that unless a case involved a purely local matter the federal courts were not required to follow state common law. Common law consists of the rules and principles developed over time by judges in order to resolve legal disputes. Common law generally developed when there was no applicable statute passed by the legislature to guide the courts. The key issue in *Swift v. Tyson* was whether the federal courts were required to follow the common-law rules developed by judges in state courts or whether they could rely on a distinct common law based on principles developed in federal courts.

An important original justification for creating a separate FEDERAL COURT SYSTEM was the need for an authoritative way to resolve the inevitable disputes between citizens of different states. New Yorkers did not necessarily trust Maine courts to treat them fairly, and the distrust was mutual. So the new federal courts were explicitly given "diversity jurisdiction"—the authority to hear disputes between individuals from different states. The creation of the federal courts was also motivated by the perceived importance of uniform interpretation of laws in promoting trade and commerce among the states. Opponents, however, feared that the federal courts would become a tool of the new federal government to overpower the states and overturn state laws.

Swift v. Tyson involved exactly the kind of complex commercial law dispute with transactions crossing state lines that motivated the desire for uniform rules. John Swift sued in New York to obtain money promised to him there by George Tyson. In arguing that he should not have to pay the money, Tyson submitted evidence that his promise of money to Swift was based on a previous fraudulent transaction involving property in Maine. Tyson's defense was relevant according to judicial rulings by New York courts but not under commercial law principles developed by the Supreme Court and most other state courts.

Under Section 34 of the JUDICIARY ACT OF 1789, if there was no applicable provision of the Constitution or federal law then the federal courts were required to apply state law. Justice Joseph STORY, the author of the Court's opinion in *Swift*, interpreted "state law" in Section 34 to apply only to formal laws or state statutes passed by legislatures. The term *state law* did not include state common law or "general principles of commercial law" developed in decisions of the New York courts, which Justice Story described as "often reexamined, reversed, and qualified by the Courts themselves" [*Swift v. Tyson*, 41 U.S. 1, 35 (1842)].

While the Supreme Court would give "the most deliberate attention" to what the state courts had decided, it was not to be "bound up and governed" by their decisions [*Swift v. Tyson*, 41 U.S. 1, 37 (1842)]. Instead, federal courts could rely on federal common law. Relying, therefore, on its own prior precedents and interpretation of commercial law principles, the Court held that the "equities between the antecedent parties" were not relevant to the enforcement of the agreement between Swift and Tyson. [*Swift v. Tyson*, 41 U.S. 1, 38 (1842)]. Justice Story asserted that this interpretation was preferable "for the benefit and convenience of the commercial world" [*Swift v. Tyson*, 41 U.S. 1, 39 (1842)].

The Supreme Court's decision in *Swift v. Tyson* allowed the federal courts to play a significant role in nationalizing commercial and trade rules and avoiding conflicting rules that would have hampered economic growth. However, it also tipped the FEDERALISM balance of power in favor of the federal courts over the states.

Swift was reversed in ERIE RAILROAD V. TOMPKINS, 304 U.S. 64, 79 (1938), when the Supreme Court, in an opinion written by Justice Louis BRANDEIS, declared that Justice Story's interpretation of Section 34 was not only erroneous but "an unconstitutional assumption of powers by the courts of the United States which no lapse of time or respectable array of opinion should make us hesitate to correct."

For more information: Freyer, Tony. *Harmony and Dissonance: The Swift and Erie Cases in American Federalism.* New York: New York University Press, 1981; Jackson, Robert H. "The Rise and Fall of *Swift v. Tyson*." *American Bar Association Journal* 24 (1938): 609.

—Lori A. Johnson

symbolic speech

Symbolic speech is a form of expression protected under the First Amendment to the Constitution.

The earliest case to protect this type of speech came in the 1931 case of *Stromberg v. California,* 283 U.S. 359. In *Stromberg,* the Supreme Court struck down a California law that had forbidden the flying of red flags as a symbol of political allegiance. A children's camp, affiliated with an international group, had flown a red flag in support of Communist Party philosophies. In the majority opinion, Chief Justice HUGHES reasoned that "The maintenance of opportunity for free political discussion to the end that government may be responsive to the will of the people, and that changes may be obtained by lawful means, is a fundamental principle of our constitutional system."

Later, in *Thornhill v. Alabama,* 310 U.S. 88 (1940), this form of unspoken expression was expanded to include the act of picketing matters "of public concern." It was not until 1969 that the term *symbolic speech* would become a well-established form of speech shielded by First Amendment protections. It was then, in *TINKER V. DES MOINES,* 393 U.S. 503, that symbolic speech was defined as "conduct that expresses an idea." This opinion came at a time of great historical moment for the United States, then deeply embroiled in the Vietnam War amid growing public doubt over the conflict. In *Tinker,* the Court invalidated a rule prohibiting students from wearing black armbands in protest of the war.

However, the most controversial symbolic speech ruling, to date, came in 1989 when the Supreme Court struck down a Texas flag-burning law in *TEXAS V. JOHNSON,* 491 U.S. 397 (1989). Ruling in favor of the right to burn the flag, Justice BRENNAN's majority opinion stressed the fundamental rationale behind protected speech. He wrote that "if there's a bedrock principle underlying the first amendment, it is that the government may not prohibit the expression of an idea simply because society finds the idea offensive or disagreeable." This does not mean, however, that all types of symbolic speech are protected in all cases.

In *U.S. V. O'BRIEN,* 391 U.S. 367 (1968), the Court upheld a federal law that prohibited the burning of one's draft card. The losing party in *O'Brien* argued that the draft card had been burned to voice opposition to the Vietnam War. In rejecting this point, the Court ruled that the object of protest must be meant to clearly communicate an idea to another, and that burning this federal document, a draft card, did not satisfy this criterion. Similarly, the Court has limited the right to picket when picketers are too noisy or disruptive in a setting (in this case a medical clinic) where privacy or quiet is required. (*Grayned v. City of Rockford,* 408 U.S. 104 [1972]).

Most recently, this type of "obtrusive" picketing behavior has been restricted outside of abortion clinics where the Court has created a 36 foot "buffer zone" to separate picketers from patients seeking access to medical services [*MADSEN V. WOMEN'S HEALTH,* 512 U.S. 753 (1994)]. The Court has also limited symbolic speech when it is used as a means of silencing another's right to free expression. This issue arose in the case of *Hurley v. Irish-American Gay Group of Boston,* 515 U.S. 557 (1995). In *Hurley,* the Court was faced with a parade organizer who did not want to include marchers, as a separate group, conveying a pro-homosexuality message during the organizer's annual St. Patrick's Day parade.

In supporting the parade organizer's view, the Court wrote that it was wrong for the state to compel private parade organizers to allow marchers to convey a message that the parade was not designed to represent. In essence, the issue was not centered on the expressive rights of the marchers but was focused on the expressive right of the parade organizers and the suppression of that right through compulsory participation laws. Overall, the test used to determine whether symbolic speech may be restricted by state action comes from the *Tinker* case (1969): "In order to convince a court that symbolic conduct should be punished and not protected as speech, the government must show that it has an important reason. However, the reason cannot be that government disapproves of the message conveyed by the symbolic conduct."

For more information: Weaver, Russell L., and Donald E. Lively. *Understanding the First Amendment.* Newark, N.J.: LexisNexis, 2003.

—Patricia E. Campie

T

Taft, William Howard (1857–1930) *president of the United States, chief justice of the United States*

William Howard Taft is the only person to have served both as president and CHIEF JUSTICE of the United States.

In addition to serving in both of these roles, Taft was also an assistant prosecuting attorney for Cincinnati, Ohio (1881–83), collector of internal revenue (1882–83), assistant county solicitor (1885–87), Ohio Superior Court judge (1887–90), U.S. solicitor general (1890–92), U.S. Circuit Court judge (1892–1900), governor-general of the Philippines (1901–04), secretary of war under Theodore Roosevelt (1904–08), provisional governor of Cuba (1907), twenty-seventh president of the United States (1909–13), and tenth Chief Justice of the U.S. Supreme Court (1921–30).

Born in Cincinnati, Ohio, William Howard Taft was one of five children in a wealthy, ideologically conservative and Republican family. Taft was exposed to public life early. His father (Alphonso) was a prominent lawyer and judge, the secretary of war and attorney general for Ulysses S. Grant, and an ambassador to Austria-Hungary and Russia for Chester A. Arthur. Taft himself was well-educated, attending Cincinnati public schools. He graduated from Woodward High School in 1874. He attended Yale College and graduated with distinction in 1878, and later Cincinnati Law School where he graduated in 1880, the same year he was admitted to the bar. He authored several articles for the *Cincinnati Commercial* as a part-time court reporter during law school. A member of the Unitarian religion, Taft married Helen Herron (1861–1943) in 1886, and they later had three children: Robert Alphonso Taft (1889–1953), Helen Herron Taft (1891–1987), and Charles Phelps Taft (1897–1983). His wife was very influential in steering him more toward a political career than one solely based on legal practice.

After completing law school, his first public post was as assistant prosecuting attorney from 1881 to 1883. For a short tenure, he also served as a collector of internal revenue for Cincinnati in 1882, and then became assistant county solicitor from 1885 to 1887. Governor Joseph Foraker appointed him in 1887 to fill an unexpired term in the Ohio Superior Court in Cincinnati, a post he held for three years. He successfully ran for election but was asked to serve as the U.S. solicitor general in 1890 by President Benjamin Harrison.

During his service in Washington, D.C., Taft became acquainted with Theodore Roosevelt, who was then serving as a civil service commissioner. Roosevelt became a mentor for Taft at that point and was particularly influential in the early stages of his career. Two years later, Harrison appointed him to the U.S. Circuit Court in the sixth district, where he served for eight years until President William McKinley asked him to stabilize conditions in the newly acquired Philippines. Taft accepted the challenge of heading the Second Philippine Commission and became their first American governor in 1901. Later, Roosevelt sent Taft to handle the turmoil following the 1906 election in Cuba and to supervise the building of the Panama Canal.

Soon after Roosevelt decided not to run for another term, he formally disclosed his desire to have Taft as his successor and enthusiastically campaigned on Taft's behalf. Taft was perceptibly more absorbed in debating matters of legal discourse than pursuing executive power, telling Roosevelt in his 1906 letter that he "would much prefer to go on the Supreme Bench for life than to run for the Presidency."

Nevertheless, with Roosevelt's endorsement, Taft defeated William Jennings Bryan to win the presidency in 1908, with 321 electoral votes to Bryan's 162. While Taft was revered for his shrewd understanding of the legal system and performance as a lawyer and judge, his skills as an executive were not as exemplary. In fact, the Taft presidency was characterized by many as a failure. He was often considered as being alienated, inarticulate, and unable to carry his objectives to meaningful conclusions. Members from the Republican Party had difficulty relating to him, particularly when Roosevelt, his mentor, departed for Africa and backing from Rooseveltian followers subsided.

Taft became even more estranged from his mentor when a conservation policy debacle attracted public scrutiny. Taft's secretary of the interior, Richard H. Ballinger, opened for sale land in Alaska previously reserved by Roosevelt under public domain. Taft sided with Ballinger despite his long-time friendship with Roosevelt.

Taft's defense of the Payne-Aldrich Tariff Act was also criticized by many fellow Republicans. Further, he had the backing of the autocratic speaker in the House of Representatives, Joseph G. Cannon. Cannon was notorious for unilaterally manipulating committee assignments to punish Republican party dissonants who did not emphatically vote according to partisan lines. This strategy was designed to maintain partisan discipline, but along with Cannon's ardent defense of Taft administration policies, the Republican Party instead became more fractionalized. This resultantly expanded the divide between pro-Taft supporters and insurgents who were disenchanted with both the president's programs and the speaker's autonomous control of the House of Representatives.

Roosevelt's growing indifference for Taft became increasingly apparent as time elapsed and the election of 1912 approached. Taft captured the Republican party nomination, at which point Roosevelt withdrew from the party and reemerged as a Progressive "Bull Moose" Party candidate. Woodrow Wilson challenged them as the Democratic Party's candidate. Wilson easily won the election with 435 electoral votes, over Roosevelt and Taft who had 88 and 8 electoral votes respectively. While Wilson did not have a majority of the popular votes with 41.8 percent, the margin of victory was still almost twice as much as his two opponents. The Taft presidency was not an entire failure. Taft's efforts to advance international cooperation, enhance fair competition by battling large monopolies, and promote portions of his legislative agenda were successful. Also during his administration, Congress proposed by a two-thirds vote the Sixteenth Amendment (ratified in 1913 to grant Congress the power to lay and collect taxes on incomes without apportionment in the states) and Seventeenth Amendment (ratified in 1913 to provide for the popular election of U.S. senators) to the Constitution.

The intense three-way battle between the three candidates, one of which was a former mentor, left Taft disenchanted with politics. Accordingly, he became a professor of law at Yale. He was a staunch supporter of peace, particularly during World War I, and later accepted the position of president of the League to Enforce Peace. In 1921, without any previous experience serving on the Supreme Court, Taft was nominated by President Warren G. Harding to become chief justice, where he served until his death in 1930.

One of Taft's notable accomplishments on the bench was his successful lobbying of Congress to pass the 1925 Judges Act, which greatly expanded the Supreme Court's discretion to decide which cases it will hear, thus giving priority to ones of national importance. His role as chief justice was a much more suitable role for him to perform given his impressive legal talents but seemingly deficient stamina for politics. In comparison to Roosevelt, Taft was increasingly placid in his use of presidential powers. Taft's image suffered due to the innate comparisons that many drew between him and his former mentor. Hence, Roosevelt's accomplishments often overshadowed Taft's. However, Taft's predilection for law rather than politics made him a better lawyer and legal scholar than politician.

For more information: Anderson, Judith L. *William Howard Taft: An Intimate History.* New York: W. W. Norton, 1981; Coletta, Paolo. *The Presidency of William Howard Taft.* Lawrence: University Press of Kansas, 1973; Mason, Alpheus T. *William Howard Taft: Chief Justice.* Lanham, Md.: University Press of America, 1983; Pringle, Henry F. *The Life and Times of William Howard Taft.* 2 vols. New York: Farrar and Rinehart, 1939; Steamer, Robert J. *Chief Justice: Leadership and the Supreme Court.* Columbia: University of South Carolina Press, 1986.

—Daniel Baracskay
—Paul J. Weber

takings clause

The takings clause of the Fifth Amendment to the UNITED STATES CONSTITUTION requires that private property that is acquired by the government through EMINENT DOMAIN can only be taken for a valid public use, and only if the owner is given just compensation for the value of the property acquired.

The Fifth Amendment, often remembered for its civil protections against DOUBLE JEOPARDY and self incrimination, also provides that government may not take land for "public use" without providing the owner "just compensation." Consistent with the English common law, government retained the power to seize private property. The text of the takings clause merely compels the government to reimburse the owner the value of the loss.

Originally, the Constitution's takings clause was understood to apply only to the federal government. In *BARRON V. BALTIMORE* (1833), the Supreme Court ruled that a takings claim made against the state of Maryland could not be supported by the text of the Fifth Amendment, as the restrictions in the BILL OF RIGHTS did not apply to states. It was not until the *Chicago, Burlington & Quincy Railroad Co. v. Chicago* (1897) case, that the Supreme Court applied the just compensation standard of the takings clause to the states themselves.

In cases concerning eminent domain, the application of the takings clause is fairly straightforward. Intending to serve some public need, the government physically takes possession over private property and, subsequently, compensates the owner for the fair market value of the assets seized. Most of the controversies surrounding the application of the takings clause arise from governmental actions that fall short of a physical invasion of private property. As governments become increasingly inclined to regulate the use of private property, the definition of a "taking" becomes less clear.

The notion of a regulator taking first surfaced in *Pennsylvania Coal Co. v. Mahon* (1922). Shortly after selling the surface rights of their mining property to private concerns, the Pennsylvania legislature enacted laws prohibiting the plaintiffs from exercising their contractual rights to mine the land beneath. Recognizing the government's right to enact laws regulating the use of private lands, the Supreme Court, nonetheless, ruled that, without just compensation, such restrictions were unconstitutional.

In PENN CENTRAL TRANSPORTATION CO. V. NEW YORK CITY (1978), the Supreme Court set limits on the extent of a regulatory claim by linking the definition of a takings to the concept of "investment-backed expectations." Concerned that the landmark status conferred upon Grand Central Station would interfere with the economic exploitation of the property, Penn Central Transportation Company brought suit against the City of New York, claiming that the development restitutions constituted a taking. The Supreme Court reasoned that, although the LAND USE restrictions undoubtedly precluded the expansion of the plaintiff's property, the city regulations did not interfere with the investors' initial profit expectations. In establishing a taking, courts must determine whether valid governmental regulations undermine the overall worth of a property, rather than focusing upon any one facet of its potential value. In the case of Grand Central Station, the designation as a historic landmark may have undermined its potential for further development, but overall the regulation did not interfere with the manner in which the property had been historically used.

The precise application of the takings clause was further refined in LUCAS V. SOUTH CAROLINA COASTAL COUNCIL (1992). Shortly after David Lucas purchased a $900,000 beachfront lot on the Isle of Palms, the state of South Carolina passed the Beachfront Management Act, prohibiting construction on the property. Lucas filed suit arguing that, unlike the Penn Central claim, the newly enacted beachfront regulations completely undermine the express purpose for which the property was procured.

Although the government regulations did not alter the use of the existing land, as an investor, he could not have known he would be forced to leave the lot vacant. The Supreme Court ultimately agreed with Lucas, again relying on the investment-backed expectations standard as the basis for determining the regulation constituted a taking. The Court further argued that, in its capacity to safeguard the interests of the public, the state was not prohibited from establishing regulations over the use of private lands. Rather, when such regulations provide a common benefit at the expense to an individual, just compensation is required.

The meaning of the takings clause is further complicated when governments use private property to create a public benefit at no apparent cost to the individual. Here, too, the Supreme Court rulings provide some guidance. In *Brown v. Legal Foundation of Washington* (2003), the high court was asked to consider whether the interest on legal retainers that is generated in accounts created by state government could be taken to provide legal services to the poor. The plaintiffs argued that, since the money provided to support legal services was generated using private funds, the fruits of that investment belonged to the individual. The Court disagreed, arguing that the Fifth Amendment protects persons against the seizure of property and private citizens are not entitled to be compensated when they can show no tangible loss.

For more information: Hubbard, F. Patrick. "Palazzolo, Lucas, and Penn Central: The Need for Pragmatism, Symbolism, and Ad Hoc Balancing." *Neb. L. Rev.* 80 (2001): 465; Wildenthal, Bryan H. "The Lost Compromise: Reassessing the Early Understanding in Court and Congress on Incorporation of the Bill of Rights in the Fourteenth Amendment." *Ohio St. L. J.* 61 (2000): 1,051.

Taney, Roger Brooke (1777–1864) *chief justice of the United States*

Roger Taney was the fifth CHIEF JUSTICE of the United States (1836–64), best remembered as the author of the Court's opinion in DRED SCOTT V. SANDFORD, 60 U.S. 393 (1857), one of the precipitating events of the Civil War (1861–65). Taney, however, made important and lasting contributions to constitutional jurisprudence. He established the doctrine that the public good has higher value than private property rights and that unfair laws violate the guarantee of "due process of law." He also warned against the imperial presidency.

Taney was born on a plantation in Calvert County in southern Maryland, into a Roman Catholic family, the son of a substantial owner of slaves. He graduated valedictorian from Dickinson College in Carlisle, Pennsylvania. In 1799 he won a seat in the Maryland legislature as a Federalist and was admitted to the Maryland bar. He practiced law in Frederick, Maryland, near the Pennsylvania border. He represented the Reverend Jacob Gruber in a criminal case where he was charged with giving a sermon denouncing slavery, a felony under Maryland law. Taney asked the jury

Justice Roger Brooke Taney *(United States Supreme Court)*

to ignore the law and acquit his client because slavery was evil. Subsequent slave revolts and the increasing stridency of abolitionist denunciation of the South, however, caused Taney to become a defender of black slavery. He allied with that faction of the Federalist Party that supported the War of 1812. He was elected to the Maryland senate in 1816. Sensing that the Federalists were in irreversible decline, he switched his loyalty to the Democratic Party in 1824. From 1827 to 1831, he was the attorney general of Maryland.

A longtime supporter of General Andrew Jackson, he chaired the Jackson Central Committee of Maryland in the 1828 election. In 1831 Jackson appointed him U.S. attorney general and acting secretary of war. Taney agreed with Jackson that the Bank of the United States was a dangerous concentration of economic power and threatened the rights of both the common people and the states. In 1832 Taney authored the message delivered by Jackson vetoing a congressional act renewing the bank's charter. After reelection in 1832, Jackson appointed Taney secretary of the treasury so that he could dismantle the bank and distribute its funds to state banks. The Senate, however, blocked the appointment. When Jackson appointed Taney as an associate justice of the Supreme Court in 1835, the Senate again declined to support the president's choice. The Senate,

however, did confirm Taney's appointment by Jackson as chief justice in 1836 despite continued opposition by the Whig Party.

Taney succeeded John MARSHALL as chief justice. He disagreed with Marshall on two significant constitutional issues—protection for vested property interests and the extent of national power. In 1785 the Massachusetts legislature chartered the Charles River Bridge Company to construct a bridge and collect tolls. In 1828 the legislature established the Warren Bridge Company to build a free bridge nearby, thereby depriving the owners of the toll bridge of their revenues. The Charles River Bridge Company filed suit, claiming the Massachusetts legislature had impaired the 1785 contract in violation of Article I, Section 10 of the U.S. Constitution. In *Charles River Bridge v. Warren Bridge,* 36 U.S. 420 (1837), Taney ruled for the Court that the public interest in encouraging economic growth was of higher value than the rights of private property. President Franklin D. Roosevelt adopted Taney's reasoning during the Great Depression in the 1930s to justify federal government incursions on the rights of private corporations in order to promote economic recovery that would benefit all Americans. A majority of the Supreme Court agreed with Roosevelt and Taney's approach beginning in 1937.

In *Dred Scott v. Sandford,* 60 U.S. 393 (1857), the Court held that Congress had no power to prohibit slavery in the territories of the United States. Taney, in a 7 to 2 decision, ruled that the due process clause of the Fifth Amendment protected the right of an owner to take his slave into territories held by the United States in trust for all Americans, Southerners and Northerners. He invalidated the Missouri Compromise of 1820. This was the second time in its history that the Supreme Court declared an act of Congress unconstitutional. The first was *MARBURY V. MADISON,* 5 U.S. 137 (1803), in which Chief Justice Marshall found a portion of the JUDICIARY ACT OF 1789 repugnant to the Constitution. Through his opinion in *Dred Scott,* Taney attempted to end the most bitter controversy then dividing the country—whether slavery would be confined to the states where it existed or would expand into the West. Taney further held that black persons of African descent were not and never could be citizens of the United States. America, said Taney, was a country founded by whites for whites. Blacks were forcibly brought to America, he said, for the sole purpose of serving as slaves to white masters. Taney alleged that the dominant opinion at the time of the Constitution's ratification in 1788 was that blacks had no rights which white men were bound to respect.

Taney's use of the language "nor shall any person be deprived of life, liberty or property without due process of law" to strike down an act of Congress was the first application of the doctrine of SUBSTANTIVE DUE PROCESS. Later

Courts made frequent use of this novel interpretation, after the due process language was incorporated in the Fourteenth Amendment in 1868. Under the substantive, as opposed to the procedural, interpretation, the due process clauses of the Fifth and Fourteenth Amendments do not simply require fair trials, they demand just laws. The Court under Chief Justice Earl WARREN in the 1950s and 1960s frequently found state laws infringing on individual rights void under substantive due process.

During the Civil War, President Abraham Lincoln, whom Taney regarded as a tyrant, suspended the privilege of the writ of habeas corpus, guaranteed by Article I, Section 9 of the Constitution. The military commander of Maryland ordered John Merryman, a Confederate sympathizer, arrested and indefinitely confined to Ft. McHenry. Merryman petitioned Taney, in his capacity as a circuit justice, to issue a writ of habeas corpus to the commander of the fort. Taney in *Ex parte Merryman*, Circuit Court, District of Maryland (1861), issued the writ but when the general failed to produce the prisoner Taney wrote an opinion declaring that Lincoln had no power to suspend the right of habeas corpus, one of the great protections for liberty under the English common law. Lincoln ignored Taney's ruling. The Supreme Court later held in *EX PARTE MILLIGAN*, 71 U.S. 2 (1866), that only Congress, not the president, has the power to suspend the writ of habeas corpus. Taney remained chief justice until his death on October 12, 1864.

For more information: Freedman, Suzanne. *Roger Taney: The Dred Scott Legacy.* Berkeley Heights, N.J.: Enslow, 1995; Renstrom, Peter G., ed. *The Taney Court: Justices, Rulings and Legacy.* Santa Barbara, Calif.: ABC-CLIO, 2003; Smith, Charles. *Roger B. Taney: Jacksonian Jurist.* New York: Da Capo Press, 1973.

—Kenneth Holland
—Matthew Woessner

tax and spend powers

The dual powers to tax and to spend are two of the enumerated powers the Constitution grants to the federal government. They are found in Article I, Section 8, clause 1, which states that "the Congress shall have power to lay and collect taxes, duties, imposts and excises, to pay the debts and provide for the common defense and general welfare of the United States; but all duties, imposts and excises shall be uniform throughout the United States." The government's power to tax is independent of the government's other powers delineated by the Constitution; the taxing power is not confined to the pursuit of other enumerated powers, such as the commerce clause's power to regulate trade between the states.

The federal government's ability to tax is broad, but there are a few limitations on the power. A general limitation found within the language of the power, is that "duties, imposts and excises shall be uniform throughout the United States." The term *uniform* refers only to equality among the states and not individuals. The tax structure cannot discriminate among the states by applying special taxes against some but not others. Making distinctions between individuals of different means is crucial to our system of INCOME TAX, which employs a progressive rate structure. Furthermore, the uniformity requirement has been interpreted to refer only to the taxation of activities (sometimes referred to as indirect taxes) rather than the taxation of property.

A past limitation, which has since been nullified, upon the government's power to tax arises in Article I, Section 9, clause 4, which states that "direct taxes shall be apportioned among the several states which may be included within this Union, according to their respective numbers. . . ." This article was once interpreted to require "direct taxes," the exact definition of which has never been clear, to be arranged in such a way that the revenue collected from each state is in direct proportion to that state's population. When the income tax was first passed by the Congress in 1894, it was challenged as unconstitutional on multiple grounds, primarily as not being apportioned among the states by population. The Supreme Court struck down the tax as unconstitutional. In response, Congress, in need of the revenue an income tax would generate, passed the Sixteenth Amendment creating the power to "lay and collect taxes on incomes, from whatever source derived, without apportionment among the several states. . . ." The Sixteenth Amendment has virtually nullified the apportionment requirement of Article I, Section 9. The confusion over direct taxes has been set aside, and the government has since developed a comprehensive income tax system.

While the primary purpose of a tax is to raise money, almost all taxes will have incidental effects on how people act. This is called a "regulatory effect." Since the grant of power is to tax, and not to regulate, taxes that appear to be regulations in disguise are vulnerable to challenge. If a tax were challenged as a regulation, a court would consider various factors in deciding whether the measure was on the whole a tax or a regulation. Usually, as long as a tax produces substantial revenue, it will be upheld. Additionally, if a tax regulates a subject matter that the government could achieve through another enumerated power, such as through the commerce clause, the tax's regulatory effect has no constitutional significance and will be allowed to stand. However, the true relevance of these limiting factors is unclear due to the Court's more recent deference to Congress in tax matters.

The power to spend the money raised through tax is also independent of the other enumerated powers. The historic case of *U.S. V. BUTLER*, 279 U.S. 1 (1936), established the spending power's independence, further stating that

Congress can spend for any purpose which serves the "general welfare." At issue in *Butler* was the use of "conditional appropriations," whereby the government will spend money only if certain conditions are met. Butler was challenging the Agricultural Adjustment Act of 1933 as a regulation. The act allowed the secretary of Agriculture to form agreements with farmers to reduce the amount of land they farmed in exchange for money, which was raised by taxes on the processing of agriculture. The Court declared that Congress had the power only to tax and spend for the general welfare. It did not have the power to regulate for the general welfare. The act was an attempt to coercively purchase compliance through a regulatory scheme. This was an impermissible regulation, beyond the federal government's enumerated powers. *Butler* continues to stand for the principle that Congress cannot regulate but can tax and spend for the general welfare. The judiciary gives Congress great deference in defining what is the general welfare.

The only other limits on the power to tax and spend are those contained in the BILL OF RIGHTS and the Constitution's other safeguards such as state sovereignty. Congress cannot violate the individuals' constitutional rights through a tax and spending program. For an illustration of how these other constitutional issues interact with tax and spend programs, and to learn how Congress, through the use of conditional spending, made the national drinking age 21, see SOUTH DAKOTA V. DOLE, 483 U.S. 203 (1987).

For more information: Nowak, John E., and Ronald D. Rotunda. *Constitutional Law.* 5th ed. St. Paul, Minn.: West, 1995; Tribe, Laurence H. *American Constitutional Law.* 2nd ed. Mineola, N.Y.: Foundation Press, 1988.

—Amy-Marie Culver

taxpayer suits

Taxpayer suits are cases brought by federal taxpayers to challenge the constitutionality of federal taxing and spending programs. Under certain limited circumstances, federal taxpayers may have STANDING to sue the federal government, however taxpayer status alone does not meet the requirement for standing.

In the first case to address the issue of taxpayer standing, FROTHINGHAM V. MELLON, 262 U.S. 447 (1923), the Court denied standing to the litigant, arguing that she failed to show actual or immediate danger of direct injury. Justice Joseph SUTHERLAND, writing for the majority, argued that a taxpayer's interest and potential injury from federal expenditures is "comparatively minute and indeterminable, and the effect upon future taxation, of any payment out of the funds, so remote, fluctuating and uncertain, that no basis is afforded for an appeal to the preventive powers of a court of equity." Given the difficulty of showing direct injury, the *Frothingham* decision effectively prevented taxpayers from challenging the constitutionality of federal spending until the WARREN Court modified the standard for taxpayer standing in FLAST V. COHEN, 392 U.S. 83 (1968). In *Flast,* the Court awarded standing to a group of seven taxpayers who challenged the constitutionality of the Elementary and Secondary Education Act of 1965. The act provided federal education grants, which states could use to support instruction in religious schools. In his opinion for the majority, Chief Justice Earl Warren created a two-prong nexus test for taxpayer standing: The taxpayer must be challenging an exercise of Congress's taxing and spending power, and the taxpayer must show that Congress exceeded specific limitations of its taxing and spending power, such as the First Amendment's establishment clause.

The Court has been reluctant to expand taxpayer standing beyond the limits established by *Flast,* often denying standing to taxpayers challenging executive branch actions. In *Valley Forge Christian College v. Americans United for Separation of Church and State, Inc.,* 454 U.S. 464 (1982), the litigants were trying to prevent the Department of Health, Education, and Welfare from donating surplus government property to a religious educational institution. The government claimed their authority to dispose of property was derived from Article IV, Section 3 and was not an exercise of power under the taxing and spending clause. The Court agreed, ruling the taxpayers failed the first prong of the *Flast* test for taxpayer standing.

The Court ruled similarly in *Schlesinger v. Reservists Committee to Stop the War,* 418 U.S. 208 (1974), where litigants challenged the military reserve commissions held by members of Congress during the Vietnam War, charging that they violated Article I, Section 6, and in *U.S. v. Richardson,* 418 U.S. 166 (1974), where taxpayers argued nondisclosed funding for the CIA violated Article I, Section 9. In cases that do not involve congressional power under the taxing and spending clause, the Court has typically relied on *Frothingham's* "direct injury" standard. However, it has adhered to *Flast* and granted standing in the limited cases where taxpayers have shown that congressional spending exceeded specific limitations of the establishment clause [*Bowen v. Kendrick,* 487 U.S. 589 (1988)].

For more information: Bianco, Christine F. "A Hard and Flast Rule for Taxpayer Standing: *Valley Forge Christian College v. Americans United for Separation of Church & State, Inc.*" *St. John's Law Review* 57 (1982–83); Rowland, C. K., and Bridget Jeffery Todd. "Where You Stand Depends on Who Sits: Platform Promises and Judicial Gatekeeping in the Federal District Courts." *The Journal of Politics* 53, no. 1 (February 1991): 175–185.

—Michelle D. Christensen

Terminiello v. Chicago, 337 U.S. 1 (1949)

The case of *Terminiello v. Chicago* helped define the field of FIGHTING WORDS in First Amendment law. The case came only a few years after the doctrine was announced in CHAPLINSKY V. NEW HAMPSHIRE and significantly narrowed the scope of when fighting words could be punished.

The case itself involved a shadowy figure named Father Arthur Terminiello, a priest from Birmingham, Alabama. Father Terminiello was under suspension from his bishop for his frequent inflammatory speeches against Jews and African Americans. Gerald L. K. Smith, a notorious anti-Semite rabble-rouser, brought him to Chicago. Terminiello's speech was widely publicized and drew a crowd of at least 800 active listeners and more than a thousand protesters. According to his testimony "They called us 'God damned Fascist, Nazis, ought to hang the so and sos.' When I entered the building I heard the howls of the people outside. . . ."

The protest did not deter Father Terminiello however, and he made a typically inflammatory speech to the assembled crowd. He attacked Eleanor Roosevelt and said, "Now, this danger we face—let us call them Zionist Jews if you will, let's call them atheistic, communistic Jewish or Zionist Jews, then let us not fear to condemn them." Several members of crowd reportedly responded enthusiastically calling out, "kill the Jews," and "Dirty kikes." As the crowd outside the auditorium became more unruly, the police arrested several protesters and Father Terminiello, charging him with a breach of the peace. He was convicted and sentenced to pay a fine of $100. He took his APPEAL to the Supreme Court.

On May 16, 1949, the Supreme Court released its 5 to 4 decision reversing Terminiello's conviction. Justice William O. DOUGLAS wrote the majority opinion and said in part, "a function of free speech under our system of government is to invite dispute. It may indeed best serve its high purpose when it induces a condition of unrest, creates dissatisfaction with conditions as they are, or even stirs people to anger."

In recent years the principles that Douglas articulated have become known as a "heckler's veto." Courts have rejected the idea that mobs or individuals can prevent others from speaking by their threats of violence.

Chief Justice VINSON and Justice FRANKFURTER dissented on relatively technical grounds while Justices JACKSON and BURTON dissented vigorously. Justice Jackson's dissent presented a long recitation of facts about the case and compared the situation to that of Germany as Hitler was coming to power. Jackson argued that the Court's clear and present danger test was PRECEDENT and said, "these wholesome principles are abandoned today and in their place is substituted a dogma of absolute freedom for irresponsible and provocative utterance which almost completely sterilizes the power of local authorities to keep the peace as against this kind of tactics."

Terminiello was the first case to challenge the range of the fighting words doctrine. This discussion would take several more cases to be settled. Cases such as *Gooding v. Wilson* and COHEN V. CALIFORNIA would eventually establish new rules for the fighting words doctrine that would significantly limit its application.

For more information: Kalven, Harry, Jr. *A Worthy Tradition: Freedom of Speech in America.* New York: Harper and Row, 1988.

—Charles C. Howard

Terry v. Ohio, 392 U.S. 1 (1968)

In *Terry v. Ohio*, the Supreme Court upheld the decision of a police officer to STOP AND FRISK two individuals suspected of planning a crime. The case is important because of the Court's endorsement of broad POLICE POWERS to stop and search individuals.

"Investigative stop," "investigative detention," "temporary detention," or "stop and frisk" are terms utilized by law enforcement officers to describe what has become known as a "*Terry* stop." The *Terry* stop is known as the legal stopping of a citizen for a brief time period in order to determine whether the person being stopped has a weapon. This legal stopping and frisking (different from a searching, which is more involved) has to be based upon the police officer's reasonable belief that the person being stopped either has committed a crime or is about to commit a crime. This type of law enforcement activity was held constitutional with the *Terry* case but can trace its roots to the English common law.

In the English common law a police officer could stop a citizen because they had a "right to inquiry" privilege. This general inquiry into whatever the person being questioned was doing could be done without any legal justification. The American legal system adaptation of this common law privilege is the "voluntary contact" with the officer that is legally supported by the courts. This kind of stop required no fact gathering or suspicion by the officer that is conducting the stop, and thus there is no Fourth Amendment rights violation to this conduct. In addition the conduct by the officer must be reasonable and be of a short duration.

Terry and another man were observed by a detective/police officer who had 30 years police experience in the particular area where Terry and the other man were. Detective McFadden was in plain clothes outside of a store, observing the men who took turns walking up and down the street looking inside the store and then walking back and conversing. The two men performed this action many times and then a third man was introduced to the mix. The officer thought the men were "casing" the store—that is, getting ready to conduct a stickup. The police officer intervened and found weapons on two of the three men, one being Terry and the other being Chilton.

Terry was convicted by an Ohio court of carrying a concealed weapon and sentenced to a felony with a term of three years in jail. The concern by the Terry legal team was that the officer legally had no right to stop and then seize the men that he was observing because they had committed no crime as of the time they were stopped. The Supreme Court thought otherwise and affirmed the lower court's decision, allowing the court to introduce the weapon into evidence against Terry.

The Supreme Court believed that the officer was acting on a bit more than just a hunch. The Court believed that the officer acted in a reasonable manner, specifically "a reasonably prudent man would have been warranted in believing Terry was armed and thus presented a threat to the officer's safety while he was investigating Terry's suspicious behavior." The officer's protection was the underlying reason and rationale for the pro–law-enforcement decision. The officer's job is inherently dangerous, and therefore the Court was supporting the effort of the officer to conduct his duties while attempting to protect himself in the process. This conduct of patting down someone that the officer had stopped to inquire about possible criminal behavior was a common practice, but the *Terry* case set the stage for further precedence. Though the conditions for the legal stop had to be based upon more than just experience, there had to be other factors that when taken in totality equaled a reasonable inquiry.

To search anywhere but the outermost clothing has usually been determined to be an unreasonable search, but that depends specifically upon the kind of weapon and where the weapon was retrieved on the person being searched by the officer. The Court left the door open for officers to make reasonable decisions in this area and made no real effort to decide what is reasonable in an absolute manner. By doing so, the Court has allowed the law-enforcement community to conduct their business in a responsive manner to the needs of society. Thusly, the stop by an officer is typically done without the affirmation of having "probable cause"—which is a much higher standard to address in the courts and calls for a more finite focus of the court.

For more information: Heumann, Milton, and Lance Cassak. *Good Cop, Bad Cop: Racial Profiling and Competing Views of Justice.* New York: Peter Lang, 2003.

—Ernest Alexander Gomez

Texas v. Johnson, 491 U.S. 397 (1989)

In *Texas v. Johnson*, the Supreme Court ruled that burning the American flag as a protest was a form of expression protected by the First Amendment guarantee of freedom of speech. In an opinion written by Justice William J. BRENNAN Jr., the Court invalidated a state law that made it a crime to desecrate the flag.

The 5-4 ruling triggered a firestorm, both inside the Court where dissenting justices expressed strong objections, and outside the Court where politicians and patriotic groups decried the ruling, pushed new flag-burning laws, and spent more than a decade-and-a-half seeking a constitutional amendment to protect the flag.

The case arose when Gregory Lee Johnson burned an American flag as part of demonstrations against the 1984 Republican National Convention in Dallas, Texas, where President Ronald Reagan was being nominated to run for a second term. The incident took place outside the Dallas City Hall. Johnson was convicted for violating a Texas law that made it a crime to deface an American flag in a manner that will seriously offend those who observe the incident. His conviction was reversed in the Texas Court of Criminal Appeals, and the state carried the case to the Supreme Court.

The Supreme Court said the Texas law was an attempt to suppress expression simply because it was unpopular or offensive. "If there is a bedrock principle underlying the First Amendment, it is that the government may not prohibit the expression of an idea simply because society finds the idea itself offensive or disagreeable," Justice Brennan wrote. Justice Brennan suggested that the best way to show respect for the flag was not to punish protesters but to wave it proudly in response to the flag-burner. "We do not consecrate the flag by punishing its desecration, for in doing so we dilute the freedom that this cherished emblem represents," he wrote.

In dissent Chief Justice William H. REHNQUIST, quoting the first verse of Francis Scott Key's *Star-Spangled Banner* and the full text of the poem *Barbara Frietchie* by John Greenleaf Whittier, called this a regrettably patronizing civics lecture. He said the Court was wrong to disallow special protection for the flag.

It took Congress less than four months to pass new federal legislation to protect the flag. Congress feared that the prior law, punishing those who cast contempt on the flag, was unconstitutional in light of *Texas v. Johnson* because, like the Texas law, the federal statute focused on the content of the expression. The new Flag Protection Act of 1989 eliminated the direct reference to content and punished mutilating or defacing the flag.

To test the new federal law, individuals burned flags on the steps of the U.S. Capitol and in Seattle, Washington.

Neither group was convicted because federal judges declared the new law unconstitutional. In *U.S. v. EICHMAN*, 496 U.S. 310 (1990), the Supreme Court agreed, 5 to 4, that the new federal law still singled out the content of the expression in flag-burning in violation of the First Amendment.

Since the two rulings, numerous constitutional amendments have been introduced in Congress. The proposals have passed the U.S. House but have failed in the U.S. Senate. Numerous state legislatures have urged adoption of a constitutional amendment, and many states still have old and possibly invalid flag desecration laws on the books.

For more information: Goldstein, Robert Justin. *Flag Burning and Free Speech: The Case of Texas v. Johnson.* Lawrence: University Press of Kansas, 2000.

—Stephen Wermiel

Thomas, Clarence (1948–) *Supreme Court justice*
One of the most controversial figures in both contemporary political life and Supreme Court history, Clarence Thomas has been an associate U.S. Supreme Court justice since his controversial Senate confirmation process in 1991 to replace Thurgood MARSHALL, the first African-American justice on the Court. Having been confirmed at a young age as the 106th Supreme Court justice, he could have one of the longest tenures on the court.

To his critics, like columnist Maureen Dowd of *the New York Times*, he is "barking mad." For his defenders, like the *Wall Street Journal*, his opinions are "clear and well-reasoned (and) honor our constitutional traditions." One of the more complicated and controversial figures of contemporary America and certainly in the history of the U.S. Supreme Court, his October 1991 second Senate confirmation hearings were observed by huge television audiences. In particular, the accusations of SEXUAL HARASSMENT of a former subordinate, Professor Anita Hill of the University of Oklahoma Law School, were not only dramatic but led to a development of U.S. law in this substantive area.

Thomas was nominated with among the fewest qualifications for a Court justice, having served on the Washington, D.C. Circuit of Appeals for only one and a half years from his March 12, 1990, appointment to the Circuit to his October 23, 1991, swearing in to the Supreme Court. He ironically has been one of the Court's strongest opponents of AFFIRMATIVE ACTION, an opposition which some view as hypocritical. That President George Herbert Walker Bush called him the "most qualified person in the country for the position" only added to the resentment of many, though others wanted revenge for the earlier rejection of the nomination of Robert Bork, who had been replaced by a more moderate judge, David SOUTER, the previous nom-

ination to the bench in 1991. Souter then became even more moderate on the bench. Thomas's famous reaction to the accusations by Hill and others against him was that he had been subjected to a "high-tech lynching," which denied him his public reputation and respect. Following this and other final statements, he was confirmed by a 52-48 vote. The Court marshals insisted that he wear a bulletproof vest at his confirmation vote in the Senate.

Jurisprudence
Thomas's views polarize the country perhaps as much as any figure in U.S. life. Critics call them rigid; defenders, principled. His constitutional interpretations are based largely on "originalism," the doctrine that any constitutional ambiguity should be viewed through the optic of the framers' original intention. Critics state the original intent is often unknowable (e.g., on issues of little importance then such as abortion or public education) or were nonexistent technologies (e.g., the Internet) or irrelevant (many were racist slave owners). Critics also assert that originalism is not more consistent or predictable methodology for rendering constitutional interpretations.

To critics, originalism produces judgments that are just as political and self-serving as the "politically activist" judgments that originalism charges are typical of the WARREN Court. Samuel Marcosson has concluded that Justices Thomas and Antonin SCALIA make assertions from contemporary Republican Party ideology and discount the possibility that greater FEDERALISM, emphasis on the TAKINGS CLAUSE, and emphasis on color blindness to oppose affirmative action are not based on specific policies or doctrines from the late 18th-century debates.

Critics also assert that opposing affirmative action, which benefited his career, is hypocritical. Defenders counter that his only obligation is to reach an honest conclusion about the constitutionality of a policy. They also wonder why a black justice should be singled out for more criticism than other opponents of affirmative action such as Justice Scalia.

Finally, Associate Justice Stephen BREYER and Thomas have had a rather heated set of exchanges on the relevance of foreign court decisions on U.S. jurisprudence. Thomas was left in the minority in the 2003 *Lawrence v. Texas* case, which declared its sodomy law to be unconstitutional, citing decisions of the European Court of Human Rights as evidence of what civilized states should emulate.

Among defenders of Thomas, Scott Gerber has concluded that it is a mistake to combine the views of Thomas and Scalia, even though that is conventional wisdom. Gerber calls Thomas a "liberal originalist" on CIVIL RIGHTS and a "conservative originalist" on CIVIL LIBERTIES and federalism. On the latter, Thomas rejects any idea of group rights and relies on the Declaration of Independence. Gerber finds Thomas to be a more consistent thinker than Scalia, who is more apt to justify a desired result with whatever logic is persuasive, however illogical compared with other decisions rendered. Thomas, on the other hand, implicitly believes that the Constitution's framers were dedicated to the ends of the Declaration and therefore would have approved of their inclusion as goals in CONSTITUTIONAL INTERPRETATION. Thomas answered Senator Orrin Hatch in his confirmation hearing that he had been interested in natural rights theory, presumably drawn from John Locke and Thomas Jefferson, since his time as chair of the EQUAL EMPLOYMENT OPPORTUNITY COMMISSION.

In fact, Thomas rarely makes separate opinions. More frequently, he votes with other judges. So, perhaps, his reputation as a maverick is undeserved.

On the Court, he has joined Chief Justice William Rehnquist and other conservatives in reviving the federalism doctrine, that more powers ought to be federated from the central or federal government to the states. He argues that the First Amendment's ESTABLISHMENT CLAUSE was not intended to deny a role to RELIGION in public life, including the access of religious groups to public and government facilities. He has taken the view that there is no constitutional basis for an abortion, criticizing the holding in *ROE V. WADE* as based on an imputed right to PRIVACY not found in the Constitution, from which an imputed right to abortion is found.

In his 6 to 3 majority opinion in *Good News Bible Club v. Milford,* he wrote that a Christian youth group could meet after school hours in public-school facilities. He wrote a minority dissent against applying the *Americans with Disabilities Act* to Casey Martin, a disabled professional golfer whom the majority allowed to use a golf cart.

Not all of his views are routinely conservative. For example, in *Desert Palace v. Costa,* the Supreme Court ruled unanimously in an opinion written by Justice Thomas that an employee does not need direct evidence of bias in order to bring a lawsuit against an employer. He argued that if Congress intended to require a standard of direct evidence, it would have said so. Justice Thomas said that Congress's "failure to do so is significant, for Congress has been unequivocal when imposing heightened proof requirements in other circumstances."

However, the more typical view would be in *GRUTTER V. BOLLINGER,* where Thomas was in the minority in opposing race preferences and the goal of diversity in university admissions. He quoted Frederick Douglass: "And if the Negro cannot stand on his own legs, let him fall also. . . . Let him alone. . . . Your interference is doing him positive injury." Thomas also asked why so much more emphasis is placed on the interests of the elites to gain education than in the problems of the underclass that so much afflict the country.

Justice Clarence Thomas *(United States Supreme Court)*

Personal Background

At a speech at the 2003 University of Georgia Law School graduation, Thomas said that he was rejected by every law firm to which he applied in Atlanta, after graduating from Yale Law School. He got his first job as assistant Missouri attorney general in Jefferson City, in 1974–77 through John Danforth, who later became a U.S. Senator and was one of his most eloquent advocates in his SUPREME COURT CONFIRMATION debates. He worked for Monsanto from 1977 to 1979 in the pesticide and agriculture division, was legislative assistant to Senator Danforth from 1979 to 1981, assistant secretary for Civil Rights in the U.S. Department of Education (1981–82), and chairman for the Equal Employment Opportunity Commission (1982–90).

The grandson of a sharecropper, he was born on June 28, 1948, in the Pin Point, near Savannah, the second child of M. C. Thomas and Leola Williams. The media and critics often portray him as stupid and quiet, based on what they see in the Court. In fact, those who know him report that he has a prodigious memory and talks for hours with friends. He greatly resents the press and greatly restricts its access to him. He feels that the news media hardly ever even tried to portray his life accurately.

He was raised after a few years, when his parents divorced, by a disciplinarian grandfather Anderson and grandmother in Savannah, who owned a 75-acre farm and demanded that he work hard in school. His grandfather died in 1983, and Thomas keeps a bust of him in his office.

Thomas has said that he does not speak because as a child, he learned an English patois based on the African dialect near parts of Savannah. As a result, he has long emphasized listening more than speaking out in public. He was educated in Catholic schools in Savannah, graduating from St. John Vianney Minor Seminary in 1968. He graduated ninth in his class at Holy Cross in 1971 and received a J.D. from Yale in 1974. At the latter, he was known as a political activist with some left-wing views. When and how he became a conservative activist is hardly known in any detail, other than that it emerged during his time as chair of the EEOC. Yet, even there, his investigations found that Alabama's state universities were still segregated.

He helps young black students and others; meets schoolchildren weekly, apparently more than any other justice. He gives speeches mostly to conservative legal associations and to schools and universities—often for two days—with whom he has a personal connection. Though quiet on the bench, he is loquacious with friends and associates. He knows all the Supreme Court employees by name, as well as members of their families and where they attend school. He possibly gives more volunteer time than any Supreme Court justice, particularly with underprivileged black students, with whom he meets weekly.

A NASCAR fan, in 1999 he probably became the only Supreme Court justice to be grand marshal at the Daytona 500. A regular weight lifter, perhaps the most athletic since Byron WHITE and William O. DOUGLAS, he keeps portraits of Booker T. Washington and Frederick Douglass in his office, as well as the bust of his grandfather. He attends daily mass at St. Joseph's Catholic Church on days when he attends the Court.

He urges others in speeches, such as at the 2003 UGA Law School graduation, not to make themselves feel like "victims," no matter how many trials and tribulations they might face: "Today as the fabric of society is saturated with complaint and protest, each of you has the opportunity to be a hero," he said. "Do what you know must be done."

For more information: Foskett, Ken. *Judging Thomas: the Life and Times of Clarence Thomas.* New York: William Morrow, 2004; Gerber, Scott D. *First Principles: The Jurisprudence of Clarence Thomas.* New York: New York University Press, 2002; Marcosson, Samuel A. *Original Sin: Clarence Thomas and the Failure of the Constitutional Conservatives.* New York: New York University Press, 2002; Smith, Christopher E., and Joyce A. Baugh. *The Real*

Clarence Thomas: Confirmation Veracity Meets Performance Reality. New York: Peter Lang, 2000; Thomas, Andrew Peyton. *Clarence Thomas: A Biography.* San Francisco, Calif.: Encounter Books, 2001.

—Henry F. Carey

Thornburg v. Gingles, 478 U.S. 30 (1986)

Thornburg v. Gingles is the leading case interpreting Section 2 of the VOTING RIGHTS ACT (1965), which guarantees members of minority groups equal opportunity to "elect representatives of their choice" [42 U.S.C. § 1973(b)]. *Gingles* held that a minority group could make out a *prima facie* case under Section 2 by showing three "preconditions": (1) the minority group is sufficiently large and geographically compact to constitute a majority in a district; (2) the members of the minority group vote similarly; and (3) the majority votes as a block to defeat the candidate preferred by the minority group. A violation of Section 2 is termed "vote dilution" and rests on the conclusion that even though a person's vote has been freely cast and duly counted, the electoral system was engineered in such a way as to make that person's vote less valuable than another's. Vote dilution need not be motivated by racial animus to violate the act, but it occurs whenever a voting procedure "results in" a member of a minority group being given unequal voting power [42 U.S.C. § 1973(a)].

One effect of the *Gingles* preconditions has been to jeopardize the use of multimember districts in jurisdictions where minority groups form a substantial portion of the population. Multimember districts, unless voters are permitted to devote multiple votes to a single candidate, may allow a group with a slight overall majority to control a much greater percentage of legislative seats, limiting the influence of minority populations. Application of *Gingles* often requires the dissolution of multimember districts and the institution of a system of single-member districting where the minority group will comprise a majority in one or more single-member "remedial" districts. Accordingly, *Gingles* has been forcefully criticized as the imposition by the Court of a theory of political philosophy under which (certain) cohesive groups should be entitled to representation in the legislature.

Gingles has not been confined to merely multimember districts, however. It has also required that single-member districts be drawn to reflect minority voting strength, meaning that racial gerrymandering that packs minorities into a few districts or spreads their numbers across several districts could violate the act. Taking account of minority voting strength to comply with Section 2 has often caused difficulty, because a line of Supreme Court cases beginning with SHAW V. RENO, 509 U.S. 630 (1993), has held that it violates the EQUAL PROTECTION CLAUSE for states to draw district lines where the predominant consideration is race.

Apart from the equal-protection problems in race-based districting, *Gingles* and Section 2 suffer from a conceptual difficulty in defining the appropriate influence minority groups should have on the political process. Perhaps it would appear most sensible to award minority groups a share of legislative representation proportionate to the group's population in the community. If a minority group has 20 percent of the population, it should have 20 percent of the representation. Whatever intuitive appeal this option may have, it would appear to be explicitly *foreclosed* by Section 2: "nothing in this section establishes a right to have members of a protected class elected in numbers equal to their proportion in the population" [42 U.S.C. § 1973(b)]. What other way was there to ensure that minority groups have an equal opportunity to elect candidates of their choice? The Court has effectively conceded that there is no answer to that question, and proportionality has become the touchstone for vote dilution claims despite the text of Section 2.

No individual person has any realistic chance of electing the candidate of his choice. For Section 2 to mean much, then, it must require that minority *groups* be given an equal chance to elect candidates, but the Voting Rights Act, the Fifteenth Amendment, and the court decisions interpreting Section 2 have all phrased the rights at issue as belonging to individuals. Moreover, it is not clear who the "other members of the electorate," who form the point of comparison for relative electoral influence, are. While nonminorities broadly speaking typically have more electoral power than a minority group, a democratic majoritarian system is *supposed* to give more power to larger groups. If, on the other hand, Section 2 gives minorities the right not to have their votes diluted relative to other groups of voters defined by nonracial characteristics, it would seem that no court could compare the electoral influence of an infinite number of groups to make sure that minority groups were not being disadvantaged.

The Voting Rights Act sought to protect the political influence of minority groups, but the statute itself contains conflicts about how that goal is to be achieved. *Gingles* imposed a doctrinal framework over top of the act but has not resolved the theoretical questions inherent in an attempt to make an electoral system "fair."

For more information: Gerken, Heather K. "Understanding the Right to an Undiluted Vote." *Harv. L. Rev.* 114 (2001): 1,663; Issacharoff, Samuel. "Groups and the Right to Vote." *Emory L.J.* 44 (1995): 869.

—Michael Richard Dimino, Sr.

Timmons v. Twin Cities Area New Party, 520 U.S. 351 (1997)

In *Timmons v. Twin Cities Area New Party*, a 6 to 3 majority of the Court upheld Minnesota's law banning fusion, the tactic in which more than one political party nominates the same candidate for a partisan office.

Once common in the United States, fusion can be attractive to minor parties. Fusion lets minor parties nominate candidates who have been or will be nominated by another party, typically either the Democratic or Republican party candidate. Because these fusion candidates enjoy major-party support, they are more likely to win office than is the typical nominee of a minor party. The fusion nominations allow voters to register their support for the minor-party platform while still backing a potential winning candidate. Fusion thus addresses two major problems facing minor-party candidates in a plurality election system (where a majority of votes is not required): wasted votes and spoiling.

In districts in which one of the two dominant parties is much stronger than the other, votes for minor-party candidates are often said to be wasted because they do not have any bearing on the result. In districts where the two major parties are more evenly matched, the presence of even relatively few minor-party voters can have the paradoxical effect of spoiling the race.

Timmons emerged as a test case brought by the New Party strategists as part of a multistate plan to eliminate anti-fusion laws nationally by winning a ruling against them in the Supreme Court. Instead, the case served as a milestone to mark the end point of a series of decisions that first expanded and then sharply limited opportunities for minor parties in the United States. The high-water mark of the expansion was ANDERSON V. CELEBREZZE, 460 U.S. 780 (1983), in which the Court struck down a restrictive ballot access law that would have kept independent presidential candidate John Anderson off the Ohio ballot in 1980. The majority opinion cited an earlier ruling that noted "an election campaign is a means of disseminating ideas as well as attaining political office." However, then-Justice REHNQUIST, in the minority in *Anderson*, gave a dissent that foreshadowed the *Timmons* decision. Those views prevailed in *Burdick v. Takushi*, 504 U.S. 428 (1992).

In *Burdick*, the Court held that states need not count or even permit write-in votes, and that bans on write-in votes placed only a reasonable, minimal burden on voters' First and Fourteenth Amendment rights. Thus, after *Burdick*, it was clear that the Court was not receptive to claims that individual voters should be allowed to express themselves via the ballot. So the New Party's claim in *Timmons* was founded directly on the right of association: the claim was that groups of voters organized into minor political parties had the same right to nominate the candidates of their choice as the major parties did, regardless of whether a major party had or would nominate the same candidate. The New Party could make a strong claim that Minnesota's arguments against fusion were speculative and unfounded, because the party could point to New York, where decades of legal fusion had neither destabilized the state nor even enabled minor parties to threaten the dominance of the Democratic and Republican parties.

Chief Justice Rehnquist, now writing for the Court, found that states could decide that political stability is best served through a healthy two-party system and that the states could pass laws that hampered minor parties such as bans on fusion, so long as the laws did not completely insulate the two-party system from challenges.

The *Timmons* opinion even included a quote from Justice O'CONNOR, the only justice then serving who had also been an elected partisan politician: "There can be little doubt that the emergence of a strong and stable two-party system in this country has contributed enormously to sound and effective government."

As a result of *Timmons*, the New Party has almost entirely disappeared, joining the hundreds of minor parties in American political history who have found the power of the Democratic and Republican parties and the Supreme Court of the United States to be an unbeatable combination.

For more information: Argersinger, Peter H. "A Place on the Ballot: Fusion Politics and Antifusion Laws." *American Historical Review* 85, no. 2 (April 1980); Disch, Lisa Jane. *The Tyranny of the Two-Party System.* New York: Columbia University Press, 2002.

—John Gear

Tinker et al. v. Des Moines Independent School District, 393 U.S. 503 (1969)

In *Tinker et al. v. Des Moines Independent School District,* the U.S. Supreme Court affirmed the First Amendment rights to free speech of high school students wearing black armbands. While holding that the rights of students (and teachers) to free speech are different from those of adults, the key test is disruption of the educational process. Their wearing of armbands in a Des Moines, Iowa, high school, in a silent protest against U.S. involvement in the Vietnam War, constituted constitutionally protected speech. While certain rights were held to be possessed only by adult citizens and not students, wearing armbands was not among them.

A dozen of the students were from a Unitarian youth group, including Mary Beth and John Tinker, two siblings,

and a few more joined them. The actual petitioners were two high school students (John Tinker and Christopher Tinker) and one junior high student (Mary Beth Tinker). The school had heard about their plan to protest the war and issued a rule against wearing armbands under punishment of suspension. The students appeared with their armbands a few days later. The high school principal tried but failed to convince the students that they were wrong. After that, he suspended them and sent them home and told them not to return with the armbands on, though he apparently did so respectfully. The case drew much attention after some of their supportive parents informed the news media of this alleged violation of the U.S. Constitution.

The Tinker parents sued the school but lost in the district court for southern Iowa, which upheld the prerogative of school authorities to regulate speech in order to prevent the disruption of discipline. [258 F Supp 971.] Then, the Eighth Circuit of the Court of Appeals upheld the decision without writing an opinion. The parents appealed all the way to the Supreme Court, which granted a WRIT OF CERTIORARI. By a vote of 7 to 2, Justice Abe FORTAS wrote that the armbands were close to PURE SPEECH. He emphasized:

> In our system, state-operated schools may not be enclaves of totalitarianism. School officials do not possess absolute authority over their students. Students in school as well as out of school are "persons" under our Constitution. They are possessed of FUNDAMENTAL RIGHTS which the State must respect, just as they must respect their obligations to the State.

While the authorities said that they feared that violence would result, the Supreme Court held that this was an unreasonable assertion and that no disruption was caused by the protest. It held that the students:

> Neither interrupted school activities nor sought to intrude in the school affairs or the lives of others. They caused discussion outside of the classrooms, but no interference with work and no disorder. In the circumstances, our Constitution does not permit officials of the State to deny their form of expression.

Thus, an objective test of disruption was established, rather than relying on the subjective, if sincere views of school officers:

> We properly read [the Constitution] to permit reasonable regulation of speech-connected activities in carefully restricted circumstances. But we do not confine the per-

missible exercise of First Amendment rights to a telephone booth or the four corners of a pamphlet, or to supervised and ordained discussion in a school classroom.

Furthermore, the Court inferred that the censorship and suspension were designed primarily to suppress particular views, rather than to avoid disruption of educational processes. Justice Fortas wrote, "It appeared that the authorities' action was based upon an urgent wish to avoid controversy." Rather, the majority concluded that discussion of politics, with which the armbands were consistent, was part of schools' educational mission, both in the short run and in developing democratic citizens.

The case upheld somewhat similar issues in MEYER V. NEBRASKA, 262 U.S. 390 (1923), and *Bartels v. Iowa*, 262 U.S. 404 (1923), where courts held that the due process clause of the Fourteenth Amendment prevented states from encroaching on student liberty by forbidding the teaching of foreign languages. The majority quoted Mr. Justice Blackman in *Keyishian v. Board of Regents*, 385 U.S. 589, 603 (1967), who wrote,

> The vigilant protection of constitutional freedoms is nowhere more vital than in the community of American schools. [*Shelton v. Tucker*, 364 U.S. 479, at 487.] The classroom is peculiarly the 'marketplace of ideas.' The Nation's future depends upon leaders trained through wide exposure to that robust exchange of ideas which discovers truth 'out of a multitude of tongues, [rather] than through any kind of authoritative selection.'"

In *Tinker,* the court also extended protections of student speech to the wearing of buttons, flags, decals, or other badges of SYMBOLIC SPEECH or expression, so long as this does not interfere with the orderly process of the school or with the rights of others. For example, the Court held in this case that the distribution of materials on school property must be in conformity with existing rules.

In their dissents, Justice Hugo BLACK noted that he did not agree with all of the Court's conclusions about free speech, which was not disruptive to discipline in general but took the students' mind off their work. A more comprehensive dissent came from Justice John Marshall HARLAN who held that the burden of proof was on the plaintiffs to disprove the presumption that school authorities were not acting in good faith, such as by suppressing an unpopular viewpoint. Unlike the Court majority, he saw no evidence that this was so.

However, in HAZELWOOD SCHOOL DISTRICT V. KUHLMEIER, 484 U.S. 260, 108 S. Ct. 562 98 L.Ed 592 (1988), the Court noted that a student-run press could still be censored by school authorities, even though it is more directly like speech, because, unlike these passive examples, this active form of speech could be disruptive in particular instances.

For more information: Farish, Leah. *Tinker v. Des Moines: Student Protest.* Berkeley Heights, N.J.: Enslow, 1997; Johnson, John W. *The Struggle for Student Rights:* Tinker v. Des Moines *and the 1960s.* Lawrence: University Press of Kansas, 1997.

—Henry F. Carey

Title IX

Title IX, enacted as part of the Education Amendments of 1972, provides that "No person in the United States shall, on the basis of sex, be excluded from participation in, be denied the benefits of, or be subjected to discrimination under any education program or activity receiving Federal financial assistance."

Title IX applies to both public and private schools, from kindergarten through graduate school, so long as the educational program receives any form of federal funding. The then Department of Health, Education and Welfare (HEW)—which is today's Department of Education (DOE)—was charged with regulating Title IX, and the Office for Civil Rights (OCR) was charged with enforcing its provisions. In 1975 HEW issued a set of regulations that made Title IX applicable to a range of areas within education, including student recruitment, admissions, course offerings, housing, financial aid, and athletics.

The history of Title IX and the Supreme Court essentially begins with the ruling in *Cannon v. University of Chicago*, 441 U.S. 677 (1979). Here, the Court said that Title IX is enforceable through an implied private right of action, thereby permitting individuals to bring lawsuits under the statute. However, since Title IX did not explicitly provide for the availability of compensatory damages, its effectiveness was limited. The Supreme Court's decision in GROVE CITY COLLEGE V. BELL, 465 U.S. 555 (1984), further limited the scope of Title IX. Here, the Court interpreted the statue to authorize the withholding of funds only from specific programs that discriminated against women, rather than from the educational institution as a whole. In 1988 Congress passed the Civil Rights Restoration Act, which overrode the Court's ruling in GROVE CITY. It was not until *Franklin v. Gwinnett County Public Schools*, 503 U.S. 60 (1992), that the Court ruled that students in schools receiving federal funds may sue for and win damages in SEXUAL DISCRIMINATION cases under Title IX.

Title IX has also been extended to cases involving SEXUAL HARASSMENT within schools. *Gebser v. Lago Vista Independent School District*, 524 U.S. 274 (1998), held that damages for student-teacher sexual harassment cannot be recovered unless school officials have actual notice of, and are "deliberately indifferent" to, the teacher's conduct. In *Davis v. Monroe County Board of Education*, 526 U.S. 629 (1999), the Court held that, in cases of student-on-student sexual harassment, individuals may recover damages when the educational institution receiving federal funding has actual knowledge of and is deliberately indifferent to the harassment, and where the harassment is so severe, pervasive, and offensive that it deprives individuals of educational opportunities.

Even though Title IX is applicable to many areas within education, such as student recruitment and admissions, today it has become predominantly associated with athletics. In 1979 HEW issued a Policy Interpretation in order to assess educational institutions' compliance with Title IX in the realm of athletics. Schools could demonstrate compliance if they met any one of the following criteria: (1) whether athletic opportunities for male and female students are "provided in numbers substantially proportionate to their respective enrollments"; (2) whether the institution can demonstrate a continuing expansion of their programs to match the developing interest of the members of the underrepresented sex; (3) whether it can be shown that current programs have fully accommodated "the interest and abilities" of the underrepresented sex.

One of the most well-known cases involving Title IX and athletics is a federal appeals court ruling in *Cohen v. Brown University*, 101 F.3d 155 (1st Cir. 1996). The court held that Brown, which had eliminated some women's sports teams, had violated Title IX, as women made up 51 percent of the student body but only 39 percent of all Brown's athletes. Notably, regarding the third prong of the test for Title IX compliance, the court reasoned that women could not be presumed to be less interested than men in athletic participation, thereby leaving proportionality as the primary indicator of Title IX compliance. The Supreme Court decided not to hear Brown's APPEAL, so the ruling remains as nonbinding legal PRECEDENT.

Title IX has received mixed support from the American public. Its proponents argue that the legislation has been essential for the movement toward gender equity in education, while its critics argue that it is essentially a quota system, particularly as applied to athletic programs, and is discriminatory against men. Moreover, the debate over the implementation of Title IX has generated much controversy and spurred costly legal action in recent years. Therefore, Title IX remains an important battleground in the fight for women's equality, and there exists potential for future reform of its provisions.

For more information: Gavora, Jessica. *Tilting the Playing Field: Schools, Sports, Sex and Title IX.* San Francisco, Calif.: Encounter Books, 2002.

—Jill Abraham

Title VII of the Civil Rights Act of 1964

Title VII of the CIVIL RIGHTS ACT OF 1964 prohibits discrimination by employers on the basis of race, color, RELIGION, sex, or national origin. Later amendments to Title VII have expanded its scope to include pregnant and disabled workers as protected classes, as well. The provisions of this law apply to labor unions; public employers at the municipal, state, or federal levels; employment agencies; and organizations that employ 15 or more people. As part of Title VII, Congress created the EQUAL EMPLOYMENT OPPORTUNITY COMMISSION (EEOC) to provide for enforcement.

The Civil Rights Act of 1964 is widely considered the most important federal legislation for protecting CITIZENSHIP rights since Reconstruction. This law empowered the United States DEPARTMENT OF JUSTICE with extensive investigatory rights and enabled it to prosecute cases of discrimination. While a large number of federal and state laws have been passed to fight employment discrimination, Title VII has had the greatest impact.

Originally introduced to Congress in 1963, the bill was suspended in a purgatory of floor and committee debate. Five days after the assassination of President John F. Kennedy, President Lyndon Johnson made his first presidential address in a joint session of Congress. In that address, he challenged Congress to pass this law as a memorial to President Kennedy, which Congress quickly did.

Since 1964, women and minority groups have been able to use Title VII as their primary statutory support in challenging discriminatory employment practices in the courts. While the statute does not clearly define discrimination, the federal courts have developed two liability classifications—disparate treatment and disparate impact. These approaches to demonstrating discrimination were first articulated by the Supreme Court in a footnote to a RACIAL DISCRIMINATION case, *International Brotherhood of Teamsters v. United States*, 431 U.S. 324 (1977).

> "Disparate treatment". . . . is the most easily understood type of discrimination. The employer simply treats some people less favorably than others because of their race, color, religion, sex, or national origin. Proof of discriminatory motive is critical, although it can in some situations may be distinguished from claims that stress "disparate impact." The latter involve employment practices that are facially neutral in their treatment of different groups but that in fact fall more harshly on one

group than another and cannot be justified by business necessity. Proof of discriminatory motive, we have held, is not required under disparate impact theory.

These two theories of discrimination immediately place the burden on the employee to demonstrate that they legitimately fit into one of the two classification schemes. In these cases, the employee must initially demonstrate a prima facie case of discrimination, this allows the court to eliminate the most common nondiscriminatory reasons for the disparate treatment or action. To do this under Title VII, the employee must demonstrate the claimed discrimination as being either intentional (disparate treatment) or as a neutral policy that has "an adverse impact on a specific class because of class members' race, religion, color, sex, national origin, or pregnancy" (disparate impact). After this prima facie case has been made, an employer has two opportunities for demonstrating a legitimate reason for engaging in discriminating behavior: a business necessity (the discrimination is necessary for the business to exist) or a bona fide occupational qualification defense (BFOQ) where the nature of the job excludes the protected class.

Because the purpose of Title VII was to increase opportunities for women and minorities in jobs from which they had been traditionally excluded, the Supreme Court has interpreted this statute as allowing employer-created AFFIRMATIVE ACTION programs [UNITED STEELWORKERS V. WEBER, 443 U.S. 193 (1971); Johnson v. Transportation Agency of Santa Clara, 480 U.S. 616 (1987)], and court-imposed hiring and promotion programs to remedy past discrimination [United States v. Paradise, 480 U.S. 149 (1987)]. Sexual discrimination, prohibited by Title VII, has been interpreted by the Supreme Court to include SEXUAL HARASSMENT in the workplace. Such harassment includes the creation of a hostile work environment in which an employer does not protect the employee from behavior so sexually objectionable that a reasonable person would find it difficult to be successful [HARRIS V. FORKLIFT SYSTEMS, INC., 510 U.S. 17 (1993)], or for quid pro quo discrimination where sexual actions are demanded in exchange for the giving or withholding of employee benefits such as promotion or employment.

In 1991 Congress passed a new Civil Rights Act in response to a series of Supreme Court decisions that had weakened the effectiveness of Title VII. These decisions had shifted the burden of discriminatory proof from the employer (who had to demonstrate they had committed no illegal discrimination) to the employee (who had to demonstrate there was illegal discrimination). The Civil Rights Act of 1991 reversed the rulings of five 1989 Supreme Court cases; the text of the law itself noted that this "legislation is necessary to provide additional protections against unlawful discrimination in employment."

For more information: Davis, Abraham L., and Barbara Luck Graham. *The Supreme Court, Race, and Civil Rights.* Thousand Oaks, Calif.: Sage, 1995; Mezey, Susan Gluck. *Elusive Equality: Women's Rights, Public Policy, and the Law.* Boulder, Colo.: Lynne Rienner, 2003; Zimmer, Michael J., Charles A. Sullivan, Richard F. Richards, and Deborah A. Calloway. *Cases and Material on Employment Discrimination.* 5th ed. New York: Aspen Law and Business, 2000.

—Michelle Donaldson Deardorff

tobacco liability

The liability of tobacco companies for damages as a result of people smoking is a major source of legal controversy.

After the publication of the 1964 U.S. surgeon general's report, a document that definitively linked cigarette smoking with lung cancer and other terminal diseases, both the tobacco companies and the general public became very eager to determine the U.S. Supreme Court's stance on this matter. If the Court found that the tobacco companies were liable for damages due to smoking-related injuries, ill smokers and their families would have a basis for suing the cigarette manufacturers to recover lost compensation and medical expenses. However, a deluge of similar lawsuits could force the companies into BANKRUPTCY.

In 1969, for the first time ever, the Court found tobacco companies liable for injuries caused by cigarettes. By refusing to hear an APPEAL from a lower court decision, the Court demonstrated its agreement with the trial court's determination that cigarettes were inherently dangerous when used for their intended purpose in *Banzhaf v. Federal Communications Commission,* 405 F.2d 1082 (1968); cert. den., 396 U.S. 842 (1969).

During the 1970s, while Congress progressively increased the warnings required on cigarette packaging and in advertisements, the Court was also hard at work. In its 1975 decision in *U.S. v. Park,* 421 U.S. 658, the Court held that if a manufacturer knows or suspects that one of its products presents some type of hazard, a consumer injured by the product has the right to sue the manufacturer for monetary damages.

During the 1980s, thousands of ill smokers and/or their families throughout the United States sued cigarette manufacturers. The outcomes of these cases were inconsistent, since some courts interpreted the federal law that mandated warning labels for cigarette packaging as providing cigarette manufacturers with immunity from ill smokers' personal injury and/or product liability cases based on state law. Finally, in *CIPOLLONE V. LIGGETT GROUP,* 505 U.S. 504 (1992), the Court established a consistent, national standard regarding the rights of injured smokers and their families, cigarette manufacturers, and any other parties involved in similar lawsuits in the future.

The federal law allows ill smokers or their representatives to sue cigarette manufacturers under state products liability laws. However, the federal labeling laws prohibit individuals from suing cigarette manufacturers under state laws regulating advertising of cigarettes. The Court also stated that for cases pertaining to smoking-related injuries, decisions regarding amount and recipients of monetary damages (if any) are best decided in the trial courts.

States' product liability laws are fairly standard throughout the United States. If a manufacturer knew or suspected that one of its products presented some type of hazard and an individual was harmed by such a hazard, the manufacturer is susceptible to lawsuits for monetary damages. To protect itself from such lawsuits, the manufacturer must be absolutely certain that the hazard is removed from the product prior to marketing it, or provide easy-to-find, clearly written and/or diagrammed, highly precise information about the hazard so that consumers will be aware of the magnitude and type of risk they will assume when using the product. Most states' products liability or consumer protection laws also allow injured individuals to sue manufacturers that failed to disclose SCIENTIFIC EVIDENCE linking cigarette smoking to lung cancer and circulatory system diseases or conspired with other companies to misrepresent or conceal material facts concerning the health hazards of smoking.

Since *Cipollone,* the Court has continued to support the right of injured smokers to sue cigarette manufacturers under state product liability statutes. Additionally, in agreements with the attorneys general of all 50 states, the major cigarette manufacturers have admitted withholding scientific evidence of detrimental health effects of smoking and lying to the public about links between smoking and life-threatening diseases, and they have paid each state millions of dollars to settle the states' claims for health-care costs necessitated by smoking.

Since 1997, the Court has been careful to avoid intervention in tobacco cases. For instance, in *U.S. Food and Drug Administration v. Brown and Williamson,* 529 U.S. 120 (2000), the Court prevented the Food and Drug Administration (FDA) from imposing stringent, new regulations on tobacco products. The Court rejected the FDA's argument that the Food, Drug, and Cosmetic Act (FDCA) that created the FDA would classify nicotine as a drug and cigarettes as drug-administering devices. FDA could claim regulatory authority over tobacco products only if Congress had passed a law giving the agency that power. Instead, specific provisions of the FDCA denied FDA the power to regulate tobacco.

The Court's position with respect to cigarette smoking has remained virtually unchanged since the 1969 declaration that this practice was inherently hazardous. In *Cipollone,* the Court said that cigarettes were the only currently legal, generally available product in the United States that causes serious health problems when used as the manufacturer intended. Hence, the availability of cigarettes should continue only if those who profit from manufacturing, advertising, or selling cigarettes are very cautious about the manner in which they present this product to the public. The Court's policy statement in *Cipollone* served as a warning to cigarette manufacturers that their continued existence is dependent upon strict compliance with all federal and state statutes and common law.

For more information: Centers for Disease Control and Prevention. "Tobacco Overview." U.S. Department of Health and Human Services. Available online. URL: http://www.cdc.gov/tobacco/overview/chron96.htm. Downloaded May 20, 2004.

—Beth S. Swartz

Toyota Motors v. Williams, 534 U.S. 184 (2002)

In *Toyota Motors v. Williams,* the Supreme Court ruled that carpal tunnel syndrome was not a disability under the Americans with Disabilities Act (ADA) and that an employer did not have to make special accommodations for individuals with this ailment.

Specifically the Court addressed the issue of what constitutes a "major life activity" that has been "substantially limited" for purposes of recovery under the ADA. Williams was an employee of Toyota's automotive assembly plant in Kentucky, beginning her employment in August 1990. Eventually work-related injuries, bilateral carpal tunnel syndrome and bilateral tendonitis, led to a workers compensation recovery and Williams returned to work with other duties. Her new duties were altered, leading to additional injuries. Eventually Williams's employment was terminated. She filed suit against Toyota, making claims for recovery under the ADA, among other statutes, asserting that her disabilities sustained while working for Toyota substantially limited her ability to perform manual tasks, housekeeping, gardening, playing with her children, lifting and working, all of which she identified as major life activities.

The district court rejected her claims for disability, a decision reversed by the Sixth Circuit. The Sixth Circuit reasoned that in order to prove her case the petitioner had to show she could not perform a "class of manual activities associated with her work," and this she had done.

Writing for a unanimous Court, Justice O'CONNOR reversed the Sixth Circuit, holding that it erred in focusing upon Williams's ability to perform the manual tasks associated with her job. Rather, the Court directed that the focus should be upon whether there has been a substantial limitation to major life activities, that is, those tasks central to most people's daily lives (e.g., bathing, dressing, housework, etc.) and not simply upon the requirements of a specific occupation.

The Sixth Circuit had ruled that Ms. Williams was disabled and substantially limited in performing manual tasks associated with her assembly line job but disregarded evidence that Williams could tend to her personal hygiene and perform household chores. The Sixth Circuit had also ruled that Williams was entitled to partial SUMMARY JUDGMENT.

Justice O'Connor argued that this was inappropriate. The Sixth Circuit should not have considered only Williams's ability to do the specialized manual work associated with her assembly job as sufficient proof that she was substantially limited to performing manual tasks and should not have granted partial summary judgment.

The importance of this case is that the Supreme Court's decision substantially raises the bar and makes it more difficult for workers to prove disabilities.

For more information: Americans with Disabilities Act. "Information and Technical Assistance on the Americans with Disabilities Act." U.S. Department of Justice (2004). Available online. URL: http://www.usdoj.gov/crt/ada/adahom1.htm. Downloaded May 20, 2004; National Organization on Disability. Available online. URL: http://www.nod. org.

—Charlsey T. Baumeier

treaties

Treaties are any international agreements, whether called a Treaty (e.g., Strategic Arms Limitation Treaty), Covenant (e.g., the International Covenant on Civil and Political Rights), Pact (e.g., Kellogg-Brian Pact), Protocol (1977 Geneva Protocols to the 1949 Geneva Conventions), Convention (e.g., Genocide Convention), or agreement (Reagan-Duvalier interdiction agreement). All of these terms are synonyms in international law (though not in U.S. law, see below).

Treaties may be multilateral (regional or universal, typically) or bilateral (between two countries, the more common type). Bilateral treaties tend to be negotiated by the foreign ministries of two or a few more countries. Multilateral treaties are usually negotiated through the auspices of an international organization like the UN or the World Health Organization and/or can result from a convention of states. An example of a multilateral treaty combining both processes was the International Criminal Court (ICC) statute, which convened a conference of states in Rome in 1998, but which held UN-managed preparatory

commissions during several years both before and after the Rome conference. Bilateral treaties generally state when the treaty will bind the two countries. Multilateral treaties usually state how many treaties must ratify a treaty before it comes into force. The ICC came into force on the fourth anniversary of the Rome conference on July 1, 2002, after 60 countries had ratified it. As of Nov. 28, 2003, 93 countries had ratified this treaty.

Treaties are one of the four main sources of international law, the other important one being custom, as well as peremptory norms, and judicial rulings and teachings [Article 38 (1) of the statute of the International Court of Justice]. The rules on using and interpreting treaties come from a treaty, the Vienna Convention on the Law of Treaties [155 UN Treaty Series, 331, May 23, 1969]. Though the United States has not ratified this treaty, the provisions of this Vienna Convention are generally regarded as binding under customary international law.

Generally, states are under no obligation to enter into treaties. Nor is there any prejudice for or against states ratifying treaties with reservations, which are qualifications or exceptions on the enforceability in the ratifying country to particular provisions in a given treaty [Article 2 (1) (d) of the Vienna Convention]. However, a reservation is not permitted in treaties which expressly forbid reservations, such as the Law of the Sea Treaty, the statute of the ICC, and the proposed Framework Convention for Tobacco Control. Such restrictions often induce countries like the United States not to ratify them, as in the case of these three treaties. Reservations also cannot be so broad as to defeat the overall purpose of a treaty.

Treaties are binding because of the freely granted consent conferred to the other states. The Latin dictum *Pacta sunt servanda* is said to apply: that states must fulfill their legal obligations. Article 26 of the Vienna Convention asserts that "(E)very treaty in force is binding upon the parties to it and must be performed by them in good faith." This is true, it is argued by one school of thought, even if it subsequently changes its mind about whether to feel bound by it. However, the United States has frequently altered its commitment to treaties, such as withdrawing from the compulsory jurisdiction of the International Court of Justice [Article 36 (2)], the "optional clause" of its statute. Thus, another view is that under customary international law, the meaning of treaties themselves can evolve if there is sufficient state practice and a sense of legal obligation to sanction this change.

Thus, the meaning of Article 2 (7) of the UN Charter has evolved since that treaty came into force in 1945. It reads, "Nothing contained in the present Charter shall authorize the United Nations to intervene in matters which are essentially within the domestic jurisdiction of any state." However, human rights have come to be "internationalized," that is, regarded, at least in terms of criticizing other states, as no longer inherently domestic issues. However, remedies for human rights violations have not been internationalized under this treaty provision.

Because of the ambiguity of so many treaty provisions, and the absence on most issues of definitive interpretations from authoritative courts and the division of academic opinion, treaties cannot be said to impose law as such. Rather, they are indications of what that law is. Reference to other sources of international law, especially customary law, becomes necessary to ascertain what rules in treaties and what interpretation in them should be given. Of course, this opens up many issues and ambiguities for the comprehension and enforcement of treaties.

A treaty in the United States can have a specific meaning distinct from the generic one above. It is an international agreement requiring the advice and consent of the U.S. Senate. Furthermore, while Article Six of the U.S. Constitution ostensibly makes treaties the "supreme law" of the United States, the Court has not taken that interpretation literally, often assuming that obligations in treaties are often not "self-executing" and therefore require enabling legislation to be binding under U.S. law. (By contrast, the Court has often held that customary international law, when definable, is binding).

Since 1829, the Court under Chief Justice MARSHALL and later under Justice STORY, has distinguished between self-executing, which are seen as contracts with binding promises exchanged, and non-self-executing treaties, which require congressional interpretation. This sometimes referred to the distinction between self-fulfilling and declaratory treaties. The first specify the obligations of the ratifying state. The second only represent statements of principle.

Article VI of the U.S. Constitution makes treaties "the supreme law" of the United States. Though there is little or no evidence of any original intent by the framers to make such a distinction, "originalist" justices today like Justices Rehnquist, SCALIA, and THOMAS, ignore the clear meaning of Article VI, as do most of the remaining justices. While the judges support the validity of the distinction, there is disagreement over whether a treaty fits into either category, or even whether what parts of a treaty do. This leaves the other country (countries) without a clear understanding of what commitments the United States makes in signing treaties, especially if the content is not determined in the ratification process and requires enabling legislation. When provisions or an entire treaty is held to be not self-executing, enabling legislation is required to make claims actionable in U.S. courts. The Court held in *Sale v. the Haitian Centers Council,* 509 U.S. 918; 113 S. Ct. 3028 (1993), that the United Nations Protocol Relating to the Status of Refugees (1967) was only a nonbinding declaration of principles, in this case against non-*refoulement,* the forced return of refugees with a well-founded fear of persecution, to their countries. Instead, the Court held that the treaty had no extraterritorial jurisdiction, and the U.S. Coast Guard was free to continue interdicting Haitian boat people inside the Haitian territorial sea.

Since World War II, the United States has been reluctant to ratify many important treaties. It did not ratify the Genocide Convention until 1988, 40 years after the December 9, 1948, promulgation of that treaty for ratification at the UN. President Ronald Reagan apparently wanted to atone for his 1985 visit, prior to the Bonn summit, to lay a wreath at the Bitburg Cemetery, where some Nazi special forces were buried. (He had wanted to cancel the visit, but West German Chancellor Helmut Kohl was afraid of a furor in Germany if the visit was cancelled.) The most important human rights treaty, the International Covenant on Civil and Political Rights, was not ratified by the U.S. Senate until 1992 in the final year of President George H. W. Bush's presidency. The United States has never ratified the Kyoto Protocol, the ICC, the Convention on the Elimination of Discrimination against Women, the Children's Convention, and the International Covenant on Economic, Social and Cultural Rights. With such limited participation in treaties, the United States has the capability to undermine the efficacy of the system of multilateral treaties and thus the rule of international law.

When the United States ratified one of the most important human rights treaties, the International Covenant on Civil and Political Rights, it imposed a reservation that held the treaty not to be self-executing. More recently, the Court seems to be assuming that treaties, particularly in human rights, are assumed to be non-self-executing, even when there is no reservation stating such. This Court view is at odds with conventional views of international law.

The Clinton administration ultimately signed the ICC statute on Dec. 31, 2000, but never submitted it to the Senate for ratification. It had opposed the ICC treaty because a state like the United States could theoretically be subjected to this treaty, even if that state had not ratified it. The Bush administration opposed the ICC treaty on more general grounds and took the unprecedented step of "unsigning" a treaty. Then, the Bush administration initiated dozens of bilateral treaties with countries receiving U.S. foreign aid, which bound the recipient country to promise never to extradite a U.S. soldier or official to the ICC. Many of these countries, however, have not ratified these agreements signed with the United States. The question of whether so many countries that have ratified the ICC treaty could interject a provision is open to debate.

For more information: Aust, Anthony. *Modern Treaty Law and Practice*. Cambridge: Cambridge University Press, 2000; International Criminal Court. Available online. URL: http://www.icc-cpi.int/php/show.php?id=home&l=EN. Downloaded May 20, 2004; Reuter, Paul. *Introduction to the Law of Treaties*. London: Kegan Paul, 1995.

—Henry F. Carey

U

unenumerated rights

Unenumerated rights are rights not explicitly stated in the text of the Constitution. The justices of the Supreme Court have implied them by reviewing the language and history of the BILL OF RIGHTS along with the Fourteenth Amendment. Unenumerated rights are controversial because interpretations of the Constitution vary among the justices.

The controversy primarily revolves around the ambiguity of the NINTH AMENDMENT: "The enumeration, in the Constitution, of certain rights, shall not be construed to deny or disparage others retained by the people." The resulting ambiguity is twofold. On the one hand, it can be read as protecting individual liberties that are not explicitly stated in the first Eight Amendments. On the other hand, it can be read as protecting the states from intrusion if the national government were to assume powers not explicitly delegated to it by the Constitution. The Tenth Amendment furthers this second interpretation by stating, "The powers not delegated to the United States by the Constitution, nor prohibited by it to the States, are reserved to the States respectively, or to the people." Unfortunately, the framers did not provide a distinction that clarified the meaning of the Ninth Amendment.

The Supreme Court of the United States first gave a judicial interpretation of the Ninth Amendment in *GRIS-WOLD V. CONNECTICUT*, 381 U.S. 479 (1965). The case involved the opening of a birth control clinic in 1961 in the state of Connecticut, which at that time prohibited the use of birth control. Estelle Griswold was arrested for giving CONTRACEPTIVES to a married couple. Griswold's attorney challenged the Connecticut law by arguing that it intruded upon an individual's privacy. The Court ruled in favor of Griswold, ruling that the restriction on the use of contraceptives by married couples violated their right to privacy. The Court found this unenumerated right within the meaning of the First, Third, Fourth, Fifth, Ninth, and Fourteenth Amendments.

A concurring opinion written by Justice Goldberg gave an interpretation of the Ninth Amendment, "The language and history of the Ninth Amendment reveal that the Framers of the Constitution believed that there are FUNDAMENTAL RIGHTS, protected from government infringement, which exist alongside those fundamental rights specifically mentioned in the first eight constitutional amendments." Furthermore, "It was proffered to quiet expressed fears that a bill of specifically enumerated rights could not be sufficiently broad to cover all essential rights and that the specific mention of certain rights would be interpreted as a denial that others were protected. . . ." Justice Goldberg concluded that the right to privacy is a fundamental right belonging to the people according to the meaning of the Ninth Amendment. This case created a constitutional right to privacy.

The Court applied the right to privacy rule in *Griswold* to succeeding cases, most famously in *ROE V. WADE*, 410 U.S. 113 (1973). *Roe* involved a Texas law making it illegal to obtain an abortion unless the mother's life was at risk. At the district court level, a three-judge panel ruled that the Texas law violated the Ninth Amendment right to privacy. The Court agreed to hear the case on APPEAL. It held that the right to privacy protects the decision to have an abortion. The Court majority opinion found that the due process clause of the Fourteenth Amendment protects this right, not necessarily the Ninth Amendment.

Roe is important for unenumerated rights because the Constitution does not explicitly state a right to privacy. The Court opinion explains that the right stems from the First, Fourth, Fifth, Ninth, and Fourteenth Amendments. Specifically, the Court favored the Fourteenth Amendment's concept of liberty.

Recently, the Supreme Court of Massachusetts held that withholding the benefits of marriage to couples of the same sex violated the Massachusetts Constitution. No matter how this issue is eventually resolved, it is another example of the development of an unenumerated right.

For more information: Massey, Calvin R. *Silent Rights: The Ninth Amendment and the Constitution's Unenumerated Rights.* Philadelphia, Pa.: Temple University Press, 1995.

—Matthew R. Doyle

United Public Workers of America v. Mitchell, 330 U.S. 75 (1947)

In *United Public Workers of America v. Mitchell,* the U.S. Supreme Court held that Section 9(a) of the Hatch Act, which prohibits federal executive officers and employees from taking an active part in political management or campaigns, did not violate the Constitution. George P. Poole, a roller at the U.S. Mint in Philadelphia, Pennsylvania, had served at the 1940 general election as the ward executive committeeman for the Democratic Party in Philadelphia. The Civil Service Commission entered a proposed order for his discharge, alleging a violation of the Hatch Act. In response, Poole charged that the act deprived him of his constitutional rights under the First, Ninth, and Tenth Amendments and the due process clause and was therefore void.

The Court acknowledged at the outset that the restriction placed on civil servants by the Hatch Act resulted in "a measure of interference" with the rights ordinarily secured by the Constitution but also asserted that "these fundamental human rights are not absolutes." [*United Public Workers,* 330 U.S. at 95.] For guidance, the Court looked to two precedents. In *Ex parte Curtis,* 106 U.S. 371 (1882), a case decided one year after the assassination of President Garfield by a partisan office seeker, the Court had upheld a law prohibiting federal employees who were not appointed by the president and confirmed by the Senate from giving money to or receiving money from other federal employees for political purposes. According to the Court, the rule set forth in *Ex parte Curtis* was that Congress may, "within reasonable limits," regulate the political activities of federal employees "as it might deem necessary." [*United Public Workers,* 330 U.S. at 96.] Similarly, in *United States v. Wurzbach,* 280 U.S. 396 (1930), the Court had affirmed the constitutionality of an act that prohibited members of Congress from receiving political contributions from federal employees.

In light of these cases, the Court, speaking through Justice Reed, reasoned that if Congress had the constitutional power to regulate political contributions of money by federal employees, it also had the power to regulate their "political contributions of energy." [*United Public Workers,* 330 U.S. at 98.] Deferring to the judgment of Congress, the Court noted the dangers with which the political activity of federal employees threatened the efficiency and integrity of the public administration. Promotions might be awarded not on the basis of official performance but as rewards for partisanship. Government favor might be exercised on political grounds. Political parties might be less devoted to the public good, or a one-party system might evolve. The Court concluded that the Constitution does not prevent Congress from addressing "what many . . . believe is a material threat to the democratic system." [*United Public Workers,* 330 U.S. at 99.]

The Court rejected the arguments that the Hatch Act is more restrictive than necessary and that there is no justification for regulating industrial workers, such as a roller at the Mint, as well as administrative employees. On both counts the Court again deferred to Congress, stating that the reasonable judgment of Congress exercised in support of the public service, and not strict necessity, defines the scope of Congress's constitutional power over political activity. Distinctions between industrial and administrative employees were "all matters of detail for Congress." [*United Public Workers,* 330 U.S. at 102.] The Court would interfere only when a law regulating the political activity of federal employees "passes beyond the general existing conception of governmental power." [*United Public Workers,* 330 U.S. at 102.]

Justices BLACK and DOUGLAS dissented in separate opinions. Justice Black argued that laws curtailing First Amendment freedoms should not be upheld unless they are "narrowly drawn . . . to prevent a grave and imminent danger to the public." [*United Public Workers,* 330 U.S. at 110.] In his view, the Hatch Act, by depriving the public of the political participation, interest, and activity of three million federal employees, violated this rule and punished a whole class of citizens to prevent the misdeeds of a few. Justice Douglas distinguished administrative employees, who influence policy and interact with the public, from industrial workers. Although partisanship among industrial workers in the executive department might also be harmful—they may be mobilized into a political machine, or promotion may depend on loyalty to a party—the dangers are fewer and of a different kind than those associated with administrative employees. Justice Douglas concluded that, because legislation restricting constitutional rights ought to be narrowly drawn, only prohibitions selectively aimed at specific abuses would, in respect to the industrial workers of the government, be constitutional.

For more information: Schultz, David, and Robert Maranto. *The Politics of Civil Service Reform.* New York: Peter Lang, 1998.

—Andy V. Bardos
—Nicole M. James

United States Constitution

Drafted in convention in 1787 and subsequently ratified by conventions called within each of the states, the U.S. Constitution was a major departure from the previous government under the Articles of Confederation, under which states exercised primary sovereignty. In place of the unicameral Congress under the Articles of Confederation, the delegates settled on a bicameral Congress and balanced it against two coordinate branches, the executive and the judicial. The first three articles of the Constitution respectively outline the organization and powers of the legislative, executive, and judicial branches.

In listing the powers of the president, Article II, Section 2 assigns the executive the power to appoint judges with the advice and consent of the Senate. The appointment and confirmation processes are extremely political, and the Senate has been far from a rubber stamp. The process resulted from a compromise at the Constitutional Convention between advocates of the Virginia Plan, who favored vesting appointment in Congress, and the New Jersey Plan, who wanted to vest this power in the executive.

Article III specifies that "the judicial power" of the United States "shall be vested in one supreme Court, and in such inferior Courts as the Congress may from time to time ordain and establish." The U.S. Supreme Court is thus the only court mentioned by name in the document (and the CHIEF JUSTICE, who is given authorization in Article I, Section 3 to preside over impeachment trials of the President, is the only judge so designated). The Constitution does not specify how many justices there will be. This number has ranged from six to 10; Congress set the current number of nine (the chief and eight associates) just after the Civil War. Congress rejected the last major attempt to change this number—Franklin D. Roosevelt's so-called COURT-PACKING PLAN of 1937—as a political ploy designed to fill it with members more sympathetic to the New Deal. In addition to serving as the symbolic head of the Court, the chief justice presides over conferences of the Court and, by tradition, writes or assigns opinions when in the majority.

The Constitution grants Congress the authority to establish lower federal courts but did not require that it did so (it could simply have relied on state courts). Significantly, the very first Congress, in which many delegates to the convention participated, settled on a system very much like that in existence today—that is, a system of lower district and circuit courts under the authority of the Supreme Court. Although lower court structures are subject to change, since the JUDICIARY ACT OF 1789, there have been three rungs on the federal ladder. U.S. district courts act as trial courts, and the circuit courts of appeal and the U.S. Supreme Court mostly hear appellate arguments. Cases may advance either up this ladder, or they may get to the Supreme Court from a state's highest court of appeal, generally designated its supreme court.

Article III attempts to protect the independence of judges in two fashions. First, it specifies that they serve "during good behavior," meaning until they die, resign, or are impeached and convicted. Convictions of impeachment require a two-thirds vote of the Senate. The Constitution specifically limits the grounds of impeachment in Article II, Section 4 to "Treason, Bribery, or other high Crimes and Misdemeanors." Although the latter phrase is vague, early precedents—most notably the unsuccessful impeachment trial of Justice Samuel CHASE during the Jefferson administration—indicate that political disagreements do not qualify. Second, the Constitution prohibits the salaries of judges from being lowered during their tenure. Recognizing that life tenure could be quite lengthy, the delegates to the Constitutional Convention wisely allowed, but did not require, Congress to raise judicial salaries.

Section 2 of Article III of the Constitution outlines the jurisdiction of federal courts, which extends to cases of both law and equity (two different areas of law developed in British). This jurisdiction is based on the parties to the suit or on the subject matter of the suit. Thus, to cite but a few examples, the federal judiciary is designated to hear cases involving ambassadors and disputes among the states as well as all cases arising under the Constitution or laws of the United States. Similarly, the Constitution grants the Supreme Court ORIGINAL JURISDICTION in a limited number of cases; it exercises appellate jurisdiction in all others.

Articles I and II outline minimal age, CITIZENSHIP, and residency requirements for members of the legislative and executive branches. Recognizing that the president would appoint and the Senate would confirm members of the judicial branch, Article III has no similar requirements for judges. Today, a law degree is considered a sine qua non for judicial service.

The Constitutional Convention rejected proposals to ally the president and members of the national judiciary in a Council of Revision with power to veto congressional laws. Although a number of delegates to the Constitutional Convention indicated that they expected the judiciary to exercise the power of JUDICIAL REVIEW, that is, the power to declare state and federal laws to be unconstitutional, the Constitution does not specify such a power. Such authority is consistent with the idea of a written Constitution superior to other laws and enforceable by a branch less immediately accountable to public opinion. In *MARBURY V. MADISON*, 1 Cranch (5 U.S.) 137 (1803), Chief Justice John MARSHALL convincingly argued that if the Supreme Court were to examine and interpret laws, it was reasonable for it to look both at the language of these laws and of the Constitution under which they were adopted.

The power to invalidate state laws is arguably a necessary concomitant to maintenance of a federal system. This latter power is further enhanced by the supremacy clause in the second paragraph of Article VI. This clause asserts the supremacy of "This Constitution, and the Laws of the United States which shall be made in Pursuance thereof; and all TREATIES made, or which shall be made, under the Authority of the United States" and binds state judges to the U.S. Constitution "any Thing in the Constitution of Laws of any State to the Contrary notwithstanding." The next paragraph binds all officeholders in the United States, including judges, to support the Constitution.

Many judicial powers have developed through legislation, PRECEDENT, and judicial assertions of authority. Consistent with the language of Article III, American courts have confined themselves to "cases and controversies," but as Alexis de Tocqueville observed in *Democracy in America,* there are few political questions in the United States that do not eventually find their way into court.

Today the Court rules in areas as diverse as FEDERALISM, the SEPARATION OF POWERS, the respective powers to be exercised by each of the three branches of government, the rights specified in the BILL OF RIGHTS, the Fourteenth Amendment, and in other constitutional amendments, and even over matters, like privacy and the right to travel, that, while not specifically listed in the Constitution, are thought to be implicit in other rights listed there. Arguably on firmest ground when it can site specific constitutional authority for its decisions, the Court has long since passed the stage where it confines itself to the interpretation of specific provisions.

For more information: Abraham, Henry J. *The Judicial Process.* 7th ed. New York: Oxford University Press, 1998; Vile, John R. *A Companion to the United States Constitution and Its Amendments.* 3rd ed. Westport, Conn.: Praeger, 2001.
—John R. Vile

United States Constitution, application overseas

The ideas for governance laid out by the UNITED STATES CONSTITUTION have been borrowed, adapted, and used in many diverse countries. Few documents have had as much impact on the governments of the world as the Constitution of the United States of America. In some cases the Constitution has been used directly as a template for other constitutions; in other cases the same philosophical ideas that influenced the founders who wrote the U.S. Constitution influenced the governments of other countries.

The most basic principles of the Constitution have been used in framing the constitutions of a majority of free countries. These principles are the rule of law and considering the constitution as the supreme law of the land. These concepts were especially important for Germany's constitution post-World War II. Germany also adopted provisions for equality for all people and the principles of fundamental human rights for all. Similarly, at the end of World War II, drafters of the Japanese and Korean constitutions imitated the U.S. Constitution in providing protection for individual rights.

The system of FEDERALISM prescribed by the Constitution has been adapted and used in several countries in the 20th century. Dual sovereignty of state and federal governments was a novel concept introduced in the United States Constitution in Article IV, Section 4. Although the original idea came from the French political philosopher Baron de Montesquieu, the implementation of a system of SEPARATION OF POWERS between the legislative, executive, and judicial branches of the government, rather than a parliamentary system such in Great Britain, is another widely copied American innovation.

Another uniqueness of the system was a result of a pragmatic compromise in the original Constitutional Convention—a legislature with a House of Representatives elected directly by citizens and a Senate originally representing the states. Russia, Switzerland, and Austria are major European nations that adopted the federal model, with Switzerland and Russia as the most decentralized. Switzerland also modeled its two-house legislature on the House and Senate.

The Constitution also provides for a presidential system of government which is distinguished from a parliamentary system in that the executive and legislative branches are separate. The presidential system has been adopted by Russia, South Korea, Mexico, and several nations in South America. The Constitution was also innovative in providing procedures by which it could be amended. This has been an important concept integrated into many constitutions written since the founding of the United States.

Finally, the United States also exported the idea of JUDICIAL REVIEW to evaluate conformity to the Constitution. In the American model the entire court system, the judicial branch, oversees the system of checks and balances; in the modified European model only one specialized court performs this function. Among the nations that follow the U.S. model are Sweden, Switzerland, Greece, Japan, and South Korea. The Japanese system of judicial review most closely resembles that of the United States. France, Germany, Spain, and Russia follow the European model by having a specialized court perform this function.

Whether directly or indirectly, the Constitution has had a widespread and lasting impact on the world. The Constitution has stood the test of time for more than 200 years. Nations continue to view it as a working model, borrowing, adapting, and implementing its basic principles.

For more information: Friedrich, Carl J. *The Impact of American Constitutionalism Abroad.* Boston: Boston University Press, 1967; Henkin, Louis, and Albert J. Rosenthal, eds. *Constitutionalism and Rights: The Influence of the United States Constitution Abroad.* New York: Columbia University Press, 1989.

—Mariya Chernyavskaya

U.S. Term Limits, Inc. v. Thornton, 514 U.S. 779 (1995)

In *U.S. Term Limits, Inc. v. Thornton*, the Supreme Court held that individual states cannot impose term limits on members of Congress, and that congressional term limits can be established only through an amendment to the federal Constitution.

The case arose in response to the term limits movement of the early 1990s. At the time, term limits advocates argued that incumbency advantages had produced too many entrenched, long-term members, and that Congress as a whole had become remote, unresponsive to changes in public opinion, and corrupt. The movement sought to replace long-term incumbents with "citizen legislators" by imposing limits of three terms (6 years) in the House of Representatives and two terms (12 years) in the Senate. During this period, public opinion polls consistently indicated widespread dissatisfaction with Congress and support for the term limits proposal.

The movement's problem was how to achieve this goal. Under the standard Article V process for constitutional amendment, Congress must approve an amendment by a two-thirds vote of both houses before it can be submitted to the states for ratification. It was unlikely Congress would ever approve a term limits amendment, in large part because most members of Congress had no desire to restrict their own careers.

Recognizing this problem, term limit activists, led by an organization called U.S. Term Limits, Inc., developed a strategy to impose limits on members of Congress state-by-state. Between 1990 and 1994, 23 states imposed term limits on members of Congress. In almost every instance, the limits were approved through direct voter initiatives, and often by large margins. After losing at the polls, term limits opponents turned to the courts to invalidate these measures. In Arkansas the state courts invalidated the voter-approved congressional term limits measure, and the Supreme Court granted certiorari to settle the constitutional question of whether individual states could establish term limits for members of Congress.

By a narrow 5 to 4 vote, the Court declared state-imposed limits on congressional terms unconstitutional. Writing for the majority, Justice STEVENS, joined by Justices SOUTER, BREYER, GINSBURG, and Kennedy, reasoned that term limit laws create new qualifications for congressional office. Article I of the Constitution lists only three qualifications for members of Congress—relating to age, residency, and CITIZENSHIP. Although the text does not *expressly* state that this list of qualifications is exclusive, the Court argued that such a reading is implied, based on the text and structure of the Constitution, the history surrounding its drafting and ratification, and the nature of federal system. To support this view, the Court argued that allowing individual states to impose separate term limit requirements on their congressional representatives would create a "patchwork" of state qualifications that would undermine "the uniformity and national character that the Framers envisioned and sought to ensure." [514 U.S. 779, 822.]

In a separate concurrence, Justice Anthony Kennedy asserted that citizens have a federal right of citizenship—a direct relationship with the national government, unmediated by the states. Citing Chief Justice John MARSHALL in *McCulloch v. Maryland,* 17 U.S. 316 (1819), Kennedy argued that this connection dates to the ratification of the Constitution, because it was the people, not the states, who established the national government. Consequently, Kennedy argued, states cannot encroach on the relationship between citizens and the national government by placing restrictions on the citizens' rights to select their national representatives. [514 U.S. 779, 845.]

The Court's decision provoked a vigorous and lengthy (88-page) dissent. Justice THOMAS, joined by Chief Justice REHNQUIST and Justices O'CONNOR and SCALIA, attacked the majority's interpretation of the constitutional text and history, as well as its view of the federal system. Asserting the priority of state citizenship over national citizenship, the dissenters contended that the people, acting through the states, have a reserved power, guaranteed by the Tenth Amendment, to impose term limits on their respective members of Congress. The dissenters emphasized that the Constitution nowhere prevents states from establishing additional eligibility requirements for members of Congress. "The Constitution is simply silent on this question," the dissenters argued. "And where the Constitution is silent, it raises no bar to action by the States or the people." [514 U.S. 779, 845.]

U.S. Term Limits, Inc. v. Thornton will be remembered for two things: First, it provided the Court an occasion to debate first principles regarding the nature of the federal system, but more consequentially, it reversed a massive grass-roots, state-level movement to limit congressional terms that, for better or worse, would have significantly altered the institutional arrangements and culture of Congress and the rest of the federal government.

For more information: Nagel, Robert F. "Theoretical and Constitutional Issues: The Term Limits Dissent: What Nerve." *Ariz. L. Rev.* 38 (Fall 1996): 843; Sullivan, Kathleen M. "Dueling Sovereignties: *U.S. Term Limits, Inc. v. Thornton.*" *Harv. L. Rev.* 109 (November 1995): 78.

—Kenneth P. Miller
—Sarah Bishop

United States Trust Co. v. New Jersey, 431 U.S. 1 (1977)

In *United States Trust Co. v. New Jersey,* for the first time in 40 years, the United States Supreme Court used the contract clause of the Constitution to strike down a state law. The decision can be seen as part of a gradual movement by a more conservative Court to breathe new life into the constitutional protection of economic rights.

Article I, Section 10, clause 1 of the Constitution provides that "No State shall . . . pass any Law impairing the Obligation of Contracts." While the meaning may seem plain on its face, the Supreme Court's interpretation of this clause has shifted over time. Early in the Court's history, the Supreme Court, under Chief Justice John MARSHALL, used the clause to strike down state action in such cases as *DARTMOUTH COLLEGE V. WOODWARD,* 4 Wheat. 518 (1819). Beginning with *HOME BUILDING & LOAN ASSOCIATION V. BLAISDELL,* 290 U.S. 398 (1934), the Court balanced the contract clause with state police power. The result was that the Court deferred to state legislative judgment in regulating their economic affairs.

In *United States Trust Co.,* the Court signaled a new shift away from the deferential approach of previous decades. The case involved a 1921 compact between the states of New York and New Jersey to form the Port Authority of New York. The Port Authority's mission was to develop and coordinate transportation and commerce. It was a private organization with funds coming primarily from investors. It could mortgage its facilities and pledge its revenues as payment for bonds issued to its investors. In 1962 the Port Authority bought the Hudson & Manhattan Railroad and agreed that it would no longer use its profits to finance rail expenditures. In 1974, with the United States in the midst of an energy crisis, the Port Authority looked to expand its system. Both state legislatures passed statutes repealing the previous agreements not to spend profits on rail. The U.S. Trust Co., which held the bonds secured by the profits, sued under the contracts clause.

In a 4 to 3 opinion, Justice Harry A. BLACKMUN wrote, "Mass transportation, energy conservation, and environmental protection are goals that are important and of legitimate public concern. Appellees contend that these goals are so important that any harm to bondholders from repeal

The George Washington Bridge, managed by the Port Authority of New York and New Jersey *(Library of Congress)*

of the 1962 covenant is greatly outweighed by the public benefit. We do not accept this invitation to engage in a utilitarian comparison of public benefit and private loss. . . . A state cannot refuse to meet its legitimate financial obligations simply because it would prefer to spend the money to promote the public good rather than the private welfare of its creditors." [*United States Trust Co. v. New Jersey,* 431 U.S. 1, 28–29 (1977).] The Court held that the state had other means of achieving its goals without repealing the covenant and said that circumstances had not changed so drastically between 1962 and 1974 as to make this repeal statute reasonable.

In dissent, Justice William J. BRENNAN wrote that the Court's decision was contrary to "decisions of the court [that] for at least a century have construed the Contract Clause largely to be powerless in binding a State to contracts limiting the authority of successor legislatures to enact laws in furtherance of the health, safety, and similar collective interests of the polity." [*United States Trust Co. v. New Jersey,* 431 U.S. 1, 33 (1977).] Brennan recognized and was critical of what he saw as the Court's conservative shift, "I might understand, though I do not accept, this revival of the Contract Clause were it in accordance with some coherent and constructive view of public policy. But elevation of the Clause to the status of regulator of the municipal bond market at the heavy price of frustration of sound legislative policymaking is as demonstrably unwise as it is unnecessary. The justification for today's decision, therefore, remains a mystery to me, and I respectfully dissent." [*United States Trust Co. v. New Jersey* 431 U.S. 1, 33 (1977).]

Did this case revitalize the contract clause? While the Court did make it more difficult for states to defend the abrogation of contracts they had made, thereby reducing the level of deference to state legislatures they had previously showed since *Blaisdell,* subsequent cases such as *Allied Structural Steel Co. v. Spannaus,* 438 U.S. 243 (1978), showed that the Court was unwilling to restore the contract clause to the prominence it had in the nation's early history under Chief Justice Marshall. Under Chief Justices Warren BURGER and William REHNQUIST, modern Courts have taken a more moderate approach.

For more information: Scheiber, Harry N., ed. *The State and Freedom of Contract.* Stanford, Calif.: Stanford University Press, 1999; Wright, Benjamin F. *The Contract Clause of the Constitution.* Cambridge, Mass.: Harvard University Press, 1938.

United States v. American Library Association, 123 S. Ct. 2297 (2003)

In the *United States v. American Library Association,* the United States Supreme Court upheld a federal law that required libraries receiving federal money to install Internet filters on their computer terminals. In reaching this decision, the Court rejected arguments that this was a form of censorship and a violation of the First Amendment free speech clause.

The invention and rise of the INTERNET AND THE WORLDWIDE WEB have had an important impact upon American society. One area where the impact has been most felt is in terms of the amount of information that is stored on or retrievable from the Web. Because government statistics, newspapers, and other public and private information are often available over the Web, the Internet has become an important research tool used by scholars, students, and members of the general public. The information available over the Web has also made it a great research tool that is used in libraries alongside more conventional ways to gather information, such as in hardbound encyclopedias and books.

However, in addition to all the valuable information found on the Web, a lot of information objectionable to many can also be found there. Among this material is that which is considered sexually explicit, pornographic, or obscene. The presence of this material creates two problems for libraries: First, children may be able to access this material on its terminals and, second, adults may wish to view it while at the library and this viewing could be visible to minors. In an effort to prevent minors from accessing sexually explicit material on the Web in libraries, Congress passed in 1999 the Child Internet Protection Act (CIPA) that barred libraries from receiving federal money unless they installed filters on their computer terminals that blocked images that constitute obscenity or which contained child pornography. Critics contended that the law

was a form of censorship, that it constituted a form of content-based regulation that violated the First Amendment, or that it was overly inclusive in that it restricted patron access to images that were protected by the Constitution. Several libraries objected to CIPA, and a three-judge district court ruled the filtering requirement unconstitutional in that it was a content-based restriction of the First Amendment. The Supreme Court accepted the case for review and upheld the law.

In writing for the Court, Chief Justice REHNQUIST acknowledged the important role that libraries played in American society in terms of facilitating learning and sharing knowledge. He described libraries as a traditional PUBLIC FORUM, meaning that they enjoyed broad First Amendment protection. However, Rehnquist argued that the Internet is not a traditional public forum and instead is simply an extension of the more traditional resources offered by the library. Thus, libraries may decide to permit patrons the use of computer terminals and the Internet much as they may decide which books to allow patrons to use when they make purchase selections. This means that in not buying certain books the library is not violating the First Amendment rights of its patrons, and therefore in not allowing access to certain Web sites it similarly is not infringing on the rights of its users.

More importantly, the Court, relying upon its decision in *SOUTH DAKOTA V. DOLE,* 483 U.S. 203 (1987), where it upheld the reception of highway funds upon states raising their minimum drinking age, contended that Congress has broad discretion under its spending power to condition that reception of federal money upon the compliance with specific mandates. Thus, in this case, Congress could require libraries to install the Internet filter even if it denied some patrons access to material that was constitutionally protected. If libraries did not wish to block access they could simply refuse the federal money.

In dissent, Justices STEVENS, SOUTER, and GINSBURG contended that CIPA did violate the First Amendment. They saw the law as compromising the traditional role of libraries as providing public access to ideas and information that is constitutionally protected. Thus, the law was overbroad and content-specific in its application.

As a result of this case many libraries around the country now block access to many sexually explicit Web sites. On the other hand, some libraries have refused federal money on principle, arguing that it is not their job to censor information that their patrons may wish to access.

For more information: Kalven, Harry, Jr. *A Worthy Tradition: Freedom of Speech in America.* New York: Harper and Row, 1988.

—David Schultz

United States v. Belmont, 301 U.S. 324 (1937)

In *United States v. Belmont,* the United States Supreme Court reversed the decisions made by both the U.S. District Court and the U.S. Circuit COURT OF APPEALS, granting the U.S. federal government the right to recover moneys deposited by a Russian corporation in a New York City bank. This case is important in that it reiterates the supremacy of a treaty, compact, or agreement between the president of the United States and foreign government officials. These external powers of the United States are to be exercised without regard to state laws or policies. In respect of all international negotiations and compacts, state lines disappear. This means that no state policy overrides or supersedes foreign relations established by the federal government.

United States v. Belmont pinpointed one major exception to our Constitution's Fifth Amendment, stating that private property shall not be taken without just compensation. The Supreme Court decided that our Constitution and its policies have no extraterritorial operation unless our own citizens are involved. The opinion of the Court stated that what another country has done in the way of taking over property of its nationals is not questionable in the courts of the United States. This means that it is not for the judicial branch of the U.S. government to decide whether or not another country has acted legally, regarding their citizens and the taking of their property.

Prior to 1918, Petrograd Metal Works, a Russian corporation, deposited a sum of money with August Belmont, a private banker doing business in New York City under the name of August Belmont & Co. In 1918 the Soviet government nationalized the corporation and divided all of its assets, including the funds in the deposit account. This meant that the deposit was now property of the Soviet government.

However, in November of 1933, President Roosevelt and representatives of the Soviet Union established diplomatic relations with each other in an effort to finalize claims and counterclaims between the two governments. In this international compact, it was agreed that the Soviet government would release and assign to the United States all amounts due to them from American nationals; therefore, the deposited sum of money now, arguably, belonged to the United States. In the years between, however, August Belmont died and the executors of his will would not respond to the United States' request for the money.

The two lower courts held that the deposit was within the state of New York, that it could not be considered intangible property within Soviet territory, and that the nationalization decree, if enforced, would put into effect an act of confiscation, violating the Fifth Amendment of the U.S. Constitution. These courts decided in favor of the respondents, ruling that a judgment for the United States would in fact be contrary to the controlling public policy of the state of New York. Further, the public policy of the United States would be infringed by such a judgment.

These rulings brought about two questions for the Court to consider. First: Was any policy of the state of New York being infringed upon? It was stated that the recognition and establishment of relations and agreements between the Soviet government and the president of the United States were all part of one transaction, resulting in an international compact. These negotiations were within the competence of the president and his agreements could not be doubted. Their answer was that no state policy can prevail against the international compact that was involved in this case. Moreover, the external powers of the United States are to be exercised without regard to state laws or policies. The supremacy of such (TREATIES, compacts, etc.) has been recognized since the days of our founding fathers. Mr. James Madison stated that if a treaty is not held superior to existing state laws, then the treaty would be ineffective in regards to uniformity.

Second: Was private property taken without just compensation? The Court again answered, no. The Court stated that our Constitution, laws, and policies have no extraterritorial operation, unless in respect of our own citizens. What another country has done in the way of seizing property of its nationals and/or corporations is not a matter for our courts to decide upon. The Court continued to state that such parties should look to their own governmental officials for potential redress. In this particular case, only the rights of the Russian corporation were in fact affected by the international compact and request for the deposit. The right to these moneys once belonged to the Soviet government as successor of the corporation, but that right had now been passed to the United States. Therefore, Belmont's executors had no legal interest in the specified deposit account and the Fifth Amendment had not been violated.

With all aforementioned considerations addressed, the Court held that the U.S. federal government did allege facts sufficient to constitute a cause of action against Belmont's executors.

For more information: Ducat, Craig R. *Constitutional Interpretation.* 8th ed. Belmont, Calif.: Thompson Learning, 2004.

—Amanda B. Sears
—Michelle L. Dempsey

United States v. Butler, 297 U.S. 1 (1936)

In *United States v. Butler,* the Supreme Court held that "certain provisions of the Agricultural Adjustment Act, 1933, conflict with the Federal Constitution." The case is important because of its characterization of the judicial process and its discussion of taxing and spending power of the U.S. government.

Justice Roberts settled the dispute on the general welfare clause of the Constitution, and Justice STONE's dissenting remarks were voiced by other Court minorities in the years to come. This case is important to the study of constitutional law and the Supreme Court because it decided how far the national government could go with taxing and Court minorities pleading for JUDICIAL RESTRAINT. It dealt with the appealed case by the U.S. government versus Butler, the receiver for Hoosac Mills, which processed cotton and refused to pay a tax set up by the Agricultural Adjustment Act (AAA). The act was one of the early attempts of the Roosevelt administration to upturn the agricultural market, specifically cotton. They believed the Depression was taking hold throughout the country because of overproduced products, therefore the government wished to raise commodity prices, subsidize farmers for unplanted acres, and tax the processors.

When one processor, Butler, refused, he was taken to court where the U.S. district court ordered him to pay it, the U.S. Circuit COURT OF APPEALS reversed it, and the U.S. Supreme Court, by a vote 6 to 3, upheld the circuit court's order for reasons Justice Roberts outlines. He agrees with Hamilton's view of taxing and spending, for which government has the right as long at it is for the general welfare and this was not limited by the enumerated powers. This AAA tax was not for the general welfare for three main reasons. The first was that the federal government tried to regulate and control agricultural production, an area reserved to states. The second reasoning was as Justice Roberts points out, although the U.S. government does have the power to tax and spend, it was using these means for an unconstitutional end, meaning the government was using an appropriate power—taxing and spending—however, they could not justify the spending and taxing of this money for the general welfare. Lastly the act violated the Tenth Amendment; powers not expressly granted or reasonably applied to the U.S. government are reserved to the states and people. This as explained above is where exactly the AAA went wrong, taking power away from the states for a just means, however, the end was not justified. It is not within the federal powers to contract reduced acreage or production of agricultural products or force farmers to comply; this is a power reserved to the states.

So according to these three reasons expressed by Justice Roberts, the Court upheld the U.S. circuit court's decision. Butler did not have to pay the tax because the tax was unconstitutional. His opinion on Article I, Section 8 of the Constitution finally settled a long-standing dispute on the authorization of Congress to levy taxes. James Madison and Alexander Hamilton first expressed the two sides of the debate. Justice Roberts accepts Hamilton's view that in this section, the powers to tax and spend were separate powers and were only restricted if the general welfare was served.

The second reason was not questioning whether the act was unconstitutional or not but the way which the court came about its decision. This act was unconstitutional because they disapproved of how the taxes were to be spent. Noting the serious depression within the nation, it is hard not to believe that levying taxes for farmers is not in the best interest of the general welfare. Their final dissent was that while the Agricultural Adjustment Act may fail, any or all of its provisions may not.

For more information: Mason, Alpheus Thomas, and Donald Grier Stephenson, Jr. "National Taxing and Spending Power: *United States v. Butler* (1936)." In *American Constitutional Law: Introductory Essays and Selected Cases,* Englewood Cliffs, N.J.: Prentice Hall, 1993, 245–258; Pritchett, Herman, C. "Butler, United States v.," in *The Oxford Guide to United States Supreme Court Decisions,* edited by Kermit L. Hall. Oxford: Oxford University Press, 1999.

United States v. Carolene Products Co., 304 U.S. 144 (1938)

In an otherwise unremarkable case in which the Court upheld a law passed by Congress regulating commerce, there emerges what is arguably the most significant footnote in American judicial history. The footnote, known as "Footnote Four," suggests the appropriateness of applying varying degrees of judicial scrutiny to different types of legislation.

The Filled Milk Act of 1923 declared "filled milk"— milk that has been altered so that the resulting product is an imitation of milk—to be injurious to the public health and prohibited the shipment of such milk in INTERSTATE COMMERCE. The Carolene Products Company, located in southern Illinois, was indicted for violating the act. The company had obtained a demurrer to the indictment which was sustained by the U.S. District Court for the Southern District of Illinois, a decision the United States appealed to the Supreme Court.

The Court—in a 6 to 1 decision with Justice Harlan Fiske STONE writing for the Court and Justice James C. McReynolds dissenting—reversed the lower court's decision. The Court held that a RATIONAL BASIS for the legislation was all the Fifth Amendment required. Additionally, the Court held that nothing in the due process clause of the Fifth Amendment prohibited a national or state legislature from enacting laws for the protection of its citizens. Furthermore, it noted the presumption of constitutionality—a practical rule of government holding that the people and their representatives should be allowed to correct their own mistakes wherever possible—inherent in legislative acts.

By 1938 the conflict between economic reformers and conservative justices was becoming a battle of the past, and the Court was starting to embrace a posture of deference to the policy judgments of Congress and state legislatures. While economic questions or disputes were becoming less of a concern to the judiciary compared to the first part of the 20th century, CIVIL LIBERTIES and rights were starting to make their way onto the Court's DOCKET with increasing frequency. A decisive moment in this transformation from economic rights to civil liberties and rights was Footnote Four in *United States v. Carolene Products*. It appeared one year after the Court had abandoned its previous position of JUDICIAL ACTIVISM in defense of economic rights of businesses and employers. Prior to *Carolene Products,* the Court had rigidly scrutinized legislation affecting property rights to decide if the legislation served a desirable public purpose.

Stone, in his opinion, stated that Congress had the power to regulate interstate commerce and if it chose to set minimal standards for milk quality, that was the business of the legislative and not the judicial branch. Immediately after this statement, a footnote was inserted suggesting that, in noneconomic regulation cases, the Court could adopt a higher level of scrutiny.

The first paragraph of the footnote holds that whenever a statute or regulation appears on its face to be in conflict with a specific constitutional prohibition the usual presumption that laws are constitutional should be reduced or waived altogether. The second paragraph suggests that the judiciary has a special responsibility, or that greater scrutiny may be appropriate to defend those rights vital to the effective functioning of the political process, such as limiting the rights to vote, to express political viewpoints, to organize politically, or to assemble. The third paragraph indicates that the presumption of constitutionality may be inappropriate for statutes or regulations that affect "discrete and insular minorities." Because a bias against racial or religious minorities may skew and alter the political process, more intensive scrutiny many be appropriate when laws are targeted at such minorities.

The standard put forth in Footnote Four in *Carolene Products* has become known as the "preferred freedoms" doctrine and has special significance for First Amendment claims as it means that the courts will proceed with a special scrutiny when faced with laws restricting freedom of expression, particularly those communicating unpopular views.

The opinion, and more directly Footnote Four, clearly showed Stone's growing concern for civil liberties and that the Court had a responsibility to protect them.

For more information: Ely, John Hart. *Democracy and Distrust.* Cambridge, Mass.: Harvard University Press, 1980; Epstein, Lee. *Constitutional Law for a Changing America: Rights Liberties, and Justice.* 3rd ed. Washington, D.C.: Congressional Quarterly Press, 1998; Mason, Alpheus Thomas. *Harlan Fiske Stone: Pillar of the Law.* New York: Viking, 1956.

—Mark Alcorn

United States v. Curtiss Wright Export Corporation, 299 U.S. 304 (1936)

The Supreme Court in *United States v. Curtiss Wright Export Corporation* upheld a congressional delegation of legislative authority to the president by distinguishing between the limited nature of domestic legislative power and the more expansive nature of the foreign affairs power. Yet the Court's opinion strayed far beyond the narrow issue to become a critical source of presidential power in foreign affairs.

A dispute between Bolivia and Paraguay impelled Congress to pass a joint resolution authorizing President Roosevelt to embargo arms sales to the two nations should he determine it necessary to force a settlement. The president ordered the embargo almost immediately, yet it was alleged that the Curtiss Wright Corporation had continued to sell its warplanes to Bolivia in violation of the order. In their defense, Curtiss Wright argued—in part—that the joint resolution was an unconstitutional delegation of legislative authority to the president because it gave him uncontrolled discretion in making law. At issue, then, was a fundamental question regarding the SEPARATION OF POWERS: Is it legal for Congress to delegate legislative power to the president?

Writing for the Court, Justice George SUTHERLAND— through an examination of the origin and nature of domestic and foreign legislative power—upheld the actions of Congress and the president's subsequent order of embargo. However, in making the distinction between delegations of power used internally versus externally, Sutherland penned a broad opinion that remains a key source for those arguing for executive dominance of foreign policy.

In a complicated and questionable passage, Sutherland maintains that the nation's "power over foreign affairs" is different in origin and "essential character" than its power in domestic affairs, and that, consequently, "participation in the exercise of the power is significantly limited." Also invoking past delegations by Congress, the character of the presidency, and the historic words of Chief Justice MARSHALL, Sutherland found that the president had the most legitimate claim to its exercise, noting his "very delicate, plenary, and exclusive power . . . as the sole organ of the federal government in the field of international relations— a power which does not require as a basis for its exercise an act of Congress. . . ."

The legacy of *Curtiss* remains contested; some note that Sutherland's theory of the origin of the foreign affairs power, which he locates outside the Constitution, makes it difficult for judge or justice to locate any proper boundaries to its exercise. Equally important is the opinion's effect on the presidency; critics see it as the basis for a modern presidency of such power in foreign policy that it threatens fundamental republican principles, with its "sole organ" doctrine "trotted out . . . whenever [the Court] has required a rationale to support a constitutionally doubtful presidential action in foreign affairs." Others see *Curtiss* as merely an acknowledgment of what history and common sense make clear—the unique qualities of the president, his capacity for secrecy, and the dispatch that is a consequence of his singular nature, make him ideally suited for the exercise of the nation's foreign affairs power.

Today, however, in the wake of September 11 and the continuing War on Terror, the *Curtiss* decision may be taking on a new significance. Indeed, it has been employed in the lower federal courts by the Bush administration in support of its detention of certain American citizens as military combatants. For example, In *Hamdi v. Rumsfeld,* 296 F.3d 282 (2002), the Fourth Circuit relied heavily on *Curtiss* in deferring to the president's decision to classify an American citizen captured in Afghanistan, Yaser Hamdi, as an enemy combatant. Thus the sharp distinction that *Curtiss* created between the president's limited domestic authority and his far more expansive power in foreign relations is, in an increasingly interdependent world, far more difficult to maintain.

For more information: Adler, David Gray, and Robert George, eds. *The Constitution and the Conduct of American Foreign Policy.* Lawrence: University Press of Kansas, 1996; Henkin, Louis. *Foreign Affairs and the United States Constitution.* Oxford: Clarendon Press, 1996.

—Patrick F. Campbell

United States v. Darby, 312 U.S. 100 (1941)

In the landmark case *United States v. Darby,* the Supreme Court voted unanimously to uphold the Fair Labor Standards Act in an effort to distinguish unfair labor laws. The impact of this case rested in the concept of New Deal legislation. Congress in the 1930s passed a series of legislative measures to overcome the Great Depression, and this case was one of the first to be considered under this new legislation. The foundation for the state's case was based primarily off of the Supreme Court case GIBBONS V. OGDEN, 22 U.S. 1 (1824). According to the Supreme Court Historical Society, Congress's power of commerce is the power *"to prescribe the rule by which commerce is governed."* Gibbons v. Ogden was the landmark case that declared Congress's right to regulate trade in the interest of national well-being.

The counsel started out by outlining the rights that Congress had under the commerce clause. The need for the commerce clause existed because states were producing different labor laws. The variance in these laws proved to damage INTERSTATE COMMERCE. According to Solicitor General Biddle, "those labor conditions among the States, burdened interstate commerce, led to labor disputes obstructing that commerce, and constituted an unfair method of competition." He further said that when the commerce clause was adopted, that the term *interstate commerce* was interpreted by Congress to mean the same as "the interrelated business of other states." Biddle then went on to prove through the case of *Baldwin v. Seelig,* 294 U.S. 511, that these ideas of low labor and substandard wages have already been addressed and that interstate regulations cannot and should not be controlled at the state level.

Mr. Archibald B. Lovett, interceding for the appellee, argued that the Fair Labor Standards Act attempted to regulate the production of goods as well as conditions that affect the aforementioned subject. Because of this regulation, it should not have been Congress's right to control such commerce. He then further argued that only in certain cases does Congress have the power to prohibit shipping. Archibald said, for example, if the goods in shipment were harmful, Congress has the right to control and or prohibit the shipment of these damaging products. Finally, he said "Conditions in production like those involved here have always been held to affect interstate commerce only indirectly. Their control is therefore subject solely to the reserved powers of the States." In other words, Congress did in fact have the right to control certain aspects of interstate commerce, but with the exception of special circumstances, it lacked the power to control shipment of goods.

According to Chief Justice Stone, who published an opinion of the case, "The two principal questions raised by the record in this case are, first, whether Congress has constitutional power to prohibit the shipment in interstate commerce of lumber manufactured by employees whose wages are less than a prescribed minimum or whose weekly hours of labor at that wage are greater than a prescribed maximum, and, second, whether it has power to prohibit the employment of workmen in the production of goods 'for interstate commerce' at other than prescribed wages and hours. A subsidiary question is whether in connection with such prohibitions Congress can require the employer subject to them to keep records showing the hours worked each day and week by each of his employees including those engaged 'in the production and manufacture of goods to-wit, lumber, for interstate commerce.'"

In response to these two questions, the justices deduced that the Fair Labor Standards Act was logical as it set up a comprehensive legislative scheme for prohibiting shipments of products and commodities in the United

States if their respective companies did not adhere to the labor and wage standards set up under Sec. 2 (a) of the Fair Labor Standards Act. Furthermore, Justice STONE indicated that several instances existed where the appellee shipped goods and/or commodities from the state of Georgia to points outside of the state (therefore engaging in interstate commerce) and in many instances paying less than minimum wage or requiring more than the prescribed maximum hour limit. In addition, according to evidence, Stone concluded the appellee failed to keep documentation of the hours worked and wages paid.

This case was monumental for two reasons: First, it established a stronger sense of FEDERALISM. According to the U.S. Federalism Web site, *U.S. v. Darby* was a landmark case because it finally marked the concession of commerce to be controlled by Congress. Had the ruling not been overturned, the decision of the U.S. district court of Alabama would have been upheld, giving the states reason to not adhere to the regulations set up by the Fair Labor Standards Act. Second, this case represented the constitutionality of New Deal legislation. Again as stated in the U.S. Federalism Web site, much of the New Deal legislation was declared unconstitutional until this point. However the conservative Supreme Court conceded and thereby gave the Franklin Roosevelt administration, as well as future administrations to come, more power to control the economy.

For more information: Stephenson, Mason. *American Constitutional Law Introductory Essays and Selected Cases.* Englewood Cliffs, N.J.: Prentice Hall, 1993; Young, James V. *Landmark Constitutional Law Decisions.* Lanham, Md.: University Press of America, 1993.

United States v. E. C. Knight Co., 156 U.S. 1 (1895)

In *United States v. E. C. Knight Co.,* the Court decided that the Sherman Antitrust Act of 1890 was not intended by Congress to restrict monopolies, so long as those monopolies did not directly affect INTERSTATE COMMERCE. In so ruling, the Court differentiated "transportation and its instrumentalities, and articles bought, sold, or exchanged for purposes of . . . transit among the states" from manufacturing and other localized processes, prior to the transportation and sale of goods. The products of manufacturing, it was found, are not necessarily transferred across state lines and, even if they are, affect interstate commerce "only incidentally and indirectly."

In early 1892, the American Sugar Refining Company (ASRC) controlled 65 percent of the American sugar refinery industry, the products of which were transported throughout the United States. Charges brought against the company in the Circuit Court for the Eastern District of

Pennsylvania claimed that the company undertook an "unlawful and fraudulent scheme to purchase the stock, machinery, and real estate" of the four remaining large sugar refineries (totaling an additional 33 percent of the market) in order to "restrain trade among the several states, or with foreign nations" and monopolize the American sugar industry. Charges were brought against ASRC and each of the four companies with which they entered into such agreements on March 4, 1892, which included E. C. Knight, a sugar manufacturer registered in Pennsylvania. ASRC and E. C. Knight, it was argued, monopolized the Pennsylvania sugar industry and conspired to increase the price of sugar, with the intent of exacting "large sums of money from the state of Pennsylvania, and from the other states of the United States." Bills were issued by the United States requesting that the agreements of March 4 be declared void, the stock transferred back to the original owners, and that an injunction be issued preventing further breech of the terms of the Sherman Act. Finally, the bills, which were issued against the other four companies in their respective district courts, called for relief "as equity and justice may require."

The Circuit Court for Eastern District of Pennsylvania dismissed the bill on the grounds that no "contract, combination, or conspiracy to restrain or monopolize trade or (interstate) commerce" had been found. The decision was appealed to the Supreme Court after the COURT OF APPEALS for the Third Circuit affirmed the decision.

Justice FULLER's majority opinion distinguished the prosecution of monopolies operating within a state from the controlling of interstate commerce. The latter, he found, was the intent of the Sherman Act while the former was a matter to be left to the states. Recalling MARSHALL's twofold requirement that interstate commerce involve both "traffic" and "intercourse," Fuller found that E. C. Knight's actions remained "within the jurisdiction of the police power of the state."

While the claimants charged that the manufacture of refined sugar constituted a "necessary of life," Fuller found that manufacturing determines only a secondary "disposition" of the good, even though the act of manufacturing certainly does constitute the initiation of a process that could, but need not necessarily, result in interstate commerce. Manufactured products, therefore, enter the stream of interstate commerce when they are transported, and neither ASRC nor E. C. Knight was involved in transporting sugar between states.

To place manufacturing under the jurisdiction of Congress, Fuller argued, would be to afford the federal government "the power to regulate, not only manufactures, but also agriculture, horticulture, stock-raising, domestic fisheries, mining; in short, every branch of human industry." Furthermore, Fuller argued that the "rules of production" were best left under the jurisdiction of localized industries and that for Congress to regulate such industries would clearly be in contradiction to the spirit of the Sherman Act.

Fuller clarified the purpose of the Sherman Act, which he found was not intended to deal with monopolies "directly as such," or to otherwise control, "limit or restrict the rights of corporations," but was instead intended to prevent "combinations, contracts and conspiracies to monopolize trade and commerce among the several states or with foreign nations." The claims made against E. C. Knight, on the contrary, dealt exclusively with acts and contracts within the state of Pennsylvania "and bore no direct relation" to interstate commerce.

For more information: Adams, Walter, and James W. Brock. *The Bigness Complex: Industry, Labor, and Government in the American Economy.* New York: Pantheon Books, 1986.

—Daniel Skinner
—Garret M. Knull

United States v. Eichman, 496 U.S. 310 (1990)

In *United States v. Eichman,* the Supreme Court, by a 5 to 4 vote, reaffirmed the Court's commitment set forth in TEXAS V. JOHNSON to protecting extremely provocative expression. Justices REHNQUIST, WHITE, STEVENS, and O'CONNOR were in dissent.

During the 1984 Republican convention held in Dallas, demonstrators marched through the city to protest the Reagan administration's policies. One of the demonstrators, Gregory Lee Johnson, burned an American flag and chanted "America, the red, white, and blue, we spit on you." Johnson was arrested and convicted for violating the Texas statute criminalizing desecration of an American flag in such a way that the actor knew the action would seriously offend onlookers. However, the Court's decision in *Texas v. Johnson,* 491 U.S. 397 (1989), held that the Texas flag desecration statue was unconstitutional because it punished expressive conduct. The U.S. Congress then reacted by passing the Flag Protection Act of 1989 with the intent to have the Court reconsider its decision in the *Texas v. Johnson* case. The Flag Protection Act prohibited the knowing mutilation, defacement, physical defilement, burning of, or trampling on, any American flag. The government's interest becomes implicated when a person's treatment of the flag communicates a message inconsistent with the flag's identified ideals.

On October 30, 1989, two days after the new law took effect, a small group of demonstrators gathered on the steps of the Capitol in Washington to protest the Flag Protection Act. Advance notice had been provided to the media that flags were to be burned as part of the demonstration. Police reacted quickly to four men who had separated themselves from the crowd and began to burn American flags. Police arrested three demonstrators. Ironically, the fourth man arrested was Gregory Lee Johnson, the namesake of the original Texas flag desecration case. However, the police stopped him before he could get his flag ignited, and he failed to be included in the indictment that followed.

The resultant case, *United States v. Eichman,* quickly challenged the new flag protection law and involved two consolidated appeals by the United States in cases in which appellees had been prosecuted for publicly burning American flags in violation of the 1989 Flag Protection Act. Appellees' consul, William Kunstler, moved to dismiss the charges on the grounds that the Flag Protection Act violates the First Amendment and that the Flag Protection Act was as constitutionally flawed as the Texas statute in that FLAG BURNING cannot be regulated without some reference to the context of the flag burning which is a manner of expressive conduct.

The government's consul, Solicitor General Kenneth Starr, contended that unlike the Texas statute, the Flag Protection Act was not intended to abridge offensive expressive conduct but rather to prevent all forms of flag desecration. By taking this line of legal reasoning, the government wanted to prevent the Court from adopting a more exacting constitutional scrutiny of the Flag Protection Act as the Court had done regarding the Texas statute argued in the *Texas v. Johnson* flag burning case.

However, the Court held that the precise language of the Flag Protection Act confirmed Congress's intent to be the communicative impact of flag destruction and its inconsistency with the identified ideals of the flag's symbolic value. Consequently, the Court in a 5 to 4 vote with Justice BRENNAN speaking for the Court said the Flag Protection Act of 1989 suffered from the same fundamental flaw as the Texas statute. The Court reasoned that although the Flag Protection Act contained no explicit content-based limitation on the scope of prohibited conduct, it was clear to the Court that the interest of the government was to limit a form of free expression. The Court clearly indicated that it would continue viewing with exacting scrutiny any law aimed at preventing flag desecration as constitutionally suspect because any such law is viewed by the Court to be inescapably linked to the government's disapproval of the message conveyed by an act of flag mistreatment. The Court added that the increasing popular approval for the Flag Protection Act fails to provide enhanced justification for the government's infringement on First Amendment rights.

For more information: Thompson, Tracy. "Three Charged in Capitol Flag Burning," *Washington Post,* November 1, 1989; Wheeler, Linda. "4 Arrested in Buring of Flag on Capitol Steps," *Washington Post,* October 31, 1989.

—William W. Riggs

United States v. Leon, 468 U.S. 902 (1984)

In *United States v. Leon,* the Supreme Court established a "good faith" exception to the Fourth Amendment EXCLUSIONARY RULE that illegally obtained evidence cannot be used against a defendant at trial. Justice WHITE wrote the opinion of the Court and was joined by Justices BURGER, POWELL, REHNQUIST, and O'CONNOR. Justice BLACKMUN filed a concurring opinion. Justice BRENNAN wrote a dissenting opinion and was joined by Justice MARSHALL. Justice STEVENS authored a separate dissenting opinion.

In 1981 Alberto Leon and others were targeted by the police for trafficking illegal drugs. After extensive investigation and observation, the police applied for a warrant to search several residences, including Leon's. The warrant was granted and the police seized a large quantity of drugs. All the suspects were then charged with conspiracy to possess and distribute cocaine and other drugs.

Leon, however, filed a motion to quash the evidence, arguing that the police had failed to establish probable cause when applying for the warrant. A judge agreed with Leon and suppressed the evidence. At the same time, the judge rejected an argument from the government that an exception to the exclusionary rule should be granted because the police were acting in good faith with a warrant they believed to be valid. This ruling was subsequently upheld by the COURT OF APPEALS. The Reagan administration then appealed the decision to the Supreme Court, asking the Court to decide whether there should be a good-faith exception to the Fourth Amendment exclusionary rule.

Justice White began the majority opinion by reflecting that the case featured a clash of competing public goods. On one hand, the Fourth Amendment exclusionary rule is necessary to deter "official misconduct and remove inducements to unreasonable invasions of privacy." On the other hand, however, society has a vested interest in "establishing procedures under which criminal defendants are acquitted or convicted on the basis of all the evidence which exposes the truth." Thus if the Court is to find a remedy in the case, that remedy must attempt to find a balance between these conflicting interests.

Accordingly, Justice White explained that the Court would use a cost-benefit analysis to determine whether a good-faith exception should be authorized. As for costs, there can be little doubt that disallowing a good-faith exception would result in great harm to society. Excluding evidence seized in good faith would "impede unacceptably the truth-finding functions of judge and jury . . . [allow] some guilty defendants to go free or receive reduced sentences . . . and generat[e] disrespect for the law and administration of justice." The benefits of disallowing a good-faith exception, however, are few. The purpose of having the exclusionary rule is to deter illegal police conduct. Would allowing a good-faith exception further this end? Justice

White argued that it would not. Since the mistake in most of these cases lies with the magistrate issuing the warrant, the police, being unaware of the error, will not alter their behavior in the slightest. Consequently, "in the absence of an allegation that the magistrate abandoned his detached and neutral role, suppression is appropriate only if the officers were dishonest in preparing their affidavit or could not have harbored an objectively reasonable belief in the existence of probable cause."

In his concurring opinion, Justice Blackmun voiced his agreement with the majority's decision in the case, but, according to Blackmun, the Court must also make clear that the ruling is provisional and not "cast in stone." If, Blackmun explained, "it should emerge from experience that, contrary to our expectations, the good-faith exception to the exclusionary rule results in a material change in police compliance with the Fourth Amendment, we shall have to reconsider what we have undertaken here."

Justice Brennan, writing in dissent, protested that the Court's ruling is the most recent step in a long chain of efforts to "strangle" the Fourth Amendment. In this instance, the Court has used the language of "deterrence and of cost/benefit analysis" to weaken personal constitutional rights. According to the majority, the purpose of the exclusionary rule is deterrence of illegal police action. Thus government action which does not contribute to this deterrence goal can legitimately be excluded from the requirement of exclusion. What the majority fails to realize, however, is that the purpose of the exclusionary rule is not only deterrence, but also to protect individual rights, namely the "right of the people to be secure in the persons, houses, papers, and effects, against unreasonable searches and seizures." This Fourth Amendment guarantee, therefore, requires that "all evidence secured by means of unreasonable searches and seizures" must be excluded regardless of what the results of a cost/benefit analysis might be.

In his separate dissenting opinion, Justice Stevens argued that the Court's ruling resulted in a logical absurdity. The Fourth Amendment stipulates that two conditions must be met for legal searches and seizures. First, the searches and seizures must be reasonable; and, second, they must be the result of warrants that are supported by probable cause and are particular in terms of the persons and places to be searched and the things to be seized. The Constitution, not to mention the rules of logic, demands that the Court speak with one voice on these requirements. The Court cannot, for instance, "intelligibly assume, arguendo, that a search was constitutionally unreasonable but that the seized evidence is admissible because the same search was reasonable." As such the majority's decision to create a good-faith exception to the exclusionary rule cannot stand.

For more information: Griswold, Erwin. *Search and Seizure*. Lincoln: University of Nebraska Press, 1975; Schlesinger, Stephen. *Exclusionary Injustice*. New York: Dekker, 1977.

—Eric C. Sands

United States v. Libellants and Claimants of the Schooner Amistad, 40 U.S. 518 (1841)

In *United States v. the Amistad,* it was held by the Supreme Court that the Africans of the *Amistad* schooner were free individuals. Justice STORY delivered the opinion of the Court and declared that Africans of the *Amistad* have never been slaves, were natives of Africa, and were kidnapped there, and were unlawfully transported. The Court ordered the immediate release of the Africans from the custody, and discharged them from the suit. Justice Baldwin alone dissented, without comment.

Fifty-three Africans who were aboard *Amistad* were among a large group of Africans who were abducted from Eastern Africa by Portuguese slave hunters in 1839 and were transferred to Havana, Cuba, by Spanish slave traders through a ship named the *Tecora* and were placed in barracoons or slave marts, in violation of the TREATIES between Spain and Great Britain for the abolition of slave trade and Spanish laws that forbade slave trafficking at the time. Two Spanish sugar plantation owners in Cuba, Jose Ruiz and Pedro Montez, purchased Africans of the *Amistad,* the former 49 and the latter four of them, from the mentioned slave marts in Cuba and put them on board the *Amistad* on June 27, 1839, and the schooner left Havana, Cuba, for Puerto Príncipe, Cuba. While en route, the Africans revolted under the leadership of Sengbe Pieh (called Cinqué by the Spanish), and one of the Africans on board, on July 1, 1839, seized the ship and killed Raymon Ferrer, captain of the schooner and his cook.

Due to their ignorance in navigation, they spared the lives of Ruiz and Montez in exchange for their help in steering the *Amistad* back to where they were initially shipped from, the coast of Africa, or to some place where slavery was not permitted. Taking advantage of the ignorance of the Africans, Ruiz and Montez managed to navigate the *Amistad* for the United States, succeeded in coming around Montauk Point, and the schooner anchored within half a mile of the shore off Long Island, State of New York, where it was discovered by the U.S. Navy brig, *Washington.*

Captain Navy Lieutenant Gedney and his crew seized the *Amistad* on August 26, 1839, and brought the vessel, the cargo, and the Africans into the port of New London, Connecticut, for salvage. Ruiz and Montez were freed, and the Africans were imprisoned in New Haven, Connecticut. The murder charges against the Africans during the takeover of the schooner were initially dismissed, but they remained in confinement due to the libels for salvage presented by Lieutenant Gedney in the name of the crew of the *Washington* for saving the *Amistad,* its cargo, and the Africans with great difficulty and considerable danger; by Henry Green and Pelatiah Fordham, of Sag Harbour, Long Island, for capturing the Africans who set foot on shore for water and supplies, and eventually contributing to the possession of the *Amistad,* its cargo, and the Africans by the *Washington,* and finally by Ruiz and Montez for possession of the Africans and parts of the cargo, before the District Court of the Connecticut. Ruiz and Montez claimed that the Africans were their slaves and property and should be returned to them along with the cargo according to the treaty between Spain and the United States and denied salvage to any other persons claiming salvage.

This engraving depicts Joseph Cinqué and about 50 other enslaved Africans rising up against the captain and crew of the *Amistad. (Library of Congress)*

In the meantime, the Spanish minister to the United States presented a claim to the State Department stating that the *Amistad,* its cargo, and the slaves were the property of the Spanish subjects and should be restored to the owners according to the treaty between the United States and Spain. William Bolabird, attorney of the District Court of Connecticut, argued that the claim of the Spanish minister was well founded and proposed that Court release the *Amistad,* its cargo, and the slaves to Ruiz and Montez, in line with the treaty. However, he also suggested that if the slaves were transported from Africa in violation of the laws of the United States, they should be returned to the coast of Africa. The Africans on the other hand were defended by Roger Baldwin, grandson of an American revolutionary who signed the Declaration of Independence and a supporter of the anti-slavery cause, and he claimed that the Africans were unlawfully kidnapped from Africa and were transported to Cuba, and Ruiz and Montez made a pretended purchase of them from persons who had no right on the Africans and produced false and fraudulent papers to transport them to an unknown location to be enslaved for life. He wanted the court to set the Africans free, unconditionally.

The District Court, led by Judge Judson, ruled in favor of the Africans and decided to put them under the authority of the president of the United States, to be transported to Africa. While making this ruling, the District Court recited the decree of the government of Spain of December 1817, prohibiting the slave trade, and declaring all Negroes brought into the dominions of Spain by slave traders to be free; and enjoining the execution of the decree on all the officers of Spain in the dominions of Spain [40 U.S. 518 (1841)]. In this context, it rejected claims by Captain Gedney, Green, and Fordam to salvage on the alleged slaves. The claims of property on the Africans by Ruiz and Montez were included under the claim of the minister of Spain to the United States and were dismissed. Only the claims of property on the *Amistad* and the cargo on board, by Cuban merchants including Ruiz and Montez, were sustained, and one-third of the gross value of the schooner and the merchandise on it was decided to be given to Captain Gedney and his crew as salvage.

The United States "claiming in pursuance of a demand by the duly accredited minister of her Catholic Majesty, the Queen of Spain, to the United States, moved an appeal from the whole and every part of the said decree, to the Circuit Court" of Connecticut [40 U.S. 518 (1841)]. The Circuit Court of Connecticut in due course affirmed the ruling of the lower court. The United States, claiming in pursuance of a demand by the Spanish minister, then appealed to the Supreme Court from the whole and every part of the said decree.

Although Attorney General Gilpin vehemently argued for the Spanish side and claimed that there was due proof concerning the legality of the property, concerning the Africans as property of Spanish subjects, and the Africans should be delivered in entirety to their Spanish owners, the Supreme Court affirmed the decision of the District Court. They stated that the Africans were free men and women, illegally taken from Africa and unlawfully transported to Cuba, and never the lawful slaves of Ruiz or Montez, or of any other Spanish subject.

It was maintained that the African slave trade was abolished by the laws, treaties, and edicts of Spain, so the Africans delivered into the dominions of Spain were also declared to be free. It was held that although public documents of the government accompanying the property were found on board, the papers could not establish that the Africans were slaves, because the Africans were not slaves but illegally detained people onboard the *Amistad.* It was also held that the papers of property regarding to Africans found onboard the *Amistad* were fraudulent, and for this reason any asserted title founded upon them was void. The deposition of the British subject Robert Madden, who held the office of superintendent of liberated Africans in Havana, Cuba, at the time, regarding the illegal transactions concerning the slave trade in the island of Cuba and the involvement of public officials in this game played a certain role in this ruling.

It was also stated that the Africans were not guilty of murder for the deaths of the crewmen during the *Amistad* takeover, and their rise against their captors did not make them pirates or robbers; that the treaty between the United States and Spain did not apply; and, consequently, that the Africans were entitled to their freedom. Although his argument was omitted by the court, former President John Quincy Adams joined the defense team and defended the right of the Africans to fight to regain their freedom. Mentioning the ideals of the American Revolution, he attacked then President Van Buren's collaboration with the Spanish monarchy. He argued that if the judges ruled in favor of the Spanish government, it would mean that they ruined the democratic ideals on the basis of which the American republican form of government had been formed. Conclusive establishment of the fact that the Africans had been illegally transported to Cuba, by Mr. Baldwin and Mr. Adams, led to the freedom of the 35 Africans of the *Amistad* and their return to their homeland. The remaining 18 either died at sea or in prison while awaiting trial.

Although the *United States v. Amistad* had nothing to say about the ongoing slavery in the United States at the time, it is arguably the very first human rights case successfully defended at the Supreme Court level concerning the Africans, which makes it significant for all the practical political and legal reasons in American history.

For more information: The Basic Afro-American Reprint Library. *The* Amistad *Case: The Most Celebrated Slave*

Mutiny of the Nineteenth Century. New York: Johnson Reprint Corporation, 1968; Freedman, Suzanne. *United States v. Amistad: Rebellion on a Slave Ship.* Berkeley Heights, N.J.: Enslow, 2000.

—M. Murat Yasar
—Michelle L. Dempsey
—Amanda B. Sears

United States v. Morrison, 529 U.S. 598 (2000)

In *United States v. Morrison,* the Supreme Court held that the provision in the VIOLENCE AGAINST WOMEN ACT (VAWA) allowing victims of gender-based violence to sue their assailants in federal court was unconstitutional.

When Christy Brzonkala was a freshman at Virginia Tech in 1994 she alleged that two football players, Antonio Morrison and James Crawford, raped her. Although she brought charges through the university's judicial system, Crawford was acquitted and Morrison was given only a nominal sanction. Brzonkala then sued her assailant under VAWA. The law provided that freedom from violence based on gender is a civil right, and that victims of crimes such as rape and domestic violence could turn to the federal courts for a remedy. Congress had included VAWA in the package of anticrime legislation passed in 1994.

For three years prior to its passage, the legislators heard testimony about the effects of violence against women on the economy. Specifically they learned that the fear of rape or domestic violence often limits women's job opportunities, curtails their freedom to travel for business or pleasure, and has a negative effect on their educational pursuits. In addition, gender-based violence costs public and private health-care providers millions of dollars each year. Thus Congress concluded that such crimes have a significant economic impact and passed VAWA under their power to regulate INTERSTATE COMMERCE.

In addition, the lawmakers were presented with substantial testimony that the states failed to respond adequately to violence against women, to afford necessary protection against rape or domestic violence. A majority of state attorneys general agreed that the right to sue an assailant in federal court would provide a needed additional remedy to victims of gender-based violence. Thus the second constitutional basis for VAWA was the Fourteenth Amendment, which requires states to provide citizens with equal protection of the law and allows Congress to enforce that guarantee with appropriate legislation.

The Court found the relevant provision of VAWA unconstitutional on both grounds. The majority—Chief Justice REHNQUIST, who wrote the opinion, joined by Justices O'CONNOR, Kennedy, SCALIA, and THOMAS—held that Congress had exceeded its power by including the law

under the commerce clause. As they read the Constitution, only economic activities or noneconomic activities that had a substantial effect on the economy came within the commerce power. The Court refused to accept the judgment of the legislators that the connection between violence against women and its economic impact was sufficient.

Nor did the Court agree with Congress that women have a civil right to be free from gender-based violence and that if states were not safeguarding that right, it was justice to allow such victims to go into federal court to claim damages from their assailants. The Court threw out the Fourteenth Amendment claim, holding that the remedy was not congruent with the offense. They believed that if the states were not protecting victims, suing assailants was not the appropriate remedy.

Some argue that the supporters of VAWA see violence against women as a systemic problem, growing out of deep gender inequities in American society. Thus it falls, like racial violence, within the purview of the federal government. Opponents of this view, including the Court majority, seem to view violence against women as discrete, individual crimes that are best handled through the traditional procedures of the criminal justice system.

For more information: Atwell, Mary Welek. *Equal Protection of the Law? Gender and Justice in the United States.* New York: Peter Lang, 2002; Schneider, Elizabeth M. *Battered Women and Feminist Lawmaking.* New Haven, Conn.: Yale University Press, 2000.

—Mary Welek Atwell

United States, et al. v. National Treasury Employees Union, 513 U.S. 454 (1995)

In *United States, et al. v. National Treasury Employees Union,* the United States Supreme Court struck down a federal ban on employees accepting honoraria as a violation of the First Amendment. This decision had an impact on efforts to regulate corruption in government.

Under a provision of the Ethics Reform Act of 1989 [Section 501(b)] federal employees were prohibited from accepting payment for any appearance, speech, or article. To offset this honoraria ban, federal employees above a specific salary range were granted a 25 percent salary increase. Several executive branch employees and two labor unions filed suit in the U.S. District Court claiming §501(b) was an infringement on freedom of speech under the First Amendment of the Constitution. They pointed out that past appearances, speeches, and/or articles for which these employees had received honoraria pertained to outside matters not relating to their official duties. The district court held that the honoraria ban was unconstitutional as applied to executive branch employees and enjoined the government from enforcing it against these employees.

The question addressed by the Supreme Court was whether Section 501(b) violates the First Amendment. Justice STEVENS writing for a majority found that §501(b) did violate the First Amendment since it unduly restricted freedom of speech. The government had not established sufficient evidence that a blanket ban on speaking for pay was the appropriate response to anticipated harms from employees receiving honoraria. The government must demonstrate that harms are real, not merely speculative; fear of possible harms cannot by itself justify suppressing free speech. The Court also found that the speculative benefits that the honoraria ban may provide the government do not justify the infringement on freedom of speech.

Stevens continued that although §501(b) neither prohibits any speech nor discriminates on the content or viewpoint of the message, the honoraria ban directly affects the activities of certain federal employees, as well as restricts the public's right to hear and read their messages. Federal employees often seek to exercise their right as citizens to freely express opinions on matters that are of public interest and not as employees speaking on personal matters. Even though federal employees work for the government, they do not surrender the First Amendment rights they would otherwise exercise as citizens. The compensation federal employees receive for any expressive activity is in their capacity as citizens and not as government employees.

Nor was the majority persuaded by the government's concern that employees receiving honoraria may abuse or misuse power by accepting compensation for unofficial and nonpolitical appearances or speeches. The vast majority of appearances or speeches neither involves the subject matter of government employment nor takes place within the workplace. Therefore, there is no workplace disruption.

Justice O'CONNOR concurred in part to argue that discriminating between lower and upper echelons is unconstitutional and that a total ban on honoraria is too broad a remedy for the perceived problem.

Justices Rehnquist, SCALIA, and THOMAS dissented, arguing that a honoraria ban is consistent with the First Amendment.

For more information: Allen, David, and Robert Jensen, eds. *Freeing the First Amendment: Critical Perspectives on Freedom of Expression.* New York: New York University Press, 1995; O'Brien, David. *The Public's Right to Know: The First Amendment and the Supreme Court.* New York: Praeger, 1981.

—Eric C. Sands
—R. Nanette Nazaretian

United States v. O'Brien, 391 U.S. 367 (1968)

In *United States v. O'Brien*, the Supreme Court upheld the conviction of David O'Brien, who set his draft card on fire in protest of the United States' involvement in Vietnam during a 1966 rally in Boston. In so doing, the Court for the first time conceded that so-called SYMBOLIC SPEECH qualified for First Amendment protection.

O'Brien had been convicted of violating a hastily passed 1965 amendment to the Selective Service Act criminalizing the knowing destruction or mutilation of a draft card. Up until his case, the constitutional status of expressive conduct was in limbo, and it was unclear whether the Court was prepared to immunize certain modes of behavior merely because they conveyed a message, political or otherwise. Chief Justice Earl WARREN had previously voiced skepticism that conduct could be considered speech worthy of First Amendment shelter. During ORAL ARGUMENT, he noted that one potential implication of protecting "symbolic speech" would be to provide cover for a soldier who broke his rifle in protest.

Notwithstanding his unease, Warren's 7 to 1 majority opinion reluctantly carved out a middle ground providing some protection for expressive conduct while simultaneously enabling prosecution of violent or disruptive action, no matter how expressive.

The solution was a four-part test: "[A] government regulation is sufficiently justified if it is within the constitutional power of the Government; if it furthers an important or substantial governmental interest; if the governmental interest is unrelated to the suppression of free expression; and if the incidental restriction on alleged First Amendment freedoms is no greater than is essential to the furtherance of that interest."

Unfortunately for David O'Brien, he won the larger war but lost his own battle. While his case was the trailblazing pronouncement that symbolic speech could be protected by the First Amendment, the Court concluded that his symbolic speech was not protected, holding that his prosecution was a bureaucratic imperative to keep the SELECTIVE SERVICE system functioning, and not a reaction to his opinion on the war. The Court arrived at this conclusion, however, in the face of a mountain of contrary evidence, including the truculent pronouncements by the 1965 amendment's sponsors that the new rules were specifically implemented with the goal of curbing antiwar protests, and the testimony of the head of the Selective Service Agency in which he admitted that the rule mandating the preservation of the physical integrity of the draft card was unnecessary. O'Brien would eventually serve two years in federal prison.

The *"O'Brien test"* would shortly break its symbolic speech moorings. The "important or substantial interest" prong of the test would later be used as a baseline for other

Court attempts to finesse what would otherwise be hard-and-fast distinctions. Most notably, in *CRAIG V. BOREN,* 429 U.S. 190 (1976), the Court adapted this language as the test to evaluate gender discrimination claims. Unwilling to elevate gender discrimination to the level of race discrimination (which would require the use of the "compelling interest" test inherent in STRICT SCRUTINY), yet also unwilling to subject gender discrimination to the undemanding requirements of RATIONAL BASIS, the Court fell back on the *O'Brien* language and required that "classifications by gender must serve important governmental objectives and must be substantially related to achievement of those objectives."

For more information: Cray, Ed. *Chief Justice: A Biography of Earl Warren.* New York: Simon and Schuster, 1997; Greenawalt, Kent. *Fighting Words.* Princeton, N.J.: Princeton University Press, 1995; Schweber, Howard. *Speech, Conduct, and the First Amendment.* New York: Peter Lang, 2003.

—Steven B. Lichtman

United States v. Pink, 315 U.S. 203 (1942)

In *United States v. Pink,* the Supreme Court reversed the earlier ruling and held in favor of the United States in their attempt to assist the Soviet Union in recovering assets of the First Russian Insurance Company which the New York superintendent of insurance refused to release. The court required New York to release the assets. The Court debated the ruling of *UNITED STATES V. BELMONT,* 301 U.S. 324 (1937), in which the Court recognized the executive agreement, made by President Franklin Roosevelt, known as the Litvinov Assignment, and agreed to take control of the assets and distribute them among American claimants. This ultimately was meant to normalize relations with the Soviet Union.

This case was brought to the Supreme Court when a New York court looked to recover the assets of the Litvinov Assignment. New York rejected the government's claim of ownership of the assets, by saying that to enforce the Litvinov Assignment would violate New York public policy against the confiscation of private property. The Supreme Court reversed the decision of the New York court in a decision of 5 to 2 (two of the justices did not participate in the ruling). The Fifth Amendment of the UNITED STATES CONSTITUTION states that state matters, no matter how noble, do not trump the federal government's exclusive foreign affairs powers, and that aliens as well as citizens are protected.

The importance of this case is that *United States v. Pink* states that any executive agreement, such as a treaty, is part of the supreme law of the land, and no state has the right to interfere with the federal government's rulings on

foreign affairs. Justice William DOUGLAS said that if the Litvinov Assignment had been a treaty, there would be no doubt about its validity, and the same result should appear in both. This showed that the supremacy of an executive agreement rules over all state laws or policies. New York's actions were an attempt to reject part of the policy of an agreement made between the United States and the Soviet Union. *United States v. Pink* made it known that in decisions dealing with foreign policy, the national government has complete control. This case stated that state governments could not, without the permission of the national government, make or enforce policies with other nations even if they do not take any formal form. If state laws and policies did not yield to the national government, then our foreign policies would not work. Justice Douglas stated that New York could not "rewrite our foreign policy to conform to its own domestic policies." Power over external affairs is vested in the national government exclusively.

For more information: Levy, Leonard Williams, Kenneth Karst, and Dennis Mahoney. *Encyclopedia of the American Constitution.* New York: Macmillan, 1990; Renstrom, Peter. *The Stone Court: Justices, Rulings, and Legacy.* Santa Barbara, Calif.: ABC-CLIO, 2001.

United States v. Schechter Poultry Corporation, 295 U.S. 495 (1935)

In *United States v. Schechter Poultry Corporation,* the Court struck down the National Industrial Recovery Act (NIRA) as being unconstitutional on two bases. The NIRA was a key part of President Franklin D. Roosevelt's economic recovery plan following the Great Depression of 1929. The NIRA gave the president authority to regulate the live poultry industry, resulting in a code of regulations which included the authority to determine what constituted "fair competition." The regulations also attempted to establish minimum wages and limitations on hours for workers in the industry.

Schechter Poultry bought live poultry, slaughtered it, and sold it locally. They were charged with 18 violations of the live poultry code including wage and hour violations. Even though Schechter Poultry purchased poultry from suppliers outside New York State, they slaughtered and sold it locally. Because Schechter Poultry conducted its business within New York State, the Court ruled that the matter did not *directly* impact INTERSTATE COMMERCE and therefore Congress exceeded its constitutional authority in passing the NIRA, which constituted an unconstitutional infringement upon states' rights. The Court placed great weight on the lack of direct impact upon interstate commerce in their determination that Congress had surpassed its constitutional authority.

The Court also noted that the NIRA gave the president nearly unlimited discretion in creating the regulations and determining the meaning of the term *fair competition.* In delivering the opinion of the Court, Chief Justice HUGHES observed that the Constitution places all legislative power with Congress, and that such power was not transferable. The CHIEF JUSTICE stated that in leaving the definition of the term *fair competition* as well as the power to create codes regulating "fair competition" to the president's discretion, Congress had attempted to transfer legislative power to the president, resulting in an unconstitutional delegation of legislative authority violating the constitutional principle of SEPARATION OF POWERS. Known as the "Schechter rule," the case became a standard for those who oppose Congress delegating legislative authority.

The opinion was delivered May 27, 1935, which came to be known as "Black Monday," as it signaled what proved to be a series of cases in which the Supreme Court struck down legislation passed as part of the New Deal. While the decision in *Schechter* was unanimous, five of the nine Supreme Court justices on the Court at the time favored protecting private property rights and states rights and proved to be hostile to much of the New Deal legislation designed to stimulate economic recovery through federal regulation.

For more information: Biskupic, Joan, and Elder Witt. *The Supreme Court and the Powers of the American Government.* Washington, D.C.: Congressional Quarterly, 1997; Epstein, Lee, and Thomas G. Walker. *Constitutional Law for a Changing America: Institutional Powers and Constraints.* Washington, D.C.: Congressional Quarterly, 1997; Woll, Peter. *Constitutional Law: Cases and Comments.* Englewood Cliffs, N.J.: Prentice Hall, 1981.

—Karen L. Jarratt-Ziemski

United States v. Virginia, 518 U.S. 515 (1996)

In *United States v. Virginia,* the Supreme Court ruled that a Virginia same-sex school of higher learning violated the EQUAL PROTECTION CLAUSE of the Fourteenth Amendment.

The Virginia Military Institute (VMI), established in 1839, allowed only men to participate in its rigorous and prestigious "adversative model" of education. This egalitarian program functioned much like a Marine boot camp, featuring harsh physical rigors, absence of privacy, and mental stress. VMI's mission was to prepare "citizen-soldiers" for future leadership in public and private life. It was Virginia's sole same-sex public institution of higher learning and had always been financially supported by the state. In 1990 a female high school student seeking admission to VMI filed a complaint. The United States sued Virginia, alleging an equal protection violation under the Fourteenth Amendment.

The COURT OF APPEALS gave Virginia three options: first, admit women to VMI; second, establish a parallel institution for women; third, abandon state support. Virginia chose the second option and created the Virginia Women's Institute for Leadership (VWIL). VWIL, however, was not designed as a military school. Rather, Virginia determined that women perform better in a more cooperative environment and designed the institute accordingly. The United States brought suit on behalf of the women who could handle the rigors of VMI and thrive under them, arguing that the decree for a remedial plan and the plan itself were "pervasively misguided." The United States argued that any acceptable remedial plan must alter the situation as though the barrier had not existed.

Virginia argued in favor of keeping VMI a same-sex institution on the grounds that it provided important educational benefits and diversity in educational approaches. Furthermore, Virginia asserted that the school's adversative approach would have to be modified if women were allowed admission, destroying the core of the program and benefiting neither men nor women. Simply, women would not be able to do as well at VMI due to basic gender differences.

The Court sided with the United States. Justice GINSBURG restated that in cases of gender-based discrimination the burden of justification is on the state and must be exceedingly persuasive. Post hoc explanations or overbroad generalizations about the differences of the sexes would not be sufficient to provide that exceedingly persuasive justification.

First, Virginia had not shown that diversity in educational approaches was ever a motive in the creation of VMI. Second, she rejected Virginia's argument based on role stereotypes. The state cannot force women to attend VMI, but it also cannot deny admission to those with the will and capacity to do so. Finally, Justice Ginsburg rejected Virginia's contention that VWIL provided an equal alternative avenue for women. The student body, faculty, courses, and facilities paled in comparison to VMI. Furthermore, no new women's institution could hope to offer the prestige and alumni network that VMI offered. She likened the absence of these final benefits to the separate-but-equal situation in *Sweatt v. Painter,* 339 U.S. 629 (1950), upholding and reiterating that decision.

This case is also noteworthy because it muddied the Court's doctrine on gender-based classifications. Prior to *United States v. Virginia,* the Court had relied on a rationale of "heightened" or "intermediate" in such cases. Justice Ginsburg's addition of "exceedingly persuasive justification" as a determinant of constitutionality drew criticism from Justices REHNQUIST and SCALIA in their separate opinions.

For more information: Brodie, Laura F. *Breaking Out: VMI and the Coming of Women.* New York: Random

House, 2000; Strum, Philippa. *Women in the Barracks: The VMI Case and Equal Rights.* Lawrence: University Press of Kansas, 2002.

—Scott Cody

United Steelworkers of America v. Weber, 443 U.S. 193 (1979)

In *United Steelworkers of America v. Weber,* the Supreme Court held that TITLE VII OF THE CIVIL RIGHTS ACT of 1964, prohibiting RACIAL DISCRIMINATION, does not condemn all private, voluntary race-conscious AFFIRMATIVE ACTION plans.

The case arose when the United Steelworkers union and an employer, Kaiser Aluminum and Chemical Company, entered into an agreement to eliminate a long-standing pattern of discrimination against black workers in a Gramercy, Louisiana, plant. The problem was that although 39 percent of plant workers were black, only 1.83 percent of skilled (and higher paid) workers were black. Generally employees were either hired with the appropriate craft skills or gained skilled worker status through training programs from which blacks had been excluded. The voluntary plan called for the company to reserve 50 percent of the openings in the training program for blacks until the ratio of black skilled to unskilled workers equaled the ratio of white skilled to unskilled workers. Brian Weber, a white worker, was denied entry in the training program while some black workers with less seniority were admitted. He sued, claiming that the program violated Title VII of the Civil Rights Act of 1964.

Justice BRENNAN, writing for a 5 to 2 majority, argued that in passing the Civil Rights Act, Congress "did not intend to prohibit the private sector from taking effective steps to implement the goals of Title VII." He added that this was an effort of private parties to overcome the results of an admittedly discriminatory pattern of promotions, did not prohibit white employees from advancing in the company, and was for a limited time. Therefore the agreement was consistent with the intent of the Civil Rights Act.

Writing vigorous dissents, Chief Justice BURGER and Justice REHNQUIST accused the majority of going against the clear, explicit language of Title VII. Justice Burger argued that the Court abandoned the normal principles of statutory interpretation to effectively rewrite Title VII. Justice Rehnquist sarcastically stated that the majority was five years ahead of its time. It should be writing in 1984 because it uses doublespeak to achieve its desired results. [Rehnquist was referring to George Orwell's futuristic novel *1984.*] Neither Justices STEVENS nor POWELL participated or voted in the case.

United Steelworkers was important as a follow-up to *REGENTS OF THE UNIVERSITY OF CALIFORNIA V. BAKKE,* 438 U.S. 265 (1978), decided just one year earlier. It established the principle that a benign racial classification could be used to correct a history of racial discrimination, and the principle that private employers and unions could use race as a factor in promotion and training in order to overcome "archaic patterns of racial segregation and hierarchy." The Court later used *United Steelworkers* as a PRECEDENT to extend the constitutionality of affirmative action programs to women in *JOHNSON V. TRANSPORTATION AGENCY OF SANTA CLARA COUNTY, CALIFORNIA,* 480 U.S. 646 (1987).

However, it should also be noted that in a later case, *GRUTTER V. BOLLINGER,* 539 U.S. 306 (2003), the Court explicitly rejected "patterns of past discrimination" as a basis for affirmative action in favor of a "diverse student body" rationale. The *Grutter* majority expressed its clear expectation that this rationale was for a limited time only.

For more information: Epstein, Lee, and Thomas G. Walker. *Constitutional Law for a Changing America: Rights, Liberties, and Justice.* 5th ed. Washington, D.C.: CQ Press, 2004.

—Paul J. Weber

Vacco v. Quill, 521 U.S. 793 (1997)

In *Vacco v. Quill,* the United States Supreme Court held that there is no constitutional right to commit suicide. The Court upheld a New York statute criminalizing physician-assisted suicide against a challenge brought by doctors who sought to aid patients suffering from terminal conditions in dying.

The state statute provided that manslaughter in the second degree was the appropriate charge for a person who assisted another person in committing suicide. The petitioners claimed that the N.Y. statute violated equal protection and due process of law. The argument forwarded by the physicians was that in New York a competent person had the right to refuse life-sustaining medical treatment and this in essence was the same thing. Chief Justice Rehnquist wrote for the Court, which did not agree with petitioners, instead holding that the statute survived constitutional scrutiny. Because the statute's ban did not "burden a fundamental right nor target a suspect class," it was subject only to "rational basis review." Rational basis review requires only that a rational relationship exist between a legitimate governmental interest and the statute in question. In this case, the Court recognized a legitimate governmental interest in the sanctity of human life and a rational relationship between the New York statute and that interest.

The Court explained that the right to refuse medical treatment does not equate with the right to commit suicide. The Court's opinion reflects the intent to draw a clear distinction between the right of a mentally competent person to refuse medical treatment or the right to DIE and committing suicide or assisting another person in doing so.

Justice O'CONNOR concurring in *Quill* wrote that the "state's interest in protecting those who are not truly competent or facing imminent death, or those whose decisions to hasten death would not truly be voluntary, are sufficiently weighty enough to justify a prohibition against physician-assisted suicide." [521 U.S. 793, at 809.] She explained that the argument of respondents misstates the legal question

and that there is no doubt as to the fact that suffering patients have a constitutional right to obtain relief from suffering and to palliative care even when that care may hasten their deaths. The difficulty lies in defining "terminal illness," and the risk is so great that a dying patient's request to end his or her life may not be voluntary that the law will not allow doctors to assist patients in committing suicide.

On the same day that the Court heard ORAL ARGUMENT in *Quill,* the Court also heard and decided *Washington v. Glucksberg.* In *Glucksberg* the petitioner's claims rested on similar constitutional grounds but in the end also failed to convince the Court that a right to commit suicide should be recognized. The argument in *Glucksberg* was that there was either a violation of equal protection of the law, or of due process of law under the Fourteenth Amendment. Petitioners asserted that based on the Court's reasoning in PLANNED PARENTHOOD V. CASEY and CRUZAN V. MISSOURI DEPARTMENT OF HEALTH, the right to "self-sovereignty" was the foundation on which the Court could establish the right to physician-assisted suicide. As in *Quill,* the Court disagreed with petitioners, holding instead that a right to physician-assisted suicide is not protected by the Fourteenth Amendment and involves no fundamental right protected by the due process clause. The question of whether or not "the right to die" encompasses the right for mentally competent adults to physician-assisted suicide was closed in *Vacco v. Quill,* but the Court may return in the years to come as medical advances allow doctors to better define illnesses as "terminal," enabling them to equip patients with a more precise understanding of the illness they are facing. This in turn may enable patients to make a medically informed choice about whether or not they wish to continue living.

For more information: Arestad, Kim. "*Vacco v. Quill* and the Debate Over Physician-Assisted Suicide: Is the Right to Die Protected by the Fourteenth Amendment?" *New York Law School Journal of Human Rights* 15 (Spring 1999):

511; Feinberg, Brett. "The Court Upholds a State Law Prohibiting Physician-Assisted Suicide." *Journal of Criminal Law & Criminology* 88 (Spring 1998): 847; Moore, Paul. "Physician-Assisted Suicide: Does 'The End' Justify the Means?" *University of Arizona Law Review* 40 (Winter 1998): 1,471; *Village of Euclid, Ohio v. Ambler Realty Co.*, 272 U.S. 365 (1926).

—Laurie M. Kubicek

Van Devanter, Willis (1859–1941) *Supreme Court justice*

Willis Van Devanter, who served as associate justice of the U.S. Supreme Court from 1910 until 1937, was born on April 17, 1859, in Marion, Indiana. After receiving his law degree from the University of Cincinnati Law School in 1881, he returned to Marion to work for his father's law firm. Three years later, Van Devanter moved to Cheyenne, Wyoming Territory, established his own law office, and became active in Republican politics.

Van Devanter's political participation led to his rapid climb through a series of increasingly important public offices. Between 1886 and 1888, Van Devanter was appointed to serve on the Wyoming Territory Statutory Revision Commission, appointed city attorney of Cheyenne, and elected to the territorial legislature. In 1889, in recognition of Van Devanter's work on behalf of the Republican Party, President Benjamin Harrison appointed the 30-year-old attorney and legislator as chief justice of the Wyoming Territorial Supreme Court.

Van Devanter resigned from his prestigious position one year after his appointment in order to return to his very lucrative law practice. He remained active in Republican politics but did not hold public office again until 1897, when he was appointed to the position of assistant U.S. attorney general for the Department of the Interior. Van Devanter resigned from that position in 1903 and returned to Wyoming to accept his appointment to the U.S. COURT OF APPEALS for the Eighth Circuit by President Theodore Roosevelt.

During his seven-year stint on the Eighth Circuit, Van Devanter authored few opinions. His most significant work was his concurrence with some of the senior, more conservative Eighth Circuit justices in several decisions that interpreted the interstate commerce clause (U.S. Constitution, Article I, Section 8) as strictly limiting the power of the federal government to intervene in matters that might affect the economies of two or more states.

The death of the chief justice of the U.S. Supreme Court, Melville FULLER, in July of 1910, allowed President William H. TAFT to seize the opportunity to add Conservative justices to the Court. On December 15, 1910, the Senate confirmed Justice Edward D. WHITE's promotion from the position of associate justice to that of chief justice, and Van Devanter's appointment to fill White's newly vacated position.

As an associate justice of the Supreme Court, Van Devanter continued the PRECEDENT he established while on the Court of Appeals, disfavoring federal regulation of the economy. He concurred in decisions that established precedents limiting Congress's ability to pass laws concerning issues such as child labor and "yellow dog" contracts that allowed employers to require, as a precondition to employment, that workers sign away their right to unionize. The other salient prejudice that Van Devanter took to the high court was an interpretation of the due process clause of the Fourteenth Amendment that prevented state regulation of maximum work hours and minimum rate of pay.

During his term on the Supreme Court, Van Devanter did not write many opinions and may have actually suffered from writer's block. However, he was influential in group decision-making, because he was extremely intelligent, had a near-photographic memory, and knew a great deal of obscure and arcane federal law. Chief Justices Taft and White readily admitted that they tapped Van Devanter's knowledge in order to arrive at key decisions in cases before the Court.

Van Devanter's conservative interpretation of the Constitution resulted in his unofficial alliance with the other, similarly inclined Justices Butler, McReynolds, SUTHERLAND, and Roberts. This group concurred in *U.S. v. Schechter Poultry Corporation*, 295 U.S. 495 (1935), and *U.S. v. BUTLER*, 297 U.S. 1 (1936), two landmark cases that found two key components of the New Deal, the *National Industrial Recovery Act*, 40 U.S.C. §§401–444 (1933); and the *Agricultural Adjustment Act*, 7 U.S.C. §§601–640 (1933), unconstitutional.

These decisions were unusual in that they did not focus on specific, defective portions of these laws but instead presented policy statements that demonstrated that the Court had, in essence, returned to its 19th century policy of prohibiting Congress from enacting laws that might have even the slightest effect upon INTERSTATE COMMERCE. FDR believed that adherence to this policy would plunge the nation into Depression once again. In February 1937 he sent Congress the "court-packing bill," that in essence would have forced the retirement of the six Supreme Court justices who were more than 70 years old.

Partly in response to the threat presented by this bill, between March and May of 1937, the Supreme Court handed down decisions evidencing a switch in their interpretation of the Constitution that allowed the majority of the justices to uphold New Deal legislation.

Additionally, several of the elderly justices had actually delayed retirement in anticipation of Congress's passing the long-awaited law that granted retired justices a reasonable government pension. Justice Van Devanter announced his retirement, effective June 2, 1937, soon after the retirement bill passed. He died nearly three years later, at his home in Wyoming, on February 8, 1941.

For more information: Ariens, Michael. "American Legal History." Michaelariens.com. Available online. URL: http://www.michaelariens.com/ConLaw/justices/vandevanter.htm. Downloaded May 20, 2004; Legal Information Institute. "Biographies of Associate Justices of the U.S. Supreme Court." Cornell University Law School (1999). Available online. URL: http://www2.law.cornell.edu/cgi-bin/foliocgi.exe/justices/query=°/doc/{t140}. Downloaded May 20, 2004; The OYEZ Project. "Biographies." U.S. Supreme Court Multimedia. Available online. URL: http://www.oyez.org/oyez/resource/legal_entity/63/biography. Downloaded May 20, 2004.

—Beth S. Swartz

Village of Euclid, Ohio v. Ambler Realty Co., 272 U.S. 365 (1926)

In *Village of Euclid, Ohio v. Ambler Realty Co.,* Justice SUTHERLAND, writing for the Court, upheld the validity of comprehensive ZONING laws and declared that zoning restrictions on the use of private property did not unconstitutionally deprive individuals of the use of their property without "due process."

In 1922 the Village of Euclid, Ohio, enacted a comprehensive zoning law to regulate the location of businesses, industry, apartment complexes, and single and double family houses within the limits of the village. The ordinance created a building inspector and an office of zoning appeals to enforce the provisions of the law. Meetings of the appeals board were open, and a written record of its proceedings was kept for the public record. Ambler Realty filed suit claiming the law deprived it of property "without due process of law" and denied it the "equal protection of the law" guaranteed in the Fourteenth Amendment. Specifically, Amber Realty maintained that property it had purchased to resell for industrial development had lost significant potential value because of the zoning law. For example, land that could be sold for industrial usage had a market value of approximately $10,000 per acre, while that same land, limited to residential usage, had a maximum market value of only $2,500 per acre.

The question before the Supreme Court was whether the village's zoning ordinance was an unreasonable use of the police power and violated the constitutional protection to property. Justice Sutherland addressed the authority for enacting zoning regulations, the questions of a "living constitution," and the specific issue in the *Ambler* case.

Sutherland noted that while zoning laws "are of modern origin," their justification is found in "the police power, asserted for the public welfare," a power traditionally reserved to the states. Zoning laws grew out of the changing nature of life in the United States: "Until recent years, urban life was comparatively simple; but with the great increase and concentration of population, problems have developed, and constantly are developing, which require, and will continue to require, additional restrictions in respect to the use and occupation of private lands in urban communities." What at one time would have been rejected as "fatally arbitrary and unreasonable" restrictions on property rights had become wise, necessary, and "uniformly sustained."

Sutherland explained the Constitution as an elastic document that can and must meet the challenges presented by changing conditions in order to remain relevant to our society. While the meaning of the Constitution and its guarantees do not change, "the scope of their application must expand or contract to meet the new and different conditions which are constantly coming within the field of their operation. In a changing world it is impossible that it should be otherwise."

However, this concept of elasticity applies only to the application of constitutional principles and not to their meaning. An ordinance that attempts to address new conditions must still remain within the bounds of the Constitution; new solutions to new situations may not always be constitutional. There is not a precise line separating "the legitimate from the illegitimate assumption of power," and, therefore, "the circumstances and the locality" must be considered. To assist in the determination of legitimate from illegitimate, Sutherland suggested that we consult the "law of nuisances," which considers the circumstances of the situation in balancing conflicting rights. As Sutherland points out, "A nuisance may be merely a right thing in the wrong place, like a pig in the parlor instead of the barnyard." To make this determination, the courts should defer to the state's legislative judgment since it is the legislative branch that is more attuned to local conditions and circumstances. Their decision is, however, still subject to the guarantees in the Constitution and any determination "found clearly not to conform to the Constitution, of course, must fall."

Zoning laws dealing with height of buildings, construction materials used, occupancy limits, etc., fall with the legitimate use of the police power. Sutherland refused to address the broader question of "the creation and maintenance of residential districts, from which business and trade of every sort . . . are excluded." He did, however, note that the majority of decisions in the state courts had upheld such regulations.

For more information: Haar, Charles, and Jerold Kayden. *Landmark Justice: The Influence of William J. Brennan on America's Communities.* Washington, D.C.: Preservation Press, 1989.

—Alex Aichinger

Vinson, Fred M. (1890–1953) *chief justice of the Supreme Court*

Fred M. Vinson, a former congressman from Kentucky, former circuit court judge and secretary of the Treasury, was appointed to the Supreme Court in 1946 by President Truman to replace Chief Justice Harlan Fiske STONE. He served until 1953.

Historians of the Court have sometimes speculated that Vinson was appointed simply because he was the president's poker buddy. That is too facile an explanation. The Supreme Court was sharply divided during Stone's last years, and Truman worried that the justices' ever more open battles were undermining public confidence. In view of Vinson's outstanding record in the executive and legislative branches, as well as his five years as a circuit court judge, many Washington leaders saw him as an ideal candidate to bring harmony to the Court. Yet he has been almost universally rated a failure as CHIEF JUSTICE. What happened?

The reasons appear to be a combination of personal, institutional, and contextual. On a personal level, the very strengths that served Vinson so well in the political branches may have undermined him in the judicial branch. Vinson was a negotiator and peacemaker without a particular agenda of his own beyond striving for harmony among the brethren. His easygoing style was inadequate to overcome the huge egos and ideological passions that split Justices FRANKFURTER and BLACK. As a firm believer in JUDICIAL RESTRAINT and deference to the legislature, Vinson could have been a soul mate of Justice Frankfurter. The latter's pedantic concurring opinions and unwillingness to work for consensus except on his own terms gradually drove the justices apart. [After the funeral Frankfurter wrote to a former clerk that Vinson's death was the one true indicator he had of the existence of a God!] Apparently Justice JACKSON was sorely disappointed that he had not been selected as chief justice. He, along with several of the other justices, saw the new chief as intellectually inferior. Vinson's cautious writing style (he had a reverence for the legislature and PRECEDENT not shared even by Frankfurter), his reluctance to pen concurring opinions, and his willingness to assign major cases to other justices did nothing to enhance his personal reputation. In brief, he was too nice a guy.

On an institutional level Vinson also had difficulty. One of the keys to Chief Justice John MARSHALL's success had been his ability to persuade his colleagues to abandon the custom of writing individual opinions in each case and issue

Chief Justice Fred Vinson *(United States Supreme Court)*

one majority opinion with limited concurrences and dissents. Vinson understood this and tried in vain to limit concurrences. As chief justice he could assign majority opinions, but he still had only one vote and no power to limit concurrences and dissents. One measure of the Court's divisions is the number of concurring and dissenting opinions. As one expert writes, "in the 1950 term when the Court had only 88 majority opinions, it also handed down 23 concurring opinions and a whopping 60 dissenting opinions." Nor could Vinson force the justices to accept and decide more cases than they were willing to. Before World War II the Court had sometimes taken up to 200 cases a year.

During Vinson's first year the Court accepted 142. The decisions issued also dropped to 94 in 1949, to 88 in 1950, and to 89 in 1951. In some respects Vinson can be held personally responsible for this. He firmly believed the Court should reserve its judgments "for cases of high national importance or clear conflict below." In no event should it merely be a revisory board to correct lower court errors and second-guess the legislature. Or perhaps with justices intent on scoring points against one another through concurrences and dissents they simply did not have the time to decide more cases. Vinson's leadership could not overcome their divisions.

Finally, the historical context in which Vinson served might well have been such that no one could have led the Court successfully until the nation had a chance to settle down after the war and the threat of Communist infiltration was properly assessed. One should recall that during the first half of the century most liberals, confronted with a conservative activist court, were passionate defenders of judicial restraint and more interested in economic rights than CIVIL RIGHTS. One of Vinson's problems, in the eyes of his critics, is that he never moved beyond that position. He was a New Deal liberal who for the most part trusted government, but he was not a civil libertarian in the mode of Earl WARREN, who followed him as chief justice. He was a man behind his times.

On the other hand, Vinson's record in the areas of individual rights and due process in light of contemporary scholarship provides a more nuanced and sympathetic picture. In the late '40s and early '50s the extent of Communist influence in government was simply an unknown, and both Senator McCarthy and the House Un-American Activities Committee were riding high. Research from Soviet archives in the 1990s shows that there were indeed efforts to infiltrate American government, although nowhere near the extent or with the success administration critics alleged. Vinson's political philosophy was that "order must be secured for freedom to exist." When he had to balance society's need for order and stability against an individual's freedom of speech, Vinson usually came down on the side of order. His majority opinions in *American Communications Association v. Douds,* 339 U.S. 382 (1950), and *Dennis v. United States,* 341 U.S. 494 (1951), reflected this value. In the political climate resulting from the war on terrorism his opinions will be viewed more favorably.

The second area needing reconsideration is Vinson's approach to the rights of racial minorities. While often castigated for his cautious adherence to precedent, he did indeed believe that segregation was wrong and worried about how best to attack it. One can make a strong argument that the Vinson court's undermining of *PLESSY V. FERGUSON,* 163 U.S. 537 (1896), through a series of cases, made its eventual overturning possible. Vinson's first opinion in this area, *SHELLEY V. KRAEMER,* 334 U.S. 1 (1948), struck down the power of states to enforce restrictive racial covenants. Three cases decided in 1950, *Henderson v. United States,* 339 U.S. 816 (segregating dining tables based on race violates the interstate commerce clause); *Sweatt v. Painter,* 339 U.S. 629 (rejecting separate law schools for blacks in Texas on the basis that they were inherently unequal), and *McLaurin v. Oklahoma,* 339 U.S. 637 (keeping a black student separated from his peers in a graduate program), each weakened *Plessy* and prepared the country for the Court's sweeping rejection of "separate but equal" in *Brown v. Board of Education,* 347 U.S. 483,

four years later. Vinson wrote the opinions in both *Sweatt* and *McLaurin.* They may have been cautiously written, but the intent was clear and their impact significant.

Chief Justice Vinson died suddenly of a heart attack on September 8, 1953. In the light of his successor, Earl Warren, he was judged a failure. Yet he accomplished many things in his lifetime, and contemporary scholars are reassessing that first evaluation.

For more information: St. Clair, James, and Linda C. Guigin. *Chief Justice Fred M. Vinson of Kentucky: A Political Biography.* Lexington: University Press of Kentucky, 2002.
—Paul J. Weber

Violence Against Women Act of 1994 (42 U.S.C. §13981)

In 1994 Congress passed the Violence Against Women Act (VAWA) in reaction to increased public awareness of domestic violence and rape in the aftermath of several high-profile cases in the 1990s, such as that of O. J. Simpson, who was accused of killing his wife Nicole and her friend Ronald Goldman on June 12, 1994.

VAWA provided for increased federal penalties for acts of violence against women and set aside funds to establish grants for domestic violence and rape crisis programs. VAWA appropriated funds to increase public awareness of violence against women and to increase police protection. The provision of VAWA that attracted the most attention was the section that allowed women who were victims of gender-related crimes to sue their victims for punitive and compensatory damages and to ask for federal court-ordered injunctions to keep their attackers away. The compensatory damages included recovery of lost earnings and reimbursement for medical expenses.

Before the women's movement, violence against women was taken for granted. The American legal basis for such violence had its roots in English common law wherein *coverture* dictated that a married woman's identity was literally "covered" by her husband. Most states allowed a man to beat his wife as long as the item used was no thicker than his thumb. The phrase "rule of thumb" originated from this concept. As society changed, victims of acceptable violence expanded to include female partners and girlfriends. It was assumed that males were naturally aggressive. The women's movement, however, drew attention to the problem and led to a public understanding that violence was not normal behavior.

The VAWA went into effect on September 13, 1994. Shortly thereafter events took place that challenged congressional authority to provide for CIVIL RIGHTS remedies under VAWA. Christy Brzonkala, a first-year student at Virginia Polytechnic Institute, was allegedly raped by two football players, Antonio Morrison and James Crawford. Morrison later admitted to a school judiciary committee that the two men had indeed had sex with her and that Brzonkala had said "no" at least twice. Morrison was suspended for two semesters, a verdict which he challenged. Brzonkala sued both Morrison and the school, who had never reported the rape to authorities, under VAWA.

The United States Supreme Court heard the case of UNITED STATES V. MORRISON ET AL., 529 U.S. 598 (2000), in January 2000. The constitutional basis for the challenge was derived from congressional dependence on its INTERSTATE COMMERCE powers (Article I, Section 8) and on the EQUAL PROTECTION CLAUSE of the Fourteenth Amendment. On May 15, 2000, in a 5 to 4 decision, the Court struck down the civil rights section of VAWA.

Interpreting the right of Congress to legislate VAWA, the Court determined that on the basis of FEDERALISM Congress had no constitutional power to usurp the powers of the states to deal with violence. They argued that allowing Congress to do so would open the door to federal intrusion in other areas of family law, a province of state and local governments. The state of Illinois responded to the decision by passing its own bill to give victims the right to sue in gender-related crimes. Other provisions of VAWA were allowed to stand.

Justices SOUTER, STEVENS, GINSBURG, and BREYER issued a scathing dissent in *United States v. Morrison et al.*, arguing that Congress had documented the need for federal legislation in the matter of violence against women with a "mountain of evidence." The dissenters pointed out that the NECESSARY AND PROPER CLAUSE, Section 8, clause 18, had historically given Congress the power to supplement its interstate commerce powers.

Those who supported the Court's decision generally agreed that the case was rightfully decided on the basis of federalism. Critics, however, argued that violence against women was indeed an economic issue and that Congress acted within its constitutional powers. Throughout the 1990s as Congress was in the process of preparing to enact legislation on violence against women, they heard firsthand evidence of the economic aspects of violence against women. They learned from employers that battered women are often absent from work and are less productive that other women when they are doing their jobs. Experts on rape told them about the economic impact on rape victims, including the fact that many victims of rape are so traumatized they lose their jobs.

In 2003, 88 members of the House of Representatives sponsored HR 494, the Violence Against Women Civil Rights Restoration Act, to reinstate the civil rights provision of the 1994 act. The bill remains in committee.

For more information: Noonan, John T., Jr. *Narrowing the Nation's Power: The Supreme Court Sides with the States.* Berkeley: University of California Press, 2002; Renzetti, Claire M., et al., eds. *Sourcebook on Violence Against Women.* Thousand Oaks, Calif.: Sage Publications, 2001.

—Elizabeth Purdy

Virginia v. Hicks, 539 U.S. 113 (2003)

In an attempt to control escalating crime and drug dealing in a Richmond, Virginia, housing project, the RICHMOND REDEVELOPMENT AND HOUSING AUTHORITY (RRHA) enacted a policy limiting access to the streets of the RRHA to persons with "a legitimate business or social purpose." Persons violating this policy were subject to notification by the Richmond police that they were guilty of trespass and, if they remained on the premises or returned, were subject to arrest. Mr. Hicks, not a resident, was informed of the policy and received a written notice barring him from the housing project; he disregarded the notice and was arrested and convicted of the crime of trespass. Hicks appealed his conviction on the grounds that the law was facially invalid, that is, the law is simply too broad to be constitutional. While the RRHA does have a legitimate interest in controlling criminal activities and can enact policies designed to reduce those activities, that policy cannot be so broad in scope as to prohibit and punish other noncriminal, constitutionally protected, activities such as demonstrating or engaging in political activities, or simply exercising one's legitimate freedom of speech.

Justice SCALIA cites *Broadrick v. Oklahoma,* 413 U.S. 601 (1973), in explaining OVERBREADTH doctrine: "The showing that a law punishes a 'substantial' amount of protected free speech, 'judged in relation to the statute's plainly legitimate sweep' suffices to invalidate *all* enforcement of that law" until the application is narrowed to remove the potential threat to freedom of speech. That is, a law punishing unprotected speech or conduct will be voided if its application can also punish constitutionally protected speech or conduct.

Scalia admits that use of the overbreadth doctrine is "strong medicine" because of the social costs created by its use, but it is required in certain instances "out of concern that the threat of enforcement of an overbroad law may deter or 'chill' constitutionally protected speech." Because of this, the Court will only resort to facial invalidation when the law specifically addresses "speech or conduct necessarily associated with speech." The law in question must threaten legitimate freedom of speech but in a substantial way and in a way relative to the legitimate application of that law. In other words, the Court will balance the social costs of a legitimate policy with the potential but real threat to constitutionally protected freedoms.

In this case, Hicks was convicted under the trespass provisions of the law, and it was his "nonexpressive *conduct . . .* not his speech, for which he is punished as a trespasser." This case is not about freedom of speech, rather it is concerned with the legitimate application of anticrime legislation in general and criminal trespass in particular. The RRHA trespass policy does not violate the First Amendment's overbreadth doctrine.

For more information: Aronson, Baron. "The Supreme Court Rightly Rejects a Free Speech Challenge In *Virginia v. Hicks,* Which Is, at Heart, a Simple Trespassing Case." FindLaw Commentary. Available online. URL: http://writ.news.findlaw.com/aronson. Downloaded May 20, 2004.

—Alex Aichinger

Voting Rights Act

A landmark piece of legislation passed by Congress in 1965 after prior federal antidiscrimination laws proved insufficient in overcoming barriers to voting rights based on race or ethnic background. Despite several historical attempts to prevent discrimination, universal suffrage was not realized in the United States until the second half of the 20th century.

Efforts first emerged in the post-Civil War Reconstruction Era. The Fifteenth Amendment to the Constitution was ratified in 1870 to ensure that voting would not be abridged "on account of race, color, or previous condition of servitude." However, it proved ineffective in preventing intimidation tactics to exclude potential African-American voters from the election process. This led to the rise of the white primary, particularly in southern states. It was not until years later that the Supreme Court ruled the white primary to be unconstitutional in *Smith v. Allwright,* 321 U.S. 649 (1944), making primary elections subservient to the Fifteenth Amendment. Obstructionist tactics still persisted despite the Court's verdict. The use of complex literacy tests and poll taxes, which were primarily administered only to African-American voters, continued the atmosphere of discrimination.

The CIVIL RIGHTS ACT OF 1964 declared the application of unequal standards in voter registration procedures illegal. It required that literacy tests be administered in a written format at a sixth-grade level of education. This became the norm until Congress outlawed the tests entirely in 1970. The Twenty-fourth Amendment to the Constitution, ratified in 1964, declared poll taxes unconstitutional as a requirement for voting in national elections, and the Court extended this provision to state and local elections in the case *HARPER V. VIRGINIA STATE BOARD OF* Elections, 383 U.S. 663 (1966).

Despite these efforts, African-American voters remained disenfranchised as resistance to universal suffrage persisted, especially in the South. Registrars circumvented prior congressional legislation and Court decisions by limiting the number of applications processed, sabotaging vote cards submitted by African-American voters, and delaying vote counts to taint election results, to name a few tactics. Early in 1965, Martin Luther King, Jr., led a CIVIL RIGHTS demonstration in Selma, Alabama, to protest continued discrimination. In response to the demonstration, President Lyndon B. Johnson persuaded Congress to pass the Voting Rights Act of 1965, which he symbolically signed in the same room where Abraham Lincoln had written the Emancipation Proclamation in 1862. While opposition was intense, primarily by politicians in southern states, the Voting Rights Act still rallied the necessary votes in the House of Representatives by 333 to 48 and the Senate by 77 to 19 for passage. The legislation granted the U.S. attorney general new powers, including the authority to replace local registrars with federal registrars if evidence of discrimination existed. It also simplified registration procedures to expand suffrage. The impact of the act was rapid as both the number of African Americans who registered to vote and the rate for those elected to office skyrocketed nationwide.

Congress deemed the Voting Rights Act to be effective, so much so that it has been renewed and expanded several times. The act was first extended for five years in 1970. New provisions set residency requirements at 30 days and prohibited states from disqualifying voters in presidential elections if they did not meet residency requirements beyond that time frame, and also provided uniform federal rules for absentee registration and voting in presidential elections.

The minimum voting age was lowered from 21 to 18 years of age, which was upheld in the Supreme Court's ruling in *Oregon v. Mitchell,* 400 U.S. 112, for national elections only. The Twenty-sixth Amendment expanded this age requirement to the state and local levels. The act was extended in 1975 for seven years, and several new requirements were added such as bilingual ballots in all states. Also required was the approval of changes in state election laws falling under the act by the DEPARTMENT OF JUSTICE or a federal court, and the broadening of protections to other races including Hispanic Americans, Asian Americans, and Native Americans. Congress extended the Voting Rights Act for 25 years in 1982. The act was strengthened when the effects test replaced the intent test, where the intent to discriminate did not need to be proved if the effects were clearly demonstrated. The law also gave judges greater power to redraw voting districts to ensure minimum minority representation.

The Voting Rights Act and its subsequent amendments made universal suffrage possible by establishing a federal standard to prevent discrimination at the state and local levels. It tempered the effects of passive and sometimes noncompliant subnational governments, and it provided recompense for the sluggish nature of implementing judicial decisions. Women's suffrage likewise faced an uphill battle until voting rights were secured by ratification of the Nineteenth Amendment in 1920.

For more information: Ball, Howard, Dale Krane, and Thomas P. Lauth. *Compromised Compliance: Implementation of the 1965 Voting Rights Act.* Westport, Conn.: Greenwood Press, 1982; Hudson, David Michael. *Along Racial Lines: Consequences of the 1965 Voting Rights Act.* New York: Peter Lang, 1998; Laney, Garrine P. *The Voting Rights Act of 1965: Historical Background and Current Issues.* New York: Nova Science, 2003.

Waite, Morrison Remick (1816–1888) *chief justice of the Supreme Court*

Morrison Remick Waite was appointed by President Ulysses Grant in 1874 to the Supreme Court, where he served as CHIEF JUSTICE until his death in 1888.

Morrison Waite was born in Lyme, Connecticut, on November 29, 1816. After graduating from Yale College in 1837, he worked briefly as a law clerk for his father, who was chief justice of the Connecticut Supreme Court. Later that year, Waite moved to Maumee City, Ohio, to clerk for an attorney there. After Waite was admitted to the Ohio bar in 1839, he opened his own law office in Maumee and worked there for the next 11 years.

In September 1840, Waite was married to another native of Lyme, his second cousin, Amelia C. Warner. During the next dozen years, the couple had four children.

In 1850 Waite, his wife, and their growing family moved to Toledo, Ohio, where Waite immediately established a new law practice and also accepted an invitation to run for the lower house of the Ohio legislature on the Whig Party ticket. Waite's late-1850 victory at the polls may have erased some of the frustration generated by his unsuccessful 1846 run for the U.S. House of Representatives.

Only two years later, after deciding that he was far better suited to practicing law than to legislating, Waite declined the Whigs' invitation to run for a second term in the Ohio House and returned to Toledo to practice law full-time. He also found time to maintain some political contacts and activities, because he was a key participant in founding the Ohio Republican Party in 1856. Six years later, at the invitation of the Republicans, Waite ran for the House of Representatives but again lost his bid for national office. In 1863 Waite declined the Ohio Republicans' offer of an appointment to the Ohio Supreme Court.

In 1871 President Ulysses S. Grant appointed Waite to be a delegate to an international arbitration board established to settle claims for damages incurred when Great Britain assisted the Confederacy during the Civil War. Waite's intelligence and patience enabled him to quickly earn respect of the European negotiators and allowed him to become a dominant figure in the negotiations. On his return to the United States, Waite received nationwide publicity for being a key player in the arbitration board's decision to award $15.5 million to the United States.

In 1873 Waite won a popular election to become a delegate to the Ohio Constitutional Convention and was then unanimously elected by his fellow delegates to preside over

Chief Justice Morrison Remick Waite *(Library of Congress)*

the event. While this Convention was in session on January 19, 1874, President Grant nominated Waite to become chief justice of the United States Supreme Court. As soon as Waite was sure that the Senate had confirmed this appointment, he walked away from the Constitutional Convention and a successful law practice that was the result of 34 years of hard work in order to assume his new position.

Waite's adjustment to his new job was made difficult by the animosity of some of the associate justices who had hoped to win promotion to chief justice themselves. Fortunately, Joseph BRADLEY, an associate justice who did not have higher aspirations and was acknowledged by his peers to be the most intelligent and astute of all the justices, decided to become Waite's unofficial mentor.

Bradley was an unusually generous man as well as a facile writer, while Waite was reputed to be a competent legal researcher but a clumsy writer. After Waite became chief justice, when the Court was faced with an important and/or complex decision, it was not unusual for Bradley to do the lion's share of writing of an opinion to which Waite then signed his name. While Waite was not inclined to correct the public's belief that he wrote all of the opinions to which he signed his name, he always gave Bradley credit for his important role when they were in the company of the other justices.

Most legal scholars agree that the most important case decided during Waite's tenure as chief justice (hereinafter, "the Waite Court") was *MUNN v. ILLINOIS*, 94 U.S. 113 (1877). In that case, the Waite Court held that the Fourteenth Amendment's due process clause allowed states to regulate the economies only of those businesses that had an impact on the lives of a broad cross section of the local community, or, in the Court's terminology, businesses that "were affected (or "clothed") with a public interest."

In practice, in *Munn*, the Court verified the propriety of using state-established rates for businesses such as grain elevators, since this type of business affected factors important to the entire local population, such as food prices, unemployment, and ability to conduct INTERSTATE COMMERCE. However, the Waite Court held that it would be unconstitutional for a state to establish economic controls on a privately owned and operated clothing store or other small business, because this sort of niche business did not affect a significant portion of the community. Although Waite signed his name to the *Munn* case, Supreme Court historians agree that Bradley probably did most of the research and wrote most of the opinion.

In the *Civil Rights Cases,* 109 U.S. 3 (1883), the Court found that the Civil Rights Act of 1875, 18 Stat. 433 (1875), which attempted to prohibit RACIAL DISCRIMINATION in inns, public transportation, and places of amusement, was unconstitutional. The Waite Court reasoned that the Civil Rights Act attempted to prohibit discriminatory action that

was purely private in nature, and therefore not within the scope of the EQUAL PROTECTION CLAUSE of the Fourteenth Amendment. The Court further held that the due process clause of the Fourteenth Amendment applied only to the rights of black men in the post–Civil War era, and not to any other privileges and immunities guaranteed in the Constitution. This restrictive interpretation of the Fourteenth Amendment prevailed for more than 10 years after the decision in the *Civil Rights Cases.*

Morrison Remick Waite served as Chief Justice until his death, on March 23, 1888, at the age of 71.

For more information: Ariens, Michael. "Notable Persons and Events in American Legal History, Chief Justices of the Supreme Court." Michaelariens.com. Available online. URL: http://www.michaelariens.com/ConLaw/justices/waite.htm. Downloaded May 20, 2004; The OYEZ Project. "Morrison Remick Waite." U.S. Supreme Court Multimedia. Available online. URL: http://www.oyez.org/oyez/resource/legal_entity/43/biography. Downloaded May 20, 2004.

—Beth S. Swartz

Wallace v. Jaffree, 472 U.S. 38 (1985)

In *Wallace v. Jaffree,* the U.S. Supreme Court addressed the constitutionality of a state statute authorizing voluntary prayer in public schools. The majority of the Court in this case ruled that the statute was unconstitutional.

The state of Alabama had three statutes addressing prayer in public schools. The first statute authorized teachers in public schools to provide a "period of silence" of one minute or less for quiet meditation. The second statute authorized the same period of silence but stated that the period was for ". . . meditation or voluntary prayer." The third statute provided that state teachers or professors

> . . . may pray, may lead willing students in prayer, or may lead the willing students in the following prayer to God: Almighty God, you alone are our God. We acknowledge you as the Creator and Supreme Judge of the world. May Your justice, Your truth and Your peace abound this day in the hearts of our countrymen, in the counsels of our government, in the sanctity of our homes and in the classrooms of our schools in the name of our Lord. Amen.

Jaffree challenged the statutes as unconstitutional under the ESTABLISHMENT CLAUSE of the First Amendment of the United States Constitution, which states "Congress shall make no law respecting an establishment of RELIGION. . . ." In an extremely unusual ruling, the federal trial judge decided that although the state's SCHOOL PRAYER statutes might be unconstitutional based upon previous Court decisions, the Court had erred in those decisions. The trial judge ruled the statutes constitutional because the state of Alabama had the right to establish a state religion, contrary to existing Court PRECEDENT. [*Jaffree v. Board of School Commissioners,* 554 F. Supp. 1104 (1983).]

The Eleventh Circuit COURT OF APPEALS reversed the trial court decision, holding that the school prayer statutes prescribing a state prayer and the authorization of voluntary prayer were unconstitutional. [*Jaffree v. Wallace,* 705 F.2d 1526 (1983).]

The state of Alabama appealed that portion of the Court of Appeals decision finding unconstitutional a period of silence for "mediation and voluntary prayer" (Ala. Code 16-1-20.1). The Court applied the *Lemon* test, from *LEMON V. KURTZMAN,* 403 U.S. 602 (1971), which requires the following analysis of statutes challenged under the Establishment Clause of the First Amendment: (1) Does the statute have a secular legislative purpose? (2) Is the principal or primary effect of the statute one that neither advances nor inhibits religion? (3) Does the statute foster an excessive government entanglement with religion? The Court held that Alabama's voluntary prayer statute failed the first prong of the test since the express purpose of the statute was to place prayer back in public schools. State endorsement of voluntary prayer is unconstitutional. The Court did not address the Alabama statute providing for a "moment of silence" which made no reference to religion or prayer.

For more information: Schultz, David. "Church State Relations and the First Amendment." In *Law and Politics: Unanswered Questions,* edited by David Schultz, 235–266. New York: Peter Lang, 1994.

—Scott Childs

Walz v. Tax Commission of the City of New York, 397 U.S. 664 (1970)

In *Walz v. Tax Commission of the City of New York,* the Supreme Court upheld the constitutionality of tax exemptions for property owned by religious organizations and used for religious purposes.

Appellant Frederick Walz, a citizen of New York, sued to disallow such exemptions. He argued that since religious groups reap the benefits of government programs such as fire and police protection but pay no property taxes, the taxpaying public is effectively forced to subsidize the group by paying for such services on their behalf. According to Walz, this de facto subsidy is unconstitutional under the ESTABLISHMENT CLAUSE of the First Amendment, which prohibits laws "respecting an establishment of religion." The New York State Court granted the City's motion for SUMMARY JUDGMENT. Both the Appellate Division of the

New York Supreme Court and the New York COURT OF APPEALS affirmed. In a 7 to 1 decision, the Supreme Court concurred with the State courts.

Chief Justice BURGER wrote the opinion of the Court, joined by Justices BLACK, STEWART, WHITE, and MARSHALL. Acknowledging the complexity of the issues at hand the CHIEF JUSTICE ruled that a delicate balance must be struck between the seemingly conflicting establishment and free exercise clauses of the First Amendment. His argument was threefold. First, he made a purely historical argument, arguing that the PRECEDENT for tax exemption for religious institutions is a long-standing tradition that supports a governmental policy of "benevolent neutrality" toward churches and has clearly not promoted any form of state-sponsored RELIGION.

Second, churches and other religious organizations are part of a larger group of nonprofit charitable organizations that are granted tax-exempt status due to their positive "moral and mental" contributions to society. These, he argued, should not be undercut by the burden of taxation. Since tax-exempt status is granted to this category of charitable organizations as a whole, religious institutions are not being granted special and unique consideration or privilege. Finally, Burger recognized the precedent established in *LEMON V. KURTZMAN,* which states that laws must discourage an "excessive government entanglement" with religious organizations. Burger argues that taxation of religious institutions would violate this clause, resulting in a more intimate relationship between church and state than currently exists. He does concede, however, that a total separation between the two institutions is impossible given the complexity of modern society.

Justice BRENNAN's concurring opinion generally follows Burger's opinion but expands upon the historical reasons for allowing religious tax exemptions and emphasizes the dual roles played by religious establishments. While he is clearly cognizant of their primary function as houses of worship, he is also quick to extol the contributions to society made by churches, which not only serve as centers of morality but also contribute to the diversity of the nation.

Justice HARLAN concurs to emphasize the theoretical ideals of "neutrality and voluntarism" which must be recognized by the state. Since the government is universal in granting tax exemption to institutions that exist to promote charitable works in a not-for-profit environment, the government preserves its own neutrality in refusing to grant any organization within that category a preferred or special status.

Justice DOUGLAS writes the lone dissent. In it, he discredits the reliance upon historical precedent in this case, offering counterexamples that demonstrate that the historical relationship between church and state is not as unambiguous as the majority supposes. Further, Douglas argues that the basis of tax exemption for charitable organizations revolves around their performance of a function that the government would assume in their absence. Because religious institutions perform non-secular functions that cannot constitutionally be assumed by the state, Douglas argues that they must be categorized separately from other charitable organizations. As such, they should not be afforded the same tax-exempt status, which, according to Douglas, amounts to little more than a state subsidy of religion that is clearly unconstitutional.

For more information: Miller, Robert, and Ronald Flowers. *Toward Benevolent Neutrality: Church, State and the Supreme Court.* Waco, Tex.: Baylor University Press, 1992.
—Jacob Fowles

Ward's Cove Packing Company v. Atonio, 490 U.S. 642 (1989)

In 1989 in *Ward's Cove Packing Company v. Atonio,* the United States Supreme Court rejected the argument of nonwhite workers in an Alaskan salmon cannery who accused their employer of violating TITLE VII OF THE CIVIL RIGHTS ACT of 1964, which prohibited the practice of discrimination in hiring and promoting employees. Despite the fact that the workers had gathered a substantive body of information documenting the alleged discrimination by Ward's Cove Packing Company, the Court determined that the absence of minorities in skilled jobs within the company reflected "a dearth of qualified nonwhite applicants" rather than overt discrimination.

Frank Atonio and other minorities who worked for the Ward's Cove Packing Company insisted that minorities were relegated to unskilled, lower-paying jobs within the company, while white workers were assigned to higher-paying skilled jobs that provided greater opportunity for advancement. The plaintiffs claimed that this practice was discriminatory in light of Title VII of the Civil Rights Act of 1964, which banned all discrimination in employment on the basis of race, sex, color, RELIGION, and national origin.

Atonio and his colleagues introduced evidence that the Ward's Cove Packing Company had created two separate levels of jobs: *unskilled cannery jobs* that were mostly filled by nonwhites, Filipinos, and Alaskan natives, and *skilled non-cannery positions* that were filled for the most part by white workers. The plaintiffs argued that the company discriminated through a pattern of nepotism, rehiring preferences, a lack of objective hiring criteria, separate hiring channels, and a reluctance to promote from within the company. They insisted that the discrimination was made even more repulsive by racially segregated housing and dining facilities.

The REHNQUIST Court dealt a major blow to supporters of AFFIRMATIVE ACTION by declaring in *Ward's Cove* that the burden of proof "remains with the plaintiff *at all times,*" making it more difficult for individuals to prove discrimination against employers. Shifting the burden of proof to the plaintiff was a direct withdrawal from the position the Court had established in 1971 in *GRIGGS V. DUKE POWER COMPANY,* 401 U.S. 424, in which the Court had stated that it was not necessary for plaintiffs in job discrimination cases to prove intentional discrimination by employers because Title VII mandated that employers to be responsible for the *consequences* as well as the *motivations* of discriminatory practices.

In a harsh dissent to the majority opinion in *Ward's Cove Packing Company v. Atonio,* Justice Harry BLACKMUN contended that his colleagues had taken "three major strides backwards in the battle against race" with their decision to upset "the longstanding distribution of burdens of proof in Title VII disparate-impact cases." In his dissent, Blackmun accused his colleagues of ignoring both history and present-day reality. He pondered "whether the majority still believes that race discrimination—or, more accurately, race discrimination against nonwhites—is a problem in our society, or even remembers that it ever was."

President Lyndon B. Johnson first established affirmative action as a means of ending discrimination in 1965 with Executive Order 11246. Subsequently, the Office of Federal Contract Compliance (OFCC) issued guidelines that spelled out the responsibilities of employers to conform to federal guidelines. Three months before the *Ward's Cove* decision, the Court struck a major blow to affirmative action in *CITY OF RICHMOND V. J. A. CROSON COMPANY,* 488 U.S. 469 (1989) when it rejected the City of Richmond's efforts to promote diversity by requiring that 30 percent of all government contracts be set aside for minorities. Retreating from the decades-long position on affirmative action, Justice O'CONNOR, writing for the Court in the case, declared that preferential programs that attempted to legislate remedies for past societal discrimination were inherently suspect.

A number of other affirmative action cases in 1989 seemed to foreshadow a governmental retreat from the past decades. In *Martin v. Wilks,* 490 U.S. 755, the Court gave firefighters in Birmingham, Alabama, permission to reopen earlier discrimination cases and challenge their findings. The Court also rejected an employee's claim of racial harassment in *Patterson v. McLean Credit Union,* 491 U.S. 164, and in *Lorance v. AT&T Technologies, Inc.,* 490 U.S. 900 (1989), the Court further restricted the rights of employees to charge employers with discrimination under Title VII.

In direct response to the Court's retreat from affirmative action, the U.S. Congress introduced new CIVIL

RIGHTS legislation that reiterated the national government's earlier position on affirmative action. President George Bush originally called the legislation a "quota bill" and withheld his support. However, Bush's position on affirmative action made him more vulnerable to attacks by the Democratic party in the upcoming 1992 election. He subsequently shifted position, expressing support for the new legislation that became the Civil Rights Act of 1991. Despite the efforts of Congress, the issue of affirmative action has continued to haunt the Supreme Court into the 21st century.

For more information: Barker, Lucius J., and Twiley W. Barker, Jr. *Civil Liberties and the Constitution.* Englewood Cliffs, N.J.: Prentice Hall, 1990; Nieman, Donald G. *Promises to Keep: African-Americans and the Constitutional Order, 1776 to the Present.* New York and Oxford: Oxford University Press, 1991; Simon, James F. *The Center Holds: The Power Struggle Inside the Rehnquist Court.* New York: Simon and Schuster, 1995.

—Elizabeth Purdy
—Nathan A. Strum

Ward v. Rock Against Racism, 491 U.S. 781 (1989)

In *Ward v. Rock Against Racism,* the United States Supreme Court upheld New York City's sound-amplification guidelines against a First Amendment challenge.

After a series of complaints and problems associated with sound levels at the Naumberg Acoustic Bandshell in New York City's Central Park, the city adopted use guidelines for the bandshell that required performers in the space to use both sound-amplification equipment and a sound technician provided by the city. Respondent Rock Against Racism, an unincorporated association that had sponsored a series of concerts in the bandshell in the past, challenged the guidelines on First Amendment grounds. After the Second Circuit reversed the district court's decision upholding the guidelines, the Supreme Court granted certiorari and upheld the guidelines as a reasonable regulation of the place and manner of protected speech. Justice Kennedy delivered the opinion of the Court, with Justice MARSHALL filing a dissenting opinion, in which Justices BRENNAN and STEVENS joined.

The Court began its analysis by deeming the bandshell to be "a public forum for performances in which the government's right to regulate expression is subject to the protections of the First Amendment." [*Ward v. Rock Against Racism,* 491 U.S. 781, 791 (1989).] The Court noted that "even in a public forum the government may impose reasonable restrictions on the time, place, or manner of protected

speech," provided that: (1) the restrictions "are justified without reference to the content of the regulated speech"; (2) "they are narrowly tailored to serve a significant governmental interest"; and (3) "they leave open ample alternative channels for communication of the information." [*Ward v. Rock Against Racism,* 491 U.S. 781, 791 (1989).] The Court then considered each of these three requirements.

With respect to the first prong—namely, content neutrality, the Court framed the inquiry as "whether the government has adopted a regulation of speech because of disagreement with the message it conveys." [*Ward v. Rock Against Racism,* 491 U.S. 781, 791 (1989).] In this instance, the Court concluded, the guidelines were justified without reference to the substance or message of the regulated speech and, as such, were content neutral. Moreover, the Court rejected Rock Against Racism's argument that the guidelines were effectively (even if not expressly) content based as a result of the discretion accorded the city officials charged with enforcing them. In so doing, the Court concluded that the Guidelines, "[w]hile . . . undoubtedly flexible," had to be interpreted to forbid city officials from treating performers differently based upon the message those performers were delivering.

The principal dispute in this case, however, concerned the second requirement—namely, that the challenged regulation be "narrowly tailored" to serve a significant governmental interest. In deciding this issue, the Court expressly rejected the analysis adopted by the COURT OF APPEALS, which was drawn from the Supreme Court's earlier decision in UNITED STATES V. O'BRIEN, 391 U.S. 367, 377 (1968), and which required that the city's solution be the least restrictive alternative of furthering this goal. Rather, the Court concluded, the requirement of narrow tailoring would be satisfied "so long as the . . . regulation promotes a substantial government interest that would be achieved less effectively absent the regulation" and did not "burden substantially more speech than is necessary to further the government's legitimate interests."

As the Court held, so "long as the means chosen are not substantially broader than necessary to achieve the government's interest . . . the regulation will not be invalid simply because a court concludes that the government's interest could be adequately served by some less-speech restrictive alternative." In passing, the Court then addressed the third requirement, holding that the regulation also met the final requirement that it leave open ample alternative channels of communication.

Justice Marshall dissented sharply, arguing that the majority had effectively abandoned the requirement that time, place, and manner regulations be narrowly tailored, and that the guidelines at issue constituted an impermissible PRIOR RESTRAINT. Noting the "availability of less intrusive but effective means of controlling volume," Marshall argued that the majority's decision "deprive[d] the narrow tailoring requirement of all meaning" and eliminated the requirement that the government balance the effectiveness of a particular regulation with the burdens on free speech.

—Anne M. Voigts
—Carrie A. Schneider
—Stanley M. Morris

war powers

The war powers refer to the ability of the president and Congress to commit troops abroad in situations where United States interests are challenged. Over time, the Supreme Court has issued several rulings regarding war powers.

The abilities of the office and of the Congress are enumerated within the Constitution in Article II for the president, and Article I for the Congress. These two branches of the government can combine to wage a war, fund it, and allow other related needs to be addressed. The original ability for the United States of America to allow the president to wage war and the Congress to assist was derived from the formation of the U.S. Bank. By having a bank, the government could then raise an army and fund the defense of the nation.

The SEPARATION OF POWERS originally allowed for the courts to decide only questions of constitutionality and understandings of power. The thought was for the president to have the ability to send troops to war, but only a war approved by the Congress, thus keeping the president in check if the people's representatives disagreed over foreign policy. Mostly, the courts addressed these issues after the fact, but they would decide the exacting appropriate nature of which branch maintained which abilities. The framers of the Constitution did not want troops committed by the stroke of a pen based upon one man's inclination—that was too imperial an idea for a developing democracy—but the country needed to be able to defend itself when attacked, so the president did need some latitude. In the case *Bas v. Tingy* (1800), the Supreme Court believed that the Congress could engage the American troops sans the official declaration of war document; thereby giving the nation an opportunity to defend their interests in the short run.

Lincoln was the first president to enact the "war power" as a means of protecting the union, in that he was allowed by the courts to do so because Congress was out of session at the time. In his Message to Congress, on July 4, 1861, President Lincoln first referred to the abilities of the office in terms of a unification of those capabilities by calling the broad powers the "war power."

The courts supported President Lincoln with the *PRIZE CASES* of 1863. By allowing the president to blockade the rebellious Southern insurgency at the onset of the Civil War, the courts had effectively enforced the war power that Lincoln addressed in his message to the Congress. Later Presidents Wilson, Roosevelt, and Truman all utilized the Army and Navy to address the protection of the United States' properties and interests abroad. The courts in 1936 defined the war powers rationale for giving such sweeping powers to the federal government as a whole. The Congress and the president have debated as to which branch has the authority to solely wage war, and the courts for the most part have excluded themselves from the debate. In the late sixties, there were many calls for the nation's top court to pass a decision condemning the war in Vietnam. The social peace movements battled the government politically in various high profile events, but for the most part the courts did not pass opinions in regard to the validity of the war.

The War Powers Resolution (1973), which was passed over President's Nixon's veto, restricted the abilities of the president and set new reporting standards for the presidential branch of the United States in terms of war. Basically, the president could send troops to war in certain circumstances, must report and discuss the deployment with the Congress, and must abide by the congressional decisions in regard to the time length of the war involvement. Post this initial expiration date, which allows the president to engage in the war for 60 days (with an extension of another 30 days), the Congress must officially draft an act of war document that then allows for funds to be made available for completion of the military endeavors. Thus, a president must set a time length for the war, and the Congress must give the power and the funding to the war in order for the president to run the war as the commander in chief of the U.S. armed forces.

Opponents to the results of the 1973 act professed that the act did not go far enough to curb possible abuses by the president. In addition, the belief was that anything the Congress would be able to stop would be post the commission of troops to an unpopular war that would result in U.S. casualties. Proponents of the act offered that the president was still free to develop foreign policy and defend the nation from attack without having to deal with big meetings and possible leakage of security information that could compromise decisive victories. Most presidents have claimed that a limited amount of time to perform the necessary functions is unrealistic due to possible unforeseen advents. In more recent times, the relative balance between the two branches has been a little less challenging due to the fervent patriotism that has at times enveloped the country.

In 2001, after the terrorist attacks on the World Trade Towers, the president called the nation into a state of war against "terrorists"—but not against another country directly. The retributive application of the U.S. troops into foreign countries such as Afghanistan was done based upon facts and fears that were believed by some to have been not entirely affirmed. The Congress passed special legislation allowing for the continuation of activities into a second nation, Iraq, based partly upon the nation's involvement in the support of terrorist activities. Opponents to these invasions have professed that the president had been given too much latitude by the Congress, but once done, the actions of the president and the powers granted could not be popularly undone. It remains to be seen if the years following the involvement within Iraq and Afghanistan will force the Congress to yet again request a constitutional analysis of the war power; but one thing is almost assured, the courts will make the decision.

For more information: *Immigration and Naturalization Service v. Chadha*, 462 U.S. 919 (1983); War Powers Act (War Powers Resolution) of 1973.

—Ernest Alexander Gomez

Warren, Earl (1891–1974) *chief justice of the Supreme Court*

Earl Warren was appointed CHIEF JUSTICE of the United States Supreme Court by President Dwight Eisenhower in 1953, and he served until 1969.

Earl Warren is considered by many experts to be one of the great chief justices, second only to John MARSHALL in his impact on the Constitution. Yet he is also reviled for his liberal JUDICIAL ACTIVISM.

Warren was raised in Bakersfield, California, in a working-class family. His father was a laborer for the Southern Pacific Railroad who eventually became a foreman. Earl attended public schools and enrolled at the University of California-Berkeley where he earned both his undergraduate and law degrees. After a brief stint in the army he found a job as deputy district attorney of Alameda County, which encompassed the city of Oakland. He proved to be a very successful prosecutor and eventually was elected district attorney. From there he won election as attorney general of California, running as the nominee of the Democratic, Republican, and Progressive parties. His honesty and anticrime stance made him a very popular figure in California politics. One popular action he later regretted was leading the effort to remove citizens of Japanese ancestry from major cities and the California coast. Following the attack on Pearl Harbor, people were uncertain whether there were saboteurs among the Japanese. In 1942 Warren ran as a Republican against an incumbent Democratic governor and won.

Warren served 10 successful years as governor. He was reelected twice by large pluralities, the first Republican star since Roosevelt had swept the Republicans out of power in

Chief Justice Earl Warren *(United States Supreme Court)*

1932. Was he liberal or conservative? In fact, he was a bit of both, and a commonsense visionary as well. He began as governor by cutting taxes and establishing a financial reserve for emergencies. He also worked for prison reform, increased spending for higher education, assistance for the elderly and the mentally ill, and pioneered a compulsory health insurance system. Warren was a pragmatist who saw government as a means to help those in need, but he knew from his years as district attorney that government power can be abused. Thus while he joined in the anticommunist crusades after World War II, he tried to protect academic freedom, freedom of speech, and due process.

Much to his astonishment, Earl Warren was asked to run for vice president on the 1948 Republican ticket with Governor Thomas Dewey of New York. They lost to Harry Truman, but Warren was now seen as a potential presidential candidate. The 1952 Republican National Convention was filled with uncertainties. There was potential for a deadlock between the two main candidates, Dwight Eisenhower and Robert Taft. Warren was seen as a compromise candidate or at least someone who could pledge California's votes to either candidate, but deadlock was avoided and Eisenhower was nominated on the first ballot. Warren campaigned actively for him. Eisenhower respected Warren's administrative abilities. Either he or one of his aides promised Warren "the first available seat" on the court. Chief Justice Fred VINSON died of a heart attack on September 8, 1953. Warren's nomination was announced on September 30.

The "Warren Court" was one of the most activist courts since the founding of the Republic. It had as profound and comprehensive an impact on American society as any court in history. Indeed, the Warren Court practically defined political liberalism in the postwar era and set much of the national agenda for the next half century. It began with an assault on racial segregation. The Court's unanimous decision in *Brown v. Board of Education,* 347 U.S. 483 (1954), declaring that legally segregated schools are inherently unequal, is arguably the most important event in race relations since passage of the Fourteenth amendment in 1868. It overruled a 58-year PRECEDENT in *PLESSY V. FERGUSON,* 163 U.S. 537 (1896), and signaled the Court's willingness to plunge into political thickets where state and federal legislators feared to tread. Technically *Brown* dealt only with education, but its principled argument was sweeping, and dozens of cases followed that outlawed segregated public transportation, public accommodations, housing, employment, and even marital relations.

Segregation was only the first problem the Warren Court addressed. Other issues included (a) forcing state legislatures to reapportion so that each citizen's vote counts as much as every other citizen's [*Baker v. Carr,* 369 U.S. 186 (1962) and *REYNOLDS V. SIMS,* 377 U.S. 533 (1964)]; (b) limiting the federal government's ability to intimidate and destroy careers and reputations by using their investigative powers [*Watkins v. United States,* 354 U.S. 178 (1957) and *Greene v. McElroy,* 360 U.S. 474 (1957)]; (c) limiting common prayer in public schools [*Engel v. Vitale,* 370 U.S. 421 (1962) and *Abington School District v. Schempp,* 374 U.S. 203 (1963)]; (d) enhancing the government's power to regulate economic activities to enhance safety, honesty, fairness [*NLRB v. Gissel Packing Co.,* 395 U.S. 575 (1969) and *Brown Shoe Co. v. United States,* 370 U.S. 294 (1962)]; and most controversial, (e) protecting the rights of those accused of crimes.

Aside from race relations, no initiatives of the Warren Court triggered more public reaction than its largely successful effort to protect the rights of criminal defendants. Earl Warren had more experience in criminal justice than all other justices combined. Indeed, of the 235 opinions Warren authored, 69 or nearly a third concerned criminal law and procedure. No case caused more controversy than his opinion in *MIRANDA V. ARIZONA,* in which he laid out the famous Miranda warnings that must be read to every criminal suspect at the time of their arrest and before they can be questioned. "You have the right to remain silent; anything you say can be used against you in court; you have the right to talk to a lawyer before questioning and to have a lawyer with you during questioning. You may stop questioning at any time. If you cannot afford a lawyer, one will be provided for you." Warren also made clear that evidence gathered in violation of these stipulations could not be used as evidence in a court, the so-called EXCLUSIONARY RULE.

Conservatives were apoplectic, and "Impeach Earl Warren" signs went up across the country. With the passage of time scholars have been able to evaluate the impact of the changes in criminal process initiated by the Warren Court: neither convictions nor the number of confessions declined measurably. Rarely did a guilty person go free. The most important result of the Warren Court's jurisprudence was increased education and training of police forces across the country.

Shortly after President Kennedy was assassinated in 1963, President Lyndon Johnson asked the chief justice to chair a commission and investigate the tragedy. Warren hoped to publish a definitive report that would allay American fears of an international conspiracy. The "Warren Commission Report" had the opposite effect. Much of the blame can be laid on Warren. Because he wanted a quick report, the commission staff did not vigorously pursue evidence collected by the FBI and CIA, did not follow up on alternative theories that more than one bullet was fired, possibly from different locations, and refused to allow graphic pictures to accompany the report. Warren also insisted on a unanimous opinion by committee members and was willing to water down statements to get it. The Warren report was widely attacked as a cover-up or, at best, a sloppy, unprofessional piece of work. Although the commission's results have never been proved wrong, the damage to Warren's reputation was significant.

Earl Warren was a liberal, activist justice. He saw his role as guiding the courts to promote the ethical values imbedded in the Constitution—equality of opportunity, liberty for individuals to speak, read, write, and associate as they saw fit without government censorship, and the right of government to regulate businesses for the common good, and protection of those minorities most vulnerable to abusive government power, African Americans and people accused of crime. Warren retired from the Supreme Court in 1969 and died of congestive heart failure in 1974. What he accomplished on the Supreme Court continues to be controversial, but no one denies he had a major impact on constitutional law and CIVIL LIBERTIES.

For more information: Cray, E. *Chief Justice: A Biography of Earl Warren.* New York: Simon and Schuster, 1997; Katcher, L. *Earl Warren: A Political Biography.* New York: McGraw-Hill, 1967; Pollack, J. *Earl Warren: The Judge*

Who Changed America. Englewood Cliffs, N.J.: Prentice Hall, 1979; White, G. Edward. *Earl Warren: A Public Life.* New York: Oxford University Press, 1982.

—Paul J. Weber

Warth v. Seldin, 422 U.S. 490 (1975)

In *Warth v. Seldin,* the Court held that the instant CLASS ACTION suit against the suburban town of Penfield, New York, and its town officials was unconstitutional. The importance of this decision rests primarily in that it set the PRECEDENT that a plaintiff must make out a clear "case of controversy" for the Court to take action.

According to the Court's ruling, the plaintiffs in the case did not produce any concrete facts that proved that the ZONING ordinance passed by Penfield directly harmed them. In addition, the third-party groups involved failed to assert that the passing of the ordinance infringed on their rights as third-party contractors. Finally, the individual plaintiffs failed to produce evidence confirming an "injury" resulting from the ordinance. Through this process, the Court determined that in any civil suit, it is the plaintiff's responsibility to present the Court with a direct line of causation between the plaintiff's injury and the defendant's action.

The Court rejected the petition that the townships' zoning ordinance indirectly excluded those citizens being of low and moderate income from living within the township's limits and therefore not violating the plaintiff's federal constitutional rights and of the CIVIL RIGHTS statues in 42 USCS 1981–1983. Justice POWELL, representing the perspectives of five members of the Court, affirmed that none of the plaintiffs or third-party participants had a STANDING for the class action suit for the following reasons: (1) the four plaintiffs who were of low or moderate incomes who, incidentally, were of a minority or ethnic group status, had failed to produce evidence stating that they were directly hampered or injured by the ordinance; (2) there is no clear line of causation between the town's ordinance and its enforcement and the plaintiff's claimed injuries; (3) residents of Penfield who are of low and moderate income have raised no complaints stating that their constitutional rights have been denied due to this ordinance; (4) the third-party building contractors who claimed damages for infringements against their members failed to produce evidence supporting their claim adequately enough to award judicial involvement; (5) the Housing Council of Monroe County Area Inc., composed of numerous area housing organizations, has not alleged, with one exception that is no longer relevant, that any of its members has made strides toward building homes in Penfield.

Furthermore, the Court asserted that persons of low or moderate income who incidentally are members of a minority or ethnic group have zero standing to contest, as plaintiffs in a federal class suit, a town's zoning ordinance which supposedly excludes such individuals as a violation of their rights under the federal Constitution and the civil rights statutes in 42 USCS 1981–1983, where the plaintiffs failed to produce evidence supporting their claims, whereas if these restrictions were not in place by the ordinance, these individuals would have been treated unfairly by the township. Also, the Court also declared that city taxpayers and residents have no position to challenge a suburb's zoning ordinance as long as there is no direct line of causation between the suburban town's ordinance and the individual's way of life within the city.

This case is of significance because it sets the precedent for future civil suits since it states that there must be a direct line of causation between the plaintiff and the infraction caused by the defendant. Without this direct line, the case has no standing within the civil courts. Therefore, the burden of proof is laid upon the plaintiff, and it is the plaintiff's responsibility to provide facts sustaining the complaint and invoking the powers of the Court. In addition, this case sets future precedent when dealing with the zoning rights of townships and city residents. In essence, the Court deems that it is the responsibility of local governments to resolve such matters and have the lower courts handle the appeals.

For more information: Friedenthal, Jack H. *Civil Procedure.* St. Paul, Minn.: West Group, 1999.

Washington, Bushrod (1762–1829) *Supreme Court justice*

George Washington's favorite nephew, Bushrod Washington, was appointed by President John Adams to the Supreme Court in 1798, serving until his death in 1829.

Bushrod Washington was born on June 5, 1762, the son of the first president's younger brother, Brigadier General John Augustine Washington. The first president's nephew was only a toddler when his obvious intelligence and quick wit caught his uncle's attention. This academic talent allowed Bushrod Washington ("Washington") to matriculate at the College of William and Mary when he was 13 years old, to become a member of the first chapter of Phi Beta Kappa in the United States, and to graduate only a few days after his 16th birthday in June 1778.

At William and Mary, Washington befriended a classmate who shared his passionate interest in law, John MARSHALL, who later became the first CHIEF JUSTICE of the Supreme Court. Washington, who was much younger than most of the students, very short, and perpetually carelessly attired, was usually overlooked by classmates and was grateful for Marshall's friendship. Marshall apparently enjoyed Washington's intellect and sense of humor so much that he found it easy to ignore his classmate's physical appearance.

Three months after Washington received his baccalaureate degree, he enlisted in the Continental Army. He was given the rank of Private of the Dragoons and sent off to war. During the next three years, Washington, who was younger than nearly all of his comrades, consistently demonstrated leadership that belied his age. He was brave in combat situations and earned additional respect from his superior officers when he showed an uncanny ability to anticipate British tactics. The Dragoons' efforts were key to the American victory in the last major confrontation of the Revolution, the Battle of Yorktown. This conflict began in late September 1781 and finally ended on October 19, 1781, with the surrender of the British commander, General Cornwallis. When the smoke cleared, Washington and his comrades watched as his uncle, George Washington, supervised the British surrender. Bushrod Washington's three years of exemplary military work in the Dragoons were officially recognized with the presentation of a citation for distinguished service to his country.

Soon after Bushrod Washington's discharge from the army, George Washington sponsored his nephew's apprenticeship with James Wilson, a well-known Philadelphia attorney. After being admitted to the Virginia bar in 1783, Bushrod Washington opened his own law office in Alexandria, Virginia. One year later, his mentor, James Wilson, was appointed to the U.S. Supreme Court.

In 1788 Washington served as a delegate to the Virginia Convention to ratify the U.S. Constitution. During the next 10 years, Washington appeared frequently in Virginia's trial and appellate courts, where his intellect and mastery of legal strategy earned him the respect of both the judiciary and his legal opponents. He also socialized with members of the bar, since many of them shared Washington's interest in and constant involvement with politics. Washington was a staunch Federalist throughout his adult life, and he remained hardworking and loyal to the party throughout the mid- and late-1790s, when the ranks of the Federalists were wracked by internal dissension.

Subsequent to George Washington's death in 1797, Bushrod Washington was appointed executor of the estate and also inherited his uncle's entire Mount Vernon plantation and the slaves who worked there. In Bushrod Washington's first, and possibly only practical and noncontroversial exercise of his authority as his uncle's executor, he loaned all of his uncle's journals, letters, and other documents to John Marshall, who had requested these materials to research a planned biography of George Washington.

In autumn of 1798, while his uncle's will was still in probate, Bushrod Washington's mentor, Supreme Court Justice James Wilson, died. President John Adams appointed Washington to fill this vacancy on the bench, partly because of his excellent military record and his work for the Federalists, but mostly because of his extraordinary intellectual ability and excellent record in the courts. On February 4, 1799, 37-year-old Bushrod Washington was sworn in as an associate justice of the U.S. Supreme Court. (The only justice who was younger at the time of his appointment was Joseph Story, who was 32 when he was appointed to the Supreme Court in 1812.)

George Washington had undoubtedly intended to honor his nephew, Bushrod Washington, by designating him as heir to his real estate. The elder Washington probably did not realize that the property had become terribly dilapidated during his years of absence, while he was fighting the Revolution and presiding over the United States, first from New York City, then from Philadelphia. In fact, when Bushrod Washington visited Mount Vernon, he found that only one room in the mansion was livable.

George Washington's will mandated that all of the Mount Vernon slaves be emancipated after his death. Bushrod Washington shared his uncle's idea that slavery was wrong but believed that emancipation would only result in racial wars within the United States. His ideas were expressed in the goals of an organization that he had created and in which he had the title of lifetime president, the American Colonization Society. This organization aimed to eliminate slavery in the United States by freeing all slaves and resettling them in Africa.

After following his uncle's instructions regarding emancipation of the Mount Vernon slaves, Bushrod Washington brought his own slaves back to the estate. They were untrained for country living and proved to be of very limited assistance. Washington soon realized that the very meager salary of an early-19th-century justice of the Supreme Court was inadequate to cover the cost of feeding and lodging the nonworking slaves and hiring carpenters or handymen to make the most essential repairs to the plantation buildings. Eventually, Washington found himself on the brink of bankruptcy. He attempted to sell some of the nonworking slaves at auction and was immediately attacked by abolitionists either for being unfaithful to his own cause or for not following his uncle's example of freeing his slaves.

Unfortunately, at that point, three male slaves escaped and found a newspaper reporter willing to believe their largely falsified story. After publication of that story, another reporter visited Mount Vernon while Bushrod Washington was in the District of Columbia, fulfilling his responsibilities at the Supreme Court. For weeks, reporters at newspapers throughout the colonies carried on a vicious verbal assault, the jist of which was that Bushrod Washington was a lesser human being than his famous uncle.

Throughout his 30 years as a justice of the Supreme Court, Washington strongly supported the nationalist jurisprudence of Marshall and could usually be counted among the supporters of Marshall's opinions. Washington was solicitous of private property claims, using the contracts clause of Article I, Section 10 of the U.S. Constitution, and also advocated a fairly broad concept of federal power when presented with competing claims made by the states. Washington wrote a concurring opinion in DARTMOUTH COLLEGE V. WOODWARD, 4 Wheat. 518 (1819), in which he tempered the language in Marshall's majority opinion regarding the contracts clause of the U.S. Constitution, and voted with the majority in *Ogden v. Saunders,* 25 U.S. 213 (1827), the only constitutional law case in which Marshall wrote a dissenting opinion. During his 30 years as a justice, Washington aired his differences of opinion with his fellow justices in only one dissenting opinion, *Mason v. Haille,* 25 U.S. 270 (1827).

Why did Washington leave such a meager written record of his 30 years on the bench? It has been suggested that he signed his name to so few Court opinions because he did not want to leave behind materials that could be used to compare his accomplishments to those of his famous uncle, George Washington. While he undoubtedly loved his famous uncle, it is abundantly clear that Bushrod Washington hated having every iota of his being compared with his uncle's and found lacking.

Bushrod Washington died while working as an associate justice of the U.S. Supreme Court on November 26, 1829. He was laid to rest beside his famous uncle in the Washington family plot.

For more information: Ariens, Michael. "American Legal History—Justices of the Supreme Court." Michaelariens.com. Available online. URL: http://www.michaelariens.com/ConLaw/justices/washington.htm. Downloaded May 20, 2004; Supreme Court Historical Society. "Bushrod Washington." United States Supreme Court. Available online. URL: http://www.supremecourthistory.org/02_history/subs_timeline/images_associates/008.html. Downloaded May 20, 2004.

—Beth S. Swartz

Washington v. Davis, 426 U.S. 229 (1976)

In *Washington v. Davis,* the Supreme Court held that the disproportionate impact of a qualifying test administered to all applicants for the police force in the District of Columbia did not violate their equal protection rights within the Fifth and Fourteenth Amendments. Instead, only intentional discrimination constituted a violation of these constitutional clauses.

The Civil Service Commission developed a qualifying test known as "Test 21" for general examination use throughout the federal service. The test examined the verbal skills, vocabulary, reading, and comprehension abilities of applicants. To pass, applicants needed to score at least 40 out of 80. The police department in Washington, D.C., administered the test to all applicants. Afterward, results revealed that four times more blacks than whites failed. Some unsuccessful black applicants contested the validity of Test 21 on the grounds that it adversely affected black candidates in violation of their right to equal protection under the law.

The district court did not agree. It held that the requirements of the qualifying test are a valid recruiting procedure for the police department, noting that the design and administration of the exam lacked a discriminatory intent. In addition, it pointed out that the test did not discriminate against those blacks who passed the exam. The Federal Appeals Court heard the case and reversed, holding that the test unfairly disadvantaged black applicants. It pointed to the disproportionately large number of blacks failing the test as compared to whites; this was the critical factor to focus upon, not whether the design or administration of the test lacked a discriminatory intent.

The Supreme Court reversed the decision of the Appeals Court. Writing for the Court, Justice Byron White explained that the government has a legitimate objective ". . . to upgrade the communicative abilities of its employees . . . particularly where the job requires special ability to communicate orally and in writing." Furthermore, ". . . our cases have not embraced the proposition that a law or other official act . . . is unconstitutional solely because it has a racially disproportionate impact." The Court acknowledged that a disproportionate number of blacks failed. However, the issue to consider was whether there was a showing that the design or administration of the test was discriminatory.

The significance of *Washington v. Davis* lies in its refusal to investigate motives that might uncover discriminatory intent. This ruling made success in future "disparate impact" cases harder for CIVIL RIGHTS groups. Justice WHITE also rejected the more rigorous JUDICIAL REVIEW, STRICT SCRUTINY, called for in the CIVIL RIGHTS ACT OF 1964. He perceived strict scrutiny as an inappropriate encroachment on the duties of administrators and executives.

Overall, the Court ruled that showing a disproportionate impact was insufficient by itself to prove discrimination. To do that, petitioners must show discriminatory intent.

For more information: Lamb, Charles M., and Stephen C. Halpern, eds. *The Burger Court: Political and Judicial Profiles.* Urbana: University of Illinois Press, 1991.

—Matthew R. Doyle

Watchtower Bible & Tract Society v. Village of Stratton, 536 U.S. 150 (2002)

In *Watchtower Bible & Tract Society v. Village of Stratton,* the Supreme Court struck down a municipal ordinance requiring those wishing to engage in door-to-door advocacy of a political cause or religious proselytizing to first register with the mayor's office and obtain a permit as a violation of the free speech clause of the First Amendment. In an 8 to 1 decision delivered by Justice STEVENS, the Court found that the Village of Stratton ordinance was overbroad since it affected religious proselytizing and ANONYMOUS POLITICAL SPEECH.

Stratton, Ohio, is a village of 278 people. The village enacted an ordinance prohibiting "canvassers" from going door-to-door promoting any cause without first obtaining a "Solicitation Permit" from the office of the mayor. There is no monetary cost for the permit, and permits are regularly given out when requested. The canvassers are allowed to go on the premises that are listed on the registration form and must carry the permit to show to residents who request to see it.

For more than 50 years the Court has invalidated restrictions on door-to-door canvassing. Most of these cases have involved the Jehovah's Witnesses since their RELIGION mandates proselytizing door-to-door. The Jehovah's Witnesses take literally the Scriptures which state, "Go ye into all the world, and preach the gospel to every creature." They follow the example of Paul, teaching "publicly, and from house to house."

The Sixth Circuit COURT OF APPEALS found the municipal ordinance to be content-neutral and upheld it under INTERMEDIATE SCRUTINY. The Supreme Court reversed the lower court's decision, determining that the municipal ordinance was overbroad since it did not only apply to religious but also political causes. The ordinance was not narrowly tailored to the Village of Stratton's interests of protecting the privacy of its residents and preventing fraud and crime. The amount of speech covered under the ordinance raised the concern of the Court. If the provisions of the municipal ordinance had only pertained to COMMERCIAL SPEECH it would have been narrowly tailored to the village's interests.

The Supreme Court also found that the municipal ordinance interferes with speakers maintaining anonymity; places a burden on those holding certain political and religious beliefs that may prevent them from seeking a permit; and effectively bans spontaneous speech. The Court did not determine what level of scrutiny (RATIONAL BASIS, intermediate, or strict) was necessary for determining the constitutionality of the ordinance since the ordinance was determined to be overbroad.

Chief Justice REHNQUIST was the lone dissenter in *Watchtower.* Rehnquist contends that the municipal ordinance passes the relevant test of intermediate scrutiny. The ordinance is content-neutral and merely regulates the manner of canvassing door-to-door. Crime prevention, fraud prevention, and protection of privacy are legitimate governmental interests. Rehnquist focused a large portion of his dissenting opinion on crime prevention, citing several examples of crimes committed under the guise of door-to-door canvassing.

For more information: Greenhouse, Linda. "Court Strikes Down Curb on Visits by Jehovah's Witnesses," *The New York Times,* June 18, 2002; Pelham, Zachary E. "Constitutional Law—Freedom of Speech: Door-to-Door Permit Requirements for Noncommercial Canvassers, Domestic Threat or Freedom of Speech?" *North Dakota Law Review* 79 (2003): 369—390; Symposium. "Leading Cases: I. Constitutional Law: 3. Door-to-Door Canvassing." *Harvard Law Review* 116 (November 2002): 282–292; *Watchtower Bible & Tract Society of New York v. Village of Stratton,* 536 U.S. 150 (2002).

—Carrie A. Schneider

Webster v. Reproductive Health Services, 492 U.S. 490 (1989)

In *Webster v. Reproductive Health Services,* the Supreme Court of the United States ceded control of access to abortion to the individual states as long as they did not totally prevent access to abortions as established under *ROE V. WADE,* 410 U.S. 113 (1973). While the conservative members of the Court tend to abhor the *Roe* decision, their own conservatism often binds them to the doctrine of STARE DECISIS ("let the past decision stand"). An astounding 78 "friends of the court" briefs were filed in *Webster,* representing both sides of the abortion debate.

The instrument for severely restricting ABORTION RIGHTS was a Missouri law that had been designed with the sole purpose of promoting "childbirth over abortions." The law banned the use of public facilities for the performance of abortions and made it illegal for staff at public hospitals to perform abortions even if private funds were used. The only exception was to save the mother's life. All use of public funds for abortion counseling was also banned. Because of *Roe,* Missouri could not totally restrict abortions, so the law set up a required test of viability on all women seeking abortions who were deemed to be at least 20 weeks into their pregnancies. The testing included gestational age, weight, and lung maturity of the fetus. Viability is generally assumed to take place at 24 weeks, the point at which a fetus might conceivably survive outside the womb with medical assistance. In the preamble to the law, the Missouri legislature determined that human life begins at conception. The battle lines in *Webster* included Missouri attorney William L. Webster and a host of antiabortion "friends of the court" versus health-care professionals backed by a host of pro-choice "friends of the court."

The *Webster* decision was a product of an extremely divided Court. From the nine justices, six separate opinions emerged. On the extreme right, Justice SCALIA wanted to overturn *Roe v. Wade.* For what ultimately constituted the majority in Webster, Chief Justice REHNQUIST argued that *Roe* forced the Supreme Court to serve as an *"ex officio medical board"* and referred to *Roe's* "rigid trimester analysis" as "unsound in principle and unworkable in practice." Rehnquist was joined in this opinion by Associate Justices WHITE and Kennedy, arguing for rejection of *Roe's* trimester system.

The majority of the Court argued that there was "no reason why the State's compelling interest in protecting potential human life should not extend throughout pregnancy rather than coming into existence only at the point of viability." The lone female on the Court and usually the crucial fifth vote, Justice Sandra Day O'CONNOR accepted the restrictions of *Webster* but was against overturning *Roe,* maintaining that "a woman has a right to choose abortion before viability and to obtain it without undue interference from the state." She argued for a new "undue burden test" to replace the trimester system of *Roe.* The Court refused to decide on the constitutionality of the preamble.

The liberal pro-choice bloc of Justices BLACKMUN, BRENNAN, STEVENS, and MARSHALL voted to strike down the Missouri law in its entirety. Justice Blackmun, the author of *Roe v. Wade,* staunchly defended the "sphere of liberty" established in *Roe* that granted women the right to make personal reproductive choices. Blackmun had been assigned the task of developing an argument for *Roe* because of his background in medical law, and he stood by the trimester system that he had developed as responsive to existing medical technology in 1973. Blackmun insisted that the trimester system was a "fair, sensible, and effective way of safeguarding the freedom of a woman, while accommodating the state's interest in potential human life." In an unpublished dissenting opinion to *Webster,* Blackmun wrote, "I rue this day. I rue the violence that has been done to the liberty and equality of women. I rue the violence that has been done to our legal fabric and to the integrity of the Constitution. I rue the inevitable loss of public esteem for this Court."

Webster was a major victory for abortion opponents who had expected *Webster* to overturn *Roe* and a triumph for the Reagan/Bush administrations that had made overturning *Roe* a major priority. The response from the states was immediate. In the months following the July 3 decision in *Webster,* more than 40 bills were introduced in various state legislatures, although most of the bills bogged down in debate. The language of the legislation shifted away from carefully worded support for fetal rights and attempts to limit freedom of choice to articulated support for family cohesion, taxpayers' rights in public funding, prevention of fetal pain, informed consent, and outright bans of so-called birth control abortions.

For more information: Alderman, Ellen, and Caroline Kennedy. *The Right to Privacy.* New York: Alfred A. Knopf, 1995; Boyle, Mary. *Re-thinking Abortion: Psychology, Gender Power, and the Law.* London and New York: Routledge, 1997; Simon, James F. *The Center Holds: The Power Struggle Inside The Rehnquist Court.* New York: Simon and Schuster, 1995.

—Elizabeth Purdy

Weeks v. United States, 232 U.S. 383 (1914)

In *Weeks v. United States,* the Court held that the Fourth Amendment barred the prosecution from introducing evidence seized by federal officials during illegal searches. This rule is commonly called the EXCLUSIONARY RULE. Based on the *Weeks* decision, the exclusionary rule only applied to federal cases. The Court later extended the exclusionary rule to state cases in *MAPP V. OHIO,* 367 U.S. 643 (1961).

The Court distinguished the *Weeks* case from its prior decision in *Adams v. New York,* 192 U.S. 585 (1904), in which it stated, "[E]vidence which is pertinent to the issue is admissible, although it may have been procured in . . . an illegal manner." [*Adams v. New York,* 192 U.S. 585, 596 (1904).] The Court distinguished the *Weeks* case, in part, because Weeks did not wait until trial, as Adams had done, to object to the manner in which the evidence was seized. Weeks alleged "in due season" that the seizure of evidence from his home without a warrant was a constitutional violation. [*Weeks v. United States,* 232 U.S. 383, 396 (1914).] Weeks objected to the manner of the seizure before trial, immediately after the trial began, and when the evidence was offered.

The Court based its decision to exclude the evidence on "the fundamental law in the Fourth Amendment, that a man's house [is] his castle and not to be invaded" by the government absent specific legal authority. [*Weeks v. United States,* 232 U.S. 383, 390 (1914).] The record indicated that Weeks was arrested without a warrant at his place of employment. Other police officers searched his house and removed various items, which they turned over to the United States Marshal. Later that day, the marshal returned to the residence with police officers to search for additional evidence. The marshal was admitted by a person, possibly a boarder, and conducted a warrantless search of Weeks's room. The marshal removed letters, which were used as evidence in prosecuting Weeks for using the mail for an illegal lottery. [*Weeks v. United States,* 232 U.S. 383, 386 (1914).]

The Court stated that the Fourth Amendment places limitations on the courts of the United States and federal officials. It creates a duty to protect people against unreasonable searches and seizures. "The tendency of those who execute the criminal laws of the country to obtain conviction by means of unlawful seizures . . . should find no sanction in the judgments of the courts which are charged at all times with the support of the Constitution. . . ." [*Weeks v. United States,* 232 U.S. 383, 392 (1914).] Thus, the Court held that the letters could not be used as evidence.

The Court did not address the actions of the local police officers, stating that the Fourth Amendment was not directed to misconduct of state and local officials. [*Weeks v. United States,* 232 U.S. 383, 398 (1914).] The Court later held that the exclusionary rule did not apply to prosecutions in state courts for state crimes although the Fourth Amendment applied to the states through the Fourteenth Amendment. [*Wolf v. Colorado,* 338 U.S. 25, 33 (1949).] However, the Court eventually extended the exclusionary rule to conduct of state and local officials, recognizing that it "makes very good sense." [*Mapp v. Ohio,* 367 U.S. 643, 657 (1961).]

For more information: LaFave, Wayne R. *Search and Seizure: A Treatise on the Fourth Amendment.* 3rd ed. St. Paul, Minn.: West, 1996; Stuntz, William J. "The Substantive Origins of Criminal Procedure." *Yale L. J.* 105 (1995): 393.

—Mason Byrd

welfare benefit rights

The United States Supreme Court has addressed issues surrounding welfare benefits on several occasions. Often these rulings have been concerned with the right to welfare or specific benefits, or issues regarding the termination of these benefits.

Social welfare refers to government aid to individuals who lack the ability or resources to provide for themselves or their families. Social welfare programs are designed to support a minimal living condition for individuals and families. There are several social welfare programs in place such as those that provide income support, subsidized housing, health care, and nutrition support. The modern American welfare system began with the Social Security Act of 1935. This act allowed the federal government to assist the states in providing economic assistance to needy adults such as the elderly, blind, and disabled. It was also designed to provide for the care of dependent children, and thus authorized the Aid to Families with Dependent Children (AFDC) program.

Aid to Families with Dependent Children was established as a joint federal and state program. The federal government provided most of its funding and wrote the rules under which it was administered. However, states had some

discretion as to how they operated the program. In 1996 Congress passed and President Clinton signed the Personal Responsibility and Work Opportunity Reconciliation Act. This legislation changed AFDC to Temporary Assistance for Needy Families (TANF). The act placed restrictions on aid in that it cannot be used for adults who have received welfare for more than five years. In addition it requires that adults receiving aid must begin working within two years of receiving aid. There have been several Supreme Court cases relative to the receipt of welfare benefits under AFDC and TANF.

In *SHAPIRO V. THOMPSON,* 394 U.S 618 (1969), the Court determined that basing AFDC aid on various residency requirements violated the EQUAL PROTECTION CLAUSE of the Fourteenth Amendment. Thompson was a 19-year-old mother with one child and pregnant with a second child. She applied for assistance under the AFDC program after moving to Connecticut from Massachusetts but was denied assistance on the grounds that she did not meet the state's one-year residency requirement. This case was decided along with *Washington v. Legrant* (1969) and *Reynolds v. Smith* (1969). In *Washington,* three people applied for and were denied AFDC aid on the ground that they had not resided in the District of Columbia for one year immediately preceding the filing of their application. In *Reynolds,* two people were denied AFDC aid because they had not been residents of Pennsylvania for at least one year prior to their applications. The Court ruled that Connecticut, Washington, D.C., and Pennsylvania failed to present any compelling administrative or social reasons for their residency requirements, thus the waiting period requirements denied equal protection of the law as guaranteed by the Fourteenth Amendment.

In *Goldberg v. Kelly,* 397 U.S. 254 (1970), the Court held that states must afford public aid recipients a pre-termination evidentiary hearing before discontinuing their aid. The Court determined that states that terminate public aid without allowing a hearing prior to termination violate notions of due process as guaranteed by the Fourteenth Amendment. Kelly, acting on behalf of New York residents receiving financial assistance from AFDC or New York's state welfare program, challenged the constitutionality of procedures for notice and termination of such aid. New York terminated public aid without affording the beneficiaries a hearing prior to termination. The Court found New York's hearings deficient in that they did not permit recipients to present evidence, be heard orally or through counsel, or cross-examine adverse witnesses, and thus the hearings denied PROCEDURAL DUE PROCESS as established in the Fourteenth Amendment's due process clause.

In *Bowen v. Roy,* 476 U.S. 693 (1986), the Court held that the government could require welfare recipients to provide it with their Social Security numbers as a condition of receiving aid. Stephen Roy and Karen Miller applied for and received benefits under the AFDC program and the food stamp program in Pennsylvania. They refused to comply with federal rules which required recipients to provided state welfare agencies with their and other family members' Social Security numbers as a condition of receiving benefits. Roy and Miller believed that obtaining a Social Security number for their two-year-old daughter would violate their religious beliefs. As such, the Pennsylvania Department of Public Welfare terminated AFDC benefits paid to them on the child's behalf and began proceedings to reduce the level of food stamps that the family was receiving. They filed an action against the Pennsylvania Department of Public Welfare in federal district court on the grounds that the free exercise clause of the First Amendment entitled them to an exemption from the Social Security number requirement.

The district court determined that an efficient and fraud-resistant system could be maintained without requiring a Social Security number for the child. The Supreme Court, however, reversed this decision and found that requiring a Social Security number does not violate the free exercise clause of the First Amendment on the basis that the Social Security number requirement does not prohibit the exercise of religious freedom. Further, the Court found that the requirement for supplying the Social Security number, as a condition of eligibility for benefits, is legitimate and important in preventing fraud.

In SAENZ V. ROE, 526 U.S. 489 (1999), the Court barred states from paying lower welfare benefits to families who have lived in the state for less than one year. Thirty years before this decision, in *Shapiro v. Thompson*, 394 U.S 618 (1969), the Court found that the basing of aid on residency requirements violates the equal protection clause of the Fourteenth Amendment. However, this case is different in that the Court relied on the privileges and immunities clause of the Fourteenth Amendment rather than its equal protection clause.

Under the Personal Responsibility and Work Opportunity Act of 1996, states receiving TANF funding could pay the benefit amount of another state's TANF program to residents who have lived in the state for less than 12 months. Brenda Roe filed a CLASS ACTION suit against Rita Saenz, director of California's Department of Social Services, on behalf of other first-year residents when California decided that would enforce the TANF provision. The Court explained that by paying first-year residents the same TANF benefits they received in their state of origin, states treated new residents differently than others who have lived in that state for more than one year. As such, enforcement of the durational residency requirement of the Personal Responsibility and Work Opportunity Reconciliation Act of 1996 unconstitutionally discriminated among residents.

For more information: Bussiere, Elizabeth. *(Dis)entitling the Poor: The Warren Court, Welfare Rights, and the American Political Tradition.* University Park: Pennsylvania State University Press, 1997; Dye, Thomas R. *Understanding Public Policy.* 9th ed. Upper Saddle River, N.J.: Prentice Hall, 1998; Janda, K., J. M. Berry, and J. Goldman. *The Challenge of Democracy: Government in America.* Boston: Houghton Mifflin, 1997; Jasper, Margaret C. *Welfare: Your Rights and the Law.* Dobbs Ferry, N.Y.: Oceana Publications, 2002; Welch, S., J. Gruhl, M. Steinman, J. Comer, and J. P. Vermeer. *Understanding American Government.* Belmont, Calif.: Wadsworth, 1997.

—Marcus D. Mauldin

Wesberry v. Sanders, 376 U.S. 1 (1964)

Wesberry v. Sanders held that all congressional districts within a state must, "as nearly as practicable," contain equal numbers of people.

Though one-person, one-vote is now an unchallenged axiom for drawing congressional and state legislative districts, it was not until the 1960s that the Supreme Court interpreted the Constitution to impose such a requirement. Before BAKER V. CARR, 369 U.S. 186 (1962), the Court refused even to consider constitutional claims relating to inequality in the sizes of districts, believing them to be nonjusticiable political questions. Once *Baker* removed the jurisdictional obstacle to hearing the cases, *Wesberry* and REYNOLDS V. SIMS, 377 U.S. 533 (1964), were able to hold that districts of unequal size violated the Constitution, with *Wesberry* applying to congressional districts and *Reynolds* applying to districts electing state legislators.

Wesberry found the one-person, one-vote requirement in Article I, Section 2 of the Constitution, which provides that members of Congress shall be chosen "by the People of the several States." By contrast, *Reynolds* rested on the Fourteenth Amendment, which prohibits states from denying persons "the equal protection of the laws." According to the *Wesberry* Court, "the command of Art. I, § 2, that Representatives be chosen 'by the People of the several States' means that as nearly as is practicable one man's vote in a congressional election is to be worth as much as another's." [376 U.S. at 7–8.] *Wesberry* itself did not attempt to clarify what it meant by "as nearly as is practicable" beyond saying that "equal representation for equal numbers of people" was a "plain objective" and a "fundamental goal" of the Constitution. Subsequent cases have established, however, that districts are vulnerable to constitutional challenge even when differences in population are quite minimal. Thus, the "as nearly as is practicable" rule has become a mandate of precise mathematical equality.

Because the constitutional provision did not by its terms prohibit the challenged district arrangement—representatives were elected by the "people," but by unequal numbers of people—Justice BLACK, writing for the seven-member Court, relied heavily on historical analysis. The Court noted the controversy over representation during the Constitution's framing, and concluded that the framers deliberately created a House of Representatives to reflect the populace, as contradistinguished from the Senate, which was to represent the states. According to the Court, "[i]t would defeat the principle solemnly embodied in the Great Compromise—equal representation in the House for equal numbers of people—for us to hold that, within the States, legislatures may draw the lines of congressional districts in such a way as to give some voters a greater voice in choosing a Congressman than others."

As Justice HARLAN pointed out in dissent, and as commentators agree, however, the Court's historical analysis was problematic. While the framers to some degree wanted to apportion representatives equally *among* the states, there was no evidence that they wanted to ensure equitable apportionment *within* the states. Justice Harlan noted that historical practice had seen plenty of examples of congressional districts of varying sizes, and indeed out of the 435 members of the House of Representatives then sitting, at least 398 were elected from districts that would have failed *Wesberry's* equality-of-population principle. Moreover, Justice Harlan called attention to the provisions of the Constitution setting forth the distribution of representatives among the states, and argued that even there, population equality was subsumed to other interests. Justice Harlan noted that such provisions as the three-fifths compromise and Article I, Section 2's requirement that each state receive at least one representative violated the *Wesberry* principle that representation in the House was to be based solely on population.

Justice Harlan also leveled a powerful attack on the Court's refusal to acknowledge Congress's role in regulating congressional elections, pursuant to Article I, Section 4. As Justice Harlan noted, and the Court ignored, Congress had in the past exercised its power to regulate the drawing of district lines but had *removed* a statutory requirement that districts be of approximately equal population.

Regardless of *Wesberry's* loose relationship to both the constitutional text and the history surrounding its adoption and application, the one-person, one-vote standard has taken a firm hold in constitutional law. Current disputes brought under the EQUAL PROTECTION CLAUSE or the VOTING RIGHTS ACT center not on the number of people in a district, but on the racial and partisan composition of districts.

For more information: Auerbach, Carl A. "The Reapportionment Cases: One Person, One Vote—One Vote, One Value." *Sup. Ct. Rev.* (1964): 1, 5; Kelly, Alfred H.

"Clio and the Court: An Illicit Love Affair." *Sup. Ct. Rev.* 119 (1965): 135–136; Tribe, Laurence H. *American Constitutional Law.* 2nd ed. Mineola, N.Y.: Foundation Press, 1988.

—Michael Richard Dimino, Sr.
—J. Michael Bitzer

West Coast Hotel Co. v. Parrish, 300 U.S. 379 (1937)

In *West Coast Hotel Co. v. Parrish,* the Supreme Court upheld a Washington state statute imposing minimum wages for women. In so doing, the Court directly overruled *ADKINS V. CHILDREN'S HOSPITAL,* 261 U.S. 525 (1923), and cleared the way for both state legislatures and Congress to engage in the extensive regulation of business practices.

Along with *NATIONAL LABOR RELATIONS BOARD V. JONES & LAUGHLIN,* 301 U.S. 1 (1937), *West Coast* is usually considered a watershed case which ushered in a new relationship between the judicial and legislative branches over the issue of economic regulation.

For almost 40 years prior to *West Coast,* the Court had been reluctant to allow either Congress or state legislatures to restrain the actions of businesses, particularly in reference to labor practices. Though the Court had upheld some statutes aimed at preserving the health and safety of workers as reasonable exercises of the government's police power, most attempts to regulate employers were struck down as violations of the LIBERTY OF CONTRACT. This liberty, while not explicitly in the Constitution, was said to be implicit in the "life, liberty, and property" protected from arbitrary governmental action by the due process clause of the Fourteenth Amendment.

In the 1923 *ADKINS* case, the Court struck down a federal statute imposing a minimum wage for women and children in the District of Columbia. The majority extended the concept of "liberty of contract" to include women, arguing that the Nineteenth Amendment had made them fully equal to men. Women therefore should have the same liberty as men to work for whatever wages employers offered. Though the government's police power allowed for some regulation in the name of protecting health, safety, and morals, the Court said there was no evidence that setting a minimum wage would protect any woman's morals. Finally, wrote Justice SUTHERLAND for the majority, allowing the government to set a minimum wage implied the power to set a maximum wage as well, and then the police power would know no limits.

Progressives decried the Court's rigidity and lack of deference to the decisions made by the elected branches. Disenchantment with the Court became more fierce with the onset of the Great Depression in the 1930s. Franklin

Delano Roosevelt was elected in 1932 and, with a willing Congress, proceeded to introduce the large-scale economic regulations known as the New Deal. The Court continued to strike down many of these new federal statutes, saying the political branches had exceeded their constitutional limits and were trampling on the liberties of employers.

Significantly, however, the Court's majority in these cases had fallen to a mere five justices. Following his landslide reelection in 1936, FDR proposed changing the composition of the Court in a manner that would, in effect, allow him to pack the Court with justices likely to uphold New Deal legislation. As Congress was debating FDR's COURT-PACKING PLAN, the Court handed down *West Coast Hotel*. It involved a statute from Washington State, which, as in *Adkins*, established minimum wages for women. In a 5 to 4 decision, the Court upheld the statute and directly overruled *Adkins*. Justice Owen Roberts had changed his vote. No longer espousing "liberty of contract," Roberts now sided with those who upheld the government's authority to regulate business for the general welfare.

Writing for the majority in *West Coast Hotel*, Chief Justice Charles Evans HUGHES argued that "liberty of contract" was a fiction. Not only was it not to be found in the text of the Constitution, but it presupposed an equality between employer and employee that simply did not exist. In addition, the majority said that women remained more vulnerable than men to unscrupulous employers who would underpay them if possible. Finally, Hughes pointed to the economic conditions of the time. If employers failed to pay a reasonable wage, it would fall on taxpayers to relieve the suffering of multitudes of workers. In his dissent, Sutherland was shocked that the majority would be swayed by the economic climate, arguing that the CONSTITUTIONAL INTERPRETATION should not be subject to "ebb and flow" of such events. He reiterated the logic of *Adkins*, asserting it remained properly decided.

FDR's plan to pack the Court died in Congress, for *West Coast* made it unnecessary. Not only was "liberty of contract" dead, but the Court retreated from the battle over economic regulation. For the most part, the extent to which the government should and will regulate business practices is now a matter left to the elected branches to be decided on political, not constitutional, grounds.

For more information: Cushman, Barry. *Rethinking the New Deal Court: The Structure of a Constitutional Revolution.* New York: Oxford University Press, 1998; Leuchtenburg, William E. *The Supreme Court Reborn: The Constitutional Revolution in the Age of Roosevelt.* New York: Oxford University Press, 1995; White, G. Edward. *Who Killed Lochner?: The Constitution and the New Deal.* Cambridge, Mass.: Harvard University Press, 2000.

—Gwyneth I. Williams

Justice Byron White

White, Byron (1917–2002) *Supreme Court justice*

Byron White was a multifaceted justice appointed to the Supreme Court by President John Kennedy in 1962, serving until 1993.

Associate Justice White was multifaceted, liberal on economic issues, conservative on criminal law and privacy issues. Born in Fort Collins, Colorado, in 1917, White worked in the sugar beet fields near his home of Wellington. An academic natural, White took to athletics, excelling at football and basketball. White attended the University of Colorado and became an All-American halfback and the leading scorer on the basketball team. A trip to the National Invitational Tournament in New York brought intense media scrutiny and soured White toward the media for the rest of his life. White won a Rhodes scholarship and would go on to play football professionally for the Pittsburgh Pirates of the NFL while attending Yale Law School.

At the outbreak of World War II, White put off law school, enlisted in the Navy, and served in the South Pacific. White's duties as an intelligence officer were notable because he wrote the report on John F. Kennedy's heroics in the aftermath of the crash of PT-109.

Following the war, White finished law school at Yale and accepted a clerkship under Supreme Court Justice Fred VINSON. White displayed extraordinary legal talents at Yale, graduating magna cum laude in 1946. Returning to Denver following the clerkship, White dove into contract law and soon established his firm in the Denver business community.

The notoriety of being a Colorado sports hero brought a wide range of business clients in Denver. It also made White an obvious choice for public office, which he consistently rebuffed. While White rejected opportunities to run for public office, he did help Colorado Democrats, and when John F. Kennedy ran for president in 1960, White was engaged to deliver Colorado's Democratic votes for Kennedy's nomination.

While Kennedy and White's paths had crossed before, the battle for the Democratic nomination created close ties to both John and Bobby Kennedy. Kennedy's victory in 1960 brought White to Washington as a deputy attorney general under Bobby. When the CIVIL RIGHTS movement exploded in Montgomery, Alabama, Kennedy sent White to ensure that the freedom riders were protected. White stood up to Alabama Governor John Patterson and made certain that the freedom riders were protected. He refrained from framing the question as one of civil rights, instead insisting it was a question of protecting INTERSTATE COMMERCE. White's success in Alabama solidified and elevated his status in the Kennedy administration.

The retirement of Justice Charles Whitaker in 1962 created a crisis for the Kennedy administration. Kennedy's impulse was to appoint the first black Supreme Court justice, but the political situation would ensure a Southern filibuster of any such nomination. Kennedy considered his options and finally settled on White. White was confirmed as an associate justice in April of 1962. Among his most important opinions were *Broadrick v. Oklahoma* [413 U.S. 601 (1973)], dealing with political work by state employees, *WASHINGTON V. DAVIS* [426 U.S. 229 (1976)], dealing with a setback to AFFIRMATIVE ACTION, and *California v. Greenwood* [486 U.S. 35 (1988), dealing with search and seizure of evidence.

The *New York Times* called White "Kennedy's greatest mistake" and White indeed proved to be on the opposite side of Kennedy on many issues that were becoming important on the Court. White clearly felt that judging someone by the color of one's skin was repugnant, but he rejected remedies that provided an advantage to minorities. White's record on criminal procedure was generally conservative. Indicative of White's attitude was his dissent in *MIRANDA V. ARIZONA* [384 U.S. 436 (1966)], in which he exhibits a career-long reservation toward JUDICIAL ACTIVISM: "The proposition that the privilege against self-incrimination forbids in-custody interrogation without the warnings specified in the majority opinion and without a clear waiver of counsel has no significant support in the history of privilege or in the language of the Fifth Amendment."

Even more antithetical to the liberal attitude embodied by the Kennedy administration, White was extremely conservative with regard to issues of personal privacy. In *BOWERS V. HARDWICK* [478 U.S. 186 (1986)], White concluded that states' rights to legislate on issues related to public morality could not be undermined on the basis of a right to privacy. His dissent in *ROE V. WADE* [410 U.S. 113 (1973)], is emphatic: "I find nothing in the language or history of the Constitution to support the Court's judgment. The Court simply fashions and announces a new constitutional right for pregnant mothers and, with scarcely any reason or authority for its action, invests that right with sufficient substance to override most existing state abortion statutes."

White resigned in 1993 and returned to Denver, where he died at his home in 2002.

For more information: Hutchinson, Dennis J. *The Man Who Once Was Whizzer White.* New York: Free Press, 1998.
—Tim Hundsdorfer

White, Edward Douglass (1845–1921) *chief justice of the Supreme Court*

Edward D. White was appointed by President William Howard TAFT to be CHIEF JUSTICE (1910–21), and before that, by President Grover Cleveland to be an associate justice (1894–1910) of the U.S. Supreme Court. In addition, White was U.S. senator from Louisiana (1891–94), and he contributed to legal thought in decisions he wrote in antitrust matters and in determining how constitutional protections should be applied to overseas U.S. possessions.

White was born into a wealthy and politically connected Catholic family. His father, Edward Douglass White, Sr., was a sugar planter, five-term U.S. representative, and Louisiana governor. The younger White was educated on the family plantation and, later, received a Jesuit education at several schools, including Georgetown College in Washington, D.C. At age 16, he left Georgetown to enlist in the Confederate Army. Captured by Union forces in 1863, White subsequently described Southern secession as a mistake. He read law in New Orleans, passed the bar in 1868, and became active in Louisiana Democratic politics.

White won election to the state senate in 1874, allied himself with Governor Francis T. Nicholls, and, in 1878, was appointed a state supreme court justice. When Nicholls was turned out of office in 1880, White was removed from the court and returned to private practice. In 1890, after Nicholls returned to power, he appointed White to a U.S. Senate vacancy. During White's term in the Senate, he was an ardent defender of Louisiana's sugar industry and a popular figure among his colleagues.

In late 1893, after the Senate had rejected two of Grover Cleveland's appointees to a Supreme Court vacancy, President Cleveland nominated White as an associate justice—confident that the Senate would not reject one of its own. White, a conservative who sided with big business, supported segregation, and generally opposed labor reforms, was quickly confirmed by the Senate. In 1910 President William Taft elevated White to chief justice to stabilize the Court which, since 1909, had lost five justices to death and retirement. Taft broke with tradition, for it marked the first time an associate had been promoted. The Republican president and his new chief justice accorded in their support for business interests and mistrust of Progressive reforms.

White's most significant contribution to constitutional thought was his development of the "Insular Doctrine," during a series of cases in the early 20th century in which the Supreme Court grappled with the issue: Do constitutional guarantees apply to American territories and protectorates as they do in domestic society? Writing for the minority in *Downes v. Bidwell*, 182 U.S. 244 (1901), and *Hawaii v. Mankichi*, 190 U.S. 197 (1903), White laid out a theory of INCORPORATION, i.e., that a territory could only claim constitutional protections to the degree that Congress had conferred them. In *Dowdell v. U.S.*, 221 U.S. 325 (1911), the Supreme Court adopted the insular doctrine for overseas territories. The court applied this same interpretation to Alaska in *Rasmussen v. U.S.*, 197 U.S. 516 (1905), and to Native Americans in *Lone Wolf v. Hitchcock*, 187 U.S. 553 (1903). Thus, it provided Congress a free hand in managing peoples that fell outside constitutional protection.

In statutory law, White's most lasting opinion was rendered in STANDARD OIL V. UNITED STATES, 221 U.S. 1 (1911). White wrote the unanimous opinion that upheld the federal government's decision to break up the mammoth oil monopoly, but he construed the definition of combinations in restraint of trade so narrowly that he weakened the Sherman Antitrust Act. White's "rule of reason" rejected a literal reading of the law which prohibited all monopolies that restricted trade. Ever since, the Sherman Antitrust Act has been read to permit "reasonable" monopolies.

In both constitutional and statutory law, White strove to give the Supreme Court a great deal of latitude in making subjective interpretations. He was productive, writing more than 700 opinions during his 27 years on the high court. He also was an exceedingly popular public figure in capital social circles—and this influence extended to the bench where he enhanced COMITY among the justices. Against the legacy left by his famous contemporaries—Oliver Wendell HOLMES and Louis BRANDEIS—White, however, remains a relatively obscure figure in the Court's history.

For more information: Baer, Judith A. "Edward Douglass White." In *The Supreme Court Justices: A Biographical Directory*, edited by Melvin Urofsky. New York: Garland, 1994; Friedman, Leon, and Fred Israel, eds. *The Justices of the United States Supreme Court*. New York: Chelsea House, 1980; Highsaw, Robert B. *Edward Douglass White: Defender of the Conservative Faith*. Baton Rouge: Louisiana State University Press, 1981.

—Matthew Wasniewski

Whren v. United States, 517 U.S. 806 (1996)

In *Whren v. United States*, the United States Supreme Court upheld the conviction of an individual for crack cocaine possession after his vehicle was stopped by the police for apparently routine driving infractions and subsequently searched for drugs. The case was an important Fourth Amendment search and seizure opinion, but it has also been described as giving the police significant ability to use racial profiling in the stopping of motorists.

In *Whren*, two plainclothes police officers were in an unmarked car patrolling an area considered to be a high drug area. They observed a truck sitting at an intersection for what they described as an unusually long time—20 seconds. Suddenly the truck made a U-turn and drove away at what the officers described as "unreasonable speed." The police pursued to warn the drivers about the traffic violations they had observed. When they approached the vehicle they saw some bags of crack cocaine in Whren's hands; the drivers were arrested. Whren contended that the drug evidence should be suppressed under the Fourth Amendment because the initial stop was illegal as there was neither probable cause nor reasonable suspicion to stop their vehicle. The Supreme Court disagreed.

Writing for a unanimous Court, Justice SCALIA indicated that police clearly had the authority to stop the truck based upon their observed violations of local traffic laws. However, Whren argued that in this case the use of the traffic laws to stop his vehicle was simply pretextual. That is, the police were using the traffic laws as a way of establishing probable cause to do a warrantless search that would not have been permitted otherwise under the Fourth Amendment. In response, Scalia dismissed this claim, stating that the actual motivations of the police for stopping the vehicle were immaterial except in cases of challenges of RACIAL DISCRIMINATION under the EQUAL PROTECTION CLAUSE. It is under this clause, and not the Fourth Amendment, that claims on intentional discrimination are to be raised.

Scalia argued that past cases had established that police motivation for engaging in a search was not a critical factor in determining whether a search was legal. Instead, in those cases, as here with Whren, the critical factor was not whether a reasonable officer would have generally stopped a vehicle like this under the conditions they described, but whether a reasonable officer could have stopped the vehicle. The importance of this distinction was that so long as police see some violation of the law, they are justified in stopping the vehicle and doing a search because they have probable cause based upon the observed traffic violations.

Whren v. United States is a controversial decision. Some argue that it gives police officers too much discretion to use routine traffic violations as a basis of stopping individuals whom they suspect of other illegal activity. Given how complex the traffic laws are and the fact that many of us often violate some law, such as having a broken tail light, on occasion, *Whren* seems to allow police to stop almost anyone they want. Critics of racial profiling argue that police often use violations of minor traffic laws as ways to stop people of color and then use these stops as a way to search vehicles for other illegal activity.

For more information: Heumann, Milton, and Lance Cassak. *Good Cop, Bad Cop: Racial Profiling and Competing Views of Justice.* New York: Peter Lang, 2003.

—David Schultz

Wickard v. Filburn, 317 U.S. 111 (1942)

In *Wickard v. Filburn,* the Supreme Court expanded Congress's power to regulate the economy by holding that its authority under Article I "to regulate commerce among the states" extends to activities that are local in character.

In 1941 Congress amended the Agricultural Adjustment Act of 1938 to authorize the Department of Agriculture to establish marketing quotas for certain agricultural commodities, including wheat. The department gave Filburn a wheat acreage allotment of 11.1 acres. Filburn, however, harvested nearly 23 acres of wheat. He claimed that he intended to use the wheat on his farm in order to feed his family, poultry, and livestock. The government imposed a penalty on Filburn of $117.11 for exceeding his allotment. Filburn argued that the law regulated production and consumption, activities local in character. Congress, he said, can regulate only INTERSTATE COMMERCE or activities that directly affect interstate commerce.

The Court rejected the contention that the commerce power did not reach production and consumption. Speaking for a unanimous court, Justice Robert JACKSON laid down the rule that even if an activity is local and not commercial, "it may still, whatever its nature, be reached by Congress if it exerts a substantial economic effect on interstate commerce, and this irrespective of whether such effect is what might at some earlier time have been defined as 'direct' or 'indirect.'" [*Wickard v. Filburn,* 317 U.S. 111, 125 (1942).] By growing wheat in excess of his allotment, Filburn did not need to purchase wheat for consumption on his farm. His failure to purchase on the open market meant that the national demand for wheat was lower than it otherwise would have been. When demand falls, so does the price of wheat. The main purpose of the Agricultural Adjustment Act was to raise the price of commodities by reducing the supply. High prices for crops and livestock mean higher incomes for farmers. Raising farmers' incomes was President Franklin D. Roosevelt's principal solution to the crisis faced by American farmers during the Great Depression.

Wickard v. Filburn represented the culmination of a process of broadening the scope of the federal government's power to regulate commerce that began in 1937. In *NATIONAL LABOR RELATIONS BOARD V. JONES & LAUGHLIN STEEL CORPORATION,* 301 U.S. 1 (1937), the Court ruled that Congress could regulate labor relations because strikes reduce production and therefore threaten interstate commerce. In previous cases, a conservative Court had held that because production preceded commerce, defined as buying and selling, Congress had no power to regulate it.

In accordance with the principle of FEDERALISM, said the Court in *UNITED STATES V. E. C. KNIGHT COMPANY,* 156 U.S. 1 (1895), the Constitution recognizes the sole power of the states to regulate manufacturing, oil production, agriculture, and mining. In *SWIFT AND COMPANY V. UNITED STATES* (1905), the Court held that Congress could only regulate intrastate activities that had a "direct effect" on interstate commerce. In *UNITED STATES V. BUTLER,* 297 U.S. 1 (1936), the Court declared the Agricultural Adjustment Act of 1933 unconstitutional because it encroached on the powers of the states and because growing of crops was not a commercial activity.

Following the reelection of President Roosevelt by a popular landslide in November 1936, the Court's two moderate justices, Chief Justice Charles Evans HUGHES and Justice Owen Roberts, joined the three liberals to give Congress the power to pass laws regulating manufacturing, mining, and agriculture. The Supreme Court returned to the broad reading of congressional commerce power first articulated by Chief Justice John MARSHALL *in GIBBONS V. OGDEN,* 9 Wheat. 1, 194 (1824).

For more information: Hall, Kermit, ed. *A Nation of States: Federalism at the Bar of the Supreme Court.* New York: Garland, 2000; Stephenson, Donald Grier, Jr. *Campaigns and the Court.* New York: Columbia University Press, 1999; Twight, Charlotte. *Dependent on DC: The Rise of Federal Control over the Lives of Ordinary Americans.* New York: Palgrave, 2002.

—Kenneth Holland

wiretapping

Wiretapping, the interception, generally through electronic means, of communications between two or more persons without their knowledge, presents a legal question with which the Supreme Court has wrangled for nearly 80 years.

Beginning with the case of *Olmstead v. United States,* 277 U.S. 438 (1928), the Supreme Court permitted the wide, discretionary use of wiretaps by law-enforcement officials, finding that there was no physical trespass in the "seizure" of a conversation and, therefore, no violation of the Fourth Amendment. Just six years later, with the enactment of the Federal Communications Act, Congress imposed significant limits on the interception of electronic communications, undoubtedly altering the Court's wiretapping jurisprudence forever.

Ultimately, in 1967, in KATZ V. UNITED STATES, 389 U.S. 347 (1967), the Court observed that its many rulings over 39 years had so dramatically eroded the principles of *Olmstead* as to render the case not controlling. The following year, Congress enacted Title III of the Omnibus Crime Control and Safe Streets Act of 1968 ("Title III"), which prohibited the misuse of intercepted oral, wire, or electronic communications, dramatically impacting the jurisprudence of wiretapping. The Court has subsequently redefined wiretapping jurisprudence and has come face-to-face with the difficulties of judicial regulation of a steadily developing and evolving technology.

In 1928 Chief Justice TAFT wrote the majority opinion for the Supreme Court in *Olmstead,* holding that wiretapping did not violate the Fourth Amendment for two reasons. First, the Fourth Amendment protects citizens within their premises; however, there is no trespass in the "seizure" of a conversation and therefore no search. Second, the Fourth Amendment prohibits the seizure of an individual's personal effects; however, the subject of wiretapping is a conversation, an intangible object therefore not subject to seizure. Thus, conversations, as intangible objects that may be overheard without a physical trespass were not considered to be protected by the Fourth Amendment's protections against search and seizure.

With the enactment of the Federal Communications Act, Congress attempted to protect conversations from wiretapping. The Court responded in *Nardone v. United States,* 302 U.S. 379 (1937), by denying the admissibility of information gleaned from wiretaps at trial, while refusing to disallow wiretaps as a means of legal surveillance. In numerous cases over the next 30 years, the Court reexamined its rulings and modified the rules it applied to law enforcement's use of wiretaps. Importantly, the Court concluded evidence obtained through wiretaps could be used if one party consented to the interception of the conversations. [*Rathburn v. United States,* 355 U.S. 107 (1957).]

The Court handed down a seminal decision in 1967 in a case called *Katz v. United States,* 389 U.S. 347 (1967). In *Katz,* the Court was asked to consider whether an intercepted conversation in a phone booth was protected by the Fourth Amendment. Most important, the Court held that the Fourth Amendment protects people, not places. Further, as had been the case since the passage of the Federal Communications Act, the federal government had expressed a clear concern for protecting the conversations of citizens, not just their tangible possessions. The *Katz* ruling introduced the Court's consideration of a two-prong standard for evaluating wiretapping concerns. First, the Court sought to determine whether the individual exhibited a subjective expectation of privacy. That is, did an individual take measures to ensure his or her privacy in the communication at question? Second, is that expectation of privacy one that society would *objectively* find reasonable? For roughly 30 years to follow, that standard would shape Supreme Court decisions and dictate the standard for permissible wiretaps.

The following year, Congress enacted Title III, which set out specific requirements for the granting of wiretap SEARCH WARRANTS, but it did not end the dispute over when a wiretap violates the Fourth Amendment. In fact, because it authorized wiretapping given certain conditions, the legislation often found itself in conflict with both settled case law and the Fourth Amendment in general. For example, in *Dalia v. United States,* 441 U.S. 238 (1979), the Court found that the issuance of a warrant for a wiretap necessarily includes the authorization of covert entry into an individual's premises in order to install the electronic equipment. The particularity requirement of the Fourth Amendment, that a search warrant specify exactly what is subject to the search warrant, that no "general" warrants may be issued, has also been a source of litigation, as it is difficult to particularize what conversation or what parts of a conversation may be "searched."

In 2001 the Supreme Court handed down a seminal decision in *Kyllo v. United States,* 533 U.S. 21 (2001). There, the Court, speaking through Justice Scalia, sought to create a "bright-line" rule for determining when the use of electronic surveillance equipment may be used by law enforcement authorities without a search warrant. The Court ruled that technology "in the general public use" may be used without a search warrant. While "general public use" has not been defined by the courts, a reasonable interpretation of that phrase might well include wiretapping technology. Given such an interpretation, the new *Kyllo* rule may have significant implications for the future of wiretapping jurisprudence. How the *Kyllo* rule will be played out remains to be seen.

For more information: Lasson, Nelson B. *The History and Development of the Fourth Amendment to the United*

States Constitution. New York: Da Capo Press, 1970; Polyviou, Polyvios, G. *Search & Seizure: Constitutional and Common Law.* London: Duckworth, 1982.

—Tom Clark

Wisconsin v. Yoder, 406 U.S. 205 (1972)

In *Wisconsin v. Yoder,* the U.S. Supreme Court granted an exemption from the compulsory school attendance law of children before the age of 16 on the basis of the First Amendment's religious freedom clause, PARENTAL RIGHTS and duties in upbringing their children, and the Fourteenth Amendment.

The case revolved around the refusal of Amish parents to send their 14- and 15-year-old children to school, in violation of Wisconsin law. The parents claimed that the law infringes upon their First Amendment right to freedom of RELIGION and their right under the Fourteenth Amendment as compulsory secondary education, public or private, contradicts the Amish values and way of life and thus endangers the community's survival. They were tried, convicted, and fined in Wisconsin's trial court, and Wisconsin's COURT OF APPEALS approved the convictions. Wisconsin's Supreme Court reversed, and, on certiorari, the U.S. Supreme Court affirmed the Wisconsin court.

Delivering the Court's opinion, Justice BURGER characterized the question as one of balancing interests. On the one hand, the state's interest in universal education, which, while it is important to prepare politically involved and self-reliant citizens, is not absolute [*Sherbert v. Verner,* 374 U.S. 398 (1963); *Prince v. Massachusetts,* 321 U.S. 158, 165 (1944)]. Conversely lies the parent's fundamental right to freedom of religion and their traditional interest in raising their children in accordance with their religious beliefs. Balancing these claims, the Court found that Wisconsin's interests are less substantial than those of the parents.

The Court observed that the neutral appearance of the law might offend the constitutional requirement of neutrality if it unduly burdens the free exercise of religion. It further rules that, in contrast to the state's claim, religious practices are not essentially outside the protection of the First Amendment. This is particularly so, as Justice WHITE, joined by Justices STEWART and BRENNAN, stressed in a concurring and separate opinion, considering the minor deviation from the compulsory law and the high value of religious freedom in American society.

Given the parents' well-established religious convictions and the evidence of the endangerment in secondary education to the community's way of life, the Court further dismissed the argument that the State has a *parens patriae* role to advance the child's interest in education regardless of the parents' wishes. Addressing the parents as the only relevant parties to the proceedings due to their possible criminal liability and citing *PIERCE V. SOCIETY OF THE SISTERS* (268 U.S., 510), the Court ruled that the primary role of parents in raising their children includes both their right and duty to direct the child and prepare him for additional obligations. These obligations, however, include also moral standards, religious beliefs, and elements of good CITIZENSHIP. Thus, the Court concludes that the combination of parenthood interests and a free exercise claim as presented in the case triumphed over the state's justifications for undermining the parents' religious rights.

Justice DOUGLAS, in a partly dissenting opinion, expressed the view that further emphasis should be placed on the freedom of religion of the child, separate from the parents, as granting the exception to the parents' request simultaneously imposes religious beliefs on the child.

For more information: Schultz, David. "Church State Relations and the First Amendment." In *Law and Politics: Unanswered Questions,* 235–266. New York: Peter Lang, 1994.

—Maya Sabatello

women and the Constitution

From its origination, the Constitution has provided limited protections for women. As basic CITIZENSHIP rights have been expanded to women, it has been the interpretation of the Constitution that has evolved, not the explicit language of the text. Although the Constitution originally made vague references to "persons" and "citizens" without specifying gender, people of color and white women were generally not included as part of the understood meaning. With its changes in interpretation over time, the Court now understands women to be citizens under the Constitution, but men and women are not provided identical constitutional treatment.

Common law, as practiced in most western European countries and in many American colonies, deemed a woman to be the property of her father, husband, or liege lord. After Independence, most states adapted this interpretation into their legal codes, providing women limited political and economic power. Women who were impoverished, indentured, or enslaved had even fewer legal protections.

Under most state laws, women could not own, buy, or sell property, earn money that they could control, or make binding contracts. While some state constitutions gave women basic citizenship rights, the federal Constitution left the legal position of women up to the states. A small group of women advocated continuously for inclusion within the language of the Constitution; however, it was not until the passage of the Fourteenth Amendment in 1868 that the Court began to formally consider the constitutionally protected rights of women. The Fourteenth Amendment, in part, requires the states to provide equal protection of the laws and to protect the privileges and immunities of citizenship.

Soon after the passage of the Fourteenth Amendment, the Supreme Court determined that the transformed Constitution still did not protect the rights of women. *BRADWELL V. ILLINOIS,* 83 U.S. 130 (1873), found that the right of women to practice law the same as men was not guaranteed by their status as a "citizen" of the United States. The case of *Minor v. Happersett,* 88 U.S. 627 (1875), made it clear that citizenship does not necessarily mean the right to vote; the Court argued that the Fourteenth Amendment only protects the rights that people already possessed in 1868, it did not create new ones. The Court believed that states could extend additional citizenship rights to women, such as voting, but the federal Constitution did not. It was up to the states to ensure that women were understood to be citizens.

At the beginning of the 20th century, the industrial revolution and additional waves of immigration brought heightened attention to the role of women in the workplace. As the concurring opinion by Justice BRADLEY in the *Bradwell* case demonstrates, CONSTITUTIONAL INTERPRETATION had seen women primarily in the role of mothers and wives. He stated "the civil law, as well as nature herself, has always recognized a wide difference in the respective spheres and destinies of man and woman. . . . The paramount destiny and mission of woman are to fulfill the noble and benign office of wife and mother."

As women entered the workforce in larger numbers, state legislatures wanted to protect these mothers. They began to regulate the number of hours that women could work, delineate what occupations were acceptable for women, and supervise other aspects of female employment. The justification for this protective legislation was found in *MULLER V. OREGON* (1908), where the Court found that since "healthy mothers are essential to vigorous offspring, the physical well-being of women becomes an object of public interest and care in order to preserve the strength and vigor of the race." This legal interpretation became the norm, and the Court upheld legislation designed to protect women from the civic sphere into the 1980s.

A series of Supreme Court decisions illustrates the range of protective legislation that states passed and the Constitution was interpreted as allowing. In *Goesaert v. Cleary,* 335 U.S. 464 (1948), the Court found that states could ban women from bartending, unless they worked at an establishment owned by their husbands or fathers. The *Hoyt v. Florida,* 368 U.S. 57 (1961), majority decided that women have the right to serve on juries, but because women are "the center of home and family life" they do not have the civic obligation to serve that men have.

The Court in the 1981 case of *MICHAEL M. V. SUPERIOR COURT OF SONOMA COUNTY,* 450 U.S. 464 (1981),

determined that males may be liable for statutory rape charges, even if similarly situated women are not. In the same year, *ROSTKER V. GOLDBERG,* 453 U.S. 57 (1981), made it clear that women's exemption from the draft is not unconstitutional discrimination "but rather realistically reflects the fact that the sexes are not similarly situated." The Court later changed its rulings regarding waitresses and juries, the state changed its mind regarding gender distinctions in statutory rape, but *Rostker* is still current constitutional interpretation. So while protective legislation is less acceptable today, it is still constitutional and considered good policy under specific circumstances (e.g., pregnancy protections).

While some activists fought to protect women through legislation that reflected their unique political and social situation, other advocates sought to have citizenship equalized through the extension of voting rights. Many states had changed their own constitutions to provide women the franchise; in 1920, the Nineteenth Amendment to the federal Constitution passed. Despite the guarantee that the right to vote cannot be denied on the basis of gender, many women of color were not able to exercise this right due to racial oppression.

The Court, under pressure from feminist activists, was subsequently forced to consider the relationship between the EQUAL PROTECTION CLAUSE of the Fourteenth Amendment and protective legislation. Although protective legislation recognizes the unique circumstances of women, does such legislation prevent women from having equal employment opportunities or from being recognized as an equal citizen?

In cases such as *Hoyt,* the Court had argued that laws distinguishing between men and women only had to have a rational foundation for such discrimination. Because women are mothers, they cannot be expected to spend time away from their families on juries, but in 1971 the Supreme Court, for the first time ever, found a law that treated men and women differently to be unconstitutional. The Court in *Reed v. Reed,* 404 U.S. 71 (1971), determined that if a law that discriminates on the basis of gender meets an important governmental purpose and is substantially related to that goal—it is constitutional. If such a law does not meet an important purpose or is not substantially related—it is unconstitutional. This standard, known as INTERMEDIATE SCRUTINY, has generally been the test the Court uses to evaluate laws that treat men and women differently.

However, beginning in the *UNITED STATES V. VIRGINIA,* 518 U.S. 515 (1996), case, the Court decided that the state must now show "exceedingly persuasive justification" for differential treatment of women and men. This heightened standard makes it more difficult for the government to treat men and women differently for purposes of protection or discrimination.

It is during this time of legal transition that the Court began asking what the Constitution could mean for the lives of women. In *Griswold v. Connecticut*, 381 U.S. 479 (1965), the Court discovered a right to privacy in the Constitution. This right guarantees people legal access to birth control and, eventually the Court determined, access to other means of controlling reproduction, including abortion. These decisions by the Court have been very controversial and continue to be debated well into the 21st century. Simultaneously, a movement to change the Constitution gained momentum. The goal was to clearly indicate what the Court was slowly beginning to interpret the Constitution as saying: "Equality of rights under the law shall not be denied or abridged by the United States or by any State on account of sex." The EQUAL RIGHTS AMENDMENT or ERA was a very controvertible issue. Many people were afraid that if it passed women would lose the few protections they had—the ability not to be drafted, their special protections as wives and mothers, and the recognition of their special role in society. The ERA failed to get the necessary votes to amend the Constitution.

To this day, the Constitution does not explicitly guarantee equality based on gender. The guarantee of equal rights for women has been provided by federal statutes, state laws and constitutions, and federal and state court decisions, but not by the explicit language of the Constitution.

For more information: Cushman, Clare, ed. *Supreme Court Decisions and Women's Rights: Milestones to Equality.* Washington, D.C.: Congressional Quarterly Press, 2001; Kerber, Linda K. *No Constitutional Right to Be Ladies: Women and the Obligation of Citizenship.* New York: Hill and Wang, 1998; VanBurkleo, Sandra F. *"Belonging to the World:" Women's Rights and American Constitutional Culture.* New York: Oxford University Press, 2001.

—Michelle Donaldson Deardorff

writ of certiorari

Writ of certiorari is a court order that commands a lower court to send the official papers in a case to the appellate court that issued the writ. This writ is most famously used by the Supreme Court of the United States when it decides whether to review cases from lower courts. Although the Supreme Court has ORIGINAL JURISDICTION in a narrow range of cases and must hear appeals in some other classes of cases, the vast majority of its caseload arrives at the Court when it grants a petition for a writ of certiorari. This petition typically is sought by a party who lost in the lower court, which usually will be a U.S. COURT OF APPEALS or a state high court, or occasionally some other court.

In recent years, the Supreme Court received some 8,000 petitions for a writ of certiorari from the losing party but granted fewer than 100 per year. Under the RULE OF FOUR, granting a petition requires the affirmative vote of four of the justices, all nine of whom have reviewed the arguments for why the Court should accept the case and decide it on the merits. Because of the thousands of petitions each year, most of the justices participate in the "cert pool," in which the thousands of cert petitions are divided among the justices' law clerks for review and a recommendation as to the disposition of the petition.

The order deciding the petition usually is perfunctory, merely noting whether the writ is granted or denied. Dissents from a decision on a petition for a writ of certiorari are uncommon but not unknown and occasionally can be rather strongly worded. This occurs because cases in which "cert," as the writ is known colloquially, is granted generally present disputes in which there are disagreements among the lower courts or in which there are very important issues of constitutional or statutory interpretation. For example, Justice Harry BLACKMUN notably dissented from a decision denying a petition for a writ of certiorari in a death penalty case, thereby signifying his strong feelings against CAPITAL PUNISHMENT, which culminated a dramatic personal shift from supporting the death penalty earlier in his time on the high court.

Upon granting the petition and issuing the writ, the Supreme Court will establish the schedule for briefs to be submitted and for ORAL ARGUMENT to take place. The denial of a petition for a writ of certiorari has no precedential value, meaning that the Supreme Court cannot be cited as preferring a particular result, regardless of the outcome of the case in the court below. As a practical matter, however, the Court's cert decision has the effect of permitting the lower court's decision to stand, which can have significant practical implications. Scholars, lawyers, and others study carefully the justices' decisions on petitions for certiorari, seeking clues to the Court's decision-making practices and dynamics.

For more information: Perry, H. W., Jr. *Deciding to Decide: Agenda Setting in the United States Supreme Court.* Cambridge, Mass.: Harvard University Press, 1991; Segal, Jeffrey A., and Harold J. Spaeth. *The Supreme Court and the Attitudinal Model.* New York: Cambridge University Press, 1993.

—Luke Bierman
—Brett Peach

Wyman v. James, 400 U.S. 309 (1971)

In *Wyman v. James*, the Supreme Court reversed the decision of the district court, holding that the home visitation provided for by New York law in connection with the AFDC (Aid to Families with Dependent Children) program is a reasonable administrative tool and does not violate any right guaranteed by the Fourth Amendment.

Barbara James, a mother applying for assistance through AFDC, initially allowed a visit to her home, and following that visit benefits were issued to Barbara James for her son Maurice. Approximately two years later another home visit was requested, but James refused saying that she would provide all reasonable and relevant information but she would not permit a visit within her home.

The Fourth Amendment affords people the right to be secure in their persons, houses, papers, and effects. Although the Court held this to be a basic right to a free society, the Court ultimately rejected James's claim that the home visitation was a search and, when not consented to or when not supported by a warrant based on probable cause, violated her Fourth Amendment rights. Responding to this claim the Court held that this is not a search in the traditional sense that is covered by the Fourth Amendment. Because the search is not forced or compelled, the decision to deny the search is not criminal. Therefore if consent was withheld, there was no visitation, and there was no search.

The Fourth Amendment's standard is unreasonableness, and the Court concluded that the proposed visit did not descend to that level of unreasonableness. In doing so the Court also provided a number of reasons why the search was not unreasonable. In this case the public interest is providing needed assistance to the child, and these needs were viewed as more important than the rights claimed by the mother. In providing this assistance the Court noted that "The search is at the heart of the welfare administration, affording a more personal, rehabilitative orientation, unlike that of most federal programs." In addition, the program is funded through public tax dollars and it is a legitimate request of the agency representing the public that there be at least a limited way to ensure the proper usage of those funds.

The Court also recognized that the steps taken by the agency were appropriate and followed the guidelines that are set forth in the New York Social Services Law. Mrs. James received advanced written notice; there was no suggestion of forcible entry, entry at an awkward time, or reprehensible behavior such as snooping. Finally, the Court concluded that all reasonable and relevant information to the case could not be obtained by the agency through other means and that the home visitation was not only legitimate but the best way for the agency to verify residence of the beneficiary.

For more information: Davis, Martha F. *Brutal Need: Law, Lawyers, and the Welfare Rights Movement, 1960–1973.* New Haven, Conn.: Yale University Press, 1993; Munger, Frank. "Poverty, Welfare, and the Affirmative State." *Journal of Law and Society* 37, Issue 3 (September 2003): 659–685

—Carrie A. Schneider

Y

Yates v. United States, 354 U.S. 298 (1957)

In *Yates v. United States*, the Supreme Court set aside the convictions of 14 members of the Communist Party convicted of violating the Smith Act. In the decision the Court differentiates between the advocacy of abstract doctrine and the advocacy of unlawful action. Advocacy of abstract doctrine is constitutionally protected speech while the latter is not.

In 1940 the U.S. Congress passed the Smith Act making it illegal for anyone in the United States to advocate or teach the forcible overthrow of the government. Following the end of World War II the Smith Act was used to prosecute leaders of the Communist Party in the United States. The first case to reach the Supreme Court was *DENNIS V. UNITED STATES* in 1951. The Court upheld the convictions of the 11 Communist Party members. Applying the clear and present danger test, the Court found that even though the possibility of overthrow was remote, significant harm would result from any attempt. If the government is aware that a group is advocating and teaching the necessity of overthrow, the government is required to act.

The Court's decision in *Yates v. United States* modified its ruling in *Dennis* increasing protections given to POLITICAL SPEECH. Six years had passed since the Court's ruling in *Dennis*. During this time the political climate underwent some changes. Senator Joseph McCarthy had died and anticommunist sentiment had somewhat abated.

Yates involved the 1951 convictions of 14 "second string" members of the Communist Party in California. The Court's decision was based on interpreting the Smith Act instead of addressing First Amendment issues. Justice HARLAN delivered the opinion of the Court. The Court found that the trial judge's instructions to the jury did not adequately distinguish between advocacy and teaching of abstract doctrine and advocacy of unlawful action either now or at some point in the future. The Smith Act prohibits advocacy of action and not advocacy of ideas. Advocacy and teaching addressed at taking action, whether or not incitement, is punishable. Advocacy addressed at merely believing in something is not punishable. In *Dennis*, the Court was concerned with the presence of advocacy aimed at taking forcible action in the future and not with a conspiracy to engage in seditious advocacy at some point in the future.

In writing for the majority, Harlan stated that the decision was clarifying *Dennis;* however, many scholars believe that the Court's opinion in *Yates* was actually an evolution in the Court's First Amendment jurisprudence. The Court began to incorporate elements of District Court Judge Learned Hand's incitement approach. Hand's approach in *Masses Publishing Co. v. Patten* (1917) was to focus on the speaker's words. If the language used incited those who heard it to action, the speech was not protected under the First Amendment.

For more information: Gunther, Gerald. "Learned Hand and the Origins of Modern First Amendment Doctrine: Some Fragments of History." *Stanford Law Review* 27 (February 1975): 719–773; Redish, Martin H. "Advocacy of Unlawful Conduct and the First Amendment: In Defense of Clear and Present Danger." *California Law Review* 70 (September 1982): 1,159–1,200; Sullivan, Kathleen, and Gerald Gunther. *Constitutional Law.* 14th ed. New York: Foundation Press, 2001.

Yick Wo v. Hopkins, 118 U.S. 351 (1886)

In *Yick Wo v. Hopkins*, the Supreme Court held unconstitutional a San Francisco ordinance that made it illegal to operate a laundry in a wooden building. This case is about the discriminatory administration of the law.

Yick Wo, a Chinese plaintiff, had been operating a laundry in a wooden building in San Francisco for 22 years. More than two-thirds of the laundries in San Francisco were operated in wooden buildings similar to Yick Wo's. The ordinance in effect banned all these laundries. Wooden laundries could continue operating only if city officials issued a permit.

Yick Wo and several hundred other wooden laundry operators applied for a permit. Virtually every non-Chinese applicant was granted a permit. Every Chinese applicant was denied. While the non-Chinese residents were allowed to continue operating their wooden laundries, Yick Wo was convicted of violating the ordinance and imprisoned. It was this discrimination in the application of the law that gave rise to Yick Wo's successful petition for writ of habeas corpus.

All people within the United States, regardless of race, are ensured the equal protection of the laws under the Fourteenth Amendment. This means that laws cannot unjustifiably discriminate based on race. Laws that do discriminate do so in different ways. Discrimination can be expressly incorporated into the law, called "de jure" ("as a matter of law") discrimination. Alternatively, the discrimination may be in the form of discriminatory administration of an ostensibly nondiscriminatory law, called "de facto" ("in point of fact") discrimination.

Yick Wo is an example of de facto discrimination. Although the language of the ordinance in *Yick Wo* did not treat races differently, the ordinance was administered in a racist manner. The Court unanimously reversed Yick Wo's conviction. "No reason for [the discrimination] is shown," the Court reasoned, "and the conclusion cannot be resisted that no reason for it exists except hostility to [Chinese people]." Since the law was unjustifiably discriminatory as administered, the law violated the EQUAL PROTECTION CLAUSE of the Fourteenth Amendment.

For more information: Tribe, L. H. *American Constitutional Law.* Mineola, N.Y.: Foundation Press, 1988.

—Daniel J. Singel

Younger v. Harris, 401 U.S. 37 (1971)

In *Younger v. Harris,* the United States Supreme Court held that federal courts cannot prohibit pending state criminal proceedings except under extraordinary circumstances where the danger of irreparable harm to the defendant is both great and immediate.

Defendant Harris had been indicted for violation of California's Criminal Syndicalism Act for distributing leaflets promoting change in industrial ownership via political action. Although the U.S. Supreme Court had held the Criminal Syndicalism Act constitutional in *Whitney v. California,* 274 U.S. 357 (1927), the Court had struck down an identical act in *Brandenburg v. Ohio,* 395 U.S. 444 (1969). Harris filed suit in federal district court seeking to prevent Younger, the district attorney of Los Angeles County, from prosecuting him on the grounds that the Criminal Syndicalism Act was a violation of his free speech rights as guaranteed by the First and Fourteenth Amendments. Harris further claimed that the Court's ruling in *Dombrowski v.*

Pfister, 380 U.S. 479 (1965), allowed federal intervention in the state case. The district court held that the Criminal Syndicalism Act was unconstitutional and void for vagueness and OVERBREADTH and enjoined Harris's prosecution.

At the district court level, three other plaintiffs were allowed to intervene in the case. Although none of these plaintiffs had been indicted or threatened with prosecution under the act, two of them claimed that the mere presence of the act inhibited their ability to engage in free speech as members of the Progressive Labor Party. The third, a college history instructor, claimed that the act made him uncertain as to whether he could continue to teach about Karl Marx or read from the *Communist Manifesto* in classroom instruction. On APPEAL, the Supreme Court ruled that the three intervening parties did not present a live controversy as required for review by Article III of the U.S. Constitution, unlike Harris. According to the Court, persons having only imaginary or speculative fears of state criminal prosecution are not appropriate plaintiffs.

In regard to Harris's suit, the Supreme Court reversed the district court's ruling and lifted the injunction against Harris's prosecution in state court. Justice Hugo BLACK's majority decision rested on policy grounds tied to notions of FEDERALISM. The Court held that, according to longstanding public policy and proper respect for state functions, federal courts should not restrain state criminal proceedings unless the defendant will suffer great and immediate irreparable injury, even if the state statute is possibly unconstitutional. According to the Court, the cost, anxiety, and inconvenience of defending oneself in a single criminal prosecution, as Harris would face, do not constitute great and immediate irreparable injury. Likewise, federal court intervention should occur only when a state defendant's federal rights cannot be protected in the pending prosecution. In this case, Harris could raise his constitutional claims in his state criminal trial.

The Court distinguished Harris's situation from the one faced by defendants in *Dombrowski.* In that case, the defendants faced harassment and bad-faith prosecutions on the part of state officials. Those circumstances establish the kind of irreparable injury necessary for federal intervention in state criminal proceedings. In contrast, Harris had not suggested that the prosecution against him was brought in bad faith or that he was being harassed.

Justice Black acknowledged that when state laws restricting free speech are possibly unconstitutional on their face, their continued enforcement might create a "chilling effect" in the area of First Amendment rights. Yet, he held that any possible "chilling effect" was not sufficient, in itself, to warrant federal intervention in state criminal proceedings.

In its majority decision in *Younger,* the Supreme Court declined to consider whether a federal anti-injunction statute, 28 U.S.C. 2283, applied in the case. The anti-injunction statute prohibits federal court intervention in state court proceedings except "as expressly authorized by Act of Congress, or where necessary in aid of its jurisdiction, or to protect or effectuate its judgments." In the sole dissent in *Younger,* Justice William O. DOUGLAS argued that in adopting 42 U.S.C. 1983 as part of the Civil Rights Act of 1871, Congress had expressly authorized federal courts to intervene in state criminal proceedings involving prosecutions under statutes that deprived defendants of their constitutional rights. As such, according to Justice DOUGLAS, federal court intervention in the state case was appropriate under 28 U.S.C. 2283. In *Mitchum v. Foster,* 407 U.S. 225 (1972), the Supreme Court adopted Justice Douglas's argument and held that 42 U.S.C. 1983 was one of the instances where Congress had expressly authorized federal courts to enjoin pending state actions.

For more information: Matasar, Richard A., and Gregory S. Bruch. "Procedural Common Law, Federal Jurisdictional Policy, and Abandonment of the Adequate and Independent State Grounds Doctrine." *Columbia Law Review* 86 (1986): 1,291–1,390; Soifer, Aviam, and Hugh C. Macgill. "The Younger Doctrine: Reconstructing Reconstruction." *Texas Law Review* 55 (1977): 1,141–1,215.

—Mahalley D. Allen

Youngstown Co. v. Sawyer, 343 U.S. 579 (1952)

In *Youngstown Co. v. Sawyer,* the Supreme Court found that President Truman did not have authority to seize the nation's steel mills, an action he had attempted in an effort to settle a labor dispute during the Korean War.

The president had directed the secretary of Commerce to seize the mills following a strike announcement by labor leaders. Seizing the mills would ensure that steel production would remain adequate for the nation's war efforts, thus the president claimed that his INHERENT POWERS as chief executive and his position as commander in chief made his actions necessary to prevent national disaster should the mills close. In response, the mill owners claimed that the president's actions were an unconstitutional exercise by the executive of lawmaking power reserved for Congress.

Justice Hugo BLACK delivered the Court's opinion. The key question, Black begins, is to "decide whether the President was acting within his constitutional power" when he ordered the seizure. Black first finds that there is no constitutional basis for his order; indeed, what the Constitution expressly grants the president implies a limit to his actions in certain areas: "the President's power to see that the laws are faithfully executed refutes the idea that he is to be a lawmaker." Further, there is no congressional authorization for the seizure; instead, the president's order, argues Black, "directs that a presidential policy be executed

Steel mill in Youngstown, Pennsylvania *(Library of Congress)*

in a manner prescribed by the President." In short, while it is "beyond doubt" that the seizure could be ordered by Congress, the Constitution does not allow the president to act as a lawmaker.

While the Court's opinion is an important affirmation of Congress's power in the domestic arena, and of the limits of domestic executive power, it is Justice Robert JACKSON's concurring opinion that arguably has had more influence. Jackson took the opportunity presented the Court and penned a uniquely sober opinion that listed the "practical situations in which a President may doubt, or others may challenge, his powers." When a president's actions are "pursuant to an express or implied authorization of Congress," he is at his maximum authority; when Congress is silent on a matter on which the president acts, the branches are said to have concurrent authority, though its ultimate distribution remains "uncertain"; finally, when Congress has expressed its disagreement with the president's action, "his power is at its lowest ebb."

The *Youngstown* decision, and particularly Jackson's concurring opinion, has stood as a compelling statement on the SEPARATION OF POWERS and of the proper limits of government action, being cited numerous times in cases ranging in topic from EXECUTIVE PRIVILEGE and immunity to the supremacy of the national government in foreign affairs. For Jackson, however, the issue was clear: free government can only be sustained if the executive is "under the law" made by legislators, not free to spin his will into statute. For those that embrace this axiom, *Youngstown* remains a judicial landmark.

For more information: Bellia, Patricia L., et al. "Youngstown at Fifty: A Symposium." *Constitutional Commentary* 19, no. 1 (Spring 2002).

—Patrick F. Campbell

Z

Zadvydas v. Davis, 533 U.S. 678 (2001)

In *Zadvydas v. Davis,* the United States Supreme Court ruled that resident aliens held by the government beyond the 90-day removal period were entitled to a habeas corpus hearing if held more than six months beyond expiration of this time period. The significance of this case resided in a limitation upon the power of the Immigration and Naturalization Service (INS) to indefinitely detain aliens awaiting deportation.

Aliens are individuals who are not citizens but nonetheless reside in the United States. In some cases, these individuals have entered the country illegally, or they have been convicted of a crime or otherwise have failed to comply with the conditions that allow them to remain in the United States. When that occurs, these individuals may be deported if a final order has been issued. If that occurs, federal law states that the INS may hold in custody the person subject to deportation up to 90 days. This 90 days is known as a removal period. During this time the INS prepares the alien for removal, seeking to determine to what country to send that person, for example.

In some situations, the 90-day period expires before the individual is ready to be deported. In these situations, federal law allows the U.S. attorney general to detain the person beyond the 90-day period if it is felt that the person is a risk to the community, a security threat, or in danger of flight if released. This post removal period detention has no time limit on it, suggesting that the INS may hold an alien for an indefinite period of time. It is this indefinite holding of an alien by the INS that is the subject of the dispute in *Zadvydas v. Davis.*

In this case, Kestutis Zadvydas was a resident alien who was born in Germany of Lithuanian parents and immigrated to the United States with his parents when he was eight years old. Zadvydas had a long criminal record including burglaries and drug convictions, and in 1974 after a conviction for the possession and sale of cocaine, he was taken in custody by the INS and ordered deported. However,

Germany refused to accept Zadvydas that year, the Dominican Republic refused in 1996, and in 1998 Lithuania also rejected him.

Beginning in 1995, Zadvydas filed petitions in court seeking habeas corpus, or release from detention by the INS. His claim was that he was being illegally detained beyond the 90-day removal period. In 1997 a federal district court granted his habeas petition and ordered him released, but the Fifth Circuit COURT OF APPEALS reversed, indicating that his detention was not unconstitutional because his deportation was impossible and because the government was making good faith efforts to remove him from the United States. The Supreme Court accepted the case for review and reversed the Fifth Circuit opinion.

Writing for the Court, Justice BREYER first noted that habeas corpus in federal court is available to review post removal period detentions. However, the main issue in the case was whether the government could detain someone for an indefinite period of time beyond the 90-day removal period. The INS argued that the statute permitted this, but the Court stated that an indefinite detention raised serious constitutional questions, especially when the deportation hearings were supposed to be civil and nonpunitive.

Moreover, Breyer questioned whether Congress really had intended to allow this indefinite detention, indicating that the fact that it had changed the law to place a limit of 90 days on the removal period suggested that they intended to limit how long the government may hold someone. Breyer also rejected arguments by the government that issues of detention of aliens were inherently executive department and security issues and that the president and attorney general should be given significant leeway in making these types of decisions. Overall, the majority concluded that there had to be some reasonable limit regarding how long a person could be held, and they concluded that six months beyond the expiration of the 90-day removal period was it. At that point the person being detained could petition for release, and the burden would be on the government to show why continued detention was required.

Overall, *Zadvydas v. Davis* was considered an important victory for the rights of aliens. The case was decided in June 2001, but it took on even more importance after the terrorist attacks on the United States later that year on September 11. With the United States cracking down on individuals suspected of being terrorists, it placed limits upon the ability of the government to detain individuals indefinitely simply because they were aliens.

For more information: Reckers, Rob. "The Future of Aliens Ordered Removed from the United States in the Wake of *Zadvydas v. Davis*." *Houston Journal of International Law* 25 (Fall 2002): 195.

—David Schultz

Zobrest v. Catalina Foothills School District, 509 U.S. 1 (1993)

In *Zobrest v. Catalina Foothills School District,* the Supreme Court required a public school district that provided sign language interpreters to its public school students to also provide them to students of religious schools. It is one of several cases reflecting the REHNQUIST Court's transition to a non-preferentialist reading of the First Amendment's ESTABLISHMENT CLAUSE from the strict separationist approach that had begun to crystallize in the 1970s and '80s.

James Zobrest was deaf from birth. Through fifth grade he was educated in a school for the deaf. From sixth through eighth grade he attended a public school and was provided with a sign-language interpreter under the terms of the federal Individuals with Disabilities in Education Act (IDEA) and a similar Arizona statute. As he entered high school, his parents chose to send him to a Catholic school and requested that the Arizona public school district in which they resided continue to provide him with an interpreter under IDEA. The Catalina Foothills School District believed that provision of a state-funded interpreter to Mr. Zobrest would violate the Constitution's establishment clause. The district therefore declined to provide the interpreter. Zobrest's parents took legal action to secure an interpreter; they were denied at the U.S. District Court and the U.S. COURT OF APPEALS before appealing to the Supreme Court.

The Court reversed lower court rulings. Writing for the majority, Chief Justice Rehnquist defined the program in question as a general benefit provided by government for the public welfare. Because the translator was provided to the student rather than to the school, the benefit did not give any direct or indirect aid to a religious institution. Rehnquist explained that "[w]hen the government offers a

neutral service on the premises of a sectarian school as part of a general program that 'is in no way skewed towards religion,' it follows under our prior decisions that provision of that service does not offend the Establishment Clause."

In his opinion, Chief Justice Rehnquist attempted to clarify distinctions between programs allowing government aid to parochial schools that the Court had found acceptable and those it had invalidated. *MUELLER V. ALLEN,* 463 U.S. 388 (1983), and *Witters v. Washington Dept. of Services for the Blind* (1986) upheld programs in which citizens used general benefits provided by states to finance religious educations. Because the programs in question both had a clear secular purpose and advanced RELIGION indirectly and insignificantly, they were not held to be in violation of the establishment clause. On the other hand, *Meek v. Pittenger,* 421 U.S. 349 (1976), and *School Dist. of Grand Rapids v. Ball,* 473 U.S. 373 (1985), invalidated programs which provided direct aid to educational institutions, including parochial schools. [*Meek* and *Ball* would both subsequently be overturned; *Ball* was partially overturned in *Agostini v. Felton,* 521 U.S. 203 (1997), *Meek* in *MITCHELL V. HELMS,* 530 U.S. 793 (2000).]

In dissent, Justice BLACKMUN argued, "even a general welfare program may have specific applications that are constitutionally forbidden under the Establishment Clause." Yet his dissent centered on the argument that it was a violation of the establishment clause for the state to provide an interpreter who served as "the medium for communication of a religious message." According to Blackmun, the Court had consistently "prohibit[ed] the provision of any instructional materials or equipment that could be used to convey a religious message, such as slide projectors, tape recorders, record players, and the like. . . ." Chief Justice Rehnquist, in contrast, distinguished the interpreter, who provided a neutral service in translating a message, from the message itself.

The principle of non-preferentialism or government neutrality toward religion that Chief Justice Rehnquist began to clarify in *Zobrest* would be even more clearly articulated in the *Agostini v. Felton* and *Mitchell v. Helms* cases, which ultimately introduced the framework of an entirely new establishment clause doctrine.

For more information: Levy, Leonard W. *The Establishment Clause.* Chapel Hill: University of North Carolina Press, 1994.

—Jason Ross

zoning

Zoning, which is a use of a local government's police power to ensure the public's environmental quality in terms of health, safety and welfare, requires that government strike a delicate balance between the public's privilege of enjoying their environment and the private property owners' right to use their land as they choose.

Generally, municipalities base zoning decisions on the intensity of use of a parcel of realty. Hence, different types of property use, such as commercial, industrial, residential, or mixed uses, are usually subject to different zoning regulations or ordinances.

During the 18th and 19th centuries, the United States was primarily an agricultural country and was very sparsely populated. Hence, there was no need to worry about the quality of the living environment in densely populated areas. However, as the population of the United States grew and became increasingly urban, the concept of zoning evolved. The idea of some governmental control of land utilization in cities for purposes of health, hygiene, safety, and of the simple enjoyment of life became increasingly acceptable. The rationale for allowing such control was based on the idea that cities are "creatures of the state." This means that cities exist only because state laws and constitutions define them as such. If a state decides that the health and welfare of a city's population depends on compliance with a state-promulgated rule, the city must adhere to the rule or lose privileges or funds that otherwise would be concomitant with the area's status under state law.

A state's power over a city is counterbalanced by the provisions of the Fifth and Fourteenth Amendments to the Constitution that prohibit government from taking private property away from its owner without just compensation and due process of law. These countervailing forces allowed only very gradual evolution of governmental control over private property. The Supreme Court began to concede to the necessity of this type of governmental control when a local ordinance imposed height limits on buildings in the District of Columbia in 1899 and established safety and fire regulations in Boston in 1904 and in Los Angeles in 1909.

In the landmark case of EUCLID V. AMBLER, 272 U.S. 365 (1926), the Court upheld the constitutionality of a zoning law that prevented a property owner from building a commercial structure in a residential zoning district. This case demonstrated that if a city was to remain tolerable as a living environment, it was necessary for zoning laws to keep pace with the evolving complexity of cities. After the validity of the concept of zoning laws passed the high court's muster, more cities were encouraged to adopt zoning plans. In an effort to help cities avoid problems that would interfere with public health and welfare, in 1926 the U.S. Department of Commerce promulgated a standard zoning act that all cities could utilize.

In several cases decided by the Court during the 1980s and 1990s, it appeared that private property owners had the upper hand when zoning regulations were questioned. In LUCAS V. SOUTH CAROLINA COASTAL COUNCIL, 505 U.S. 1003 (1992), regulations that denied the property owner all "economically viable use of his land" constituted one of the discrete categories of regulatory deprivations that required compensation without the usual case-specific inquiry into the public interest advanced in support of the restraint. Although the Court has never set forth the justification for this categorical rule, the practical—and economic—equivalence of physically appropriating and eliminating all beneficial use of land counsels its preservation.

In *Dolan v. City of Tigard,* 512 U.S. 374 (1994), the Court held that a "rough proportionality test best described the avoidance of taking without compensation" under the Fifth Amendment. The high court said that the rough proportionality test did not require mathematical calculations. Instead, this test required that the city must make some sort of individualized determination that the required dedication is related both in nature and extent to the impact of the proposed development.

Palazzolo v. Rhode Island Coastal Resources Management Council, 533 U.S. 606 (2001), arose out of a coastal situation rather than in a city. In 1971 a certain portion of coastal Rhode Island in which salt marshes were located was declared to be a federally protected wetland. In 1978 the plaintiff purchased two parcels within the coastal salt marsh, with the intention of filling the marshland and creating a beach club. The council refused to grant a construction permit, since Palazzolo's plans did not serve a compelling public purpose. In response to this refusal to grant the permit, Palazzolo sued the council for compensation for the land they had taken without affording him due process of law. The Supreme Court reversed the highest state court, finding that the landowner's parcels had been rendered useless to him and worthless on resale.

Palazzolo, above, is indicative of the Court's tendency, over the last 15 years, to act more favorably toward a property owner than toward a governmental entity in cases where the owner's right to enjoy his or her property was infringed by a municipality. However, at the end of the 2002 term, the Court issued an important opinion that many have hailed as a major victory for government regulators who seek to slow or restrict the land development industry.

In *Monterey v. Del Monte Dunes at Monterey, Ltd.,* 119 S. Ct. 1624 (1999), the Court found that if a municipality has withheld use of a landowner's property without substantially advancing a legitimate public interest, the municipality must compensate the owner under the "takings" clause of the Fifth Amendment to the U.S. Constitution. Hence, the question here was whether the city took the property outright by exercising its power of EMINENT DOMAIN, or took the property temporarily and for a legitimate purpose.

In this case, the City of Monterey was doing a time-consuming, statutorily mandated study on the property.

Since that zoning ordinance is intended to protect the public from improper utilization of the property, the time spent to complete the study to determine the legality of the planned property use was not a "taking," hence Monterey had no obligation to compensate Del Monte Dunes.

In February 2002 the Court declined to review a decision by a federal appeals court, thereby allowing the so-called *Voyeur Dorm* Web site to remain in operation. In this case, the question was whether a city adult entertainment law applied to a residence that housed the women featured on the *Voyeur Dorm* Web site who allowed every moment of their lives to be televised. The house itself is located in a residential section of Tampa, Florida, which, like most cities, forbids adult entertainment establishments in residential areas. When one of *Voyeur Dorm*'s attorneys sent a letter to Tampa's zoning coordinator, asking her interpretation of the city's zoning code as it applied to his client, the coordinator wrote that the city zoning code was applicable to the Web site.

On APPEAL, the U.S. COURT OF APPEALS for the Eleventh Circuit found that zoning restrictions are indelibly anchored in particular geographic locations. Hence, the zoning law was inapplicable, since the *Voyeur Dorm*'s public offering was located not in a physical space but in virtual space. As a result of this decision, the Web site was allowed to continue broadcasting, *Voyeur Dorm, L.C. v. City of Tampa*, 121 F. Supp. 2d 1373 (M.D. Fla. 2000), *City of Tampa v. Voyeur Dorm, Inc.*, cert. denied, 534 U.S. 1161 (2002).

The more recent case of *Tahoe-Sierra Preservation Council, Inc. v. Tahoe Regional Planning Agency*, 122 S. Ct. 1465 (2002), was occasioned by a similar situation. While it worked at formulating a comprehensive LAND USE plan for the Lake Tahoe area, the Tahoe Regional Planning Agency (TRPA) imposed two moratoria, totaling 32 months, on development in the Lake Tahoe Basin. Real estate owners affected by the moratoria sued the TRPA, claiming that the agency's actions constituted a "taking" of their property without just compensation. The district court found that the moratoria ordered by TRPA are not per se "takings" of property requiring compensation per the Fifth Amendment's "takings" clause. However, it concluded that the moratoria did constitute a "taking" under the categorical rule announced in *Lucas v. South Carolina Coastal Council*, 505 U.S. 1003 (1992), because TRPA's action deprived petitioners of all economically viable use of their land for only a short period of time. On appeal, TRPA successfully challenged the district court's "takings" determination.

In *Tahoe-Sierra Preservation Council, Inc. v. Tahoe Regional Planning Agency*, the Court held that a temporary moratorium on land development around Lake Tahoe did not amount to a "taking" that automatically required the payment of compensation under the Fifth Amendment's "takings" clause. The high court found that moratoria or "interim development controls" are essential to successful real estate development. However, the Court carefully clarified the narrow scope of its holding to assure landowners that government regulators must have a valid reason to delay land use planning or make decisions regarding construction permits.

For about a decade prior to 2002, the Court appeared to be inclined to offer individuals the benefit of the doubt in zoning disputes. After the 2002 *Tahoe* decision, while the justices may have appeared to step away from their pro-individual stance, they have actually simply decided to take these matters on a case-by-case basis, rather than allow a trend to sway their judgment.

For more information: American Planning Association. "Supreme Court Upholds Land-Use Planning Authority." 2002 http://www.planning.org/newsreleases/1999/ftp0525. htm. Downloaded May 20, 2004.

—Beth S. Swartz

Zorach v. Clauson, 343 U.S. 306 (1952)

Zorach v. Clauson upheld the constitutionality of a program implemented in New York City public schools that allowed students to be released from school at designated times during the school day to receive religious instruction off campus.

In this case, parents requested in writing that their children be released for this instruction, and the teachers of these private religious classes (who were not public school teachers) reported attendance to the public school. Students who did not attend off-campus religious classes remained in classes at the public school.

Zorach v. Clauson followed *McCollum v. Board of Education,* 333 U.S. 203 (1948), which held unconstitutional a similar "released time" program in Illinois. This Illinois program permitted public schools to allow private religious organizations to provide religious instruction during regular school hours in public school facilities. Summarizing the holding in the *McCollum* case, Justice BLACK wrote: "Here not only are the State's tax-supported public school buildings used for the dissemination of religious doctrines. The state also affords sectarian groups an invaluable aid in that it helps to provide pupils for their religious classes through use of the state's compulsory public school machinery."

Justice DOUGLAS, writing the opinion in *Zorach,* argued that the program at issue was substantially different from the program invalidated by *McCollum* and that it did not violate the establishment clause. He pointed out that the New York program did not permit the use of public school facilities for religious instruction during the school day, nor did it require any public funding. Further, he famously argued: "We are a religious people whose institutions presuppose a Supreme Being. . . . When the state encourages religious instruction or cooperates with religious authorities . . . it then respects the religious nature of our people and accommodates the public service to their spiritual needs. To hold that it may not would be to find in the Constitution a requirement that the government show a callous indifference to religious groups."

Dissent from the majority opinion focused on the compulsory nature of public education. The majority opinion in *Zorach* did not directly address this issue because the decision to participate in religious education was voluntarily made by the parents and was conducted off public school grounds in private facilities. Justice Black's dissent, echoed in a separate dissent by Justice FRANKFURTER, turned on the argument that religious groups benefited from the New York program, taking advantage of the "compulsory school machinery so as to channel children into sectarian classes." Thus the program served as an unconstitutional state aid to RELIGION. Justice JACKSON argued that the program was coercive to those students who do not participate in off-campus religious education: "Schooling is more or less sus-pended during the 'released time' so the nonreligious attendants will not forge ahead of the churchgoing absentees. But it serves as a temporary jail for a pupil who will not go to Church."

Ultimately, what separated the majority opinion from the dissents in *Zorach* was a fundamentally different understanding of what the ESTABLISHMENT CLAUSE requires. The majority clearly adhered to a non-preferential or accommodationist interpretation, one that would permit some mingling of religious belief and practice with public services and functions as long as the government does not prefer one religion or denomination to another. According to this logic, government actions that have the effect of aiding religion are acceptable if that effect is indirect and as long as all sects are aided equally. The dissents advanced a strict separationist interpretation that would make unconstitutional any and all contact between religion and public life.

For more information: Levy, Leonard W. *The Establishment Clause.* Chapel Hill: University of North Carolina Press, 1994.

—Jason Ross

Chronology

1787
Constitutional Convention.

1788
Constitution is ratified by requisite number of states.

1789
JUDICIARY ACT OF 1789 establishes the Supreme Court with six members and allows for cases from a state's highest court to be appealed to the United States Supreme Court.

   President Washington appoints the first six justices. John JAY becomes the first CHIEF JUSTICE.

1791
First 10 amendments to the Constitution, known as the BILL OF RIGHTS, are ratified.

1796
Oliver ELLSWORTH becomes chief justice.

1800
John MARSHALL becomes chief justice.

1803
In *MARBURY V. MADISON*, the Supreme Court states it has the power to declare laws unconstitutional.

1810
In *FLETCHER V. PECK*, the Supreme Court declares it has the power to review the constitutionality of state laws.

1811
Samuel CHASE is the only Supreme Court justice impeached by the House of Representatives. The Senate refuses to convict him.

1819
In *MCCULLOCH V. MARYLAND*, the Supreme Court upholds the constitutionality of the Bank of the United States and indicates that the federal government has expansive power under the "necessary and proper" clause.

1824
In *GIBBONS V. OGDEN*, the Supreme Court upholds expansive power for the U.S. government to regulate commerce.

1831
In *Cherokee Nation v. Georgia*, the Supreme Court issues the first of several decisions regarding the status of Native Americans in the United States.

1833
In *BARRON V. BALTIMORE*, the Supreme Court states that the Bill of Rights does not apply to the states.

1836
Roger TANEY becomes chief justice.

1857
In *Dred Scott v. Sandford*, the Supreme Court declares the Missouri Compromise unconstitutional and also rules that blacks are property, not citizens.

1864
Salmon P. CHASE becomes chief justice.

1865
The Thirteenth Amendment, abolishing slavery, is ratified.

1868
The Fourteenth Amendment is ratified, overturning *Dred Scott v. Sandford*. The amendment prevents states from

denying the privileges and immunities of U.S. citizens, equal protection of the law, or due process of law.

1870

The Fifteenth Amendment is ratified, prohibiting discrimination in voting on the basis of race.

1873

In the SLAUGHTER-HOUSE CASES, the Supreme Court limits the meaning of the privileges and immunities clause of the Fourteenth Amendment.

1874

Morrison R. WAITE becomes chief justice.

1875

Supreme Court rules in *Minor v. Happersett* that states may deny women the right to vote.

1883

In the *Civil Rights Cases,* the Supreme Court declares that Congress lacks the authority to prevent discrimination in private establishments.

1888

Melville W. FULLER becomes chief justice.

1895

Supreme Court upholds the use of injunctions to halt labor strikes in IN RE DEBS.

Supreme Court narrows the application of the Sherman Antitrust Act and the power of Congress to regulate commerce in *United States v. E. C. Knight Company.*

1896

In PLESSY V. FERGUSON, the Supreme Court upholds segregation and the "separate but equal" doctrine.

1897

In *Chicago, Burlington & Quincy Railroad Company v. Chicago,* the Supreme Court begins the process of incorporating the Bill of Rights to the states by holding that the Fifth Amendment just compensation clause applies to the states.

In ALLGEYER V. LOUISIANA, the Supreme Court strikes down a state law regulating a private contract.

1905

In LOCHNER V. NEW YORK, the Supreme Court strikes down a state law regulating the working hours of bakers, holding that it violated the due process clause of the Fourteenth Amendment.

1908

In MULLER V. OREGON, the Supreme Court upholds laws limiting the working hours for women. Louis BRANDEIS introduces the famous "BRANDEIS BRIEF" in the case.

1910

Edward D. WHITE becomes chief justice.

1918

In HAMMER V. DAGENHART, the Supreme Court strikes down child labor laws as an unconstitutional regulation of commerce.

1919

The Nineteenth Amendment is ratified, giving women the right to vote.

In ABRAMS V. UNITED STATES, the Supreme Court upholds the convictions of five Russian immigrants who circulated antiwar leaflets.

1921

Former president William Howard TAFT becomes chief justice.

1925

In GITLOW V. NEW YORK, the Supreme Court incorporates the First Amendment free speech clause to apply to the states through the due process clause of the Fourteenth Amendment.

1930

Charles Evans HUGHES becomes chief justice.

1932

In the Scottsboro case of *Powell v. Alabama,* the Supreme Court rules that the state must provide legal counsel to those accused of capital crimes.

Supreme Court upholds the power of states to issue a moratorium on mortgage repayments in HOME BUILDING AND LOAN ASSOCIATION V. BLAISDELL.

1935

SUPREME COURT BUILDING is completed and the Court moves into it.

1936

In a trio of cases including UNITED STATES V. SCHECHTER POULTRY, the Supreme Court invalidates much of the New Deal, contending that it involved an unconstitutional delegation of power.

1937

President Roosevelt issues his "COURT-PACKING PLAN."

Supreme Court begins to uphold the constitutionality of the New Deal.

1938

In the famous footnote number four of *United States v. Carolene Products*, the Supreme Court indicates that it will no longer give heightened scrutiny to economic legislation but instead will afford more protection to civil rights. This case marks the beginning of the "New Deal" Court.

1940

In *Minersville School District v. Gobitis*, the Supreme Court upholds a compulsory FLAG SALUTE law.

1941

Harlan Fiske STONE becomes chief justice.

1942

In *WICKARD V. FILBURN*, the Supreme Court broadens the commerce clause power of Congress to regulate wheat production for personal use.

In *BETTS V. BRADY*, the Supreme Court creates the EXCLUSIONARY RULE that prevents the use of illegally obtained evidence federal court to convict an individual.

The Court declares in *SKINNER V. OKLAHOMA* that individuals have a fundamental right to procreate.

1943

In *West Virginia v. Barnette*, the Supreme Court holds that compulsory flag saluting in school is unconstitutional. This decision overturns *Minersville School District v. Gobitis*.

1944

In *KOREMATSU V. UNITED STATES*, the Supreme Court upholds the forced and mass detaining of Japanese Americans. In the same case the Court also declares any policy that categorizes individuals by race is suspect.

1946

Fred M. VINSON becomes chief justice.

In *COLEGROVE V. GREEN*, the Supreme Court says it will not hear reapportionment cases.

1951

In *DENNIS V. UNITED STATES*, the Supreme Court upholds the conviction of 11 members of the Communist Party for violating the Smith Act.

1952

In *YOUNGSTOWN SHEET & TUBE CO., V. SAWYER*, the Supreme Court declares that President's Truman's seizing of the steel mills during the Korean War was unconstitutional.

1953

Earl WARREN becomes chief justice.

1954

"Separate but equal" doctrine is declared unconstitutional in *BROWN V. BOARD OF EDUCATION*.

1958

Supreme Court declares it is the final word on the meaning of the Constitution in *Cooper v. Aaron*.

1961

In *MAPP V. OHIO*, the Supreme Court extends the exclusionary rule to apply to the states.

1962

In *BAKER V. CARR*, the Court reverses its decision in *Colegrove v. Green* and rules that reapportionment challenges can be heard in federal court.

In *ENGEL V. VITALE*, the Supreme Court declares that state-sponsored prayer in public schools is unconstitutional.

1963

In *GIDEON V. WAINWRIGHT*, the Supreme Court rules that individuals accused of felonies must receive an attorney if they cannot afford one.

In *Abington v. Schempp*, the Supreme Court declares Bible reading in public schools to be unconstitutional.

1964

The CIVIL RIGHTS ACT OF 1964 is passed by Congress.

In *HEART OF ATLANTA MOTEL V. UNITED STATES*, the Supreme Court upholds the constitutionality of the 1964 Civil Rights Act.

In *NEW YORK TIMES V. SULLIVAN*, the Supreme Court establishes a higher standard that must be met in order to sue a public official for libel.

In *REYNOLDS V. SIMS*, the Supreme Court establishes the "ONE PERSON, ONE VOTE" standard for redistricting.

1965

The VOTING RIGHTS ACT OF 1965 is passed by Congress.

In *Griswold v. Connecticut*, the Supreme Court declares unconstitutional a state law making it illegal to sell CONTRACEPTIVES to married couples.

1966

In *MIRANDA V. ARIZONA,* the Supreme Court rules that those suspected of a crime must be read their rights when they are taken into custody.

1967

Thurgood MARSHALL becomes the first African American on the Supreme Court.

1969

In *Brandenburg v. Ohio,* the Supreme Court rules that mere advocacy of violence is protected under the First Amendment.

Warren BURGER becomes chief justice.

1971

In *LEMON V. KURTZMAN,* the Supreme Court issues a constitutional test to determine when state aid to parochial schools violates the establishment clause.

In *SWANN V. CHARLOTTE-MECKLENBURG BOARD OF EDUCATION,* the Supreme Court upholds the use of busing to achieve racial integration of schools.

1972

In *FURMAN V. GEORGIA,* the Supreme Court strikes down all death penalty laws as unconstitutional.

1973

Laws outlawing abortion are struck down in *Rowe v. Wade.*

Supreme Court establishes a new test for obscenity in *Miller v. California.*

Supreme Court declares in *SAN ANTONIO INDEPENDENT SCHOOL DISTRICT V. RODRIGUEZ* that education is not a fundamental right and wealth is not a SUSPECT CLASSIFICATION.

1974

In *United States v. Nixon,* the Supreme Court orders President Nixon to turn over his private White House taped recorded conversations to a special prosecutor.

1976

In *Buckley v. Valeo,* the Supreme Court upholds portions of the new Federal Election Campaign Act that regulates campaign contributions. The Court strikes down the regulations on campaign spending.

In *GREGG V. GEORGIA,* the Supreme Court upholds the Georgia death penalty law.

In *CRAIG V. BOREN,* the Supreme Court states that a higher level of scrutiny is needed when individuals are classified by gender.

1978

In *REGENTS OF THE UNIVERSITY OF CALIFORNIA V. BAKKE,* the Supreme Court upholds the use of affirmation action in education admissions so long as race is one of several factors used in evaluating candidates.

1981

Sandra Day O'CONNOR becomes the first woman on the Supreme Court.

1986

William REHNQUIST becomes chief justice.

In a contentious confirmation process, the U.S. Senate refuses to confirm Robert BORK to be on the Supreme Court.

In *BOWERS V. HARDWICK,* the Supreme Court rules that private, consensual homosexual sodomy is not protected by the Constitution.

In *MERITOR SAVINGS BANK V. VINSON,* the Supreme Court declares SEXUAL HARASSMENT to be sexual discrimination.

1989

In *TEXAS V. JOHNSON,* the Supreme Court declares unconstitutional a law making FLAG BURNING illegal.

1990

In *CRUZAN V. DIRECTOR, MISSOURI DEPARTMENT OF HEALTH,* the Supreme Court rules that individuals have a right to DIE and withhold medical treatment.

1992

In *PLANNED PARENTHOOD V. CASEY,* the Supreme Court reaffirms *ROE V. WADE* but also upholds several restrictions upon women seeking abortions.

The Supreme Court strikes down a CROSS BURNING law as a violation of the First Amendment in *R.A.V. v. St. Paul.*

1995

In *United States v. Lopez,* the Supreme Court strikes down Congress's authority under the commerce clause to regulate guns near schools.

1996

In *Seminole Tribe of Florida v. Florida,* the Supreme Court strikes down as unconstitutional the Indian Gaming Regulatory Act provision which authorizes Indian tribes to sue state governments, claiming that the law violates state SOVEREIGN IMMUNITY. This case is the beginning of several Rehnquist Court decisions that limit the ability of individuals to sue state governments.

2000

In *Bush v. Gore*, the Supreme Court halts the Florida presidential recount, making George Bush the winner of the 2000 presidential race.

2003

Supreme Court overrules *Bowers v. Hardwick* in *Lawrence v. Texas*.

In a pair of cases, *Gratz v. Bollinger* and *Grutter v. Bollinger*, the Supreme Court upholds the use of AFFIRMATIVE ACTION to promote educational diversity.

In *United States v. Virginia*, the Supreme Court upholds a state cross burning law as constitutional.

In *McConnell v. FEC*, the Supreme Court upholds soft money ban in the Bipartisan Campaign Finance Reform Act of 2002.

Selected Bibliography

Baker, Leonard. *Back to Back: The Dual Between F.D.R. and the Supreme Court.* New York: Macmillan, 1967.

Baker, Liva. *Felix Frankfurter.* New York: Coward-McCann, 1969.

———. *The Justice from Beacon Hill: The Life and Times of Oliver Wendell Holmes.* New York: HarperCollins, 1991.

Baum, Lawrence. *The Supreme Court.* Washington, D.C.: CQ Press, 2000.

Beth, Loren P. *John Marshall Harlan: The Last Whig Justice.* Lexington: University Press of Kentucky, 1992.

Bickel, Alexander M. *Politics and the Warren Court.* New York: Harper and Row, 1965.

Bickel, Alexander. *The Least Dangerous Branch: The Supreme Court at the Bar of Politics.* New Haven, Conn.: Yale University Press, 1962.

Blasi, Vincent. *The Burger Court: The Counter-Revolution That Wasn't.* New Haven, Conn.: Yale University Press, 1986.

Bork, Robert. *The Tempting of America: The Political Seduction of the Law.* New York: Touchstone Books, 1990.

Brigham, John. *The Cult of the Court.* Philadelphia, Pa.: Temple University Press, 1987.

Cardozo, Benjamin N. *The Nature of the Judicial Process.* New Haven, Conn.: Yale University Press, 1964.

Choper, Jesse. *Judicial Review and the National Political Process: A Functionalist Reconsideration of the Supreme Court.* Chicago: University of Chicago Press, 1980.

Clinton, Robert L. *Marbury v. Madison and Judicial Review.* Lawrence: University Press of Kansas, 1989.

Cox, Archibald. *The Court and the Constitution.* Boston: Houghton Mifflin, 1987.

———. *The Role of the Supreme Court in American Government.* New York: Oxford University Press, 1976.

Currie, David P. *The Constitution in the Supreme Court: The Second Hundred Years, 1888–1986.* Chicago: University of Chicago Press, 1990.

———. *The Constitution in the Supreme Court: The First Hundred Years, 1789–1888.* Chicago: University of Chicago Press, 1985.

Cushman, Clare. *The Supreme Court Justices: Illustrated Biographies, 1789–1995.* Washington, D.C.: Congressional Quarterly, 1995.

Davis, Michael D., and Hunter R. Clark. *Thurgood Marshall: Warrior at the Bar, Rebel on the Bench,* Updated and Revised Edition. New York: Citadel Press, 1994.

Douglas, William O. *The Court Years 1939–1975.* New York: Random House, 1980.

Eisler, Kim Isaac. *A Justice for All: William J. Brennan, Jr., and the Decisions that Transformed America.* New York: Simon and Schuster, 1993.

Elsmere, Jane Shaffer. *Justice Samuel Chase.* Muncie, Ind.: Janevar, 1980.

Ely, James W., Jr. *The Guardian of Every Other Right: A Constitutional History of Property Rights.* New York: Oxford University Press, 1998.

Ely, John Hart. *Democracy and Distrust: A Theory of Judicial Review.* Cambridge, Mass.: Harvard University Press, 1980.

Epstein, Lee, and Joseph F. Kobylka. *The Supreme Court and Legal Change: Abortion and the Death Penalty.* Chapel Hill: University of North Carolina Press, 1992.

Fairman, Charles. *History of the Supreme Court of the United States: Reconstruction and Reunion 1864–88.* New York: Macmillan, 1971.

———. *Mr. Justice Miller and the Supreme Court 1862–1890.* Cambridge, Mass.: Harvard University Press, 1939.

Farrand, Max. *The Records of the Federal Convention of 1787.* New Haven, Conn.: Yale University Press, 1966.

Frankfurter, Felix. *The Commerce Clause under Marshall, Taney and Waite.* Chicago: Quadrangle Books, 1964.

———. *Felix Frankfurter Reminisces.* New York: Doubleday, 1962.

Gillman, Howard. *The Constitution Besieged: The Rise and Demise of Lochner Era Police Powers Jurisprudence.* Chicago: University of Chicago Press, 1993.

Gottlieb, Stephen E. *Morality Imposed: The Rehnquist Court and Liberty in America.* New York: New York University Press, 2000.

Greenberg, Jack. *Crusaders in the Courts: How a Dedicated Band of Lawyers Fought for the Civil Rights Revolution.* New York: Basic Books, 1994.

Haines, Charles Grove. *The Role of the Supreme Court in American Government and Politics, 1789–1835.* New York: Russell and Russell, 1960.

Hall, Kermit L. *The Magic Mirror: Law in American History.* New York: Oxford University Press, 1989.

Hobson, Charles F. *The Great Chief Justice: John Marshall and the Rule of Law.* Lawrence: University of Kansas Press, 1996.

Holmes, Oliver W., Jr. *The Common Law* (ed. Mark DeWolfe Howe). Boston: Little Brown, 1963.

Howard, J. Woodford. *Mr. Justice Murphy: A Political Biography.* Princeton, N.J.: Princeton University Press, 1968.

Hughes, Charles Evans. *The Supreme Court of the United States.* New York: Columbia University Press, 1938.

Hutchison, Dennis. *The Man Who Once Was Whizzer White: A Portrait of Justice Byron R. White.* New York: Free Press, 1998.

Jeffries, John C., Jr. *Justice Lewis F. Powell, Jr.* New York: Charles Scribner's Sons, 1994.

Kahn, Ronald. *The Supreme Court & Constitutional Theory.* Lawrence: University of Kansas Press, 1994.

Kalman, Laura. *Abe Fortas: A Biography.* New Haven, Conn.: Yale University Press, 1990.

Kelly, Alfred H., Winfred A. Harbison, and Herman Belz. *The American Constitution: Its Origins and Development.* 2 vols. New York: W. W. Norton, 1991.

Klarman, Michael J. *From Jim Crow to Civil Rights: The Supreme Court and the Struggle for Racial Equality.* New York: Oxford University Press, 2004.

Kluger, Richard. *Simple Justice.* New York: Random House, 1975.

Latham, Frank Brown. *The Great Dissenter: John Marshall Harlan, 1833–1911.* New York: Cowles, 1970.

Leuchtenburg, William E. *The Supreme Court Reborn: The Constitutional Revolution in the Age of Roosevelt.* New York: Oxford University Press, 1995.

Lewis, Anthony. *Gideon's Trumpet.* New York: Random House, 1964.

Maltese, John Anthony. *The Selling of Supreme Court Nominees.* Baltimore: Johns Hopkins University Press, 1995.

Mason, Alpheus Thomas. *Harlan Fiske Stone: Pillar of the Law.* New York: Viking, 1956.

McCann, Michael W. *Rights at Work: Pay Equity Reform and the Politics of Legal Mobilization.* Chicago: University of Chicago Press, 1994.

McClellan, James. *Joseph Story and the American Constitution.* Norman: University of Oklahoma Press, 1990.

Morris, Richard Brandon. *John Jay, the Nation, and the Court.* Boston: Boston University Press, 1967.

Muir, William K., Jr. *Prayer in Public Schools: Law and Attitude Change.* Chicago: University of Chicago Press, 1967.

Murphy, Bruce Allen. *Wild Bill: The Legend and Life of William O. Douglas.* New York: Random House, 2003.

Murphy, Paul, L. *The Constitution in Crisis Times, 1918–1969.* New York: Harper and Row, 1972.

Pacelle, Richard L., Jr. *The Transformation of the Supreme Court's Agenda.* Boulder, Colo.: Westview, 1991.

Pederson, William D., and Norman W. Provizer. *Leaders of the Pack: Polls & Case Studies of Great Supreme Court Justices.* New York: Peter Lang, 2003.

Perry, H. W., Jr. *Deciding to Decide: Agenda Setting in the United States Supreme Court.* Cambridge, Mass.: Harvard University Press, 1991.

Pound, Roscoe. *The Formative Era of American Law.* Glouchester, Mass.: Peter Smith, 1938.

Pringle, Henry F. *Life and Times of William Howard Taft.* 2 vol. Hamden, Conn.: Shoe String Press, 1965.

Pritchett, Charles Herman. *The Roosevelt Court: A Study in Judicial Politics and Values, 1937–1947.* New York: Macmillan, 1948.

Provine, Doris Marie. *Case Selection in the United States Supreme Court.* Chicago: University of Chicago Press, 1980.

Pusey, Merlo L. *Charles Evans Hughes.* 2 vol. New York: Macmillan, 1951.

Rehnquist, William H. *The Supreme Court: How It Was, How It Is.* New York: Quill, 1987.

Rosenberg, Gerald N. *The Hollow Hope: Can Courts Bring About Social Change?* Chicago: University of Chicago Press, 1991.

Savage, David G. *Turning Right: The Making of the Rehnquist Supreme Court.* New York: John Wiley, 1992.

Schultz, David A., and Christopher E. Smith. *The Jurisprudential Vision of Justice Antonin Scalia.* Lanham, Md.: Rowman and Littlefield, 1996.

Schwartz, Bernard. *Super Chief, Earl Warren and His Supreme Court: A Judicial Biography.* New York: New York University Press, 1983.

———. *The New Right and the Constitution: Turning Back the Legal Clock.* Boston: Northeastern University Press, 1990.

———. *A History of the Supreme Court.* New York: Oxford University Press, 1993.

Segal, Jeffrey A., and Harold J. Spaeth. *The Supreme Court and the Attitudinal Model.* New York: Cambridge University Press, 1993.

Sickels, Robert J. *John Paul Stevens and the Constitution: The Search and the Balance.* University Park: Pennsylvania State University Press, 1988.

Silverstein, Mark. *Constitutional Faiths: Felix Frankfurter, Hugo Black and the Process of Judicial Decision Making.* Ithaca, N.Y.: Cornell University Press, 1984.

Simon, James F. *The Center Holds: The Power Struggle Inside the Rehnquist Court.* New York: Simon and Schuster, 1995.

Strum, Phillippa. *Louis D. Brandeis: Justice for the People.* Cambridge, Mass.: Harvard University Press, 1984.

Swisher, Carl Brent. *Stephen J. Field: Craftsman of the Law.* Hamden, Conn.: Archon Books, 1963.

———. *Roger B. Taney.* New York: Macmillan, 1935.

Warren, Charles. *The Supreme Court in United States History.* 3 vol. Boston: Little, Brown, 1924.

Wasby, Stephen L. *The Impact of the United States Supreme Court: Some Perspectives.* Homewood, Ill.: Dorsey Press, 1970.

White, G. Edward. *The Marshall Court & Cultural Change: 1815–1835.* New York: Oxford University Press. 1991.

Woodward, Bob, and Scott Armstrong. *The Brethren.* New York: Simon and Schuster, 1979.

Index

A

Abington School District v. Schempp (1963) 353–354, 510
Abood v. Detroit Board of Education (1977) **1–2,** 42–43, 437
abortion rights **2–4,** *3,* 243, 326, 386–388
  birth defects and 387–388
  Blackmun on 39–40
  Bork on 45–46
  contraceptives and 68–69
  fundamental rights and 176–177
  Medicaid funding of 201, 391–392
  mootness and 296
  parental consent and 204, 339–340
  partial-birth abortions and 248, 340
  protest of 52, 267–268, 306, 383–384, *387,* 453
  restricted access to 340–341, 514–515
  RICO Act as weapon of 368, 383–384
  Scalia on 398
  Souter on 420–421
Abrams v. Johnson (1997) 286
Abrams v. U.S. (1919) **4,** 399
abstention **4–5,** 96
Accardi v. Shaughnessy (1954) 213
access tax
  Internet and 228–229
accommodationists 144–146, 377
actual innocence **5–6,** 399–400
  capital punishment and 204
Adair v. U.S. (1908) 108
Adams, John 75–76, 233, 268
  appointments of 271
Adams, John Quincy 489
Adamson Act (1916) 251
Adamson v. California (1947) **6,** 38, 327, 360
Adams v. New York (1904) 515
Adams v. Williams (1972) 408

Adarand Constructors, Inc. v. Pena (1995) **6–7,** 45, 80, 282, 421
Adkins v. Children's Hospital of D.C. (1923) **7–8,** 162, 261, 450, 518–519
administrative due process 276–277
administrative law and decision-making 7, **8–9,** 196
advertising
  commercial speech and 108–109
  Eleventh Amendment and 310–311
  lawyers and 256–257
  political speech and 348–350
  tobacco industry and 169–170
Aetna Life Insurance Co. v. Haworth (1937) 302
affirmative action **9–10,** *10,* 84, 236–237, 366–367, 374–375, 435, 506, 520
  Blackmun and 39
  Bork and 45–46
  Brennan and 54
  broadcast licenses and 282
  equal protection clause and 141
  Equal Rights Amendment and 142
  federal contracts and 6–7, 176, 421
  intermediate scrutiny and 223
  minority contracts and 80–81
  Native Americans and 218
  O'Connor and 320
  Powell and 353
  reverse discrimination and 186, 193
  suspect classification and 449
  Thomas and 462
  Title VII and 469
  voluntary compliance with 494
Afroyim v. Rusk (1967) **10–11**
age discrimination **11–12,** 248–249, 424

Age Discrimination in Employment Act (1967) 11–12, 140, 239, 252, 311
Agee, Philip 194
agency shop arrangement 1–2
Agostini v. Felton (1997) 260, 294, 421, 532
Agricultural Adjustment Act of 1933 111, 230, 309, 459, 481, 496, 522
Aguilar v. Felton (1985) 294
Air Carriers Access Act of 1986 125
airport solicitations
  religious freedoms and 224
Akins v. Virginia (2002) 334
Akron v. Akron Center for Reproductive Health (1983) 3, 352–353
Alabama v. Garrett (2001) 424
Alabama v. Shelton (2002) **12–13**
Alaska Native Claims Settlement Act (1971) 217
Alaska v. Native Village of Venetie (1998) 217
Albertson v. Subversive Activities Control Board 98
Albertsons, Inc. v. Kirkingburg (1999) 87, 126
Alden v. Maine (1999) 87, 178, 310–311
Alderman v. U.S. (1969) 268
Alien and Sedition Acts (1798) 399
Alien Registration Act (Smith Act) (1940) 98
Alien Tort Claims Act 444
alienage 13, 15–16, 213–214, 220, 395
  education and 344
  habeas corpus rights and 531–532
  plenary power and 341–342
Allegheny County v. ACLU (1989) **14,** 145, 378
Allegheny Pittsburgh Coal Co. v. County Commission (1989) 141
Allen v. Wright (1984) 427

Allgeyer v. Louisiana (1897) **14–15,** 260, 262, 419
Allied Structural Steel Co. v. Spannaus (1978) 479–480
Almeida-Sanchez v. U.S. (1973) 273
Amalgamated Food Employees Union v. Logan Valley Plaza (1968) 274
Ambah v. Norwich (1979) **15–16**
amendments, constitutional 325, 445–446
American Civil Liberties Union (ACLU)
  campaign finance reform and 279
  cross-burning, defense of 115
  establishment clause and 378
  Frankfurter and 172
  school prayer and 139
American Communications Assn. v. Douds (1950) 499
American Insurance Assn. et al. v. Garamendi, Insurance Commissioner, State of California (2003) 443
American Medical Association (AMA)
  abortion rights and 2–4
Americans with Disabilities Act (ADA) (1990) 86–87, 125, 140, 311, 463, 470–471
  PGA golf tour and 337–338
amicus curiae brief 56
Amistad 488, 488–490
amnesty. *See* pardon
anarchists 4
Anderson, John 16–17
Anderson v. Celebrezze (1983) **16–17,** 429, 465
announce clause 380
anonymous political speech **17,** 280–281
  registration permit for 514
Anti-Injunction Act (1932) 252

Antiterrorism and Effective Death
    Penalty Act of 1996 102, 358
antitrust laws **17–18**
    Department of Justice and 121
    RICO Act patterned on 368
Apex Hosiery Co. v. Leader (1940)
    252
Apodaca v. Oregon (1972) 242, 353
appeal **19**
appellate courts *156*
appointments clause
    independent counsel statute and
    297
apportionment clause 458
Apprendi v. New Jersey (2000)
    384–385
arbitration 59
Argersinger v. Hamilton (1972) 13
*Arizonans for Official English v.
    Arizona* (1997) 296
Arizona v. Evans (1995) 149
Arizona v. Fulminante (1991)
    19–20, 198–199
Arizona v. Hicks (1987) 339
Arizona v. Rumsey (1984) 130
*Arlington Heights v. Metropolitan
    Housing Development Corp.* (1977)
    20–21, 337
Armstrong, Scott 60
Armstrong v. U.S. (1871) 98, 328
Ashcroft v. ACLU (2002) 225–226
Ashcroft v. Free Speech Coalition
    (2002) 248, 314
Ashton v. Kentucky (1966) 33
Ashwander rules 21–22
*Ashwander v. Tennessee Valley
    Authority* (1936) **21–22**
assembly, right to 173
assisted suicide 125
*Assn. of American Physicians and
    Surgeons, Inc. v. Clinton* (1993)
    150
Associated Press v. U.S. (1945) 283
athletics
    Title IX and 467–468
Atkins v. Virginia (2002) **22–23**
attainder, bill of 36
attorney, right to 143–144
*Austin v. Michigan State Chamber of
    Commerce* (1990) **23–24**
automobile stops and searches
    24–25, 25
Avery v. Midland County (1968)
    189

B
Baehr v. Lewin (1993) 270
bail, right to **26–28**
Bail Reform Act of 1984 27
Bailey v. Drexel Furniture (1922)
    28
Baker v. Carr (1962) **28–29,** 53, 69,
    88, 94, 131, 197, 238, 259, 348,
    372, 381, 429, 510, 517
Baker v. Vermont (1999)
    180, 270

Balanced Budget and Emergency
    Deficit Control Act of 1985 46–47,
    429
Baldus Study 278
Baldwin v. Seelig (1935) 208, 484
ballot access 16–17
bankruptcy **29–30,** 162
Bankruptcy Code 29–30
Bankruptcy Courts 29–30
Bantam Books, Inc. v. Sullivan
    (1963) 357
Banzhaf v. FCC (1968, 1969) 469
Barenblatt v. U.S. (1959) **30**
Barker v. Wingo (1967) 425
Barnes v. Glen Theatre (1991)
    30–31, 317
Barron v. Baltimore (1833) **31–32,**
    215, 353–355, 455
Bartels v. Iowa (1923) 467
Bas v. Tingy (1800) 508
Bates v. State Bar of Arizona (1977)
    256
Batson challenge 32
Batson v. Kentucky (1986) **32,** 234,
    335–336
Beachfront Management Act (1988)
    264, 456
Beauharnais v. Illinois (1952)
    32–33
*Bedford Cut Stone Co. v.
    Journeymen Stone Cutters' Assn.,
    et al.* (1927) 251
Bell v. Wolfish (1979) 358
Belle Terre v. Boraas (1974) **33–34**
Bellotti v. Baird (1979) 69
Benton v. Maryland (1969)
    129–130, 328
Berman v. Parker (1954) **34–35,**
    138, 202
Bethel School District v. Fraser
    (1986) 203
Betts v. Brady (1942) **35–36,** 38,
    327–328
Bias-Motivated Crime Ordinance
    (1989) 115
Biddle v. Perovich (1927) 99, 328
bigamy 269, 376, 381–382, 389
bill of attainder clause **36–37,** 168
    land fraud and 168
bill of pain and penalties 36
Bill of Rights (1791) **37–38,** 60,
    81–82. *See also* incorporation
    Brennan and 53–54
Bipartisan Campaign Finance
    Reform Act (2002) 279
birth control 2, 135–136, 191–192,
    474, 526
birth defects
    abortion rights and 387–388
*Bivens v. Six Unknown Named
    Agents of Federal Bureau of
    Narcotics* (1971) 315
Black, Hugo 38, **38–39**
    Communist infiltration and 30
    dissents of 120, 166, 200, 208,
    466–467, 475, 535
    due process dissent of 6

incorporation and 360
    majority opinions of 139, 144,
    146, 162, *182*, 198, 246, 249,
    353, 366, 529, 530, 534
    right to counsel and 35–36
    Vinson and 498
*Black & White Taxicab Co. v. Brown
    & Yellow Taxicab Co.* (1928) 143
black codes 408
Blackburn v. Alabama (1960) 19
Blackmun, Harry 39, **39–40**
    alien rights and 15–16
    concurrences of 487
    dissents of 113, 164, 185, 204,
    331, 391–392, 526, 532
    majority opinions of 61, 100, 170,
    178, 225, 234, 378, 388, 467,
    479, 506
    religious displays and 14
    sexual privacy and 46
Blackstone, William M. 336
Black v. Commonwealth of Virginia
    (2001) 115
Blasi, Vincent 60
*BMW of North America, Inc. v.
    Gore* (1996) 363–364
*Board of County Commissioners,
    Wabaunsee County, Kansas v.
    Umbehr* (1996) **40–41**
*Board of Directors of Rotary Intl. v.
    Rotary Club of Duarte* (1987) 353
*Board of Education of Independent
    School District No. 992 of
    Pottawatomie County v. Earls*
    (2002) 440
*Board of Education of the Westside
    Community Schools v. Mergens*
    (1990) 16, 145, 263, 355
Board of Education v. Pico (1982)
    41
*Board of Regents of State Colleges et
    al. v. Roth* (1972) **42**
*Board of Regents of University of
    Wisconsin v. Southworth* (2000)
    1–2, **42–43,** 437
*Board of Trade of the City of
    Chicago v. Olsen* (1923) 452
*Board of Trustees of the University
    of Alabama v. Garrett* (2001) 87
Bob Jones University v. U.S. (1983)
    43–44
Boerne v. Flores (1997) **44,** 248, 311
Bolger v. Young Drugs Prods. Corp.
    (1983) 105–106
Bolling v. Sharpe (1954) **44–45,** 56
bona fide occupational qualification
    defense (BFOQ) 225, 469
books, banning of 41
Booth v. Maryland (1987) 330–331
Bork, Robert H. **45–46,** 447–448
Bowen v. Kendrick (1988) 459
Bowen v. Roy (1986) 516–517
Bowers v. Hardwick (1986) 39–40,
    46, 179, 255, 353, 359, 418
Bowsher v. Synar (1986) **46–47,** 60,
    429
Boyd v. U.S. (1886) 411

Boy Scouts of America v. Dale
    (2000) 179, 247–248, 338
Bradfield v. Roberts (1899) 376
Bradley, Joseph **47–48**
    dissents of 95, 419
    Waite, mentor to 504
Bradwell v. Illinois (1873) **48–49,**
    142, 525
Brady Handgun Violence Protection
    Act (1993) 239
Bragdon v. Abbott (1998) 126
Brandeis, Louis Dembitz 49, **49–50**
    dissents of 50, 312, 358–359
    majority opinions of 143, 452
    privacy opinion argued by 358
Brandeis Award 50
Brandeis brief **50–51,** 298
Brandenburg test 114–115
Brandenburg v. Ohio (1969)
    114–115, 529
Branti v. Finkel (1980) 321
Branzburg v. Hayes (1972) **51–52,**
    283
*Bray v. Alexandria Women's Health
    Clinic* (1993) **52,** 267
Breedlove v. Suttles (1937) 199
Breed v. Jones (1975) 245
Breithaupt v. Abram (1957) 400
Brennan, William, Jr. 52, **52–53**
    book banning in schools and 41
    concurrences of 505
    dissents of 105, 114, 116, 122,
    185, 190, *192*, 194, 201, 203,
    278, 284–285, 285, 312, 379,
    410, 479, 487
    education for illegal aliens and 15
    legislative districts and 28–29
    majority opinions of 54, 68, 107,
    136, 159, 165, 189, 236, 246,
    282, 288, 313, 344, 348, 351,
    394, 415, 421–422, 452, 461,
    486, 494
    zoning restrictions and 34
*The Brethren: Inside the Supreme
    Court* (Woodward, Armstrong) 60
Brewer, David J.
    majority opinions of
        hours in workday and 51
Breyer, Stephen Gerald **54–55,** 55,
    448
    dissents of 148, 500
    majority opinions of 382–383,
    531
Bridges v. Wixon (1945) 342
brief **55–56**
Briggs v. Elliott (1954) 56
bright-line rule 523
Broadrick v. Oklahoma (1973) 325,
    500, 520
Brockett v. Spokane Arcades, Inc.
    (1985) 96
Brown, Henry Billings
    majority opinions of 343
Brown Shoe Co. v. U.S. (1962) 510
*Brown v. Board of Education of
    Topeka* (1954) 10, 44, **56–57,** 62,
    82, 88, 103–104, 107, 119, 141,

Brown v. Board of Education of Topeka (1954) *(continued)* 189, 200, 232, 274, 315, 344, 366–367, 439, 446, 449, 499, 510

Brown v. Board of Education of Topeka II (1955) 56–57, 450–451

Brown v. Legal Foundation of Washington (2003) 456

Brown v. Maryland (1827) 272–273

Brown v. Texas (1979) 432

Brown v. Thomson (1983) 323

Brown v. Walker (1896) 411

Bruner v. U.S. (1952) 102

Bryant v. Zimmerman (1928) 303

Buchanan v. Warley (1917) **57**

Buckley Amendment (1974) 439

Buckley v. Valeo (1976) 158–159, 159, 278, 280, 349

Buck v. Bell (1927) **57–58,** 105–106, 206, 418

Bullington v. Missouri (1981) 130

Bunting v. Oregon (1917) 173

Burdick v. Takushi (1992) 465–466

Burford abstention 4–5

Burford v. Sun Oil Co. (1943) 5

Burger, Warren Earl **58–61,** 59, 74
    book banning in schools and 41
    dissents of 65, 93, 114, 494
    majority opinions of 176, 194, 220, 260, 265, 283, 287–288, 329–330, 354, 377, 378, 410, 450, 505–506, 524
    obscenity and 352
    race at religious schools and 43

The Burger Court: The Counter-Revolution That Wasn't (Blasi) 60

Burr, Aaron 149

Burson v. Freeman (1992) **61**

Burton, Harold **61–62**

Bush, George H. W.
    abortion rights and 2
    appointments of 420, 448
    flag burning and 165

Bush, George W.
    election of 62–63

Bush v. Gore (2000) **62–63,** 69–70, 248

Bush v. Vera (1996) 286–287, 373, 416

Business—A Profession (Brandeis) 50

business necessity defense 225

busing 287–288, 450–451

Butchers' Benevolent Ass. v. Crescent City Livestock Landing and Slaughterhouse Co. (1873). *See Slaughter-House Cases*

C

Caban v. Mohammed (1979) 329

Calder v. Bull (1798) **64–65,** 72, 152, 269

California Democratic Party v. Jones (2000) 338, 346

California Dental Association v. Federal Trade Commission (1999) 256

California Federal Savings and Loan v. Guerra (1987) 356

California v. Cabazon Band of Mission Indians (1987) 217–218

California v. Green (1970) 113

California v. Greenwood (1988) 520

California v. LaRue (1972) 317

Callins v. Collins (1994) 39

campaign finance laws 158–159, 278–279, 348–349
    corporations and 23–24
    nonprofits and 159
    political parties and 347, 348–350

campaigning near polls 61

Canada Packers, Ltd. v. Atchison, Topeka and Santa Fe Railroad (1966) 355

Cannon v. Green (1970) 43

Cannon v. University of Chicago (1979) 467

Cantwell v. Connecticut (1940) 33, **64,** 138, 235, 377

capital punishment **64–65,** 93, 177
    actual innocence and 5–6, 204
    Blackmun and 39
    commutation and 99
    double jeopardy and 130
    juveniles and 243–244
    mental retardation and 22–23, 333–334
    prisoners' rights and 357–358
    racial bias and 277–278
    rape and 369–370
    right to counsel and 182
    sentencing and 190, 384–385
    Stewart and 430
    victim-impact evidence and 330–331
    writ of certiorari and 526

Capitol Square Review and Advisory Board v. Pinette (1995) 253

Cardozo, Benjamin Nathan **66–68,** 67
    majority opinions of 327

Carey v. Population Service International (1977) **68–69,** 105

Carlin, George 154–155

carpal tunnel syndrome
    disabilities and 470–471

Carrington v. Rash (1965) 199

Carter, Jimmy 185

Carter v. Carter Coal Co. (1936) 304

cases and controversies clause **69,** 242–243, 265, 326, 347, 427, 511
    Native American rights and 301–302
    standing and 174–175

casinos
    Indian rights and 217–218

censorship
    Internet and 225
    music and 300–301
    school press and 202–203

Central Hudson v. New York Public Service Commission (1980) 76, 96, 109

centralized federalism 161

certification **69–70**

certiorari, writ of 19

Chabad v. ACLU Greater Pittsburgh Chapter (1989) 14

Chae Chan Ping v. U.S. (1889) 341

Chandler v. Miller (1997) 134

Chaplinsky v. New Hampshire (1942) 32–33, **70–71,** 162–163, 460

Chapman v. California (1967) 198

Chapman v. Scott (1925) 99

Chapter 11 bankruptcy 29–30

Chapter 13 bankruptcy 29–30

Charles River Bridge v. Warren Bridge Co. (1837) 433, 457

Chase, Salmon P. **71**
    impeachment of 476
    majority opinions of 64, 151, 269, 292

Chase, Samuel **71–72**

checks and balances 239, 259, 269, 413

Cherokee majority opinions (1823, 1831, 1832) **72–73**

Cherokee Nation v. Georgia (1832) 72–73, 216–217, 433

Cherokee Nation v. Hitchcock (1902) 217

Chevron, Inc. USA v. Natural Resources Defense Council, Inc. (1984) 9, **73**

Chicago, Burlington & Quincy Railroad Co. v. Chicago (1897) 175, 184, 215, 455

chief justice of the United States **73–74**

child abuse
    social services culpability in 122

Child Internet Protection Act (1999) 480

Child Labor Act of 1915 194–195

child labor laws 28, 194–195, 251–252, 252, 496

Child Labor Tax Act (1919) 28

child pornography 314, 352

Child Pornography Prevention Act of 1996 314

Children's Internet Protection Act (2000) 226, 227

Children's Online Privacy Protection Act (COPPA) (1998) 225

Chimel v. California (1969) **74–75**

Chinese Exclusion Case (1889) 341

Chisholm v. Georgia (1793) **75–76,** 248, 324, 424, 446

church and state, separation of 38

Church Arson Prevention Act of 1996 182

CIA 194

CIA finding 459

cigarette advertising **76–77**

cigarette warning labels 77–78

Cipollone v. Liggett Group, Inc. (1984, 1990) 77–78, 469–470

Circuit Courts 156

circuit riding 157

citizenship 10–11, 13, 15–16, **78–79,** 246, 468, 476
    education of illegal aliens and 344
    equal protection clause and 140–141
    Holmes and 206
    plenary powers and 341–342
    women's rights and 48–49

City of Boerne v. Flores (1997) 138

City of Chicago v. Morales (1999) **79–80**

City of Cleburne v. Cleburne Living Center (1985) **89**

City of Richmond v. J. A. Croson Co. (1989) **80–81,** 141, 176, 274, 320, 376, 506

civil liberties 18, 62, **81–82,** 220, 240
    communism and 97–98
    drug searches and 168–169
    Frankfurter and 171–172
    gay and lesbian rights and 388
    Miranda warning and 122–123, 290
    Murphy and 299, 300
    prisoners' rights and 357–358
    states' rights and 31–32, 184
    substantive due process and 441
    Warren Court and 510

civil rights **82–84,** 238, 246, 449
    abortion protests and 52
    application abroad 135
    Bork and 45–46
    Brennan and 53–54
    Brown v. Board of Education and 56–57
    cross burnings and 114–115
    defamation of character and 418
    disabilities and **86–87,** 125–127
    District of Columbia and 44–45
    education and 192–193
    EEOC and 140
    Frankfurter and 172
    freedom of the press and 313
    Fuller and 175
    gay rights and 179–180
    interpretation of 103
    Japanese internment and 249–250
    limitations on 310–311
    Marshall (Thurgood) and 273–275
    mentally retarded and 89
    NAACP membership disclosure and 303
    Native Americans and 216–218
    pardons and 328
    preferred freedoms and 99
    public accommodations and 203
    Rehnquist and 376
    voting and 501

Civil Rights Act of 1866 82, 408, 417, 430

Civil Rights Act of 1871 315, 530

Civil Rights Act of 1875 48, 57, 84, 203, 235–236, 504

Civil Rights Act of 1964 45, 57, *83*,
84–85, 84, 85, 252, 390
   interstate commerce clause and
      18, 230
   sexual discrimination and
      281–282
   sexual harassment and 200, 414
   Title II of
      public accommodations and 203
   Title VI of
      affirmative action and 374
      college admissions and 193
      federal contracts and 176
      reverse discrimination and 186
   Title VII of 11–12, 135, 236–237,
      366–367, **468–469**, 494
      affirmative action, voluntary, and
         494
      EEOC and 139–140
      employment and 190–191
      fetal protection rights and
         224–225
      pregnancy and 181
      pregnancy in the workplace and
         356
      racial discrimination and
         506–507
      rights of minors and 289
      voting rights and 501
Civil Rights Act of 1983 185
Civil Rights Act of 1991 140, 469,
   507
Civil Rights Acts (1866, 1870, 1871,
   1875) **85–86**
Civil Rights Cases (1883) 48, 203,
   446, 504
Civil Rights Division 121
Civil Rights Restoration Act of 1988
   192, 467
Civil War Amendments 82
Clark, Thomas 4, **87–88**
   majority opinions of 88, 268
class action suits **88–89**, 186, 435,
   459, 511, 517
   punitive damages and 363
   tobacco industry and 469–470
Clayton Act (1914) 17–18, 251
Clean Air Act (1963) 73
clear and present danger doctrine 4,
   460
   cross burning and 114–115
   Holmes and 206
   political speech and 399
Cleburne v. Cleburne Living Center
   371
clemency. *See* pardon
Cleveland, Grover
   appointments of 175, 520
   railroad strike and 221
Clinton, Bill
   appointments of 54, 182, 448
   as defendant 90–91
   Rust v. Sullivan rescinded by 392
Clinton v. City of New York (1998)
   89–90
Clinton v. Jones (1997) 54, **90–91**
Coasting Act 128

Coercing Virtue (Bork) 45
coercion test 14, 19–20
   harmless error doctrine and 199
Cohen v. Brown University (1999)
   468
Cohens v. Virginia (1821) **91–92**, 276
Cohen v. California (1971) 70–71,
   92–93, 163, 197, 460
Coit v. Green (1971) 43
Coker v. Georgia (1977) **93**, 370
Coleman v. Miller (1939) 445
*Coles v. Cleveland Board of
   Education* (1999) 402
Colgrove v. Green (1946) **94**, 348
collateral
   bail and 26
Collector v. Day (1870) **94–95**
college charter
   state jurisdiction over 118–119
*College Savings Bank v. Florida
   Prepaid Postsecondary Education
   Expense Board* (1999) 310
colonial courts 157
Colonnade Catering Corp. v. U.S.
   (1970) 273
Colorado I (1997). *See Colorado
   Republican Federal Campaign
   Committee et al. v. FEC* (1997)
Colorado II (2001). *See FEC v.
   Colorado Republican Federal
   Campaign Committee* (2001)
*Colorado Republican Federal
   Campaign Committee et al. v. FEC*
   (1997) **95**, 158
*Columbia Broadcasting System, Inc.
   v. Democratic National Committee*
   (1973) 283
comity **96**
*Commentaries on the Constitution of
   the U.S.* (Story) 433
commerce. *See* interstate commerce
commercial speech 70, **96–97**,
   364–365. *See also* advertising; corporate speech
   cigarette advertising and 76–77
   contraceptives and 105–106
The Common Law (Holmes) 206
Commonwealth v. Allison (1917) 136
Commonwealth v. Hunt (1842) 251
Communications Act (1934) 154
Communications Decency Act
   (1996) 225, 352
communism 30, 120
   bills of attainder and 36
   free speech and 62
   self-incrimination and 131, 411
Communist Control Act (1954) 98
Communist Party
   convictions of overturned 528
   rights of **97–98**
   Scottsboro boys, benefactors of
      405–406
*Communist Party of the U.S. v.
   Subversive Activities Control Board*
   (1961) 36
community standards 60
   pornography and 351

commutation **98–99**
compartmentalization of funding
   Title IX and 192
compelling state interest 49, **99**
   Ku Klux Klan ruling and 303
compensatory damages 362–363
Complete Auto Transit v. Brady
   (1977) **100**
Comstock Law (1873)
   contraceptives and 191–192
concurrent opinions
   as judicial leverage 323
condemnation. *See* eminent domain
confessions, coerced 19–20
confrontation clause. *See* Sixth
   Amendment
Congress *101*
Congress and the Supreme Court
   100–102, *101*
congressional districts
   population and 94
congressional term limits 478–479
*Connecticut Dept. of Public Safety et
   al. v. Doe* (2003) 226
consensual searches 168–169
conspiracy
   communism and 98, 120
constitutional interpretation
   102–104
constitutionalism 442
constitutionality
   discretion in considering 21–22
constructionists 102–104
constructive speech 173
Continental TV v. GTE Sylvania
   (1977) **104–105**
contraceptives 68–69, **105–106**,
   135–136, 191–192, 317, 344–345,
   418, 474
   fundamental rights and 176–177
contract clause 513
   history of 479–480
   price-fixing and 306–307
   property foreclosure and 207–208
   property rights and 433
   women's labor rights and 298
contract law. *See* tort law
constructivism 238
Cook v. Gralike (2001) 445
Cooley v. Board of Wardens (1851)
   106–107, 128, 409
Coolidge, Calvin
   appointments of 430
   tariff on barium dioxide and
      195–196
Coolidge v. New Hampshire (1971)
   339
cooperative federalism 161
Coopers & Lybrand v. Livesay
   (1978) 412
Cooper v. Aaron (1958) 104,
   107–108
Cooper v. Pate (1964) 357
coordinated expenditures 158–159
   political campaigns and 95
   political parties and 347
Coppage v. Kansas (1915) **108**

copyright
   Internet and 226
Copyright Extensions Act (1998)
   226
corporate speech **108–109**
corporations
   rights as individuals 395–396
corruption of blood 36
Counselman v. Hitchcock (1892)
   411
*County Commissioners, Wabaunsee
   County, Kansas v. Umbehr* (1996)
   321
Court of Appeals, U.S. **109–111**
court-packing plan 38, 101–102,
   111, **111–112**, 208, 230, 232, 261,
   304–305, 307, 309–310, 371,
   435–436, 450, 476, 496, 519
   Hughes and 209–210
court system *436*
covenants
   racial discrimination and 417
Cox, Archibald 45
Coyle v. Smith (1911) **112**
Coy v. Iowa (1988) **112–113**
Craig v. Boren (1976) **113–114**,
   141, 181, 223, 291, 390, 413–414,
   434, 492
creative federalism 161
credit. *See* bankruptcy
criminal defendants' rights
   Warren Court and 510
criminal procedure
   Bill of Rights and 37
Criminal Syndicalism Act
   (California) 529
criminal syndicalism laws
   communism and 97–98
*Crosby v. Natl. Foreign Trade
   Council* (2000) 444
cross burning **114–115**
cross-examination
   confrontation and 112–113
cruel and unusual punishment
   execution of the mentally retarded
      and 22–23
Cruzan v. Missouri Dept. of Health
   (1990) **115–116**, 124, 495
Cruz v. Beto (1972) 357
culpability
   ex post facto laws and 152
Cummings v. Missouri (1866) 36
curator, office of the **116–117**
current of commerce theory 451
custodial interrogation
   122–123

D

Dalia v. U.S. (1979) 523
Dames & Moore v. Regan (1981)
   443
Darrow, Clarence
   railroad strike and 221
Dartmouth College v. Woodward
   (1819) **118–119**, 272, 479,
   513

Daubert v. Merrell-Dow Pharmaceuticals (1993) **119**, 261, 404
Davis-Bacon Act (1931) 252
Davis v. Alaska (1974) 245
Davis v. Monroe County Board of Education (1999) 468
Davis v. Prince Edward County (1954) 56
Day, William
  majority opinions of 57, 194–195, 301
death penalty. *See also* capital punishment
  innocence as appeals basis 5–6
De Canas v. Bica (1976) 213
Debs v. U.S. (1919) 4
debt. *See* bankruptcy
declaratory judgment **119–120**
defamation of character 313, **418**
  parody and 211–212
Defense of Marriage Act (1996) 270
DeJonge v. Oregon (1937) 97
Delaware v. Van Arsdall (1986) 198–199
Democracy in America (Tocqueville) 477, xii
Demore v. Kim (2003) 342
Dennis v. U.S. (1951) 62, 98, **120**, 499, 528
Department of Justice **120–122**
Dept. of Revenue of Montana v. Kurth Ranch 130
Desert Palace v. Costa 463
Deshaney v. Winnebago County Social Services Dept. (1989) **122**
Dickerson v. U.S. (2000) **122–123**
dicta **123–124**
die, right to **124–125**
Dies Committee 97–98
Diggs v. Shultz (1973) 259
Dillon v. Gloss (1921) 445
direct injury standard 459
disability rights **125–127**
  civil rights and 86–87
  EEOC and 140
  pregnancy and 181
  Title VII and 468–469
disestablishment clause. *See* establishment clause
disparate impact 513
dissenting opinions
  as judicial leverage 323
District Courts 156
diversity jurisdiction 142, 452
Dobbins v. The Commissioners of Erie (1842) 94
docket **127**
Doe v. Commonwealth's Attorney (1976) 46
Dolan v. City of Tigard (1994) 253–254, 533
domain names 227
Dombrowski v. Pfister (1965) 529
Domestic Security Enhancement Act 11

do not resuscitate orders (DNRs) 125
dormant commercial clause **127–129**
double jeopardy **129–130**, 327–328
  juveniles and 245
Douglas, William O. 33, **130–132**, *131*
  dissents of 51–52, 120, 166, 475, 505–506, 524, 530
  majority opinions of 144–145, 188–189, 199, 317, 322, 359, 408, 417, 460, 492, 534
  zoning restrictions and 34
Dowdell v. U.S. (1911) 521
Downes v. Bidwell (1901) 175, 521
draft 409–410, 410–411
  Stevens and 429
  women's rights and 390–391, 525
draft card burning 491–492
  as symbolic speech 452
Dred Scott v. Sanford (1857) 84, 96, **132–133**, 269, 408, 446, 449, 456–457
drinking age
  gender and 113–114
Drug Enforcement Administration (DEA) 182
drugs 315, 385–386
  compulsory medication and 412
  cruel and unusual punishment clause and 197–198
  exclusionary rule, exceptions, to 487
  music censorship and 300–301
  Native Americans and 218
  racial profiling and 521–522
  religious freedoms and 138–139, 377, 382, 398
  RICO Act and 367–368
  sentencing guidelines and 293–294
  students and 439, 440
  vagrancy laws to combat 500–501
  voluntary searches for 168–169
drug testing **133–134**
  students and 440
dual federalism 161, 195
due process clause. *See* Fifth Amendment; Fourteenth Amendment
Durham v. U.S. (1954) 171
DVD Copy Control Assn. v. Andrew Bunner (2003) 226, 365

E

Edelman v. Jordan (1974) 152, 424
Edenfield v. Fane (1993) 76
Edge Broadcasting v. U.S. 97
Edmonson v. Leesville Concrete Co. (1991) 335–336
education
  affirmative action in 374–375
  Brown v. Board of Education and 56–57
  busing and 287–288

Communist infiltration of 30
D.C. racial discrimination and 44–45
desegregation and 107
disabilities and 86
drug testing and 133
due process and 186
employment and 190–191
establishment clause and 144–145
federal funding of parochial schools and 294–295
fees as compelled speech in 42–43
free speech and 41
gender discrimination and 291
illegal aliens and 15–16, 213, 344
parental rights and 329
religious freedom and 139, 185–186
religious instruction and 534
religious school tax deductions and 297–298
separation of church and state and 459
state funding of religious schools and 259–260
student press and 438
student protest and 466–467
student searches and 311–312
Education Amendments (1972) 415
  Title IX of 467–468
  federal funding and 192–193
Education Consolidation Improvement Act (1981) 294
Education of All Handicapped Children Act (EAHCA). *See* IDEA
Edwards v. California (1941) 232
Edwards v. Carter (1978) 259
Edwards v. South Carolina (1963) 173
EEOC v. Arabian American Oil Co. (1991) **135**
Eighteenth Amendment 445
Eighth Amendment
  bail, right to, and 26–28
  Bill of Rights and 37–38
  cruel and unusual punishment clause of
    capital punishment and 65–66, 93, 177, 190, 278, 384
    capital punishment of rape and 369–370
    capital punishment of the mentally retarded and 22–23, 333–334
    drugs and 197–198
    minors' rights and 289
    prisoners' rights and 358
    prisoners' transfer and 322
    three strikes laws and 147–148
    victim-impact evidence and 330–331
  excessive bail protections of incorporation and 216
  prisons and 39
  sexual privacy and 46

Eisenhower, Dwight D.
  appointments of 53, 58–59, 197, 429, 509
Eisenstadt v. Baird (1972) 2, 68, 105, **135–136**, 284–285, 345, 359
Eldred v. Ashcroft (2003) 226
elections
  political spending and 95
elections, presidential 62–63
electoral law 16–17
Elementary and Secondary Education Act of 1965 459
Eleventh Amendment 308–309, 445, 446
  age discrimination and 248
  citizens of another state clause
  disabilities and 87
  federal jurisdiction and 91–92
  land fraud and 167–168
  new federalism and 310–311
  original jurisdiction and 324
  sovereign immunity and 75–76, 151–152, 424
  states' rights and 238–239
Ellsworth, Oliver **136–137**, *137*
Elrod v. Burns (1976) 40, 321
Emergency Price Control Act (1942) 102
eminent domain 34–35, **137–138**, 202
  takings clause and 455–456
  zoning and 533–534
Employee Polygraph Protection Act (2001) 262
Employee Retirement Income Security Act (1974) 252
Employment Division, Dept. of Human Resources of Oregon v. Smith (1990) **138–139**, 218, 377, 382, 398
Enabling Act of 1906 112
Endangered Species Act 265
endorsement test 14
Engel v. Vitale (1962) **139**, 145, 353–354, 396, 401, 429, 510
Engine Manufacturers' Association v. South Coast Air Quality (2003) 121
English Bill of Rights (1689) 26–28
Environmental Protection Agency v. Mink (1973) 259
Environmental Protection Agency 9, 73
Epperson v. Arkansas (1968) 171
Equal Access Act (1984) 355
Equal Employment Opportunity Commission (EEOC) 12, 84, 135, **139–140**
  pregnancy in the workplace and 356
  Thomas as chair of 463
  Title VII, created by 468
equal justice under law doctrine
  segregation and 107
Equal Pay Act (1963) 140

equal protection clause **140–141.**
See also Fifth Amendment;
Fourteenth Amendment
Equal Rights Amendment
141–142, 174, 445, 526
equal time rule. *See* Fairness
Doctrine
Erdman Act (1889) 251
Erie Railroad Co. v. Tompkins
(1938) 50, **142–143,** 452
Escanaba Co. v. Chicago (1882) 112
Escobedo v. Illinois (1964)
143–144, 290
Espionage Act of 1917 4, 50
establishment clause 14, 15–16,
144–146
Estelle v. Gamble (1976) 122
Ethics in Government Act of 1978
296
Euclid v. Ambler Realty Co. (1926)
34, 533
eugenics 417–418
euthanasia 495–496
Evarts Act (1891) 110, 157
Everson v. Board of Education
(1947) 144, **146–147,** 232,
353–355
evidentiary rulings
disability rights and 276–277
ex post facto laws and 152
evolving standards of decency test
22–23, 243
Ewing v. California (2003)
147–148, 198
Ex parte Crouse (1838) 244
Ex parte Curtis (1882) 475
Ex parte Garland (1866) 36, 328
Ex parte McCardle (1869) 101
Ex parte Merryman (1861) 458
Ex parte Milligan (1866) **151,** 458
Ex parte Wells (1865) 98, 328
Ex parte Young (1908) **151–152,**
424
ex post facto laws 64, **152–153,** 168
sex offender registries and 420
exacting scrutiny test 141
excise tax 214
exclusionary rule 74, **148–149,** 268,
400, 515–516
exceptions to 487–488
procedural due process and 360
student searches and 312
Warren and 510
Executive Order 9835 (1947) 98
executive privilege **149–150**
Nixon and 60
exemplary damages. *See* punitive
damages
expert testimony 404–405
standards governing 119
express advocacy 159,
278–279

F

Fair Employment Practices Agencies
140

Fairfax's Devisee v. Hunter's Lessee
(1813) 275
Fair Housing Act of 1968 21
Fair Housing Amendments of 1988
125
Fair Labor Standards Act 178, 195,
305, 484
fair market value 137
Fairness Doctrine **154,** 373–374
faith-based organizations
establishment clause and 145
Falwell, Jerry 211–212
Family and Medical Leave Act
(1993) 311, 368–369
Family Educational Rights and
Privacy Act (1974) 439
Faragher v. City of Boca Raton
(1998) 281, 415
Fare v. Michael C. (1979) 245
Farrington v. Tokushiga (1927) 338
Faubus, Orville 107
FCC 373–374
FCC v. Pacifica Foundation (1978)
154–155, 301, 374
*FDA v. Brown & Williamson
Tobacco Corp.* (1998) 169,
169–170
FEC v. Beaumont (2003) 160
*FEC v. Colorado Republican Federal
Campaign Committee* (2001) 95,
158–159
*FEC v. Massachusetts Citizens for
Life, Inc.* (1986) **159–160**
Federal Age Discrimination Act
(1975) 248
Federal Bureau of Investigation 121
communism and 98
surveillance and 246–247
Federal Communications Act (1934)
523
Federal Communications
Commission 154, 282
music censorship and 300–301
federal court system **155–158,** *156,*
240
original jurisdiction and 324–325
origins of 452
states' rights v. 4–5
Federal Election Campaign Act
(1974) 95, 158, 159, 278, 280
*Federal Election Commission v.
Massachusetts Citizens for Life,
Inc.* (1986) 24
federalism **160–162,** 178, 238, 485
Breyer and 54
Chase (Samuel) and 72
disabilities and 87
emulated abroad 477–478
immunity from state prosecution
222–223
Marshall and 272–273
necessary and proper clause and
308–309
rational basis test and 371
revival as new federalism
310–311
segregation laws and 107

The Federalist Papers (Madison,
Hamilton, Jay) 75, 233, 239, 269,
281, 371, xii
Federal Rules of Civil Procedure
143, 326, 441
Federal Rules of Evidence 404
expert testimony and 119
Federal Tort Claims Act of 1946 423
Federal Trade Commission Act
(1914) 17–18, 210
federal *vs.* state law
Bill of Rights and 37
Felker v. Turpin (1996) 102
FERC v. Mississippi (1982) 422
Ferguson v. Charleston (2001) 134
Ferguson v. Skrupa (1963) **162**
fetal protection rights 357
women's labor and 224–225
Fiallo v. Bell (1977) 342
Field, Stephen
dissents of 419
Field v. Clark (1892) 90
Fifteenth Amendment 215,
366–367, 445, 446, 449
city elections and 295–296
one person, one vote and 188
racial gerrymandering and
464–465
slavery ended by 132–133
voting rights clause of 501–502
school admissions and 56–57
voting rights established by 85
Fifth Amendment
double jeopardy clause of
129–130
state exceptions to 327–328
due process clause of 366–367
abortion rights and 201, 387
D.C. school admissions and 56
disability rights and 276–277
Dred Scott decision and 457
federal contracts and 176
interstate commerce and 482
Japanese internment and
249–250
military benefits and 174
minority broadcast licenses and
282
natural law and 72
slavery, interstate recognition of,
and 132
substantive due process and 440
welfare residency requirements
and 415–416
eminent domain and 34–35
equal protection clause of 492
age discrimination and 11–12
aliens and 13
automobile searches and 24–25
Bill of Rights and 37
coerced confessions and 19–20
D.C. schools and 44–45
draft and 410
police qualifying exam and 513
fair hearing clause and
illegal aliens and 213–214
federal contracts and 6–7

federal *vs.* state enforcement of
31–32
grand jury clause of
incorporation and 216
grand jury requirement of 211
jury of one's peers clause
Scottsboro cases and 405
just compensation clause of
eminent domain and 137–138
temporary public use and
163–164
treaties' supersession of 481
minimum wage and 7–8
privacy and 359
procedural due process and 360
passport revocation and 194
public use clause
eminent domain and 137–138,
202
incorporation and 215
self-incrimination clause of 131,
411–412
communism and 98
compulsory DWI blood test and
400–401
draft requirements and 410
harmless error doctrine and 198
Miranda ruling and 143–144,
290, 520
rights of minors and 289
state court exemption from 6
takings clause of 455–456
compensation and 332–333
land use and 253, 264–265
states and 184
zoning and 533
fighting words doctrine 70–71, 92,
162–163, 460
Filled Milk Act of 1923 482
firearms 407–408
First Amendment
assembly clause of
school organizations and
252–253
Bill of Rights and 37
Black and 39
communism and 30
contractors and 40–41
corporate campaign finance laws
and 23–24
employment and 42
establishment clause of 376–378,
378–379, 396–397, 505
federal funding of parochial
schools and 294–295
freedom of assembly and 173
freedom of speech and 389–390
nativity scene and 265–266
off-premises religious classes
and 535
private school funding and 167
religious school entitlements and
532
religious taxation and
505–506
Scalia and 398
scholarships and 263

First Amendment (continued)
  school busing and 146–147
  school deductions and 297–298
  school organizations and
    252–253
  school prayer and 139, 257,
    353–355, 401–402, 504–505
  school vouchers and 403
  separation of church and state
    and 81–82
  student press and 438
  students and 439
  taxpayer suits and 459
  Thomas and 463
  freedom of association clause of
  political endorsements and 321
  students and 438
  freedom of the press clause
    grand jury testimony and 51–52
    prior restraint and 357
    right to trial and 362
    states and 184
    Stewart and 430
  freedom of the press clause of
    fairness doctrine and 373–374
    libel and 276
    libel law and 313
    political criticism of candidates
      and 283–284
    prior restraint and 307
    schools and 202–203
    slander and libel and 418
  free exercise clause of 376–378
    bigamy and 381–382
    commutation conditions and
      98–99
    compulsory school attendance
      and 524
    corporate speech and 108–109
    drugs and 138–139, 398
    establishment clause and
      145–146
    fighting words doctrine and
      162–163
    flag burning and 164–165
    flag salute and 165–166
    footnote four and 483
    hate speech and 115
    Jehovah's Witnesses and 235
    parental rights and 329
    political speech and 95
    private school funding and 167
    radio and 154–155
    religious solicitation and 64
    scholarships and 263
    school organizations and 185,
      252–253
    students and 438
  free speech clause of
    abortion protests and 52, 267
    adult theaters and 379
    amplification and 507–508
    anonymity and 280–281
    antiabortion activists and 306
    campaign finance reform and
      279
    campaigning near polls and 61

  child pornography and 314
  cigarette advertising and 76–77
  commercial speech and 96–97
  communism and 98, 528
  draft-card burning and 491–492
  Fairness Doctrine and 154,
    373–374
  federal employees and 475
  fighting words doctrine and 460
  flag burning and 461, 486
  honoraria and 490–491
  Internet and 225–226
  Internet filters in libraries and
    480
  Jehovah's Witnesses and 235
  judicial elections and 380
  lawyer advertising and 256
  legal counseling and 257–258
  libel law and 53–54
  limitations on 70
  music censorship and 300–301
  nude dancing and 317–318
  obscenity and 92–93, 197
  overbreadth and 325
  pamphleteering and 529
  parody and 211
  political endorsements and 321
  political speech and 348–349
  pornography and 329–330,
    351–352
  prior restraint and 307
  public forum and 360–362
  pure speech and 364–365
  registration permit and 514
  religious school organizations
    and 185
  religious solicitation and 224
  school prayer and 402
  school press censorship and
    202–203
  sedition and 206, 399
  slander and libel and 418
  states and 184
  student activity fees and 437
  student newspapers and 438
  student protest and 466–467
  substantive due process and 441
  symbolic speech and 452
  union advocacy and 1–2
  white supremacy and 170
illegal aliens and 213
juvenile delinquents and 245
nudity and 30–31
overbreadth doctrine and 501
political parties' rights and
  346–347
presidential candidates and 16–17
privacy and 359
racial discrimination and 32–33
religious displays and 14
religious freedoms clause of
  saluting the flag and 104
rights of minors and 289
right to assembly clause 173
  white supremacy and 170
schools and 41
sexual privacy and 46

student activity fees and 1–2
student fees and 42–43
wartime restrictions of 4
zoning restrictions and 34
First Bank of the U.S. 279–280, 280
First English Lutheran Church v.
  County of Los Angeles (1987)
  163–164
First Military Reconstruction Act of
  1867 82
first Monday in October 164, 324
First Monday in October (film) 164
First National Bank of Boston v.
  Bellotti (1978) 24
Fladell v. Palm Beach County
  Canvassing Board (2000) 62
flag burning 54, 164–165, 364,
  461–462, 486
  Kennedy (Anthony) and 247
  as symbolic speech 452
Flag Protection Act of 1989 165,
  461–462, 486
flag salute 165–166, 235
  Frankfurter and 173
  Jackson (Robert H.) and 232
  Murphy and 300
  Stone and 430–431
Flast v. Cohen (1968) 166–167,
  175, 459
Fleming v. Page (1850) 219
Fletcher v. Peck (1810) 36,
  167–168, 272, 433
Flint v. Stone Tracy Co. (1911) 214
Flood v. Kuhn (1972) 40
Florida Democratic Party v. Palm
  Beach County Canvassing Board
  (2000) 62
Florida Prepaid Postsecondary
  Education Expense Board v.
  College Savings Bank (1999) 310
Florida v. Bostick (1991) 168–169
Florida v. Royer (1983) 432
Flynt, Larry 211–212
Foley Bros. 135
Foley v. Connelie (1978) 15
Fong Yue Ting v. U.S. (1893) 341–342
Food, Drug and Cosmetic Act
  (FDCA) 169, 470
Footnote Four 140, 184, 371, 434,
  482
  Stone and 431
Ford, Gerald 328
  appointments of 428
Ford v. Wainwright 333
foreign affairs powers
  executive supremacy of 483–484
foreign policy 443–444
  treaties and 471–473
Foreign Sovereign Immunity Act
  (1976) 423
forma pauperis 55
Forsyth County v. Nationalist
  Movement (1992) 170
Fortas, Abe 171, 447–448
  capital punishment and 182
  majority opinions of 221, 364,
    438–439, 466

forum shopping 143
  tobacco lawsuits and 77–78
Four Horsemen 450
Fourteenth Amendment 141, 215,
  446, 449, 510
  affirmative action and 9–10
  age discrimination and 11–12
  aliens and 13
  automobile searches and 24–25
  Black, Hugo, and 39
  citizenship and 10–11
  coerced confessions and 19–20
  corporate campaign finance laws
    and 23–24
  D.C. schools and 44–45
  due process clause of 400–401
    abortion rights and 204–205,
      388, 474
    adult theaters and 379
    assisted suicide and 495
    business regulation of 312–313
    capital punishment and 65–66
    Civil Rights Act of 1875 and 203
    civil rights and 84
    compulsory physical evidence
      and 386
    compulsory school attendance
      and 338
    contraceptives and 344–345
    debt reduction and 162
    denial of paternal visitation and
      284–285
    disabilities and 86–87
    double jeopardy and 327–328
    exclusionary rule and 148
    ex post facto laws and 152
    First Amendment and 173, 184
    First through Eighth
      Amendments and 327–328
    freedom of the press and
      283–284
    fundamental rights and
      176–177
    gang congregation and 79–80
    gay rights and 179–180, 255
    gender-based violence and 490
    grand jury indictment and 211
    illegal aliens and 213
    incorporation and 214–216
    incorporation of Second
      Amendment and 407–408
    interstate commerce and 230
    Jehovah's Witnesses and 235
    juvenile offenders and 220–221
    juveniles and 244, 245
    labor conditions and 260–261
    land use and 253
    maximum hour law and 251
    minimum wage and 496
    monopolies and 48
    NAACP membership disclosure
      and 303
    natural law and 72
    pamphleteering and 529
    parental rights and 329
    police powers and
      282–283

police powers v. property rights and 298–299
press prior restraint and 307
price-fixing and 307, 504
prisoners' transfer and 321–322
privacy and 68
public use 175
religion and 377
right to a speedy trial and 424–425
search and seizure and 268
separate but equal doctrine and 343
sexual discrimination and 413–414
sovereign immunity and 151–152
statistical evidence and 277–278
student activity fees and 437
students and 186, 467
substantive due process and 440
substantive rights under 122
Taney and 458
taxation and 146–147
unions and 108
welfare termination and 516–517
zoning and 57, 497–498, 533
due process in state courts 6
Eleventh Amendment immunity and 311
employment and 42
equal protection clause of 140–141
abortion rights and 204–205, 387
affirmative action and 53–54
assisted suicide and 495
businesses and 48
city elections and 295–296
compulsory school attendance and 524
congressional districts and 94
contraceptives and 136
corporations protected by 396
debt reduction and 162
disabilities and 86–87
exclusionary rule and 516
federal contracts and 176
fundamental rights and 176–177
gay and lesbian rights and 388–389
gay rights and 179–180, 255–256
gender and 113–114
gender-based school admissions and 291
gender discrimination and 424
gender in jury selection and 234
gender violence and 500
immigrant education and 344
interracial marriage and 263–264, 269–270
interstate commerce and 230
involuntary sterilization and 417–418

judicial bias and 278
mentally retarded and 89
one person, one vote and 188
peremptory challenges 335
police qualifying exam and 513
poll tax and 199
poverty and 395
presidential elections and 62, 69–70
pregnancy and 181
public accommodations and 82
race as suspect classification and 449
racial covenants and 417
racial discrimination and 366–367, 504, 529
racial profiling and 521
racial redistricting and 416
reapportionment and 517
redistricting and 322, 372–373, 381
religious school organizations and 185
reverse discrimination and 186, 193, 374–375
rights of minors and 289
same-sex colleges and 493–494
school admissions and 56–57
school busing and 287–288
school organizations and 252–253
segregation ended by 107
sexual discrimination and 413–414
state enforcement and 288–289
statutory rape and 285–286
sterilization and 57–58, 105–106
students and 439
veteran hiring preference and 336
voting rights and 53, 246, 464–465
welfare residency requirements and 394, 415–416
women and 524–526
women's labor rights and 298
women's rights and 49, 183
zoning and 57
federal contracts and 6–7
freedom of association
NAACP membership disclosure and 303
history of 85
incorporation and 345–346
indigents and 35–36
jury selection and 32
labor and 206–207
legislative districts and 28–29
libel and 53–54
liberty of contract clause of 14–15, 262
new federalism and 310–311
origin of 31–32
privacy and 359
contraceptives and 105
obscenity and 91

privileges and immunities clause of
incorporation and 215
monopolies and 419
women's rights and 48–49
procedural due process and 360
public use clause of
eminent domain and 202
racial discrimination and 32–33
religious freedom and 44
resident aliens and 15–16
right to die and 125
self-incrimination and 198
separate but equal doctrine in 236
constitutional interpretation and 103
sexual privacy and 46
slavery ended by 132–133
takings clause and 163–164, 332
union advocacy and 1–2
voting rights and 246
zoning and 20–21, 33–34
Fourth Amendment
abortion rights and 387
automobile searches and 24–25
Bill of Rights and 37
probable cause requirement
drug testing and 133
right to privacy in 359
exclusionary rule and 268
search and seizure clause of
compulsory DWI blood test and 400–401
drug testing and 133
due process and 268
electronic surveillance and 246–247
exclusionary rule, exceptions to 487–488
exclusionary rule and 148–149, 515–516
gang congregation and 79–80
home welfare inspections and 526–527
judicial review and 286
pamphleteering and 224
plain view doctrine and 339
privacy and 411
racial profiling and 521–522
rights of minors and 289
search warrants and 406–407
stop and frisk and 432
students and 311–312, 439, 440
Terry stops and 460–461
voluntary drug search 168–169
warrants and 74–75
wiretapping and 358, 523
workplaces and 273
Frankfurter, Felix 171–173, 172, 197
dissents of 208, 460, 535
libel and 33
majority opinions of 94, 166, 345, 386, 399
as Powell's mentor 352
Vinson and 498
Franklin, Benjamin 233

Franklin v. Gwinnett County Public Schools (1992) 415, 467
Frank v. Mangum (1915) 206
Freedom of Access to Clinic Entrances Act (1993) 52, 306, 383
freedom of assembly and association 173
freedom of contract 7–8
Freedom of Information Act 150
mootness and 296
freedom of the press
racial prejudice and 32–33
Freeman v. Pitts (1992) 189
free speech
government employees and 40–41
racial prejudice and 32–33
students and 41
wartime restrictions of 4
friends of the court briefs 21–22
Frohwerk v. U.S. (1919) 4
Frontiero v. Richardson (1973) 174, 181, 183, 390
Frost v. Corporation Commission (1929) 312
Frothingham v. Mellon (1923) 166, 174–175, 459
Frye v. U.S. (1923) 119, 261, 404
Fuller, Melville Weston 175
dissents of 222
majority opinions of 350, 485
full faith and credit clause
divorce and 96
gay marriage and 270
Fullilove v. Klutznick (1980) 7, 80, 176
fundamental rights 89, 176–177, 317, 474
civil rights and 83
poll tax and 199
strict scrutiny and 434
Furman v. Georgia (1972) 65, 93, 177, 352, 369, 430
fusion 465

G
gag order 307–308
Gallegos v. Colorado (1962) 244
gambling
commercial speech and 97
Indian rights and 217–218
Gang Congregation Ordinance (Chicago) 79–80
Garcia v. San Antonio MTA (1985) 178–179, 305, 422
Garner v. City of L.A. Board of Public Works 98
Garrett v. University of Alabama at Birmingham (2001) 311
Garrison v. Louisiana (1964) 33
gatekeeper function of judges
expert testimony and 119
gay and lesbian rights 179–180, 180, 255–256, 388–389
Kennedy (Anthony) and 247–248

gay and lesbian rights (continued)
   substantive due process and
      440–441
   symbolic speech and 453
gay marriage amendment 180,
   255–256, 270
G.E. v. Joiner (1997) 119
Gebser v. Lago Vista ISD (1998)
   468
Geduldig v. Aiello (1974) **181**
gender-based violence 490
gender discrimination 311, 424, 492,
   499–500. See also sexual discrimination; women's rights
   draft and 414
   drinking age and 113–114
   equal protection clause and 141
   Equal Rights Amendment and
      141–142
   intermediate scrutiny and 223
   jury selection and 234
   Native American rights and 218
   peremptory challenges and 335
   same-sex colleges and 493–494
   statutory rape and 285–286
   Title IX and 467–468
   Title VII and 469
   university admissions and 290–291
   workplace and 298
General Allotment Act of 1887 301
General Electric Co. v. Gilbert
   (1976) 356
General Electric Co. v. Joiner (1997)
   404
Georgia v. McCollum (1992) 335
Gephardt v. Beldon (1954) 56
gerrymandering 373, 464–465
   Frankfurter and 172
   racial discrimination and 286–287
   racial redistricting and 416
Gertz v. Welch (1974) 284
Gibbons v. Ogden (1824) 106,
   127–128, 161, **181–182,** 229, 272,
   433, 484, 522, 4099
Gideon v. Wainwright (1963) 12,
   35–36, 38, 171, **182,** 328, 429
Ginsburg, Ruth Bader 13, **182–184,**
   183
   dissents of 380, 420, 500
   majority opinions of 141,
      384–385, 493
Gitlow v. New York (1925) **184,**
   215, 380, 399
Gloucester Ferry Co. v.
   Pennsylvania (1885) 205
Goesaert v. Cleary (1948) 142, 181,
   525
gold standard 309
Goldberg, Arthur
   concurring opinion of 317, 474
Goldberg v. Kelly (1970) 276–277,
   516
Goldwater v. Carter (1979)
   184–185, 259
Gomillion v. Lightfoot (1960) 172,
   295
Gompers v. Bucks Stove and Range
   Co. (1911) 251

Gooding v. Wilson 460
Good News Club v. Milford Central
   School District (2001) **185–186,**
   402, 463
Gore, Al 62–63
Gore v. Harris (2000) 62
Goss v. Lopez (1975) **186,** 353, 439
government agencies 8–9
Graham v. Richardson (1971) 342
Gramm-Rudman-Hollings Act of
   1985 60
Grand Inquests: The Historic
   Impeachments of Justice Samuel
   Chase and President Andrew
   Johnson (Rehnquist) 376
grand juries 211
   press and 51–52
grandparents
   parental rights and 329
Grant, Ulysses S.
   appointments of 47–48, 503
Gratz v. Bollinger (2003) 10,
   186–187
Gravel v. U.S. (1972) **187–188**
Grayned v. City of Rockford (1972)
   453
Gray v. Sanders (1963) 29, 88, 131,
   188–189, 322, 372
Greater New Orleans Broadcasting
   v. U.S. (1999) 97
Green factors 189
Greene v. McElroy (1957) 510
Green v. County School Board of
   New Kent County, Virginia (1968)
   189–190
Gregg v. Georgia (1976) 22, 65,
   190, 369, 384, 430
Gregory v. Ashcroft (1991) 434
Griffin v. California (1965) 131, 411
Grifiths (1973) 15
Griggs v. Duke Power (1971)
   190–191, 506
Griswold v. Connecticut (1965) 2,
   39, 45, 105, 131, 135–136, 162,
   191–192, 238, 284–285, 317, 345,
   359, 386–387, 418, 429, 474, 526
Grove City College v. Bell (1984)
   192–193, 467
Grovey v. Townsend (1935) 431
Grutter v. Bollinger (2003) 10, 176,
   186, **193,** 375, 463, 494
Guffney v. Cummings (1973) 189
Gun Free School Zones Act (1990)
   239, 310, 372, 421, 423

H

habeas corpus 101–102, 400, 529
   aliens and 531–532
   innocence impacting 5–6
   Lincoln suspension of 458
   prisoners' rights and 358
Haig v. Agee (1981) **194**
Haley v. Ohio (1948) 244
Hamadi v. Rumsfeld (2002) 483
Hamilton, Alexander 17, 67–68,
   103, 136, 239, 269, 281, 371, 442,
   xii

Hammer v. Dagenhart (1918) 28,
   194–195
Hampton intelligible principle 196
Hand, Learned 120, 528
Hansberry v. Lee (1940) 88
Hans v. Louisiana (1890) 424
Harding, Warren G.
   appointments of 449, 455
Harisiades v. Shaughnessy (1952)
   341
Harlan, John Marshall 196,
   196–197
   Communist infiltration and 30
   concurrences of 427, 505
   dissents of 200, 262, 268, 344,
      345, 360, 366, 389, 415–416, 518
   majority opinions of 92, 303, 528
Harmelin v. Michigan (1991)
   197–198
harmless error rule 19–20, **198–199**
Harper v. Virginia State Board of
   Elections (1966) 131, **199–200,**
   501
Harris v. Florida Elections
   Canvassing Commission (2000) 62
Harris v. Forklift Systems, Inc.
   (1993) **200–201,** 414, 469
Harris v. McRae (1980) **201,** 430,
   434
Harris v. U.S. (1947) 75
Hatch Act 475
Hawaii Housing Authority v. Midkiff
   (1984) **202**
Hawaii v. Mankichi (1903) 521
Hawke v. Smith (1920) 445
Hayes-Cooper Act (1929) 251
Hazelwood School District v.
   Kuhlmeier (1988) 16, **202–203,**
   438, 467
Heart of Atlanta Motel v. U.S. (1964)
   18, 84, 86, **203**
heckler's veto 460
heightened judicial scrutiny. See
   strict scrutiny
Helms v. Cody (1985) 294
Helvering v. Davis (1937) 68
Henderson v. U.S. (1950) 499
Hepburn Act (1906) 231
Hepburn v. Griswold (1870) 47–48,
   71
Herrera v. Collins (1992) 5, **204**
Hicklin test 351
Hill, Anita 462
Hill v. Colorado (2000) 248
Hines v. Davidowitz (1941) 356
Hirabayashi v. U.S. (1943) 300, 431
Hirota v. MacArthur (1948) 220
History of the U.S. Decision-Making
   Process on Vietnam Policy
   (Pentagon Papers) 187
HIV
   disability rights and 126
Hobbs Act (1951) 383
Hodel v. Virginia Surface Mining
   and Reclamation Assn. (1981) 305
Hodgeson et al. v. Minnesota et al.
   (1990) **204–205**
Hoffa v. Saxbe (1974) 98–99

Hoffman Plastic Compounds, Inc. v.
   National Labor Relations Board
   (2002) 213
Hoke v. U.S. (1913) **205**
Holden v. Hardy (1898) 8, 50, 260
Holland v. Illinois (1990) 336
Hollingsworth v. Virginia (1798)
   445
Holmes, Oliver Wendell, Jr. 37, 47,
   50, **205–207**
   dissents of 108, 143, 328
   free speech dissent of 4
   Hughes and 209
   majority opinions of 57–58, 293,
      399, 451
Home Building and Loan
   Association v. Blaisdell (1934)
   207–208, 220, 479
homosexuality 46. See gay and les-
   bian rights
honoraria 490–491
Hoover, Herbert
   appointments of 66, 209
Hoover, J. Edgar
   communism and 98
Hopkins v. U.S. (1898) 451
Horton v. California (1990) 339
House Un-American Activities
   Committee 30, 98, 499
housing discrimination 20–21
   Stewart and 430
Hoyt v. Florida (1961) 142, 181, 525
H. P. Hood & Sons v. DuMond
   (1949) **208–209**
Hughes, Charles Evans 74,
   209–210
   interstate commerce clause and
      230
   majority opinions of 207, 215,
      304, 307, 309, 357, 493, 519
human rights law
   Native Americans and 73
Humphrey's Executor v. U.S.
   210–211
Hunt v. Cromartie (1999) 416
Hunt v. Washington Apple
   Advertising Commission (1977) 129
Hurley v. Irish-American Gay and
   Lesbian Group of Greater Boston
   (1995) 179, 453
Hurtado v. California (1884) **211,**
   215, 360
Hustler Magazine v. Falwell (1988)
   211–212
Hutto v. Davis (1982) 197
Hutto v. Finney (1978) 358
Hyde Amendment 201
Hylton v. U.S. (1796) 72

I

Ibanez v. Florida Dept. of Business
   and Professional Regulation (1994)
   70
Idaho v. Freeman (1981) 445
illegal aliens 13, 15–16, 84,
   213–214, 435
   education of 344

Illegal Immigrant Responsibility and Immigration Reform Act of 1996 (IIRIRA) 102, 313
illegitimacy
  intermediate scrutiny and 223
Illinois Central Railroad v. Bosworth (1890) 328
Illinois ex rel. McCollum v. Board of Education (1948) 172
Illinois v. Krull (1987) 148–149
Illinois v. Wardlow (2000) 432
immigration 13, 394
  education and 344
  illegal aliens and 213–214
Immigration and Nationality Act of 1940 11, 79
Immigration and Naturalization Service (INS) 102, 121, 220
Immigration and Naturalization Service v. Chada (1983) 60
immigration law
  plenary power and 341–342
immunity
  prisoners' rights and 382–383
impeachment 73–74
  Chase (Samuel) and 71–72
  of Clinton 90–91
  Rehnquist and 376
  Fortas and 171
  political question doctrine and 348
  Warren threatened with 510
imperial presidency
  Taney's warnings of 456–457
income tax **214**, 350–351
  bearer bonds subject to 421
  educational deductions for religious schools and 297–298
  Fuller and 175
  multistate businesses and 100
incorporation 31–32, 184, **214–216**
  Bill of Rights and 37–38
  Fifth Amendment and 411
  preemption and 355–356
  procedural due process and 360
  school prayer and 353–355
independent counsel provision 296–297
independent expenditures 158–159
  political campaigns and 95
Indian Civil Rights Act of 1968 218
Indian Gaming Regulatory Act (1990) 218, 310
Indian rights **216–218**
Individuals with Disabilities Education Act (IDEA) (1975) 86, 125, 532
inferior officer clause
  independent counsel statute and 297
informed consent 3
inherent powers **218–221**, 292–293
inheritance tax 214
In re Debs (1895) 219, **220**
In re Gault (1967) 171, **220–221**, 245
In re Neagle (1890) 219, **222–223**
In re Winship (1970) 245

In re Yamashita (1946) 300
instrumentalists 103
insular doctrine 521
INS v. Chadha (1983) 90, 220
INS v. St. Cyr (2001) 342
intelligible principle 196
intermediate scrutiny 49, 99, 114, **223**
Internal Security Act (McCarran Act) (1950) 98
International Brotherhood of Teamsters v. U.S. (1977) 468–469
International Society for Krishna Consciousness, Inc. v. Lee (1992) **224**
International Union, United Auto Workers v. Johnson Controls (1991) **224–225**
Internet
  anonymity and 17
  compulsory filters in federally funded libraries 480
  pornography and 352
Internet and censorship 225
Internet and the Worldwide Web **226–228**
Internet Corporation for Assigned Names and Numbers (ICANN) 227
Internet taxation **228–229**
Internet Tax Freedom Act of 1998 226, 227, 229
interracial marriage 418
Interstate Commerce Act (1887) 231
interstate commerce clause 17–18, 181–182, **229–231**, 231, 452, 484, 492–493, 520
  child labor and 28, 194–195
  Civil Rights Act of 1964 and 203
  civil rights and 84
  dormant commerce clause and 127–129
  expansion of federal government by 308–309
  federal taxation on 28
  judicial scrutiny and 482–483
  local marketing quotas and 522
  meat monopoly and 451–452
  monopolies, regulation of 426–427, 485–486
  national minimum drinking age and 423
  new federalism and 310–311
  NLRB establishment and 303–305
  original package doctrine and 272
  police powers and 298–299, 345–346
  price-fixing and 504
  prison labor and 251
  prostitution and 205
  railroad strike and 219, 221
  rational basis test and 372
  regulation of nuclear waste and 314–315
  selected exclusiveness and 408–409

separate but equal laws and 342–344
  shipping facilities and 208–209
  sovereign immunity and 424
  state business tax and 100
  state employees and 178
  state regulation of 106–107
  states' jurisdiction over 127–129, 288–289
  state sovereignty and 305
  Tenth Amendment and 422
  Violence Against Women Act and 490, 500
Interstate Commerce Commission 196, **231**
Intl. Longshoreman's Union v. Boyd (1954)
  ripeness and 385
Intl. Society for Krishna Consciousness v. Lee (1992) 362
Iredell, James 239
issue advocacy 278–279
It Is So Ordered: A Constitution Unfolds (Burger) 61

J

Jackson, Andrew
  Indian rights and 217
  Story as nemesis 433
Jackson, Robert H. **232–233**
  concurring opinions of 219, 418, 443, 530
  dissents of 146, 250
  majority opinions of 166, 208, 522
  Rehnquist clerkship with 375–376
Jacobellis v. Ohio (1964) 351, 430
Jacob Wetterling Crimes Against Children and Sexually Violent Offender Registration Act (1994) 419
Jaffree v. Board of School Commissioners (1983) 505
Jaffree v. Wallace (1983) 505
Jager v. Douglas County School District (1989) 401
Japanese internment camps *249*, *249*–250, 366, 434, 449
  Frankfurter and 173
  Murphy and 300
  Stone and 431
Japan Line, Ltd. v. County of Los Angeles (1979) 444
Jay, John 17, 75, *233*, **233**, 281, 301
Jean v. Nelson (1985) 213
J.E.B. v. Alabama (1994) 32, **234**
Jefferson, Thomas 103, 144, 147, 149, 268, 376, 463
Jehovah's Witnesses **235**, 377, 514
  flag salute and 165–166, 431
Jim Crow laws 9–10, 82, **235–236**, 342–344. *See also* separate but equal doctrine
Johnson, Andrew *291*
  veto of Reconstruction Acts 291
Johnson, Lyndon B. *83*
  affirmative action and 367, 506

appointments of 171, 274, 447
  civil rights and 84–85, 203, 468
  Voting Rights Act and 501
  Warren Commission and 510
Johnson v. Avery (1969) 357
Johnson v. Louisiana (1972) 242, 353
Johnson v. McIntosh (1823) 72, 216–217
Johnson v. Transportation Agency of Santa Clara County (1987) 142, 236, **236–237**, 469, 494
Johnson v. Zerbst (1938) 12
Jones v. City of Opelika (1942) 166, 235
Jones v. City of Opelika II (1943) 235
Jones v. Mayer (1968) 430
Jones v. Wolf (1979) 377
Judges Act (1925) 455
judicial activism and restraint 45–46, **237–239**
  Brandeis briefs and 50–51
  Warren Court and 509–511
judicial administration
  Burger and 58–61
judicial bypass
  abortion rights and 204
judicial immunity 316
Judicial Procedure Reform Act (1937) 112
judicial restraint 482
judicial review 72, 82, 89, 102, 237, **239–240**, 268–269, 413, 446, 476
  exacting scrutiny test and 141
  expansion of individual rights and 286
  Marshall and 272
  ripeness and 385
judicial scrutiny
  Stone and 431
Judiciary Act of 1789 110, 121, 143, 157, **240–242**, 271, 324, 435, 444, 452, 457, 476
  Ellsworth and 136
  federal jurisdiction and 275–276
  Story and 433
Judiciary Act of 1801 435
Judiciary Act of 1867 271
Judiciary Act of 1925 391
jurisdiction
  federal 69
  federal *vs.* state 96
  states' rights and 91–92
jury selection 32
  peremptory challenges and 334–336
jury size and voting **241–242**
just compensation 34–35, 137–138
justiciability 69, **242–243**. *See also* cases and controversies
juvenile offenders 220–221
  capital punishment and 22–23, **243–244**
juvenile rights **244–245**
juveniles 289–290
J. W. Hampton, Jr., & Co. v. U.S. (1928) **195–196**

K

Kadrmas v. Dickinson (1988) 344
Kansas v. Hendricks (1997) 130, 420
Karcher v. Daggett (1983) 189, 323, 429
Katzenbach v. McClung (1964) 84, 86, 203
Katzenbach v. Morgan (1966) **246**
Katz v. U.S. (1967) **246–247**, 358–359, 407, 523
Keating-Owens Bill (1916) 28
Keller v. State Bar of California (1990) 42–43, 437
Kennedy, Anthony **247–248**
  concurrences of 478
  majority opinions of 189–190, 255, 258, 276, 369, 377, 388, 389, 420, 421, 507
  religious freedom and 44
  student fees and 42–43
Kennedy, John F.
  affirmative action and 9
  appointments of 519
  assassination of 468, 510
Kennedy v. Sampson (1973) 259
Kent v. Dulles (1958) 194
Kent v. U.S. (1966) 244–245
Kevorkian, Dr. Jack 125
Keyishian v. Board of Regents (1967) 467
Kimel v. Board of Regents (2000) 239, **248–250**, 311
King, Martin Luther, Jr. 313, 501
Klopfer v. North Carolina (1967) 426
Knauff v. Shaughnessy (1950) 13
Kohl v. U.S. (1876) 137–138
Korematsu v. U.S. (1944) 173, 249, **249–250**, 300, 366, 431, 434–435, 449
Kovacs v. Cooper (1949) 173
Kremen v. NSI (2003) 227
Ku Klux Klan 338, 378
  cross burning and 114–115
  membership disclosure of 303
  Second Amendment and 408
Ku Klux Klan Act (1871) 52, 315
Kumho Tire Co., Ltd. v. Carmichael (1999) 119, 404
Kurzban (2000) 213
Kyllo v. U.S. (2001) 523

L

La Abra Silver Mining Co. v. U.S. (1899) 219
labor
  illegal aliens and 213–214
labor contracts 103, 260–261
labor laws
  women's rights and 298
labor practices
  gender discrimination and 224–225
labor union rights **251–252**
Lafollete Seamen's Act (1915) 251

Lamar, L. Q. C.
  dissents of 222
Lamb's Chapel v. Center Moriches School District (1993) 145, 185–186, **252–253**, 263, 389–390, 402
land fraud 167–168
Landmarks Preservation Law (1965) 332
Landon v. Plasencia (1982) 342
Land Reform Act of 1967 202
Landrum-Griffin Act (1959) 252
land use **253–255**
  1983 lawsuits and 316
  Native American rights 301–302
  takings clause and 456
  zoning restrictions and 33–34
Lassiter v. Northampton County Board of Elections (1959) 130–131
The Laura (1885) 328
Lawrence, Jerome 164
Lawrence v. Texas (2003) 46, 105, 179, **255–256**, 270, 359, 372, 418, 440–441, 462
lawyer advertising **256–257**
"layered cake federalism" 161
laying of taxes clause 195
Lee, Robert E. (playwright) 164
Lee M. Till v. SCS Credit Corp. (2004) 121
Lee v. International Society for Krishna Consciousness, Inc. (1992) 224
Lee v. Weisman (1992) 145, 248, **257**, 355, 377, 396, 398, 401–402
legal insanity 171
Legal Services Corp. v. Velazquez (2001) **257–258**
legal tender cases (1871) 47
legislative apportionment 94
legislative standing **258–259**
legislative veto 60
Lehr v. Robertson (1983) 329
Leisy v. Hardin (1890) 175
Lemmon v. The People (1860) 96
Lemon test 253, 259–260, 265, 297, 354–355, 377, 505
  school vouchers and 403
Lemon v. Kurtzman (1971) 14, 144, 253, **259–260**, 265, 297, 354, 377, 403, 505
Lewis, John L. *304*
libel **418**
  Hustler Magazine v. Falwell 211–212
  political criticism and 283–284
  press and 276
  racial discrimination and 32–33
libel law 313
  free speech and 53–54
liberty interest 124–125
  paternal visitation rights and 284–285
liberty of contract 14–15, 108, **260–261**, 262, 371, 419, 518
  Sutherland and 450
License Cases (1847) 229–230

lie detector tests **261–262**
Lincoln, Abraham 151
  appointments of 71
  suspension of habeas corpus 458
  war powers and 359, 508
Line Item Veto Act (1996) 89–90
liquidation (Chapter 7) 29
liquor industry
  commercial speech in 96–97
Liquormart 44 v. Rhode Island (1996) 96–97, 109
literacy tests 236, 449, 501
Little Rock 9 107
Litvinov Assignment 492
Lloyd v. Tanner (1972) 353
Lochner v. New York (1905) 14, 50, 103, 108, 140–141, 162, 175, 206–207, 208, 238, 240, 251, 260, **262**, 298, 299, 306, 419, 441
Locke, John 463
Locke v. Davey (2004) **263**
Lockyer v. Andrade (2003) 198
loitering
  gang congregation and 79–80
Lone Wolf v. Hitchcock (1903) 521
Lorance v. AT&T Technologies, Inc. (1989) 506
Lorillard Tobacco Co. v. Reilly (2001) 76–77
lotteries
  commercial speech and 97
Lovell v. Griffin (1938) 165
Loving v. Virginia (1967) **263–264**, 270, 418
loyalty oaths 36
  communism and 98
Lucas v. South Carolina Coastal Council (1992) 253, **264–265**, 456, 533
Ludlow massacre 251
Lujan v. Defenders of Wildlife (1992) **265**, 302
Lunney v. Prodigy Services Co. 226
Luther v. Borden (1849) 347
Lynch v. Donnelly (1984) 14, 145, **265–266**, 378

M

Machinists v. Street (1961) 1
MacPherson v. Buick Motor Company (1916) 67
Madison, James 17, 147, 233, 272, 280, 281, 364, 442
  Bill of Rights and 316
  on inherent powers 218–219
  one person, one vote and 322
Madsen v. Women's Health Center, Inc. (1994) 248, **267–268**, 453
Malloy v. Hogan (1964) 6, 328, 400, 411
mandatory sentencing 147–148
Mann Act 205
manufacturers rights over retail 104
Mapp v. Ohio (1961) 74, 88, 148, **268**, 360, 400, 515
"marble cake federalism" 161

Marbury v. Madison (1803) 72, 92, 107, 239, 240–241, **268–269**, 272, 292, 324, 371, 413, 457, 476
marriage, right to **269–270**
  fundamental rights and 176–177
Marshal, office of the **270–271**
Marshall, John 74, 149, **271–273**, *271*, 275
  civil liberties and 31
  concurrent opinions of 335
  dissents of 168, 169, 190, 194, 507
  Indian rights and 216
  interstate commerce clause and 229
  majority opinions of 72–73, 91, 128, 168, 181, 215, 239, 268–269, 270, 292, 308, 328, 409, 413, 457, 476, 478, 479
  state taxation of federal agencies and 279–280
  Story and 433
  Washington (Bushrod), mentor to 511–513
Marshall, Secretary of Labor, et al. v. Barlow's, Inc. (1978) **273**
Marshall, Thurgood **273–275**, 274
  corporate campaign finance laws and 23–24
  dissents of 288, 295, 297–298, 312, 331, 337, 410
  jury selection and 32
  majority opinions of 322
  zoning restrictions and 34
Marsh v. Chambers (1983) 402
Martinez v. Bynum (1983) 344
Martin v. Hunter's Lessee (1816) **275–276**, 433
Martin v. Wilks 506
Maryland v. Buie (1990) 407
Maryland v. Craig (1990) 113
Mason v. Haille (1827) 513
Massachusetts v. Murgia (1976) 249
Massachusetts v. Sheppard (1984) 148, 268
Masses Publishing Co. vs. Patten (1917) 528
Masson v. New Yorker (1991) **276**
Maternity Act 174
Mathews v. Diaz (1976) 13, 341
Mathews v. Eldridge (1976) **276–277**
Mathis v. U.S. (1968) 290
McCain-Feingold Act 278, 281
McCarran Act (1950) 98
McCarthyism 30, 499, 528
McClesky v. Zant (1991) 204
McCollum v. Board of Education (1948) 139, 232, 534
McConnell v. Federal Election Commission (2003) 24, **278–279**, 281
McCorvey, Norma *(Roe v. Wade)* 386–388
McCulloch v. Maryland (1819) 94, 103, 161, 207–208, 272, **279–280**, 308, 433, 478

McIntyre v. Ohio Elections Commission (1995) 17, 280–281
McKiever v. Pennsylvania (1971) 245
McKleskey v. Kemp (1987) 65, **277–278**
McLaurin v. Oklahoma (1950) 499
McNary v. Haitian Refugee Center, Inc. (1991) 213
McReynolds, James Clark
    dissents of 304, 309, 482
    majority opinions of 338
Meachum v. Fano (1976) 322
meat monopoly 451–452
mediation 59
medical treatment, refusal of
    evidence of intent required for 116
Meek v. Pittenger (1975) 145, 294, 532
Megan's Law (1994) 226, 419–420
"Memorial and Remonstrance Against Religious Assessments" (Madison) 147
mental illness
    capital punishment and 22–23
mental retardation 89
    capital punishment and 22–23, 333–334
    disability rights and 126–127
    sterilization and 105–106, 206
    as suspect classification 371
Meredith v. Winter Haven (1943) 5
Meritor Savings Bank v. Vinson (1986) **281–282,** 414
Metro Broadcasting, Inc. v. FCC (1990) **282**
Meyer v. Nebraska (1923) 105–106, **282–283,** 329, 338, 467
Miami Herald Publishing Co. v. Tornillo (1974) **283–284,** 374
Michael H. et al. v. Gerald D. (1989) **284–285,** 329
Michael M. v. Superior Court of Sonoma County (1981) 223, **285–286,** 390, 525
Michigan v. Long (1983) **286**
Michigan v. Tucker (1974) 123
Migratory Bird Treaty Act (1918) 292–293
military benefits 174
Military Selective Service Act of 1967 409, 410, 414
military trials 151
Milk Control Board v. Eisenberg Farm Products (1939) 208
Miller, Samuel F.
    majority opinions of 48–49, 215, 222, 419
Miller v. California (1973) 60, 314, 329–330, 352
Miller v. Johnson (1995) **286–287,** 373, 416
Milliken v. Bradley (1974) **287–288,** 451
Minersville School District v. Gobitis (1940) 104, 166, 173, 235, 300, 430–431

minimum drinking age 422–423
minimum wage 7–8, 178, 252, 307
    Van Devanter and 496
Minnesota v. Cloverleaf Creamery Co. (1981) **288–289**
Minnesota v. Dickerson (1993) 432
minority contracts 6–7
minors, rights of **289–290**
Minor v. Happersett (1875) 142, 525
Miranda v. Arizona (1966) 143–144, 197, **290,** 429, 510, 520
    juveniles and 245
    statutory relief from 122–123
Mississippi University for Women v. Hogan (1982) 223, **290–291**
Mississippi v. Johnson (1867) **291–292**
Missouri Compromise. *See Dred Scott v. Sanford*
Missouri v. Holland (1920) **292–293**
Missouri v. Jenkins (1995) 421
Mistretta v. U.S. (1989) **293–294**
Mitchell v. Helms (2000) 145, **294–295,** 326, 532
Mitchell v. Laird (1973) 258–259
Mitchell v. Wells (1859) 96
Mitchum v. Foster (1972) 530
Mobile v. Bolden (1980) **295–296**
monopolies 17–18, 312, 426–427, 451–452. *See also Slaughter-House Cases*
    Brandeis and 49
Montayne v. Haymes (1976) 322
Monterey v. Del Monte Dunes at Monterey, Ltd. (1999) 533
Montesquieu, Charles-Louis de Secondat, baron de La Brède et de
    separation of powers and 413
Moore v. Dempsey (1923) 206
Moore v. East Cleveland (1977) 371
moot 243, **296–297**
Morehead v. New York ex rel. Tipaldo (1936) 307
Morehead v. Tipaldo (1936) 261
Morey v. Doud (1957) 141
Mormons 376, 381–382, 389
    religious freedom and 269
Morrison v. Olson (1988) **296–297**
Morton v. Mancari (1974) 218
Motor Carriers Act (1980) 231
M. Patterson v. Texas (2002) 23
Mueller v. Allen (1983) 145, 260, **297–298,** 403, 532
Mugler v. Kansas (1887) 14
Muller v. Oregon (1908) 49–50, 50–51, 181, 251, **298,** 306, 525
Munn v. Illinois (1876) 8, **298–299,** 504
Murdock v. Commonwealth of Pennsylvania (1943) 235
Murphy, Frank 299, **299–300**
    dissents of 166, 208, 250
    majority opinions of 70, 325
Murphy v. United Parcel Service, Inc. (1999) 87, 126

Murray v. Curlett (1963) 353–354
Murray v. Hoboken Land Improvement Co. (1855) 211
music censorship **300–301**
Muskrat v. U.S. (1911) **301–302**
Myers v. U.S. (1926) 210

N

NAACP v. Alabama (1958) **303**
Nader v. Bork (1973) 259
Naim v. Naim (1955) 264
Nardone v. U.S. (1937) 523
Nash v. Florida Industrial Commission (1967) 356
National Association for the Advancement of Colored People (NAACP) 236
    Legal Defense Fund of
        capital punishment and 278
        Marshall (Thurgood) and 274
        membership disclosure of 303
        Murphy and 299
        Scottsboro boys, benefactors of 405–406
national bank 103
National Consumers' League 50–51
National Environmental Policy Act (1969) 9
National Firearms Act of 1934 408
National Industrial Recovery Act (1935) 111, 230, 309, 492–493, 496
National Labor Relations Act (1937) 230, 303–304, 309
National Labor Relations Board (NLRB) 303–304
National Labor Relations Board (NLRB) v. Jones & Laughlin Steel Corporation (1937) 18, 230, 252, **303–304,** 304, 310, 452, 510, 518, 522
National League of Cities v. Usery (1976) 178, **305,** 376, 422
National Organization of Women v. Scheidler (1994) 3–4, **306,** 384
National Probation Cases 445
National Recovery Act 50
National Rifle Association
    campaign finance reform and 279
national supremacy clause 161
    federalism and 161
Native Americans 72–73, 216–218
    land use and 301–302
    sovereign immunity and 423
nativity scene 378
naturalization 78–79
natural law 72
natural rights theory
    Thomas and 463
Near v. Minnesota ex rel. Olsen (1931) 210, 215, 308, 357
Nebbia v. New York (1934) **306–307**
Nebraska Press Assn. v. Stuart (1976) **307–308**
necessary and proper clause 103, 161, **308–309**

federal jurisdiction and 279–280
federalism and 161
income tax on state bearer bonds and 422
Violence Against Women Act and 500
Nelson, Justice
    dissents of 359
    majority opinions of 94–95
Nevada Dept. of Human Resources v. Hibbs (2003) 311, 424
New Deal 230, 482, 492–493
    Cardozo and 68
    court-packing plan and 111–112
    curb on 305
    judicial review and 240
    labor regulation and 303–305
    liberty of contract and 261
    rational basis test and 371
    Sutherland opposed to 450
New Deal constitutionality **309–310**
new federalism 161, 305, **310–311**
New Jersey v. T.L.O. (1985) 133, 245, **311–312,** 439, 440
New Jersey Welfare Rights Organization v. Cahill (1973) 223
Newport News Shipbuilding and Dry Dock Co. v. EEOC (1983) 356
New State Ice Co. v. Liebmann (1932) **312–313**
New York Times Co. v. Sullivan (1964) 53–54, 211, 276, **313,** 418
New York Times Co. v. Tasini (2001) 226
New York Times v. U.S. (1971) 308, 357
New York v. Ferber (1982) **314,** 352
New York v. Quarles (1984) 123, 290
New York v. U.S. (1992) **314–315**
Nguyen v. INS (2001) 342
Nike, Inc. v. Kasky (2003) 109
1983 lawsuits **315–316**
Nineteenth Amendment 445
    Equal Rights Amendment and 141–142
    one person, one vote and 188
    women's labor rights and 261
    women's suffrage and 525
Ninth Amendment **316–317**
    Bill of Rights and 37–38
    contraceptives and 191–192
    federal employees, political speech of, and 475
    fundamental rights and 176–177
    individual rights guarantee
        abortion rights and 387
        privacy and 46, 359
        unenumerated rights and 474–475
Nishimura Ekiu v. U.S. (1892) 13
Nixon, Richard M.
    appointments of 39, 58–59, 352, 375
    Bork and 45
    campaign finance abuses and 278
    executive privilege and 149–150
    independent counsel provision and 296

Nixon, Richard M. *(continued)*
  litigation of 60
  pardon of 328
  tapes and 36
Nixon v. Administrator of General Services (1977) 36
Nixon v. Shrink Missouri Govt. PAC (2000) 349
Nixon v. U.S. 348
NLRB. *See* National Labor Relations Board (NLRB)
non-preferentialism
  establishment clause and 146
Norris v. Alabama (1935) 405–406
North Carolina v. Pearce (1969) 130
Noto v. U.S. (1961) 98
nude dancing 30–31, **317–318**

O

O'Brien test 491–492
obscenity 92–93, **351–352**
  adult movie theaters and 329–330
  Burger and 60
  child pornography and 314
  Internet and 225–226, 227
  Internet filters in libraries and 480
  music censorship and 300–301
  prior restraint and 357
  radio and 154–155
  zoning ordinances and 379–380
Occupational Safety and Health Act (1970)
  search and seizure clause and 273
O'Connor, Sandra Day 164, **319–321,** *320*
  abortion rights and 2
  affirmative action and 10
  concurrences of 234, 495
  dissents of 164, 369, 423
  majority opinions of 96, 113, 115, 138, 141, 148, 168, 176, 193, 200, 202, 279, 286, 291, 315, 333, 355, 416, 421, 422, 470–471, 506
  racial discrimination and 7
Ogden v. Saunders (1827) 513
O'Hare Truck Service, Inc. v. City of Northlake (1996) 40–41, **321**
Oklahoma
  relocation of capital of 113
Oklahoma City v. Dowell (1992) 451
Oklahoma Criminal Sterilization Act 130
Older Workers Benefit Protection Act (OWBPA) 12
Olim v. Wakinekona (1983) **321–322**
Olmstead v. L.C., by Zimring (1999) 87, 126
Olmstead v. U.S. (1928) 50, 358, 523
Omnibus Consolidated Rescissions and Appropriations Act (1996) 258
Omnibus Crime Control and Safe Streets Act of 1968 122, 310, 523

Oncale v. Sundowner Offshore Svcs. (1998) 414–415
one person, one vote 29, 53, 88, 94, 131, 188–189, **322–323,** 517–518
  redistricting and 372, 381, 416
operation of law 78–79
opinion writing **323**
oral arguments 74, **323–324**
Oregon v. Elstad (1985) 290
Oregon v. Mitchell (1970) 246, 446, 501
Oregon v. Smith (1990) 44, 138
Organized Crime Control Act of 1970 367
  RICO statute of 306
originalism 397, 472
  Thomas and 462–463
originalists 103
original jurisdiction 19, 75–76, 100–102, 127, 239, 240, **324–325,** 476, 526
original package doctrine 272
Orozco v. Texas (1969) 290
Orr v. Orr (1979) 390
Osborne v. Ohio (1990) 314
Osborn v. U.S. (1875) 328
Other People's Money: And How the Bankers Use It (Brandeis) 50
overbreadth doctrine **325,** 500
overturning Supreme Court decisions **325–326**

P

Pacific Gas & Electric Co. v. State Energy Resources Conservation and Development Commission (1983) 356
PACs
  campaign expenditures and 158–159
  campaign finance laws and 159–160
  spending limitations of 95
Palazzolo v. Rhode Island Coastal Resources Mgmt. Council (2001) 254, 533
Palko v. Connecticut (1937) 129–130, **327–328**
Palmer Raids 97
pamphleteering 17, 165–166, 349, 529
Panama Refining v. Ryan (1935) 309
Papish v. University of Missouri Curators (1973) 438
Pap's A.M. v. City of Erie (2000) 317
Parden v. Terminal Railway (1964) 424
pardon 328, **328–329**
pardoning power
  commutation and 98–99
parens patriae 244
parental consent 68–69
  abortion rights and 204–205
parental rights **329**
  religious exemption from school attendance and 524

Parents Music Resource Center
  music censorship and 301
Paris Adult Theater I v. Slaton (1973) **329–330**
parody
  defamation and 211–212
Partial-Birth Abortion Funding Ban Act of 2003 3
Pasadena v. Spangler (1976) 451
Passenger Cases (1849) 230
Passport Act of 1926 194
paternal visitation rights 284–285
Patient Self-Determination Act (1991) 125
PATRIOT Act (2001) 11
  citizenship and 79
  RICO Act and 368
PATRIOT Act II. *See* Domestic Security Enhancement Act 11
  citizenship and 79
patronage 321
Patterson v. McLean Credit Union (1989) 506
Patterson v. Texas (2002) 244
Payne-Aldrich Tariff Act 455
Payne v. Tennessee (1991) **330–331**
Peckham, Rufus
  majority opinions of 262
Peel v. Attorney Registration and Disciplinary Commission of Illinois (1990) 70
Penn Central test 254
Penn Central Transportation Co. v. New York City (1978) 254, **332–333,** 456
Pennhurst State School and Hospital v. Halderman (1984) 152
Pennsylvania Coal Co. v. Mahon (1922) 456
Pennsylvania Dept. of Corrections v. Yeskey (1998) 126
Pennsylvania v. Union Gas (1989) 424
Penry v. Lynaugh (1989) **333–334**
Pentagon Papers 38, 187, 308, 357
per curiam opinions
  Bush v. Gore as 62–63
peremptory challenges 32, 234, **334–336**
Perez v. Brownell (1958) 10–11
Perry Educational Assn. v. Perry Local Educational Assn. (1983) 399
Perry v. Lynaugh (1989) 22
Personal Responsibility and Work Opportunity Reconciliation Act (1996) 516–517
Personnel Administrator of Massachusetts et al. v. Feeney (1979) **336–337**
PGA Tour, Inc. v. Casey Martin (2001) 126, **337–338,** 463
Phillips Petroleum Co. v. Shutts (1985) 88
Pierce v. Hill Military Academy (1925) 338
Pierce v. Society of the Sisters (1925) 146, 329, 338, **338,** 524

Pitney, Justice
  majority opinions of 108
plain view doctrine **339**
Planned Parenthood Assn. of Kansas City, Missouri v. Ashcroft (1983) 352–353
Planned Parenthood of Missouri v. Danforth (1976) **339–340**
Planned Parenthood of Southeastern Pennsylvania v. Casey (1992) 3, 125, 248, 320, 326, 340, **340–341,** 388, 398, 420–421, 441, 495
Pledge of Allegiance 235
plenary power 195, 323–324, **341–342,** 443–444
  political powers and 346
Plessy v. Ferguson (1896) 56, 103, 140, 175, 200, 236, **342–344,** *343,* 366, 389, 446, 449, 499, 510
plurality 14
Plyler v. Doe (1982) 15, **344,** 353, 395, 435
pocket veto 259
Poe v. Ullman (1961) 162, 191, **344–345,** 408
police powers 202, 262, **345–346,** 460–461
  contract clause and 207
  individual liberty and 282–283
  property rights and 298–299
  strict scrutiny and 434–435
police searches 74–75
political parties, rights of **346–347**
political question doctrine 29, 220, 259, **347–348**
political rights
  civil rights and 82
political speech 17, 158–159, 159–160, 280–281, **348–349**
  communism and 528
  draft-card burning and 491–492
  election spending and 95
  federal employees prohibited from 475
  flag burning and 164–165
  judicial elections and 380
  pamphleteering and 529
  public forums and 362
  student protest and 466–467
  union dues and 437
  white supremacy and 170
Pollock v. Farmers Loan and Trust Co. (1895) 175, 214, **350–351,** 421, 446
poll taxes 199–200, 236, 501
polygraphs 261–262
Pope v. Williams (1904) 199
pornography **351–352**
  adult movie theaters and 329–330
  child 314, 352
  commercial speech and 109
  Internet and 225–226, 227
  Internet filters in libraries and 480
  Stewart and 430
  zoning ordinances and 379–380, 534

Port Authority of New York and New
Jersey 479
poverty
    as prospective suspect class
    395
Powell, Lewis F., Jr. 15, 20–21,
    352–353
    affirmative action and 10
    dissents of 186, 291, 370
    majority opinions of 66, 104, 191,
    277, 278, 374–375, 511
Powell v. Alabama (1932) 210,
    405–406, 450
Powell v. McCormack (1969) 259
Powers v. Ohio (1991) 336
prayer in school **353–355,** 354
    sporting events and 396–397
    voluntary 504–505
precedent. See stare decisis
preemption **355–356**
    interstate commerce and 230
preferred freedoms doctrine 99
pregnancy
    Title VII and 468–469
Pregnancy Discrimination Act
    (1978) 181, **356–357**
presentment clause
    line-item veto and 90
presidential candidates 16–17
presidential immunity
    civil lawsuits and 90–91
presidential powers 218
presidential removal powers 210–211
press
    grand jury testimony and 51–52
press censorship
    schools and 202–203
pretext stops 25
price controls 102
price fixing 17–18, 451–452
    milk monopoly and 306–307
Prigg v. Pennsylvania (1842) 434
Primary Colors (Anonymous) 17
Prince v. Massachusetts (1944) 235,
    524
Printz v. U.S. (1997) 239, 408, 423
prior restraint **357**
    abortion counseling and 391–392
    amplified speech and 507–508
    press and 307
    student newspapers and 438
prisoners
    sterilization and 106
prisoners of war 220
prisoners' rights **357–358**
    1983 lawsuits and 316
    interstate transfer and 321–322
    qualified immunity of guards and
    382–383
Prison Litigation Reform Act of 1996
    102, 358
prison terms
    Kennedy (Anthony) and 248
privacy 317, **358–359,** 418, 474
    abortion rights and 2–4, 339–340,
    387
    Brandeis Award and 50

compulsory school attendance and
    338
    contraceptives and 68, 136,
    191–192, 345
    Douglas and 131
    drug sentencing and 197–198
    fundamental rights and 176–177
    marriage rights and 270
    obscenity and 329–330
    search warrants and 406–407
    sexual freedoms and 46
    surveillance and 246–247
    women's rights and 526
privileges and immunities clause
    446. See also Fourteenth
    Amendment
    right to travel and 394
Prize Cases (1862) 219, **359,** 508
probable cause
    automobile searches and 24–25
    search warrants and 406–407
    stop and frisk and 432
    student searches and 312, 439
pro bono tradition
    Brandeis and 49
procedural due process 194, **360,** 440
    juveniles and 220–221
    prisoners' rights and 321–322
procreation
    contraceptives and 105
Procunier v. Martinez (1974) 357,
    383
product liability
    cigarettes and 77–78
property clause 167
property interest
    education and 186
property rights 167–168, 254,
    264–265, 433
    foreclosure and 207–208
    police powers and 299
    private college charter and
    118–119
    zoning laws and 497–498
prostitution
    interstate commerce and 205
psychiatric evaluations
    capital punishment and 22–23
Public Contracts Act (1936) 252
public forum 4, **360–362,** 389
    libraries as 480
    religious freedom and 224
    student newspapers and 438
    white supremacy and 170
Public Health Service Act 391
public indecency
    nude dancing and 30–31
public trial **362**
public use 34–35, 137
Public Works Employment Act 176
Publius 17, 281
Pullman abstention 4–5
punishment of individuals 36
punitive damages **362–363**
pure speech **364–365,** 466
    overbreadth and 325
Purkett v. Elem (1995) 336

Q
quickening 2
quid pro quo
    campaign finance laws and
    158–159
    political corruption and 348–350
    sexual harassment and 414, 469
Quill Corp. v. North Dakota (1992)
    129, 228
Quilloin v. Walcott (1977) 329
Quinlan, Karen Ann 124

R
racial discrimination 9–10, 62,
    82–84, **366–367,** 468, 506
    affirmative action, voluntary, and
    494
    age discrimination and 11–12
    Bradley and 48
    Bureau of Indian Affairs and 218
    businesses and 48
    busing and 287–288
    city elections and 295–296
    Civil Rights Act of 1964 and 84–85
    covenants and 417
    cross burning and 114–115
    in D.C. schools 44–45
    death penalty and 66
    EEOC and 140
    employment and 190–191
    federal contracts and 6–7, 176
    free speech and 32–33
    hiring preferences and 337
    housing and 21
    judicial bias and 277–278
    jury selection and 32
    marriage and 263–264
    NAACP membership disclosure
    and 303
    peremptory challenges and
    334–336
    police qualifying exam as 513
    precedents of 205
    primary voting and 346
    public accommodations and 203
    rational basis test and 371
    redistricting and 286–287
    religious freedom vs. 43–44
    school admission and 56–57
    school desegregation and
    189–190
    Second Amendment and 408
    strict scrutiny and 483
    suspect classification and 449
    voting rights and 501
    Warren Court and 510
    zoning laws and 57
racial profiling 521–522
Racketeer Influenced and Corrupt
    Organizations Act (RICO) (1970)
    abortion rights and 306
Ragsdale et al. v. Wolverine World
    Wide, Inc. (2002) **368–369**
Railroad Commission v. Pullman Co.
    (1941) 4–5
Railroad Retirement Act (1935) 111

Railway Employees' Dept. v. Hanson
    (1956) 1
Railway Labor Act (1926) 251
Raines v. Byrd (1997) 90, 259
railroad strike 221
Rankin v. McPherson (1987) 40
rape 490
    capital punishment and 93
    death penalty and **369–370**
    Roe v. Wade and 387
    Scottsboro boys and 405–406
Rasmussen v. U.S. (1905) 521
Rathburn v. U.S. (1957) 523
rational basis 15, 82, 89, 99, 114,
    370–372
    state jurisdiction and 288–289
R.A.V. v. City of St. Paul (1992) 115
Reagan, Ronald
    abortion rights and 2–3
    appointments of 45–46, 164, 247,
    320, 375, 397, 447
    veto of Title IX 192
reapportionment **372–373,** 502,
    517. See also redistricting
reasonable person standard 169
recidivist statutes 148
Reconstruction
    Civil Rights Acts and 85–86
Reconstruction Acts 101, 291–292
redistricting 28–29, 94, 172, 322,
    372–373, 381, 517
    one person, one vote and
    188–189
    political question doctrine and
    348
    race and 286–287, 421
    racial gerrymandering and
    464–465
    Stevens and 429
Red Lion Broadcasting v. FCC
    (1969) 154, 284, **373–374**
Reed v. Reed (1971) 34, 49, 142,
    181, 183, 223, 298, 390, 434, 525
Regents of the University of
    California v. Bakke (1978) 10, 54,
    141, 187, 193, 223, 275, 353,
    374–375, 494
Regents' Prayer Case 139
Regina v. Hicklin (British law)
    (1868) 351
Rehabilitation Act of 1973 86–87,
    125–126, 140
Rehnquist, William 375, **375–376**
    capital punishment and 22–23
    dissents of 113, 119, 160, 165,
    176, 220, 332, 397, 461, 465,
    493, 494, 514
    free speech and 17
    majority opinions of 116, 122,
    123, 163–164, 174, 187, 197,
    199, 204, 263, 267, 285, 286,
    297, 305, 306, 317, 331, 379,
    403, 422, 480, 490, 495, 515,
    532
    obscenity and 352
    race at religious schools and
    43

religious freedom 44, 146–147, 252–253, **376–378,** 514
display of on state property 14
drugs and 138–139
education and 139, 185–186
establishment clause and 144–146
federal education grants and 459
freedom of speech and 70–71
Jehovah's Witnesses and 235
Native Americans and 218
property taxes and 505–506
public displays of **378–379**
public forums and 224
public school attendance and 338
public schools and 60
Scalia and 398
school funding and 259–260, 535
school prayers at sporting events and 396–397
school tax deductions and 297–298
school vouchers and 403
solicitation for 64
student press and 438
Religious Freedom Restoration Act (1993) 44, 138, 248
religious schools
race and tax status in 43–44
Reno v. ACLU (1997) 225, 352, 374
Reno v. American Arab Anti-Discrimination Committee (1999, 2000) 214
Renton v. Playtime Theaters (1986) **379–380**
reorganization
for businesses (Chapter 13) 29
for consumers (Chapter 11) 29
for farmers (Chapter 12) 29
reporter's privilege 51–52
Republican Party of Minnesota v. White (2002) **380**
residency requirements 394
restraint of trade 17–18, 104–105, 230, 451–452
Standard Oil monopoly and 426
White (Edward) and 521
retail restrictions 104
retained rights 316–317
retroactive guilt. *See* ex post facto laws
reverse discrimination 186, 193, 374–375, 494. *See also* affirmative action
Reynolds v. Sims (1964) 29, 189, 372–373, **381,** 510, 517
Reynolds v. Smith 516
Reynolds v. U.S. (1879) 64, 138–139, 269–270, 376, **381–382**
Richardson v. McKnight (1997) **382–383**
RICO Act **367–368**
abortion and **383–384**
Riggins v. Nevada (1992) 412
right of access 284
right to counsel 12–13, 35–36

right to die 116. *See also* suicide, assisted
right-to-reply laws 283–284, 373–374
right-to-work laws 252
Rindge Co. v. Los Angeles (1923) 202
Ring v. Arizona (2002) **384–385**
ripeness **385**
abortion rights and 386
Roberts, Owen J. 35
majority opinions of 64, 307, 309
Robinson-Patman Act (1936) 17–18
Rochin v. California (1952) 360, **385–386**
Roe v. Wade (1973) 2–4, 45, 88, 105, 201, 248, 315, 326, 339–340, 340–341, 352, 359, 376, **386–388,** 387, 418, 421, 429, 441, 463, 474, 514–515, 520
antiabortion activists and 306
Blackmun and 39–40
contraceptives and 68–69
declaratory judgments and 119
Ninth Amendment and 317
privacy and 131, 192
Rogers v. U.S. (1951) 411
Romer v. Evans (1996) 141, 179, 247, 372, **388–389**
Roosevelt, Franklin D. 309–310
appointments of 38, 130, 171, 232, 299, 430
Brandeis and 50
court-packing plan and 111–112, 371, 437
embargo of arms sales to Bolivia and Paraguay 483–484
Japanese internment and 249–250, 366
New Deal and 101–102, 230
presidential removal powers and 210–211
Roosevelt, Theodore
appointments of 205, 454–455
Rosebud Sioux Tribe v. Kneip (1977) 217
Rosenberger v. Rector and Visitors of the University of Virginia (1995) 145–146, 185–186, 248, 253, **389–390,** 421, 437, 438
Rostker v. Goldberg (1981) **390–391,** 414, 429, 525
Roth v. U.S. (1957) 92, 351
Rubin v. Coors (1995) 96
rule of four **391,** 526
Rummel v. Estelle (1980) 148, 197
Rust v. Sullivan (1991) 258, **391–392**
Rutan v. Republican Party of Illinois (1990) 321
Rutledge, John **392–393**
dissents of 146, 208
Rutledge, Wiley
Stevens clerked with 429
Ryan, George
capital punishment and 66

S
Sacco and Vanzetti
Frankfurter and 172
Saenz v. Roe (1999) **394,** 517
sales tax
Internet and 228
Sale v. The Haitian Centers Council (1993) 472
San Antonio Independent School District v. Rodriguez (1973) 274, 353, **395,** 435, 439
San Diego Gas & Electric Co. (1986) 164
Sanford, Edward
majority opinions of 184
Santa Clara County v. Southern Pacific Railroad (1886) **395–396**
Santa Clara Pueblo v. Martinez (1978) 218
Santa Fe Independent School District v. Doe (2000) 145, 248, 355, **396–397,** 401–402
Sattazahn v. Pennsylvania (2003) 130
Sawyer v. Whitley (1992) 5–6
Scales v. U.S. (1961) 98
Scalia, Antonin 397, **397–399**
capital punishment and 22–23
dissents of 90, 123, 180, 234, 236, 255, 263, 294, 297, 321, 337–338, 383, 388, 493, 515
free speech and 17, 40–41
majority opinions of 52, 113, 115, 138, 197, 264, 284, 339, 380, 382, 500, 521, 523
racial discrimination and 7
right to counsel and 13
Thomas and 462–463
Schall v. Martin (1984) 245
Schechter Poultry Corp. v. U.S. (1935) 304, 309
Scheidler v. Natl. Org. of Women, Inc. (2003) 368, 384
Schenck v. U.S. (1919) 4, 206, **399**
Schick v. Reed (1974) 99
Schlesinger v. Reservists Committee to Stop the War (1974) 459
Schlup v. Delo (1994) 5, **399–400**
Schmerber v. California (1966) 400
Schneider v. Irvington (1939) 165–166
school attendance
religious freedoms and 524
school censorship
press and 202–203
school desegregation 107, 189–190, 236
School District of Abington Township v. Schempp (1963) 88, 401
School District of Grand Rapids v. Ball (1985) 294, 532
school prayer 139, 257, 354, 377, **401–402**
establishment clause and 145
sporting events and 396–397
voluntary 504–505

school searches 311–312
school vouchers **402–404**
scientific evidence **404–405**
Scopes trial
Darrow and 221
Frankfurter and 172
Scottsboro boys 210, **405–406,** 450
Scott v. Illinois (1979) 13
Scott v. Sanford (1857) 240
search and seizure clause 24–25
juveniles and 245
search warrants 74–75, 148, **405–406,** 406
drug testing and 133
plain view doctrine and 339
students and 311–312
Second Amendment **407–408**
Bill of Rights and 37
incorporation and 216
rights of minors and 289
secularity 14
Sedima v. Imrex Co. (1985) 368
Sedition Act 206
segregation 236. *See also* racial discrimination
Marshall (Thurgood) and 273–275
school busing and 287–288
selected exclusiveness doctrine **408–409**
interstate commerce and 106–107
Selective Service **409–410**
Selective Service Act of 1917 409–410
Selective Service Commission v. Minnesota Public Interest Research Group (1984) **410–411**
self-incrimination, right against **411–412**
Sell v. U.S. (2003) **412**
Seminole Tribe v. Florida (1996) 152, 310–311, 424
sentencing guidelines 293–294
Sentencing Reform Act (1984) 293
separate but equal doctrine 56–57, 236, 342–344, 343, 366–367, 446, 499. *See also* Jim Crow laws
equal protection clause and 140
suspect classification and 449
separationists
establishment clause and 144–146
separation of church and state 146–147, 376
civil liberties and 81–82
establishment clause and 144–146
Frankfurter and 172
school funding and 294–295
school vouchers and 403
Souter and 421
separation of powers 46–47, 54, 60, 237, 280, **413,** 493
executive privilege and 149
imitated abroad 477–478

independent counsel statute and 297
line-item veto and 90
political question doctrine and 347
Reconstruction Acts and 291–292
segregation laws and 107–108
sentencing guidelines and 293–294
speech and debate clause and 187
steel seizure case and 530
war powers and 508
Serbian Eastern Orthodox Diocese for the USA and Canada v. Milivojevich (1976) 377
"Seven Dirty Words You Can't Say on Television" 154–155
Seven Star, Inc. v. U.S. (1989) 214
Seventh Amendment 445
Bill of Rights and 37–38
right to jury and
rights of minors and 289
Taft and 455
trial by jury clause
incorporation and 216
sex discrimination 236, 390
military benefits and 174
pregnancy in the workplace and 356
sex offenders registry
Internet and 226
sexual abuse
confrontation clause and 112–113
online registry of 419–420
sexual discrimination **413–414**
jury selection and 234
pregnancy and 181
sexual harassment and 281–282, 414–415
Title IX and 467–468
Title VII and 469
sexual freedoms 46
sexual harassment 281–282, **414–415**
Clinton and 54, 90–91
Thomas and 462
Title IX and 468
Title VII and 469
workplace and 200–201
The Shape of the River (Bowen and Bok) 9
Shapiro v. Thompson (1969) 394, **415–416,** 516–517
Shaughnessy v. U.S. ex rel. Mezei (1953) 13, 213
Shaw v. Hunt (1996) 286, 416
Shaw v. Reno (1993) 286–287, 373, **416,** 421, 464–465
Shelley v. Kraemer (1948) 62, **416,** 499
Shelton v. Tucker (1960) 430, 467
Sheppard v. Maxwell (1966) 308
Sherbert v. Verner (1963) 138, 524
Sherman Antitrust Act (1890) 17–18, 230, 252, 426, 451–452, 485–486, 521
Fuller and 175
retail restrictions and 104–105

shocks the conscience rule 385–386
Sibron v. New York (1968) 432
Sierra Club v. Morton (1972) 427
Simopoulis v. Virginia (1983) 352–353
Sixteenth Amendment 445, 446
apportionment clause nullified by 458
income tax and 214
income tax established by 350
Taft and 455
taxation powers 95
Sixth Amendment
Bill of Rights and 37
confrontation clause
facing one's accuser and 112–113
harmless error doctrine and 199
indigents and 35–36
jury selection and 32
right to counsel clause of 12–13
compulsory DWI blood test and 400–401
Miranda ruling and 143–144
rights of minors and 289
state criminal trials and 182
right to present evidence in
exclusionary rule and 261–262
right to trial clause of
freedom of the press and 362
press prior restraint and 307
speedy trial and 424–425
state exceptions to 327
trial by jury clause of
capital punishment sentencing and 385
Skinner v. Railway Labor Executives' Assn. (1989) 133
Skinner v. State of Oklahoma ex rel. Williamson (1942) 58, 105–106, 130, **417–418,** 434
slander and libel **418**
Slaughter-House Cases (1873) 6, 14, 47–48, 48–49, 71, 140, 173, 215, 236, 394, **419,** 446
slavery 132–133
comity and 96
Slouching Towards Gomorrah (Bork) 45
Smiley v. Holm (1932) 94
Smith Act (1940) 98, 120, 528
Smith et al. v. Doe et al. (2003) 226
Smith v. Allwright (1944) 346, 431, 501
Smith v. Daily Mail Publishing Co. (1979) 245
Smith v. Doe (2003) **419–420**
social rights
civil rights and 82
Social Security Act of 1935 112, 201, 309–310, 516–517
welfare restrictions and 415
sodomy 46, 105, 179, 255–256, 353, 389, 418
soft money donations 278–279
Solem v. Helm (1983) 147, 197
solicitor general 121

Souter, David **420–421,** *421,* 448
dissents of 62, 187, 295, 416, 420, 500
majority opinions of 443
South Carolina v. Baker (1988) **421–422**
South Carolina v. Gathers (1989) 330–331
South Dakota v. Dole (1987) **422–423,** 459, 480
Southern Pacific Co. v. Arizona (1945) 128
sovereign immunity 54, 75–76, 151–152, 310–311, **423–424,** 446
Indian rights and 216–218
special circumstances rule
capital punishment and 182
special education 86–87
speech and debate clause 187
members of Congress and 187
speedy trial **424–426**
Speedy Trial Act of 1974 425–426
Springer v. U.S. (1881) 350
Stafford v. Wallace (1922) 452
Staggers Rail Act (1980) 231
Standard Oil Co. of New Jersey v. U.S. (1911) 230, **426–427,** 521
standing 69, 174–175, 243, **427,** 511
mootness and 296
Stanford v. Kentucky (1989) 243
Stanley v. Georgia (1969) 330, 359
Stanley v. Illinois (1972) 329
Stanton v. Baltic Mining Co. (1916) 350
stare decisis 238, 248, 325–326, 331, 340, **427–428**
precedent and 355
State Farm Mutual Automobile Insurance Co. v. Campbell (2003) 364
state income tax
businesses and 100
State Intermediate Courts of Appeal 436
statement and account clause 167
CIA funding and 167
State of Washington v. Heckel (2001) 227
state sovereignty
interstate commerce limits and 305
jurisdiction over
Oklahoma capital relocation and 113
regulation of nuclear waste and 314–315
states' rights 75–76, 279–280, 423–424
civil liberties and 81–82
cotton monopoly and 482
federal courts *vs.* 4–5
incorporation and 216
Supreme Court *vs.* 14–15
U.S. taxation of judges and 94–95
State Supreme Courts of Appeal 436
State Trial Courts 436

statutory rape 223, 525
gender discrimination and 285–286
steel seizure case (1952) 38, 219, **530**
Jackson (Robert H. and) 232
Stephenson v. Dow Chemical Co. (2003) 88
sterilization, involuntary 57–58, 105–106, 434
criminals and 417–418
Douglas and 130
Holmes and 206
prisoners and 106
Sternberg v. Carhart (2000) 248
Stevens, John Paul **428–429,** *429*
capital punishment and 22–23
dissents of 148, 164, 187, 273, 288–289, 312, 317, 331, 420, 487, 500
free speech and 17
majority opinions of 79–80, 90, 204, 225, 254–255, 279, 281, 337, 355, 377, 394, 396, 478, 491
racial discrimination and 7
Steward Machine Co. v. Davis (1937) 310
Stewart, Potter **429–430**
dissents of 51–52, 139, 176
majority opinions of 74, 190, 201, 295–296, 336, 339
Stogner v. California (2003) 153
Stone, Harlan 74, *430,* **430–431,** 482
concurrences of 418
dissents of 166
"footnote four" of *U.S. v. Carolene Products* and 140, 434
majority opinions of 128, 184, 371, 484
Stone v. Gurham (1980) 354
stop and frisk **431–433,** 460–461
Story, Joseph **433–434**
majority opinions of 275, 452, 488
Strauder v. West Virginia (1880) 142
Streamlined Sales and Use Tax Agreement (SSUTA) 229
stream of commerce theory 451
strict constructionism 102–104
strict scrutiny 6–7, 89, 99, **434–435**
civil liberties and 81–82
civil rights and 82
racial prejudice and 483
rational basis test and 371
suspect classification and 449
strict separationism
establishment clause and 146
Stromberg v. California (1931) 210, 215, 452
structure of the court **435–436,** *436*
student activity fees 1–2, **437**
as compelled speech 42–43
student newspapers **438,** 439
student searches **440**
students, rights of **438–439**
Sturgis v. Crowninshield (1819) 433

substantive due process 14–15, 72, 108, 122, 132, 162, 238, 262, 299, 306–307, 338, 360, **440–441**
  contraceptives and 191–192
  Tanney and 457–458
Sugarman v. Dougall (1973) 15
Sugar Trust Case (1895) 230
suicide, assisted 495–496
  right to die and 116
suicide machine 125
Sullivan Act (1911) 408
summary judgment **441–442**
sunset provisions
  affirmative action and 193
supremacy clause
  preemption and 355–356
  racial segregation and 107
  regulation of nuclear waste and 315
Supreme Court and foreign policy **442–444**
Supreme Court and the constitutional amending process **445–446**
Supreme Court building 270–271, 324, **447**
  office of the curator and 116–117
Supreme Court confirmation **447–448**
The Supreme Court: How It Was, How It Is (Rehnquist) 376
Sure-Tan, Inc. v. National Labor Relations Board (2002) 213
surveillance 246–247, 358, 523–524
suspect classification 12, 44–45, 99, **449**
  civil rights and 82
  equal protection clause and 141
  intermediate scrutiny and 223
  poverty and 395
  rational basis test and 371
  strict scrutiny and 434
Sutherland, George 7–8, **449–450**
  dissents of 207
  majority opinions and 167, 174–175, 210, 261, 312, 442, 459, 483, 497, 518
Sutton Rulings 87
Sutton v. United Air Lines (1999) 87, 126
Swain v. Alabama (1965) 32, 334–335
Swann v. Charlotte-Mecklenburg Board of Education (1971) **450–451**
Sweatt v. Painter (1950) 499
Swift and Co. v. U.S. (1905) 18, **451–452**, 522
Swift v. Tyson (1842) 142–143, 434, **452**
"switch in time that saved nine" 68, 112, 209–210, 307, 437. *See also* court-packing plan
symbolic speech 30–31, 364–365, **452**
  draft-card burning and 491–492
  students and 466–467

T
Taft, William Howard 8, **454–455**
  appointments of 496, 520
  child labor laws and 28
  majority opinions of 195, 210, 358, 523
  Supreme Court building and 447
Taft-Hartley Act (1947) 252
Tahoe Sierra Preservation Council v. Tahoe Regional Planning Agency (2002) 254, 534
Taiwan, treaty with 184
take title clause
  regulation of nuclear waste and 315
takings clause 163–164, **455–456**
Taney, Roger B. **456–457**, 457
  majority opinions of 132, 347, 408
Tariff Act 195–196
tax and spend clause 167, **458–459**
taxation 214
  child labor, used to regulate 28
  dormant commerce clause and 129
  establishment clause and 146
  of income invalidated 350–351
  Internet and 226, 227, 228
  New Deal legislation and 309
  property rights and 166–167
  religious exemptions and 505–506
  religious school deductions and 297–298
  school vouchers and 403
  states' rights and 280
  Tariff Act and 195–196
taxation, federal
  of state judges' salaries 94–95
Tax Equity and Fiscal Responsibility Act of 1982 (TEFRA) 421
taxpayer suits 167, 174–175, **459–460**
Taylor v. Louisiana (1975) 142
Taylor v. Martin County Canvassing Board (2000) 62
The Tempting of America (Bork) 45
Ten Commandments
  establishment clause and 379
Tenth Amendment 482
  Bill of Rights and 37–38
  child labor and 195
  federal employees and political opinions under 475
  federalism and 161
  local activities and 18
  national minimum drinking age and 423
  regulation of nuclear waste and 315
  reserved powers clause of
    taxing state judges' salaries and 94–95
    term limits and 478
  state powers defined by
    strict constructionists and 103
  state sovereignty and 421–422
  states' rights and 238–239
  treaties and 292–293

Terminiello v. Chicago (1949) 70–71, 232, **460**
term limits 478–479
Terry stops 24–25, 346, 460–461.
  See also stop and frisk
Terry v. Adams (1953) 172
Terry v. Ohio (1968) 24, 407, 432, **460–461**
Texas v. Johnson (1989) 54, 163, 165, 247, 364, 452, **461–462**, 486
Third Amendment
  Bill of Rights and 37–38
  privacy and 359
  quartering soldiers clause of
    incorporation and 216
Thirteenth Amendment 215, 366–367, 446, 449
  abolition of slavery clause of
    school admissions and 56–57
  involuntary servitude clause of
    monopoly practices and 419
  separate but equal doctrine and 343
  slavery ended by 85, 132–133
Thomas, Clarence 448, **462–463**, 463
  dissents of 193, 321, 478
  free speech of contractors and 40–41
  majority opinions of 159, 294, 408
Thomas v. Network Solutions, Inc. (1998) 227
Thompson v. Oklahoma (1988) 243, 333
Thompson v. Utah (1898) 242
Thornburgh v. Gingles (1986) 373, **464–465**
Thornburgh v. the American College of Obstetrics and Gynecology (1985) 2
Thornhill v. Alabama (1940) 325, 452
three strikes laws 147–148, 198
Tileston v. Ullman (1943) 105, 191
Timmons v. Twin Cities Area New Party (1997) **465–466**
Tinker et al. v. Des Moines Independent School District (1969) 41, 92, 171, 186, 203, 364–365, 438–439, 452, **466–467**
Title IX 84, **467–468**
Title VI
  federal contracts and 176
Title VII **468–469**. *See also* Civil Rights Act of 1964
tobacco industry 76–77, 77–78
  RICO Act and 368
  Sherman Antitrust Act and 230
  taxation and 214
tobacco liability **469–470**
tobacco settlements 169–170
Tocqueville, Alexis de xii, 477
Toll v. Moreno (1982) 15
tort law
  Cardozo and 67–68
  punitive damages and 362–363

Toyota Motors v. Williams (2002) 126, **470–471**
Transportation Act of 1920 231
travel, right to
  fundamental rights and 176–177
Treasury Employees v. Von Raab (1989) 133–134
treaties 72, 100–102, 241, **471–473**, 477, 492
  Indian rights and 216–218, 301–302
  inherent powers and 292–293
  legislative standing and 259
  Taiwan and 184–185
  U.S. supremacy of 481
trial by jury clause 241–242
Trop v. Dulles (1958) 22, 333
Truman, Harry S.
  appointments of 62, 87, 498
  steel seizure case and 219, 530
Trust Cases (1911) 230
Turner Broadcasting System I v. FCC (1994) 374
Turner Broadcasting System II v. FCC (1997) 374
Turner v. Safley (1987) 270, 358
Twelfth Amendment
  electoral college and 445
Twentieth Amendment 445
Twenty-fifth Amendment 445
Twenty-first Amendment 445
  national minimum drinking age and 422–423
  nude dancing and 317
  ratification method of 445
Twenty-fourth Amendment 445
  poll taxes outlawed by 131, 199, 501
Twenty-second Amendment 445
Twenty-seventh Amendment 445
Twenty-sixth Amendment 246, 445, 446
  voting rights at the state level and 501
Twenty-third Amendment
  electoral college and 445
Twining v. New Jersey (1908) 6, 215

U
Ullman v. U.S. (1956) 131
Ultramares Corporation v. Touche (1931) 67–68
unanimous decisions 107, 115, 189, 205, 252, 263–264, 292, 301, 306, 309, 314, 338, 381, 450, 463, 470–471, 484, 493, 510, 521, 522
unenumerated rights 317, 359, **474–475**
Uniform Declaratory Judgments Act (YR.?) 120
unions 251–252
  "agency shop" arrangement 1–2
  campaign finance laws and 24
  dues 1–2
  political speech and 437

prohibition of 108
right to organize and 303–305
United Jewish Organizations of Williamsburgh, Inc. v. Carey (1977) 416
United Public Workers of America v. Mitchell (1947) **475**
United Steelworkers of America v. Weber (1979) 236, 469, **494**
unlawful combatants 220
unprotected speech 70–71
unwed fatherhood cases
parental rights and 329
urban renewal 34–35
U.S., et al. v. National Treasury Employees Union (1995) **490–491**
U.S. Capitol building *101*
U.S. Circuit Courts of Apppeal *436*
U.S. Claims Court *156, 436*
U.S. Constitution **476–477**
U.S. Constitution, application overseas **477–478**
U.S. Court of Appeals 19, 109–111, *156*
U.S. Court of Appeals for the Federal Circuit *156, 436*
U.S. Court of International Trade *156, 436*
U.S. Court of Military Appeals *156*
U.S. Court of Veterans Appeals *156*
U.S. Courts of Military Review (by service) *156*
U.S. District Courts *436*
U.S. FDA v. Brown and Williamson (2000) 470
U.S. Steel Workers of America v. Weber (1979) 376
U.S. Tax Court *156*
U.S. Term Limits, Inc. v. Thornton (1995) 478–479
U.S. Trust Co. v. New Jersey (1977) 479
U.S. v. Adair (1908) 251
U.S. v. American Library Assn. (2003) 225, 227, 263, **480**
U.S. v. American Tobacco Co. (1911) 230
U.S. v. Amistad (1841) 433–434
U.S. v. Arnold Schwinn & Co. (1967) 104
U.S. v. Belmont (1937) 443, **481,** 492
U.S. v. Biswell (1972) 273
U.S. v. Brown (1965) 36
U.S. v. Butler (1936) 230, 309, 430–431, 458–459, **481–482,** 496, 522
U.S. v. Calandra (1974) 268
U.S. v. Carolene Products (1938) 99, 140, 371, 399, 431, 434, **482–483**
U.S. v. Chadwick (1977) 273
U.S. v. Classic (1941) 431
U.S. v. Cruikshank (1875) 236, 408
U.S. v. Curtiss Wright Export Corp. (1936) 219, 442–443, **483–484**
U.S. v. Darby (1941) 195, **484–485**
U.S. v. Dickerson (1999) 122

U.S. v. Dion (1986) 218
U.S. v. E. C. Knight Co. (1895) 18, 175, 451, **485–486,** 522
U.S. v. Edge Broadcasting Co. (1993) 76
U.S. v. Eichman (1990) 165, 364, 461–462, **486**
U.S. v. Ewell (1966) 424
U.S. v. French (2000) 358
U.S. v. Johns (1985)
plain view doctrine and 339
U.S. v. Leon (1984) 268, **487–488**
U.S. v. Libellants and Claimants of the Schooner Amistad (1841) **488–490**
U.S. v. Lopez (1995) 161, 178, 231, 239, 310, 346, 372, 421, 422–423
U.S. v. Lovett (1943) 36
U.S. v. Mary Elizabeth Blue Hull Memorial Presbyterian Church (1970) 377
U.S. v. Miller (1939) 408
U.S. v. Morrison (2000) 86, 231, 239, 310, **490,** 500
U.S. v. Nixon (1974) 59, 149
U.S. v. O'Brien (1968) 30, 452, **491–492,** 507
U.S. v. One Book Entitled "Ulysses" by James Joyce (1933) 351
U.S. v. Paradise (1987) 469
U.S. v. Park (1975) 469
U.S. v. Pink (1942) 443, **492**
U.S. v. Rabinowitz (1950) 75
U.S. v. Radio TV News Directors Assn. (1969) 373–374
U.S. v. Reese (1876) 236
U.S. v. Richardson (1974) 459
U.S. v. Salerno (1987) 27
U.S. v. Schechter Poultry Corp. (1935) 230, **492–493,** 496
U.S. v. Sharpe (1985) 432
U.S. v. Sheffer (1998) 261
U.S. v. Turkette (1981) 367
U.S. v. Usery (1996) 130
U.S. v. Virginia (1996) 141, 183, 223, 413–414, **493–494,** 525
U.S. v. Weatherhead (1999) 296
U.S. v. Wilson (1833) 328
U.S. v. Wise (1962) 43
U.S. v. Witkovich (1957) 342
U.S. v. Wong Kim Ark (1898) 175
U.S. v. Wurzbach (1930) 475

V

Vacco v. Quill (1997) 125, **495–496**
valid secular policy test 64
Valley Forge College v. Americans United for Separation of Church and State (1982) 167, 427, 459
Van Devanter, Willis **496–497**
Vegelahn v. Guntner (1896) 206
Vernonia v. Acton (1995) 439
Veronica School District 47J v. Acton (1995) 133

veterans
civil service hiring preference of 336
veto 89–90
victim-impact evidence
capital punishment and 330–331
Village of Euclid, Ohio v. Ambler Realty Co. (1926) **497–498**
Vinson, Fred 498, **498–499**
dissents of 460
majority opinions of 120, 417
White (Byron), clerk for 520
Violence Against Women Act (1994) 239, 310, 490, **499–500**
Violence Against Women Civil Rights Restoration Act (proposed) 500
"Virginia Bill for Establishing Religious Freedom" (Jefferson) 147
Virginia State Board of Education v. Barnette (1943) 232
Virginia State Board of Pharmacy v. Virginia Consumer Council (1976) 76, 108–109
Virginia v. Black (2003) 115
Virginia v. Hicks (2003) **500–501**
Vitek v. Jones (1980) 284–285
voir dire
peremptory challenges and 334–336
voluntary searches 168–169
vote dilution 464
voting rights 28–29, 342–344
freedom of the press and 313
fundamental rights and 176–177
one person, one vote and 188–189
poll tax and 199–200
Voting Rights Act of 1964 236
racial redistricting and 416
Voting Rights Act of 1965 82, 236, 246, 373, 464–465, **501–502**
city elections and 295–296
Voyeur Dorm, L.C. v. City of Tampa (2000) 534

W

Wagner Labor Relations Act (1935) 112, 252, 304
Waite, Morrison Remick 503, **503–504**
majority opinions of 298–299, 376, 381–382, 395–396
Wallace v. Jaffree (1985) 354, 377, 401, **504–505**
Waller v. Georgia (1984) 362
Walton v. Arizona (1990) 384–385
Walz v. Tax Commission of the City of New York (1970) **505–506**
Ward v. Rock Against Racism **507–508**
Ward's Cove Packing Co. v. Atonio (1989) **506–507**
Ware v. Hylton (1796) 72

war powers 151, 359, 443–444, **508–509**
political question doctrine and 348
War Powers Act 443–444
War Powers Resolution (1973) 508
war revenue tax 214
warrants. See search warrants
Warren, Earl **509–511**
D.C. schools and 44–45
dissents of 416
majority opinions of 56–57, 167, 263–264, 290, 491
obscenity and 351
Warren, Samuel D. 358
Warren Commission Report 510
Warth v. Seldin (1975) **511**
Washington, Bushrod **511–513**
Washington, George 511–512
appointments of 72–73, 136, 233, 392
Washington v. Davis (1976) 20, 337, **513–514,** 520
Washington v. Glucksberg (1997) 116, 125, 495
Washington v. Legrant 516
Washington v. Washington State Commercial Passenger Fishing Vessel Assn. (1979) 217
Watchtower Bible & Tract Society v. Village of Stratton (2002) 235, **514**
Watergate 60, *328*
Bork, Robert, and 45
campaign finance abuses and 278
independent counsel provision and 296
Watkins v. U.S. (1957) 510
Webster, Daniel 118–119
Webster v. Reproductive Health Services (1989) 3, 326, **514–515**
Weeks v. U.S. (1914) 74, 148, 268, **515–516**
Weems v. U.S. (1910) 197
weighted voting 189
welfare 166–167, 394, **516–517**
legal challenges to 258
residency requirements and 415–416
Wesberry v. Sanders (1964) 29, 189, 322, 372, **517–518**
West Coast Hotel v. Parrish (1937) 238, 261, 307, **518–519**
West Virginia Board of Education v. Barnette (1943) 104, 166, 173, 235, 300, 431
Westside Community Schools v. Mergens (1990) 145
White, Byron **519–520**
dissents of 198, 220, 236, 288, 520
majority opinions of 89, 93, 97, 186, 192, 202–203, 252, 273, 314, 350, 370, 374, 416, 426–427, 438, 487, 513
press before grand juries and 51–52
sexual privacy and 46

White, Edward Douglass **520–521**
white primaries 431, 501
white supremacy movement 170
White v. Regester (1973) 295
Whitney v. California (1927) 529
Whren v. U.S. (1996) **521–522**
Wickard v. Filburn (1942) 28, 203, **522**
Widmar v. Vincent (1981) 145, 354–355, 390
Williamson v. Lee Optical (1955) 162
Williams v. Florida (1970) 242
Wilson, James 239
Wilson, Woodrow
    appointments of 49–50, 358
    communism and 97
    labor conditions and 251
Wilson v. Blackbird Marsh Creek Co. (1829) 128
Wilson v. Seiter (1991) 358
Wimberly v. Labor and Industrial Relations Commission (1987) 356–357
wiretapping 50, 358, **523–524**
Wisconsin v. Yoder (1972) 60, 138, 329, **524**

Witters v. Washington Dept. of Services for the Blind (1986) 145, 403, 532
Wolf v. Colorado (1949) 148, 268, 300, 357–358, 360, 516
Wolman v. Walter (1977) 294
women and the Constitution **524–526**
women's rights 48–49, 141–142, 499–500
    abortion counseling and 391–392
    abortion protest and 267–268
    RICO prosecution of 306
    civil rights and 82
    college athletic programs and 192–193
    fetal protection rights and 224–225
    gender-based violence and 310
    maximum hours laws and 251
    military draft and 390–391
    minimum wage and 307
    pregnancy in the workplace and 356
    same-sex colleges and 493–494
    wage discrimination and 140
    workplace and 298

Wong Kim Ark v. U.S. (1898) 13
Wong Wing v. U.S. (1896) 13, 213, 342
Wood v. Broom (1932) 94
Woodward, Bob 60
Wooley v. Maynard (1977) 235
Worcester v. Georgia (1832) 73, 216–217
writ of certiorari 391, **526**
Wyatt v. Cole (1992) 382–383
Wyman v. James (1971) **526–527**

Y

Yakus v. U.S. (1942) 101–102
Yamataya v. Fisher (1903) 341–342
Yates v. U.S. (1957) 120, **528**
yellow dog contracts 108
    Van Devanter and 496
Yick Wo v. Hopkins (1886) 199, 342, **528–529**
Youngberg v. Romeo (1982) 122
Younger v. Harris (1971) 96, **529–530**
Youngstown Sheet & Tube Co. v. Sawyer (1952) 232, 443, **530**. *See* steel seizure case

Young v. American Mini Theaters, Inc. (1976) 109, 379

Z

Zablocki v. Redhail (1978) 269–270, 418
Zadvydas v. Davis (2001) 342, **531–532**
Zelman v. Simmons-Harris (2002) 145, 263, 403
Zemel v. Rusk (1965) 194
Zionism
    Brandeis and 49–50
Zobrest v. Catalina Foothills School District (1993) 145, 263, 403, **532**
zoning laws 33–34, 57, 511, **532–533**
    adult theaters and 379–380
    pornography and 109
    property rights and 497–498
    rational basis test and 371
Zorach v. Clauson (1952) 139, 144–145, 232, **534–535**
Zwickler v. Koota (1967) 325